MOTTOES

Related Gale Titles

Allusions—Cultural, Literary, Biblical, and Historical: A Thematic Dictionary. 2nd edition. More than 8,700 literary, biblical, and cultural allusions and metaphors are identified by source in this dictionary. Entries are arranged alphabetically under more than 700 thematic headings.

Dictionary of Collective Nouns and Group Terms. 2nd edition. Furnishes definitions, usage examples, and source notes for 1,800 terms. Ancient phrases, general terms, modern punning terms, and terms of quantity and number are covered.

Idioms and Phrases Index. Contains over 400,000 entries identifying some 140,000 idioms, phrases, and expressions in the English language. Each entry guides users to one or more of 30 dictionaries that define the term.

Modifiers. Presents some 16,000 English adjectives derived from, or relating to, over 4,000 selected common and technical nouns.

Slogans. This work collects more than 6,000 slogans, rallying cries, and other exhortations from such fields as advertising, politics, and everyday speech, and arranges them under appropriate thematic headings, along with a discussion of each slogan's origin and use.

-Ologies and -Isms. 3rd edition. A lexicon of more than 15,000 words containing such suffixes as -ology, -ism, -ic, -cide, -phobia, -mancy, etc., that are not easily accessible in standard dictionaries. Words are arranged under thematic headings.

Picturesque Expressions: A Thematic Dictionary. 2nd edition. Explains 7,000 expressions. Entries give the expression, an explanation of its origin, its approximate date of appearance in written English, and, in most cases, usage notes and illustrative quotations.

Prefixes and Other Word-Initial Elements of English. For each of 3,000 common and technical prefixes, the dictionary gives examples of use, a description of its origin and meaning, and variant and related forms.

Suffixes and Other Word-Final Elements of English. Provides definitions, usage notes, examples, and variant and related forms of 1,500 suffixes.

The Private Lives of English Words. Identifies and explains the etymologies of some 400 words that exemplify various processes of linguistic change. Most of these words have had their meanings drastically changed over the course of their history.

MOTTOES

A Compilation of More Than 9,000 Mottoes from
Around the World and Throughout History, with Foreign
Examples Identified and Translated into English, the
Entries Arranged in the Text under Thematic Categories,
Supplemented by Alphabetic Indexes of All Mottoes and
of the Families, Institutions, Individuals, &c.,
to Which They Are Attributed

FIRST EDITION

Laurence Urdang, Editorial Director

Ceila Dame Robbins, Editor

Frank R. Abate, Associate Editor

GALE RESEARCH COMPANY
BOOK TOWER · DETROIT, MICHIGAN 48226

Editorial Staff

Editorial Director: Laurence Urdang
Editor: Ceila Dame Robbins
Associate Editor: Frank R. Abate
Consulting Editor: John K. Bollard

Editorial Associates: Peter M. Gross, Linda M. D. Legassie,
  Charles F. Ruhe

Gale Research Company

Publisher: Frederick G. Ruffner
Editorial Director: Dedria Bryfonski
Associate Editorial Director: Ellen T. Crowley

Production Supervisor: Mary Beth Trimper
Senior Production Associate: Dorothy Kalleberg
Art Director: Arthur Chartow

Library of Congress Cataloging-in-Publication Data

Mottoes: a compilation of more than 9,000 mottoes
  from around the world and throughout history . . .

  Bibliography: p. 13
  Includes indexes.
  1. Mottoes. I. Urdang, Laurence. II. Robbins,
Ceila Dame. III. Abate, Frank R.
PN6309.M68   1986   080   86-12122
ISBN 0-8103-2076-2

Data Processing and Composition by
Shepard Poorman Communications Corp., Indianapolis, Indiana

Typographic and Systems Design by Laurence Urdang Inc.

Printed in the United States of America

Contents

Foreword

Mottoes evoke a bygone era, that of Europe in the Middle Ages, when feudalism was the reigning social principle and heraldry a prime means of denoting well-born status. The coat of arms began as a strictly graphic device, a practical method of personal identification. The use of full-body armor made it difficult to recognize individual knights in battle, so the coat of arms, displayed on shield, surcoat, or pennant, afforded a colorful and effective solution. Associated as it was with the age of chivalry, it is no wonder that the use of coats of arms became a matter of individual, then family pride. Armorial bearings passed through generations, a symbol of a family's continuity, a link with one's ancestors and their deeds.

As the coat of arms came to be regarded more as a badge of family honor than a simple means of identification, its appropriateness for relaying, in words, some general sentiment became obvious; hence the ubiquity of mottoes on coats of arms and the close association of mottoes with heraldry. Most mottoes are attributed to families or branches of families, with a significant minority being of institutional origin. Most are brief, easily fitting on a coat of arms. The bulk of them are Latin, reflecting the fact that it was the Western *lingua franca* until relatively recent times.

Common Themes

Close scrutiny of many thousands of mottoes reveals a number of recurrent themes, a fact that suggested to the editors the usefulness of organizing the text according to thematic categories. Most obvious, perhaps, is the fact that so many have a religious basis or reference. The categories DIVINE GUIDANCE and DIVINITY each contain more than 300 mottoes, not to mention numerous mottoes in the categories BLESSING; CHRIST, JESUS; CROSS, THE; DIVINE GIFTS; FAITH; and SCRIPTURES, or in related groups such as FIDELITY, HOPE, PIETY, and VIRTUE. It is also clear—and not surprising—that mottoes tend to stress positive themes: note the categories KINDNESS, ENJOYMENT, FRIENDSHIP, PROSPERITY, RECTITUDE, and many others. Quite common, too, are mottoes that emphasize upright character, devotion to duty, reliability, and the like; for example, the categories COURAGE, DEDICATION, DEPENDABILITY, DILIGENCE, FIDELITY, HONOR, LEADERSHIP, OBEDIENCE, PATRIOTISM, SELF-CONTROL, and WORTHINESS offer hundreds of instances.

Mottoes of Interest

Though thousands of mottoes in this collection hint of a religious theme or speak of right action, with many, indeed, proud or sententious in tone, this does not mean that variety is lacking or that there is little of broader interest, even amusement. We may note as an example of the lighter or more imaginative use of mottoes a few that involve play on words:

Conanti nihil difficile est *Latin* 'Nothing is difficult for one who tries.' (*or* 'for a Conant')

—Conant.

Sumus *Latin* 'We are.'

—Weare.

Der Nagel hält fest. *German* 'The nail (*or* 'Nagel') holds fast.'

—Nagel.

Tout zèle *French* 'All zeal.'

—Touzel.

Cruce duce *Latin* 'With the Cross for a leader.'

—Adams.

A good number are peculiar, quite difficult to imagine as tokens of family pride:

Faint yet pursuing.

—Dickinson.

Fugiendo vincimus *Latin* 'We conquer by fleeing.'

—Ogg.

Qui non ciconia tigris *Latin* 'He who is not a stork is a tiger.'

—Browne.

Perhaps some incident in family history explains them?

8

Famous Mottoes; Quotations

There are, of course, the truly famous mottoes, familiar to many:

Honi soit qui mal y pense *French* 'Woe to him who thinks evil of
it.' —Order of the Garter.

Dieu et mon droit *French* 'God and my right.'
—United Kingdom of Great Britain and Northern Ireland.

Annuit coeptis *Latin* 'He nods on these beginnings.'
—Great Seal of the United States of America.

A great number of others are based on or quoted directly from literature
or the Bible, whether well known:

Fiat lux *Latin* 'Let there be light.' [Genesis 1:3]
— Rollins College, Winter Park, Florida.

Arma virumque cano *Latin* 'I sing of arms and a man.' [Vergil,
Aeneid i.1] —Gabriel.

or obscure:

Omne solum forti patria *Latin* 'Every soil is a fatherland to the
brave man.' [Ovid, *Fasti* i.493]
—Julius Heinrich, Duke of Saxony-Lauenburg (1586–1665).

Intaminatis fulget honoribus *Latin* 'He shines with unstained
honors.' [Horace, *Car.* iii.2.17] — Seton, Winton (E.).

Among mottoes based on literature, the author whose works seem to be
most quoted is Vergil. In general, the Bible was unquestionably the
source most widely utilized of all books.

As for other observations and significance that can be gained by a
perusal of *Mottoes*, we suggest that each user will find something of
value, no matter what his particular interest or intent.

The Editorial Approach

In compiling *Mottoes* the editors have tried to ensure that the fullest
and most accurate information is presented. The language of the motto is
identified (with rare exceptions), and foreign mottoes are accompanied by
translations into English. Including these features has presented some difficulties, as mottoes are frequently pithy to the point of obscurity (some,
doubtless, would be clearer if seen along with the coat of arms, to which
they may directly refer), written in an exotic tongue, or burdened by or-
thographic and grammatical peculiarities—occasionally all of the above.

9

It is hoped that the results of our editorial effort herein presented will not be faulted for having occasionally favored correctness over tradition.

Organization of the Collection

The collection includes more than 9,000 mottoes, notable for its size alone, yet made much more useful by the organization into thematic categories. Through this feature it is possible to study a group of mottoes that are related by their content or subject. The full list of 345 categories, complete with their cross references, may be consulted in the **Table of Thematic Categories** beginning on page 15. In addition to the access by category, the two indexes, one for mottoes and the other for source information, enable the user to find a particular motto already in mind or look for the motto of a particular family, institution, or individual.

It is the express desire of the editors that *Mottoes* be put to close, critical use and that users favor us with their comments and suggestions.

Frank R. Abate

How to Use This Book

Entries in *Mottoes* are organized by thematic categories, in a structure similar to that of a thesaurus, bringing together material of related meaning. This allows for association of related entries that is difficult or impossible using an alphabetic format. Still, the advantages of alphabetic order are not overlooked—**Index I** gives a complete alphabetic list of all mottoes, with reference to their category and entry number in the text.

The **Table of Thematic Categories**, pp. 15–38, gives a complete list of the 345 categories in the text. One may check the **Table** for the particular area or areas of interest, then turn to the text itself, where, under each category, mottoes are listed alphabetically and numbered sequentially. The **Table** also provides cross references for greater convenience. Note the inclusion of the category **UNCLASSIFIED**, containing mottoes that were difficult or impossible to categorize thematically.

Alphabetic access to the mottoes in the text is provided by **Index I**, as mentioned above; the thematic categories have also been included in this index to enhance ease of reference. In addition, **Index II** presents an alphabetic list of all sources—family names, individuals, institutions, etc.—to which the mottoes are attributed. Both indexes give reference to specific entries in the text by showing category name and entry number.

Many of the mottoes are attributed to a surname that is followed by an abbreviation, in parentheses, that indicates a title of peerage. The abbreviations and their significance are as follows:

(B.) = Baron   (E.) = Earl
(Bt.) = Baronet   (M.) = Marquis, Marquess
(D.) = Duke   (V.) = Viscount

Mottoes of various local councils in the United Kingdom are listed with their source, frequently including an abbreviation for the specific type of council. These abbreviations and their significance are as follows:

B.C.   = Borough Council
C.B.C. = County Borough Council
C.C.   = County Council
R.D.C. = Rural District Council

Bibliography

Numerous sources have been consulted during the compilation of this book, including dictionaries, encyclopedias, and other general works of reference. Listed here are those works that deal specifically with mottoes and that have been of greatest value:

Caulfield, S. F. A. *House Mottoes and Inscriptions: Old and New.* Detroit, Singing Tree Press, 1968 (reprint; originally published in 1908).

Elvin, C. N. *Elvin's Handbook of Mottoes,* revised with Supplement and Index by R. Pinches. London, Heraldry Today, 1971.

Pine, L. G. *A Dictionary of Mottoes.* London, Routledge & Kegan Paul, 1983.

Scott, C. Wilfrid. *Civic Heraldry of England & Wales.* New York, Giles Arno Press, 1972 (reprint of the 1953 edition).

Shankle, George Earlie. *American Mottoes and Slogans.* New York, H. W. Wilson Co., 1941.

Table of Thematic Categories

N.B. *In the following table, both actual categories used in the text and synonyms that are references to categories are listed in one alphabetic order. The categories are set in* **BOLD FACE CAPITAL LETTERS,** *while synonyms are in bold face with only their first letter capitalized.*

Please note the inclusion of the category **UNCLASSIFIED,** *which contains many mottoes that were difficult or impossible to categorize thematically.*

ABILITY
   See also POWER.
   Abundance . . . See PROSPERITY.
ACCEPTANCE
   See also PATIENCE.
   Acclaim . . . See PRAISE.
ACCOMPLISHMENT
   See also SUCCESS.
   Accord . . . See ORDER.
   Achievement . . . See ACCOMPLISHMENT.
ACQUISITION
ACTION
   See also WILL.
   Acts . . . See DEEDS.
ADMIRATION
   See also PRAISE.
   Adornment . . . See DECORATION.
ADVANCE
   See also IMPROVEMENT.
ADVERSITY
   See also DANGER; FORTITUDE; HOSTILITY; SUFFERING.
   Affection . . . See LOVE.

Affluence . . . See PROSPERITY.

Afterlife . . . See PARADISE.

AGE

AGGRESSION

See also CONFLICT; FIERCENESS; FORCE; HOSTILITY; WAR.

AGRICULTURE

See also COMMERCE; FLORA; GROWTH; HARVEST.

Aid . . . See ASSISTANCE.

Aims . . . See GOALS.

Alert . . . See WARNING.

Allegiance . . . See PATRIOTISM.

AMBITION

See also SELF-RELIANCE.

ANCESTRY

See also PARENTS; PAST, THE.

ANGER

See also AGGRESSION; HOSTILITY.

ANIMALS

See also BIRDS.

Antagonism . . . See HOSTILITY.

Antiquity . . . See AGE; PAST, THE.

Appearance . . . See COUNTENANCE.

Appeasement . . . See CONCILIATION.

Appreciation . . . See GRATITUDE.

Aptitude . . . See ABILITY.

Arising . . . See RISING.

Arms . . . See WEAPONS.

Aroma . . . See FRAGRANCE.

Arrogance . . . See PRIDE.

ART

Ascent . . . See RISING.

ASPIRATION

See also AMBITION; DESTINATION; EFFORT; GOALS.

ASSISTANCE

See also DIVINE GUIDANCE.

Athletics . . . See SPORT.

ATTEMPT

See also RISK.

ATTENTIVENESS

See also LISTENING; VIGILANCE; WAKEFULNESS.

Attractiveness . . . See BEAUTY.

Thematic Categories

AUDACITY
  See also COURAGE.
AUTHORITY
  See also GOVERNMENT; LEADERSHIP.
  Autumn . . . See SEASONS.
  Awareness . . . See ATTENTIVENESS.
  Badness . . . See EVIL.
  Battle . . . See WAR.
  Beasts . . . See ANIMALS.
BEAUTY
  See also GRACEFULNESS.
  Beginning . . . See ORIGIN.
  Behavior . . . See ACTION; MANNERS.
BEING, SELF
  Belief . . . See FAITH.
  Benediction . . . See BLESSING.
BENEFITS
  See also REWARD.
  Betterment . . . See IMPROVEMENT.
  Bible . . . See SCRIPTURES.
BIRDS
BIRTH
  See also LIFE; REBIRTH.
  Blackness . . . See DARKNESS.
  Blamelessness . . . See INNOCENCE.
  Blasphemy . . . See PROFANITY.
BLESSING
  See also DIVINE GIFTS; GOODNESS; GRACE.
BOASTFULNESS
  See also PRIDE.
  Boldness . . . See COURAGE.
  Bravery . . . See COURAGE.
BRIGHTNESS
  See also SHINING; STARS; SUN.
  Brotherhood . . . See FRIENDSHIP; HUMANITY.
  Business . . . See COMMERCE.
  Calmness . . . See EQUANIMITY; TRANQUILLITY.
  Capability . . . See ABILITY.
  Care . . . See CONCERN.
CAUSATION

CAUTION
>See also PRUDENCE; VIGILANCE.

Celebrity . . . See FAME.

CERTAINTY
>See also CLARITY.

Chance . . . See FORTUNE.

CHANGE
>See also TRANSIENCE.

Charm . . . See GRACEFULNESS.

Cheating . . . See DECEPTION.

Children . . . See OFFSPRING.

CHRIST, JESUS
>See also DIVINITY; RELIGION; SACRIFICE; SALVATION.

Chronology . . . See TIME.

Church . . . See RELIGION.

Cities . . . See LOCAL GOVERNMENT.

CLARITY

Cleanliness . . . See PURITY.

Clemency . . . See MERCY.

CLEVERNESS

Combat . . . See WAR.

Command . . . See AUTHORITY.

COMMERCE

Companionship . . . See FELLOWSHIP.

Completion . . . See FINISH.

Composure . . . See EQUANIMITY.

CONCERN
>See also KINDNESS.

CONCILIATION
>See also HEALING and HEALTH; PEACE.

Conclusion . . . See FINISH.

Conduct . . . See ACTION; MANNERS.

CONFIDENCE
>See also SELF-RELIANCE; TRUST.

CONFLICT
>See also AGGRESSION; ENEMIES; HOSTILITY; OPPOSITION; WAR.

Confrontation . . . See HOSTILITY; WAR.

CONQUEST
>See also VICTORY.

CONSCIENCE
>See also RECTITUDE.

18

CONSERVATION
  See also PERMANENCE.
CONSISTENCY
CONTEMPT
  Contest . . . See SPORT.
CONVENIENCE
  See also USEFULNESS.
  Corruption . . . See EVIL.
COUNTENANCE
COUNTRY
  See also HOME; NATIONAL MOTTOES; PATRIOTISM.
COUNTRYSIDE
COURAGE
  See also AUDACITY; FORTITUDE; MILITARY DISTINCTION.
COURTESY
  See also HOSPITALITY.
  Craftiness . . . See CLEVERNESS.
CROSS, THE
  See also CHRIST, JESUS; RELIGION; SACRIFICE; SALVATION.
CROWN
  See also LEADERSHIP; PRINCELINESS; ROYALTY.
  Crucifix . . . See CROSS, THE.
  Cultivation . . . See AGRICULTURE.
  Cunning . . . See CLEVERNESS.
  Curing . . . See HEALING and HEALTH.
  Custom . . . See TRADITION.
DANGER
  See also ADVERSITY.
  Daring . . . See COURAGE.
DARKNESS
  See also OBSCURITY.
  Dawn . . . See DAY; SUN.
DAY
  See also LIGHT; SUN.
DEATH
  See also LIFE; REBIRTH.
DECEPTION
  See also ENTRAPMENT.
DECISION
DECORATION

DEDICATION
See also FIDELITY; STEADFASTNESS.
DEEDS
See also ACCOMPLISHMENT; ACTION.
DEFENSE
See also FORTIFICATIONS; PROTECTION; VIGILANCE; WEAPONS.
DEFIANCE
See also FORTITUDE; OPPOSITION.
Deity . . . See DIVINITY.
Delight . . . See HAPPINESS.
Deliverance . . . See SALVATION.
DEPENDABILITY
See also STEADFASTNESS; TRUSTWORTHINESS.
DEPRIVATION
Descendants . . . See OFFSPRING.
DESIRE
See also WILL.
DESPAIR
See also SADNESS; SUFFERING.
Despotism . . . See OPPRESSION.
DESTINATION
See also FATE; GOALS.
Destiny . . . See FATE; FORTUNE.
DESTRUCTION
DEVOTION
See also DEDICATION; FIDELITY; PATRIOTISM; PIETY; REVERENCE.
Dew . . . See WATER.
Dignity . . . See NOBILITY.
DILIGENCE
See also DEDICATION; PERSEVERANCE.
DIRECTION
See also DESTINATION; DIVINE GUIDANCE; PURPOSE; WAY.
DIRECTNESS
Discernment . . . See WISDOM.
DISCIPLINE
See also ORDER; SELF-CONTROL.
Discord . . . See CONFLICT.
DISCRETION
See also PRUDENCE.
Disdain . . . See CONTEMPT.

DISGRACE
  Dishonesty . . . See DECEPTION.
  Dishonor . . . See DISGRACE.
  Distinction . . . See EXCELLENCE.
  Distress . . . See SUFFERING.
DIVINE GIFTS
  See also BLESSING; DIVINITY; GIFTS and GIVING; GRACE; PROVIDENCE;
    RELIGION.
DIVINE GUIDANCE
  See also GUIDANCE; RELIGION.
DIVINITY
  See also BLESSING; CHRIST, JESUS; CROSS, THE; DIVINE GIFTS; DIVINE
    GUIDANCE; GRACE; PROVIDENCE; RELIGION.
  Dominance . . . See AUTHORITY; POWER; PRIMACY.
  Donations . . . See GIFTS and GIVING.
  Dread . . . See FEAR.
DUE
  Durability . . . See ENDURANCE; PERMANENCE.
DUTY
  Eagerness . . . See ZEALOUSNESS.
EARTH
  See also WORLD.
  Education . . . See KNOWLEDGE.
EFFORT
  See also DILIGENCE.
EMERGENCE
  Eminence . . . See FAME; GREATNESS; NOBILITY.
  Emotions . . . See FEELINGS.
  Encouragement . . . See EXHORTATION.
  End . . . See FINISH.
  Endeavor . . . See ATTEMPT.
ENDURANCE
  See also PERMANENCE; STRENGTH; SUFFERING.
ENEMIES
  See also CONFLICT; HOSTILITY; OPPOSITION; WAR.
ENJOYMENT
  See also HAPPINESS; LAUGHTER.
ENLIGHTENMENT
  See also KNOWLEDGE; WISDOM.
ENTRAPMENT
  See also DECEPTION; HUNTING.

ENVY
EQUALITY
EQUANIMITY
See also MODERATION.
Esteem . . . See ADMIRATION.
ETERNITY
Etiquette . . . See MANNERS.
EVIL
See also DECEPTION.
EXALTATION
EXCELLENCE
See also PERFECTION.
Exclusiveness . . . See UNIQUENESS.
Exertion . . . See EFFORT.
EXHORTATION
Existence . . . See BEING, SELF; LIFE.
EXPECTATION
Exploits . . . See ACCOMPLISHMENT; DEEDS.
EXPLORATION
See also SEARCH and DISCOVERY.
Extent . . . See SIZE.
Face . . . See COUNTENANCE.
FACTUALITY
See also TRUTH.
FAILURE
FAIRNESS
See also EQUALITY; JUSTICE; RECTITUDE; RIGHTEOUSNESS.
FAITH
See also RELIGION; TRUST.
Faithfulness . . . See DEVOTION; FIDELITY.
Fall . . . See SEASONS.
Falsity . . . See DECEPTION.
FAME
See also HONOR; REPUTATION.
Family . . . See ANCESTRY; OFFSPRING; PARENTS.
Family names . . . See PROPER NAMES.
Farming . . . See AGRICULTURE.
FATE
See also DESTINATION.
Father . . . See PARENTS.
Fatherland . . . See COUNTRY.

FEAR
FEELINGS
　　See also HEART; LOVE.
FELLOWSHIP
　　See also FRIENDSHIP.
　　Fervor . . . See ZEALOUSNESS.
FIDELITY
　　See also DEDICATION; DEVOTION; FAITH; PATRIOTISM; STEADFASTNESS;
　　　　SUPPORT; TRUSTWORTHINESS.
FIERCENESS
　　See also AGGRESSION; DEFIANCE.
　　Fighting . . . See CONFLICT; WAR.
FINISH
FIRE
　　Flame . . . See FIRE.
FLEXIBILITY
　　See also CONCILIATION.
FLORA
　　See also AGRICULTURE.
FLOURISHING
　　See also FRUIT; GROWTH; OFFSPRING; PROSPERITY; REBIRTH; SUCCESS.
　　Flowers . . . See FLORA.
FOLLOWING
　　See also LEADERSHIP; PURSUIT.
　　Fondness . . . See LOVE.
FORCE
　　See also FIERCENESS; HOSTILITY; POWER; STRENGTH.
　　Foreigner . . . See STRANGER.
　　Foreshadowing . . . See WARNING.
FORESIGHT
　　See also FUTURE, THE; PREPAREDNESS; PRUDENCE; WARNING.
FORGETTING
　　See also MEMORY; PAST, THE.
　　Forgiveness . . . See MERCY.
FORTIFICATIONS
　　See also DEFENSE.
FORTITUDE
　　See also COURAGE; SPIRIT; STEADFASTNESS; STRENGTH.
FORTUNE
　　See also GLORY; PROSPERITY; SUCCESS.

Thematic Categories

FRAGRANCE

Frankness . . . See HONESTY.

Freedom . . . See LIBERTY.

Friendliness . . . See HOSPITALITY.

FRIENDSHIP

See also FELLOWSHIP; LOVE.

FRUIT

See also AGRICULTURE; FLORA; FLOURISHING.

FULLNESS

Function . . . See OFFICE.

Fury . . . See ANGER.

FUTURE, THE

See also POSSIBILITY; TIME; VISION.

Gaining . . . See ACQUISITION.

Game . . . See SPORT.

GENEROSITY

See also GIFTS and GIVING; UNSELFISHNESS.

GENIUS

See also ABILITY; WISDOM.

GENTLENESS

See also KINDNESS; MERCY.

GIFTS and GIVING

See also GENEROSITY.

Gladness . . . See HAPPINESS.

GLORY

See also FAME; HONOR; SUCCESS; VICTORY.

Glowing . . . See SHINING

GOALS

See also DESTINATION; DIRECTION.

God . . . See BLESSING; DIVINE GIFTS; DIVINE GUIDANCE; DIVINITY; GRACE; PROVIDENCE; RELIGION.

GOOD NEWS

GOODNESS

See also HONOR; KINDNESS; NOBILITY; RIGHTEOUSNESS; WORTHINESS.

GOVERNMENT

GRACE

See also BLESSING; DIVINE GIFTS; MERCY; RELIGION; SALVATION.

GRACEFULNESS

See also BEAUTY.

Graciousness . . . See COURTESY.

GRADUALNESS
  See also MODERATION.
GRATITUDE
GREATNESS
  See also EXCELLENCE.
GROWTH
  See also FLOURISHING; INCREASE.
GUIDANCE
  See also ASSISTANCE; DIVINE GUIDANCE; GOVERNMENT; LEADERSHIP.
GUILT
  See also CONSCIENCE.
  Guiltlessness . . . See INNOCENCE.
HANDS
HAPPINESS
  See also ENJOYMENT; FORTUNE; LAUGHTER.
  Hardship . . . See ADVERSITY.
HARMLESSNESS
  See also GENTLENESS; INNOCENCE.
  Harmony . . . See ORDER; UNITY.
HARVEST
  See also AGRICULTURE; FRUIT.
  Hatred . . . See HOSTILITY.
  Hazard . . . See DANGER.
HEALING and HEALTH
  Hearing . . . See LISTENING.
HEART
  See also FEELINGS; LOVE.
  Heaven . . . See PARADISE.
  Heavenly bodies . . . See STARS.
  Help . . . See ASSISTANCE.
  Heredity . . . See PARENTS.
  Heritage . . . See ANCESTRY.
  Homage . . . See REVERENCE.
HOME
  Homeland . . . See COUNTRY.
HONESTY
  See also FAIRNESS; INTEGRITY; RECTITUDE; RIGHTEOUSNESS; SINCERITY;
    TRUSTWORTHINESS; TRUTH; VIRTUE.
HONOR
  See also DUTY; MILITARY DISTINCTION; RECTITUDE; REPUTATION;
    TRUSTWORTHINESS; VIRTUE.

HOPE

Hopelessness . . . See DESPAIR.

HOSPITALITY

See also ACCEPTANCE; FRIENDSHIP.

HOSTILITY

See also AGGRESSION; CONFLICT; ENEMIES; FIERCENESS; OPPOSITION; WAR.

HUMANITY

See also KINDNESS; UNSELFISHNESS.

HUMILITY

See also MODERATION; OBSCURITY; SIMPLICITY; UNSELFISHNESS.

HUNTING

See also ENTRAPMENT; PERSECUTION; PURSUIT; SPORT.

Hurt . . . See INJURY.

Ideals . . . See PRINCIPLES.

IDENTITY

See also SELF-KNOWLEDGE.

IDLENESS

Illumination . . . See LIGHT.

IMITATION

IMMORTALITY

Impartiality . . . See FAIRNESS.

Impediment . . . See OPPOSITION.

Impermanence . . . See TRANSIENCE.

IMPROVEMENT

See also ADVANCE.

Inactivity . . . See IDLENESS.

INCENTIVE

INCREASE

See also FULLNESS; GROWTH; PROSPERITY.

Independence . . . See LIBERTY; SELF-RELIANCE.

Indestructibility . . . See IMMORTALITY.

INDUSTRIOUSNESS

Ingenuity . . . See CLEVERNESS.

INJURY

INNOCENCE

See also GOODNESS; PURITY.

INSIGNIFICANCE

See also HARMLESSNESS.

Instruction . . . See GUIDANCE.

INTEGRITY
See also HONESTY; HONOR; NOBILITY; PURITY; RECTITUDE; REPUTATION; RIGHTEOUSNESS; TRUSTWORTHINESS; VIRTUE.

Intellect . . . See MIND.

Intelligence . . . See CLEVERNESS; GENIUS.

INTENTION
See also AMBITION; WILL.

INTER-RELATEDNESS
See also UNITY.

Investigation . . . See SEARCH and DISCOVERY.

IRONY

Jealousy . . . See ENVY.

Jesus . . . See CHRIST, JESUS.

Joy . . . See ENJOYMENT.

Joy . . . See HAPPINESS.

Joy . . . See LAUGHTER.

JUDGMENT

Judiciousness . . . See DISCRETION.

Jurisdiction . . . See AUTHORITY.

JUSTICE
See also FAIRNESS; LAW; RIGHTS.

KINDNESS
See also GENTLENESS; GOODNESS; HUMANITY; LOVE; UNSELFISHNESS.

Kings . . . See ROYALTY.

KNOWLEDGE
See also MIND; SELF-KNOWLEDGE; WISDOM.

Labor . . . See INDUSTRIOUSNESS.

Language . . . See WORDS.

Last names . . . See PROPER NAMES.

LAUGHTER
See also ENJOYMENT; HAPPINESS.

LAW
See also GOVERNMENT; JUSTICE.

LEADERSHIP
See also AUTHORITY; CROWN; GUIDANCE; ROYALTY.

LIBERTY
See also SELF-DETERMINATION.

LIFE
See also BIRTH; DEATH; REBIRTH.

Thematic Categories

LIGHT
>See also DAY; SHINING; SUN.

>Likeness . . . See SIMILARITY.

LIMITATION
>See also MODERATION; SELF-CONTROL.

>Lineage . . . See ANCESTRY.

LISTENING
>See also ATTENTIVENESS.

LIVELINESS
>See also SPIRIT.

LOCAL GOVERNMENT
LOCATION
LOFTINESS
>See also RISING.

>Logic . . . See REASON.

>Longing . . . See DESIRE.

LOVE
>See also FEELINGS; HEART; KINDNESS.

>Loveliness . . . See BEAUTY.

>Loyalty . . . See DEVOTION; FIDELITY; TRUSTWORTHINESS.

>Luck . . . See FORTUNE.

>Lying . . . See DECEPTION.

>Magnitude . . . See SIZE.

MAINTENANCE
>See also CONSERVATION; SUPPORT.

>Majesty . . . See GREATNESS.

MANLINESS
MANNER
MANNERS
>Means . . . See MANNER.

MEASURE
>See also LIMITATION.

>Meekness . . . See HUMILITY.

>Melody . . . See MUSIC.

MEMORY
>See also PAST, THE.

MERCY
>See also KINDNESS.

>Method . . . See MANNER.

>Might . . . See POWER; STRENGTH.

MILITARY DISTINCTION

See also REWARD; WAR.

Mimicry . . . See IMITATION.

MIND

See also KNOWLEDGE; SPIRIT; THOUGHT; WISDOM.

Misery . . . See SUFFERING.

Misfortune . . . See FORTUNE.

MODERATION

See also EQUANIMITY; LIMITATION; PRUDENCE; SELF-CONTROL.

Modesty . . . See HUMILITY.

Modification . . . See CHANGE.

Mother . . . See PARENTS.

Municipalities . . . See LOCAL GOVERNMENT.

MUSIC

NAME

See also PROPER NAMES.

Nation . . . See COUNTRY.

NATIONAL MOTTOES

Nationalism . . . See PATRIOTISM.

Nature . . . See ANIMALS; EARTH; FLORA.

NAVIGATION

See also DIRECTION; SEA.

NECESSITY

Need . . . See DEPRIVATION.

News . . . See GOOD NEWS.

Night . . . See DARKNESS.

NOBILITY

See also GOODNESS; PRINCELINESS; RIGHTEOUSNESS; ROYALTY; STATUS; VIRTUE.

Notoriety . . . See FAME.

NOURISHMENT

OBEDIENCE

See also FOLLOWING.

Objectives . . . See GOALS.

Obligation . . . See DUTY.

OBSCURITY

See also DARKNESS.

Obtaining . . . See ACQUISITION.

Ocean . . . See SEA.

OFFICE

OFFSPRING
    Oldness . . . See AGE.
    Omnipresence . . . See UBIQUITY.
    Opportuneness . . . See TIMELINESS.
OPPORTUNITY
    See also POSSIBILITY.
OPPOSITION
    See also DEFIANCE.
OPPRESSION
ORDER
    See also DISCIPLINE.
ORIGIN
    Ornamentation . . . See DECORATION.
    Outcome . . . See RESULTS.
    Ownership . . . See POSSESSION.
PARADISE
    See also SALVATION.
PARENTS
    See also ANCESTRY.
    Parity . . . See EQUALITY.
    Passion . . . See DESIRE; LOVE.
PAST, THE
    See also ANCESTRY; TIME.
PATIENCE
    See also ACCEPTANCE; EQUANIMITY; SELF-CONTROL; SUFFERING.
PATRIOTISM
    See also COUNTRY; DEVOTION.
    Payment . . . See REWARD.
PEACE
    See also TRANQUILLITY; WAR.
PEOPLE
    See also HUMANITY.
PERFECTION
    See also EXCELLENCE.
    Perfume . . . See FRAGRANCE.
    Peril . . . See DANGER.
PERMANENCE
    See also ENDURANCE.
    Perpetuity . . . See ETERNITY.
PERSECUTION
    See also HUNTING; SUFFERING.

PERSEVERANCE
>   See also FORTITUDE; STEADFASTNESS.

PIETY
>   See also DEVOTION; RELIGION; REVERENCE.

>   Plainness . . . See SIMPLICITY.

>   Plants . . . See AGRICULTURE; FLORA; FRUIT.

>   Pleasure . . . See ENJOYMENT; HAPPINESS; LAUGHTER.

>   Plenty . . . See PROSPERITY.

>   Politeness . . . See COURTESY; MANNERS.

POSSESSION

POSSIBILITY
>   See also FUTURE, THE.

>   Potential . . . See POSSIBILITY.

POWER
>   See also ABILITY; FORCE; STRENGTH.

PRAISE
>   See also ADMIRATION; HONOR; MILITARY DISTINCTION.

PREPAREDNESS
>   See also FORESIGHT.

PRESENT, THE
>   See also TIME.

>   Presents . . . See GIFTS and GIVING.

>   Preservation . . . See CONSERVATION.

PRIDE
>   See also BOASTFULNESS.

PRIMACY

PRINCELINESS
>   See also CROWN; NOBILITY; ROYALTY.

PRINCIPLES
>   See also LAW; RECTITUDE.

>   Privileges . . . See RIGHTS.

PROFANITY
>   Proficiency . . . See ABILITY.

>   Progress . . . See ADVANCE.

PROPER NAMES
>   See also NAME.

>   Prophecy . . . See FORESIGHT; FUTURE, THE.

PROSPERITY
>   See also FLOURISHING; INCREASE; SUCCESS.

PROTECTION
>   See also DEFENSE; SUPPORT.

Thematic Categories

PROVIDENCE

See also DIVINE GIFTS; DIVINE GUIDANCE; DIVINITY; SALVATION.

PROVOCATION

PRUDENCE

See also CAUTION; DISCRETION; FORESIGHT; MODERATION; WISDOM.

PURITY

See also INNOCENCE; INTEGRITY; RECTITUDE; VIRTUE.

PURPOSE

See also DIRECTION; INTENTION.

PURSUIT

See also FOLLOWING; HUNTING; SEARCH and DISCOVERY.

Queens . . . See ROYALTY.

Quickness . . . See SPEED.

Quietness . . . See SILENCE.

Rain . . . See WATER.

Rapidity . . . See SPEED.

Rashness . . . See AUDACITY.

Rationality . . . See REASON.

Readiness . . . See PREPAREDNESS.

REASON

See also MIND; THOUGHT.

REBIRTH

See also BIRTH; DEATH; LIFE; PARADISE; SALVATION.

Recollection . . . See MEMORY.

RECTITUDE

See also FAIRNESS; HONESTY; HONOR; INTEGRITY; PRINCIPLES; PURITY; RIGHTEOUSNESS; RIGHTS; TRUSTWORTHINESS; VIRTUE; WORTHINESS.

Redemption . . . See SALVATION.

Reflection . . . See THOUGHT.

Regard . . . See ADMIRATION.

Regulation . . . See LAW.

Relatedness . . . See INTER-RELATEDNESS.

Reliability . . . See DEPENDABILITY; TRUSTWORTHINESS.

Reliance . . . See TRUST.

RELIGION

See also CHRIST, JESUS; CROSS, THE; DIVINITY; FAITH; GRACE; SALVATION.

Remembrance . . . See MEMORY.

Remuneration . . . See REWARD.

Renewal . . . See REBIRTH.

Renown . . . See FAME.

REPUTATION
See also FAME; INTEGRITY; PURITY.

Requirement . . . See NECESSITY.

Resignation . . . See ACCEPTANCE.

Responsibility . . . See DUTY.

REST
RESTRAINT
Restriction . . . See LIMITATION.

RESULTS
Revenge . . . See VENGEANCE.

REVERENCE
See also DEVOTION; PIETY.

Revival . . . See REBIRTH.

REWARD
See also MILITARY DISTINCTION.

RIGHTEOUSNESS
See also FAIRNESS; GOODNESS; HONESTY; INTEGRITY; NOBILITY; PURITY; RECTITUDE.

RIGHTS
RISING
RISK
Rivers . . . See WATER.

ROYALTY
See also CROWN; LEADERSHIP; PRINCELINESS.

Rule . . . See GOVERNMENT; LAW.

RUNNING
SACRIFICE
SADNESS
See also DESPAIR; SUFFERING.

Safety . . . See SECURITY.

Sailing . . . See NAVIGATION.

SALVATION
See also CHRIST, JESUS; CROSS, THE; GRACE; PROVIDENCE; RELIGION.

SATISFACTION
SCHOOL MOTTOES
Scope . . . See SIZE.

Scorn . . . See CONTEMPT.

SCRIPTURES
See also DIVINE GUIDANCE; RELIGION.

SEA
See also WATER; WAVES.

SPEED
See also RUNNING.

SPIRIT
See also MIND.

Spiritedness . . . See LIVELINESS.

SPORT
See also HUNTING.

Spring . . . See SEASONS.

Stability . . . See PERMANENCE.

Standards . . . See PRINCIPLES.

STARS
See also BRIGHTNESS.

STATE MOTTOES

Statecraft . . . See GOVERNMENT.

STATUS

Statute . . . See LAW.

STEADFASTNESS
See also FIDELITY; FORTITUDE; PERMANENCE; PERSEVERANCE.

Stillness . . . See SILENCE.

STRANGER

STRENGTH
See also FORCE; POWER; STEADFASTNESS.

Strife . . . See WAR.

Subjugation . . . See OPPRESSION.

SUCCESS
See also ACCOMPLISHMENT; FLOURISHING; FORTUNE; GLORY;
PROSPERITY; VICTORY.

SUFFERING
See also DESPAIR; ENDURANCE; PATIENCE; PERSECUTION; SADNESS.

Summer . . . See SEASONS.

SUN
See also BRIGHTNESS; DAY; LIGHT; SHINING.

SUPPORT
See also PROVIDENCE.

Sureness . . . See CERTAINTY.

Surnames . . . See PROPER NAMES.

Swiftness . . . See SPEED.

Symbol . . . See SIGN.

Talk . . . See WORDS.

Temperance . . . See MODERATION; SELF-CONTROL.

Temporariness . . . See TRANSIENCE.

Tenderness . . . See GENTLENESS.

Terror . . . See FEAR.

Thankfulness . . . See GRATITUDE.

THOUGHT

See also JUDGMENT; MIND; REASON.

Thriving . . . See FLOURISHING.

TIME

See also FUTURE, THE; PAST, THE; PRESENT, THE; SEASONS; TIMELINESS; TRANSIENCE.

TIMELINESS

See also TIME.

Timidity . . . See FEAR.

Title . . . See NAME; NOBILITY.

Today . . . See PRESENT, THE.

Toil . . . See INDUSTRIOUSNESS.

Tomorrow . . . See FUTURE, THE.

Tools . . . See UTENSILS.

TOUCH

Towns . . . See LOCAL GOVERNMENT.

Trade . . . See COMMERCE.

TRADES

TRADITION

See also ANCESTRY.

TRANQUILLITY

See also PEACE.

TRANSIENCE

See also CHANGE; TIME.

Trickery . . . See DECEPTION.

Triumph . . . See CONQUEST; VICTORY.

Triviality . . . See INSIGNIFICANCE.

TRUST

See also CONFIDENCE; FAITH; TRUSTWORTHINESS.

TRUSTWORTHINESS

See also FIDELITY; HONESTY; INTEGRITY; REPUTATION.

TRUTH

See also FACTUALITY; HONESTY.

Tyranny . . . See OPPRESSION.

UBIQUITY

UNCLASSIFIED

Understanding . . . See WISDOM.

Unfriendliness . . . See HOSTILITY.

Unimportance . . . See INSIGNIFICANCE.

UNIQUENESS
UNITY
UNSELFISHNESS
  See also GENEROSITY; HUMANITY; KINDNESS.
USEFULNESS
  See also SERVICE.
UTENSILS
  Utility . . . See USEFULNESS.
  Valor . . . See COURAGE.
VENGEANCE
VICTORY
  See also CONQUEST; SUCCESS.
VIGILANCE
  See also DEFENSE; WAKEFULNESS; WARNING.
VIRTUE
  See also GOODNESS; HONESTY; INTEGRITY; NOBILITY; PIETY; PURITY;
    RECTITUDE; WORTHINESS.
  Visage . . . See COUNTENANCE.
VISION
  Vitality . . . See LIVELINESS.
WAKEFULNESS
  See also VIGILANCE.
WALKING
WAR
  See also AGGRESSION; CONFLICT; ENEMIES; HOSTILITY; OPPOSITION;
    PEACE; WEAPONS.
WARNING
  See also FORESIGHT; VIGILANCE.
  Watchfulness . . . See ATTENTIVENESS; VIGILANCE.
WATER
  See also SEA; WAVES.
WAVES
  See also SEA; WATER.
WAY
  See also DIRECTION.
  Wealth . . . See PROSPERITY.
WEAPONS
  See also DEFENSE; WAR.
  Well-being . . . See HEALING and HEALTH.
  Wickedness . . . See EVIL.

WILL

See also ACTION; DESIRE; DIVINE GUIDANCE; INTENTION; SELF-DETERMINATION.

WILLINGNESS

Winter . . . See SEASONS.

WISDOM

See also KNOWLEDGE; MIND; PRUDENCE; SELF-KNOWLEDGE.

WORDS

See also SCRIPTURES.

Work . . . See INDUSTRIOUSNESS; TRADES.

WORLD

See also EARTH.

WORTHINESS

See also RECTITUDE; VIRTUE.

Wound . . . See INJURY.

Yesterday . . . See PAST, THE.

Youth . . . See AGE.

ZEALOUSNESS

See also DILIGENCE.

MOTTOES

ABILITY (*See also* POWER.)

1. **Ambo dexter**   *Latin* 'Skillful with both hands'
   —Hewetson.

2. **Arte, Marte, vigore**   *Latin* 'By skill, valour, and energy'
   —Wednesbury B. C., U.K.

3. **Arte conservatus**   *Latin* 'Preserved by skill'
   —Christopher.

4. **Arte et animo**   *Latin* 'By skill and courage'
   —Ferguson.

5. **Arte et labore**   *Latin* 'By skill and toil'
   —Blackburn C. B. C., U.K.

6. **Arte et Marte**   *Latin* 'By skill and valor'
   —Middleton, Hunter.

7. **Arte faventi nil desperandum**   *Latin* 'Supported by skill, there is no cause to despair'
   —Leek U. D. C., U.K.

8. **Arte non impetu**   *Latin* 'By skill, not force'
   —Hunter.

9. **Arte non vi**   *Latin* 'By skill, not force'
   —Jordan.

10. **Arte vel Marte**   *Latin* 'By art or force'
    —Deans, Dundas.

11. **Artibus et armis**   *Latin* 'By arts and arms'
    —Elton (Bt.).

12. **Artis vel Martis**   *Latin* 'Of skill or valor'
    —Eastoft, Eure.

13. **Et arte et Marte**   *Latin* 'Both by skill and valor'
    —Bain.

14. **Gnaviter**   *Latin* 'Skillfully'
    —Anderson (of Broughton, Bt.).

15. **Ingenio ac labore**   *Latin* 'By ability and toil'
    —Kerr, Worrall.

16. **Ingenio et merito**   *Latin* 'By ability and desert'
    —Grout.

41

17. **Ingenio et viribus** *Latin* 'By ability and strength'
—Huddlestone.

18. **Knowledge/ Skill**
—Terra Technical College, Fremont, Ohio.

19. **Lux veritas peritia populo nostro** *Latin* 'Light, truth, and skill for our people'
—Coastal Carolina Community College, Jacksonville, North Carolina.

20. **Non omnia possumus omnes** *Latin* 'We are not all able to do all things'
—Palazzo Borghese, Rome.

21. **Non solum ingenii, verum etiam virtutis** *Latin* 'Not only talent, but also virtue'
—Liverpool College, U.K.

22. **Omnia conando docilis solertia vincit** *Latin* 'Apt ability conquers all things it attempts'
—[Manilius, *Astronomicon*, i. 95.] Johann, Duke of Saxony-Weimar (1570–1605).

23. **Patet ingeniis campus** *Latin* 'The field lies open to talent'
—Tucker.

24. **Possunt quia posse videntur** *Latin* 'They are able because they seem to be'
—Goodere, Keightley.

25. **Potius ingenio quam vi** *Latin* 'Rather by skill than by force'
—Edgar, Young.

26. **Scienter utor** *Latin* 'I use it skillfully'
—Forbes (of Auchreddy).

27. **Scite, citissime, certe** *Latin* 'Expertly, most swiftly, surely'
—Havergal.

28. **Scribere scientes** *Latin* 'Men skilled in writing'
—Scriveners' Company.

29. **Tam arte quam Marte** *Latin* 'As much by art as strength'
—McLea, Wright.

30. **Tam in arte quam Marte** *Latin* 'As much in skill as in force'
—Milne.

31. **Tractent fabrilia fabri** *Latin* 'Let smiths handle smiths' tools'
—Smiths' Company, Exeter.

32. **Valens et volens** *Latin* 'Able and willing'
—Fetherston (of Bracklyn), Fetherstonhaugh.

33. **Vi et arte**   *Latin* 'By strength and skill'
—Ferguson, Stevens.

34. **Virtute et ingenio**   *Latin* 'By virtue and ability'
—Master.

35. **Vivitur ingenio**   *Latin* 'He lives by skill'
—Darley, Copen.

ACCEPTANCE   (*See also* PATIENCE.)
1. **Che sarà sarà**   *Italian* 'What will be will be'
—Bedford (D.), Russell (Bt.).

2. **Ego accedo**   *Latin* 'I assent'
—Orr.

3. **Esto**   *Latin* 'Be it so'
—Hill.

4. **Prend moi tel que je suis**   *French* 'Take me as I am'
—Bell, Ely (M.), Loftus, Ricketts (Bt.).

5. **Prenez en gré**   *French* 'Take in good will'
—Ogle (Bt.).

6. **Qui sera sera**   *French* 'What will be, will be'
—Edgell, Betteason (of Seven Oakes), Wolferstan (co. Suffolk).

7. **Quodcunque evenerit optimum**   *Latin* 'Whatever happens is best'
—Lloyd.

ACCOMPLISHMENT   (*See also* SUCCESS.)
1. **Age aut perfice**   *Latin* 'Act or achieve'
—McMillan.

2. **A posse ad esse**   *Latin* 'From possibility to being'
—Carter.

3. **Ardua vinco**   *Latin* 'I overcome difficulties'
—Stratton (of Montrose).

4. **Aut nunquam tentes aut perfice**   *Latin* 'Either never attempt or accomplish'
—Bennet, Creswell, Crouch, Day, Dorset (D.), Hustler, Sackville.

5. **Benefacere et laetari**   *Latin* 'To do well and be glad'
—Duc de Gallo.

6. **Bene factum** *Latin* 'Well done'
   —Weldon.

7. **Cursum perficio** *Latin* 'I accomplish the race'
   —Hunter.

8. **Exegi** *Latin* 'I have accomplished it'
   —Lees (Bt.).

9. **In ardua petit** *Latin* 'He searches after things difficult of attainment'
   —Malcolm (of Poltalloch).

10. **Knowledge/ Understanding/ Achievement/ Citizenship**
    —S. D. Bishop State Junior College, Mobile, Alabama.

11. **Ne tenta vel perfice** *Latin* 'Attempt not or accomplish'
    —Hill.

12. **Ne tentes aut perfice** *Latin* 'Attempt not or accomplish'
    —Downshire (M.), Faunce, Hill (Bt.), Hill.

13. **Nostra quae fecimus** *Latin* 'What we have done is our own'
    —Kenan.

14. **Nunquam tentes aut perfice** *Latin* 'Either never attempt, or accomplish'
    —Bennet.

15. **Peperi** *Latin* 'I have brought forth'
    —Peperell (Bt.).

16. **Plus d'effet que de bruit** *French* 'More effect than noise'
    —Friedrich I, Duke of Saxony-Gotha and Altenburg (1646–91).

17. **Pour y parvenir** *French* 'To accomplish it'
    —Canterbury (V.), Rutland (D.), Manners (B.), Manners (of Goadby Marwood Park).

18. **Pret d'accomplir** *French* 'Ready to accomplish'
    —Aston (Co. Chester).

19. **Suscipere et finire** *Latin* 'To undertake and accomplish'
    —Bolckow.

20. **Tua puta quae tute facis** *Latin* 'Think those things to be yours which you yourself have done'
    —over a door in the Palazzo Borghese, Rome.

21. **Tutto si fa** *Italian* 'Everything gets done'
    —La Trobe-Bateman.

22. **Va outre marque** *French* 'Go beyond the mark'
    —Utermarck.

ACQUISITION

1. **Bene paratum dulce** *Latin* 'That which is rightly acquired is sweet'
                                                —Ogilvy (of Inchaven).

2. **Certamine parata** *Latin* 'Acquired by strife'
                                                —Cairncross.

3. **Honeste parata** *Latin* 'Things honorably got'
                                                —Whyte.

4. **Labore parta** *Latin* 'Acquired by labor'
                                                —White.

5. **Parta tueri** *Latin* 'Defend your acquisitions'
                          —Jacob (of Bromley), Lilford (B.), Powys.

6. **Qui vult capere capiat** *Latin* 'Who wishes to take, let him take'
                                                —Gloag.

7. **Quod transtuli retuli** *Latin* 'What I have taken I have restored'
                                                —Woodrooffe.

8. **Sume superbiam quaesitam mentis** *Latin* 'Assume the pride of mind which you have acquired'
                                                —Seaver.

9. **Venale nec auro** *Latin* 'Not to be bought with gold'
                          —[Horace, *Car.* ii. 16. 1.] Jervis.

ACTION (*See also* WILL.)

1. **Action**
                                —Bognor Regis U. D. C., U.K.

2. **Age aut perfice** *Latin* 'Act or achieve'
                                                —McMillan.

3. **Agite pro viribus** *Latin* 'Act according to your strength'
                                                —Campbell.

4. **Aut tace aut face** *Latin* 'Either be silent or act'
                                                —Scott (of Comeston).

5. **Celer atque fidelis** *Latin* 'Active and faithful'
                                                —Duine.

6. **Diu delibera cito fac** *Latin* 'Think long, act fast'
                                                —Davie (U.S.).

7. **Fac justa** *Latin* 'Act justly'
                                                —Newington.

8. **Firm, vigilant, active**
                                        —Muncaster (B.).

9. **Fortis agendo**   *Latin* 'Strong in action'
                                        —Pittman (U.S.).

10. **Grand venteurs petits faiseurs**   *French* 'Great boasters, small
    doers'
            —Anna Auguste, Princess of Nassau-Dillenburg (1612–56).

11. **Impetueux**   *French* 'Impetuous'
                                        —Poyntz.

12. **Innocent courageous activity**
                                        —White.

13. **In recto decus**   *Latin* 'Honor in acting right'
            —Ferrier, Scott, Brunswick and Luenburg, Syme,
                                    Simmons, Hoseason.

14. **Moveo et propitior**   *Latin* 'I move and am appeased'
                            —Knox, Ranfurley (E.), Wells.

15. **Non cantu sed actu**   *Latin* 'Not by singing but by acting'
                                        —Gillman.

16. **Pensa poi fa**   *Italian* 'Consider, then act'
            —August, Duke of Braunschweig-Wolfenbüttel
                                        (1579–1666).

17. **Perge coepisti**   *Latin* 'Proceed and you have begun'
                            —Ten Broeck (U.S.).

18. **Plus d'effet que de bruit**   *French* 'More effect than noise'
            —Friedrich I, Duke of Saxony-Gotha and Altenburg
                                        (1646–91).

19. **Prius quam factum considera**   *Latin* 'Think before you act'
                                        —Reeves.

20. **Prosecute or perish**
                                        —Buchanan.

21. **Spectemur agendo**   *Latin* 'Let us be viewed by our actions'
            —[Ovid, *Met.* xiii. 120.] Agar, Brown, Browne, Drumson,
                    Duckett, Ellis, Elvin (of East Dereham), Lloyd, Mott,
                        Montague (B.), Montague, Moore, Morris, McLeur,
                            Reynolds, Rutson, Shannon (E.), Scholefield.

22. **Virtus, laus, actio**   *Latin* 'Virtue, glory, action'
                                        —Frazer.

23. **Virtus actione consistit**   *Latin* 'Virtue consists of action'
                                        —Craven (U.S.).

24. **Virtus constat in actione**　*Latin* 'Virtue consists in action'
　　　　　　　　　　　　　　　　　　　　—Norgate.

25. **Virtus in actione consistit**　*Latin* 'Virtue consists in action'
　　　　　　—Craven (E.), Clayton (Bt.), Halford, Sier.

26. **Virtutis laus actio**　*Latin* 'The praise of virtue is action'
　　　　　　—Corbet (Bt.), Rumbold (Bt.), Tansley.

27. **Vivere est agere**　*Latin* 'To live is to act'
　　　　　　　　　　　　　　　　　　　—Sewall (U.S.).

28. **Wrth ein ffrwythau ein hadnabyddir**　*Welsh* 'Let us be known by our actions'
　　　　　　　　　　　　　—Ellis (of Merinoth).

29. **Wrth ein ffrwyth yr adnabyddir**　*Welsh* 'We are known by our actions'
　　　　　　　　　　　　　　　　　　　　　—Ellis.

ADMIRATION (*See also* PRAISE.)

1. **Nil admirari**　*Latin* 'Not to admire'
　　　　　　—Bolingbroke, Clare (E.), Carew (B.).

3. **Pauca suspexi, pauciora despexi**　*Latin* 'I have admired few things, I have despised fewer'
　　　　　　　　　　　　　　　　　　　—Berkeley.

4. **Postera laude recens**　*Latin* 'Ever fresh in the admiration of posterity'
　　　　　　　　　　　　　　　　　—Hardinge (V.).

5. **Suspice Teucro**　*Latin* 'Admire Teucer'
　　　　　　　　　　　　　　　　　—Tucker (U.S.).

ADVANCE (*See also* IMPROVEMENT.)

1. **Advance**
　　　—Brand; Ferrier; Goole B. C., U.K., Spiers (of Eldershe).

2. **Advance with courage**
　　　　　　　　　　　　　　　—Marjoribanks (Bt.).

3. **Aequo pede propera**　*Latin* 'Hasten with steady pace'
　　　　　　　　　　　　　　　　　　—East (Bt.).

4. **Avance!**　*French* 'Advance!'
　　　　—Collyr (of Norwich), Long, Portman (E.).

5. **Avancez!** *French* 'Advance!'
—Chalmers (of Culto), Chambers (of Scotland), Churton, Hill (Bt.).

6. **Avant!** *French* 'Forward!'
—Stewart (Bt.), Stuart (Bt.).

7. **Avant sans peur** *French* 'Forward without fear'
—Seton-Karr.

8. **Avauncez et archez bien** *French* 'Advance and shoot well'
—Swinnerton.

9. **Ay, forward**
—Brand (of Baberton).

10. **Bonne espérance et droit en avant** *French* 'Forward, good hope and right!'
—Nugent.

11. **Boutez en avant** *French* 'Push forward'
—Barry (Co. Chester), Barrymore (E.), Fowle (co. Wilts).

12. **Cadernid, cyfiawnder, cynnydd** *Welsh* 'Stability, justice, progress'
—Barry B. C., U.K.

13. **Cum progressu cantus** *Latin* 'Singing while advancing'
—Seaton, Seton.

14. **Droyt et devaunt** *Old French* 'Right and forward'
—Drury.

15. **En avant** *French* 'Forward'
—D'Eyncourt, Lucy.

16. **En avant si je puis** *French* 'Forward, if I am able'
—Warren-Warren.

17. **For-d-ward**
—Strachen (Bt.).

18. **Fordward**
—Balfour.

19. **Forward**
—Castle-Steuart (E.), Stewart (of Athenry, Bt.), Queensbury (M.), Ker, Ogilvie, Ogilvy (Bt.), Carrel, Douglas, Sandby, Howales, Strachan, Stirling (Bt.), Campbell, Balfour, Speir, Wemyss (E.), Ward.

20. **Forward, kind heart**
—Bell.

21. **Forward, non temere**   *Eng. and Latin* 'Forward, not rashly'
—Balfour.

22. **Forward in the name of God**
—Lothian (M.).

23. **Forward ours**
—Seton (of Culbeg and Tough, Scotland).

24. **Forward without fear**
—Gordon (of Embo, bt.).

25. **Gang forrit**   *Scots Dialect*
—Kennedar.

26. **Gang forward**   *Scots Dialect*
—Stirling (Bt.), Stirling (of Achoyle), Keir.

27. **Gang through**   *Scots Dialect*
—Sterling.

28. **Go on, and persevere**
—Nichol.

29. **Go straight, and fear not**
—Le Hart.

30. **Go through**
—Brenton (Bt.).

31. **Hazard, zet (yet) forward**
—Seton, Winton (E.).

32. **I press forward**
—Croall.

33. **Ire in adversa**   *Latin* 'To advance against adversity'
—Stokes (Bt.).

34. **J'avance**   *French* 'I advance'
—Bartram, East, Ker (of Abbot Rule).

35. **J'avance. Foy en Dieu**   *Old French* 'I go forward. Faith in God'
—Bartram (U.S.).

36. **Muthig vorwartz**   *German* 'Forward boldly'
—Prance.

37. **Onward**
—Atherton, Bowring, Fraser-Mackintosh, Lorimer.

38. **Onward ever**
—Bessemer.

39. **On with you**
—Nagle.

40. **Passez avant**   *French* 'Pass forward'
—Carter, Waldegrave.

41. **Pass forward**
—Stewart.

42. **Per**   *Latin* 'Through'
—Bindlosse.

43. **Perge coepisti**   *Latin* 'Proceed and you have begun'
—Ten Broeck (U.S.).

44. **Perge et valeas**   *Latin* 'Proceed and you may succeed'
—Hutchinson (U.S.).

45. **Perge sed caute**   *Latin* 'Advance but cautiously'
—Jenkins (of Bicton).

46. **Pergo sursum**   *Latin* 'I advance upward'
—Romans.

47. **Poussez en avant**   *French* 'Push forward'
—Barry.

48. **Press forward**
—Grissell, Mortimer.

49. **Press through**
—Borelands, Cockburn, Young (of Marlow, bt.).

50. **Progredere ne regredere**   *Latin* 'Advance, do not retreat'
—Honyman (Bt.).

51. **Progredi non regredi**   *Latin* 'To advance and not retreat'
—Rutledge (U.S.).

52. **Progredior**   *Latin* 'I advance'
—Sharp.

53. **Right onward**
—Doane (U.S.).

54. **Si j'avance, suivez-moi; si je fuis, tuez-moi; si je meurs, vengez-moi**   *French* 'If I advance, follow me; if I flee, kill me; if I die, avenge me'
—La Roche-Jaquelin.

55. **Tendimus**   *Latin* 'We go forward'
—Craik.

56. **Through**
—Hamilton (D.), Hamilton (of Silverston, bt.), Hamilton (of the Mount, Co. Middlesex, bt.), Hamilton (of Woodbrook, bt.), Hamilton (of Brecon, bt.), Hamilton (Co. Meath, etc.), Abercorn (M.).

57. **Thrust on**
—Thruston (of Cranbrook).

58. **Ultra pergere** *Latin* 'To advance farther'
—Lyndhurst (B.).

59. **Virtute promoveo** *Latin* 'I advance by virtue'
—Sideserf (of Rochlaw).

ADVERSITY (*See also* DANGER; FORTITUDE; HOSTILITY; SUFFERING.)

1. **Ad astra per ardua** *Latin* 'To the stars through difficulties'
—Drummond (of Midhope).

2. **Ad astra per aspera** *Latin* 'To the stars through difficulties'
—State of Kansas.

3. **Adversa virtute repello** *Latin* 'I repel adversity by virtue'
—Denison, Dennistoun, Londesborough (B.), Medhurst.

4. **Adversis major, par secundis** *Latin* 'Greater than adversity, a match for prosperity'
—Bulwer, Forbes.

5. **Adverso fortior** *Latin* 'Stronger than adversity'
—Clifton-Dicconson, Dicconson.

6. **Ardua difficilia ascensu** *Latin* 'Heights are hard to climb'
—Anna Dorothee, Duchess of Saxony (1657–1704).

7. **Arduis saepe, metu nunquam** *Latin* 'Often in difficulties, never in fear'
—Brassey (B.).

8. **Aspera me juvant** *Latin* 'Difficulties delight me'
—Low.

9. **A tribulacione** *Latin* 'By tribulation'
—Cokain.

10. **Constantia in ardua** *Latin* 'Perseverance against difficulty'
—Harland (Co. York).

11. **Dabunt aspera rosas** *Latin* 'Rough ground will produce roses'
—Mushet.

12. **Difficiles sed fructuosae** *Latin* 'Difficulties, but rewarding ones'
—Appleton (U.S.).

13. **Difficilia quae pulchra** *Latin* 'Things which are beautiful are difficult'
—Elford (Bt.).

14. **Dulcius ex asperis** *Latin* 'The sweeter because obtained by hardships'
—Fergusson (Bt.), Ferguson.

15. **Dura pati virtus** *Latin* 'Suffering hardships is a virtue'
—August, Duke of Saxony-Lauenburg (1577–1656).

16. **Dura placent fortibus** *Latin* 'Strong men love hardships'
—Friedrich Karl, Duke of Württemberg (1652–98).

17. **Duris non frangor** *Latin* 'I am not disheartened by difficulties'
—Mure (of Caldwell), Muir, Moore (of Corswall).

18. **E spinis** *Latin* 'From among thorns'
—Delap, Dunlop (of Garnkirk).

19. **Fidelis in adversis** *Latin* 'Faithful in adversity'
—Hamilton

20. **Fidelitas in adversis** *Latin* 'Fidelity in adversity'
—Fuller.

21. **Fides in adversis** *Latin* 'Faith in adversity'
—Wolf, Woolfe.

22. **Fixus adversa sperno** *Latin* 'Firm, I despise adversity'
—Hamerton (of Hellifield).

23. **Forti et fidele nihil difficile** *Latin* 'For the strong and faithful nothing is difficult'
—Allen (U.S.).

24. **Fortis in arduis** *Latin* 'Strong in difficulties'
—Middleton B. C., U.K.

25. **Haec aspera terrent** *Latin* 'These hardships terrify'
—Moubray.

26. **Hic labor** *Latin* 'This is the difficulty'
—[after Virgil, *Aen.* vi. 129.] Dee.

27. **Hic labor, hoc opus** *Latin* 'This is the difficulty, this the task'
—[after Vergil, *Aen.* vi. 129.] Mortlake.

28. **Hoc ardua vincere docet** *Latin* 'This teaches us to overcome difficulties'
—Winchester.

29. **Impelle obstantia** *Latin* 'Thrust aside obstacles'
—Arthur.

30. **In adversis idem** *Latin* 'The same in adversity'
—Duke (U.S.).

31. **In ardua nitor** *Latin* 'I contend against difficulties'
—Halkerston.

32. **In ardua petit** *Latin* 'He searches after things difficult of attainment'
—Malcolm (of Poltalloch).

33. **In ardua tendit** *Latin* 'He reaches towards things difficult of attainment'
—McAllum, McCallem, Malcolm (of Burnfort).

34. **In ardua virtus** *Latin* 'Virtue against difficulties'
—Leathes (of Herringfleet), Wolstenholme.

35. **In arduis fortis** *Latin* 'Strong in adversity'
—Fordyce.

36. **In arduis viget virtus** *Latin* 'Virtue flourishes in adversity'
—Gurdon (of Letton, Cranworth, and Barnham Broom, Co. Norfolk), Gurdon-Rebow, Dorien, Magens.

37. **In prosperis time, in adversis spera** *Latin* 'In prosperity, fear, in adversity, hope'
—Gabriel.

38. **In rebus arctis** *Latin* 'In straitened circumstances'
—Frye.

39. **Ire in adversa** *Latin* 'To advance against adversity'
—Stokes (Bt.).

40. **Juvant aspera fortes** *Latin* 'Difficulties delight the brave'
—Steuart.

41. **Juvant aspera probum** *Latin* 'Misfortunes benefit the good man'
—Denham (Bt.), Steuart (of Coltness, bt.), Stewart.

42. **Labor omnia vincit** *Latin* 'Perseverance overcomes all difficulties'
—Brown, Cutler, Chaplin, Burder, Daniel (Co. Stafford), Eddington, McNair, Prattman.

43. **Luctor, at emergam** *Latin* 'I struggle, but I shall recover'
—Maitland.

44. **Luctor, non mergor** *Latin* 'I struggle, but am not overwhelmed'
—Glass.

45. **Mal au tour** *French* 'Misfortune to the tower'
—Patten.

46. **Malis obsta** *Latin* 'Resist misfortunes'
—Urmston (of Warrington).

47. **Nec aspera terrent** *Latin* 'Nor do hardships cause us fear'
—Hanoverian Guelphic Order, 3rd (King's Own) Hussars,
8th Foot (King's Liverpool Regt.), 14th Foot (Prince of
Wales' Own), 23rd Foot (Royal Welsh Fusiliers), 25th
Foot (King's Own Scottish Borderers), 27th Foot (1st
Batt. Inniskilling Fusiliers).

48. **Nec aspera terrent** *Latin* 'Difficulties do not daunt'
—Order of the Guelph (Britain), Tyler.

49. **Ne cede arduis** *Latin* 'Yield not to difficulties'
—Troubridge (Bt.).

50. **Ne cede malis** *Latin* 'Yield not to misfortunes'
—Albemarle (E.); Doig; Keppel; Herne Bay U. D. C.,
U.K.

51. **Ne cede malis; sed contra** *Latin* 'Yield not to misfortunes; but
oppose them'
—Canning (V.), Garvagh (B.), Stratford (B.).

52. **Nil arduum** *Latin* 'Nothing is difficult'
—Gordon (of Banff).

53. **Nil mihi tollit hyems** *Latin* 'No bad weather takes anything from
me'
—Irvine.

54. **Nil mortalibus arduum** *Latin* 'Nothing is too hard for mortals'
—Kater.

55. **Nitor in adversum** *Latin* 'I contend against adversity'
—Gooding, Horner.

56. **Nos aspera juvant** *Latin* 'Difficulties benefit us'
—Louis, Lowis.

57. **Par ardua liberi** *Latin* 'Free through difficulties'
—Pitt.

58. **Per angusta ad augusta** *Latin* 'Through difficulties to honors'
—Christall, Massareene (V.), Skiffington.

59. **Per ardua** *Latin* 'Through difficulties'
—Curtis (of Gatcombe, bt.), Clarkson, Crookshank, Berry
(Bt.), Drake (Bt.), McIntyre, McEntire, Stubbert,
Masterton, Tailour.

60. **Per ardua ad alta** *Latin* 'Through straits to heights'
—Achany; Birmingham University, U.K.; Hannay (Bt.);
Hall; Hanman.

61. **Per ardua ad summa** *Latin* 'Through difficulties to the heights'
—Beddington and Wallington B. C., U.K.

62. **Per ardua fama**   *Latin* 'Through difficulties, fame'
—Whyte.

63. **Per ardua stabilis**   *Latin* 'Firm in adversity'
—Henshaw, Mann (of Ditchingham, co. Suffolk).

64. **Per ardua stabilis esto**   *Latin* 'Be firm through difficulties'
—Dendy.

65. **Per ardua surgo**   *Latin* 'I rise through difficulties'
—Fenton, Mahon.

66. **Per aspera ad astra**   *Latin* 'Through hardships to the stars'
—Christian Albert, Duke of Holstein-Gottorp (1641–94);
Friedrich I, Duke of Saxony-Gotha and Altenburg
(1646–91); August, Count von der Lippe (d. 1701).

67. **Per damna per caedes**   *Latin* 'Through losses, through carnage'
—Bosanquet, Boyton.

68. **Per juga, per fluvios**   *Latin* 'Across precipices, through torrents'
—Harland.

69. **Per mille ardua**   *Latin* 'Through a thousand difficulties'
—Millerd.

70. **Per pericula ad decus ire juvat**   *Latin* 'He delights to go through
adversity to glory'
—Scarborough B. C., U.K.

71. **Per tela per hostes**   *Latin* 'Through arrows and enemies'
—Brymer.

72. **Per tot discrimina**   *Latin* 'Through so many crises'
—[Vergil, *Aen.* i. 204.] Maximilian I, Emperor of
Germany (1459–1519).

73. **Plus spinis quam ferro**   *Latin* 'More by thorns than the sword'
—Richardson.

74. **Praeclarius quo difficilius**   *Latin* 'The more difficult, the more
honorable'
—Fountain.

75. **Prudentia in adversos**   *Latin* 'Prudence in adversity'
—Tollet (of Betley), Wickstead.

76. **Pulchrior ex arduis**   *Latin* 'The brighter from difficulties'
—Mackenzie (of Coul, bt.).

77. **Quid nobis ardui**   *Latin* 'What is hard for us?'
—Kensington B. C., U.K.

78. **Rebus in adversis spes mea Christus erit** *Latin* 'In adversity Christ shall be my hope'
— Bernhard, Prince of Anhalt (1572–96).

79. **Recta sed ardua** *Latin* 'Proper but difficult'
— Lindsay (U.S.).

80. **Rien sans peine** *French* 'Nothing without difficulty'
— Johnson (U.S.).

81. **Secure vivere mors est** *Latin* 'To live without trouble is death'
— Dayrell (of Lillingston).

82. **Sperat infestis** *Latin* 'He hopes in adversity'
— [Horace, *Car*. ii. 10, 13.] Colborne, Seaton (B.).

83. **Spero infestis, metuo secundis** *Latin* 'I hope in adversity, I fear in prosperity'
— Ellerton, Ludlow (E.), Stewart.

84. **Sub onere crescit** *Latin* 'He thrives under the burden'
— Fergusson.

85. **There is no difficulty to him that wills**
— Hains (U.S.).

86. **Troimh chruadal** *Scots Gaelic* 'Through hardships'
— McIntyre.

87. **Tu ne cede malis** *Latin* 'Yield not to misfortunes'
— Amery, Damer, De Meuron, Parry, Riddock, Steere, Turner.

88. **Tu ne cede malis, sed contra audentior ito** *Latin* 'Yield not to misfortunes, but go the more boldly against them'
— [Vergil, *Aen*. vi. 95.] Cooke (of Cordangan).

89. **Virescit in arduis virtus** *Latin* 'Virtue flourishes in difficulties'
— Keir.

90. **Virtus viget in arduis** *Latin* 'Virtue flourishes in difficulties'
— Gurdon.

AGE

1. **Cur senio praelata juventus'** *Latin* 'Why is youth preferred to old age?'
— Louis de la Trémouille (1460–1525).

2. **Gottes furcht die schönste Tugend, Gewöhnt das Alter, zeirt die Jugend** *German* 'Fear of God is the fairest virtue; it reconciles old age, and adorns youth'
— Sophie, Princess of Anhalt (1654–1724).

3. **L'antiquité ne peut pas l'abolir**   *French* 'Antiquity cannot abolish it'

—Conroy.

4. **Maturity**

—Bartlett (U.S.).

5. **Nunquam senescit**   *Latin* 'It never grows old'

—Gloag.

6. **Old age is a virtue**

—Van Rensselaer (U.S.).

7. **Omnia orta occidunt et aucta senescunt**   *Latin* 'All that is passes away, and all that grows grows old'
—[Sallust, *Bellum Jugurth*, ii.] Casimir, Margrave of Brandenburg-Baireuth (1481–1527).

8. **To rock the cradle of reposing age**

—Foster (U.S.).

9. **Toujours jeune**   *French* 'Always young'

—Young.

10. **Vetustas dignitatem generat**   *Latin* 'Age begets dignity'
—East Retford B. C., U.K.

AGGRESSION (*See also* CONFLICT; FIERCENESS; FORCE; HOSTILITY; WAR.)

1. **Ainsi je frappe**   *French* 'Thus I strike'
—Charles the Bold (1433–77).

2. **Bualim se**   *Gaelic* 'I strike him'

—MacCartan.

3. **Certo dirigo ictu**   *Latin* 'I aim with a sure blow'

—Thurburn.

4. **Ferio**   *Latin* 'I strike'

—Littlejohn.

5. **Ferio sed sano**   *Latin* 'I strike, but I heal'

—Sharpe.

6. **Feros ferio**   *Latin* 'I strike the fierce'
—Chisholm, Gooden-Chisholm.

7. **Frappe fort**   *French* 'Strike hard'
—Thackwell, Wodehouse (B.), Wodehouse.

8. **Frappez avec raison**   *French* 'Strike with reason'
—Parry-Mitchell.

9. **Frappez fort**   *French* 'Strike hard'
—Netherwood.

10. **Grossos qui rodit roditur**   *Latin* 'Who smiteth the Grouse is smit'
—Growse (of Beldeston, co. Suffolk).

11. **His calcabo gentes**   *Latin* 'By these I will trample on the nations'
—Colclough.

12. **Ictus non victus**   *Latin* 'Struck, not conquered'
—Shute.

13. **Quis accursabit?**   *Latin* 'Who shall assail?'
—Hamilton.

14. **Recte ferio**   *Latin* 'I strike straight'
—Bedell-Sivright, Sivright.

15. **Smite on, quoth Smith**
—Smith.

16. **Strike**
—Hawke (B.).

17. **Strike alike**
—Lauder.

18. **Strike Dakyns, the devil's in the hempe**
—Dakyns (of Derbyshire).

19. **Strike sure**
—Greig.

AGRICULTURE (*See also* **COMMERCE; FLORA; GROWTH; HARVEST.**)

1. **Agriculture and commerce**
—Maidstone B. C., U.K.; State of Tennessee.

2. **Evertendo faecundat**   *Latin* 'It renders fruitful by turning over'
—Imbrie.

3. **Non omnis fert omnia tellus**   *Latin* 'Not every soil gives every fruit'
—[Vergil, Georg. iv. 39.] August, Duke of Braunschweig-Wolfenbüttel (1579–1666).

4. **Oni heuir ni fedir**   *Welsh* 'Without sowing one cannot reap'
—Carmarthen R. D. C., U.K.

5. **Pylkington Polledowne**   *Middle English* 'Pilkington polls (mows) downe (meadows)'
—Pilkington (of Blackburn).

6. **Qui plantavit curabit** *Latin* 'He who planted it will care for it'
—Roosevelt (U.S.).

7. **Trade and plantations**
—Commissioners of Trade and Plantations.

AMBITION (*See also* SELF-RELIANCE.)

1. **Alienus ambitioni** *Latin* 'Averse to ambition'
—Hawkins.

2. **Ambition sans envie** *French* 'Ambition without envy'
—Walch.

ANCESTRY (*See also* PARENTS; PAST, THE.)

1. **Avi numerantur avorum** *Latin* 'A long train of ancestry is enumerated'
—Grantley (B.), Norton, Hitch, Perton, Pryce, Rede, Turberville.

2. **Avitae gloriae memor** *Latin* 'Mindful of ancestral glory'
—Acton.

3. **Avito evehor honore** *Latin* 'I am exalted by ancestral honor'
—Holmes, Burnes.

4. **Avito jure** *Latin* 'By ancestral right'
—Wheeler.

5. **Avito non sine honore** *Latin* 'Not without ancestral honor'
—Leppington.

6. **Avitos juvat honores** *Latin* 'He maintains his ancestral honors'
—Wishart.

7. **Avitos novit honores** *Latin* 'He knows his ancestral honors'
—Gusthart.

8. **Avito viret honore** *Latin* 'He flourishes through the honor of his ancestors'
—Bute (M.), Stuart de Decies (B.), Stewart de Rothsay (B.), Mackenzie, Wharncliffe (B.), Turner.

9. **Avorum honor** *Latin* 'The honor of my ancestors'
—Ryland.

10. **Avorum honori** *Latin* 'For the honor of our ancestors'
—Barne.

11. **Cultui avorum fidelis** *Latin* 'Faithful in honoring my ancestors'
—Trappes.

12. **Dat decus origini**   *Latin* 'He gives honor to his ancestry'
—Hamilton.

13. **Decori decus addit avito**   *Latin* 'He adds honor to that of his ancestors'
—Erskine, Kelly.

14. **Drwy rynwedd gwaed**   *Welsh* 'By virtue of blood'
—Walwyn.

15. **Et patribus et posteritati**   *Latin* 'For both ancestors and posterity'
—Hitchin U. D. C., U.K.

16. **Exempla suorum**   *Latin* 'The examples of his ancestors'
—Innes (Bt.).

17. **Gronwi hil Gwernimon**   *Welsh* 'Gronow's of the race of princes'
—Gronow.

18. **Heroum filii**   *Latin* 'Sons of heroes'
—Wellington College, U.K.

19. **Hoc majorum opus**   *Latin* 'This is the work of my ancestors'
—Eliot, Eliot-Lockhart, Elliot.

20. **Hoc majorum virtus**   *Latin* 'The valor of my ancestors (won) this'
—Logan.

21. **Honestate vetustas stat**   *Latin* 'Ancestry is established by honor'
—Stewart (of Edinglassie).

22. **Macte virtute patrum**   *Latin* 'Honored for the valor of your fathers'
—Mackrell.

23. **Majores sequor**   *Latin* 'I follow my ancestors'
—Gordon.

24. **Majorum vestigia premo**   *Latin* 'I follow close on the footsteps of my ancestors'
—Seaton.

25. **Memor virtutis avitae**   *Latin* 'Mindful of ancestral virtue'
—De Windt.

26. **Multa virum durando saecula vincit**   *Latin* 'The many, enduring generations of men prevail'
—Gandolfi (D.).

27. **Non melior patribus**   *Latin* 'Not better than my ancestors'
—Hardinge.

28. **Paterni nominis patrimonium**   *Latin* 'The patrimony of a paternal name'
—Oakley (Bt.).

29. **Paternis suppar** *Latin* 'Nearly equal to ancestral glory'
—Rushout.

30. **Paterno robore tutus** *Latin* 'Safe in my ancestral strength'
—Scott.

31. **Pietate parentum** *Latin* 'By the piety of my forefathers'
—Tulloch.

32. **Prisco stirpe Hibernico** *Latin* 'Of an ancient Irish stock'
—Lennon.

33. **Repetens exempla suorum** *Latin* 'Following the example of his ancestors'
—Granville.

34. **Retinens vestigia famae** *Latin* 'Still treading in the footsteps of an honorable ancestry'
—Lister (of Armytage Park), Lloyd (of Leaton-knolls), Riblesdale (B.).

35. **Sequitur vestigia patrum** *Latin* 'He follows the footsteps of his ancestors'
—Irvine (of Inchray).

36. **Stare super vias antiquas** *Latin* 'To stand in the track of my ancestors'
—Bayning (B.).

37. **Stat religione parentum** *Latin* 'He continues in the religion of his forefathers'
—De Grey, Lucas (of Castle Thane).

38. **Stemmata quid faciunt?** *Latin* 'What avail pedigrees?'
—Baggalay, Hickman, Meyrick (of Goodrick Court).

39. **Suffibulatus majores sequor** *Latin* 'Having buckled on my armaments, I follow my ancestors'
—Hathorn, Stewart.

40. **Tam genus quam virtus** *Latin* 'As much lineage as virtue'
—Lunden.

41. **Vestigia premo majorum** *Latin* 'I tread in the footsteps of my ancestors'
—Ludwig Rudolf, Duke of Braunschweig in Blankenburg (1671–1735).

42. **Virtus durat avorum** *Latin* 'The virtue of my ancestors remains'
—Seton.

43. **Virtute avorum** *Latin* 'By the virtue of ancestors'
—Watkins.

44. **Virtute dignus avorum** *Latin* 'Worthy of the virtue of his ancestors'

—Worthinton.

45. **Virtutem avorum aemulus** *Latin* 'Rivalling the virtue of the ancestors'

—Mortimer (U.S.).

46. **Virtutis avorum praemium** *Latin* 'The reward of my ancestors valor'

—Templeton (V.), Upton.

ANGER (*See also* AGGRESSION; HOSTILITY.)

1. **Est nobilis ira leonis** *Latin* 'The rage of the lion is noble'

—Stuart.

2. **Furor arma ministrat** *Latin* 'Rage furnishes arms'
   —[Vergil, *Aen.* i. 150.] Baynes (Bt.).

3. **Ira leonis nobilis** *Latin* 'The anger of the lion is noble'

—Croome.

4. **Iram leonis nole timere** *Latin* 'Fear not the anger of the lion'

—Long.

5. **Nobilis est ira leonis** *Latin* 'The wrath of the lion is noble'
   —Inglis (Bt.), Inglis (of Stewart, Buchanan, etc.), Broome.

6. **Nobilis ira** *Latin* 'Noble in anger'
   —Creighton-Stuart, Stewart (of Tillicoultry, bt.).

7. **Nobilis ira leonis** *Latin* 'The lion's anger is noble'

—Ross.

8. **Prenez en ire** *French* 'Take in ire'

—La Fout.

9. **Ratione, non irâ** *Latin* 'By reason, not by rage'

—Small (of Curriehill).

ANIMALS (*See also* BIRDS.)

1. **Addit frena feris** *Latin* 'He puts bridles on wild beasts'

—Milner (Bt.).

2. **Agnus Dei salvator meus** *Latin* 'The Lamb of God, my savior'

—Haslam.

3. **Agnus in pace, leo in bello** *Latin* 'A lamb in peace, a lion in war'
   —Edmonds.

4. **Anguis in herba**   *Latin* 'A snake in the grass'
    —Anguish (Co. Norfolk).

5. **Be wise as a serpent, harmless as a dove**
    —[Matt. x. 16.] Lewis.

6. **Cabar feidh**   *Scots Gaelic* 'The antler of the deer'
    —Seaforth Highlanders.

7. **Cautus metuit foveam lupus**   *Latin* 'The cautious wolf fears the snare'
    —Caton (of Binbrook).

8. **Cave cervum**   *Latin* 'Beware the stag'
    —Ridgeley (U.S.).

9. **Cave Leam**   *Latin* 'Beware the lioness'
    —Lea.

10. **Cave lupum**   *Latin* 'Beware the wolf'
    —Hubbard.

11. **Cervus non servus**   *Latin* 'A stag not enslaved'
    —Goddard (of Swindon), Thorold (Bt.).

12. **Christus pelicanus et agnus**   *Latin* 'Christ my pelican and my lamb'
    —Godfrey.

13. **Cruce non leone fides**   *Latin* 'My trust is in the cross, not in the lion'
    —Matthew (of Coggeshall, Co. Essex).

14. **Deo adverso, leo vincitur**   *Latin* 'God opposing, the lion is conquered'
    —Newenham.

15. **Dinna waken sleeping dogs**
    —Robertson (of Lude).

16. **Ecce Agnus Dei, qui tollit peccata mundi**   *Latin* 'Behold the Lamb of God, which taketh away the sin of the world'
    —[John i. 29.] Tallow-Chandlers' Company.

17. **Est nobilis ira leonis**   *Latin* 'The rage of the lion is noble'
    —Stuart.

18. **Esto bonus et pius ne sit leo te magis impavidus**   *Latin* 'Be good and pious, let not the lion be more undaunted than thou'
    —Wintringham.

19. **Ex cruce leo**   *Latin* 'From the cross a lion'
    —Terry.

20. **Ex unguibus leonis** *Latin* 'From the claws of the lion'
            —Ogilvie.

21. **Feed ye my sheep**
            —Shepherd.

22. **Feroci fortior** *Latin* 'Bolder than the ferocious (boar)'
            —Lockhart (of Birkhill).

23. **Fides leone fortior** *Latin* 'Faith is mightier than the lion'
            —Motley (U.S.).

24. **Floreo in ungue leonis** *Latin* 'I bloom in the lion's claw'
            —King.

25. **Fortior leone justus** *Latin* 'The just man is stronger than a lion'
            —Goodricke (of Ribstone Hall).

26. **Fortis ceu leo fidus** *Latin* 'Strong as a lion and faithful'
            —McBrayne.

27. **Homo homini vulpes** *Latin* 'Man is a fox towards his fellow man'
            —Wolseley (of Wolseley, bt.).

28. **In cruce non in leone fides** *Latin* 'In the cross not in the lion is my faith'
            —Lisle.

29. **Ira leonis nobilis** *Latin* 'The anger of the lion is noble'
            —Croome.

30. **Iram leonis nole timere** *Latin* 'Fear not the anger of the lion'
            —Long.

31. **Latet anguis in herba** *Latin* 'The snake lurks in the grass'
            —Anguish.

32. **Leo de Juda est robur nostrum** *Latin* 'The Lion of Judah is our strength'
            —Borlase, Warren.

33. **Leo inimicis amicis columba** *Latin* 'The lion for my enemies, the dove for my friends'
            —Dilke.

34. **Leoni non sagittis fido** *Latin* 'I trust to the lion not to my arrows'
            —Egerton.

35. **Mauvais chiens** *French* 'Wicked dogs'
            —Machell.

36. **Mors lupi agnis vita** *Latin* 'The death of the wolf is life to the lambs'
            —Ouseley (Bt.), Rendell.

37. **Morte leonis vita**   *Latin* 'Life by the death of the lion'
           —Vaux (B.).

38. **Na bean d'on chat gun lamhainu**   *Scots Gaelic* 'Touch not a cat but with a glove'
           —Macpherson (of Cluny).

39. **Nobilis est ira leonis**   *Latin* 'The wrath of the lion is noble'
     —Inglis (Bt.), Inglis (of Stewart, Buchanan, etc.), Broome.

40. **Nobilis ira leonis**   *Latin* 'The lion's anger is noble'
           —Ross.

41. **Noli irritare leonem**   *Latin* 'Irritate not the lion'
           —Abbs, Underwood.

42. **Noli irritare leones**   *Latin* 'Do not exasperate the lions'
           —Lyons (B.), Lyons (of Ledestown).

43. **Non leoni sed Deo**   *Latin* 'Not for the lion, but for God'
           —Maddock.

44. **Omnia subjecisti sub pedibus—oves et boves**   *Latin* 'Thou hast put all things under his feet: all sheep and oxen'
     —[after Ps., viii. 6–7.] Butchers' Company.

45. **Prudens sicut serpens**   *Latin* 'Wise as the serpent'
           —Pole.

46. **Quercus glandifera amica porcis**   *Latin* 'The acorn-bearing oak is kind to pigs'
           —Allen.

47. **Quid leone fortius?**   *Latin* 'What is braver than a lion?'
           —Clayton (Bt.).

48. **Qui non ciconia tigris**   *Latin* 'Who is not a stork is a tiger'
           —Browne.

49. **Ramosa cornua cervi**   *Latin* 'The branching horns of the stag'
           —Woodstock B. C., U.K.

50. **Satis est prostrasse leoni**   *Latin* 'It is enough to a lion to have laid low'
           —Salusbury (Bt.).

51. **Sic mihi si fueris tu leo qualis ens**   *Latin* 'If thus you, lion, do to me, what a lion you will be!'
           —Rant.

52. **Sionnach aboo**   *Gaelic* 'The fox defying'
           —Fox.

53. **Taurum cornibus prende**   *Latin* 'Take the bull by the horns'
           —Kettlewell.

54. The righteous are bold as a lion
                                        —McBrayne.

55. Touch not the cat bot (i.e., without) a glove
                          —Gillies, MacPherson, McGilleray, Grant, Gillespie,
                              McBean, Mackintosh, McIntosh, McCrombie,
                                                          Macpherson.

56. Ut aquila versus coelum   *Latin* 'As an eagle towards the sky'
                                        —Bowdoin (U.S.).

57. Ut aspirat cervus   *Latin* 'As the hart panteth'
                                        —Staveley.

58. Vellera fertis oves   *Latin* 'Sheep, ye bear the wool'
                                        —Elliot.

59. Vivit Leo de Tribu Juda   *Latin* 'The Lion of the Tribe of Judah
     lives'
                                        —Ethiopia.

60. Y blaidd nid ofnaf   *Welsh* 'I fear not the wolf'
                                        —Jennings.

61. Y cyfiawn sydd hy megis llew   *Welsh* 'The righteous is bold like a
     lion'
                                        —Hughes (of Alltwyd).

ART

1. Arcus, artes, astra   *Latin* 'The bow, arts, and stars'
                                        —Birney (of Salin), Burmey.

2. Ars bona violentia   *Latin* 'Violence is a fine art'
                                        —Baker.

3. Ars longa, vita brevis   *Latin* 'Art is long, life is short'
                                        —Millais (Bt.).

4. Ars mercede viget   *Latin* 'Art flourishes by patronage'
                                        —Reading School, U.K.

5. Art, industry, contentment
                                        —Basildon Development Corp.

6. Arte et industria   *Latin* 'By art and industry'
                                        —Baynes.

7. Arte et labore   *Latin* 'By art and labor'
                                        —Smythe.

8. Arte fideque   *Latin* 'By art and faith'
                                        —Orrock.

9. **Arte firmus**   *Latin* 'Firm by art'
           —Mason.

10. **Artes honorabit**   *Latin* 'He will do honor to the arts'
           —Hanger.

11. **Artes/scientias/humanitates**   *Latin* 'Arts/sciences/humanities'
       —New Mexico Highlands University, Las Vegas, New Mexico.

12. **Arte utile facio**   *Latin* 'I make what is useful by my art'
           —Craig.

13. **Arte vel Marte**   *Latin* 'By art or force'
           —Deans, Dundas.

14. **Artibus et armis**   *Latin* 'By arts and arms'
           —Elton (Bt.).

15. **Arts and trades united**
           —Fanmakers' Company.

16. **Deo adjuvante arte et industria floret**   *Latin* 'With God's help, it flourishes by art and industry'
           —Kidderminster B. C., U.K.

17. **Honor alit artes**   *Latin* 'Honor fosters the arts'
           —Burton-upon-Trent C. B. C., U.K.

18. **Honor nourishes the arts**
       —International Fine Arts College, Miami, Florida.

19. **Honos alit artes**   *Latin* 'Honor nourishes arts'
           —Greenhill.

20. **In scientia veritas in arte honestas**   *Latin* 'Truth in science, honesty in art'
           —Wells (Bt.).

21. **Kunst, Macht, Kunst**   *German* 'Art, might, art'
           —Papworth.

22. **Language/ Art/ Science**
       —Newcomb College, New Orleans, Louisiana.

23. **Marte et arte**   *Latin* 'By valor and skill'
       —Drummond (of London), Maguire, Nevoy, Jones (of Cranmer Hall, Co. Norfolk, bt.).

24. **Marte non Arte**   *Latin* 'By arms not art'
           —Neasmith.

25. **Marte vel arte**   *Latin* 'By force or by art'
       —Barnim XII, Duke of Pomerania zu Rügenwalde (1549–1603).

26. **Non minor est virtus quam quaerere, arte tueri**   *Latin* 'Nor is it less valor to defend by art than to obtain'
—Master.

27. **Pro arte non marte**   *Latin* 'For art, not strength'
—Blagrave.

28. **Prosunt gentibus artes**   *Latin* 'Arts benefit the people'
—Bermondsey B. C., U.K.

29. **Quae prosunt omnibus artes**   *Latin* 'Arts that are beneficial to all'
—Surgeons' Company.

30. **Quaesita marte tuenda arte**   *Latin* 'Things obtained by war must be defended by art'
—Luttrell.

31. **Scientiis/ artibus/ religioni**   *Latin* 'By knowledge, by art, by religion'
—Mercer University, Macon, Georgia.

32. **Vel arte vel Marte**   *Latin* 'Either by art or strength'
—Baines, Deans (of Loeg).

33. **Vires/ artes/ mores**   *Latin* 'Strength/ arts/ morals'
—Florida State University, Tallahassee, Florida.

ASPIRATION (*See also* AMBITION; DESTINATION; EFFORT; GOALS.)

1. **A bonis ad meliora**   *Latin* 'From good things to better'
—Goodwright.

2. **Ad alta**   *Latin* 'To high things'
—Cairnie.

3. **Ad ardua tendit**   *Latin* 'He attempts difficult things'
—McOlum.

4. **Ad astra**   *Latin* 'To the stars'
—Moorson, Bigsby.

5. **Ad astra nitamur semper ad optima**   *Latin* 'To the stars, to the best things, always our aim'
—Bigsby.

6. **Ad astra per ardua**   *Latin* 'To the stars through difficulties'
—Drummond (of Midhope).

7. **Ad astra per aspera**   *Latin* 'Through adversity to the stars'
—Campbell University, Buies Creek, North Carolina.

8. **Ad astra per aspera**   *Latin* 'To the stars through difficulties'
—State of Kansas.

9. **Ad astra sequor** *Latin* 'I follow to the stars'
—Tottenham (Co. Wexford).

10. **Ad coelos volans** *Latin* 'Flying to the heavens'
—Clavering, Cayton.

11. **Ad coelum tendit** *Latin* 'He directs his course towards heaven'
—Booker.

12. **Ad summum** *Latin* 'To the highest'
—University of Alaska, Fairbanks, Alaska.

13. **Affectat Olympo** *Latin* 'He aspires to heaven'
—Bell.

14. **Aim high**
—Minn.

15. **Ainsi et peut estre meilleur** *French* 'Thus and perhaps better'
—Rolleston, Stafford.

16. **Alis aspicit astra** *Latin* 'On wing he looks towards the stars'
—Carnegie.

17. **Alta pete** *Latin* 'Aim at high things'
—Glen, Fletcher.

18. **Alta petit** *Latin* 'He aims at high things'
—Marshall, Stott.

19. **Alta peto** *Latin* 'I aim at high things'
—Greenall, Smethurst, Sotherne.

20. **Altiora in votis** *Latin* 'Higher things are the object of my wishes'
—Des Voeux.

21. **Altiora petamus** *Latin* 'Let us strive for loftier things'
—University of Salford, Salford, U.K.

22. **Altiora pete** *Latin* 'Seek higher things'
—Gordon (of Tichmurie).

23. **Altiora petenda** *Latin* 'Higher things must be aimed at'
—Burke.

24. **Altiora petimus** *Latin* 'We seek higher things'
—Finsbury B. C., U.K.

25. **Altiora peto** *Latin* 'I seek higher things'
—Oliphant (of Newton, co. Perth), Warwick School, U.K.

26. **Altiora sequimur** *Latin* 'We follow after higher things'
—Pode.

27. **Altiora spero** *Latin* 'I hope higher things'
—Torr.

28. **Altiora videnda** *Latin* 'We must look to higher things'
                                                    —Honor.

29. **Altius ibunt qui ad summa nituntur** *Latin* 'They will rise highest
    who strive for the highest place'
                                        —Forbes (Bt.), Fordyce.

30. **Altius tendo** *Latin* 'I aim higher'
                                                    —Kinlock.

31. **Always to excel**
                                —Belgrave, Manningham, Neve.

32. **Aquila petit solem** *Latin* 'The eagle seeks the sun'
                                                    —Kendall.

33. **Ardua petit ardea** *Latin* 'The heron seeks high places'
                                                —Heron (Bt.).

34. **Ardua tendo** *Latin* 'I attempt difficult things'
                                                —Malcolm (Bt.).

35. **Ascendam** *Latin* 'I shall rise'
                                            —Kennaway (Bt.).

36. **Ascendo** *Latin* 'I rise'
                                                    —Catty.

37. **Aspira** *Latin* 'Aspire'
                                                    —Feld.

38. **Aspire, persevere, and indulge not**
                                                    —Adam.

39. **Aspire, persevere, trust**
                                                —Adams (U.S.).

40. **Aspiro** *Latin* 'I aspire'
                            —Bolton, Curry, M'Fell, Ramsay (Bt.).

41. **Caelestia sequor** *Latin* 'I follow heavenly things'
                                            —McDonald, Monro.

42. **Capta majora** *Latin* 'Seek greater things'
                                            —Geddes, or Geddeis.

43. **Cupio meliora** *Latin* 'I desire better things'
                                                    —Melliar.

44. **De mieux je pense en mieux** *French* 'From better I think to bet-
    ter'
                                                    —Brooke.

45. **Esto quod audes** *Latin* 'Be what you dare'
                                                    —Delway.

46. **Ewch yn uchaf** *Welsh* 'Go the highest'
—Wynn-Williams.

47. **Ewch yn uwch** *Welsh* 'Go higher'
—Radnorshire C. C., U.K.

48. **Excelsior** *Latin* 'Ever upward'
—State of New York, Steinthal.

49. **Haulte emprise** *Old French* 'High endeavor' or 'Noble undertaking'
—Haltemprice U. D. C., U.K.

50. **He seeks high deeds**
—Marshall.

51. **Higher**
—Galloway.

52. **In alta tende** *Latin* 'Aim at things on high'
—Webb.

53. **In sublime** *Latin* 'Upwards'
—Reid.

54. **Itur ad astra** *Latin* 'Our way is to the stars'
—Mackenzie, Mulchinock.

55. **Levavi oculos meos in montes** *Latin* 'I lifted up my eyes to the hills'
—Malvern U. D. C., U.K., Workington B. C., U.K.

56. **Majora sequor** *Latin* 'I pursue greater things'
—Haliburton.

57. **Majora tenta praesentibus aequus** *Latin* 'When equal to the present, attempt greater things'
—Lynch.

58. **Meliora sequentur** *Latin* 'They will pursue better things'
—Kelsall.

59. **Monte dessus** *French* 'Soar upward'
—Bunny.

60. **Montez toujours** *French* 'Aspire always'
—Walsham (Bt.).

61. **Non inferiora sequenda** *Latin* 'We must not follow meaner things'
—Butler.

62. **Onwards, upwards**
—Cox.

63. **Onward upward**
   —Kentucky State University, Frankfort, Kentucky.

64. **Per ardua ad alta** *Latin* 'Through straits to heights'
   —Achany; Birmingham University, U.K.; Hannay (Bt.);
   Hall; Hanman.

65. **Per ardua ad summa** *Latin* 'Through difficulties to the heights'
   —Beddington and Wallington B. C., U.K.

66. **Per aspera ad astra** *Latin* 'Through hardships to the stars'
   —Christian Albert, Duke of Holstein-Gottorp (1641–94);
   Friedrich I, Duke of Saxony-Gotha and Altenburg
   (1646–91); August, Count von der Lippe (d. 1701).

67. **Per castra ad astra** *Latin* 'Through the camp to the stars'
   —Nicholson.

68. **Petimus altiora** *Latin* 'We seek loftier things'
   —Cattley.

69. **Petit alta** *Latin* 'He seeks high things'
   —Abercrombie (Bt.).

70. **Quod sis esse velis nilque malis** *Latin* 'May you be what you wish
   to be and be far from evil'
   —Champion (U.S.).

71. **Quod sursum volo videre** *Latin* 'I would see what is above'
   —Dunraven (E.), Quin.

72. **Reach for the stars**
   —University of Central Florida, Orlando, Florida.

73. **Semper sursum** *Latin* 'Ever upwards'
   —Barrow-in-Furness C. B. C., U.K., Graham.

74. **Sublime petimus** or **Sublimia petimus** *Latin* 'We seek what is on
   high'
   —Cleghorn.

75. **Sublimiora petamus** *Latin* 'Let us seek higher things'
   —Biddulph (of Ledbury, Amroth Castle, Barton, etc.),
   Biddulph (Bt.).

76. **Sublimiora peto** *Latin* 'I seek higher things'
   —Jackson.

77. **Sublimiora quaero** *Latin* 'I seek higher things'
   —Wright.

78. **Sublimiora spectemus** *Latin* 'Let us regard loftier things'
   —Warren.

79. **Sublimis per ardua tendo** *Latin* 'I reach out through difficulty to the sublime'
—Chauncy (U.S.).

80. **Sub pondere sursum** *Latin* 'Beneath my load (I look) upward'
—Porterfield.

81. **Supera alta tenere** *Latin* 'To reach the lofty heavens'
—Seabury (U.S.).

82. **Superiora sequor** *Latin* 'I follow higher things'
—Ramsay.

83. **Sursum** *Latin* 'Upwards'
—Calandrine, Douglas, Hutchinson, Pringle, Scott.

84. **Sursum corda** *Latin* 'Hearts upwards'
—Howison, McGillycuddy.

85. **Tache sans tâche** *French* 'Strive (to be) without reproach'
—Carnagie (of North and Southesk), Patterson (of Kelvin Grove).

86. **Tende bene et alta pete** *Latin* 'Strive on well and seek high place'
—Entrance to Benthall Hall, Shropshire, England.

87. **Tendit ad astra** *Latin* 'He directs his gaze towards the stars'
—Maxwell.

88. **To each his farthest star**
—Surry Community College, Dobson, North Carolina.

89. **Together we aspire, together we achieve**
—Trinidad and Tobago.

90. **Video alta sequorque** *Latin* 'I see lofty objects and pursue them'
—Carnagie.

91. **Yet higher**
—Kinlock (of Gourdie).

ASSISTANCE (*See also* DIVINE GUIDANCE.)

1. **Always helping**
—Gravine (of Edinburgh).

2. **Audio et juvo** *Latin* 'I hear and assist'
—Harker.

3. **Auxilium** *Latin* 'Aid'
—Machin, Prickett.

4. **Cadenti porrigo dextram** *Latin* 'I extend my right hand to the falling'
—Pearse, King (Co. Somerset).

5. **Cuidich an righ** *Scots Gaelic* 'Assist the king'
—McDonnel, Seaforth Highlanders, U.K.

6. **Help**
—Foundling Hospital.

7. **Help at hand, brother**
—Muire.

8. **Help only those who help themselves**
—Andrew Carnegie.

9. **His nitimur et munimur** *Latin* 'We are supported and strengthened by these'
—Maconochie (of Meadowbank).

10. **Infirmis opitulare** *Latin* 'To help the weak'
—Kildahl.

11. **J'ayme porter secours** *Old French* 'I love to bring help'
—Porter (Bt.).

12. **Juvat dum lacerat** *Latin* 'It helps while it tears'
—Kroye.

13. **Juvat lacerat** *Latin* 'It helps (while) it tears'
—Knoye, Koehler.

14. **Juvo audaces clarior hinc honos** *Latin* 'I help the brave; hence, honor is more distinct'
—Buchanan (U.S.).

15. **Miseris auxilium (or) opem fero** *Latin* 'I bring help to the wretched'
—Malden.

16. **Miseris succurrere** *Latin* 'To help the unfortunate'
—Prince, Smyth (Co. Clare).

17. **Miseris succurrere disco** *Latin* 'I learn to succor the unfortunate'
—Dramond, Hinde, Hodgson, MacMillan, Soltau.

18. **Miseris succurro** *Latin* 'I succor the wretched'
—Macmillan-Scott, Scott.

19. **Non ignarus mali miseris succurrere disco** *Latin* 'Not unacquainted with misfortune, I learn to succor the wretched'
—Savage.

20. **Opiferque per orbem dicor** *Latin* 'I am called a bringer of help throughout the world'
>—Apothecaries' Company; Kadie, Kadle, Keddie.

21. **Pauperum solatio** *Latin* 'For consolation of the poor'
>—Order of St. Elizabeth (Brazil).

22. **To help people learn**
>—Leeward Community College, Pearl City, Hawaii.

23. **Utriusque auxilio** *Latin* 'By the help of both'
>—Spottiswood.

ATTEMPT (*See also* RISK.)

1. **Aut nunquam tentes aut perfice** *Latin* 'Either never attempt or accomplish'
>—Bennet, Creswell, Crouch, Day, Dorset (D.), Hustler, Sackville.

2. **Frisch gewagedt ist halb gewonnen** *German* 'Boldly ventured is half won'
>—Franz Albert, Duke of Saxony (1598–1642).

3. **Frisch gewagt und treu gemeint** *German* 'Boldly ventured and honestly intended'
>—Eberhard Ludwig, Duke of Württemberg (1676–1733).

4. **Nunquam tentes aut perfice** *Latin* 'Either never attempt, or accomplish'
>—Bennet.

5. **Tentanda via est** *Latin* 'The way must be tried'
>—Peckham (of Nyton), Stronge (Bt.), Wildman (of Newstead Abbey).

6. **Virtute experiamur** *Latin* 'We will attempt it with virtue'
>—Philipp, Duke of Schleswig-Holstein (1584–1663).

ATTENTIVENESS (*See also* LISTENING; VIGILANCE; WAKEFULNESS.)

1. **Age quod agis** *Latin* 'Attend to what you are doing'
>—Prevost (Bt.).

2. **Be ever mindful**
>—Campbell (of Moy).

3. **Be mindful**
>—Cawdor (E.), Campbell (Bt.), Calder, Clyde.

4. **Esto memor**   *Latin* 'Be mindful'
—Keats.

5. **Memor**   *Latin* 'Mindful'
—Russell.

6. **Memor esto**   *Latin* 'Be mindful'
—Campbell, Graham (of Killern), Hutchinson (of Edinburgh), McFell, McPhail.

7. **Memor et fidelis**   *Latin* 'Mindful and faithful'
—Selsey (B.), Reed, Peachy.

8. **Regard bien**   *French* 'Attend well'
—Milligan, Milliken (of Renfrew).

9. **Tak tent**   *Scots Dialect* 'Take heed'
—Crockatt.

AUDACITY *(See also* COURAGE.)

1. **Armé de foi hardi**   *French* 'Bold, being armed with faith'
—Cranbrook (V.).

2. **Audacem juvant fata**   *Latin* 'The fates assist the bold'
—Somerville

3. **Audaces fortuna juvat**   *Latin* 'Fortune favors the bold'
—Barron, Bloxham, Burroughes, Carpenter, Chamberlaine, Davenport (of Bramall), King (Bt.), Hayes, Cosby (of Stradbally), Turnbull, Morgan, Stewart, Costello (of Ireland).

4. **Audaces juvat**   *Latin* 'She (Fortune) favors the bold'
—Cleveland (Co. Devon), Campbell, Goodge, Googe.

5. **Audaces juvo**   *Latin* 'I assist the bold'
—Campbell (of Jurd and Achteny), McCausland, Buchanan-Hamilton.

6. **Audacia**   *Latin* 'Boldness'
—Grant (of Auchrraine).

7. **Audacia et industria**   *Latin* 'Boldness and diligence'
—Buchanan.

8. **Audacia et virtute adepta**   *Latin* 'Gained by daring and valor'
—Paton.

9. **Audaci favet fortuna**   *Latin* 'Fortune favors the bold'
—Turnbull.

10. **Audaciter** *Latin* 'Boldly'

—Ewen (of Craigton).

11. **Audacter et aperte** *Latin* 'Boldly and openly'

—Campbell (Bt.).

12. **Audacter et sincere** *Latin* 'Boldly and sincerely'
—Castleford U. D. C., U.K.; Clive, Powes (E.).

13. **Audacter et strenue** *Latin* 'Boldly and earnestly'

—Blyth, Pollock (Bt.).

14. **Audax** *Latin* 'Bold'

—Erth.

15. **Audax at cautus** *Latin* 'Bold but cautious'

—Jenks (U.S.).

16. **Audax bona fide** *Latin* 'Bold with good faith'

—Bull (U.S.).

17. **Audax ero** *Latin* 'I will be bold'

—Boldero.

18. **Audax et celer** *Latin* 'Bold and quick'

—Pearce (Bt.).

19. **Audax et justus** *Latin* 'Bold and just'

—Wright.

20. **Audax et promptus** *Latin* 'Bold and ready'

—Douglas (Bt.).

21. **Audax et vigilans** *Latin* 'Bold and vigilant'

—Currie.

22. **Audax ingenii** *Latin* 'Of a bold disposition'

—Woodburne.

23. **Audax in recto** *Latin* 'Bold in the right'

—Stewart.

24. **Audax justum perficere** *Latin* 'Bold to perform what is just'

—Strathy.

25. **Audax omnia perpeti** *Latin* 'Daring to endure all things'

—Harding.

26. **Audax pro suis** *Latin* 'Bold for his own'

—Howitt.

27. **Audax vincendo** *Latin* 'Bold by overcoming'

—Ashburn.

28. **Aude, incipe** *Latin* 'Dare, begin'

—Anderton.

29. **Aude et prevalebis** *Latin* 'Dare, and thou shalt prevail'
—Frend.

30. **Audemus dum cavemus** *Latin* 'We dare though we are wary'
—Wallasey C. B. C., U.K.

31. **Audentes fortuna juvat** *Latin* 'Fortune favours the bold'
—[Vergil, *Aen.* x. 284.] Mackinnon, Mowbray, Turing
(Bt.).

32. **Audentior** *Latin* 'Bolder'
—Watford B. C., U.K.

33. **Audentior ibo** *Latin* 'I will go more boldly'
—Oliveira.

34. **Audeo** *Latin* 'I dare'
—Rose (of Houghton Conquest, Co. Beds.).

35. **Be bolde, be wyse**
—Gollop (of Strode).

36. **Be hardie**
—Edmonston, Edmonstoun.

37. **Be hardy**
—Edmonston (of Newton, Scotland).

38. **Bold**
—Spence.

39. **Cautus in consiliis, in facto audax** *Latin* 'Cautious in counsel,
bold in deed'
—Ewig Friedrich, Duke of Württemberg (1657–85).

40. **Celer et audax** *Latin* 'Quick and bold'
—Jackson; 60th (King's Royal) Rifle Corps, U.K.

41. **Consulto et audaciter** *Latin* 'With prudence and daring'
—Plummer.

42. **Contra audentior** *Latin* 'Bolder, being opposed'
—Mount Stephen (B.).

43. **Dare**
—Darley, Warren-Darley.

44. **Decide and dare**
—Dyce.

45. **Faithful and brave**
—Uniacke (U.S.).

46. **Feroci fortior** *Latin* 'Bolder than the ferocious (boar)'
—Lockhart (of Birkhill).

47. **Fidelis et audax**   *Latin* 'Faithful and bold'
—Russell.

48. **Fidelis et in bello fortis**   *Latin* 'Faithful and brave in war'
—Gillespie.

49. **Fideliter, fortiter, feliciter**   *Latin* 'Faithfully, bravely, and successfully'
—Scourfield (Bt.).

50. **Fidus et audax**   *Latin* 'Faithful and bold'
—Callaghan, Lismore (V.), Slade (Bt.).

51. **Fortes adjuvat ipse Deus**   *Latin* 'God himself aids the brave'
—Davenport.

52. **Fort et fidèle**   *French* 'Bold and faithful'
—Heaton-Ellis.

53. **Fort et loyal**   *French* 'Bold and loyal'
—Selby.

54. **Fortis et astutus**   *Latin* 'Bold and crafty'
—Pott (of Bentham).

55. **Fortis et egregius**   *Latin* 'Bold and excellent'
—Dowling.

56. **Fortiter, fideliter, feliciter**   *Latin* 'Boldly, faithfully, successfully'
—Hutchinson, Jackson, Monck (V.), Rathdowne (E.).

57. **Fortiter, sed apte**   *Latin* 'Boldly, but appropriately'
—Falconer.

58. **Fortiter et celeriter**   *Latin* 'Boldly and quickly'
—Mather (of Lauton).

59. **Fortiter et constanter**   *Latin* 'Boldly and steadfastly'
—Johann Georg III, Count of Mansfield in Eisleben (1640–1710); Johann Wilhelm, Duke of Saxony (1677–1707).

60. **Fortiter et feliciter**   *Latin* 'Boldly and fortunately'
—White.

61. **Fortiter et fide**   *Latin* 'Boldly and faithfully'
—Bunten (of Kilbride).

62. **Fortiter et fideliter**   *Latin* 'Boldly and faithfully'
—Armitage, Briggs, Browne (of Browneshill), Cox, Fallous, Norton (of Kings-Norton), O'Fallon, Pennyman (Bt.), Peperrell, Wilson (of Knowle Hall), Oranmore and Browne (B.).

63. **Fortiter et honeste** *Latin* 'Boldly and honorably'
—Abney.

64. **Fortiter et recte** *Latin* 'Boldly and rightly'
—Crayford U. D. C., U.K., Drake (Bt.), Rankin, Anderson.

65. **Fortiter et sincere** *Latin* 'Boldly and sincerely'
—Johnson.

66. **Fortiter et strenue** *Latin* 'Boldly and earnestly'
—Dempster, McLean.

67. **Fortiter et suaviter** *Latin* 'Boldly and mildly'
—Ogilvie (of Milltoun).

68. **Fortiter et vigilanter** *Latin* 'Boldly and vigilantly'
—Tyson.

69. **Fortitudine et decore** *Latin* 'By boldness and gracefulness'
—Ballinghall.

70. **Hardiment et bellement** *French* 'Boldly and handsomely'
—Stuckley (Bt.).

71. **Honeste audax** *Latin* 'Honorably bold'
—Edingtown, Parkyns, Rancliffe (B.), Wolley (of Allen Hill).

72. **I dare**
—Carnwarth (E.), Adair, Dalziell, Dalsiel, Dalyell.

73. **In periculis audax** *Latin* 'Bold in danger'
—Maher.

74. **Integer audax promptus** *Latin* 'Sound, bold, ready'
—Williams (U.S.).

75. **Juvabitur audax** *Latin* 'The bold will be helped'
—Buchanan.

76. **Liber et audax** *Latin* 'Free and bold'
—Freeman (of Castle Cor).

77. **Mitis et audax** *Latin* 'Mild and bold'
—Markham.

78. **Non temere, sed fortiter** *Latin* 'Not rashly, but boldly'
—Bloxsome, Wallington.

79. **Non timere sed fortiter** *Latin* 'Not with fear, but boldly'
—Bloxsome, Wallington.

80. **Perspicax, audax** *Latin* 'Quickwitted, bold'
—Erskine.

81. **Pro cruce audax**   *Latin* 'Bold for the cross'
—Squarey.

82. **Propria virtute audax**   *Latin* 'Bold in his own virtue'
—Madden.

83. **Pro rege ac fide audax**   *Latin* 'Bold for king and faith'
—Bideford B. C., U.K.

84. **Prudens, fidelis, et audax**   *Latin* 'Prudent, faithful, and bold'
—Leigh.

85. **Recte faciendo audax**   *Latin* 'Bold in doing justly'
—Grundy.

86. **Ripis rapax, rivis audax**   *Latin* 'On the banks rapacious, in the streams daring'
—O'Halloran.

87. **Sae bauld**   *Scots Dialect* 'So bold'
—Sibbald.

88. **Sagax et audax**   *Latin* 'Shrewd and bold'
—O'Naghten.

89. **Secret et hardi**   *French* 'Secret and bold'
—Dynevor (B.), Rice.

90. **Sedulus et audax**   *Latin* 'Diligent and bold'
—Rutherfurd.

91. **Strenuè et audacter**   *Latin* 'Strenuously and daringly'
—Wood.

92. **Suaviter, fortiter**   *Latin* 'Gently, boldly'
—Smith (of Gloucestershire).

93. **Temeraire**   *French* 'Rash'
—Harvey (of Chigwell).

94. **The righteous are bold as a lion**
—McBrayne.

95. **Tout hardi**   *French* 'Quite bold'
—McHardie.

96. **Trop hardi**   *French* 'Too bold'
—Hardie.

97. **Tu ne cede malis, sed contra audentior ito**   *Latin* 'Yield not to misfortunes, but go the more boldly against them'
—[Vergil, *Aen.* vi. 95.] Cooke (of Cordangan).

98. **Vigila et aude**   *Latin* '(Be) vigilant and dare'
—Campbell (Bt.).

99. **Vigilans et audax** *Latin* 'Vigilant and bold'
—Bradley (of Co. Worcester), Corrie, Cockburn (Bt.), Campbell (Bt.), Dunn.

100. **Virtus insignit audentes** *Latin* 'Virtue renders the bold illustrious'
—Beamish.

101. **Watchful and bold**
—Coats.

102. **Who dares wins**
—Yerburgh.

103. **Y cyfiawn sydd hy megis llew** *Welsh* 'The righteous is bold like a lion'
—Hughes (of Alltwyd).

AUTHORITY (*See also* GOVERNMENT; LEADERSHIP.)

1. **Imperio** *Latin* 'By command'
—Murray (of Broughton).

2. **Imperio regit unus aequo** *Latin* 'One only rules with unbiased sway'
—[Horace, *Od.* iv. 3. 47.] Gunning (Bt.).

3. **Impero** *Latin* 'I command'
—Murray, Stewart.

4. **Mihi jussa capessere** *Latin* 'To execute my commands'
—Masham.

5. **Nisi paret imperat** *Latin* 'Unless he obeys, he commands'
—Bernard.

6. **Sfida e commanda** *Italian* 'He challenges and commands'
—Metaxa-Anzolato.

7. **Veritas securis** *Latin* 'Truth has authority'
—Scribner (U.S.).

BEAUTY (*See also* GRACEFULNESS.)

1. **All this beauty is of God**
—Isle of Wight C. C., U.K.

2. **Beauty and grace**
—Smith (U.S.).

3. **Beauty surrounds, health abounds**
—Morecambe and Heysham B. C., U.K.

4. **Bonitas/veritas/pulchritas** *Latin* 'Goodness ruth/beauty'
—Marycrest College, Davenport, Iowa.

5. **Candide comme la fleur** *French* 'Fair as the flower'
—Fenton.

6. **Dat virtus quod forma negat** *Latin* 'Virtue gives what beauty denies'
—Bertrand Du Guesclin (D. 1380).

7. **Decor integer** *Latin* 'Perfect comeliness'
—Mounsey.

8. **Difficilia quae pulchra** *Latin* 'Things which are beautiful are difficult'
—Elford (Bt.).

9. **Forma flos, fama flatus** *Latin* 'Beauty is a flower, fame a breath'
—Bagshawe (of Wormhill, co. Derby).

10. **Forma perit, virtus remanet** *Latin* 'Beauty perishes; virtue remains'
—August, Count von der Lippe (D. 1701).

11. **Formosa quae honesta** *Latin* 'What is honorable is beautiful'
—Tarton, Turton.

12. **Iechyd, harddwch, heddwch** *Welsh* 'Health, beauty and tranquility'
—Colwyn Bay B. C., U.K.

13. **Jewel of the Thames**
—Maidenhead B. C., U.K.

14. **Le beau est le splendeur du vrai** *French* 'Beauty is the splendor of truth'
—Doulton.

15. **Pulchritudo et salubritas** *Latin* 'Beauty and health'
—Bournemouth C. B. C., U.K.

16. **Sic oculos, sic ille genas, sic ora ferebat** *Latin* 'Such eyes, such cheeks, such a mouth had he'
—[Vergil, *Aen.* iii. 490.] Albert, Margrave of Brandenburg (1490–1545).

17. **Sua gratia parvis** *Latin* 'Little things have a beauty of their own'
—Little.

18. **Tempore candidior** *Latin* 'Become fairer by time'
—Mair.

19. **Tout pour la belle, laquelle j'aime le plus** *French* 'Everything for the beautiful, which I love the best'
> —Julius Heinrich, Duke of Saxony-Lauenburg (1586–1665).

20. **Truth and beauty**
> —Eccles (V.).

21. **Tutamen pulchris** *Latin* 'A protection for the fair'
> —Chambre.

22. **Vertu embellit** *French* 'Virtue beautifies'
> —Kunigunde Juliane, Princess of Anhalt (1608–56); Kunigunde Juliane, Landgravine of Hesse (1608–56).

23. **Virtus admixta decori** *Latin* 'Virtue combined with beauty'
> —Emanuel Leberecht, Prince of Anhalt-Plötzkau (1671–1704).

BEING, SELF

1. **Homo sum** *Latin* 'I am a man'
> —Homan (Bt.), Mann, Manns.

2. **I am, I am**
> —Ricketson.

3. **Si je n'estoy** *French* 'If I were not'
> —Curwen.

4. **Sum quod sum** *Latin* 'I am what I am'
> —Coldicott, Foresight.

5. **Sumus** *Latin* 'We are'
> —Weare (of Hampton), Bishop.

BENEFITS (*See also* REWARD.)

1. **Aliena insania frui optimum** *Latin* 'To benefit from the folly of others is best'
> —[Pliny, *Nat. Hist.* xviii. 15.] Ernst Ludwig, Duke of Pomerania zu Wolgast (1545–92).

2. **Beneficii memor** *Latin* 'Mindful of a benefit'
> —Butler.

3. **Beneficiorum memor** *Latin* 'Mindful of benefits'
> —Nicholson, Kelham.

4. **Pro mundi beneficio**   *Latin* 'For the benefit of the world'
—Republic of Panama.

5. **Ut prosim aliis prosim**   *Latin* 'Let me prosper that I may benefit others'
—Ferguson.

BIRDS

1. **Accipiter praedam sequitur, nos gloriam**   *Latin* 'The hawk seeks prey, we (seek) glory'
—Hawker, Strother (of Shooter's Hill, Kent).

2. **Addicunt aves**   *Latin* 'Birds augur it'
—Lutefoot (of Scotland).

3. **Ales volat propriis**   *Latin* 'The bird flies to its kind'
—Tufton (Bt.).

4. **Alte fert aquila**   *Latin* 'The eagle bears on high'
—Monteagle (B.).

5. **Aquila non captat muscas**   *Latin* 'The eagle catcheth not flies'
—Bedingfield (Bt.), Bedingfield (of Ditchingham, Co. Norfolk), Buller (of Cornwall), Chinn (of Gloucester), Drake, Graves (B.), Greaves (of Mayfield), Gothard (of Newcastle), Illidge, Steel (Bt.), Trant, Weddeburn, Weston, Wright.

6. **Aquila petit solem**   *Latin* 'The eagle seeks the sun'
—Kendall.

7. **Ardua petit ardea**   *Latin* 'The heron seeks high places'
—Heron (Bt.).

8. **Aviumque volatus**   *Latin* 'And a flight of birds'
—Wilson.

9. **Be wise as a serpent, harmless as a dove**
—[Matt. x. 16.] Lewis.

10. **Christus pelicano**   *Latin* 'Christ is like the pelican'
—Lechmere (Bt.).

11. **Christus pelicanus et agnus**   *Latin* 'Christ my pelican and my lamb'
—Godfrey.

12. **Craggan phithich**   *Scots Gaelic* 'The rock of the raven'
—Macdonnel, Macdonell.

13. **De hirundine**   *Latin* 'From the swallow'
—Arundel.

14. **Duw a ddarpar i'r brain** *Welsh* 'God provides for the crows'
—Hughes (of Plas Coch).

15. **Effingit phoenix Christum reparabilis ales** *Latin* 'The phoenix with its recurrent appearance recalls Christ'
—Mayer (U.S.).

16. **Eryr eryrod Eryri** *Welsh* 'The eagle of the eagles (*or* ridges) of Snowdon'
—Wynne (of Pengwern), Wynn-Williams.

17. **Ferant mea serta columbae** *Latin* 'Let doves bear my garland'
—Hodgson.

18. **Frisch gewagedt ist halb gewonnen** *German* 'Boldly ventured is half won'
—Franz Albert, Duke of Saxony (1598–1642).

19. **God feeds the crows**
—Crawfurd.

20. **Insontes ut columbae** *Latin* 'Innocent as doves'
—Francis.

21. **La merle aime la liberté** *French* 'The blackbird (or merle) loves liberty'
—Merle.

22. **Leo inimicis amicis columba** *Latin* 'The lion for my enemies, the dove for my friends'
—Dilke.

23. **Let the hawk shaw**
—Porteous.

24. **Non generant aquilae columbas** *Latin* 'Eagles do not beget doves'
—Lempriere, Rodney (B.).

25. **Pullis corvorum invocantibus eum** *Latin* 'When the young ones of the crows call upon him'
—[Ps., cxlvii. 9.] Sir Griffith Ap Rice (South Wales).

26. **Quis preparet corvo escam suam?** *Latin* 'Who can prepare his food for the ravens?'
—Ravens.

27. **Renovabitur ut aquilae juventus tua** *Latin* 'Thy youth shall be renewed as the eagles'
—Barlow.

28. **Renovatur aetas ejus sicut aquilae** *Latin* 'His age is renewed like the eagle's'
—Raymond.

29. **Secundâ alite** *Latin* 'With prosperous omen' or 'By favor of the bird'
                                        —Lathom, or Latham.

30. **Sicut aquilae pennis** *Latin* 'As on eagle's wings'
                                        —Niblett.

31. **Vespertilionis** *Latin* 'Of the bat'
                                        —Batson.

BIRTH (*See also* LIFE; REBIRTH.)

1. **Genitum se credere mundo** *Latin* 'To believe oneself born for the world'
                                        —Saunders.

2. **Non omnibus nati** *Latin* 'Not born for all'
                                        —Frank.

3. **Rupto robore nati** *Latin* 'We are born from the broken oak'
                                        —Aikenhead.

BLESSING (*See also* DIVINE GIFTS; GOODNESS; GRACE.)

1. **A blessing to the aged**
                                        —Spectacle-makers' Company.

2. **An Gottes Segen ist alles gelegen** *German* 'Everything rests on God's blessing'
          —Heinrich II, Count Reuss (1575–1639); Friedrich Ulrich,
                Duke of Braunschweig-Wolfenbüttel (1591–1634);
                        Christian, Duke of Wohlau (1618–72).

3. **Beatus qui implevit** *Latin* 'Blessed is he who has finished (his task)'
                                        —Bingley.

4. **Benedic fontes, Domine** *Latin* 'Bless the wells, O Lord!'
                          —John Wells, last Abbot of Croyland.

5. **Benedicite fontes Dominum** *Latin* 'Oh, ye wells, bless the Lord'
                                        —Wells.

6. **Benedic nobis Domine** *Latin* 'Bless us, O Lord'
                                        —Bain.

7. **Benedictio Domini divites facit** *Latin* 'The blessing of the Lord, it maketh rich'
                  —[Prov. x. 22.] Wenzel Adam Posthumus, Duke of
                                        Teschen (1524–79).

8. **Benedicto Dei ditat** *Latin* 'He enriches with the blessing of God'
—Laurie.

9. **Bona benemerenti benedictio** *Latin* 'A good blessing to the well-deserving'
—Bradshaw.

10. **Durch Gottes Segen** *German* 'Through God's blessing'
—August, Count von der Lippe (d. 1701).

11. **Ecce sic benedicitur vir qui timet Deum** *Latin* 'Behold, that thus shall the man be blessed that feareth the Lord'
—[Ps., cxxviii. 4.] Christian Ernst, Margrave of Brandenburg-Baireuth (1644–1712).

12. **In Einem Stehet Vnsere Seligkeit** *German* 'Our blessedness lies in One'
—Luise Amalie, Princess of Anhalt (1606–35).

BOASTFULNESS (*See also* PRIDE.)

1. **Crow not, croke not**
—Crockett.

2. **Et si ostendo non jacto** *Latin* 'And if I show what I am, I do not boast'
—Oakden, Ogden.

3. **Grand venteurs petits faiseurs** *French* 'Great boasters, small doers'
—Anna Auguste, Princess of Nassau-Dillenburg (1612–56).

4. **I show not boast**
—Nimmo.

5. **Non ostento, sed ostendo** *Latin* 'I boast not, but give proof'
—Fowell.

6. **Ostendo non ostento** *Latin* 'I show, not boast'
—Isham (Bt.), Betts, Ritchie.

BRIGHTNESS (*See also* SHINING; STARS; SUN.)

1. **Clareo foveoque** *Latin* 'I am bright, and I cherish'
—Clare.

2. **Clarescam** *Latin* 'I shall become bright'
—Hebbert.

3. **Clariora sequor** *Latin* 'I follow brighter things'
—Buchanan (of Ardock).

4. **Clarior astris** *Latin* 'Brighter than the stars'
—Baillie.

5. **Clarior e flammis** *Latin* 'Brighter from the flame'
—Gray.

6. **Clariores e tenebris** *Latin* 'Men are brighter from previous obscurity'
—Puleston (Bt.), Polden, Leeson.

7. **Clarior e tenebris** *Latin* 'The brighter from previous obscurity'
—Bright, Gray, Lightbody, Miltown (E.), Purves, Purvis.

8. **Clarior ex obscuro** *Latin* 'Brighter from obscurity'
—Sanderson.

9. **Claritate dextra** *Latin* 'With a bright light on the right'
—Brady, Geale-Brady.

10. **Longo splendescit in usu** *Latin* 'It acquires brilliance by long use'
—Heinrich II, Duke of Münsterberg (1507–48).

11. **Pristinum spero lumen** *Latin* 'I hope for pristine luster'
—Preston (Bt.).

12. **Refulgent in tenebris** *Latin* 'They glitter in the dark'
—Stodart, Studdert.

CAUSATION

1. **Cause caused it**
—Elphinstone (B.).

2. **J'ai bonne cause** *French* 'I have good reason'
—Bath (M.), Thynne.

3. **J'ay bonne cause** *French* 'I have good reason'
—Botfield.

4. **Nil sine causa** *Latin* 'Nothing without a cause'
—Brown.

5. **Non sine causa** *Latin* 'Not without a cause'
—Justice.

6. **Ratio mihi sufficit** *Latin* 'The reason is sufficient for me'
—Graham (of Drumgoon).

7. **Rerum cognoscere causas** *Latin* 'To understand the causes of things'
—The London School of Economics and Political Science.

8. **Sans cause** *French* 'Without cause'
—Geer (U.S.).

CAUTION (*See also* PRUDENCE; VIGILANCE.)

1. **Allezeit mit Hut**   *German* 'At all times with caution'
—Maximilian I, Emperor of Germany (1459–1519).

2. **Audax at cautus**   *Latin* 'Bold but cautious'
—Jenks (U.S.).

3. **Audemus dum cavemus**   *Latin* 'We dare though we are wary'
—Wallasey C. B. C., U.K.

4. **Candide, sed caute**   *Latin* 'Candidly, but cautiously'
—Sinclair (Bt.).

5. **Candide et caute**   *Latin* 'Candidly and cautiously'
—Elliot, Grieve.

6. **Cate at caute**   *Latin* 'Carefully and cautiously'
—Gatty.

7. **Catus [sic] semper viret**   *Latin* 'The cunning man always flourishes'
—Caton.

8. **Caute, sed impavide**   *Latin* 'Cautiously, but without fear'
—Cayzer.

9. **Caute nec timide**   *Latin* 'Cautiously, not fearfully'
—Fearon (of Hunstanton).

10. **Caute non astute**   *Latin* 'Cautiously, not craftily'
—Ross (of Kindies).

11. **Caute sed intrepide**   *Latin* 'Cautiously, but fearlessly'
—Drummond.

12. **Cautus a futuro**   *Latin* 'Cautious as to the future'
—Bowen.

13. **Cautus in consiliis, in facto audax**   *Latin* 'Cautious in counsel, bold in deed'
—Ewig Friedrich, Duke of Württemberg (1657–85).

14. **Cautus metuit foveam lupus**   *Latin* 'The cautious wolf fears the snare'
—Caton (of Binbrook).

15. **Cautus sed strenue**   *Latin* 'Cautiously, but strenuously'
—Hamlyn.

16. **Cave, paratus**   *Latin* 'Prepared, be cautious'
—Johnston.

17. **Cavendo**   *Latin* 'By taking care'
—Crowfoot (of Beccles).

18. **Cavendo tutus**   *Latin* 'Safe by being cautious'
—Cavendish, Burlington (E.), Devonshire (D.),
Cruickshank, Hardwick, Waterpark (B.),
Waring.

19. **Cura dat victoriam**   *Latin* 'Caution gives victory'
—Denham.

20. **Curae cedit fatum**   *Latin* 'Fate gives way to caution'
—Thomson.

21. **Curae testimonium**   *Latin* 'A testimony of caution'
—Taunton.

22. **Ehe wiegs dann wags**   *German* 'Rather weigh than venture'
—Bogislaus XIII, Duke of Pomerania zu Barth
(1544–1606).

23. **Expende primo**   *Latin* 'Weigh first'
—August, Duke of Braunschweig-Wolfenbüttel
(1579–1666).

24. **Festina lente**   *Latin* 'Make haste slowly'
—Barnard, Blaauw, Brookes, Campbell, Colquhon,
Dunsany (B.), Everett, Fingall (E.), Fletcher,
Louth (B.), Mewburn (of Darlington), Onslow
(Bt.), Onslow, Plunket (B.), Rigge, Rawlinson
(knt.), Rothery, Swift (of Rotherham), Trotter
(Bt.), Trotter, Westcombe, Whittaker.

25. **Fortiter qui sedulo**   *Latin* '(He acts) bravely, who (acts) carefully'
—Keith (of Craig).

26. **In copia cautus**   *Latin* 'Careful amid plenty'
—Dod (of Edge).

27. **Je gardye bien**   *Old French* 'I am careful'
—Pickering.

28. **Non cate sed caute**   *Latin* 'Not cunningly but cautiously'
—Gatty.

29. **Non timeo, sed caveo**   *Latin* 'I fear not, but am cautious'
—Hewitson, Oakeley, Strachan (Bt.), Strachan,
Symmonds.

30. **Parat et curat**   *Latin* 'He prepares and is cautious'
—Stewart (of Blacaskie).

31. **Perseverando et cavendo**   *Latin* 'By perseverance and caution'
—Moore.

32. **Prenez garde**   *French* 'Take care'
—Elmsley, Emslie, Emsley, Elmsly.

33. **Propere et provide**   *Latin* 'Quickly and cautiously'
                                                    —Robinson.
34. **Propero sed curo**   *Latin* 'I make haste, but am cautious'
                                                    —Graham.
35. **Provide qui laboriose**   *Latin* 'Take care, who are hard-working'
                                                    —Innes.
36. **Secundo, curo**   *Latin* 'I prosper and am cautious'
                                                    —Buchanan.
37. **Vincit qui curat**   *Latin* 'He conquers who is cautious'
                                                    —White.

CERTAINTY (*See also* CLARITY.)
 1. **Bien sûr**   *French* 'Certainly'
                                                    —De Tuch.
 2. **Lock sick**   *Scots Gaelic* 'Be sure'
                                                    —Erwin.
 3. **Lock sicker**   *Scots Gaelic* 'Be sure'
                          —Douglas (Bt.), Megget, Morton (E.).
 4. **Omnia certa fac**   *Latin* 'Make everything certain'
                                                    —Ashpitel.

CHANGE (*See also* TRANSIENCE.)
 1. **Antes muerto que mutado**   *Spanish* 'Rather dead than changed'
                —Wilhelm V, Landgrave of Hesse-Cassel (1602–37).
 2. **Caelum non animum**   *Latin* 'You may change your climate, but
     not your disposition'
          —Comyn, Strachey (Bt.), Rhodes (of Bellair), Waldegrave
                                                          (E.).
 3. **Coelum non animum mutat**   *Latin* 'Change of climate does not
     change the mind'
                                                    —Ramsden.
 4. **Disponendo me, non mutando me**   *Latin* 'By influencing me, not
     by changing me'
                               —Manchester (D.), Montague.
 5. **Dum varior**   *Latin* 'Until I am changed'
                                     —Ramsay (of Idington).
 6. **Fluctuo sed affluo**   *Latin* 'I fluctuate, but I flow on'
                                                    —Arbuthnot.

7. **Haud muto factum**   *Latin* 'I do not change the thing done'
    —Broughton (Bt.).

8. **Je ne change qu'en mourant**   *French* 'I change but in death'
    —Salvin.

9. **Mutabimur**   *Latin* 'We shall be changed'
    —Brinkley.

10. **Mutare non est meum**   *Latin* 'It is not mine to change'
    —Frewen (of Northiam).

11. **Mutare sperno**   *Latin* 'I scorn to change'
    —Hobhouse, Lefroy, Singleton (Co. Clare).

12. **Mutare vel timere sperno**   *Latin* 'I scorn to change or to fear'
    —Beaufort (D.), Barnes, Bythesea, Somerset.

13. **Nec mutandus, nec metus**   *Latin* 'Neither change nor fear'
    —Rawlins.

14. **Not always so**
    —Barrell (U.S.).

15. **Omnium rerum vicissitudo**   *Latin* 'All things are subject to change'
    —[Terence, *Eunuchus*, ii. 276.] August, Duke of Braunschweig-Wolfenbüttel (1579–1666); Ford (Bt.).

16. **Revise**
    —Dundas.

17. **Sans changer**   *French* 'Without changing'
    —Clarke (of Ashgate, Co. Derby), Derby (E.), Enery, Grove (Bt.), Lefevre, Musgrave (Bt.), Musgrave (of Myrtle), Nigon, Stanley (of Alderley, B.), Stanley (of Dalegarth).

18. **Sans variance, et à mon droit**   *French* 'Without change, and for my right'
    —Bowes.

19. **Sans varier**   *French* 'Without changing'
    —Charlton (of Lea Hall).

20. **Traducere aevum leniter**   *Latin* 'To reform the age mildly'
    —Browne.

21. **Varietas est propria fortunae**   *Latin* 'Change is natural to fortune'
    —Ernest VI, Count of Mansfeld (1561–1609).

22. **Vertitur in diem** *Latin* 'It is changed into day'
> —Farquhar.

23. **Vertitur in lucem** *Latin* 'It is changed into light'
> —Baillie.

CHRIST, JESUS (*See also* DIVINITY; RELIGION; SACRIFICE; SALVATION.)

1. **A. B. C. D. E. F. (Allein bei Christo die ewige Freude)** *German* 'With Christ alone is eternal joy'
> —Albrecht Günther, Count Schwarzburg (1582–1634).

2. **Agnus Dei salvator meus** *Latin* 'The Lamb of God, my savior'
> —Haslam.

3. **Arbor vitae Christus, fructus per fidem gustamus** *Latin* 'Christ is the tree of life, the fruit whereof we taste through faith'
> —Fruiterers' Company.

4. **Auspice Christo** *Latin* 'Under the guidance of Christ'
> —Davie (Bt.), Lawley (Bt.), Wenlock (B.).

5. **Building Christian character**
> —Southwestern Christian College, Terrell, Texas.

6. **Christ above all**
> —William Jennings Bryan College, Dayton, Tennessee.

7. **Christ for the world**
> —Yankton College, Yankton, South Dakota.

8. **Christianity and culture**
> —Franklin College, Franklin, Indiana.

9. **Christi pennatus sidera morte peto** *Latin* 'Furnished with wings (feathers), by the death of Christ I seek the stars'
> —Fetherston.

10. **Christo duce** *Latin* 'With Christ for leader'
> —Richard I.

11. **Christo duce feliciter** *Latin* 'Happily, under the guidance of Christ'
> —Binning.

12. **Christo et humanitati** *Latin* 'For Christ and humanity'
> —Blackburn College, Carlinville, Illinois.

13. **Christo suavis odor** *Latin* 'A sweet savor to Christ'
> —Ross.

14. **Christ preeminent**
> —Messiah College, Grantham, Pennsylvania.

15. **Christum diligere melius est omnibus scire**   *Latin* 'To love Christ is better than to know all things'
— [after Ephesians iii. 19.] Johann, Prince of Anhalt-Zerbst (1621–67).

16. **Christus dux solus**   *Latin* 'Christ is my only guide'
—Christiane, Duchess of Saxony-Eisenberg (1659–79).

17. **Christus meine Hoffnung**   *German* 'Christ is my hope'
—Joachim, Margrave of Brandenburg (1583–1600).

18. **Christus meum asylum**   *Latin* 'Christ is my refuge'
—Philipp Ludwig, Count of Palatinate of Rhein zu Neuburg (1547–1614).

19. **Christus mihi lucrum**   *Latin* 'Christ is my gain'
—Stewart.

20. **Christus mihi vita**   *Latin* 'Christ is my life'
—Bigg.

21. **Christus mihi vita, mors lucrum**   *Latin* 'For me to live is Christ, and to die is gain'
—[Phil. i. 21.] Heinrich Julius, Duke of Braunschweig-Wolfenbüttel (1564–1613).

22. **Christus nobiscum, state!**   *Latin* 'Christ is with us: stand firm!'
—Casimir, Margrave of Brandenburg-Baireuth (1481–1527).

23. **Christus omnia, mundus nihil**   *Latin* 'Christ is everything, the world nothing'
—Johann, Prince of Anhalt-Zerbst (1621–67).

24. **Christus pelicano**   *Latin* 'Christ is like the pelican'
—Lechmere (Bt.).

25. **Christus pelicanus et agnus**   *Latin* 'Christ my pelican and my lamb'
—Godfrey.

26. **Christus primatum tenens**   *Latin* 'Christ holding the first place'
—Westmont College, Santa Barbara, California.

27. **Christus providebit**   *Latin* 'Christ will provide'
—Thomson.

28. **Christus servatus vera libertas**   *Latin* 'To serve Christ is true liberty'
—Vaughan.

29. **Christus sit regula vitae**   *Latin* 'Let Christ be the rule of life'
—Samwell (of Upton Hall).

30. **Corona mea Christus**   *Latin* 'Christ is my crown'
                              —Chetwode (Bt.), Lapsley, Webb.

31. **Credo Christi cruce**   *Latin* 'I trust in the cross of Christ'
                              —Darit.

32. **Deo duce Christo luce**   *Latin* 'God my guide, Christ my light'
                              —Butler.

33. **Disce mori et vivere Christo**   *Latin* 'Learn to die and to live in Christ'
                              —Friedrich Wilhelm I, Duke of Saxony-Weimar
                              (1562–1602).

34. **Distinctively Christian**
                              —Tennessee Temple University, Chattanooga, Tennessee.

35. **Ecce Agnus Dei, qui tollit peccata mundi**   *Latin* 'Behold the Lamb of God, which taketh away the sin of the world'
                              —[John i. 29.] Tallow-Chandlers' Company.

36. **Effingit phoenix Christum reparabilis ales**   *Latin* 'The phoenix with its recurrent appearance recalls Christ'
                              —Mayer (U.S.).

37. **Excellence for Christ**
                              —St. Andrews Presbyterian College, Laurinburg, North Carolina.

38. **Firmus in Christo**   *Latin* 'Firm in Christ'
                              —Firmin.

39. **Have faith in Christ**
                              —Glendoning (of Partoun), Glendonwyn.

40. **In Christo fratres**   *Latin* 'Brothers in Christ'
                              —Tonbridge School, U.K.

41. **In Christo omnia**   *Latin* 'In Christ is everything'
                              —August, Duke of Saxony (1589–1615).

42. **In Christo salus**   *Latin* 'Salvation is in Christ'
                              —Abernethy.

43. **In Christo speravi**   *Latin* 'In Christ I have hoped'
                              —Peckover.

44. **In vulneribus Christi triumpho**   *Latin* 'In the wounds of Christ I triumph'
                              —Bernhard, Duke of Saxony-Meiningen (1649–1706).

45. **In vulneribus Jesu meum auxilium**   *Latin* 'In the wounds of Jesus is my help'
                              —Johann Wilhelm, Duke of Saxony-Eisenach (1666–1729).

46. **Jesu, esto mihi Jesus** *Latin* 'Jesus, be Jesus unto me'
—Swale.

47. **Jesu est prêt** *French* 'Jesus is ready'
—Frizell (U.S.).

48. **Jesus**
—Chippenham, Chipman.

49. **Jesus Hominum Salvator** *Latin* 'Jesus the Savior of mankind'
—Legat, Order of the Seraphim (Sweden).

50. **Jesus meine Zuversicht** *German* 'In Jesus is my trust'
—Luise Henriette, Electress of Brandenburg (1627–67).

51. **Jesus seul bon et bel** *French* 'Jesus alone good and fair'
—Breary.

52. **Lucrum Christi mihi** *Latin* 'To me Christ is gain'
—Forde.

53. **Lux mea Christus** *Latin* 'Christ is my light'
—Newman, Rogers.

54. **Mea anchora Christus** *Latin* 'Christ is my anchor'
—Mayor.

55. **Mihi vita Christus** *Latin* 'Christ is my life'
—Kaye.

56. **Mihi vivere Christus est** *Latin* 'For me, Christ is life'
—St. Joseph's Seminary, Yonkers, New York.

57. **Mors Christi mors mortis mihi** *Latin* 'Christ's death is to me the death of death'
—Boothby (Bt.).

58. **Navem tuam Christe tuere** *Latin* 'Protect Thy ship, O Christ!'
—Friedrich II, the Wise, Elector of the Palatinate of Rhein (1483–1556).

59. **Nemo nisi Christus** *Latin* 'No one if not Christ'
—Apthorp (U.S.).

60. **Nescitur Christo** *Latin* 'He is not known by Christ'
—Rous.

61. **Nisi Christus nemo** *Latin* 'Christ or no one'
—Parkin.

62. **Omnia in Christo** *Latin* 'Everything in Christ'
—August, Prince of Anhalt-Plötzkau (1575–1653).

63. **Omnia mihi Christus** *Latin* 'Christ is my all'
—Christian August, Count of the Palatinate of Sulzbach (1622–1708).

64. **One in Christ Jesus**
—Interdenominational Theological Center, Atlanta,
Georgia.

65. **Per Jesum Christum** *Latin* 'Through Jesus Christ'
—Luther Theological Seminary, St. Paul, Minnesota.

66. **Pro Christo et humanitate** *Latin* 'For Christ and humanity'
—Olivet College, Olivet, Michigan.

67. **Pro Christo et patria dulce periculum** *Latin* 'For Christ and my country danger is sweet'
—Carr, Roxburghe (D.).

68. **Pro Christo et Republica** *Latin* 'For Christ and the Republic'
—Birmingham-Southern College, Birmingham, Alabama.

69. **Quid non cor saepius pro Immanueli?** *Latin* 'Why is the heart not oftener for Immanuel?'
—Wishart.

70. **Rebus in adversis spes mea Christus erit** *Latin* 'In adversity Christ shall be my hope'
—Bernhard, Prince of Anhalt (1572–96).

71. **Salus mea Christus** *Latin* 'Christ is my salvation'
—Forbes.

72. **Salus per Christum** *Latin* 'Salvation through Christ'
—Abernethy, Christian, Forbes (of Culloden), Hare (of Docking, Co. Norfolk), Gordon, Leith (of Whitehaugh).

73. **Salus per Christum Redemptorem** *Latin* 'Salvation through Christ the Redeemer'
—Moray (E.), Stewart, Stuart (of Duncarn).

74. **Sanguine Christe tuo** *Latin* 'By thy blood, O Christ'
—Bramhall.

75. **Scopus vitae Christus** *Latin* 'The goal of my life is Christ'
—August, Margrave of Brandenburg (1580–1601); Menzies.

76. **Solus Christus mea rupes** *Latin* 'Christ alone is my rock'
—Orrock.

77. **Solus per Christum Redemptorem** *Latin* 'Alone through Christ the Redeemer'
—Stewart.

78. **Solus spes mea Christus** *Latin* 'Christ is my only hope'
—Johann the Wise, Margrave of Brandenburg-Küstrin (1513–71).

79. **Spes mea Christus**   *Latin* 'Christ is my hope'
—Anton Heinrich, Count Schwarzburg (1571–1638); Bruno
III, Count of Mansfeld (1576–1644); Sibylle Elisabeth,
Duchess of Braunschweig (1576–1630); Ludwig Philipp,
Count of the Palatinate of Veldenz (1577–1601);
Christian Wilhelm, Margrave of Brandenburg
(1587–1665); Johann, Margrave of Brandenburg
(1597–1628); Elisabeth Sophie, Duchess of Saxony-
Lauenburg (1599–1627); Friedrich Ludwig, Count of the
Palatinate of Landsberg (1619–81); Ernst, Duke of
Saxony-Hildburghausen (1655–1715); Clanmorris (B.),
Lucan (E.), Bingham (of Melcombe).

80. **Spes mea Christus erit**   *Latin* 'Christ shall be my hope'
—Powell.

81. **Stella Christi duce**   *Latin* 'With the star of Christ for guide'
—Sohier.

82. **Unica spes mea Christus**   *Latin* 'Christ is my only hope'
—Georg, Duke of Braunschweig-Lüneburg (1582–1641);
Dishington.

83. **Vescitur Christo**   *Latin* 'He feeds on Christ'
—Rous (of Devon).

84. **Vespera iam venit; nobiscum Christe maneto, Extingui lucem nec
patiare tuam**   *Latin* 'The evening has come; stay by us, O
Christ, and let not thy light be extinguished'
—Johann Georg I, Prince of Anhalt-Dessau (1567–1618).

85. **Victoriam coronat Christus**   *Latin* 'Christ crowns the victory'
—Campbell (of Abernchill, bt.).

86. **zV ChrIsto Ist MeIn VerDraVen**   *German* 'In Christ is my trust.'
—(The capital letters, rearranged, give the year 1618).
Johann Georg I, Prince of Anhalt-Dessau
(1567–1618, in somewhat modified Roman
numerals: MDCVVVIII).

CLARITY

1. **Clarior alter**   *Latin* 'Another (that is) clearer'
—Peronneau (U.S.).

2. **Denuo fortasse lucescat**   *Latin* 'Perchance it may become clear
again'
—Spurdens.

CLEVERNESS

1. **Animo, non astutia** *Latin* 'By courage, not by craft'
   —Gordon (D.), Gordon (Bt.), Gordon (co. Down), Pedlar (of Hoo Mavey).

2. **By cunning not by craft**
   —Todd (U.S.).

3. **Caute et sedulo** *Latin* 'Cautiously and carefully'
   —Atkins, Brown (of Bonnington), Hamlyn.

4. **Est nec astu** *Latin* 'Nor is it by craft'
   —Brook, Brooke.

5. **Marte et ingenio** *Latin* 'By war and wit'
   —Smith (Co. Essex, Bt.).

6. **Non astutia** *Latin* 'Not by craft'
   —Gordon, Oswald.

7. **Si non consilio impetu** *Latin* 'If not by stratagem, by assault'
   —Agnew.

8. **Virtute doloque** *Latin* 'By valor and craft'
   —Binning.

COMMERCE

1. **Agriculture and commerce**
   —Maidstone B. C., U.K.; State of Tennessee.

2. **Courage, humanity, commerce**
   —South Shields C. B. C., U.K.

3. **Pannus mihi panis** *Latin* 'Wool is my bread'
   —Kendal B. C., U.K.

4. **Par commerce** *French* 'By commerce'
   —French.

5. **Pro libertate et commercio** *Latin* 'For liberty and commerce'
   —Hicks (U.S.).

6. **Regio floret patrocinio commercium commercioque regnum**
   Latin 'Commerce flourishes by royal protection, and the kingdom by commerce'
   —African Company.

7. **The field is the world**
   —Free Trade Club of New York.

8. **Trade and navigation**
   —Royal Exchange Assurance.

9. **Trade and plantations**
    —Commissioners of Trade and Plantations.

CONCERN (*See also* KINDNESS.)

1. **Alterum non laedere** *Latin* 'Not to injure another'
    —Keir.

2. **Amicis prodesse, nemini nocere** *Latin* 'To do good to my friends, to injure nobody'
    —Lowton.

3. **Curandum omnium bonum** *Latin* 'We must care for the good of all'
    —Garstang R. D. C., U.K.

4. **Sublimia cures** *Latin* 'Care for high things'
    —Bowman.

5. **The college that cares**
    —Capital City Junior College, Little Rock, Arkansas.

6. **To reach out**
    —Golden Valley Lutheran College, Minneapolis, Minnesota.

CONCILIATION (*See also* HEALING and HEALTH; PEACE.)

1. **Ad faedera cresco** *Latin* 'I grow in accordance with treaties'
    —Oliver.

2. **Aversos compono animos, et secula cogo** *Latin* 'I reunite estranged hearts, and bring together distant ages'
    —Loseley House, near Guildford, Surrey, England.

3. **Bello palmam fero** *Latin* 'I bear the palm in war'
    —Bell.

4. **Divisa conjungo** *Latin* 'I heal divisions'
    —Gordon (of Glastirim).

5. **Hostes nunc amici** *Latin* 'Foes now friends'
    —Abergavenny B. C., U.K.

6. **Me juvat ire per altum** *Latin* 'I delight to bridge an abyss'
    —Bridge.

7. **Moveo et propitior** *Latin* 'I move and am appeased'
    —Knox, Ranfurley (E.), Wells.

CONFIDENCE (*See also* SELF-RELIANCE; TRUST.)

1. **All's well**
—Camberwell B. C., U.K.; Mudge.

2. **Ausim et confido** *Latin* 'I am brave and confident'
—Areskine, Erskine (of Kirkbuddo).

3. **Certior dum cerno** *Latin* 'More sure while I discern'
—Lundin.

4. **Confide** *Latin* 'Be confident'
—Gen. Sir R. Gardiner, G. C. B.

5. **Confide recte agens** *Latin* 'Doing rightly, be confident'
—Broadhead, Glanville, Fellows, Long, Newdigate, Newdigate.

6. **Confisus viribus** *Latin* 'Confident in my own powers'
—Watson.

7. **Cui fides fide** *Latin* 'Place full confidence in whom you trust'
—Peard.

8. **Far and sure**
—Hunter.

9. **Fida clavo** *Latin* 'Made sure with a nail'
—Carr.

10. **Fide et fiducia** *Latin* 'By fidelity and confidence'
—Blackman, Gilchrist, Harnage (Bt.), Primrose, Roseberry (E.), Thorlby, Watt.

11. **Fiducia creat fidem** *Latin* 'Confidence gives rise to fidelity'
—Ingoldsby.

12. **Fiducia et labore** *Latin* 'By confidence and industry'
—Jockel.

13. **Fiducia et vi** *Latin* 'By confidence and strength'
—Slough B. C., U.K.

14. **Labore et fiducia** *Latin* 'By industry and confidence'
—Litster.

15. **Per crucem confido** *Latin* 'By the cross I have confidence'
—Crosley.

16. **Pie repone te** *Latin* 'Repose with pious confidence'
—Pierrepont, Manvers (E.), Mordey.

17. **Recta ubique** *Latin* 'Things right everywhere'
—Gaury.

18. **Recte agens confido**   *Latin* 'While acting uprightly I am confident'
> —Perry (of Avon Dasset).

19. **Silendo et sperando**   *Latin* 'In quietness and in confidence'
> —[Isa., xxx. 15.] August, Duke of Saxony-Weissenfels (1614–80).

20. **Union, justice, confidence**
> —State of Louisiana.

21. **Union, justice and confidence**
> —Northwestern State University, Natchitoches, Louisiana; Alexandria Vocational-Technical Institute, Alexandria, Louisiana.

22. **Union/ confidence/ justice**
> —Louisiana Technical University, Ruston, Louisiana.

CONFLICT (*See also* AGGRESSION; ENEMIES; HOSTILITY; OPPOSITION; WAR.)

1. **Consilio absit discordia**   *Latin* 'Let discord be absent from counsel'
> —Whitehaven B. C., U.K.

2. **Discordiae fomes injuria**   *Latin* 'Injustice breeds discord'
> —Johann Ernst I, Duke of Saxony-Weimar (1594–1626).

3. **Discordia frangimur**   *Latin* 'By discord we are broken'
> —Glass-sellers' Company.

4. **Discordia maxima dilabuntur**   *Latin* 'The greatest things are brought to naught by discord'
> —Tailors' Company, Exeter.

5. **Discordia praecursor ruinae**   *Latin* 'Discord is the forerunner of ruin'
> —Johann Philipp, Duke of Saxony-Altenburg (1597–1639).

6. **J'aspire**   *French* 'I aspire'
> —Devizmes.

7. **Nil agit, litem quod lite resolvit**   *Latin* 'He does no good, because he settles strife by strife'
> —[Horace, *Sat.* ii. 3. 103.] Field.

CONQUEST (*See also* VICTORY.)

1. **A rege et victoria**   *Latin* 'From the king and by conquest'
> —Barry, Ligonier, Thatchell.

2. **Bis vincit qui se vincit** *Latin* 'He conquers twice who conquers himself'

—Bysse.

3. **Certavi et vici** *Latin* 'I have fought and conquered'

—O'Flanaghan.

4. **Conquer or die**

—Crosthwaite.

5. **Curre ut vincas** *Latin* 'Run that you may conquer'

—Warren.

6. **Expugnare** *Latin* 'To conquer'

—Crawfurd.

7. **Expugnavi** *Latin* 'I have conquered'

—Pollock.

8. **Fugiendo vincimus** *Latin* 'We conquer by fleeing'

—Ogg.

9. **Gradatim vincimus** *Latin* 'We conquer by degrees'

—Browne, Curtis (Bt.), Duke (Bt.).

10. **Hactenus invictus** *Latin* 'Hitherto unconquered'

—Crawfurd, Gallightly, Gellatly.

11. **His vinces** *Latin* 'With these you will conquer'

—MacDonnell.

12. **Hoc vinco** *Latin* 'With this I conquer'

—Hay.

13. **I conquer by the wound**

—Bartholomew.

14. **I conquer or die**

—Lumsden.

15. **Igne et ferris vicimus** *Latin* 'We conquer by fire and swords'

—Hodder.

16. **Ille vincit ego mereo** *Latin* 'He conquers, I deserve'

—Sinclair.

17. **In bono vince** *Latin* 'Conquer by the good'

—Ramsgate College, U.K.

18. **In hoc signo vincam** *Latin* 'Under this sign I shall conquer'

—Order of St. Mary the Glorious.

19. **In hoc signo vinces** *Latin* 'Under this sign you shall conquer'
—Arran (E.), Aiscough, Burtee (Bt.), Berrie, Booth (Bt.),
Burke, Cavan, D'Urban, Dickens, Gore (Bt.),
Glasham, Glasbern, Ironside, Kuyfton, Langton (of
Newton Park), Knox (of Belleck Abbey), Macadam,
McCarlie, McKerlie, Mosse, Newling, Stanhope (Bt.),
Taylor, Turney, Watson, O'Donnell (Bt.), Order of
St. Constantine, Waltham U. D. C., U.K.

21. **In hoc vinces** *Latin* 'In this shall you conquer'
—Cross.

22. **In victos** *Latin* 'Against the conquered'
—Cracknell.

23. **Invigila sic vinces** *Latin* 'Watch, so shall you conquer'
—Price.

24. **In vigilia sic vinces** *Latin* 'In watchfulness thus will you conquer'
—Price.

25. **Mars denique victor es** *Latin* 'You Mars at length are the conqueror'
—Marsden.

26. **Me vincit, ego mereo** *Latin* 'He has conquered me I am the gainer'
—Sinclair.

27. **Nec me qui caetera vincit** *Latin* 'Nor does he who conquers all other things conquer me'
—Bruce.

28. **Per ignem ferris vicimus** *Latin* 'Even through fire have we conquered with our sword'
—Hodder.

29. **Persevera et vince** *Latin* 'Persevere and conquer'
—Smith.

30. **Perseverantia omnia vincit** *Latin* 'Perseverance conquers all things'
—Cooper.

31. **Perseverantia vincit** *Latin* 'Perseverance conquers'
—Kesteven C. C., U.K.; Burnes.

32. **Qui nos vincet?** *Latin* 'Who shall conquer us?'
—Beugo.

33. **Qui patitur vincit** *Latin* 'He conquers who endures'
—Kinnard (B.), Kinaird.

34. **Semper victor** *Latin* 'Always conqueror'
—Ramsay (of Whitehill).

35. **Sine sanguine victor** *Latin* 'A bloodless conqueror'
—Smith.

36. **Tandem vincitur** *Latin* 'At last it is conquered'
—Morris (U.S.).

37. **Tanquam despicatus sum vinco** *Latin* 'Although I am despised I conquer'
—Grant.

38. **Te duce vincimus** *Latin* 'With thee as leader, we conquer'
—Scots Guards.

39. **Tenax propositi vinco** *Latin* 'Being firm of purpose I conquer'
—Grimshaw.

40. **Tentando superabis** *Latin* 'You will conquer by trying'
—Kingdom.

41. **Traditus, non victus** *Latin* 'Betrayed, not conquered'
—Howden (B.).

42. **Ut vidi ut vici** *Latin* 'As I saw, so I conquered'
—Naunton.

43. **Vae victis** *Latin* 'Woe to the conquered'
—Senhouse (of Nether Hall).

44. **Venabulis vinco** *Latin* 'I conquer with hunting-spears'
—Venables.

45. **Vici** *Latin* 'I have conquered'
—Cooke, Raines.

46. **Vicimus** *Latin* 'We have conquered'
—Brett, White.

47. **Vicisti et vivimus** *Latin* 'Thou hast conquered and we survive'
—Johnson (of Bath, Bt.).

48. **Vicit, pepercit** *Latin* 'He conquered, he spared'
—Draper.

49. **Victor** *Latin* 'Conqueror'
—James (of Eltham), Linskill.

50. **Victor in arduis** *Latin* 'A conqueror amid difficulties'
—McConnel.

51. **Victrix prudentia** *Latin* 'Prudence is conqueror'
—Gordon.

52. **Victus in arduis** *Latin* 'Conquered in difficulties' or 'Their abode is in steep places'
—Harrison.

53. **Vidi, vici** *Latin* 'I saw, I conquered'
—Scurfield, Twiselton.

54. **Vincam** *Latin* 'I shall conquer'
—Griffen.

55. **Vincam vel moriar** *Latin* 'I will conquer or die'
—Caton, McDougall, McDowall.

56. **Vincendo victus** *Latin* 'Conquered in conquering'
—Lee.

57. **Vincenti dabitur** *Latin* 'It shall be given to the conqueror'
—Vincent (Bt.).

58. **Vincenti dabitur laurea** *Latin* 'The laurel is given to the conqueror'
—Vincent (U.S.).

59. **Vincent qui se vincent** *French* 'They shall conquer who conquer themselves'
—Vincent.

60. **Vincere** *Latin* 'To conquer'
—McCoul.

61. **Vincere aut mori** *Latin* 'To either conquer or die'
—McNeill, O'Hagan, Tuthill.

62. **Vincere est vivere** *Latin* 'To conquer is to live'
—Smyth.

63. **Vincere vel mori** *Latin* 'To conquer or die'
—McDowall, McGougan, McNeil, McNelly, Macneill (of Barra), Maclaine, Neil, Neill.

64. **Vincet vel mori** *Latin* 'He shall conquer or die'
—McDowall.

65. **Vincet virtute** *Latin* 'He shall conquer by virtue'
—Smart.

66. **Vincit liberavit** *Latin* 'He conquers, he has set free'
—Slingsby.

67. **Vincit omnia** *Latin* 'He conquers all things'
—O'Conry.

68. **Vincit qui devincit** *Latin* 'He conquers who endears'
—Griffen.

69. **Vincit qui patitur** *Latin* 'He conquers who endures'
—Berea College, Berea, Kentucky.

70. **Vincit qui se vincit** *Latin* 'He conquers who conquers himself'
—Ellis, Wilson (Co. York), Holland.

71. **Virtute et fide vinco** *Latin* 'I conquer by bravery and fidelity'
—Fenton.

72. **Vita vel morte triumpha** *Latin* 'Triumph in life or death'
—Allen.

73. **Vivere sat vincere** *Latin* 'To conquer is to live enough'
—Attwood, Molyneux, DeMolines, Sefton (E.), Ventry
(B.).

CONSCIENCE (*See also* RECTITUDE.)

1. **A good conscience is a sure defence**
—Paruck.

2. **Asgre lan diogel ei phercen** *Welsh* 'Secure is he with a pure heart'
—Herbert (of Llanarth Court), Jones, Vaughan.

3. **Conscientia virtuti satis amplum theatrum est** *Latin* 'A good conscience is a sufficient sphere of activity for virtue'
—Friedrich V, Margrave of Baden-Durlach (1594–1659).

4. **God and my conscience**
—Roberts.

5. **Gott, Vaterland, Gewissen** *German* 'God, fatherland, conscience'
—Albrecht, Duke of Saxony-Eisenach (1599–1644).

6. **Milita bonam militiam retinens fidem et bonam conscientiam** *Latin* 'War a good warfare, holding faith, and a good conscience'
—[1 Tim., i. 18–19.] Rudolf, Prince of Anhalt-Zerbst
(1576–1621); Wilhelm, Duke of Saxony
(1596–1622).

7. **Murus aeneus, conscientia sana** *Latin* 'A sound conscience is a wall of brass'
—Lumley, Scarborough (E.), Williamson.

8. **Nil conscire sibi** *Latin* 'To have a conscience free from guilt'
—[Horace, *Ep.* i. 1. 61.] Biss, Bullock (of Faulkbourn),
Carew (Bt.), Collingwood, French, Michel (of
Dewlish), Rothwell, Rogers, Sibthorp, Winchelsea
(E.), Walker, Webb.

9. **Proba conscientia** *Latin* 'A good conscience'
—Bacon.

10. **Stabit conscius aequi** *Latin* 'Conscious of what is just he shall stand'
—Charlton, Grant-Dalton.

CONSERVATION (*See also* PERMANENCE.)

1. **Aliis reposita** *Latin* 'Laid by for others'
—Cant.

2. **Condidi** *Latin* 'I have stored up'
—Stewart.

3. **Conservabo ad mortem** *Latin* 'I will preserve it till death'
—Jennings.

4. **Et custos et pugnax** *Latin* 'Both a preserver and a champion'
—Marjoribanks.

5. **Gardez le capron** *French* 'Preserve Capron'
—Hollist.

6. **Stet** *Latin* 'Let it stand'
—Standbridge.

7. **Waste not**
—Green.

CONSISTENCY

1. **Aequabiliter et diligenter** *Latin* 'By consistency and diligence'
—Mitford, Moore, Redesdale (B.).

2. **Always the same**
—Freebairn.

3. **Feror unus et idem** *Latin* 'I am borne along one and the same'
—Collingwood, Mitchell.

4. **In adversis idem** *Latin* 'The same in adversity'
—Duke (U.S.).

5. **Maneo qualis manebam** *Latin* 'I remain such as I was remaining'
   —Pendleton (U.S.).

6. **Nec devius unquam** *Latin* 'Never varying'
   —Wallace.

7. **Qualis ab incepto** *Latin* 'The same as from the beginning'
   —De Grey (E.), Hamilton (of Abbotstown), Majendie, Mirehouse, Weddell.

8. **Sans changer ma vérité** *French* 'Without changing my word'
   —Le Strange, L'Estrange.

9. **Semper eadem** *Latin* 'Always the same'
   —Collmore, Forrester (Bt.), Fairburn, Hollingsworth, Hornsey, Panton, Reid.; Leicester City and C. B. C., U.K.; Queen Elizabeth I.

10. **Semper idem** *Latin* 'Always the same'
    —Anton Ulrich, Duke of Braunschweig-Wolfenbüttel (1633–1714); Garfit, Harvey.

11. **Semper sic** *Latin* 'Always thus'
    —Bedwell.

12. **Sempre in un modo** *Italian* 'Always in one way'
    —Loftus.

13. **The same**
    —Skeen.

14. **Toujours le même** *French* 'Always the same'
    —Georg Wilhelm, Margrave of Brandenburg-Baireuth (1678–1726); Tait; Order of the Red Eagle (Brandenburg).

15. **Tout un durant ma vie** *Old French* 'Always the same during my life'
    —Barrington, Pelham-Clay.

16. **Un durant ma vie** *French* 'The same during my life'
    —Barrington (Bt.).

CONTEMPT

1. **Calco sub pedibus** *Latin* 'I trample it under my feet'
   —Alcock.

2. **Despicit quae vulgus suspicit** *Latin* 'He despises what the crowd admires'
   —Ryland.

3. **Immeritas temnere minas**   *Latin* 'To scorn undeserved threats'
—Thores.

4. **Nil admirari**   *Latin* 'Not to admire'
—Bolingbroke, Clare (E.), Carew (B.).

5. **Parva contemnimus**   *Latin* 'We despise small things'
—Gernon.

6. **Spernit humum**   *Latin* 'He spurns what is base'
—[Horace, *Odes* 3. 2. 24] Forbes (of Pittencrief), Mitchell, McKindley.

7. **Sperno**   *Latin* 'I reject'
—Elleis.

8. **Temere ne sperne**   *Latin* 'Do not scorn rashly'
—Bramble.

CONVENIENCE (*See also* USEFULNESS.)

1. **Commodum non damnum**   *Latin* 'A benefit, not an injury'
—Backie, Baikie (of Tankerness).

2. **Ex usu commodum**   *Latin* 'Advantage from its use'
—Smith (of Dirleton).

3. **Fungor fruor**   *Latin* 'I use, I enjoy'
—Pybus (U.S.).

4. **His utere mecum**   *Latin* 'Use these things with me'
—Twogood.

5. **Illustrans commoda vitae**   *Latin* 'Illustrating the conveniences of life'
—Royal Institution of Great Britain.

6. **Utitur ante quaesitis**   *Latin* 'He uses what has been gained before'
—Draghorn.

COUNTENANCE

1. **Facies qualis mens talis**   *Latin* 'As the face so is the mind'
—Blair (of Balmill).

2. **Facie tenus**   *Latin* 'Even to the face'
—Wheler (Co. Warwick).

COUNTRY (*See also* HOME; NATIONAL MOTTOES; PATRIOTISM.)

1. **All for our country**

   —State of Nevada.

2. **Amor patriae vincit** *Latin* 'The love of country conquers'

   —Meyler.

3. **Amor vincit patriae** *Latin* 'The love of country conquers'

   —Gibbes (U.S.).

4. **Cara patria carior libertas** *Latin* 'Dear country, dearer liberty'

   —Clinton (U.S.).

5. **Cara vita, carior patria, carissima libertas** *Latin* 'Dear life, dearer country, dearest liberty'

   —Kettle (U.S.).

6. **Decorum pro patria mori** *Latin* 'It is honorable to die for our country'

   —[after Horace, *Odes* III. ii. 13.] Ellis.

7. **Delectat amor patriae** *Latin* 'The love of country delights'

   —Smith (Co. Meath).

8. **Deo, patriae, amicis** *Latin* 'To God, my country and my friends'

   —Cooper.

9. **Deo, patriae, proximo** *Latin* 'For God, my Country, my neighbor'

   —Christian, Duke of Saxony-Eisenberg (1653–1707).

10. **Deo, patriae, regi** *Latin* 'For God, my country and my king'

    —Cooper.

11. **Deo, patriae, tibi** *Latin* 'For God, my native land and thee'

    —Laimboro.

12. **Deo, regi, et patriae** *Latin* 'To God, my king, and my country'

    —Irvine.

13. **Deo, regi, patriae** *Latin* 'To God, my king, my country'

    —Duncombe (of Cassgrove), Feversham (B.), Irvine (of Kinconssie).

14. **Deo, reipublicae, et amicis** *Latin* 'To God, our country, and our friends'

    —Levant Company.

15. **Deo et patriae** *Latin* 'For God and country'

    —Friedrich Ulrich, Duke of Braunschweig-Wolfenbüttel (1591–1634); Johann Georg I, Elector of Saxony (1613–80); Friedrich Heinrich, Count of the Palatinate (1614–29); Adolf Wilhelm, Duke of Saxony-Eisenach (1632–68); Outhwaite.

16. **Deo et patriae fidelis** *Latin* 'Faithful to God and country'
—Atkinson.

17. **Deo patriae, scientiis, artibus** *Latin* 'For God and country through sciences and arts'
—Gonzaga University School of Law, Spokane, Washington.

18. **Deo patriaeque fidelis** *Latin* 'Faithful to God and my country'
—Fagan.

19. **Deo Reipublicae et amicis esto semper fidelis** *Latin* 'Be ever faithful to God, the state, and friends'
—Duffield (U.S.).

20. **Deus, patria, rex** *Latin* 'God, native land, and king'
—Phillipps, Phillips, Tarlton.

21. **Dias mo dhuthaich** *Scots Gaelic* 'For God and my country'
—Mackenzie (Bt.), MacKenzie.

22. **Dieu et ma patrie** *French* 'God and my country'
—Marton.

23. **Dieu et mon pays** *French* 'God and my country'
—McKirdy.

24. **Dieu et mon roi** *French* 'God and my king'
—Rawlinson.

25. **Dios, patria, libertad** *Spanish* 'God, fatherland and liberty'
—Dominican Republic.

26. **Dulce est pro patria mori** *Latin* 'It is sweet to die for one's country'
—[after Horace, *Odes* III. 2. 13.] Van Rensselaer (U.S.).

27. **Dulce pro patriâ periculum** *Latin* 'Danger is sweet for one's country'
—Ker (of Moristoun).

28. **Dulcis amor patriae** *Latin* 'The love of one's country is sweet'
—Clifford, Fitzwygram (Bt.), Robinson.

29. **Dulcis pro patria labor** *Latin* 'Labor for one's country is sweet'
—McKerrell (of Hill House).

30. **Duty, honor, country**
—West Point U.S. Military Academy, West Point, New York.

31. **Faithful to my unhappy country**
—Molyneux.

32. **For God, Queen, and country**
—Harleyford, Buckinghamshire, England.

33. **For God and my country**
—Uganda.

34. **For my country**
—Jobling.

35. **France et sans dol** *French* 'For France and without sorrow'
—Cartier.

36. **Fy Nuw a Chymru** *Welsh* 'My God and Wales'
—Philipps, Walters.

37. **Gott, Vaterland, Gewissen** *German* 'God, fatherland, conscience'
—Albrecht, Duke of Saxony-Eisenach (1599–1644).

38. **Haec manus ob patriam** *Latin* 'This hand for my country'
—Mactier, Shuckburgh (Bt.).

39. **Home and country**
—National Society of the Daughters of the American Revolution.

40. **Honestum pro patria** *Latin* 'What is honorable and just should be done for one's country'
—Heinrich Julius, Duke of Braunschweig-Wolfenbüttel (1564–1613).

41. **Honestum pro patriâ** *Latin* 'What is honorable for my country'
—Hamilton.

42. **Honneur et patrie** *French* 'Honor and my country'
—Order of the Legion of Honor (France).

43. **Instat vi patriae** *Latin* 'He rushes on with the strength of his country'
—Tichburn.

44. **J'aime mon Dieu, mon roi, et ma patrie** *French* 'I love my God, my king, and my country'
—Kirvin.

45. **Le roy et l'estat** *Old French* 'The king and the state'
—Ashburnham (E.), Sherard.

46. **L'homme vrai aime son pays** *French* 'The true man loves his country'
—Homfray (Co. Stafford).

47. **Libertas et natale solum** *Latin* 'Liberty and my native soil'
—Adams (of Bowden), Freeman, Sanderson.

48. **Libertas et patria** *Latin* 'Liberty and country'
—Giles (U.S.).

49. **Libertas et patria mea** *Latin* 'Liberty and my country'
—Giles (U.S.).

50. **Mon Dieu, mon roi, et ma patrie** *French* 'My god, my king, and my country'
—Kerwan (Co. Galway).

51. **Natale solum dulce** *Latin* 'Our native soil is sweet'
—Taylor (of Todmorden Hall, Co. Lancaster, and Burghfield, Co. Berks).

52. **Nil nisi patria** *Latin* 'Nothing without one's country'
—Hindmarsh.

53. **No country, no fatherland that does not keep faith**
—Confederate States of America.

54. **Non mihi sed patriae** *Latin* 'Not for myself, but for my country'
—Hippisley (Co. Berks, Bt.), Spring, Springe.

55. **Non mutat genus solum** *Latin* 'Country does not change the race'
—Hamilton.

56. **Non sibi, patriae** *Latin* 'Not for himself, for his country'
—Tomlinson.

57. **Non sibi, sed patriae** *Latin* 'Not for himself, but for his country'
—Baker, Heppesley, Romney (E.), Marsham, Thomlinson.

58. **Non sibi, sed patriae natus** *Latin* 'Not born for himself, but for his country'
—Jodrell (Bt.).

59. **Numini et patriae asto** *Latin* 'I stand by God and my country'
—Aston (B.).

60. **Ob ducem, ob patriam** *Latin* 'For (our) leader, for (our) country'
—Waddy.

61. **Ob patriam vulnera passi** *Latin* 'Having endured wounds for their country'
—Burnes (of Montrose).

62. **Omne solum forti patria** *Latin* 'Every soil is a fatherland to the brave man'
—[Ovid, *Fasti*, i. 493.] Julius Heinrich, Duke of Saxony-Lauenburg (1586–1665); Balfour (of Burleigh, Bruges (co. Wilts); D'Oy (bt.); Tounley-Balfour (of Tounley Hall).

63. **Omne solum patria** *Latin* 'Every land is our native country'
—Bill.

64. **Omne solum viro patria est** *Latin* 'Every country is a home for a man'
—Matthews.

65. **Omnia relinquit servare rempublicam** *Latin* 'He leaves everything to save the state'
—Turberville (U.S.).

66. **Par l'amour et la fidélité envers la patrie** *French* 'By love and fidelity towards our country'
—Order of St. Catharine (Russia).

67. **Patria cara, carior fides** *Latin* 'My country is dear, my faith dearer'
—Nicolas, Nicholas, Thomson.

68. **Patria cara, carior libertas** *Latin* 'My country is dear, but liberty is dearer'
—Bouverie, Cay, Lindon, Pleydell-Bouverie-Campbell-Wyndham.

69. **Patriae et Deo sursum deorsum** *Latin* 'For my country and my God, upwards and downwards'
—Johann Georg II, Elector of Saxony (1613–80).

70. **Patriae et religioni fidelis** *Latin* 'Faithful to country and religion'
—Teevan.

71. **Patriae fidelis** *Latin* 'Faithful to my country'
—Tiffin, Wood.

72. **Patriae fidus** *Latin* 'Faithful to my country'
—Lewis (Co. Glamorgan).

73. **Patriae infelici fidelis** *Latin* 'Faithful to my unhappy country'
—Courtown (E.), Molyneux, Montgomery, Stopford.

74. **Patriae non sibi** *Latin* 'For his country, not for himself'
—Argles.

75. **Patria fidelis** *Latin* 'A faithful country'
—Tiffin.

76. **Patriam amo** *Latin* 'I love my country'
—Scott.

77. **Patriam hinc sustinet** *Latin* 'Hence he sustains his country'
—Higgins.

78. **Patria veritas fides**. *Latin* 'Country, truth, faith'
—Everett (U.S.).

79. **Patrie est où bien on est** *French* 'Our country is wherever we are well off'
   —[Teucer, *Fragm.* 21.] Ernst, Margrave of Brandenburg (1617–42).

80. **Pie vivere, et Deum et patriam diligere** *Latin* 'To live piously, and to love (both) God and our country'
   —Redmond.

81. **Pour Dieu et mon pays** *French* 'For God and my country'
   —De Lantour.

82. **Pour ma libertay pour ma patree** *Old French* 'For my liberty, for my country'
   —Vaudin.

83. **Pour ma patrie** *French* 'For my country'
   —Cooper, Dalgairns.

84. **Pro amore patriae** *Latin* 'For love of country'
   —Scot, Scott.

85. **Pro Christo et patria** *Latin* 'For Christ and country'
   —Geneva College, Beaver Falls, Pennsylvania; Gilbert, Ker, Verner.

86. **Pro Christo et patria dulce periculum** *Latin* 'For Christ and my country danger is sweet'
   —Carr, Roxburghe (D.).

87. **Pro Christo et Republica** *Latin* 'For Christ and the Republic'
   —Birmingham-Southern College, Birmingham, Alabama.

88. **Pro Deo, patriâ, et rege** *Latin* 'For God, my country, and my king'
   —Blades (of High Paull), Beugo, James (of Dublin, Bt.).

89. **Pro Deo, pro Rege, pro patria, et lege** *Latin* 'For God, for the King, for the country, and the law'
   —Blakemore.

90. **Pro Deo, rege, et patriâ** *Latin* 'For God, my king, and my country'
   —Blaydes (of Rawby), McDowall.

91. **Pro Deo et nobilissima patria Batavorum** *Latin* 'For God and the exalted country of the Batavians'
   —Van Nest (U.S.).

92. **Pro Deo et patria** *Latin* 'For God and country'
   —University of Dayton School of Law, Dayton, Ohio; Loras College, Dubuque, Iowa, Maguire.

93. **Pro Deo et pro patria** *Latin* 'For God and for country'
—Stackpole.

94. **Pro fide ac patria** *Latin* 'For my faith and country'
—Longe.

95. **Pro fide et patria** *Latin* 'For faith and my country'
—Daniell, Johann Georg II, Elector of Saxony (1613–80).

96. **Pro fide rege et patria pugno** *Latin* 'I fight for the faith, king, and country'
—Lentaigne, O'Neill.

97. **Pro lege et patria** *Latin* 'For law and country'
—Daniel.

98. **Pro libertate et patriâ** *Latin* 'For liberty and my country'
—Michie.

99. **Pro libertate patriae** *Latin* 'For the liberty of my country'
—Evans, Clarina (B.), Massy (B.), Massey (Bt.), Maysey.

100. **Pro patria** *Latin* 'For my country'
—Bannerman (Bt.), Betson, Bulman, Bonsall, Cooke, Carbery (B.), Douglas (of Carnoustie, Bt.), Douglas, Groseth, Hay (Bt.), Higgins, Hamilton (of Preston), Hastie, James (Bt.), Kay, Newlands, Newton (of Newton), Ogilvie, Provan, Rochead, Scott, Turner, Warrington, Wood (of Holm Hull), Widdrington, Order of the Sword (Sweden).

101. **Pro patria auxilio Deo** *Latin* 'For my country with God's help'
—Grossett (Co. Wilts).

102. **Pro patria consumor** *Latin* 'I exhaust myself for my country'
—Heinrich Julius, Duke of Braunschweig-Wolfenbüttel (1564–1613).

103. **Pro patriâ ejusque libertate** *Latin* 'For my country and its freedom'
—Joy.

104. **Pro patria et gloria** *Latin* 'For country and honor'
—7th Regiment of National Guard, State of New York (U.S. Civil War).

105. **Pro patria et libertate** *Latin* 'For country and liberty'
—Michie.

106. **Pro patria et religione** *Latin* 'For country and religion'
—Shanly.

107. **Pro patria et virtute** *Latin* 'For country and virtue'
—Higgins.

108. **Pro patria mori** *Latin* 'To die for my country'
—Gardiner (U.S.), Manly.

109. **Pro patria non timidus perire** *Latin* 'Not afraid to die for my country'
—Champneys (Bt.).

110. **Pro patria saepe, pro Rege semper** *Latin* 'For my country often, for my king always'
—Ainslie.

111. **Pro patria sanguis** *Latin* 'My blood for my country'
—Splatt.

112. **Pro patria semper** *Latin* 'For my country ever'
—Callow, Power (Bt.).

113. **Pro patria uro** *Latin* 'I burn for my country'
—Costerton.

114. **Pro patria vivere et mori** *Latin* 'To live and die for our country'
—Grattan.

115. **Pro rure pro patria** *Latin* 'For countryside and country'
—Hertford R. D. C., U.K.

116. **Pro virtute patria** *Latin* 'For his valor, his country (gave it)'
—Order of the Two Sicilies.

117. **Pugna pro patria** *Latin* 'Fight for the country'
—Georg, Duke of Braunschweig-Lüneburg (1582–1641), Aldershot B. C., U.K.

118. **Pugna pro patria, 1625** *Latin* 'Fight for the country, 1625'
—Reynolds (U.S.).

119. **Pugna pro patria, & (Paul Revere)** *Latin* 'Fight for the country, & (Paul Revere)'
—Revere (U.S.).

120. **Quid non pro patria?** *Latin* 'What would not one do for his country?'
—Campbell (of Perthshire), Mathew.

121. **Qui non patriam amat?** *Latin* 'Who does not love his country?'
—Quinan.

122. **Quod non pro patria?** *Latin* 'What would one not do for his country?'
—Bowie, Bowhie.

123. **Quo me cunque vocat patria** *Latin* 'Whithersoever my country calls me'
—Arden (of Longcroft).

124. **Regi et patriae fidelis** *Latin* 'Faithful to king and country'
—Norbury (B.).

125. **Regi patriaeque fidelis** *Latin* 'Faithful to king and country'
—Scott (of Great Barr, bt.).

126. **Regis et patriae tantum valet amor** *Latin* 'So much does love of king and country avail'
—Tyldesley.

127. **Religioni reipublicae** *Latin* 'For religion and the state'
—King Henry VIII School, Coventry, U.K.

128. **Rhyddid gwerin ffyniant gwlad** *Welsh* 'The freedom of the people is the prosperity of the land'
—Carmarthenshire C. C., U.K.

129. **Semper paratus pugnare pro patriâ** *Latin* 'Always ready to fight for my country'
—Lockhart (B.).

130. **Semper praesto patriae servire** *Latin* 'I am ever ready to serve my country'
—O'Neil.

131. **The Fatherland is worth more than the Kingdom of Heaven**
—Kingdom of Nepal.

132. **Tout pour Dieu et ma patrie** *French* 'Wholly for God and my country'
—Winn (of Nostell Priory, Co. York).

133. **Travail, liberté, patrie** *French* 'Work, freedom, fatherland'
—Republic of Togo.

134. **Ubi bene ibi patria** *Latin* 'One's country is where one is well'
—Baillie.

135. **Ubi libertas ibi patria** *Latin* 'Where liberty prevails there is my country'
—Beverley, Baillie, Darch, Dinwiddie, Garrett, Hugar.

136. **Ubique patriam reminisci** *Latin* 'Everywhere to remember one's country'
—Cass (of East Barnet), Harris, Malmesbury (E.).

137. **Veritas et patria** *Latin* 'Truth and my country'
—Hoadly.

138. **Verus amor patriae** *Latin* 'The true love of country'
—Hughes (of Wexford).

139. **Vicit amor patriae** *Latin* 'Love of country has conquered'
—Holles.

140. **Vincit amor patriae** *Latin* 'The love of my country exceeds everything'
>—Chichester (E.), Cooper, Gun, Hargreaves, James, Molesworth (V.), Muncaster (B.), Pennington.

141. **Vincit amor patriae** *Latin* 'Love of country prevails'
>—Sunderland R. D. C., U.K.

142. **Virtus libertas et patria** *Latin* 'Virtue, liberty, and country'
>—Wetmore (U.S.).

143. **Virtuti pro patria** *Latin* 'For valor in behalf of our country'
>—Order of Maximilian Joseph of Bavaria.

COUNTRYSIDE

1. **Pax hospita ruris** *Latin* 'Peace, the hostess of the countryside'
>—Jones (U.S.).

2. **Rura mihi placent** *Latin* 'Things of the countryside please me'
>—Congleton R. D. C., U.K.

3. **Ruris amator** *Latin* 'Lover of the countryside'
>—Friern Barnet U. D. C., U.K.

4. **Rus gratiis musisque dignum** *Latin* 'A countryside worthy of the Graces and Muses'
>—Bathavon R. D. C., U.K.

5. **Urbs in rure** *Latin* 'The town in the countryside'
>—Solihull U. D. C., U.K.

COURAGE (*See also* AUDACITY; FORTITUDE; MILITARY DISTINCTION.)

1. **Abest timor** *Latin* 'Fear is absent'
>—Ewart, Ker (of Sutherland Hall).

2. **Absque metu** *Latin* 'Without fear'
>—Dalmahoy (of Ravelridge).

3. **A coeur vaillant rien d'impossible** *French* 'To a valiant heart nothing is impossible'
>—Jeanne d'Albret, mother of Henry IV of Navarre; Henry IV of Navarre; Hartcup.

4. **Adest prudenti animus** *Latin* 'Courage belongs to the prudent'
>—Hamilton (of Mount Hamilton).

5. **Ad summa virtus** *Latin* 'Courage to the last'
>—Bruce (of Wester-Kinloch).

6. **Advance with courage**
—Marjoribanks (Bt.).

7. **Alis et animo** *Latin* 'On wings and with courage'
—Munro.

8. **Animis et fato** *Latin* 'By courageous acts and good fortune'
—Thriepland (Bt.).

9. **Animo** *Latin* 'With courage'
—Gordon.

10. **Animo, non astutia** *Latin* 'By courage, not by craft'
—Gordon (D.), Gordon (Bt.), Gordon (co. Down), Pedlar (of Hoo Mavey).

11. **Animo et fide** *Latin* 'By courage and faith'
—Burroughs (of Burlingham and Long Stratton, Co. Norfolk), Cornock (Co. Wexford), Guildford (E.), North, Phillips, Turner, Carshalton U. D. C., U.K., Stockport C. B. C., U.K.

12. **Animo et prudentia** *Latin* 'By courage and prudence'
—Howett, Jowett, Lyon, Mellor.

13. **Animo et scientia** *Latin* 'With courage and knowledge'
—Clark.

14. **Animose certavit** *Latin* 'He hath striven courageously'
—Pryme (of Cambridge).

15. **Animum fortuna sequitur** *Latin* 'Fortune follows courage'
—Bedford (Co. Warwick), Craik (of Arbigland).

16. **Animum ipse parabo** *Latin* 'I myself will provide courage'
—[Horace, *Ep.* i. 18, 111.] Nibbert.

17. **Animum prudentia firmat** *Latin* 'Prudence strengthens courage'
—Brisbane (of Scotland).

18. **Animus et fata** *Latin* 'Courage and fortune'
—Thriepland.

19. **Animus valet** *Latin* 'Courage availeth'
—Bosworth.

20. **Ardet virtus, non urit** *Latin* 'Valor inflames, but consumes not'
—Fyers, Fyres.

21. **Armis et animis** *Latin* 'By arms and courage'
—Carnagie, Carnegie, Gilfillan.

22. **Arte, Marte, vigore** *Latin* 'By skill, valour, and energy'
—Wednesbury B. C., U.K.

23. **Arte et animo** *Latin* 'By skill and courage'
                                                —Ferguson.

24. **Arte et Marte** *Latin* 'By skill and valor'
                                        —Middleton, Hunter.

25. **Artis vel Martis** *Latin* 'Of skill or valor'
                                            —Eastoft, Eure.

26. **At vincet pauperiem virtus** *Latin* 'But bravery will conquer poverty'
                                                    —Brey.

27. **Au coeur vaillant rien impossible** *French* 'To the valiant heart nothing is impossible'
              —Georg Wilhelm, Elector of Brandenburg (1595–1640).

28. **Audacia et virtute adepta** *Latin* 'Gained by daring and valor'
                                                    —Paton.

29. **Ausim et confido** *Latin* 'I am brave and confident'
                              —Areskine, Erskine (of Kirkbuddo).

30. **Au valeureux coeur rien impossible** *French* 'To the brave heart nothing is impossible'
                                                —Messeury.

31. **Aux armes vaillant, en amour constant** *French* 'In arms valiant, in love constant'
                              —Friedrich, Duke of Saxony (D. 1586).

32. **Avant sans peur** *French* 'Forward without fear'
                                              —Seton-Karr.

33. **A virtute orta** *Latin* 'Sprung from courage'
                                                  —Stewart.

34. **Bellicae virtutis praemium** *Latin* 'The reward of military valor'
              —Order of St. Louis and The Legion of Honour (France).

35. **Be strong and of good courage**
                                              —Beddington.

36. **Bonae virtutis amore** *Latin* 'From love for true valor'
                                              —Le Conteur.

37. **Bono animo esto** *Latin* 'Be of good courage'
                                                  —Morrell.

38. **By courage and faith**
                                        —Seaham U. D. C., U.K.

39. **By valour**
                                            —Hern, or Heron.

40. **Clementia et animis**   *Latin* 'By clemency and courage'
                                    —Panmure (B.), Maule.

41. **Conjuncta virtuti fortuna**   *Latin* 'Good fortune is allied to bravery'
                                    —McBeth.

42. **Consilio ac virtute**   *Latin* 'By prudence and valor'
                                    —Lewin.

43. **Consilio et anima**   *Latin* 'By wisdom and courage'
                                    —Wanstead and Woodford B. C., U.K.

44. **Consilio et animis**   *Latin* 'By wisdom and courage'
                —Gibson, Lauderdale (E.), Maitland (Bt.), Ramadge;
                          Kiveton Park R. D. C., Surbiton B. C., U.K.

45. **Constantia, virtus**   *Latin* 'Constancy and valor'
                                    —Fitz-William.

46. **Courage!**
                —Cummin, Cuming (of Reluglas), Cumming (of Pitully),
                          Cumming (of Coulter, bt.).

47. **Courage, humanity, commerce**
                                    —South Shields C. B. C., U.K.

48. **Courage à la mort**   *French* 'Courage till death'
                                    —Hutchins.

49. **Courage à l'Ecosse**   *French* 'Courage after the manner of the Scotch'
                                    —Spense.

50. **Courage avance le homme**   *French* 'Courage advances the man'
                                    —Vaughan (of Lettleton, kt.).

51. **Courage et esperance**   *French* 'Courage and hope'
                                    —Storie.

52. **Courage sans peur**   *French* 'Courage without fear'
                          —Aynesworth, Gage (V.), Willoughby.

53. **Courageux**   *French* 'Courageous'
                                    —Lee.

54. **Detur forti palma**   *Latin* 'Let the palm be given to the brave'
                                    —Sinclair (of Brimmes).

55. **Diofn diymffrost**   *Welsh* 'Fearless, boastless'
                                    —Wynne (of Pengwern).

56. **Drogo nomen, et virtus arma dedit**   *Latin* 'Drogo is my name, and valor gavė me arms'
                          —Drew (descendant of the family of Drogo).

57. **Ense et animo**   *Latin* 'With sword and courage'
—Grant (Bt.).

58. **Et agere et pati fortiter, Romanum est**   *Latin* 'Both to do and to endure bravely is a Roman's part'
—Romer.

59. **Et arte et Marte**   *Latin* 'Both by skill and valor'
—Bain.

60. **Et Marte et arte**   *Latin* 'Both by valor and skill'
—Bain, Bayn, Bayne, Drummond (of Pilkellanie).

61. **Et suavis et fortis**   *Latin* 'Pleasant and brave'
—Harper.

62. **Exemple brave et louable**   *French* 'A brave and praiseworthy example'
—Palliser.

63. **Fide et animus**   *Latin* 'Courage with faith'
—Howard.

64. **Fide et virtute**   *Latin* 'By fidelity and valor'
—Brandling, Gladstone (Bt.), Goodwin, Ramsbottom, Rochead.

65. **Fidus et fortit**   *Latin* 'Faithful and brave'
—Scott (of Castle House, bt.).

66. **Forte non ignave**   *Latin* 'Brave not cowardly'
—Lee.

67. **Fortes fideles**   *Latin* 'Brave and faithful'
—Stenhouse.

68. **Fortes semper monstrant misericordiam**   *Latin* 'The brave always show mercy'
—Baldwin.

69. **Forti et fideli nihil difficile**   *Latin* 'To the brave and faithful man nothing is difficult'
—Deane, McCarthy, Muskerry (B.), O'Keefe.

70. **Forti favet caelum**   *Latin* 'Heaven favors the brave'
—Oswald.

71. **Forti nihil difficile**   *Latin* 'Nothing is difficult to the brave'
—Disraeli.

72. **Forti non ignavo**   *Latin* 'To the brave man, not to the dastard'
—Lyell, Lyle, Lyde.

73. **Fortiorum fortia facta**   *Latin* 'The brave deeds of brave men'
—Stark, Stork.

74. **Fortis atque fidelis** *Latin* 'Brave and faithful'
—Savage (of Dublin).

75. **Fortis cadere, cedere non potest** *Latin* 'The brave man may fall, but cannot yield'
—Drogheda (M.), Moore (Bt.), Moore (Co. Kent and Berks.).

76. **Fortis cadere, non cedere potest** *Latin* 'The brave man may fall, but cannot yield'
—Moore.

77. **Fortis esto, non ferox** *Latin* 'Be brave, not ferocious'
—Wintringham (Bt.).

78. **Fortis est qui se vincit** *Latin* 'He is brave who conquers himself'
—Woods.

79. **Fortis et aequus** *Latin* 'Brave and just'
—Livingstone (of Aberdeen).

80. **Fortis et fide** *Latin* 'Brave and faithfully'
—Carfrae (of Edinburgh).

81. **Fortis et fidelis** *Latin* 'Brave and faithful'
—Close, Beton, Bryan, Douglas, Dunbar, D'Alton, Finlay, Findlay, Fletcher, May, Hind, Fitzgerald, Orme, Lalor, Middleton.

82. **Fortis et fidus** *Latin* 'Brave and trusty'
—Flint, Loughnan, McClauchlan, McLachlan (of Kilchoan), McLauchlan.

83. **Fortis et hospitalis** *Latin* 'Brave and hospitable'
—Murphy.

84. **Fortis et lenis** *Latin* 'Brave and gentle'
—Curry.

85. **Fortis et placabilis** *Latin* 'Brave and placable'
—Scot (of Bonholm).

86. **Fortis et stabilis** *Latin* 'Brave and steadfast'
—Killikelley.

87. **Fortis et vigilans** *Latin* 'Brave and vigilant'
—Orr.

88. **Fortis fidelis** *Latin* 'Brave, faithful'
—Stenhouse.

89. **Fortis in arduis** *Latin* 'Brave under difficulties'
—McDougall, McDowall, Middleton, Lord, Thompson, Beaton, Betune, Findlay.

90. **Fortis in bello**   *Latin* 'Brave in war'
—Cantillon de Ballyluge.

91. **Fortis in teipso**   *Latin* 'Brave in thyself'
—Ogle.

92. **Fortis non ferox**   *Latin* 'Brave, not fierce'
—Stockes, Stokes.

93. **Fortis qui prudens**   *Latin* 'He is brave who is prudent'
—Ormsby.

94. **Fortis sub forte**   *Latin* 'The brave under the brave'
—Fitz-Patrick.

95. **Fortis sub forte fatiscet**   *Latin* 'The brave shall grow weary beneath the brave'
—Robeck.

96. **Fortis valore et armis**   *Latin* 'Strong in courage and arms'
—Hatch.

97. **Fortiter**   *Latin* 'Bravely'
—Beauman (of Wexford), Boswell, Clipsham, Elliott (of Harwood), Longbottom, McCray, McAlister, McLachlan, Wright, Warrand.

98. **Fortiter, sed apte**   *Latin* 'Boldly, but appropriately'
—Falconer.

99. **Fortiter ac sapienter**   *Latin* 'Bravely and wisely'
—Hordern.

100. **Fortiter agendo**   *Latin* 'By acting bravely'
—Pitman.

101. **Fortiter! Ascende!**   *Latin* 'Bravely! Ascend!'
—Caldwell (U.S.).

102. **Fortiter defendit**   *Latin* 'He defends bravely'
—Andrews.

103. **Fortiter et aperte**   *Latin* 'Bravely and openly'
—Yatman.

104. **Fortiter et honeste**   *Latin* 'Bravely and uprightly'
—Hawkes (U.S.).

105. **Fortiter et sapienter ferre**   *Latin* 'To bear bravely and wisely'
—Porritt.

106. **Fortiter in angustis**   *Latin* 'Bravely in straits'
—Hartshorn.

107. **Fortiter in re**   *Latin* 'Bravely in action'
—Nunn.

108. **Fortiter qui fide** *Latin* '(He acts) bravely, who (acts) faithfully'
—Hamilton.

109. **Fortiter qui sedulo** *Latin* '(He acts) bravely, who (acts) carefully'
—Keith (of Craig).

110. **Fortiter sed feliciter** *Latin* 'Bravely but happily'
—White.

111. **Fortiter sed suaviter** *Latin* 'Bravely but gently'
—Lee, Muntz, Willsher.

112. **Fortiter ubique** *Latin* 'Bravely everywhere'
—Clerk.

113. **Fortitudine, doctrina, sapientia** *Latin* 'By bravery, by knowledge, by wisdom'
—Friedrich II, Duke of Saxony-Gotha and Altenburg (1676–1732).

114. **Fortitudine et ense** *Latin* 'By valor and the sword'
—Crossdell.

115. **Fortitudine et velocitate** *Latin* 'With courage and celerity'
—Balnaves, Balneaves.

116. **Fortitudini** *Latin* 'For courage'
—Hoste (Bt.); Order of Maria Theresa, founded 1757; Military Order of Maria Theresa (Austria).

117. **Fortunâ, virtute** *Latin* 'By good fortune and valor'
—Beath, Beith.

118. **Fortuna virtuti comes** *Latin* 'Fortune the companion of valor'
—Ferguson.

119. **For valor**
—The Victoria Cross.

120. **Functa virtute fides** *Latin* 'Faith having exhibited valor'
—Murray.

121. **Furth and fear nocht** *Scots Dialect*
—Farside.

122. **Generosa virtus nihil timet** *Latin* 'Generous valor fears nothing'
—Dunphy.

123. **Generosus et animosus** *Latin* 'Generous and courageous'
—Glennon.

124. **Gladio et virtute** *Latin* 'By the sword and by valor'
—Garstin.

125. **Haec fructus virtutis** *Latin* 'These are the fruit of valor'
—Waller (Bt.).

126. **Hic fructus virtutis** *Latin* 'This is the fruit of valor'
—Waller (Bt.).

127. **Honestas et fortitudo** *Latin* 'Honor and courage'
—Dunckerley.

128. **Impavide** *Latin* 'Fearlessly'
—B. Bond-Cabbell.

129. **Impavido pectore** *Latin* 'With undaunted heart'
—Murchison.

130. **Impavidum ferient ruinae** *Latin* 'Dangers shall strike me unappalled'
—Mundell.

131. **Industria, virtus, et fortitudo** *Latin* 'Industry, valor, and fortitude'
—Derby C. B. C., U.K., Smellie (of Slindon, co. Sussex).

132. **Inest clementia forti** *Latin* 'Mercy is inherent in the brave'
—Gent, Maule.

133. **Innocent courageous activity**
—White.

134. **In officio impavidus** *Latin* 'Fearless in office'
—Falshaw.

135. **In silentio fortitudo** *Latin* 'Courage in silence'
—Hardress, Thoresby.

136. **Intrepide et constanter** *Latin* 'Fearlessly and with constancy'
—Karl Wilhelm, Prince of Anhalt-Zerbst (1652–1718).

137. **Intrepidus** *Latin* 'Fearless'
—Scots Guards, U.K.

138. **Intrepidus et benignus** *Latin* 'Intrepid and benign'
—Mackennal.

139. **Invia virtuti pervia** *Latin* 'Pathless ways may be trodden by valor'
—Hamilton.

140. **In via virtuti pervia** *Latin* 'In the road which is accessible to valor'
—Hamilton.

141. **In virtute et fortuna** *Latin* 'In valor and fortune'
—Gardner.

142. **Irrideo tempestatem** *Latin* 'I laugh at the storm'
—Wood (of Mount House).

143. **Juncta virtuti fides** *Latin* 'Fidelity joined to valor'
—Murray.

144. **Juste et fortiter** *Latin* 'Justly and bravely'
—Blaxland.

145. **Juvant aspera fortes** *Latin* 'Difficulties delight the brave'
—Steuart.

146. **L'anticho valor non è anchor morto** *Italian* 'The ancient valor is not yet dead'
—Joachim Ernst, Prince of Anhalt (1592–1615).

147. **Macte virtute** *Latin* 'Honored for your valor'
—Murray.

148. **Macte virtute patrum** *Latin* 'Honored for the valor of your fathers'
—Mackrell.

149. **Marte et arte** *Latin* 'By valor and skill'
—Drummond (of London), Maguire, Nevoy, Jones (of Cranmer Hall, Co. Norfolk, bt.).

150. **Miles et fortis** *Latin* 'A soldier and a brave one'
—Ord.

151. **Misenach** *Scots Gaelic* 'Courage'
—Campbell.

152. **Mitis et fortis** *Latin* 'Gentle and brave'
—Ord.

153. **Mitis sed fortis** *Latin* 'Mild but brave'
—Orde, Phipson-Wybrants.

154. **Mox virtute se tollit ad auras** *Latin* 'Soon he will raise himself by his valor to the heavens'
—Swettenham, Warren.

155. **Munifice et fortiter** *Latin* 'Bountifully and bravely'
—Handyside.

156. **Muthig vorwartz** *German* 'Forward boldly'
—Prance.

157. **Nec deficit animus** *Latin* 'Courage does not fail me'
—Eccles.

158. **Nec desit virtus** *Latin* 'Nor let valor be wanting'
—Furse.

159. **Nec minus fortiter** *Latin* 'Not less bravely'
—Cuthbert, Cuthbertson.

160. **Nil metuens superavi** *Latin* 'Fearing nothing I have overcome'
—Bushe.

161. **Nil time** *Latin* 'Fear nothing'
—Man.

162. **Nil timeo** *Latin* 'I fear nothing'
—Drummond.

163. **Nil timere nec temere** *Latin* 'To fear nothing nor to act thought-lessly'
—Combe.

164. **Non metuo** *Latin* 'I do not fear'
—Hamilton (of Little Ernock).

165. **Non minor est virtus quam quaerere, arte tueri** *Latin* 'Nor is it less valor to defend by art than to obtain'
—Master.

166. **Non minor est virtus quam quaerere parta tueri** *Latin* 'To defend what you have gained is no less valor than to gain'
—Master.

167. **Ohne Furcht** *German* 'Without fear'
—Teschemaker.

168. **Omne solum forti patria** *Latin* 'Every soil is a fatherland to the brave man'
—[Ovid, *Fasti*, i. 493.] Julius Heinrich, Duke of Saxony-Lauenburg (1586–1665); Balfour (of Burleigh, Bruges (co. Wilts); D'Oyly (bt.); Tounley-Balfour (of Tounley Hall).

169. **Omnia fortitudine vincit** *Latin* 'He conquers everything by his bravery'
—Wiehe.

170. **Omni liber metu** *Latin* 'Free from every fear'
—Birley.

171. **Ornat fortem prudentia** *Latin* 'Prudence adorns the brave'
—Dunbar.

172. **Par valeur** *French* 'By valor'
—Heron, White.

173. **Patientia et magnanimitas** *Latin* 'Patience and courage'
—Kirby.

174. **Per saxa per ignes fortiter et recte** *Latin* 'Through rocks, through fires, bravely and rightly'
—Elliot (U.S.).

175. **Per tela per hostes impavidi** *Latin* 'Undaunted through arrows and enemies'
—Borron.

176. **Per vim et virtutem** *Latin* 'By strength and valor'
—Youl.

177. **Per virtutem scientiamque** *Latin* 'By valor and knowledge'
—MacNeil.

178. **Pie et fortiter** *Latin* 'Piously and bravely'
—Bennet.

179. **Pietate et bellica virtute** *Latin* 'By piety and martial valor'
—Order of St. Henry (Saxony).

180. **Post hominem animus durat** *Latin* 'After a man our courage is strengthened'
—Bridge.

181. **Pretium virtutis** *Latin* 'The prize of bravery'
—Welsh.

182. **Preux quoique pieux** *French* 'Valiant though pious'
—Long.

183. **Pristinae virtutis memores** *Latin* 'Mindful of our former valor'
—The Eighth Hussars.

184. **Provide et fortiter** *Latin* 'With prudence and with courage'
—Johann Georg I, Elector of Saxony (1585–1656).

185. **Pro virtute et fidelitate** *Latin* 'For valor and fidelity'
—Order of Military Merit (Hesse Cassel).

186. **Pro virtute patria** *Latin* 'For his valor, his country (gave it)'
—Order of the Two Sicilies.

187. **Prudentiâ et animis** *Latin* 'By prudence and courage'
—Steel.

188. **Prudentiâ et animo** *Latin* 'By prudence and courage'
—Antram, Ochterlony (Bt.).

189. **Prudentia et marte** *Latin* 'With prudence and courage'
—Mylne.

190. **Prudentia et virtute** *Latin* 'By prudence and valor'
—Rankin.

191. **Quid leone fortius?** *Latin* 'What is braver than a lion?'
—Clayton (Bt.).

192. **Quod agis fortiter** *Latin* 'Which you do bravely'
—Oliphant.

193. **Quo virtus vocat**   *Latin* 'Whither valor calls'
—Yate (of Whimper, Co. Suffolk), Yate (of Bromesberrow), Peacock-Yate.

194. **Rebus angustis fortis**   *Latin* 'Brave in adversity'
—Cobbold (of Ipswich).

195. **Reddunt aspera fortem**   *Latin* 'Dangers render brave'
—Scot, Scott.

196. **Revocate animos**   *Latin* 'Rouse your courage'
—Hay.

197. **Saigeadoir collach a buadh**   *Gaelic* 'The valiant archer forever'
—O'Hanly.

198. **Sans crainte**   *French* 'Without fear'
—Gordon-Cumming, Miles, Petre, Sanderson, Tyrell (Bt.).

199. **Sans peur**   *French* 'Without fear'
—Hogart, Karr, Sutherland.

200. **Sans peur et sans reproche**   *French* 'Without fear and without reproach'
—Baynard.

201. **Sapienter et fortiter**   *Latin* 'Wisely and bravely'
—Ludwig Günther, Count Schwarzburg-Ebeleben (1621–81).

202. **Semper fidelis et audax**   *Latin* 'Always faithful and brave'
—Moore, O'More.

203. **Sera deshormais hardi**   *French* 'He will be forevermore courageous'
—Hardie.

204. **Sine metu**   *Latin* 'Without fear'
—Jameson, Meres.

205. **Sine timore**   *Latin* 'Without fear'
—Cormack, McCormack, McCormick.

206. **Sis fortis**   *Latin* 'Be thou brave'
—Lindsay (of Cavill).

207. **Son courage dompter c'est la grand [*sic*] victoire**   *French* 'To subdue one's valor is the greatest conquest'
—Heinrich V, Count Reuss (1602–67).

208. **Spei bonae atque animi**   *Latin* 'Of good hope and courage'
—Millar.

209. **Sperate et vivite fortes**   *Latin* 'Hope and live bold(ly)'
—Bland (of Kippax Park).

210. **Stet non timeat**   *Latin* 'Let him stand and not fear'
—Bindon.

211. **Still without fear**
—Sutherland.

212. **Tam audax quam fidelis**   *Latin* 'As brave as faithful'
—Roxburgh.

213. **Teneat, luceat, floreat, vi, virtute, et valore**   *Latin* 'May it hold, shine, and flourish, by valor, virtue, and worth'
—Kenny (of Kilcloghar and Correndos, Co. Galway), Kenny (of Ballyflower, Co. Roscommon).

214. **Tharros, Dynamis, Philosophia**   *(transliterated from Greek)* 'Courage, strength and love of wisdom'
—Grossmont College, El Cajon, California.

215. **The reward of valor**
—Moodie.

216. **Timere sperno**   *Latin* 'I scorn to fear'
—Salle, Wason.

217. **Timoris nescius**   *Latin* 'Ignorant of fear'
—Scots Guards.

218. **Timor omnis abest**   *Latin* 'All fear is away'
—Craigie (of Cairsay).

219. **Timor omnis abesto**   *Latin* 'Away with all fear'
—Macnab (Bt.), Craigge, Craigy.

220. **Tutus si fortis**   *Latin* 'Safe if brave'
—Fairborne, Raeburn.

221. **Vaillant et veillant**   *French* 'Valiant and vigilant'
—Cardwell.

222. **Vaillaunce avance le homme**   *Old French* 'Valor advances the man'
—Acton (Co. Worcester).

223. **Valore et virtute**   *Latin* 'By valor and virtue'
—Salle.

224. **Valor e lealdad**   *Spanish* 'Valor and loyalty'
—Order of the Tower and Sword; Croft.

225. **Valor et fortuna**   *Latin* 'Valor and good fortune'
—Rollo (of Powhouse).

226. **Valour and loyalty**
—Grant.

227. **Veillant et vaillant** *French* 'Watchful and valiant'
—Erskine (Bt.).

228. **Vi et animo** *Latin* 'By strength and courage'
—Hankinson, McCulloch.

229. **Vi et virtute** *Latin* 'By strength and valor'
—Baird (Bt.), Baird, Bolton, Barnes, Chisholm, Hurst, McTaggart, Smart, Spoight, White; Farriers' Company.

230. **Vif, courageux, fier** *French* 'Spirited, courageous, proud'
—Falcon.

231. **Vigilantia et virtute** *Latin* 'By vigilance and valor'
—Porter.

232. **Virescit vulnere virtus** *Latin* 'Valor increases with wounds'
—[Quoted by Nonius from the Annals of the Roman poet, Furius Antias. Also see Aulus Gellius, xviii, 11.] David, Count of Mansfeld (1573–1628).

233. **Virtus ardua petit** *Latin* 'Valor seeks for difficulties'
—Cooke.

234. **Virtus dabit, cura servabit** *Latin* 'Valor will give, care will keep'
—Brown (of Clonboy).

235. **Virtus in ardua** *Latin* 'Courage against difficulties'
—Pottinger (Bt.).

236. **Virtus in arduis** *Latin* 'Courage in difficulties'
—Ashburton (B.), Cockain, Cullen, Cockane, Gamon, Macqueen.

237. **Virtus in arduo** *Latin* 'Valor in difficulty'
—Howell.

238. **Virtus in caducis** *Latin* 'Valor amid the ruin of things'
—McDowal.

239. **Virtus nihil inexpertum omittit** *Latin* 'Manliness leaves nothing untried'
—Karl Ludwig, Duke of Holstein-Sonderburg-Wiesenburg (1654–90).

240. **Virtute doloque** *Latin* 'By valor and craft'
—Binning.

241. **Virtute duce, comite fortunâ** *Latin* 'With valor my leader and good fortune my companion'
—Davies, Shand, Visme.

242. **Virtute et constantia**   *Latin* 'By valor and constancy'
—Auld (or Aulde).

243. **Virtute et fide**   *Latin* 'By valor and faith'
—Collins, Beauvale (B.), Harley, Lamb, Melbourne (V.),
Oxford (E.), Marriott.

244. **Virtute et fidelitate**   *Latin* 'By valor and fidelity'
—Order of the Golden Lion (Hesse-Cassel); Blaikie, Crofts,
Goodsir, Lyons, Reeves.

245. **Virtute et fortitudine**   *Latin* 'By bravery and fortitude'
—Morris, Whettnall, Cooper.

246. **Virtute et fortuna**   *Latin* 'By valor and good fortune'
—Andrew.

247. **Virtute et labore**   *Latin* 'By valor and exertion'
—Allan, Cochran, Dundonald (E.), Foster (of Norwich,
bt.), Headley (B.), Heddle, M'Clintock (of Drumcar),
McKenzie, Rig, Rigg, Winn.

248. **Virtute et merito**   *Latin* 'By bravery and merit'
—Order of Charles III (Spain).

249. **Virtute et valare luceo non uro**   *Latin* 'By virtue and valor I
shine, but do not burn'
—Mackenzie.

250. **Virtute et valore**   *Latin* 'By virtue and valor'
—Stamer (Bt.), Batt, McKenzie, Peppard, Noble,
Mackenzie (of Ganloch, co. Ross, Bt.),
Waldron.

251. **Virtute excerptae**   *Latin* 'Plucked by valor'
—Cary.

252. **Virtute gloria parta**   *Latin* 'Glory is obtained by valor'
—Napier.

253. **Virtute maenia cedant**   *Latin* 'Let walls yield to valor'
—Wilder.

254. **Virtute nihil obstat et armis**   *Latin* 'Nothing resists valor and
arms'
—Adlborough (E.).

255. **Virtute non astutia**   *Latin* 'By courage not by craft'
—Limerick (E.), Thomas, Whitbread.

256. **Virtute non ferocia**   *Latin* 'By courage not by cruelty'
—Forbes.

257. **Virtute non verbis**   *Latin* 'By valor not by boasting'
—Baxter, Coulthart (of Collyn), Fitz-Morris, Lansdowne (M.), Petty, Robinson, Sawers.

258. **Virtute parta tuemini**   *Latin* 'Defend what is acquired by valor'
—Blackwood, Pepperell.

259. **Virtute quies**   *Latin* 'Repose through valor'
—Normanby (M.), Phipps.

260. **Virtute vici**   *Latin* 'By valor I conquered'
—Ingram, Meynell.

261. **Virtuti fortuna comes**   *Latin* 'Fortune is companion to valor'
—Potter (of Buile Hill, Lancashire), Ferguson, Mayne (of Powis, etc.), Orr, Stewart, Wren.

262. **Virtuti in bello**   *Latin* 'To bravery in war'
—Order of St. Henry of Saxony.

263. **Virtuti nihil invium**   *Latin* 'Nothing is impervious to valor'
—Chamberlayne, Hillary (Bt.).

264. **Virtuti pro patria**   *Latin* 'For valor in behalf of our country'
—Order of Maximilian Joseph of Bavaria.

265. **Virtutis fortuna comes**   *Latin* 'Fortune is the companion of valor'
—Ashtown (B.), Brook, Clancarty (E.), Ferguson (of Raith), Hughes, Harberton (V.), Trench, Wellington (D.); Wellington College, U.K.

266. **Virtutis gloria merces**   *Latin* 'Glory is the reward of valor'
—Gyll, Deuchar, Lorimer, McDonagh, McDonegh, Macgregor, Robertson (of Strowan, Ladykirk and Kindeace, co. Ross).

267. **Virtutis in bello praemium**   *Latin* 'The reward of valor in war'
—Steuart (of Allanton).

268. **Virtutis Namurcensis praemium**   *Latin* 'The reward of valor displayed at Namur'
—18th Foot (Royal Irish) Regiment.

269. **Virtutis regio merces**   *Latin* 'A country the recompense of bravery'
—Blackadder, Duff.

270. **Vis et virtus**   *Latin* 'Strength and bravery'
—Chisalme.

271. **Vis fortibus arma**   *Latin* 'Strength is arms to the brave'
—Cruikshank.

272. **Vitae faciendo nemini timeas** *Latin* 'Fear no one in performing the duties of life'
　　　　　　　　　　　　　　　—Robertson.

273. **Vite, courageux, fier** *French* 'Swift, courageous, proud'
　　　　　　　　　　　　　　　—Harrison.

274. **Vivite fortes** *Latin* 'Live bravely'
　　　　　　　　　　　　　　　—Allen.

275. **Voor moed, beleid, trouw** *Dutch* 'For courage, prudence, and fidelity'
　　　　　　　　　　　—Order of Wilhelm (Netherlands).

276. **Without fear**
　　　　—Campbell (of Gartsford, bt.), Duffus (B.), Sutherland.

277. **With wisdom and courage**
　　　　　　　　　　　　　—St. Pancras B. C., U.K.

278. **Woksape / Woohitika / Wacantognaka / Wowacintanka** *Lakota* 'Wisdom/ bravery/ fortitude/ generosity'
　　　　　—Sinte Gleska College, Rosebud, South Dakota.

279. **Y blaidd nid ofnaf** *Welsh* 'I fear not the wolf'
　　　　　　　　　　　　　　　—Jennings.

COURTESY (*See also* HOSPITALITY.)

1. **Comiter sed fortiter** *Latin* 'Courteously but firmly'
　　　　　　　　　　　　　　—Sheffield (Bt.).

2. **Courtoisie, bonne aventure** *French* 'Courtesy, good fortune'
　　　　　　　　　　　　　　—Musset (France).

3. **Obsequens non servilis** *Latin* 'Courteous not servile'
　　　　　　　　　　　　　—Henslowe, White.

4. **Obsequio non viribus** *Latin* 'By courtesy not by force'
　　　　　　　　　　　　　　—Hamilton.

5. **Soyez compatissant soyez courtois** *French* 'Be pitiful, be courteous'
　　　　　　　　　　　　　　—Curtoys.

6. **Soyez courtois** *French* 'Be courteous'
　　　　　　　　　　　　　　—Curtoys.

7. **Truth, honor, and courtesy**
　　　　　　　　　　　　　　—Gentleman.

CROSS, THE (*See also* CHRIST, JESUS; RELIGION; SACRIFICE; SALVATION.)

1. **Absit ut glorier nisi in cruce** *Latin* 'May I glory in nothing but the cross'
   —Clarke (of Ardington).

2. **A cruce salus** *Latin* 'Salvation from the cross'
   —Burgh, Bourke, De Burgho, Downes (B.), Jefferson (Co. York), Mayo (E.).

3. **Believe in the cross**
   —Weaver-Hazelton.

4. **Benedictus qui tollit crucem** *Latin* 'Blessed is he who bears the cross'
   —Bennet, Wooldridge.

5. **Certa cruce salus** *Latin* 'Sure salvation through the cross'
   —Garritte, Kinnaird (B.).

6. **Christi crux est mea lux** *Latin* 'The cross of Christ is my light'
   —Northcote (Bt.).

7. **Crede cruci** *Latin* 'Believe in the Cross'
   —Cross (V.).

8. **Credo cruci Christi** *Latin* 'I trust in the cross of Christ'
   —Wood.

9. **Cresco per crucem** *Latin* 'I increase by the cross'
   —Davis, Rowan.

10. **Creta cruce salus** *Latin* 'Salvation born from the cross'
    —Kinnaird (B.), Waterhouse.

11. **Cruce delector** *Latin* 'I delight in the cross'
    —Sinclair.

12. **Cruce duce** *Latin* 'With the cross for guide'
    —Adams.

13. **Cruce dum spiro spero** *Latin* 'While I breathe I hope in the cross'
    —Cross, Darlington.

14. **Cruce glorior** *Latin* 'I glory in the cross'
    —Pye.

15. **Cruce insignis** *Latin* 'Illustrious from the cross'
    —Beck.

16. **Crucem ferre dignum** *Latin* 'Worthy to bear the cross'
    —Newenham, Worth.

17. **Cruce non hasta** *Latin* 'By the cross, not the spear'
—Taylor-Whitehead.

18. **Cruce non leone fides** *Latin* 'My trust is in the cross, not in the lion'
—Matthew (of Coggeshall, Co. Essex).

19. **Cruce non prudentia** *Latin* 'By the cross, not by prudence'
—Topham.

20. **Cruce salus** *Latin* 'Through the cross salvation'
—Shee.

21. **Cruce spes mea** *Latin* 'My hope is in the cross'
—Bird.

22. **Cruce vide et festina** *Latin* 'See by the cross and make haste'
—Trendall.

23. **Cruce vincimus** *Latin* 'We conquer by the cross'
—Newbigging.

24. **Cruciata cruce junguntur** *Latin* 'Crosses are joined to the cross'
—Gairden, Gardyne.

25. **Cruci dum fido spiro** *Latin* 'While I trust in the cross I live'
—Douw (U.S.).

26. **Cruci dum spiro fido** *Latin* 'Whilst I have breath I confide in the cross'
—Dyson, D'Urban, Galway (V.).

27. **Cruci dum spiro spero** *Latin* 'Whilst I breathe my hope is in the cross'
—Darlington, Metterville (V.).

28. **Crucifixa gloria mea** *Latin* 'My glory is in the cross'
—Knatchbull-Hugessen.

29. **Crux auctrix et tutrix** *Latin* 'The Cross my help and protection'
—Friedrich II, Duke of Saxony-Gotha and Altenburg (1676–1732).

30. **Crux Christi lux caeli** *Latin* 'The cross of Christ is the light of Heaven'
—Pettiward.

31. **Crux Christi mea salus** *Latin* 'The Cross of Christ is my salvation'
—Johann Georg, Duke of Saxony-Weissenfels (1677–1712).

32. **Crux Christi nostra corona** *Latin* 'The cross of Christ is our crown'
—Barclay (Bt.), Mercer, Mersar.

33. **Crux Christi nostra salus** *Latin* 'The Cross of Christ is our salvation'
    —Friedrich the Wise, Elector of Saxony (1463–1525).

34. **Crux Christi salus mea** *Latin* 'My salvation is the cross of Christ'
    —Peck.

35. **Crux Christi solamen offert** *Latin* 'The cross of Christ gives consolation'
    —Barclay.

36. **Crux dat salutem** *Latin* 'The cross gives salvation'
    —Sinclair.

37. **Crux et praesidium et decus** *Latin* 'The cross is both an honor and a defense'
    —Andros.

38. **Crux fidei calcar** *Latin* 'The cross is the spur of faith'
    —Brooking.

39. **Crux mea lux** *Latin* 'The cross is my light'
    —Brockett (U.S.).

40. **Crux mea stella** *Latin* 'The cross is my star'
    —Devlin.

41. **Crux mihi anchora** *Latin* 'The cross is my anchor'
    —Page.

42. **Crux mihi grata quies** *Latin* 'The cross is my pleasing rest'
    —Adam, Edie, McAdam.

43. **Crux nostra corona** *Latin* 'The cross is our crown'
    —Austin.

44. **Crux praesidium et decus** *Latin* 'The cross is (my) guard and honor'
    —Tyler.

45. **Crux salutem confert** *Latin* 'The cross confers salvation'
    —Barclay.

46. **Crux scutum** *Latin* 'The cross is my shield'
    —Gregory.

47. **Crux spes unica** *Latin* 'The cross is my only hope'
    —Collas.

48. **Cum cruce salus** *Latin* 'Salvation with the cross'
    —Mountain.

49. **Dextra cruce vincit** *Latin* 'His right hand conquers with the cross'
    —Hurley.

50. **Dux vitae ratio in cruce victoria**   *Latin* 'Reason the guide of life, victory in the cross'

—Fanshaw.

51. **Except in the cross**   *(from Greek)*

—Scalter, Thorp.

52. **Ex cruce leo**   *Latin* 'From the cross a lion'

—Terry.

53. **Fidei coticula crux**   *Latin* 'The cross is the test of truth'
—Chevallier, Clarendon (E.), Baker (Bt.), Jersey (E.), Villers, Whatton.

54. **Floreat crux**   *Latin* 'May the cross flourish'
—Ladbrooke (Lynn, co. Norfolk).

55. **Fortiter gerit crucem**   *Latin* 'He bravely supports the cross'
—Allan, Donoughmore (E.), Hutchinson (Bt.), Tritton.

56. **Gardez la croix**   *French* 'Keep the cross'
—Ward (Co. Wilts).

57. **Glorior in cruci Christi**   *Latin* 'I glory in the cross of Christ'
—Burder (U.S.).

58. **In cruce confido**   *Latin* 'I trust in the cross'

—Thrale.

59. **In cruce et lachrymis spes est**   *Latin* 'There is hope in the cross and in tears'
—Hincks (of Breckenbrough).

60. **In cruce fides**   *Latin* 'Faith in the cross'
—Rudge, Glendening.

61. **In cruce glorior**   *Latin* 'I glory in the cross'
—Cliffe (Co. Wexford), Douglas (of Rosehill), Pye.

62. **In cruce mea fides**   *Latin* 'In the cross is my faith'
—Billairs.

63. **In cruce mea spes**   *Latin* 'My hope is in the cross'
—Tryon (U.S.).

64. **In cruce non in leone fides**   *Latin* 'In the cross not in the lion is my faith'

—Lisle.

65. **In cruce salus**   *Latin* 'In the cross is salvation'
—Aiken, Abercromby, Brigham, Bourke, Langholme, Mountem, Marr, Lawrence, Tailour, Tailyour.

66. **In cruce spero**   *Latin* 'I trust in the cross'
—Allardic, Barclay.

67. **In cruce spes mea**   *Latin* 'In the cross is my hope'
—De la Field.

68. **In cruce triumphans**   *Latin* 'Triumphing in the cross'
—Raffles.

69. **In cruce victoria**   *Latin* 'Victory through the cross'
—Snell.

70. **In cruce vincam**   *Latin* 'I shall conquer in the cross'
—Oldfield.

71. **In cruce vinco**   *Latin* 'Through the cross I conquer'
—Copley.

72. **In crucifixa gloria mea**   *Latin* 'My glory is in the cross'
—Knatchbull (Bt.).

73. **Inter cruces triumphans in cruce**   *Latin* 'Amongst crosses, triumphing in the cross'
—Dalton.

74. **Inter feros per crucem ad coronam**   *Latin* 'Among the untamed, through the cross, to the crown'
—Stowe (U.S.).

75. **Le croix de hors mais pais dedans**   *Old French* 'The cross without, but peace within'
—Surdevile.

76. **Magnanimiter crucem sustine**   *Latin* 'Sustain the cross with magnanimity'
—Kenyon (B.), Whitney.

77. **Mea gloria crux**   *Latin* 'The cross is my glory'
—Heald.

78. **Mors crucis mea salus**   *Latin* 'The death of the cross is my safety'
—Blount (of Orletory).

79. **Nemo sine cruce beatus**   *Latin* 'No one is happy but by the cross'
—Baker.

80. **Nihilo nisi cruce**   *Latin* 'With nothing but the cross'
—Barbour.

81. **Nihil sine cruce**   *Latin* 'Nothing without the cross'
—Beresford.

82. **Nil desperandum crux scutum**   *Latin* 'Nothing to be despaired under shield of the cross'
—Gregory.

83. **Nil nisi cruce** *Latin* 'Nothing unless by the cross'
—Beresford (Bt.), Beresford (V.), Decies (Bt.), Gully, Waterford (M.).

84. **Nil sine cruce** *Latin* 'Nothing without the cross'
—Gully.

85. **Non crux, sed lux** *Latin* 'Not the cross, but (its) light'
—Black, Blair, Cramer, Griffiths.

86. **Per aspera ad dulcia crucis** *Latin* 'By rugged paths to the sweet joys of the cross'
—Bretherton.

87. **Per crucem ad castra** *Latin* 'Through the cross to the camp'
—Davies.

88. **Per crucem ad coelum** *Latin* 'Through the cross to heaven'
—Paul.

89. **Per crucem ad coronam** *Latin* 'By the cross to a crown'
—Power (Co. of Dublin, bt.), Power (of Edinburgh), Poer.

90. **Per crucem ad lucem** *Latin* 'Through the cross to the light'
—Campbell.

91. **Per crucem ad stellas** *Latin* 'By the cross to heaven'
—Legard (Bt.).

92. **Per crucem confido** *Latin* 'By the cross I have confidence'
—Crosley.

93. **Pro cruce audax** *Latin* 'Bold for the cross'
—Squarey.

94. **Qui croit en Dieu croix** *French* 'He who believes in God believes in the cross'
—Vail (U.S.).

95. **Robur in cruce** *Latin* 'Strength in the cross'
—Anketill.

96. **Sine cruce sine luce** *Latin* 'Without the cross without light'
—Close, Maxwell.

97. **Sola cruce** *Latin* 'In the cross only'
—Best.

98. **Sola cruce salus** *Latin* 'The only salvation is through the cross'
—Barclay, Brookbank.

99. **Spes mea in cruce unica** *Latin* 'My hope is in the cross alone'
—Martin.

100. **Sub cruce candida** *Latin* 'Under the white cross'
—Arden (B.), Egmont (E.), Perceval (Co. Sligo).

101. **Sub cruce canto**   *Latin* 'Under the cross I sing'
—Percival (U.S.).

102. **Sub cruce copia**   *Latin* 'Plenty under the cross'
—Cross.

103. **Sub cruce floreamus**   *Latin* 'May we flourish beneath the cross'
—Poulton-le-Fylde U. D. C., U.K.

104. **Sub cruce glorior**   *Latin* 'I glorify under the cross'
—Astell.

105. **Sub cruce lux**   *Latin* 'Light under the cross'
—Donaldson.

106. **Sub cruce salus**   *Latin* 'Salvation under the cross'
—Fletcher (Co. Stafford), Bangor (V.), Ward (of Willey), Capron.

107. **Sub cruce semper viridis**   *Latin* 'Always vigorous under the cross'
—Shrubb.

108. **Sub cruce veritas**   *Latin* 'Truth under the cross'
—Adams, Crosse.

109. **Sub cruce vinces**   *Latin* 'Under the cross you shall conquer'
—Norwood, Perceval.

110. **The cross our stay**
—Parkhouse.

111. **Via crucis via lucis**   *Latin* 'The way of the cross is the way of life'
—Sinclair.

112. **Viget sub cruce**   *Latin* 'He flourishes under the cross'
—Colquhon.

113. **Vigueur l'amour de croix**   *French* 'The love of the cross gives strength'
—Andrews, Darnol.

114. **Virtus sub cruce crescit**   *Latin* 'Virtue increases under the cross'
—Bury.

115. **Virtus sub cruce crescit, ad aethera tendens**   *Latin* 'Virtue grows under the cross, and looks to heaven'
—Charleville (E.).

CROWN (*See also* LEADERSHIP; PRINCELINESS; ROYALTY.)

1. **A cuspide corona**   *Latin* 'By a spear a crown'
—Broderick, Chapman, Midleton (V.).

2. **Alla corona fidissimo**   *Italian*   'To the crown most faithful'
>—Leche (of Carden).

3. **Caelestem spero coronam**   *Latin*   'I hope for a heavenly crown'
>—Blake-Humfrey.

4. **Coronabitur legitime certans**   *Latin*   'He shall be crowned after a fair contest'
>—Order of the Royal-Crown, founded 802.

5. **Corona mea Christus**   *Latin*   'Christ is my crown'
>—Chetwode (Bt.), Lapsley, Webb.

6. **Crux Christi nostra corona**   *Latin*   'The cross of Christ is our crown'
>—Barclay (Bt.), Mercer, Mersar.

7. **Crux nostra corona**   *Latin*   'The cross is our crown'
>—Austin.

8. **Cuspis fracta causa coronae**   *Latin*   'A spear broken in the cause of the crown' or, 'A spear broken is the cause of a crown'
>—Rolt (Co. Kent).

9. **De bon vouloir servir le roy**   *Old French*   'To serve the king with right good will'
>—Bennet, Grey (E.), Grey (Bt.), Tankerville (E.).

10. **Deo regique liber**   *Latin*   'Free to serve God and the king'
>—Johnson (of Twickenham, Bt.).

11. **His regi servitium**   *Latin*   'With these we render service to the king'
>—Neilson.

12. **Inclytus perditae recuperator coronae**   *Latin*   'The famous recoverer of a lost crown'
>—Seton.

13. **Inter feros per crucem ad coronam**   *Latin*   'Among the untamed, through the cross, to the crown'
>—Stowe (U.S.).

14. **Justitia stabilitur thronus**   *Latin*   'By justice is the throne upheld'
>—Friedrich, Count of the Palatinate of Vohenstrauss (1557–97).

15. **Laidir ise lear Righ**   *Gaelic*   'Strong is the king of the sea'
>—O'Learie.

16. **Libertas sub rege pio**   *Latin*   'Liberty under a pious king'
>—Addington, Packe, Sidmouth (V.).

17. **Opes regum, corda subditorum** *Latin* 'The riches of kings are the hearts of their subjects'
—Order of Leopold (Austria).

18. **Pacem, sed coronatam pacem** *Latin* 'Peace, but crowned peace'
—Nott.

19. **Per crucem ad coronam** *Latin* 'By the cross to a crown'
—Power (Co. of Dublin, bt.), Power (of Edinburgh), Poer.

20. **Point de couronne sans peine** *French* 'No crown without effort'
—Albrecht, Duke of Saxony-Coburg (1648–99).

21. **Praeclarum regi et regno servitium** *Latin* 'Honorable service to king and country'
—Ogilvie (of Barras, Bt.).

22. **Pretium victoribus corona** *Latin* 'The reward to the conquerors is a crown'
—Knapton.

23. **Pro corona et foedere Christi** *Latin* 'For the crown and Christ's covenant'
—Cedarville College, Cedarville, Ohio.

24. **Pro lege, Rege, grege** *Latin* 'For the law, the king, the people'
—Shield.

25. **Pro lege, Rege (et) grege** *Latin* 'For the law, the king, (and) the people'
—Christian Wilhelm, Margrave of Brandenburg (1587–1665).

26. **Pro lege et Rege** *Latin* 'For law and the king'
—Hicks (U.S.), Whitebread (U.S.).

27. **Pro mitra coronam** *Latin* 'A crown for a mitre'
—Sharpe.

28. **Pro patria saepe, pro Rege semper** *Latin* 'For my country often, for my king always'
—Ainslie.

29. **Regis et patriae tantum valet amor** *Latin* 'So much does love of king and country avail'
—Tyldesley.

30. **Sui victoria indicat regem** *Latin* 'Victory over self marks the king'
—Rye.

31. **Tutamen tela coronae** *Latin* 'Our weapons are the defense of the crown'
—Tisdall.

DANGER (*See also* ADVERSITY.)

1. **Aspera juvant** *Latin* 'Dangers delight'
—Stewart.

2. **Cum periculo lucrum** *Latin* 'Gain with danger'
—Ogilvie.

3. **Danger I court**
—Wright.

4. **Discrimine salus** *Latin* 'Safety in danger'
—Trail.

5. **Dulce periculum** *Latin* 'Danger is sweet'
—McAlla, McCall, Macauley (B.).

6. **Dulce pro patriâ periculum** *Latin* 'Danger is sweet for one's country'
—Ker (of Moristoun).

7. **Ex unguibus leonis** *Latin* 'From the claws of the lion'
—Ogilvie.

8. **Fertur discrimine fructus** *Latin* 'Profit is gained by danger'
—Gordon (of Aberdeenshire).

9. **In dubiis constans** *Latin* 'Firm amid dangers'
—Cockburn.

10. **In periculis audax** *Latin* 'Bold in danger'
—Maher.

11. **Inter hastas et hostes** *Latin* 'Among spears and enemies'
—Powell.

12. **Mihi lucra pericula** *Latin* 'Dangers are profitable to me'
—Suttie.

13. **Non sine periculo** *Latin* 'Not without danger'
—McKenzie, Fraser.

14. **Per angustam** *Latin* 'Through danger'
—Fletcher.

15. **Principiis obsta** *Latin* 'Meet the danger at its approach'
—Ffolkes (of Hillington Hall, co. Norfolk, bt.).

16. **Reddunt aspera fortem** *Latin* 'Dangers render brave'
—Scot, Scott.

17. **Secundis dubiisque rectus** *Latin* 'Upright both in prosperity and in perils'
—[after Horace, *Car.* iv. 9, 35.] Camperdown (E.), Cleveland (D.), Lippincott.

18. Secure amid perils
> —Henderson.

19. Spernit pericula virtus   *Latin* 'Virtue despises danger'
> —Carpenter, Ramsay (of Banff House, Bt.), Forrester.

20. Terrena pericula sperno   *Latin* 'I despise earthly dangers'
> —Ogilvie (Bt.).

21. Vincit pericula virtus   *Latin* 'Virtue overcomes dangers'
> —Maine, Thornton.

DARKNESS (*See also* OBSCURITY.)
1. After darkness comes light
> —Hewitt.

2. E tenebris lux   *Latin* 'Light out of darkness'
> —Lightbody.

3. Ex caligine veritas   *Latin* 'Truth out of darkness'
> —Claverly.

4. In caligine lucet   *Latin* 'It shines in darkness'
> —Baillie (Bt.).

5. In tenebris lucidior   *Latin* 'The brighter in darkness'
> —Inglis.

6. In tenebris lux   *Latin* 'Light in darkness'
> —Scott.

7. Lucent in tenebris   *Latin* 'In darkness they let their light shine'
> —O'Moran.

8. Lux in tenebris   *Latin* 'Light in darkness'
> —Fullerton (of Westwood).

9. Noctes diesque   *Latin* 'Nights and days'
> —Stacy.

10. Nocte volamus   *Latin* 'We fly by night'
> —Bateson, Yarburgh.

11. Nox nulla secuta est   *Latin* 'No night followed'
> —Tupper.

12. Out of darkness cometh light
> —Wolverhampton C. B. C., U.K.

13. **Per lucem ac tenebras mea sidera sanguine surgent** *Latin* 'Through light and darkness my star will arise in blood'
> —Cayley.

14. **Phoebus, lux in tenebris**   *Latin* 'Phoebus, light in darkness'
—Jeffrey.

15. **Post tenebras lucem**   *Latin* 'After darkness, light'
—Bright.

16. **Post tenebras lux**   *Latin* 'After darkness light'
—on the first Eddystone Lighthouse, Devonshire, England;
Hewatt.

17. **Post tenebris speramus lumen de lumine**   *Latin* 'After the darkness we hope for light upon light'
—Coffin (U.S.).

18. **Refulgent in tenebris**   *Latin* 'They glitter in the dark'
—Stodart, Studdert.

19. **Tenebras meas**   *Latin* 'My darkness'
—Abney-Hastings.

20. **Tenebris lux**   *Latin* 'Light in darkness'
—Scott (of Pitlochie).

21. **Vespera iam venit; nobiscum Christe maneto, Extingui lucem nec patiare tuam**   *Latin* 'The evening has come; stay by us, O Christ, and let not thy light be extinguished'
—Johann Georg I, Prince of Anhalt-Dessau (1567–1618).

DAY (*See also* LIGHT; SUN.)

1. **Cum prima luce**   *Latin* 'With the dawn of day'
—Loveday.

2. **Face the dawn**
—Kingswood U. D. C., U.K.

3. **Jour de ma vie**   *French* '(Most glorious) day of my life'
—West, (of Delawarr, e.).

4. **La vita al fin e'l di loda la sera**   *Italian* 'Praise life when it is at an end, and the day when it is night'
—Le Couteur.

5. **Le matin et le soir le premier jour**   *French* 'The morning and the evening, the first day'
—[after Genesis, 1. 5.] Day (U.S.).

6. **Mane diem**   *Latin* 'Await the day'
—Mayne.

7. **Noctes diesque**   *Latin* 'Nights and days'
—Stacy.

8.   **Noctes diesque praesto**   *Latin* 'Ready by night or day'
—Murray.

9.   **Point du jour**   *French* 'Daybreak'
—Lowestoft B. C., U.K.

10.   **Redde diem**   *Latin* 'Restore the day'
—Foster.

11.   **The day of my life**
—West (of Tonbridge Wells, Co. Kent).

12.   **Vertitur in diem**   *Latin* 'It is changed into day'
—Farquhar.

DEATH   (*See also* LIFE; REBIRTH.)

1.   **Antes muerto que mutado**   *Spanish* 'Rather dead than changed'
—Wilhelm V, Landgrave of Hesse-Cassel (1602–37).

2.   **Ast necas tu**   *Latin* 'But thou killest'
—Brook.

3.   **Aut mors aut libertas**   *Latin* 'Either death or liberty'
—Wall.

4.   **Aut mors aut victoria**   *Latin* 'Death or victory'
—Jackson (Bt.).

5.   **Aut mors aut vita decora**   *Latin* 'Either death or honourable life'
—Gordon (of Carnousie), Shaw.

6.   **Aut vincam aut peream**   *Latin* 'I will either conquer or perish'
—Purcell.

7.   **Better deathe than shame**
—Pearsall.

8.   **Bua noo bawse**   *Gaelic* 'Victory or death'
—O'Hagan.

9.   **Candidus cantabit moriens**   *Latin* 'The pure man will die cheerfully'
—Cawdor (E.).

10.   **Conquer death by virtue**
—Sherman (U.S.).

11.   **Conquer or die**
—Crosthwaite.

12.   **Cuimhnich bas Alpin**   *Scots Gaelic* 'Remember the death of Alpin'
—Alpin, McAlpin.

13. **Decorum pro patria mori** *Latin* 'It is honorable to die for our country'
— [after Horace, *Odes* III. ii. 13.] Ellis.

14. **Disce mori et vivere Christo** *Latin* 'Learn to die and to live in Christ'
— Friedrich Wilhelm I, Duke of Saxony-Weimar (1562–1602).

15. **Disce mori mundo** *Latin* 'Learn to die to the world'
— Moore.

16. **Dulce est pro patria mori** *Latin* 'It is sweet to die for one's country'
— [after Horace, *Odes* III. 2. 13.] Van Rensselaer (U.S.).

17. **Dulce meum terra tegit** *Latin* 'Gently doth the earth cover my loved one'
— Mary Queen of Scots, after the death of her first husband, Francis II.

18. **Dum exspiro spero** *Latin* 'While I die I hope'
— Lace.

19. **Finis dat esse** *Latin* 'Death gives us (real) being'
— Burgrave, Brograve.

20. **Fragrat post funera virtus** *Latin* 'Virtue smells sweet after death'
— Chiesly.

21. **Frisch gewagt und treu gemeint** *German* 'Boldly ventured and honestly intended'
— Eberhard Ludwig, Duke of Württemberg (1676–1733).

22. **Gwell angau na chywilydd** *Welsh* 'Better death than shame'
— Lloyd (of Ferney Hall), Mackworth (Bt.).

23. **Gwell angau na gwarth** *Welsh* 'Better death than disgrace'
— Fenton.

24. **Gwell angeu na chwylydd** *Welsh* 'Better death than shame'
— Williams.

25. **Gwell marw** *Welsh* 'Better die'
— Price.

26. **Haud timet mortem qui vitam sperat** *Latin* 'He who hopes for life fears not death'
— Christian I, Elector of Saxony (1560–91).

27. **Honorat mors** *Latin* 'Death confers honor'
— Bragge, Broigg.

28. **Honor post funera vivit** *Latin* 'Honor lives after death'
—Broadly.

29. **I conquer or die**
—Lumsden.

30. **I die for those I love**
—Patterson, Stacpole, Stewart.

31. **Il vant [sic] mieux mourir que vivre sans honeur** *French* 'Tis better to die than to live dishonorably'
—Friedrich, Duke of Württemberg (1615–82).

32. **In morte quies** *Latin* 'In death peace'
—Cust.

33. **Je meurs ou je m'attache** *French* 'I die or I cling'
—Lewis (Bt.).

34. **Je mourrai pour ceux que j'aime** *French* 'I will die for those I love'
—Blenkinsopp, Coulson.

35. **Labes pejor morte** *Latin* 'A dishonoring stain is worse than death'
—Durrant (Bt.).

36. **Laetitia per mortem** *Latin* 'Joy through death'
—Luther.

37. **La mort me suit** *French* 'Death follows me'
—Bolton.

38. **Liberty or death**
—2nd Regiment of Infantry of South Carolina; Virginia.

39. **Mallem mori quam foedari** *Latin* 'I would rather die than be disgraced'
—Gilbert (Bt.).

40. **Malo mori quam foedari** *Latin* 'I prefer death to dishonor'
—Order of Ermine, Athlone (E.), Barnewell (Bt.), Beale, Boucher, Casley, Carson (of Scarning, co. Norfolk), Chetham Strode (of South Hill), Daeg, De Freyne (Bt.), Esmond (Bt.), French (B.), French, Ginkell, Gingle, Harty (Bt.), Higginson, Jackson (of Preston), Kingsland (V.), Lister, Mulloy, Menzes, Murray, O'Mulley, Prior (of Rathdowney), Poe (of Harley Park), Payne (Bt.), Payne (of Jersey), Pain, Ryan (of Inch), Surtees, Strode (of Shipton Mallet), Trimelstowne (B.), Tenison.

41. **Manes non fugio** *Latin* 'I do not shun death'
—Gordon.

42. **Me certum mors certa facit** *Latin* 'Certain death makes me resolute'
—Sibbald (of Kips, Scotland).

43. **Meditatio mortis optima philosophia** *Latin* 'Meditation on death is the truest philosophy'
—Philipp II, Duke of Pomerania (1573–1618).

44. **Memento mori** *Latin* 'Remember thou must die'
—Gumbleton; Order of Death's Head, Heinrich Julius, Duke of Braunschweig-Wolfenbüttel (1564–1613); Rudolf, Prince of Anstalt-Zerbst (1576–1621); Sylvius Nimrod, Duke of Württemberg (1622–64).

45. **Memorare novissima** *Latin* 'To remember death'
—Hanford.

46. **Moriendo modulor** *Latin* 'Dying I sing'
—Mitchell.

47. **Moriendo vivam** *Latin* 'I shall live by dying'
—Shakerley (Bt.).

48. **Moriendo vivo** *Latin* 'In dying I live'
—Yaldwyn.

49. **Moriendum** *Latin* 'We must die'
—Van der Kemp (U.S.).

50. **Moriens, sed invictus** *Latin* 'Dying, but unconquered'
—Gammell.

51. **Moriens cano** *Latin* 'Dying I sing'
—Cobbe.

52. **Mori quam faedari** *Latin* 'To die rather than be defiled'
—Savage (U.S.).

53. **Mors, aut honorabilis vita** *Latin* 'Death, or life with honor'
—Joyce.

54. **Mors aerumnarum requies** *Latin* 'Death is rest from afflictions'
—Rumney.

55. **Mors aut vita decora** *Latin* 'Either death or honorable life'
—Dempster.

56. **Mors in vita** *Latin* 'Death in life'
—Smith.

57. **Mors janua vitae** *Latin* 'Death is the gate of life'
—Brograve.

58. **Mors lupi agnis vita**   *Latin* 'The death of the wolf is life to the lambs'
—Ouseley (Bt.), Rendell.

59. **Mors meta laborum**   *Latin* 'Death is the goal of our labors'
—Cromwell.

60. **Mors mihi lucrum**   *Latin* 'Death is gain to me'
—Jones, Lluellyn.

61. **Mors mihi vitae fide**   *Latin* 'Death to me by faith in life'
—Ellis.

62. **Mors mihi vita est**   *Latin* 'Death is life to me'
—Wolseley, Wolseley (Bt.).

63. **Mors non timenda est**   *Latin* 'Death is not to be feared'
—Coleman.

64. **Mors omnibus communis**   *Latin* 'Death is common to all'
—Luscombe.

65. **Mors potior macula**   *Latin* 'Death rather than infamy'
—Chamberlayne.

66. **Mort dessus**   *French* 'Death is hanging over us'
—Bunney, Bunny.

67. **Mortem aut triumphum**   *Latin* 'Death or victory'
—Clifton (of Lytham and Clyfton).

68. **Mort en droit**   *French* 'Death in the right'
—Drax, Earle-Drax.

69. **Morte triumpho**   *Latin* 'With death as a triumph'
—Arnold (U.S.).

70. **Non moritur cujus fama vivit**   *Latin* 'He dies not whose fame survives'
—Congreave (Bt.), Congreave.

71. **Non omnis moriar**   *Latin* 'I shall not all die'
—[Horace, *Odes*, iii. 30. 6.] Wilhelm Ernst, Duke of
Saxony-Weimar (1662–1728).

72. **Nosse Deum et bene posse mori sapientia summa est**   *Latin* 'To know God and to be able to die happily is the highest wisdom'
—Ernst, Duke of Braunschweig-Lüneburg (1564–1611);
August, Duke of Braunschweig-Lüneburg
(1568–1636).

73. **Pejus letho flagitium**   *Latin* 'Disgrace is worse than death'
—[Horace, *Car.* iv. 9–50.] Martin (of Ham Court),
Sampson (of Henbury).

74. **Per funera vitam**   *Latin* 'Through death, life'
—Scots Guards, U.K.

75. **Perimus licitis**   *Latin* 'We perish by what is lawful'
—Teignmouth (B.).

76. **Perit ut vivat**   *Latin* 'He dies that he may live'
—Fenwick, Phin.

77. **Per mortem vinco**   *Latin* 'I conquer through death'
—Waterlow.

78. **Plustost mourier que changer**   *Old French* 'Rather die than change (my faith)'
—Hermann Fortunatus, Margrave of Baden-Rodemachern (1596–1664); Barbara Agnes, Duchess of Liegnitz (d. 1631).

79. **Plustot mourire que vivere sans vertu**   *Old French* 'Rather die than live without virtue'
—Johann, Margrave of Brandenburg (1597–1628); Friedrich, Duke of Saxony (1599–1625); Elisabeth, Margravine of Baden (1620–96).

80. **Post funera faenus**   *Latin* 'An interest after death'
—Mow.

81. **Post funera virtus**   *Latin* 'Virtue survives death'
—Bogislaus XIII, Duke of Pomerania zu Barth (1544–1606); Robertson.

82. **Post mortem triumpho, et morte vici; multis despectus magna feci**   *Latin* 'I triumph after death, and in death I have conquered: despised by many, I have achieved great things'
—Order of Maria Eleonora.

83. **Post mortem virtus virescit**   *Latin* 'Virtue flourishes after death'
—Tyssen-Amherst (of Didlington Hall, Co. Norfolk), Tyssen (of Hackey).

84. **Potius mori quam foedari**   *Latin* 'Better to die than be disgraced'
—Gifford.

85. **Prius mori quam fidem fallere**   *Latin* 'Rather die than break faith'
—Drummond (of Uxbridge).

86. **Pro patria mori**   *Latin* 'To die for one's country'
—Gardiner (U.S.), Manly.

87. **Pro patria non timidus perire**   *Latin* 'Not afraid to die for my country'
—Champneys (Bt.).

88. **Regarde à la mort**   *French* 'Consider death'
—Milward, Minchin.

89. **Regardez mort**   *French* 'Consider death'
—Bastable.

90. **Ser libre o morir**   *Spanish* 'Freedom or death'
—Hamilton.

91. **Si j'avance, suivez-moi; si je fuis, tuez-moi; si je meurs, vengez-moi**   *French* 'If I advance, follow me; if I flee, kill me; if I die, avenge me'
—La Roche-Jaquelin.

92. **Stricta parata neci**   *Latin* 'Drawn and ready for death'
—Budge.

93. **Tod**   *German* 'Death'
—Futroye.

94. **Triumpho morte tam vitâ**   *Latin* 'I triumph equally in death as in life'
—Allen (V.).

95. **Un bel mourir toute la vie honore**   *French* 'A glorious death honors the whole life'
—Georg III, son of Bogislaus XIII, Duke of Pomerania (1528–1617).

96. **Usque ad mortem**   *Latin* 'Even to death'
—Parks (U.S.).

97. **Victoria vel mors**   *Latin* 'Victory or death'
—Macdonald, McDowall.

98. **Victory or death**
—O'Hagan.

99. **Viget in cinere virtus**   *Latin* 'Virtue flourishes after death'
—Davidson.

100. **Vincam vel moriar**   *Latin* 'I will conquer or die'
—Caton, McDougall, McDowall.

101. **Vincere aut mori**   *Latin* 'To either conquer or die'
—McNeill, O'Hagan, Tuthill.

102. **Vincere vel mori**   *Latin* 'To conquer or die'
—McDowall, McGougan, McNeil, McNelly, Macneill (of Barra), Maclaine, Neil, Neill.

103. **Vincet vel mori**   *Latin* 'He shall conquer or die'
—McDowall.

104. **Virtus post fata superstes**   *Latin* 'Virtue survives death'
       —Johann Casimir, Duke of Saxony-Coburg (1564–1633).

105. **Virtus post funera vivit**   *Latin* 'Virtue lives after the tomb'
       —Stansfield.

106. **Vita vel morte triumpha**   *Latin* 'Triumph in life or death'
       —Allen.

107. **Vive memor Lethi**   *Latin* 'Live mindful of death'
       —Johann, Duke of Schleswig-Holstein (1545–1622); Johann
       Friedrich, Count of the Palatinate of Hilpoltstein
       (1587–1644).

108. **Vive memor lethi, fugit hora**   *Latin* 'Live mindful of death; time
     flies'
       —Bailhache.

109. **We shall die all**
       —Sundial in a London courtyard.

DECEPTION (*See also* ENTRAPMENT.)

  1. **Absit fraus**   *Latin* 'Let all deception be far off'
       —Gordon.

  2. **Bedhoh fyr ha heb drok**   *Cornish* 'Be wise and without evil'
       —Carthew (of East Dereham).

  3. **Errantia lumina fallunt**   *Latin* 'Wandering lights deceive'
       —Kinnaird.

  4. **Est nulla fallacia**   *Latin* 'There is no deceit'
       —Carr (of Cocken).

  5. **I'll deceive no man**
       —Hamilton (of Somelston).

  6. **Nil falsi audeat**   *Latin* 'Let him dare nothing false'
       —Nicholl.

  7. **Noli mentiri**   *Latin* 'Do not lie'
       —Notley.

  8. **Non deludere**   *Latin* 'Not to delude'
       —De Luders.

  9. **Non fallor**   *Latin* 'I am not deceived'
       —Kennedy (of Clowburn).

 10. **Nulla fraus tuta latebris**   *Latin* 'No fraud is safe in its hiding-
     place'
       —Ellacombe.

11. **Practise no fraud**
>—Henderson.

12. **Prudentia, fraudis nescia**   *Latin* 'Prudence, which knows not deceit'
>—Elphinston.

13. **Vae duplici cordi**   *Latin* 'Woe to the deceitful heart'
>—Fitton.

DECISION

1. **Decide**
>—Davis (of Leytonstone).

2. **Decide and dare**
>—Dyce.

3. **In bivio dextra**   *Latin* 'In a forked path choose the right hand'
>—Rokeby.

DECORATION

1. **Hâc ornant**   *Latin* 'With this they adorn'
>—Scougall.

2. **Haec ornant**   *Latin* 'These things adorn'
>—Scrugall.

3. **Ornatur radix fronde**   *Latin* 'The root is adorned by the foliage'
>—Innes.

4. **Stimulat sed ornat**   *Latin* 'It stimulates but it adorns'
>—McCartnay, MacCartney, Mackartney.

DEDICATION (*See also* FIDELITY; STEADFASTNESS.)

1. **A pledge of better times**
>—Samuel (Bt.).

2. **Auspicium melioris aevi**   *Latin* 'A pledge of better times'
>—St. Albans (D.).

3. **Consagracion/ educacion**   *Spanish* 'Consecration/ education'
>—Antillian Coll., Mayagüez, Puerto Rico.

4. **Cor meum tibi offero Domine**   *Latin* 'I offer my heart to you, Lord'
>—Calvin Theological Seminary, Grand Rapids, Michigan.

5. **Institutae tenax**   *Latin* 'Holding by the arrangement'
—Astley, Parke.

6. **Je m'y oblige**   *French* 'I bind myself to it'
—Eyton.

7. **Juravi et adjuravi**   *Latin* 'I have sworn, and sworn solemnly'
—Moores.

8. **Nunc mihi nunc alii**   *Latin* 'Now for myself, now for another'
—Wormeley (U.S.).

9. **Praesta et persta**   *Latin* 'Promise and persevere'
—Walker.

10. **Praestando praesto**   *Latin* 'While I promise I perform'
—Hamilton.

11. **Praesto ut praestem**   *Latin* 'I promise to perform'
—Preston.

12. **Servata fides cineri**   *Latin* 'The promise made to the ashes (i.e., of the departed) has been kept'
—Harrowby (E.).

13. **Servate fidem cineri**   *Latin* 'Keep the promise made to the ashes (of your forefathers)'
—Harvey.

14. **Sit Tibi sancta cohors comitum**   *Latin* 'To Thee be the band of comrades dedicated'
—Congleton B. C., U.K.

15. **Sustento sanguine signa**   *Latin* 'I support the standard with my blood'
—Seton.

16. **Ut vinclo vir verbo ligitur**   *Latin* 'A man is bound by his word as by a chain'
—Clover.

17. **Votis et conamine**   *Latin* 'By vows and exertion'
—Kirk.

18. **Vows shall be respected**
—Vowe (of Hallaton).

DEEDS (*See also* ACCOMPLISHMENT; ACTION.)

1. **Actio virtutis laus**   *Latin* 'The deed is the commendation of the virtue'
—Ashburne.

2. **Bien est qui bien fait**   *French* 'Well is he that does well'
   —Wells.

3. **Bien faire et ne rien dire**   *French* 'To do good and to say nothing' sometimes **Bien faire, et ne rien craindre** 'To do good, and to fear nothing'
   — Du Rien, or Durien.

4. **Chi la fa l'aspetti**   *Italian* 'As a man does, so let him expect to be done by'
   —Mazzinghi (of London, originally from Germany).

5. **Claris dextra factis**   *Latin* 'A right hand employed in glorious deeds'
   —[Vergil, *Aen.* vii. 474.] Burgh, Byam.

6. **Concordant nomine facta**   *Latin* 'Our deeds agree with our name'
   —Grace (Bt.).

7. **Dant priscae decorum**   *Latin* 'Deeds of antiquity confer renown'
   —Stewart.

8. **Deeds not words**
   —Dawson (of Low Wray), Rickford (of Aylesbury), Sainthill, Pirie, Combs.

9. **Deeds shaw**
   —Rutherford.

10. **Deeds show**
    —Ruthven (B.).

11. **Dictis factisque simplex**   *Latin* 'Simple in words and deeds'
    —Sawrey, Gilpin.

12. **Do a good turn (deed) daily**
    —Boy Scouts of America; Girl Scouts of America.

13. **Do ever good**
    —Dover.

14. **Do good**
    —Spence (of Kerbuster).

15. **Do it with thy might**
    —Buxton.

16. **Do not for to repent**
    —Boteler.

17. **Do no ylle, quoth D'Oylle**
    —D'Oyley (Bt.), D'Oyley (co. Norfolk).

18. **Do or die**
— Douglas (of Springwood (Bt.), Douglas (of Cavers).

19. **Do that ye come fore**
— Broughton.

20. **Do well, doubt not**
— Tunbridge Wells B. C., U.K.; Kingsmill, Bruce.

21. **Do well, doubt nought**
— Bruce (of Killroot).

22. **Do well and doubt not**
— Tottenham B. C., U.K.; Blakeston (Bt.), Bruce, Houston.

23. **Do well and let them say**
— Elphinston, Scot (of Orkney), Scott.

24. **Do ye next thyng**
— Everett (U.S.).

25. **Dum tempus habemus operemur bonum**   *Latin* 'Whilst we have time let us do good'
— Crisp.

26. **Eadhan dean agus na caomhain**   *Scots Gaelic* 'Even do, and spare not'
— Macgregor, Peter.

27. **E'en do**   *Scots dialect*
— McHud.

28. **E'en do, boit spair nocht**   *Scots dialect*
— Murray, McGregor.

29. **E'en do, but spare nocht**   *Scots dialect*
— Murray (Bt.), Macgregor (Bt.).

30. **E'en do and spare noighte**   *Scots dialect*
— McAlpine.

31. **E'in do and spare not**   *Scots dialect*
— Gregorson, McGregor, Peters, MacPeter.

32. **Extant rectè factis praemia**   *Latin* 'The rewards of good deeds endure'
— Coffin (Bt.).

33. **Fac alteri ut tibi vis**   *Latin* 'Do unto others as you would have them do to you'
— Hatch (U.S.).

34. **Face aut tace**   *Latin* 'Do or be silent'
— Veel.

35. **Fac et spera**   *Latin* 'Do and hope'
>>> —Askew, Ayscough, Caldwell, Campbell, Crommelin, Donald, Delacherois, Fea, Heathcote, Hyatt, Ledsam, Macknight, McGee, Matherson, Mynors, Scepter.

36. **Fac simile**   *Latin* 'Do thou the like'
>>> —Sick and Hurt Office, London.

37. **Fac similiter**   *Latin* 'Do likewise'
>>> —Oliver.

38. **Facta non verba**   *Latin* 'Deeds not words'
>>> —Hoyle (Co. York), De Rinzey, De Renzey, Wells (of Sporle, co. Norfolk), Wilson (of Beckenham).

39. **Facta probant**   *Latin* 'Let deeds prove'
>>> —Stepney (Bt.).

40. **Factis non verbis**   *Latin* 'By deeds not words'
>>> —Dumergue, Money.

41. **Facto non verbo**   *Latin* 'By deed not word'
>>> —Day.

42. **Factum est**   *Latin* 'It is done'
>>> —Plasterers' Company.

43. **Faire sans dire**   *French* 'To do without speaking'
>>> —Fox, Fielder, Heyes (Co. Chester), Ilchester (E.), Par, Todd, Kingsford, Warr (of Grappenhall).

44. **Fais bien, crains rien**   *French* 'Do well, fear nothing'
>>> —Jornlin, Zornlin.

45. **Faitz proverount**   *Old French* 'Deeds will prove'
>>> —Grimston.

46. **Famam extendere factis**   *Latin* 'To extend fame by deeds'
>>> —[Vergil, *Aen.* x. 467.] Galway (V.).

47. **Far and tacer**   *Italian* 'To do and keep silence'
>>> —Wilhelm V, Landgrave of Hesse-Cassel (1602–37).

48. **Fatti maschi, parole femmine**   *Italian* 'Deeds are masculine, words feminine'
>>> —Calvert.

49. **Fatti maschii parole femine**   *Italian* 'Deeds are masculine, words feminine'
>>> —State of Maryland.

50. **Fay bien, crain rien**   *Old French* 'Do well, fear nothing'
>>> —Benson.

51. **Fay ce que doy advienne que pourra** *Old French* 'Do what you ought, come what may'
—Ireton.

52. **Gesta verbis praeveniunt** *Latin* 'Their deeds go before their words'
—Eckley, Harcourt, Swanston, Woodcock.

53. **Go, and do thou likewise**
—[Luke, x. 37.] Colston.

54. **Good deeds shine clear**
—Minshull.

55. **He seeks high deeds**
—Marshall.

56. **Hoc age** *Latin* 'Do this'
—Paris.

57. **Ito tu et fac similiter** *Latin* 'Go thou and do likewise'
—[Luke, x. 37.] Oliver.

58. **Je feray ce que je diray** *Old French* 'I'll do what I say'
—Jefferay.

59. **Je le feray durant ma vie** *Old French* 'I will do it so long as I live'
—Fairfax (of Gilling Castle).

60. **Judge us by our deeds**
—Dagenham B. C., U.K.

61. **Laus virtutis actio** *Latin* 'The deed commends the virtue'
—Rawson.

62. **Let the deed shaw**
—Addison, Fleming, Mowbray.

63. **Man do it**
—Edgar (of Wadderly).

64. **Nil penna, sed usus** *Latin* 'Not the quill, but its use'
—Gilmer.

65. **Nomen extendere factis** *Latin* 'To perpetuate one's name by deeds'
—Neeld (Bt.).

66. **Non fecimus ipsi** *Latin* 'We have not done these things ourselves'
—Duncombe (of Brickhill).

67. **Opera bona effulgent** *Latin* 'Good works shine forth'
—Jacoby.

68. **Presto et spero** *Latin* 'I perform and hope'
—Merry.

69. **Quae fecimus ipsi** *Latin* 'Things which we ourselves have done'
—Fulton.

70. **Quid tibi fieri non vis alteri ne feceris** *Latin* 'Do not to another what you wish not to be done to yourself'
—Ram.

71. **Quid tibi vis fieri facias** *Latin* 'Do what you wish to be done to you'
—Ram.

72. **Quod eorum minimi [sic] mihi** *Latin* 'What (ye do) to the least of these (ye do) to me'
—[Matt., xxv. 40.] Corporation of the Sons of the Clergy.

73. **Quod facio, valde facio** *Latin* 'What I do I do with energy'
—Sikes (of Berwick), Sykes (of Highbury, Leeds, etc.).

74. **Quod fieri non vis alter [sic] ne feceris** *Latin* 'Do not do what you do not wish to be done to another'
—Cock (U.S.).

75. **Quod potui perfeci** *Latin* 'I have done what I could do'
—Melville (V.).

76. **Quod tibi fieri non vis alteri ne feceris** *Latin* 'You should not do to another what you do not wish done to yourself'
—Boyle.

77. **Quod tibi hoc alteri** *Latin* '(Do) to another what thou (wouldst have done) to thee'
—[Luke, vi. 31.] Crawfurd (of Cartsburn), Fleetwood (Bt.), Hesketh.

78. **Quod tibi id alii** *Latin* '(Do) that to another which thou (wouldst have done) to thee'
—Lopes.

79. **Quod tibi ne alteri** *Latin* 'What (injurys is done to thee, do not to another'
—Alexander (of Auchmull).

80. **Quod tibi vis alteri feceris** *Latin* 'Do to another what you wish to be done to yourself'
—Bathurst (U.S.).

81. **Quod tibi vis fieri fac alteri** *Latin* 'Do to another what you wish done to yourself'
—[Luke, vi. 31.] Ram.

82. **Quod tibi vis fieri facias** *Latin* 'Do what you wish to be done to yourself'
—Philipse.

83. **Recte fac noli timere**   *Latin* 'Do right and fear not'
    —Prestwich B. C., U.K.

84. **Refulget labores nostros coelum**   *Latin* 'The sky reflects our works'
    —Scunthorpe B. C., U.K.

85. **Res non verba quaeso**   *Latin* 'I seek deeds, not words'
    —Mountford.

86. **Sermoni consona facta**   *Latin* 'Deeds agreeing with words'
    —Collins (Co. Devon), Trelawney.

87. **Spectemur agendo**   *Latin* 'Let us be judged from our deeds'
    —1st Royal Dragoons, 101st Foot (Royal Munster Fusiliers), 102nd Foot (Royal Dublin Fusiliers), Chorley R. D. C., Barnsley C. B. C., Lambeth B. C., Hammersmith B. C., U.K.

88. **Stat gratia facti**   *Latin* 'It stands for the sake of the deed'
    —Taylour.

89. **Suaviter in modo, fortiter in re**   *Latin* 'Gentle in manner, firm in act'
    —Newborough (B.), Nunn, Wynn.

90. **Suaviter in modo fortiter in re**   *Latin* 'Gentle in manner, strong in deed'
    —General Dwight D. Eisenhower.

91. **Usque fac et non parcas**   *Latin* 'E'en do and spare not'
    —Peters (of Aberdeen).

92. **Ut sibi sic alteri**   *Latin* 'Do to another as to thyself'
    —Letchworth.

93. **Ut tibi sic aliis**   *Latin* 'As to yourself so to others'
    —Hussey.

94. **Ut tibi sic alteri**   *Latin* 'As to yourself so to another'
    —Bowles, Kingsdon (B.).

95. **Virtutem extendere factis**   *Latin* 'To increase virtue by deeds'
    —[Vergil, *Aen.* vi. 806.] Fisher.

96. **Whatsoever thy hand findeth to do, do it with thy might**
    —Buxton (Bt.).

DEFENSE (*See also* FORTIFICATIONS; PROTECTION; VIGILANCE; WEAPONS.)

1. **Acquirit qui tuetur**   *Latin* 'He obtains who defends'
              —Mortimer (of Auchenbody).

2. **A good conscience is a sure defence**
              —Paruck.

3. **Armat et ornat**   *Latin* 'For defense and ornament'
              —Brown (of Gorgymill).

4. **Armat spina rosas**   *Latin* 'The thorn is the defense of the rose'
              —Rose.

5. **Asgre lan diogel ei phercen**   *Welsh* 'Secure is he with a pure heart'
              —Herbert (of Llanarth Court), Jones, Vaughan.

6. **Audemus jura nostra defendere**   *Latin* 'We dare defend our rights'
              —State of Alabama.

7. **Crux et praesidium et decus**   *Latin* 'The cross is both an honor and a defense'
              —Andros.

8. **Crux praesidium et decus**   *Latin* 'The cross is (my) guard and honor'
              —Tyler.

9. **Crux scutum**   *Latin* 'The cross is my shield'
              —Gregory.

10. **Defend**
              —Wood (of Boneytown), Wood (of co. Gloucester, bt.).

11. **Defendamus**   *Latin* 'Let us defend'
              —Taunton B. C., U.K., Town of Taunton.

12. **Defend and spare not**
              —MacConachie.

13. **Defendendo vinco**   *Latin* 'By defending I conquer'
              —Graham (of Braco).

14. **Defend the fold**
              —Cartwright (of co. Notts, Northampton and Suffolk).

15. **Defensio non offensio**   *Latin* 'Defense not offense'
              —Mudie.

16. **Deus praesidium**   *Latin* 'God is our defense'
              —Bevan.

17. **En Dieu mon esperance et l'espee [*sic*] pour ma defense**
French 'In God is my hope and the sword of my defence'
—Johann Ernst, Duke of Saxony-Saalfield (1658–1729).

18. **Et regem defendere victum** *Latin* 'To defend the king even in his defeat'
—Whitgreave (of Moseley Court).

19. **Ferio, tego** *Latin* 'I strike, I defend'
—Hawdon, Herklott, Howdon, McAul, McCall, Sims, Syme.

20. **Fortiter defendit, triumphans** *Latin* 'Triumphing, it bravely defends'
—Town of Newcastle-on-Tyne.

21. **Fortiter defendit triumphans** *Latin* 'She bravely defends and triumphs'
—Newcastle-upon-Tyne City and C. B. C., U.K.

22. **Haec manus pro patriae pugnando vulnera passa** *Latin* 'This hand has been wounded in defense of my country'
—O'Neill, Gealagh.

23. **I'll defend**
—Kincaid, Lennox.

24. **In defence**
—Williamson, Allardice (of Dunotter).

25. **In defence of the distressed**
—Allardice.

26. **In ferro tutamen** *Latin* 'Defense in the sword'
—Ferrier.

27. **In libertate sociorum defendenda** *Latin* 'In defending the liberty of our companions'
—Macgregor.

28. **In malos cornu** *Latin* 'With my horn against the bad'
—Dadley.

29. **I will defend**
—Kincaid.

30. **Je garderay** *Old French* 'I will guard'
—Bridges.

31. **Littore sistam** *Latin* 'I shall take my stand on the shore'
—Hamilton.

32. **Maneo et munio** *Latin* 'I remain and defend'
—Dalrymple.

33. **Maximum proeli impetum et sustinere** *Latin* 'Even to hold off the greatest onslaught in battle'
      —White (U.S.).

34. **Mihi parta tueri** *Latin* 'To defend the things acquired by me'
      —North, Styleman-Le Strange.

35. **Moneo et munio** *Latin* 'I advise and defend'
    —Dalrymple, Elphinstone (Bt.), Elphinstone (of Horn and Logie).

36. **Munit haec et altera vincit** *Latin* 'This hand defends, the other conquers'
      —Nova Scotia Knights.

37. **My defense**
      —Allardice.

38. **Non minor est virtus quam quaerere parta tueri** *Latin* 'To defend what you have gained is no less valor than to gain'
      —Master.

39. **Parta tueri** *Latin* 'Defend your acquisitions'
    —Jacob (of Bromley), Lilford (B.), Powys, [Terence, *Phormio*, v. 3, 5.] August Wilhelm, Duke of Braunschweig-Wolfenbüttel (1662–1731).

40. **Pax aut defensio** *Latin* 'Peace or defense'
      —Laudale.

41. **Primum tutare domum** *Latin* 'First defend home'
      —Watkins.

42. **Regem defendere victum** *Latin* 'To defend the conquered king'
      —Whitgreave.

43. **Se defendendo** *Latin* 'In his own defense'
      —Beebee (of Willey Court), Eccles, Ekles.

44. **Sic nos, sic sacra tuemur** *Latin* 'Thus we defend ourselves and sacred rights'
      —McMahon (Bt.).

45. **S'ils te mordent, mords les** *French* 'If they bite thee, bite them'
      —Morley (of Marrick Park, Yorkshire).

46. **They ryght defend**
      —Southwold B. C., U.K.

47. **This I'll defend**
    —McFarlane, Macfarlan, MacPharlin, Durnard.

48. **Tuebor**   *Latin* 'I will defend'
—Byng, Torrington (V.); Strafford (B.).; State of Michigan.

49. **Tuemur**   *Latin* 'We defend'
—Higgins.

50. **Tutamen**   *Latin* 'A defense'
—Skrine (of Warleigh).

51. **Tutela**   *Latin* 'A defense'
—Lyle, Lyell (of Dysart).

52. **Tutemur**   *Latin* 'Let us defend'
—Higgins.

53. **Vigilando munio**   *Latin* 'I defend by being vigilant'
—Kirkaldie.

54. **Virtus tutamen**   *Latin* 'Virtue is a defense'
—Germon.

55. **Virtute parta tuemini**   *Latin* 'Defend what is acquired by valor'
—Blackwood, Pepperell.

56. **With fort and fleet for home and England**
—Gillingham B. C., U.K.

DEFIANCE (*See also* FORTITUDE; OPPOSITION.)

1. **A youth over his enemies defying**   (*from Gaelic*)
—O'Donovan.

2. **Butleirach abú**   *Gaelic* 'Butlers defying'
—Butler.

3. **Crom abú**   *Gaelic* 'Crom defying'
—Geraldine (Co. Kildare), Fitzgerald, Leinster (D.), DeRus (B.).

4. **Grassagh abú**   *Gaelic* 'Graces defying'
—Grace and Geraldines (of Courtstoun).

5. **In defiance**
—MacBrain, Macbraire (of Tweedhill, etc.).

6. **Lamh dearg Eirinn abú**   *Gaelic* 'The red hand for Ireland defying'
—O'Neill.

7. **Lamh derg aboo**   *Gaelic* 'The red hand defying'
—Magawly.

8. **Lamh foistenach abu**   *Gaelic* 'The gentle hand defying'
   —O'Sullivan.

9. **Lamh laider an nachter**   *Gaelic* 'The strong hand defying'
   —O'Brien.

10. **Mullac aboo**   *Gaelic* 'The chief defying'
    —Dunne, Doyne.

11. **Resistite usque ad sanguinem**   *Latin* 'Resist even to the death'
    —Keogh.

12. **Shanet aboo**   *Gaelic* 'Shanet defying'
    —Fitzgerald and Vesci (B.), Fitzgerald (of Castle Ishen (Bt.), Fitzgerald (the Knight of Glyn and the Knight of Kerry).

13. **The swarthy stranger defying** or **The red stranger defying**   *(from Gaelic)*
    —Burke, DeBurgos.

14. **The yellow (haired) man defying**   *(from Gaelic)*
    —Fitz Maurice (Kerry Geraldines).

DEPENDABILITY (*See also* STEADFASTNESS; TRUSTWORTHINESS.)

1. **Be sure**
   —Pasley (of Craig).

2. **Build sure**
   —McAlpine (Bt.).

3. **Sure**
   —Macdonald.

4. **Sure and steadfast**
   —Martin (of Anstey Pastures).

5. **Tout jour**   *French* 'Always'
   —Ogilvie.

DEPRIVATION

1. **Semper sitiens**   *Latin* 'Always thirsty'
   —Drought.

2. **Thou shalt want ere I want**
   —Cranstoun (B.).

3. **Ut deficiar**   *Latin* 'That I may be destitute'
   —Auchinleck.

DESIRE (*See also* WILL.)

1. **Appetitus rationi pareat** *Latin* 'Let your desires obey your reason'
   —[Cicero, *de Off.* I. 39. 10.] Custance (of Weston, Co. Norfolk).

2. **Cupio, credo, habeo** *Latin* 'I desire, I believe, I have'
   —Cawley (Bt.).

3. **I desire not to want**
   —Cranston.

4. **Insignia fortuna paria** *Latin* 'My desire and my fortune are matched'
   —De La Field.

5. **Invitum sequitur honor** *Latin* 'Honor follows one who desires it not'
   —Donegal (M.), Chichester, Templemore (B.).

6. **Je le vueil** *French* 'I wish it'
   —Binet.

7. **Je veux le droict** *Old French* 'I desire that which is just'
   —Duckett (Bt.).

8. **Je veux le droit** *French* 'I desire that which is just'
   —Duckett.

9. **Marbu mhiann leinn** *Scots Gaelic* 'As we would desire'
   —Campbell.

10. **Mercie is my desire**
    —Abercrombie.

11. **Mercy is my desire**
    —Abercrombie, Laing, Lang, Wishart.

12. **M. V. Z. G. (Mein Verlangen zu Gott)** *German* 'My desires (I give) to God'
    —Anna Marie, Margravine of Brandenburg (1609–80).

13. **Nec cupias, nec metuas** *Latin* 'Neither desire nor fear'
    —Hardwicke (E.), York, Yorke (of Erddig).

14. **Nec metuas, nec optes** *Latin* 'Neither fear nor desire'
    —Coddington.

15. **N. E. M. Q. O. (Non est mortale quod opto)** *Latin* 'It is no mortal thing I desire'
    —Friedrich III, Duke of Schleswig-Holstein-Gottorp (1597–1659).

16. **Non est mortale quod opto** *Latin* 'It is no mortal thing that I desire'
—[Ovid, *Met.* ii. 56.] Johann Albert II, Duke of Mecklenburg-Güstrow (1590–1636); Christian Ludwig, Duke of Mecklenburg-Schwerin (1632–92); Bernhard, Duke of Saxony-Meiningen (1649–1706); Johann Wilhelm, Duke of Saxony-Eisenach (1666–1729); Christian Ernst, Duke of Saxony-Coburg-Saalfeld (1683–1745).

17. **Non vox, sed votum** *Latin* 'Not the voice, but the wish'
—Nagle (Bt.).

18. **Quae sursum volo** *Latin* 'I wish those things which are above'
—McQuinn.

19. **Quae vult valde vult** *Latin* 'What things he wishes, he wishes fervently'
—Wilmot; Motteux.

20. **Quod volo erit** *Latin* 'What I wish will be'
—Wright.

21. **Quod vult, valde vult** *Latin* 'What he wishes, he wishes fervently'
—Maunsell (Bt.), Holt, Horton.

22. **Sitivit in te anima mea** *Latin* 'My soul has thirsted for thee'
—[after Ps., lxiii. 1.] Johann Georg I, Elector of Saxony (1585–1656).

23. **Super sidera votum** *Latin* 'My wishes are above the stars'
—Rattray (of Craighill).

24. **Velis id quod possis** *Latin* 'May you wish for that which you can (have)'
—Brett.

25. **Volo et valeo** *Latin* 'I wish and I prevail'
—Charles (U.S.), Clarke (U.S.).

26. **Votis, tunc velis** *Latin* 'By wishes, then by sails'
—Martin.

DESPAIR (*See also* SADNESS; SUFFERING.)
1. **Despair not**
—East Land Company.

2. **Never despair**
   —Colton (U.S.), Pintard (U.S.).

3. **Nihil desperandum** *Latin* 'Never despair'
   —Walley.

4. **Nil desperando** *Latin* 'Nothing by despairing'
   —Moat (U.S.).

5. **Nil desperandum** *Latin* 'Never despair'
   —Anson (Bt.), Anson, Chard, Chawner, Cookson (of
   Whitehill), Crosbie, Gardiner, Hay, Horn,
   Hawkins, Hawkswell, Heron (Bt.), Heron, Imry,
   Jones, Lichfield (E.), Musgrove (Bt.), Ogilvy (of
   Ruthven), Parry, Stewart, Simpson, Silver,
   Walker (Bt.), Tucker.

6. **Nil desperandum auspice Deo** *Latin* 'Nothing to be despaired of
   under the auspices of God'
   —Anderson.

7. **Nil desperandum est** *Latin* 'We must never despair'
   —Stewart (Bt.).

8. **Turpiter desperatur** *Latin* 'Despaired is base'
   —Hall (Bt.).

DESTINATION (*See also* FATE; GOALS.)

1. **Ad diem tendo** *Latin* 'I journey towards the dayspring'
   —Stein, Stevens.

2. **Ad littora tendit** *Latin* 'It makes for the shore'
   —Quatherine, Jamieson.

3. **Ad littora tendo** *Latin* 'I make for the shore'
   —Watson.

4. **Dove andate?** *Italian* 'Whither are you going?'
   —Barchard.

5. **Huc tendimus omnes** *Latin* 'We are all traveling to this bourne'
   —Paterson.

6. **Qua tendis?** *Latin* 'Whither do you steer?'
   —Roy.

7. **Quocunque ferar** *Latin* 'Whithersoever I may be carried'
   —Sinclair.

8. **Whither will ye**
   —Stewart (U.S.).

DESTRUCTION

1. **Concussae cadent urbes**   *Latin* 'Shattered, the cities fall'
—Scots Guards.

2. **Extermination**
—Frederick Douglass.

3. **Frango**   *Latin* 'I destroy'
—M'Laren.

4. **Fried ernehrt Unfried verzehrt**   *German* 'Peace nourishes, strife destroys'
—Friedrich, Duke of Braunschweig-Lüneburg (1574–1648).

5. **Hic vastat telis moenia facta suis**   *Latin* 'He destroys with his own bolts the walls he has made'
—Georg Friedrich, Margrave of Brandenburg-Anspach (1539–1603).

6. **Non ad perniciem**   *Latin* 'Not to destruction'
—Carleton.

7. **Non omnis frangar**   *Latin* 'I shall not be all broken'
—Colby.

8. **Superba frango**   *Latin* 'I destroy superb things'
—Macklellan (of Bombay).

DEVOTION (*See also* DEDICATION; FIDELITY; PATRIOTISM; PIETY; REVERENCE.)

1. **Commit thy work to God**
—[Prov., xvi. 3.] Caithness (E.), Sinclair.

2. **Deum cole, regem serva**   *Latin* 'Worship God, revere the king'
—Cole (Earl of Enniskillen), Cole (of Twickenham), Townshend (co. Cork), Coleridge, Jones.

3. **Devouement sans bornes**   *French* 'Devotion without limits'
—Prodgers.

4. **Dias mo dhuthaich**   *Scots Gaelic* 'For God and my country'
—Mackenzie (Bt.).

5. **Dieu et ma patrie**   *French* 'God and my country'
—Marton.

6. **Dieu et mon pays**   *French* 'God and my country'
—McKirdy.

7. **Dieu et mon roi**   *French* 'God and my king'
—Rawlinson.

8. **In sanguine foedus** *Latin* 'A covenant by blood'
—Order of the Two Sicilies, Order of St. Januarius (of Naples).

9. **Knowledge, devotion, wisdom, service**
—Pembroke State University, Pembroke, North Carolina.

10. **Scientia/ Pietas que vitalis** *Latin* 'Learning and devotion are vital'
—Texas Wesleyan College, Fort Worth, Texas.

DILIGENCE (*See also* DEDICATION; PERSEVERANCE.)

1. **Aequabiliter et diligenter** *Latin* 'By consistency and diligence'
—Mitford, Moore, Redesdale (B.).

2. **Aequaliter et diligenter** *Latin* 'Calmly and diligently'
—Moore.

3. **Aequitate ac diligentia** *Latin* 'With fair play and diligence'
—Ashbury.

4. **Armis et diligentia** *Latin* 'By arms and diligence'
—Baskin (of Scotland).

5. **Assiduitas** *Latin* 'Assiduity'
—Beck, Quayles.

6. **Assiduitate** *Latin* 'By assiduity'
—Johnston (of Anstruther), Skeen.

7. **Assiduitate, non desidia** *Latin* 'By industry, not sloth'
—King William's College, Isle of Man, U.K.

8. **Assiduitate non desidiâ** *Latin* 'By assiduity, not by sloth'
—Loch (of Drylaw and Rachan).

9. **Audacia et industria** *Latin* 'Boldness and diligence'
—Buchanan.

10. **Be trwgh and delygent** *Middle English* 'Be true and diligent'
—Lucy (of Co. Warwick).

11. **By assiduity**
—Byass.

12. **By truth and diligence**
—Lucy.

13. **Cada uno es hijo de sus obras** *Spanish* 'Scarce one is the son of his works' *or* 'Raised by his own exertions'
—Boss.

14. **Concordia et sedulitate** *Latin* 'By union and diligence'
—Goldsmid(Bt.).

15. **Constantia et diligentia** *Latin* 'By perseverance and diligence'
—Spence.

16. **Cum prudentia sedulus** *Latin* 'Diligent with prudence'
—Beatson, Betson.

17. **Diligence/ Discipline/ Integrity**
—Steed College, Johnson City, Tennessee.

18. **Diligence/ Integrity/ Knowledge**
—McNeese State University, Lake Charles, Louisiana.

19. **Diligenter** *Latin* 'Diligently'
—Bramwell (Bt.).

20. **Diligenter et fideliter** *Latin* 'Diligently and faithfully'
—Allen.

21. **Diligentes Deus ipse juvat** *Latin* 'God Himself helps the diligent'
—Hartill.

22. **Diligentia** *Latin* 'Diligence'
—Dickman.

23. **Diligentia cresco** *Latin* 'I rise by industry'
—Moncrief (of Edinburgh).

24. **Diligentia ditat** *Latin* 'Industry renders rich'
—Ferrier, Newell.

25. **Diligentia et candore** *Latin* 'By diligence and fairness'
—Dick.

26. **Diligentia et honeste** *Latin* 'By diligence and honorable dealing'
—Garnett-Orme.

27. **Diligentia et honore** *Latin* 'With diligence and honor'
—Garnett.

28. **Diligentia et vigilantia** *Latin* 'Diligence and watchfulness'
—Semple.

29. **Diligentia fit ubertas** *Latin* 'Plenty is caused by diligence'
—Hay.

30. **Diligentia fortior** *Latin* 'Stronger by diligence'
—Truell.

31. **Diligentia fortunae mater** *Latin* 'Diligence is the mother of fortune'
—Barkham.

32. **Favente Deo et sedulitate** *Latin* 'God and assiduity favoring'
—Collins.

33. **Fide et diligentia** *Latin* 'By faith and diligence'
—Crawford, Crawfurd, Woking U. D. C., U.K.

34. **Fide et sedulitate** *Latin* 'With faith and diligence'
—Elwood.

35. **Fideliter et diligenter** *Latin* 'Faithfully and diligently'
—Graham (Bt.).

36. **Fiducia et labore** *Latin* 'By confidence and industry'
—Jockel.

37. **Honestas et diligentia** *Latin* 'Honesty and diligence'
—Suffolk University Law School, Boston, Massachusetts.

38. **Industria, virtus et fortitudo** *Latin* 'Diligence, courage, and strength'
—Derby C. B. C., U.K.

39. **Juvant Deus impigros** *Latin* 'God assists the diligent'
—Strachan.

40. **Juvat impigros Deus** *Latin* 'God aids the diligent'
—Huddersfield C. B. C., U.K.

41. **Labore et diligentia** *Latin* 'With labor and diligence'
—Binns.

42. **Lente in voto** *Latin* 'Deliberate in my vow'
—Thomson.

43. **Lente sed attente** *Latin* 'Slowly but carefully'
—Roberts.

44. **Lente sed opportune** *Latin* 'Slowly, but opportunely'
—Campbell.

45. **Lento sed certo et recto gradu** *Latin* 'With a slow but sure and straight step'
—Knowlys (of Heysham).

46. **Omnia superat diligentia** *Latin* 'Diligence surmounts all difficulties'
—Mitchell.

47. **Opes parit industria** *Latin* 'Industry begets plenty' *or* 'Industry produces riches'
—Bingley U. D. C., U.K.; Benson.

48. **Perseverantia et cura quies** *Latin* 'Rest by perseverance and care'
—Hall.

49. **Procurata industria** *Latin* 'Attended to through hard work'
—Fraunces (U.S.).

50. **Scientia et industria cum probitate** *Latin* 'Knowledge and diligence with uprightness'
—Lincoln College, Canterbury, New Zealand.

51. **Sedule et prospere** *Latin* 'Diligently and prosperously'
—White.

52. **Sedule et secunde** *Latin* 'Diligently and prosperously'
—Lookyer.

53. **Sedulitate** *Latin* 'By diligence'
—Divire, Elphingston.

54. **Sedulo et honeste** *Latin* 'Diligently and honestly'.
—Lyall.

55. **Sedulo et honeste tutela** *Latin* 'Guardianship with honor and diligence'
—Lyell.

56. **Sedulo numen** *Latin* 'God is with the diligent'
—Harrower, Harrowing.

57. **Sedulus et audax** *Latin* 'Diligent and bold'
—Rutherfurd.

58. **Tam virtute quam labore** *Latin* 'As much by virtue as by exertion'
—Hamilton.

59. **Verus et sedulus** *Latin* 'True and diligent'
—McCulloch.

60. **With truth and diligence**
—Lucy (of Charlecote).

DIRECTION (*See also* DESTINATION; DIVINE GUIDANCE; PURPOSE; WAY.)

1. **A Gadibus usque auroram** *Latin* 'From West to East'
—South Sea Company.

2. **Je me tourne vers l'occident** *French* 'I turn towards the west'
—Westropp.

3. **Je tourne vers l'occident** *French* 'I turn towards the west'
—O'Callaghan-Westropp.

4. **Nec ab oriente, nec ab occidente** *Latin* 'Neither from the east nor from the west'
—Botesham, Jermyn.

5. **Ni dessus, ni dessous** *Latin* 'Neither above nor below'
—Grove.

6. **Quihidder will ye?** *or* **Quidhidder will zie?** *Scots dialect* 'Whither will ye?'
> —Stewart (of Appin).

7. **Recta sursum** *Latin* 'Right upwards'
> —Graham (of Duntroon).

8. **Recto cursu** *Latin* 'In a right course'
> —Corser.

9. **Sursum deorsum** *Latin* 'Upwards and downwards'
> —Johann Georg II, Elector of Saxony (1613–80).

10. **Tourne vers l'occident** *French* 'Turn towards the west'
> —Dawson, Westropp-Dawson.

11. **Versus** *Latin* 'Towards'
> —Peters.

DIRECTNESS

1. **Ad rem** *Latin* 'To the point'
> —Wright.

2. **Aperto vivere voto** *Latin* 'To live without a wish concealed'
> —Aylesford (E.), Finch, Chamer, Wright.

3. **Candide** *Latin* 'Candidly'
> —Stewart (of Binny).

4. **Candide, sed caute** *Latin* 'Candidly, but cautiously'
> —Sinclair (Bt.).

5. **Candide, sincere** *Latin* 'With candor and sincerity'
> —Grieve.

6. **Candide et caute** *Latin* 'Candidly and cautiously'
> —Elliot, Grieve.

7. **Candide et secure** *Latin* 'Candidly and safely'
> —Graham, Lynedoch (B.).

8. **Candider et constanter** *Latin* 'Candidly and constantly'
> —Coventry (E.).

9. **Candore** *Latin* 'By candor'
> —Robe.

10. **Droit comme ma flêche** *French* 'Straight as my arrow'
> —Fletcher.

11. **Go straight, and fear not**
> —Le Hart.

12. **In candore decus** *Latin* 'There is honor in sincerity'
    —Chadwick (of Pudleston Court).
13. **Omnes fremant licet dicam quod sentio** *Latin* 'Though all may grumble I will say what I feel'
    —Smith (U.S.).
14. **Recto gradu** *Latin* 'Straightforwardly'
    —August Ludwig, Prince of Anhalt-Plötzkau (1697–1755).
15. **Sine dolo** *Latin* 'Without guile'
    —Lewis.
16. **Turn nor swerve**
    —Turnor.

DISCIPLINE (*See also* ORDER; SELF-CONTROL.)
1. **Bonitatem et disciplinam et scientiam doce me** *Latin* 'Teach me goodness and discipline and knowledge'
    —College of Mount Saint Vincent, Riverdale, New York.
2. **Diligence/ Discipline/ Integrity**
    —Steed College, Johnson City, Tennessee.
3. **Disciplina, fide, perseverantia** *Latin* 'By discipline, fidelity, and perseverance'
    —Duckworth (Bt.).
4. **Disciplina praesidium civitatis** *Latin* 'Discipline, the guardian of the state'
    —University of Texas, Austin, Texas.
5. **Faith, unity, discipline** *(from Urdu and Bengali)*
    —Republic of Pakistan.
6. **Suaviter et fortiter** *Latin* 'Mildly and firmly'
    —Daubeney, Minto (E.), Rathbone.
7. **Suaviter sed fortiter** *Latin* 'Mildly, but firmly'
    —Busk, Dennis, Williams (of Lee).

DISCRETION (*See also* PRUDENCE.)
1. **Audi, vide, sile** *Latin* 'Hear, see, be silent'
    —Tillard.
2. **Audio sed taceo** *Latin* 'I hear, but say nothing'
    —Trollop (of Durham).
3. **Audito et gradito** *Latin* 'Listen, and walk on'
    —Cruikshanks (of London).

4. **Constant et discret et ang amour secret** *Old French* 'Constant and discreet, and secret in love'
—Bernhard, Duke of Saxony-Weimar (1604–39).

5. **Discretio moderatrix virtutum** *Latin* 'Discretion is the moderator of virtues'
—Quincy (U.S.).

6. **Video et taceo** *Latin* 'I see and say nothing'
—Fox (of Eppleton).

7. **Virtus dedit, cura servabit** *Latin* 'What virtue has given, discretion will preserve'
—Browne.

DISGRACE

1. **Craignez honte** *French* 'Fear shame'
—Bentinck, Dillwyn (of Burroughes-Lodge), Portland (B.), Weston.

2. **Degeneranti, genus opprobrium** *Latin* 'To a degenerate man his family is a disgrace'
—Ashurst.

3. **Dread shame**
—Leighton (Bt.), Leighton (of Shrewsbury).

4. **Extremos pudeat rediisse** *Latin* 'Let it shame us to have come back last'
—Westmacott.

5. **Gwell angau na chywilydd** *Welsh* 'Better death than shame'
—Lloyd (of Ferney Hall), Mackworth (Bt.).

6. **Gwell angau na gwarth** *Welsh* 'Better death than disgrace'
—Fenton.

7. **Honi soit qui mal y pense** *French* 'Dishonored be he who thinks ill of it'
—Crown of England, Order of the Garter (Britain).

8. **Labes pejor morte** *Latin* 'A dishonoring stain is worse than death'
—Durrant (Bt.).

9. **Mallem mori quam foedari** *Latin* 'I would rather die than be disgraced'
—Gilbert (Bt.).

10. **Malo mori quam foedari** *Latin* 'I prefer death to dishonor'
—Order of Ermine, Athlone (E.), Barnewell (Bt.), Beale, Boucher, Casley, Carson (of Scarning, Co. Norfolk), Chetham Strode (of South Hill), Daeg, De Freyne (Bt.), Esmond (Bt.), French (B.), French, Ginkell, Gingle, Harty (Bt.), Higginson, Jackson (of Preston), Kingsland (V.), Lister, Mulloy, Menzes, Murray, O'Mulley, Prior (of Rathdowney), Poe (of Harley Park), Payne (Bt.), Payne (of Jersey), Pain, Ryan (of Inch), Surtees, Strode (of Shipton Mallet), Trimelstowne (B.), Tenison.

11. **Malo pati quam foedari** *Latin* 'I prefer suffering to disgrace'
—Duckett.

12. **Nec lusisse pudet, sed non incidere lusum** *Latin* 'It does not shame me to have played, but that I have not left off playing'
—Bond.

13. **Pejus letho flagitium** *Latin* 'Disgrace is worse than death'
—[Horace, *Car.* iv. 9–50.] Martin (of Ham Court), Sampson (of Henbury).

14. **Potius mori quam foedari** *Latin* 'Better to die than be disgraced'
—Gifford.

15. **Quod pudet hoc pigeat** *Latin* 'Let that which is shameful be displeasing to you'
—Dobyns.

16. **Timet pudorem** *Latin* 'He dreads shame'
—Downe (V.).

DIVINE GIFTS (*See also* BLESSING; DIVINITY; GIFTS and GIVING; GRACE; PROVIDENCE; RELIGION.)

1. **A Deo data** *Latin* 'Given by God'
—Friedrich Wilhelm, Elector of Brandenburg (1620–88).

2. **A deo et patre** *Latin* 'From God and my father'
—Thomas.

3. **A Deo et rege** *Latin* 'From God and the king'
—Chesterfield (E.), Fawkes, Hampton, Harrington (E.), Lewis, Scudmore (Bt.), Stanhope (E.), Strachy (Bt.).

4. **A deo in Deo** *Latin* 'From God in God'
—Troyte.

5. **A Deo lux nostra** *Latin* 'Our light is from God'
—Holloway.

6. **Caelitus datum**   *Latin* 'Given by God'
       —Borthwick, Finlason, Finlay, Finlayson.

7. **Comme Dieu grantit**   *French* 'As God grants'
       —Grantham.

8. **Dabit otia Deus**   *Latin* 'God will give times of leisure'
       —Brisbane, Brisbane-McDougall.

9. **Dante Deo**   *Latin* 'By the gift of God'
       —Wolff (Bt.), Van Wolff.

10. **Dat Deus incrementum**   *Latin* 'God giveth the increase'
       —Crofton (B.), Crofton (Bt.), Muggeridge, Westminster
School, U.K.

11. **Dat Deus originem**   *Latin* 'God gives birth (high or low)'
       —Hamilton.

12. **Dat et sumit Deus**   *Latin* 'God giveth and taketh away'
       —Ethelston.

13. **De Dieu est tout**   *French* 'From God everything'
       —Mervyn.

14. **De Dieu tout**   *French* 'From God everything'
       —White, Beckford.

15. **Dei dono sum quod sum**   *Latin* 'By the bounty of God I am what
I am'
       —Lumsden (of Pitcaple and Cushnie), Lundin.

16. **Dei donum**   *Latin* 'The gift of God'
       —Town of Dundee.

17. **D'en haut**   *French* 'From on high'
       —Whitefoord.

18. **Deo donum**   *Latin* 'A gift from God'
       —Darling.

19. **Deus dabit**   *Latin* 'God will give'
       —More (of Iunernytie).

20. **Deus dat incrementum**   *Latin* 'God giveth the increase'
       —Warrington C. B. C., U.K.

21. **Deus dat qui vult**   *Latin* 'God gives what He wishes'
       —Stacey.

22. **Deus dedit**   *Latin* 'God gave'
       —Moir.

23. **Deus haec otia**   *Latin* 'God has given us this ease'
       —[after Vergil, *Ec.* i. vi.] Lambert.

24. **Deus haec otia fecit** *Latin* 'God hath given this tranquillity'
—[after Vergil, *Ec.* i. vi.] Williams (Co. Brecon and
Herts.).

25. **Deus incrementum dedit** *Latin* 'God has given increase'
—Firth.

26. **Deus nobis haec otia fecit** *Latin* 'God hath given us this tranquillity'
—[Vergil, *Ec.* i. vi.] Town of Liverpool, Liverpool City
and C. B. C., U.K., Bolger, Burrow, Hide.

27. **Dieu donne** *French* 'God gives'
—Colpoys.

28. **Dii moresque dabunt** *Latin* 'The gods and (our own) habits will
give it'
—O'Beirne.

29. **Ditat Deus** *Latin* 'God enriches'
—McTaggart.

30. **Dominus dedit** *Latin* 'The Lord hath given'
—Harries.

31. **Dona dantur desuper** *Latin* '(All) gifts are given from on high'
—Christian I, Prince of Anhalt-Bernburg (1568–1630).

32. **God give grace**
—Tait.

33. **God gives increase**
—[1 Cor., iii. 6.] Balfour (Bt.).

34. **God giveth all**
—House in Axmouth, Devonshire, England.

35. **God giveth the victory**
—Simon.

36. **God grant grace**
—Grocers' Company.

37. **God grant unity**
—Wheelwrights' Company.

38. **God send grace**
—Erne (E.), Dalrymple, Crichton.

39. **Gott gibt, Gott nimmt** *German* 'The Lord giveth, and the Lord
taketh away'
—[after Job, i. 21.] Philipp II, last Duke of Braunschweig-
Grubenhagen (1533–96); Friedrich Ulrich, Duke of
Braunschweig-Wolfenbüttel (1591–1634).

40. **Gratis a Deo data** *Latin* 'Given freely by God'
—Skeen, Skene.

41. **Incrementum dat Deus** *Latin* 'God gives increase'
—Moseley (of Owsden).

42. **O Gott gewähr was ich begehr** *German* 'O God grant what I desire'
—Richard, Count of the Palatinate (1521–98).

43. **Omne bonum Dei donum** *Latin* 'Every good is the gift of God'
—Boughton (Bt.), Edwards, Powell.

44. **Omne bonum desuper** *Latin* 'Every good is from above'
—Burney.

45. **Omnia bona desuper** *Latin* 'All good things are from above'
—Goodlake.

46. **Omnia desuper** *Latin* 'All things are from above'
—Embroiderers' Company.

47. **Omnia mei dona Dei** *Latin* 'All my goods are the gift of God'
—Done.

48. **Pulchra terra Dei donum** *Latin* 'This fair land is the gift of God'
—Herefordshire C. C., U.K.

49. **Sapientia donum Dei** *Latin* 'Wisdom is the gift of God'
—Field.

50. **Tout d'en haut** *French* 'All from above'
—Bellew (Bt.), Bellew.

51. **Was Gott beschertt, Bleibt vnerwehrtt** *German* 'What God bestows, remains preserved'
—Ernst, Margrave of Brandenburg (1583–1613).

DIVINE GUIDANCE (*See also* GUIDANCE; RELIGION.)

1. **A Deo, non fortuna** *Latin* 'By God, not by fortune'
—Greaves, Greaves-Banning.

2. **A Deo victoria** *Latin* 'Victory from God'
—Graham, Graeme.

3. **Adjuva, o Virgo, res tua agitur** *Latin* 'Help, O Virgin (Mary), thy matter is in hand'
—Albrecht, Margrave of Brandenburg (1490–1568).

4. **Adjuvante Deo** *Latin* 'God my helper'
—Phillips, Malins.

5. **Adjuvante Deo, quid timeo?** *Latin* 'God helping me, what do I fear?'
   —Bridgman.

6. **Adjuvante Deo in hostes** *Latin* 'God aiding against enemies'
   —Donovan, O'Donovan.

7. **A Domino auxilium meum** *Latin* 'From God is my help'
   —Ernst Ludwig, Duke of Pomerania zu Wolgast (1545–92).

8. **Adsit Deus** *Latin* 'God be with me'
   —Balfour.

9. **Adsit Deus non demovebor** *Latin* 'God with me, I shall not be removed'
   —Baird.

10. **A fyno Duw a fydd** *Welsh* 'What God wills will be'
    —Hughes, Matthew, Walsham (Bt.).

11. **Aides Dieu!** *French* 'Help, O God!'
    —Aubert, Mill (Bt.), Mills.

12. **Aide toi et le ciel t'aidera** *French* 'Help yourself and heaven shall help you'
    —Sylvester (U.S.).

13. **A la garde de Dieu** *French* 'In God's keeping'
    —Alphonse de Lamartine (1792–1869).

14. **A la volonté de Dieu** *French* 'At the will of God'
    —Strickland (Bt.).

15. **Alles Nach Gotes Willen** *German* 'Everything after the will of God'
    —Johann Georg, Elector of Brandenburg (1525–98); Albert, Count of Nassau-Weilburg (1537–93); Ludwig, Prince of Anhalt-Köthen (1579–1650); Johann Christian, Duke of Brieg (1591–1639); Georg Friedrich, Margrave of Brandenburg (1539–1603); Georg III, Duke of Brieg (1611–64); Karl Wilhelm, Prince of Anhalt-Zerbst (1652–1718); Emanuel Leberecht, Prince of Anhalt-Plötzkau (1671–1704).

16. **Allons, Dieu ayde** *Old French* 'Let us go on, God assists us'
    —Blakely.

17. **Altiora in votis** *Latin* 'I pray for the higher things'
    —Highgate School, U.K.

18. **A. M. A. D. (Auxilium meum a Deo)** *Latin* 'My help cometh from the Lord'
—[Ps., cxxi. 2.] Christian, Margrave of Brandenburg-Baireuth (1581–1655).

19. **Angelis suis praecepit de te** *Latin* 'He has given his angels charge of thee'
—Power.

20. **An Gottes Segen ist alles gelegen** *German* 'Everything rests on God's blessing'
—Heinrich II, Count Reuss (1575–1639); Friedrich Ulrich, Duke of Braunschweig-Wolfenbüttel (1591–1634); Christian, Duke of Wohlau (1618–72).

21. **A. N. G. W. (Alles nach Gottes Willen)** *German* 'Everything according to the will of God'
—Heinrich Julius, Duke of Braunschweig-Wolfenbüttel (1564–1613); Marie, Margravine of Brandenburg (1579–1649); Sophie, Duchess of Schleswig-Holstein (1579–1618); Elisabeth, Duchess of Schleswig-Holstein (1580–1653); Christian, Margrave of Brandenburg-Baireuth (1581–1655); Erdmann August, Margrave of Brandenburg-Baireuth (1615–51).

22. **Annuit coeptis** *Latin* 'God has favored our undertaking'
—Great Seal of United States of America.

23. **Arctaeos Numine fines** *Latin* '(I reached) the limits of the north by (the help of) God'
—Ross.

24. **Ardentibus votis** *Latin* 'With earnest prayer'
—Anton Ulrich, Duke of Braunschweig-Wolfenbüttel (1633–1714).

25. **Ar Duw y gyd** *Welsh* 'All depend on God'
—Phillips; Price (Bt.).

26. **Arx et anchora mihi Deus** *Latin* 'God is a stronghold and a security for me'
—Rawson.

27. **As God wills**
—Winterstoke (B.).

28. **As God wills, so be it**
—Blacksmiths' Company, London.

29. **Astra castra, numen, lumen munimen**   *Latin* 'The stars are my camp, the Deity is my light and guard'
—Belcarres (E.), Lindsay (Bt.), Lindsey.

30. **At all times God me defend**
—Lyell.

31. **Au plaisir fort de Dieu**   *French* 'At the all-powerful disposal of God'
—Mount Edgecumbe (E.).

32. **Auspice Christo**   *Latin* 'Under the guidance of Christ'
—Davie (Bt.), Lawley (Bt.), Wenlock (B.).

33. **Auspice Deo**   *Latin* 'Under God's direction'
—Speid.

34. **Auspice Deo extule mari**   *Latin* 'God being my leader, I brought him out of the sea'
—Phillips-Marshall, Phillips.

35. **Auspice Deo vinces**   *Latin* 'Under the guidance of God you will conquer'
—Beley.

36. **Auspice Numine**   *Latin* 'Under Divine direction'
—Welsh.

37. **Auspice summo Numine**   *Latin* 'Under direction of Almighty God'
—Irvine.

38. **Auxilio ab alto**   *Latin* 'By aid from on high'
—Martin.

39. **Auxilio Dei**   *Latin* 'By the help of God'
—Erisby, Morehead, Muirhead (of Bredisholm).

40. **Auxilio Dei supero**   *Latin* 'I overcome with the help of God'
—Chapin (U.S.).

41. **Auxilio Divino**   *Latin* 'By divine aid'
—Drake (Bt.), Devon C. C., U.K.

42. **Auxilium ab alto**   *Latin* 'Aid from above'
—Clonbrock (B.), Dillon (Bt.), Killett, Normand, Ordell, King, Martin (Bt.), Roscommon (E.).

43. **Auxilium meum ab alto**   *Latin* 'My help is from above'
—Blakeney.

44. **Auxilium meum a Domino**   *Latin* 'My help is from the Lord'
—Collyer, Lloyd, Price (Bt.), Mostyn (B.).

45. **Ave Maria plena gratia** *Latin* 'Hail, Mary, full of grace'
—[after Luke, i. 28.] Cusack.

46. **A vino Duw dervid** *Welsh* 'What God wills will happen.'
—Edwards (Bt.), Lloyd.

47. **A vonno Div dervid** *Welsh* 'What God wills will happen.'
—Lloyd.

48. **Be as God will**
—Bracebridge (of Atherstone), Bracebridge (Co. Warwick).

49. **Benefac, Domine, bonis et rectis corde** *Latin* 'Do good, O Lord, unto those that be good, and to them that are upright in their hearts'
—[Ps. cxxv. 4.] Wilhelm V, Duke of Bavaria (1548–1626).

50. **Benigno numine enisus** *Latin* 'Under a propitious Deity I have ascended'
—Monk Bretton (B.).

51. **By the grace of God**
—Login.

52. **Christo duce feliciter** *Latin* 'Happily, under the guidance of Christ'
—Binning.

53. **Christus dux solus** *Latin* 'Christ is my only guide'
—Christiane, Duchess of Saxony-Eisenberg (1659–79).

54. **Cio che Dio vuole, io voglio** *Italian* 'What God wills, I will'
—Dormer (B.).

55. **Conserva me, Domine** *Latin* 'Preserve me, O Lord'
—Tayler.

56. **Conserva nos Domina** *Latin* 'Uphold us, blessed Virgin!'
—Bogislaus X, Duke of Pomerania (1454–1523).

57. **Contre fortune bon coeur, Dieu tourne tout en bonheur** *French* 'Against fortune a stout heart: may God direct everything for the best'
—Dorothee Sophie, Duchess of Saxony (1587–1645).

58. **Cruce duce** *Latin* 'With the cross for guide'
—Adams.

59. **Custodi civitatem Domine** *Latin* 'Keep the city, O Lord'
—Westminster City Council, U.K.

60. **Dabit Deus his quoque finem** *Latin* 'God will put an end even to these (griefs)'
—[Vergil, *Aen.* i. 199.] Karl Wilhelm, Prince of Anhalt-Zerbst (1652–1718).

61. **Dabit Deus vela** *Latin* 'God will fill the sails'
—Tennant.

62. **Da nobis lucem, Domine** *Latin* 'Give us light, O Lord!'
—Glaziers' Company.

63. **Dante Deo reddam** *Latin* 'God giving me, I shall restore'
—Mitchell.

64. **Dei beneficio sum quod sum** *Latin* 'By the grace of God I am what I am'
—Russell.

65. **Dei gratia** *Latin* 'By the grace of God'
—Kingston.

66. **Dei gratia sumus quod sumus** *Latin* 'By the grace of God, we are what we are'
—Barking B. C., U.K.

67. **Dei Providentia juvat** *Latin* 'The providence of God is our help'
—Welman (of Poundsford Park).

68. **Deo ac bello** *Latin* 'By God and war'
—Chambers.

69. **Deo adjuvante** *Latin* 'By the help of God'
—Wellington U. D. C., U.K.

70. **Deo adjuvante** *Latin* 'With God assisting'
—Pellew (Viscount Exmouth), Jones, Salmons, Williams.

71. **Deo adjuvante, fortuna sequatur** *Latin* 'With God assisting, good fortune may follow'
—Roberts (of Crofton Hall, Co. Salop).

72. **Deo adjuvante arte et industria floret** *Latin* 'With God's help, it flourishes by art and industry'
—Kidderminster B. C., U.K.

73. **Deo adjuvante labor proficit** *Latin* 'By God's help labor succeeds'
—Sheffield City and C. B. C., U.K.

74. **Deo adjuvante non timendum** *Latin* 'With God assisting we must not fear'
—Coyne, Fitzwilliams, Hamlet, Peters, Williams.

75. **Deo adjuvante vincam**   *Latin* 'God helping I shall conquer'
—Hart.

76. **Deo adverso, leo vincitur**   *Latin* 'God opposing, the lion is conquered'
—Newenham.

77. **Deo aspirante virescit**   *Latin* 'With God's help he flourishes'
—Ulrich, Duke of Pomerania (1587–1622).

78. **Deo dirigente**   *Latin* 'Under the direction of God'
—Bogislaus XIV, Duke of Pomerania (1580–1637).

79. **Deo dirigente crescendum est**   *Latin* 'It increases under God's direction'
—Lowell (U.S.).

80. **Deo duce**   *Latin* 'God my guide'
—Town of Pettinween (Scotland), Hennidge, Ricketts, Hooper.

81. **Deo duce, comite industria**   *Latin* 'God being my guide, industry my companion'
—Slaney (Co. Salop), Nicoll.

82. **Deo duce, ferro comitante**   *Latin* 'God my guide, and my sword my companion'
—Caulfield, Charlemont (E.).

83. **Deo duce, fortunâ comitante**   *Latin* 'With God as my guide, good fortune as companion'
—Merchants of Exeter, Sladen.

84. **Deo duce, sequor**   *Latin* 'I follow, God being my guide'
—Wheelton.

85. **Deo duce Christo luce**   *Latin* 'God my guide, Christ my light'
—Butler.

86. **Deo duce comite fortuna**   *Latin* 'God for guide, fortune for companion'
—Palles.

87. **Deo duce decrevi**   *Latin* 'Under God's direction I have determined'
—Harnage (Bt.).

88. **Deo ducente, nil nocet**   *Latin* 'God leading, nothing hurts'
—Pelly.

89. **Deo ducente nil nocet**   *Latin* 'With God as leader, nothing can injure'
—East India Company.

90. **Deo duce perseverandum** *Latin* 'With God as our leader we must persevere'
—Jay (U.S.).

91. **Deo et gladio** *Latin* 'By God and my sword'
—Crealock, Crealocke.

92. **Deo et labore** *Latin* 'By God and by labour'
—Sebag.

93. **Deo favente** *Latin* 'By the favor of God'
—Alves, Dingwall.

94. **Deo favente cresco** *Latin* 'I go on increasing by the favor of God'
—Bartlett.

95. **Deo favente florebo** *Latin* 'By the favor of God, I shall prosper'
—Blenshell.

96. **Deo favente progredior** *Latin* 'I go forward by the favor of God'
—Pyke.

97. **Deo favente supero** *Latin* 'Being favored by God, I overcome'
—Cooke.

98. **Deo inspirante, rege favente** *Latin* 'By the inspiration of God and the king's favor'
—Stahlschmidt.

99. **Deo juvante** *Latin* 'With God's help'
—Principality of Monaco, Duff, Fife (e.), Groze, Grimaldi, Maitland, Shatt, Tawse, Wodderspoon, Kirkburton U. D. C., U.K.

100. **Deo juvante consilio et armis** *Latin* 'By counsel and arms with the aid of God'
—Maitland.

101. **Deo juvante gero** *Latin* 'By the help of God I carry on'
—Galloway.

102. **Deo juvante vinco** *Latin* 'By God's assistance I conquer'
—Stewart.

103. **Deo protectori meo** *Latin* 'For God, my protector'
—Christian, Duke of Saxony-Eisenburg (1653–1707).

104. **Deo regnat** *Latin* 'He rules through God'
—Judd (U.S.).

105. **Deo vindice** *Latin* 'God maintains'
—Great Seal of the Confederate States of America.

106. **Deo volente** *Latin* 'God willing'
—Reeves, Palliser.

107. **Der Herr ist mein Schild auf den ich traue** *German* 'The Lord is my shield, on which I trust'
—[after 2 Sam., xxii. 3.] Joachim Ernst, Margrave of Brandenburg-Anspach (1583–1625); his son, Friedrich, Margrave of Brandenburg-Anspach (1616–34).

108. **Deum posui adjutorem** *Latin* 'I have taken God for my helper'
—Kingston.

109. **Deus ab inimicis me defendit** *Latin* 'God defends me from my enemies'
—Le Touzel.

110. **Deus adesto** *Latin* 'Let God stand by us'
—Brown.

111. **Deus adjutor et liberator meus** *Latin* 'God is my help and deliverer'
—[after Ps., xl. 17.] Heinrich the Pious, Duke of Saxony (1473–1541).

112. **Deus adjutor meus** *Latin* 'God is mine helper'
—[Ps., liv. 4.] Bogislaus XIV, Duke of Pomerania (1580–1637).

113. **Deus adjuvabit** *Latin* 'God will assist (us)'
—Taylor (U.S.).

114. **Deus adjuvat nos** *Latin* 'God assists us'
—Booth (Bt.).

115. **Deus alit eos** *Latin* 'God feeds them'
—Croker (of Trevillas), James.

116. **Deus aspiret coeptis** *Latin* 'May God favor the enterprise'
—[after Ovid, *Met.* i. 2.] Friedrich, Duke of Württemberg (1557–1608).

117. **Deus clypeus meus** *Latin* 'God is my shield'
—Biddle.

118. **Deus dabit vela** *Latin* 'God will fill the sails'
—Campbell, Norman (Co. Sussex).

119. **Deus dat incrementum** *Latin* 'God gives increase'
—Bancroft (U.S.).

120. **Deus dexter meus** *Latin* 'God is my right hand'
—Dobbyn.

121. **Deus dux certus** *Latin* 'God is a sure leader'
—Bromage.

122. **Deus est nobis sol et ensis**   *Latin* 'God is a sun and sword to us'
                                                —Powell.

123. **Deus est noster refugium**   *Latin* 'God is our refuge'
                                                —Tailor.

124. **Deus est petra et fortitudo mea**   *Latin* 'The Lord is my rock and my fortress'
     —[2 Sam., xxii. 2.] Christian, Duke of Saxony (1652–89).

125. **Deus est super domo**   *Latin* 'God is over the household'
                                                —Straker.

126. **Deus fortioribus adest**   *Latin* 'God is on the side of the strongest'
     —Bogislaus XIV, Duke of Pomerania (1580–1637).

127. **Deus fortissima turris**   *Latin* 'God is a very strong tower'
                                                —Le Bailly.

128. **Deus fortitudo mea**   *Latin* 'God is my strength'
     —Friedrich Wilhelm, Elector of Branderburg (1620–88),
                                     Jones (of Bealanamore).

129. **Deus gubernat navem**   *Latin* 'God steers the vessel'
                                     —Town of Renfrew, Leckie.

130. **Deus in auxilium meum**   *Latin* 'God to my help'
     —Friedrich Achilles, Duke of Württemberg (1591–1630).

131. **Deus indicat**   *Latin* 'God discovers'
                                     —East India Company.

132. **Deus industriam beat**   *Latin* 'God blesses industriousness'
                                                —Harborne.

133. **Deus juvat**   *Latin* 'God assists'
                                                —McDuff.

134. **Deus me audit**   *Latin* 'God hears me'
                                     —Lawford, Mauduit.

135. **Deus me sustinet**   *Latin* 'God sustains me'
                                                —Arbuthnot.

136. **Deus meum solamen**   *Latin* 'God is my comfort'
                                     —Keir (of Linlithgow).

137. **Deus meus dux meus**   *Latin* 'My God is my guide'
                                                —St. Albyn.

138. **Deus mihi adjutor**   *Latin* 'God is my helper'
                                                —Ochterlonie.

139. **Deus mihi munimen**   *Latin* 'God is my fortress'
                                                —Hardcastle.

140. **Deus mihi providebit** *Latin* 'God will provide for me'
—Goold (Bt.), Keane (B.), Jerrney.

141. **Deus mihi spes et tutamen** *Latin* 'God is my hope and safeguard'
—Bradshaw.

142. **Deus nobis** *Latin* 'God with us'
—Pinkney.

143. **Deus nobiscum** *Latin* 'God with us'
—Darnell.

144. **Deus nobiscum, quis contra?** *Latin* 'If God be with us, who can be against us?'
—Baron de Bliss (Brandon Park).

145. **Deus nobis quis contra?** *Latin* 'God for us, who shall be against us?'
—De Montmorency, Morres, Carter, Robins.

146. **Deus noster refugium** *Latin* 'Our God is our refuge'
—Barnes.

147. **Deus noster refugium et virtus** *Latin* 'God is our refuge and strength'
—Dewsbury C. B. C., U.K.

148. **Deus pascit corvos** *Latin* 'God feeds the ravens'
—Corbet (Bt.), Corbet, Johnes, Jones, Williams (of Temple House), Cornish, Corbin, Corbyn, Protheroe, Ravenshaw.

149. **Deus pastor meus** *Latin* 'God is my shepherd'
—[Ps., xxiii. 1.] Bogie, or Boggie.

150. **Deus praesidium** *Latin* 'God is our defense'
—Bevan.

151. **Deus prosperat justos** *Latin* 'God prospers the just'
—Aveland (B.), Heathcote.

152. **Deus protector meus** *Latin* 'God is my protector'
—Humphery, Berens, Ulrich, Duke of Pomerania (1587–1622).

153. **Deus protector noster** *Latin* 'God is our protector'
—Emerson-Tennent (of Tempo), Order of the Lamb of God (Sweden).

154. **Deus providebit** *Latin* 'God will provide'
—Berton (Bt.), Bolger (of Wexford), Brummind (of Blair), Lesly (of Aberdden), Marshall, Matherm Mein, Mundy, Prideaux (Bt.), Dominican School of Philosophy and Theology, California.

155. **Deus quis contra**   *Latin* 'God with us, who can be against us?'
    —Hutton.

156. **Deus refugium nostrum**   *Latin* 'God our refuge'
    —Malcolm.

157. **Deus robur meum**   *Latin* 'God is my strength'
    —Wood (of Brownhills).

158. **Deus salutem disponit**   *Latin* 'God orders salvation'
    —Archer.

159. **Deus scutum et cornu salutis**   *Latin* 'God my shield and the horn of my salvation'
    —Thoroton.

160. **Deus si monet**   *Latin* 'If God directs'
    —Simonet.

161. **Deus solamen**   *Latin* 'God is my comfort'
    —Der, Kerr.

162. **Deus solus auget aristas**   *Latin* 'God alone increaseth the harvest'
    —Riddell (of Felton).

163. **Deus tuetur**   *Latin* 'God defends'
    —Davies (of Elmley Park).

164. **Deus veritatem protegit**   *Latin* 'God protects the truth'
    —Roper.

165. **De vultu tuo Domine meum prodeat judicium**   *Latin* 'From thy countenance, O Lord, may my justice issue!'
    —Friedrich II, Elector of the Palatinate (1483–1556).

166. **Die Gnad Gottes weirt ewig**   *German* 'The grace of God is everlasting'
    —Ernest II, Duke of Braunschweig-Grubenhagen (1518–67).

167. **Dieu aidant**   *French* 'God helping'
    —Balfour (of Forret).

168. **Dieu aide au premier Chrestien**   *French* 'God assists the first Christian'
    —Montmorency.

169. **Dieu aide au premier Chretien (Chrestien) et baron de France**   *French* 'God assists the first Christian and baron of France'
    —Order of the Dog and Cock, Montmorency (France).

170. **Dieu avec nous**   *French* 'God with us'
　　　—Berkeley (E.), Berkeley (of Spetchley), Segrave (B.),
　　　　　　　　　　　　　　　　　　　Calcraft, Calcott.

171. **Dieu ayde**   *Old French* 'God assists'
　　　—DeMontmorency, Frankfort de Montmorency (V.),
　　　　　　　　　　　　　　　　　　　Mountmorres (V.).

172. **Dieu defend le droit**   *French* 'God defends the right'
　　　—Churchill (B.), Blenkinsop, Hunter, Seaton, Spencer
　　　　　　　　　　　　　　　　　　　　　　(E.).

173. **Dieu en soit garde**   *French* 'God be its keeper'
　　　　　　　　　　　　　　—Town of Rheims, France.

174. **Dieu est ma roche**   *French* 'God is my rock'
　　　　　　　　　　　　—Roche (Bt.), Fermoy (B.).

175. **Dieu est mon aide**   *French* 'God is my help'
　　　　　　　　　　　　—Band (of Wookey House).

176. **Dieu et ma main droite**   *French* 'God and my right hand'
　　　　　　　　　　　　　　　　　　　—Bate.

177. **Dieu garda Le Moyle**   *French* 'God protects Le Moyle'
　　　　　　　　　　　　　　　　　　　—Moyle.

178. **Dieu gouverne ma vie**   *French* 'God rule my life!'
　　　—Elisabeth, Duchess of Braunschweig (1553–1617).

179. **Dieu le veut**   *French* 'God wills it'
　　　　　　　　　　　　　　　　　　—Lermitte.

180. **Dieu m'a fait fort**   *French* 'God has made me strong'
　　　　　　　　　　　　　　　　　　—Scott.

181. **Dieu me conduise**   *French* 'God guide me!'
　　　　　　　　　　　　　—Hayes (Bt.), Delaval.

182. **Dieu me garde**   *French* 'God keep me'
　　　　　　　　　　　　　　　　　—Agardes.

183. **Dieu mon appui**   *French* 'God is my stay'
　　　　　　　　　　　　　　　　　　—Oliver.

184. **Dieu nous aventure donne bonne**   *French* 'May God give us good
　　　fortune'
　　　　　　　　　　　　　—Hamburgh Merchants.

185. **Dieu pour la Tranchée, qui contre?**   *French* '(If) God (be) for the
　　　Trenches, who shall be against them?'
　　　　　　　　　　　—Le-Poer-Trench, Clancarty (E.).

186. **Dieu pour nous**   *French* 'God for us'
　　　　　　　　　—Fletcher (of Ashford), Peters.

187. **Dieu te garde et regarde** *French* 'God watches out for you and watches over you'
—Bernon (U.S.).

188. **Dii facientes adjuvant** *Latin* 'The gods help those who exert themselves'
—Broughton-Rouse.

189. **Dii rexque secundent** *Latin* 'The Gods and the king will favor us'
—Soapmakers' Company.

190. **Diis bene juvantibus** *Latin* 'By the good help of the gods'
—Middleton.

191. **Diligentes Deus ipse juvat** *Latin* 'God Himself helps the diligent'
—Hartill.

192. **Dios mi amparo y esperanza** *Spanish* 'God is my support and hope'
—Gibbs.

193. **Diovolendo lo faro** *Italian* 'God willing I will do it'
—Wharton.

194. **Dirigat Deus** *Latin* 'May God direct us'
—Allen.

195. **Diriget Deus** *Latin* 'God will direct it'
—Butter.

196. **Ditat Deus** *Latin* 'God enriches'
—State of Arizona.

197. **Divino robore** *Latin* 'By divine strength'
—Galiez, Gellie.

198. **Divinum auxilium maneat nobiscum** *Latin* 'May God's help remain with us'
—Johann Georg I, Prince of Anhalt-Dessau (1567–1618).

199. **Doce me, Domine, statuta tua** *Latin* 'Teach me, Lord, thy commandments'
—[after Ps., cxix. 66.] Wilhelm Ludwig, Prince of Anhalt-Köthen (1638–65).

200. **Domine, dirige me in verbo tuo** *Latin* 'Lord, direct me in thy Word!'
—Johann, Duke of Saxony-Weimar (1570–1605).

201. **Domine, dirige nos** *Latin* 'O Lord, direct us'
—[Eccles., xxxvi. 19.] Brome (of West Malling), City of London.

202. **Domini est dirigere**   *Latin* 'It is for the Lord to direct'
—Gipping R. D. C., U.K.

203. **Domini factum est**   *Latin* 'It is the Lord's doing'
—[Ps., cxviii. 23.] Corbet, Scott (of Moreton), Sibbald (Co. Berks.).

204. **Dominus a dextris**   *Latin* 'The Lord is on my right hand'
—Batt.

205. **Dominus adjutor meus**   *Latin* 'God is my helper'
—Johann Ernst I, Duke of Saxony-Weimar (1594–1626).

206. **Dominus bonus propitiabitur**   *Latin* 'The good Lord will be propitious'
—Bonus.

207. **Dominus dux noster**   *Latin* 'The Lord is our guide'
—Stuart.

208. **Dominus fecit**   *Latin* 'The Lord hath done it'
—Baird, Jackson.

209. **Dominus fortissima turris**   *Latin* 'The Lord is the strongest tower'
—Dettavilland, Tower.

210. **Dominus illuminatio mea**   *Latin* 'The Lord is my light'
—University of Oxford, Leycester (of White Place).

211. **Dominus ipse faciet**   *Latin* 'The Lord himself will do it'
—Adam.

212. **Dominus mihi adiutor**   *Latin* 'The Lord is a helper unto me'
—Kingdom of Denmark.

213. **Dominus mihi adjutor, quem timebo?**
—[after Ps., xxvii. 1.] King of Denmark; Pope Paul IV (1476–1559); Albert, Margrave of Brandenburg (1490–1545).

214. **Dominus nobis solet scutum**   *Latin* 'The Lord is our sun and shield'
—Banbury B. C., U.K.

215. **Dominus petra mea**   *Latin* 'The Lord is my rock'
—Dampier.

216. **Dominus protector meus**   *Latin* 'God my protector'
—[after Ps., xviii. 2.] Karl I, Duke of Münsterberg (1476–1536); Karl Friedrich, Duke of Oels (1593–1647).

217. **Dominus providebit**   *Latin* 'The Lord will provide'
—[Gen., xxii. 8.] Boyle, Burton (of Burton Hall and Longner), Glasgow (E.), Masson, McLaws, McVicar, Maximilian II, Emperor of Germany (1527–76); Friedrich V, King of Bohemia (1532–96); Wilhelm, Duke of Braunschweig-Lüneburg-Harburg (1564–1642); Christian, Count of the Palatinate of Bischweiler (1598–1654); Karl Ludwig, Elector of the Palatinate (1617–80).

218. **Dominus salus mea**   *Latin* 'The Lord is my safety'
—Smith.

219. **Dominus virtutum meum scutum**   *Latin* 'The Lord of valor is my shield'
—Sigismund, Margrave of Brandenburg (1592–1640).

220. **Duce Deo**   *Latin* 'With God for leader'
—De Massue, Massue.

221. **Ducente Deo**   *Latin* 'God guiding'
—Lepper.

222. **Ducit Dominus**   *Latin* 'The Lord leads'
—Dezom.

223. **Ductore Deo**   *Latin* 'With God for leader'
—Peckitt.

224. **Duw a ddarpar i'r brain**   *Welsh* 'God provides for the crows'
—Hughes (of Plas Coch).

225. **Duw a'n bendithio**   *Welsh* 'God bless us'
—Pryce (Bt.).

226. **Duw fyddo ein cryfdwr**   *Welsh* 'God be our strength'
—Edwards.

227. **Duw ydi ein cryfdwr**   *Welsh* 'God is our strength'
—Edwards (of Manchester).

228. **El hombre propone, Dios dispone**   *Spanish* 'Man proposes, God disposes'
—Davy.

229. **Est voluntas Dei**   *Latin* 'It is the will of God'
—Baldwin, Oliffe.

230. **Et Dieu mon appui**   *French* 'And God my support'
—Hungerford.

231. **Except the Lord keep the city**
—Halifax C. B. C., U.K.

232. **Favente Deo** *Latin* 'By God's favor'
—Pawson, Reynolds (of Great Yarmouth and Necton, Co. Norfolk), Wilkie, Fisher.

233. **Favente Deo et sedulitate** *Latin* 'God and assiduity favoring'
—Collins.

234. **Favente Deo supero** *Latin* 'By God's favor I conquer'
—Mitchell.

235. **Favente Numine regina servatur** *Latin* 'By the favor of the Deity the Queen is preserved'
—Micklethwait (Bt.).

236. **Favore Altissimi** *Latin* 'By the grace of the Highest'
—Ferdinand Albert, Duke of Braunschweig-Bevern (1680–1735).

237. **Felici numine crescat** *Latin* 'May he grow under God's grace'
—Georg Friedrich, Margrave of Brandenburg-Anspach (1678–1703).

238. **Fiat Dei voluntas** *Latin* 'God's will be done'
—Meredyth (Bt.).

239. **Fiat divina voluntas** *Latin* 'The divine will be done'
—August, Duke of Braunschweig-Lüneburg (1568–1636).

240. **Fiat secundum Verbum Tuum** *Latin* 'Let it be done according to Thy Word'
—St. Marylebone B. C., U.K.

241. **Fiat voluntas Dei** *Latin* 'God's will be done'
—Salwey.

242. **Fiat voluntas Domini** *Latin* 'The Lord's will be done'
—[after Matt., vi. 10.] Erdmuthe Sophie, Margravine of Brandenburg (1644–70).

243. **Fiat voluntas tua, Domine** *Latin* 'May Thy will be done, O Lord!'
—Joachim Ernst, Prince of Anhalt (1536–86); Johann Georg I, Prince of Anhalt-Dessau (1567–1618).

244. **Floresco favente Deo** *Latin* 'God helping me, I flourish'
—Neill.

245. **Fortes adjuvat ipse Deus** *Latin* 'God himself aids the brave'
—Davenport.

246. **Fortissimus clypeus Dominus** *Latin* 'The strongest shield is the Lord'
—Franz Karl, Duke of Saxony (1594–1669).

247. **Fortis turris mihi Deus** *Latin* 'God is my strong tower'
—O'Kelly.

248. **Fortiter Deo juvante** *Latin* 'Bravely, God helping'
—Pollard.

249. **Fortitudo mea Deus** *Lat* 'God is my strength'
—Channing (Bt.).

250. **Fortitudo mea Dominus** *Latin* 'God is my strength'
—Ferdinand Maria, Elector of Bavaria (1636–79).

251. **G. H. M. E. (Gott hilf mir Elenden)** *German* 'God help miserable me'
—Eleonore, Electress of Brandenburg (1583–1607).

252. **God be guide**
—Kennedy.

253. **God be my bede** *Middle English* 'God be my aide'
—Geedham.

254. **God be my guide**
—Blair, Butler, Glengall (E.).

255. **God be our friend**
—Staple Merchants' Company.

256. **God be our good guide**
—Russia Merchants' Company.

257. **God careth for us**
—Mitford (of Pitshill).

258. **God caryth for us**
—Pits.

259. **Goddes grace governe Garneys**
—Garneys.

260. **God feedeth ye land**
—Leyland.

261. **God feeds the crows**
—Crawfurd.

262. **God for us**
—Douglas.

263. **God fried (Gott-friede) German**
—Godfrey (Bt.).

264. **God guide all**
—Lesly (of Aberdeen).

265. **God is my defender**
—Breame.

266. God is my health
—Hadley.

267. God is my help
—Hadley (U.S.).

268. God is my safety
—Craw (of Nether-Byer).

269. God is my shield
—Rosborough, Rosborough-Colclough.

270. God is our strength
—Ironmongers' Company.

271. God me guide
—Crichton (of Easthill).

272. God send me wel to kepe
—Anne of Cleves, fourth wife of Henry VIII.

273. God shaw the right
—Craufurd (of Newfield, Drumsog, etc.).

274. God shield the right
—Crawfurd.

275. God's providence is my inheritance
—Boyle.

276. God the only founder
—Founders' Company.

277. God will provide
—Stewart.

278. God with my right
—Bryson, Buchanan (of Drumakill).

279. God with us
—Gordon, Moodie.

280. **Gofal Dyn Duw ai gwared** *Welsh* 'God will release man from care'
—Parry.

281. **Good God increase**
—Goodale, Goodalle.

282. **Got mit uns** *German* 'God with us'
—King of Prussia.

283. **Gottes fügunck mein begnügung** *German* 'God's dispensation is my contentment'
—Joachim Ernst, Margrave of Brandenburg-Anspach (1583–1625).

284. **Gottes Heill ist mein Erbteil**   *German* 'God's grace is my inheritance'
     —Heinrich III, Count Reuss (1578–1616).

285. **Gottes Heil mein einzig Theil**   *German* 'God's grace is my only portion'
     —Marie Eleonore, Margravine of Brandenburg (1599–1655).

286. **Gottes hort pleibt ebiglich**   *German* 'God's grace remains forever'
     —Albrecht, Margrave of Brandenburg (1490–1568).

287. **Gottes Rath am besten**   *German* 'God's counsel is best'
     —Karl, Margrave of Baden-Durlach (1529–77).

288. **Gottes Wort mein Hort**   *German* 'God's Word is my shield'
     —Ernst VI, Count of Mansfeld (1561–1609); Anna, Electress of Brandenburg (1576–1625); Agnes, Duchess of Saxony (1584–1629); Eva Katharine, Princess of Anhalt (1613–79); Agnes, Margravine of Brandenburg (d. 1629).

289. **Gott führe Mych Auff Ebner Bhan**   *German* 'God, lead me into the land of uprightness'
     —[Ps., cxliii. 10.] Marie Eleonore, Margravine of Brandenburg (1550–1608).

290. **Gott gibt als ich hoffe**   *German* 'God grant as I hope'
     —Georg the Pious, Margrave of Brandenburg-Anspach (1484–1543).

291. **Gott hilft aus Not**   *German* 'God helps us from need'
     —Heinrich II, the Younger, Duke of Braunschweig-Wolfenbüttel (1489–1568); Johann Friedrich, Elector of Saxony (1503–54).

292. **Gott mit uns**   *German* 'God with us'
     —King of Prussia; Johann Georg I, Elector of Saxony (1585–1656); Wilhelm, Duke of Saxony-Weimar (1598–1662).

293. **Gott verläszt die Seinen nicht**   *German* 'God forsakes not his own'
     —Franz, Duke of Braunschweig-Lüneburg (1572–1601); Dorothee, Electress of Brandenburg (1636–89).

294. **Gott verlest niemant, der auf ihn vertrawt**   *German* 'God forsakes none who trust in him'
     —Anna, Margravine of Baden (D. 1621).

295. **Gott waltts** *German* 'God disposes'
—Johann Georg, Margrave of Brandenburg (1577–1624).

296. **Gratia Dei cibus animae** *Latin* 'The grace of God is the food of the soul'
—Moritz, Count of the Palatinate of Rhein (B. 1620).

297. **Gratia Dei servatus** *Latin* 'He is protected by the favor of God'
—Sons of Veterans of the United States of America.

298. **Gubernat navem Deus** *Latin* 'God steers the ship'
—Lecky.

299. **G. W. G. (Gottes Wille Geschehe)** *German* 'God's will be done'
—[after Matt., vi. 10.] Juliane Ursula, Margravine of Baden (D. 1614).

300. **H. D. H. D. (Hilf du heilige Dreifaltigkeit)** *German* 'Help thou holy Trinity'
—Johann Georg I, Prince of Anhalt-Dessau (1567–1618).

301. **Heb nefol nerth, nid sicr saeth** *Welsh* 'Without heavenly aid no arrow is sure'
—Jones (of Hartsheath, co. Flint).

302. **H. G. H. G. H. G. (Hilf Gott, hilf Gott, hilf Gott)** *German* 'God help, God help, God help'
—Sophie Elisabeth, Countess of Schwarzenburg (1565–1621).

303. **H. G. Z. G. (Hilf Gott zu Glück)** *German* 'May God help us to fortune'
—Magdalene, Princess of Anhalt (1585–1657).

304. **H. H. H. H. H. (Hilf, himmlischer Herr, höchster Hort)** *German* 'Help, heavenly Father, highest treasure'
—Elisabeth, Duchess of Saxony-Coburg (1540–94).

305. **Hoc duce sub cruce non sine luce** *Latin* 'Under whose guidance beneath the cross not without light'
—Emilie, Countess of Schwarzburg (1614–70).

306. **Homo proponit, Deus disponit** *Latin* 'Man proposes, God disposes'
—Starkey.

307. **H. R. M. D. D. H. G. (Herr, regiere mich durch deinen heiligen Geist)** *German* 'Lord, rule me through Thy holy spirit'
—Eva Christine, Margravine of Brandenburg (1590–1657);
Elisabeth, Electress of Brandenburg (1563–1607);
Eleonore, daughter of Prince Rudolf of Anhalt-Zerbst (1608–81).

308. **Ich wags, Gott walts** *German* 'I venture, God disposes'
—Johann Georg, Margrave of Brandenburg (1577–1624);
Julius Heinrich, Duke of Saxony-Lauenburg
(1586–1665).

309. **Ich wags mit Gott** *German* 'With God I venture'
—Ulrich, Duke of Württemberg (1617–71).

310. **If God will**
—Samson, Scheffeld (kt. of Rhodes, reign of Henry VIII).

311. **If you aid God, he will aid you** *(from Arabic)*
—Morocco.

312. **In Deo faciemus virtutem** *Latin* 'Through God we shall do valiantly'
—Karl Wilhelm, Prince of Anhalt-Zerbst (1652–1718).

313. **In Deo robur meum** *Latin* 'In God is my strength'
—Armstrong.

314. **In Deo solum (or solo) robur** *Latin* 'In God alone is strength'
—Harris.

315. **In Deo tutamen** *Latin* 'In God is my defense'
—Oldfield.

316. **In manibus Dei sortes meae** *Latin* 'In the hands of God is my fate'
—Gustav Christoph, Margrave of Baden (1566–1609).

317. **In manibus Domini sorsque salusque mea** *Latin* 'In the hands of the Lord are my fate and salvation'
—Marie Elisabeth, Countess of Oldenburg (1581–1619);
Anton Günther, last Count of Oldenburg and
Delmenhorst (1583–1667).

318. **In manibus Domini sortes meae** *Latin* 'In the hands of the Lord is my fate'
—Georg III, Duke of Brieg (1611–64).

319. **In manu Dei cor principis** *Latin* 'In the hand of God is the heart of the prince'
—Johann Philipp, Duke of Saxony-Altenburg (1597–1639).

320. **In nomine tuo Domine laxabo rete meum** *Latin* 'At Thy word, O Lord, will I let down my net'
—[after Luke, v. 5.] Johann Philipp, Duke of Saxony-
Altenburg (1597–1639).

321. **In potentatibus salus dextera Domini** *Latin* 'The right hand of the Lord is a saving strength'
—[after Ps., xx. 6.] Albert, Margrave of Brandenburg (1490–1545).

322. **Jehovah-Jireh** *Hebrew* 'The Lord will provide'
—Grant (of Monymusk, bt.).

323. **Juvant Deus impigros** *Latin* 'God assists the diligent'
—Strachan.

324. **Juvante Deo** *Latin* 'By God's assistance'
—Layard.

325. **Juvat impigros Deus** *Latin* 'God aids the diligent'
—Huddersfield C. B. C., U.K.

326. **Laboranti numen adest** *Latin* 'God is with him that endeavors'
—Macfarlane.

327. **Lasz Gott walten** *German* 'Let God dispose'
—Friedrich, Margrave of Brandenburg (1588–1611).

328. **Lehremich dein Wortt meiner Seelen Hort** *German* 'Teach me thy word, refuge of my soul!'
—Wilhelm Ludwig, Prince of Anhalt-Köthen (1638–65).

329. **L'homme propose, Dieu dispose** *French* 'Man proposes, God disposes'
—[Thomas à Kempis, *Imitatio Christi*, i. 19, 2.] Sophie, Margravine of Brandenburg (1614–46); Elisabeth Henriette, Landgravine of Hesse (1661–83).

330. **Meditare** *Latin* 'Meditate well'
—Fairlie.

331. **Me fortem reddit Deus** *Latin* 'God makes me strong'
—Scott.

332. **Mein Anfang und Ende steht in Gottes händen** *German* 'My beginning and my end are in God's hands'
—Anna Sophie, Princess of Anhalt (1584–1652); Friedrich, Duke of Braunschweig-Lüneberg (1574–1648).

333. **Mein Gott, füg es zum Besten (M. G. F. Z. B.)** *German* 'My God, order it for the best'
—Sophie, consort of Georg Friedrich, Margrave of Brandenburg-Anspach (1563–1639).

334. **Meor ras tha Dew** *Cornish* 'Gracious is thy God'
—Willyams.

335. **Mon heur et salut gist en mains de Dieu**   *Old French* 'My fortune and health lie in God's hands'
—Dorothee, Margravine of Brandenburg (1596–1649).

336. **Na fyno Duw na fyd**   *Welsh* 'What God wills not will not be'
—Price.

337. **Nil amplius oro**   *Latin* 'I pray for nothing more'
—Cox.

338. **Nil desperandum auspice Deo**   *Latin* 'With God as our leader there is no cause for despair'
—Sunderland C. B. C., U.K.

339. **Nil facimus non sponte Dei**   *Latin* 'We do nothing without God's will'
—Atkinson (U.S.).

340. **Nisi per te**   *Latin* 'Through Thee alone'
—August, Duke of Schleswig-Holstein-Sonderburg-Norburg (1635–99).

341. **Non ego sed gratia Dei**   *Latin* 'Not I but the grace of God'
—McGrea.

342. **Non obstante Deo**   *Latin* 'If God oppose not'
—Cunningham.

343. **Non sola mortali luce gradior**   *Latin* 'I advance not by mortal light alone'
—Mascarène (U.S.).

344. **Nos pascit Deus**   *Latin* 'God feeds us'
—Rooke.

345. **Not laws of man but laws of God**
—Balch.

346. **Numine et arcu**   *Latin* 'By the Deity and my bow'
—Bowman.

347. **Numine et virtute**   *Latin* 'By God's providence and by virtue'
—Yule.

348. **Ohn Gottes Gunst Alles umsonst**   *German* 'Without the grace of God all is in vain'
—Christian I, Prince of Anhalt-Bernburg (1568–1630).

349. **O Maria, ora pro nobis**   *Latin* 'O Mary, pray for us!'
—Ferdinand Maria, Elector of Bavaria (1636–79).

350. **Omnia debeo Deo**   *Latin* 'I owe all things to God'
—Grenehalgh.

351. **Omnia Deo juvante** *Latin* 'I can do all things with God's help'
—Crawfurd.

352. **Omnia Deo pendent** *Latin* 'Everything depends on God'
—Stockton.

353. **Omnia ex voluntate Dei** *Latin* 'Everything according to the will of God'
—Rudolf II, Emperor of Germany (1552–1612); Adolf Wilhelm, Duke of Saxony-Jena (1632–68).

354. **Omnia providentia Dei** *Latin* 'All things by the providence of God'
—Graham.

355. **Omnis a deo potestas** *Latin* 'All power is from God'
—Griffith (U.S.).

356. **Opitulante Deo** *Latin* 'By God's help'
—Brereton (Co. Norfolk).

357. **O. P. N. J. C. (Ora pro nobis Jesu Christe)** *Latin* 'Pray for us, Jesus Christ'
—Ernst, Duke of Bavaria (1554–1612).

358. **Ora et ara** *Latin* 'Pray and plough'
—South Kesteven R. D. C., U.K.

359. **Ora et labora** *Latin* 'Pray and labor'
—Dalhousie (E.), Holburton.

360. **Orando laborando** *Latin* 'By prayer and by labor'
—Rugby School, U.K.

361. **Orando te aspiciam** *Latin* 'In praying I will look to thee'
—Foster (Bt.).

362. **Orate et vigilate** *Latin* 'Pray and watch'
—Hewlett.

363. **Par Dieu est mon tout** *French* 'My all is from God'
—Margetson.

364. **Par la volonté de Dieu** *French* 'By the will of God'
—Gunman, Wyvill (Bt.).

365. **Pax multa diligentibus legem tuam, Domine** *Latin* 'Great peace have they which love Thy law, O Lord'
—[after Ps., cxix. 165.] Johann Georg, Elector of Brandenburg (1525–98); August, Elector of Saxony (1526–86); Albrecht, Margrave of Brandenburg (1490–1568).

366. **Per ardua Deo favente**　*Latin* 'Through difficulties, God helping'
　　　　　　　　　　　　　　　　　　　　—Butterworth.

367. **Per Dei providentiam**　*Latin* 'Through the providence of God'
　　　　　　　　　　　　　　　　　　　　—Dennett.

368. **Per Deum et ferrum obtinui**　*Latin* 'By God and my sword have I prevailed'
　　　　　　　　　　　　　　　　　　　　—Hill.

369. **Per Deum meum transilio murum**　*Latin* 'Through my God I leap over a wall'
　　　　　　　　　　　　　　　　　　　　—Pemberton.

370. **Plena dabit Deus vela**　*Latin* 'God will fill our sails'
　　　　　　　　　　　　　　　　　　　　—Bontine, Tennant.

371. **Prece et labore**　*Latin* 'By prayer and toil'
　　　—Christian Ernst, Margrave of Brandenburg-Baireuth
　　　　　　　　　　　　　　　　　　　　(1644–1712).

372. **Propitio Deo securus ago**　*Latin* 'With the grace of God I live secure'
　　　—Franz II, Duke of Saxony-Lauenburg (1547–1619).

373. **Providentiâ Dei**　*Latin* 'The providence of God'
　　　　　　　　　　　　　　　　　　　　—Nicholson.

374. **Providentia Dei conservet**　*Latin* 'May the providence of God preserve'
　　　　　　　　　　　　　　　　　　　　—De la Motte.

375. **Providentiâ Dei stabiliuntur familiae**　*Latin* 'Families are established by the providence of God'
　　　　　　　　　　　　　　　　　　　　—Lamplugh.

376. **Providentiâ divinâ**　*Latin* 'By divine providence'
　　　　　—Keating, Keching, Sangster, or Songster.

377. **Quem te Deus esse jussit**　*Latin* 'What God commands thee to be'
　　　　　　　　　　　　　　　　　　　　—Sheffield (E.).

378. **Quidni tandem?**　*Latin* 'What, pray, tell me?'
　　　　　　　　　　　　　　　　　　　　—Hatton.

379. **Quid non Deo juvante**　*Latin* 'What (can we) not (do) with God's aid'
　　　　—Chalmers (of Gaitgarth), Salt (Co. York).

380. **Quod Deus vult fiat**　*Latin* 'God's will be done'
　　　　　　　　　　　　　　　　　　　　—Chetwynd (Bt.).

381. **Quod Deus vult hoc semper fit** *Latin* 'What God wills always happens'
—Bernhard, Duke of Saxony-Weimar (1604–39).

382. **Quod Deus vult volo** *Latin* 'What God wishes I wish'
—Mountford.

383. **Recte omnia duce Deo** *Latin* 'God being my guide all things will be rightly done'
—Rodd.

384. **Recte omnia duce Deo** *Latin* 'With God for guide all is right'
—Rodd.

385. **R. M. H. D. D. H. G. (Regiere mich Herr durch dienen heiligen Geist)** *German* 'Rule me, Lord, through Thy holy spirit'
—Ann, Margravine of Brandenburg (1575–1612).

386. **Robur in Deo** *Latin* 'Strength in God'
—Raeburn.

387. **Robur meum Deus** *Latin* 'God is my strength'
—Rhodes.

388. **Rupes mea Dominus** *Latin* 'The Lord is my rock'
—[2 Sam., xxii. 2.] Rudolf Maximilian, Duke of Saxony (1595–1647).

389. **Salvet me Deus** *Latin* 'May God help me!'
—Spiers.

390. **Sans Dieu le ne puis** *French* 'Without God I cannot do it'
—Skipworth, Skipwith (Bt.).

391. **Sapit qui Deo sapit** *Latin* 'He is wise who is wise through God'
—Wiseman.

392. **Save me, Lord!**
—Corbet (of Towcross).

393. **Scuto amoris Divini** *Latin* 'By the shield of God's love'
—Scudamore (of Ditchingham, co. Norfolk).

394. **Scuto bonae voluntatis tuae coronasti nos** *Latin* 'With the shield of Thy good-will Thou hast covered us'
—State of Maryland.

395. **Scuto divino** *Latin* 'With the divine shield'
—Day (Bt.).

396. **Scutum impenetrabile Deus** *Latin* 'An impenetrable shield is God'
—Dongan (U.S.).

397. **Scutum meum Jehova** *Latin* 'Jehovah is my shield'
—Corry.

398. **Secundum voluntatem Dei** *Latin* 'According to the will of God'
—Ludwig Friedrich, Duke of Württemberg (1586–1631).

399. **Sedulo numen** *Latin* 'God is with the diligent'
—Harrower, Harrowing.

400. **Seigneur, je te prie garde ma vie** *French* 'Lord, I beseech thee save my life'
—Brettell, Henzey, Pidcock, Tyzack.

401. **Semni ne semni** *(language unknown; supposed somehow to mean* 'I can do nothing without God')
—Dering (Bt.).

402. **Servabit me semper Jehovah** *Latin* 'The Lord will always preserve me'
—Barclay.

403. **Si Deus nobiscum** *Latin* 'If God be with us'
—Hughes, Parry.

404. **Si Deus nobiscum quis contra nos?** *Latin* 'If God be with us, who can be against us?'
—Mairis, Mountmorres, Otway.

405. **Si Deus pro nobis quis contra nos?** *Latin* 'If God be for us, who shall be against us?'
—Georg the Pious, Margrave of Brandenburg-Anspach (1484–1543); Johann Friedrich, Elector of Saxony (1503–54); Philipp I, Landgrave of Hesse (1504–67); Albrecht Alcibiades, Margrave of Brandenburg-Baireuth (1522–51); Georg Friedrich, Margrave of Brandenburg-Anspach (1539–1603); Johann Georg, Margrave of Brandenburg (1577–1624); Georg Rudolf, Duke of Liegnitz (1595–1653); Wilhelm, Duke of Saxony-Weimar (1598–1662); Christian Ludwig, Duke of Mecklenburg-Schwerin (1632–92); Heinrich, Duke of Saxony-Römhild (1650–1710); Caldicote.

406. **Si Deus quis contra?** *Latin* 'If God (be with us) who can be against us?'
—Benson (of Parkside), Spence, Spens (of Lathallan).

407. **Si Dieu est pour nous, qui sera contre nous?** *French* 'If God be for us, who shall be against us?'
—Charlotte Dorothee Sophie, Duchess of Saxony-Weimar (1669–1708).

408. **Si Dieu ne veut, Fortune ne peut** *French* 'If God will not, fortune cannot'
—Albrecht, Margrave of Brandenburg-Anspach (1620–67).

409. **Si Dieu veult** *French* 'If God wills it'
—Preston (of Lancashire).

410. **Sine Deo frustra** *Latin* 'Without God, in vain'
—Gill, Gull.

411. **Sit Deus in studiis** *Latin* 'May God be with me in my studies'
—Sydenham.

412. **Sit vult Deus** *Latin* 'Be it, God wills it'
—Kempsey.

413. **S. M. D. (Susceptor Meus Dominus)** *Latin* 'God is my protector'
—Jacob, Margrave of Baden-Hochberg (1562–90); Georg Friedrich, Margrave of Baden-Hochberg (1573–1638).

414. **Sola meus turris Deus** *Latin* 'God is my only fortress'
—Baker.

415. **Sol et pastor Deus** *Latin* 'God, our sun and shepherd'
—Sunbury-on-Thames U. D. C., U.K.

416. **Sol et scutum Deus** *Latin* 'God is our sun and shield'
—Pearson.

417. **Stant innixa Deo** *Latin* 'They stand supported by God'
—Craufurd.

418. **St. Callawy ora pro me** *Latin* 'St. Callawy pray for me'
—Callaway (U.S.).

419. **Sub tutela Domini** *Latin* 'Under the protection of God'
—Spode.

420. **Sustentante Deo** *Latin* 'With the help of God'
—Karl, Elector of the Palatinate (1651–85).

421. **T. A. N. D. E. M. (Tibi aderit numen divinum, expecta modo)** *Latin* 'God will help thee—only wait'
—Elisabeth Ernestine Antonie, Duchess of Saxony (1681–1766).

422. **Tarde non fur mai grazie diuine** *Italian* 'Divine grace never comes too late'
—Ludwig the Elder, Prince of Anhalt-Köthen (1579–1650).

423. **The Lord is my only support**
—Over a stairway in a house in Edinburgh, Scotland.

424. **The Lord will provide**
—Botfield.

425. **Through God revived**
> —Hamilton (of Binning).

426. **Tout à la volonté de Dieu**   *French* 'Everything according to the will of God'
> —Christiane Wilhelmine, Duchess of Saxony-Weissenfels (D. 1707).

427. **Tout en la conduicte de Dieu**   *French* 'Everything in God's guidance'
> —Friedrich Ulrich, Duke of Braunschweig-Wolfenbüttel (1591–1634).

428. **Tu Deus ale flammam**   *Latin* 'Thou, God, nourish the flame'
> —Flavel.

429. **Turris fortis mihi Deus**   *Latin* 'God is a strong tower to me'
> —Clugstone, Kelly, MacQuarie, McGuarie, O'Kelly, Peter.

430. **Turris fortissima Deus**   *Latin* 'God is the strongest tower'
> —Torre.

431. **Turris fortissima nomen Domini**   *Latin* 'A very strong tower the name of the Lord'
> —[Prov., xviii. 10.] Bernhard, Duke of Saxony-Meiningen (1649–1706); Johann Georg I, Elector of Saxony (1585–1656).

432. **Turris mihi Deus**   *Latin* 'God is my tower'
> —Towers, Kelly.

433. **Tutamen Deus**   *Latin* 'God is my defense'
> —Bent, Hooper.

434. **Ubi desint vires hominum ibi incipit divinum auxilium**   *Latin* 'Where human strength ceases divine aid begins'
> —Sibylle Elisabeth, Duchess of Braunschweig (1576–1603).

435. **Ut conchas auge nostra metalla Deus**   *Latin* 'O God, multiply our metals like shells'
> —Friedrich Ulrich, Duke of Braunschweig-Wolfenbüttel (1591–1634), motto on a coin of 1633.

436. **Ut fert divina voluntas**   *Latin* 'As the Divine Will directs'
> —Albrecht, Duke of Saxony-Eisenach (1599–1644); Emanuel Leberecht, Prince of Anhalt-Plötzkau (1671–1704).

437. **Velle vult quod Deus**   *Latin* 'To wish what God wishes'
> —Bankes.

438. **Vi divina**   *Latin* 'By Divine power'
> —Pearse.

439. **Vill God I sall** *Middle English*
—Menzies (Bt.).

440. **Vi martiali Deo adjuvante** *Latin* 'By force of war, God helping'
—Marshall.

441. **Virebo proficiente Deo** *Latin* 'Through God's grace shall I flourish'
—Friedrich Wilhelm, Elector of Brandenburg (1620–88).

442. **Volonté de Dieu** *French* 'The will of God'
—Tyler.

443. **Vota vita mea** *Latin* 'Prayers are my life'
—Brabazon (Bt.), Meath (E.).

444. **Was Gott bewahrt ist wohl verwahrt** *German* 'What God guards is well preserved'
—Ludwig the Elder, Prince of Anhalt-Köthen (1579–1650).

445. **Was Gott will Ist mein Ziel** *German* 'What God wills is my goal'
—Christian Wilhelm, Margrave of Brandenburg (1587–1665).

446. **Wer auf Gott vertraut, der hat auf einen Fels gebaut** *German* 'Whoso upon God relies, hath built upon a rock'
—Over a door in a house in Clontra Shankill, Ireland.

447. **Wie es Gott feugt myhr genueget** *German* 'As God disposes is sufficient for me'
—Eleonore Sophie, Princess of Anhalt (1603–75).

448. **Wie Gott will** *German* 'As God wills'
—Dorothee, Duchess of Saxony (1601–75).

449. **Will God, I shall**
—Menzies.

450. **Will God and I shall**
—Ashburnham (of Sussex and Suffolk).

451. **Will God I shall**
—Torrey (U.S.).

452. **With God, all things are possible**
—State of Ohio.

453. **Without help from above the arrow flies in vain**
—Jones.

454. **Z. G. M. T. (Zu Gott mein Trost)** *German* 'In God my comfort'
—Ernst, Duke of Braunschweig-Lüneburg (1564–1611).

DIVINITY (*See also* BLESSING; CHRIST, JESUS; CROSS, THE; DIVINE GIFTS; DIVINE GUIDANCE; GRACE; PROVIDENCE; RELIGION.)

1. **Absque Deo nihil** *Latin* 'Nothing without God'
—Peters (of Newcastle).

2. **A deo et Rege** *Latin* 'From God and the King'
—Richmond B. C., U.K.

3. **Ad majorem Dei gloriam** *Latin* 'To the greater glory of God'
—Society of Jesus.

4. **Ad te, Domine** *Latin* 'To thee, O Lord'
—Newman.

5. **Allein in Gott mein Vertrauen** *German* 'My trust is in God alone'
—Sigismund, Margrave of Brandenburg (1592–1640).

6. **Alles in Gottes Gewalt** *German* 'Everything is in the power of God'
—Magnus, Duke of Braunschweig-Lüneburg (1577–1632).

7. **Alles mit Gott, nichts ohn Ursach** *German* 'Everything with God: nothing without reason'
—Elisabeth, Duchess of Saxony (1593–1650).

8. **Alles mit Gott, und der Zeit** *German* 'Everything is with God and with time'
—Erdmuthe Sophie, Margravine of Brandenburg (1644–70).

9. **Alles von Gott** *German* 'Everything from God'
—Friedrich, Duke of Braunschweig-Lüneburg (1574–1648).

10. **Alles zur Ehre Gottes** *German* 'Everything for the honor of God'
—Joachim, Prince of Anhalt (1509–61).

11. **All is in God**
—Clovyle, Colvile, Colvell (Co. Essex).

12. **All my hope is in God**
—Frazer, Undey, Udney.

13. **All things for the glory of God**
—Chingford B. C., U.K.

14. **All this beauty is of God**
—Isle of Wight C. C., U.K.

15. **A. M. G. (Alles mit Gott)** *German* 'Everything with God'
—Georg Albrecht, Margrave of Brandenburg-Baireuth (1619–66).

16. **Anchora spei Cereticae est in te, Domine**   *Latin* 'The anchor of
    Cardigan's hope is in Thee, O Lord'
    —Cardigan B. C., U.K.

17. **Arx fortissima nomen Domini**   *Latin* 'The name of the Lord is a
    very strong citadel'
    —[after Prov., xviii. 10.] Johann Georg, Duke of
    Schleswig-Holstein (1594–1613).

18. **Aspiciunt oculis superi mortalia justis**   *Latin* 'The gods look down
    on mortal deeds with just eyes'
    —Eberhard Ludwig, Duke of Württemberg (1676–1733).

19. **Auf deinen Wegen leit Herr Gott mich allezeit**   *German* 'In Thy
    ways, O God, lead me at all times'
    —Ludwig the Elder, Prince of Anhalt-Köthen (1579–1650).

20. **Auf Gott meine Hoffnung**   *German* 'On God my hope'
    —Magdalene Sibylle, Electress of Saxony (1612–87).

21. **Aut mors aut vita Deus**   *Latin* 'God is either death or life'
    —Gordon (of Edinglassie).

22. **Aut mors aut vita Deus**   *Latin* 'God is either death or life'
    —Gordon (of Edinglassie).

23. **Befiehl dem Herrn deine Wege**   *German* 'Commit thy way unto
    the Lord'
    —[Ps., xxxvii. 5.] Heinrich, Duke of Braunschweig and
    Danneberg (1533–98).

24. **Benedictus es, O Domine: doce me Statuta Tua**   *Latin* 'Blessed
    art thou, O Lord: teach me Thy statutes'
    —Bradfield College, U.K.

25. **Calton wrth calton Duw a digon**   *Welsh* 'Heart to heart God over
    all'
    —Robert (U.S.).

26. **Cari Deo nihilo carent**   *Latin* 'Those dear to God want nothing'
    —Weekes.

27. **Clamamus, Abba, Pater**   *Latin* 'Whereby we cry, Abba, Father'
    —[Rom., viii. 15.] Abbott.

28. **Cole credeque Deum**   *Latin* 'Worship and believe God'
    —Hodilow.

29. **Cole Deum**   *Latin* 'Worship God'
    —Coull.

30. **Colens Deum et regem**   *Latin* 'Honouring God and the King'
    —Collins.

31. **Comme à Dieu playra**   *Old French* 'As shall please God'
—Thorp.

32. **Compositum jus fasque animi**   *Latin* 'A mind which respects alike the laws of mutual justice and of God'
—Ellenborough (E.), Law, Laws, Nightingale.

33. **Crains Dieu tant que tu viveras**   *French* 'Fear God as long as thou shalt live'
—Athlumney (B.).

34. **Crede Deo**   *Latin* 'Trust in God'
—Atkinson.

35. **Cum Deo bene faciendo bene faciet**   *Latin* 'If we do well for God, he will do well for us'
—Wilhelm, Duke of Saxony-Weimar (1598–1662).

36. **Cum Deo et die**   *Latin* 'With God and time'
—Eduard, Count of the Palatinate of Rhein (1625–63); Friedrich III, Duke of Saxony-Gotha and Altenburg (1699–1772); Christian, Duke of Saxony-Merseburg (1615–91); Eberhard Ludwig, Duke of Württemberg (1676–1733).

37. **Cum Deo salus**   *Latin* 'With God salvation'
—Christian, Duke of Saxony-Weissenfels (1682–1736).

38. **Da gloriam Deo**   *Latin* 'Give glory unto God'
—Dyers' Company.

39. **Dei gratia grata**   *Latin* 'The grace of God is grateful'
—Dixie (Bt.).

40. **Dei memor, gratus amicis**   *Latin* 'Mindful of God, grateful to friends'
—Antrobus (Bt.).

41. **Dei omnia plena**   *Latin* 'All things are full of God'
—Hinds.

42. **Delectare in Domino**   *Latin* 'To rejoice in the Lord'
—[Ps., xxxvi. 4.] Bampfylde, Poltimore (B.).

43. **Deo, non sagittis fido**   *Latin* 'I trust in God, not in arrows'
—Cuyler (Bt.).

44. **Deo, patriae, amicis**   *Latin* 'To God, my country and my friends'
—Cooper.

45. **Deo, patriae, proximo**   *Latin* 'For God, my Country, my neighbor'
—Christian, Duke of Saxony-Eisenberg (1653–1707).

46. **Deo, patriae, regi** *Latin* 'For God, my country and my king'
—Cooper.

47. **Deo, patriae, tibi** *Latin* 'For God, my native land and thee'
—Laimboro.

48. **Deo, regi, et patriae** *Latin* 'To God, my king, and my country'
—Irvine.

49. **Deo, regi, patriae** *Latin* 'To God, my king, my country'
—Duncombe (of Cassgrove), Feversham (B.), Irvine (of Kinconssie).

50. **Deo, regi, vicino** *Latin* 'To God, my king, my neighbor'
—Bromsgrove Grammar School, Cookes, Worcester Coll. Oxon.

51. **Deo, regi fidelis** *Latin* 'Faithful to God and the king'
—Atkinson, O'Daly.

52. **Deo, reipublicae, et amicis** *Latin* 'To God, our country, and our friends'
—Levant Company.

53. **Deo ac veritati** *Latin* 'For God and truth'
—Colgate University, Hamilton, New York.

54. **Deo cari nihilo carent** *Latin* 'Those dear to God want nothing'
—Weekes.

55. **Deo confide** *Latin* 'Trust in God'
—Fison (Bt.).

56. **Deo confidimus** *Latin* 'We trust in God'
—West Ham C. B. C., U.K.

57. **Deo confido** *Latin* 'I trust in God'
—Fison.

58. **Deo date** *Latin* 'Give unto God'
—Arundel (of Wardour, b.).

59. **Deo (Domino) optimo maximo (D. O. M.)** *Latin* 'To God the best and greatest'
—Monastic Order of St. Benedict.

60. **Deo et amicitiae** *Latin* 'For God and friendship'
—Forman (U.S.).

61. **Deo et patriae** *Latin* 'For God and country'
—Friedrich Ulrich, Duke of Braunschweig-Wolfenbüttel
(1591–1634); Johann Georg I, Elector of Saxony
(1613–80); Friedrich Heinrich, Count of the
Palatinate (1614–29); Adolf Wilhelm, Duke of
Saxony-Eisenach (1632–68); Outhwaite.

62. **Deo et patriae fidelis** *Latin* 'Faithful to God and country'
—Atkinson.

63. **Deo et principe** *Latin* 'With God and the prince'
—Lamb (Bt.).

64. **Deo et principi** *Latin* 'For God and the prince'
—Montolien.

65. **Deo et regi** *Latin* 'For God and the king'
—Stanhope.

66. **Deo et regi asto** *Latin* 'I stand by God and the king'
—Deacon.

67. **Deo et regi fidelis** *Latin* 'Faithful to God and the king'
—Daly.

68. **Deo et virtuti** *Latin* 'For God and virtue'
—Lackerstein.

69. **Deo fidelis et regi** *Latin* 'Faithful to God and king'
—Dunsandle (B.).

70. **Deo fidens** *Latin* 'Trusting in God'
—Gordon.

71. **Deo fidens persistas** *Latin* 'Trusting in God, persevere'
—Kinahan.

72. **Deo fidens proficio** *Latin* 'Trusting to God I go forward'
—Chadwick.

73. **Deo fisus labora** *Latin* 'Work while trusting in God'
—William Jewell College, Liberty, Missouri.

74. **Deo fretus erumpe** *Latin* 'Trust God and sally'
—Newark-on-Trent B. C., U.K.

75. **Deo gloria** *Latin* 'Glory to God'
—Gennys.

76. **Deo gratias** *Latin* 'Thanks to God'
—Senhouse.

77. **Deo honor et gloria** *Latin* 'Unto God be honor and glory'
—Leather Sellers' Company.

78. **Deo lux nostra** *Latin* 'God is our light'
—Holloway (U.S.).

79. **Deo non arce spes** *Latin* 'My hope is in God, not in my fortress'
—Castell.

80. **Deo non armis fido** *Latin* 'I trust in God, not in arms'
—Boycott, Morse, Morse-Boycott.

81. **Deo omnia** *Latin* 'All things to God'
—Harter.

82. **Deo omnia plena** *Latin* 'All things are full of God'
—Gourgas (U.S.).

83. **Deo pagit** *Latin* 'He covenants with God'
—Pagit (of Hadley).

84. **Deo patriae, scientiis, artibus** *Latin* 'For God and country through sciences and arts'
—Gonzaga University School of Law, Spokane, Washington.

85. **Deo patriaeque fidelis** *Latin* 'Faithful to God and my country'
—Fagan.

86. **Deo Reipublicae et amicis esto semper fidelis** *Latin* 'Be ever faithful to God, the state, and friends'
—Duffield (U.S.).

87. **Deo semper confido** *Latin* 'In God I trust ever'
—James (of Otterburn).

88. **Deo spes mea** *Latin* 'My hope is in God'
—Thornton.

89. **Deo spes meo** *Latin* 'My hope is my God'
—Thornton (U.S.).

90. **Deo tum patria** *Latin* 'For God, then the homeland'
—Morton (U.S.).

91. **De praescientiâ Dei** *Latin* 'From the foreknowledge of God'
—Barbers' Company (London), Barbers-Surgeons' Company, Exeter.

92. **Der Menschen Spot ist ein Greuel vor Got** *German* 'Man's mockery is an abomination before God'
—Friedrich Ulrich, Duke of Braunschweig-Wolfenbüttel (1591–1634).

93. **Der Welt entfliehen ist zu Gott Ziehen** *German* 'To flee the world is to draw nigh to God'
—Ernst, Prince of Anhalt (1608–32).

94. **Detur gloria Deo**   *Latin* 'Glory be to God'
—Robertson.

95. **Detur gloria soli Deo**   *Latin* 'To God alone be the glory given'
—Dulwich College, U.K.

96. **Deum cole, regem serva**   *Latin* 'Worship God, revere the king'
—Cole (Earl of Enniskillen), Cole (of Twickenham),
Townshend (co. Cork), Coleridge, Jones.

97. **Deum et regem**   *Latin* 'God and king'
—Collins.

98. **Deum qui habet omnia habet**   *Latin* 'Who has God has all'
—August, Duke of Saxony-Weissenfels (1614–80).

99. **Deum time**   *Latin* 'Fear God'
—Murray (of Blackbarony, bt.), Murray (of Clairemont,
bt.).

100. **Deum time, Caesarem honora**   *Latin* 'Fear God, honor the king'
—[1 Peter, ii. 17.] Christian II, Elector of Saxony
(1583–1611).

101. **Deum time, regem honora**   *Latin* 'Fear God, honor the king'
—[1 Peter, ii. 17.] Otto Heinrich, Count of the Palatinate
of Sulzbach (1556–1604); Armstrong (B.).

102. **Deum verere**   *Latin* 'Reverence God'
—August, Count von der Lippe (d. 1701).

103. **Deus, patria, rex**   *Latin* 'God, native land, and king'
—Phillipps, Phillips, Tarlton.

104. **Deus amici et nos**   *Latin* 'God, friends, and ourselves'
—Pell (U.S.).

105. **Deus amicus**   *Latin* 'God is (my) friend'
—Pell (U.S.).

106. **Deus est pax**   *Latin* 'God is my peace'
—Godfray.

107. **Deus est spes**   *Latin* 'God is our hope'
—Ridsdale.

108. **Deus et libertas**   *Latin* 'God and liberty'
—Godfrey (Bt.).

109. **Deus intersit**   *Latin* 'Let God be in our midst'
—Stephens.

110. **Deus lumen meum**   *Latin* 'God is my light'
—Torrens.

111. **Deus major columnâ**   *Latin* 'God is stronger than a column'
     —Henniker (B.).

112. **Deus mihi principium et finis**   *Latin* 'God my beginning and my end'
     —Heinrich, Duke of Saxony (d. 1585).

113. **Deus mihi sol**   *Latin* 'God is my sun'
     —Nicholson (of Ballow).

114. **Deus non ego**   *Latin* 'God, not I'
     —Newton (U.S.).

115. **Deus non reliquit memoriam humilium**   *Latin* 'God hath not forgotten the humble'
     —Meynell (of North Kilvington).

116. **Deus per omnia**   *Latin* 'God pervades all things'
     —Islington B. C., U.K.

117. **Deus spes mea**   *Latin* 'God is my hope'
     —Herbertstone.

118. **Deus spes nostra**   *Latin* 'God our hope'
     —Friedrich Karl, Duke of Württemberg (1652–98).

119. **Deus vivat**   *Latin* 'God lives'
     —Black (U.S.).

120. **Dias mo dhuthaich**   *Scots Gaelic* 'For God and my country'
     —Mackenzie (Bt.).

121. **Dias mo dhuthaich**   *Scots Gaelic* 'For God and my country'
     —MacKenzie.

122. **Die den Herrn suchen, haben keinen mangell an irgend einem gutt**   *German* 'Those who seek the Lord have no need for any other good'
     —Ludwig the Younger, Prince of Anhalt (1607–27).

123. **Dieu, un roi, une foi**   *French* 'God, one king, one faith'
     —Rush.

124. **Dieu a la mer**   *French* 'God owns the sea'
     —Dennis.

125. **Dieu est mon espoir**   *French* 'God is my hope'
     —Cusack.

126. **Dieu est tout**   *French* 'God is everything'
     —Allington.

127. **Dieu et la réligion**   *French* 'God and religion'
     —Bondier.

128. **Dieu et ma fiancée** *French* 'God and my affianced'
—Latimer.

129. **Dieu et ma foi** *French* 'God and my faith'
—Favil.

130. **Dieu et ma patrie** *French* 'God and my country'
—Marton.

131. **Dieu et mon devoir** *French* 'God and my duty'
—Bradshaw, Willet.

132. **Dieu et mon droit** *French* 'God and my right'
—Sovereigns of Great Britain (since Henry VI); United Kingdom of Great Britain and Northern Ireland; Georg Wilhelm, Elector of Brandenburg (1595–1640); Sherborne School, U.K. (founded 1550).

133. **Dieu et mon espée [*sic*]** *French* 'God and my sword'
—Norton (of Elmham, Co. Norfolk), Rickinghall (Co. Suffolk).

134. **Dieu et mon pays** *French* 'God and my country'
—McKirdy.

135. **Dieu sait tout** *French* 'God knows everything'
—Lewin.

136. **Dios, patria, libertad** *Spanish* 'God, fatherland and liberty'
—Dominican Republic.

137. **Dios union y libertad** *Spanish* 'God, union and liberty'
—Republic of El Salvador.

138. **Domine, speravi** *Latin* 'O Lord, I have hoped'
—Lloyd.

139. **Domine in virtute tua** *Latin* 'Lord, in Thy strength'
—Cochrane.

140. **Domini factum** *Latin* 'The work of the Lord'
—Sibthorpe.

141. **Domino quid reddam?** *Latin* 'What shall I render unto the Lord?'
—[Ps., cxvi. 12.] Blofield.

142. **Dominus exultatio mea** *Latin* 'The Lord is my delight'
—Stubs.

143. **Dominus illuminatio mea** *Latin* 'The Lord, my illumination'
—Oxford University, Oxford, U.K.

144. **Dread God**
—Carnegie (Bt.), Carnegie (of Kinnard), Gordon (of Earlston, Bt.), Gordon (of Aston and Craighlaw), Hay, Hodgson, Monro (Bt.), Macdougal.

145. **Ducat amor Dei** *Latin* 'Let the love of God lead us'
—Battye.

146. **Duw a Digon** *Welsh* 'God is enough'
—Vaughan, Prytherch, Nicholl (of Dimlands); Denbighshire C. C., U.K.

147. **Duw a fydd** *Welsh* 'God will be'
—Jones (Co. of Carmarthen).

148. **Duw ar fy rhan** *Welsh* 'God for my portion'
—Pryce.

149. **Duw dy Ras** *Welsh* 'God thy grace'
—Kemeys-Tynte (of Haleswell).

150. **En Dieu affie** *French* 'Trust in God'
—Mallet.

151. **En Dieu est ma fiance** *French* 'In God is my trust'
—Luttrell.

152. **En Dieu est mon esperance** *French* 'In God is my hope'
—Gerard (Bt.), Gerard (of Prescot), Walmsley, Ashton-in-Makerfield U. D. C., U.K.

153. **En Dieu est mon espoir** *French* 'In God is my hope'
—Smith (Bt.), Trevanion (of Caerhays).

154. **En Dieu est tout** *French* 'In God is everything'
—Davies, Chambre, Conolly (of Castletown), Wentworth (co. York), Watson, Watson-Wentworth (of Rockingham, M.); Wentworth Military Academy, Lexington, Missouri.

155. **En Dieu et mon roy** *Old French* 'In God and my king'
—Churchyard.

156. **En Dieu gist ma confiance** *French* 'In God lies my trust'
—Johann Georg, Margrave of Brandenburg (1577–1624).

157. **En Dieu mon esperance** *French* 'In God my hope'
—Dorothee, Margravine of Brandenburg (1596–1649); Sophie Eleonore, Landgravine of Hesse (1609–71); Anna Marie, Duchess of Saxony-Weissenfels (1627–69); Eleonore Erdmuthe Luise, Margravine of Brandenburg (1662–96); Anna, Countess of Oldenburg (b. 1605).

158. **En Dieu mon esperance et l'espee** [*sic*] **pour ma defense**
    French 'In God is my hope and the sword of my defence'
    —Johann Ernst, Duke of Saxony-Saalfield (1658–1729).

159. **En Dieu se fie** *French* 'Trust in God'
    —Verdon.

160. **En Dieu seul gist ma confiance** *French* 'In God alone rests my trust'
    —Sophie Ursula, Countess of Oldenburg (1601–41).

161. **En Dieu sont nos espèrances** *French* 'In God are all our hopes'
    —Whalley.

162. **En vain espère, qui ne craint Dieu** *French* 'He hopes in vain, who fears not God'
    —Janssen.

163. **Esperance en Dieu** *French* 'Hope in God'
    —Bullock, Beverly (E.), Greathead, Northumberland (D.),
    Prudhoe (B.), Percy.

164. **Espère en Dieu** *French* 'Hope in God'
    —Edgelow.

165. **Es stehet Alles in Gottes Händen** *German* 'Everything is in God's hands'
    —Heinrich Julius, Duke of Braunschweig-Wolfenbüttel (1564–1613).

166. **Est Deo gratia** *Latin* 'Thanks are to God'
    —Searle.

167. **Exaltum cornu in Deo** *Latin* 'The horn is exalted in God'
    —Truro C. C., U.K.

168. **Fear God**
    —Crombie, Cheyne, Brisbane (Bt.), Gordon, Huddart,
    McAndrew, McDowell, McDougal, Munro.

169. **Fear God, fear nought**
    —Locker.

170. **Fear God, honor the king**
    —Wrexham B. C., U.K.; Bromley-Davenport, Davenport,
    Porter.

171. **Fear God and dread nought**
    —Wingrove.

172. **Fear God and fight**
    —McClambroch, McLandsborough.

173. **Fear God and live**
—Sinclair.

174. **Fear God and spare nought**
—Grassick.

175. **Fear God in life**
—Somerville (B.), Somerville (of Drum).

176. **Fear God in love**
—Somerville.

177. **Fear God only**
—Spence.

178. **Fide, sed cui vide** *Latin* 'Trust, but in whom take care'
—Astley (Bt.), Astell, Beaumont (of Whitley), Coyney (of Weston Coyney), Birkbeck, Astley (of Everleigh), Bankes (of Winstanley), Greensugh, Holme, Prickett, Reynolds, Stapleton.

179. **Fido Deo et ipse** *Latin* 'I myself, too, trust in God'
—Gibbons.

180. **Fidus Deo et Regi** *Latin* 'Faithful to God and the King'
—De Bary.

181. **For God, Queen, and country**
—Harleyford, Buckinghamshire, England.

182. **For God and my country**
—Uganda.

183. **Forward with God**
—Douglass.

184. **Fy Nuw a Chymru** *Welsh* 'My God and Wales'
—Philipps, Walters.

185. **G. I. M. T: (Gott ist mein Teil)** *German* 'God is my portion'
—Friedrich IV, Duke of Liegnitz (1552–96).

186. **G. I. M. T. (Gott ist mein Trost)** *German* 'God is my comfort'
—Anna, Duchess of Wohlau (1561–1616); August, Duke of Braunschweig-Wolfenbüttel (1579–1666); Karl III, Duke of Münsterberg and Oels (D. 1617); August, Duke of Saxony-Lauenburg (1577–1656).

187. **Gloria Deo!** *Latin* 'Glory to God'
—Challen (of Shermanbury), Henn.

188. **Gloria Deo in excelsis** *Latin* 'Glory to God in the highest'
—[Luke, ii. 14.] Leake.

189. **Gloria Deo in profundis** *Latin* 'Glory to God in the heavens'
—Whalley.

190. **Gloria in excelsis Deo** *Latin* 'Glory to God on high'
—Killock.

191. **Gloria Patri** *Latin* 'Glory to the Father'
—Dewar.

192. **Gloria sat Deus unus** *Latin* 'God alone is sufficient glory'
—Weston.

193. **Gloria soli Deo** *Latin* 'Glory to God alone'
—Penruddocke (of Compton Park).

194. **G. M. G. (Gott mein Gut)** *German* 'God is my good'
—Karl, Margrave of Baden-Durlach (1529–77); Ernst
Friedrich, (1560–1604).

195. **God, Our Father—Christ, Our Redeemer—Man, Our Brother**
—Morris Brown College, Atlanta, Georgia.

196. **God and my conscience**
—Roberts.

197. **God can raise to Abraham children of stones**
—Paviours' Company.

198. **God in his least creatures**
—Silk Trowersters' Company.

199. **God is all**
—Fraser (of Fraserfield).

200. **God is love**
—[1 John, iv. 8.] Wesley.

201. **God my trust**
—Mason (of Necton Hall, co. Norfolk).

202. **Godt ist mein Trost** *German* 'God is my comfort'
—Margarethe, Countess of Mansfeld (b. 1534).

203. **God with us**
—Dursley R. D. C., U.K.

204. **Got regiert alles** *German* 'God governs everything'
—Anna, Princess of Anhalt (d. 1624).

205. **Gott, Vaterland, Gewissen** *German* 'God, fatherland, conscience'
—Albrecht, Duke of Saxony-Eisenach (1599–1644).

206. **Gott allein die Ehre** *German* 'To God alone the honor'
—Johann Georg IV, Elector of Saxony (1668–94).

207. **Gott mein Trost**   *German* 'God my comfort'
   —Anna Marie, Duchess of Saxony (1589–1626).

208. **Gott vermag alle Dinge**   *German* 'God can do all things'
   —[after Matt., xix. 26.] Emilie, Margravine of
   Brandenburg (1516–91).

209. **Gott vertraut, wohl gebaut**   *German* 'Entrusted to God is well
   built'
   —Philibert, Margrave of Baden (1536–69).

210. **Gott weiz die Zeit**   *German* 'God knows the time'
   —Georg, Count of the Palatinate of Simmern (1518–69).

211. **Gratias Deo agere**   *Latin* 'Give thanks to God'
   —Sidney.

212. **Gud og Kongen**   *Danish* 'God and the king'
   —Order of the Danebrog (Denmark).

213. **G. V. D. S. N. (Gott verläszt die Sienen nicht)**   *German* 'God
   forsakes not his own'
   —Dorothee, Duchess of Braunschweig-Wolfenbüttel
   (1607–34).

214. **G. W. A. Z. B. (Gott wende Alles zum Besten)**   *German* 'May
   God turn everything to the best'
   —Amöne Amalie, Princess of Anhalt (d. 1626).

215. **G. W. W. S. (Gott wirds wohl schaffen)**   *German* 'God will
   arrange'
   —Dorothee Auguste, Duchess of Braunschweig
   (1577–1625).

216. **Hab Gott vor Augen**   *German* 'Have God before thine eyes'
   —Christoph, Count of the Palatinate of Simmern
   (1551–74).

217. **Heb Dduw heb ddim**   *Welsh* 'Without God, nothing'
   —Price.

218. **Heb Dduw heb ddim, Duw a digon**   *Welsh* 'Without God, noth-
   ing; God is enough'
   —Davies, Edwards (Co. Wicklow), Hopkins, Hughes (of
   Kinmel), Jones (of Ystrad), Lloyd (of Dan-yr-alt),
   Meredith (Bt.), Meyrick, Morgan, Mostyn (B.),
   Williams.

219. **Hoc in loco Deus rupes**   *Latin* 'Here God is a rock'
   —Hockin.

220. **Honour God**
   —Carpenters' Company.

221. **Hope in God**
—Harkness.
222. **I. B. A. G. (Ich bau auf Gott)** *German* 'I build on God'
—Heinrich Posthumus, Count Reuss (1572–1635).
223. **Ich trawe Gott in aller noht** *German* 'I trust God in every need'
—Sibylle Christine, Princess of Anhalt (1603–86).
224. **I Dduw bo'r diolch** *Welsh* 'To God be thanks'
—Lloyd.
225. **I. D. F. N. (In Domino fiducia nostra)** *Latin* 'In the Lord is our trust'
—August, Prince of Anhalt-Plötzkau (1575–1653).
226. **I. D. F. V. (In Deo faciemus virtutem)** *Latin* 'Through God we shall do valiantly'
—[Ps., lx. 12.] August, Prince of Anhalt-Plötzkau (1575–1653).
227. **I hope in God**
—Macnaghten, McNaughten, Naughten.
228. **Il principio e il fine mio stà nelle mani di Dio** *Italian* 'My beginning and my end stand in God's hands'
—Anna, Countess of Schwarzburg (1584–1652).
229. **In Deo confidemus** *Latin* 'In God is our trust'
—Pryce.
230. **In Deo confido** *Latin* 'I trust in God'
—Kirkman, Tovy, Lawford, Moore.
231. **In Deo confido, nil desperandum** *Latin* 'Trust in God, nothing is to be despaired of'
—Kelly.
232. **In Deo confiteor** *Latin* 'My confession is in God'
—Lodder.
233. **In Deo est mihi omnis fides** *Latin* 'In God is my whole trust'
—Palmer (Bt.).
234. **In Deo et in ipso confido** *Latin* 'In God and in myself I trust'
—Richardson.
235. **In Deo et veritate fido** *Latin* 'I trust in God and in truth'
—Hooper (U.S.).
236. **In Deo fidemus** *Latin* 'We trust in God'
—Brighton C. B. C., U.K.
237. **In Deo fides** *Latin* 'My trust is in God'
—Chapple.

238. **In Deo fides, lux in tenebris** *Latin* 'Faith in God is light in darkness'
—Unkown.

239. **In Deo fido** *Latin* 'I trust in God'
—Medley.

240. **In Deo manuque fides** *Latin* 'In God and my hand is my trust'
—Mackesy.

241. **In Deo mea consolatio** *Latin* 'In God is my consolation'
—Wolfgang Wilhelm, Count of the Palatinate of Rhein zu Neuburg (1578–1653).

242. **In Deo mea spes** *Latin* 'My hope is in God'
—Hesketh (of Gwyrch Castle), Neate.

243. **In Deo non armis fido** *Latin* 'I trust in God, not in arms'
—Morse (U.S.).

244. **In Deo nostra spes est** *Latin* 'In God is our hope'
—Rocke.

245. **In Deo omnia** *Latin* 'In God are all things'
—Bluett, Huxley, Reed.

246. **In Deo solo confido** *Latin* 'I trust in God alone'
—Converse (U.S.).

247. **In Deo solo speravi** *Latin* 'In God alone have I trusted'
—Allen.

248. **In Deo solo spes mea** *Latin* 'My hope is in God alone'
—Kay, Key.

249. **In Deo speramus** *Latin* 'We trust in God'
—Brown University, Providence, Rhode Island.

250. **In Deo speravi** *Latin* 'In God have I trusted'
—Clark (Bt.).

251. **In Deo spero** *Latin* 'I place my hope in God'
—De Saumarez (B.).

252. **In Deo spes** *Latin* 'In God is hope'
—Mitchell.

253. **In Deo spes est** *Latin* 'In God is hope'
—Harvard.

254. **In Deo spes mea** *Latin* 'In God is my hope'
—Elizabeth of Austria, wife of Charles IX of France (1554–92); Sigismund, Margrave of Brandenburg (1592–1640); Wilhelm Ludwig, Duke of Württemberg (1647–77), Couran.

255. **In Domino confido**   *Latin* 'I trust in the Lord'
—[Ps., xi. 1.] Asheton, Cargill, Cockburn, Erskin, Erskine, Newdigate, McGill, Williams, Walker, Willyams, Ernst the Pious, Duke of Saxony-Gotha (1601–75); Friedrich Wilhelm, Duke of Saxony (1603–19).

256. **In Domino et non in arcu meo sperabo**   *Latin* 'I will rest my hope on the Lord, and not in my bow'
—Molony (Co. Clare).

257. **In Domino fiducia nostra**   *Latin* 'In the Lord is our trust'
—Karl Wilhelm, Prince of Anhalt-Zerbst (1652–1718).

258. **In God is all**
—Fraser, Frazer, Saltoun (B.).

259. **In God is all my hope**
—Plumbers' Company.

260. **In God is all my trust**
—Pewterers' Company, Grant.

261. **In God is all our trust**
—Brewers' Company, Bricklayers and Tilers' Company.

262. **In God I trust**
—Frazer, Thompson.

263. **In God we trust**
—State of Florida, Scott (U.S.), on coins of the United States.

264. **In Gott allein**   *German* 'In God alone'
—Schuster (Bt.).

265. **In Gott meine Hoffnung**   *German* 'In God my hope'
—Anna Marie, Duchess of Saxony-Weimar (1575–1643).

266. **Initium sapientiae est timor Domini**   *Latin* 'The fear of the Lord is the beginning of wisdom'
—[Ps. cxi. 10.] Martin (of Long Melford, Bt.).

267. **In Jehovah fides mea**   *Latin* 'In Jehovah is my trust'
—Brailsford.

268. **In te, Domine, confido**   *Latin* 'In thee, Lord, I confide'
—Knyfton, Wayne.

269. **In te, Domine, speravi**   *Latin* 'In Thee, O Lord, have I put my trust'
—Abbs, Greenhill, Haire, Lyon (of Auldabar), Prestwich, Rouse, Strathmore (E.), Vale.

270. **In te, Domine, spes nostra** *Latin* 'In thee, Lord, is our hope'
—Gill.

271. **In te Deus speravi** *Latin* 'In thee, O God, I have hoped'
—Browne.

272. **Intento in Deum animo** *Latin* 'With mind intent on God'
—Bosvile.

273. **In te spectant, domine, oculi omnium** *Latin* 'To thee, O Lord, the eyes of all are turned'
—Town of Nantes, France.

274. **In the Lord is all our trust**
—Masons' Company (London).

275. **I trust in God**
—Richardson, Wheatly.

276. **J'aime mon Dieu, mon roi, et ma patrie** *French* 'I love my God, my king, and my country'
—Kirvin.

277. **Je crains Dieu** *French* 'I fear God'
—Whitehurst.

278. **Jehovah**
—Whetham.

279. **Jehova portio mea** *Latin* 'The Lord is my portion'
—Mercer.

280. **Jehova vexillum meum** *Latin* 'Jehova is my banner'
—Johann Georg II, Elector of Saxony (1613–80); Johann Georg III, his son (1647–91).

281. **Je me fie en Dieu** *French* 'I trust in God'
—Blois (Bt.), Plymouth (E.), Windsor.

282. **J'espère en Dieu** *French* 'I hope in God'
—Ray (U.S.).

283. **Jovi confido** *Latin* 'I confide in Jove'
—Gairdner.

284. **Jovi praestat fidere quam homine** *Latin* 'It is preferable to trust in Jove rather than in a man'
—Stuyvesant (U.S.).

285. **Jovis omnia plena** *Latin* 'All things are full of Jove'
—[Vergil, *Ecl.* iii. 60.] Westby, Godden.

286. **Kar Duw, res pub. tia** *Cornish and Latin* 'Love God above the Commonwealth'(?)
—Harris.

287. **Kensol tra Tonkein ouna Diu mathern yn** *Welsh* 'Before all things, Tonkin, fear God in the king'
—Tonkin.

288. **La bonté de Dieu** *French* 'The goodness of God'
—D'Olier.

289. **Laudans invocabo Dominum** *Latin* 'I will call upon the Lord with praise'
—Palgrave.

290. **Laus Deo** *Latin* 'Praise be to God'
—Arbuthnott (V.).

291. **Lippen to God** *Scots dial.* 'Trust God'
—Watson.

292. **Lord, have mercy!**
—[Matt. xvii. 15.] Drummond, Strathallan (v.).

293. **Lux Dei ibi salus** *Latin* 'In the light of God there is safety'
—Dixwell.

294. **Lux mihi Deus** *Latin* 'God my light'
—Prescott (Bt.).

295. **Mea Deus gloria** *Latin* 'God is my glory'
—Bernhard, Duke of Saxony-Weimar (1604–39).

296. **Mea spes est in Deo** *Latin* 'My hope is in God'
—Smith, Miller.

297. **Mein End und Leben ist Gott ergeben** *German* 'My end and life are given to God'
—Ludwig the Elder, Prince of Anhalt-Köthen (1579–1650);
Ludwig the Younger (1607–27).

298. **Mein Thun und Leben ist Gott ergeben** *German* 'My deeds and life are given up to God'
—Georg Albrecht, Margrave of Brandenburg (1591–1615).

299. **Mi camokah baalim Yehowah** *Hebrew* 'Who is like unto thee of the gods, O Jehovah?'
—[Od. xv. 11.] Goldsmid.

300. **Mihi consulit Deus** *Latin* 'God careth for me'
—Bennett.

301. **Mihi gravato Deus** *Latin* 'Let God lay the burden on me'
—Ridgeway.

302. **Mit Gott und mit der Zeit** *German* 'With God and with time'
—Philipp, Duke of Saxony-Lauchstädt (1657–90).

303. **Mon Dieu, mon roi, et ma patrie** *French* 'My god, my king, and my country'
—Kerwan (Co. Galway).

304. **Mon Dieu est ma roche** *French* 'My God is my rock'
—Roche, Fermoy (B.).

305. **M. V. S. Z. G. A. (Mein Vertrauen steht zu Gott allein)** *German* 'My trust is in God alone'
—Johann Adolf II, Duke of Saxony-Weissenfels (1649–97).

306. **My hope is in God**
—Middleton.

307. **My trust is in God alone**
—Cloth-workers' Company, London.

308. **My trust is in the Lord**
—Unwin.

309. **Nid da onid Duw** *Welsh* 'No good but God'
—Williams.

310. **Nihil sine Deo** *Latin* 'Nothing without God'
—Peterson.

311. **Nil sine Deo** *Latin* 'Nothing without God'
—Reeves.

312. **Nil sine numine** *Latin* 'Nothing without the Deity'
—State of Colorado; Regis College, Denver, Colorado; Blundell, Banner, Weld (of Lulworth).

313. **Nisi Dominus** *Latin* 'Except the Lord'
—[Ps., cxxvii. 1.] Compton (Bt.), Compton (of Carham), Hartbury.

314. **Nisi Dominus frustra** *Latin* 'It is in vain without the Lord'
—Hinde, Inglis, Towers; City of Edinburgh, Chelsea B. C., U.K.

315. **Non haec sine numine** *Latin* 'These things are not without the Deity'
—Baker, Clifden (V.).

316. **Non leoni sed Deo** *Latin* 'Not for the lion, but for God'
—Maddock.

317. **Non mihi, sed Deo et regi** *Latin* 'Not for myself, but for god and the king'
—Booth (of Salford).

318. **Non mihi Domine sed nomini tuo da gloriam** *Latin* 'Not unto me, O Lord, but unto Thy name, give glory'
—[after Ps., cxv. 1.] Friedrich II, the Wise, Elector of the Palatinate (1483–1556).

319. **Non nobis, Domine, non nobis, sed nomini tuo da gloriam** *Latin* 'Not to us, Lord, not to us, but to Thy name, give the glory'
—[Ps., cxv. 1.] Knights Templars; Albert V, Duke of Bavaria (1528–79).

320. **Non nostraque Deo** *Latin* 'Not our affairs, (but) for God'
—Rogers (U.S.).

321. **Non sine Deo** *Latin* 'Not without God'
—Eliot.

322. **Non sine numine** *Latin* 'Not without the Deity'
—Gifford (B.).

323. **Nos nostraque Deo** *Latin* 'We and ours to God'
—Rogers (Bt.).

324. **Nosse Deum et bene posse mori sapientia summa est** *Latin* 'To know God and to be able to die happily is the highest wisdom'
—Ernst, Duke of Braunschweig-Lüneburg (1564–1611); August, Duke of Braunschweig-Lüneburg (1568–1636).

325. **Numen et lumen effugio** *Latin* 'I shun the Deity and light'
—Hewson.

326. **Numen flumenque** *Latin* 'Divinity and the river'
—Marquette University, Milwaukee, Wisconsin.

327. **Numine** *Latin* 'Through divinity'
—Bowie (U.S.).

328. **Numini et patriae asto** *Latin* 'I stand by God and my country'
—Aston (B.).

329. **Obligatam redde Jove** *Latin* 'Pay what is due to Jove'
—[Horace, *Odes* ii. 7. 17.] Ward.

330. **Oculi mei semper respiciunt ad Dominum** *Latin* 'Mine eyes are ever toward the Lord'
—[Ps., xxv. 15.] Elisabeth Sophie, Duchess of Saxony-Gotha (1619–80).

331. **Ofwn yr arglwydd** *Welsh* 'We fear the Lord'
—Williams (Co. Cardigan).

332. **Omnia cum Deo** *Latin* 'All things with God'
—Eberhard III, Duke of Württemberg (1614–74); Johann
Friedrich, Duke of Württemberg (1637–59).

333. **Omnia cum Deo et nihil sine eo** *Latin* 'Everything with God,
and nothing without him'
—Wilhelm Ernst, Duke of Saxony-Weimar (1662–1728).

334. **Omnia cum Deo et tempore** *Latin* 'Everything with God and
with time'
—Wilhelm Ludwig, Duke of Württemberg (1647–77).

335. **Omnia Deo confido** *Latin* 'I trust all things to God'
—McNeight.

336. **Opera Dei mirifica** *Latin* 'The works of God are wonderful'
—Barniston, Garmston, Hustwick (of Hull).

337. **Our trust is in God**
—Sadlers' Company, London.

338. **Permitte caetera divis** *Latin* 'Leave the rest to the gods'
—[Horace, *Od.* i. 9. 9.] McCrummin.

339. **Portio mea Dominus** *Latin* 'The Lord is my portion'
—Johann Ernst, Prince of Anhalt (1578–1602).

340. **Pour Dieu, pour terre** *French* 'For God, for earth'
—Leigh (Co. Chester).

341. **Pour Dieu et mon pays** *French* 'For God and my country'
—De Lantour.

342. **Pour Dieu et mon Roi** *French* 'For God and my King'
—Bagot.

343. **Pour mon Dieu** *French* 'For my God'
—Peitere, Peter, McPeter.

344. **Praise God**
—Kerr; Kerr (of Kerrislande).

345. **Praise God for all**
—Bakers' Company (of London and Exeter).

346. **Pro Deo, patriâ, et rege** *Latin* 'For God, my country, and my
king'
—Blades (of High Paull), Beugo, James (of Dublin, Bt.).

347. **Pro Deo, pro Rege, pro patria, et lege** *Latin* 'For God, for the
King, for the country, and the law'
—Blakemore.

348. **Pro Deo, rege, et patriâ** *Latin* 'For God, my king, and my country'
—Blaydes (of Rawby), McDowall.

349. **Pro Deo certo** *Latin* 'I strive for God'
—Anderson.

350. **Pro Deo et Caesare** *Latin* 'For God and the emperor'
—Franz Ludwig, Count of the Palatinate (b. 1664); Johann Ernst, Duke of Saxony-Saalfeld (1658–1729).

351. **Pro Deo et catholica fide** *Latin* 'For God and the Catholic faith'
—Altham.

352. **Pro Deo et ecclesia** *Latin* 'For God and church'
—Friedrich, Landgrave of Hesse (1616–82); Bisshopp (Bt.).

353. **Pro Deo et grege** *Latin* 'For God and the flock'
—Paterson.

354. **Pro Deo et libertate** *Latin* 'For God and liberty'
—Wilson.

355. **Pro Deo et meo** *Latin* 'For God and mine own'
—Moritz, Duke of Saxony-Zeitz (1619–81).

356. **Pro Deo et nobilissima patria Batavorum** *Latin* 'For God and the exalted country of the Batavians'
—Van Nest (U.S.).

357. **Pro Deo et patria** *Latin* 'For God and country'
—University of Dayton School of Law, Dayton, Ohio; Loras College, Dubuque, Iowa.

358. **Pro Deo et patriâ** *Latin* 'For God and our country'
—Maguire.

359. **Pro Deo et populo** *Latin* 'For God and the people'
—Friedrich Wilhelm, Elector of Brandenburg (1620–88); Ferdinand IV, King of Rome (1633–54); Bishop's Stortford U. D. C., U.K.

360. **Pro Deo et pro patriâ** *Latin* 'For God and my country'
—Stackpole.

361. **Pro Deo et rege** *Latin* 'For God and the king'
—Bickerton, Blacker, Golding, Hawkins, Masterton, Rosse (E.).

362. **Pro omnibus laus Deo** *Latin* 'Praise God for all things'
—Manders.

363. **Quand fortune me tourmente, L'Espoire en Dieu me contente**
      French 'When fortune torments, hope in God contents'
                              —Luise Amalie, Princess of Anhalt (1606–35).

364. **Qui a Dieu, il a tout**   *French* 'Who has God, has all'
                              —August, Duke of Saxony-Weissenfels (1614–80).

365. **Quid reddam Domino?**   *Latin* 'What shall I render to the Lord?'
                              —Calthorpe.

366. **Quis similis tui in fortibus, Domine?**   *Latin* 'Who is like unto
      Thee, O Lord, among the mighty ones?'
                              —[Od. xv. 11.] Goldmid (Bt.), Goldsmid.

367. **Quis ut Deus?**   *Latin* 'Who is like God?'
                  —Joseph Clemens, Duke of Bavaria (1671–1723); Order of
                              Merit of St. Michael (Bavaria); Wing.

368. **Quo Deus et gloria ducunt**   *Latin* 'Where God and glory lead'
                  —Friedrich Wilhelm, Duke of Mecklenburg-Schwerin
                                                        (1675–1713).

369. **Reddite Deo**   *Latin* 'Render unto God' *or* 'Redditch for God'
                              —Redditch U. D. C., U.K.

370. **Rere Vaka Na Kaloo Ka Doka Na Tui**   *Fijian* 'Fear God, honor
      the king'

                                                            —Fiji.

371. **Resistit Deus superbis**   *Latin* 'God resisteth the proud'
                  —[1 Peter, v. 5.] Philipp, Landgrave of Hesse-Butzbach
                                                        (1581–1643).

372. **Rhad Duw a ryddid**   *Welsh* 'God's grace and liberty'
                              —Dinorben (B.).

373. **Rien sans Dieu**   *French* 'Nothing without God'
                              —Kerrison (Bt.), Peters.

374. **Robur in vita Deus**   *Latin* 'God is our strength in life'
                              —Jadewine.

375. **Sacrificium Dei cor contritum**   *Latin* 'The sacrifice of God is a
      contrite heart'
                              —[Ps., li. 17.] Corker (of Ballimaloe).

376. **Salutem disponit Deus**   *Latin* 'God dispenses salvation'
                              —Edgar.

377. **Samoa Muamua le Atua**   *Samoan* 'In Samoa, God is first'
                              —American Samoa.

378. **Sancta trinitas mea haereditas** *Latin* 'The sacred Trinity is my heredity'
— August, Duke of Saxony-Weissenfels (1614–80).

379. **Sans Dieu rien** *French* 'Without God nothing'
— Godley (Co. Leitrim), Hodgkinson, Petre (B.), Peter (of Harlyn), Saunderson; Worksop B. C., U.K.

380. **Sapit qui Deum sapit** *Latin* 'He is a wise man who has the knowledge of God'
— Wiseman.

381. **Sedulo numen adest** *Latin* 'The deity is present with the careful man'
— Cunninghame.

382. **Sicut oliva virens laetor in aede Dei** *Latin* 'As the flourishing olive, I rejoice in the house of God'
— [after Ps., lii. 8.] Oliver.

383. **Sine Deo careo** *Latin* 'Without God I am wanting'
— Cary (U.S.).

384. **Sine Deo nihil** *Latin* 'Without God nothing'
— Litster.

385. **Sine numine nihilum** *Latin* 'Nothing without the divinity'
— Jones.

386. **Sola in Deo salus** *Latin* 'Safety alone in God'
— Robinson (Bt.), Robinson, Rokeby (B.).

387. **Sola salus servire Deo** *Latin* 'The only safe course is to serve God'
— Gore (Bt.), Ware (of Edinburgh), Magenis.

388. **Soli Deo** *Latin* 'To God alone'
— Alloway.

389. **Soli Deo gloria** *Latin* 'To God alone be the glory!'
— Ernst, Archduke of Austria (1553–95); Georg Gustav, Count of the Palatinate of Rhein zu Lautereck (1564–1634); Philipp II, Duke of Pomerania (1573–1618); Anna, Duchess of Pomerania (1590–1660); Johann Wilhelm, Duke of Saxony-Eisenach (1666–1729); Glovers' and Skinners' Company; Bonteine; Lesly; Eustace.

390. **Soli Deo gloria et honor** *Latin* 'Glory and honor for God alone'
— Boudinot.

391. **Soli Deo honor** *Latin* 'Honor to God alone'
— Stewart.

392. **Soli Deo honor et gloria** *Latin* 'Honor and glory be to God alone'
—Huddleston (of Sawston).

393. **Soli Deo victoria** *Latin* 'To God alone the victory'
—Johann Friedrich, Elector of Saxony (1503–54).

394. **Solo Deo gloria** *Latin* 'Glory through God only'
—Beste, Digby-Beste.

395. **Speravi in Domino** *Latin* 'I have placed my hope in the Lord'
—Hay.

396. **Spero in Deo** *Latin* 'I trust in God'
—Blackie.

397. **Spes est in Deo** *Latin* 'My hope is in God'
—Bagge (of Stradsett).

398. **Spes in Deo** *Latin* 'My hope is in God'
—Boultbee.

399. **Spes in Domino** *Latin* 'My hope is in the Lord'
—Hardy.

400. **Spes magna in Deo** *Latin* 'Great hope is in my God'
—Meiklejohn.

401. **Spes mea Deus** *Latin* 'God is my hope'
—Friedrich II, the Wise, Elector of the Palatinate
(1483–1556); O'Farrell, Brooke (Bt.); Curriers'
Company; Varty.

402. **Spes mea in Deo** *Latin* 'My hope is in God'
—Brooke, Dewhurst, Gosker, Greaves, Gaskell, Guiness,
Kirkwood, Lewin, Leithbridge (Bt.), Roper, Teynham
(B.), Saunders, Wainwright, Johann Friedrich,
Elector of Saxony (1503–54).

403. **Stella futura micat divino lumine** *Latin* 'The star of the future
twinkles with a divine light'
—Taylour.

404. **Thy hand, O Lord, hath been glorified in strength** *(from Greek)*
—Order of the Redeemer (Greece); Emerson.

405. **Time Deum** *Latin* 'Fear God'
—Ross.

406. **Timor Domini fons vitae** *Latin* 'The fear of the Lord is the fountain of life'
—Butler, Dunboyne (B.).

407. **To God only be all glory**
—Goldsmiths' Company, Skinners' Company.

408. **To know Him and to make Him known**
—Columbia Bible College, Columbia, South Carolina.

409. **Tota mea fiducia est in deo** *Latin* 'My whole trust is in God'
—Pewterers' Company.

410. **Tout à la gloire de Dieu** *French* 'Everything to the glory of God'
—Eleonore, daughter of Prince Rudolf of Anhalt-Zerbst
(1608–81).

411. **Tout avec Dieu** *French* 'Everything with God'
—Christian, Duke of Braunschweig-Lüneburg
(1566–1633); Frederike Elisabeth, Duchess
of Saxony-Weissenfels (1669–1730);
Eberhard III, Duke of Württemberg
(1614–74).

412. **Tout avec Dieu, rien sans raison** *French* 'Everything with God,
nothing without reason'
—Christian II, Prince of Anhalt-Bernburg (1599–1656);
Friedrich, Duke of Saxony (1599–1625).

413. **Tout est de Dieu** *French* 'All is from God'
—Gage.

414. **Tout par et pour Dieu** *French* 'All by and for God'
—Du Bois de Ferrieses.

415. **Tout pour Dieu et ma patrie** *French* 'Wholly for God and my
country'
—Winn (of Nostell Priory, Co. York).

416. **Tout vient de Dieu** *French* 'All comes from God'
—Clinton (B.), Leigh (B.), Leahy (of Cork), Pinchard,
Trefusis.

417. **Traue Gott, thue recht, scheue niemand** *German* 'Trust God, do
right, fear nobody'
—Wilhelm, Duke of Saxony-Weimar (1596–1622).

418. **Trust in God**
—Davis, Hardness, Husdell.

419. **Trust in God and not in strength**
—Renton.

420. **Tu, Domine, gloria mea** *Latin* 'Thou, O Lord, art my glory'
—Leicester, de Tabley (B.).

421. **Tua est o Deus gloria** *Latin* 'Thine is the glory, O God!'
—Albert V, Duke of Bavaria (1528–79).

422. **Turris fortissima est nomen Jehovae** *Latin* 'The name of Jehovah is the strongest tower'
—Plymouth City and C. B. C., U.K.

423. **Un Dieu, un roi** *French* 'One God, one king'
—D'Arcy, Lyttleton.

424. **Un Dieu, un roy, un coeur** *Old French* 'One God, one king, one heart'
—Lake (Bt.).

425. **Un Dieu, un roy, un foy** *Old French* 'One God, one king, one faith'
—Curle, Rush.

426. **Un Dieu et un Roi** *French* 'One God and one king'
—De Jersey.

427. **Ung Dieu, ung loy, ung foy** *Old French* 'One God, one law, one faith'
—Burke (of St. Cleras).

428. **Ung Dieu, ung roy, une loy** *Old French* 'One God, one king, one law'
—Town of Lyons, France.

429. **Ung Dieu et ung roy** *Old French* 'One God and one king'
—Daray, Hatherton (B.).

430. **Unto God only be honor and glory**
—Drapers' Company (London).

431. **Ut cunque placuerit Deo** *Latin* 'Howsoever it shall have pleased God'
—Darby, How, Howe.

432. **Vertrau Gott, tue Recht, scheu Niemandt** *German* 'Trust in God, do right, fear no man'
—Bernhard, Prince of Anhalt (1572–96).

433. **Virtus prae numine** *Latin* 'Virtue under the presence of the Divinity'
—Price.

434. **Vis in vita Deus** *Latin* 'God the strength in life'
—McConnel.

435. **Vive Deo** *Latin* 'Live to God'
—Durham.

436. **Vive Deo ut vivas** *Latin* 'Live to God that you may live'
—Craig (Bt.).

437. **Walk in the way of God**
—Walker-Heneage.

438. **Was Gott erquickt kein neyd erstickt** *German* 'What God creates no spite can choke'
—Gisela Agnes, consort of Prince Emanuel Leberecht of Anhalt-Plötzkau (d. 1670).

439. **Wer sich verleszet auf Gott, Der kan nicht werden zu spott** *German* 'Who gives himself up to God can come to no scorn'
—Amöne Amalie, Princess of Anhalt (d. 1626).

440. **Wer will uns scheiden von der Liebe Gottes?** *German* 'Who shall part us from the love of God?'
—Elisabeth Charlotte, consort of Georg Wilhelm, Elector of Brandenburg (1597–1660).

441. **Whyll God wyll** *Middle English*
—Treffry.

442. **Without God castles are nothing**
—Castleman.

443. **Yet in my flesh shall I see God**
—[Job, xix. 26.] Surman.

DUE

1. **Jus suum cuique** *Latin* 'To every man his own'
—Noel, Perrot.

2. **Nil aequo plus** *Latin* 'Nothing more than my due'
—Hawkins.

3. **Redde suum cuique** *Latin* 'Give to each his own'
—Waddington (U.S.).

4. **Reddite cuique suum** *Latin* 'Render to each his own'
` —[after Mark, xii. 17 and Luke, xx. 25.] New French Merchant Adventurers' Company; Order of the Black Eagle of Prussia; Every (Bt.); Don (of Spittal); Grant (Bt.); Grant (of Monymusk); Thomson (of Banchory).

5. **Suum cuique tribue** *Latin* 'Give to every man his own'
—Dunbar.

6. **Suum cuique tribuens** *Latin* 'Assigning to each his own'
—Walford.

7. **Suum cuique tribuere** *Latin* 'To assign to each his own'
—Wrexham R. D. C., U.K.

DUTY

1. **Aequat munia comparis** *Latin* 'She fully discharges the duties of a partner'
—Order of Saint Catherine (Russia).

2. **Age officium tuum** *Latin* 'Perform your duty'
—Abbott (of Darlington, formerly of Suffolk and East Dereham, Norfolk).

3. **Au roy donne devoir** *Old French* 'Give duty to the king'
—Royden (Bt.).

4. **Chescun son devoir** *Old French* 'Every one his duty'
—Cox.

5. **Deo regique debeo** *Latin* 'I owe duty to God and the king'
—Johnson.

6. **Devoir** *French* 'Duty'
—Footner.

7. **Dieu et mon devoir** *French* 'God and my duty'
—Bradshaw, Willet.

8. **Do your duty and leave the rest to Providence**
—General Thomas Jonathan (Stonewall) Jackson.

9. **Duty**
—Brouncker (of Boveridge).

10. **Duty, honor, country**
—West Point U.S. Military Academy, West Point, New York.

11. **Faire mon devoir** *French* 'To do my duty'
—Jocelyn, Roden (E.).

12. **Faire son devoir** *French* 'To do his duty'
—Boulton.

13. **Fais qui doit, arrive qui pourra** *French* 'Do your duty, happen what may'
—Cure (of Blake Hall).

14. **Fides cum officio** *Latin* 'Faith with duty'
—Newton.

15. **Foy, roi, droit** *Old French* 'Faith, king, duty'
—Lynes (of Tooley Park).

16. **Foy pour devoir** *Old French* 'Faith for duty'
—Somerset (D.), Seymour.

17. **Gwna a ddylit doed a ddel** *Welsh* 'Do thy duty come what may'
—Lewis (Bt.).

18. **Knowledge/ Duty/ Honor**
—South Carolina State College, Orangeburg, South
Carolina.

19. **Le jong tyra bellement** *French* 'He bore the yoke well'
—Trosham.

20. **Loyal devoir** *French* 'Loyal duty'
—Carteret (B.), Grenfell.

21. **Mon devoir fait mon plaisir** *French* 'My duty is my pleasure'
—Sophie Charlotte, Queen of Prussia (1668–1705).

22. **Mon privilege et mon devoir** *French* 'My privilege and my duty'
—Shevill.

23. **Officio et fide** *Latin* 'By duty and fidelity'
—Fawcett.

24. **Officium praesto** *Latin* 'I perform my duty'
—Pownall (of Pownall).

25. **Quae Caesaris Caesari, quae Dei Deo** *Latin* 'Unto Caesar the
things which are Caesar's; and unto God the things which are
God's'
—[Matt., xxii. 21.] Johann the Wise, Margrave of
Brandenburg-Küstrin (1513–71).

26. **Quo fas et gloria ducunt** *Latin* 'Whither duty and glory lead'
—Royal Artillery, U.K.; Royal Engineers, U.K.; Queen's
Own (Roy. West Kent) Regiment, U.K.

27. **Quo fas et gloria ducunt** *Latin* 'Whither duty and glory lead'
—Friedrich Magnus, Margrave of Baden-Durlach
(1647–1709); Georg Wilhelm, Duke of
Braunschweig-Lüneburg-Zelle (1624–1705).

28. **Servare munia vitae** *Latin* 'To observe the duties of life'
—Oglander (Bt.).

29. **Spartam nactus es: hanc exorna** *Latin* 'Sparta is thy lot: do her
credit'
—[after Euripides, *Fragmenta*, 695.] Loretto School, U.K.

30. **Tantum nobis creditum** *Latin* 'So much has been entrusted to us'
—Erindale College of the University of Toronto,
Mississauga, Ontario, Canada.

31. **The buck stops here**
—Harry S. Truman.

32. **Vitae faciendo nemini timeas** *Latin* 'Fear no one in performing
the duties of life'
—Robertson.

EARTH (*See also* WORLD.)

1. **Despicio terrena**   *Latin* 'I despise earthly things'
   —Bedingfield (of Ditchingham), McCrobie.

2. **Despicio terrena et solem contemplor**   *Latin* 'I despise earthly things and contemplate the sun'
   —Bedingfield (Bt.).

3. **E tellure effodiuntur opes**   *Latin* 'Our wealth is dug out of the earth'
   —Aston (of Bescot).

4. **E terra divitiae**   *Latin* 'From the earth, riches'
   —Swadlincote U. D. C., U.K.

5. **E terra germino ad coelum expando**   *Latin* 'I sprout out of the earth, I expand to heaven'
   —Frost.

6. **Ex terra copiam e mari salutem**   *Latin* 'From the land fullness and from the sea health'
   —Worthing B. C., U.K.

7. **Linquenda tellus**   *Latin* 'The earth must be left behind'
   —Boucher (U.S.).

8. **Non sufficit orbis**   *Latin* 'The world does not suffice'
   —Bond.

9. **Omnia mundana fluxa**   *Latin* 'All earthly things are fleeting'
   —Ludwig VI, Elector of the Palatinate (1539–83).

10. **Omnia mundana turbida**   *Latin* 'All things of earth are troublesome'
    —White.

11. **Orbe circum cincto**   *Latin* 'The world being girt around'
    —Saumarez.

12. **Per orbem**   *Latin* 'Through the world'
    —Clay (Bt.).

13. **Pour Dieu, pour terre**   *French* 'For God, for earth'
    —Leigh (Co. Chester).

14. **Quae regio in terris nostri non plena laboris?**   *Latin* 'What spot in the earth is not full of our labors?'
    —[Vergil, *Aen.* i. 460.] Royal Engineers, U.K.

15. **Spanning the world**
    —Community College of the Air Force, Alabama.

16. **Terra, aqua, ignis, sal, spiritus, sulphur, Sol, Venus, Mercurius** *Latin* 'Land, water, fire, salt, spirit, sulphur, Sun, Venus, Mercury'
—Irvine.

17. **Terra, mare, fide** *Latin* 'By the earth, sea, and faith'
—Campbell.

18. **Terra aut mari** *Latin* 'By land or by sea'
—Parke (U.S.).

19. **Terra marique** *Latin* 'On land and sea'
—Thornton Cleveleys U. D. C., U.K.

20. **Terra marique** *Latin* 'By land and sea'
—Cuninghame.

21. **Terrena per vices sunt aliena** *Latin* 'All earthly things by turns are foreign to us'
—Fust.

22. **The Earth is the Lord's, and the fulness thereof**
—Royal Exchange, London.

23. **Ubi solum ibi coelum** *Latin* 'Where there is land there is sky'
—Anderson.

24. **Urbi et orbi** *Latin* 'For the city and the world'
—Long Island University, Brooklyn, New York.

25. **Utere mundo** *Latin* 'Use the world'
—Blackly (U.S.).

26. **Vir vita terra** *Latin* 'Man, life, earth'
—Delaware Valley College, Doyleston, Pennsyvania.

EFFORT (*See also* DILIGENCE.)

1. **Assaye** *French* 'Try'
—Dundas; Highland Light Infantry.

2. **By design and endeavour**
—Crawley Development Corp., U.K.

3. **Certanti dabitur** *Latin* 'It shall be given to him who strives for it'
—Oldershaw.

4. **Conabimur** *Latin* 'We will try'
—Birt, Gwynne.

5. **Conamine** *Latin* 'Make the attempt'
—Kirke.

6. **Conamine augeor** *Latin* 'By effort I am advanced'
   —Lesly (of Colpnay).

7. **Conanti dabitur** *Latin* 'It will be given to him who strives'
   —Conant, Pigott.

8. **Conanti nihil difficile est** *Latin* 'Nothing is difficult for one who strives'
   —Conant (U.S.).

9. **Endeavour**
   —Hendon B. C., U.K.

10. **Essayez** *French* 'Try'
    —Dundas (Bt.), Dundas, Zetland (E.).

11. **Essayez hardiment** *French* 'Try boldly'
    —Dundas (of Keukevil).

12. **Fortitudine et labore** *Latin* 'By fortitude and exertion'
    —Reid.

13. **Fortunâ et labore** *Latin* 'By good fortune and exertion'
    —Sym.

14. **Fortuna vectem [sic] sequitur** *Latin* 'Fortune follows effort'
    —Wight.

15. **Honeste progrediemur conando** *Latin* 'Let us progress by honest endeavor'
    —Seisdon R. D. C., U.K.

16. **I'll try**
    —Newbigging.

17. **Insolitos docuere nisus** *Latin* 'Taught unwonted exertions'
    —[Horace, *Car.* iv. 4. 8.] Babington.

18. **Insolitos docuere nisus** *Latin* 'They have shown unusual efforts'
    —Babington.

19. **In the name of God try**
    —Woolnough (of London).

20. **I will try**
    —Norwich University, Northfield, Vermont.

21. **Laboro fide** *Latin* 'I strive faithfully'
    —Readhead (Bt.).

22. **Nitamur semper ad optima** *Latin* 'Let us always strive for the best'
    —Bigsby.

23. **Niti facere, experiri** *Latin* 'To strive to do is to experience'
    —Caldwell (of Lindley Wood).

24. **Nitimur et munitur**   *Latin* 'We strive and are protected'
—Wellwood.

25. **Nitor donec supero**   *Latin* 'I strive until I overcome'
—Russell (of Charlton Park, co. Gloucester, bt.).

26. **Per actus conamine**   *Latin* 'You attempt by doing it'
—Kersey.

27. **Petimus credimus**   *Latin* 'We strive, we believe'
—Bob Jones University, Greenville, South Carolina.

28. **Point de couronne sans peine**   *French* 'No crown without effort'
—Albrecht, Duke of Saxony-Coburg (1648–99).

29. **Probando et approbando**   *Latin* 'By trying and approving'
—Ramsay.

30. **Quant je puis**   *French* 'As much as I can'
—Stonyhurst College.

31. **Qui nucleum vult nucem frangat**   *Latin* 'Let him break the nut who wants the kernel'
—Hasler (Co. Sussex).

32. **Qui stadium currit eniti debet ut vincat**   *Latin* 'Who runs a race must strive if he wish to win'
—[Cicero, *De Off*. iii. 10.] Friedrich Christoph, Count of Mansfeld (1564–1631).

33. **Strive for the gain of all**
—Gainsborough U. D. C., U.K.

34. **Struggle**
—Ruggles-Brise (of Spains Hall).

35. **Try**
—Gethin (Bt.), O'Hara, Parker (Bt.).

36. **Try and tryst**
—Clark.

37. **Vincit labor**   *Latin* 'Exertion will conquer'
—Campbell (of Blythswood).

EMERGENCE

1. **Emergo**   *Latin* 'I emerge'
—Glass, Webster.

2. **Migro et respicio**   *Latin* 'I come forth and look back'
—Ramsay.

3. **Pandite**   *Latin* 'Open'
—Gibson.

ENDURANCE   (*See also* PERMANENCE; STRENGTH; SUFFERING.)
1. **A ddioddefws a orfu**   *Welsh* 'He who suffered was victorious'
—Glamorgan C. C., U.K.
2. **Agere et pati**   *Latin* 'To do and endure'
—Shiell.
3. **A lo hecho pecho**   *Spanish* 'What can't be cured must be endured'
—Frankland.
4. **Assez dure**   *French* 'Sufficiently hard'
—Ironmongers' Company.
5. **Audax omnia perpeti**   *Latin* 'Daring to endure all things'
—Harding.
6. **Bear thee well**
—Bardwell.
7. **Bear up**
—Fulford (of Fulford).
8. **Beati qui durant**   *Latin* 'Blessed are (the Durants) they who endure'
—Durant.
9. **Byde**
—Gordon (of Cockclarochie).
10. **Byde be**
—Gordon (of Ardmellie).
11. **Byde together**
—Gordon (of Auchendown).
12. **Byde tyme**
—Stevens (U.S.).
13. **Chi dura vince**   *Italian* 'He who endures overcomes'
—Spiers.
14. **Disce ferenda pati**   *Latin* 'Learn to endure what must be borne'
—Hollingworth (of Hollingworth).
15. **Disce pati**   *Latin* 'Learn to endure'
—Camperdown (E.), Donkin (of Ripon), Duncan.
16. **Durat, ditat, placet**   *Latin* 'It endures, it enriches, and it pleases'
—Ged.

17. **Endure and hope**
—Wright, Wyatt.

18. **Endure fort** *French* 'Endure boldly'
—Crawford, Balcarres (E.), Lindsay.

19. **Endurer faiet durer** *Old French* 'Endurance makes firm'
—Friedrich, Count of the Palatinate of Vohenstrauss (1557–97).

20. **Esto perpetua** *Latin* 'May she exist forever'
—Royal Naval School, Eltham, U.K.

21. **Esto perpetua** *Latin* 'Be perpetual'
—Amicable Life Insurance Society.

22. **Esto perpetua** *Latin* 'May it endure forever'
—State of Idaho.

23. **Expectes et sustineas** *Latin* 'Thou mayest hope and endure'
—Gwyn (of Ford Abbey), Wharton.

24. **Ferendo et feriendo** *Latin* 'By bearing and striking'
—Harrison (of Copford Hall).

25. **Ferendo feres** *Latin* 'Thou wilt bear it by endurance'
—Irvine (of Cairnfield).

26. **Ferendo non feriendo** *Latin* 'By bearing not by striking'
—Deane.

27. **Ferendum et sperandum** *Latin* 'We must endure and hope'
—Mackenzie (of Redcastle).

28. **Fer et perfer** *Latin* 'Bear and forbear'
—Barnard.

29. **Fer fortiter** *Latin* 'Bear bravely'
—Barnes.

30. **Ferre non ferto** *Latin* 'Bear not to bear'
—Steel.

31. **Fideque perennant** *Latin* 'And they endure through faith'
—Irvine.

32. **Fortitudo et spes** *Latin* 'Endurance and hope'
—Stockton-on-Tees B. C., U.K.

33. **Have patience and endure**
—Rushton.

34. **He conquers who endures**
—Bath.

35. **He yt tholis overcumms** *Old English* 'He that endures overcomes'
    —over the entrance door of a house in Edinburgh,
    Scotland.

36. **Immersabilis** *Latin* 'Not to be overwhelmed'
    —Hamilton (of Bangour).

37. **Indure but Hope**
    —Barrell (U.S.).

38. **Indure furth**
    —Lindsey.

39. **Manet in aeternum** *Latin* 'It endureth forever'
    —Sprewell, Warner (of Ardeer, co. Ayr).

40. **Mens immota manet** *Latin* 'The steadfast mind endures'
    —Meldrum, Shaw; [Vergil, *Aen.* iv. 449.] Elizabeth,
    Daughter of James I (1595–1662).

41. **Multa tuli fecique** *Latin* 'I have endured and done much'
    —Arkwright.

42. **Multa virum durando saecula vincit** *Latin* 'The many, enduring
    generations of men prevail'
    —Gandolfi (D.).

43. **Non extinguar** *Latin* 'I shall not be extinguished'
    —The Antiquarian Society, London; Fraser.

44. **Patior, potior** *Latin* 'I endure, I enjoy'
    —Peyton (Bt.), Peyton.

45. **Patior ut potior** *Latin* 'I endure as I enjoy'
    —Spottiswood.

46. **Per undas et ignes fluctuat nec mergitur** *Latin* 'Through waters
    and fires she tosses but is not overwhelmed'
    —City of Paris, France.

47. **Pro veritate suffer fortiter** *Latin* 'Endure bravely for the truth'
    —Sharpless (U.S.).

48. **Qui transtulit sustinet** *Latin* 'He who transplanted still sustains'
    —State of Connecticut.

49. **Scripta manent** *Latin* 'What is written remains'
    —Young.

50. **Sustine et abstine** *Latin* 'Bear and forbear'
    —Garden, Kemey.

51. **Sustineo** *Latin* 'I endure'
    —Ten Broeck (U.S.).

52. **Sustinere** *Latin* 'To endure'
—Brooks (U.S.).

53. **Te stante virebo** *Latin* 'Whilst thou endurest I shall flourish'
—Temple.

54. **Thole (Endure) and think on**
—Tweedy.

55. **Thol (Endure) and think**
—Tweedie.

56. **Toleranda et speranda** *Latin* 'We must endure and hope'
—Wright.

57. **Unita durant** *Latin* 'Things united endure'
—Heinrich Julius, Duke of Braunschweig-Wolfenbüttel
(1564–1613); Friedrich August I, Elector of Saxony
(1670–1733).

58. **Vincit qui patitur** *Latin* 'He conquers who endures'
—Ackworth, Amphlett, Addenbrooke, Ashurst, Colt (Bt.),
Chester (of Royston), Harrison, Homfrey, Shaw (Bt.),
Smerdon, Turberville, Wire, Gildea, Whitgift.

59. **We long endure**
—Colne B. C., U.K.

ENEMIES (*See also* CONFLICT; HOSTILITY; OPPOSITION; WAR.)

1. **Leo inimicis amicis columba** *Latin* 'The lion for my enemies, the
dove for my friends'
—Dilke.

ENJOYMENT (*See also* HAPPINESS; LAUGHTER.)

1. **Amoenitas, salubritas, urbanitas** *Latin* 'Amenity, salubrity, and
urbanity'
—Ryde.

2. **Amoenitas salubritas urbanitas** *Latin* 'Pleasantness, health,
urbanity'
—Ryde B. C., U.K.

3. **C'est mon plaisir** *French* 'It is my pleasure'
—Gaude de Martainville, La Rochefoucault, Simon
(Brittany).

4. **Delectando pariterque monendo** *Latin* 'By pleasing as well as by
warning'
—McKay (U.S.).

5. **Delectant domi non impediunt foris** *Latin* 'They delight at home and do not hinder abroad'

—Hoblyn.

6. **Delectat et ornat** *Latin* 'It is both pleasing and ornamental'
—Brown (of Edinburgh), Cree, McCrae, McCree, Macrea, Harvie.

7. **Delectatio** *Latin* '(My) delight'

—Forbes (of Riris).

8. **Delectatio mea** *Latin* 'My delight'

—Pollock (of Roxburgh).

9. **Deliciae mei** *Latin* 'My delight'

—Dalgleish (of Scotscraig).

10. **Dulcedine capior** *Latin* 'I am captivated by sweetness'

—Howlastone.

11. **Dulces ante omnia Musae** *Latin* 'The Muses are delightful above all things'

—Lowes (of Ridley Hall).

12. **E labore dulcedo** *Latin* 'Pleasure arises out of labor'

—Boyle, Innes, McInnes.

13. **Et suavis et fortis** *Latin* 'Pleasant and brave'

—Harper.

14. **Ex sudore voluptas** *Latin* 'Pleasure out of hard labor'

—Swettenham.

15. **Ex usu commodum** *Latin* 'Advantage from its use'

—Smith (of Dirleton).

16. **Hinc delectatio** *Latin* 'Hence delight'

—Forbes.

17. **Jouir en bien** *French* 'To enjoy innocently'

—Beckwith (of Thurcroft).

18. **Jucunditate afficior** *Latin* 'I am greatly delighted'

—Hunter.

19. **Juvant arva parentum** *Latin* 'The lands of my forefathers delight me'

—Cassan (Queen's County).

20. **Nihil potest placere quod non et decet** *Latin* 'Nothing can please which is not also becoming'
—[Quintilian, *De Instit. Oratoria*, i. 11, 11.] Franz Erdmann, Duke of Saxony-Lauenburg (1629–66).

21. **Non aspera juvant**   *Latin* 'Rough things do not delight'
—Lowis.

22. **Omnes arbusta juvant**   *Latin* 'Groves (Underwood) delight all men'
—Underwood.

23. **Parce qu'il me plaît**   *French* 'Because it pleases me'
—Sprot.

24. **Patior, potior**   *Latin* 'I endure, I enjoy'
—Peyton (Bt.), Peyton.

25. **Patior ut potior**   *Latin* 'I endure as I enjoy'
—Spottiswood.

26. **Placeam**   *Latin* 'I will please'
—Murray (of Priestfield).

27. **Placeat nobis quod Deo placet**   *Latin* 'May that please us which pleases God'
—Johann Georg II, Elector of Saxony (1613–80).

28. **Playsyr vaut Payn**   *Old French* 'Pleasure costs pain'
—Payn.

29. **Pungit, sed placet**   *Latin* 'It pricks, but pleases'
—Rome.

30. **Recreat et alit**   *Latin* 'It amuses and nourishes'
—Duddingstoun.

31. **Sapienter uti bonis**   *Latin* 'Wisely to enjoy blessings'
—Butler.

32. **Semper hilaris**   *Latin* 'Always merry'
—Merry.

33. **Si non felix**   *Latin* '(Merry) if not happy'
—Merry.

34. **Sors mihi grata cadit**   *Latin* 'A pleasant lot devolves to me'
—Skeen.

35. **Utere dum potes**   *Latin* 'Enjoy while you may'
—Lecky.

36. **Vigilantia, robur, voluptas**   *Latin* 'Vigilance, strength, pleasure'
—Arundell, Blair (Bt.), Hunter.

ENLIGHTENMENT (*See also* KNOWLEDGE; WISDOM.)
1. 'And the glow from that fire can truly light the world'
—John F. Kennedy University, Orinda, California.

2. **Hinc illuminabimur** *Latin* 'Hence we shall be enlightened'
—Oliphant (of Clasbury, Langtoun, etc.).

3. **Illumino** *Latin* 'I enlighten'
—Farquharson (of Houghton).

4. **Loisgim agus soilleirghim** *Scots Gaelic* 'I will burn and enlighten'
—McLeod, Macleod (of Cadboll).

5. **Me Minerva lucet** *Latin* 'Minerva illumines me'
—Le Marchant (Bt.).

6. **Radii omnia lustrant** *Latin* 'His rays illuminate all things'
—Brownhill.

7. **Terras irradient** *Latin* 'They will enlighten (many) lands'
—Amherst College, Amherst, Massachusetts.

ENTRAPMENT (*See also* DECEPTION; HUNTING.)

1. **I will secure him**
—Kirkpatrick

2. **Ne cadam insidiis** *Latin* 'Lest I fall into snares'
—Cleland.

3. **Qui capit capitur** *Latin* 'He who takes is taken'
—Smyth (Bt.).

4. **Quid capit, capitur** *Latin* 'What takes is taken'
—Smith.

5. **Vinctus sed non victus** *Latin* 'Chained but not conquered'
—Galway.

6. **Vincula temno** *Latin* 'I despise bonds'
—Sinclair.

7. **Voici nos liens** *French* 'See our bonds'
—Mazyck (U.S.).

ENVY

1. **Hostis honori invidia** *Latin* 'Envy is an enemy to honor'
—Dickens; Market Harborough U. D. C., U.K.

2. **Indignante invidia florebit justus** *Latin* 'The just man will flourish in spite of envy'
—Crosbie.

3. **Invidere sperno** *Latin* 'I scorn to envy'
—Davies, Saunders.

4. **Invidia assecla integritatis** *Latin* 'Envy waits on integrity'
—Heinrich Julius, Duke of Braunschweig-Wolfenbüttel
(1564–1613).

5. **Invidiae claudor, pateo sed semper amico** *Latin* 'I am closed to envy, but am always open to a friend'
—over a bedroom door in Loseley House, near Guildford,
Surrey, England.

6. **Invidia major** *Latin* 'Superior to envy'
—Drago, Inwards.

7. **Malgré l'envie** *French* 'In spite of envy'
—Thirley.

8. **Nec invideo, nec despicio** *Latin* 'I neither envy nor despise'
—Raymond.

9. **Qui invidet minor est** *Latin* 'He that envies is inferior'
—Cadogan (E.), Pugh.

10. **Spero invidiam** *Latin* 'I hope for envy'
—Erich II, the Younger, Duke of Braunschweig-Kalenberg
(1528–84).

11. **Virtus invidiae scopus** *Latin* 'Virtue is the mark of envy'
—Methuen (B.).

12. **Virtus vincit invidium** *Latin* 'Virtue overcometh envy'
—Cornwallis (E.), Clibborn, Mann.

13. **Virtute invidiam vincas** *Latin* 'May you overcome envy by virtue'
—Cleborne.

14. **Virtute vincit invidiam** *Latin* 'He conquers envy by virtue'
—Mann.

15. **Virtuti comes invidia** *Latin* 'Envy is companion to virtue'
—Cunninghame.

16. **Virtutis comes invidia** *Latin* 'Envy is the companion of virtue'
—Devereux, Hereford (V.).

EQUALITY

1. **Ce m'est égal** *French* 'This is equal to me'
—Phillips-Treby.

2. **Equality**
—University of Wyoming, Laramie, Wyoming.

3. **Equality before the law**
—State of Nebraska.

4. **Equal rights**
—State of Wyoming.

5. **Liberté, egalité, fraternité**   *French* 'Liberty, equality, fraternity'
—French Republic.

6. **Nec pluribus impar**   *Latin* 'Not unequal to many'
—Philip II of Spain; Louis XIV of France.

7. **Non major alio non minor**   *Latin* 'Not greater than another, not less'
—Clark.

8. **Par pari**   *Latin* 'Equal to my equal'
—Sicklemore (of Wetheringsett).

9. **Primus inter pares**   *Latin* 'First among equals'
—Columbus College, Columbus, Georgia.

10. **Zo kwe zo**   *Sangho* 'All men are equal'
—Central African Republic.

EQUANIMITY (*See also* MODERATION.)

1. **Aequaliter et diligenter**   *Latin* 'Calmly and diligently'
—Moore.

2. **Aequam servare mentem**   *Latin* 'To preserve an equal mind'
—[after Horace, *Od.*, ii. 3.] Green (Bt.), Hoyle (of Denton Hall), Mathew, Raymond, Rivers (B.), Treacher, Moon (Bt.).

3. **Aequanimiter**   *Latin* 'With equanimity'
—Harboro, Shuttleworth (Bt.), Suffield (B.).

4. **Aequo animo**   *Latin* 'With equanimity'
—Pennant, Repton.

5. **Animus non deficit aequus**   *Latin* 'Equanimity is not wanting'
—[After Horace, Ep. i. 11, 30.] Burrell, Willoughby de Eresby (B.).

6. **Be steady**
—Butcher (U.S.).

7. **Calm**
—McAdam (of Ballochmorrie).

8. **Equanimiter**   *Latin* 'With equanimity'
—Suffield (B.).

9. **Mens aequa in arduis**   *Latin* 'An equal mind in difficulties'
—Hastings.

10. **Mens aequa in arduis** *Latin* 'A stable mind amid difficulties'
—Crosby (U.S.).

11. **Mens aequa rebus in arduis** *Latin* 'An equal mind in difficulties'
—Hardinge (V.).

12. **Mens in arduis aequa** *Latin* 'A stable mind amid difficulties'
—Abercrombie (U.S.).

13. **Nec elata, nec dejecta** *Latin* 'Neither overjoyed nor dejected'
—Northmore.

14. **Never elated never dejected**
—Thomas.

15. **Pari animo** *Latin* 'With equal mind'
—Leake.

16. **Placidus semper timidus nunquam** *Latin* 'Placid always, timid never'
—Catlin (U.S.).

17. **Steady**
—Aylmer (B.), Bridport (B.), Hood, McAdam, Northen, Neill, Norris, Tonge, Verelst, Weller.

18. **Steer steady**
—Donaldson, Strachan (Bt.).

19. **Stire steddie**
—Donaldson.

20. **Summum nec metuam diem nec optem** *Latin* 'May I neither dread nor desire the last day'
—Tighe (of Woodstock).

ETERNITY

1. **Aeternitas** *Latin* 'Eternity'
—Rayson.

2. **Age in aeternum** *Latin* 'Strive to eternity'
—Conwell.

3. **Eternitatem cogita** *Latin* 'Think on eternity'
—Boyd (of Trochrig).

4. **L'esperensse de l'eternel disipe tous mes ennuis** *Old French* 'The hope of eternal life disperses all my cares'
—Luise Henriette, Electress of Brandenburg (1627–67).

5. **L'éternel regne** *French* 'The everlasting kingdom'
—La Serre.

6. **Pour jamais** *French* 'Forever'
—Bolden, Evers, Gurwood.

7. **Praestant aeterna caducis** *Latin* 'Eternal things are better than perishable'
—Johann Wilhelm, Duke of Saxony-Jena (1675–90).

EVIL (*See also* DECEPTION.)

1. **Mala praevisa pereunt** *Latin* 'Evils foreseen are destroyed'
—Hodges.

2. **Malis fortiter obsta** *Latin* 'Bravely block evil'
—Appleton (U.S.).

3. **Malum bono vince** *Latin* 'Subdue evil by good'
—Hay (of Linplum).

4. **Nocentes prosequor** *Latin* 'I prosecute the bad'
—Dumbreck, Savary.

5. **Non recedet malum a domo ingrati et seditiosi** *Latin* 'Evil shall not depart from the house of the ungrateful and the disturber of peace'
—[after Prov., xvii. 13.] Heinrich Julius, Duke of
Braunschweig-Wolfenbüttel (1564–1613).

6. **N. R. M. A. D. I. (Non recedet malum a domo ingrati)** *Latin* 'Evil shall not depart from the house of the ungrateful'
—[after Prov., xvii. 13.] Julius, Duke of Braunschweig-
Wolfenbüttel (1529–89).

7. **Sans mal** *French* 'Without evil'
—Strickland.

8. **Sin not**
—Synnott.

9. **Vince malum patientia** *Latin* 'Overcome evil with patience'
—Lee, Townshend.

10. **Weapon forefendeth evil**
—Mitford.

11. **Wer gutes u boses nit kan ertragan wirt kein grose chre erjagen** *German* 'Who cannot bear good and evil shall not obtain great honors'
—Brander (Co. Hants).

EXALTATION

1. **Depressus extollor**   *Latin* 'I am exalted after being depressed'
   —Butler, Kilkenny.
2. **Erectus, non elatus**   *Latin* 'Exalted, but not elated'
   —Beaumont (Bt.), Beaumont (of Barrow), Clarke, Phillips.
3. **Exaltavit humiles**   *Latin* 'He hath exalted the humble'
   —Holte (of Erdington).
4. **Industria evehit**   *Latin* 'Industry promotes'
   —Warrender.

EXCELLENCE   (*See also* PERFECTION.)

1. **Always to excel**
   —Belgrave, Manningham, Neve.
2. **A tradition of excellence**
   —New York State University College at Potsdam, New York.
3. **Commitment to excellence**
   —U.S. Air Force Academy, Colorado Springs, Colorado.
4. **Education for excellence**
   —Durham Technical Institute, Durham, North Carolina.
5. **Emphasis excellence**
   —Kilgore College, Kilgore, Texas.
6. **Excellence**
   —University of Wisconsin, Eau Claire, Wisconsin.
7. **Excellence for Christ**
   —St. Andrews Presbyterian College, Laurinburg, North Carolina.
8. **Excellence through education**
   —Naval Postgraduate School, Monterey, California.
9. **Excellentia**   *Latin* 'Excellence'
   —University of Tennessee at Martin, Martin, Tennessee.
10. **Fortis et egregius**   *Latin* 'Bold and excellent'
    —Dowling.
11. **In order to excel**
    —Henniker (B.).
12. **Not quantity —but quality**
    —Stowe State College, St. Louis, Missouri.

13. **Que je surmonte**   *French* 'May I excel'
—Chaceler (of Shieldhill).

14. **Sine crimine fiat**   *Latin* 'Be it done without reproach'
—Innes (Bt.).

15. **Studio optimae doctrinae et saluti sanitatis**   *Latin* '(Dedicated) to the pursuit of educational excellence and the preservation of health'
—Logan College of Chiropractic, Chesterfield, Missouri.

16. **Tempora mutantur permanet praestantia**   *Latin* 'The times change but excellence prevails'
—Mitchell Community College, Statesville, North Carolina.

17. **Unitate praestans**   *Latin* 'Excelling by unity'
—Preston R. D. C., U.K.

18. **Va outre marque**   *French* 'Go beyond the mark'
—Utermarck.

EXHORTATION

1. **Avauncez et archez bien**   *French* 'Advance and shoot well'
—Swinnerton.

2. **Macte**   *Latin* 'Bravo!'
—Smith.

EXPECTATION

1. **Ab alto speres alteri quod feceris**   *Latin* 'Expect from Heaven what you have done to another'
—Wyndham.

2. **Accidit in puncto quod non speratur in anno**   *Latin* 'What you do not expect in a year often happens in a moment'
—Charles V, Emperor of Germany (1500–58).

3. **Ante expectatum diem**   *Latin* 'Before the wished-for day'
—Steinman.

4. **Expecta cuncta supernè**   *Latin* 'Expect all things from above'
—Wilson (of Inverness).

5. **Expecto**   *Latin* 'I expect'
—Hepburn.

6. **Inopinum sed gratum**   *Latin* 'Unexpected but welcome'
—Worthington.

7. **I wait my time**
—Porteous.

8. **Le maître vient**   *French* 'The master comes'
—Peck.

9. **Meliora speranda**   *Latin* 'Better fortunes in expectancy'
—Douglass.

10. **Redit expectata diu**   *Latin* 'The long expected returns'
—Starkey.

11. **U. K. O. (Unverhofft Kommt Oft)**   *German* 'The unexpected often happens'
—Franz, Duke of Pomerania (1577–1620).

EXPLORATION   (*See also* SEARCH and DISCOVERY.)

1. **Caelis exploratis**   *Latin* 'For the heavens explored'
—Herschel (Bt.).

2. **Inspice**   *Latin* 'Examine'
—Davis.

3. **Je ne cherche qu'un**   *French* 'I seek but one'
—Compton (Northampton, m.),

4. **Remember there are two sides to every question. Get both.**
—Warren G. Harding.

FACTUALITY   (*See also* TRUTH.)

1. **Ainsi il est**   *French* 'Thus it is'
—Bellingham (Bt.).

2. **Au fait**   *French* 'In fact'
—Shaw.

3. **Naturam primum cognoscere rerum**   *Latin* 'First to learn the nature of things' or 'Above all to find out the way things are'
—Australian National University, Canberra, Australia.

4. **Res non verba**   *Latin* 'Facts not words'
—Duberly, Jarrett, McRorie, Wilson (Bt.), Wilson (of Eshton Hall).

FAILURE

1. **Deficiam aut efficiam**   *Latin* 'I will fail, or I will perform'
—Storie.

2. **Il n'est si ferré qui ne glisse** *French* 'No one is so well shod that he does not slip'
   —Friedrich Ulrich, Duke of Braunschweig-Wolfenbüttel (1591–1634).

3. **Qui modo scandit corruet statim** *Latin* 'Who quickly climbs will suddenly fall'
   —Moreton Hall, Cheshire, England.

4. **Qui stat caveat ne cadat** *Latin* 'Let him who standeth take heed lest he fall'
   —[1 Cor., x. 12.] Domville.

5. **Ubi lapsus? Quid feci?** *Latin* 'Whither have I fallen? What have I done?'
   —Courtenay, Devon (E.).

FAIRNESS (*See also* EQUALITY; JUSTICE; RECTITUDE; RIGHTEOUSNESS.)

1. **Aequitas actionem regulam** *Latin* 'Equity (makes) action the rule'
   —Montague.

2. **Aequitas actionum regula** *Latin* 'Equity is the rule of actions'
   —Bradbury.

3. **Aequitate ac diligentia** *Latin* 'With fair play and diligence'
   —Ashbury.

4. **Candide et constanter** *Latin* 'Fairly and firmly'
   —Irwine, Warner.

5. **Chacun sa part** *French* 'Each his share'
   —Gwilt.

6. **Diligentia et candore** *Latin* 'By diligence and fairness'
   —Dick.

7. **Equity**
   —Handley.

8. **Je veux bonne guerre** *French* 'I wish fair play'
   —Thomson, Thompson.

9. **Je veux de bonne guerre** *French* 'I wish fair play'
   —Wenlock (B.).

10. **Ne parcas nec spernas** *Latin* 'Neither spare nor scorn'
    —Lamond, Lamont.

11. **Nunquam praeponens** *Latin* 'Never preferring'
    —Duntz (Bt.).

FAITH (*See also* RELIGION; TRUST.)

1. **Accipe daque fidem**   *Latin* 'Receive and give faith'
     —Crickett.

2. **A foye**   *Old French* 'To faith'
     —Sir Richard Tempest.

3. **Amantibus justitiam, pietatem, fidem**   *Latin* 'To the lovers of justice, piety, and faith'
     —Order of St. Anne (Sleswick).

4. **Amantibus justitiam, pietatem, fidem**   *Latin* 'To those who love justice, piety, and faith'
     —Order of St. Anne (Schleswig-Holstein).

5. **Animo et fide**   *Latin* 'By courage and faith'
     —Burroughes (of Burlingham and Long Stratton, Co. Norfolk), Cornock (Co. Wexford), Guildford (E.), North, Phillips, Turner, Carshalton U. D. C., U.K.

6. **Animo et fide**   *Latin* 'By faith and courage'
     —Stockport C. B. C., U.K.

7. **Animo et fide**   *Latin* 'Through soul and faith'
     —Pensacola Jr. College, Pensacola, Florida.

8. **Ardens fide**   *Latin* 'Burning with faith'
     —Brentwood U. D. C., U.K.

9. **Armé de foi hardi**   *French* 'Armed with hardy faith'
     —Cranbrook (E.), Hardy (Bt.).

10. **Arte fideque**   *Latin* 'By art and faith'
     —Orrock.

11. **Au Dieu foy, aux amis foyer**   *Old French* 'To god faith, to friends home'
     —Hall of Farnham Castle, Hampshire, England.

12. **By courage and faith**
     —Seaham U. D. C., U.K.

13. **By faith I obtain**
     —Turners' Company, London.

14. **By faith we are saved**
     —[Gal., ii. 20.] Cathcart (Bt.).

15. **Celeriter nil crede**   *Latin* 'Believe naught hastily'
     —Stringer.

16. **Chassé pour foi**   *French* 'Persecuted for the faith'
     —Andovier, Lamb.

17. **Color fidesque perennis** *Latin* 'Its color and our faith are imperishable'
    —Irvine.

18. **Constans fidei** *Latin* 'Steady to my faith'
    —Cogan, Coggan, Colborne (B.), Ridley (Bt.), Ridley (V.).

19. **Constans fides et integritas** *Latin* 'Constant faith and integrity'
    —Brinckerhoff (U.S.).

20. **Coronat fides** *Latin* 'Faith crowns all'
    —Dall, Pringle (Bt.).

21. **Crede et vince** *Latin* 'Believe and conquer'
    —Gildowrie, Toash.

22. **Crede mihi** *Latin* 'Believe me'
    —Fitz-Marmaduke.

23. **Credo** *Latin* 'I believe'
    —Kirsopp, Sinclair.

24. **Credo, amo et regno** *Latin* 'I believe, love, and rule'
    —Clive.

25. **Credo Deo** *Latin* 'Believe in God'
    —Atkinson.

26. **Credo et amo** *Latin* 'I believe and love'
    —Crossley (of Scaitcliffe).

27. **Credo et videbo** *Latin* 'I believe, and I shall see'
    —Chresly.

28. **Crux fidei calcar** *Latin* 'The cross is the spur of faith'
    —Brooking.

29. **Culpari metuit fides** *Latin* 'Faith fears to be blamed'
    —[Horace, Od. iv. 5. 20.] Whitfield.

30. **Dieu, un roi, une foi** *French* 'God, one king, one faith'
    —Rush.

31. **Dieu et ma foi** *French* 'God and my faith'
    —Favil.

32. **Domino fides immobilis** *Latin* 'An immovable faith in God'
    —Barry.

33. **Eh kopf ab, als von der lehr abstehn** *German* 'Rather lose your head than give up your faith'
    —Georg the Pious, Margrave of Brandenburg-Anspach (1484–1543).

34. **En bon foy** *Old French* 'In good faith'
    —Chadwick, Sacheverell.

35. **En Dieu est ma foy**   *Old French* 'In God is my faith'
—Cheevers, Legh-Keck, Mauleverer (Co. York), Staunton (co. Warwick).

36. **En Dieu ma foi**   *French* 'My faith is in God'
—Favill.

37. **En Dieu ma foy**   *Old French* 'My faith is in God'
—Staunton, Sampson.

38. **En foi prest**   *French* 'Ready in faith'
—Barlow (of Ryde); Isle of Wight.

39. **En pure foi**   *French* 'In pure faith'
—Hewitt.

40. **Et fide et virtute**   *Latin* 'By both faith and virtue'
—Porter.

41. **Et servata fides perfectus amorque ditabunt**   *Latin* 'Both tried faith and perfect love will enrich'
—Younge.

42. **Ex fide fortis**   *Latin* 'Strong through faith'
—Beauchamp (E.), Lygon, Pindar.

43. **Faith**
—Billingham U. D. C., U.K.

44. **Faith, Hope, Charity**
—Order of the Royal Red Cross.

45. **Faith, unity, discipline**   *(from Urdu and Bengali)*
—Republic of Pakistan.

46. **Faith, work, service**
—Calne B. C., U.K.

47. **Faith and hope**
—Lindsey.

48. **Faith and works**
—Nelson (E.).

49. **Faith in industry**
—Edmonton B. C., U.K.

50. **Fayth hathe no feare**
—Rycroft (Bt.)

51. **Fe med'um buen hidalgo**   *Spanish* 'Faith measures a good gentleman'
—Bockenham.

52. **Ferme en foy**   *Old French* 'Strong in faith'
—Chichester, Haydon, Sanford.

53. **Fert lauream fides**   *Latin* 'Faith bears the laurel'
—Hay (of Lethim).

54. **Fey e fidalgia**   *Spanish* 'Faith and fidelity'
—Shelley (Bt.).

55. **Fide, labore, et virtute**   *Latin* 'By faith, labor, and virtue'
—Maryott.

56. **Fide et animus**   *Latin* 'Courage with faith'
—Howard.

57. **Fide et bello fortis**   *Latin* 'Strong in faith and war'
—Carritt.

58. **Fide et caritate laboro**   *Latin* 'I labor with faith and charity'
—Bovier.

59. **Fide et clementia**   *Latin* 'By faith and clemency'
—Martin (Co. Sussex).

60. **Fide et diligentia**   *Latin* 'By faith and diligence'
—Woking U. D. C., U.K.

61. **Fide et fortitudine**   *Latin* 'With faith and fortitude'
—Aubert, Brickdale, Cox, Capel, Essex (E.), Farquharson (of Invercauld), Hickson, Lawrence (of Llanelweth), McFarquhar, Noble (of Reresbie), Madan, Lloyd (of Coedmore).

62. **Fide et fortitudine**   *Latin* 'By faith and fortitude'
—Penrith U. D. C., U.K.

63. **Fide et in bello fortis**   *Latin* 'Strong in faith and in war'
—Carrot.

64. **Fide et industria**   *Latin* 'By faith and industry'
—Whittingham.

65. **Fide et labore**   *Latin* 'By faith and industry'
—Allen, Harpenden U. D. C., U.K.

66. **Fide et literis**   *Latin* 'By faith and by letters'
—St. Paul's School, London.

67. **Fide et opera**   *Latin* 'By faith and work'
—McArthur, Stewart.

68. **Fide et perseverantia**   *Latin* 'By faith and perseverance'
—Lumsden.

69. **Fide et sedulitate**   *Latin* 'With faith and diligence'
—Elwood.

70. **Fide et spe**   *Latin* 'With faith and hope'
—Borthwick.

71. **Fide et vigilantia** *Latin* 'By faith and vigilance'
—Stepney (Bt.).

72. **Fidei constans** *Latin* 'Steadfast in faith'
—Colegrave.

73. **Fidei signum** *Latin* 'The emblem of faith'
—Murray (of Deuchar).

74. **Fidei tenax** *Latin* 'Strong in faith'
—Wolverton (B.).

75. **Fidei virtutem adde** *Latin* 'Add to your faith virtue'
—Lee.

76. **Fide laboro** *Latin* 'I labor with faith'
—Bovier.

77. **Fidelis exsulatae** *Latin* 'Faithful, though exiled'
—Manbey.

78. **Fidelitate et industria stat Bilstonia** *Latin* 'Bilston stands by faith and industry'
—Bilston B. C., U.K.

79. **Fidem libertatem amicitiam retinebis** *Latin* 'You will keep faith, liberty, and friendship'
—Adams (U.S.).

80. **Fidem meam servabo** *Latin* 'I will keep my faith'
—Sheddon.

81. **Fidem rectam qui colendo** *Latin* 'Who by cultivating right faith'
—Hibbert.

82. **Fidem respice** *Latin* 'Regard faith'
—Hoskins (U.S.).

83. **Fidem servabo** *Latin* 'I will keep faith'
—Emerson (U.S.), Haskins (U.S.).

84. **Fidem servabo genusque** *Latin* 'I will preserve (be true to) my faith and my race'
—Massey (of Watton, co. Norfolk).

85. **Fidem servare** *Latin* 'To keep faith'
—Osmand.

86. **Fidem servat, vinculaque solvit** *Latin* 'He keeps faith and loosens the bonds'
—Velasquez de la Cadena (U.S.).

87. **Fidem servo** *Latin* 'I keep faith'
—Alexander (of Boghall).

88. **Fidem tene**   *Latin* 'Keep faith'
    —Hornyold.

89. **Fide non armis**   *Latin* 'By faith not arms'
    —Gambier.

90. **Fide parta, fide aucta**   *Latin* 'By faith obtained, by faith increased'
    —McKenzie (of Kilcoy, bt.), Mackenzie (of Fairburn).

91. **Fide patientia labore**   *Latin* 'By faith, patience, and work'
    —Pilter.

92. **Fideque perennant**   *Latin* 'And they endure through faith'
    —Irvine.

93. **Fides**   *Latin* 'Faith'
    —Maxton, Petree, Roster, Wyllie (of Forfar).

94. **Fides cum officio**   *Latin* 'Faith with duty'
    —Newton.

95. **Fides et amor**   *Latin* 'Faith and love'
    —Graham.

96. **Fides et fortitudo**   *Latin* 'Faith and fortitude'
    —Moreland (U.S.); Ropner (Bt.).

97. **Fides et honor**   *Latin* 'Faith and honor'
    —De Forest (B.).

98. **Fides et justitia**   *Latin* 'Faith and justice'
    —Farnborough U. D. C., U.K.; Webster (Bt.).

99. **Fides in adversis**   *Latin* 'Faith in adversity'
    —Wolf, Woolfe.

100. **Fides invicta triumphat**   *Latin* 'Unconquered faith triumphs'
    —Gloucester City and C. B. C., U.K.

101. **Fides leone fortior**   *Latin* 'Faith is mightier than the lion'
    —Motley (U.S.).

102. **Fides lumen praebeat**   *Latin* 'May faith grant light'
    —St. Gregory's College, Shawnee, Oklahoma.

103. **Fides mihi panoplia**   *Latin* 'Faith is my panoply'
    —Aries.

104. **Fides montium Deo**   *Latin* 'The faith of the hills is in God'
    —Hills.

105. **Fides non timet**   *Latin* 'Faith fears not'
    —Harvey, Lee, Monteagle (B.), Rice.

106. **Fides nudaque veritas**   *Latin* 'Faith and naked truth'
    —Lushington.

107. **Fides praestantior auro**   *Latin* 'Faith is more estimable than gold'
—Clapperton, Gibb.

108. **Fides praevalebit**   *Latin* 'Faith will prevail'
—Morris (U.S.).

109. **Fides probata coronat**   *Latin* 'Tried faith crowns'
—Campbell (of Purvis, bt.), Laidlaw, Roch.

110. **Fides puritas**   *Latin* 'Faith, purity'
—Webster.

111. **Fides scutum**   *Latin* 'Faith is a shield'
—Bruen (U.S.), Gleim (U.S.).

112. **Fides Stephani**   *Latin* 'Stephen's faith'
—Stephens.

113. **Fides sufficit**   *Latin* 'Faith sufficeth'
—Halket (Bt.), Halkett (co. Fife), Halket (co. Warwick).

114. **Fides unit**   *Latin* 'Faith unites'
—McKenzie.

115. **Fides vincit et veritas custodit**   *Latin* 'Faith conquers and truth guards'
—Story (U.S.).

116. **Fide tenes anchoram**   *Latin* 'You hold anchor by faith'
—Malim.

117. **Fight and faith**
—St. Clair.

118. **Firma nobis fides**   *Latin* 'Faith is strong to us'
—Vilant, Waterhous.

119. **Firm en foi**   *French* 'Firm in faith'
—Chichester (V.).

120. **Firmor ad fidem**   *Latin* 'I am true to the faith'
—Chippendall.

121. **Foi, roi, droit**   *French* 'Faith, king, right'
—Lynes.

122. **Foi en loyalté**   *French* 'Faith in loyalty'
—D'Anvers.

123. **Foi est tout**   *French* 'Faith is all'
—Robinson.

124. **Fortitudini juncta fidelitas**   *Latin* 'Faith joined with fortitude'
—Bogart (U.S.).

125. **Foy**   *Old French* 'Faith'
—Gilpin (of Bungay, Suffolk).

126. **Foy, roi, droit**   *Old French* 'Faith, king, duty'
                                    —Lynes (of Tooley Park).

127. **Foy en tout**   *Old French* 'Faith in everything'
                                    —Yelverton, Sussex (E.), Sutcliffe.

128. **Foy est tout**   *Old French* 'Faith is everything'
                                    —Ripon (E.), Robinson, Babington.

129. **Foy pour devoir**   *Old French* 'Faith for duty'
                                    —Somerset (D.), Seymour.

130. **Foys sapience et chevalerie**   *Old French* 'Faith, wisdom, and chivalry'
                                    —A'Beckett.

131. **Fructus per fidem**   *Latin* 'Advantages through faith'
                                    —Fructuozo.

132. **Functa virtute fides**   *Latin* 'Faith having exhibited valor'
                                    —Murray.

133. **Garde la foi**   *French* 'Keep the faith'
                                    —Kensington (B.), Rich (Bt.).

134. **Garde la foy**   *Old French* 'Keep the faith'
                                    —De la Beche.

135. **Garde ta foy**   *Old French* 'Guard thy faith'
                                    —Rich.

136. **Gardez la foy**   *Old French* 'Keep the faith'
                                    —Poulett (E.), Dymocke.

137. **Guarde la foy**   *Old French* 'Keep the faith'
                                    —Rich.

138. **Ha persa la fide, ha perso l'honore**   *Italian* 'Faith lost, honor is lost'
                                    —Lewis (of St. Pierre).

139. **Have faith in Christ**
                                    —Glendoning (of Partoun), Glendonwyn.

140. **Honor et fides**   *Latin* 'Honor and faith'
                                    —Sears.

141. **Ich weis das mein Erlöser lebt**   *German* 'I know that my Redeemer liveth'
                                    —[Job xix. 25.] Katherine, Duchess of Braunschweig (d. 1537); Dorothee Susanne, Duchess of Saxony-Weimar (1544–92); WDorothee Sophie, Duchess of Saxony (1587–1645).

142. **Immota fides** *Latin* 'Immoveable faith'
—The Ducal Order of Brunswick, of Henry the Lion.

143. **In adversis etiam fide** *Latin* 'With faith even in adversity'
—Dandridge.

144. **Incorrupta fides** *Latin* 'Uncorrupted faith'
—Whitmore.

145. **Incorrupta fides, nudaque veritas** *Latin* 'Uncorrupted faith and the naked truth'
—Forde, Myers (Bt.), Waskett (of Hingham).

146. **In cruce fides** *Latin* 'Faith in the cross'
—Rudge, Glendening.

147. **In cruce mea fides** *Latin* 'In the cross is my faith'
—Billairs.

148. **In cruce non in leone fides** *Latin* 'In the cross not in the lion is my faith'
—Lisle.

149. **Indubitata fides** *Latin* 'Undoubted faith'
—Reynell.

150. **In fide, justitia, et fortitudine** *Latin* 'In faith, justice, and strength'
—Order of St. George (Bavaria).

151. **In fide et in bello fortis** *Latin* 'Strong both in faith and war'
—Bagwell (of Marlfield), Carroll, or O'Carroll (of Ballymore).

152. **In fide fiducia** *Latin* 'There is trust in faith'
—Leys School, Cambridge, U.K.

153. **In fide fortis** *Latin* 'Strong in faith'
—Chambers.

154. **In fide vestra virtutem in virtute autem scientiam** *Latin* '(Have) virtue in your faith but knowledge in your virtue'
—Agnes Scott College, Decatur, Georgia.

155. **Intaminata fide** *Latin* 'With spotless faith'
—Scots Guards.

156. **Intemerata fides** *Latin* 'Faith undefiled'
—Aberdeen, Robertson.

157. **I trow aright**
—Trower.

158. **I trow aught**
—Trower (of St. Albans).

159. **J'avance. Foy en Dieu** *Old French* 'I go forward. Faith in God'
—Bartram (U.S.).

160. **J'ay ma foi tenu à ma puissance** *French* 'I have kept my faith as far as I am able'
—Croker.

161. **Je garde ma foi** *French* 'I defend my faith'
—Le Cronier.

162. **Je tiendray ma puissance par ma foi** *French* 'I will maintain my power by my faith'
—Croker.

163. **Je tiens foi** *French* 'I keep faith'
—Russell.

164. **Justitiae soror fides** *Latin* 'Faith is the sister of justice'
—Thurlow (B.), Thurlow.

165. **Justus ex fide vivit** *Latin* 'The just lives by his faith'
—[after Habakkuk, ii. 4.] Albrecht, Margrave of Brandenburg (1490–1568); Georg Friedrich, Margrave of Brandenburg-Anspach (1539–1603).

166. **Keep faith**
—Crewkerne U. D. C., U.K.

167. **Keep firm in the faith**
—Order of Hubert.

168. **La foi me guide** *French* 'Faith guides me'
—Deane.

169. **Le roy, la loy, la foy** *Old French* 'King, law, faith'
—Grover.

170. **Libertatem, amicitiam, retinebis et fidem** *Latin* 'You will hold on to liberty, friendship, and faith'
—Boylston (U.S.).

171. **Lux et fides** *Latin* 'Light and faith'
—Taylor University, Upland, Indiana.

172. **Mea gloria fides** *Latin* 'Faith is my glory'
—Gilchrist, Watson.

173. **Milita bonam militiam retinens fidem et bonam conscientiam** *Latin* 'War a good warfare, holding faith, and a good conscience'
—[1 Tim., i. 18–19.] Rudolf, Prince of Anhalt-Zerbst (1576–1621); Wilhelm, Duke of Saxony (1596–1622).

174. **Mors mihi lucrum**   *Latin* 'Death is gain to me'
—Jones, Lluellyn.

175. **Mors mihi vitae fide**   *Latin* 'Death to me by faith in life'
—Ellis.

176. **Ne doubtero**   *Old French* 'I will not doubt'
—Strangways (of Well).

177. **Nostre roy et nostre foy**   *Old French* 'Our king and our faith'
—Neel.

178. **One faith, one king, one law**
—Bourk.

179. **Ore lego, corde credo**   *Latin* 'I read with my face (i.e., eyes), I believe with my heart'
—Hamilton (of Cairness).

180. **Patria cara, carior fides**   *Latin* 'My country is dear, my faith dearer'
—Nicolas, Nicholas, Thomson.

181. **Patria veritas fides**   *Latin* 'Country, truth, faith'
—Everett (U.S.).

182. **Per fidem et constantiam**   *Latin* 'Through faith and constancy'
—Schiefflin (U.S.).

183. **Per fidem et patientiam**   *Latin* 'Through faith and patience'
—Broomhead-Colton-Fox.

184. **Per fidem omnia**   *Latin* 'All through faith'
—Howard.

185. **Per fidem vinco**   *Latin* 'I conquer through faith'
—Eastwood.

186. **Persevera Deoque confido**   *Latin* 'Persevere and trust in God'
—Brown.

187. **Pour la foi**   *French* 'For the faith'
—Lawes.

188. **Pride in our past, faith in our future**
—Hertford B. C., U.K.

189. **Pride in the past/ Faith in the future**
—Hastings College, Hastings, Nebraska.

190. **Prisca fides**   *Latin* 'Ancient faith'
—Glasford.

191. **Prist en foyt**   *Old French* 'Ready in faith'
—Barlow.

192. **Prius mori quam fidem fallere** *Latin* 'Rather die than break faith'
— Drummond (of Uxbridge).

193. **Pro avitâ fide** *Latin* 'For the faith of our forefathers'
— Brooke.

194. **Pro fide** *Latin* 'For the faith'
— Howard.

195. **Pro fide, lege, et rege** *Latin* 'For faith, laws, and king'
— Order of the White Eagle (Polish).

196. **Pro fide ac patria** *Latin* 'For my faith and country'
— Longe.

197. **Pro fide et patria** *Latin* 'For faith and country'
— Daniell, Johann Georg II, Elector of Saxony (1613–80).

198. **Pro fide rege et patria pugno** *Latin* 'I fight for the faith, king, and country'
— Lentaigne, O'Neill.

199. **Pro rege ac fide audax** *Latin* 'Bold for king and faith'
— Bideford B. C., U.K.

200. **Pro rege et religione** *Latin* 'For my king and faith'
— Boycott (Co. Salop).

201. **Pure foy ma joye** *Old French* 'True faith is my delight'
— Purefoy (of Leicestershire).

202. **Qui croit en Dieu croix** *French* 'He who believes in God believes in the cross'
— Vail (U.S.).

203. **Qui perde la foye n'a plus de perdre** *Old French* 'Who loses faith has no more to lose'
— Hart.

204. **Robur atque fides** *Latin* 'Strength and faith'
— Whitaker.

205. **Salus in fide** *Latin* 'Salvation through faith'
— Magrath.

206. **Sancta clavis coeli fides** *Latin* 'The sacred key of heaven is faith'
— Sankey.

207. **Scientia vera cum fide pura** *Latin* 'True knowledge with pure faith'
— Beloit College, Beloit, Wisconsin.

208. **Scio cui credidi** *Latin* 'I know whom I have believed'
—Gaskell (of York), Milnes; Heinrich Julius, Duke of Braunschweig- Wolfenbüttel (1564–1613).

209. **Scuto fidei** *Latin* 'By the shield of faith'
—Morris (Bt.).

210. **Secundat vera fides** *Latin* 'True faith prospers'
—Ogilvy (of Banff).

211. **Servabo fidem** *Latin* 'I will keep the faith'
—Dutton, Johnson (of Runcorn), Sherborne (B.).

212. **Serva fidem** *Latin* 'Keep faith'
—Corfield, Sandberg.

213. **Signum fidei** *Latin* 'The sign of faith'
—Saint Mary's College of California, Moraga, California.

214. **Sincera fide agere** *Latin* 'To act with faith sincere'
—Birch.

215. **Sine fraude fides** *Latin* 'Faith without deceit'
—Johnston.

216. **Sine labe fides** *Latin* 'Faith unspotted'
—Lockhart (of Cleghorn).

217. **Sit sine labe fides** *Latin* 'Let faith be unspotted'
—Peters.

218. **Spero ut fidelis** *Latin* 'I hope as being faithful'
—Mynors, Baskerville.

219. **Spes et fides** *Latin* 'Hope and faith'
—Chamberlain (Bt.).

220. **Stat fortis in fide** *Latin* 'He stands firm in faith'
—Rochfort.

221. **Stat promissa fides** *Latin* 'Promised faith abides'
—Leslie, Lesley.

222. **Sto cado fide et armis** *Latin* 'I stand and fall by faith and arms'
—Farquhar.

223. **Sto pro fide** *Latin* 'I stand firm for my faith'
—Stow.

224. **Tenax et fide** *Latin* 'Persevering and with faith'
—Smith (of East Stoke, Bt.).

225. **Tenax in fide** *Latin* 'Steadfast in faith'
—Smith.

226. **Tendit ad astra fides** *Latin* 'Faith reaches towards heaven'
—Burns.

227. **Terra, mare, fide** *Latin* 'By the earth, sea, and faith'
—Campbell.

228. **Terra marique fide** *Latin* 'With faith by land and sea'
—Campbell (of Ardintenny), Billing (co. Norfolk).

229. **Tiens ta foy** *Old French* 'Keep your faith'
—Bathurst (E.),. Kemp, Mignon.

230. **Tout en foy** *Old French* 'All in faith'
—Sutcliffe.

231. **Tristis et fidelis** *Latin* 'Sad and faithful'
—D'Alton.

232. **Ubi amor ibi fides** *Latin* 'Where there is love there is faith'
—Duckinfield (Bt.), Garratt, Newman (co. Devon, Bt.),
Aubrey (co. Hereford).

233. **Ubi fides ibi lux et robur** *Latin* 'Where there is faith there is light
and strength'
—Birkenhead C. B. C., U.K.

234. **Ubi fides ibi vires** *Latin* 'Where faith is there is strength'
—Hussey.

235. **Un Dieu, un roy, un foy** *Old French* 'One God, one king, one
faith'
—Curle, Rush.

236. **Une foi** *French* 'One faith'
—Curle.

237. **Une foy, une loy** *Old French* 'One faith, one law'
—Sorel.

238. **Une foy mesme** *Old French* 'One same faith'
—Gilpin.

239. **Une pure foi** *French* 'A pure faith'
—Hewitt (Co. Glamorgan).

240. **Ung Dieu, ung loy, ung foy** *Old French* 'One God, one law, one
faith'
—Burke (of St. Cleras).

241. **Ung roy, ung foy, ung loy** *Old French* 'One king, one faith, one
law'
—Burke (of Marble Hill, Bt.), Burke (of Kilcoran, Owen,
and Clongowna), Clanricarde (M.), De Burgo (Bt.),
Rush.

242. **Ung sent ung soleil** *Old French* 'One faith, one sun'
—Lloyd-Verney, Verney.

243. **Unity and faith**
—Federation of Nigeria.

244. **Un peuple, un but, une foi**   *French* 'One people, one goal, one faith'
—Republic of Mali, Republic of Senegal.

245. **Un roy, une foy, une loy**   *Old French* 'One king, one faith, one law'
—De Burgh.

246. **Unser glaub ist der sieg, der die welt überwunden hatt**   *German* 'The victory that overcometh the world, even our faith'
—[1 John, v. 4.] August, Prince of Anhalt-Plötzkau (1575–1653).

247. **Vera trophaea fides**   *Latin* 'Faith is our true trophy'
—Swabey.

248. **Vi et fide**   *Latin* 'By force and faith'
—Campbell.

249. **Vi et fide vivo**   *Latin* 'I live by force and faith'
—Nihell.

250. **Vince fide**   *Latin* 'Conquer by faith'
—Parry.

251. **Vires et fides**   *Latin* 'Strength and faith'
—Cowan.

252. **Virtute et fide**   *Latin* 'By valor and faith'
—Collins, WBeauvale (B.), Harley, Lamb, Melbourne (V.), Oxford (E.), Marriott.

253. **Virtute fideque**   *Latin* 'By virtue and faith'
—Elibank (B.), Murray, McMurray.

254. **Vis et fides**   *Latin* 'Strength and faith'
—Campbell (of Co. Hants and Dunoon, Scotland), Wyndham.

255. **Vita more fide**   *Latin* 'By hope, custom, and faith'
—Hanercroft.

256. **Vraye foy**   *Old French* 'True faith'
—Boswell (Bt.).

FAME   (*See also* HONOR; REPUTATION.)

1. **Chi semini vertu racoglia fama**   *Italian* 'Who sows virtue gathers fame'
—Coore (of Scruton Hall).

2. **Dant priscae decorum** *Latin* 'Deeds of antiquity confer renown'
—Stewart.

3. **Fama candidâ rosâ dulcior** *Latin* 'Fame is sweeter than the white rose'
—Taylor.

4. **Famae studiosus honestae** *Latin* 'Desirous of honourable fame'
—Browne.

5. **Famae venientis amore** *Latin* 'With the love of future fame'
—[Vergil, *Aen.* vi. 889.] Starky (of Spye Park and Bromham).

6. **Famae vestigia retinens** *Latin* 'Keeping to the footsteps of fame'
—Ennishowen.

7. **Famam extendere factis** *Latin* 'To extend fame by deeds'
—[Vergil, *Aen.* x. 467.] Galway (V.).

8. **Famam extendimus factis** *Latin* 'We extend our fame by our deeds'
—Vach (of Dawyck), Veitch.

9. **Fama perennis erit** *Latin* 'Thy fame shall be enduring'
—Wyborn.

10. **Fama sed virtus non moriatur** *Latin* 'Fame perishes, but not virtue'
—Ingersoll (U.S.).

11. **Fama semper vivet** *Latin* 'Our renown shall live forever'
—Liddell, Ravensworth (B.).

12. **Fama semper vivit** *Latin* 'Fame lives forever'
—Gason.

13. **Fama volat** *Latin* 'Rumor has wings'
—Town of Marseilles, France.

14. **Forma flos, fama flatus** *Latin* 'Beauty is a flower, fame a breath'
—Bagshawe (of Wormhill, co. Derby).

15. **Gloria principum felicitas seculi** *Latin* 'The fame of princes is the fortune of the century'
—Johann Friedrich, Duke of Braunschweig-Lüneburg (1625–79).

16. **Hwy peri clod na golud** *Welsh* 'Fame lasts longer than riches'
—Lloyd (of Rosindale and Aston).

17. **Non arbitrio popularis aurae** *Latin* 'Not by the caprice of popular applause'
—[after Horace, *Car.* iii. 2. 17.] Dale (of Ashborne).

18. **Non moritur cujus fama vivit**   *Latin* 'He dies not whose fame survives'
—Congreave (Bt.), Congreave.

19. **Palladia fama**   *Latin* 'Palladian fame'
—Inchbold.

20. **Per ardua fama**   *Latin* 'Through difficulties, fame'
—Whyte.

21. **Virtutem sequitur fama**   *Latin* 'Fame follows virtue'
—Dance.

FATE (*See also* DESTINATION.)

1. **Che sarà sarà**   *Italian* 'What will be will be'
—Bedford (D.), Russell (Bt.).

2. **Conduct is fate**
—De Beauvoir (Bt.).

3. **Curae cedit fatum**   *Latin* 'Fate gives way to caution'
—Thomson.

4. **Data fata secutus**   *Latin* 'Following my destiny'
—[Vergil, *Aen.* i. 382.] Archdale, Porter, St. John (B.), Streatfield.

5. **Every bullet has its billet**
—Vassall (of Milford Co. Southampton).

6. **Fata consiliis potiora**   *Latin* 'Fate is mightier than human plans'
—Wilhelm V, Landgrave of Hesse-Cassel (1602–37).

7. **Fata sequar**   *Latin* 'I shall pursue my fate'
—Van Brunt (U.S.), Van Buren (U.S.).

8. **Fata viam invenient**   *Latin* 'The fates will find a way'
—Spange, Van Sittart.

9. **Fata viam invenient**   *Latin* 'Fate will find a way'
—[Vergil, *Aen.* iii. 395.] Heinrich Julius, Duke of Braunschweig-Wolfenbüttel (1564–1613); Albrecht, Margrave of Brandenburg-Anspach (1620–67).

10. **Fata vim invenient**   *Latin* 'Fate will find the power'
—Ernst, Margrave of Brandenburg (1583–1613).

11. **Fato, nec fraude, nec astu**   *Latin* 'By fate, neither by fraud nor craft'
—Maximilian, Elector of Bavaria (1573–1651).

12. **Fato fortior virtus**   *Latin* 'Virtue is stronger than fate'
—Hertslet.

13. **Fato non merito**   *Latin* 'By fate not desert'
—Fitz-George.

14. **Fato prudentia major**   *Latin* 'Prudence is greater than fate'
—[Vergil, *Geor.* i. 416.] Cheney, Lomax (of Clayton);
Catherine de Medicis (1519–89).

15. **Fortuna mea in bello campo**   *Latin* 'My lot is in fair ground'
—Beauchamp (E.).

16. **Inevitabile fatum**   *Latin* 'Inevitable destiny'
—Kramer.

17. **In manibus Dei sortes meae**   *Latin* 'In the hands of God is my fate'
—Gustav Christoph, Margrave of Baden (1566–1609).

18. **In manibus Domini sorsque salusque mea**   *Latin* 'In the hands of the Lord are my fate and salvation'
—Marie Elisabeth, Countess of Oldenburg (1581–1619);
Anton Günther, last Count of Oldenburg and
Delmenhorst (1583–1667).

19. **In manibus Domini sortes meae**   *Latin* 'In the hands of the Lord is my fate'
—Georg III, Duke of Brieg (1611–64).

20. **Ino [*sic*] virtus et fata vocant**   *Latin* 'Thence virtue and fate call'
—Jones (U.S.).

21. **Invita sortem fortuna**   *Latin* 'Fate in spite of fortune'
—Knightley.

22. **Invitis ventis**   *Latin* 'In reluctant winds'
—Duport.

23. **Nil fatalia terrent**   *Latin* 'Things decreed by fate do not dismay us'
—Carse.

24. **Nunquam deorsum**   *Latin* 'Never downward'
—Graham (of Monargan).

25. **Ou le sort appelle**   *French* 'Where destiny calls'
—Francis.

26. **Qui sera sera**   *French* 'What will be, will be'
—Edgell, Betteason (of Seven Oakes), Wolferstan (co.
Suffolk).

27. **Quo fata trahunt** *Latin* 'Whither the fates lead'
—Albert, Archduke of Austria (1559–1621).

28. **Quo fata trahunt retrahuntque sequamur** *Latin* 'Whither the fates lead, forwards and backwards, let us follow'
—[Vergil, *Aen.* v. 709] Bernhard, Prince of Anhalt (1572–96).

29. **Quo fata vocant** *Latin* 'Whithersoever the fates call'
—De Lisle (B.), Bland, Russell (of Handsworth), Sidney (Bt.), Thurlow (B.).

30. **Quo virtus et fata vocat** *Latin* 'Where virtue and the fates call (me)'
—Ffolliott.

31. **Sic volvere parcas** *Latin* 'So the Fates determine'
—Reeves.

32. **Sit fors ter felix** *Latin* 'May your fate be thrice happy'
—Forster.

33. **Sors est contra me** *Latin* 'Fate is against me'
—Lewis.

34. **Sors mea a Domino** *Latin* 'My fate is from the Lord'
—Georg III, Duke of Brieg (1611–64).

35. **Sors omnia versat** *Latin* 'Fate whirls everything about'
—Philip.

36. **Tyde what may**
—Haig (of Bemerside).

37. **Victrix fortunae sapientia** *Latin* 'Wisdom overcomes fate'
—Friedrich, Duke of Saxony (1596–1622).

38. **Virtus superat fortunam** *Latin* 'Virtue prevails over fate'
—Johann Ernst, Prince of Anhalt (1578–1602).

FEAR

1. **Aimer sans crainte** *French* 'Love without fear'
—De Massue.

2. **Amor sine timore** *Latin* 'Love without fear'
—Reade.

3. **Be just, and fear not**
—Ashby, Atkins, Coleman, Hewitt, Lilford (V.), Payne, Peacock, Strange, Warren; Carlisle City and C. B. C., Pudsey B. C., U.K.

4. **Byddwch gyfiawn ac nag ofnwch** *Welsh* 'Be righteous, and fear not'

—Lewis (of Gilfach).

5. **Crainte refrainte** *French* 'Fear restrained'

—Poyntz.

6. **Das Weib so fürchtet Gott, nicht werden kan zu spot** *German* 'The woman who fears God can come to no scorn'

—Ludwig the Elder, Prince of Anstalt-Köthen (1579–1650).

7. **Deum time et dedecus** *Latin* 'Fear God and dishonor'

—Baddeley.

8. **D. F. D. H. I. D. W. A. (Die Furcht des Herrn ist der Weisheit Anfang)** *German* 'Fear of the Lord is the beginning of wisdom'

—[Ps., cxi. 10.] Dorothee Hedwig, Princess of Anhalt (1587–1608); Johann Sigismund, Elector of Brandenburg (1572–1619).

9. **Die Furcht des Herrn ist die Krone der Weisheit** *German* 'Fear of the Lord is the crown of wisdom'

—Bernhard VII, Prince of Anhalt (1540–70).

10. **Drede God and honour the king**

—Banquet room of Haddon Hall, Cheshire, England.

11. **Fac recte et nil time** *Latin* 'Do right and fear nothing'

—Jeffries, Hill.

12. **Fac recte nil time** *Latin* 'Do right, fear nothing'

—Ashworth.

13. **Fear not**

—Dawes.

14. **Fear nought**

—Ramsay.

15. **Fear one**

—Cozens-Hardy (Co. Norfolk).

16. **Fear to transgress**

—Clonmel (E.), Scott.

17. **Fido non timeo** *Latin* 'I trust, I do not fear'

—Hermon.

18. **Gottes furcht die schönste Tugend, Gewöhnt das Alter, zeirt die Jugend** *German* 'Fear of God is the fairest virtue; it reconciles old age, and adorns youth'

—Sophie, Princess of Anhalt (1654–1724).

19. **Gottes Furcht meine höchste Burg** *German* 'Fear of God is my highest stronghold'
  —Katherine, Duchess of Saxony (1602–49).

20. **Honorate, diligite, timete** *Latin* 'Honor, love, fear'
  —Moseley.

21. **Honore timore** *Latin* 'With honor and with fear'
  —Friedrich August I, Elector of Saxony (1670–1733).

22. **Horror ubique** *Latin* 'Terror everywhere'
  —Scots Guards, U.K.

23. **Ich fürchte and traue Gott in allen Dingen** *German* 'I fear and trust God in all things'
  —Katharine, Electress of Brandenburg (1541–1602).

24. **I force no friend, I fear no foe**
  —Farquharson.

25. **I. M. C. M. (In medio currere metuo)** *Latin* 'I fear to go in the middle'
  —Julius, Duke of Braunschweig-Wolfenbüttel (1529–89).

26. **Initium sapientiae timor Domini** *Latin* 'The fear of the Lord is the beginning of wisdom'
  —[Ps., cxi. 10.] Eberhard I, Duke of Württemberg (1445–95); Friedrich, Margrave of Brandenburg (1530–52); Johann August, Count of the Palatinate of Veldenz (1575–1611); Christian II, Elector of Saxony (1583–1611); Joachim, Margrave of Brandenburg (1583–1600); Johann Philipp, Duke of Saxony-Altenburg (1597–1639); Sophie, Princess of Anhalt (1654–1724); Karl Emil, Margrave of Brandenburg (1655–74).

27. **In prosperis time, in adversis spera** *Latin* 'In prosperity, fear, in adversity, hope'
  —Gabriel.

28. **Justam perficito nihil timeto** *Latin* 'Do what is just, fear nothing'
  —Kelly.

29. **Juste nec timide** *Latin* 'Be just and fear not'
  —Farnworth B. C., U.K.

30. **Justum perficito, nihil timeto** *Latin* 'Act justly, and you will fear nothing'
  —Rogers (of Yarlington Lodge).

31. **Justus esto, et non metue** *Latin* 'Be just, and fear not'
—Robson.

32. **Love every man, fear no man**
—Cropper, Thornburgh.

33. **Metuenda corolla draconis** *Latin* 'The dragon's crest is to be feared'
—Londonderry (M.), Stewart.

34. **Metuo secundis** *Latin* 'I am fearful in prosperity'
—Hodgeson, Uppleby (of Wootton).

35. **Mutare vel timere sperno** *Latin* 'I scorn to change or to fear'
—Beaufort (D.), Barnes, Bythesea, Somerset, Little Lever U. D. C., U.K.

36. **Nec cupias, nec metuas** *Latin* 'Neither desire nor fear'
—Hardwicke (E.), York, Yorke (of Erddig).

37. **Nec metuas, nec optes** *Latin* 'Neither fear nor desire'
—Coddington.

38. **Nec mutandus, nec metus** *Latin* 'Neither change nor fear'
—Rawlins.

39. **Nec spe, nec metu** *Latin* 'Neither in hope, nor in fear'
—Otto the Younger, Duke of Braunschweig-Lüneburg-Harburg (1528–1603).

40. **Nec spe nec metu** *Latin* 'Neither with hope nor fear'
—Read (U.S.).

41. **Nec sperno, nec timeo** *Latin* 'I neither despise nor fear'
—Ellames.

42. **Nec timeo, nec sperno** *Latin* 'I neither fear nor despise'
—Boyne (V.), Glover, Green (of Lichfield), Pagen, Shippard (Bt.).

43. **Nec timet, nec tumet** *Latin* 'He is neither timid nor arrogant'
—Lloyd.

44. **Nec timidè, nec temerè** *Latin* 'Neither timidly nor rashly'
—Forbes.

45. **Nec timidus, nec ferus** *Latin* 'Neither fearful nor brutal'
—Trotter.

46. **Nec timidus nec ferus** *Latin* 'Neither timid nor fierce'
—Trotter.

47. **Nec triste, nec trepidum** *Latin* 'Neither sad nor fearful'
—Trist.

48. **Nec tumidus, nec timidus**   *Latin* 'Neither tumid nor timid'
    —Guthrie.

49. **Nec vi standum, nec metu**   *Latin* 'We must stand neither by force nor fear'
    —Rawlins.

50. **Ne timeas recte faciendo**   *Latin* 'Fear not when acting right'
    —Hadderwick.

51. **Never fear**
    —Stewart (of Castlestewart and St. Fort).

52. **Nil temere, neque timore**   *Latin* 'Nothing rashly, nor with fear'
    —Berney (Bt.).

53. **Not rashly, nor with fear**
    —Harrison.

54. **Ofner na ofno angau**   *Welsh* 'Let him be feared who fears not death'
    —Lewis (of Greenmeadow, Co. Glamorgan), Bruce.

55. **Pelle timorem**   *Latin* 'Drive off fear'
    —Whatley.

56. **Pur sans peur**   *French* 'Pure without fear'
    —White.

57. **Qui craint Dieu, fort du tout**   *French* 'Who fears God is strong to resist everything'
    —Marie Elizabeth, Duchess of Saxony-Coburg (1638–87).

58. **Quis timet?**   *Latin* 'Who fears?'
    —Price (of Saintfield).

59. **Recte faciendo, neminem timeo**   *Latin* 'Acting justly, I fear nobody'
    —Cairncross.

60. **Recte faciendo neminem timeas**   *Latin* 'In acting justly fear no one'
    —Harvey (of Ickwell Bury), Robertson, Scott (of Betton).

61. **Richt do and fear na**
    —King.

62. **Semi mortuus qui timet**   *Latin* 'He is half dead who fears'
    —Cromwell.

63. **Semper in metu**   *Latin* 'At all times in fear'
    —Johann Casimir, Prince of Anhalt-Dessau (1596–1660).

64. **Sis justus, et ne timeas**   *Latin* 'Be just and fear not'
    —White.

65. **Sis justus nec timeas**   *Latin* 'Be just, fear not'
                                                —Garvey.

66. **Sperare timere est**   *Latin* 'To hope is to fear'
                                                —Ratcliff.

67. **Terrere nolo, timere nescio**   *Latin* 'I wish not to intimidate, and know not how to fear'
                                                —Dering (Bt.).

68. **Terrorem affero**   *Latin* 'I bring terror with me'
                                                —Scots Guards.

69. **Thue Recht scheu Nimant**   *German* 'Do right and fear nobody'
                    —Johann Friedrich III, Duke of Saxony (1538–65); Julius
                                Franz, Duke of Saxony-Lauenburg (1641–89).

70. **Time Deum, honora Caesarem**   *Latin* 'Fear God; honor the emperor'
                    —[after 1 Peter, ii. 17.] Julius Ernst, Duke of
                                Braunschweig-Lüneberg-Danneburg
                                (1571–1636); August, Duke of Saxony
                                (1589–1615).

71. **Time Deum et ne timeas**   *Latin* 'Fear God and fear no other'
                                                —Burnham.

72. **Timenti Dominum non deerit ullum bonum**   *Latin* 'To him that fears the Lord no good will be wanting'
                    —Philipp Sigismund, Duke of Braunschweig (1568–1623).

73. **Timor Dei nobilitas**   *Latin* 'The fear of God is nobility'
                                                —Lempriére.

74. **Timor Dei summa securitas**   *Latin* 'The fear of God is the greatest security'
                                —On a building in Louvigny, France.

75. **Timor Domini initium sapientiae (est)**   *Latin* 'The fear of the Lord is the beginning of wisdom'
                    —[Ps., cxi. 10.] Georg Wilhelm, Count of the Palatinate of
                                Birkenfeld (1591–1669); Magdalene Auguste, Duchess of
                                Saxony-Gotha and Altenburg (1679–1740).

76. **Tue Recht und Scheiwe niemand**   *German* 'Do right, and fear no man'
                    —Karl, Margrave of Baden (1598–1625).

77. **Tuta timens**   *Latin* 'Fearing safe things'
                                                —Leadbetter.

78. **Vae timido**   *Latin* 'Woe to the timid'
                                                —Maddison.

79. **Veritas sine timore**   *Latin* 'Truth without fear'
—Phelps (U.S.).

80. **Vérité sans peur**   *French* 'Truth without fear'
—Bedford, Gunning, Middleton (B.), Willoughby.

81. **Virtus sine metu**   *Latin* 'Virtue without fear'
—Howard.

82. **Walk in the fear of God**
—Walker.

83. **Who's afear'd?**
—Dorset C. C., U.K.

FEELINGS (*See also* HEART; LOVE.)

1. **Angliae cor**   *Latin* 'The heart of England'
—Hinckley U. D. C., U.K.

2. **Cor ad cor loquitur**   *Latin* 'Heart speaks to heart'
—Cardinal Newman College, St. Louis, Missouri.

3. **Corda serata fero**   *Latin* 'I bear a locked heart'
—Lockhart.

4. **Corda serata pando**   *Latin* 'I lay open locked hearts'
—Lockhart (Bt.).

5. **Corde et manu**   *Latin* 'With heart and soul'
—Clayhills.

6. **Corde et manu**   *Latin* 'With heart and hand'
—Steuart (of Auchlunkart), Stewart (of Carnousie), Goffdon.

7. **Corde fixam**   *Latin* 'Fixed in my heart'
—Godfrey.

8. **Corde manuque**   *Latin* 'With heart and hand'
—Gorden (of Invergordon).

9. **Corde mente manu**   *Latin* 'With heart, mind, and hand'
—Farie.

10. **Cor et manus**   *Latin* 'Heart and hand'
—McManus.

11. **Cor vulneratum**   *Latin* 'A wounded heart'
—Mack.

12. **Cuislean mo cridhe**   *Scots Gaelic* 'The beating of my heart'
—McDonnel.

13. **Cum corde** *Latin* 'With the heart'
—Drummond (of Cultmalundy).

14. **De bon cuer** *Old French* 'With good heart'
—Walton-le-Dale U. D. C., U.K.

15. **Heart and hand**
—Matheson.

16. **Heart of oak**
—Weyland (of Woodrising, Co. Norfolk).

17. **Manu et corde** *Latin* 'With heart and hand'
—Bates (of Denton).

18. **Mens et manus** *Latin* 'Heart and hand'
—Duncanson.

19. **Mente et manu** *Latin* 'With heart and hand'
—Glassford, Patrickson.

20. **Mente manuque** *Latin* 'With heart and hand'
—Farquhar (Bt.), Benshaw, Borthwick (of Stow).

21. **Mente manuque praesto** *Latin* 'Ready with heart and hand'
—Foulis (Bt.).

22. **Nolite cor opponere** *Latin* 'Do not oppose your heart'
—Wilhelm V, Duke of Bavaria (1548–1626).

23. **Semper cor caput Cabot** *Latin* 'Ever the heart, the head, and Cabot'
—Cabot (U.S.).

24. **Tam corde quam manu** *Latin* 'With the heart as well as with the hand'
—Maynard.

25. **Tout coeur** *French* 'All heart'
—Tuckerman (U.S.).

26. **With heart and hand**
—Dudgeon, Rule.

FELLOWSHIP (*See also* FRIENDSHIP.)

1. **Bon accord** *French* 'Good fellowship'
—Town of Aberdeen.

2. **Eruditio/ ductus/ societas** *Latin* 'Learning/ leadership/ fellowship'
—Indian River Community College, Ft. Pierce, Florida.

3. **Fellowship is life**
   —Walthamstow B. C., Coseley U. D. C., U.K.
4. **Fraternité, justice, travail** *French* 'Fraternity, justice, work'
   —Republic of Dahomey.
5. **Mecum habita** *Latin* 'Dwell with me'
   —Dun.
6. **Nid cadarn ond brodyrdde** *Welsh* 'No strength but in fellowship'
   —Merthyr Tydfil C. B. C., U.K.
7. **Quidni pro sodali?** *Latin* 'Why not for a companion?'
   —Burnet.
8. **Reddunt commercia mitem** *Latin* 'Social interchanges render (men) civilised'
   —Stewart (of Dundee).
9. **Societas scientia virtus** *Latin* 'Fellowship, knowledge, virtue'
   —Milner (U.S.).

FIDELITY (*See also* DEDICATION; DEVOTION; FAITH; PATRIOTISM; STEADFASTNESS; SUPPORT; TRUSTWORTHINESS.)

1. **Ab origine fidus** *Latin* 'Faithful from the first'
   —Maclaurin.
2. **Ad finem fidelis** *Latin* 'Faithful to the end'
   —Colville, Gilroy, Howson, Kerslake (of Banner Hall, co. Norfolk), Peto (Bt.), Wedderburn, Whitehead.
3. **Adhaereo** *Latin* 'I adhere'
   —Burrell.
4. **Ad mortem fidelis** *Latin* 'Faithful till death'
   —Candler (of Acomb).
5. **Aimez loyaulté** *French* 'Love loyalty'
   —Bolton (B.), Cowan (Bt.), Paulet (Bt.), Winchester (M.).
6. **A l'amy fidèle pour jamais** *Old French* 'Faithful forever to my friend'
   —Seymour.
7. **Alla corona fidissimo** *Italian* 'To the crown most faithful'
   —Leche (of Carden).
8. **Always**
   —Stevens.
9. **Always faithful**
   —M'Kenzie (Co. Inverness).

10. **A ma vie** *French* 'For my life'
—Order of the Ear of Corn and Ermine.

11. **Amico fidus ad aras** *Latin* 'Faithful to my friend as far as conscience permits, or even to death', lit., 'even to the altar'
—Rutherford (of Fairningtoun).

12. **Amour avec loyaulté** *French* 'Love with loyalty'
—Parr (of Kendal, co. of Westmoreland).

13. **Ancient and loyal**
—Wigan C. B. C., U.K.

14. **Armis et fide** *Latin* 'By arms and fidelity'
—Campbell (of Auchawilling).

15. **A toujours loyale** *French* 'Forever loyal'
—Fenwick (of Longframlington).

16. **A tout jour loill** *Old French* 'Always loyal'
—Fenwick.

17. **At servata fides perfectus amorque ditabunt** *Latin* 'But faith kept, and perfect love will enrich'
—Younge (Co. Stafford).

18. **Autre n'auray** *French* 'I will have none other'
—Order of the Golden Fleece (Spain).

19. **A vous entier** *French* 'For you entirely'
—John, Duke of Bedford, son of Henry IV.

20. **Aymez loyaulté** *Old French* 'Love loyalty'
—Bolton (B.), Cowan, Paulett, Stratton, Winchester (M.).

21. **Basis virtutum constantia** *Latin* 'Constancy is the foundation of virtue'
—Devereux, Hereford(V.).

22. **Be faithful**
—Adnew, Vans.

23. **Be traist** *Scots dialect* 'Be faithful'
—Innes (Bt.), Innes, Roxburghe (B.), Shiels.

24. **Be treist** *Scots dialect* 'Be faithful'
—Innes (of Innes).

25. **Be trewe**
—Hamilton-Tyndal-Bruce.

26. **Be true**
—M'Guarie.

27. **Be true and you shall never rue**
—Duff.

28. **Be trwgh and delygent**   *Middle English* 'Be true and diligent'
—Lucy (of Co. Warwick).

29. **Caesar aut nullus**   *Latin* 'Caesar or none'
—Wall.

30. **Celer atque fidelis**   *Latin* 'Active and faithful'
—Duine.

31. **Celeritas virtus fidelitas**   *Latin* 'Speed, virtue, and fidelity'
—Carpenter (U.S.).

32. **Cito fideliterque**   *Latin* 'Quickly and faithfully'
—Gutch.

33. **Civitas in bello in pace fidelis**   *Latin* 'In war and in peace a faithful city'
—Worcester City and C. B. C., U.K.

34. **Coeur Fidèle**   *French* 'A faithful heart'
—Hart.

35. **Conservata fides perfectus amorque ditabunt**   *Latin* 'Constant fidelity and perfect love will enrich'
—Yonge.

36. **Constancy**
—McKowan.

37. **Constans et fidelis**   *Latin* 'Constant and faithful'
—Arnett.

38. **Constans et fidelitate**   *Latin* 'Constant and with fidelity'
—Order of St. Hubert.

39. **Constans et prudens**   *Latin* 'Constant and prudent'
—Campbell (of Skerrington).

40. **Constans fidei**   *Latin* 'Constant to my faith'
—Cogan, Coggan, Colborne (B.), Ridley (Bt.), Ridley (V.).

41. **Constant**
—Gray.

42. **Constant and faithful**
—Macqueen.

43. **Constant and true**
—Rose (of Kilravock), Ross (of Belfast).

44. **Constant be**
—Bedfordshire C. C., U.K.

45. **Constant en tout**   *French* 'Constant in everything'
—Standish (of Duxburg).

46. **Constanter** *Latin* 'With constancy'
—Anton Ulrich, Duke of Braunschweig-Wolfenbüttel (1633–1714).

47. **Constanter ac non timide** *Latin* 'Constantly and fearlessly'
—Hemphill (B.).

48. **Constanter et pie** *Latin* 'With constancy and with piety'
—Christian II, Prince of Anhalt-Bernburg (1599–1656).

49. **Constanter et sincere** *Latin* 'With constancy and with sincerity'
—Johann Casimir, Count of the Palatinate of Lantern (1543–92); Joachim, Margrave of Brandenburg (1583–1600); Johann Casimir, Prince of Anhalt-Dessau (1596–1660); Rupert, Count of the Palatinate of Rhein (1619–82); Johann Ernst, Duke of Saxony-Saalfeld (1658–1729).

50. **Constant et discret et ang amour secret** *Old French* 'Constant and discreet, and secret in love'
—Bernhard, Duke of Saxony-Weimar (1604–39).

51. **Constantia** *Latin* 'By constancy'
—Goodall.

52. **Constantia et fidelitate** *Latin* 'By constancy and fidelity'
—Clarke (of Rossmore, bt.).

53. **Constantia et virtute** *Latin* 'By constancy and virtue'
—Amherst (E.).

54. **Cor unum et anima una** *Latin* 'Of one heart and of one soul'
—[Acts, iv. 32.] Wilhelm V, Duke of Bavaria (1548–1626).

55. **Cui debeo fidus** *Latin* 'Faithful to whom I owe faith'
—Craw.

56. **Cura et constantia** *Latin* 'By care and constancy'
—Cunningham, Cunninghame.

57. **Dat tela fidelitas** *Latin* 'Fidelity supplies weapons'
—Tipping.

58. **Deo, regi fidelis** *Latin* 'Faithful to God and the king'
—Atkinson, O'Daly.

59. **Deo et patriae fidelis** *Latin* 'Faithful to God and country'
—Atkinson.

60. **Deo et regi asto** *Latin* 'I stand by God and the king'
—Deacon.

61. **Deo et regi fidelis** *Latin* 'Faithful to God and the king'
—Daly.

62. **Deo fidelis et regi** *Latin* 'Faithful to God and king'
—Dunsandle (B.).

63. **Deo patriaeque fidelis** *Latin* 'Faithful to God and my country'
—Fagan.

64. **Deo Reipublicae et amicis esto semper fidelis** *Latin* 'Be ever faithful to God, the state, and friends'
—Duffield (U.S.).

65. **De tout mon coeur** *French* 'With all my heart'
—Boileau (Bt.), Pollen.

66. **Dextra fideque** *Latin* 'By my right hand and my fidelity'
—Bell.

67. **Die da treu sindt in der Liebe Gottes die list ihr [*sic*] ihm nicht nehmen** *German* 'Those who are faithful in the love of God he lets not be taken from him'
—Ludwig the Elder, Prince of Anhalt-Köthen (1579–1650).

68. **Diligenter et fideliter** *Latin* 'Diligently and faithfully'
—Allen.

69. **Disciplina, fide, perseverantia** *Latin* 'By discipline, fidelity, and perseverance'
—Duckworth (Bt.).

70. **Ditat servata fides** *Latin* 'Tried fidelity enriches'
—Archbald, Innes (of Edinburgh), Papillon.

71. **Either forever**
—Whitmore.

72. **En sincerité et fidelité ma vie je finiray** *Old French* 'In sincerity and fidelity shall I end my life'
—Anna Sophie, Duchess of Braunschweig-Wolfenbüttel (1598–1659).

73. **En tout fidèle** *French* 'Faithful in all things'
—Van Allen (U.S.).

74. **En tout loyale** *French* 'In all loyal'
—Carne.

75. **Esto fidelis** *Latin* 'Be faithful'
—Aubertin, Whitter.

76. **Esto fidelis usque ad finem** *Latin* 'Be faithful even to the end'
—Fydell.

77. **Esto fidelis usque ad mortem** *Latin* 'Be faithful unto death'
—Jones.

78. **Esto miles fidelis**   *Latin* 'Be thou a faithful soldier'
—Miles.

79. **Esto semper fidelis**   *Latin* 'Be ever faithful'
—Duffield (of Coverdale, Co. York), Yea (Bt.).

80. **Estote fideles**   *Latin* 'Be ye faithful'
—De Winton.

81. **Ever faithful**
—Gordon (of Tacachie).

82. **Expertus fidelem**   *Latin* 'Having found him faithful'
—Lewis (Bt.).

83. **Expertus fidelem Jupiter**   *Latin* 'Jove found him faithful'
—Cardinal Richelieu (1585–1642).

84. **Faithful**
—Robinson.

85. **Faithful and brave**
—Uniacke (U.S.).

86. **Faithful and true**
—Higgins.

87. **Faithful in adversity**
—Hamilton (of Barns, Scotland).

88. **Faithful to my unhappy country**
—Molyneux.

89. **Feal pero desdecado**   *Old Spanish* 'Faithful though fallen'
—Churchill.

90. **Ferme et fidèle**   *French* 'Firm and faithful'
—Le Maistre.

91. **Fey e fidalgia**   *Spanish* 'Faith and fidelity'
—Shelley (Bt.).

92. **Ffyddlawn beunydol**   *Welsh* 'Always faithful'
—Watkins (of Woodfield, near Droitwich).

93. **Ffyddlon at y gorfen**   *Welsh* 'Faithful to the end'
—James.

94. **Fide et amore**   *Latin* 'By fidelity and love'
—Carden (Bt.), Conway, Dicey, Gardiner (of Ely), Heart, Hertford (M.), Sadler, Chadwick (of Lynn, Co. Norfolk).

95. **Fide et armis**   *Latin* 'By fidelity and arms'
—Fairquhar.

96. **Fide et constantia**   *Latin* 'By fidelity and constancy'
—James (Co. Kent), Dixon.

97. **Fide et diligentia**   *Latin* 'With fidelity and diligence'
—Crawford, Crawfurd.

98. **Fide et fiducia**   *Latin* 'By fidelity and confidence'
—Blackman, Gilchrist, Harnage (Bt.), Primrose, Roseberry (E.), Thorlby, Watt.

99. **Fide et firme**   *Latin* 'Faithfully and firmly'
—Fairholm.

100. **Fide et integritate**   *Latin* 'By fidelity and integrity'
—Venning.

101. **Fide et Marte**   *Latin* 'By fidelity and military service'
—Ralston.

102. **Fide et virtute**   *Latin* 'By fidelity and valor'
—Brandling, Gladstone (Bt.), Goodwin, Ramsbottom, Rochead.

103. **Fidele**   *Latin* 'Faithfully'
—Roupell, Roussell.

104. **Fidèle et constant**   *French* 'Faithful and steadfast'
—Ernst Ludwig I, Duke of Saxony-Meiningen (1672–1724).

105. **Fidèle pour toujours**   *French* 'Trusty always'
—Longworth.

106. **Fideli certa merces**   *Latin* 'To the faithful there is certain reward'
—Bottomly, Bottomley, Morley (E.), Parker.

107. **Fideli certe merces**   *Latin* 'To the faithful man there is assuredly a reward'
—Saul or Saule.

108. **Fideli distillant sanguine corde**   *Latin* 'Their heart bleeds drop by drop for the faithful'
—Fayting.

109. **Fideli quod obstat?**   *Latin* 'What hinders the faithful?'
—Firebrace.

110. **Fidelis**   *Latin* 'Faithful'
—Crichton, Hill (of Oxon), Kenah, Shepherd, Waldy.

111. **Fidelis ad mortem**   *Latin* 'Faithful unto death'
—Buckler (U.S.).

112. **Fidelis ad urnam**   *Latin* 'Faithful to the tomb'
—Malone.

113. **Fidelis esto** *Latin* 'Be faithful'
—Fox.

114. **Fidelis et audax** *Latin* 'Faithful and bold'
—Russell.

115. **Fidelis et constans** *Latin* 'Faithful and steadfast'
—Bragge.

116. **Fidelis et generosus** *Latin* 'Faithful and generous'
—Durell.

117. **Fidelis et in bello fortis** *Latin* 'Faithful and brave in war'
—Gillespie.

118. **Fidelis et paratus** *Latin* 'Faithful and ready'
—Soote.

119. **Fidelis et suavis** *Latin* 'Faithful and gentle'
—Emery.

120. **Fidelis in adversis** *Latin* 'Faithful in adversity'
—Hamilton

121. **Fidelis in omnibus** *Latin* 'Faithful in all things'
—Collins.

122. **Fidelis inter perfidos** *Latin* 'Faithful amongst the unfaithful'
—Street.

123. **Fidelis morte** *Latin* 'Faithful in death'
—Paxton (U.S.).

124. **Fidelisque ad mortem** *Latin* 'And faithful to death'
—Taylor.

125. **Fidelissimus semper** *Latin* 'Most faithful always'
—Keating.

126. **Fidelis usque ad mortem** *Latin* 'Faithful even unto death'
—Sutton (of Elton).

127. **Fidelitas** *Latin* 'Fidelity'
—Purdie, Scot, Scott (of Edinburgh).

128. **Fidelitas et veritas** *Latin* 'Fidelity and truth'
—Peters.

129. **Fidelitas in adversis** *Latin* 'Fidelity in adversity'
—Fuller.

130. **Fidelitas regi et justitia mihi** *Latin* 'Fidelity to the king and justice to myself'
—Dawson.

131. **Fidelitas urbis salus regis** *Latin* 'The faithfulness of the city is the safety of the king'
— Bridgnorth B. C., U.K.

132. **Fidelitas/ veritas/ integritas** *Latin* 'Fidelity/ truth/ integrity'
— Salmon P. Chase College of Law of Northern Kentucky University, Covington, Kentucky.

133. **Fidelitas vincit** *Latin* 'Fidelity prevails'
— Cotton, Dunscombe.

134. **Fidelitate** *Latin* 'By fidelity'
— Newman.

135. **Fidelitate et amore** *Latin* 'By fidelity and love'
— Hathorn.

136. **Fidélité est de Dieu** *French* 'Fidelity is of God'
— Mellor, Powerscourt (V.), Wingfield.

137. **Fideliter** *Latin* 'Faithfully'
— Cunliffe (Bt.), Hamilton, Havelock (Bt.), Henry, Muckleston, Ralph, Ogilvy, Symonds, Teale.

138. **Fideliter, fortiter, feliciter** *Latin* 'Faithfully, bravely, and successfully'
— Scourfield (Bt.).

139. **Fideliter amo** *Latin* 'I love faithfully'
— Goldie-Scott.

140. **Fideliter et alacriter** *Latin* 'Faithfully and cheerfully'
— Walker.

141. **Fideliter et constanter** *Latin* 'Faithfully and with constancy'
— Fredriedrich I, Duke of Saxony-Gotha and Altenburg (1646–91); Order of Prince Ernst of Saxe-Coburg-Gotha.

142. **Fideliter et diligenter** *Latin* 'Faithfully and diligently'
— Graham (Bt.).

143. **Fideliter et recte** *Latin* 'Faithfully and uprightly'
— Pitches.

144. **Fideliter serva** *Latin* 'Perform faithfully'
— Norris (Co. Norfolk).

145. **Fideli tuta merces** *Latin* 'To a faithful man the reward is sure'
— Thornton.

146. **Fidem meam observabo** *Latin* 'I will keep my faith'
— Sheddon.

147. **Fides culpari metuens** *Latin* 'Fidelity fearful of blame'
—Yeldham.

148. **Fides fortuna fortior** *Latin* 'Fidelity is stronger than fortune'
—Hoey.

149. **Fides invicta triumphat** *Latin* 'Invincible fidelity triumphs'
—City of Gloucester.

150. **Fides servata ditat** *Latin* 'Tried fidelity enriches'
—Baillie.

151. **Fides servata secundat** *Latin* 'Tried fidelity makes prosperous'
—Napier (Bt.), Stirling.

152. **Fiducia creat fidem** *Latin* 'Confidence gives rise to fidelity'
—Ingoldsby.

153. **Fidus ad extremum** *Latin* 'Faithful to the last'
—Leith (of Whitehaugh).

154. **Fidus ad finem** *Latin* 'Faithful to the last'
—Jenkins.

155. **Fidus confido** *Latin* 'I as a faithful man confide'
—Pack.

156. **Fidus Deo et Regi** *Latin* 'Faithful to God and the King'
—De Bary.

157. **Fidus et audax** *Latin* 'Faithful and bold'
—Callaghan, Lismore (V.), Slade (Bt.).

158. **Fidus et fortit** *Latin* 'Faithful and brave'
—Scott (of Castle House, bt.).

159. **Fidus et suavis** *Latin* 'Faithful and agreeable'
—Emery.

160. **Fidus in arcanis** *Latin* 'Faithful in secret affairs'
—Stevenson.

161. **Fidus in arcanum** *Latin* 'Faithful in a secret affair'
—Stevenson.

162. **Fiel pero desdichado** *Spanish* 'Faithful, though unfortunate'
—Davis (U.S.), Marlborough (D.), Thanet (E.), Tufton.

163. **Firinneach gus a chrich** *Scots Gaelic* 'Faithful to the last'
—Macgregor.

164. **Firm and faithful**
—Cassidy.

165. **Firmè dum fide** *Latin* 'Firmly while faithfully'
—Heignie.

166. **Firmiter et fideliter** *Latin* 'Steadfastly and faithfully'
—Newman.

167. **Firmus et fidelis** *Latin* 'Steadfast and faithful'
—Marwick.

168. **Floreat semper fidelis civitas** *Latin* 'Let the faithful city ever flourish'
—Worcester City and C. B. C., U.K.

169. **Foi en loyalté** *French* 'Faith in loyalty'
—D'Anvers.

170. **Fort en loyalté** *French* 'Strong in loyalty'
—D'Anvers.

171. **Fortes fideles** *Latin* 'Brave and faithful'
—Stenhouse.

172. **Fort et fidèle** *French* 'Bold and faithful'
—Heaton-Ellis.

173. **Fort et loyal** *French* 'Bold and loyal'
—Selby.

174. **Forti et fidele nihil difficile** *Latin* 'For the strong and faithful nothing is difficult'
—Allen (U.S.).

175. **Forti et fideli nihil difficile** *Latin* 'To the brave and faithful man nothing is difficult'
—Deane, McCarthy, Muskerry (B.), O'Keefe.

176. **Fortis atque fidelis** *Latin* 'Brave and faithful'
—Savage (of Dublin).

177. **Fortis ceu leo fidus** *Latin* 'Strong as a lion and faithful'
—McBrayne.

178. **Fortis et fide** *Latin* 'Brave and faithfully'
—Carfrae (of Edinburgh).

179. **Fortis et fidelis** *Latin* 'Brave and faithful'
—Close, Beton, Bryan, Douglas, Dunbar, D'Alton, Finlay, Findlay, Fletcher, May, Hind, Fitzgerald, Orme, Lalor, Middleton.

180. **Fortis fidelis** *Latin* 'Brave, faithful'
—Stenhouse.

181. **Fortiter, fideliter, feliciter** *Latin* 'Boldly, faithfully, successfully'
—Hutchinson, Jackson, Monck (V.), Rathdowne (E.).

182. **Fortiter et fide** *Latin* 'Boldly and faithfully'
—Bunten (of Kilbride).

183. **Fortiter et fideliter** *Latin* 'Boldly and faithfully'
—Armitage, Briggs, Browne (of Browneshill), Cox, Fallous, Norton (of Kings-Norton), O'Fallon, Pennyman (Bt.), Peperrell, Wilson (of Knowle Hall), Oranmore and Browne (B.).

184. **Fortiter qui fide** *Latin* '(He acts) bravely, who (acts) faithfully'
—Hamilton.

185. **Fortitudine et fidelitate** *Latin* 'By fortitude and fidelity'
—Brown, Stuckey.

186. **Fortitudo et fidelitas** *Latin* 'Fortitude and fidelity'
—Town of Dumbarton.

187. **Franche, leal, et oyé** *Old French* 'Free, loyal, and open'
—Leeds (D.).

188. **Franco leale toge** *Spanish* 'Free and loyal is to thee'
—Dolphin.

189. **Germana fides candorque** *Latin* 'Genuine fidelity and sincerity'
—Falconberg.

190. **Gratitude and loyalty**
—Nagle.

191. **Haec generi incrementa fides** *Latin* 'Fidelity (gave) these honors to our race'
—Townshend (M.).

192. **Hold to the Most High**
—Seabury (U.S.).

193. **Honor fidelitatis praemium** *Latin* 'Honor is the reward of fidelity'
—Boston (B.), Irby.

194. **Hora è sempre** *Latin* 'Now and always'
—Denys (Bt.), Farmer, Pomfret (E.).

195. **Huic generi incrementa fides** *Latin* 'Faithfulness caused the increase of this family'
—Townshend (Co. Denbigh).

196. **I keep traist**
—Forbes.

197. **Impegerit fidus** *Latin* 'The faithful man may have stumbled'
—Constable.

198. **Impiger et fidus** *Latin* 'Alert and faithful'
—Constable.

199. **In arduis fidelis**   *Latin* 'Faithful in difficulties'
      —Balfour, Riverdale (B.).

200. **In constantia decus**   *Latin* '(There is) honor in constancy'
      —Coppard.

201. **In loyalty**
      —Semple.

202. **In recto fides**   *Latin* 'Faith in rectitude'
      —Dixon.

203. **In treu vast**   *O. German* 'Firm in fidelity'
      —Order of the Hospitallers of St. Hubert (Bavaria).

204. **In utroque fidelis**   *Latin* 'Faithful in either case'
      —Carey, Falkland (V.), Nash.

205. **Invictae fidelitatis praemium**   *Latin* 'The reward of faithfulness unconquered'
      —Hereford City Council, U.K.

206. **Invicta fidelitas praemium**   *Latin* 'The reward of invincible fidelity'
      —Hereford (E.).

207. **Irrupta copula**   *Latin* 'The tie unbroken'
      —Morris.

208. **Juncta virtuti fides**   *Latin* 'Fidelity joined to valor'
      —Murray.

209. **Justus et fidelis**   *Latin* 'Just and faithful'
      —Bomford.

210. **Labore et fide**   *Latin* 'By labor and loyalty'
      —Pritchard.

211. **L'amour et loyauté**   *French* 'Love and loyalty'
      —Swayne.

212. **Legi regi fidelis**   *Latin* 'Faithful to the king and law'
      —Barry, Sautry.

213. **Le nom, les armes, la loyauté**   *French* '(My) name, (my) arms, (my) loyalty'
      —Newland.

214. **Libera deinde fidelis**   *Latin* 'Free, therefore faithful'
      —Godalming B. C., U.K.

215. **Libertas et fidelitate**   *Latin* 'Freedom and loyalty'
      —Seal of State of West Virginia.

216. **Love and loyalty**
      —Crompton, Stansfield.

217. **Loyal, confidential** *French* 'Loyal, secret'
—Lawson.

218. **Loyal à la mort** *French* 'Loyal to death'
—Adair, Chatterton (Bt.), Ely (M.), Hepworth (of
Pontefract), Laforey (Bt.), Loftus; Loftus (Bt.),
Lyster (of Rowton Castle), Loftus (Co.
Norfolk), Shadwell.

219. **Loyal and industrious**
—Rowley Regis B. C., U.K.

220. **Loyal and true**
—Chatham B. C., U.K.

221. **Loyal au mort** *French* 'Loyal to the dead'
—Adair (Bt.), Atterbury (Bt.), Barwell, Drummond (of
Innermay), Laforey, Langton, Belsher, Loftus,
Roberson, Lyster, Pendrill.

222. **Loyal en tout** *French* 'Loyal in everything'
—Brown, Kenmare (E.).

223. **Loyal in adversity**
—Gerrard.

224. **Loyal je serai durant ma vie** *French* 'I will be loyal as long as I
live'
—Stourton (B.).

225. **Loyalle suys** *Old French* 'Be loyal'
—Ferrers.

226. **Loyalment je sers** *French* 'I serve loyally'
—Jephson, Norreys.

227. **Loyal suis je** *French* 'I am loyal'
—Shirley.

228. **Loyalté me lie** *Old French* 'Loyalty binds me'
—Margesson; Richard III.

229. **Loyal until death**
—White (Bt.).

230. **Loyaulte n'a honte** *Old French* 'Loyalty knows no shame'
—Clinton, Newcastle (D.).

231. **Loyauté me oblige** *French* 'Loyalty obliges me'
—Heathcote-Drummond-Willoughby.

232. **Loyauté m'oblige** *French* 'Loyalty binds me'
—Bertie, Lindsey (E.).

233. **Loyauté mon honneur**   *French* 'Loyalty my honor'
—Walker.

234. **Loyauté sans tache**   *French* 'Loyalty without defect'
—Dare.

235. **Loywf as thow fynds**   *Middle English* [sic]
—Tempest (of Broughton), Greenly.

236. **Magna vis fidelitatis**   *Latin* 'The force of fidelity is great'
—Newman.

237. **Mea culpa fides**   *Latin* 'Fidelity is my fault'
—Lawlor.

238. **Meliore fide quam fortuna**   *Latin* 'With better fidelity than fortune'
—Gresley (Bt.).

239. **Memor et fidelis**   *Latin* 'Mindful and faithful'
—Selsey (B.), Reed, Peachy.

240. **Mutare fidem nescio**   *Latin* 'I cannot break faith'
—Outram (Bt.).

241. **Nautae fida**   *Latin* 'Faithful to the sailor'
—Sirr.

242. **No country, no fatherland that does not keep faith**
—Confederate States of America.

243. **No heart more true**
—Hamilton (of Daichmont).

244. **Nunquam non fidelis**   *Latin* 'Never unfaithful'
—Moultrie, Moultray, Moutray, Moutrie.

245. **Officio et fide**   *Latin* 'By duty and fidelity'
—Fawcett.

246. **Paratus et fidelis**   *Latin* 'Ready and faithful'
—Carruthers, Hamond (Bt.), Walford.

247. **Par l'amour et la fidélité envers la patrie**   *French* 'By love and fidelity towards our country'
—Order of St. Catharine (Russia).

248. **Patriae et religioni fidelis**   *Latin* 'Faithful to country and religion'
—Teevan.

249. **Patriae fidelis**   *Latin* 'Faithful to my country'
—Tiffin, Wood.

250. **Patriae fidus**   *Latin* 'Faithful to my country'
—Lewis (Co. Glamorgan).

251. **Patriae infelici fidelis** *Latin* 'Faithful to my unhappy country'
—Courtown (E.), Molyneux, Montgomery, Stopford.

252. **Pen aur a chalon wir** *Welsh* 'A golden head and true heart'
—Watkins.

253. **Per constanza et speranza** *Italian* 'Through constancy and hope'
—Gomm.

254. **Perseverantia industria et fidelitas** *Latin* 'Perseverance, industry, and fidelity'
—Ravenscroft.

255. **Pietate, fide, et justicia** *Latin* 'With piety, fidelity, and justice'
—Wilhelm VI, Landgrave of Hesse-Cassel (1629–63).

256. **Pour loyaulté maintenir** *French* 'For maintaining loyalty'
—De Massue.

257. **Prisca constantia** *Latin* 'With ancient constancy'
—Newcastle-under-Lyme B. C., U.K.

258. **Prisca virtute fideque** *Latin* 'With ancient virtue and fidelity'
—Johann Adolf, Duke of Schleswig-Holstein-Sonderburg-Plön (1634–1704).

259. **Prius mori quam fidem fallere** *Latin* 'Rather die than break faith'
—Christian Wilhelm, Margrave of Brandenburg (1587–1665).

260. **Pro fide ablectus** *Latin* 'Chosen for fidelity'
—Ablett.

261. **Pro fide et merito** *Latin* 'For fidelity and merit'
—Order of St. Ferdinand and of Merit (Sicily).

262. **Promptus et fidelis** *Latin* 'Ready and faithful'
—Carruthers, Crondace.

263. **Pro virtute et fidelitate** *Latin* 'For valor and fidelity'
—Order of Military Merit (Hesse Cassel).

264. **Prudens, fidelis, et audax** *Latin* 'Prudent, faithful, and bold'
—Leigh.

265. **Prudentiâ et constantiâ** *Latin* 'With prudence and constancy'
—Denman (B.).

266. **Prudhomme et loyale** *French* 'Prudent and loyal'
—Prudham.

267. **Pure et loyale** *French* 'Pure and loyal'
—Amalie Elisabeth, Landgravine of Hesse-Cassel (1619–51).

268. **Quia fidem servasti**   *Latin* 'Because you have kept faith'
—Grieve.

269. **Rather die than be disloyal**
—Pearson (of Kippenrose).

270. **Ready and faithful**
—Gorham, Walker.

271. **Rebus in arduis constans**   *Latin* 'Constant in difficulties'
—Pembroke.

272. **Recte et fideliter**   *Latin* 'Rightly and faithfully'
—Gibson, Spode.

273. **Regi et patriae fidelis**   *Latin* 'Faithful to king and country'
—Norbury (B.).

274. **Regi fidelis**   *Latin* 'Faithful to the king'
—Moulson.

275. **Regi legi fidelis**   *Latin* 'Faithful to king and law'
—Barry.

276. **Regi patriaeque fidelis**   *Latin* 'Faithful to my king and country'
—Scott (of Great Barr, bt.).

277. **Regi regnoque fidelis**   *Latin* 'Faithful to king and kingdom'
—Pocock (Bt.), Simpson.

278. **Regi semper fidelis**   *Latin* 'Ever faithful to the king'
—Smythe (Bt.).

279. **Sagaciter, fideliter, constanter**   *Latin* 'Sagaciously, faithfully, constantly'
—Ward (B.).

280. **Scroghal an dhream**   *Scots Gaelic* 'The clan is loyal'
—McAlpin.

281. **Scroghal mo dhream**   *Scots Gaelic* 'My clan is loyal'
—McÀlpin, McGregor (of Camden Hill, Bt.), Macgregor, Mallet.

282. **Semel et semper**   *Latin* 'Once and always'
—Allcard, Swinburne (Bt.).

283. **Semper**   *Latin* 'Always'
—Dunfermline (E.), Seton, Grand Duchy of Tuscany.

284. **Semper constans**   *Latin* 'Always constant'
—Dymond.

285. **Semper constans et fidelis**   *Latin* 'Ever constant and faithful'
—Irton (of Irton), Lynch, Spoor.

286. **Semper constanter**   *Latin* 'Always with constancy'
—Greenhut.

287. **Semper et ubique fidelis**   *Latin* 'Always and everywhere faithful'
—Fitz-James.

288. **Semper fidelis**   *Latin* 'Ever faithful'
—Exeter City and C. B. C., U.K.

289. **Semper fidelis**   *Latin* 'Always faithful'
—Bonner, Broadmead, Bruce, Chesterman (of Wilts and
Beds), Dick, Edge (of Exeter), Formby, Garrett,
Houlton (of Farley Castle), Lynch (Bt.), Marriott,
Nicholas (Bt.), Nicholls, Newill, Onslow (E.),
Richardson, Smith (of Sydling, Bt.), Stirling (of
Gorat, Bt.), Stewart, Steuart (of Ballechin), Taylor;
Devonshire Regiment; United States Marine Corps.

290. **Semper fidelis, mutare sperno**   *Latin* 'Ever faithful, I scorn to
change'
—Worcester City and C. B. C., U.K.

291. **Semper fidelis esto**   *Latin* 'Be always faithful'
—Spence.

292. **Semper fidelis et audax**   *Latin* 'Always faithful and brave'
—Moore, O'More.

293. **Semper fidus**   *Latin* 'Always faithful'
—Leith (of Over-Barns).

294. **Sempre fidèle**   *French* 'Always faithful'
—Du Boulay.

295. **Senzillo y leal**   *Spanish* 'Upright and loyal'
—Wilhelm, Prince of Anhalt-Bernburg-Harzgerode
(1643–1709).

296. **Servatum sincere**   *Latin* 'Kept faithfully'
—Prevost (Bt.).

297. **Seur et loyal**   *French* 'Sure and loyal'
—Colbarne.

298. **Sic fidem teneo**   *Latin* 'Thus I keep faith'
—Molesworth (Bt.), Welford.

299. **Sic fidus ut robur**   *Latin* 'True as oak'
—Stirling.

300. **Sincere et constanter**   *Latin* 'With sincerity and constancy'
—Georg Friedrich Karl, Margrave of Brandenburg-Baireuth (1688–1735); Christian Ludwig, Duke of Braunschweig-Lüneburg-Zelle (1622–65); Ernst August, Duke of Saxony-Weimar (1688–1741).

301. **Soyez fiel**   *Old French* 'Be faithful'
—Yates.

302. **Stolz und treu**   *German* 'Proud and true'
—Cram (U.S.).

303. **Suis ducibus ubique fidelis**   *Latin* 'Faithful everywhere to his chiefs'
—Le Quesne.

304. **Sur et loyal**   *French* 'Sure and loyal'
—Wild.

305. **Swift and true**
—Fust.

306. **Tam audax quam fidelis**   *Latin* 'As brave as faithful'
—Roxburgh.

307. **Tam fidus quam fixus**   *Latin* 'Equally faithful as steadfast'
—Stewart.

308. **Tenax et fidelis**   *Latin* 'Steadfast and faithful'
—Abdy (Bt.), Carrington (B.), Dartford B. C., U.K., Smith, Tennant (of Skipton).

309. **Tenax et fidus**   *Latin* 'Persevering and faithful'
—Hebbert.

310. **Ter fidelis**   *Latin* 'Thrice faithful'
—Slack.

311. **Toujours**   *French* 'Always'
—Le Feuvre.

312. **Toujours fidèle**   *French* 'Always faithful'
—Bladen, Beauchamp, Hickman, Hairstanes, Mercier, Mill, Proctor (Bt.), Holford (of Buckland), Fenwick, Wallington, Waters.

313. **Toujours loyale**   *French* 'Always loyal'
—Fenwicke, Perkins (of Sutton Coldfield), Stule.

314. **Tous jours loyal**   *Old French* 'Always loyal'
—Craufurd, Benwick-Clennell; Fenwick.

315. **Tout jour fidèle**   *Old French* 'Always faithful'
—Ogilvie.

316. **Touts jours fidèle**   *Old French* 'Always faithful'
—Talbot.

317. **Treu und fest**   *German* 'Faithful and steadfast'
—Prince Albert, husband of Queen Victoria I; 11th (Prince Albert's Own) Hussars.

318. **Trow to you**
—Darell.

319. **True**
—Bruce (of Pittarthie), Horne.

320. **True and trusty**
—Heriot.

321. **True as the dial to the sun**
—Hyndman.

322. **True to the end**
—Home (E.), Home, Hume (Bt.), Campbell (of Powis, Bt.), Ferguson, Hume (of Humewood), Orr, Binning, Foreman.

323. **True to the last**
—Ferguson.

324. **True unto death**
—Baker.

325. **T. V. B. (Treu und beständig)**   *German* 'Faithful and steadfast'
—Johann Georg, Margrave of Brandenburg (1577–1624).

326. **Tyme tryeth troth**
—Trevellyn (Bt.).

327. **Ubique fidelis**   *Latin* 'Everywhere faithful'
—Hamilton (of Udstoun).

328. **Unity and loyalty**
—Borough of Chippenham.

329. **Usque ad mortem fidus**   *Latin* 'Faithful even to death'
—Ward (of Salhouse).

330. **Usque fidelis**   *Latin* 'Always faithful'
—Napier (of Balwhaple).

331. **Utrique fidelis**   *Latin* 'Faithful to both'
—Monmouthshire C. C., U.K.

332. **Valor e lealdad**   *Spanish* 'Valor and loyalty'
—Order of the Tower and Sword; Croft.

333. **Valour and loyalty**
—Grant.

334. **Verax et fidelis** *Latin* 'True and faithful'
—Peareth.

335. **Verus et fidelis** *Latin* 'True and faithful'
—Parkin.

336. **Verus et fidelis semper** *Latin* 'True and faithful ever'
—Aylward.

337. **Via una cor unum** *Latin* 'One way, one heart'
—Hart, McCorda.

338. **Vigilans et fidelis** *Latin* 'Watchful and faithful'
—Wilson.

339. **Virtus fides fortitudo** *Latin* 'Virtue, fidelity, and fortitude'
—Spens.

340. **Virtute et fidelitate** *Latin* 'By valor and fidelity'
—Order of the Golden Lion (Hesse-Cassel); Blaikie, Crofts,
Goodsir, Lyons, Reeves.

341. **Virtuti et fidelitati** *Latin* 'For virtue and fidelity'
—Order of the Golden Lion.

342. **Vir tutus et fidelis** *Latin* 'A man safe and faithful'
—Bomford.

343. **Voor moed, beleid, trouw** *Dutch* 'For courage, prudence, and
fidelity'
—Order of Wilhelm (Netherlands).

344. **Vrai à la fin** *French* 'True to the end'
—Pike.

FIERCENESS (*See also* AGGRESSION; DEFIANCE.)

1. **Feroci fortior** *Latin* 'Bolder than the ferocious (boar)'
—Lockhart (of Birkhill).

2. **Ferox inimicis** *Latin* 'Fierce to his enemies'
—Sykes (of Leeds).

3. **Fortis esto, non ferox** *Latin* 'Be brave, not ferocious'
—Wintringham (Bt.).

4. **Fortis ferox et celer** *Latin* 'Strong, fierce, and swift'
—McCarthy.

5. **Fortis non ferox** *Latin* 'Brave, not fierce'
—Stockes, Stokes.

6. **Luceo et terreo** *Latin* 'I shine and terrify'
—Allan.

7. **Nec timidus, nec ferus** *Latin* 'Neither fearful nor brutal'
—Trotter.

8. **Nec timidus nec ferus** *Latin* 'Neither timid nor fierce'
—Trotter.

9. **Redoubtable et Fougueux** *French* 'Formidable and Fiery'
—Harvey (of Chigwell).

FINISH

1. **A. B. D. E. (Anfang bedenk das Ende)** *German* 'At the beginning consider the end'
—Bruno II, Count of Mansfeld (1545–1615).

2. **Beatus qui implevit** *Latin* 'Blessed is he who has finished (his task)'
—Bingley.

3. **Bon fin** *French* 'A good end'
—Graham.

4. **Completur** *Latin* 'It is finished'
—Arnot.

5. **Consider the end**
—Milroy, Rosher.

6. **Finem prospiciens** *Latin* 'Looking to the end'
—Turner.

7. **Finem respice** *Latin* 'Consider the end'
—Bligh, Brooke, Collis, Darnley (E.), Hall (of Grappenhall), Pattenson.

8. **Finis coronat opus** *Latin* 'The end crowns the work'
—Finnis, Baker (of Ashcombe, Bt.), Barnet, Bayle, Crosthwaite.

9. **La fin couronne les oeuvres** *French* 'The end crowns the works'
—Yarker (of Leyburn).

10. **Look to the end, saith Kennedy**
—Kennedy.

11. **Regard the end**
—Ripley (U.S.).

12. **Respice finem** *Latin* 'Regard the end'
—Fisher, Lucas, Priestly; Newmarket U. D. C., U.K.

13. **Respice fines** *Latin* 'Consider the end'
—Ovington.

14. **Sine fine** *Latin* 'Without end'
—Crichton, McGill, Makgill, Maitland.

15. **Tout fin fait** *French* 'Everything comes to an end'
—St. Hill.

16. **Vise à la fin** *French* 'Look to the end'
—Calder, Home (Bt.).

FIRE

1. **And the bush was not consumed**
—Jewish Theological Seminary of America, New York City, New York.

2. **Ferte cito flammas** *Latin* 'Bear fire quickly'
—Grant.

3. **Feu sert et sauve** *French* 'Fire presses on and saves'
—Fels (U.S.).

4. **Flagror non consumor** *Latin* 'I am burned but not consumed'
—Guerrant (U.S.).

5. **I burn weil, I see**
—McLeod.

6. **Igne constricto, vita secura** *Latin* 'Fire being restrained life is secure'
—Sir Humphrey Davy (1778–1829).

7. **Igne et ferro** *Latin* 'Fire and iron'
—Hickman (Bt.).

8. **Lampada tradam** *Latin* 'I will pass on the torch'
—Whewell.

9. **Nec ferro, nec igne** *Latin* 'Neither by sword nor fire'
—McKaile.

10. **Nec ferro nec igni** *Latin* 'Neither by sword nor by fire'
—Appleby B. C., U.K.

11. **Per ignem per gladium** *Latin* 'By fire and sword'
—Welbey (Bt.).

12. **Per saxa per ignes** *Latin* 'By rocks, by fires'
—Smith.

13. **Per saxa per ignes fortiter et recte** *Latin* 'Through rocks, through fires, bravely and rightly'
—Elliot (U.S.).

14. **Salvus in igne** *Latin* 'Safe in fire'
—Trivett (of Penshurst).

15. **Terra, aqua, ignis, sal, spiritus, sulphur, Sol, Venus, Mercurius** *Latin* 'Land, water, fire, salt, spirit, sulphur, Sun, Venus, Mercury'
—Irvine.

FLEXIBILITY (*See also* CONCILIATION.)

1. **Flectar non frangar** *Latin* 'I shall bend, not break'
—Garneys.

2. **Flectas non frangas** *Latin* 'Bend, you will not break'
—Hoole.

3. **Flecti non frangi** *Latin* 'To be bent not to be broken'
—Palmerston (V.), Phillips.

4. **Salix flectitur sed non frangitur** *Latin* 'The willow bends but does not break'
—De Salis.

5. **Sto, mobilis** *Latin* 'I stand, but am easily moved'
—Drummond.

FLORA (*See also* AGRICULTURE.)

1. **Amantes ardua dumos** *Latin* 'The thorns which love the hills'
—[from Vergil, *Georg.* III. 315.] Thornhill.

2. **Amicta vitibus ulmo** *Latin* 'An elm covered with vine'
—Elmsall.

3. **Ante omnia sylvae** *Latin* 'The woods (*or* forests) before all things'
—Forrester, Forster, Woods.

4. **Archoille** 'The woody hill'
—McGregor (Bt.).

5. **Armat spina rosas** *Latin* 'The thorn is the defense of the rose'
—Rose.

6. **Armat spina rosas** *Latin* 'The thorn is the arms of the rose'
—Rose.

7. **Auch Tulpen darf man lieben** *German* 'One may even love tulips'
—Updike (U.S.).

8. **Candide comme la fleur** *French* 'Fair as the flower'
—Fenton.

9. **Dabunt aspera rosas** *Latin* 'Rough ground will produce roses'
—Mushet.

10. **De marisco** *Latin* 'From the bulrush (marsh)'
—Marsh.

11. **Dum in arborem** *Latin* 'Until grown into a tree'
—Hamilton.

12. **Ecce ferunt calathis musae mihi lilia plenis** *Latin* 'Look, the muses bring lilies to me in full baskets'
—[after Vergil, *Eclogues* 2. 46.] Cram (U.S.).

13. **En la rose je fleurie** *French* 'I flourish in the rose'
—Lennox, Richmond (D.).

14. **Fama candidâ rosâ dulcior** *Latin* 'Fame is sweeter than the white rose'
—Taylor.

15. **Flores curat Deus** *Latin* 'God careth for the flowers'
—Flowers.

16. **Floriferis ut apes in saltibus** *Latin* 'Flowery like a bee in the glades'
—[Lucretius, *De Rerum Natura*, iii. 11.] Williams (U.S.).

17. **Floruit fraxinus [*sic*]** Latin
—Ashcroft.

18. **Forma flos, fama flatus** *Latin* 'Beauty is a flower, fame a breath'
—Bagshawe (of Wormhill, co. Derby).

19. **Lauro resurgo** *Latin* 'I rise again with the laurel'
—Lorain.

20. **Laurus crescit in arduis** *Latin* 'The laurel grows in steep places'
—Rainier.

21. **Lilia candorem pectus Leo nobile monstrat** *Latin* 'Lilies show a bright white, the lion a noble heart'
—Goodwin.

22. **Liliae praelucent telis** *Latin* 'Lilies outshine weapons of war'
—Webber.

23. **Lux mihi laurus** *Latin* 'The laurel is my light'
—Chambers.

24. **Mare ditat, rosa decorat**   *Latin* 'The sea enriches and the rose adorns'
—Town of Montrose.

25. **Mare ditat flores decorant**   *Latin* 'The sea enriches and the flowers adorn'
—Exmouth U. D. C., U.K.

26. **Nulla rosa sine spinis**   *Latin* 'No rose without thorns'
—Ilbert (Co. Devon).

27. **Nunc cinis, ante rosa**   *Latin* 'Now ashes, formerly a rose'
—August, Count von der Lippe (d. 1701).

28. **Nunquam fallentis termes olivae**   *Latin* 'A branch of the never-failing olive'
—Oliver.

29. **Oriens sylva**   *Latin* 'Rising from the wood'
—Eastwood.

30. **Quercus**   *Latin* 'The oak'
—Wright.

31. **Quercus glandifera amica porcis**   *Latin* 'The acorn-bearing oak is kind to pigs'
—Allen.

32. **Rosa concordiae signum**   *Latin* 'A rose, the emblem of harmony'
—Northamptonshire C. C., U.K.

33. **Rosam ne rode**   *Latin* 'Gnaw not the rose'
—Cashen, Ross.

34. **Rosam qui meruit ferat**   *Latin* 'Let him bear the rose who has deserved it'
—Price.

35. **Rosa petit coelum**   *Latin* 'The rose seeks heaven'
—Rose, Rous.

36. **Rosario**   *Latin* 'In a bed of roses'
—Harvey.

37. **Rosa sine spina**   *Latin* 'The rose without a thorn'
—Penrose, Wadman.

38. **Rosis coronat spina**   *Latin* 'The thorn crowns with roses'
—Forbes (of Corse).

39. **Rutilans rosa sine spina**   *Latin* 'A glittering rose without a thorn'
—Queen Elizabeth I.

40. **Saepe creat pulchras aspera spina rosas**   *Latin* 'The sharp thorn often bears beautiful roses'
         —Thorn.

41. **Sicut lilium**   *Latin* 'Like the lily'
     —[after Matt., vi. 28.] Magdalen College School, Oxford, U.K.

42. **Sit sine spina**   *Latin* 'Let it be without thorn'
         —Cay (of Charlton).

43. **The tree drops acorns**
         —Bally.

44. **Tot rami quot arbores**   *Latin* 'As many trees as there are branches'
         —Royal Asiatic Society.

45. **Veritas quasi rosa resplendet**   *Latin* 'The truth shows forth like a rose'
         —Trew (U.S.).

46. **Woodnotes wild**
         —Burns.

FLOURISHING (*See also* FRUIT; GROWTH; OFFSPRING; PROSPERITY; REBIRTH; SUCCESS.)

1. **Abscissa virescit**   *Latin* 'By pruning it grows green'
         —Bisset.

2. **Adhuc viresco**   *Latin* 'I am still growing strong'
         —Smollett.

3. **Alnus semper floreat**   *Latin* 'May the alder always flourish'
         —Aldersey.

4. **Amore floresco**   *Latin* 'I flourish with love'
         —Moore.

5. **A more floresco**   *Latin* 'I flourish according to my custom'
         —Moore.

6. **Antiquo decore virens**   *Latin* 'Flourishing by ancient glory'
     —Johann Georg II, Prince of Anhalt-Dessau (1627–93).

7. **Antiquum decus floreat**   *Latin* 'May its ancient glory flourish'
         —Oldbury B. C., U.K.

8. **Crescitur cultu**   *Latin* 'It is increased by cultivation'
     —Barton (of Swinton and Stapleton Park).

9. **Deo aspirante virescit**   *Latin* 'With God's help he flourishes'
     —Ulrich, Duke of Pomerania (1587–1622).

10. **Diu virescit**   *Latin* 'He keeps fresh and green for a long time'
—Wood.

11. **Dum vivo, vireo**   *Latin* 'While I live I flourish'
—Latta.

12. **Efflorescent**   *Latin* 'They will flourish'
—Hirst.

13. **Efflorescent cornices dum micat sol**   *Latin* 'Rooks will flourish while the sun shines'
—Rooke (of Carlisle, Akenhead and Wigtoun).

14. **Effloresco**   *Latin* 'I bloom greatly'
—Cairns (of Pilmor).

15. **Elvenaca floreat vitis**   *Latin* 'May the vine of Elvion flourish'
—Elvin (of East Dereham).

16. **En la rose je fleurie**   *French* 'I flourish in the rose'
—Lennox, Richmond (D.).

17. **Et neglecta virescit**   *Latin* 'Even though neglected, it flourishes'
—Hamilton (of Kilbrackmont).

18. **Excisa viresco**   *Latin* 'Though cut off, I flourish green'
—Watson.

19. **Fecunditate**   *Latin* 'By fruitfulness'
—Hunter.

20. **Fecunditate afficior**   *Latin* 'I am blessed with fruitfulness'
—Hunter.

21. **Feliciter floret**   *Latin* 'It flourishes prosperously'
—Crawfurd.

22. **Floreant lauri**   *Latin* 'May the laurels flourish'
—Lowry.

23. **Floreat**   *Latin* 'May it flourish'
—Uttoxeter U. D. C., U.K.

24. **Floreat Actona**   *Latin* 'Let Acton flourish'
—Acton B. C., U.K.

25. **Floreat Ailesburia**   *Latin* 'May Aylesbury flourish'
—Aylesbury B. C., U.K.

26. **Floreat Bathon**   *Latin* 'May Bath flourish'
—Bath City and C. B. C., U.K.

27. **Floreat crux**   *Latin* 'May the cross flourish'
—Ladbrooke (Lynn, co. Norfolk).

28. **Floreat Ecclesia Anglicana**   *Latin* 'May the Church of England flourish'
      —Glastonbury B. C., U.K.

29. **Floreat Etona**   *Latin* 'May Eton flourish'
      —Eton U. D. C., U.K.; Eton College, U. K.

30. **Floreat Hova**   *Latin* 'May Hove flourish'
      —Hove B. C., U.K.

31. **Floreat imperii portus**   *Latin* 'Let the port of empire flourish'
      —Port of London Authority, U.K.

32. **Floreat industria**   *Latin* 'May industry flourish'
      —Batley B. C., Darlington C. B. C., U.K.

33. **Floreat majestas**   *Latin* 'Let majesty flourish'
      —Brown (Bt.).

34. **Floreat Rugbeia**   *Latin* 'May Rugby flourish'
      —Rugby B. C., U.K.

35. **Floreat Salopia**   *Latin* 'Let Shropshire flourish'
      —Salop C. C., Shrewsbury B. C., U.K., Taylor.

36. **Floreat semper fidelis civitas**   *Latin* 'Let the faithful city ever flourish'
      —Worcester City and C. B. C., U.K.

37. **Floreat Swansea**   *Latin* 'May Swansea flourish'
      —Swansea C. B. C., U.K.

38. **Floreat usque Leo**   *Latin* 'May the Lion ever flourish'
      —St. Mark's School, Windsor, U.K.

39. **Florens suo orbe monet**   *Latin* 'Flourishing it gives warning in its own circle'
      —Monnet (U.S.).

40. **Floreo in ungue leonis**   *Latin* 'I bloom in the lion's claw'
      —King.

41. **Florescit**   *Latin* 'He is flourishing'
      —Watson.

42. **Floruit floreat**   *Latin* 'May it flourish as it has flourished'
      —Newbury B. C., U.K.

43. **Flourish**
      —Rose.

44. **Flourish in all weathers**
      —Erving (U.S.).

45. **Fodina revirescens**   *Latin* 'A newly flourishing mine'
—Johann Friedrich, Duke of Braunschweig-Lüneburg
(1625–79).

46. **Holme semper viret**   *Latin* 'Holme always flourishes'
—Holme (of Paull-Holme).

47. **Hyeme viresco**   *Latin* 'I flourish in winter'
—Strode (of Strode).

48. **Indignante invidia florebit justus**   *Latin* 'The just man will flourish in spite of envy'
—Crosbie.

49. **Insperata floruit**   *Latin* 'It has flourished beyond expectation'
—Cleghorn, Watson.

50. **In tempestate floresco**   *Latin* 'I flourish in the tempest'
—Coffin, Pine.

51. **It shall flourish**
—Palmer.

52. **Jus floruit**   *Latin* 'Right has flourished'
—Taylor.

53. **Justus ut palma florebit**   *Latin* 'The righteous shall flourish like a palm tree'
—Friedrich, Margrave of Brandenburg (1588–1611);
Order of St. George (Bavaria).

54. **Labore omnia florent**   *Latin* 'All things flourish through industry'
—Drinkwater, Huntingdonshire C. C., U.K., Eccles B. C.,
U.K.

55. **Laeti acie florent**   *Latin* 'They flourish joyful in their keenness of mind'
—Eyre.

56. **Laeto aere florent**   *Latin* 'They flourish in glad air'
—Ayre.

57. **Let Glasgow flourish**
—Borough of Glasgow.

58. **Lord, let Glasgow flourish**
—Town of Glasgow.

59. **Me stante virebunt**   *Latin* 'While I exist they shall flourish'
—Tirwhit, Tyrwhitt (of Ketilly, Co. Lincoln).

60. **Non semper viret**   *Latin* 'It does not always thrive'
—Varnum (U.S.).

61. **Olim florebat** *Latin* 'It flourished at one time'
—Landel.

62. **Optivo cognomine crescit** *Latin* 'He flourishes under his adopted name'
—[Horace, *Ep.* iii. 2. 101.] Larpent (Bt.).

63. **Revirescam** *Latin* 'I shall flourish again'
—Dalgleish.

64. **Revirescat** *Latin* 'May it flourish again'
—Gould, Maxwell.

65. **Revirescimus** *Latin* 'We flourish again'
—Burnes, Glenelg (B.), Maxwell (of Everingham).

66. **Revirescit** *Latin* 'It flourishes again'
—Belches, Belshes (of Invernay).

67. **Reviresco** *Latin* 'I flourish again'
—Clarke, Mackenan, Maxwell (Bt.), Maxwell (of Maxwell), Rushton (of Elswick).

68. **Semper floreat** *Latin* 'Let it flourish forever'
—Inverarity.

69. **Semper virens** *Latin* 'Always flourishing'
—Broadwood.

70. **Semper virescens** *Latin* 'Always flourishing'
—Hamilton.

71. **Semper viridis** *Latin* 'Always flourishing'
—Green, Maxwell.

72. **Sepulto viresco** *Latin* 'I flourish for the one buried'
—Adml. Sir G. Eden-Hamond (Bt. G.C.B.).

73. **Sicut iris florebit** *Latin* 'He will be bright as the rainbow'
—Bor.

74. **Sicut quercus virescit industria** *Latin* 'Industry flourishes like the oak'
—Mansfield B. C., U.K.

75. **Sic virescit industria** *Latin* 'Thus industry flourishes'
—Stewart, Rotherham C. B. C., U.K.

76. **Sic viresco** *Latin* 'Thus I flourish'
—Christie (of Craigtoun), Christy.

77. **Soirbheachadh le Gleann Amuinn** *Gaelic* 'May Glenalmond flourish!'
—Glenalmond College, U.K.

78. **Sub cruce floreamus** *Latin* 'May we flourish beneath the cross'
—Poulton-le-Fylde U. D. C., U.K.

79. **Sub sole, sub umbra, virescens** *Latin* 'In sun or in shade, thriving'
—Erving (U.S.).

80. **Sub sole, sub umbra virens** *Latin* 'Flourishing both in sunshine and in shade'
—Irvine, Irving, Irwine, Winter-Irving.

81. **Sub sole viresco** *Latin* 'I flourish under the sun'
—Irvine (of Artamford).

82. **Te favente virebo** *Latin* 'Under thy favor I shall flourish'
—Grant (of Dalvey, bt.).

83. **Teneat, luceat, floreat, vi, virtute, et valore** *Latin* 'May it hold, shine, and flourish, by valor, virtue, and worth'
—Kenny (of Kilcloghar and Correndos, Co. Galway), Kenny (of Ballyflower, Co. Roscommon).

84. **Te stante virebo** *Latin* 'Whilst thou endurest I shall flourish'
—Temple.

85. **Velut arbor aevo** *Latin* 'May the tree thrive'
—University of Toronto, Toronto, Ontario, Canada.

86. **Vernon serper viret** *Latin* 'Vernon always flourishes'
—Vernon (B.), Vernon (of Hanbury Hall).

87. **Viget sub cruce** *Latin* 'He flourishes under the cross'
—Colquhon.

88. **Virebo** *Latin* 'I shall flourish'
—Hamilton.

89. **Virebo proficiente Deo** *Latin* 'Through God's grace shall I flourish'
—Friedrich Wilhelm, Elector of Brandenburg (1620–88).

90. **Virescit** *Latin* 'He flourishes'
—Moncrief, Moncrieff (Bt.), Stewart.

91. **Virescit vulnere** *Latin* 'It flourishes from a wound'
—Stewart.

92. **Viresco** *Latin* 'I flourish'
—Greenless, Monteath, Smellet, Stewart, Tailefer.

93. **Viresco et surgo** *Latin* 'I flourish and rise'
—Maxwell.

94. **Viret in aeternum** *Latin* 'It flourishes forever'
—13th Hussars.

95. **Viridis et fructifera** *Latin* 'Verdant and fruitful'
    —Hamilton.

96. **Viridis semper** *Latin* 'Always green'
    —Mathison.

97. **Vir non semper floret** *Latin* 'A man does not always flourish'
    —Davidson.

98. **Virtute viget** *Latin* 'He flourishes by virtue'
    —Keirie, Paton.

99. **Virtute viresco** *Latin* 'I flourish by virtue'
    —Paterson.

100. **Vivant dum virent** *Latin* 'Let them live while they flourish'
    —Forrest.

101. **Vivat Greatrakes, semper virescat** *Latin* 'Let Greatorex live and always flourish'
    —Greatorex.

102. **Vulnere viresco** *Latin* 'I flourish from a wound'
    —Stewart.

FOLLOWING (*See also* LEADERSHIP; PURSUIT.)

1. **Caelestia sequor** *Latin* 'I follow heavenly things'
    —McDonald, Monro.

2. **Duce natura sequor** *Latin* 'With nature as leader I follow'
    —Holyoke (U.S.).

3. **Duc me, sequar** *Latin* 'Lead on; I will follow'
    —Friedrich I, Duke of Saxony-Gotha and Altenburg (1646–91).

4. **Et suivez moi** *French* 'And follow me'
    —Hawley.

5. **Follow me**
    —Breadalbane (M.), Campbell (Bt.), Gurwood.

6. **I will follow**
    —Campbell.

7. **Lumen coeleste sequamur** *Latin* 'May we follow heavenly inspiration'
    —Beatie.

8. **Meliora sequimur** *Latin* 'We follow better things'
    —Eastbourne C. B. C., U.K.

9. **Non minima sed magna prosequor**   *Latin* 'I follow not trivial, but important things'
—Dobie.

10. **Our lamb has conquered: Let us follow him**
—Moravian Theological Seminary, Bethlehem, Pennsylvania.

11. **Praecedentibus insta**   *Latin* 'Press hard upon those who go before you'
—St. Germains (E.).

12. **Prosequor alis**   *Latin* 'I follow with wings'
—Graham (of Dumblane).

13. **Quo duxeris adsum**   *Latin* 'I attend whithersoever you lead'
—Ogilvy.

14. **Quo Minerva ducit, sequor**   *Latin* 'Where Minerva leads, I follow'
—Tayloe (U.S.).

15. **Semper ut te digna sequare**   *Latin* 'That you may always follow things worthy of you'
—Vernon.

16. **Sequamur**   *Latin* 'Let us follow'
—Oswald.

17. **Sequere me est voluntas Dei**   *Latin* 'Follow me, it is the will of God'
—Baldwin.

18. **Sequitando si giunge**   *Italian* 'By following, he comes up'
—Lambert (Bt.).

19. **Sequitur patrem non passibus aequis**   *Latin* 'He follows his father, but not with equal steps'
—Wilson.

20. **Sequor**   *Latin* 'I follow'
—Campbell, Mackinray, Mac Inroy.

21. **Sequor nec inferior**   *Latin* 'I follow, but am not inferior'
—Crewe (B.).

22. **Si j'avance, suivez-moi; si je fuis, tuez-moi; si je meurs, vengez-moi**   *French* 'If I advance, follow me; if I flee, kill me; if I die, avenge me'
—La Roche-Jaquelin.

23. **Strenue insequor**   *Latin* 'I follow strenuously'
—Luke.

24. **Suivant St. Pierre** *French* 'According to (*or* following) St. Peter'
—Knight.

25. **Suivez de l'ange** *French* 'Follow the angel'
—Long.

26. **Suivez moi** *French* 'Follow me'
—Brough (Bt.), Hawley.

27. **Summa rerum vestigia sequor** *Latin* 'I follow the highest tracks of things'
—Allan.

28. **Superna sequor** *Latin* 'I follow heavenly things'
—Ramsay (of Methven), Wardrop (of Strathavon).

29. **Te digna sequere** *Latin* 'Follow things worthy of you'
—Borlase, Parnell.

30. **Tu digna sequere** *Latin* 'Follow worthy things'
—Knight.

FORCE (*See also* FIERCENESS; HOSTILITY; POWER; STRENGTH.)

1. **Aut suavitate aut vi** *Latin* 'Either by gentleness or by force'
—Hopkins (Bt.).

2. **Aut vi aut suavitate** *Latin* 'Either by force or mildness'
—Griffith.

3. **Cogi qui potest nescit mori** *Latin* 'He who can be compelled knows not how to die'
—Norton.

4. **Comitate quam viribus** *Latin* 'By mildness rather than force'
—Hall.

5. **Consilio non impetu** *Latin* 'By counsel, not by force'
—Agnew (Bt.), Agnew (of Barnbarroch, Dalreagle, and Lochryan).

6. **I force no friend, I fear no foe**
—Farquharson.

7. **Inutilis vis est** *Latin* 'Force is useless'
—Owens.

8. **Marte vel arte** *Latin* 'By force or by art'
—Barnim XII, Duke of Pomerania zu Rügenwalde (1549–1603).

9. **My might makes my right**
—Mackey (U.S.).

10. **Nec vi, nec astutia** *Latin* 'Not by force nor by cunning'
—Waring.

11. **Nec vi standum, nec metu** *Latin* 'We must stand neither by force nor fear'
—Rawlins.

12. **No force alters their fashion**
—King Stephen, of England (1097–1154).

13. **Non invita** *Latin* 'Not by constraint'
—Smith.

14. **Non robore, sed vi** *Latin* 'Not by strength, but by force'
—Tippet (of Truro).

15. **Non vi, sed voluntate** *Latin* 'Not by force, but by good will'
—Boucher.

16. **Non vi sed mente** *Latin* 'Not by force but by mind'
—Lincolne.

17. **Obsequio non viribus** *Latin* 'By courtesy not by force'
—Hamilton.

18. **Ratione, non vi** *Latin* 'By reason, not by force'
—McTaggart (Bt.).

19. **Sapientia non violentia** *Latin* 'By wisdom, not by force'
—Philipp II, Duke of Pomerania (1573–1618).

20. **Tam in arte quam Marte** *Latin* 'As much in skill as in force'
—Milne.

21. **Valde et sapienter** *Latin* 'With force and wisdom'
—Musgrave, Sagar-Musgrave.

22. **Vi at tamen honore** *Latin* 'By force, yet with honor'
—Wyatt.

23. **Vi aut virtute** *Latin* 'By force or virtue'
—Chisholm.

24. **Via vi** *Latin* 'A way by force'
—Hayter.

25. **Vi corporis et animi** *Latin* 'By force of body and mind'
—Boddy.

26. **Vi et armis** *Latin* 'By force and arms'
—Armstrong.

27. **Vi et consiliis** *Latin* 'By force and counsels'
—Merewether.

28. **Vi et fide** *Latin* 'By force and faith'
—Campbell.

29. **Vi et fide vivo** *Latin* 'I live by force and faith'
—Nihell.

30. **Vi et libertate** *Latin* 'By force and liberty'
—Vibert.

31. **Vi et veritate** *Latin* 'By force and by truth'
—Sloan.

32. **Vim da vi honestae** *Latin* 'Give strength to honorable force'
—Davy.

33. **Vim vincit virtus** *Latin* 'Virtue prevails over force'
—Julius Friedrich, Duke of Württemberg (1588–1635).

34. **Vim vi repellere licet** *Latin* 'It is lawful to repel force by force'
—Gwyn (of Pant-y-cored), Gwyn-Holford.

35. **Vim vi repello** *Latin* 'I repel force by force'
—Baldwin.

36. **Vi non astutia** *Latin* 'By force, not cunning'
—Rumford.

37. **Vi nulla invertitur ordo** *Latin* 'Our order is not overthrown by any violence'
—Cordwainers' Company, Exeter.

38. **Virtute, non viribus** *Latin* 'By virtue, not by force'
—Derrick.

39. **Virtute, non viribus vincent** *Latin* 'They shall conquer by virtue, not by force'
—Vincent.

40. **Virtute non vi** *Latin* 'By virtue not by force'
—Barneby, Chivas, Shivez, Coppinger, Derrick, Rumsey.

41. **Vi si non consilio** *Latin* 'By force, if not by contrivance'
—Sherbrooke.

42. **Vis veritatis magna** *Latin* 'The force of truth is great'
—Hall.

43. **Vi vel suavitate** *Latin* 'By force or by mildness'
—Rochfort.

44. **Vi victus non coactus** *Latin* 'Overcome by force not compelled'
—Warter.

45. **Vi vivo et armis** *Latin* 'I live by force and arms'
—Hennessy, O'Hennessy.

FORESIGHT (*See also* FUTURE, THE; PREPAREDNESS; PRUDENCE; WARNING.)

1. **Alles mit Bedacht** *German* 'Everything with foresight'
   —August, Duke of Braunschweig-Wolfenbüttel (1579–1666).

2. **Foresight**
   —Hambrough (of Steephill Castle, Isle of Wight).

3. **Foresight is all**
   —Lidderdale (of St. Mary Isle, Scotland).

4. **Praevide, ne praeveniare** *Latin* 'Look forward, lest you be forestalled'
   —Timperley.

5. **Praevisa mala pereunt** *Latin* 'Foreseen misfortunes perish'
   —Hodges (of Hemsted), Twysden (Bt.), Winterbotham.

6. **Prospice** *Latin* 'Look forward'
   —Luard.

7. **Prospice, respice** *Latin* 'Look forward, look back'
   —Gossip.

8. **Providentia in adversis** *Latin* 'Foresight in difficulties'
   —Tollet.

9. **Sapiens qui prospicit** *Latin* 'He is wise who looks ahead'
   —Malvern College, U.K.

10. **Ultra aspicio** *Latin* 'I look beyond'
    —Melville.

11. **Video meliora** *Latin* 'I see better things'
    —Montefiore.

12. **Video meliora proboque** *Latin* 'I see and approve of better things'
    —Smythe-Owen.

FORGETTING (*See also* MEMORY; PAST, THE.)

1. **I forget not**
   —Campbell.

2. **Irreparabilium felix oblivio rerum** *Latin* 'Oblivion of the irretrievable is a boon'
   —Friedrich, Duke of Saxony (1599–1625).

3. **Jucunda oblivia vitae** *Latin* 'It is pleasant to forget (the calamities of) life'
   —Balguy.

4. **Lest ye forget**
   —95th (Derbyshire) Regiment, U.K.

5. **Nec beneficii immemor injuriae** *Latin* 'Forgetful of an injury, not of a kindness'
   —Walrond.

6. **Ne m'oubliez** *French* 'Forget me not'
   —Carsair.

7. **Ne obliviscaris** *Latin* 'Do not forget'
   —Campbell (Bt.), McTavish.

8. **Ne oubliez** *French* 'Do not forget'
   —Montrose (D.), Graham.

9. **Non oblitus** *Latin* 'Not forgetful'
   —McTavish.

10. **Non obliviscar** *Latin* 'I will not forget'
    —Colvil.

11. **N'oublie** *French* 'Do not forget'
    —Graham, Moure, Moir, Moil.

12. **N'oublies** *French* 'Do not forget'
    —Grehan.

13. **N'oubliez** *French* 'Do not forget'
    —Graham.

14. **Nunquam obliviscar** *Latin* 'I shall never forget'
    —McIver, Simpson (of Sittingbourn).

15. **Oblier ne puis** *French* 'I cannot forget'
    —Sir Henry Wyat (reign of Henry VIII).

16. **Obliviscar** *Latin* 'I shall forget'
    —Colvil, Colville.

17. **Obliviscaris** *Latin* 'Forget'
    —Campbell.

18. **Oublier ne puis** *French* 'I cannot forget'
    —Colville (B.), Colvil.

19. **Pour appendre oublier ne puis** *French* 'In order to learn, I cannot forget'
    —Palmer.

FORTIFICATIONS (*See also* DEFENSE.)

1. **Castra et nemus Strivilense** *Latin* 'The castle and wood of Stirling'

—Stirling.

2. **Er codiad y caer** *Welsh* 'From (since) the foundation of the fortress'

—Heaton.

3. **Hic murus aheneus** *Latin* 'Let this be your wall of brass'

—Macleod.

4. **It is fortified**

—MacConach.

5. **Moenibus crede ligneis** *Latin* 'Trust to wooden walls'

—Clarke.

6. **Turris tutissima virtus** *Latin* 'Virtue is the safest fortress'

—Carlyon.

FORTITUDE (*See also* COURAGE; SPIRIT; STEADFASTNESS; STRENGTH.)

1. **Animi fortitudo** *Latin* 'Fortitude of mind'

—Mecham.

2. **Constantia et fortitudine** *Latin* 'By constancy and fortitude'

—Herbert.

3. **Fide et fortitudine** *Latin* 'With faith and fortitude'

—Aubert, Brickdale, Cox, Capel, Essex (E.), Farquharson (of Invercauld), Hickson, Lawrence (of Llanelweth), McFarquhar, Noble (of Reresbie), Madan, Lloyd (of Coedmore), Penrith U. D. C., U.K.

4. **Fides et fortitudo** *Latin* 'Faith and fortitude'

—Moreland (U.S.); Ropner (Bt.).

5. **Fortitude in adversity**

—Parker (U.S.).

6. **Fortitudine** *Latin* 'With fortitude'

—Barry, D'Warris, Duerryhouse, Erskine (Bt.), Fairlie-Cunninghame (Bt.), McCray, McCrae, Hobson, Hall, Mowbray.

7. **Fortitudine crevi** *Latin* 'I have thrived by fortitude'

—Craven.

8. **Fortitudine et fidelitate** *Latin* 'By fortitude and fidelity'

—Brown, Stuckey.

9. **Fortitudine et labore**   *Latin* 'By fortitude and exertion'
    —Reid.

10. **Fortitudine et prudentiâ**   *Latin* 'By fortitude and prudence'
    —Hargreaves, Herbert, Hacket, Lighton (Bt.), O'Reilly (of
    Knock Abbey), Powis (E.), Younge (of Bassingbourn).

11. **Fortitudine et sapientia**   *Latin* 'With fortitude and wisdom'
    —Fox.

12. **Fortitudine victor**   *Latin* 'A victor by fortitude'
    —Taylor.

13. **Fortitudine vincit**   *Latin* 'He conquers by fortitude'
    —Doyle (Bt.).

14. **Fortitudini juncta fidelitas**   *Latin* 'Faith joined with fortitude'
    —Bogart (U.S.).

15. **Fortitudo**   *Latin* 'Fortitude'
    —Clark (of Belford and Werk).

16. **Fortitudo et fidelitas**   *Latin* 'Fortitude and fidelity'
    —Town of Dumbarton.

17. **Fortitudo et justitia**   *Latin* 'Fortitude and justice'
    —Judah (U.S.).

18. **Fortitudo et justitia invictae sunt**   *Latin* 'Fortitude and justice are
    invincible'
    —Maguire.

19. **Fortitudo et prudentia**   *Latin* 'Fortitude and prudence'
    —Egan.

20. **Fortitudo fidelis honore munerata**   *Latin* 'Faithful fortitude is
    rewarded with honor'
    —Russell.

21. **Fortitudo in adversis**   *Latin* 'Fortitude in adversity'
    —Cox.

22. **In arduis fortitudo**   *Latin* 'Fortitude in adversity'
    —Hamilton.

23. **Industria, virtus, et fortitudo**   *Latin* 'Industry, valor, and forti-
    tude'
    —Smellie (of Slindon, co. Sussex).

24. **Justitia et fortitudo invincibilia sunt**   *Latin* 'Justice and fortitude
    are invincible'
    —Maguire.

25. **Periculum fortitudine evasi** *Latin* 'I have escaped danger by fortitude'
—Harland (Bt.), Mahon.

26. **Probitas cum fortitudine** *Latin* 'Honesty with fortitude'
—Brewster.

27. **Spes et fortitudo** *Latin* 'Hope and fortitude'
—Mair.

28. **Victoria, fortitudo, virtus** *Latin* 'Victory, fortitude, and virtue'
—Young.

29. **Virtus et fortitudo invincibilia sunt** *Latin* 'Virtue and fortitude are invincible'
—McGuire.

30. **Virtus fides fortitudo** *Latin* 'Virtue, fidelity, and fortitude'
—Spens.

31. **Virtute et fortitudine** *Latin* 'By bravery and fortitude'
—Morris, Whettnall, Cooper.

32. **Woksape / Woohitika / Wacantognaka / Wowacintanka** *Lakota* 'Wisdom/ bravery/ fortitude/ generosity'
—Sinte Gleska College, Rosebud, South Dakota.

FORTUNE (*See also* GLORY; PROSPERITY; SUCCESS.)

1. **A Deo, non fortuna** *Latin* 'By God, not by fortune'
—Greaves, Greaves-Banning.

2. **Alles steht bei glvck und Zeit** *German* 'Everything comes with luck and with time'
—Ferdinand II, Emperor of Germany (1578–1637); Friedrich Ulrich, Duke of Braunschweig-Wolfenbüttel (1591–1634).

3. **Animis et fato** *Latin* 'By courageous acts and good fortune'
—Thriepland (Bt.).

4. **Animose certavit** *Latin* 'He hath striven courageously'
—Pryme (of Cambridge).

5. **Animus et fata** *Latin* 'Courage and fortune'
—Thriepland.

6. **Assaj ben' balla à chi la fortuna suona** *Italian* 'He dances well for whom fortune plays'
—Friedrich, Count of the Palatinate of Vohenstrauss (1557–97); Franz, Duke of Braunschweig-Lüneburg (1572–1601).

7. **Audaces fortuna juvat timidosque repellit**   *Latin* 'Fortune favors the brave and repels the fearful'
—Ambler (U.S.).

8. **Bon fortune**   *French* 'Good luck'
—Ferrier.

9. **Civitatis fortuna cives**   *Latin* 'The fortune of the state depends on the citizens'
—Bebington B. C., U.K.

10. **Conjuncta virtuti fortuna**   *Latin* 'Good fortune is allied to bravery'
—McBeth.

11. **Contra fortuna bon coeur**   *Latin & French* 'A stout heart against fortune'
—Bernhard, Duke of Saxony-Weimar (1604–39).

12. **Contre fortune bon coeur**   *French* 'Face fortune with a stout heart'
—Wright.

13. **Contre fortune bon coeur, Dieu tourne tout en bonheur**   *French* 'Against fortune a stout heart: may God direct everything for the best'
—Dorothee Sophie, Duchess of Saxony (1587–1645).

14. **Cum secundo flumine**   *Latin* 'With the favoring stream'
—Lund.

15. **Deo adjuvante, fortuna sequatur**   *Latin* 'With God assisting, good fortune may follow'
—Roberts (of Crofton Hall, Co. Salop).

16. **Deo duce, fortunâ comitante**   *Latin* 'With God as my guide, good fortune as companion'
—Merchants of Exeter, Sladen.

17. **Deo duce comite fortuna**   *Latin* 'God for guide, fortune for companion'
—Palles.

18. **Deo non fortunae**   *Latin* 'To God not fortune'
—Gardiners.

19. **De vertu bonheur**   *French* 'From virtue fortune'
—Sophie, Electress of Hanover (1630–1714).

20. **Diligentia fortunae mater**   *Latin* 'Diligence is the mother of fortune'
—Barkham.

21. **Eamus quo ducit fortuna** *Latin* 'Let us go where fortune leads'
—Atty, James.

22. **Faveat fortuna** *Latin* 'Let fortune favor'
—Newton.

23. **Faventibus auris** *Latin* 'By favorable gales'
—Stirling (of Dundee).

24. **Favet fortuna labori** *Latin* 'Fortune favors labor'
—Turnbull.

25. **Felicior quo certior** *Latin* 'Luckier as it is surer'
—Ormiston.

26. **Fides fortuna fortior** *Latin* 'Fidelity is stronger than fortune'
—Hoey.

27. **Fors et virtus** *Latin* 'Fortune and virtue'
—Lotbiniere (U.S.).

28. **Fors non mutat genus** *Latin* 'Fortune does not change race'
—Maughan.

29. **Forte** *Latin* 'By chance'
—Fortick.

30. **Fortem fors juvat** *Latin* 'Fortune favors the bold'
—Menzies.

31. **Fortes fortuna adjuvat** *Latin* 'Fortune favors the brave'
—Moritz, Elector of Saxony (1521–53).

32. **Fortes fortuna juvat** *Latin* 'Fortune favors the bold'
—Blennerhasset (Bt.), Bloomfield (B.), Dickson, Doller, Murray, Troyte.

33. **Forti fors bona** *Latin* 'Fortune is favorable to the bold'
—Watson.

34. **Fortunâ, virtute** *Latin* 'By good fortune and valor'
—Beath, Beith.

35. **Fortuna audaces juvat** *Latin* 'Fortune favors the bold'
—Cleveland, Colmore, Cregoe, Barron (of Kilkenny).

36. **Fortuna audaces juvat timidosque repellit** *Latin* 'Fortune assists the daring but baffles the timid'
—Cregol.

37. **Fortuna comes** *Latin* 'Fortune is my companion'
—Ferguson.

38. **Fortuna et honos ab alto** *Latin* 'Fortune and honor are from above'
—Rydon.

39. **Fortunâ et labore**   *Latin* 'By good fortune and exertion'
—Sym.

40. **Fortuna faveat**   *Latin* 'May fortune favor us'
—O'Flaherty.

41. **Fortunâ favente**   *Latin* 'With fortune in my favor'
—Falkiner (Bt.), Pudsey.

42. **Fortuna favet**   *Latin* 'Fortune favors'
—Whyte.

43. **Fortuna favet audaci**   *Latin* 'Fortune favors the daring'
—Turnbull.

44. **Fortuna favet fortibus**   *Latin* 'Fortune favors the brave'
—O'Flaherty.

45. **Fortuna juvat**   *Latin* 'Fortune furthers'
—McAndrew.

46. **Fortuna juvat audaces**   *Latin* 'Fortune favors the bold'
—Baron.

47. **Fortunam honestent virtute**   *Latin* 'Let them make honorable their fortune by their virtue'
—Brandreth.

48. **Fortunam reverenter habe**   *Latin* 'Enjoy fortune intelligently'
—[Ausonius, *Epigrammata*, viii. 8.] Philipp, Duke of Schleswig-Holstein (1584–1663).

49. **Fortuna parcet labori**   *Latin* 'Fortune will save trouble'
—Buchanan.

50. **Fortuna rotunda**   *Latin* 'Fortune is round'
—Ernst VI, Count of Mansfeld (1561–1609).

51. **Fortuna sequatur**   *Latin* 'Let fortune be attendant'
—Aberdeen (E.), Gordon, Warren.

52. **Fortuna sequitur**   *Latin* 'Fortune follows'
—Dickinson.

53. **Fortuna ut Luna**   *Latin* 'Fortune (changes) like the moon'
—Günther, Count Schwarzburg (1570–1643); Alexander Heinrich, Duke of Schleswig-Holstein (1608–67).

54. **Fortuna vectem [sic] sequitur**   *Latin* 'Fortune follows effort'
—Wight.

55. **Fortuna viam ducit**   *Latin* 'Fortune leads the way'
—Hassard.

56. **Fortuna virtuti comes**   *Latin* 'Fortune the companion of valor'
—Ferguson.

57. **Fortune, infortune, une fort une**   *French* 'Fortune, misfortune, one strong one'
—Brewster (U.S.).

58. **Fortune and opportunity forever**
—O'Mulloy.

59. **Fortune de guerre**   *French* 'The fortune of war'
—Chute.

60. **Fortune helps the forward**
—Carmichael.

61. **Fortune infortune fort une**   *French* 'Fortune and ill fortune are one'
—Adolf Friedrich I, Duke of Mecklenburg-Schwerin (1588–1658).

62. **Fortune le veut**   *French* 'Fortune so wills it'
—Chaytor (Bt.).

63. **Furth fortune**
—Murray (of Edinburgh).

64. **Furth fortune, and fill the fetters**
—Athol (D.), Dunmore (E.), Glenlyon (B.), Murray (Bt.), Murray, Stewart.

65. **Indulge fortune**
—Bover.

66. **Industriâ atque fortunâ**   *Latin* 'By industry and good fortune'
—Lawrie.

67. **In omnes casus**   *Latin* 'For all chances'
—Walker.

68. **In pede fausto**   *Latin* 'With a step of good omen'
—Rutherford.

69. **In utraque fortuna paratus**   *Latin* 'Prepared for either good or bad fortune'
—Cotton, Combermere (V.).

70. **In virtute et fortuna**   *Latin* 'In valor and fortune'
—Gardner.

71. **Invita fortuna**   *Latin* 'Though fortune be unwilling'
—Knightley (Bt.).

72. **Invita sortem fortuna**   *Latin* 'Fate in spite of fortune'
—Knightley.

73. **Je defie fortune**   *French* 'I defy fortune'
—Delves.

74. **Juvant aspera probum**   *Latin* 'Misfortunes benefit the good man'
—Denham (Bt.), Steuart (of Coltness, bt.), Stewart.

75. **La fortune passe par tout**   *French* 'The vicissitudes of fortune are common to all'
—Lewis, Rollo (B.).

76. **La vita al fin e'l di loda la sera**   *Italian* 'Praise life when it is at an end, and the day when it is night'
—Le Couteur.

77. **Luck to Loyne**
—Lancaster City Council, U.K.

78. **Meliora speranda**   *Latin* 'Better fortunes in expectancy'
—Douglass.

79. **Melior fortunâ virtus**   *Latin* 'Virtue is better than fortune'
—Mellor.

80. **Me meliora manent**   *Latin* 'Better fortunes await me'
—Mossman.

81. **Merci, fortune**   *French* 'Thank you, fortune'
—The Lord Audley (reign of Henry VIII).

82. **Mon heur et salut gist en mains de Dieu**   *Old French* 'My fortune and health lie in God's hands'
—Dorothee, Margravine of Brandenburg (1596–1649).

83. **Mores fingunt fortunam**   *Latin* 'Manners mold fortune'
—Rogerson.

84. **Nec sorte, nec fato**   *Latin* 'Neither by chance nor destiny'
—Rutherford (of Edgerston).

85. **Nec tempore, nec fato**   *Latin* 'Neither by time nor fate'
—McDonald.

86. **Ni affligé par malheur, ni rejouis par bonheur**   *French* 'Neither afflicted by misfortune nor exalted by good fortune'
—Johann Ernst, Duke of Saxony-Eisenach (1566–1638).

87. **Non abest virtuti sors**   *Latin* 'Fortune deserts not virtue'
—Nisbet.

88. **Non mutat fortuna genus**   *Latin* 'Fortune does not change the race'
—Oliphant.

89. **Omine secundo**   *Latin* 'With favorable omen'
—Mac-Murdoch.

90. **Omnia fortunae committo**   *Latin* 'I commit all things to fortune'
—Duff, McNaught, Macknyghte.

91. **Per varios casus** *Latin* 'By various fortunes'
—Douglas, Drysdale, Hamilton, Lammie, L'Amy (Co. Forfar), Walker.

92. **Placeam dum peream** *Latin* 'Let me find favor as long as I live'
—Murray.

93. **Quam sibi sortem** *Latin* 'Which fortune for himself'
—Fraser.

94. **Quand fortune me tourmente, L'Espoire en Dieu me contente**
French 'When fortune torments, hope in God contents'
—Luise Amalie, Princess of Anhalt (1606–35).

95. **Quod sors fert ferimus** *Latin* 'We have what fortune brings'
—Clayton (of Enfield).

96. **Secundâ alite** *Latin* 'With prosperous omen' or 'By favor of the bird'
—Lathom, or Latham.

97. **Sidus adsit amicum** *Latin* 'Let my propitious star be present'
—Bateman (Co. Derby).

98. **Sidus adsit amicum** *Latin* 'Let my propitious star be present'
—Bateman (Co. Derby).

99. **Spem fortuna alit** *Latin* 'Good fortune nourishes hope'
—Kinnear, Petree.

100. **Spes et fortuna** *Latin* 'Hope and fortune'
—Chelmsford (B.).

101. **Stat fortuna domus** *Latin* 'The fortune of the house remains'
—Gay (of Bath), Howes (of Morningthorpe, Co. Norfolk), Wintle, White.

102. **Stat fortuna domus virtute** *Latin* 'The fortune of our house endures through virtue'
—Molyneux (Bt.).

103. **Stet fortuna** *Latin* 'Let fortune be stable'
—Cullingford (of Bayswater).

104. **Stet fortuna domus** *Latin* 'May the fortunes of the House stand!'
—Harrow School, U.K., Holdich (of Mardwell, co. Northampton).

105. **Toujours propice** *French* 'Always propitious'
—Dawson (of Castle Dawson), Cremorne (B.).

106. **Valor et fortuna** *Latin* 'Valor and good fortune'
—Rollo (of Powhouse).

107. **Varietas est propria fortunae** *Latin* 'Change is natural to fortune'
　　　　　　—Ernest VI, Count of Mansfeld (1561–1609).

108. **Ventis secundis** *Latin* 'By favorable winds'
　　　　　　—Hood (V.), Rowley (Bt.).

109. **Victrix fortunae sapientia** *Latin* 'Wisdom the conqueror of fortune'
　　　　　　—Andrews (Bt.), Calthrop (of Stanhoe Hall, Co. Norfolk).

110. **Victrix fortuna sapientiae** *Latin* 'Fortune is the conqueror of wisdom'
　　　　　　—Chalmers.

111. **Virtus fortunae victrix** *Latin* 'Virtue conquers fortune'
　　　　　　—Sandes.

112. **Virtute duce, comite fortunâ** *Latin* 'With valor my leader and good fortune my companion'
　　　　　　—Davies, Shand, Visme.

113. **Virtute et fortuna** *Latin* 'By valor and good fortune'
　　　　　　—Andrew.

114. **Virtute superanda fortuna** *Latin* 'Fortune is to be overcome by virtue'
　　　　　　—Whiteford.

115. **Virtuti et fortunae** *Latin* 'To virtue and fortune'
　　　　　　—Gardiner.

116. **Virtuti fortuna comes** *Latin* 'Fortune is companion to valor'
　　　　　　—Potter (of Buile Hill, Lancashire), Ferguson, Mayne (of Powis, etc.), Orr, Stewart, Wren.

117. **Virtutis fortuna comes** *Latin* 'Fortune is the companion of valor'
　　　　　　—Ashtown (B.), Brook, Clancarty (E.), Ferguson (of Raith), Hughes, Harberton (V.), Trench, Wellington (D.); Wellington College, U.K.

FRAGRANCE

1. **Decerptae dabunt odorem** *Latin* 'Plucked they will emit fragrance'
　　　　　　—Aiton.

2. **Diuturnitate fragrantior** *Latin* 'The more fragrance with lapse of time'
　　　　　　—Rind, Rynd.

3. **Et decerptae dabunt odorem**   *Latin* 'Even when plucked they will give out scent'
—Aiton (of Kippo).

4. **Fragrat, delectat, et sanat**   *Latin* 'It smells sweet, is pleasing, and healthful'
—Clelland.

5. **Hinc odor et sanitas**   *Latin* 'Hence fragrance and health'
—Liddel (of Edinburgh).

6. **Olet et sanat**   *Latin* 'It smells sweet and heals'
—Dunbar (of Hillhead).

7. **Quo spinosior fragrantior**   *Latin* 'The more thorns, the greater fragrance'
—Rose, Ross.

FRIENDSHIP   (*See also* FELLOWSHIP; LOVE.)

1. **A friend to youth**
—Florida College, Temple Terrace, Florida.

2. **A l'amy fidèle pour jamais**   *Old French* 'Faithful forever to my friend'
—Seymour.

3. **Amicitia cum libertate**   *Latin* 'Friendship with liberty'
—Williams (U.S.).

4. **Amicitia cum virtute**   *Latin* 'Friendship with virtue'
—Bradbury.

5. **Amicitiae virtutisque faedus**   *Latin* 'The league of friendship and virtue'
—Grand Order of Wurtemburg; Hippisley (Bt.), Nelson (of Beeston, co. Norfolk).

6. **Amicitiam trahit amor**   *Latin* 'Love draws on friendship'
—Wire-drawers' Company.

7. **Amicitia permanens et incorrupta**   *Latin* 'Friendship constant and incorruptible'
—Harrison.

8. **Amicitia praesidium firmissimum**   *Latin* 'Friendship is the surest protection'
—Ernst, Margrave of Brandenburg (1583–1613).

9. **Amicitia reddit honores**   *Latin* 'Friendship gives honors'
—Pringle.

10. **Amicitia sine fraude** *Latin* 'Friendship without deceit'
—Allen.

11. **Amico fidus ad aras** *Latin* 'Faithful to my friend as far as conscience permits, or even to death', lit., 'even to the altar'
—Rutherford (of Fairningtoun).

12. **Amicos semper amat** *Latin* 'He always loves his friends'
—Culley.

13. **Amicum proba hostem scito** *Latin* 'Test a friend, you will know an enemy'
—Fraser.

14. **Amicus** *Latin* 'Friend'
—Pert.

15. **Amicus amico** *Latin* 'A friend to a friend'
—Bellingham.

16. **Amicus certus** *Latin* 'A sure friend'
—Peat (of Sevenoaks), Peit.

17. **Amicus vitae solatium** *Latin* 'A friend is the solace of life'
—Burton.

18. **Amitié** *French* 'Friendship'
—Pitt.

19. **Anima in amicis una** *Latin* 'One feeling among friends'
—Powell.

20. **Caraid'an am feym** *Scots Gaelic* 'A friend in time of need'
—Gow, Smith, Smyth, Steuart.

21. **Crescat amicitia** *Latin* 'Let friendship increase'
—Michell.

22. **Deo, patriae, amicis** *Latin* 'To God, my country and my friends'
—Cooper.

23. **Deo, reipublicae, et amicis** *Latin* 'To God, our country, and our friends'
—Levant Company.

24. **Deo et amicitiae** *Latin* 'For God and friendship'
—Forman (U.S.).

25. **Deo Reipublicae et amicis esto semper fidelis** *Latin* 'Be ever faithful to God, the state, and friends'
—Duffield (U.S.).

26. **Deus amici et nos** *Latin* 'God, friends, and ourselves'
—Pell (U.S.).

27. **Deus amicus** *Latin* 'God is (my) friend'
—Pell (U.S.).

28. **Die Lieb der Freund macht Furcht dem Feind** *German* 'The love of friends fills the foe with fear'
—Joseph I, Emperor of Germany (1678–1711).

29. **Fear not friendship**
—Thompson.

30. **Fidem libertatem amicitiam retinebis** *Latin* 'You will keep faith, liberty, and friendship'
—Adams (U.S.).

31. **Fides amicitiae periculosa libertas** *Latin* 'Liberty, a faith dangerous to friendship'
—Dockwra.

32. **Fidus amicus** *Latin* 'A faithful friend'
—Campbell (of Islay).

33. **Freund in der Noth gehen wenig auf ein Loth** *German* 'Friends in need go not far towards the ounce'
—Sibylle, Electress of Saxony (1512–54).

34. **Friendship**
—Carr; State of Texas.

35. **Good friend**
—Godfrey.

36. **Honor et justitia manet amicitia florebit semper que** *Latin* 'Honor and justice remain, and friendship will always flourish'
—Bayard (U.S.).

37. **Invidiae claudor, pateo sed semper amico** *Latin* 'I am closed to envy, but am always open to a friend'
—over a bedroom door in Loseley House, near Guildford, Surrey, England.

38. **Ipse amicus** *Latin* 'I am my own friend'
—Baron.

39. **Junxit amicos amor** *Latin* 'Love hath united friends'
—Order of St. Joachim (Germany).

40. **L'amour et l'amitié** *French* 'Love and friendship'
—Day (of Kirby, Bedon, co. Norfolk).

41. **Leo inimicis amicis columba** *Latin* 'The lion for my enemies, the dove for my friends'
—Dilke.

42. **Libertatem, amicitiam, retinebis et fidem**   *Latin* 'You will hold on to liberty, friendship, and faith'
—Boylston (U.S.).

43. **Manet amicitia florebitque semper**   *Latin* 'Friendship remains and ever will flourish'
—Francis (U.S.), Pierpont (U.S.).

44. **Memor amici**   *Latin* 'Mindful of my friend'
—Russell.

45. **Omnibus amicus**   *Latin* 'A friend to everybody'
—Chatto.

46. **Pax et amicitia**   *Latin* 'Peace and friendship'
—Cowell (U.S.).

47. **Progressio et concordia**   *Latin* 'Progress and concord'
—Kettering B. C., U.K.

48. **Pro patriae amicis**   *Latin* 'For the friends of my country'
—Granville.

49. **Sapientia/ virtus/ amicitia**   *Latin* 'Knowledge/ virtue/ friendship'
—Central Michigan University, Mt. Pleasant, Michigan.

50. **Sat amico si mihi felix**   *Latin* 'Enough for a friend if he be kind to me'
—Law (of Lawbridge).

51. **Usque ad aras amicus**   *Latin* 'A friend even to the altar'
—Griffiths.

52. **Virtute et amicitia**   *Latin* 'By virtue and friendship'
—Jervis.

53. **Virtute et labore verum amicum cole**   *Latin* 'Nurture a true friend through virtue and hard work'
—Cunningham (U.S.).

54. **When friends meet, hearts warm**
—Stone mantelpiece in Lower Soughton, Flintshire, Wales.

FRUIT (*See also* AGRICULTURE; FLORA; FLOURISHING.)

1. **Ein jedweder Baum wird ahn seinen früchten erkandt**   *German* 'Every tree is known by its fruit'
—Wilhelm V, Landgrave of Hesse-Cassel (1602–37).

2. **Fructu arbor cognoscitur**   *Latin* 'The tree is known by its fruit'
—[Matt., vii. 16.] Purton.

3. **Fructu non foliis** *Latin* 'By the fruit, not the leaves'
—Bushby.

4. **Fructu noscitur** *Latin* 'It is known by its fruits'
—Newbigging.

5. **Fruges ecce paludis** *Latin* 'Behold the fruits of the marsh'
—Mirfield U. D. C., U.K.

6. **Inter folias fructus** *Latin* 'Fruit among the leaves'
—Hapgood (U.S.).

7. **Known by their fruits**
—Sittingbourne and Milton U. D. C., U.K.

8. **Non deerit alter aureus** *Latin* 'Another golden fruit will not be wanting'
—Don (Bt.).

9. **The fruit is as the tree**
—Kennedy.

FULLNESS

1. **Cum plena magis** *Latin* 'Rather when she is full'
—Smith (of Giblston).

2. **Donec impleat orbem** *Latin* 'Until it fill its orb'
—Kidd, Kyd (of Craigie).

3. **Donec rursus impleat orbem** *Latin* 'Until it again fill its orb'
—Scott (Bt.), Somervil, Sommerville.

4. **Donec totum impleat orbem** *Latin* 'Until it fill the whole world'
—Order of the Crescent.

5. **Ex terra copiam e mari salutem** *Latin* 'From the land fullness and from the sea health'
—Worthing B. C., U.K.

6. **Plena refulget** *Latin* 'The full moon shines'
—Pitcairn.

7. **Tandem implebitur** *Latin* 'It will be full at last'
—Scougal, Simpson.

8. **Ut implear** *Latin* 'That I may be filled'
—Mikieson.

FUTURE, THE (*See also* POSSIBILITY; TIME; VISION.)

1. **Alteri prosis saeculo** *Latin* 'May you be a blessing to the generation to come'
—Graham.

2. **Carpe diem postero ne crede** *Latin* 'Seize the present opportunity, trust not to the future'
—[after Horace, *Odes*, I. xi. 8.] Cutting (U.S.).

3. **Cautus a futuro** *Latin* 'Cautious as to the future'
—Bowen.

4. **Clavis ad futura** *Latin* 'Key to the future'
—Greenville Technical College, Greenville, South Carolina.

5. **Cras mihi** *Latin* 'Tomorrow for me'
—Parbury.

6. **Désormais** *French* 'Hereafter'
—Clifford.

7. **Erimus** *Latin* 'We shall be'
—Middlesbrough C. B. C., U.K.

8. **From henceforth**
—Poore.

9. **Futuri cautus** *Latin* 'Wary of the future'
—Raikes.

10. **Futurum invisibile** *Latin* 'The future is inscrutable'
—Beville.

11. **Il buon tempo verra** *Italian* 'Bright days will come'
—Jennings (of Hartwell).

12. **In futura spector** *Latin* 'I am seen in the future'
—Pierce (U.S.).

13. **Key to the future**
—University of Wisconsin-Milwaukee, Milwaukee, Wisconsin.

14. **La promesse du futur** *French* 'The promise of the future'
—Duryee (U.S.).

15. **Le jour viendra** *French* 'The day will come'
—Durham (E.), Lambton.

16. **Mihi cura futuri** *Latin* 'My care is for the future'
—Ongley (B.).

17. **Mihi solicitudo futuri** *Latin* 'I have a care for the future'
—Thackwell.

18. **Ne incautus futuri**   *Latin* 'Not incautious of the future'
—Hagerstown Business College, Hagerstown Business College.

19. **North to the future**
—State of Alaska.

20. **Pour l'advenir**   *French* 'For the future'
—Duc de Broglie.

21. **Pride in our past, faith in our future**
—Hertford B. C., U.K.

22. **Pride in the past/ Faith in the future**
—Hastings College, Hastings, Nebraska.

23. **Prudens futuri**   *Latin* 'Prudent for the future'
—Letchworth U. D. C., U.K.

24. **Quod ero spero**   *Latin* 'What I shall be, I hope'
—Booth (Bt.), Booth, Barton (of Grove and Clonelly), Gowans, Haworth.

25. **Respice futurum**   *Latin* 'Regard the future'
—Reece.

26. **Sic donec**   *Latin* 'Thus until'
—Bridgewater (E.), Egerton (of Tatton, co. Chester).

27. **Sic olim**   *Latin* 'So hereafter'
—Humfrey.

28. **Sperate futurum**   *Latin* 'Hope for the future'
—Altree.

29. **The time will come**
—Clarke.

30. **Till then thus**
—Jones (Co. Lancaster).

31. **Where women create their future**
—Barat College, Lake Forest, Illinois.

GENEROSITY (*See also* GIFTS and GIVING; UNSELFISHNESS.)

1. **Accipe quantum vis**   *Latin* 'Take as much as you wish'
—Brown.

2. **Bis dat qui cito dat**   *Latin* 'He gives twice who gives quickly'
—Bisson.

3. **Fidelis et generosus**   *Latin* 'Faithful and generous'
—Durell.

4. **Generositate**   *Latin* 'By generosity'
   —Nicolson (Bt.), Nicholson.

5. **Generosity with justice**
   —Smith.

6. **Generosus et animosus**   *Latin* 'Generous and courageous'
   —Glennon.

7. **Generosus et paratus**   *Latin* 'Generous and prepared'
   —Harwood.

8. **Habere et dispertire**   *Latin* 'To have and to share with others'
   —Aveland (B.).

9. **Industry and liberality**
   —Jejeebhoy (Bt.).

10. **Justitiae comes magnanimitas**   *Latin* 'Generosity is the companion of justice'
    —Town of Dijon, France.

11. **La générosité**   *French* 'Generosity'
    —Order of Generosity (Prussia).

12. **Liberalitas**   *Latin* 'Liberality'
    —Furlong.

13. **Munifice et fortiter**   *Latin* 'Bountifully and bravely'
    —Handyside.

14. **Qui vult capere capiat**   *Latin* 'Who wishes to take, let him take'
    —Gloag.

15. **Spare not**
    —Giffard, Macgregor.

16. **Spare nought**
    —Brisbane (Bt.), Hay, Tweeddale (M.), Yester.

17. **Spare when you have nought**
    —Gifford.

18. **Woksape / Woohitika / Wacantognaka / Wowacintanka**
    Lakota 'Wisdom/ bravery/ fortitude/ generosity'
    —Sinte Gleska College, Rosebud, South Dakota.

GENIUS (*See also* ABILITY; WISDOM.)

1. **Ingenium superat vires**   *Latin* 'Genius surpasses strength'
   —Adams.

2. **Nihil invitâ Minervâ**   *Latin* 'Nothing contrary to one's genius'
   —Academy of the Muses.

3. **Nil invita Minerva** *Latin* 'Nothing contrary to one's genius'
—Prime.

4. **Non invita Minerva** *Latin* 'Not against the bent of your genius'
—[Cicero, *de Off.* i. 31. 3.] Scott.

GENTLENESS (*See also* KINDNESS; MERCY.)

1. **Aut suavitate aut vi** *Latin* 'Either by gentleness or by force'
—Hopkins (Bt.).

2. **Aut vi aut suavitate** *Latin* 'Either by force or mildness'
—Griffith.

3. **Dulcidine** *Latin* 'By sweetness'
—Bogle.

4. **Felis demulcta mitis** *Latin* 'A stroked cat is gentle'
—Kane, Keane (Bt.).

5. **Fidelis et suavis** *Latin* 'Faithful and gentle'
—Emery.

6. **Fortis et lenis** *Latin* 'Brave and gentle'
—Curry.

7. **Fortiter in re, et suaviter in modo** *Latin* 'Firmly in act and gently in manner'
—Beaufort.

8. **Fortiter sed suaviter** *Latin* 'Bravely but gently'
—Lee, Muntz, Willsher.

9. **Gentle birth and virtue** *(from Greek)*
—Nicholl.

10. **Mitis et audax** *Latin* 'Mild and bold'
—Markham.

11. **Mitis et fortis** *Latin* 'Gentle and brave'
—Ord.

12. **Mitis sed fortis** *Latin* 'Mild but brave'
—Orde, Phipson-Wybrants.

13. **Recte et suaviter** *Latin* 'Justly and mildly'
—Curzon, Scarsdale (B.), Wyborn.

14. **Suaviter** *Latin* 'Gently'
—Cawood.

15. **Suaviter, fortiter** *Latin* 'Gently, boldly'
—Smith (of Gloucestershire).

16. **Suaviter et fortiter**   *Latin* 'Mildly and firmly'
—Daubeney, Minto (E.), Rathbone.

17. **Suaviter in modo**   *Latin* 'Gently in manner'
—Churchward.

18. **Suaviter sed fortiter**   *Latin* 'Mildly, but firmly'
—Busk, Dennis, Williams (of Lee).

19. **Vi vel suavitate**   *Latin* 'By force or by mildness'
—Rochfort.

GIFTS and GIVING   (*See also* GENEROSITY.)

1. **Abstulit qui dedit**   *Latin* 'He who gave hath taken away'
—Howard, Jerningham.

2. **Ab uno ad omnes**   *Latin* 'From one to all'
—Perth and Melfort (E.).

3. **Après donner it [sic] faut prendre**   *French* 'After giving it is necessary to take'
—Cameren (Brittany).

4. **A te pro te**   *Latin* 'From thee, for thee'
—Savage, Morton.

5. **Auctor pretiosa facit**   *Latin* 'The Giver makes them valuable'
—Buckinghamshire (E.), Hobart, Lubbock (Bt.), Raymond.

6. **Auctor pretiosa fecit**   *Latin* 'The Giver made them valuable'
—Barlee.

7. **Beau don**   *French* 'A beautiful gift'
—Bowdon U. D. C., U.K.

8. **Dabit qui dedit**   *Latin* 'He will give who gave'
—Smith (Bt.).

9. **Dando conservat**   *Latin* 'He keeps by giving'
—Harpending (U.S.).

10. **Dant Deo**   *Latin* 'They give to God'
—Wood.

11. **Dare quam accipere**   *Latin* 'Rather to give than to receive'
`                                      ` —Guy.

12. **Date eleemosynam et ecce omnia munda sunt vobis**   *Latin* 'Give alms and lo! all pure things are yours'
—Wyggesden School, Leicester, U.K.

13. **Dedit meliora dabitque** *Latin* 'He has given better things and will give them'
> —Ormerod.

14. **Donner et pardonner** *French* 'To give and forgive'
> —Hicks.

15. **Favente des supero** *Latin* 'May you give with divine favor'
> —Hardenbrook (U.S.).

16. **Freely ye received, freely give**
> —Pepperdine University, Malibu, California.

17. **Give and forgive**
> —Andrews.

18. **Giving and forgiving**
> —Biggar (of Wolmet).

19. **Industriae munus** *Latin* 'The gift of industry'
> —Leechaman.

20. **Je reçois pour donner** *French* 'I receive to give'
> —Innes.

21. **Ke ne dune Ke ne tiens ne pret Ke desire** *Old French* 'He who does not give what he has does not gain what he desires'
> —King Henry III

22. **Naturae donum** *Latin* 'The gift of nature'
> —Peacock.

23. **Non rapui, sed recepi** *Latin* 'I have not taken by violence, but received'
> —Cotterell (Bt.).

24. **Non sino, sed dono** *Latin* 'I do not permit, but I give'
> —Siddon.

25. **Quid retribuam?** *Latin* 'What shall I render?'
> —Parsons.

26. **Qui non dat quod habet non occupat ille quod optat** *Latin* 'He who does not give what he has, does not gain what he desires'
> —King Henry III.

27. **Sibi quisque dat** *Latin* 'Everyone gives to himself'
> —Harper.

28. **Tibi soli** *Latin* 'To thee alone'
> —Kyle.

GLORY (*See also* FAME; HONOR; SUCCESS; VICTORY.)

1. **Accipiter praedam sequitur, nos gloriam** *Latin* 'The hawk seeks prey, we (seek) glory'
    —Hawker, Strother (of Shooter's Hill, Kent).

2. **Ad gloriam per spinas** *Latin* 'To glory through thorns'
    —Thorn.

3. **A Dieu seul la gloire** *French* 'To God alone the glory'
    —Magdalene Sibylle, Electress of Saxony (1612–87).

4. **Antiquo decore virens** *Latin* 'Flourishing by ancient glory'
    —Johann Georg II, Prince of Anhalt-Dessau (1627–93).

5. **Antiquum decus floreat** *Latin* 'May its ancient glory flourish'
    —Oldbury B. C., U.K.

6. **Aucto splendore resurgo** *Latin* 'I rise again with increased glory'
    —85th Foot (Shropshire Light Infantry).

7. **Chi semina virtu raccologie fama** *Italian* 'He who sows virtue, reaps glory'
    —Johann Friedrich, Duke of Württemberg (1585–1628).

8. **Con la virtu e l'arme s'acquista gloria** *Italian* 'With virtue and arms is glory won'
    —Johann Wilhelm II, Duke of Saxony (1600–32).

9. **Cruce glorior** *Latin* 'I glory in the cross'
    —Pye.

10. **Crucifixa gloria mea** *Latin* 'My glory is in the cross'
    —Knatchbull-Hugessen.

11. **Dat gloria vires** *Latin* 'Glory gives strength'
    —Hog, Hogg, 2Hogue.

12. **Decus et veritas** *Latin* 'Glory and truth'
    —Rockford College, Rockford, Illinois.

13. **Deo honor et gloria** *Latin* 'Unto God be honor and glory'
    —Leather Sellers' Company.

14. **Ex adverso decus** *Latin* 'Glory comes from opposition'
    —Ludwig Rudolf, Duke of Braunschweig in Blankenburg (1671–1735).

15. **Ex duris gloria** *Latin* 'From hardships, glory'
    —Erich II, the Younger, Duke of Braunschweig-Kalenberg (1528–84); Joachim Ernst, Duke of Schleswig-Holstein (1595–1671); Johann Friedrich, Duke of Braunschweig-Lüneburg (1625–79).

16. **Ex duris gloria** *Latin* 'From suffering ariseth glory'
—Bentham.

17. **Fax mentis honestae gloria** *Latin* 'Glory is the light of a noble mind'
—Forbes (Bt.), Lauder, Molleson, The Nova-Scotia Baronets.

18. **Fax mentis incendium gloriae** *Latin* 'The torch of glory inflames the mind'
—Forbes, Granard (E.).

19. **Gloria calcar habet** *Latin* 'Glory has a spur'
—Knight (of Clopton).

20. **Gloria finis** *Latin* 'Glory is the end'
—Brooke.

21. **Gloria non praeda** *Latin* 'Glory, not plunder'
—Murray (of Lochnaw).

22. **Gloria sat Deus unus** *Latin* 'God alone is sufficient glory'
—Weston.

23. **Gloria virtutis merces** *Latin* 'Glory is the reward of virtue'
—Robertson (of Auchleeks).

24. **Gloria virtutis umbra** *Latin* 'Glory is the shadow of virtue'
—Eters, Longford (E.), Pakenham.

25. **Glorior in cruci Christi** *Latin* 'I glory in the cross of Christ'
—Burder (U.S.).

26. **His gloria reddit honores** *Latin* 'Glory confers honor on these men'
—Drummond.

27. **Honestae gloria fax mentis** *Latin* 'Glory the torch of the honorable mind'
—Pilkington (Bt.).

28. **Immortalis virtutis et gloriae fama perpetim post fata superstes** *Latin* 'The imperishable renown of virtue and glory survive death forever'
—Johann Georg II, Prince of Anhalt-Dessau (1627–93).

29. **In cruce glorior** *Latin* 'I glory in the cross'
—Cliffe (Co. Wexford), Douglas (of Rosehill), Pye.

30. **In crucifixa gloria mea** *Latin* 'My glory is in the cross'
—Knatchbull (Bt.).

31. **In Deo salus mea et gloria mea** *Latin* 'In God my salvation and my glory'
    —Johann Adolf I, Duke of Saxony-Weissenfels (1649–97).

32. **In moderation placing all my glory**
    —Fitzhugh.

33. **In robore decus** *Latin* 'Glory in strength'
    —Clerk.

34. **Labore quaeritur gloria** *Latin* 'Glory is sought through labor'
    —Dowse (U.S.).

35. **Mea gloria crux** *Latin* 'The cross is my glory'
    —Heald.

36. **Mea gloria fides** *Latin* 'Faith is my glory'
    —Gilchrist, Watson.

37. **Mihi gloria sursum** *Latin* 'My glory is above'
    —Arnold (U.S.).

38. **Mutus inglorius** *Latin* 'The dumb is without glory'
    —Halford.

39. **Mutus inglorius artis** *Latin* 'The dumb in an art is without glory'
    —Halford.

40. **Non mihi sed tibi gloria** *Latin* 'Glory to thee, not to me'
    —Warren, Wilkinson.

41. **On things transitory resteth no glory**
    —Isham (Bt.).

42. **'Or glory'**
    —17th (Duke of Cambridge's Own) Lancers.

43. **Per angusta ad augusta** *Latin* 'Through difficulties to glory'
    —Ernst, Margrave of Brandenburg (1617–42).

44. **Per pericula ad decus ire juvat** *Latin* 'He delights to go through adversity to glory'
    —Scarborough B. C., U.K.

45. **Praemium, virtus, gloria** *Latin* 'Reward, virtue, glory'
    —Crosane.

46. **Proprium decus et patrium** *Latin* 'One's own glory and that of one's ancestors'
    —Morris (U.S.).

47. **Prudentia gloriam acquirit** *Latin* 'Prudence obtains glory'
    —Litton.

48. **Quo Deus et gloria ducunt** *Latin* 'Where God and glory lead'
—Friedrich Wilhelm, Duke of Mecklenburg-Schwerin
(1675–1713).

49. **Quo fas et gloria** *Latin* 'Whither law and glory (lead)'
—Robertson (of Glasgow).

50. **Quo fas et gloria ducunt** *Latin* 'Whither duty and glory lead'
—Friedrich Magnus, Margrave of Baden-Durlach
(1647–1709); Georg Wilhelm, Duke of
Braunschweig-Lüneburg-Zelle (1624–1705).

51. **Resurgit ex virtute vera gloria** *Latin* 'True glory rises from virtue'
—Albert V, Duke of Bavaria (1528–79).

52. **Salus et decus** *Latin* 'Salvation and glory'
—Lloyd (U.S.).

53. **Salus et gloria** *Latin* 'Our salvation and our glory'
—Eleonore, third consort of Emperor Ferdinand III (d.
1686), Order of the Star of the Cross (Austria).

54. **Sola gloriosa quae justa** *Latin* 'The just alone is glorious'
—Johann Georg IV, Elector of Saxony (1668–94).

55. **Un bel mourir toute la vie honore** *French* 'A glorious death honors the whole life'
—Georg III, son of Bogislaus XIII, Duke of Pomerania
(1528–1617).

56. **Unto God only be honor and glory**
—Drapers' Company (London).

57. **Victoria gloria merces** *Latin* 'Victory, glory, reward'
—Berwick-upon-Tweed B. C., U.K.

58. **Virtus, laus, actio** *Latin* 'Virtue, glory, action'
—Frazer.

59. **Virtus invicta gloriosa** *Latin* 'Unconquered virtue is glorious'
—Thomas (Bt.), Bentham (of Lincoln's Inn).

60. **Virtute gloria parta** *Latin* 'Glory is obtained by valor'
—Napier.

61. **Virtutis gloria merces** *Latin* 'Glory is the reward of virtue'
—Friedrich III, Duke of Schleswig-Holstein-Gottorp
(1597–1659), Gyll, Deuchar, Lorimer,
McDonagh, McDonegh, Macgregor, Robertson
(of Strowan, Ladykirk and Kindeace, co. Ross).

62. **Vita brevis gloria aeterna** *Latin* 'Life is short, glory eternal'
—Price.

GOALS (*See also* DESTINATION; DIRECTION.)

1. **Ad metam** *Latin* 'To the mark'
—Bower, Combrey, Comrie, Comrey, Comry.

2. **Certum pete finem** *Latin* 'Aim at a sure end'
—[Horace, *Ep.* i. ii. 56.] Corse, Crosse, Bundy, Howard, Evans, Bissland, Thompson (Bt.), Wicklow (E.).

3. **Ettle weel** *Scots dialect* 'Aim well'
—Smart.

4. **Frapper au but** *French* 'To hit the mark'
—Gibbs.

5. **Pour parvenir au bout il faut souffrir tout** *French* 'To reach the goal we must suffer all things'
—Wilhelm V, Landgrave of Hesse-Cassel (1602–37).

6. **Quod petis hic est** *Latin* 'Here is what you seek'
—Smith (U.S.).

7. **Scopus vitae Christus** *Latin* 'The goal of my life is Christ'
—August, Margrave of Brandenburg (1580–1601); Menzies.

8. **Un peuple, un but, une foi** *French* 'One people, one goal, one faith'
—Republic of Mali, Republic of Senegal.

GOOD NEWS

1. **Gaudium adfero** *Latin* 'I bring good tidings'
—Campbell.

2. **Good news**
—Tattersall.

GOODNESS (*See also* HONOR; KINDNESS; NOBILITY; RIGHTEOUSNESS; WORTHINESS.)

1. **Amour de la bonté** *French* 'Love of goodness'
—Cowell.

2. **Bona bonis** *Latin* 'Goods to the good'
—Hurd (U.S.).

3. **Bonis omnia bona** *Latin* 'All things are good to the good'
—Orr (of Barrowfield).

4. **Bonitas/veritas/pulchritas** *Latin* 'Goodness ruth/beauty'
—Marycrest College, Davenport, Iowa.

5. **Bonitatem et disciplinam et scientiam doce me**   *Latin* 'Teach me goodness and discipline and knowledge'
   —College of Mount Saint Vincent, Riverdale, New York.

6. **Bonne et belle assez**   *French* 'Good and handsome enough'
   —Bellasyse.

7. **Bono vince malum**   *Latin* 'Overcome evil through good'
   —Gerrard, Finch, Kettle.

8. **Bonus justus et utilis**   *Latin* 'Good, just, and useful'
   —Lerrier.

9. **C(a)eteris major qui melior**   *Latin* 'Who is better is greater than the rest'
   —Radcliffe.

10. **Crescam ut prosim**   *Latin* 'I will increase, that I may do good'
    —Mitchelson, Order of St. Joachim.

11. **Ecce quam bonum**   *Latin* 'Behold how good'
    —The University of the South, Sewanee, Tennessee.

12. **Esto bonus et pius ne sit leo te magis impavidus**   *Latin* 'Be good and pious, let not the lion be more undaunted than thou'
    —Wintringham.

13. **Ex malo bonum**   *Latin* 'Good out of evil'
    —Appleton (U.S.).

14. **La bondad para la medra**   *Spanish* 'Goodness produces success'
    —Lennard.

15. **La bonté de Dieu**   *French* 'The goodness of God'
    —D'Olier.

16. **Miserere mei, Deus, secundum magnam misericordiam tuam**   *Latin* 'Have mercy on me, O God, after thy great goodness'
    —[Ps. li. 1.] On coronet of Garter King-at-Arms.

17. **Nec degenero**   *Latin* 'I do not degenerate'
    —Lane.

18. **Nec mireris homines mirabiliores**   *Latin* 'Wonder not at wonderful men'
    —Lambert.

19. **Nid da onid Duw**   *Welsh* 'No good but God'
    —Williams.

20. **Nil magnum nisi bonum**   *Latin* 'Nothing is great unless good'
    —Cooper (Bt.).

21. **Nil nisi bonum**   *Latin* 'Nothing if not good'
    —Simpson (U.S.).

22. **Non degener**   *Latin* 'Not degenerated'
     —Grindley, Kinlock, Kinglake (of Saltmoor), Wedderburn
     (Bt.).

23. **None is truly great but he that is truly good**
     —Packwood.

24. **Non nisi bonis placere cupio**   *Latin* 'The good alone I desire to
     please'
     —Ernst, Landgrave of Hesse-Rheinfels (1623–93).

25. **Omne bonum ab alto**   *Latin* 'All good from above'
     —Crossley.

26. **Omne bonum superne**   *Latin* 'All good from above'
     —Miller.

27. **Omnia bona bonis**   *Latin* 'To the good all things (are) good'
     —Harwich B. C., U.K.; Wenman, Wainman.

28. **Omnia probate, quod bonum est tenete**   *Latin* 'Prove all things:
     hold fast that which is good'
     —[1 Thess., v. 21.] Dorothee, Electress of Brandenburg
     and Duchess of Braunschweig-Lüneburg-Zelle
     (1636–89).

29. **Omnia pro bono**   *Latin* 'All things for good'
     —Murdoch, Murdock.

30. **Omnibus optimus**   *Latin* 'The best for all'
     —Aveling.

31. **Optimum quod evenit**   *Latin* 'The best is what has happened'
     —Laurens (U.S.).

32. **Pensez en bien**   *French* 'Think on good'
     —Noel, Wentworth.

33. **Probis, non pravis**   *Latin* 'To the good, not to the wicked'
     —over the drawing-room door, Loseley House, near
     Guildford, Surrey, England.

34. **Prodesse quam conspici**   *Latin* 'To do good rather than to be con-
     spicuous'
     —Buck (of Agecroft), Cocks, Chamberlayne, Grote (of
     Surrey), Leigh, Somers (E.).

35. **Quam plurimis prodesse**   *Latin* 'To do good to as many as you
     can'
     —Worsley (Bt.).

36. **Quod improbum terret probo prodest**   *Latin* 'To the dread and
     terror of the bad and to the reward of the good'
     —Penzance B. C., U.K.

37. **Rara bonitas** *Latin* 'Goodness is rare'

—Bennet.

38. **Sans mauvais désir** *French* 'Without evil desire'

—Constable.

39. **Sola bona quae honesta** *Latin* 'Those things only are good which are honest'

—Archer (Co. Warwick), Colebrooke (Bt.); Ernst August, Elector of Hanover (1629–98); Neave (Bt.).

40. **Sola bona quae honesta** *Latin* 'Only those things that are honorable are good'

—Leamington B. C., U.K.

41. **Terar dum prosim** *Latin* 'May I be worn out provided I do good'

—Merrman (of Kensington).

42. **Viditque Deus hanc lucem esse bonam** *Latin* 'And God saw the light that it was good'

—Rundle.

43. **Vincam malum bono** *Latin* 'I will overcome evil by good'

—Robinson.

44. **Vince malum bono** *Latin* 'Overcome evil by good'

—[Rom., xii. 21.] Jones (Co. Lancaster).

45. **Wer gutes u boses nit kan ertragan wirt kein grose chre erjagen** *German* 'Who cannot bear good and evil shall not obtain great honors'

—Brander (Co. Hants).

GOVERNMENT

1. **Constitution/ Wisdom/ Justice/ Moderation**

—University System of Georgia.

2. **Hic regit, ille tuetur** *Latin* 'This governs, that protects'

—Philipp II, Duke of Pomerania (1573–1618).

3. **Imperium in imperio** *Latin* 'An empire within an empire'

—Early motto of State of Ohio (1866–1868), Wetherby R. D. C., U.K.

4. **Per antiquam cartam** *Latin* 'By an ancient charter'

—Adlington.

5. **Pietas et justitia principatus columnae** *Latin* 'Piety and justice are the supports of government'

—Adolf Friedrich I, Duke of Mecklenburg-Schwerin (1588–1658).

6. **Pro Magna Charta** *Latin* 'For Magna Charta'
—Le Despencer (B.), Stapleton (Bt.), Stapleton.

7. **Reget et defendet** *Latin* 'He will rule and protect'
—Friedrich August I, Elector of Saxony (1670–1733).

8. **Republique** *Latin* 'The commonwealth'
—Harris.

9. **Rule be ours**
—Byres.

10. **Serviendo guberno** *Latin* 'By serving I govern'
—O'Rourke.

11. **The state, the home, the farm**
—Abraham Baldwin Agricultural College, Tifton, Georgia.

12. **This is our charter**
—Chartres.

13. **Tout pour l'empire** *French* 'All for the empire'
—Order of Re-Union.

14. **Violenta nemo imperia continuit diu: Moderata durant** *Latin* 'A violent rule has been long maintained by no one: moderation endures'
—[Seneca, *Troades*, l. 256.] Ernst VI, Count of Mansfeld (1561–1609).

GRACE (*See also* BLESSING; DIVINE GIFTS; MERCY; RELIGION; SALVATION.)

1. **Beauty and grace**
—Smith (U.S.).

2. **By the grace of God**
—Login.

3. **Dei beneficio sum quod sum** *Latin* 'By the grace of God I am what I am'
—Russell.

4. **Dei gratia** *Latin* 'By the grace of God'
—Kingston.

5. **Dei gratia grata** *Latin* 'The grace of God is grateful'
—Dixie (Bt.).

6. **Dei gratia sumus quod sumus** *Latin* 'By the grace of God, we are what we are'
—Barking B. C., U.K.

7. **Der Menschen Gunst ist umsonst** *German* 'Human grace is in vain'
— Friedrich Ulrich, Duke of Braunschweig-Wolfenbüttel (1591–1634).

8. **Die Gnad Gottes weirt ewig** *German* 'The grace of God is everlasting'
— Ernest II, Duke of Braunschweig-Grubenhagen (1518–67).

9. **En espoir je vive attendant grace** *French* 'I live in hope awaiting grace'
— Scrope.

10. **En grace affie** *French* 'On grace depend'
— Brudenel, Cardigan (E.), Grace (Bt.).

11. **Favore Altissimi** *Latin* 'By the grace of the Highest'
— Ferdinand Albert, Duke of Braunschweig-Bevern (1680–1735).

12. **God give grace**
— Tait.

13. **God grant grace**
— Grocers' Company.

14. **God send grace**
— Erne (E.), Dalrymple, Crichton.

15. **Gottes Heill ist mein Erbteil** *German* 'God's grace is my inheritance'
— Heinrich III, Count Reuss (1578–1616).

16. **Gottes Heil mein einzig Theil** *German* 'God's grace is my only portion'
— Marie Eleonore, Margravine of Brandenburg (1599–1655).

17. **Gottes hort pleibt ebiglich** *German* 'God's grace remains forever'
— Albrecht, Margrave of Brandenburg (1490–1568).

18. **Grace me guide**
— Forbes (B.), Pownall (of Hounslow); Forbes.

19. **Gratia Dei cibus animae** *Latin* 'The grace of God is the food of the soul'
— Moritz, Count of the Palatinate of Rhein (B. 1620).

20. **Gratia et veritas** *Latin* 'Grace and truth'
— Luther Theological Seminary, St. Paul, Minnesota.

21. **Gratia naturam vincit** *Latin* 'Grace conquers nature'
— Edwards (Bt.).

22. **Meor ras tha Dew** *Cornish* 'Gracious is thy God'
—Willyams.

23. **Non ego sed gratia Dei** *Latin* 'Not I but the grace of God'
—McGrea.

24. **Ohn Gottes Gunst Alles umsonst** *German* 'Without the grace of God all is in vain'
—Christian I, Prince of Anhalt-Bernburg (1568–1630).

25. **Par la grace et par les armes** *French* 'By grace and by arms'
—Ludwig Friedrich, Duke of Schleswig-Holstein-Sonderburg-Beck (1654–1728).

26. **Peace and grace**
—Graham (of Gartur).

27. **Propitio Deo securus ago** *Latin* 'With the grace of God I live secure'
—Franz II, Duke of Saxony-Lauenburg (1547–1619).

28. **Prudentia decus innocentia** *Latin* 'Prudence, grace, innocence'
—Ramsay.

29. **Tarde non fur mai grazie diuine** *Italian* 'Divine grace never comes too late'
—Ludwig the Elder, Prince of Anhalt-Köthen (1579–1650).

30. **Virebo proficiente Deo** *Latin* 'Through God's grace shall I flourish'
—Friedrich Wilhelm, Elector of Brandenburg (1620–88).

GRACEFULNESS (*See also* BEAUTY.)
1. **Debonnaire** *French* 'Graceful'
—Balfour, Bethune (Bt.), Bethune.

2. **Decore** *Latin* 'With grace'
—Baltingall.

3. **Fortitudine et decore** *Latin* 'By boldness and gracefulness'
—Ballinghall.

GRADUALNESS (*See also* MODERATION.)
1. **By degrees**
—Brey.

2. **Gradatim** *Latin* 'By degrees'
—Anderson, Hopwood, Kilgour.

3. **Gradatim plena**   *Latin* 'Full by degrees'
　　　　　　　　　　—Burnside (of Whitlaw), Gordon.

4. **Paullatim sed firmiter**   *Latin* 'Gradually but surely'
　　　　　　　　　　—University College School, London.

5. **Peu a peu**   *French* 'Little by little'
　　　　　　　　　　—Moseley (U.S.).

GRATITUDE

1. **Deo gratias**   *Latin* 'Thanks to God'
　　　　　　　　　　—Senhouse.

2. **Est Deo gratia**   *Latin* 'Thanks are to God'
　　　　　　　　　　—Searle.

3. **Give the thankys that are due**
　　　　　　　　　　—Plumer (of Gilston).

4. **Gratâ manu**   *Latin* 'With a grateful hand'
　　　　　　　　　　—Call (Bt.).

5. **Grata quies**   *Latin* 'Rest is grateful'
　　　　　　　　　　—Bexley.

6. **Grata sume manu**   *Latin* 'Take with a grateful hand'
　　　　　　　　　　—Brisco (of Coghurst), Winnington (Bt.).

7. **Gratias Deo agere**   *Latin* 'Give thanks to God'
　　　　　　　　　　—Sidney.

8. **Gratitude**
　　　　　　　　　　—Bigland (Co. Lancaster).

9. **Gratitude and loyalty**
　　　　　　　　　　—Nagle.

10. **Grato animo**   *Latin* 'With grateful mind'
　　　　　　　　　　—Barker, Blayds.

11. **Ingratis servire nefas**   *Latin* 'It is impossible to serve the ungrateful'
　　　　　　　　　　—Martin.

12. **Memor et gratus**   *Latin* 'Mindful and grateful'
　　　　　　　　　　—Gooch.

13. **Non immemor beneficii**   *Latin* 'Grateful for kindness'
　　　　　　　　　　—Broadley, Fitzgerald, Graham, Quantock, Leinster (D.).

14. **Nunquam ingratus**   *Latin* 'Never ungrateful'
　　　　　　　　　　—Friedrich August I, Elector of Saxony (1670–1733).

15. **Thankful**

—Hamilton, Stephenson-Hamilton.

GREATNESS (*See also* EXCELLENCE.)

1. **Cum magnis vixisse** *Latin* 'To have lived with the great'

—Swift.

2. **Magnanimus esto** *Latin* 'Be great of mind'

—Ingram, Irvine.

3. **Magni animi pretium** *Latin* 'The reward of magnanimity'

—Order of the White Elephant.

4. **Magnus Hippocrates; tu nobis major!** *Latin* 'Great Hippocrates! thou art greater than we'

—Dimsdale.

5. **Majora, uberiora, pulchriora** *Latin* 'Greater, more fruitful, and more beautiful'

—Hemel Hempstead Development Corp., U.K.

6. **Nil magnum nisi bonum** *Latin* 'Nothing is great unless good'

—Cooper (Bt.).

7. **None is truly great but he that is truly good**

—Packwood.

8. **Qui s'estime petyt deviendra grand** *Old French* 'He who thinks himself little shall become great'

—Petyt (of Ackworth, co. York).

9. **Quo major eo utilior** *Latin* 'The greater the more useful'

—Neilson.

10. **Sic parvis magna** *Latin* 'Thus great things arise from small'

—Drake (Bt.).

GROWTH (*See also* FLOURISHING; INCREASE.)

1. **'A place to grow'**

—Los Angeles Baptist College, Newhall, California.

2. **Couper fait grandir** *French* 'Cutting causes growth'

—Cooper.

3. **Crescit eundo** *Latin* 'It grows as it goes'

—New Mexico.

4. **Cresco sub jugo** *Latin* 'I grow under the yoke'

—Hay.

5. **Dum cresco spero** *Latin* 'While I grow I hope'
—Bromley B. C., U.K.

6. **Dum in arborem** *Latin* 'Until grown into a tree'
—Hamilton.

7. **E terra germino ad coelum expando** *Latin* 'I sprout out of the earth, I expand to heaven'
—Frost.

8. **Ex glande quercus** *Latin* 'From the acorn, the oak'
—Southgate B. C., U.K.

9. **Felici numine crescat** *Latin* 'May he grow under God's grace'
—Georg Friedrich, Margrave of Brandenburg-Anspach (1678–1703).

10. **Growing**
—Fergusson.

11. **His parva crescunt** *Latin* 'Little things grow great by these'
—Hyslop.

12. **I grow and wither both together**
—Wither.

13. **Injussi virescunt** *Latin* 'They grow green unbidden'
—Greenfield.

14. **Iterum virescit** *Latin* 'Again it grows green'
—Bisset.

15. **Luceat et crescat** *Latin* 'Let it shine and grow'
—Blackwood.

16. **Mutuo amore cresco** *Latin* 'By mutual love I grow'
—Lindsay.

17. **Quae vernant crescent** *Latin* 'Things which are green will grow'
—Burnet.

18. **Quicquid crescit in cinere perit** *Latin* 'Whatever grows perishes in ashes'
—Ashburner (of Cockermouth).

19. **Repullulat** *Latin* 'It buds afresh'
—Bisset, Lauder (of Bellhaven), Laurie (of Portsburgh).

20. **Sub pondere** *Latin* 'Beneath a weight (I grow)'
—Gustav Adolf, Margrave of Baden-Durlach (1631–77).

21. **Sub pondere cresco** *Latin* 'I grow under a weight'
—Fleming.

22. **Tandem fit arbor** *Latin* 'At last it becomes a tree'
—Hamilton.

23. **Tandem fit surculus arbor**   *Latin* 'A shoot (or bush) at length becomes a tree'
    —Bush, Burnet, Beresford, Douglas.

24. **Veteri frondescit honore**   *Latin* 'It puts forth leaves with ancient honor'
    —The Buffs (East Kent Regiment).

25. **We grow by industry**
    —Bedworth U. D. C., U.K., Blyth B. C.

GUIDANCE   (*See also* ASSISTANCE; DIVINE GUIDANCE; GOVERNMENT; LEADERSHIP.)

1. **Audi consilium**   *Latin* 'Heed counsel'
    —West Riding C. C., U.K.

2. **Auxilia auxiliis**   *Latin* 'Helps with the help of helps'
    —Helps.

3. **Auxiliante resurgo**   *Latin* 'When he helps I rise again'
    —Graham (of Merickle).

4. **Bene consulendo**   *Latin* 'By good counsel'
    —Derbyshire C. C., U.K.

5. **Concilio et labore**   *Latin* 'By counsel and by labor'
    —Manchester City and C. B. C., U.K.

6. **Consilio et prudentia**   *Latin* 'By counsel and by wisdom'
    —Atherton U. D. C., U.K.

7. **Dirige**   *Latin* 'Direct us'
    —Aldrige.

8. **Dirigo**   *Latin* 'I guide'
    —State of Maine.

9. **Dirigo et defendo**   *Latin* 'I direct and protect'
    —Sheppard.

10. **Duce et auspice**   *Latin* 'Under guidance and auspices (of the Holy Ghost)'
    —Order of the Holy Ghost (France).

11. **Dux mihi veritas**   *Latin* 'Truth is my guide'
    —Haggard.

12. **El honor es mi guia**   *Spanish* 'Honor is my guide'
    —Lousada.

13. **For the spiritual and educational guidance of youth**
    —Paul Quinn College, Waco, Texas.

14. **Heaven's light our guide**
—Order of the Star of India (founded 1861); Portsmouth City and C. B. C., U.K.

15. **Honneur me guide** *French* 'Honor guides me'
—Lousada.

16. **Honor me guide**
—Lusado.

17. **In concilio consilium** *Latin* 'In council is wisdom'
—Lancashire C. C., U.K.

18. **Monemus et munimus** *Latin* 'We counsel and protect'
—Monmouth B. C., U.K.

19. **Moneo et munio** *Latin* 'I advise and defend'
—Dalrymple, Elphinstone (Bt.), Elphinstone (of Horn and Logie).

20. **Mone sale** *Latin* 'Advise with wit'
—Monsell (of Tervoe).

21. **Montes unde auxilium meum** *Latin* 'The hills whence cometh my help'
—Keswick U. D. C., U.K.

22. **Opus nostrum dirige** *Latin* 'Direct our work'
—East Suffolk C. C., U.K.

23. **Passus rege meos** *Latin* 'Guide my steps'
—Walker.

24. **Prodesse civibus** *Latin* 'To benefit my fellow-citizens'
—Denison, Beckett (Co. York).

25. **Raison pour guide** *French* 'Reason for guide'
—Gascoyne.

26. **Solamen** *Latin* 'Consolation'
—Hope.

27. **Te duce gloriamur** *Latin* 'We glory under thy guidance'
—Sinclair (Bt.).

28. **Vicinas urbes alit** *Latin* 'It nurtures neighboring cities'
—Spalding U. D. C., U.K.

29. **Virtus duxit avorum** *Latin* 'The virtue of our ancestry was our guide'
—Seton.

30. **Virtute duce** *Latin* 'With virtue for guide'
—Elder, Shannon, Shand (of the Burn, co. Forfar).

31. **Vitam dirigit**   *Latin* 'It guides my life'
          —Christison.

GUILT   (*See also* CONSCIENCE.)
1. **Nemo sine crimine vivit**   *Latin* 'No one lives without blame'
          —Hope (U.S.).
2. **Nil conscire sibi**   *Latin* 'To have a conscience free from guilt'
    —[Horace, *Ep.* i. 1. 61.] Biss, Bullock (of Faulkbourn),
    Carew (Bt.), Collingwood, French, Michel (of
    Dewlish), Rothwell, Rogers, Sibthorp, Winchelsea
    (E.), Walker, Webb.
3. **Purus sceleres [sic]**   *Latin* 'Free from crime'
          —Carter (U.S.).
4. **Quis accusabit?**   *Latin* 'Who shall accuse?'
          —Hamilton.

HANDS
1. **Ambo dexter**   *Latin* 'Skillful with both hands'
          —Hewetson.
2. **Bella dextra**   *Latin* 'Wars with the right hand'
          —Ellis.
3. **By hammer and hand all arts do stand**
          —Blacksmiths' Company.
4. **Corde et manu**   *Latin* 'With heart and hand'
    —Steuart (of Auchlunkart), Stewart (of Carnousie),
    Goffdon.
5. **Corde manuque**   *Latin* 'With heart and hand'
          —Gorden (of Invergordon).
6. **Corde mente manu**   *Latin* 'With heart, mind, and hand'
          —Farie.
7. **Cor et manus**   *Latin* 'Heart and hand'
          —McManus.
8. **Dedicated to training hand, mind, heart**
          —Snead State Junior College, Boaz, Alabama.
9. **Dextra fideque**   *Latin* 'By my right hand and my fidelity'
          —Bell.
10. **Et manu et corde**   *Latin* 'Both with hand and heart'
          —Bates.

11. **Fit manus aliena sua**   *Latin* 'Another's hand becomes his'
　　　　　　　　　　　　　　　　　　　　　—Thornton.

12. **Forti tene manu**   *Latin* 'Hold with a firm hand'
　　　　　　　　　　　　　　　　　　　　　—Corry.

13. **Haec manus ob patriam**   *Latin* 'This hand for my country'
　　　　　　　　　　　　　　　—Mactier, Shuckburgh (Bt.).

14. **Head/ Heart/ Hand**
　　　　　　　—Bethune-Cookman College, Dayton Beach, Florida.

15. **Heart and hand**
　　　　　　　　　　　　　　　　　　　　　—Matheson.

16. **Lamh dearg Eirinn abú**   *Gaelic* 'The red hand for Ireland defy-
　　　ing'
　　　　　　　　　　　　　　　　　　　　　—O'Neill.

17. **Lamh derg aboo**   *Gaelic* 'The red hand defying'
　　　　　　　　　　　　　　　　　　　　　—Magawly.

18. **Lamh foistenach abu**   *Gaelic* 'The gentle hand defying'
　　　　　　　　　　　　　　　　　　　　　—O'Sullivan.

19. **Lamh laider an nachter**   *Gaelic* 'The strong hand defying'
　　　　　　　　　　　　　　　　　　　　　—O'Brien.

20. **Manu et corde**   *Latin* 'With heart and hand'
　　　　　　　　　　　　　　　　　　—Bates (of Denton).

21. **Manu forti**   *Latin* 'With a strong hand'
　　　　—Boyd, Jesham, Mackay, McCay, McCasker, Reay (B.).

22. **Manuque**   *Latin* 'And by the hand'
　　　　　　　　　　　　　　　　　　　　　—Jossey.

23. **Manus haec inimica tyrannis**   *Latin* 'This hand is hostile to
　　　tyrants'
　　　　　　　—Carysfort (E.), Dossey, Hemsworth (of Shropham, co.
　　　　　　　　Norfolk), Manley, Probyn, Riversdale (B.), Tonson.

24. **Manus justa nardus**   *Latin* 'A just hand is a precious ointment'
　　　　　　　　—Maynard (V.), Maynard (of Harlesey Hall).

25. **Mens et manus**   *Latin* 'Mind and hand'
　　　　　　　—Duncanson, North Carolina Agricultural and Technical
　　　　　　　　State University, Greensboro, North Carolina.

26. **Mente et manu**   *Latin* 'With heart and hand'
　　　　　　　　　　　　　　　—Glassford, Patrickson.

27. **Mente manuque**   *Latin* 'With heart and hand'
　　　　　　　—Farquhar (Bt.), Benshaw, Borthwick (of Stow).

28. **Mente manuque praesto**   *Latin* 'Ready with heart and hand'
—Foulis (Bt.).

29. **Quae habet manus tenebit**   *Latin* 'My hand will hold fast what it has'
—Templeman.

30. **Signantur cuncta manu**   *Latin* 'All things are sealed with the hand'
—Greig.

31. **Suprema manus validior**   *Latin* 'A hand stronger than the highest'
—Merry.

32. **Tam corde quam manu**   *Latin* 'With the heart as well as with the hand'
—Maynard.

33. **The red hand of Ireland**
—O'Neill (of Bunowen).

34. **The strongest hand uppermost**
—Kennedy.

35. **Thy right hand, O Lord, hath been glorified in strength**   *(from Greek)*
—Emerson-Tennant.

36. **With heart and hand**
—Dudgeon, Rule.

HAPPINESS (*See also* ENJOYMENT; FORTUNE; LAUGHTER.)

1. **A clean heart and cheerful spirit**
—Portman (B.).

2. **Amor Dei et proximi summa beatitudo**   *Latin* 'The love of God and our neighbour is the highest happiness'
—Dobbs.

3. **Art, industry, contentment**
—Basildon Development Corp.

4. **Avec ce que je tiens, je suis content**   *French* 'I am content with that which I have'
—Bradshaw.

5. **Coeur content grande talent**   *French* 'A contented heart is a great treasure'
—Marie Elisabeth, Landgravine of Hesse (1634–65).

6. **Comfort (confort) et liesse** *French* 'Comfort and joy'
—Doncaster C. B. C., U.K.

7. **Conquiesco** *Latin* 'I am contented'
—Metcalfe (Bt.).

8. **Contentement passe richesse** *French* 'Contentment is preferable to riches'
—Bowyer (Bt.).

9. **Contentus paucis** *Latin* 'Content with few things'
—Lea.

10. **Cordi dat animus alas** *Latin* 'My spirit gives wings to my heart'
—Falconer.

11. **En Dieu ma joye** *French* 'In God my joy'
—Magdalene Sibylle, Duchess of Saxony-Gotha and Altenburg (1648–81).

12. **Exaltatio mea** *Latin* 'My exaltation'
—Stubbs.

13. **Felice che puo** *Italian* 'Happy who can'
—Carew.

14. **Felicem reddet religio** *Latin* 'Religion will render happy'
—Millar.

15. **Felicitate restituta** *Latin* 'With happiness restored'
—Order of the Two Sicilies.

16. **Felix qui pacificus** *Latin* 'He is happy who is peaceful'
—Spence.

17. **Felix qui prudens** *Latin* 'He is happy who is prudent'
—Ashcombe (B.).

18. **Filey et felicitas** *Latin* 'Filey and felicity'
—Filey U. D. C., U.K.

19. **Fortis que felix** *Latin* 'Strong and happy'
—Minshull (U.S.), Walter (U.S.).

20. **Fortiter sed feliciter** *Latin* 'Bravely but happily'
—White.

21. **Gaude, Maria Virgo!** *Latin* 'Rejoice, O Virgin Mary'
—Coopers' Company.

22. **Gaudebunt campi, et omnia quae in iis sunt** *Latin* 'Let the fields rejoice and all that is therein'
—[Ps., xcvi. 12.] Campi.

23. **Gaudeo** *Latin* 'I rejoice'
—Brown (Bt.), Browne (of Westminster).

24. **Gaudere et epulari oportet**　*Latin* 'It is fitting to rejoice and feast'
    —Stalying.
25. **Gaudia magna nuncio or Gaudia nuncio magna**　*Latin* 'Joyous things, great things, I announce'
    —Scott (U.S.).
26. **Hallelujah**
    —Aylmer (Bt.), Aylmer (of Lyons, Co. Kildare).
27. **Hallelujah! Hallelujah! Hallelujah!**
    —Tuite.
28. **Happiness and prosperity through unity**　*(from Burmese)*
    —Union of Burma.
29. **Health and happiness**
    —Kaye (of Dalton Hall).
30. **Hic habitat felicitas**　*Latin* 'Here dwells happiness'
    —Baker's shop in Pompeii, Italy.
31. **Ich lasz mich genügen am göttlichen Fügen**　*German* 'I am content with God's decrees'
    —Sophie, Margravine of Brandenburg (1684–1752).
32. **Inest jucunditas**　*Latin* 'There is cheerfulness in it'
    —Elliot.
33. **Je me contente**　*French* 'I am content'
    —Sparrow.
34. **Joy sans fin**　*Old French* 'Joy without end'
    —Widdington.
35. **Jubilee**
    —Stamer.
36. **Kein Freud ohne Leid**　*German* 'No joy without sorrow'
    —Albert Friedrich, Margrave of Brandenburg (1582–1600).
37. **Laetavi**　*Latin* 'I have rejoiced'
    —Jolly.
38. **Laetitia et spe immortalitatis**　*Latin* 'With joy and hope of immortality'
    —Lyte, Shaw.
39. **Laetitia per mortem**　*Latin* 'Joy through death'
    —Luther.
40. **Laetus in praesens animus**　*Latin* 'A happy spirit in the present'
    —Powell (U.S.).
41. **Laetus sorte mea**　*Latin* 'Contented with my lot'
    —Sympson.

42. **Laetus sorte vives sapienter**   *Latin* 'You will live wisely contented with your lot'
—Kelk.

43. **Laugh lader an aughter**   'Laugh harder and louder'
—Kennedy.

44. **Licet esse beatis**   *Latin* 'It is allowed (to men) to be happy'
—Warde.

45. **Lux, salubritas, felicitas**   *Latin* 'Light, health, happiness'
—Clacton U. D. C., U.K.

46. **Ma joye en Dieu seulement**   *Old French* 'My joy is in God alone'
—Mompesson (Co. Norfolk).

47. **Make a clean heart and a cheerful spirit**
—Portman (B.).

48. **Nec placida contenta quiete est**   *Latin* '(The family) is not content with quiet repose'
—Mordaunt, Shipley.

49. **Nemo sine cruce beatus**   *Latin* 'No one is happy but by the cross'
—Baker.

50. **Nid cyfoeth ond boddlonrwydd**   *Welsh* 'No wealth without contentment'
—Garnons (Co. Denbigh and Co. Herts.).

51. **Omne bene**   *Latin* 'All's well'
—Harvey.

52. **Omnia bene**   *Latin* 'All's well'
—Harvey.

53. **Qui seminant in lachrymis, in exultatione metent**   *Latin* 'Who sow in tears, shall reap in joy'
—[Ps., cxxvi. 5.] Kemp.

54. **Qui vit content tient assez**   *French* 'He who lives contentedly has enough'
—Bradshaw (of Barton), Bradshaigh.

55. **Rident florentia prata**   *Latin* 'The flowery meadows laugh'
—Pratt (of Ryston Hall, co. Norfolk).

56. **Salus et felicitas**   *Latin* 'Health and happiness'
—Torquay B. C., Sale B. C., U.K.

57. **Sapientia felicitas**   *Latin* 'Wisdom is happiness'
—University of Oxford.

58. **Sicut oliva virens laetor in aede Dei** *Latin* 'As the flourishing olive, I rejoice in the house of God'
—[after Ps., lii. 8.] Oliver.

59. **Sit fors ter felix** *Latin* 'May your fate be thrice happy'
—Forster.

60. **Soies content** *French* 'Be content'
—Charnock.

61. **Son comfort et liesse** *French* 'His comfort and joy'
—Town of Doncaster (U.K.).

62. **Sorte contentus** *Latin* 'Content with one's lot'
—Welby.

63. **Sorte sua contentus** *Latin* 'Content with his lot'
—Hartwell (Bt.).

64. **Soyez content** *French* 'Be content'
—Charnocke.

65. **Stat felix amico Domino** *Latin* 'His happiness is sure when the Lord is his friend'
—Steuart.

66. **Sursum corda** *Latin* 'Lift up your hearts'
—Haileybury College, U.K.

67. **Tout mon contentement est en Dieu** *French* 'All my happiness is in God'
—Elisabeth, Duchess of Saxony (1593–1650).

68. **Utraque fortuna contentus** *Latin* 'Content with either fortune'
—Vosper.

69. **Vinum exhilarat animum** *Latin* 'Wine cheers the heart'
—Vintners' Company.

70. **Virtus sola felicitas** *Latin* 'Virtue is the only happiness'
—Bliss.

71. **Virtutis praemium felicitas** *Latin* 'Happiness the reward of virtue'
—Jones.

72. **Vive la joye** *Old French* 'Joy forever'
—Joy.

HARMLESSNESS (*See also* GENTLENESS; INNOCENCE.)

1. **Be wise as a serpent, harmless as a dove**
—[Matt. x. 16.] Lewis.

2. **Innocue ac provide**   *Latin* 'Harmlessly and providently'
   —Arbuthnot (of Montrose), Lapington.

3. **Prudens et innocuus**   *Latin* 'Prudent and harmless'
   —Kingsbury.

4. **Simplices sicut pueri, sagaces sicut serpentes**   *Latin* 'Harmless as boys, wise as serpents'
   —Vaughan.

5. **Wise and harmless**
   —Grant (of Carron).

HARVEST (*See also* AGRICULTURE; FRUIT.)

1. **Et mea messis erit**   *Latin* 'My harvest will also arrive'
   —Denny (Bt.).

2. **Hinc garbae nostrae**   *Latin* 'Hence our sheaves'
   —Cummin (of Brunthill).

3. **Messis ab altis**   *Latin* 'Harvest from the deeps'
   —Tynemouth C. B. C., U.K.

4. **Messis ab alto**   *Latin* 'Our harvest is from the deep'
   —Whittuck; Royal Fishery Company.

5. **Parva seges satis est**   *Latin* 'A small harvest is enough'
   —Cole (U.S.).

HEALING and HEALTH

1. **Amoenitas, salubritas, urbanitas**   *Latin* 'Amenity, salubrity, and urbanity'
   —Ryde.

2. **Amoenitas salubritas urbanitas**   *Latin* 'Pleasantness, health, urbanity'
   —Ryde B. C., U.K.

3. **Beauty surrounds, health abounds**
   —Morecambe and Heysham B. C., U.K.

4. **Body, mind, spirit**
   —Point Loma College, San Diego, California.

5. **By wounding I cure**
   —Stirling (of Calden).

6. **Curandum est ut sit mens sana in corpore sano** *Latin* 'Take care to have a sound mind in a sound body'
—[Juvenal, *Sat.* x. 356.] Ludwig V, Landgrave of Hesse-Darmstadt (1577–1626).

7. **Ex terra copiam e mari salutem** *Latin* 'From the land fullness and from the sea health'
—Worthing B. C., U.K.

8. **Ex vulnere salus** *Latin* 'Health from a wound'
—Borthwick.

9. **Firmitas et sanitas** *Latin* 'Strength and health'
—Griffith.

10. **Fragrat, delectat, et sanat** *Latin* 'It smells sweet, is pleasing, and healthful'
—Clelland.

11. **Health and happiness**
—Kaye (of Dalton Hall).

12. **Hinc odor et sanitas** *Latin* 'Hence fragrance and health'
—Liddel (of Edinburgh).

13. **Iechyd, harddwch, heddwch** *Welsh* 'Health, beauty and tranquility'
—Colwyn Bay B. C., U.K.

14. **Incidendo sano** *Latin* 'I cure by cutting'
—Kincaid.

15. **Lux, salubritas, felicitas** *Latin* 'Light, health, happiness'
—Clacton U. D. C., U.K.

16. **Medicine—To Teach, To Serve, To Search**
—University of Arkansas for Medical Sciences, Arkansas.

17. **Mens sana in corpore sano** *Latin* 'A sound mind in a sound body'
—McKean (U.S.).

18. **Nid meddyg ond meddyg enaid** *Welsh* 'No physician but the Physician of the soul'
—Fraser, Pughe (of Ty Gwyn).

19. **Non est vivere sed valere vita** *Latin* 'Not living, but health is life'
—Walker.

20. **Olet et sanat** *Latin* 'It smells sweet and heals'
—Dunbar (of Hillhead).

21. **Per scientiam ad salutem publicam** *Latin* 'Through knowledge to public health'
—Johns Hopkins School of Hygiene and Public Health, Baltimore, Maryland.

22. **Physical/ Mental/ Spiritual/ Social**
—University of Science and Arts of Oklahoma, Chickasha, Oklahoma.

23. **Physical/ Spiritual/ Social/ Mental**
—Florida College, Temple Terrace, Florida.

24. **Porta maris portus salutis** *Latin* 'A gate of the sea and a haven of health'
—Margate B. C., U.K.

25. **Pulchritudo et salubritas** *Latin* 'Beauty and health'
—Bournemouth C. B. C., U.K.

26. **Quarta saluti** *Latin* 'The fourth to health'
—Halliday.

27. **Qui panse** *French* 'Who heals'
—St. Lawrence.

28. **Quod me mihi reddit amicum** *Latin* 'What restores me to myself befriends me'
—Haslewood.

29. **Salubritas et eruditio** *Latin* 'Health and learning'
—Cheltenham B. C., U.K.

30. **Salubritas et industria** *Latin* 'Health and industry'
—Swindon B. C., U.K.

31. **Salus et felicitas** *Latin* 'Health and happiness'
—Torquay B. C., Sale B. C., U.K.

32. **Salus et gloria** *Latin* 'Health and glory'
—Eleonore, third consort of Emperor Ferdinand III (d. 1686).

33. **Sanitas/ scientia/ sanctitas** *Latin* 'Health/ knowledge/ holiness'
—Gannon University, Erie, Pennsylvania.

34. **Sanitate crescamus** *Latin* 'May we grow in health'
—Croydon C. B. C., U.K.

35. **Signum salutis semper** *Latin* 'Ever the sign of health'
—Bridlington B. C., U.K.

36. **Sol et salubritas** *Latin* 'Sun and health'
—Bexhill B. C., U.K.

37. **Studio optimae doctrinae et saluti sanitatis** *Latin* '(Dedicated) to the pursuit of educational excellence and the preservation of health'
—Logan College of Chiropractic, Chesterfield, Missouri.

38. **Ut sanem vulnero** *Latin* 'I wound to heal'
—Holt.

39. **Vulnere sano** *Latin* 'I cure by a wound'
—Balderston.

HEART (*See also* FEELINGS; LOVE.)

1. **A clean heart and cheerful spirit**
—Portman (B.).

2. **Bene praeparatum pectus** *Latin* 'A heart well prepared'
—[Horace, *Car.* ii. 10, 12.] Jex-Blake.

3. **Coeur content grande talent** *French* 'A contented heart is a great treasure'
—Marie Elisabeth, Landgravine of Hesse (1634–65).

4. **Cordi dat animus alas** *Latin* 'My spirit gives wings to my heart'
—Falconer.

5. **Cor unum** *Latin* 'One heart'
—Soke of Peterborough C. C., U.K.

6. **Cor unum, via una** *Latin* 'One heart, one way'
—Cecil, Exeter (M.), Mountsandford (B.), Sandford, Wills.

7. **Dedicated to training hand, mind, heart**
—Snead State Junior College, Boaz, Alabama.

8. **Et manu et corde** *Latin* 'Both with hand and heart'
—Bates.

9. **Make a clean heart and a cheerful spirit**
—Portman (B.).

10. **One heart, one way**
—Stourbridge B. C., U.K.

11. **Un Dieu, un roy, un coeur** *Old French* 'One God, one king, one heart'
—Lake (Bt.).

12. **Vita et pectore puro** *Latin* 'With pure life and heart'
—Beloe.

HOME

1. **A Home! A Home! A Home!**
   —Home (E.).

2. **Apto cum lare** *Latin* 'With a fit abode'
   —Elliot.

3. **Au Dieu foy, aux amis foyer** *Old French* 'To god faith, to friends home'
   —Hall of Farnham Castle, Hampshire, England.

4. **Certior in caelo domus** *Latin* 'A surer home in heaven'
   —Adams.

5. **Ches moy** *Old French* 'At home'
   —Honywood.

6. **Cornu exaltabitur honore** *Latin* 'The horn shall be exalted in honor'
   —Smyth (of Drumcree).

7. **Domi ac foris** *Latin* 'At home and abroad'
   —Norie.

8. **Domus grata** *Latin* 'A pleasing home'
   —Denison (U.S.).

9. **Et domi et foris** *Latin* 'Both at home and abroad'
   —Mack, Livingstone.

10. **Home**
    —Girvan.

11. **Home, industry, leisure**
    —Bracknell Development Corp., U.K.

12. **Home and country**
    —National Society of the Daughters of the American Revolution.

13. **Nobis habitatio felix** *Latin* 'A happy dwelling place for us'
    —Wilmslow U. D. C., U.K.

14. **Non domo dominus, sed domino domus** *Latin* 'Not the master for the house, but the house for the master'
    —House of Rossini, Bologna, Italy.

15. **Omne solum viro patria est** *Latin* 'Every country is a home for a man'
    —Matthews.

16. **Primum tutare domum** *Latin* 'First defend home'
    —Watkins.

17. **Pro ara et focis** *Latin* 'For hearth and home'
   —Johann Wilhelm, Duke of Saxony-Eisenach (1666–1729).

18. **Pro aris et focis** *Latin* 'For hearth and home'
   —[Cicero, *De. Nat.* Deo. iii. 40.] Heinrich Julius, Duke of
   Braunschweig-Wolfenbüttel (1564–1613); Johann
   Ludwig, Count of Palatinate of Zweibrücken
   (1609–47); Anton Günther, Count of Schwarzburg-
   Sondershausen (1620–66); Dessoffy de Cserneck,
   (Hungary).

19. **Pro aris et focis** *Latin* 'For our altars and our homes'
   —Blomfield, Campbell (of Shirven), Hazlerigge (Bt.),
   Kirkland, McNaught, Purdon, Phelips, Snell,
   Wait, Woodford.

20. **The state, the home, the farm**
   —Abraham Baldwin Agricultural College, Tifton, Georgia.

21. **Un [sic] corpus animo sic domus corpori** *Latin* 'As the body is to
   the soul, so is the house to the body'
   —House in Stoke Bishop, Gloucestershire, England.

22. **With fort and fleet for home and England**
   —Gillingham B. C., U.K.

HONESTY (*See also* FAIRNESS; INTEGRITY; RECTITUDE; RIGHTEOUSNESS;
SINCERITY; TRUSTWORTHINESS; TRUTH; VIRTUE.)

1. **Aut mors aut vita decora** *Latin* 'Either death or honourable life'
   —Gordon (of Carnousie), Shaw.

2. **Bona fide sine fraude** *Latin* 'In good faith without fraud'
   —Singleton.

3. **Bona quae honesta** *Latin* 'Good things which are honest'
   —Jackson (U.S.).

4. **Confido in probitate** *Latin* 'I trust in my probity'
   —Cadell.

5. **Cupressus honores peperit** *Latin* 'The cypress has procured us
   honor'
   —Duff.

6. **Diligentia et honeste** *Latin* 'By diligence and honorable dealing'
   —Garnett-Orme.

7. **Fortiter et honeste** *Latin* 'Boldly and honorably'
   —Abney.

8. **Fortiter et honeste** *Latin* 'Bravely and uprightly'
—Hawkes (U.S.).

9. **Honest and fast**
—Anderson.

10. **Honestas** *Latin* 'Honesty'
—Faal, Goadie, Goudie.

11. **Honestas optima politia** *Latin* 'Honesty is the best policy'
—Goff, Granger, Owen (Bt.), Sparrow (of Redhill).

12. **Honeste** *Latin* 'Honestly'
—Laing.

13. **Honestè vivo** *Latin* 'I live honestly'
—Halket (Bt.), Halkett.

14. **Honestie is good policie**
—Thomson.

15. **Honesto vivo** *Latin* 'I live by honesty'
--Halket.

16. **Honestum praeferre utili** *Latin* 'To prefer the honest to the profitable'
—Raikes (of Welton).

17. **Honesty is better than riches**
—Ray-Clayton (of Norwich).

18. **Honesty is good policy**
—Thomson (of Edinburgh).

19. **Honesty is the best policy**
—Thomas (of Yapton, bt.).

20. **Honesty without fear**
—Kelvin (B.).

21. **Honor et honestas** *Latin* 'Honor and honesty'
—Patriarche, Tremayne.

22. **Honos vitâ clarior** *Latin* 'Honor more glorious than life'
—Innes.

23. **Il vant [sic] mieux mourir que vivre sans honeur** *French* 'Tis better to die than to live dishonorably'
—Friedrich, Duke of Württemberg (1615–82).

24. **In scientia veritas in arte honestas** *Latin* 'Truth in science, honesty in art'
—Wells (Bt.).

25. **Integra mens augustissima possessio**   *Latin* 'An honest mind is the most glorious possession'
   —Blayney (B.).

26. **Juste et droit**   *French* 'Just and frank'
   —Whichcote (Bt.).

27. **Keep clean the game**
   —Henry Chadwick, (re. baseball).

28. **Malim esse probus quam haberi**   *Latin* 'I had rather be honest than be thought so'
   —Kennedy (of Kirkmichael).

29. **Mentis honestae gloria**   *Latin* 'The glory of an honest mind'
   —Grey.

30. **Merui candore favorem**   *Latin* 'I have deserved favor from my fairness'
   —White.

31. **Nihil utile quod non honestum**   *Latin* 'Nothing dishonorable is useful'
   —Dovers, Moor, Moore (of Fawley).

32. **Perduret probitas**   *Latin* 'Let honesty endure'
   —Pearson.

33. **Pietate et probitate**   *Latin* 'By piety and honesty'
   —Rees.

34. **Probitas cum fortitudine**   *Latin* 'Honesty with fortitude'
   —Brewster.

35. **Probitas et firmitas**   *Latin* 'Honesty and firmness'
   —Lesly.

36. **Probitas laudatur et alget**   *Latin* 'Honesty is praised and neglected'
   —Antill (U.S.).

37. **Probitas optimum est consilium**   *Latin* 'Honesty is the best policy'
   —Koecker (U.S.).

38. **Probitas verus honos**   *Latin* 'Honesty is true honor'
   —Barrett, Bateson (Bt.), Chetwynd (V.), Lacon (Bt.), Newman, Vicary.

39. **Probitate**   *Latin* 'By honesty'
   —Rennie, Renny.

40. **Probitate et industria**   *Latin* 'By honesty and industry'
   —Bridgen (U.S.).

41. **Probitate et labore**   *Latin* 'By honesty and toil'
                                                    —Gould.

42. **Probitate et virtute**   *Latin* 'By probity and valor'
                                                    —Rose.

43. **Probitatem quam divitias**   *Latin* 'Honesty rather than riches'
                          —Clayton (of Adlington Hall, Bt.), Claydon.

44. **Probum non paenitet**   *Latin* 'The honest man repents not'
                                                    —Sandys (B.).

45. **Qui honeste fortiter**   *Latin* 'He who (acts) honestly acts bravely'
                                          —Anderson (of Edinburgh).

46. **Quod honestum est decet**   *Latin* 'What is honorable is becoming'
                                                    —Richardson.

47. **Quod honestum utile**   *Latin* 'What is honest is useful'
                          —Lawson (Bt.), Annand (of Annandale).

48. **Recte quod honeste**   *Latin* 'That is rightly which is honestly done'
                                          —Anderson (of Glasgow).

49. **Sedulo et honeste**   *Latin* 'Diligently and honestly'
                                                    —Lyall.

50. **Simplex vigilum veri**   *Latin* 'An honest one of the sentinels of truth'
                                          —Perkins (Co. Warwick).

51. **Verax atque probus**   *Latin* 'Trustworthy and honest'
                                                    —Ruttledge.

52. **Verus honor honestas**   *Latin* 'Honesty is true honor'
                                                    —Lacock.

53. **Veteri frondescit honore**   *Latin* 'It puts forth leaves with ancient honor'
                                  —The Buffs (East Kent Regiment).

54. **Virtute et probitatè**   *Latin* 'By virtue and honesty'
                                                    —Magan.

55. **Vivat honestas**   *Latin* 'May honesty flourish'
                                                    —Sproston.

HONOR (*See also* DUTY; MILITARY DISTINCTION; RECTITUDE;
    REPUTATION; TRUSTWORTHINESS; VIRTUE.)

1. **A cuspide honos**   *Latin* 'Honor by the spear'
                                                    —Swindley.

2. **Addecet honeste vivere** *Latin* 'It much becomes us to live honourably'

—Addison.

3. **Antiquum assero decus** *Latin* 'I claim ancient honor'

—Arrot.

4. **Antiquum obtinens (honorem)** *Latin* 'Possessing our ancient honor'

—Bagot (B.), Beaumont, Cotgreave (of Netherleigh), Shakerly (Bt.).

5. **Aut mors aut vita decora** *Latin* 'Either death or honourable life'

—Gordon (of Carnousie), Shaw.

6. **Avita et aucta** *Latin* '(Honors) Inherited and acquired'

—Order of the Iron Crown (Austria).

7. **Avitos juvat honores** *Latin* 'He maintains his ancestral honors'

—Wishart.

8. **By industry and honor**

—Hall.

9. **Calcar honeste** *Latin* 'A spur with honor'

—Crawford.

10. **Callide et honeste** *Latin* 'Wisely and honourably'

—Calley (of Burderop).

11. **Clarior hinc honos** *Latin* 'Hence the brighter honour'

—Buchanan, Mac Causland.

12. **Cornu exaltabitur honore** *Latin* 'The horn shall be exalted in honor'

—Smyth (of Drumcree).

13. **Crux et praesidium et decus** *Latin* 'The cross is both an honor and a defense'

—Andros.

14. **Crux praesidium et decus** *Latin* 'The cross is (my) guard and honor'

—Tyler.

15. **Cum toga honoris** *Latin* 'With the cloak of honor'

—Robe.

16. **Cupressus honores peperit** *Latin* 'The cypress has procured us honor'

—Duff.

17. **Decens et honestum** *Latin* 'Becoming and honorable'

—Fyffe (of Dron).

18. **Decori decus addit avito** *Latin* 'He adds honor to that of his ancestors'
—Erskine, Kelly.

19. **Decus et tutamen** *Latin* 'An honor and a protection'
—Gravesend B. C., U.K.

20. **Decus recte peto** *Latin* 'I seek honor honorably'
—Jenks (Bt.).

21. **Decus summum virtus** *Latin* 'Virtue is the highest honor'
—Holburne (Bt.), Hulburn.

22. **Denique decus** *Latin* 'Honor at length'
—Stoddart.

23. **Deo honor et gloria** *Latin* 'Unto God be honor and glory'
—Leather Sellers' Company.

24. **Dignitas et libertas a Deo et Caesare** *Latin* 'Honors and freedom come from God and from the emperor'
—Christian II, Prince of Anhalt-Bernburg (1599–1656).

25. **Diligentia et honore** *Latin* 'With diligence and honor'
—Garnett.

26. **Ducitur hinc honos** *Latin* 'Hence honor is derived'
—Buchanan (of Miltown).

27. **Dum spiro spero** *Latin* 'While I have breath I hope'
—Aschmaty, Asscotti, Auchmuty (of Brianstown), Bainbridge, Baker, Bannatyne (of Newhall), Bloxam, Brooke, Bushell, Colquhon, Compton, Cottee, Cotter (Bt.), Davies (of Marrington Hall), Dearden, Deardon, Dillon (V.), Doran, Drummond, Elrick, Glazebrook, Going, Gordon, Gurney, Hoare (Bt.), Hoare, Hunter, Learmouth, Lee, Monk-Mason (of Mason-Brook), Moore, Morice, Morris, Oldfield, O'Reilly, Partridge (of Hockham, co. Norfolk), Pearson, Price, Roberts (of Beechfield), Rodwell, Sharp, Smith, Stanton, Stretton, Spearman (of Thornley), Spry, Symonds, Tatlock, Thompson (co. Durham), Walker, Westerman.

28. **Dum vivo, spero** *Latin* 'While I live I hope'
—Stuart-Menteith (Bt.), Monteath, Thom, Latta, Whiteway.

29. **Duty, honor, country**
    —West Point U.S. Military Academy, West Point, New York.

30. **Ehr und Eid gilt mehr als Land und Leut** *German* 'Honor and oath are worth more than country and people'
    —Christoph, Margrave of Baden-Rodemachern (1537–75).

31. **El honor es mi guia** *Spanish* 'Honor is my guide'
    —Lousada.

32. **En espérance je vis** *French* 'In hope I live'
    —Carew.

33. **E perseverantia honor** *Latin* 'Honor from perseverance'
    —Davey.

34. **Et decus et pretium recti** *Latin* 'Both the honor and the reward of rectitude'
    —Fitz-Roy, Grafton (D.), Southampton (B.), Disney.

35. **Exaltabit honore** *Latin* 'It will exalt with honor'
    —Smyth (of Graybrook).

36. **Ex armis honos** *Latin* 'Honor gained by arms'
    —Ogilvy (of Logie).

37. **Ex candore decus** *Latin* 'Honor from sincerity'
    —Keith (of Craig).

38. **Ex recto decus** *Latin* 'Honor through rectitude'
    —Durno.

39. **Ex sola virtute honos** *Latin* 'Honor springs from virtue alone'
    —Johnston, Johnstone.

40. **Ex vero decus** *Latin* 'Honor from the truth'
    —Jones.

41. **Ex virtute honos** *Latin* 'Honor from virtue'
    —Jardin.

42. **Fama proclamat honorem** *Latin* 'Reputation proclaims honor'
    —Perot (U.S.).

43. **Fides et honor** *Latin* 'Faith and honor'
    —De Forest (B.).

44. **Formosa quae honesta** *Latin* 'What is honorable is beautiful'
    —Tarton, Turton.

45. **Fortuna et honos ab alto** *Latin* 'Fortune and honor are from above'
    —Rydon.

46. **Gardez l'honneur** *French* 'Preserve honor'
—Broadley (Bt.), Hanmer.

47. **Hinc decus inde tegmen** *Latin* 'From this quarter honor, from that protection'
—Graham.

48. **Hinc ducitur honos** *Latin* 'Hence honor is derived'
—Nisbet.

49. **Hinc honor et opes** *Latin* 'Hence honor and wealth'
—Hay (of Cardenie).

50. **Hinc honor et salus** *Latin* 'Hence honor and safety'
—Lindsay.

51. **Hinc laus et honos** *Latin* 'Hence praise and honor'
—Rae.

52. **Hoc signum non onus, sed honor** *Latin* 'This banner is no burden, but an honor'
—Stoughton.

53. **Honesta peto** *Latin* 'I seek honorable things'
—Oliphant.

54. **Honesta quam magna** *Latin* 'How great are honorable things'
—Walker.

55. **Honesta quam splendida** *Latin* 'Honor rather than splendor'
—Barrington (V.), Hine, Dickens (knt.).

56. **Honestas et fortitudo** *Latin* 'Honor and courage'
—Dunckerley.

57. **Honestas et veritas** *Latin* 'Honor and truth'
—Kemp.

58. **Honestas quam splendida** *Latin* 'How illustrious is honorable conduct'
—Askwith.

59. **Honestate vetustas stat** *Latin* 'Ancestry is established by honor'
—Stewart (of Edinglassie).

60. **Honeste, fortiter** *Latin* 'Honorably and bravely'
—Smith.

61. **Honeste et constanter** *Latin* 'Honorably and constantly'
—Reddie.

62. **Honestum praetulit utili** *Latin* 'He has preferred honor to profit'
—Emline.

63. **Honestum pro patria**   *Latin* 'What is honorable and just should be done for one's country'
    —Heinrich Julius, Duke of Braunschweig-Wolfenbüttel (1564–1613).

64. **Honestum pro patriâ**   *Latin* 'What is honorable for my country'
    —Hamilton.

65. **Honestum utili patria**   *Latin* 'The honorable is the native soil of the useful'
    —Hamborough.

66. **Honestum utili praefer**   *Latin* 'Prefer the honorable to the agreeable'
    —Hambrough (of Steephill Castle, Isle of Wight).

67. **Honestum utili prefero**   *Latin* 'I prefer honor to profit'
    —McGell.

68. **Honneur et patrie**   *French* 'Honor and my country'
    —Order of the Legion of Honor (France).

69. **Honneur me guide**   *French* 'Honor guides me'
    —Lousada.

70. **Honneur pour objet**   *French* 'Honor for object'
    —Page.

71. **Honneur sans repos**   *French* 'Honor without repose'
    —Montgomery.

72. **Honor**
    —Lawton.

73. **Honor, pietas**   *Latin* 'Honor, piety'
    —Waters.

74. **Honor, purpose, wisdom**
    —Palo Verde College, Blythe, California.

75. **Honor, virtus, probitas**   *Latin* 'Honor, virtue, and probity'
    —Barrett.

76. **Honor alit artes**   *Latin* 'Honor fosters the arts'
    —Burton-upon-Trent C. B. C., U.K.

77. **Honorantes me honorabo**   *Latin* 'I will honor those who honor me'
    —Atthill, (Co. Norfolk), Huntingdon (E.), Mannsell.

78. **Honorate, diligite, timete**   *Latin* 'Honor, love, fear'
    —Moseley.

79. **Honorat mors**   *Latin* 'Death confers honor'
    —Bragge, Broigg.

80. **Honor Deo**   *Latin* 'Honor be to God'
—Mercers' Company.

81. **Honore et amore**   *Latin* 'With honor and love'
—Richards, Grantham (of Ketton), Hammersley,
Solosborough.

82. **Honore et armis**   *Latin* 'By honor and arms'
—Campbell.

83. **Honore et justitia**   *Latin* 'Through honor and justice'
—Jayne (U.S.).

84. **Honore et labore**   *Latin* 'By honor and labor'
—Hill.

85. **Honore et virtute**   *Latin* 'With honor and virtue'
—Gillbanks.

86. **Honore integro contemno fortunam**   *Latin* 'With honor unstained I despise fortune'
—FitzGibbon.

87. **Honore pietas**   *Latin* 'Piety with honor'
—Waters.

88. **Honores praefero**   *Latin* 'I prefer honor'
—Scots Guards, U.K.

89. **Honor et amor**   *Latin* 'Honor and love'
—Niblie.

90. **Honor et fides**   *Latin* 'Honor and faith'
—Sears.

91. **Honor et honestas**   *Latin* 'Honor and honesty'
—Patriarche, Tremayne.

92. **Honore timore**   *Latin* 'With honor and with fear'
—Friedrich August I, Elector of Saxony (1670–1733).

93. **Honor et industria**   *Latin* 'Honor and industry'
—Bacup B. C., U.K.

94. **Honor et justitia**   *Latin* 'Honor and justice'
—Antill (U.S.).

95. **Honor et justitia manet amicitia florebit semper que**
Latin 'Honor and justice remain, and friendship will always
flourish'
—Bayard (U.S.).

96. **Honor et veritas**   *Latin* 'Honor and truth'
—Waller (Bt.).

97. **Honor et virtus** *Latin* 'Honor and virtue'
—Akins, Grogan (Bt.), Morgan.

98. **Honor fidelitatis praemium** *Latin* 'Honor is the reward of fidelity'
—Boston (B.), Irby.

99. **Honor me guide**
—Lusado.

100. **Honor nourishes the arts**
—International Fine Arts College, Miami, Florida.

101. **Honor post funera vivit** *Latin* 'Honor lives after death'
—Broadly.

102. **Honor potestate honorantis** *Latin* 'Honor is in the power of him who honors'
—Edwards, Kynaston.

103. **Honor praemium virtutis est** *Latin* 'Honor is the reward of virtue'
—Flynn.

104. **Honor probataque virtus** *Latin* 'Honor and approved valor'
—Fitzgerald (of Turlough), MacDermott.

105. **Honor rewards industry**
—Gardiner.

106. **Honor sequitur fugientem** *Latin* 'Honor follows him who shuns it'
—Donegall (M.).

107. **Honor veritas et justitia** *Latin* 'Honor truth and justice'
—Southam.

108. **Honor virtutem coronat** *Latin* 'Honor crowns virtue'
—Davies.

109. **Honor virtutis praemium** *Latin* 'Honor is the reward of virtue'
—Bell, Boyle, Cork and Orrery (E.), Hawtin, Hawtyn, Hole, Ferrers (E.), Fielding, Shirley.

110. **Honor virtutis pretium** *Latin* 'Honor is the reward of virtue'
—Mills.

111. **Honos alit artes** *Latin* 'Honor nourishes arts'
—Greenhill.

112. **Honos cui honos** *Latin* 'Honor to whom honor is due'
—Brooke.

113. **Honos fidelitatis praemium** *Latin* 'Honor the reward of fidelity'
—Irby.

114. **Honos industriae praemium**   *Latin* 'Honor the reward of industry'
                                        —King (of Campsie, bt.).

115. **Honos virtutis satelles**   *Latin* 'Honor the attendant of virtue'
                                        —Baker.

116. **Honos vitâ clarior**   *Latin* 'Honor more glorious than life'
                                        —Innes.

117. **Hostis honori invidia**   *Latin* 'Envy is an enemy to honor'
                                        —Dickens; Market Harborough U. D. C., U.K.

118. **Illis honos venit**   *Latin* 'Honor comes to them'
                                        —Mitchell.

119. **Il vant [sic] mieux mourir que vivre sans honeur**   *French* 'Tis better to die than to live dishonorably'
                                        —Friedrich, Duke of Württemberg (1615–82).

120. **In candore decus**   *Latin* 'There is honor in sincerity'
                                        —Chadwick (of Pudleston Court).

121. **Incoctum pectus honesto**   *Latin* 'A bosom deeply imbued with honor'
                                        —Smedley (of Revesby, Co. Lincoln).

122. **In constantia decus**   *Latin* '(There is) honor in constancy'
                                        —Coppard.

123. **In recto decus**   *Latin* 'Honor in acting right'
                                        —Ferrier, Scott, Brunswick and Luenburg, Syme,
                                          Simmons, Hoseason.

124. **Intaminatis fulget honoribus**   *Latin* 'He shines with unstained honors'
                                        —[Horace, *Car.* iii. 2. 17.] Seton, Winton (E.), Wofford
                                          College, Spartanburg, South Carolina.

125. **Intaminatis honoribus**   *Latin* 'With unstained honors'
                                        —Fitz-Herbert, St. Helens (B.).

126. **Invitum sequitur honor**   *Latin* 'Honor follows one who desires it not'
                                        —Donegal (M.), Chichester, Templemore (B.).

127. **Invitum sequitur honos**   *Latin* 'Honor follows even the unwilling man'
                                        —Gerard (U.S.).

128. **J'aime l'honneur qui vient par la vertu**   *French* 'I love the honor which is attained through virtue'
                                        —Order of the Noble Passion.

129. **Justa sequor**   *Latin* 'I follow honorable things'
—Keith.

130. **Justum et decorum**   *Latin* 'Just and honorable'
—Friedrich Adolf, Count von der Lippe (1667–1718).

131. **Knowledge/ Duty/ Honor**
—South Carolina State College, Orangeburg, South
Carolina.

132. **Labore et honore**   *Latin* 'By industry and honor'
—Bowden, Rendlesham (B.), Thelluson, Pemberton (of
Barnes), Viner.

133. **Lauro redimita quiescam**   *Latin* 'I will rest crowned with laurels'
—Lyon.

134. **L'honneur est mon tresor, la vertu ma conduite**   *French* 'Honor is
my treasure, virtue my guide'
—Wilhelm VI, Landgrave of Hesse-Cassel (1629–63);
Hedwig Sophie, Landgravine of Hesse-Cassel
(1623–83).

135. **L'honneur me guide**   *French* 'Honor guides me'
—Lousada.

136. **L'honneur nous unit**   *French* 'Honor unites us'
—Furnival.

137. **Meritas augentur honores**   *Latin* 'Honors are enhanced by des-
serts'
—Lacy (Bt.).

138. **Mors, aut honorabilis vita**   *Latin* 'Death, or life with honor'
—Joyce.

139. **My word is my bond**
—Smallman.

140. **Nativum retinet decus**   *Latin* 'He retains his native honor'
—Livingstone.

141. **Nec quaerere, nec spernere honorem**   *Latin* 'Neither to seek nor
to despise honor'
—Bolingbroke (V.), Boughey (Bt.), St. John.

142. **Nec quaerere honorem nec spernere**   *Latin* 'Neither seek nor
spurn honor'
—Bell (U.S.), Sargent (U.S.).

143. **Nil nisi honestum**   *Latin* 'Nothing unless honorable'
—Philips.

144. **Nil nisi quod honestum**   *Latin* 'Nothing unless what is honorable'
—Leather.

145. **Non fraude sed laude**   *Latin* 'Not by deceit but with honor'
—Gordon (Co. Aberdeen and Terpersey).

146. **Nunquam nisi honorificentissimè**   *Latin* 'Never unless most honorably'
—Freeling (Bt.).

147. **Onus sub honore**   *Latin* 'There is a burden (to sustain) under honor'
—Johnson.

148. **Optima quae que honesto**   *Latin* 'To the man of honor everything best'
—Lambert.

149. **Passant cressant en honneur**   *French* 'Progressing in honor'
—Walker.

150. **Post proelia praemia**   *Latin* 'After battles honors'
—Fellows, McInnes, Nicholson, Rossmore (B.).

151. **Praemium, virtus, honor**   *Latin* 'Reward, virtue, honor'
—Brown (of Blackburn), Cox.

152. **Praemium honor**   *Latin* 'The reward is honor'
—Foster.

153. **Praemium virtutis honor**   *Latin* 'Honor is the reward of virtue'
—Cheere, Lovelace, Tetlow (of Haughton).

154. **Probitas fons honoris**   *Latin* 'Integrity is the fountain of honor'
—Gubbay.

155. **Probitas veritas honos**   *Latin* 'Integrity, truth, and honor'
—Browne.

156. **Probitas verus honos**   *Latin* 'Honesty is true honor'
—Barrett, Bateson (Bt.), Chetwynd (V.), Lacon (Bt.),
Newman, Vicary.

157. **Pro patria et gloria**   *Latin* 'For country and honor'
—7th Regiment of National Guard, State of New York
(U.S. Civil War).

158. **Prudentia et honor**   *Latin* 'Prudence and honor'
—McKinna.

159. **Quae recta sequor**   *Latin* 'I pursue things honorable'
—Campbell.

160. **Quo honestior eo tutior**   *Latin* 'The more honorable the safer'
—Guise.

161. **Recte ad ardua** *Latin* 'Honorably throughout difficulties'
—Mackenzie (of Delvin).

162. **Sed sine labe decus** *Latin* 'Moreover an honor without stain'
—Eldon (E.).

163. **Sedulo et honeste tutela** *Latin* 'Guardianship with honor and diligence'
—Lyell.

164. **Semper honos** *Latin* 'Always honor'
—Horry (U.S.).

165. **Sic rectius progredior** *Latin* 'Thus I proceed more honorably'
—Sinclair.

166. **Sine labe decus** *Latin* 'Honor without stain'
—Allen; Wimbledon B. C., U.K.

167. **Sine virtute vani sunt honores** *Latin* 'Without virtue honors are empty'
—Bozman (U.S.).

168. **Sit nomen decus** *Latin* 'May my name be an honor'
—Worsley.

169. **Sit sine labe decus** *Latin* 'May my honor be without blemish!'
—Eldon (E.).

170. **Sola bona quae honesta** *Latin* 'Only those things that are honorable are good'
—Leamington B. C., U.K.

171. **Sperate et vivite fortes** *Latin* 'Hope and live bold(ly)'
—Bland (of Kippax Park).

172. **Speratum et completum** *Latin* 'Hoped for and fulfilled'
—Arnet, Arnut.

173. **Spero et progredior** *Latin* 'I hope and proceed'
—Pringle (of Clifton, etc.).

174. **Spero et vivo** *Latin* 'I hope and live'
—Mashiter.

175. **Spes, salus, decus** *Latin* 'Hope, safety, honor'
—Nesham (of Stockton).

176. **Strenue et honeste** *Latin* 'Strenuously and honorably'
—Jackson.

177. **Studiis et rebus honestis** *Latin* 'By study and honorable pursuits'
—Dunning.

178. **Tam virtus quam honos** *Latin* 'As well virtue as honor'
—Hamilton.

179. **Truth, honor, and courtesy**

—Gentleman.

180. **Unto God only be honor and glory**

—Drapers' Company (London).

181. **Vanus est honor** *Latin* 'Honor is vain'

—Bowden.

182. **Vertu cherche honneur** *French* 'Virtue seeks honor'

—D'Arcy.

183. **Verus honor honestas** *Latin* 'Honesty is true honor'

—Lacock.

184. **Veteri frondescit honore** *Latin* 'It puts forth leaves with ancient honor'

—The Buffs (East Kent Regiment).

185. **Vi at tamen honore** *Latin* 'By force, yet with honor'

—Wyatt.

186. **Virtue is honor**

—Kenrick.

187. **Virtue is my honour**

—McLannahan.

188. **Virtue mine honor**

—Maclean (Bt.), McLean.

189. **Virtue only has claim to honour**

—Rumsey (U.S.).

190. **Virtus acquirit honorem** *Latin* 'Virtue gains honor'

—Spence.

191. **Virtus auget honorem** *Latin* 'Virtue increases honor'

—Edmounstone (Bt.).

192. **Virtus auget honores** *Latin* 'Virtue increases honors'

—Charles.

193. **Virtus et honos** *Latin* 'Virtue and honor'

—Order of St. Hubert of Loraine and of Bar, Order of Merit of the Bavarian Crown.

194. **Virtus honoris Janua** *Latin* 'Virtue, the gateway to honor'

—Burr (U.S.), Farlow (U.S.).

195. **Virtus incumbet honori** *Latin* 'Virtue will rest upon honor'

—Williams (of Eltham).

196. **Virtus intaminatis fulget honoribus** *Latin* 'Virtue shines with unspotted honors'

—[Horace, *Car.* iii. 2. 17.] Truss.

197. **Virtus nobilitat honoremque parit** *Latin* 'Virtue ennobles and brings honor'
—Friedrich, Duke of Schleswig-Holstein and Norburg (1581–1658).

198. **Virtus verus honos** *Latin* 'Virtue is true honor'
—Burr.

199. **Virtute acquiritur honos** *Latin* 'Honor is acquired by virtue'
—Richardson (Bt.), Richardson, Richie, Ritchie, Spence.

200. **Virtute et honore** *Latin* 'With virtue and honor'
—Wells.

201. **Virtute honor** *Latin* 'Honor through virtue'
—Richardson.

202. **Virtutem ante pono honorem** *Latin* 'I prefer virtue to honor'
—McPherson (U.S.).

203. **Virtutem coronat honos** *Latin* 'Honor crowns virtue'
—Drummond.

204. **Virtutibus praemium honor** *Latin* 'Honor the reward of virtues'
—Ffeilden (of Witton).

205. **Virtutis alimentum honos** *Latin* 'Honor is the food of valor'
—Parker (of Petteril Green).

206. **Virtutis honor praemium** *Latin* 'Honor is the prize of valor'
—Sparling.

207. **Virtutis praemium honor** *Latin* 'Honor is the reward of virtue'
—Denbigh (E.), Fielden, Feniscowles, Millington.

208. **Wer gutes u boses nit kan ertragan wirt kein grose chre erjagen** *German* 'Who cannot bear good and evil shall not obtain great honors'
—Brander (Co. Hants).

HOPE

1. **Ad finem spero** *Latin* 'I hope to the last'
—Ogilvie.

2. **All my hope is in God**
—Frazer, Undey, Udney.

3. **Anchora spei Cereticae est in te, Domine** *Latin* 'The anchor of Cardigan's hope is in Thee, O Lord'
—Cardigan B. C., U.K.

4. **A spe in spem** *Latin* 'From hope to hope'
—Perkin.

5. **At spes infracta** *Latin* 'Yet my hope is unbroken'
—Conyngham (Bt.), Dick, Hood, Hope (Bt.).

6. **At spes non fracta** *Latin* 'Yet hope is not broken'
—Blaenavon U. D. C., U.K., Hope, Hopetown (E.),
Kennard.

7. **At spes solamen** *Latin* 'Yet hope is my solace'
—Hope (of Balcomy).

8. **Bonne espérance et droit en avant** *French* 'Forward, good hope and right!'
—Nugent.

9. **Bon temps viendra** *French* 'The good time will come'
—Gage.

10. **Caelestem spero coronam** *Latin* 'I hope for a heavenly crown'
—Blake-Humfrey.

11. **Chéris l'espoir** *French* 'Cherish hope'
—Cherry.

12. **Christus meine Hoffnung** *German* 'Christ is my hope'
—Joachim, Margrave of Brandenburg (1583–1600).

13. **Clypeus omnibus in te sperantibus** *Latin* 'Thou art a shield to all who place their hope in thee'
—[after Prov. xxx. 5.] Maximilian, Prince-Elector of
Bavaria (1573–1651); Maximilian Emanuel,
Elector of Bavaria (1662–1726).

14. **Concipe spes certas** *Latin* 'Conceive sure hopes'
—Sealy.

15. **Courage et esperance** *French* 'Courage and hope'
—Storie.

16. **Court hope**
—Courthope.

17. **Cresco et spero** *Latin* 'I increase and hope'
—Hannay.

18. **Cruce dum spiro spero** *Latin* 'While I breathe I hope in the cross'
—Cross, Darlington.

19. **Cruce spes mea** *Latin* 'My hope is in the cross'
—Bird.

20. **Cruci dum spiro spero** *Latin* 'Whilst I breathe my hope is in the cross'
—Darlington, Metterville (V.).

21. **Crux spes unica** *Latin* 'The cross is my only hope'
—Collas.

22. **Deo non arce spes** *Latin* 'My hope is in God, not in my fortress'
—Castell.

23. **Deo spes mea** *Latin* 'My hope is in God'
—Thornton.

24. **Deo spes meo** *Latin* 'My hope is my God'
—Thornton (U.S.).

25. **De quo bene speratur** *Latin* 'Whence there is good hope'
—Hartree.

26. **Deus est spes** *Latin* 'God is our hope'
—Ridsdale.

27. **Deus mihi spes et tutamen** *Latin* 'God is my hope and safeguard'
—Bradshaw.

28. **Deus spes mea** *Latin* 'God is my hope'
—Herbertstone.

29. **Deus spes nostra** *Latin* 'God our hope'
—Friedrich Karl, Duke of Württemberg (1652–98).

30. **Dieu est mon espoir** *French* 'God is my hope'
—Cusack.

31. **Domine, speravi** *Latin* 'O Lord, I have hoped'
—Lloyd.

32. **Dum cresco spero** *Latin* 'While I grow I hope'
—Bromley B. C., U.K.

33. **Dum exspiro spero** *Latin* 'While I die I hope'
—Lace.

34. **Dum spiro caelestia spero** *Latin* 'While I have breath I hope heavenly things'
—Jones (of Thurston).

35. Dum spiro spero *Latin* 'While I have breath I hope'
—Aschmaty, Asscotti, Auchmuty (of Brianstown), Bainbridge, Baker, Bannatyne (of Newhall), Bloxam, Brooke, Bushell, Colquhon, Compton, Cottee, Cotter (Bt.), Davies (of Marrington Hall), Dearden, Deardon, Dillon (V.), Doran, Drummond, Elrick, Glazebrook, Going, Gordon, Gurney, Hoare (Bt.), Hoare, Hunter, Learmouth, Lee, Monk-Mason (of Mason-Brook), Moore, Morice, Morris, Oldfield, O'Reilly, Partridge (of Hockham, Co. Norfolk), Pearson, Price, Roberts (of Beechfield), Rodwell, Sharp, Smith, Stanton, Stretton, Spearman (of Thornley), Spry, Symonds, Tatlock, Thompson (co. Durham), Walker, Westerman, State of South Carolina.

36. Dum vivo, spero *Latin* 'While I live I hope'
—Stuart-Menteith (Bt.), Monteath, Thom, Latta, Whiteway.

37. En bon espoir *French* 'In good hope'
—Nicholas (of East Love), Willoughby.

38. En bon espoyr *Old French* 'In good hope'
—Cokaine.

39. En Dieu est mon esperance *French* 'In God is my hope'
—Gerard (Bt.), Gerard (of Prescot), Walmsley, Ashton-in-Makerfield U. D. C., U.K.

40. En Dieu est mon espoir *French* 'In God is my hope'
—Smith (Bt.), Trevanion (of Caerhays).

41. En Dieu mon esperance *French* 'In God my hope'
—Dorothee, Margravine of Brandenburg (1596–1649); Sophie Eleonore, Landgravine of Hesse (1609–71); Anna Marie, Duchess of Saxony-Weissenfels (1627–69); Eleonore Erdmuthe Luise, Margravine of Brandenburg (1662–96); Anna, Countess of Oldenburg (b. 1605).

42. En Dieu mon esperance et l'espee [sic]pour ma defense *French* 'In God is my hope and the sword of my defence'
—Johann Ernst, Duke of Saxony-Saalfield (1658–1729).

43. Endure and hope
—Wright, Wyatt.

44. **En espérance je vis**   *French* 'In hope I live'
    —Carew.

45. **En esperanza**   *Spanish* 'In hope'
    —Mack.

46. **En espoir je vive attendant grace**   *French* 'I live in hope awaiting grace'
    —Scrope.

47. **En vain espère, qui ne craint Dieu**   *French* 'He hopes in vain, who fears not God'
    —Janssen.

48. **Esperance**   *French* 'Hope'
    —Wallace (Bt.), Ellis; Order of the Thistle of Bourbon.

49. **Esperance en Dieu**   *French* 'Hope in God'
    —Bullock, Beverly (E.), Greathead, Northumberland (D.), Prudhoe (B.), Percy.

50. **Espérance sans peur**   *French* 'Hope without fear'
    —Griffith.

51. **Espêre et persévère**   *French* 'Hope and persevere'
    —Paget (Bt.).

52. **Espère mieux**   *French* 'Hope for better'
    —Heath.

53. **Esperez en Dieu**   *French* 'Hope in God'
    —Gale.

54. **Espoir me comfort**   *French* 'Hope comforts me'
    —Tilney, Straingways.

55. **Espoir me conforte**   *French* 'Hope is my comfort'
    —Johann Georg II, Count of Mansfeld (1593–1647).

56. **Et finem spero**   *French* 'And I hope for the end'
    —Bevers.

57. **Expectes et sustineas**   *Latin* 'Thou mayest hope and endure'
    —Gwyn (of Ford Abbey), Wharton.

58. **Fac et spera**   *Latin* 'Do and hope'
    —Askew, Ayscough, Caldwell, Campbell, Crommelin, Donald, Delacherois, Fea, Heathcote, Hyatt, Ledsam, Macknight, McGee, Matherson, Mynors, Scepter.

59. **Faith, Hope, Charity**
    —Order of the Royal Red Cross.

60. **Faith and hope**
—Lindsey.

61. **Ferendum et sperandum** *Latin* 'We must endure and hope'
—Mackenzie (of Redcastle).

62. **Fide et spe** *Latin* 'With faith and hope'
—Borthwick.

63. **Firma spe** *Latin* 'With strong hope'
—Lesly (of Kincraige), Leslie.

64. **Firma spes** *Latin* 'Hope is strong'
—Moncrief.

65. **Fortitudo et spes** *Latin* 'Endurance and hope'
—Stockton-on-Tees B. C., U.K.

66. **Fy ngobaith sydd yn Nuw** *Welsh* 'My hope is in God'
—Carne.

67. **Galea spes salutis** *Latin* 'Hope is the helmet of salvation'
—Cassels, Dudley.

68. **Hinc spes affulget** *Latin* 'Hence hope shines upon us'
—Innholders' Company.

69. **Hinc spes effulget** *Latin* 'Hence hope shines forth'
—Aberdour.

70. **Hope**
—State of Rhode Island.

71. **Hope and not rue**
—Oliphant, Prinlis.

72. **Hope for the best**
—Sison, Sisson.

73. **Hope in God**
—Harkness.

74. **Hope me encourageth**
—Bushe.

75. **Hope to come**
—Foliot, Foliott.

76. **Hope to share**
—Riddell.

77. **Hope well and have well**
—Bower.

78. **Hope well and love all well**
—Bower.

79. **I hope**
—Gordon, Straloch.

80. **I hope for better**
—Boswell (of Dowen).

81. **I hope in God**
—Macnaghten, McNaughten, Naughten.

82. **I hope to share**
—Nisbet, Riddell (Bt.).

83. **I hope to speed**
—Cathcart (E.), Cathcart.

84. **I live in hope**
—Kinnear.

85. **I'll hope and not rue**
—Oliphant.

86. **Immortalia spero**   *Latin* 'I hope for immortality'
—Tytler.

87. **In caelo spes mea est**   *Latin* 'My hope is in heaven'
—Micklethwaite.

88. **In Christo speravi**   *Latin* 'In Christ I have hoped'
—Peckover.

89. **In coelo spero**   *Latin* 'I hope in heaven'
—Miller.

90. **In cruce et lachrymis spes est**   *Latin* 'There is hope in the cross and in tears'
—Hincks (of Breckenbrough).

91. **In cruce mea spes**   *Latin* 'My hope is in the cross'
—Tryon (U.S.).

92. **In cruce spes mea**   *Latin* 'In the cross is my hope'
—De la Field.

93. **In Deo nostra spes est**   *Latin* 'In God is our hope'
—Rocke.

94. **In Deo solo spes mea**   *Latin* 'My hope is in God alone'
—Kay, Key.

95. **In Deo speravi**   *Latin* 'In God I have hoped'
—Clark.

96. **In Deo spero**   *Latin* 'I place my hope in God'
—De Saumarez (B.).

97. **In Deo spes**   *Latin* 'In God is hope'
—Mitchell.

98. **In Deo spes est** *Latin* 'In God is hope'
—Harvard.

99. **In Deo spes mea** *Latin* 'In God is my hope'
—Couran, Elizabeth of Austria, wife of Charles IX of
France (1554–92); Sigismund, Margrave of
Brandenburg (1592–1640); Wilhelm Ludwig, Duke
of Württemberg (1647–77).

100. **Inde spes** *Latin* 'Thence hope'
—Moncrieff.

101. **In Domino et non in arcu meo sperabo** *Latin* 'I will rest my hope
on the Lord, and not in my bow'
—Molony (Co. Clare).

102. **Indure but Hope**
—Barrell (U.S.).

103. **Industria et spe** *Latin* 'By industry and hope'
—Skipton U. D. C., U.K., Barge, Claxton, Fenouiler,
Horrocks, Sage, Warden.

104. **In God is all my hope**
—Plumbers' Company.

105. **In Gott meine Hoffnung** *German* 'In God my hope'
—Anna Marie, Duchess of Saxony-Weimar (1575–1643).

106. **In heaven is my hope**
—Huggard.

107. **In hoc signo spes mea** *Latin* 'In this sign is my hope'
—D'Urban, Taaffe (V.).

108. **In hoc spes mea** *Latin* 'In this is my hope'
—Gordon (of Beldorney).

109. **In meliora spera** *Latin* 'Hope for better things'
—Donkin.

110. **In me mea spes omnis** *Latin* 'All my hope in myself'
—Post (U.S.).

111. **In prosperis time, in adversis spera** *Latin* 'In prosperity, fear, in
adversity, hope'
—Gabriel.

112. **In silentio et spe** *Latin* 'In silence and hope'
—[after Isaiah, xxx. 15.] Ernst the Pious, Duke of Saxony-
Gotha (1601–75); Bernhard, Duke of Saxony-Weimar
(1602–39); Elisabeth Dorothee, Landgravine of Hesse
(1640–1709).

113. **In silentio et spe fortitudo mea** *Latin* 'In silence and in hope is my strength'
>—[after Isaiah, xxx. 15.] Johann the Wise, Margrave of Brandenburg-Küstrin (1513–71); Justus II, Count of Mansfeld (1558–1619).

114. **In spe et labore transigo vitam** *Latin* 'I pass my life in hope and exertion'
>—Mack.

115. **In spe et silentio** *Latin* 'In hope and in silence'
>—Joachim Ernst, Prince of Anhalt (1536–86); Otto the Younger, Duke of Braunschweig-Lüneburg-Harburg (1528–1603).

116. **In spe resto** *Latin* 'I stand firm in hope'
>—Wade.

117. **In spe spiro** *Latin* 'In hope I breathe'
>—Sharp.

118. **In te, Domine, spes nostra** *Latin* 'In thee, Lord, is our hope'
>—Gill.

119. **In te Deus speravi** *Latin* 'In thee, O God, I have hoped'
>—Browne.

120. **I. S. E. S. (In silentio et spe)** *Latin* 'In silence and in hope'
>—Bernhard, Prince of Anhalt (1572–96).

121. **J'ai bonne esperance** *French* 'I have good hope'
>—Craig, McKean.

122. **J'ai espoir mieux avoir** *French* 'I hope for better things'
>—Dine.

123. **Jamais sans espérance** *French* 'Never without hope'
>—King (B.).

124. **J'espère** *French* 'I hope'
>—Swinton (of Swinton), Hamilton.

125. **J'espère bien** *French* 'I hope well'
>—Crew (of Crew, Crewcombe, etc.).

126. **J'espère en Dieu** *French* 'I hope in God'
>—Ray (U.S.).

127. **Je vive en esperance** *French* 'I live in hope'
>—Akers.

128. **Je vive en espoir** *French* 'I live in hope'
>—Rous, Stradbroke (E.), Stephens.

129. **L'esperance du salut** *French* 'The hope of salvation'
—Grabham.

130. **L'esperance me comfort** *French* 'Hope comforts me'
—Nairne (B.), Nairn (of St. Ford).

131. **L'esperance me console** *French* 'Hope consoles me'
—De Cardonnel.

132. **L'esperance me contente** *French* 'Hope gives me content'
—Christian, Margrave of Brandenburg-Anspach (1623–43).

133. **L'esperensse de l'eternel disipe tous mes ennuis** *Old French* 'The hope of eternal life disperses all my cares'
—Luise Henriette, Electress of Brandenburg (1627–67).

134. **L'espoir est ma force** *French* 'Hope is my strength'
—Tupper.

135. **Live in hope**
—Coldstream.

136. **Lucem spero** *Latin* 'I hope for light'
—Kemp (Bt.).

137. **Lucem spero clariorem** *Latin* 'I hope for a brighter light'
—Preston (Bt.).

138. **Mea spes est in Deo** *Latin* 'My hope is in God'
—Smith, Miller.

139. **Meliora speranda** *Latin* 'Better fortunes in expectancy'
—Douglass.

140. **Meliora sperando** *Latin* 'By hoping better things'
—Douglas.

141. **Meliora spero** *Latin* 'I hope for better things'
—Walsh.

142. **Meliora spero sequorque** *Latin* 'I hope and strive for better fortunes'
—Rait.

143. **My hope is constant**
—Donaldson.

144. **My hope is constant in thee**
—Macdonald.

145. **My hope is in God**
—Middleton.

146. **My hope on high**
—Bedlow (U.S.).

147. **Nec spe, nec metu**   *Latin* 'Neither in hope, nor in fear'
—Otto the Younger, Duke of Braunschweig-Lüneburg-Harburg (1528–1603).

148. **Nec spe nec metu**   *Latin* 'Neither with hope nor fear'
—Read (U.S.).

149. **Non deest spes**   *Latin* 'Hope is not wanting'
—Forbes (of Alford).

150. **Non robore, sed spe**   *Latin* 'Not by strength, but by hope'
—Tippet.

151. **Nourissez l'espèrance**   *French* 'Cherish hope'
—White.

152. **Nous travaillerons en esperance**   *French* 'We will labor in hope'
—Blackett (Bt.), Blackett (of Wylan, Matson, etc.).

153. **Optima sperando spiro**   *Latin* 'By hoping for the best I breathe'
—Humphreys.

154. **Our hope is on high**
—Rippon (Co. Northumberland).

155. **Patientia et spe**   *Latin* 'With patience and hope'
—Duiguid, Duniguid.

156. **Patior et spero**   *Latin* 'I suffer and hope'
—Baillie.

157. **Pauper non in spe**   *Latin* 'Not poor in hope'
—Poore.

158. **Pauper sed non in spe**   *Latin* 'Poor, but not in hope'
—Poor (U.S.).

159. **Pax et spes**   *Latin* 'Peace and hope'
—Pease (Bt.).

160. **Per constanza et speranza**   *Italian* 'Through constancy and hope'
—Gomm.

161. **Persevere in hope**
—Mackinnon.

162. **Persto et spero**   *Latin* 'I stand fast and hope'
—Merry.

163. **Post tenebris speramus lumen de lumine**   *Latin* 'After the darkness we hope for light upon light'
—Coffin (U.S.).

164. **Presto et spero**   *Latin* 'I perform and hope'
—Merry.

165. **Pristinum spero lumen** *Latin* 'I hope for pristine luster'
—Preston (Bt.).

166. **Qualis ero spero** *Latin* 'I hope what I shall be'
—Quayle.

167. **Quand fortune me tourmente, L'Espoire en Dieu me contente**
French 'When fortune torments, hope in God contents'
—Luise Amalie, Princess of Anhalt (1606–35).

168. **Quis prohibeat sperare meliora?** *Latin* 'Who can forbid to hope
better things?'
—Parker.

169. **Quod ero spero** *Latin* 'What I shall be, I hope'
—Booth (Bt.), Booth, Barton (of Grove and Clonelly),
Gowans, Haworth.

170. **Re alta spero** *Latin* 'I indeed hope for lofty things'
—Riall.

171. **Semper meliora spero** *Latin* 'Always for better things I hope'
—Hughes.

172. **Semper spero meliora** *Latin* 'I constantly hope for better things'
—Pringle.

173. **Silentio et spe** *Latin* 'In silence and in hope'
—Philipp, Count of the Palatinate of Rhein (1627–50),
Brander.

174. **Singulariter in spe** *Latin* 'Specially in hope'
—Lascher.

175. **Solus spes mea Christus** *Latin* 'Christ is my only hope'
—Johann the Wise, Margrave of Brandenburg-Küstrin
(1513–71).

176. **Spe** *Latin* 'By hope'
—Horrocks, Lovett.

177. **Spe aspera levat** *Latin* 'He lightens difficulties by hope'
—Ross (of Morinchie).

178. **Spe et amore** *Latin* 'Hope and love'
—Fisher.

179. **Spe et industria** *Latin* 'By hope and industry'
—Neaves, Wallace.

180. **Spe et labore** *Latin* 'By hope and exertion'
—Jebb.

181. **Spe expecto** *Latin* 'I expect with hope'
—Forbes, Livingstone.

182. **Spe gaudeo**   *Latin* 'I rejoice in hope'
—Macartney.

183. **Spei bonae atque animi**   *Latin* 'Of good hope and courage'
—Millar.

184. **Spe labor levis**   *Latin* 'Hope makes labor light'
—Hill (of Gressenhall Hall, co. Norfolk).

185. **Spe meliore vehor**   *Latin* 'I am born along by a better hope'
—Bogle.

186. **Spe melioris alor**   *Latin* 'I am nourished by the hope of better'
—Franz Julius, Duke of Saxony (1584–1634).

187. **Spem et speravi**   *Latin* 'And I have hoped for hope'
—Markoe (U.S.).

188. **Spem fortuna alit**   *Latin* 'Good fortune nourishes hope'
—Kinnear, Petree.

189. **Spem pretio non emam**   *Latin* 'I will not purchase mere hope'
—Beck.

190. **Spem renovant alae**   *Latin* 'Its wings renew its hope'
—Norvill (of Boghall).

191. **Spem renovat**   *Latin* 'He renews his hope'
—Grierson.

192. **Spem renovat anni**   *Latin* 'It renews the hope of the year'
—Grierson.

193. **Spem sequimur**   *Latin* 'We follow hope'
—Ellison.

194. **Spem successus alit**   *Latin* 'Success nourishes hope'
—Ross (of Balnagowan, Bt.).

195. **Spem vigilantia firmat**   *Latin* 'Vigilance strengthens hope'
—Dunbar.

196. **Spe nemo ruet**   *Latin* 'With hope, no one shall fail'
—Spennymoor U. D. C., U.K.

197. **Spe posteri temporis**   *Latin* 'In hope of the latter time'
—Atcherley, Jones.

198. **Spera**   *Latin* 'Hope'
—Gaskell.

199. **Sperabo**   *Latin* 'I will hope'
—Amand (of Lutton), Pitcairn, Annand.

200. **Sperando spiro**   *Latin* 'I breathe by hoping'
—Silney, Young.

201. **Sperandum** *Latin* 'To be hoped for'
—Rait, Scot.

202. **Sperandum est** *Latin* 'It is to be hoped for'
—Wallace (Bt.), Wallace.

203. **Sperandum est esperance** *Latin and French* 'Hope is to be hoped for'
—Wallace (U.S.).

204. **Sperans** *Latin* 'Hoping'
—Ellis.

205. **Sperans pergo** *Latin* 'I advance hoping'
—Fletcher (of Kevan).

206. **Sperantes in Domino non deficient** *Latin* 'Those who hope in the Lord shall not fail'
—Niblett.

207. **Speranza é verita** *Italian* 'Hope and truth'
—Pegler.

208. **Sperare timere est** *Latin* 'To hope is to fear'
—Ratcliff.

209. **Sperate et vivite fortes** *Latin* 'Hope and live bold(ly)'
—Bland (of Kippax Park).

210. **Sperate futurum** *Latin* 'Hope for the future'
—Altree.

211. **Sperat infestis** *Latin* 'He hopes in adversity'
—[Horace, *Car.* ii. 10, 13.] Colborne, Seaton (B.).

212. **Speratum et completum** *Latin* 'Hoped for and fulfilled'
—Arnet, Arnut.

213. **Speravi** *Latin* 'I have hoped'
—Lyon, Lyons.

214. **Speravi in Domino** *Latin* 'I have placed my hope in the Lord'
—Hay.

215. **Spero** *Latin* 'I hope'
—Annand, Briscoe, Chalmers (of Blancraig and Auldbar Castle), Calderwood, Dolling (of Magheralin), Gib, Gordon, Hutton, Langlands, Learmouth, Makepeace, Menzies, Sparrow, Shanke (of Castlerig), Shank, Toole, Wakefield, Waters.

216. **Spero dum spiro** *Latin* 'I hope while I have life'
—Chambers.

217. **Spero dum spiro, mea spes est unica Christus** *Latin* 'While I breathe I hope: my sole hope is Christ'
—Philipp Ernst, Count of Mansfeld (1560–1631).

218. **Spero et captivus nitor** *Latin* 'I hope, and though a captive I strive'
—Devenish.

219. **Spero et progredior** *Latin* 'I hope and proceed'
—Pringle (of Clifton, etc.).

220. **Spero et vivo** *Latin* 'I hope and live'
—Mashiter.

221. **Spero infestis, metuo secundis** *Latin* 'I hope in adversity, I fear in prosperity'
—Ellerton, Ludlow (E.), Stewart.

222. **Spero meliora** *Latin* 'I hope for better things'
—[Cicero, *Ad Atticum*, xiv. 16. 3.], Answorth, Carrington, Douglas, Johann Georg, Margrave of Brandenburg (1598–1637), Laird, Moffat, Maxwell, Murray, Phillips, Rhet, Rait, Rodie, Sparkes, Shaw (Bt.), Scopholine, Stewart, Sanderlands, Smith, Torpichen (B.), Watson.

223. **Spero procedere** *Latin* 'I hope to prosper'
—Hopkirk.

224. **Spero suspiro donec** *Latin* 'While I breathe I hope'
—Hope (of Granton).

225. **Spero ut fidelis** *Latin* 'I hope as being faithful'
—Mynors, Baskerville.

226. **Spes** *Latin* 'Hope'
—Gaskell, Wyllie.

227. **Spes, salus, decus** *Latin* 'Hope, safety, honor'
—Nesham (of Stockton).

228. **Spes alit** *Latin* 'Hope nourishes'
—Child (of Dervil), Scaife.

229. **Spes alit agricolam** *Latin* 'Hope nourishes the farmer'
—Huskinson.

230. **Spes anchora tuta** *Latin* 'Hope is a safe anchor'
—Dunmure.

231. **Spes anchora vitae** *Latin* 'Hope is the anchor of life'
—McLeay.

232. **Spes antiqua domus** *Latin* 'The ancient hope of the house'
—Ford-Bowes.

233. **Spes aspera levat**   *Latin* 'Hope lightens dangers'
                                                         —Ross.

234. **Spes audaces adjuvat**   *Latin* 'Hope assists the brave'
                                                         —Hollis.

235. **Spes dabit auxilium**   *Latin* 'Hope will lend aid'
                                               —Dunbar (of Durn, bt.).

236. **Spes decus et robur**   *Latin* 'Hope is honor and strength'
                                               —Eardley-Smith (Bt.).

237. **Spes durat avorum**   *Latin* 'The hope of my ancestors endures'
                                      —Nassau, Rochford, Walmesley.

238. **Spes est in Deo**   *Latin* 'My hope is in God'
                                               —Bagge (of Stradsett).

239. **Spes et fides**   *Latin* 'Hope and faith'
                                               —Chamberlain (Bt.).

240. **Spes et fortitudo**   *Latin* 'Hope and fortitude'
                                                         —Mair.

241. **Spes et fortuna**   *Latin* 'Hope and fortune'
                                               —Chelmsford (B.).

242. **Spes firma**   *Latin* 'My hope is firm'
                                                         —Tytler.

243. **Spes fovet et melius cras fore semper ait**   *Latin* 'Hope consoles
      and always says tomorrow will be better'
                  —[Salvianus, *Adversus Avaritiam*, after Theocritus, *Idylls*,
                              iv. 41.] Johann Ernst, Duke of Saxony-Eisenach
                                                         (1566–1638).

244. **Spes in Deo**   *Latin* 'My hope is in God'
                                                         —Boultbee.

245. **Spes in Domino**   *Latin* 'My hope is in the Lord'
                                                         —Hardy.

246. **Spes in extremum**   *Latin* 'Hope to the last'
                                               —Short (of Borrowstoun).

247. **Spes infracta**   *Latin* 'My hope is unbroken'
                                                         —Dick.

248. **Spes in futuro**   *Latin* 'My hope is in the future'
                                                         —Wadge.

249. **Spes juvat**   *Latin* 'Hope delights'
                                                         —Rolland.

250. **Spes labor levis**   *Latin* 'Hope is light labor'
                                               —Bigland, Ochterlony (Bt.).

251. **Spes lucis aeternae** *Latin* 'The hope of eternal life'
—Pitcairn.

252. **Spes magna in Deo** *Latin* 'Great hope is in my God'
—Meiklejohn.

253. **Spes mea, res mea** *Latin* 'My hope is my estate'
—Drummond (of Monedie).

254. **Spes mea Christus** *Latin* 'Christ is my hope'
—Anton Heinrich, Count Schwarzburg (1571–1638); Bruno III, Count of Mansfeld (1576–1644); Sibylle Elisabeth, Duchess of Braunschweig (1576–1630); Ludwig Philipp, Count of the Palatinate of Veldenz (1577–1601); Christian Wilhelm, Margrave of Brandenburg (1587–1665); Johann, Margrave of Brandenburg (1597–1628); Elisabeth Sophie, Duchess of Saxony-Lauenburg (1599–1627); Friedrich Ludwig, Count of the Palatinate of Landsberg (1619–81); Ernst, Duke of Saxony-Hildburghausen (1655–1715); Clanmorris (B.), Lucan (E.), Bingham (of Melcombe).

255. **Spes mea Christus erit** *Latin* 'Christ shall be my hope'
—Powell.

256. **Spes mea coelo** *Latin* 'My hope is in heaven'
—Abbey.

257. **Spes mea Deus** *Latin* 'God is my hope'
—Friedrich II, the Wise, Elector of the Palatinate (1483–1556); O'Farrell, Brooke (Bt.); Curriers' Company; Varty.

258. **Spes mea in coelis** *Latin* 'My hope is in heaven'
—Boyd.

259. **Spes mea in cruce unica** *Latin* 'My hope is in the cross alone'
—Martin.

260. **Spes mea in Deo** *Latin* 'My hope is in God'
—Brooke, Dewhurst, Gosker, Greaves, Gaskell, Guiness, Kirkwood, Lewin, Leithbridge (Bt.), Roper, Teynham (B.), Saunders, Wainwright, Johann Friedrich, Elector of Saxony (1503–54).

261. **Spes mea in futuro est** *Latin* 'My hope is in the future'
—Robinson (Bt.).

262. **Spes mea superne** *Latin* 'My hope is from above'
—Bruce (of Cowden).

263. **Spes meliora**   *Latin* 'Better hope'
—Watmough (U.S.).

264. **Spes melioris aevi**   *Latin* 'The hope of a better age'
—Rees.

265. **Spes meum solatium**   *Latin* 'Hope is my solace'
—Cushney.

266. **Spes non confundit**   *Latin* 'Hope maketh not ashamed'
—[Rom., v. 5.] Heinrich Julius, Duke of Braunschweig-
Wolfenbüttel (1564–1613).

267. **Spes non fracta**   *Latin* 'My hope is not broken'
—Morton (of Scarborough).

268. **Spes nostra**   *Latin* 'Our hope'
—Mount Saint Mary's College, Emmitsburg, Maryland.

269. **Spes sibi quisque**   *Latin* 'Everyone has his own hope'
—Bulwer.

270. **Spes somnium vigilantis**   *Latin* 'Hope is the dream of a waking
man'
—Dixon.

271. **Spes tamen infracta**   *Latin* 'My hope nevertheless unbroken'
—Hope (of Kers).

272. **Spes tutissima coelis**   *Latin* 'The surest hope is in heaven'
—King, Kingston (E.), Lorton (V.), Price (of Glangwilly).

273. **Spes ultra**   *Latin* 'Hope is beyond'
—Nairn (of Greenyards).

274. **Spes unica**   *Latin* 'A single hope'
—Our Lady of Holy Cross College, New Orleans,
Louisiana.

275. **Spes unica virtus**   *Latin* 'Hope my only virtue'
—Price.

276. **Spes vincit thronum**   *Latin* 'Hope wins a throne'
—Winthrop.

277. **Spe tutiores armis**   *Latin* 'Safer by hope than by arms'
—Lewis.

278. **Spe verus**   *Latin* 'True in hope'
—Scott.

279. **Spe vires augentur**   *Latin* 'Our strength is increased by hope'
—Hope, Scott (of Dunninald), Scott (of Silwood Park, Bt.).

280. **Spe vitae melioris**   *Latin* 'In the hope of a better life'
—Lea.

281. **Spe vivitur** *Latin* 'We live in hope'
　　　　　　　　　　　　　　　　　　　—Dobree.

282. **Sub spe** *Latin* 'Under hope'
　　　　—Duffas (B.), Dunbar (of Boath, Bt.), Dunbar (of
　　　　Northfield, Bt.), Dunbar (of Westfield), Cairns.

283. **Supra spem spero** *Latin* 'I hope beyond hope'
　　　　　　　　　　　　　　　　　　　—Jeffreys.

284. **Sur esperance** *French* 'Upon hope'
　　　　—Graver-Browne (of Morley Hall, co. Norfolk), Moncrieff
　　　　　　　　　　　　(Bt.), Moncrieffe (Bt.), Moir.

285. **Toleranda et speranda** *Latin* 'We must endure and hope'
　　　　　　　　　　　　　　　　　　　—Wright.

286. **To travel hopefully**
　　　　—Centennial motto of Western Oregon State College,
　　　　　　　　　　　　　　Monmouth, Oregon.

287. **Tu meliora spera** *Latin* 'Hope for better things'
　　　　　　　　　　　　　　　　　　　—Donkin.

288. **Unica spes mea Christus** *Latin* 'Christ is my only hope'
　　　　—Georg, Duke of Braunschweig-Lüneburg (1582–1641);
　　　　　　　　　　　　　　　　　　Dishington.

289. **Ut ducam spero** *Latin* 'I hope that I will lead'
　　　　　　　　　　　　　　　　　　　—Seckham.

290. **Vana spes vitae** *Latin* 'Worldly hope is vain'
　　　　　　　　　　　　　　　　　　　—Paul (Bt.).

291. **Vigilo et spero** *Latin* 'I watch and hope'
　　　　　　　　　　　　　　　　　—Galbraith, Twitoe.

292. **Virtus et spes** *Latin* 'Virtue and hope'
　　　　　　　　　　　　　　　　　　　—Caldwell.

293. **Vise en espoir** *French* 'Look forward in hope'
　　　　　　　　　　　　　　　　　　　—Hassard.

294. **Vita more fide** *Latin* 'By hope, custom, and faith'
　　　　　　　　　　　　　　　　　　—Hanercroft.

295. **Vive en espoir** *French* 'Live in hope'
　　　　　　　　　　　　　　　　　　　—Starr.

296. **Vivimus in spe** *Latin* 'We live in hope'
　　　　　　　　　　　　　　　　　　　—Thorburn.

297. **Vivis sperandum** *Latin* 'Where there is life there is hope'
　　　　　　　　　　　　　　　　　　　—Niven.

298. We live in hope

—Thorburn.

HOSPITALITY (*See also* ACCEPTANCE; FRIENDSHIP.)

1. Come, ye blessed; when I was harbourless ye lodged me
   —Original motto of the Innholders' Company, London.

2. Compelle intrare   *Latin* 'Compel them to come in'
   —[Luke, xiv. 23.] Heinrich Julius, Duke of Braunschweig-Wolfenbüttel (1564–1613).

3. Fortis et hospitalis   *Latin* 'Brave and hospitable'
   —Murphy.

4. Industria veritas et hospitalitas   *Latin* 'Industry, truth, and hospitality'
   —Harris.

5. Semper acceptus   *Latin* 'Ever welcome'
   —Paignton U. D. C., U.K.

6. Welcome the coming, speed the parting guest
   —Montacute House, Somersetshire, England; Pontnewydd House, Monmouthshire, England.

HOSTILITY (*See also* AGGRESSION; CONFLICT; ENEMIES; FIERCENESS; OPPOSITION; WAR.)

1. Aut homo aut nullus   *Latin* 'Either a man or nothing'
   —Atkinson.

2. En! Ferus hostis   *Latin* 'Behold, fierce enemy!'
   —Scots Guards, 1st battalion, U.K.

3. Exemplum adest ipse homo   *Latin* 'Man himself provides an example'
   —Franklin (U.S.).

4. Haec manus inimica tyrannis   *Latin* 'This hand is hostile to tyrants'
   —Burrell (of Knepp Castle, Co. Sussex, bt.).

5. Hominem te esse memento   *Latin* 'Remember that you are a man'
   —Wybergh (of Clifton Hall).

6. Homo homini vulpes   *Latin* 'Man is a fox towards his fellow man'
   —Wolseley (of Wolseley, bt.).

7. **Homo sum**   *Latin* 'I am a man'
—Homan (Bt.), Mann, Manns.

8. **Humani nihil alienum**   *Latin* 'Nothing that relates to man is foreign to me'
—[after Terence, *Heaut.* i. 1. 25.] Talbot (E.), Talbot (Bt.), Young (kt., Garter king-at-arms).

9. **In corda inimicorum Regis**   *Latin* 'Against the hearts of the enemies of the king'
—Forstall.

10. **Inimicus inimico**   *Latin* 'Hostile to an enemy'
—Nagle.

11. **Inter hastas et hostes**   *Latin* 'Among spears and enemies'
—Powell.

12. **Leo inimicis amicis columba**   *Latin* 'The lion for my enemies, the dove for my friends'
—Dilke.

13. **Manus haec inimica tyrannis**   *Latin* 'This hand is hostile to tyrants'
—Carysfort (E.), Dossey, Hemsworth (of Shropham, co. Norfolk), Manley, Probyn, Riversdale (B.), Tonson.

14. **Minatur**   *Latin* 'He threatens'
—Maturin.

15. **Nulla inimicus ero**   *Latin* 'I will be an enemy to no one'
—Donaldson.

16. **Nullis inimica ero**   *Latin* 'I will be an enemy to none'
—Donaldson.

17. **Quis contra nos?**   *Latin* 'Who shall be against us?'
—Wilhelm IV, Duke of Bavaria-Munich (1493–1550).

18. **Vir super hostem**   *Latin* 'A man above an enemy'
—O'Donovan.

19. **Vultus in hostem**   *Latin* 'The countenance against the enemy'
—[Horace, *Car.* i. 2. 39.] Codrington.

HUMANITY (*See also* KINDNESS; UNSELFISHNESS.)

1. **A university for all the Americas**
—Pan American University, Edinburg, Texas.

2. **Auriga virtutum prudentia**   *Latin* 'Prudence is the directress of the virtues'
—Mawbey (of Surrey).

3. **Cultus animi quasi humanitatis quidam cibus** *Latin* 'Improvement of the mind is as a kind of food for humanity'
—Havemeyer (U.S.).

4. **Humani nihil alienum mihi** *Latin* 'Nothing human is alien to me'
—[after Terence, *Heant.* 77.] Jenings (U.S.).

5. **Look up and not down, look forward and not back, look out and not in, and lend a hand**
—Edward Everett Hale; Lend-a-Hand Club.

6. **Lux et humanitas** *Latin* 'Light and humanity'
—Blackwell R. D. C., U.K.

7. **Nihil alienum** *Latin* 'Nothing foreign'
—Dynevor (B.).

8. **Nihil humani alienum** *Latin* 'Nothing relating to man is foreign to me'
—[after Terence, *Heaut.* 77.] Hutchinson (of Whitton).

9. **Our country is the world—our countrymen are all mankind**
—*Liberator, The* (abolitionist journal, William Lloyd Garrison, editor).

10. **Pro bono humani generis** *Latin* 'For the good of humankind'
—The Rockefeller University, New York, New York.

11. **Pro humanitate** *Latin* 'For humanity'
—Wake Forest University, Winston-Salem, North Carolina.

HUMILITY (*See also* MODERATION; OBSCURITY; SIMPLICITY; UNSELFISHNESS.)

1. **Ante honorem humilitas** *Latin* 'Humility before honor'
—Battersby.

2. **Exaltat humiles** *Latin* 'He exalts the humble'
—Sears (U.S.).

3. **Exaltavit humiles** *Latin* 'He hath exalted the humble'
—Holte (of Erdington).

4. **Fundamentum gloriae humilitas** *Latin* 'Humility is the foundation of glory'
—Hodges.

5. **Humilitate** *Latin* 'With humility'
—Carlysle.

6. **Il n'est si ferré qui ne glisse** *French* 'No one is so well shod that he does not slip'
—Friedrich Ulrich, Duke of Braunschweig-Wolfenbüttel (1591–1634).

7. **Mutas inglorius artes** *Latin* '(To exercise) unambitious of glory, the silent arts'
—Halford (Bt.).

8. **Usurpari nolo** *Latin* 'I do not wish to usurp'
—McDowall.

HUNTING (*See also* ENTRAPMENT; PERSECUTION; PURSUIT; SPORT.)

1. **Blow, hunter, thy horn**
—Forrester (of Corstorphine, Scotland).

2. **Hunter, blow the horn**
—Forrester.

3. **Labor in venatu** *Lat* 'Work in the Chase'
—Cannock U. D. C., U.K. (a former Royal Forest and Chase).

4. **Mane proedam, vespere spolium** *Latin* 'Game in the morning and a feast at night'
—Hurt.

5. **Pro pelle cutem** *Latin* 'Skin for fur'
—Hudson's Bay Company.

IDENTITY (*See also* SELF-KNOWLEDGE.)

1. **Ferar unus et idem** *Latin* 'I will pass along one and the same'
—Michell, Collingwood (B.).

2. **Unus et idem** *Latin* 'One and the same'
—Ravensworth, Siddell.

3. **Unus et idem ferar** *Latin* 'I will be borne along one and the same'
—Blundeel.

IDLENESS

1. **Ignavis nunquam** *Latin* 'Never for the idle'
—Jenyns.

2. **Pestis patriae pigrities** *Latin* 'Sloth is the bane of a country'
—Dugdale (of Merevale).

3. **Virtute damnosa quies** *Latin* 'Inactivity inimical to virtue'
—Brisbane.

4. **Virtuti damnosa quies** *Latin* 'Inactivity is prejudicial to virtue'
—Brisbane.

5. **Virtuti inimica quies** *Latin* 'Inactivity is inimical to virtue'
—Forbes.

IMITATION

1. **Aspice et imitare** *Latin* 'Look and imitate'
—Brooks.

2. **Imitari quam invidere** *Latin* 'To imitate rather than to envy'
—Child (of Newfield Hall, Bigelly House, etc.), Pleydell.

IMMORTALITY

1. **À l'immortalité** *French* 'Immortality!'
—Académie Française.

2. **Immortalia spero** *Latin* 'I hope for immortality'
—Tytler.

3. **Labora ut in aeternum vivas** *Latin* 'Strive that you may live for ever'
—Apreece (Bt.).

4. **Laetitia et spe immortalitatis** *Latin* 'With joy and hope of immortality'
—Lyte, Shaw.

5. **Mortale non opto** *Latin* 'I do not wish for what is mortal'
—Dyson.

6. **Non est mortale quod opto** *Latin* 'What I wish is not mortal'
—Brooke, Burnett.

7. **Non mortale quod opto** *Latin* 'I do not hope for what is mortal'
—Rand (U.S.).

8. **Non omnis moriar** *Latin* 'I shall not all die'
—[from Horace, *Odes*, III. xxx. 6.] Bettescombe, Heaven.

9. **Sic itur ad astra** *Latin* 'Such is the way to immortality'
—Day, Barker, Davies, Carnac (Bt.), Kerry, Mackenzie (Bt.), Martin, Pugh.

IMPROVEMENT (*See also* ADVANCE.)

1. **A bonis ad meliora** *Latin* 'From good things to better'
—Royston U. D. C., U.K.

2. **Always advancing**
—Thornaby-on-Tees B. C., U.K.

3. **A magnis ad maiora** *Latin* 'From great things to greater'
—Stepney B. C., U.K.

4. **Angusta ad augusta** *Latin* 'From straitened circumstances to exalted'
—Sheffinham.

5. **Cynghori er llesiant** *Welsh* 'Consulting for betterment'
—Penarth U. D. C., U.K.

6. **Developing human and natural resources**
—Coahoma Junior College, Clarksdale, Mississippi.

7. **Ditat et alit** *Latin* 'It enriches and nourishes'
—Guthrie.

8. **Do it better yet**
—Alexander Hamilton.

9. **Ever forward**
—Weston-super-Mare, U.K.

10. **Every day in every way, I am getting better and better**
—Émile Coué.

11. **Ewch ymlaen** *Welsh* 'Go forward'
—Roberts.

12. **For'ard, for'ard**
—Leicestershire C. C., U.K.

13. **Forward**
—Birmingham City and C. B. C., U.K.; Hayes and Harlington U. D. C., U.K.; State of Wisconsin.

14. **Forward California**
—Sacramento City College, Sacramento, California.

15. **Go forward, always go forward**
—General George S. Patton.

16. **Honeste progrediemur conando** *Latin* 'Let us progress by honest endeavor'
—Seisdon R. D. C., U.K.

17. **In unitatem coeamus** *Latin* 'Let us go forward together'
—Feltham U. D. C., U.K.

18. **Majulah Singapura**   *Malay* 'Forward, Singapore'
                                        —Singapore.

19. **Meliora sperando**   *Latin* 'By hoping better things'
                                        —Douglas.

20. **Meliora spero**   *Latin* 'I hope for better things'
                                        —Walsh.

21. **Meliora spero sequorque**   *Latin* 'I hope and strive for better fortunes'
                                        —Rait.

22. **Meliorem lapsa locavit**   *Latin* 'He has planted one better than the one fallen'
                         —on the Seal of the State of South Carolina; on the Great
                            Seal of the Northwest Territory.

23. **Mieulx serra**   *Old French* 'Better will come'
                                        —Lord Beaumont.

24. **Mieux je sera**   *French* 'Better I will be'
                                        —Beaumont, Stapleton.

25. **Moniti meliora sequamur**   *Latin* 'Let us, being admonished, follow better things'
                         —[Vergil, *Aen.* iii. 188.] Mahon (Bt.).

26. **Moveo et proficior**   *Latin* 'I move and improve'
                                        —Knox (U.S.).

27. **Moving people forward**
                         —Sampson Technical College, Clinton, North Carolina.

28. **Non progredi est regredi**   *Latin* 'Not to go forward is to go backward'
                         —McCook Community College, McCook, Nebraska,
                            Ruislip-Northwood U. D. C., Chigwell U. D. C.,
                                        U.K., Roe, Tyson.

29. **Onward**
                         —Fleetwood B. C., U.K.; Hyde B. C., U.K.

30. **Optimum est aliena frui insania**   *Latin* 'It is best to profit by another's frenzy'
                                        —Smith (U.S.).

31. **Perstando praesto**   *Latin* 'I step ahead by standing fast'
                                        —Hamilton.

32. **Plus ultra**   *Latin* 'Thus far and further'
                         —Charles V, Emperor of Germany (1500–58).

33. **Positis meliora caducis** *Latin* 'Better things, when decaying things are laid aside'
—Johann Adolf I, Duke of Saxony-Weissenfels (1649–97).

34. **Pro bona ad meliora** *Latin* 'For good to better'
—Goodwright.

35. **Progress**
—Blackpool C. B. C., U.K.; Littlehampton U. D. C., U.K.

36. **Progress, peace, prosperity**
—The Gambia.

37. **Progressio cum populo** *Latin* 'Progress with the people'
—East Ham C. B. C., U.K.

38. **Progressio et concordia** *Latin* 'Progress and concord'
—Kettering B. C., U.K.

39. **Progress with prudence**
—Howard.

40. **Prorsum et sursum** *Latin* 'Onward and upward'
—Boker (U.S.).

41. **Prorsum semper** *Latin* 'Ever forward'
—Gloucestershire C. C., U.K.

42. **Quid prodest?** *Latin* 'What does it profit?'
—Webb.

43. **Sapienter proficiens** *Latin* 'Advancing wisely'
—Nottinghamshire C. C., U.K.

44. **Semper proficimus** *Latin* 'We progress continually'
—Leyland U. D. C., U.K.

45. **Tempori parendum** *Latin* 'We must move with the times'
—Wembley B. C., Bishop Auckland U. D. C., U.K.

46. **Ulterius** *Latin* 'Farther'
—Durham.

47. **Ulterius et melius** *Latin* 'Farther and better'
—Campbell.

48. **Video meliora** *Latin* 'I see better things'
—Montefiore.

49. **Video meliora proboque** *Latin* 'I see and approve of better things'
—Smythe-Owen.

INCENTIVE

1. **Accendit cartu**   *Latin* 'He animates by crowing'
—Cockburn (Bt.).

2. **Adde calcar**   *Latin* 'Apply the spur'
—Spurrier.

3. **Cor forte calcar non requirit**   *Latin* 'A stout heart needs no spur'
—Mappin.

4. **Cor forte suum calcar est**   *Latin* 'A stout heart is its own spur'
—Mappin.

INCREASE   (*See also* FULLNESS; GROWTH; PROSPERITY.)

1. **Annique vivesque pariter crescent**   *Latin* 'Years and lives shall increase equally'
—Sears (U.S.).

2. **Augeo**   *Latin* 'I increase'
—Trent.

3. **Augeor dum progredior**   *Latin* 'I increase as I proceed'
—Durham.

4. **Crescamus**   *Latin* 'May we increase'
—Hodges (U.S.).

5. **Crescam ut prosim**   *Latin* 'I will increase, that I may do good'
—Mitchelson, Order of St. Joachim.

6. **Crescendo prosim**   *Latin* 'Let me do good by increasing'
—Scot, Scott.

7. **Crescent**   *Latin* 'They will increase'
—Tatton.

8. **Cresco**   *Latin* 'I increase'
—Stiven, Mitchael (of Alderstoun).

9. **Cresco crescendo**   *Latin* 'I increase by increasing'
—Neville-Rolfe.

10. **Cresco et spero**   *Latin* 'I increase and hope'
—Hannay.

11. **Cresco per crucem**   *Latin* 'I increase by the cross'
—Davis, Rowan.

12. **Dat incrementum**   *Latin* 'He gives the increase'
—Stewart.

13. **Deus incrementum dedit**   *Latin* 'God has given increase'
—Firth.

14. **Dum cresco spero**   *Latin* 'While I increase I hope'
—Rider.

15. **E terra germino ad coelum expando**   *Latin* 'I sprout out of the earth, I expand to heaven'
—Frost.

16. **Ex unitate incrementum**   *Latin* 'Increase comes from unity'
—Guthrie, Guthry; Guthry, Guthrie.

17. **God gives increase**
—[1 Cor., iii. 6.] Balfour (Bt.).

18. **Hinc incrementum**   *Latin* 'Hence comes increase'
—Hay (of Woodcockdale).

19. **I increase**
—Scot.

20. **Incrementum dat Deus**   *Latin* 'God gives increase'
—Moseley (of Owsden).

21. **In hoc plenius redibo**   *Latin* 'Through this I shall become fuller'
—Minshull (Co. Chester).

22. **Je gagne**   *French* 'I gain'
—Osborn, Osbourne.

23. **Modice augetur modicum**   *Latin* 'A little is increased by degrees'
—Williamson (of Hutchinfield).

24. **Modicum modice erit magnum**   *Latin* 'A little will be much by degrees'
—Williamson (of Kirkaldy).

25. **Sub sole sub umbra crescens**   *Latin* 'Increasing both in sunshine and in shade'
—Irvine (of Murthill), Irvine.

26. **Sub solo patebit**   *Latin* 'It will expand under the sun'
—Ellies.

27. **Ut crescit clarescit**   *Latin* 'As it increases, it becomes bright'
—Menzies.

28. **Utrius auctus auxilio**   *Latin* 'Increasing by help of both'
—Rankine.

INDUSTRIOUSNESS

1. **Absque labore nihil**   *Latin* 'Nothing without labor'
—Stalybridge B. C., Darwen B. C., U.K., Steele (Bt.).

2. **Armis et industria**   *Latin* 'By arms and industry'
—Cochran (of Balbarchan).

3. **Art, industry, contentment**
—Basildon Development Corp.

4. **Arte et industria**   *Latin* 'By art and industry'
—Baynes.

5. **Arte et labore**   *Latin* 'By skill and toil'
—Blackburn C. B. C., U.K., Smythe.

6. **Bene qui sedulo**   *Latin* 'He lives well who lives industriously'
—Arkley.

7. **By concord and industry**
—Droylsden U. D. C., U.K.

8. **By hammer and hand all arts do stand**
—Blacksmiths' Company.

9. **By industry and honor**
—Hall.

10. **By industry and integrity**
—Nelson B. C., U.K.

11. **By industry we prosper**
—Gavin (of Lanton).

12. **Cedant arma labori**   *Latin* 'Let arms give place to labor'
—Stubs.

13. **Clarum reddit industria**   *Latin* 'Industry renders illustrious'
—Milne.

14. **Concilio et labore**   *Latin* 'By counsel and by labor'
—Manchester City and C. B. C., U.K.

15. **Concordia, integretate, industria**   *Latin* 'By concord, integrity, and industry'
—Baron de Rothschild, Rothschild.

16. **Concordia et industria**   *Latin* 'By concord and industry'
—Dent.

17. **Constantia et labore**   *Latin* 'By resolution and exertion'
—Kirby.

18. **Copia ex industria**   *Latin* 'Plenty from industry'
—Comyn.

19. **Cura atque industria**   *Latin* 'By carefulness and industry'
—Vair.

20. **Cura et industria**   *Latin* 'By care and industry'
—Walker (of Dalry).

21. **Deo adjuvante arte et industria floret**   *Latin* 'With God's help, it flourishes by art and industry'
>—Kidderminster B. C., U.K.

22. **Deo adjuvante labor proficit**   *Latin* 'By God's help labor succeeds'
>—Sheffield City and C. B. C., U.K.

23. **Deo duce, comite industria**   *Latin* 'God being my guide, industry my companion'
>—Slaney (Co. Salop), Nicoll.

24. **Deo et labore**   *Latin* 'By God and by labour'
>—Sebag.

25. **Deo fisus labora**   *Latin* 'Work while trusting in God'
>—William Jewell College, Liberty, Missouri.

26. **Deus industriam beat**   *Latin* 'God blesses industriousness'
>—Harborne.

27. **Disce et labora**   *Latin* 'Learn and labor'
>—Mackie.

28. **Do the day's work**
>—Calvin Coolidge.

29. **Dulcis pro patria labor**   *Latin* 'Labor for one's country is sweet'
>—McKerrell (of Hill House).

30. **Dum sedulo prospero**   *Latin* 'While engaged industriously I prosper'
>—Swinton.

31. **E labore dulcedo**   *Latin* 'Pleasure arises out of labor'
>—Boyle, Innes, McInnes.

32. **E mare ex industria**   *Latin* 'From the sea and from industry'
>—West Hartlepool C. B. C., U.K.

33. **Ex industria**   *Latin* 'Through industry'
>—Milne (of Edinburgh), Mylne.

34. **Ex sudore voluptas**   *Latin* 'Pleasure out of hard labor'
>—Swettenham.

35. **Ex sudore vultus**   *Latin* 'By the sweat of the face'
>—Swettenham (of Swettenham and Somerford).

36. **Faith in industry**
>—Edmonton B. C., U.K.

37. **Favet fortuna labori**   *Latin* 'Fortune favors labor'
>—Turnbull.

38. **Fervet opus**   *Latin* 'The work is urged on vigorously'
—Treweeke.

39. **Fide, labore, et virtute**   *Latin* 'By faith, labor, and virtue'
—Maryott.

40. **Fide et caritate laboro**   *Latin* 'I labor with faith and charity'
—Bovier.

41. **Fide et industria**   *Latin* 'By faith and industry'
—Whittingham.

42. **Fide et labore**   *Latin* 'By faith and industry'
—Allen, Harpenden U. D. C., U.K.

43. **Fide et opera**   *Latin* 'By faith and work'
—McArthur, Stewart.

44. **Fide laboro**   *Latin* 'I labor with faith'
—Bovier.

45. **Fidelitate et industria stat Bilstonia**   *Latin* 'Bilston stands by faith and industry'
—Bilston B. C., U.K.

46. **Fide patientia labore**   *Latin* 'By faith, patience, and work'
—Pilter.

47. **Fit via vi**   *Latin* 'A way is made by labor'
—Campbell, Way.

48. **Floreat industria**   *Latin* 'May industry flourish'
—Batley B. C., Darlington C. B. C., U.K.

49. **Floret qui laborat**   *Latin* 'He is prosperous who labors'
—Ross.

50. **Floret qui laborat**   *Latin* 'He prospers who labors'
—Mossley B. C., Rawtenstall B. C., U.K.

51. **Fraternité, justice, travail**   *French* 'Fraternity, justice, work'
—Republic of Dahomey.

52. **Grandescunt aucta labore**   *Latin* 'Things acquired through hard work render illustrious'
—A'Court, Heytesbury (B.).

53. **Grind well**
—Marblers' Company, London.

54. **Haec lucra laborum**   *Latin* 'These are the advantages of industry'
—Rowand.

55. **Hoc opus**   *Latin* 'This is the task'
—Dee (of Mortlake).

56. **Honore et labore** *Latin* 'By honor and labor'
—Hill.

57. **Honor et industria** *Latin* 'Honor and industry'
—Bacup B. C., U.K.

58. **Honor rewards industry**
—Gardiner.

59. **Honos industriae praemium** *Latin* 'Honor the reward of industry'
—King (of Campsie, bt.).

60. **Industria** *Latin* 'By industry'
—Calrow, Crierie, Fettes, Fiddes, Gentle, Keltie, McCrire, Ogilvy, Fettes College, U.K. Peel (Bt.).

61. **Industria, intelligentia, virtus** *Latin* 'Industry, intelligence, virtue'
—Dexter (U.S.).

62. **Industria, virtus, et fortitudo** *Latin* 'Industry, valor, and fortitude'
—Smellie (of Slindon, co. Sussex).

63. **Industriâ atque fortunâ** *Latin* 'By industry and good fortune'
—Lawrie.

64. **Industria ditat** *Latin* 'Industry enriches'
—Knottingley U. D. C., Widnes B. C., Radcliffe B. C., High Wycombe, Sideserf, Reath, Wauchop, (of Niddry), Waugh, Vanderplante. B. C., U.K.

65. **Industriae munus** *Latin* 'The gift of industry'
—Leechaman.

66. **Industriae praemium** *Latin* 'The reward of industry'
—Heath (Bt.).

67. **Industria et frugalitas** *Latin* 'Industry and frugality'
—Cheever (U.S.).

68. **Industria et labore** *Latin* 'By industry and labor'
—McGassock.

69. **Industria et perseverantia** *Latin* 'By industry and perseverance'
—Cowper.

70. **Industria et probitate** *Latin* 'By industry and probity'
—Hives, Washbourne, Browne (of Ebbw Vale, Co. Monmouth).

71. **Industria et spe** *Latin* 'By industry and hope'
    —Skipton U. D. C., U.K., Barge, Claxton, Fenouiler,
    Horrocks, Sage, Warden.

72. **Industria et virtute** *Latin* 'By industry and virtue'
    —Beaver.

73. **Industria evehit** *Latin* 'Industry promotes'
    —Warrender.

74. **Industria murus** *Latin* 'Industry is a protection'
    —Thomson.

75. **Industria omnia vincit** *Latin* 'Industry overcomes all things'
    —Morley B. C., U.K.

76. **Industria permanente** *Latin* 'By unremitting industry'
    —Neave.

77. **Industria semper crescam** *Latin* 'I will always increase through
    hard work'
    —Schermerhorn (U.S.).

78. **Industria veritas et hospitalitas** *Latin* 'Industry, truth, and hos-
    pitality'
    —Harris.

79. **Industry**
    —State of Utah.

80. **Industry and liberality**
    —Jejeebhoy (Bt.).

81. **Industry and prudence conquer**
    —Accrington B. C., U.K.

82. **Industry enriches**
    —Spenborough U. D. C., U.K.

83. **Ingenio ac labore** *Latin* 'By ability and toil'
    —Kerr, Worrall.

84. **In labore quies** *Latin* 'In labor is rest'
    —Helyer.

85. **Integrity and industry**
    —Salford City and C. B. C., U.K.

86. **In the sweat of thy brow shalt thou eat thy bread**
    —[Gen. iii. 19.] Gardeners' Company.

87. **Invicta labore** *Latin* 'Unconquered by labor'
    —Armstrong.

88. **I rise by industry**
    —Foulis (of Edinburgh).

89. **Jucundi acti labores**   *Latin* 'Past labors are pleasant'
    —Chater.

90. **Justice, paix, travail**   *French* 'Justice, peace, work'
    —Democratic Republic of the Congo.

91. **Labora**   *Latin* 'Labor'
    —McKie, Mackie.

92. **Laborare est orare**   *Latin* 'To work is to pray'
    —Willesden B. C., U.K.

93. **Laborare et studere**   *Latin* 'Work and study'
    —Lincoln University, Jefferson City, Missouri.

94. **Labore**   *Latin* 'By labor'
    —Abbot, Tenterden (B.), Walmesley.

95. **Labore et amore**   *Latin* 'By labor and love'
    —Horsfall.

96. **Labore et diligentia**   *Latin* 'With labor and diligence'
    —Binns.

97. **Labore et fide**   *Latin* 'By labor and loyalty'
    —Pritchard.

98. **Labore et fiducia**   *Latin* 'By industry and confidence'
    —Litster.

99. **Labore et honore**   *Latin* 'By industry and honor'
    —Bowden, Rendlesham (B.), Thelluson, Pemberton (of Barnes), Viner.

100. **Labore et ingenio**   *Latin* 'By labor and ingenuity'
    —Pickersgill, Smethwick C. B. C., U.K.

101. **Labore et perseverantia**   *Latin* 'By labor and perseverance'
    —Campbell, Woods.

102. **Labore et prudentia**   *Latin* 'By labor and prudence'
    —Bartolozzi, Brighouse B. C., U.K.

103. **Labore et scientia**   *Latin* 'By labor and science'
    —Jarrow B. C., U.K., Wylie (Bt.).

104. **Labore et virtute**   *Latin* 'By industry and virtue'
    —Gardner, Pigott.

105. **Labore et vivere**   *Latin* 'Live even with labor'
    —Whiteley.

106. **Labore omnia florent**   *Latin* 'All things flourish through labor'
    —Drinkwater, Huntingdonshire C. C., U.K., Eccles B. C., U.K.

107. **Labore parta** *Latin* 'Acquired by labor'
—White.

108. **Labor et industria** *Latin* 'Labor and industry'
—Tane.

109. **Labor et scientia** *Latin* 'Labor and knowledge'
—Rose-Hulman Institute of Technology, Terre Haute,
Indiana.

110. **Labor et veritas** *Latin* 'Industry and truth'
—Elliot (Bt.).

111. **Labore vinces** *Latin* 'You will overcome by toil'
—Sugden, St. Leonards (B.).

112. **Labor improbus omnia vincit** *Latin* 'Extraordinary labor surmounts all difficulties'
—Mitchell (of Landath).

113. **Labor in venatu** *Lat* 'Work in the Chase'
—Cannock U. D. C., U.K. (a former Royal Forest and
Chase).

114. **Labor ipse voluptas** *Latin* 'Toil itself is pleasure'
—Lovelace (E.).

115. **Labor omnia superat** *Latin* 'Labor conquers all things'
—Laing.

116. **Labor omnia vincit**
—Ilkeston B. C., Ashton-Under-Lyme B. C., U.K.;
Centenary College of Louisiana, Shreveport,
Louisiana; State of Oklahoma; Bradford City
and C. B. C., U.K.

117. **Labor omnia vincit improbus** *Latin* 'Incessant labor conquers all
things'
—[Vergil, *Geor.* i. 145.] Butler.

118. **Labor overcomes all things**
—Erith B. C., U.K.

119. **Labor vincit omnia** *Latin* 'Labor conquers all things'
—Richardson.

120. **Labour brings plenty**
—Horwich U. D. C., U.K.

121. **Labour to rest**
—Kempe (U.S.).

122. **Learning and labor**
—University of Illinois, Urbana-Champaign, Illinois.

123. **Lege et labore**   *Latin* 'By law and labor'
                                                        —Bell.

124. **Loyal and industrious**
                                    —Rowley Regis B. C., U.K.

125. **Marte et industria**   *Latin* 'By arms and industry'
                                                        —Ogilvy.

126. **Marte et labore**   *Latin* 'By arms and toil'
                                                        —Newgill.

127. **Mente et labore**   *Latin* 'With mind and labor'
                                                    —Lawrence (Bt.).

128. **Merces haec certa laborum**   *Latin* 'This is the sure reward of industry'
                                                    —Seton (Bt.).

129. **Meret qui laborat**   *Latin* 'He is deserving who is industrious'
                                                        —Storie.

130. **Moeret qui laborat**   *Latin* 'He is sad who labors'
                                                        —Storie.

131. **Nictz Zonder Arbyt**   *Dutch* 'Nothing without work'
                            —House near Cheltenham, Gloucestershire, England.

132. **Nihil habere sine labore**   *Latin* 'To have nothing without labor'
                                                        —Cooke.

133. **Nihil nisi labore**   *Latin* 'Nothing without labor'
                                                    —Emerton.

134. **Nihil sine labore**   *Latin* 'Nothing without labor'
                            —Berry, Eator, Templer, Thearle (of London).

135. **Nil sine labore**   *Latin* 'Nothing without labor'
                                                —Atkinson, Dax.

136. **Nil sine magno labore**   *Latin* 'Nothing without great labor'
                            —Brooklyn College (City University of New York),
                                        Brooklyn, New York; Kidd.

137. **Non pas l'ouvrage, mais l'ouvrier**   *French* 'Not the work, but the workman'
                            —Workman, Workman-Macnaghten (Bt.).

138. **Non recuso laborem**   *Latin* 'I do not refuse work'
                                            —Dover College, U.K.

139. **Non servit sed laborat**   *Latin* 'Does not serve but labors'
                                                        —Innes.

140. **Non sine industria**   *Latin* 'Not without industry'
                                                        —Bevan.

141. **Non sine labore**   *Latin* 'Not without labor'
—Milnes.

142. **Non sine pulvere palma**   *Latin* 'A reward not without labor'
—Peirse.

143. **Nothing without labor**
—Haslingden B. C., U.K.

144. **Nous travaillerons en esperance**   *French* 'We will labor in hope'
—Blackett (Bt.), Blackett (of Wylan, Matson, etc.).

145. **Nul chef-d'oeuvre sans travail**   *French* 'No masterpiece without labor'
—Home of the French architect, Puget, in Marseilles, France.

146. **Nulla dies sine linea**   *Latin* 'Not a day without a task'
—Bolton (U.S.), Lefroy, Singleton, Williams.

147. **Omnia vincit labor**   *Latin* 'Labor conquers all things'
—Cook.

148. **Opera mundi**   *Latin* 'The works of the world'
—Sanderson.

149. **Opes industria parit**   *Latin* 'Industry produces riches'
—Tomlin.

150. **Ora et labora**   *Latin* 'Pray and labor'
—Dalhousie (E.), Holburton.

151. **Orando laborando**   *Latin* 'By prayer and by labor'
—Rugby School, U.K.

152. **Otium ex labore**   *Latin* 'Rest from labor'
—Remsen (U.S.).

153. **Ours the task eternal**
—Carleton University, Ottawa, Canada.

154. **Paix, travail, patrie**   *French* 'Peace, work, fatherland'
—Federal Republic of Cameroon.

155. **Palma non sine pulvere**   *Latin* 'The palm is not obtained without labor'
—Archbald, Doughty, Lamb, Liverpool (E.).

156. **Par sit fortuna labori**   *Latin* 'Let the success be equal to the labor'
—Palmer (of Carlton, Bt.), Palmer (of Kilmare), Buchanan (of Drumhead), Lowman.

157. **Parta labore quies**   *Latin* 'Rest attained by labor'
—Fulton.

158. **Per industriam**   *Latin* 'Through industry'
                                   —Rowan, Tibbetts.

159. **Perseverantia et labore**   *Latin* 'By perseverance and labor'
                                     —Pitcher.

160. **Perseverantia industria et fidelitas**   *Latin* 'Perseverance, industry, and fidelity'
                                   —Ravenscroft.

161. **Plures labore, dulcibus quidam otiis**   *Latin* 'Many to labor, some to sweet ease'
        —Sundial on town residence of M. de Fienbet, Counsellor of State to Louis XIV.

162. **Prece et labore**   *Latin* 'By prayer and toil'
        —Christian Ernst, Margrave of Brandenburg-Baireuth (1644–1712).

163. **Pretium et causa laboris**   *Latin* 'The reward and cause of labor'
                                   —Frederick.

164. **Pretium non vile laborum**   *Latin* 'No mean reward of our labor'
        —Order of the Golden Fleece (Austria and Spain).

165. **Pretiumque et causa laboris**   *Latin* 'Both the prize and the motive of labor'
                          —Burnley C. B. C., U.K.

166. **Pride and industry**
                                   —Barbados.

167. **Probitate et industria**   *Latin* 'By honesty and industry'
                              —Bridgen (U.S.).

168. **Probitate et labore**   *Latin* 'By honesty and toil'
                                   —Gould.

169. **Prodigiose qui laboriose**   *Latin* 'Who acts laboriosly acts marvellously'
                                   —Innes.

170. **Prospere qui sedulo**   *Latin* '(He does) prosperously (who does) industriously'
                              —Cunninghame.

171. **Providentia et industria**   *Latin* 'By providence and industry'
                                   —Anderson.

172. **Prudenter qui sedulo**   *Latin* '(He does) prudently who (does) industriously'
                                   —Milne.

173. **Quae regio in terris nostri non plena laboris?** *Latin* 'What spot in the earth is not full of our labors?'
—[Vergil, *Aen.* i. 460.] Royal Engineers, U.K.

174. **Qui non laborat, non manducet** *Latin* 'Who labors not eats not'
—Philip de Commines (1445–1509).

175. **Requiesco a laboribus meis** *Latin* 'I rest from my labors'
—[after Rev. xiv. 13.] Heinrich Julius, Duke of Braunschweig-Wolfenbüttel (1564–1613).

176. **Sapiens qui assiduus** *Latin* 'He is wise who is industrious'
—Hansler (of Eastwood), Mitchell (Bt.), Mitchell (of Barry), Sperling.

177. **Sapit qui laborat** *Latin* 'He is wise who exerts himself'
—Dunbar.

178. **Scientiae et labori detur** *Latin* 'Due to knowledge and labor'
—Luton B. C., U.K.

179. **Scientiae laborisque memor** *Latin* 'Mindful of knowledge and labor'
—Hutchison.

180. **Secundis usque laboribus** *Latin* 'Continually with prosperous labors'
—[Horace, *Car.* iv. 4, 45.] Richards.

181. **Sibimet merces industria** *Latin* 'Industry is a recompense to itself'
—Miller.

182. **Sicut quercus virescit industria** *Latin* 'Industry flourishes like the oak'
—Mansfield B. C., U.K.

183. **Sic virescit industria** *Latin* 'Thus industry flourishes'
—Stewart, Rotherham C. B. C., U.K.

184. **Sine labore nihil floret** *Latin* 'Nothing prospers without industry'
—Brierley Hill U. D. C., U.K.

185. **Sine labore non paritur gloriosa victoria** *Latin* 'Without labor no glorious victory is won'
—Albrecht, Duke of Saxony-Coburg (1648–99).

186. **Spe et industria** *Latin* 'By hope and industry'
—Neaves, Wallace.

187. **Subimet merces industria** *Latin* 'Industry is its own reward'
—Miller.

188. **Sudore non sopore**   *Latin* 'By toil, not by sleep'
—St. Ives B. C., U.K.
189. **Think/ Work/ Serve**
—Tennessee State University, Nashville, Tennessee.
190. **Travail, justice, solidarité**   *French* 'Work, justice, solidarity'
—Republic of Guinea.
191. **Travail, liberté, patrie**   *French* 'Work, freedom, fatherland'
—Republic of Togo.
192. **Union, travail, justice**   *French* 'Union, work, justice'
—Gabon Republic.
193. **Unité, dignité, travail**   *French* 'Unity, dignity, work'
—Central African Republic.
194. **Unité, travail, justice**   *French* 'Unity, work, justice'
—Republic of Upper Volta.
195. **Unité, travail, progrès**   *French* 'Unity, work, progress'
—Republic of Chad, Kingdom of Burundi, Republic of Congo.
196. **Ut quiescas labora**   *Latin* 'Work so you may rest'
—Gallandet (U.S.).
197. **Vi et industria**   *Latin* 'By strength and industry'
—Falconer.
198. **Vincit labor**   *Latin* 'Labor overcomes'
—Campbell.
199. **Vincit omnia industria**   *Latin* 'Industry overcomes all things'
—Bury C. B. C., U.K.
200. **Virtus et industria**   *Latin* 'Virtue and industry'
—Browne (of London).
201. **Virtute et opera**   *Latin* 'By virtue and energy'
—Bennie, Bernie.
202. **Virtute et opere**   *Latin* 'Through virtue and work'
—Prime (U.S.).
203. **Virtutem coronat opus**   *Latin* 'The work crowns the virtue'
—Laurie.
204. **We build, we fight**
—Seabees, United States Navy.
205. **We grow by industry**
—Bedworth U. D. C., U.K., Blyth B. C.
206. **Work and wait**
—Ross.

207. Work supports all
—Worksop R. D. C., U.K.

INJURY

1. **Commodum non damnum**   *Latin* 'A benefit, not an injury'
—Backie, Baikie (of Tankerness).

2. **Doluere dente lacessiti**   *Latin* 'Bitten, they felt pain'
—Arden.

3. **Haec manus pro patriae pugnando vulnera passa**   *Latin* 'This hand has been wounded in defense of my country'
—O'Neill, Gealagh.

4. **Laedere noli**   *Latin* 'Be unwilling to hurt'
—Stewart.

5. **Lothim agus marbhaim**   *Gaelic* 'I wound and I kill'
—O'Halloran.

6. **Maigre l'injustice**   *French* 'In spite of injustice'
—Fiott.

7. **Malgré le tort**   *Latin* 'Despite of wrong'
—Davis, Houghton (Bt.), James.

8. **Sanguis et vulnera**   *Latin* 'Blood and wounds'
—Skynner.

9. **Sine injuria**   *Latin* 'Without offence'
—Watson.

10. **Transfixus sed non mortuus**   *Latin* 'Transfixed but not dead'
—Walsh.

11. **Vulnera ecclesiae liberorum vita**   *Latin* 'Wounds are the life of the children of the Church'
—Church.

12. **Vulnera temno**   *Latin* 'I despise wounds'
—Cramond.

13. **Vulnerati non victi**   *Latin* 'Wounded not conquered'
—Cooks' Company.

14. **Vulneratur, non vincitur**   *Latin* 'He is wounded, not conquered'
—Homfray.

15. **Vulneratus non victus**   *Latin* 'Wounded not conquered'
—Guillamore (V.), O'Grandy.

16. **Vulnere viresco**   *Latin* 'I flourish from a wound'
—Stewart.

17. **Vulneror non vincor**   *Latin* 'I am wounded, not conquered'
    —Homfray, Muschamp (of Brotherlee).

18. **Vulnus opemque fero**   *Latin* 'I bear a wound and wealth'
    —Addison (U.S.).

INNOCENCE   (*See also* GOODNESS; PURITY.)

1. **Immobilis innocentia**   *Latin* 'Steadfast innocence'
    —Culme.

2. **Innocence surmounts**
    —Gulland.

3. **Innocens non timidus**   *Latin* 'Innocent but not fearful'
    —Rowe.

4. **Innocent and true**
    —Arbuthnot (Bt.).

5. **Innocent courageous activity**
    —White.

6. **Innocenter patienter constanter**   *Latin* 'Innocently, patiently, steadfastly'
    —Stillé (U.S.).

7. **Innocentia quamvis in agro sanguinis**   *Latin* 'With innocence though in a field of blood'
    —Lowe.

8. **Innocentia securus**   *Latin* 'Secure in innocence'
    —Jackson (Bt.).

9. **Insontes ut columbae**   *Latin* 'Innocent as doves'
    —Francis.

10. **Intellectu et innocentia**   *Latin* 'By intellect and innocence'
    —Headlam.

11. **Neminem metue innocens**   *Latin* 'Being innocent fear no one'
    —Eyre.

12. **Nil conscire sibi**   *Latin* 'To have a conscience free from guilt'
    —[Horace, *Ep.* i. 1. 61.] Biss, Bullock (of Faulkbourn), Carew (Bt.), Collingwood, French, Michel (of Dewlish), Rothwell, Rogers, Sibthorp, Winchelsea (E.), Walker, Webb.

13. **Nil conscire sibi nulli pallescere culpae**   *Latin* 'To be conscious of (no guilt) to oneself, to grow pale for no crime'
    —[Horace, *Ep.* i. 1. 61.] Sanders.

14. **Nulla pallescere culpa** *Latin* 'To turn pale from no crime'
—Forbes, Patten, Pulleine, Mitchell, Waynflete.

15. **Prudentia decus innocentia** *Latin* 'Prudence, grace, innocence'
—Ramsay.

INSIGNIFICANCE (*See also* HARMLESSNESS.)

1. **Omnia in nihil** *Latin* 'Everything comes to nothing'
—August, Prince of Anhalt-Plötzkau (1575–1653).

2. **Omnia vanitas** *Latin* 'Everything is vanity'
—Christian, Duke of Saxony-Eisenberg (1653–1707).

3. **Plus ne m'est rien, rien ne m'est plus** *French* 'Nothing more is left to me; nothing is anything to me now'
—Valentine Visconti, after the death of her husband, Louis de Bourbon, in 1425.

4. **Quantum est in rebus inane** *Latin* 'How much insignificancy is in human things'
—Minett.

5. **Quantum in rebus inane** *Latin* 'What emptiness in all things (human)'
—Osborne (Bt.), Odell (of Carriglea).

6. **Vanitas vanitatum et omnia vanitas** *Latin* 'Vanity of vanities; all is vanity'
—[Eccles., i. 2.] Wilhelm IV, Landgrave of Hesse-Cassel (1532–92).

INTEGRITY (*See also* HONESTY; HONOR; NOBILITY; PURITY; RECTITUDE; REPUTATION; RIGHTEOUSNESS; TRUSTWORTHINESS; VIRTUE.)

1. **Armed with integrity**
—Waddilove.

2. **Be and not seem**
—Rolt.

3. **By industry and integrity**
—Nelson B. C., U.K.

4. **Concordia, integretate, industria** *Latin* 'By concord, integrity, and industry'
—Baron de Rothschild, Rothschild.

5. **Constans fides et integritas** *Latin* 'Constant faith and integrity'
—Brinckerhoff (U.S.).

6. **Diligence/ Discipline/ Integrity**
    —Steed College, Johnson City, Tennessee.

7. **Diligence/ Integrity/ Knowledge**
    —McNeese State University, Lake Charles, Louisiana.

8. **Esse et videri**   *Latin* 'To be and to seem to be'
    —Wilkinson.

9. **Esse potius quam haberi**   *Latin* 'To be rather than to seem'
    —Minturn (U.S.).

10. **Esse quam videri**   *Latin* 'To be rather than seem to be'
    —Addenbrooke, Beadon, Crawley-Boevey (Bt.), Bonham,
    Brownlow, Bunbury, Collett, Couts, Croft (Bt.),
    Deline, Flinn, Gratten, Hammerton, Hill, Hood,
    Longley, Lurgan (B.), Maitland, Maris, Mathil, Oakes,
    Round, Sheriff, St. Paul (Bt.), St. Paul, Swire (of
    Cononley), Thurston (of Weston, Co. Suffolk),
    Thurston (of Talgarth), Turner, Turnour (of
    Swaffham, Co. Norfolk), Winterton (E.), Woodcock
    (of Coventry); National College of Chiropractic,
    Lombard, Illinois.

11. **Esse quam videri**   *Latin* 'To be rather than to seem'
    —State of North Carolina.

12. **Esto quod esse videris**   *Latin* 'Be what you seem to be'
    —Aufrere, Barkworth (of Wyton), Colel, Hooke, Mills,
    Milles, Sondes (B.), Watson.

13. **Fide et integritate**   *Latin* 'By fidelity and integrity'
    —Venning.

14. **Fidelitas/ veritas/ integritas**   *Latin* 'Fidelity/ truth/ integrity'
    —Salmon P. Chase College of Law of Northern Kentucky
    University, Covington, Kentucky.

15. **Fidem parit integritas**   *Latin* 'Integrity produces confidence'
    —Kay, Kaye (Bt.).

16. **Integrias/ veritas/ dignitas**   *Latin* 'Integrity/ truth/ dignity'
    —Indiana Northern Graduate School of Professional
    Management.

17. **Integritas semper tutamen**   *Latin* 'Integrity is always a safeguard'
    —Harries.

18. **Integritas tuta virus non capit**   *Latin* 'A safe integrity does not
    take poison'
    —Holl.

19. **Integritate**   *Latin* 'By integrity'
—Edwards.

20. **Integritate et fortitudine**   *Latin* 'By integrity and bravery'
—Jones.

21. **Integritate sola**   *Latin* 'By integrity alone'
—Marrable.

22. **Integritate stabis ingenuus**   *Latin* 'You will stand free by integrity'
—Stewart.

23. **Integrity**
—Dukinfield B. C., U.K.; Freake (Bt.).

24. **Integrity and industry**
—Salford City and C. B. C., U.K.

25. **Integrity/ Quality/ Progress**
—The Louisville Technical Institute, Louisville, Kentucky.

26. **Invidia assecla integritatis**   *Latin* 'Envy waits on integrity'
—Heinrich Julius, Duke of Braunschweig-Wolfenbüttel (1564–1613).

27. **Learning/ Service/ Integrity**
—Quinsigamond Community College, Worcester, Massachusetts.

28. **Malim esse quam videri**   *Latin* 'I would rather be than seem'
—Macrae.

29. **Malle debemus Principes esse quam videri**   *Latin* 'We should prefer to be, rather than to seem, princes'
—August, Duke of Braunschweig-Wolfenbüttel (1579–1666).

30. **Mieux être que paraître**   *French* 'Better be than seem'
—Barclay.

31. **Non videri, sed esse**   *Latin* 'Not to seem, but to be'
—Hare (Bt.).

32. **Probitas fons honoris**   *Latin* 'Integrity is the fountain of honor'
—Gubbay.

33. **Probitas sibi ipsi securitas**   *Latin* 'Integrity is its own security'
—Carr.

34. **Probitas solo nobilitas**   *Latin* 'Probity is the only nobility'
—Kerrison.

35. **Probitas veritas honos**   *Latin* 'Integrity, truth, and honor'
—Browne.

36. **Probitate ac virtute**   *Latin* 'By integrity and valor'
     —Rose.
37. **Probitate consilium perficitur**   *Latin* 'By probity counsel is made perfect'
     —Renny.
38. **Pro recto**   *Latin* 'For integrity'
     —Meek.
39. **Scientia/ integritas**   *Latin* 'Knowledge/ integrity'
     —Massachusetts Bay Community College, Wellesley Hills, Massachusetts.
40. **Sermoni consona facta**   *Latin* 'Actions in harmony with our words'
     —Collins, Trelawney, Trelawny.
41. **The reward of integrity**
     —Cree.
42. **Venale nec auro**   *Latin* 'Not to be bought with gold'
     —[Horace, *Car*. ii. 16. 1.] Jervis.
43. **Virtute probitate**   *Latin* 'By virtue and integrity'
     —Magan.

INTENTION   (*See also* AMBITION; WILL.)
1. **I mean no harm**
     —Gairdner.
2. **I mean well**
     —Shaw (Bt.), Stewart (Bt.), Sutcliffe, Callender.
3. **Mean, speak, and doe well**
     —Urquhart (of Cromarty).
4. **Mean, speak, and do well**
     —Urguhart (of Meldrum).
5. **Ni ddaw da o hir arofyn**   *Welsh* 'No good comes of long intending'
     —Llanover (of Llanover and Abercarn, b.).
6. **Per actum intentio**   *Latin* 'The intention (must be judged) by the act'
     —Urquhart (of Newhall).
7. **Velle bene facere**   *Latin* 'To wish to do well'
     —Curteis, Curtis.
8. **Veuille bien**   *French* 'Wish well'
     —De Veulle.

INTER-RELATEDNESS (*See also* UNITY.)

1. God hath made of one blood all nations of men
   —Berea College, Berea, Kentucky.

2. Members one of another
   —Harlow Development Corp., U.K.

3. Nemo sibi nascitur   *Latin* 'No one is born for himself alone'
   —Coles, Scott.

IRONY

1. Non sine sente rosa   *Latin* 'The rose not without a thorn'
   —Rose.

2. Nulla rosa sine spinis   *Latin* 'No rose without thorns'
   —Ilbert (Co. Devon).

3. Qui spinosior fragrantior   *Latin* 'The more thorny the more fragrant'
   —Ross (of Marchinch).

4. Rosae inter spinas nascuntur   *Latin* 'The roses are born amid the thorns'
   —Thorndike (U.S.).

5. Saepe creat pulchras aspera spina rosas   *Latin* 'The sharp thorn often bears beautiful roses'
   —Thorn.

6. Sans espine ne se eveille la rose   *French* 'No rose without a thorn'
   —Friedrich V, Margrave of Baden-Durlach (1594-1659).

7. Ubi mel ibi fel   *Latin* 'Where honey is there is gall'
   —Adolf Wilhelm, Duke of Saxony-Jena (1632–68).

JUDGMENT

1. Barn ar agen   *Welsh* 'Wrongly judged'(?)
   —Fleming.

2. Ego de meo sensu judico   *Latin* 'I judge from my own sense of things'
   —Willson.

3. Exsurge, domine, judica causam tuam   *Latin* 'Arise, Lord, and judge thy case'
   —The Inquisition.

4. Judge
   —Menzies.

5. **Judge and avenge my cause, O Lord**
—Menzies.

6. **Judge not**
—Erskine.

7. **Judge nought**
—Buchan (E.), Erskine, Stuart, Traquair (E.).

8. **Judicemur agendo** *Latin* 'May we be judged by our action'
—Hicks (U.S.).

9. **Judicio et justitia** *Latin* 'With judgment and justice'
—Joachim I, Elector of Brandenburg (1484–1535).

10. **Judicium parium, aut leges terrae** *Latin* 'The judgment of our peers or the law of the land'
—Camden (M.), Raines.

11. **Legale judicium parium** *Latin* 'The legal judgment of my peers'
—Yates.

12. **Ne jugu libron je la kovrilo** *Esperanto* 'Do not judge a book by its cover'
—Lowell (U.S.).

13. **Spectemur agendo** *Latin* 'Let us be judged from our deeds'
—1st Royal Dragoons, 101st Foot (Royal Munster Fusiliers), 102nd Foot (Royal Dublin Fusiliers).

14. **Turpi secernere honestum** *Latin* 'To separate the honorable from the base'
—Plumpre.

JUSTICE (*See also* FAIRNESS; LAW; RIGHTS.)

1. **Addere legi justitiam decus** *Latin* 'To add justice to the law is befitting'
—Norton (B.).

2. **Amantibus justitiam, pietatem, fidem** *Latin* 'To the lovers of justice, piety, and faith'
—Order of St. Anne (Sleswick).

3. **Amantibus justitiam, pietatem, fidem** *Latin* 'To those who love justice, piety, and faith'
—Order of St. Anne (Schleswig-Holstein).

4. **Armis potentius aequum** *Latin* 'Justice is more powerful than arms'
—Falconer (of Newton, Scotland).

5. **Audax et justus** *Latin* 'Bold and just'
—Wright.

6. **Audax justum perficere** *Latin* 'Bold to perform what is just'
—Strathy.

7. **Aude fieri justum** *Latin* 'Dare to become just'
—Parker (U.S.).

8. **Barn yn uchaf** *Welsh* 'Justice above all'
—Buck.

9. **Be just, and fear not**
—Ashby, Atkins, Coleman, Hewitt, Lilford (V.), Payne, Peacock, Strange, Warren, Carlisle City and C. B. C., Pudsey B. C., U.K.

10. **Benevolentia et justitia** *Latin* 'Benevolence and justice'
—Griffiths (U.S.).

11. **Cadernid, cyfiawnder, cynnydd** *Welsh* 'Stability, justice, progress'
—Barry B. C., U.K.

12. **Compositum jus fasque animi** *Latin* 'A mind which respects alike the laws of mutual justice and of God'
—Ellenborough (E.), Law, Laws, Nightingale.

13. **Confirmat justum Dominus** *Latin* 'The Lord strengthens the just'
—Georg Albrecht, Margrave of Brandenburg (1591–1615).

14. **Constans justitiam moniti** *Latin* 'Persevering in justice with moderation'
—Russell.

15. **Constitution/ Wisdom/ Justice/ Moderation**
—University System of Georgia.

16. **Deo credito justitiam colito** *Latin* 'Practice justice, trusting in God'
—Udheraj.

17. **De vultu tuo Domine meum prodeat judicium** *Latin* 'From thy countenance, O Lord, may my justice issue!'
—Friedrich II, Elector of the Palatinate (1483–1556).

18. **Discite justitiam** *Latin* 'Learn justice'
—Nisbet (of Dirletoun).

19. **Discite justitiam moniti** *Latin* 'Learn justice, being admonished'
—[Vergil, *Aen.* vi. 620.] Russell (Bt.).

20. **Droit et avant**   *French* 'Just and forward'
—Sydney (V.).

21. **Droit et loyal**   *French* 'Just and loyal'
—Dudley, (earl of Leicester in the reign of Elizabeth I),
Huntingfield (B.).

22. **Droit et loyalté**   *French* 'Justice and loyalty'
—Vanneck.

23. **Eques sit semper aequus**   *Latin* 'Let a Knight be always just'
—Knight.

24. **Et juste et vrai**   *French* 'Both just and true'
—Ray, Wray.

25. **Fiat iustitia**   *Latin* 'Let justice be done'
—South Molton B. C., U.K.

26. **Fiat justitia**   *Latin* 'Let justice be done'
—Bryce, Coker.

27. **Fiat justitia, ruat coelum**   *Latin* 'Let justice be done, though the
heavens should fall in ruins'
—Lloyd, Ouvry.

28. **Fiat justitia et pereat mundus**   *Latin* 'Let justice be done, though
the world perish'
—Ferdinand I, Emperor of Germany (1503–64).

29. **Fiat pax fiat justitia**   *Latin* 'Let peace be made, justice be done'
—Holland.

30. **Fidelitas regi et justitia mihi**   *Latin* 'Fidelity to the king and justice to myself'
—Dawson.

31. **Fides et justitia**   *Latin* 'Faith and justice'
—Farnborough U. D. C., U.K.; Webster (Bt.).

32. **Fortior leone justus**   *Latin* 'The just man is stronger than a lion'
—Goodricke (of Ribstone Hall).

33. **Fortis et aequus**   *Latin* 'Brave and just'
—Livingstone (of Aberdeen).

34. **Fortitudo et justitia**   *Latin* 'Fortitude and justice'
—Judah (U.S.).

35. **Fortitudo et justitia invictae sunt**   *Latin* 'Fortitude and justice are
invincible'
—Maguire.

36. **Fraternité, justice, travail**   *French* 'Fraternity, justice, work'
—Republic of Dahomey.

37. **Freedom and justice**
     —Republic of Ghana.

38. **Freedom with responsibility, equal justice under law**
     —Western State University College of Law, Fullerton and
     San Diego, California.

39. **Gorau tarian cyfiawnder**   *Welsh* 'The best shield is justice'
     —Flintshire C. C., U.K.

40. **Honestum pro patria**   *Latin* 'What is honorable and just should
     be done for one's country'
     —Heinrich Julius, Duke of Braunschweig-Wolfenbüttel
     (1564–1613).

41. **Honore et justitia**   *Latin* 'Through honor and justice'
     —Jayne (U.S.).

42. **Honor et justitia**   *Latin* 'Honor and justice'
     —Antill (U.S.).

43. **Honor et justitia manet amicitia florebit semper que** *latin*
     'Honor and justice remain, and friendship will always flourish'
     —Bayard (U.S.).

44. **Honor veritas et justitia**   *Latin* 'Honor truth and justice'
     —Southam.

45. **In fide, justitia, et fortitudine**   *Latin* 'In faith, justice, and
     strength'
     —Order of St. George (Bavaria).

46. **In iustitia virtutes omnes**   *Latin* 'All virtues are in justice'
     —Sims (U.S.).

47. **Je veux le droict**   *Old French* 'I desire that which is just'
     —Duckett (Bt.).

48. **Je veux le droit**   *French* 'I desire that which is just'
     —Duckett.

49. **Je voil droyt avoyre**   *Old French* 'I will have justice'
     —Wharton.

50. **Jus dicere decus**   *Latin* 'It is honorable to dispense justice'
     —Plummer.

51. **Justam perficito nihil timeto**   *Latin* 'Do what is just, fear noth-
     ing'
     —Kelly.

52. **Juste et clementer**   *Latin* 'With justice and clemency'
     —Johann Georg, Elector of Brandenburg (1525–98).

53. **Juste et droit**   *French* 'Just and frank'
                                    —Whichcote (Bt.).

54. **Juste et fortiter**   *Latin* 'Justly and bravely'
                                    —Blaxland.

55. **Juste et vray**   *French* 'Just and true'
                                    —Ray.

56. **Juste nec timide**   *Latin* 'Be just and fear not'
                                    —Farnworth B. C., U.K.

57. **Justice, paix, travail**   *French* 'Justice, peace, work'
                                    —Democratic Republic of the Congo.

58. **Justice to all**
                                    —Brock.

59. **Justicia omnibus**   *Latin* 'Justice to all'
                                    —District of Columbia.

60. **Justi germinabunt**   *Latin* 'The just shall shoot forth'
                                    —Smithson.

61. **Justi terram incolant**   *Latin* 'Let the just inhabit the earth'
                                    —Coningsby.

62. **Justitia**   *Latin* 'Justice'
                                    —Nurse, Sibbald (of Balgony).

63. **Justitiae comes magnanimitas**   *Latin* 'Generosity is the companion of justice'
                                    —Town of Dijon, France.

64. **Justitiae propositique tenax**   *Latin* 'Tenacious of justice and of purpose'
                                    —Stuart (Bt.).

65. **Justitiae soror fides**   *Latin* 'Faith is the sister of justice'
                                    —Thurlow (B.), Thurlow.

66. **Justitia et clementia**   *Latin* 'Justice and mercy'
                                    —Horsford.

67. **Justitia et concordia**   *Latin* 'Justice and concord'
                                    —Christian, Duke of Braunschweig-Lüneburg
                                            (1566–1633).

68. **Justitiae tenax**   *Latin* 'Persevering in justice'
                                    —Astley, Hastings (B.).

69. **Justitia et fortitudo invincibilia sunt**   *Latin* 'Justice and fortitude are invincible'
                                    —Maguire.

70. **Justitia et pax** *Latin* 'Justice and peace'
—Plumbers' Company.

71. **Justitia et veritas** *Latin* 'Justice and truth'
—Charles I (1600–49); Lawriston.

72. **Justitia et virtus** *Latin* 'Justice and virtue'
—Charlesworth.

73. **Justitia stabilitur thronus** *Latin* 'By justice is the throne upheld'
—Friedrich, Count of the Palatinate of Vohenstrauss (1557–97).

74. **Justitia turris nostra** *Latin* 'Justice is our tower'
—Hackney B. C., U.K.

75. **Justitia/ veritas** *Latin* 'Justice/ truth'
—Olivet Nazarene College, Kankakee, Illinois.

76. **Justitia virtutum regina** *Latin* 'Justice is the queen of the virtues'
—Goldsmiths' Company.

77. **Justi velut lumen astrarum** *Latin* 'Just men are like the light of the stars'
—Checkley (U.S.).

78. **Justum et decorum** *Latin* 'Just and honorable'
—Friedrich Adolf, Count von der Lippe (1667–1718).

79. **Justum et tenacem** *Latin* 'Just and firm of purpose'
—Colthurst (Bt.), Macknight or McKnight.

80. **Justum et tenacem propositi** *Latin* 'Just and firm of purpose'
—Holmes.

81. **Justum perficito, nihil timeto** *Latin* 'Act justly, and you will fear nothing'
—Rogers (of Yarlington Lodge).

82. **Justus ac tenax** *Latin* 'Just and firm'
—McCammond.

83. **Justus ac tenax propositi** *Latin* 'Just and firm to my purpose'
—Jones.

84. **Justus esto, et non metue** *Latin* 'Be just, and fear not'
—Robson.

85. **Justus et fidelis** *Latin* 'Just and faithful'
—Bomford.

86. **Justus et propositi tenax** *Latin* 'Just and firm of purpose'
—Chedworth, How, Penrice (of Gt. Yarmouth).

87. **Justus et tenax** *Latin* 'Just and firm'
—Hunt-Grubbe.

88. **Justus nec timidus**   *Latin* 'Just and not timid'
—Handfield.

89. **Justus propositi tenax**   *Latin* 'The just is firm of purpose'
—Ferrand.

90. **Lex ancilla justitiae**   *Latin* 'Law, the servant of justice'
—The John Marshall Law School, Chicago, Illinois.

91. **Lex et justitia**   *Latin* 'Law and justice'
—Clarke.

92. **Lux mundi justitia**   *Latin* 'Justice is the light of the world'
—Johann Georg I, Elector of Saxony (1585–1656).

93. **Order, freedom, justice**   *(from Arabic)*
—Republic of Tunisia.

94. **Pax et justitia**   *Latin* 'Peace and justice'
—Johann Georg II, Elector of Saxony (1613–80).

95. **Pie, juste, temperanter**   *Latin* 'With piety, justice, and moderation'
—Friedrich IV, Count of the Palatinate (1594–1610).

96. **Pie at juste**   *Latin* 'With piety and justice'
—August Friedrich, Duke of Schleswig-Holstein-Gottorp
(1646–1705).

97. **Pietas et justitia principatus columnae**   *Latin* 'Piety and justice are the supports of government'
—Adolf Friedrich I, Duke of Mecklenburg-Schwerin
(1588–1658).

98. **Pietate, fide, et justicia**   *Latin* 'With piety, fidelity, and justice'
—Wilhelm VI, Landgrave of Hesse-Cassel (1629–63).

99. **Pietate, legibus, justitia**   *Latin* 'By piety, by prudence and by justice'
—Friedrich I, Duke of Saxony-Gotha and Altenburg
(1646–91).

100. **Pietate et justicia** *Latin* 'By piety and justice'
—Günther, Count Schwarzburg (1570–1643); Otto, Landgrave of Hesse (1594–1617); Ferdinand III, Emperor of Germany (1608–57); Georg Wilhelm, Duke of Braunschweig-Lüneburg-Zelle (1624–1705); Christian, Duke of Saxony (1654–63); Johann Günther, Count Schwarzburg-Arnstadt (1654–69); Johann Friedrich, Margrave of Brandenburg-Anspach (1654–86); Ernst, Duke of Saxony-Hildburghausen (1655–1715); Johann Georg II, Duke of Saxony-Eisenach (1665–98); Friedrich Heinrich, Duke of Saxony-Neustadt (1668–1713); Friedrich III, Duke of Saxony-Gotha and Altenburg (1699–1772).

101. **Pietate et justitia principes dii sunt** *Latin* 'By piety and justice princes become gods'
—Christian Ulrich, Duke of Württemberg-Oels-Bernstadt (1652–1704).

102. **Prudentia et justitia** *Latin* 'With prudence and justice'
—Kaye-Shuttleworth.

103. **Quid justum non quod utile** *Latin* 'What is just, not what is useful (expedient)'
—Phillips, Phillips (of Garendon Park).

104. **Rebus justis invigilans** *Latin* 'Watchful for justice'
—Walcot.

105. **Recte et suaviter** *Latin* 'Justly and mildly'
—Curzon, Scarsdale (B.), Wyborn.

106. **Recte faciendo, neminem timeo** *Latin* 'Acting justly, I fear nobody'
—Cairncross.

107. **Recte faciendo audax** *Latin* 'Bold in doing justly'
—Grundy.

108. **Recte faciendo neminem timeas** *Latin* 'In acting justly fear no one'
—Harvey (of Ickwell Bury), Robertson, Scott (of Betton).

109. **Recte faciendo securus** *Latin* 'Safe in acting justly'
—Inglis (Bt.).

110. **Right and reason**
—Graham (of Leitchtown).

111. **Right can never die**
—Toler.

112. **Right revere, and persevere**
—Berry.

113. **Sis justus, et ne timeas** *Latin* 'Be just and fear not'
—White.

114. **Sis justus nec timeas** *Latin* 'Be just, fear not'
—Garvey.

115. **Sola gloriosa quae justa** *Latin* 'The just alone is glorious'
—Johann Georg IV, Elector of Saxony (1668–94).

116. **Stabit conscius aequi** *Latin* 'Conscious of what is just he shall stand'
—Charlton, Grant-Dalton.

117. **Tandem justitia** *Latin* 'Justice at length'
—O'Donnelly.

118. **Thure et jure** *Latin* 'By incense and justice'
—Foulis (of Revelstoun).

119. **Travail, justice, solidarité** *French* 'Work, justice, solidarity'
—Republic of Guinea.

120. **Trial by jury**
—Erskine (B.).

121. **Unidad, paz, justicia** *Spanish* 'Unity, peace, justice'
—Republic of Equatorial Guinea.

122. **Union, justice, confidence**
—State of Louisiana.

123. **Union, justice and confidence**
—Northwestern State University, Natchitoches, Louisiana; Alexandria Vocational-Technical Institute, Alexandria, Louisiana.

124. **Union, travail, justice** *French* 'Union, work, justice'
—Gabon Republic.

125. **Union/ confidence/ justice**
—Louisiana Technical University, Ruston, Louisiana.

126. **Unité, travail, justice** *French* 'Unity, work, justice'
—Republic of Upper Volta.

127. **Unity, freedom, justice**
—Sierra Leone.

128. **Veritate et justitiâ** *Latin* 'With truth and justice'
—Ximenes.

129. **Veritatis et aequitatis tenax** *Latin* 'Persevering in truth and justice'

    —Rust.

130. **Wisdom, justice, moderation**

    —State of Georgia.

KINDNESS (*See also* GENTLENESS; GOODNESS; HUMANITY; LOVE; UNSELFISHNESS.)

1. **Agere pro aliis** *Latin* 'To act for others'

    —Ashton.

2. **Beneficio bene erit** *Latin* 'He will succeed by kindness'

    —Raisbeck.

3. **Benevolentia et justitia** *Latin* 'Benevolence and justice'

    —Griffiths (U.S.).

4. **Ben ti voglio** *Italian* 'I wish thee well'

    —Richardson.

5. **Caritas fructum habet** *Latin* 'Charity bears fruit'

    —Burnell.

6. **Ex corde charitas** *Latin* 'Out of the heart, charity'

    —Watson.

7. **Faith, Hope, Charity**

    —Order of the Royal Red Cross.

8. **Fide et caritate laboro** *Latin* 'I labor with faith and charity'

    —Bovier.

9. **Fructum habet charitas** *Latin* 'Charity bears fruit'

    —Buckston.

10. **Give a hand up—not a hand out**

    —Community Chest.

11. **In omnibus caritas** *Latin* 'In all things charity'

    —Longmore.

12. **Kind heart**

    —Duff.

13. **Miseris auxilium (or) opem fero** *Latin* 'I bring help to the wretched'

    —Malden.

14. **Miseris succurrere** *Latin* 'To help the unfortunate'

    —Prince, Smyth (Co. Clare).

15. **Miseris succurrere disco**   *Latin* 'I learn to succor the unfortunate'
—Dramond, Hinde, Hodgson, MacMillan, Soltau.

16. **Miseris succurro**   *Latin* 'I succor the wretched'
—Macmillan-Scott, Scott.

17. **Non gladio, sed gratia**   *Latin* 'Not by the sword but by kindness'
—Charters or Chartres (of Hempsfield and Kingfauns).

18. **Non ignarus mali miseris succurrere disco**   *Latin* 'Not unacquainted with misfortune, I learn to succor the wretched'
—Savage.

19. **Pauperum solatio**   *Latin* 'For consolation of the poor'
—Order of St. Elizabeth (Brazil).

20. **Pour bien désirer**   *French* 'For wishing well'
—Bolden, Dacre (B.), Barrett-Lennard (Bt.).

21. **Qui dat pauperibus numquam indigebit**   *Latin* 'Who giveth to the poor will never want'
—over the doorway of Holy Trinity Hospital at West Croydon, England.

22. **Remember the poore, and god wil bles thee and thy store**
—St. Mary's Church, Persey, Berkshire, England.

23. **Sapientia/ caritas/ prudentia**   *Latin* 'Wisdom/ charity/ prudence'
—Saint Mary of the Plains College, Dodge City, Kansas.

24. **Soyez compatissant soyez courtois**   *French* 'Be pitiful, be courteous'
—Curtoys.

25. **Trusty and kind**
—Law.

26. **Unitas, veritas, caritas**   *Latin* 'Unity, truth, charity'
—Union Theological Seminary, New York, New York.

27. **Vita hominis sine literis mors est**   *Latin* 'The life of man without letters is death'
—Derby School, U.K.

28. **Vita sine litteris mors est**   *Latin* 'Life without literature is death'
—Allen (U.S.).

KNOWLEDGE (*See also* MIND; SELF-KNOWLEDGE; WISDOM.)

1. **Academic—Vocational—Cultural—Patriotic—Spiritual**
—The School of the Ozarks, Point Lookout, Missouri.

2. **Animo et scientia** *Latin* 'With courage and knowledge'
—Clark.

3. **Bonitatem et disciplinam et scientiam doce me** *Latin* 'Teach me goodness and discipline and knowledge'
—College of Mount Saint Vincent, Riverdale, New York.

4. **Books unlike universities are open to all who would read**
—Curtin (U.S.).

5. **Chi legge regge** *Italian* 'Who reads rules'
—Amphlett.

6. **Dedicated to training hand, mind, heart**
—Snead State Junior College, Boaz, Alabama.

7. **Diligence/ Integrity/ Knowledge**
—McNeese State University, Lake Charles, Louisiana.

8. **Disce et labora** *Latin* 'Learn and labor'
—Mackie.

9. **Docendo disce** *Latin* 'Learn by teaching'
—Brown.

10. **Docendum et discendum** *Latin* 'To be taught and to be learnt'
—Blackheath Proprietary School, U.K.

11. **Doctrina ferro perennior** *Latin* 'Learning, more enduring than the sword'
—Smith.

12. **Editando et legendo** *Latin* 'By editing and reading'
—Cutbush (U.S.).

13. **Education for a democracy of excellence**
—Dutchess Community College, Poughkeepsie, New York.

14. **Education is life**
—Eastern Montana College, Billings, Montana.

15. **Education is the mother of wisdom and of virtue** *from Greek*
—Edinburgh Academy, Edinburgh.

16. **Education/ Service/ Research**
—Indiana University, Division of Allied Health Sciences, Bloomington, Indiana.

17. **Educatio pro omnibus** *Latin* 'Education for all'
—Sampson Technical College, Clinton, North Carolina.

18. **Efficiunt clarum studia** *Latin* 'Studies make him illustrious'
—Milne (of Muretoun).

19. **Erit haec quoque cognita monstris** *Latin* 'This, too, shall be learnt from portents'
—Louis XIII (1601–43).

20. **Eruditio/ ductus/ societas** *Latin* 'Learning/ leadership/ fellowship'
—Indian River Community College, Ft. Pierce, Florida.

21. **Eruditio et meritum pro omnibus** *Latin* 'Learning and reward for all'
—Isothermal Community College, Spindale, North Carolina.

22. **Et docere et rerum exquirere causas** *Latin* 'To teach and to inquire into the nature of things'
—University of Georgia, Athens, Georgia.

23. **Ex scientia tridens** *Latin* 'Out of knowledge, a trident'
—United States Naval Academy, Annapolis, Maryland.

24. **Fas est ab hoste doceri** *Latin* 'It is right to be taught by an enemy'
—Hoste (Bt.).

25. **Floreat scientia** *Latin* 'Let knowledge flourish'
—Massey University, Palmerston North, New Zealand.

26. **Fortitudine, doctrina, sapientia** *Latin* 'By bravery, by knowledge, by wisdom'
—Friedrich II, Duke of Saxony-Gotha and Altenburg (1676–1732).

27. **Get understanding**
—Ladies' Tea-room in the British House of Commons.

28. **Haec studia oblectant** *Latin* 'These studies give delight'
—Clifton College, U.K.

29. **In fide vestra virtutem in virtute autem scientiam** *Latin* '(Have) virtue in your faith but knowledge in your virtue'
—Agnes Scott College, Decatur, Georgia.

30. **'I would found an institution where any person can find instruction in any study'**
—Cornell University, Ithaca, New York.

31. **Knowledge, devotion, wisdom, service**
—Pembroke State University, Pembroke, North Carolina.

32. **Knowledge aflame**
—Liberty Baptist College, Lynchburg, Virginia.

33. **Knowledge/ Duty/ Honor**
—South Carolina State College, Orangeburg, South Carolina.

34. **Knowledge for life**
—South Mountain Community College, Arizona.

35. **Knowledge for service**
—Hannibal-LaGrange College, Hannibal, Missouri.

36. **Knowledge is power**
—Sharpe.

37. **Knowledge is structured in consciousness**
—Maharishi International University, Fairfield, Iowa.

38. **Knowledge/ Skill**
—Terra Technical College, Fremont, Ohio.

39. **Knowledge/ Understanding/ Achievement/ Citizenship**
—S. D. Bishop State Junior College, Mobile, Alabama.

40. **Labor et scientia** *Latin* 'Labor and knowledge'
—Rose-Hulman Institute of Technology, Terre Haute, Indiana.

41. **Learning and labor**
—University of Illinois, Urbana-Champaign, Illinois.

42. **Learning for earning**
—Bryant and Stratton Business Institute, Clarence, New York.

43. **Learning/ Service/ Integrity**
—Quinsigamond Community College, Worcester, Massachusetts.

44. **Lege, sapere aude** *Latin* 'Read, dare to be wise'
—Tattershall.

45. **Legite et discite** *Latin* 'Read and learn'
—Ashley.

46. **Let knowledge grow from more to more; and so be human life enriched**
—University of Chicago, Chicago, Illinois.

47. **Librum cum lampade trado** *Latin* 'I yield the book with the lamp'
—Hill.

48. **Literis et armis** *Latin* 'By letters and by arms'
—Wilhelm Ernst, Duke of Saxony-Weimar (1662–1728).

49. **Litteras ne despice** *Latin* 'Do not despise literature'
—Willard (U.S.).

50. **Lux et scientia** *Latin* 'Light and knowledge'
—Andrew College, Cuthbert, Georgia.

51. **Multi pertransibunt et augebitur scientia** *Latin* 'Many shall pass through and learning shall be increased'
—Holborn B. C., U.K.

52. **Nec sinit esse feros** *Latin* 'It (education) does not allow them to be brutal'
—Grazebrook (of Pedmore, Co. Worcester).

53. **Nell' armi e nelle lettere consiste la virtu** *Italian* 'Power consists in weapons and in knowledge'
—Franz, Duke of Braunschweig-Lüneburg (1572–1601).

54. **Patience passe science** *French* 'Patience surpasses knowledge'
—Boscawen, Falmouth (E.).

55. **Per lumen scientiae viam invenient populi** *Latin* 'Through the light of knowledge the people will find a way'
—Texas College, Tyler, Texas.

56. **Per virtutem scientiamque** *Latin* 'By valor and knowledge'
—MacNeil.

57. **Que sçay-je?** *Old French* 'What do I know?'
—Michel de Montaigne (1533–80).

58. **Religio, libertas et scientia** *Latin* 'Religion, liberty, and knowledge'
—Cedar Crest College, Allentown, Pennsylvania.

59. **Salubritas et eruditio** *Latin* 'Health and learning'
—Cheltenham B. C., U.K.

60. **Sanitas/ scientia/ sanctitas** *Latin* 'Health/ knowledge/ holiness'
—Gannon University, Erie, Pennsylvania.

61. **Sapientia Domum aedificavit** *Latin* 'Knowledge has built a Home'
—Crosier Seminary Junior College, Onamia, Minnesota.

62. **Sapientia/ virtus/ amicitia** *Latin* 'Knowledge/ virtue/ friendship'
—Central Michigan University, Mt. Pleasant, Michigan.

63. **Savoir pouvoir** *French* 'Knowledge is power'
—Hodge.

64. **Scholarship/ Participation/ Service**
—McPherson College, McPherson, Kansas.

65. **Scientia** *Latin* 'Knowledge'
—Northwestern College of Chiropractic, St. Paul, Minnesota.

66. **Scientiae cedit mare** *Latin* 'The sea yields to knowledge'
—U.S. Coast Guard Academy, New London, Connecticut.

67. **Scientiae et labori detur** *Latin* 'Due to knowledge and labor'
—Luton B. C., U.K.

68. **Scientiae laborisque memor** *Latin* 'Mindful of knowledge and labor'
—Hutchison.

69. **Scientia est potentia** *Latin* 'Knowledge is power'
—Miami-Dade Community College, Miami, Florida; Tylden (U.S.).

70. **Scientia et industria cum probitate** *Latin* 'Knowledge and diligence with uprightness'
—Lincoln College, Canterbury, New Zealand.

71. **Scientia et pietas** *Latin* 'Knowledge and piety'
—Wesleyan College, Macon, Georgia.

72. **Scientia et sapientia** *Latin* 'Knowledge and wisdom'
—Illinois Wesleyan University, Bloomington, Illinois.

73. **Scientia/ integritas** *Latin* 'Knowledge/ integrity'
—Massachusetts Bay Community College, Wellesley Hills, Massachusetts.

74. **Scientia/ Pietas que vitalis** *Latin* 'Learning and devotion are vital'
—Texas Wesleyan College, Fort Worth, Texas.

75. **Scientia vera cum fide pura** *Latin* 'True knowledge with pure faith'
—Beloit College, Beloit, Wisconsin.

76. **Scientiis/ artibus/ religioni** *Latin* 'By knowledge, by art, by religion'
—Mercer University, Macon, Georgia.

77. **Sit Deus in studiis** *Latin* 'May God be with me in my studies'
—Sydenham.

78. **Societas scientia virtus** *Latin* 'Fellowship, knowledge, virtue'
—Milner (U.S.).

79. **Studendo et contemplando indefessus** *Latin* 'Unwearied in studying and meditation'
—Cardale.

80. **Studiis et rebus honestis** *Latin* 'Through studies and upright affairs'
—University of Vermont, Burlington, Vermont.

81. **Studiis et rebus honestis** *Latin* 'By study and honorable pursuits'
—Dunning.

82. **Study quiet**
—Head (Bt.), Patrick.

83. **Teaching/ Research/ Service**
—Arkansas State University, Arkansas.

84. **That the people shall know**
—Columbia University Graduate School of Journalism, New York City, New York.

85. **The road to knowledge**
—El Camino College, Torrance, California.

86. **The torch the staff of knowledge**
—Merced College, Merced, California.

87. **Think/ Work/ Serve**
—Tennessee State University, Nashville, Tennessee.

88. **To help people learn**
—Leeward Community College, Pearl City, Hawaii.

89. **To learn/ To search/ To serve**
—State University of New York.

90. **Tota educatio** *Latin* 'Total education'
—Lenoir Community College, Kinston, North Carolina.

91. **Truth/ Knowledge/ Freedom**
—Harding University, Searcy, Arkansas.

92. **Truth/ Knowledge/ Wisdom/ Education**
—Independence Community College, Independence, Kansas.

93. **Ut omnes te cognoscant** *Latin* 'So that all may know you'
—Niagara University, Niagara Falls, New York.

94. **Veritas/ mores/ scientia** *Latin* 'Truth/ morals/ knowledge'
—East Texas Baptist College, Marshall, Texas.

95. **Vita hominis sine literis mors est** *Latin* 'The life of man without letters is death'
—Derby School, U.K.

96. **Vita sine litteris mors est** *Latin* 'Life without literature is death'
—Allen (U.S.).

97. **Vocational/ technical/ general**
—Western Wisconsin Technical Institute, Wisconsin.

98. **Where students learn by doing**
—North Dakota State School of Science, Wahpeton, North Dakota.

99. **Wisdom/ Knowledge/ Skill**
—Martin Community College, Williamston, North Carolina.

100. **Your friendly place to learn**
—Chipola Junior College, Marianna, Florida.

LAUGHTER (*See also* ENJOYMENT; HAPPINESS.)
1. **Laugh lader an aughter** 'Laugh harder and louder'
—Kennedy.

2. **Lex pro urbe et orbe** *Latin* 'Law for the city and the world'
—Vermont Law School, South Royalton, Vermont.

3. **Rident florentia prata** *Latin* 'The flowery meadows laugh'
—Pratt (of Ryston Hall, co. Norfolk).

LAW (*See also* GOVERNMENT; JUSTICE.)
1. **Addere legi justitiam decus** *Latin* 'To add justice to the law is befitting'
—Norton (B.).

2. **Bind up the testimony and seal the law**
—Westminster College, New Wilmington, Pennsylvania.

3. **Compositum jus fasque animi** *Latin* 'A mind which respects alike the laws of mutual justice and of God'
—Ellenborough (E.), Law, Laws, Nightingale.

4. **Credo legi** *Latin* 'I trust in the law'
—Hamilton.

5. **Divide et impera** *Latin* 'Divide and rule'
—Denison.

6. **Freedom with responsibility, equal justice under law**
—Western State University College of Law, Fullerton and San Diego, California.

7. **Garde la loi** *French* 'Keep the law'
—Slator.

8. **Habeo pro jus fasque** *Latin* 'I stay on the side of law and right'
—Cushman (U.S.).

9. **Haud lege peritior** *Latin* 'Not more skillful than the law'
—Read.

10. **La loi le veut, et moi ni mot** *French* 'The law wishes it and I have not a word to say'
—Barrett-Lennard (Bt.).

11. **Law**
—Bowen.

12. **Law and Right**
—Allen.

13. **Lege et labore** *Latin* 'By law and labor'
—Bell.

14. **Lege et ratione** *Latin* 'By law and reason'
—Crookshank (U.S.).

15. **Leges arma tenent sanctas** *Latin* 'Arms cause laws to be respected'
—Benson.

16. **Leges juraque serva** *Latin* 'Observe the laws and ordinances'
—Grant (of Kilgraston).

17. **Leges juraque servat** *Latin* 'He observes the laws and statutes'
—Hearne.

18. **Leges juraque servo** *Latin* 'I observe the laws and ordinances'
—Leigh (of Belmont, co. Chester).

19. **Legibus antiquis** *Latin* 'By the ancient laws'
—Leigh (of Bardon).

20. **Legibus et armis** *Latin* 'By laws and arms'
—Gordon (of Gordonbank).

21. **Legibus vivo** *Latin* 'I live by laws'
—Lisle (U.S.).

22. **Legi regi fidelis** *Latin* 'Faithful to the king and law'
—Barry, Sautry.

23. **Le roy, la loy** *Old French* 'The king, the law'
—Larcom (Bt.).

24. **Le roy, la loy, la foy** *Old French* 'King, law, faith'
—Grover.

25. **Lex** *Latin* 'Law'
—San Francisco Law School, San Francisco, California.

26. **Lex ancilla justitiae** *Latin* 'Law, the servant of justice'
    —The John Marshall Law School, Chicago, Illinois.

27. **Lex et justitia** *Latin* 'Law and justice'
    —Clarke.

28. **Lex justo non est posita** *Latin* 'Law is not made for the righteous'
    —Moritz, Landgrave of Hesse-Cassel (1572–1632).

29. **Lex pro urbe et orbe** *Latin* 'Law for the city and the world'
    —Vermont Law School, South Royalton, Vermont.

30. **Lex ratio summa** or **Lex summa ratio** *Latin* 'Law is the highest reason'
    —Law.

31. **Libertas a legibus** *Latin* 'Liberty out of law'
    —Stokes (U.S.).

32. **Libertas in legibus** *Latin* 'Liberty in the law'
    —Wynford (B.), Best.

33. **Mos legem regit** *Latin* 'Custom rules the law'
    —Mosley (Bt.).

34. **Not laws of man but laws of God**
    —Balch.

35. **One faith, one king, one law**
    —Bourk.

36. **Par loi et droit** *French* 'By law and right'
    —Trayner.

37. **Peace through law**
    —Arizona State University College of Law, Arizona.

38. **Perimus licitis** *Latin* 'We perish by what is lawful'
    —Teignmouth (B.).

39. **Pietate, legibus, et armis** *Latin* 'By piety, by law, and by arms'
    —Philipp, Landgrave of Hesse-Butzbach (1581–1643).

40. **Pro Deo, pro Rege, pro patria, et lege** *Latin* 'For God, for the King, for the country, and the law'
    —Blakemore.

41. **Pro fide, lege, et rege** *Latin* 'For faith, laws, and king'
    —Order of the White Eagle (Polish).

42. **Progressio et concordia** *Latin* 'Progress and concord'
    —Kettering B. C., U.K.

43. **Pro lege, Rege, grege** *Latin* 'For the law, the king, the people'
    —Shield.

44. **Pro lege, Rege (et) grege** *Latin* 'For the law, the king, (and) the people'
—Christian Wilhelm, Margrave of Brandenburg (1587–1665).

45. **Pro lege, senatuque rege** *Latin* 'For law, senate, and sovereign'
—Dodsworth (Bt.).

46. **Pro lege et grege** *Latin* 'For law and for the people'
—Philippi, Duke of Pomerania zu Wolgast (1515–60); Bogislaus XIII, Duke of Pomerania zu Barth (1544–1606); Georg III, his son (1582–1617); Christian Wilhelm, Margrave of Brandenburg (1587–1665); Philipp, Landgrave of Hesse-Cassel (1604–26); Johann Georg I, Elector of Saxony (1585–1656).

47. **Pro lege et patria** *Latin* 'For law and country'
—Daniel.

48. **Pro lege et pro grege** *Latin* 'For law and for the people'
—Johann Sigismund, Elector of Brandenburg (1572–1619).

49. **Pro lege et Rege** *Latin* 'For law and the king'
—Hicks (U.S.), Whitebread (U.S.).

50. **Pro legibus et regibus** *Latin* 'For laws and kings'
—Wilson (Bt.).

51. **Pro libertate lege sancta** *Latin* 'For liberty ratified by law'
—Glyn.

52. **Pro rege, lege, grege** *Latin* 'For the king, the law, and the people'
—Bessborough (E.), Brougham (B.), Ponsonby (B.), Whither.

53. **Pro rege, pro lege, pro grege** *Latin* 'For king, for law, for the common people'
—Damon (U.S.).

54. **Pro rege, pro lege, pro patriae conamur** *Latin* 'We strive for king, for law, and for country'
—18th Hussars, U.K.

55. **Pro rege et lege** *Latin* 'For king and law'
—Leeds City and C. B. C., U.K.; Horton (of Howroyde); Kidson; Mandit; Stewart (of Fincastle).

56. **Quid leges sine moribus?** *Latin* 'What are laws without morals?'
—Edwards (of Ashill, co. Norfolk).

57. **Quo fas et gloria**   *Latin* 'Whither law and glory (lead)'
                                       —Robertson (of Glasgow).

58. **Regi legi fidelis**   *Latin* 'Faithful to king and law'
                                                              —Barry.

59. **Rex et nostra jura**   *Latin* 'The king and our laws'
                                       —Great Yarmouth C. B. C., U.K.

60. **Sacrarium regis cunabula legis**   *Latin* 'The shrine of the king and
     the cradle of the law'
                                       —Bury St. Edmunds B. C., U.K.

61. **Salus populi suprema est lex**   *Latin* 'The welfare of the people is
     the highest law'
                                       —Urmston U. D. C., U.K.

62. **Salus populi suprema lex**   *Latin* 'The welfare of the people is the
     highest law'
                            —Eastleigh B. C., Harrow U. D. C., Lewisham B. C.,
                                Lytham-St. Annes B. C., Swinton and Pendlebury
                                    B. C., Tipton B. C., Tonbridge U. D. C.,
                                        Willenhall U. D. C., U.K.

63. **Salus populi suprema lex esto**   *Latin* 'The security of the people
     shall be the highest law'
                            —[Cicero *Leges*. 3. 8.] Karl Emil, Margrave of
                                Brandenburg (1655–74); Johann, Duke of
                                Saxony-Weimar (1570–1605); Johann Ernst
                                I, Duke of Saxony-Weimar (1594–1626);
                                Friedrich Wilhelm, Elector of Brandenburg
                                (1620–88); State of Missouri.

64. **Sfida e commanda**   *Italian* 'He challenges and commands'
                                                    —Metaxa-Anzolato.

65. **Strike for the laws**
                                                    —Walworth (U.S.).

66. **Sub lege libertas**   *Latin* 'Under the law, liberty'
                                                              —Daniel.

67. **Une foy, une loy**   *Old French* 'One faith, one law'
                                                              —Sorel.

68. **Ung Dieu, ung loy, ung foy**   *Old French* 'One God, one law, one
     faith'
                                                    —Burke (of St. Cleras).

69. **Ung Dieu, ung roy, une loy**   *Old French* 'One God, one king, one
     law'
                                                    —Town of Lyons, France.

70. **Ung roy, ung foy, ung loy** *Old French* 'One king, one faith, one law'
    —Burke (of Marble Hill, Bt.), Burke (of Kilcoran, Owen, and Clongowna), Clanricarde (M.), De Burgo (Bt.), Rush.

71. **Un roy, une foy, une loy** *Old French* 'One king, one faith, one law'
    —De Burgh.

72. **Vincit cum legibus arma** *Latin* 'He conquers arms by laws'
    —Atkyns.

LEADERSHIP (*See also* AUTHORITY; CROWN; GUIDANCE; ROYALTY.)

1. **Agmina ducens** *Latin* 'A leader of men'
   —Strathcona (B.).

2. **Altrincham en avant** *French* 'Altrincham leads the way'
   —Altrincham B. C., U.K.

3. **A vo penn bit pont** *Welsh* 'He who will be chief, let him be a bridge'
   —Bridgend U. D. C., U.K.

4. **Be in the van**
   —Bevan.

5. **Conduco** *Latin* 'I lead'
   —Cowper-Essex.

6. **Cum principibus** *Latin* 'With my chiefs'
   —Hale.

7. **Duci et non trahi** *Latin* 'To be led and not dragged'
   —Athy.

8. **Ducitur, non trahitur** *Latin* 'He is led, not drawn'
   —Alexander.

9. **Duc me, sequar** *Latin* 'Lead on; I will follow'
   —Friedrich I, Duke of Saxony-Gotha and Altenburg (1646–91).

10. **Ductus, non coactus** *Latin* 'Led, not forced'
    —Robertson.

11. **Eruditio/ ductus/ societas** *Latin* 'Learning/ leadership/ fellowship'
    —Indian River Community College, Ft. Pierce, Florida.

12. **Follow me**
    —Breadalbane (M.), Campbell (Bt.), Gurwood.

13. **Je conduis**   *French* 'I conduct'

—Conder.

14. **Lead on**

—Hotham (B.).

15. **Liberty and independence**

—State of Delaware.

16. **Me duce**   *Latin* 'Under my leadership'

—Innes.

17. **Me duce carpe viam**   *Latin* 'With me for leader hasten on your way'

—Burdett.

18. **Nolo servile capistrum**   *Latin* 'I am unwilling (to bear) the slavish halter'

—Marsh (Bt.).

19. **Ob ducem, ob patriam**   *Latin* 'For (our) leader, for (our) country'

—Waddy.

20. **Praesis ut prosis**   *Latin* 'Lead that you may serve'
                    —Lancaster School, U.K.

21. **Qua duxeris adsum**   *Latin* 'Where you lead there I am'

—Ogilvy.

22. **Qui conducit**   *Latin* 'One who leads'

—Borthwick.

23. **Si j'avance, suivez-moi; si je fuis, tuez-moi; si je meurs, vengez-moi**   *French* 'If I advance, follow me; if I flee, kill me; if I die, avenge me'

—La Roche-Jaquelin.

24. **Te duce libertas**   *Latin* 'Where thou art leader there is liberty'
                    —Crosby.

25. **Virtue, liberty and independence**
                    —State of Pennsylvania; Barton (U.S.).

26. **Vixi liber et moriar**   *Latin* 'I have lived a freeman and will die one'

—Gray, Ibbetson (Bt.).

27. **Y ddraig goch ddyry gychwyn**   *Welsh* 'The red dragon shall lead'
                    —Cardiff City and C. B. C., Prestatyn U. D. C., U.K.

LIBERTY (*See also* SELF-DETERMINATION.)

1. **Alenda lux ubi orta libertas** *Latin* 'Where light has arisen there liberty should be sustained'
>—Davidson College, Davidson, North Carolina; Community College of Beaver County, Monaca, Pennsylvania.

2. **Always for liberty**
>—Mawbey.

3. **Amicitia cum libertate** *Latin* 'Friendship with liberty'
>—Williams (U.S.).

4. **Aut liber aut nullus** *Latin* 'Either free or not at all'
>—Independent Company of Cadets, Prince William County, Virginia.

5. **Aut mors aut libertas** *Latin* 'Either death or liberty'
>—Wall.

6. **Be neither tyrant nor slave**
>—Eby (U.S.).

7. **Cara patria carior libertas** *Latin* 'Dear country, dearer liberty'
>—Clinton (U.S.).

8. **Cara vita, carior patria, carissima libertas** *Latin* 'Dear life, dearer country, dearest liberty'
>—Kettle (U.S.).

9. **Cervus non servus** *Latin* 'A stag not enslaved'
>—Goddard (of Swindon), Thorold (Bt.).

10. **Christi servitus vera libertas** *Latin* 'True liberty in service to Christ'
>—Merrick (U.S.), Vaughan (U.S.).

11. **Christus servatus vera libertas** *Latin* 'To serve Christ is true liberty'
>—Vaughan.

12. **Civil and religious liberty**
>—Wood (of Singleton Lodge).

13. **Deo parere libertas** *Latin* 'Obedience to God is liberty'
>—Georg Wilhelm, Elector of Brandenburg (1595–1640).

14. **Deo servire summa libertas** *Latin* 'The service of God is perfect freedom'
>—Christian II, Prince of Anhalt-Bernburg (1599–1656).

15. **Deus et libertas** *Latin* 'God and liberty'
>—Godfrey (Bt.).

16. **Deus nobis pace olim fecit** *Latin* 'God gave us this freedom'
—Seal of Virginia, 1776–1779.

17. **Dios, patria, libertad** *Spanish* 'God, fatherland and liberty'
—Dominican Republic.

18. **Dios union y libertad** *Spanish* 'God, union and liberty'
—Republic of El Salvador.

19. **Ense libertatem petit** *Latin* 'He seeks liberty by his sword'
—Caldwell.

20. **Ense libertatem petit inimico tyrannis** *Latin* 'He demands liberty from tyrants with a hostile sword'
—Caldwell.

21. **Ense petit placidam sub libertate quietam** *Latin* 'By the sword we seek peace but peace only under liberty'
—State of Massachusetts.

22. **Ex libertate veritas** *Latin* 'From liberty, truth'
—Aspland.

23. **Fidem libertatem amicitiam retinebis** *Latin* 'You will keep faith, liberty, and friendship'
—Adams (U.S.).

24. **Fides amicitiae periculosa libertas** *Latin* 'Liberty, a faith dangerous to friendship'
—Dockwra.

25. **For liberty**
—Macre.

26. **For true liberty**
—Renwick.

27. **Franche, leal, et oyé** *Old French* 'Free, loyal, and open'
—Leeds (D.).

28. **Franco leale toge** *Spanish* 'Free and loyal is to thee'
—Dolphin.

29. **Free**
—Scott.

30. **Freedom and justice**
—Republic of Ghana.

31. **Freedom and unity**
—State of Vermont.

32. **Freedom our rock**
—Tammany Society (Columbian Order).

33. **Freedom with responsibility, equal justice under law**
—Western State University College of Law, Fullerton and
San Diego, California.

34. **Free for a blast**
—Clerk (Bt.), Clark (of Courie Castle), Pennycock, Ratray.

35. **Golud gwlad rhyddid** *Welsh* 'The wealth of the land is freedom'
—Cardiganshire C. C., U.K.

36. **Habeo non habeor** *Latin* 'I hold but am not held'
—Booth.

37. **Honesta libertate** *Latin* 'By honorable liberty' or 'Hone support
liberty'
—Hone.

38. **Il n'y a rien si precieux que la liberté** *French* 'Nothing is so precious as liberty'
—Ernst the Pious, Duke of Saxony-Gotha (1601–75).

39. **Immer frey [sic]** *German* 'Always free'
—Austen-Cartmell.

40. **In ferrum libertate ruebant** *Latin* 'Through liberty they rushed
to the sword'
—Gardner.

41. **In libertate sociorum defendenda** *Latin* 'In defending the liberty
of our companions'
—Macgregor.

42. **In libertate vis** *Latin* 'Strength in freedom'
—Merton and Morden U. D. C., U.K.

43. **J'aime la liberté** *French* 'I love liberty'
—Mussenden, Ribton (Bt.).

44. **La liberté** *French* 'Liberty'
—Ackers.

45. **La merle aime la liberté** *French* 'The blackbird (or merle) loves
liberty'
—Merle.

46. **Liber ac sapiens esto** *Latin* 'Be free and wise'
—Bradley (U.S.).

47. **Libera deinde fidelis** *Latin* 'Free, therefore faithful'
—Godalming B. C., U.K.

48. **Libera nos Domine** *Latin* 'Free us, Lord'
—Rowe (U.S.).

49. **Libera terra, liberque animus** *Latin* 'A free earth and a free mind'
—Frankland (Bt.).

50. **Liber et audax** *Latin* 'Free and bold'
—Freeman (of Castle Cor).

51. **Liber et erectus** *Latin* 'Free and erect'
—Graham.

52. **Libertad y orden** *Spanish* 'Liberty and order'
—Republic of Colombia.

53. **Libertas** *Latin* 'Liberty'
—Republic of San Marino; Carbery (B.), Chatteris, Birch (Bt.), Evans (of Ash Hall), Evans (Lyng, co. Norfolk), Bailey, Gregory, Lewis.

54. **Libertas a legibus** *Latin* 'Liberty out of law'
—Stokes (U.S.).

55. **Libertas et fidelitate** *Latin* 'Freedom and loyalty'
—Seal of State of West Virginia.

56. **Libertas et natale solum** *Latin* 'Liberty and my native soil'
—Adams (of Bowden), Freeman, Sanderson.

57. **Libertas et patria** *Latin* 'Liberty and country'
—Giles (U.S.).

58. **Libertas et patria mea** *Latin* 'Liberty and my country'
—Giles (U.S.).

59. **Libertas in legibus** *Latin* 'Liberty in the law'
—Wynford (B.), Best.

60. **Libertas pretiosior auro** *Latin* 'Liberty is more precious than gold'
—Southby.

61. **Libertas res inaestimabilis** *Latin* 'Freedom is a priceless possession'
—Ernst VI, Count of Mansfeld (1561–1609).

62. **Libertas sub rege pio** *Latin* 'Liberty under a pious king'
—Addington, Packe, Sidmouth (V.).

63. **Libertas virtusque** *Latin* 'Liberty and virtue'
—Fry.

64. **Libertas virtus sunt summa potestas** *Latin* 'Liberty and virtue are the highest power'
—Richards.

65. **Libertate extincta nulla virtus**   *Latin* 'There is no virtue when liberty is dead'
—Fletcher.

66. **Libertatem, amicitiam, retinebis et fidem**   *Latin* 'You will hold on to liberty, friendship, and faith'
—Boylston (U.S.).

67. **Libertate quietem**   *Latin* 'Quiet in liberty'
—Woodford (Bt.).

68. **Liberté, coopération, progrès**   *French* 'Liberty, cooperation, progress'
—Republic of Rwanda.

69. **Liberté, egalité, fraternité**   *French* 'Liberty, equality, fraternity'
—French Republic.

70. **Liberté toute entière**   *French* 'Liberty unfettered'
—Butler-Danvers, Lane, Lanesborough (E.).

71. **Liberty above all things**
—Brewster (U.S.).

72. **Liberty and independence**
—State of Delaware.

73. **Liberty and prosperity**
—State of New Jersey.

74. **Liberty and union, now and forever, one and inseparable**
—State of North Dakota.

75. **Liberty or death**
—2nd Regiment of Infantry of South Carolina; Virginia.

76. **Live free or die**
—State of New Hampshire.

77. **Lux/ libertas**   *Latin* 'Light/ liberty'
—University of North Carolina School of Nursing, Chapel Hill, North Carolina.

78. **Montani semper liberi**   *Latin* 'Mountaineers are always free'
—State of West Virginia.

79. **Mors in vita**   *Latin* 'Death in life'
—Smith.

80. **Non alio libertas conservanda modo**   *Latin* 'By no other means can freedom be preserved'
—Christian Ernst, Margrave of Brandenburg-Baireuth (1644–1712).

81. **Nullius addictus jurare in verba magistri** *Latin* 'Not bound to take an oath to any master'
—Wolcott (U.S.).

82. **Nullius in verba** *Latin* 'At the dictation of no man'
—Banks, Gabb.

83. **Nullius in verba magistri** *Latin* 'By the words of no master'
—Walcot.

84. **Nunquam libertas gratior** *Latin* 'Never was liberty more agreeable'
—Scott (of Stourbridge).

85. **Order, freedom, justice** *(from Arabic)*
—Republic of Tunisia.

86. **Our liberties we prize and our rights we will maintain**
—State of Iowa.

87. **Par ardua liberi** *Latin* 'Free through difficulties'
—Pitt.

88. **Patria cara, carior libertas** *Latin* 'My country is dear, but liberty is dearer'
—Bouverie, Cay, Lindon, Pleydell-Bouverie-Campbell-Wyndham.

89. **Pax et libertas** *Latin* 'Peace and liberty'
—Gordon.

90. **Pour ma libertay pour ma patree** *Old French* 'For my liberty, for my country'
—Vaudin.

91. **Proclaim liberty throughout all the land unto all the inhabitants thereof**
—[from Lev. 25. 10.] Liberty Bell.

92. **Pro Deo et libertate** *Latin* 'For God and liberty'
—Wilson.

93. **Pro libertate** *Latin* 'For liberty'
—Wallace (of Kelly).

94. **Pro libertate et commercio** *Latin* 'For liberty and commerce'
—Hicks (U.S.).

95. **Pro libertate et patriâ** *Latin* 'For liberty and my country'
—Michie.

96. **Pro libertate lege sancta** *Latin* 'For liberty ratified by law'
—Glyn.

97. **Pro libertate patriae**   *Latin* 'For the liberty of my country'
    —Evans, Clarina (B.), Massy (B.), Massey (Bt.), Maysey.

98. **Pro patriâ ejusque libertate**   *Latin* 'For my country and its freedom'

    —Joy.

99. **Pro patria et libertate**   *Latin* 'For country and liberty'

    —Michie.

100. **Pulcra pro libertate**   *Latin* 'For fair liberty'

     —Vane.

101. **Religio, libertas et scientia**   *Latin* 'Religion, liberty, and knowledge'

     —Cedar Crest College, Allentown, Pennsylvania.

102. **Rhad Duw a ryddid**   *Welsh* 'God's grace and liberty'

     —Dinorben (B.).

103. **Rhyddid gwerin ffyniant gwlad**   *Welsh* 'The freedom of the people is the prosperity of the land'

     —Carmarthenshire C. C., U.K.

104. **Rhyddid hedd a llwyddiant**   *Welsh* 'Freedom, peace, and prosperity'

     —Carmarthen B. C., U.K.

105. **Semper liber**   *Latin* 'Always free'

     —Stephens (of Radnorshire).

106. **Ser libre o morir**   *Spanish* 'Freedom or death'

     —Hamilton.

107. **Sit mihi libertas**   *Latin* 'Liberty be mine'

     —Findlater.

108. **Sub lege libertas**   *Latin* 'Under the law, liberty'

     —Daniel.

109. **Sub libertate quietem**   *Latin* 'Rest under liberty'
     —Burrell, Cay, Carter, Hoblyn, Kay, Keay (of Scotland),
     Peter, Parker, Walsham (Bt.).

110. **Te duce libertas**   *Latin* 'Where thou art leader there is liberty'
     —Crosby.

111. **The love of liberty brought us here**

     —Republic of Liberia.

112. **Travail, liberté, patrie**   *French* 'Work, freedom, fatherland'
     —Republic of Togo.

113. **Truth and freedom**   *(from Greek)*

     —Wakefield.

114. **Truth and liberty**
                                            —Tylden (of Milsted).

115. **Truth/ Knowledge/ Freedom**
                        —Harding University, Searcy, Arkansas.

116. **Ubi libertas** *Latin* 'Where there is liberty'
                                            —Foster (U.S.).

117. **Ubi libertas ibi patria** *Latin* 'Where liberty prevails there is my country'
              —Beverley, Baillie, Darch, Dinwiddie, Garrett, Hugar.

118. **Uhuru na umoja** *Swahili* 'Liberty and unity'
                        —United Republic of Tanzania.

119. **Una grande libre** *Spanish* 'One great free (realm)'
                                            —The Spanish State.

120. **Unity, freedom, justice**
                                            —Sierra Leone.

121. **Unity and freedom**
                                            —Malawi.

122. **Ut homines liberi sint** *Latin* 'So that men may be free'
                                            —Egham U. D. C., U.K.

123. **Veritas, libertas** *Latin* 'Truth and liberty'
                                            —Abraham.

124. **Veritas et amicitia** *Latin* 'Truth and friendship'
                        —Jones College, Jacksonville, Florida.

125. **Veritas liberabit** *Latin* 'The truth will make you free'
              —Bodenham (of Rotherwas), Lafayette College, Easton, Pennsylvania.

126. **Veritas liberabit vos** *Latin* 'The truth will set you free'
              —Saint Augustine's College, Raleigh, North Carolina.

127. **Veritas liberavit** *Latin* 'Truth has freed me'
                                            —Slingsby.

128. **Veritas/ libertas** *Latin* 'Truth/ liberty'
                        —Manatee Jr. College, Bradenton, Florida.

129. **Vi et libertate** *Latin* 'By force and liberty'
                                            —Vibert.

130. **Vincit liberavit** *Latin* 'He conquers, he has set free'
                                            —Slingsby.

131. **Virtue, liberty and independence**
                        —State of Pennsylvania; Barton (U.S.).

132. **Virtus libertas et patria**   *Latin* 'Virtue, liberty, and country'
—Wetmore (U.S.).

133. **Virtus veritas libertas**   *Latin* 'Virtue, truth, and freedom'
—Glossop B. C., U.K.

134. **Vita potior libertas**   *Latin* 'Liberty is more important than life'
—Forster, Lumm.

135. **Vixi liber et moriar**   *Latin* 'I have lived a freeman and will die one'
—Gray, Ibbetson (Bt.).

136. **Where liberty is, there is my country**
—James Otis, American patriot.

LIFE (*See also* BIRTH; DEATH; REBIRTH.)

1. **A full and abundant life in a contemporary society**
—Abraham Baldwin Agricultural College, Tifton, Georgia.

2. **Bis vivit qui bene**   *Latin* 'He lives twice who lives well'
—Becher (Bt.).

3. **Cara vita, carior patria, carissima libertas**   *Latin* 'Dear life, dearer country, dearest liberty'
—Kettle (U.S.).

4. **Dant vulnera vitam**   *Latin* 'The wounds give life'
—Collins.

5. **Dum vivimus, vivamus**   *Latin* 'While we live let us live'
—Doddridge, Hewitt, Vyvyan.

6. **Dum vivo, vireo**   *Latin* 'While I live I flourish'
—Latta.

7. **Dum vivo cano**   *Latin* 'While I live, I sing'
—Coghill; Rigg.

8. **Ex hoc vivo**   *Latin* 'I live from this'
—Drummond.

9. **I have lived today**
—Hooper (Bt.).

10. **In sanguine vita**   *Latin* 'Life in the blood'
—Cobbe.

11. **Knowledge for life**
—South Mountain Community College, Arizona.

12. **La tête plus que l'argent**   *French* 'The head is better than riches'
—Raven.

13. **La vie durante**   *French* 'During life'
> —Aymand, Cornewall (Bt.).

14. **Live, love, think, pray, dare**
> —United Daughters of the Confederacy.

15. **Live but dread**
> —Lindsay (of The Byres, Scotland).

16. **Live in hope**
> —Coldstream.

17. **Live to live**
> —Sutton, Witeley or Whiteley, Dundas.

18. **Live while green**
> —Forrest.

19. **Look and live**
> —St. Barbe.

20. **Lux tua vita mea**   *Latin* 'Thy light is my life'
> —Blount (of Maple Durham).

21. **Lux vitae**   *Latin* 'The light of life'
> —Burton (of Lindley and Bedworth).

22. **Lybba bu te bu Lybbe**   (language unknown; said to mean 'Live that you may live')
> —Ayloffe (Bt.).

23. **Moriendo vivam**   *Latin* 'I shall live by dying'
> —Shakerley (Bt.).

24. **Morte leonis vita**   *Latin* 'Life by the death of the lion'
> —Vaux (B.).

25. **Non in vita**   *Latin* 'Not in life'
> —Smith.

26. **Odor vitae**   *Latin* 'The sweet breath of life'
> —Hutton (of Marske).

27. **Oportet vivere**   *Latin* 'It behooves us to live'
> —Todd (of Tranby).

28. **Qualis vita finis ita**   *Latin* 'As is our life, so is our end'
> —Yonge.

29. **Quorsum vivere mori? Mori vita**   *Latin* 'Wherefore live to die? To die is life'
> —Blencowe.

30. **Salt is life**
> —Northwich U. D. C., U.K.

31. **Sic vita humana** *Latin* 'So is human life'
—Capel.

32. **Sic vivere vivetis** *Latin* 'Thus you shall live, to live (hereafter)'
—Bunce.

33. **Sit vita nomini congrua** *Latin* 'May our life be like our name'
—Christie.

34. **To live is to learn**
—Elizabeth City State University, Elizabeth City, North Carolina.

35. **Tot praemia vitae** *Latin* 'So many are the rewards of life'
—Sullivan.

36. **Ut amnis vita labitur** *Latin* 'Life glides on like a brook'
—Brook.

37. **Ut te cognoscant et vitam habeant** *Latin* 'So that they may know you and have life'
—Sacred Heart School of Theology, Hales Corners, Wisconsin.

38. **Vir vita terra** *Latin* 'Man, life, earth'
—Delaware Valley College, Doyleston, Pennsyvania.

39. **Vita brevis gloria aeterna** *Latin* 'Life is short, glory eternal'
—Price.

40. **Vivant dum virent** *Latin* 'Let them live while they flourish'
—Forrest.

41. **Vive et vivas** *Latin* 'Live, and you may live'
—Abercromby.

42. **Vive et vivat** *Latin* 'Live and let live'
—Atkinson (U.S.).

43. **Vive hodie** *Latin* 'Live today'
—Green-Price, Price.

44. **Vivens canam** *Latin* 'I shall yet sing while alive'
—Morris.

45. **Vivere est agere** *Latin* 'To live is to act'
—Sewall (U.S.).

46. **Vive revicturus** *Latin* 'Live (as if) about to live again'
—Vivian.

47. **Vive ut postea vivas** *Latin* 'So live that you may live hereafter'
—Frazer, Johnston (of Johnston, Bt.), Johnston.

48. **Vive ut semper vivas** *Latin* 'To live that you may live forever'
—Bancks, Falkner, Faulkner, Hopson, Manning.

49. **Vive ut vivas** *Latin* 'Live that you may live'
    —Abercromby (B.), Abercromby (of Birkenbog, bt.),
    Bathgate, Hartley (of Bucklebury), Hall, Falconer
    (of Halkerton), Iliff (of Newington Butts),
    McKenzie, Price (of Spring Grove, bt.), Sladen (of
    Alton Barnes, co. Wilts), Vivian (of Pencalenick).

50. **Vive valeque** *Latin* 'Live and be strong'
    —Green.

51. **Vivis sperandum** *Latin* 'Where there is life there is hope'
    —Niven.

52. **Vivit Leo de Tribu Juda** *Latin* 'The Lion of the Tribe of Judah
    lives'
    —Ethiopia.

53. **Vivunt dum virent** *Latin* 'They live as long as they are green'
    —Forrest.

54. **Vixit diu, quia bene vixit** *Latin* 'He has lived long enough, since
    he has lived well'
    —Wilhelm VI, Landgrave of Hesse-Cassel (1629–63): on a
    coin struck in memory of the death of his son in 1670.

55. **Whyll lyff lastyth**
    —Cornwall (of Burford, b.).

LIGHT (*See also* DAY; SHINING; SUN.)

1. **A Deo lux nostra** *Latin* 'Our light is from God'
    —Holloway.

2. **After darkness comes light**
    —Hewitt.

3. **Alenda lux ubi orta libertas** *Latin* 'Where light has arisen there
    liberty should be sustained'
    —Davidson College, Davidson, North Carolina;
    Community College of Beaver County,
    Monaca, Pennsylvania.

4. **Christi crux est mea lux** *Latin* 'The cross of Christ is my light'
    —Northcote (Bt.).

5. **Crux mea lux** *Latin* 'The cross is my light'
    —Brockett (U.S.).

6. **Da nobis lucem, Domine** *Latin* 'Give us light, O Lord!'
    —Glaziers' Company.

7. **Dant lucem crescentibus orti**   *Latin* 'Rising from crescents they give light'
—Hodges.

8. **Deo duce Christo luce**   *Latin* 'God my guide, Christ my light'
—Butler.

9. **Deo lux nostra**   *Latin* 'God is our light'
—Holloway (U.S.).

10. **Deus lumen meum**   *Latin* 'God is my light'
—Torrens.

11. **E tenebris lux**   *Latin* 'Light out of darkness'
—Lightbody.

12. **Ex flamma lux**   *Latin* 'Light from flame'
—Ingledew.

13. **Ex lumine lucrum**   *Latin* 'Profit from light'
—Wickes.

14. **Ex terra lucem**   *Latin* 'Light out of the earth'
—St. Helens C. B. C., U.K.

15. **Fiat lux**   *Latin* 'Let there be light'
—[Genesis, i. 3.] Rollins College, Winter Park, Florida; Atlantic Union College, South Lancaster, Massachusetts, Loxton.

16. **Fides lumen praebeat**   *Latin* 'May faith grant light'
—St. Gregory's College, Shawnee, Oklahoma.

17. **Gaudet in luce veritas**   *Latin* 'Truth rejoices in the light'
—Moilliet.

18. **Gaudet luce**   *Latin* 'He rejoices in the light'
—Galton (Co. Warwick).

19. **Habebunt lumen vitae**   *Latin* 'They shall have the light of life'
—Atlantic Christian College, Wilson, North Carolina.

20. **Hinc lucem et pocula sacra**   *Latin* 'Hence light and sacred draughts'
—Cambridge University, U.K.

21. **In lumine ambulo**   *Latin* 'I walk in the light'
—Gilmour.

22. **In lumine luce**   *Latin* 'Shine in the light'
—Makins (Bt.).

23. **In lumine luceam**   *Latin* 'I may shine in the light'
—Thompson.

24. **In lumine tuo videbimus lumen** *Latin* 'In thy light we shall see the light'
    —Columbia University, New York City.

25. **In lumine tuo videmus lumen** *Latin* 'In your light we see the light'
    —College of Great Falls, Great Falls, Montana.

26. **In tenebris lucidior** *Latin* 'The brighter in darkness'
    —Inglis.

27. **In tenebris lux** *Latin* 'Light in darkness'
    —Scott.

28. **Justi velut lumen astrarum** *Latin* 'Just men are like the light of the stars'
    —Checkley (U.S.).

29. **Let light shine out**
    —Northwest College of the Assemblies of God, Kirkland, Washington.

30. **Luce** *Latin* 'With light'
    —Lucy.

31. **Lucem amat virtus** *Latin* 'Virtue loves the light'
    —Strachey.

32. **Lucem spero** *Latin* 'I hope for light'
    —Kemp (Bt.).

33. **Lucem spero clariorem** *Latin* 'I hope for a brighter light'
    —Preston (Bt.).

34. **Lucent in tenebris** *Latin* 'In darkness they let their light shine'
    —O'Moran.

35. **Lucerna pedibus meis** *Latin* 'A lamp unto my feet'
    —[Ps., cxix. 105.] Mant.

36. **Lumen accipe et imperti** *Latin* 'Receive the light and communicate it'
    —Hollingsworth.

37. **Lumen sevimus antique** *Latin* 'We sowed light of old'
    —Redwood.

38. **Lumen umbra Dei** *Latin* 'Light is the shadow of God'
    —Glaziers' Company.

39. **Lux** *Latin* 'Light'
    —University of Northern Iowa, Cedar Falls, Iowa.

40. **Lux, salubritas, felicitas** *Latin* 'Light, health, happiness'
    —Clacton U. D. C., U.K.

41. **Lux anglis, crux Francis**   *Latin* 'Light to the English, a cross to the French'
—Rooper.

42. **Lux esto**   *Latin* '(Let there) be light'
—[Genesis, i. 3.] Southwestern College in Kansas, Winfield, Kansas.

43. **Lux et fides**   *Latin* 'Light and faith'
—Taylor University, Upland, Indiana.

44. **Lux et humanitas**   *Latin* 'Light and humanity'
—Blackwell R. D. C., U.K.

45. **Lux et salus**   *Latin* 'Light and safety'
—Brunton.

46. **Lux et scientia**   *Latin* 'Light and knowledge'
—Andrew College, Cuthbert, Georgia.

47. **Lux et veritas**   *Latin* 'Light and truth'
—Yale University, New Haven, Connecticut, Waldorf College, Forest City, Iowa.

48. **Lux in tenebris**   *Latin* 'Light in darkness'
—Fullerton (of Westwood).

49. **Lux/ libertas**   *Latin* 'Light/ liberty'
—University of North Carolina School of Nursing, Chapel Hill, North Carolina.

50. **Lux mea Christus**   *Latin* 'Christ is my light'
—Newman, Rogers.

51. **Lux mentis lux orbis**   *Latin* 'Light of the mind, light of the world'
—Sonoma State University, Rohnert Park, California.

52. **Lux mihi laurus**   *Latin* 'The laurel is my light'
—Chambers.

53. **Lux mundi**   *Latin* 'Light of the world'
—Thiel College, Greenville, Pennsylvania.

54. **Lux mundi justitia**   *Latin* 'Justice is the light of the world'
—Johann Georg I, Elector of Saxony (1585–1656).

55. **Lux omnibus refulgeat**   *Latin* 'Let the light shine for all'
—Smith.

56. **Lux tua via mea**   *Latin* 'Thy light is my way'
—Blount (Bt.), Blount.

57. **Lux tua vita mea**   *Latin* 'Thy light is my life'
—Blount (of Maple Durham).

58. **Lux venit ab alto** *Latin* 'Light comes from above'
—Dallas (Bt.).

59. **Lux veritas peritia populo nostro** *Latin* 'Light, truth, and skill for our people'
—Coastal Carolina Community College, Jacksonville, North Carolina.

60. **Lux vitae** *Latin* 'The light of life'
—Burton (of Lindley and Bedworth).

61. **More light, more power**
—Shoreditch B. C., U.K.

62. **Non crux, sed lux** *Latin* 'Not the cross, but (its) light'
—Black, Blair, Cramer, Griffiths.

63. **Non lumen effugio** *Latin* 'I shun not the light'
—Hewson, Hewson (of Emusmore).

64. **Numen et lumen effugio** *Latin* 'I shun the Deity and light'
—Hewson.

65. **Out of darkness cometh light**
—Wolverhampton C. B. C., U.K.

66. **Per crucem ad lucem** *Latin* 'Through the cross to the light'
—Campbell.

67. **Per lucem ac tenebras mea sidera sanguine surgent** *Latin* 'Through light and darkness my star will arise in blood'
—Cayley.

68. **Phoebo lux** *Latin* 'Light from the sun'
—Kinnaird (B.).

69. **Phoebus, lux in tenebris** *Latin* 'Phoebus, light in darkness'
—Jeffrey.

70. **Post nubes lux** *Latin* 'After clouds light'
—Blunstone, Steddert.

71. **Post tenebras lucem** *Latin* 'After darkness, light'
—Bright.

72. **Post tenebras lux** *Latin* 'After darkness light'
—on the first Eddystone Lighthouse, Devonshire, England; Hewatt.

73. **Post tenebris speramus lumen de lumine** *Latin* 'After the darkness we hope for light upon light'
—Coffin (U.S.).

74. **Quae arguuntur a lumine manifestantur**   *Latin* 'What things are questioned light clears up'
—Tallow Chandlers' Company.

75. **Quis audeat luci aggredi**   *Latin* 'Who dare approach (near) the light'
—Prior.

76. **Sic luceat lux vestra**   *Latin* 'May your light thus shine'
—Buxton College, U.K.

77. **Sine cruce sine luce**   *Latin* 'Without the cross without light'
—Close, Maxwell.

78. **Sit lux**   *Latin* 'Let there be light'
—[Genesis, i. 3.] Tarkio College, Missouri.

79. **Sit lux et lux fuit**   *Latin* 'Let there be light and there was light'
—Free and Accepted Masons.

80. **Sub cruce lux**   *Latin* 'Light under the cross'
—Donaldson.

81. **Surgite, lumen adest**   *Latin* 'Arise, the light is near'
—Glover.

82. **Surgo, lumen adest**   *Latin* 'I arise, light is near'
—Lawson.

83. **Tenebris lux**   *Latin* 'Light in darkness'
—Scott (of Pitlochie).

84. **Truth is the light**
—Wax Chandlers' Company (London).

85. **Ubi fides ibi lux et robur**   *Latin* 'Where there is faith there is light and strength'
—Birkenhead C. B. C., U.K.

86. **Vertitur in lucem**   *Latin* 'It is changed into light'
—Baillie.

87. **Viditque Deus hanc lucem esse bonam**   *Latin* 'And God saw the light that it was good'
—Rundle.

LIMITATION   (*See also* MODERATION; SELF-CONTROL.)

1. **Acer non effrenus**   *Latin* 'Keen but not unbridled'
—Milner (V.).

2. **Addit frena feris**   *Latin* 'He puts bridles on wild beasts'
—Milner (Bt.).

3. **Licentiam refroena**   *Latin* 'Restrain licentiousness'
—MacQuay.

4. **Ne supra**   *Latin* 'Not beyond'
—Catsznellage.

5. **Ne te quaesiveris extra**   *Latin* 'Seek nothing beyond your sphere'
—Hewett (Bt.), Hewitt.

6. **Ne traverse pas le pont**   *French* 'Do not cross the bridge'
—Briggs.

7. **Ne ultra**   *Latin* 'Nothing beyond'
—Davidson College, Davidson, North Carolina.

8. **Never check**
—Hawks (U.S.).

9. **Non omnia possumus omnes**   *Latin* 'We are not all able to do all things'
—Palazzo Borghese, Rome.

10. **Sans charger**   *French* 'Without overloading'
—Eddisbury, Enery.

11. **Si non datur ultra**   *Latin* 'If (it is) not allowed beyond'
—Williams (of Colebrook).

12. **Utere loris**   *Latin* 'Use the reins'
—Darly, Waddilove.

13. **Vinctus non victus**   *Latin* 'Bound, not conquered'
—De Worms.

14. **Vincula da linguae vel tibi lingua dabit**   *Latin* 'Place restraint on your tongue, or your tongue will place it on you'
—Hoskyns.

LISTENING (*See also* ATTENTIVENESS.)

1. **Audi alteram partem**   *Latin* 'Hear the other party'
—Pemberton.

2. **Audio et juvo**   *Latin* 'I hear and assist'
—Harker.

3. **Supera audi et tace**   *Latin* 'Hear celestial things and keep silence'
—Hesse.

4. **Tandem exaudisti me**   *Latin* 'At length hast Thou listened to me'
—Ernst August, Duke of Saxony-Weimar (1688–1741).

LIVELINESS (*See also* SPIRIT.)

1. **Arte, Marte, vigore** *Latin* 'By skill, valour, and energy'
   —Wednesbury B. C., U.K.

2. **Excitari non hebescere** *Latin* 'To be spirited, not inactive'
   —De Grey, Walsingham (B.).

3. **Impiger et fidus** *Latin* 'Alert and faithful'
   —Constable.

4. **Perspicax, audax** *Latin* 'Quickwitted, bold'
   —Erskine.

5. **Toujours gai** *French* 'Ever gay'
   —Gay (of Thurning Hall, co. Norfolk).

6. **Vif, courageux, fier** *French* 'Spirited, courageous, proud'
   —Falcon.

7. **Vigore** *Latin* 'With vigor'
   —Vickers.

8. **Vigore et virtute** *Latin* 'By vigor and virtue'
   —Casey.

9. **Vite, courageux, fier** *French* 'Swift, courageous, proud'
   —Harrison.

LOCAL GOVERNMENT

1. **A bonis ad meliora** *Latin* 'From good things to better'
   —Royston U. D. C., U.K.

2. **Action**
   —Bognor Regis U. D. C., U.K.

3. **A ddioddefws a orfu** *Welsh* 'He who suffered was victorious'
   —Glamorgan C. C., U.K.

4. **A deo et Rege** *Latin* 'From God and the King'
   —Richmond B. C., U.K.

5. **Adhuc hic hesterna** *Latin* 'The things of yesterday are still with us'
   —Chichester R. D. C., U.K.

6. **Ad morem villae de Poole** *Latin* 'According to the custom of the town of Poole'
   —Poole B. C., U.K.

7. **Ad pontes prospicimus** *Latin* 'At the bridges we look forward' i.e., 'From our ancient past we look forward to the future'
   —Staines U. D. C., U.K.

8. **Advance**
   —Brand; Ferrier; Goole B. C., U.K., Spiers (of Eldershe).

9. **A good name endureth**
   —Hornchurch U. D. C., U.K.

10. **Agriculture and commerce**
    —Maidstone B. C., U.K.; State of Tennessee.

11. **All's well**
    —Camberwell B. C., U.K.; Mudge.

12. **All things for the glory of God**
    —Chingford B. C., U.K.

13. **All this beauty is of God**
    —Isle of Wight C. C., U.K.

14. **Alta sententia** *Latin* 'With high purpose'
    —Arnold U. D. C., U.K.

15. **Altiora petimus** *Latin* 'We seek higher things'
    —Finsbury B. C., U.K.

16. **Altrincham en avant** *French* 'Altrincham leads the way'
    —Altrincham B. C., U.K.

17. **Always advancing**
    —Thornaby-on-Tees B. C., U.K.

18. **Always ready**
    —Glanford Brigg R. D. C., U.K.; Hall.

19. **A magnis ad maiora** *Latin* 'From great things to greater'
    —Stepney B. C., U.K.

20. **A ma puissance** *French* 'According to my power'
    —Hale U. D. C., U.K.; Stamford (E.), Grey.

21. **Amoenitas salubritas urbanitas** *Latin* 'Pleasantness, health, urbanity'
    —Ryde B. C., U.K.

22. **Amser yw'n golud** *Welsh* 'Time is our wealth'
    —Ystradgynlais R. D. C., U.K.

23. **Anchora spei Cereticae est in te, Domine** *Latin* 'The anchor of Cardigan's hope is in Thee, O Lord'
    —Cardigan B. C., U.K.

24. **Ancient and loyal**
    —Wigan C. B. C., U.K.

25. **Angliae cor** *Latin* 'The heart of England'
    —Hinckley U. D. C., U.K.

26. **Animo et fide** *Latin* 'By courage and faith'
—Burroughs (of Burlingham and Long Stratton, Co. Norfolk), Cornock (Co. Wexford), Guildford (E.), North, Phillips, Stockport C. B. C., U.K., Turner, Carshalton U. D. C., U.K.

27. **Antiqua constans virtute** *Latin* 'Steadfast in ancient virtue'
—Arundel B. C., U.K.

28. **Antiqui colant Antiquum Dierum** *Latin* 'Let men of the ancient virtues worship the Ancient of Days'
—Chester City and C. B. C., U.K.

29. **Antiquum decus floreat** *Latin* 'May its ancient glory flourish'
—Oldbury B. C., U.K.

30. **Ardens fide** *Latin* 'Burning with faith'
—Brentwood U. D. C., U.K.

31. **Arte, Marte, vigore** *Latin* 'By skill, valour, and energy'
—Wednesbury B. C., U.K.

32. **Arte et labore** *Latin* 'By skill and toil'
—Blackburn C. B. C., U.K.

33. **Arte faventi nil desperandum** *Latin* 'Supported by skill, there is no cause to despair'
—Leek U. D. C., U.K.

34. **Arx celebris fontibus** *Latin* 'A stronghold famed for its springs'
—Harrogate B. C., U.K.

35. **Aspice, respice** *Latin* 'Look to the future and the past'
—Wellingborough U. D. C., U.K.

36. **At spes non fracta** *Latin* 'Yet hope is not broken'
—Blaenavon U. D. C., U.K.

37. **Audacter et sincere** *Latin* 'Boldly and sincerely'
—Castleford U. D. C., U.K.; Clive, Powes (E.).

38. **Audemus dum cavemus** *Latin* 'We dare though we are wary'
—Wallasey C. B. C., U.K.

39. **Audentior** *Latin* 'Bolder'
—Watford B. C., U.K.

40. **Auxilio Divino** *Latin* 'By divine aid'
—Drake (Bt.), Devon C. C., U.K.

41. **Ave Mater Angliae** *Latin* 'Hail, Mother of England'
—Canterbury City and C. B. C., U.K.

42. **A vo penn bit pont**   *Welsh* 'He who will be chief, let him be a bridge'
> —Bridgend U. D. C., U.K.

43. **Beau don**   *French* 'A beautiful gift'
> —Bowdon U. D. C., U.K.

44. **Beauty surrounds, health abounds**
> —Morecambe and Heysham B. C., U.K.

45. **Be just, and fear not**
> —Ashby, Atkins, Coleman, Hewitt, Lilford (V.), Payne, Peacock, Strange, Warren; Carlisle City and C. B. C., Pudsey B. C., U.K.

46. **Bene consulendo**   *Latin* 'By good counsel'
> —Derbyshire C. C., U.K.

47. **Benedicite fontes Domino**   *Latin* 'O all ye springs, bless the Lord'
> —Buxton B. C., U.K.

48. **Beware**
> —Cleborne; Chorley B. C., U.K.

49. **By concord and industry**
> —Droylsden U. D. C., U.K.

50. **By courage and faith**
> —Seaham U. D. C., U.K.

51. **By industry and integrity**
> —Nelson B. C., U.K.

52. **By worth**
> —Keighley B. C., Farnham U. D. C., U.K.

53. **Cadernid, cyfiawnder, cynnydd**   *Welsh* 'Stability, justice, progress'
> —Barry B. C., U.K.

54. **Cadernid Gwynedd**   *Welsh* 'The strength of Gwynedd'
> —Caernarvonshire C. C., U.K.

55. **Cambray, cité de paix**   *French* 'Cambrai, city of peace'
> —Town of Cambrai, France.

56. **Camera principis**   *Latin* 'Chamber (court) of the Prince'
> —Coventry City and C. B. C., U.K.

57. **Castello fortior concordia**   *Latin* 'Concord is stronger than a fortress'
> —Northampton C. B. C., U.K.

58. **Civitas in bello in pace fidelis** *Latin* 'In war and in peace a faithful city'
—Worcester City and C. B. C., U.K.

59. **Civitatis fortuna cives** *Latin* 'The fortune of the state depends on the citizens'
—Bebington B. C., U.K.

60. **Clamant nostra tela in regis querela** *Latin* 'Our weapons clash in the king's quarrel'
—Woolwich B. C., U.K.

61. **Comfort (confort) et liesse** *French* 'Comfort and joy'
—Doncaster C. B. C., U.K.

62. **Concilio et labore** *Latin* 'By counsel and by labor'
—Manchester City and C. B. C., U.K.

63. **Consilio absit discordia** *Latin* 'Let discord be absent from counsel'
—Whitehaven B. C., U.K.

64. **Consilio et anima** *Latin* 'By wisdom and courage'
—Wanstead and Woodford B. C., U.K.

65. **Consilio et animis** *Latin* 'By wisdom and courage'
—Gibson, Lauderdale (E.), Maitland (Bt.), Ramadge; Kiveton Park R. D. C., Surbiton B. C., U.K.

66. **Consilio et prudentia** *Latin* 'By counsel and by wisdom'
—Atherton U. D. C., U.K.

67. **Constant be**
—Bedfordshire C. C., U.K.

68. **Constantia basis virtutum** *Latin* 'Steadfastness is the foundation of the virtues'
—Andover B. C., U.K.

69. **Contranando incrementum** *Latin* 'Prosperity by swimming against the stream'
—Town of Peebles.

70. **Cor unum** *Latin* 'One heart'
—Soke of Peterborough C. C., U.K.

71. **Courage, humanity, commerce**
—South Shields C. B. C., U.K.

72. **Crede signo** *Latin* 'Trust in this sign'
—Rochdale C. B. C., U.K.

73. **Curandum omnium bonum** *Latin* 'We must care for the good of all'
—Garstang R. D. C., U.K.

74. **Custodi civitatem Domine** *Latin* 'Keep the city, O Lord'
—Westminster City Council, U.K.

75. **Cynghori er llesiant** *Welsh* 'Consulting for betterment'
—Penarth U. D. C., U.K.

76. **De bon cuer** *Old French* 'With good heart'
—Walton-le-Dale U. D. C., U.K.

77. **Defendamus** *Latin* 'Let us defend'
—Taunton B. C., U.K., Town of Taunton.

78. **Deffro mae'n Ddydd** *Welsh* 'Awake! It is day'
—Cardiff City and C. B. C., U.K.

79. **Dei gratia sumus quod sumus** *Latin* 'By the grace of God, we are what we are'
—Barking B. C., U.K.

80. **Deo adjuvante** *Latin* 'By the help of God'
—Wellington U. D. C., U.K.

81. **Deo adjuvante arte et industria floret** *Latin* 'With God's help, it flourishes by art and industry'
—Kidderminster B. C., U.K.

82. **Deo adjuvante labor proficit** *Latin* 'By God's help labor succeeds'
—Sheffield City and C. B. C., U.K.

83. **Deo confidimus** *Latin* 'We trust in God'
—West Ham C. B. C., U.K.

84. **Deo duce** *Latin* 'God my guide'
—Town of Pettinween (Scotland), Hennidge, Ricketts, Hooper.

85. **Deo fretus erumpe** *Latin* 'Trust God and sally'
—Newark-on-Trent B. C., U.K.

86. **Deo juvante** *Latin* 'With God's help'
—Principality of Monaco, Duff, Fife (e.), Groze, Grimaldi, Maitland, Shatt, Tawse, Wodderspoon, Kirkburton U. D. C., U.K.

87. **Desire the right**
—Falkland Islands.

88. **Deus dat incrementum** *Latin* 'God giveth the increase'
—Warrington C. B. C., U.K.

89. **Deus gubernat navem**   *Latin* 'God steers the vessel'
           —Town of Renfrew, Leckie.

90. **Deus nobis haec otia fecit**   *Latin* 'God hath given us this tranquil-lity'
           —[Vergil, *Ec.* i. vi.] Town of Liverpool, Bolger, Burrow, Hide.

91. **Deus noster refugium et virtus**   *Latin* 'God is our refuge and strength'
           —Dewsbury C. B. C., U.K.

92. **Deus per omnia**   *Latin* 'God pervades all things'
           —Islington B. C., U.K.

93. **Dieu en soit garde**   *French* 'God be its keeper'
           —Town of Rheims, France.

94. **Domine, dirige nos**   *Latin* 'O Lord, direct us'
           —[Eccles., xxxvi. 19.] Brome (of West Malling), City of London.

95. **Domini est dirigere**   *Latin* 'It is for the Lord to direct'
           —Gipping R. D. C., U.K.

96. **Dominus nobis solet scutum**   *Latin* 'The Lord is our sun and shield'
           —Banbury B. C., U.K.

97. **Do well and doubt not**
           —Tottenham B. C., U.K.; Blakeston (Bt.), Bruce, Houston.

98. **Ducit amor oppidi**   *Latin* 'The love of our town leads us'
           —Malden and Coombe B. C., U.K.

99. **Dum cresco spero**   *Latin* 'While I grow I hope'
           —Bromley B. C., U.K.

100. **Dum defluat amnis**   *Latin* Till the river ceases to flow'
           —Walton and Weybridge U. D. C., U.K.

101. **E mare ex industria**   *Latin* 'From the sea and from industry'
           —West Hartlepool C. B. C., U.K.

102. **Endeavour**
           —Hendon B. C., U.K.

103. **En Dieu est mon esperance**   *French* 'My hope is in God'
           —Ashton-in-Makerfield U. D. C., U.K.

104. **Erimus**   *Latin* 'We shall be'
           —Middlesbrough C. B. C., U.K.

105. **E terra divitiae**   *Latin* 'From the earth, riches'
                                    —Swadlincote U. D. C., U.K.

106. **Et patribus et posteritati**   *Latin* 'For both ancestors and posterity'
                                    —Hitchin U. D. C., U.K.

107. **Ever forward**
                                    —Weston-super-Mare, U.K.

108. **Ewch yn uwch**   *Welsh* 'Go higher'
                                    —Radnorshire C. C., U.K.

109. **Except the Lord keep the city**
                                    —Halifax C. B. C., U.K.

110. **Ex glande quercus**   *Latin* 'From the acorn, the oak'
                                    —Southgate B. C., U.K.

111. **Ex terra copiam e mari salutem**   *Latin* 'From the land fullness and from the sea health'
                                    —Worthing B. C., U.K.

112. **Ex terra lucem**   *Latin* 'Light out of the earth'
                                    —St. Helens C. B. C., U.K.

113. **Face the dawn**
                                    —Kingswood U. D. C., U.K.

114. **Faith**
                                    —Billingham U. D. C., U.K.

115. **Faith, work, service**
                                    —Calne B. C., U.K.

116. **Faith in industry**
                                    —Edmonton B. C., U.K.

117. **Fama volat**   *Latin* 'Rumor has wings'
                                    —Town of Marseilles, France.

118. **Fear God, honor the king**
         —Wrexham B. C., U.K.; Bromley-Davenport, Davenport, Porter.

119. **Fellowship is life**
                                    —Walthamstow B. C., Coseley U. D. C., U.K.

120. **Festina lente**   *Latin* 'Hasten slowly'
                                    —Audenshaw U. D. C., U.K.

121. **Fiat iustitia**   *Latin* 'Let justice be done'
                                    —South Molton B. C., U.K.

122. **Fiat secundum Verbum Tuum**   *Latin* 'Let it be done according to Thy Word'
                                    —St. Marylebone B. C., U.K.

123. **Fide et diligentia**   *Latin* 'By faith and diligence'
—Woking U. D. C., U.K.

124. **Fide et fortitudine**   *Latin* 'By faith and fortitude'
—Penrith U. D. C., U.K.

125. **Fide et labore**   *Latin* 'By faith and industry'
—Harpenden U. D. C., U.K.

126. **Fidelitas urbis salus regis**   *Latin* 'The faithfulness of the city is the safety of the king'
—Bridgnorth B. C., U.K.

127. **Fidelitate et industria stat Bilstonia**   *Latin* 'Bilston stands by faith and industry'
—Bilston B. C., U.K.

128. **Fides et justitia**   *Latin* 'Faith and justice'
—Farnborough U. D. C., U.K.; Webster (Bt.).

129. **Fides invicta triumphat**   *Latin* 'Unconquered faith triumphs'
—Gloucester City and C. B. C., U.K.

130. **Fides invicta triumphat**   *Latin* 'Invincible fidelity triumphs'
—City of Gloucester.

131. **Fiducia et vi**   *Latin* 'By confidence and strength'
—Slough B. C., U.K.

132. **Filey et felicitas**   *Latin* 'Filey and felicity'
—Filey U. D. C., U.K.

133. **Firma et stabilis**   *Latin* 'Safe and sure'
—Kirkham U. D. C., U.K.

134. **Firmior**   *Latin* 'Stronger'
—Brentford and Chiswick B. C., U.K.

135. **Floreat**   *Latin* 'May it flourish'
—Uttoxeter U. D. C., U.K.

136. **Floreat Actona**   *Latin* 'Let Acton flourish'
—Acton B. C., U.K.

137. **Floreat Ailesburia**   *Latin* 'May Aylesbury flourish'
—Aylesbury B. C., U.K.

138. **Floreat Bathon**   *Latin* 'May Bath flourish'
—Bath City and C. B. C., U.K.

139. **Floreat Ecclesia Anglicana**   *Latin* 'May the Church of England flourish'
—Glastonbury B. C., U.K.

140. **Floreat Etona**   *Latin* 'May Eton flourish'
—Eton U. D. C., U.K.; Eton College, U. K.

141. **Floreat Hova** *Latin* 'May Hove flourish'
—Hove B. C., U.K.

142. **Floreat imperii portus** *Latin* 'Let the port of empire flourish'
—Port of London Authority, U.K.

143. **Floreat industria** *Latin* 'May industry flourish'
—Batley B. C., Darlington C. B. C., U.K.

144. **Floreat Rugbeia** *Latin* 'May Rugby flourish'
—Rugby B. C., U.K.

145. **Floreat Salopia** *Latin* 'Let Shropshire flourish'
—Salop C. C., Shrewsbury B. C., U.K., Taylor.

146. **Floreat semper fidelis civitas** *Latin* 'Let the faithful city ever flourish'
—Worcester City and C. B. C., U.K.

147. **Floreat Swansea** *Latin* 'May Swansea flourish'
—Swansea C. B. C., U.K.

148. **Floreat usque Leo** *Latin* 'May the Lion ever flourish'
—St. Mark's School, Windsor, U.K.

149. **Floret qui laborat** *Latin* 'He prospers who labors'
—Mossley B. C., Rawtenstall B. C., U.K.

150. **Floruit floreat** *Latin* 'May it flourish as it has flourished'
—Newbury B. C., U.K.

151. **For all**
—Southall B. C., U.K.

152. **For'ard, for'ard**
—Leicestershire C. C., U.K.

153. **Fortior quo paratior** *Latin* 'The better prepared, the stronger'
—Hornsey B. C., U.K.

154. **Fortis est veritas** *Latin* 'Truth is strong'
—Angus; Barton (of Threxton, Co. Norfolk); Hutchon; Oxford City and C. B. C., U.K.; City of Oxford.

155. **Fortis in arduis** *Latin* 'Strong in difficulties'
—Middleton B. C., U.K.

156. **Fortiter defendit, triumphans** *Latin* 'Triumphing, it bravely defends'
—Newcastle-upon-Tyne City and C. B. C., U.K.

158. **Fortiter et recte**   *Latin* 'Boldly and justly'
—Crayford U. D. C., U.K.

159. **Fortitudo et fidelitas**   *Latin* 'Fortitude and fidelity'
—Town of Dumbarton.

160. **Fortitudo et spes**   *Latin* 'Endurance and hope'
—Stockton-on-Tees B. C., U.K.

161. **Forward**
—Birmingham City and C. B. C., U.K.; Hayes and
Harlington U. D. C., U.K.; State of Wisconsin.

162. **Fruges ecce paludis**   *Latin* 'Behold the fruits of the marsh'
—Mirfield U. D. C., U.K.

163. **Fuimus et sumus**   *Latin* 'We were and we are'
—Whitby U. D. C., U.K.

164. **God's port our haven**
—Gosport B. C., U.K.

165. **God with us**
—Dursley R. D. C., U.K.

166. **Golud gwlad rhyddid**   *Welsh* 'The wealth of the land is freedom'
—Cardiganshire C. C., U.K.

167. **Gorau tarian cyfiawnder**   *Welsh* 'The best shield is justice'
—Flintshire C. C., U.K.

168. **Hanfod tref trefn**   *Welsh* 'The essence of a (good) town is orderliness'
—Ammanford U. D. C., U.K.

169. **Haulte emprise**   *Old French* 'High endeavor' or 'Noble undertaking'
—Haltemprice U. D. C., U.K.

170. **Heaven's light our guide**
—Order of the Star of India (founded 1861); Portsmouth
City and C. B. C., U.K.

171. **Hoc fonte derivata copia**   *Latin* 'Wealth, drawn from this spring'
—Wells City Council, U.K.

172. **Hold to the truth**
—Braintree and Bocking U. D. C., U.K.

173. **Home, industry, leisure**
—Bracknell Development Corp., U.K.

174. **Honeste progrediemur conando**   *Latin* 'Let us progress by honest
endeavor'
—Seisdon R. D. C., U.K.

175. **Honor alit artes**   *Latin* 'Honor fosters the arts'
—Burton-upon-Trent C. B. C., U.K.

176. **Honor et industria**   *Latin* 'Honor and industry'
—Bacup B. C., U.K.

177. **Hostes nunc amici**   *Latin* 'Foes now friends'
—Abergavenny B. C., U.K.

178. **Hostis honori invidia**   *Latin* 'Envy is an enemy to honor'
—Dickens; Market Harborough U. D. C., U.K.

179. **Ich dien**   *German* 'I serve'
—Norfolk C. C., U.K.

180. **Iechyd, harddwch, heddwch**   *Welsh* 'Health, beauty and tranquility'
—Colwyn Bay B. C., U.K.

181. **In concilio consilium**   *Latin* 'In council is wisdom'
—Lancashire C. C., U.K.

182. **In Deo fidemus**   *Latin* 'We trust in God'
—Brighton C. B. C., U.K.

183. **Industria, virtus et fortitudo**   *Latin* 'Diligence, courage, and
strength'
—Derby C. B. C., U.K.

184. **Industria ditat**   *Latin* 'Industry enriches'
—Knottingley U. D. C., Widnes B. C., Radcliffe B. C.,
High Wycombe, Sideserf, Reath, Wauchop, (of
Niddry), Waugh, Vanderplante. B. C., U.K.

185. **Industria et spe**   *Latin* 'By industry and hope'
—Skipton U. D. C., U.K., Barge, Claxton, Fenouiler,
Horrocks, Sage, Warden.

186. **Industria omnia vincit**   *Latin* 'Industry overcomes all things'
—Morley B. C., U.K.

187. **Industry and prudence conquer**
—Accrington B. C., U.K.

188. **Industry enriches**
—Spenborough U. D. C., U.K.

189. **In libertate vis**   *Latin* 'Strength in freedom'
—Merton and Morden U. D. C., U.K.

190. **Integrity**
—Dukinfield B. C., U.K.; Freake (Bt.).

191. **Integrity and industry**
—Salford City and C. B. C., U.K.

192. **Inter sylvas et flumina habitans**   *Latin* 'Dwelling 'twixt woods and rivers'
—Morpeth B. C., U.K.

193. **In te spectant, domine, oculi omnium**   *Latin* 'To thee, O Lord, the eyes of all are turned'
—Town of Nantes, France.

194. **In unitatem coeamus**   *Latin* 'Let us go forward together'
—Feltham U. D. C., U.K.

195. **In unity progress**
—Ilford B. C., U.K.

196. **In veritate victoria**   *Latin* 'Victory is in truth'
—Loughborough B. C., U.K.

197. **Invicta**   *Latin* 'Unconquered'
—Kent C. C., U.K.

198. **Invictae fidelitatis praemium**   *Latin* 'The reward of faithfulness unconquered'
—Hereford City Council, U.K.

199. **Jewel of the Thames**
—Maidenhead B. C., U.K.

200. **Judge us by our deeds**
—Dagenham B. C., U.K.

201. **Jure et dignitate gladii**   *Latin* 'By the right and dignity of the sword'
—Cheshire C. C., U.K.

202. **Juste nec timide**   *Latin* 'Be just and fear not'
—Farnworth B. C., U.K.

203. **Justitiae comes magnanimitas**   *Latin* 'Generosity is the companion of justice'
—Town of Dijon, France.

204. **Justitia turris nostra**   *Latin* 'Justice is our tower'
—Hackney B. C., U.K.

205. **Juvat impigros Deus**   *Latin* 'God aids the diligent'
—Huddersfield C. B. C., U.K.

206. **Keep faith**
—Crewkerne U. D. C., U.K.

207. **Known by their fruits**
—Sittingbourne and Milton U. D. C., U.K.

208. **Labore et ingenio**   *Latin* 'By industry and ingenuity'
—Smethwick C. B. C., U.K.

209. **Labore et prudentia**   *Latin* 'By industry and prudence'
—Brighouse B. C., U.K.

210. **Labore et scientia**   *Latin* 'By labor and science'
—Jarrow B. C., U.K.

211. **Labore omnia florent**   *Latin* 'All things flourish by labor'
—Drinkwater, Huntingdonshire C. C., U.K., Eccles B. C., U.K.

212. **Labor omnia vincit**
—Ilkeston B. C., Ashton-Under-Lyme B. C., U.K.; Centenary College of Louisiana, Shreveport, Louisiana; State of Oklahoma; Bradford City and C. B. C., U.K.

213. **Labor overcomes all things**
—Erith B. C., U.K.

214. **Labour brings plenty**
—Horwich U. D. C., U.K.

215. **Let Glasgow flourish**
—Borough of Glasgow.

216. **Libera deinde fidelis**   *Latin* 'Free, therefore faithful'
—Godalming B. C., U.K.

217. **Like as the oak**
—Uckfield R. D. C., U.K.

218. **Looking backward, looking forward**
—Twickenham B. C., U.K.

219. **Lord, let Glasgow flourish**
—Town of Glasgow.

220. **Loyal and industrious**
—Rowley Regis B. C., U.K.

221. **Loyal and true**
—Chatham B. C., U.K.

222. **Luck to Loyne**
—Lancaster City Council, U.K.

223. **Lux, salubritas, felicitas**   *Latin* 'Light, health, happiness'
—Clacton U. D. C., U.K.

224. **Many minds, one heart**
—Chelmsford B. C., U.K.

225. **Mare ditat, rosa decorat**   *Latin* 'The sea enriches and the rose adorns'
—Town of Montrose.

226. **Mare ditat flores decorant** *Latin* 'The sea enriches and the flowers adorn'
—Exmouth U. D. C., U.K.

227. **Mare et ferro** *Latin* 'By sea and steel'
—Redcar B. C., U.K.

228. **Meliora sequimur** *Latin* 'We follow better things'
—Eastbourne C. B. C., U.K.

229. **Messis ab altis** *Latin* 'Harvest from the deeps'
—Tynemouth C. B. C., U.K.

230. **Ministrando dignitas** *Latin* 'Dignity in service'
—Leyton B. C., U.K.

231. **Monemus et munimus** *Latin* 'We counsel and protect'
—Monmouth B. C., U.K.

232. **Mon Mam Cymru** *Welsh* 'Anglesey, mother of Wales'
—Anglesey C. C., U.K.

233. **Montes unde auxilium meum** *Latin* 'The hills whence cometh my help'
—Keswick U. D. C., U.K.

234. **More light, more power**
—Shoreditch B. C., U.K.

235. **Multi pertransibunt et augebitur scientia** *Latin* 'Many shall pass through and learning shall be increased'
—Holborn B. C., U.K.

236. **Mutare vel timere sperno** *Latin* 'I scorn either to change or fear'
—Little Lever U. D. C., U.K.

237. **Ne cede malis** *Latin* 'Yield not to misfortunes'
—Albemarle (E.); Doig; Keppel; Herne Bay U. D. C., U.K.

238. **Nec ferro nec igni** *Latin* 'Neither by sword nor by fire'
—Appleby B. C., U.K.

239. **Nec virtus nec copia desunt** *Latin* 'Neither virtue nor plenty are lacking'
—Macclesfield B. C., U.K.

240. **Never behind**
—Crewe B. C., U.K.

241. **Nid cadarn ond brodyrdde** *Welsh* 'No strength but in fellowship'
—Merthyr Tydfil C. B. C., U.K.

242. **Nil desperandum auspice Deo**   *Latin* 'With God as our leader there is no cause for despair'
—Sunderland C. B. C., U.K.

243. **Nisi Dominus frustra**   *Latin* 'If not the Lord, (it is) in vain'
—Chelsea B. C., U.K.

244. **Nisi Dominus frustra**   *Latin* 'It is vain without the Lord'
—Hinde, Inglis, Towers; City of Edinburgh.

245. **Nobis habitatio felix**   *Latin* 'A happy dwelling place for us'
—Wilmslow U. D. C., U.K.

246. **None such**
—Epsom and Ewell B. C., U.K.

247. **Non mihi, non tibi, sed nobis**   *Latin* 'Not for me, nor for thee, but for us'
—Battersea B. C., U.K.

248. **Non nobis sed communitati**   *Latin* 'Not for ourselves but for the community'
—Bexley B. C., U.K.

249. **Non nobis sed omnibus**   *Latin* 'Not for ourselves, but for all mankind'
—Ashe (of Ashfield, etc.); North Walsham U. D. C., U.K.

250. **Non nobis solum**   *Latin* 'Not for ourselves alone'
—Beckenham B. C., U.K.

251. **Non progredi est regredi**   *Latin* 'Not to go forward is to go backward'
—Ruislip-Northwood U. D. C., Chigwell U. D. C., U.K.

252. **Non sanz droict**   *Old French* 'Not without right'
—Shakespear; Warwickshire C. C., U.K.

253. **Non sibi sed toti**   *Latin* 'Not for self but for all'
—Hampstead B. C., U.K.

254. **Non solum ingenii, verum etiam virtutis**   *Latin* 'Not only talent, but also virtue'
—Liverpool College, U.K.

255. **Nostrum viret robur**   *Latin* 'Our strength is as a green tree' *or* 'Wood Green flourishes'
—Wood Green B. C., U.K.

256. **Not for ourselves alone**
—Barnes B. C., U.K.

257. **Nothing without labor**
—Haslingden B. C., U.K.

258. **Oculis in coelum** *Latin* 'The eye in heaven'
—Eye B. C., U.K.

259. **O lector salve celi pateant tibi valve** *Latin* 'Greeting, reader! May heaven's doors open to thee'
—Haverfordwest B. C., U.K.

260. **Omnia bona bonis** *Latin* 'To the good all things (are) good'
—Harwich B. C., U.K.; Wenman, Wainman.

261. **One and all**
—Cornwall C. C., U.K.

262. **One heart, one way**
—Stourbridge B. C., U.K.

263. **Oni heuir ni fedir** *Welsh* 'Without sowing one cannot reap'
—Carmarthen R. D. C., U.K.

264. **Onward**
—Fleetwood B. C., U.K.; Hyde B. C., U.K.

265. **Opes consilium parit** *Latin* 'Wisdom begets wealth'
—Bridgwater B. C., U.K.

266. **Opes parit industria** *Latin* 'Industry begets plenty' *or* 'Industry produces riches'
—Bingley U. D. C., U.K.; Benson.

267. **Opus nostrum dirige** *Latin* 'Direct our work'
—East Suffolk C. C., U.K.

268. **Ora et ara** *Latin* 'Pray and plough'
—South Kesteven R. D. C., U.K.

269. **Out of darkness cometh light**
—Wolverhampton C. B. C., U.K.

270. **Pannus mihi panis** *Latin* 'Wool is my bread'
—Kendal B. C., U.K.

271. **Perfero** *Latin* 'I carry through'
—Cumberland C.C., U.K.

272. **Per mare et per terram** *Latin* 'By sea and land'
—Boston B. C., U.K.

273. **Per mare per ecclesiam** *Latin* 'By sea and church'
—Southend-on-Sea C. B. C., U.K.

274. **Per pericula ad decus ire juvat** *Latin* 'He delights to go through adversity to glory'
—Scarborough B. C., U.K.

275. **Perseverantia vincit** *Latin* 'Perseverance succeeds'
—Kesteven C. C., U.K.; Burnes

276. **Persevere**
>   —Denton U. D. C., U.K.; Congreve (Bt.), Colvile, Greig,
>   Gardiner, Gibbs, Fearon, Fordyce, Farnall, Oakes
>   (Bt.), Phillips (of Reigate Lodge, Co. Surrey), Smythe,
>   Whittall.

277. **Per undas, per agros**   *Latin* 'Through the waves, through the
      fields'
>   —Cambridgeshire C. C., U.K.

278. **Point du jour**   *French* 'Daybreak'
>   —Lowestoft B. C., U.K.

279. **Porta maris portus salutis**   *Latin* 'A gate of the sea and a haven of
      health'
>   —Margate B. C., U.K.

280. **Powys Paradwys Cymru**   *Welsh* 'Powys, paradise of Wales'
>   —Montgomeryshire C. C., U.K.

281. **Praecepta non homines**   *Latin* 'Principles, not men'
>   —Newport Pagnell U. D. C., U.K.

282. **Prae salem notanda**   *Latin* 'The well-known place by the sea' *or*
      'Famed for salt'
>   —Preesall U. D. C., U.K.

283. **Prêt d'accomplir**   *French* 'Ready to achieve'
>   —Nuneaton B. C., U.K.

284. **Pretiumque et causa laboris**   *Latin* 'Both the prize and the motive
      of labor'
>   —Burnley C. B. C., U.K.

285. **Pride in our past, faith in our future**
>   —Hertford B. C., U.K.

286. **Priora cole meliora sequere**   *Latin* 'Cherish the past but strive for
      better things in the future'
>   —Enfield U. D. C., U.K.

287. **Prisca constantia**   *Latin* 'With ancient constancy'
>   —Newcastle-under-Lyme B. C., U.K.

288. **Pro bono oppido**   *Latin* 'For a good town'
>   —Horbury U. D. C., U.K.

289. **Pro civibus et civitate**   *Latin* 'For the citizens and the city'
>   —Fulham B. C., U.K.

290. **Pro Deo et populo**   *Latin* 'For God and the people'
>   —Friedrich Wilhelm, Elector of Brandenburg (1620–88);
>   Ferdinand IV, King of Rome (1633–54); Bishop's
>   Stortford U. D. C., U.K.

291. **Prodesse** *Latin* 'To serve'
—Hindley U. D. C., U.K.

292. **Progress**
—Blackpool C. B. C., U.K.; Littlehampton U. D. C., U.K.

293. **Progressio cum populo** *Latin* 'Progress with the people'
—East Ham C. B. C., U.K.

294. **Pro rege ac fide audax** *Latin* 'Bold for king and faith'
—Bideford B. C., U.K.

295. **Pro rege et lege** *Latin* 'For king and law'
—Leeds City and C. B. C., U.K.; Horton (of Howroyde);
Kidson; Mandit; Stewart (of Fincastle).

296. **Prorsum semper** *Latin* 'Ever forward'
—Gloucestershire C. C., U.K.

297. **Pro rure pro patria** *Latin* 'For countryside and country'
—Hertford R. D. C., U.K.

298. **Prosunt gentibus artes** *Latin* 'Arts benefit the people'
—Bermondsey B. C., U.K.

299. **Proudly we serve**
—Horsham U. D. C., U.K.

300. **Prudens futuri** *Latin* 'Prudent for the future'
—Letchworth U. D. C., U.K.

301. **Pulchra terra Dei donum** *Latin* 'This fair land is the gift of God'
—Herefordshire C. C., U.K.

302. **Pulchritudo et salubritas** *Latin* 'Beauty and health'
—Bournemouth C. B. C., U.K.

303. **Quanti est sapere** *Latin* 'How great it is to be wise'
—Shardlow R. D. C., U.K.

304. **Quid nobis ardui** *Latin* 'What is hard for us?'
—Kensington B. C., U.K.

305. **Ramosa cornua cervi** *Latin* 'The branching horns of the stag'
—Woodstock B. C., U.K.

306. **Recte fac noli timere** *Latin* 'Do right and fear not'
—Prestwich B. C., U.K.

307. **Reddite Deo** *Latin* 'Render unto God' *or* 'Redditch for God'
—Redditch U. D. C., U.K.

308. **Refulget labores nostros coelum** *Latin* 'The sky reflects our works'
—Scunthorpe B. C., U.K.

309. **Regnant qui servirent**   *Latin* 'They rule who serve'
—Finchley B. C., U.K.

310. **Respice aspice prospice**   *Latin* 'Look to the past, the present, and the future'
—Tettenhall U. D. C., Bootle C. B. C., Halesowen B.C., U.K.

311. **Respice finem**   *Latin* 'Look to the end'
—Newmarket U. D. C., U.K.

312. **Respice prospice**   *Latin* 'Look to the past and to the future'
—Trowbridge U. D. C., Stoke Newington B. C., Ealing B. C., U.K.

313. **Reviresco**   *Latin* 'I grow green again'
—Rishton U. D. C., U.K.

314. **Rex et nostra jura**   *Latin* 'The king and our laws'
—Great Yarmouth C. B. C., U.K.

315. **Rhyddid gwerin ffyniant gwlad**   *Welsh* 'The freedom of the people is the prosperity of the land'
—Carmarthenshire C. C., U.K.

316. **Rhyddid hedd a llwyddiant**   *Welsh* 'Freedom, peace, and prosperity'
—Carmarthen B. C., U.K.

317. **Ro an mor**   *Old Cornish* 'Gift of the sea'
—Newquay U. D. C., U.K.

318. **Rosa concordiae signum**   *Latin* 'A rose, the emblem of harmony'
—Northamptonshire C. C., U.K.

319. **Rura mihi placent**   *Latin* 'Things of the countryside please me'
—Congleton R. D. C., U.K.

320. **Ruris amator**   *Latin* 'Lover of the countryside'
—Friern Barnet U. D. C., U.K.

321. **Rus gratiis musisque dignum**   *Latin* 'A countryside worthy of the Graces and Muses'
—Bathavon R. D. C., U.K.

322. **Sacrarium regis cunabula legis**   *Latin* 'The shrine of the king and the cradle of the law'
—Bury St. Edmunds B. C., U.K.

323. **Salt is life**
—Northwich U. D. C., U.K.

324. **Salubritas et eruditio**   *Latin* 'Health and learning'
—Cheltenham B. C., U.K.

325. **Salubritas et industria**   *Latin* 'Health and industry'
—Swindon B. C., U.K.

326. **Salus et felicitas**   *Latin* 'Health and happiness'
—Torquay B. C., Sale B. C., U.K.

327. **Salus naufragis salus aegris**   *Latin* 'Safety to the shipwrecked, health to the sick'
—Ramsgate B. C., U.K.

328. **Salus populi**   *Latin* 'The welfare of the people'
—Southport C. B. C., U.K.

329. **Salus populi suprema est lex**   *Latin* 'The welfare of the people is the highest law'
—Urmston U. D. C., U.K.

330. **Salus populi suprema lex**   *Latin* 'The welfare of the people is the highest law'
—Eastleigh B. C., Harrow U. D. C., Lewisham B. C., Lytham-St. Annes B. C., Swinton and Pendlebury B. C., Tipton B. C., Tonbridge U. D. C., Willenhall U. D. C., U.K.

331. **Salve magna parens**   *Latin* 'Hail, great parent'
—Lichfield City Council, U.K.

332. **Sanitate crescamus**   *Latin* 'May we grow in health'
—Croydon C. B. C., U.K.

333. **Sans Dieu rien**   *French* 'Without God nothing'
—Godley (Co. Leitrim), Hodgkinson, Petre (B.), Peter (of Harlyn), Saunderson; Worksop B. C., U.K.

334. **Sapere aude**   *Latin* 'Dare to be wise'
—Amos, Cooper, Wise, Macclesfield (E.), Townley-Parker, Wise (of Ford House); Oxfordshire C. C., Oldham C. B. C., U.K.

335. **Sapienter proficiens**   *Latin* 'Advancing wisely'
—Nottinghamshire C. C., U.K.

336. **Scientiae et labori detur**   *Latin* 'Due to knowledge and labor'
—Luton B. C., U.K.

337. **Secundis rebus cave**   *Latin* 'In well, beware'
—Wombwell U. D. C., U.K.

338. **Semper acceptus**   *Latin* 'Ever welcome'
—Paignton U. D. C., U.K.

339. **Semper eadem**   *Latin* 'Always the same'
   —Collmore, Forrester (Bt.), Fairburn, Hollingsworth, Hornsey, Panton, Reid.; Leicester City and C. B. C., U.K.; Queen Elizabeth I.

340. **Semper fidelis**   *Latin* 'Ever faithful'
   —Exeter City and C. B. C., U.K.

341. **Semper fidelis, mutare sperno**   *Latin* 'Ever faithful, I scorn to change'
   —Worcester City and C. B. C., U.K.

342. **Semper proficimus**   *Latin* 'We progress continually'
   —Leyland U. D. C., U.K.

343. **Semper sursum**   *Latin* 'Ever upwards'
   —Barrow-in-Furness C. B. C., U.K., Graham.

344. **Serve God and be cheerful**
   —Sutton and Cheam B. C., U.K.

345. **Serve with gladness**
   —Romford B. C., U.K.

346. **Service and efficiency**
   —Stretford B. C., U.K.

347. **Service links all**
   —Leatherhead U. D. C., U.K.; Lindsey C. C., U.K.

348. **Sicut quercus virescit industria**   *Latin* 'Industry flourishes like the oak'
   —Mansfield B. C., U.K.

349. **Sic virescit industria**   *Latin* 'Thus industry flourishes'
   —Stewart, Rotherham C. B. C., U.K.

350. **Sic vos non vobis**   *Latin* 'So you are not for yourselves'
   —Baldock U. D. C., U.K., Walrond, Franks.

351. **Signum salutis semper**   *Latin* 'Ever the sign of health'
   —Bridlington B. C., U.K.

352. **Sine labe decus**   *Latin* 'Honor without stain'
   —Allen; Wimbledon B. C., U.K.

353. **Sine labore nihil floret**   *Latin* 'Nothing prospers without industry'
   —Brierley Hill U. D. C., U.K.

354. **Sit saxum firmit**   *Latin* 'May the stone be firm'
   —Stone U. D. C., U.K.; Saxby.

355. **Sit Tibi sancta cohors comitum**   *Latin* 'To Thee be the band of comrades dedicated'
   —Congleton B. C., U.K.

356. **Situ exoritur Segeduni**   *Latin* 'Arose on the site of Segudunum'
—Wallsend B. C., U.K.

357. **Sola bona quae honesta**   *Latin* 'Only those things that are honorable are good'
—Leamington B. C., U.K.

358. **Sol et pastor Deus**   *Latin* 'God, our sun and shepherd'
—Sunbury-on-Thames U. D. C., U.K.

359. **Sol et salubritas**   *Latin* 'Sun and health'
—Bexhill B. C., U.K.

360. **Son comfort et liesse**   *French* 'His comfort and joy'
—Town of Doncaster (U.K.).

361. **Spectemur agendo**   *Latin* 'Let us be judged by our deeds'
—Chorley R. D. C., Barnsley C. B. C., Lambeth B. C., Hammersmith B. C., U.K.

362. **Spe nemo ruet**   *Latin* 'With hope, no one shall fail'
—Spennymoor U. D. C., U.K.

363. **Stabit quocumque jeceris**   *Latin* 'Whichever way you throw it, it will stand'
—The Isle of Man.

364. **Stabit saxum fluet amnis**   *Latin* 'The rock will remain and the river will flow'
—Clitheroe B. C., U.K.

365. **Statio bene fida carinis**   *Latin* 'A trustworthy harbor for vessels'
—Queenstown Harbour, Cork, Ireland.

366. **Strive for the gain of all**
—Gainsborough U. D. C., U.K.

367. **Sub cruce floreamus**   *Latin* 'May we flourish beneath the cross'
—Poulton-le-Fylde U. D. C., U.K.

368. **Sudore non sopore**   *Latin* 'By toil, not by sleep'
—St. Ives B. C., U.K.

369. **Supera Moras**   *Latin* 'Over the moors' or 'Overcome delays'
—Bolton C. B. C., U.K.

370. **Surgamus ergo strenue**   *Latin* 'Let us therefore arise with vigor'
—Baildon U. D. C., U.K.

371. **Surgimus**   *Latin* 'We rise'
—Saltburn and Maske-by-the-Sea U. D. C., U.K.

372. **Suum cuique tribuere**   *Latin* 'To assign to each his own'
—Wrexham R. D. C., U.K.

373. **Tempore utimur** *Latin* 'We use time'
      —Greenwich B. C., U.K.

374. **Tempori parendum** *Latin* 'We must move with the times'
   —Wembley B. C., Bishop Auckland U. D. C., U.K.

375. **Tenax et fidelis** *Latin* 'Steadfast and faithful'
      —Dartford B. C., U.K.

376. **Terra marique** *Latin* 'On land and sea'
     —Thornton Cleveleys U. D. C., U.K.

377. **The knot unites**
      —Staffordshire C. C., U.K.

378. **They ryght defend**
      —Southwold B. C., U.K.

379. **Tra mor tra Meirion** *Welsh* 'While the sea lasts, so shall Merioneth'
      —Merioneth C. C., U.K.

380. **True worth never fails**
      —Failsworth U. D. C., U.K.

381. **Trust and triumph**
      —Gainsborough R. D. C., U.K.

382. **Turris fortissima est nomen Jehovae** *Latin* 'The name of Jehovah is the strongest tower'
     —Plymouth City and C. B. C., U.K.

383. **Tutissima statio** *Latin* 'The safest station'
      —Town of Stranrear, U.K.

384. **Ubi fides ibi lux et robur** *Latin* 'Where there is faith there is light and strength'
      —Birkenhead C. B. C., U.K.

385. **Undeb hedd llwyddiant** *Welsh* 'Unity, peace, prosperity'
      —Breconshire C. C., U.K.

386. **Ung nous servons** *Old French* 'We serve as one'
      —Pembroke B. C., U.K.

387. **Unitate fortior** *Latin* 'Stronger by union'
    —Beck; Heston and Isleworth B. C., U.K.

388. **Unitate praestans** *Latin* 'Excelling by unity'
      —Preston R. D. C., U.K.

389. **United to serve**
      —Southwark B. C., U.K.

390. **Unity and loyalty**
      —Borough of Chippenham.

391. **Unity and progress**
—Melksham U. D. C., U.K.

392. **Urbs in rure** *Latin* 'The town in the countryside'
—Solihull U. D. C., U.K.

393. **Ut homines liberi sint** *Latin* 'So that men may be free'
—Egham U. D. C., U.K.

394. **Utrique fidelis** *Latin* 'Faithful to both'
—Monmouthshire C. C., U.K.

395. **Vestigia nulla retrorsum** *Latin* 'No backward step'
—Buckinghamshire C. C., U.K.

396. **Vetustas dignitatem generat** *Latin* 'Age begets dignity'
—East Retford B. C., U.K.

397. **Vicinas urbes alit** *Latin* 'It nurtures neighboring cities'
—Spalding U. D. C., U.K.

398. **Vigilate et orate** *Latin* 'Watch and pray'
—[Matt. xxvi. 41 and Mark, xiii. 33.] Clevedon U. D. C.,
U.K.; Capron, Castlemaine (V.), Handcock,
Shuckburgh.

399. **Vincit omnia industria** *Latin* 'Industry overcomes all things'
—Bury C. B. C., U.K.

400. **Virtus veritas libertas** *Latin* 'Virtue, truth, and freedom'
—Glossop B. C., U.K.

401. **Virtute et industria** *Latin* 'By virtue and industry'
—Bristol City and C. B. C., U.K.; City of Bristol, U.K.

402. **Virtute res parvae crescunt** *Latin* 'Small things increase by virtue'
—Town of Anstruther, U.K.

403. **Vis unita fortior** *Latin* 'Strength united is stronger'
—1776 seal of New Hampshire; Brook; Flood; Hales;
Hosken; Lidwell; Moore; Mountcashel (E.);
Crosby B. C., Stoke-on-Trent City and C. B. C.,
U.K.

404. **Vivit post funera virtus**   *Latin* 'Virtue survives death'
—Nottingham City and C. B. C., U.K.; Boyle, Craig,
Shannon (E.); Wilhelm IV, Landgrave of Hesse-
Cassel (1532–92); Ernst Friedrich, Margrave of
Baden-Durlach (1560–1604); Johann Adolf, Duke
of Schleswig-Holstein-Gottorp (1575–1616);
Ludwig V, Landgrave of Hesse-Darmstadt
(1577–1626); Ludwig Günther, Count
Schwarzburg-Rudolstadt (1581–1646); Adolf
Friedrich I, Duke of Mecklenburg-Schwerin
(1588–1658).

405. **We grow by industry**
—Bedworth U. D. C., U.K., Blyth B. C.

406. **We long endure**
—Colne B. C., U.K.

407. **We serve**
—Dartford R. D. C., Wandsworth B. C., U.K.

408. **Who's afear'd?**
—Dorset C. C., U.K.

409. **With fort and fleet for home and England**
—Gillingham B. C., U.K.

410. **With wisdom and courage**
—St. Pancras B. C., U.K.

411. **Work supports all**
—Worksop R. D. C., U.K.

412. **Y ddraig goch ddyry gychwyn**   *Welsh* 'The red dragon shall lead'
—Cardiff City and C. B. C., Prestatyn U. D. C., U.K.

LOCATION

1. **Crossroads of America**
—State of Indiana.

2. **Inter sylvas et flumina habitans**   *Latin* 'Dwelling 'twixt woods and rivers'
—Morpeth B. C., U.K.

3. **Juxta Salopiam**   *Latin* 'Near to Shropshire'
—Chadwick.

4. **Là ou ailleurs**   *French* 'There or elsewhere'
—De Kergarion (Breton).

5. **Per callem collem**   *Latin* 'By the path the hill'
    —Collins (of Betterton).
6. **Qua panditur orbis**   *Latin* 'Where the world extends'
    —Campbell.
7. **Sherwoode**
    —(after Sherwood Forest, the domain of Robin Hood)
    Hood.
8. **Situ exoritur Segeduni**   *Latin* 'Arose on the site of Segudunum'
    —Wallsend B. C., U.K.
9. **Stant caetera tigno**   *Latin* 'The rest stand on a beam'
    —Huntly (M.).
10. **Sub montibus altis**   *Latin* 'Under high mountains'
    —Skeen.
11. **Supera Moras**   *Latin* 'Over the moors' or 'Overcome delays'
    —Bolton C. B. C., U.K.
12. **The college of the Keys**
    —Florida Keys Community College, Key West, Florida.
13. **Ubique aut nusquam**   *Latin* 'Everywhere or nowhere'
    —Whitefoord.

LOFTINESS (*See also* RISING.)
1. **Alte fert aquila**   *Latin* 'The eagle bears on high'
    —Monteagle (B.).
2. **Alte volat**   *Latin* 'He flies high'
    —Dawson.
3. **Alte volo**   *Latin* 'I fly high'
    —Heywood B. C., U.K., Heywood (Bt.).
4. **Altius**   *Latin* 'Higher'
    —Gregory.
5. **Arduus ad solem**   *Latin* 'Lifted up to the sun'
    —University of Manchester, Manchester, U.K.
6. **Caput inter nubila condit**   *Latin* 'It hides its head among the clouds'
    —[Vergil, *Aen.* x. 767.] Town of Gateshead.
7. **De monte alto**   *Italian* 'From a high mountain'
    —Maude.
8. **Eo altius quo profundius**   *Latin* 'The higher the deeper'
    —Lloyd.

9. **Ex monte alto**   *Latin* 'From the high mountain'
—Baker.

10. **Haut et bon**   *French* 'High and good'
—Doneraile (V.), St. Leger.

11. **I live and die for those I love**
—Lloyd.

12. **In ardua**   *Latin* 'On high'
—Hoare.

13. **I soar**
—Edidge.

14. **Monte alto**   *Latin* 'From a high hill'
—Mowat (of Inglistoun).

15. **Monte de alto**   *Latin* 'From a high hill'
—Atthill.

16. **Mox sese attolit in auris**   *Latin* 'He will soon rise in ethereal heights'
—Waring.

17. **Mox virtute se tollit ad auras**   *Latin* 'Soon he will raise himself by his valor to the heavens'
—Swettenham, Warren.

18. **Ne nimis altus**   *Latin* 'Not too high'
—Perkins.

19. **Raptim ad sidera tollar**   *Latin* 'I shall be snatched aloft to the stars'
—Guille.

20. **Se inserit astris**   *Latin* 'He places himself among the stars'
—Crosse.

21. **Semper erectus**   *Latin* 'Always exalted'
—Pepper.

22. **Sicut aquilae pennis**   *Latin* 'As on eagle's wings'
—Niblett.

23. **Tam animo mente sublimis**   *Latin* 'As lofty in spirit as in intellect'
—Forteath.

24. **Tulloch ard**   *Scots Gaelic* 'A high hill'
—McKenzie.

25. **Ut aquila versus coelum**   *Latin* 'As an eagle towards the sky'
—Bowdoin (U.S.).

26.   **Volando reptilia sperno**   *Latin* 'Flying myself I despise creeping things'

—Seras, Scarth.

LOVE (*See also* FEELINGS; HEART; KINDNESS.)

1.   **Aime le meilleur**   *French* 'Love the best'

—Sinclair (Bt.).

2.   **Aimer sans crainte**   *French* 'Love without fear'

—De Massue.

3.   **Aime ton frère**   *French* 'Love thy brother'

—Frere, Freer.

4.   **Ama gregem**   *Latin* 'Love the flock'

—Shepperd.

5.   **Amice**   *Latin* 'Lovingly'

—Russel, Watts.

6.   **Amicitiam trahit amor**   *Latin* 'Love draws on friendship'

—Wire-drawers' Company.

7.   **Amo**   *Latin* 'I love'

—Buccleugh (D.), Hoops, MacKindlay, Scott.

8.   **Amo, inspicio**   *Latin* 'I love him, I gaze upon him'

—Scot.

9.   **Amo pacem**   *Latin* 'I love peace'

—Towle.

10.   **Amor Dei et proximi summa beatitudo**   *Latin* 'The love of God and our neighbour is the highest happiness'

—Dobbs.

11.   **Amor distantia jungit**   *Latin* 'Love brings the distant near'

—Anna, Archduchess of Austria (1573–98).

12.   **Amor dulcis patriae**   *Latin* 'The love of dear homeland'

—Wigram.

13.   **Amore et prudentia**   *Latin* 'By love and by prudence'

—Friedrich II, Duke of Saxony-Gotha and Altenburg (1676–1732).

14.   **Amore floresco**   *Latin* 'I flourish with love'

—Moore.

15.   **Amorem progenerat amor**   *Latin* 'Love engenders love'

—Johann Georg II, Elector of Saxony (1613–80).

16. **Amore non vi**   *Latin* 'By love, not by violence'
    —Amory, Heathcote-Amory, Heathcoat-Amory (Bt.).

17. **Amore sitis uniti**   *Latin* 'Be ye united in love'
    —Tin-plate Workers' and Wire-workers' Company.

18. **Amor et obedientia**   *Latin* 'Love and obedience'
    —Painters' Company.

19. **Amor et pax**   *Latin* 'Love and peace'
    —Ireland.

20. **Amore vici**   *Latin* 'I have conquered by love'
    —McKenzie (Bt.).

21. **Amore vinci**   *Latin* 'To be conquered by love'
    —McKenzie.

22. **Amor patitur moras**   *Latin* 'Love endures delay'
    —Lumisden.

23. **Amor patriae vincit**   *Latin* 'The love of country conquers'
    —Meyler.

24. **Amor proximi**   *Latin* 'Love of neighbor'
    —Craney.

25. **Amor proximi**   *Latin* 'The love of our neighbor'
    —Order of Neighborly Love.

26. **Amorque et obedientia**   *Latin* 'Both love and obedience'
    —Painters' Company.

27. **Amor sine timore**   *Latin* 'Love without fear'
    —Reade.

28. **Amor vincit omnia**   *Latin* 'Love conquers all'
    —Usher.

29. **Amor vincit patriae**   *Latin* 'The love of country conquers'
    —Gibbes (U.S.).

30. **Amour avec loyaulté**   *French* 'Love with loyalty'
    —Parr (of Kendal, co. of Westmoreland).

31. **Amo ut invenio**   *Latin* 'I love as I find'
    —Perrot (Bt.).

32. **Ardenter amo**   *Latin* 'I love fervently'
    —Scot (of Harwood).

33. **At servata fides perfectus amorque ditabunt**   *Latin* 'But faith kept, and perfect love will enrich'
    —Younge (Co. Stafford).

34. **Aux armes vaillant, en amour constant**   *French* 'In arms valiant, in love constant'
>> —Friedrich, Duke of Saxony (D. 1586).

35. **Candidior**   *Latin* 'More dearly'
>> —Mair.

36. **Caritas**   *Latin* 'Love'
>> —Briar Cliff College, Sioux City, Iowa.

37. **Cedamus amori**   *Latin* 'Let us yield to love'
>> —[Vergil, *Ecl.* x. 69.] Blunden (Bt.).

38. **Cogit amor**   *Latin* 'Love compels'
>> —Joass.

39. **Conservata fides perfectus amorque ditabunt**   *Latin* 'Constant fidelity and perfect love will enrich'
>> —Yonge.

40. **Constant et discret et ang amour secret**   *Old French* 'Constant and discreet, and secret in love'
>> —Bernhard, Duke of Saxony-Weimar (1604–39).

41. **Credo, amo et regno**   *Latin* 'I believe, love, and rule'
>> —Clive.

42. **Credo et amo**   *Latin* 'I believe and love'
>> —Crossley (of Scaitcliffe).

43. **Dilige pacem**   *Latin* 'Love peace'
>> —Barlow (B.).

44. **Ducit amor oppidi**   *Latin* 'The love of our town leads us'
>> —Malden and Coombe B. C., U.K.

45. **Dulcis amor patriae**   *Latin* 'The love of one's country is sweet'
>> —Clifford, Fitzwygram (Bt.), Robinson.

46. **Est pii Deum et patriam diligere**   *Latin* 'It is the part of a pious man to love God and his country'
>> —Atkinson.

47. **Et servata fides perfectus amorque ditabunt**   *Latin* 'Both tried faith and perfect love will enrich'
>> —Younge.

48. **Excidit amor nunquam**   *Latin* 'My love never fails'
>> —Foote.

49. **Fide et amore**   *Latin* 'By fidelity and love'
>> —Carden (Bt.), Conway, Dicey, Gardiner (of Ely), Heart, Hertford (M.), Sadler, Chadwick (of Lynn, Co. Norfolk).

50. **Fidelitate et amore** *Latin* 'By fidelity and love'

—Hathorn.

51. **Fideliter amo** *Latin* 'I love faithfully'

—Goldie-Scott.

52. **Fides et amor** *Latin* 'Faith and love'

—Graham.

53. **Fovendo foveo** *Latin* 'I cherish by cherishing'

—Folville.

54. **Frere ayme frere** *Old French* 'Frere love thy brother'

—Frere.

55. **Honorate, diligite, timete** *Latin* 'Honor, love, fear'

—Moseley.

56. **Honore et amore** *Latin* 'With honor and love'
—Richards, Grantham (of Ketton), Hammersley, Solosborough.

57. **Honor et amor** *Latin* 'Honor and love'

—Niblie.

58. **Hope well and love all well**

—Bower.

59. **I live and die for those I love**

—Lloyd.

60. **In bello invictus in amore probus** *Latin* 'Unconquered in war, honorable in love'

—Steele, Steele-Graves.

61. **In te sitit anima mea** *Latin* 'My soul thirsteth for thee'
—Philipp II, Duke of Pomerania (1573–1618).

62. **J'aime à jamais** *French* 'I love forever'

—James.

63. **J'aime le meilleur** *French* 'I love the best'

—Sinclair (Bt.).

64. **J'aime qui m'aime** *French* 'I love whoever loves me'

—De Beaumanoir (Brittany).

65. **J'ayme à jamais** *Old French* 'I love forever'

—James (Bt.).

66. **J'ayme porter secours** *Old French* 'I love to bring help'

—Porter (Bt.).

67. **Je ayme** *Old French* 'I love'

—Lindsay.

68. **Je meurs pour ceux que j'aime** *French* 'I die for those whom I love'
—Paterson, Wallace.

69. **Junxit amicos amor** *Latin* 'Love hath united friends'
—Order of St. Joachim (Germany).

70. **Karanza wheelas karanza** *Cornish* 'Love worketh love'
—Polwhele (of Polwhele, Cornwall).

71. **Labore et amore** *Latin* 'By labor and love'
—Horsfall.

72. **L'amour de Dieu est pacifique** *French* 'The love of God is peaceful'
—Order of Mary Magdalen.

73. **L'amour et l'amitié** *French* 'Love and friendship'
—Day (of Kirby, Bedon, co. Norfolk).

74. **L'amour et loyauté** *French* 'Love and loyalty'
—Swayne.

75. **Let brotherly love continue**
—Plasterers' Company, Pipe-makers' Company.

76. **Let us love one another**
—Basketmakers' Company.

77. **L'homme vrai aime son pays** *French* 'The true man loves his country'
—Homfray (Co. Stafford).

78. **Live, love, think, pray, dare**
—United Daughters of the Confederacy.

79. **Love**
—McLeish, McCleish (of Maryfield).

80. **Love, but dread**
—Lindsay.

81. **Love, serve**
—Cooper, Shaftesbury (E.).

82. **Love and dread**
—Baker.

83. **Love and loyalty**
—Crompton, Stansfield.

84. **Love as brethren**
—Coopers' Company, London.

85. **Love as you find**
—Tempest.

86. **Love every man, fear no man**
                              —Cropper, Thornburgh.

87. **Lufe God abufe al: and yi nichtbors as yi self**   *Scots dialect* 'Love
    God above all: and your neighbors as yourself'
                              —the house of John Knox, Edinburgh, Scotland.

88. **Martis non Cupidinis**   *Latin* 'Of Mars not Cupid'
                              —Fletcher (Bt.).

89. **Mein Liebe is gekreuziget**   *German* 'My love is crossed'
                              —Anna Sophie, Princess of Anhalt (D. 1704).

90. **Melitae amor**   *Latin* 'Love of Malta'
                              —Rutter.

91. **Mutuo amore cresco**   *Latin* 'By mutual love I grow'
                              —Lindsay.

92. **Nescit amor fines**   *Latin* 'Love knows no end'
                              —Scot (of Vogry).

93. **Nihil amanti durum**   *Latin* 'Nothing difficult to one who loves'
                              —Reid (Bt.).

94. **Nil nequit amor**   *Latin* 'Love can do everything'
                              —Reidheugh.

95. **Omnia vincit amor**   *Latin* 'Love conquers all things'
                   —[Vergil, *Ec.* x. 59.] Bruce (of Mowance), Roderick (of
                              Gateacre).

96. **Pacem amo**   *Latin* 'I love peace'
                   —Columball (Co. Derby), Scot (of Broadmeadows), Scott
                              (of Highchester).

97. **Par l'amour et la fidélité envers la patrie**   *French* 'By love and
    fidelity towards our country'
                              —Order of St. Catharine (Russia).

98. **Patriam amo**   *Latin* 'I love my country'
                              —Scott.

99. **Pax et amor**   *Latin* 'Peace and love'
                              —Hodson (Bt.), Jessop.

100. **Per incerta certus amor**   *Latin* 'A sure love in doubtful circum-
     stances'
                              —Romanis.

101. **Pignus amoris**   *Latin* 'A pledge of love'
                              —Graham (of Douglastown).

102. **Pro amore patriae**   *Latin* 'For love of country'
                              —Scot, Scott.

103. **Qui non patriam amat?** *Latin* 'Who does not love his country?'
—Quinan.

104. **Quos amor et virtus sociant sors nulla resolvet** *Latin* 'Those whom love and virtue unite no fate shall divide'
—Johann Georg II, Prince of Anhalt-Dessau (1627–93).

105. **Quos dedit arcus amor** *Latin* 'The bows which love gave'
—Hamilton (of Colquot).

106. **Se negare est amare** *Latin* 'To love is to deny one's self'
—Roberts.

107. **Sic his qui diligunt** *Latin* 'Thus to those who love'
—Morris.

108. **Signum pacis amor** *Latin* 'Love is the token of peace'
—Bell.

109. **Sine Cerere et Baccho friget Venus** *Latin* 'Without corn and wine love grows cold'
—Longe (of Spixworth).

110. **Spe et amore** *Latin* 'Hope and love'
—Fisher.

111. **Stringit amore** *Latin* 'It binds by love'
—Order of St. Stephen.

112. **Such is love**
—Pateson (U.S.).

113. **Templa, quam dilecta** *Latin* 'Temples, how beloved'
—Buckingham (D.), Nugent (B.), Temple (Bt.), Temple.

114. **Ubi amor ibi fides** *Latin* 'Where there is love there is faith'
—Duckinfield (Bt.), Garratt, Newman (co. Devon, Bt.), Aubrey (co. Hereford).

115. **Verus amor patriae** *Latin* 'The true love of country'
—Hughes (of Wexford).

116. **Vicit amor patriae** *Latin* 'Love of country has conquered'
—Holles.

117. **Vincit amor patriae** *Latin* 'The love of my country exceeds everything'
—Chichester (E.), Cooper, Gun, Hargreaves, James, Molesworth (V.), Muncaster (B.), Pennington.

118. **Vincit amor patriae** *Latin* 'Love of country prevails'
—Sunderland R. D. C., U.K.

119. **Virtute et amore** *Latin* 'By virtue and love'
—McKenzie.

120. **Virtutis amore** *Latin* 'Through love to virtue'
—[Horace, *Ep.* i. 16. 52.] Annesley (E.), Annesley (of
Bletchingdon), Mountmorris (E.), Stephens (of
Tregenna).

121. **Viva la guèrra è l'amor** *Spanish* 'Long live war and love!'
—Franz Albert, Duke of Saxony (1598–1642).

122. **Vive la guerre et l'amor** *French* 'Long live war and love!'
—Rudolf Maximilian, Duke of Saxony (1595–1647).

123. **Vivo et morior pro quibus amo** *Latin* 'I live and die for those
whom I love'
—Chandler (U.S.).

124. **Wheare vertu lys love never dys**
—Thompson.

MAINTENANCE (*See also* CONSERVATION; SUPPORT.)
1. **Je les maintiendrai** *French* 'I will maintain them'
—Biss.

2. **Je maintiendrai** *French* 'I will maintain'
—Kingdom of the Netherlands; Malmesbury (E.), Nesbitt
(of Lismore); William III and Mary, sovereigns of
England.

3. **Je maintiendray** *Old French* 'I shall maintain'
—Hofstra University School of Law, Hempstead, New
York.

4. **Nous maintiendrons** *French* 'We will maintain'
—Suffolk(E.).

5. **Primum vir esto** *Latin* 'First, be a man'
—Baker University, Baldwin City, Kansas.

MANLINESS
1. **Christo et humanitati** *Latin* 'For Christ and humanity'
—Blackburn College, Carlinville, Illinois.

2. **Humani nihil alienum mihi** *Latin* 'Nothing human is alien to
me'
—[after Terence, *Heant.* 77.] Jenings (U.S.).

3. **Nihil humani alienum** *Latin* 'Nothing relating to man is foreign
to me'
—[after Terence, *Heaut.* 77.] Hutchinson (of Whitton).

4. **Our country is the world—our countrymen are all mankind**
   —*Liberator, The* (abolitionist journal, William Lloyd Garrison, editor).

5. **Vir/veritas/vox** *Latin* 'Man/truth/voice'
   —California State Universities and Colleges.

6. **Vir vita terra** *Latin* 'Man, life, earth'
   —Delaware Valley College, Doyleston, Pennsyvania.

MANNER

1. **Doucement, mais fermement** *French* 'Kindly but firmly'
   —Louis.

2. **Efficiency**
   —Henry Ford.

3. **Fortiter in re, et suaviter in modo** *Latin* 'Firmly in act and gently in manner'
   —Beaufort.

4. **Ita** *Latin* 'Thus'
   —Cockburn.

5. **Non modo sed quomodo** *Latin* 'Not now but how'
   —Ellis.

6. **Non quo, sed quo modo** *Latin* 'Not by whom, but in what manner'
   —Howard de Walden (B.), Suffolk (E.), Seaford (B.), Thompson (Bt.).

7. **Now thus!**
   —Trafford (of Trafford Park, Lancashire, Bt.).

8. **Now thus, now thus**
   —Pilkington (Co. Lancaster).

9. **Probando et approbando** *Latin* 'By trying and approving'
   —Ramsay.

10. **Quant je puis** *French* 'However I can'
    —Sherburne (U.S.).

11. **So fork forward**
    —Cunninghame (of Craigends).

12. **Suaviter in modo, fortiter in re** *Latin* 'Gentle in manner, firm in act'
    —Newborough (B.), Nunn, Wynn.

13. **Suaviter in modo fortiter in re** *Latin* 'Gentle in manner, strong in deed'

—General Dwight D. Eisenhower.

MANNERS

1. **Emollit mores nec sinit esse feros** *Latin* 'It softens one's manners and does not allow them to be crude'

—[Ovid, *Ex Ponto*, II. ix. 47.] University of South Carolina at Aiken, Aiken, South Carolina.

2. **Generosus nascitur non fit** *Latin* 'The gentleman is born not made'

—Wharton.

3. **Graves disce mores** *Latin* 'Learn serious manners' *or* 'Graves learn manners'

—Graves (Co. Gloucester).

4. **Ingenuas suscipit artes** *Latin* 'He fosters the polite arts'

—Long (of Carshalton).

5. **Manners makyth man**

—Hood (of Barton Park, Co. Lancaster), Wickham, Wykeham (Bishop of Winchester and Lord Chancellor of England, founder of New College, Oxford, in 1379); New College, Oxford.

6. **Mores fingunt fortunam** *Latin* 'Manners mold fortune'

—Rogerson.

7. **Mores hoc mutato** *Latin* 'Let this change manners'

—Moore.

8. **Mores meliore metallo** *Latin* 'Morals of a better character'

—Smith.

9. **Moribus antiquis** *Latin* 'With ancient manners'

—Throckmorton (Bt.).

10. **Notandi sunt tibi mores** *Latin* 'You must take note of their manners'

—Dallaway.

MEASURE (*See also* LIMITATION.)

1. **Aut omnes aut nullus** *Latin* 'Either all or none'

—Wallace (U.S.).

2. **En! dat Virginia quartum** *Latin* 'Lo! Virginia gives a fourth'

—Virginia Merchants.

3. **Est modus in rebus** *Latin* 'There is a measure in things'
   —Parnell.

4. **Guage and measure**
   —Edminston.

5. **Half is more than the whole**
   —Hillyard.

6. **Lighter than air**
   —Ayre.

7. **Multum in parvo** *Latin* 'Much in little'
   —Rutland C. C., U.K.

8. **Nil dimidium est** *Latin* 'The half is nothing'
   —Heywood.

9. **Non multa sed multum** *Latin* 'Not many, but much'
   —Caswall.

10. **Not too much**
    —Mackinlay.

11. **Numero, pondere, et mensura** *Latin* 'By numbers, weight, and measure'
    —Wren-Hoskyns (Harewood House, Herefordshire).

12. **Par ternis suppar** *Latin* 'A pair more than a match for three'
    —Northwick (B.), Rushout (Bt.).

13. **Paulatim** *Latin* 'By little and little'
    —Hatfield, Scales.

14. **Pende valde** *Latin* 'Weigh well'
    —Penfold.

15. **Poco a poco** *Italian* 'By little and little'
    —Ramage.

16. **Pour trois** *French* 'For three'
    —Latter.

17. **Tout ou rien** *French* 'All or nothing'
    —Adams.

18. **Weigh well**
    —Urquhart, Urquhart (of Byth).

MEMORY (*See also* PAST, THE.)

1. **Carn na cuimhne** *Scots Gaelic* 'The rock of remembrance'
   —Farquharson.

2. **Dolce nella memoria** *Italian* 'Sweet in the memory'
    —Order of Amaranta.

3. **Forget me not**
    —Campbell.

4. **Forget not**
    —Campbell (of Auchinbreck, Bt.).

5. **Haec olim meminisse juvabit** *Latin* 'It will hereafter delight us to remember these things'
    —[Vergil, *Aen.* i. 203.] Lewis.

6. **I beare in minde**
    —Campbell (of Barbreck).

7. **In memoriam majorum** *Latin* 'In remembrance of our ancestors'
    —Farquharson.

8. **I will not forget**
    —Campbell (of Ballochyle).

9. **Je m'en souvien-dray** *Old French* 'I will remember it'
    —Averquerque.

10. **Je me souviendrai** *French* 'I will remember'
    —Tatnall.

11. **Je ne l'oublierai jamais** *French* 'I shall never forget it'
    —Baldwin (U.S.).

12. **Je n'oublierai jamais** *French* 'I will never forget'
    —Bristol (M.), Hervey (Bt.), Hervey (of Killiane).

13. **Je n'oublierai pas** *French* 'I will not forget'
    —Baldwin.

14. **Memento Creatorem** *Latin* 'Remember thy Creator'
    —[Eccles. xii. 1.] Keith.

15. **Memento mei** *Latin* 'Remember me'
    —L'Estrange (of Moystown).

16. **Memento mori** *Latin* 'Remember that you must die'
    —Gumbleton; Order of Death's Head.

17. **Memini** *Latin* 'I remember'
    —Campbell.

18. **Meminisse juvabit** *Latin* 'We shall delight in remembering'
    —[from Vergil *Aeneid*, I. 203] Thomson.

19. **Memorare novissima** *Latin* 'To remember death'
    —Hanford.

20. **Memores fecere merendo**   *Latin* 'Their deserts made them memorable'
> —Richardson.

21. **Memoria pii aeterna**   *Latin* 'The memory of the pious man is eternal'
> —Sudeley (B.), Tracy.

22. **Nec me meminisse pigebit**   *Latin* 'Nor shall I regret to remember'
> —Wynne (Bt.).

23. **Remember**
> —Gavin, Allen, Home (of Wedderburn); Order of the White Rose.

24. **Remember and forget not**
> —Hall (of Jamaica).

25. **Remember the Alamo**
> —Seal of State of Texas.

26. **Remember thy end**
> —Keith (of Ludquhairn).

27. **Remember your oath**
> —Houlton.

28. **Souvenez**   *French* 'Remember'
> —Graham.

MERCY (*See also* KINDNESS.)

1. **Beati misericordes, quoniam ipsis misericordia tribuetur**   *Latin* '*Blessed are the merciful; for unto them mercy shall be granted*'
> —[Matt. v. 7.] Scot's Company.

2. **Clementia et animis**   *Latin* 'By clemency and courage'
> —Panmure (B.), Maule.

3. **Clementia in potentia**   *Latin* 'Clemency in power'
> —Compton.

4. **Clementia tecta rigore**   *Latin* 'Clemency concealed under (apparent) rigor'
> —Maule.

5. **Fortes semper monstrant misericordiam**   *Latin* 'The brave always show mercy'
> —Baldwin.

6. **Have mercy on us, good Lord!**
> —Sitlington (of Wigton).

7. **Inest clementia forti** *Latin* 'Mercy is inherent in the brave'
—Gent, Maule.

8. **In misericordia Dei confido** *Latin* 'I trust in the mercy of God'
—Durand.

9. **Invicta** *Latin* 'Unconquered'
—Kent C. C., U.K.; The Buffs (East Kent Regt.), U.K.;
Queen's Own (Royal West Kent Regiment), U.K.

10. **Invictus** *Latin* 'Unconquered'
—Cracknell.

11. **Invictus maneo** *Latin* 'I remain unconquered'
—Armstrong (of Gallen), Brockett, Ballycumber (of Garry
Castle), Inglis.

12. **Invictus manes** *Latin* 'You remain unconquered'
—Armstrong.

13. **Je loue Dieu grace attendant** *French* 'I praise God expecting
mercy'
—D'Arcy.

14. **Je tans grace** *Old French* 'I have mercy'
—Sir F. Bryan.

15. **Juste et clementer** *Latin* 'With justice and clemency'
—Johann Georg, Elector of Brandenburg (1525–98).

16. **Justitia et clementia** *Latin* 'Justice and mercy'
—Horsford.

17. **Mercie**
—Paterson.

18. **Mercie is my desire**
—Abercrombie.

19. **Mercy**
—Salve Regina = The Newport College, Newport, Rhode
Island.

20. **Mercy is my desire**
—Abercrombie, Laing, Lang, Wishart.

21. **Mirior invictus** *Latin* 'More wonderful unconquered'
—Garvey.

22. **Miserere mei, Deus, secundum magnam misericordiam tuam** *Latin*
'Have mercy on me, O God, after thy great goodness'
—[Ps. li. 1.] On coronet of Garter King-at-Arms.

23. **Miserere mihi Deus** *Latin* 'God be merciful to me'
—Hynde.

24. **Misericordias Domini in aeternum cantabo** *Latin* 'I will sing the mercies of the Lord forever'
—[Ps. lxxxix. 1.] Abingdon School, U.K.

25. **Misericordia temperet gladium** *Latin* 'Let pity moderate the sword'
—Mules.

26. **Nil altum quod non placidum** *Latin* 'Nothing is high which is not also merciful'
—Albert, Count of Schwarzburg-Rudolstadt (1527–1605).

27. **Nunquam victus** *Latin* 'Never conquered'
—Buchanan.

28. **Parcere prostratis** *Latin* 'To spare the fallen'
—Le Hunte.

29. **Parcere subjectis** *Latin* 'To spare the conquered'
—Longfield.

30. **Parcere subjectis et debellare superbos** *Latin* 'To spare the vanquished and subdue the proud'
—[Vergil, *Aen.* vi. 853.] Johann Friedrich, Elector of Saxony (1503–54).

MILITARY DISTINCTION (*See also* REWARD; WAR.)

1. **A la constancia militar premio** *Spanish* 'Reward of military fortitude'
—Order of St. Herminigilde (Spain).

2. **Campi fero praemia belli** *Latin* 'I bear the rewards of the battlefield'
—Campbell (of Skerrington).

3. **Miles et fortis** *Latin* 'A soldier and a brave one'
—Ord.

4. **Munus et monumentum victoriae Spures, 1513** *Latin* 'A reward and remembrance of the victory of Spurs, 1513'
—Longeville-Clarke.

5. **Pro virtute bellica** *Latin* 'For military merit'
—Order of Military Merit, Order of the Legion of Honor (France).

MIND (*See also* KNOWLEDGE; SPIRIT; THOUGHT; WISDOM.)

1. **Aequo adeste animo** *Latin* 'Be present with mind unchangeable'
—Cope (Bt.).

2. **Animis opibusque parati** *Latin* 'Prepared in mind and resources'
—State of South Carolina.

3. **Animo et corpore nitor** *Latin* 'With a strong mind and body'
—Venables.

4. **Animus, non res** *Latin* 'Mind, not circumstance'
—Huth.

5. **Caelum, non animum** *Latin* '(You may change your) climate, but not (your) mind'
—Ashworth, Finlayson, Rhodes, Waldegrave.

6. **Coelum non animum mutat** *Latin* 'Change of climate does not change the mind'
—Ramsden.

7. **Corde mente manu** *Latin* 'With heart, mind, and hand'
—Farie.

8. **Cor nobyle, cor immobyle** *Late Latin* 'A heart noble, a mind determined'
—Hussey, Hunt (of Co. Somerset), Vivian (B.).

9. **Cultus animi quasi humanitatis quidam cibus** *Latin* 'Improvement of the mind is as a kind of food for humanity'
—Havemeyer (U.S.).

10. **Dedicated to training hand, mind, heart**
—Snead State Junior College, Boaz, Alabama.

11. **Ense animus major** *Latin* 'The mind is more powerful than the sword'
—Rymer.

12. **Facies qualis mens talis** *Latin* 'As the face so is the mind'
—Blair (of Balmill).

13. **Fortem posce animum** *Latin* 'Wish for a strong mind'
—[Juvenal, *Sat.* x. 35.] Crampton (Bt.), Fynney, Phillimore, Heriot, Twisleton, Say and Sele (B.).

14. **Fortem post animum** *Latin* 'After a brave mind'
—Heriot.

15. **Head/ Heart/ Hand**
—Bethune-Cookman College, Dayton Beach, Florida.

16. **Induce animum sapientem** *Latin* 'Put on a wise mind'
—Sundial on the porch of a church in Eyam, England.

17. **Ingenium vires superat** *Latin* 'Mind overcomes force'
—Alexander.

18. **Integra mens augustissima possessio** *Latin* 'An honest mind is the most glorious possession'
—Blayney (B.).

19. **Intellectu et innocentia** *Latin* 'By intellect and innocence'
—Headlam.

20. **Libera terra, liberque animus** *Latin* 'A free earth and a free mind'
—Frankland (Bt.).

21. **Lux mentis lux orbis** *Latin* 'Light of the mind, light of the world'
—Sonoma State University, Rohnert Park, California.

22. **Magnus et animus** *Latin* 'And a great mind'
—Ross.

23. **Mens agitat molem** *Latin* 'Mind animates matter'
—Rossall School, U.K.

24. **Mens/ animus/ corpus** *Latin* 'Mind/ soul/ body'
—Colby-Sawyer College, New London, New Hampshire.

25. **Mens conscia recti** *Latin* 'A mind conscious of rectitude'
—Ashbrook (V.), Boulton, Collis, Crisp, Chrisop, Flower, Jary (of Burlingham), Kirsop, Nightingale, Phillips, Macartney (Bt.), Sillifant, Wright, Westmore, Watlington.

26. **Mens cujusque is est quisque** *Latin* 'As the mind of each, so is the man'
—[Cicero, *Rep.* vi. 24, 26.] Cottenham (B.), Leslie (of Surrey), Pepys (Bt.).

27. **Mens et manus** *Latin* 'Mind and hand'
—North Carolina Agricultural and Technical State University, Greensboro, North Carolina.

28. **Mens flecti nescia** *Latin* 'A mind that cannot be bent'
—Hulton.

29. **Mens immota** *Latin* 'A constant mind'
—Shaw.

30. **Mens pristina mansit** *Latin* 'The original mind hath remained'
—Popham (of Littlecott).

31. **Mens sibi conscia recti** *Latin* 'A mind conscious to itself of rectitude'
—Crespyny, Wright (Bt.).

32. **Mente et artificio** *Latin* 'Through mind and skill'
—Ryerson Polytechnical Institute, Toronto, Ontario, Canada.

33. **Mente et labore**   *Latin* 'With mind and labor'
                                    —Lawrence (Bt.).

34. **Mente non Marte**   *Latin* 'By the mind, not by war'
                                    —Locke.

35. **Mentes consciae recti**   *Latin* 'Minds conscious of their rectitude'
                                    —Wylie.

36. **Mentis honestae gloria**   *Latin* 'The glory of an honest mind'
                                    —Grey.

37. **Mind/ Body/ Spirit/ Educating the whole man**
                                    —Oral Roberts University, Tulsa, Oklahoma.

38. **Murus aeneus mens conscia recti**   *Latin* 'A mind conscious of rectitude is a brazen wall'
                                    —Field.

39. **Non opes, sed ingenium**   *Latin* 'Not wealth, but mind'
                                    —Ross.

40. **Non vi sed mente**   *Latin* 'Not by force but by mind'
                                    —Lincolne.

41. **Quid gens sine mente?**   *Latin* 'What would the clan do without mind?'
                                    —Muschamp.

42. **Servare mentem**   *Latin* 'To preserve the mind'
                                    —Seabright.

43. **Sume superbiam quaesitam mentis**   *Latin* 'Assume the pride of mind which you have acquired'
                                    —Seaver.

44. **Tot capita tot sententiae**   *Latin* 'So many heads, so many opinions'
                                    —Fitzalan.

45. **Ultra fert animus**   *Latin* 'The mind bears onwards'
                                    —Durham.

46. **Ut mens cujusque is est quisque**   *Latin* 'As the mind of each, so is each'
                                    —Pepys.

MODERATION (*See also* EQUANIMITY; LIMITATION; PRUDENCE; SELF-CONTROL.)

1. **Constans justitiam moniti**   *Latin* 'Persevering in justice with moderation'
                                    —Russell.

2. **Constitution/ Wisdom/ Justice/ Moderation**
                        —University System of Georgia.

3. **E medio ad mediatorem** *Latin* 'From the middle to the media-
    tor'
                        —Wilhelm, Duke of Saxony (1596–1622).

4. **Est modus** *Latin* 'There is a middle course'
                        —Lister.

5. **Fortiter et suaviter** *Latin* 'Boldly and mildly'
                        —Ogilvie (of Milltoun).

6. **Halt Mas in allem Ding** *German* 'Study moderation in every-
    thing'
                        —Maximilian I, Emperor of Germany (1459–1519).

7. **In medio tutissimus** *Latin* 'In the middle path safest'
                        —Smith (of Lydiate).

8. **In medio tutissimus ibis** *Latin* 'You will go safest in the middle'
                        —Harris.

9. **In moderation placing all my glory**
                        —Fitzhugh.

10. **Inter utrumque** *Latin* 'Between the two'
                        —Connellan.

11. **Inter utrumque tene** *Latin* 'Keep between the two'
                        —Jemmett.

12. **Mediocria firma** *Latin* 'Moderation is safe'
                —Bacon (Bt.), Grimston, Lawder, Lowndes-Stones,
                        Verulam (E.).

13. **Mediocria maxima** *Latin* 'Moderate things are the greatest'
                        —Monins.

14. **Mediocriter** *Latin* 'With moderation'
                        —Moir, Murison.

15. **Medio tutissimus** *Latin* 'Safest in the middle'
                        —Langton (of Fransham, Co. Norfolk).

16. **Medio tutissimus ibis** *Latin* 'The middle course is the safest'
                —[Ovid, *Met.* ii. 237.] Busfield, Senior, Heinrich, Count
                        Reuss zu Schleiz (1563–1616).

17. **Medio tutus** *Latin* 'Safe in the middle'
                        —McMaster.

18. **Moderata durant**   *Latin* 'Moderation endures'
    —Ernst II, Duke of Braunschweig-Grubenhagen
    (1518–67); Julius August, Duke of
    Braunschweig (1578–1617); Moritz Wilhelm,
    Duke of Saxony-Zeitz (1664–1718), Bushe,
    Irvine.

19. **Moderata manent**   *Latin* 'Moderate things remain'
    —Gillespie-Staunton.

20. **Modeste conabor**   *Latin* 'I will attempt moderately'
    —Haggard.

21. **Nec avarus nec profusus**   *Latin* 'Neither greedy nor lavish'
    —Bryan.

22. **Nec cito, nec tarde**   *Latin* 'Neither swiftly nor slowly'
    —Ballantine.

23. **Nec cupias, nec metuas**   *Latin* 'Neither desire nor fear'
    —Hardwicke (E.), York, Yorke (of Erddig).

24. **Nec temere, nec timide**   *Latin* 'Neither rashly nor timidly'
    —Aldworth, Barne, Bent, Blair, Blosse, Bradford (E.),
    Bridgeman, Buckeley (Bt.), Chinnery (Bt.),
    Cleveland (D.), Cotterel (of Hadley), Forbes,
    Guest, Graham, Holden, Ludlow, Milward,
    Mitchell, Munster (E.), Owen, Purvis, Richards,
    Sandford, Simeon (Bt.), Vane, Wakeman (Bt.),
    Walker, Western (B.).

25. **Ne nimium**   *Latin* 'Not too much'
    —Aberdeen (E.), Gordon.

26. **Ne quid nimis**   *Latin* 'Nothing in excess'
    —Christian, Duke of Braunschweig-Lüneburg
    (1566–1633); Philipp V, Count Waldeck
    (1556–67).

27. **Ne quid nimis**   *Latin* 'Not too much of anything'
    —Austen (of Shalford), Drinkwater (of Irwell), Fouler.

28. **Ne supra modum sapere**   *Latin* 'Be not over wise'
    —Newport (Bt.), Nassu.

29. **Ni plus, ni moins**   *French* 'Neither more nor less'
    —Knyvitt.

30. **Pie, juste, temperanter**   *Latin* 'With piety, justice, and moderation'
    —Friedrich IV, Count of the Palatinate (1594–1610).

31. **Quae moderata firma**   *Latin* 'Moderate things are stable'
                                                    —Ogilvy.

32. **Sans charger**   *French* 'Without overloading'
                                                    —Eddisbury, Enery.

33. **Servare modum**   *Latin* 'To keep the mean'
                                                    —Folke, Herne.

34. **Tene mensuram et respice finem**   *Latin* 'Study moderation and consider the end'
                    —Maximilian I, Emperor of Germany (1459–1519).

35. **Violenta nemo imperia continuit diu: Moderata durant**   *Latin* 'A violent rule has been long maintained by no one: moderation endures'
                    —[Seneca, *Troades*, l. 256.] Ernst VI, Count of Mansfeld (1561–1609).

36. **Wisdom, justice, moderation**
                                                    —State of Georgia.

MUSIC

1. **Cum progressu cantus**   *Latin* 'Singing while advancing'
                                                    —Seaton, Seton.

2. **Divina sibi canit**   *Latin* 'She sings divine songs to herself'
                    —Lauchlan, Lachlan, Lochlan, Loghlan.

3. **Dum vivo cano**   *Latin* 'While I live, I sing'
                                                    —Coghill; Rigg.

4. **Excutit inde canit**   *Latin* 'He shakes his wings then sings'
                                                    —Erskine.

5. **Lyrae nervos aptavi**   *Latin* 'I fitted (*or* tuned) the strings of my lyre'
                                                    —Sirr.

6. **Sol, mi, re, fa**
                    —Dr. John Bull, author of *God Save the Queen* (*King*) (temp. Elizabeth I).

7. **Vivens canam**   *Latin* 'I shall yet sing while alive'
                                                    —Morris.

NAME   (*See also* PROPER NAMES.)

1. **A favore regis nomen**   *Latin* 'A name by favor of the king'
                                                    —Kingan, Kinghan.

2. **Concordant nomine facta** *Latin* 'Our deeds agree with our name'
    —Grace (Bt.).

3. **Drogo nomen, et virtus arma dedit** *Latin* 'Drogo is my name, and valor gave me arms'
    —Drew (descendant of the family of Drogo).

4. **Ex arduis perpetuum nomen** *Latin* 'From arduous enterprises an undying name'
    —McCarthy.

5. **Haud nomine tantum** *Latin* 'Not in name alone'
    —Best.

6. **Joannes est nomen ejus** *Latin* 'John is his name'
    —Territory of Puerto Rico.

7. **Le nom, les armes, la loyauté** *French* '(My) name, (my) arms, (my) loyalty'
    —Newland.

8. **Nomen extendere factis** *Latin* 'To perpetuate one's name by deeds'
    —Neeld (Bt.).

9. **Optivo cognomine crescit** *Latin* 'He flourishes under his adopted name'
    —[Horace, *Ep.* iii. 2. 101.] Larpent (Bt.).

10. **Sit nomen decus** *Latin* 'May my name be an honor'
    —Worsley.

11. **Sit vita nomini congrua** *Latin* 'May our life be like our name'
    —Christie.

12. **Stat nominis umbra** *Latin* 'Stands the shadow of a name'
    —Stafford.

NATIONAL MOTTOES

1. **Bhinneka tunggal ika** *Malay* 'Unity through diversity'
    —Republic of Indonesia.

2. **Deo vindice** *Latin* 'God maintains'
    —Great Seal of the Confederate States of America.

3. **Dieu et mon droit**   *French* 'God and my right'
    —Sovereigns of Great Britain (since Henry VI); United
    Kingdom of Great Britain and Northern Ireland;
    Georg Wilhelm, Elector of Brandenburg
    (1595–1640); Sherborne School, U.K. (founded
    1550).

4. **Dios, patria, libertad**   *Spanish* 'God, fatherland and liberty'
    —Dominican Republic.

5. **Dios union y libertad**   *Spanish* 'God, union and liberty'
    —Republic of El Salvador.

6. **Dominus mihi adiutor**   *Latin* 'The Lord is a helper unto me'
    —Kingdom of Denmark.

7. **Freedom and justice**
    —Republic of Ghana.

8. **Happiness and prosperity through unity**   *(from Burmese)*
    —Union of Burma.

9. **Harambee**   *Swahili* 'Together'
    —Republic of Kenya.

10. **If you aid God, he will aid you**   *(from Arabic)*
    —Morocco.

11. **Joannes est nomen ejus**   *Latin* 'John is his name'
    —Territory of Puerto Rico.

12. **Libertad y orden**   *Spanish* 'Liberty and order'
    —Republic of Colombia.

13. **Libertas**   *Latin* 'Liberty'
    —Republic of San Marino; Carbery (B.), Chatteris, Birch
    (Bt.), Evans (of Ash Hall), Evans (Lyng, co. Norfolk),
    Bailey, Gregory, Lewis.

14. **Liberté, egalité, fraternité**   *French* 'Liberty, equality, fraternity'
    —French Republic.

15. **L'union fait la force**   *French* 'Unity is strength'
    —Kingdom of Belgium, Republic of Haiti.

16. **Nomine digna**   *Latin* 'May it be worthy of the name'
    —Rhodesia.

17. **Novus ordo seclorum**   *Latin* 'A new order of the ages'
    —Great Seal of United States of America.

18. **One people, one nation, one destiny**
    —Cooperative Republic Guyana.

19. **One Zambia, one nation**
—Republic of Zambia.
20. **Order, freedom, justice** *(from Arabic)*
—Republic of Tunisia.
21. **Out of many, one people**
—Jamaica.
22. **Paix, travail, patrie** *French* 'Peace, work, fatherland'
—Federal Republic of Cameroon.
23. **Pula** *Tswana* 'Rain'
—Republic of Botswana.
24. **Samoa Muamua le Atua** *Samoan* 'In Samoa, God is first'
—American Samoa.
25. **The land divided, the world united**
—Republic of Panama.
26. **The love of liberty brought us here**
—Republic of Liberia.
27. **The love of the people is my strength**
—Republic of Greece.
28. **Together we aspire, together we achieve**
—Trinidad and Tobago.
29. **Travail, justice, solidarité** *French* 'Work, justice, solidarity'
—Republic of Guinea.
30. **Travail, liberté, patrie** *French* 'Work, freedom, fatherland'
—Republic of Togo.
31. **Uhuru na umoja** *Swahili* 'Liberty and unity'
—United Republic of Tanzania.
32. **Una grande libre** *Spanish* 'One great free (realm)'
—The Spanish State.
33. **Unidad, paz, justicia** *Spanish* 'Unity, peace, justice'
—Republic of Equatorial Guinea.
34. **Union, travail, justice** *French* 'Union, work, justice'
—Gabon Republic.
35. **Unité, dignité, travail** *French* 'Unity, dignity, work'
—Central African Republic.
36. **Unité, travail, justice** *French* 'Unity, work, justice'
—Republic of Upper Volta.
37. **Unité, travail, progrès** *French* 'Unity, work, progress'
—Republic of Chad, Kingdom of Burundi, Republic of Congo.

38. **Uniti progrediemur** *Latin* 'United we shall go forward'
—Gabon Republic.

39. **Unity, freedom, justice**
—Sierra Leone.

40. **Unity and faith**
—Federation of Nigeria.

41. **Unity and freedom**
—Malawi.

42. **Uno avulso, non deficit alter** *Latin* 'When one is torn away another is not wanting'
—Kingdom of Austria.

43. **Un peuple, un but, une foi** *French* 'One people, one goal, one faith'
—Republic of Mali, Republic of Senegal.

44. **Vivit Leo de Tribu Juda** *Latin* 'The Lion of the Tribe of Judah lives'
—Ethiopia.

45. **Workers of all countries, unite!**
—Union of Soviet Socialist Republics.

46. **Zo kwe zo** *Sangho* 'All men are equal'
—Central African Republic.

NAVIGATION (*See also* DIRECTION; SEA.)
1. **Row and retake**
—Riddell.

2. **Sail through**
—Hamilton (of Rosehill).

3. **Trade and navigation**
—Royal Exchange Assurance.

4. **Velis et remis** *Latin* 'With sails and oars'
—Haynes.

NECESSITY
1. **Faut être** *French* 'It must be'
—Mumbee.

2. **Porro unum est necessarium** *Latin* 'Moreover one thing is needful'
—Cowley (B.), Mornington (E.), Wellesley (M.).

3. **Thus thou must do if thou have it**

         —Siddons.

NOBILITY (*See also* GOODNESS; PRINCELINESS; RIGHTEOUSNESS; ROYALTY; STATUS; VIRTUE.)

1. **Animus est nobilitas**   *Latin* 'The soul is the nobility'

         —Cobham.

2. **A tenir promesse vient de noblesse**   *French* 'To keep promise comes from nobleness'

         —Nevill (Lord Abergavenny).

3. **C'est la seule vertu qui donne la noblesse**   *French* 'Virtue alone confers nobility'

         —Greame (Co. York).

4. **Cor nobyle, cor immobyle**   *Late Latin* 'A heart noble, a mind determined'

         —Hussey, Hunt (of Co. Somerset), Vivian (B.).

5. **Est nobilis ira leonis**   *Latin* 'The rage of the lion is noble'

         —Stuart.

6. **Fortior quo rectior**   *Latin* 'Stronger only as much as one is nobler'

         —Sargent (U.S.).

7. **Illustribus et nobilitati**   *Latin* 'For the illustrious and the ennobled'

         —Order of the Lion of Lembourg.

8. **Ira leonis nobilis**   *Latin* 'The anger of the lion is noble'

         —Croome.

9. **La vertu est la seule noblesse**   *French* 'Virtue is the only nobility'

         —Guildford (E.), North.

10. **Nobilis est ira leonis**   *Latin* 'The wrath of the lion is noble'

         —Inglis (Bt.), Inglis (of Stewart, Buchanan, etc.), Broome.

11. **Nobilis ira**   *Latin* 'Noble in anger'

         —Creighton-Stuart, Stewart (of Tillicoultry, bt.).

12. **Nobilis ira leonis**   *Latin* 'The lion's anger is noble'

         —Ross.

13. **Nobilitas est sola virtus**   *Latin* 'Virtue is the only nobility'

         —Thackeray.

14. **Nobilitas unica virtus**   *Latin* 'Virtue is the only nobility'

         —Steward (of Nottingham).

15. **Nobilitat**   *Latin* 'It ennobles us'

         —Houghton.

16. **Nobilitatis virtus non stemma character**   *Latin* 'Virtue, not pedigree, should characterize nobility'
—Freshfield (of Stoke Newington), Westminster (M.).

17. **Noblesse oblige**   *French* 'Nobility compels'
—Duke of Lévis (France).

18. **Posse nolle nobile**   *Latin* 'To be able (but) unwilling is noble' *or* 'To be able to refuse (to do a bad action) is noble'
—Wingfield (of Tickencote).

19. **Pugilem claraverat**   *Latin* 'He had ennobled the champion'
—Newle.

20. **Sic cuncta nobilitat**   *Latin* 'Thus he ennobles all'
—Henderson.

21. **Sola nobilitas virtus**   *Latin* 'Virtue is the only nobility'
—Abercorn (M.), Blake (of Menlo, Bt.), Standish.

22. **Sola nobilitat virtus**   *Latin* 'Virtue alone ennobles'
—Hamilton (of Silverton), Hill (Bt.), Mowbray.

23. **Sola virtus nobilitat**   *Latin* 'Virtue alone ennobles'
—Henderson (Bt.).

24. **Sola virtus reddit nobilem**   *Latin* 'Virtue alone renders noble'
—Storey.

25. **The noblest motive is the public good**
—Bantry (E.), White.

26. **Timor Dei nobilitas**   *Latin* 'The fear of God is nobility'
—Lempriére.

27. **Tugendt macht Edel**   *German* 'Virtue confers nobility'
—Friedrich IV, Count of the Palatinate (1594–1610).

28. **Virtus et nobilitas**   *Latin* 'Virtue and nobility'
—Henvill, Llewellin.

29. **Virtus nobilitat**   *Latin* 'Virtue ennobles'
—Order of the Belgic Lion for Civil Merit; Gwinnett, Henderson.

30. **Virtus nobilitat honoremque parit**   *Latin* 'Virtue ennobles and brings honor'
—Friedrich, Duke of Schleswig-Holstein and Norburg (1581–1658).

31. **Virtus nobilitat omnia**   *Latin* 'Virtue ennobles all things'
—Stetson (U.S.).

32. **Virtus omnia nobilitat**   *Latin* 'Virtue ennobles all things'
—Herrick, Heyrick, Eyrick.

33. **Virtus sola nobilitas** *Latin* 'Virtue is the only nobility'
—Blake (of Menlo, bt.), Throckmorton (Bt.).

34. **Virtus sola nobilitat** *Latin* 'Virtue alone ennobles'
—Caddle, Blake (of Furbough), Henrison, Wallscourt (B.),
Watson.

35. **Virtus vera nobilitas** *Latin* 'Virtue is true nobility'
—Henville.

36. **Virtus vera nobilitas est** *Latin* 'Virtue is true nobility'
—Mather (U.S.).

37. **Virtuti si vis nobilis esse stude** *Latin* 'If you will be noble strive
after virtue'
—Friedrich IV, Count of the Palatinate (1594–1610).

NOURISHMENT

1. **Alis nutrior** *Latin* 'I am fed by my wings'
—Simpson (of Udock).

2. **Auctor** *Latin* 'The nurturer'
—Hines (U.S.).

3. **Feed ye my sheep**
—Shepherd.

4. **Non solum pane** *Latin* 'Not by bread alone'
—Drisdale.

5. **Pectore non venis** *Latin* 'With breasts, not with veins'
—Chilton.

6. **Quis preparet corvo escam suam?** *Latin* 'Who can prepare his
food for the ravens?'
—Ravens.

7. **Recreat et alit** *Latin* 'It amuses and nourishes'
—Duddingstoun.

8. **Ubique fecundat imber** *Latin* 'Everywhere the rain fertilizes'
—Higginbottom.

OBEDIENCE (*See also* FOLLOWING.)

1. **Ad aras usque obsequens** *Latin* 'Obedient as far as the altar' i.e.,
'obedience has its limits'
—Friedrich Wilhelm, Duke of Mecklenberg-Schwerin
(1675–1713).

2. **Amor et obedientia**   *Latin* 'Love and obedience'
—Painters' Company.

3. **Amorque et obedientia**   *Latin* 'Both love and obedience'
—Painters' Company.

4. **An obedient wife governs her husband**
—Harleyford, Buckinghamshire, England.

5. **Bound to obey and serve**
—Jane Seymour, 3rd wife of Henry VIII.

6. **By command of our superiors**
—Waterman's Company, London.

7. **Deo parere libertas**   *Latin* 'Obedience to God is liberty'
—Georg Wilhelm, Elector of Brandenburg (1595–1640).

8. **Nisi paret imperat**   *Latin* 'Unless he obeys, he commands'
—Bernard.

9. **Obey and rule**
—Loades.

10. **Pareo, non servo**   *Latin* 'I am obedient, not servile'
—Jenkinson (Bt.).

11. **Parere subjectus**   *Latin* 'To obey when subject'
—Glasgow.

12. **Propter obedientiam**   *Latin* 'On account of obedience'
—Hay.

13. **Rebellion to tyrants is obedience to God**
—Thomas Jefferson.

14. **Semper parere**   *Latin* 'To be obedient always'
—Hanson.

15. **Vocatus obedivi**   *Latin* 'I obeyed when called'
—Gell.

OBSCURITY (*See also* DARKNESS.)

1. **Imperium in imperio**   *Latin* 'A government within another'
—Wetherby R. D. C., U.K.

2. **Ingenium innumerata labi**   *Latin* 'My disposition is to glide along unnoticed'
—Lawrie.

3. **Lateat scintillula forsan**   *Latin* 'Some spark may perhaps lurk unseen'
—Royal Humane Society, U.K.

4. **Latet anguis in herba** *Latin* 'The snake lurks in the grass'
                                                    —Anguish.

5. **Manet alta mente repostum** *Latin* 'Deep in the heart it remains hidden'
                        —[Vergil, *Aen.* i. 26.] Ulrich, Duke of Württemberg
                                                    (1487–1550).

6. **Modico angetur modicum** *Latin* 'The smaller the less exposed'
                                                    —Williamson.

7. **Nec obscura, nec ima** *Latin* 'Neither obscure nor low'
                                                    —Law (of Burntoun).

8. **Nec parvis sisto** *Latin* 'I do not continue in obscurity'
                        —De Bathe (Bt.), De Burgh (of West Drayton).

9. **Non obscura nec ima** *Latin* 'Neither obscure nor very low'
                                                    —Law.

10. **Occultus non extinctus** *Latin* 'Hidden, not extinguished'
                                                    —Tytler.

11. **Quod improbum terret probo prodest** *Latin* 'To the dread and terror of the bad and to the reward of the good'
                                                    —Penzance B. C., U.K.

12. **Sub tegmine** *Latin* 'Under cover'
                                                    —Gordon.

13. **Sub tegmine fagi** *Latin* 'Under the cover of the beech'
                                                    —Beaufoy, Beech.

OFFICE

1. **In officio impavidus** *Latin* 'Fearless in office'
                                                    —Falshaw.

2. **Magistratus indicat virum** *Latin* 'Office shows the man'
                        —[after Sophocles, *Antigone*, 175–7.] Lonsdale (E.),
                                                    Lowther.

3. **Shenichun (Shenachie) Erin** *Gaelic* 'The historian of Erin'
                                                    —McCarthy.

4. **Toutz foitz chevalier** *Old French* 'Always a knight'
                                                    —Rideout.

OFFSPRING

1. **Bi'se mac na slaurie** *Scots Gaelic* 'Be thou the son of the crook'
                                                    —M'Laurin.

2. **Enfans du roy**   *French* 'Children of the king'
> —Infantleroy.

3. **Non generant aquilae columbas**   *Latin* 'Eagles do not beget doves'
> —Lempriere, Rodney (B.).

4. **Postera crescam laude**   *Latin* 'I will flourish in the praise of my descendants'
> —University of Melbourne, Melbourne, Australia.

5. **Pro prole semper**   *Latin* 'For my offspring ever'
> —Pendock.

6. **Reges creantur regibus**   *Latin* 'Kings are born of kings'
> —Friedrich August I, Elector of Saxony (1670–1733).

7. **Virtute et robore**   *Latin* 'By virtue and strength'
> —Borough (Co. Salop), Pillans (of East Dereham, co. Norfolk).

OPPORTUNITY   (*See also* POSSIBILITY.)

1. **Carpe diem**   *Latin* 'Seize the present opportunity'
> —[Horace, *Od.* i. 11.] Clarke, Berns, Paynter, Langford, Webster.

2. **Carpe diem postero ne crede**   *Latin* 'Seize the present opportunity, trust not to the future'
> —[after Horace, *Odes*, I. xi. 8.] Cutting (U.S.).

3. **Copiosè et opportunê**   *Latin* 'Plentifully and opportunely'
> —Bunting.

4. **Fortune and opportunity forever**
> —O'Mulloy.

5. **Occasionem cognosce**   *Latin* 'Recognize the opportunity'
> —Lowell (U.S.).

6. **Opportunity for all**
> —Kalamazoo Valley Comunity College, Kalamazoo, Michigan.

7. **Opportunity through training**
> —State Area Vocational-Technical Schools System, Tennessee.

8. **Optime quod opportune**   *Latin* 'What is done opportunely is best'
> —Campbell.

9. **Patet ingeniis campus**   *Latin* 'The field lies open to talent'
> —Tucker.

10. **Post est occasio calva**   *Latin* 'Occasion is bald behind'
—[from Dionysius, *Cato Distictiorum de Moribus* ii. 6. 26.]
Chapman.

11. **Service/ Opportunity/ Community/ Learning**
—Wayne County Community College, Detroit, Michigan.

12. **Stat sua cuique dies**   *Latin* 'Each has his day'
—Windley.

13. **To match job opportunities with job skills**
—Indiana Vocational Technical College.

OPPOSITION (*See also* DEFIANCE.)

1. **Contra audentior**   *Latin* 'Bolder, being opposed'
—Mount Stephen (B.).

2. **Defying ye field**
—Cowen.

3. **Dhandeon co heiragh ali**   *Scots Gaelic* 'In spite of who would gainsay'
—McDonald.

4. **Durum contra stimulum calcitrare**   *Latin* 'It is hard to kick against the pricks'
—[Acts, ix. 5.] Heinrich Julius, Duke of Braunschweig-
Wolfenbüttel (1564–1613); abbreviated form, D. C.
S. C., used by Julius Ernst, Duke of Braunschweig-
Lüneburg-Danneberg (1571–1636).

5. **Haec inimica tyrannis**   *Latin* 'These are adverse to tyrants'
—Riversdale.

6. **Nihil obstabit eunti**   *Latin* 'Nothing shall oppose him as he goes'
—Arden.

7. **Nil sistere contra**   *Latin* 'Nothing to oppose us'
—Nicolson (of Carnock), Stewart (of Greenock).

8. **Per il suo contrario**   *Italian* 'By its opposite'
—Anglesea (M.), Paget.

9. **Per tela per hostes**   *Latin* 'Through arrows and enemies'
—Brymer.

10. **Plus spinis quam ferro**   *Latin* 'More by thorns than the sword'
—Richardson.

11. **Rebellion to tyrants is obedience to God**
—Thomas Jefferson.

12. **Solus mihi invidus obstat** *Latin* 'Only the envious one withstands me'
—Nott.

13. **Tu ne cede me** *Latin* 'Yield not to me'
—Steere.

OPPRESSION

1. **Crescit sub pondere virtus** *Latin* 'Virtue thrives beneath oppression'
—Chapman (Bt.), Chapman (of Whitby), Denbigh (E.), Fielding, Seys, Slatter (of Chesterfield).

2. **Il n'y a rien, que soit plus difficile aux hommes, que d'estre tyrannisé en leur croyance** *French* 'Nothing is so difficult for men as to be tyrannized over in their belief'
—Ludwig the Elder, Prince of Anhalt-Köthen (1579–1650).

3. **Inimica tyrannis** *Latin* 'Unfriendly to tyrants'
—Shubrick (U.S.).

4. **Nec opprimere, nec opprimi** *Latin* 'Neither to oppress nor be oppressed'
—Sneyd (of Ashcomb), Kynnersley.

5. **Obdurum adversus urgentia** *Latin* 'Resolute against oppression'
—Bothwell (B.), Bothwell (of Gleneorse).

6. **Premi, non opprimi** *Latin* 'To be pressed, not oppressed'
—Bennet.

7. **Sic semper tyrannis** *Latin* 'Thus always to tyrants'
—State of Virginia.

ORDER (*See also* DISCIPLINE.)

1. **Cadernid, cyfiawnder, cynnydd** *Welsh* 'Stability, justice, progress'
—Barry B. C., U.K.

2. **Hanfod tref trefn** *Welsh* 'The essence of a (good) town is orderliness'
—Ammanford U. D. C., U.K.

3. **Hinc ordo, hinc copia rerum** *Latin* 'Hence order, hence abundance'
—Cardinal Mazarin (1602–61).

4. **Libertad y orden** *Spanish* 'Liberty and order'
—Republic of Colombia.

5. **Novus ordo seclorum** *Latin* 'A new order of the ages'
   —Great Seal of United States of America.

6. **Order, freedom, justice** *(from Arabic)*
   —Republic of Tunisia.

7. **Per stabilitas et per fortitudo** *Latin* 'Through stability and strength'
   —Holmes (U.S.).

8. **Sit ordo in omnibus** *Latin* 'Let there be order in all things'
   —De Teissier.

ORIGIN

1. **Dum spiro caelestia spero** *Latin* 'While I have breath I hope heavenly things'
   —Jones (of Thurston).

2. **Fons et origo** *Latin* 'The fountain and source'
   —La Fountaine (Bt.).

3. **Haec origo** *Latin* 'This origin'
   —Balnaves.

4. **Hinc origo** *Latin* 'Hence our origin'
   —Balnaves.

5. **Ipse fecit nos** *Latin* 'He himself made us'
   —Ronan.

6. **Meae memor originis** *Latin* 'Mindful of my origin'
   —Manson.

7. **Primus e stirpe** *Latin* 'The first from the stock'
   —Hay (of Leys, Co. Perth).

8. **Qui fugit molam fugit farinam** *Latin* 'He who shuns the mill, shuns the flour'
   —Coopers' Company, Exeter.

9. **Ramis micat radix** *Latin* 'The root glitters in its branches'
   —Robertson.

10. **Unde derivatur?** *Latin* 'Whence is it derived?'
    —Bloxholme.

PARADISE *(See also* SALVATION.*)*

1. **Affectat Olympo** *Latin* 'He aspires to heaven'
   —Bell.

2. **Caelestem spero coronam**   *Latin* 'I hope for a heavenly crown'
    —Blake-Humfrey.

3. **Caelestes pandite portae**   *Latin* 'Open, ye celestial gates'
    —Gibson.

4. **Caelestia canimus**   *Latin* 'We sing of heavenly things'
    —Hutchinson, Synge (Bt.).

5. **Caelestia sequor**   *Latin* 'I follow heavenly things'
    —McDonald, Monro.

6. **Caelitus mihi vires**   *Latin* 'My strength from heaven'
    —Ranelagh (V.).

7. **Caelitus vires**   *Latin* 'Strength from heaven'
    —Mallet.

8. **Caelum, non solum**   *Latin* 'Heaven, not earth'
    —Hayman (of South Abbey), Stevenson (of Newcastle-on-Tyne).

9. **Caelum quod quaerimus ultra**   *Latin* 'Heaven, which we seek beyond'
    —Godman

10. **Caelum versus**   *Latin* 'Heavenward'
    —Dickson.

11. **Certior in caelo domus**   *Latin* 'A surer home in heaven'
    —Adams.

12. **Coeli favore**   *Latin* 'By the favor of the heavens'
    —Roxburgh.

13. **Coelum ipsum petimus**   *Latin* 'We aim at heaven itself'
    —Hoste, Sawtell.

14. **Coelumque tueri**   *Latin* 'And look to heaven'
    —Ball (U.S.).

15. **Coelum tueri**   *Latin* 'Look to heaven'
    —Ball (U.S.).

16. **Collocet in caelis nos omnes vis Michaelis**   *Latin* 'May Michael's strength place us all in heaven'
    —Linlithgow (Scotland).

17. **Denique caelo fruar**   *Latin* 'I shall enjoy heaven at last'
    —Melville.

18. **Denique caelum**   *Latin* 'Heaven at last'
    —Beswicke, Bonar, Melvill (E.), Melvill, Melvile (of Raith).

19. **Denique sursum** *Latin* 'Upwards at last'
—Melvil.

20. **Divini gloria ruris** *Latin* 'The glory of the heavenly abode'
—[Vergil, *Geor.* i. 168.] Foster.

21. **E coelo lux mea** *Latin* 'My light is from heaven'
—Guille.

22. **E terra ad coelum** *Latin* 'From earth to heaven'
—Frost.

23. **Firmitas in caelo** *Latin* 'Stability in heaven'
—St. George (Bt.), Maher.

24. **Firmitas in caelo, stabilitas in terra** *Latin* 'Firmness in heaven, stability on earth'
—St. George.

25. **Forti favet caelum** *Latin* 'Heaven favors the brave'
—Oswald.

26. **Hac Iter Elysium nobis** *Latin* 'Here is our journey to Elysium'
—[Vergil, *Aen.* VI. 542.] Drayton (U.S.).

27. **Heaven's light our guide**
—Order of the Star of India (founded 1861); Portsmouth City and C. B. C., U.K.

28. **Hinc usque superna venabor** *Latin* 'Henceforth I will follow after heavenly things'
—Murray (of Philliphaugh, Danesfield, etc.).

29. **In altum** *Latin* 'Toward heaven'
—Alstone.

30. **In caelo confidemus** *Latin* 'We will trust in heaven'
—Hills.

31. **In caelo quies** *Latin* 'There is rest in heaven'
—Bewicke, Boscawen, Coldham, Dolphin (of Eyford), Horlock.

32. **In caelo spes mea est** *Latin* 'My hope is in heaven'
—Micklethwaite.

33. **In coelo spero** *Latin* 'I hope in heaven'
—Miller.

34. **In heaven is all my trust**
—Ambrose.

35. **In heaven is my hope**
—Huggard.

36. **In monte Cöeli castra Cöli** *Latin* 'On the hill of heaven is the camp of Cöel'
—Kelly.

37. **In solo regit qui degit in coelo** *Latin* 'He who lives in heaven rules on earth'
—Russell.

38. **Lumen coeleste sequamur** *Latin* 'May we follow heavenly inspiration'
—Beatie.

39. **Manent optima coelo** *Latin* 'The best things await us in heaven'
—Miller (of Glenlee, Bt.), Miller (of Collierswood).

40. **Maturus coelo non cadit ante diem** *Latin* 'He who is ripe for heaven falls not before his day'
—Bliss.

41. **Mihi coelum portus** *Latin* 'Heaven is my haven'
—Bruges.

42. **Mon repos est au ciel** *French* 'My rest is in heaven'
—Elisabeth Charlotte, Consort of Georg Wilhelm, Elector of Brandenburg (1597–1660).

43. **M. R. E. A. C. (Mon repos est au ciel)** *French* 'My rest is in heaven'
—Ludwig Philipp, Count of the Palatinate of Simmern (1602–54).

44. **Oculis in coelum** *Latin* 'The eye in heaven'
—Eye B. C., U.K.

45. **O lector salve celi pateant tibi valve** *Latin* 'Greeting, reader! May heaven's doors open to thee'
—Haverfordwest B. C., U.K.

46. **Pandite, coelestes portae** *Latin* 'Open, heavenly gates!'
—Gibson (of Durie).

47. **Paradisus in sole** *Latin* 'Paradise in the sun'
—Hubbard (U.S.).

48. **Paratus ad aethera** *Latin* 'Prepared for heaven'
—Falconer.

49. **Per coeli favorem** *Latin* 'By the favor of heaven'
—Cowie.

50. **Per crucem ad castra** *Latin* 'Through the cross to the camp'
—Davies.

51. **Per crucem ad stellas** *Latin* 'By the cross to heaven'
—Legard (Bt.).

52. **Per ecclesiam ad coelum** *Latin* 'Through the church to heaven'
—Eccles.

53. **Powys Paradwys Cymru** *Welsh* 'Powys, paradise of Wales'
—Montgomeryshire C. C., U.K.

54. **Quae supra** *Latin* 'What things are above'
—Roberts.

55. **Quae sursum volo videre** *Latin* 'I wish to see heavenly things'
—Dunraven (E.), Macqueen, Quin.

56. **Ros coeli** *Latin* 'The dew of heaven'
—Roskell (Co. Flint, Lancaster, and York).

57. **Sancta clavis coeli fides** *Latin* 'The sacred key of heaven is faith'
—Sankey.

58. **Semper sidera votum** *Latin* 'The heavens always my wish'
—Rattray.

59. **Sic itur in altum** *Latin* 'This is the way to heaven'
—Cowan.

60. **Sic vivere vivetis** *Latin* 'Thus you shall live, to live (hereafter)'
—Bunce.

61. **Strength is from heaven**
—Grubb, Whitson.

62. **Superna sequor** *Latin* 'I follow heavenly things'
—Ramsay (of Methven), Wardrop (of Strathavon).

63. **Tendimus ad coelum** *Latin* 'We press forward to heaven'
—McCowan.

64. **Vive ut postea vivas** *Latin* 'So live that you may live hereafter'
—Frazer, Johnston (of Johnston, Bt.), Johnston.

PARENTS (*See also* ANCESTRY.)

1. **Ave Mater Angliae** *Latin* 'Hail, Mother of England'
—Canterbury City and C. B. C., U.K.

2. **Mon Mam Cymru** *Welsh* 'Anglesey, mother of Wales'
—Anglesey C. C., U.K.

3. **Pietas parentum** *Latin* 'Filial affection'
—St. Edward's School, Oxford, U.K.

4. **Salve magna parens** *Latin* 'Hail, great parent'
—Lichfield City Council, U.K.

5. **Tanti talem genuere parentes**   *Latin* 'Such parents have produced such a man'
—[Vergil, *Aen.* i. 606.] Moray (of Abercairny).

PAST, THE (*See also* ANCESTRY; TIME.)

1. **Adhuc hic hesterna**   *Latin* 'The things of yesterday are still with us'
—Chichester R. D. C., U.K.

2. **Comme je fus**   *French* 'As I was'
—More (Co. Lancaster), Ward (E.).

3. **Fuimus**   *Latin* 'We have been'
—Ailesbury (M.), Bruce, Elgin (E.), Sanford, Kennedy, Were (of Wellington), Evers.

4. **Fuimus et sumus**   *Latin* 'We were and we are'
—Whitby U. D. C., U.K.

5. **Look to the past**
—Jones.

6. **Nescit abolere vetustas**   *Latin* 'Antiquity cannot abolish it'
—Oughton.

7. **Ni diothlaith rightear Seanchus le h-aimsir**   *Gaelic* 'History is not destroyed by time'
—Conroy (of Llanbrynmair, Montgomeryshire, and of Bettifield, Co. Roscommon, Bt.).

8. **Olim fecimus**   *Latin* 'We did so at one time'
—Saward, Seward.

9. **Olim sic erat**   *Latin* 'Thus it was formerly'
—Hood.

10. **Respicio sine luctu**   *Latin* 'I look back without sorrow'
—Dendy.

11. **Super antiquas vias**   *Latin* 'Upon the ancient tracks'
—Thorp.

12. **Ut olim**   *Latin* 'As formerly'
—Kinlock (of Couland).

13. **Vitâ posse priore frui**   *Latin* 'To be able to enjoy the recollections of our former life'
—[Martial, 10. 23.] Townsend.

PATIENCE (*See also* ACCEPTANCE; EQUANIMITY; SELF-CONTROL; SUFFERING.)

1. **Attendez**   *French* 'Wait'
                                        —Boyes (of Scotland).

2. **Attendez vouz**   *French* 'Wait patiently'
                                        —Boys, Boyes.

3. **Bide your time**
                                        —Bellwood.

4. **Cuivis dolori remedium est patientia**   *Latin* 'Patience is a cure for every grief'
                            —Ernst, Margrave of Brandenburg (1617–42).

5. **Dulce amarum patientia**   *Latin* 'Patience is a bitter-sweet'
                        —Wilhelm V, Duke of Bavaria (1548–1626).

6. **Durum patientia frango**   *Latin* 'I overcome hardships by patience'
                            —Crawford, Moore, Muir, Mure.

7. **Durum patientia mollit**   *Latin* 'Patience softens hardship'
                    —Christian Günther the Elder, Count of Schwarzburg and
                                        Hohenstein (1578–1642).

8. **Durum patientia vincit**   *Latin* 'Patience conquers hardship'
                —Otto the Younger, Duke of Braunschweig-Lüneburg-
                                        Harburg (1528–1603).

9. **En attendant patience**   *French* 'Meanwhile patience'
                    —Eleonore Dorothee, Duchess of Saxony-Weimar
                                        (1602–64).

10. **Fide patientia labore**   *Latin* 'By faith, patience, and work'
                                        —Pilter.

11. **Gaudet patientia duris**   *Latin* 'Patience rejoices in hardships'
                                —Grimond, O'Mallun.

12. **Have patience and endure**
                                        —Rushton.

13. **I abide my time**
                                        —Pennefather.

14. **I byde**
                                        —Taylor-Gordon.

15. **I byde it**
                                —Nisbet (Bt.), Nisbett.

16. **I byde my time**
            —Campbell (of Auchmannock), Crawfurd (of Newfield).

17. **I'll bide**
—Broadalbine Maxwell (of Teylling).

18. **Innocenter patienter constanter** *Latin* 'Innocently, patiently, steadfastly'
—Stillé (U.S.).

19. **Levius fit patientia** *Latin* 'It is rendered lighter by patience'
—Burgess, Gloster.

20. **Patience**
—Dow, Dowie.

21. **Patience and resolution**
—Muterer.

22. **Patience makes everything light**
—Lamb.

23. **Patience passe par tout** *French* 'Patience achieves all things'
—Elisabeth, Duchess of Saxony (1593–1650).

24. **Patience passe science** *French* 'Patience surpasses knowledge'
—Boscawen, Falmouth (E.).

25. **Patiens** *Latin* 'Patient'
—Dow.

26. **Patiens pulveris atque solis** *Latin* 'Patient of dust and sun'
—[Horace, *Od.* i. 8. 4.] Floyd (Bt.).

27. **Patienter** *Latin* 'Patiently'
—Bullman.

28. **Patienter et constanter** *Latin* 'Patiently and steadfastly'
—Christian Günther, the Younger, Count of Schwarzburg and Hohenstein (1616–66).

29. **Patientia casus exsuperat omnes** *Latin* 'Patience masters all chances'
—Askew.

30. **Patientia et magnanimitas** *Latin* 'Patience and courage'
—Kirby.

31. **Patientia et perseverantia** *Latin* 'With patience and perseverance'
—Dent (Co. York).

32. **Patientia et perseverantia cum magnanimitate** *Latin* 'Patience and perseverance with magnanimity'
—Fellows.

33. **Patientia et spe** *Latin* 'With patience and hope'
—Duiguid, Duniguid.

34. **Patientia victrix** *Latin* 'Patience is victorious'
—Dalton.

35. **Patientiâ vinces** *Latin* 'By patience you will conquer'
—Arden, Alvanley (B.).

36. **Patientia vincit** *Latin* 'Patience conquers'
—Chein or Cheyne, Gall, Lindesay (of Warmiston), Napier (of Tayock), Nafleur.

37. **Patientia vincit omnes** *Latin* 'Patience conquers all men'
—Friedrich Wilhelm, Elector of Brandenburg (1620–88).

38. **Patientia vincit omnia** *Latin* 'Patience conquers all things'
—Friedrich Christoph, Count of Mansfeld (1564–1631);
Anna Sophie, Landgravine of Hesse (1638–83);
Christian, Duke of Wohlau (1618–72).

39. **Patientia vinco** *Latin* 'I conquer by patience'
—Thompson.

40. **Pour qui sait attendre** *French* 'For he who knows how to wait'
—Mitchell (U.S.).

41. **Pro patria vivere et mori** *Latin* 'To live and die for our country'
—Grattan.

42. **Prudens qui patiens** *Latin* 'He is prudent who is patient'
—Coke, Leicester (E.), Lushington (of Pool and Kent).

43. **Tandem patientia victrix** *Latin* 'Patience conquers in the end'
—August, Duke of Braunschweig-Wolfenbüttel (1579–1666).

44. **Tempus et patientia** *Latin* 'Time and patience'
—Bradbury (Co. Essex).

45. **Victrix patientia** *Latin* 'Patience conquers'
—Gordon.

46. **Victrix patientia duris** *Latin* 'Patience is victorious in hardship'
—Carter.

47. **Vince malum patientia** *Latin* 'Overcome evil with patience'
—Lee, Townshend.

48. **Virtus patientia veritas** *Latin* 'Virtue, patience, truth'
—Johnson.

PATRIOTISM (*See also* COUNTRY; DEVOTION.)

1. **Academic—Vocational—Cultural—Patriotic—Spiritual**
—The School of the Ozarks, Point Lookout, Missouri.

2. **All for our country**
   —State of Nevada.

3. **Amor dulcis patriae** *Latin* 'The love of dear homeland'
   —Wigram.

4. **Amore patriae** *Latin* 'By patriotism'
   —Scott.

5. **Amor patriae vincit** *Latin* 'The love of country conquers'
   —Meyler.

6. **Amor vincit patriae** *Latin* 'The love of country conquers'
   —Gibbes (U.S.).

7. **Cara patria carior libertas** *Latin* 'Dear country, dearer liberty'
   —Clinton (U.S.).

8. **Decorum pro patria mori** *Latin* 'It is honorable to die for our country'
   —[after Horace, *Odes* III. ii. 13.] Ellis.

9. **Ducit amor patriae** *Latin* 'Patriotism leads me'
   —Blades, Philipps (Bt.), Philipps (of Dale Castle), Lechmere (of Rhyd, Co. Worcester, bt.).

10. **Dulce est pro patria mori** *Latin* 'It is sweet to die for one's country'
    —[after Horace, *Odes* III. 2. 13.] Van Rensselaer (U.S.).

11. **Dulcis amor patriae** *Latin* 'The love of one's country is sweet'
    —Clifford, Fitzwygram (Bt.), Robinson.

12. **El rey y la patria** *Spanish* 'King and country'
    —Order of St. Ferdinand.

13. **Emeritus** *Latin* 'I have served my country'
    —Emeris (of Louth, Co. Lincoln).

14. **For my country**
    —Jobling.

15. **Haec manus ob patriam** *Latin* 'This hand for my country'
    —Mactier, Shuckburgh (Bt.).

16. **He serves his party best who serves his country best**
    —Rutherford B. Hayes.

17. **L'homme vrai aime son pays** *French* 'The true man loves his country'
    —Homfray (Co. Stafford).

18. **My king and country**
    —Tyler.

19. **My prince and my country**

—Harris (B.).

20. **Natale solum dulce**   *Latin* 'Our native soil is sweet'
    —Taylor (of Todmorden Hall, Co. Lancaster, and Burghfield, Co. Berks).

21. **Nil nisi patria**   *Latin* 'Nothing without one's country'
    —Hindmarsh.

22. **Nomine et patriae asto**   *Latin* 'I stand by in name and for (my) country'
    —Fay (U.S.).

23. **Non mihi sed patriae**   *Latin* 'Not for myself, but for my country'
    —Hippisley (Co. Berks, Bt.), Spring, Springe.

24. **Non sibi, patriae**   *Latin* 'Not for himself, for his country'
    —Tomlinson.

25. **Non sibi, sed patriae**   *Latin* 'Not for himself, but for his country'
    —Baker, Heppesley, Romney (E.), Marsham, Thomlinson.

26. **Non sibi, sed patriae natus**   *Latin* 'Not born for himself, but for his country'
    —Jodrell (Bt.).

27. **Ob patriam vulnera passi**   *Latin* 'Having endured wounds for their country'
    —Burnes (of Montrose).

28. **Omnia relinquit servare rempublicam**   *Latin* 'He leaves everything to save the state'
    —Turberville (U.S.).

29. **Paix, travail, patrie**   *French* 'Peace, work, fatherland'
    —Federal Republic of Cameroon.

30. **Par l'amour et la fidélité envers la patrie**   *French* 'By love and fidelity towards our country'
    —Order of St. Catharine (Russia).

31. **Patriae et Deo sursum deorsum**   *Latin* 'For my country and my God, upwards and downwards'
    —Johann Georg II, Elector of Saxony (1613–80).

32. **Patriae fidelis**   *Latin* 'Faithful to my country'
    —Tiffin, Wood.

33. **Patriae fidus**   *Latin* 'Faithful to my country'
    —Lewis (Co. Glamorgan).

34. **Patriae infelici fidelis**   *Latin* 'Faithful to my unhappy country'
    —Courtown (E.), Molyneux, Montgomery, Stopford.

35. **Patriae non sibi**   *Latin* 'For his country, not for himself'
    —Argles.

36. **Patriam amo**   *Latin* 'I love my country'
    —Scott.

37. **Patriam hinc sustinet**   *Latin* 'Hence he sustains his country'
    —Higgins.

38. **Patria veritas fides**   *Latin* 'Country, truth, faith'
    —Everett (U.S.).

39. **Pour le roi et la patrie**   *French* 'For the king and the country'
    —Lynde (U.S.).

40. **Praeclarum regi et regno servitium**   *Latin* 'Honorable service to king and country'
    —Ogilvie (of Barras, Bt.).

41. **Praestò pro patriâ**   *Latin* 'Ready for my country'
    —Neilson.

42. **Prest pour mon pays**   *Old French* 'Ready for my country'
    —Monson (B.).

43. **Pro amore patriae**   *Latin* 'For love of country'
    —Scot, Scott.

44. **Procedamus in pace**   *Latin* 'Let us proceed in peace'
    —Montgomery.

45. **Pro ecclesia et patria**   *Latin* 'For church and country'
    —Trinity College, Hartford, Connecticut.

46. **Pro patria**   *Latin* 'For my country'
    —Bannerman (Bt.), Betson, Bulman, Bonsall, Cooke, Carbery (B.), Douglas (of Carnoustie, Bt.), Douglas, Groseth, Hay (Bt.), Higgins, Hamilton (of Preston), Hastie, James (Bt.), Kay, Newlands, Newton (of Newton), Ogilvie, Provan, Rochead, Scott, Turner, Warrington, Wood (of Holm Hull), Widdrington, Order of the Sword (Sweden).

47. **Pro patria auxilio Deo**   *Latin* 'For my country with God's help'
    —Grossett (Co. Wilts).

48. **Pro patria consumor**   *Latin* 'I exhaust myself for my country'
    —Heinrich Julius, Duke of Braunschweig-Wolfenbüttel (1564–1613).

49. **Pro patriae amore**   *Latin* 'For patriotism'
    —Wolfe.

50. **Pro patriâ ejusque libertate** *Latin* 'For my country and its free-
    dom'

    —Joy.

51. **Pro patria et gloria** *Latin* 'For country and honor'
    —7th Regiment of National Guard, State of New York
    (U.S. Civil War).

52. **Pro patria et libertate** *Latin* 'For country and liberty'
    —Michie.

53. **Pro patriâ et rege** *Latin* 'For country and king'
    —Jones, Thomas.

54. **Pro patria et religione** *Latin* 'For country and religion'
    —Shanly.

55. **Pro patria et virtute** *Latin* 'For country and virtue'
    —Higgins.

56. **Pro patria invictus** *Latin* 'Invincible for my country'
    —Odell.

57. **Pro patria mori** *Latin* 'To die for one's country'
    —Gardiner (U.S.), Manly.

58. **Pro patria non timidus perire** *Latin* 'Not afraid to die for my
    country'

    —Champneys (Bt.).

59. **Pro patria saepe, pro Rege semper** *Latin* 'For my country often,
    for my king always'

    —Ainslie.

60. **Pro patria sanguis** *Latin* 'My blood for my country'
    —Splatt.

61. **Pro patria semper** *Latin* 'For my country ever'
    —Callow, Power (Bt.).

62. **Pro patria uro** *Latin* 'I burn for my country'
    —Costerton.

63. **Pro patria vivere et mori** *Latin* 'To live and die for our country'
    —Grattan.

64. **Pro rege, pro lege, pro patriae conamur** *Latin* 'We strive for
    king, for law, and for country'

    —18th Hussars, U.K.

65. **Pro rege et patriâ** *Latin* 'For my king and country'
 —Ainslie (Bt.), Aberherdour, Bell, Carr, Cameron (of Lochiel), De Tabley (B.), Franklyn, Hamond (of St. Albans Court), Leven (E.), Leicester, Leslie, Lyon, McCubbin, Pode, Smith (of Preston, Bt.), Stewart, Wheatley.

66. **Pro rege et patriâ pugnans** *Latin* 'Fighting for my king and country'
 —Pasley (Bt.), Smith.

67. **Pro rege et pro patriâ semper** *Latin* 'Always for my king and my country'
 —Lawrence.

68. **Pro rege et republica** *Latin* 'For king and state'
 —Paul (Bt.).

69. **Pro rege saepe, pro patriâ semper** *Latin* 'For the king often, for my country always'
 —Eyre, Redington.

70. **Pro rege saepe, pro republica semper** *Latin* 'For the king often, for the commonwealth always'
 —Gibson.

71. **Pro republicâ** *Latin* 'For the state'
 —Nicholson.

72. **Pro republicâ semper** *Latin* 'For the state always'
 —Hellier.

73. **Pugna pro patria** *Latin* 'Fight for the country'
 —Georg, Duke of Braunschweig-Lüneburg (1582–1641).

74. **Pugna pro patria** *Latin* 'Fight for the country'
 —Aldershot B. C., U.K.

75. **Pugna pro patriâ** *Latin* 'Fight for your country'
 —Doughty, Tichborne (Bt.).

76. **Pugna pro patria, 1625** *Latin* 'Fight for the country, 1625'
 —Reynolds (U.S.).

77. **Pugna pro patria, & (Paul Revere)** *Latin* 'Fight for the country, & (Paul Revere)'
 —Revere (U.S.).

78. **Pugno pro patriâ** *Latin* 'I fight for my country'
 —Ogilvy (of Ragel).

79. **Quid non pro patria?** *Latin* 'What would not one do for his country?'
 —Campbell (of Perthshire), Mathew.

80. **Qui non patriam amat?** *Latin* 'Who does not love his country?'
—Quinan.

81. **Quod non pro patria?** *Latin* 'What would one not do for his country?'
—Bowie, Bowhie.

82. **Quo me cunque vocat patria** *Latin* 'Whithersoever my country calls me'
—Arden (of Longcroft).

83. **Rege et patriâ** *Latin* 'By my king and country'
—Bower.

84. **Regi patriaeque** *Latin* 'To the king and country'
—Leeper.

85. **Regis et patriae tantum valet amor** *Latin* 'So much does love of king and country avail'
—Tyldesley.

86. **Saepe pro rege, semper pro republica** *Latin* 'Often for the king, always for the commonwealth'
—Vassall (of Milford).

87. **Saepe pro rege semper pro patria** *Latin* 'Often for the king, always for the country'
—Clarke (U.S.).

88. **Semper paratus pugnare pro patriâ** *Latin* 'Always ready to fight for my country'
—Lockhart (B.).

89. **Semper patriae servire praesto** *Latin* 'Be always ready to serve your country'
—MacGeoghegan.

90. **Semper praesto patriae servire** *Latin* 'I am ever ready to serve my country'
—O'Neil.

91. **Verus amor patriae** *Latin* 'The true love of country'
—Hughes (of Wexford).

92. **Vicit amor patriae** *Latin* 'Love of country has conquered'
—Holles.

93. **Vincit amor patriae** *Latin* 'The love of my country exceeds everything'
—Chichester (E.), Cooper, Gun, Hargreaves, James, Molesworth (V.), Muncaster (B.), Pennington.

94. **Vincit amor patriae** *Latin* 'Love of country prevails'
—Sunderland R. D. C., U.K.

PEACE (*See also* TRANQUILLITY; WAR.)

1. **Amo pacem**   *Latin*   'I love peace'
    —Towle.

2. **Amor et pax**   *Latin*   'Love and peace'
    —Ireland.

3. **A vision of peace**   (*from Hebrew*)
    —Montefiore (Bt.).

4. **Beati pacifici**   *Latin*   'Blessed are the peace-makers'
    —[Matt. v. 9.] James, Stewart.

5. **Bene qui pacifice**   *Latin*   'He lives well who lives peacefully'
    —Allar-dyce.

6. **Cambray, cité de paix**   *French*   'Cambrai, city of peace'
    —Town of Cambrai, France.

7. **Comitate quam viribus**   *Latin*   'By mildness rather than force'
    —Hall.

8. **Da pacem domine**   *Latin*   'Give peace, O Lord'
    —Sanderson (B.).

9. **Deus est pax**   *Latin*   'God is my peace'
    —Godfray.

10. **Dilige pacem**   *Latin*   'Love peace'
    —Barlow (B.).

11. **Ense petit placidam sub libertate quietam**   *Latin*   'By the sword we seek peace but peace only under liberty'
    —State of Massachusetts.

12. **Est concordia fratrum**   *Latin*   'Harmony becomes brothers'
    —Brown (of Brandon).

13. **Felix qui pacificus**   *Latin*   'He is happy who is peaceful'
    —Spence.

14. **Ferant mea serta columbae**   *Latin*   'Let doves bear my garland'
    —Hodgson.

15. **Fiat pax fiat justitia**   *Latin*   'Let peace be made, justice be done'
    —Holland.

16. **Foedere non vi**   *Latin*   'By treaty, not by force'
    —Barnard (U.S.).

17. **Fried ernehrt Unfried verzehrt**   *German*   'Peace nourishes, strife destroys'
    —Friedrich, Duke of Braunschweig-Lüneburg (1574–1648).

18. **Heddwch**   *Welsh* 'Peace'
—Hart.

19. **In morte quies**   *Latin* 'In death peace'
—Cust.

20. **In pace ut sapiens**   *Latin* 'In peace as a wise man'
—Sloper.

21. **Justice, paix, travail**   *French* 'Justice, peace, work'
—Democratic Republic of the Congo.

22. **Justitia et pax**   *Latin* 'Justice and peace'
—Plumbers' Company.

23. **Khotso, pula, nala**   *Sesotho* 'Peace, rain, abundance'
—Lesotho.

24. **L'amour de Dieu est pacifique**   *French* 'The love of God is peaceful'
—Order of Mary Magdalen.

25. **La paix**   *French* 'Peace'
—Lendrum.

26. **Le croix de hors mais pais dedans**   *Old French* 'The cross without, but peace within'
—Surdevile.

27. **Nuncia pacis**   *Latin* 'A messenger of peace'
—Whannell.

28. **Nuncia pacis oliva**   *Latin* 'The olive, the messenger of peace'
—Mays, Moyes.

29. **Pacem, sed coronatam pacem**   *Latin* 'Peace, but crowned peace'
—Nott.

30. **Pacem amo**   *Latin* 'I love peace'
—Columball (Co. Derby), Scot (of Broadmeadows), Scott (of Highchester).

31. **Pacificum fert conjugium praenuncium pacis**   *Latin* 'A peaceful marriage is the harbinger of peace'
—Philipp Wilhelm, Margrave of Brandenburg-Schwedt (1669–1711), on a medal commemorating his marriage.

32. **Pacis**   *Latin* 'Of peace'
—Sloper.

33. **Pacis nuncia**   *Latin* 'A harbinger of peace'
—Murray (of Stanhope, Bt.).

34. **Paix, travail, patrie** *French* 'Peace, work, fatherland'
—Federal Republic of Cameroon.

35. **Paix et peu** *French* 'Peace and a little'
—Maitland, Walrond.

36. **Paritur pax bello** *Latin* 'Peace is obtained by war'
—Blane (Bt.).

37. **Pax** *Latin* 'Peace'
—Foulis, Hatton.

38. **Pax, copia, sapientia** *Latin* 'Peace, plenty, wisdom'
—Fleming (Bt.), Fleming (of Manchester), West.

39. **Pax, copia, virtus** *Latin* 'Peace, plenty, virtue'
—McAdam, Stewart.

40. **Pax alma redit** *Latin* 'Fair peace returns'
—Donville (of St. Albans, Bt.).

41. **Pax armis acquiritur** *Latin* 'Peace is acquired by arms'
—Arrat.

42. **Pax aut bellum** *Latin* 'Peace or war'
—Blane (Bt.), Blain, Thesiger.

43. **Pax aut defensio** *Latin* 'Peace or defense'
—Laudale.

44. **Pax copia** *Latin* 'Peace, plenty'
—Read.

45. **Pax et amicitia** *Latin* 'Peace and friendship'
—Cowell (U.S.).

46. **Pax et amor** *Latin* 'Peace and love'
—Hodson (Bt.), Jessop.

47. **Pax et copia** *Latin* 'Peace and plenty'
—Chandlee, David.

48. **Pax et justitia** *Latin* 'Peace and justice'
—Johann Georg II, Elector of Saxony (1613–80).

49. **Pax et libertas** *Latin* 'Peace and liberty'
—Gordon.

50. **Pax et spes** *Latin* 'Peace and hope'
—Pease (Bt.).

51. **Pax finis bello** *Latin* 'Peace the end of war'
—Ellis.

52. **Pax hospita ruris** *Latin* 'Peace, the hostess of the countryside'
—Jones (U.S.).

53. **Pax in bello** *Latin* 'Peace in war'
—Godolphin (B.), Leeds (D.), Osborne (of Newtown, Bt.),
Bernal-Osborne.

54. **Pax in terris** *Latin* 'Peace on earth'
—Codman (U.S.).

55. **Pax justa** *Latin* 'A just peace'
—Newington.

56. **Pax multa diligentibus legem tuam, Domine** *Latin* 'Great peace
have they which love Thy law, O Lord'
—[after Ps., cxix. 165.] Johann Georg, Elector of
Brandenburg (1525–98); August, Elector of
Saxony (1526–86); Albrecht, Margrave of
Brandenburg (1490–1568).

57. **Pax optima rerum** *Latin* 'Peace is the best of things'
—Guidott.

58. **Pax potior bello** *Latin* 'Peace preferable to war'
—Bastard (of Kitley, Co. Devon), Nemehard.

59. **Pax quaeritur bello** *Latin* 'Peace is obtained by war'
—Cromwell (of Cheshunt Park).

60. **Pax tibi, Marce, evangelista meus** *Latin* 'Peace to thee, O Mark!
my evangelist'
—Order of St. Mark.

61. **Pax tua, Domine, est requies mea** *Latin* 'Thy peace, O Lord! is
my rest'
—Umphray.

62. **Pax una triumphis innumeris potior** *Latin* 'One peace is better
than countless victories'
—Friedrich, Duke of Braunschweig-Lüneburg
(1574–1648); Friedrich Wilhelm, Elector of
Brandenburg (1620–88).

63. **Pax vobiscum** *Latin* 'Peace be with you'
—Nott.

64. **Peace**
—Dixon (of Knells), Higga.

65. **Peace and grace**
—Graham (of Gartur).

66. **Peace and plenty**
—Barnes.

67. **Peace on Earth, goodwill towards women**
—Harleyford, Buckinghamshire, England.

68. **Peace through law**
      —Arizona State University College of Law, Arizona.

69. **Peace with power**
      —Edwards (of Roby).

70. **Pietas est pax**   *Latin* 'Piety is peace'
      —Hopkins (U.S.).

71. **Piety in peace**
      —Hopkins (U.S.).

72. **Praenuntia pacis**   *Latin* 'Forerunner of peace'
      —Bell.

73. **Procedamus in pace**   *Latin* 'Let us proceed in peace'
      —Montgomery.

74. **Progress, peace, prosperity**
      —The Gambia.

75. **Rhyddid hedd a llwyddiant**   *Welsh* 'Freedom, peace, and prosperity'
      —Carmarthen B. C., U.K.

76. **Seek peace and ensure it**
      —Page.

77. **Shee ec y jerrey**   *Manx* 'Peace at the last'
      —Gell.

78. **Signum pacis amor**   *Latin* 'Love is the token of peace'
      —Bell.

79. **Sioth chain agus fairsinge**   *Gaelic* 'Peace and plenty'
      —Kavanagh.

80. **Sub pace copia**   *Latin* 'Under peace, plenty'
      —France, Franco.

81. **Tam pace quam proelio**   *Latin* 'In peace as well as in war'
      —Gordon.

82. **Tending to peace**
      —Mussenden.

83. **Undeb hedd llwyddiant**   *Welsh* 'Unity, peace, prosperity'
      —Breconshire C. C., U.K.

84. **Unidad, paz, justicia**   *Spanish* 'Unity, peace, justice'
      —Republic of Equatorial Guinea.

85. **Wo Friede, Da Freude**   *German* 'Where peace is, there is joy'
      —on a farmhouse in Lucerne, Switzerland.

PEOPLE (*See also* HUMANITY.)

1. **Civitatis fortuna cives** *Latin* 'The fortune of the state depends on the citizens'
—Bebington B. C., U.K.

2. **Haud fulsit gratior populis** *Latin* 'Never has the sun shone more kindly for the people (than in his life)'
—Georg Wilhelm, Duke of Braunschweig-Luneburg-Zelle (1624-1705).

3. **Nec rege, nec populo, sed utroque** *Latin* 'Neither for king nor people, but for both'
—Rolle (B.), Wilkinson.

4. **Non civium ardor** *Latin* 'Not the ardor of the citizens'
—[Horace, *Car.* iii. 3. 1.] Moore (of Appleby), Spurgeon (of Gressenhall, Co. Norfolk).

5. **Non pas l'ouvrage, mais l'ouvrier** *French* 'Not the work, but the workman'
—Workman, Workman-Macnaghten (Bt.).

6. **Pro civibus et civitate** *Latin* 'For the citizens and the city'
—Fulham B. C., U.K.

7. **Pro Deo et populo** *Latin* 'For God and the people'
—Friedrich Wilhelm, Elector of Brandenburg (1620-88); Ferdinand IV, King of Rome (1633-54); Bishop's Stortford U. D. C., U.K.

8. **Pro lege, Rege, grege** *Latin* 'For the law, the king, the people'
—Shield.

9. **Pro lege, Rege (et) grege** *Latin* 'For the law, the king, (and) the people'
—Christian Wilhelm, Margrave of Brandenburg (1587-1665).

10. **Pro lege et grege** *Latin* 'For law and for the people'
—Philippi, Duke of Pomerania zu Wolgast (1515-60); Bogislaus XIII, Duke of Pomerania zu Barth (1544-1606); Georg III, his son (1582-1617); Christian Wilhelm, Margrave of Brandenburg (1587-1665); Philipp, Landgrave of Hesse-Cassel (1604-26); Johann Georg I, Elector of Saxony (1585-1656).

11. **Pro lege et pro grege** *Latin* 'For law and for the people'
—Johann Sigismund, Elector of Brandenburg (1572-1619).

12. **Pro rege, lege, grege** *Latin* 'For the king, the law, and the people'
> —Bessborough (E.), Brougham (B.), Ponsonby (B.), Whither.

13. **Pro rege, pro lege, pro grege** *Latin* 'For king, for law, for the common people'
> —Damon (U.S.).

14. **Pro rege et grege** *Latin* 'For king and people'
> —Grieve, Paterson.

15. **Pro rege et populo** *Latin* 'For king and people'
> —Barrow (Bt.), Basset (B.).

16. **Regnat populus** *Latin* 'The people rule'
> —State of Arkansas.

17. **Salus populi** *Latin* 'The welfare of the people'
> —Southport C. B. C., U.K.

18. **Salus populi suprema est lex** *Latin* 'The welfare of the people is the highest law'
> —Urmston U. D. C., U.K.

19. **Salus populi suprema lex** *Latin* 'The welfare of the people is the highest law'
> —Eastleigh B. C., Harrow U. D. C., Lewisham B. C., Lytham-St. Annes B. C., Swinton and Pendlebury B. C., Tipton B. C., Tonbridge U. D. C., Willenhall U. D. C., U.K.

20. **Salus populi suprema lex esto** *Latin* 'The security of the people shall be the highest law'
> —[Cicero *Leges*. 3. 8.] Karl Emil, Margrave of Brandenburg (1655–74); Johann, Duke of Saxony-Weimar (1570–1605); Johann Ernst I, Duke of Saxony-Weimar (1594–1626); Friedrich Wilhelm, Elector of Brandenburg (1620–88), State of Missouri.

21. **Salus publica salus mea** *Latin* 'The public welfare is my welfare'
> —Karl Wilhelm Friedrich, Margrave of Brandenburg-Anspach (1712–57); Adolf Friedrich IV, Duke of Mecklenburg-Strelitz (1738–94).

22. **That the people shall know**
> —Columbia University Graduate School of Journalism, New York City, New York.

23. Under God the people rule
—State of South Dakota.

PERFECTION (*See also* EXCELLENCE.)
1. **En tout parfait** *French* 'Perfect in everything'
—Parfitt.

PERMANENCE (*See also* ENDURANCE.)
1. **Immota triumphans** *Latin* 'Triumphing unmoved'
—Forneaulex.
2. **Immotus** *Latin* 'Immoveable'
—Alston (of Herts and Suffolk).
3. **Immutabile, durabile** *Latin* 'Immutable, lasting'
—Rolland (of Disblair).
4. **Irrevocabile** *Latin* 'Irrevocable'
—Bruce (of Kinross), Bennett.
5. **Unalterable**
—Sleigh (of Haddington).

PERSECUTION (*See also* HUNTING; SUFFERING.)
1. **Chassé pour foi** *French* 'Persecuted for the faith'
—Andovier, Lamb.
2. **Cur me persequeris** *Latin* 'Why persecutest thou me?'
—[Acts, ix. 4.] Eustace, Eton.
3. **Faded, but not destroyed**
—Paver (of Braham Hall, Co. York).

PERSEVERANCE (*See also* FORTITUDE; STEADFASTNESS.)
1. **Aspire, persevere, and indulge not**
—Adam.
2. **Aspire, persevere, trust**
—Adams (U.S.).
3. **Aut viam inveniam aut faciam** *Latin* 'I will either find a road or make one'
—Cockburn (Bt.), Wightwick (of Bloxwich).
4. **Bene tenax** *Latin* 'Rightly tenacious'
—Bennet.

5. **Be right and persist**
   —Young (Co. Bucks, Bt.).

6. **Better to wear out than to rust out**
   —Frances Elizabeth Willard (referring to temperance and women's suffrage).

7. **By perseverance**
   —Cunard (Bt.).

8. **Conata perficio**   *Latin* 'I carry through what I attempt'
   —Cooper (Bt.).

9. **Constantia et diligentia**   *Latin* 'By perseverance and diligence'
   —Spence.

10. **Constantia in ardua**   *Latin* 'Perseverance against difficulty'
    —Harland (Co. York).

11. **Deo duce perseverandum**   *Latin* 'With God as our leader we must persevere'
    —Jay (U.S.).

12. **Deo fidens persistas**   *Latin* 'Trusting in God, persevere'
    —Kinahan.

13. **Disciplina, fide, perseverantia**   *Latin* 'By discipline, fidelity, and perseverance'
    —Duckworth (Bt.).

14. **E perseverantia honor**   *Latin* 'Honor from perseverance'
    —Davey.

15. **Espère et persévère**   *French* 'Hope and persevere'
    —Paget (Bt.).

16. **Familias firmat pietas**   *Latin* 'Piety strengthens families'
    —Ramsay, Wardlaw (Bt.), Wardlaw (of Tillycoultry).

17. **Fide et perseverantia**   *Latin* 'By faith and perseverance'
    —Lumsden.

18. **Fluctuo sed affluo**   *Latin* 'I fluctuate, but I flow on'
    —Arbuthnot.

19. **Fluctus fluctu**   *Latin* 'Wave on wave'
    —Flux, Maitland.

20. **Fortfahren und verharren**   *German* 'To go on and persevere'
    —Nicholl.

21. **Frango dura patientia**   *Latin* 'I break hard things by perseverance'
    —Cooper.

22. **Go on, and persevere**

—Nichol.

23. **Hirbarhad** *Welsh* 'Perseverance'

—Lewis.

24. **Illegitimi non carborundum** *Pseudo-Latin* 'Don't let the bastards grind you down'

—General Joseph W. ('Vinegar Joe') Stilwell.

25. **Incepta persequor** *Latin* 'I persevere in what I undertake'

—Wilkinson.

26. **Industria et perseverantia** *Latin* 'By industry and perseverance'

—Cowper.

27. **In pretium persevero** *Latin* 'I persevere for my reward'

—Jenner.

28. **Insiste firmiter** *Latin* 'Persevere resolutely'

—Moorside.

29. **Inveniam aut faciem** *Latin* 'I shall find a way or make one'

—Delmege.

30. **Inveniam viam aut faciam** *Latin* 'I will find a way or make one'

—Humphries (U.S.).

31. **I will never quit**

—Boulton (Bt.).

32. **Justitiae propositique tenax** *Latin* 'Tenacious of justice and of purpose'

—Stuart (Bt.).

33. **Justitiae tenax** *Latin* 'Persevering in justice'

—Astley, Hastings (B.).

34. **Labitur et labetur** *Latin* 'It flows and will go on flowing'

—Platt, Platt-Higgins.

35. **Labore et perseverantia** *Latin* 'By labor and perseverance'

—Campbell, Woods.

36. **Labor omnia vincit** *Latin* 'Perseverance overcomes all difficulties'

—Brown, Cutler, Chaplin, Burder, Daniel (Co. Stafford), Eddington, McNair, Prattman.

37. **Maneo** *Latin* 'I remain'

—Gordon.

38. **Ne cede arduis** *Latin* 'Yield not to difficulties'

—Fairbairn.

39. **Nec mons, nec subtrahit aer**   *Latin* 'Neither does the mountain diminish, nor the wind cease to blow'
—Forbes (of Brux).

40. **Never give in**
—Lawrence (Bt.).

41. **Non desistam**   *Latin* 'I will not desist'
—Row.

42. **Nulla deditio**   *Latin* 'No giving up'
—Kynsey.

43. **Ohne Hast, aber ohne Rast**   *German* 'Without haste, but without rest'
—J. W. von Goethe.

44. **Ohne Rast zum Ziel**   *German* 'Without resting to the goal'
—Abel.

45. **Patientia et perseverantia**   *Latin* 'With patience and perseverance'
—Dent (Co. York).

46. **Patientia et perseverantia cum magnanimitate**   *Latin* 'Patience and perseverance with magnanimity'
—Fellows.

47. **Patiently persevere**
—Wills.

48. **Perfero**   *Latin* 'I carry through'
—Cumberland C.C., U.K.

49. **Periissem, ni per-issem**   *Latin* 'I had perished, unless I had gone through with it'
—Anstruther (Bt.).

50. **Periissemus, nisi perstitissemus**   *Latin* 'We had perished, had we not persisted'
—Anstruther.

51. **Periissemus nisi per-iissemus**   *Latin* 'We had perished had we not persisted'
—Bermudas Company.

52. **Persevera**   *Latin* 'Persevere'
—White.

53. **Persevera Deoque confido**   *Latin* 'Persevere and trust in God'
—Brown.

54. **Persevera et vince**   *Latin* 'Persevere and conquer'
—Smith.

55. **Perseverance**
　　　　　—Burrard (Bt.), Hume, Parry, Steel, Webley.
56. **Perseverando** *Latin* 'By perseverance'
　　　　　—Seal of State of Virginia, Brinckman (Bt.), Brooks, Cope
　　　　　　　(Co. Leicester), Dugdale, Ducie (E.), Dendy,
　　　　　Frampton (of Moreton), Farnell, Flower (Bt.), Henley,
　　　　　　　Hanrott, Howell, MacGillivray, McKellar,
　　　　　Larkworthy, Morton, Roxby, Turnly, Wood (of
　　　　　　　　　　　　　　　　　Barnsley, Bt.).
57. **Perseverando et cavendo** *Latin* 'By perseverance and caution'
　　　　　　　　　　　　　　　　　　　　—Moore.
58. **Perseverantia** *Latin* 'Perseverance'
　　　　　　　　　　　　　　　　　　　　—Bell.
59. **Perseverantia ad finem optatum** *Latin* 'By perseverance to the
　wished-for end'
　　　　　　　　　　　　　　　　　　　　—Jones.
60. **Perseverantia dabitur** *Latin* 'It will be given by perseverance'
　　　　　　　　　　　　　　　　　　　　—Terry.
61. **Perseverantia et cura quies** *Latin* 'Rest by perseverance and care'
　　　　　　　　　　　　　　　　　　　　—Hall.
62. **Perseverantia et labore** *Latin* 'By perseverance and labor'
　　　　　　　　　　　　　　　　　　　　—Pitcher.
63. **Perseverantia industria et fidelitas** *Latin* 'Perseverance, industry,
　and fidelity'
　　　　　　　　　　　　　　　　　　　　—Ravenscroft.
64. **Perseverantia omnia vincit** *Latin* 'Perseverance conquers all
　things'
　　　　　　　　　　　　　　　　　　　　—Cooper.
65. **Perseverantia palma** *Latin* 'By perseverance (one gains) the
　palm'
　　　　　　　　　　　　　　　　　—Wilson (of Dulwich).
66. **Perseverantia palmam obtinebit** *Latin* 'Perseverance will obtain
　the reward'
　　　　　　　　　　　　　　　　　　　　—Tooth.
67. **Perseverantia victor** *Latin* 'Victor through perseverance'
　　　　　　　　　　　　　　　　　　　　—Campbell.
68. **Perseverantia vincit** *Latin* 'Perseverance succeeds'
　　　　　　　　　　—Kesteven C. C., U.K.; Burnes
69. **Perseveranti dabitur** *Latin* 'It will be given to the persevering'
　　　　　　—Gilmour, Robertson, Simpson (Co. Durham).

70. **Persevere**
    —Denton U. D. C., U.K.; Congreve (Bt.), Colvile, Greig, Gardiner, Gibbs, Fearon, Fordyce, Farnall, Oakes (Bt.), Phillips (of Reigate Lodge, Co. Surrey), Smythe, Whittall.

71. **Persevere in hope**
    —Mackinnon.

72. **Persevero**   *Latin* 'I persevere'
    —Baker, Pender, Waithman.

73. **Persist**
    —Humphry.

74. **Per tot discrimina rerum**   *Latin* 'Through so many critical junctures'
    —Hammond, Hickman.

75. **Praesto et persisto**   *Latin* 'I undertake and I persevere'
    —Haddington (E.), Winchester.

76. **Praesto et persto**   *Latin* 'I undertake and persevere'
    —Baillie-Hamilton-Arden, Doe, Crawhall, Hamilton.

77. **Presto et persto**   *Latin* 'I undertake and persevere'
    —Stewart.

78. **Providence and perseverance**
    —Furnaval.

79. **Right revere, and persevere**
    —Berry.

80. **Saw through**
    —Hamilton.

81. **Tenax et fide**   *Latin* 'Persevering and with faith'
    —Smith (of East Stoke, Bt.).

82. **Tenax et fidelis**   *Latin* 'Persevering and faithful'
    —Abdy (Bt.), Carrington (B.), Smith, Tennant (of Skipton).

83. **Tenax et fidus**   *Latin* 'Persevering and faithful'
    —Hebbert.

84. **Virtute et constantia**   *Latin* 'Through virtue and tenacity'
    —Malta.

PIETY (*See also* DEVOTION; RELIGION; REVERENCE.)

1. **Amantibus justitiam, pietatem, fidem** *Latin* 'To the lovers of justice, piety, and faith'
   —Order of St. Anne (Schleswig-Holstein).

2. **Caste et pie** *Latin* 'Purely and piously'
   —Johann Georg II, Elector of Saxony (1613–80).

3. **Constanter et pie** *Latin* 'With constancy and with piety'
   —Christian II, Prince of Anhalt-Bernburg (1599–1656).

4. **Cura pii diis sunt** *Latin* 'Pious men are a care to the gods'
   —Mogg.

5. **Deus evehit pios** *Latin* 'God exalts the pious'
   —Brown.

6. **Esto bonus et pius ne sit leo te magis impavidus** *Latin* 'Be good and pious, let not the lion be more undaunted than thou'
   —Wintringham.

7. **Est pii Deum et patriam diligere** *Latin* 'It is the part of a pious man to love God and his country'
   —Atkinson.

8. **Familias firmat pietas** *Latin* 'Piety strengthens families'
   —Ramsay, Wardlaw (Bt.), Wardlaw (of Tillycoultry).

9. **Gratior est a rege pio** *Latin* 'It is more agreeable coming from a pious king'
   —Gibbons (Bt.).

10. **Honor, pietas** *Latin* 'Honor, piety'
    —Waters.

11. **Honore pietas** *Latin* 'Piety with honor'
    —Waters.

12. **Memoria pii aeterna** *Latin* 'The memory of the pious man is eternal'
    —Sudeley (B.), Tracy.

13. **One on God's side is a majority**
    —Wendell Phillips, abolitionist.

14. **P. A. O. V. E. (Pietas ad omnia utilis est)** *Latin* 'Godliness is profitable unto all things'
    —[1 Tim. iv. 8.] Joachim Karl, Duke of Braunschweig (1573–1615).

15. **Philosophia pietati ancillans** *Latin* 'Philosophy in service to piety'
    —Hanover College, Hanover, Indiana.

16. **Pie, juste, temperanter** *Latin* 'With piety, justice, and moderation'
—Friedrich IV, Count of the Palatinate (1594–1610).

17. **Pie at juste** *Latin* 'With piety and justice'
—August Friedrich, Duke of Schleswig-Holstein-Gottorp (1646–1705).

18. **Pie et fortiter** *Latin* 'Piously and bravely'
—Bennet.

19. **Pie et prudenter** *Latin* 'With piety and prudence'
—Heinrich X, Count Reuss (1662–1711).

20. **Pietas cum robore conjuncta** *Latin* 'Piety combined with strength'
—Albert Friedrich, Margrave of Brandenburg (1582–1600).

21. **Pietas est optima virtus** *Latin* 'Piety is the chief virtue'
—Heinrich VIII, Count Reuss (1652–1711).

22. **Pietas est pax** *Latin* 'Piety is peace'
—Hopkins (U.S.).

23. **Pietas et frugalitas** *Latin* 'Piety and frugality'
—Guthry.

24. **Pietas et justitia principatus columnae** *Latin* 'Piety and justice are the supports of government'
—Adolf Friedrich I, Duke of Mecklenburg-Schwerin (1588–1658).

25. **Pietas praesidium firmissimum** *Latin* 'Piety is the surest protection'
—Ernst, Margrave of Brandenburg (1583–1613).

26. **Pietas summa est scientia** *Latin* 'Piety is the highest science'
—Johann Georg II, Elector of Saxony (1613–80).

27. **Pietas tutissima virtus** *Latin* 'Piety is the surest virtue'
—Ainslie.

28. **Pietas tutissima virtus** *Latin* 'Piety is the safest virtue'
—Christoph, Duke of Mecklenburg (1537–92); Friedrich Wilhelm I, Duke of Saxony-Weimar (1562–1602); Magnus, Duke of Braunschweig-Lüneburg (1577–1632); August, Duke of Saxony (1589–1615); Friedrich Wilhelm II, Duke of Saxony-Altenburg (1603–69); Georg Friedrich, Margrave of Brandenburg-Anspach (1678–1703).

29. **Pietate** *Latin* 'By piety'
—Brown.

30. **Pietate, fide, et justicia**   *Latin* 'With piety, fidelity, and justice'
—Wilhelm VI, Landgrave of Hesse-Cassel (1629–63).

31. **Pietate, legibus, et armis**   *Latin* 'By piety, by law, and by arms'
—Philipp, Landgrave of Hesse-Butzbach (1581–1643).

32. **Pietate, legibus, justitia**   *Latin* 'By piety, by prudence and by justice'
—Friedrich I, Duke of Saxony-Gotha and Altenburg (1646–91).

33. **Pietate et bellica virtute**   *Latin* 'By piety and martial valor'
—Order of St. Henry (Saxony).

34. **Pietate et justicia**   *Latin* 'By piety and justice'
—Günther, Count Schwarzburg (1570–1643); Otto, Landgrave of Hesse (1594–1617); Ferdinand III, Emperor of Germany (1608–57); Georg Wilhelm, Duke of Braunschweig-Lüneburg-Zelle (1624–1705); Christian, Duke of Saxony (1654–63); Johann Günther, Count Schwarzburg-Arnstadt (1654–69); Johann Friedrich, Margrave of Brandenburg-Anspach (1654–86); Ernst, Duke of Saxony-Hildburghausen (1655–1715); Johann Georg II, Duke of Saxony-Eisenach (1665–98); Friedrich Heinrich, Duke of Saxony-Neustadt (1668–1713); Friedrich III, Duke of Saxony-Gotha and Altenburg (1699–1772).

35. **Pietate et justitia principes dii sunt**   *Latin* 'By piety and justice princes become gods'
—Christian Ulrich, Duke of Württemberg-Oels-Bernstadt (1652–1704).

36. **Pietate et probitate**   *Latin* 'By piety and honesty'
—Rees.

37. **Pietate et prudentia**   *Latin* 'By piety and prudence'
—August, Duke of Saxony-Zörbig (1655–1715).

38. **Pietate fortior**   *Latin* 'Stronger by piety'
—Broade, Stanier-Philip-Broade.

39. **Pietatem prudentiae praefer**   *Latin* 'Prefer piety to prudence'
—Otto, Landgrave of Hesse (1594–1617).

40. **Pietate parentum**   *Latin* 'By the piety of my forefathers'
—Tulloch.

41. **Pietatis causa**   *Latin* 'In the cause of piety'
—Pye.

42. **Piety in peace**
—Hopkins (U.S.).

43. **Pieux quoique preux**   *French* 'Pious although chivalrous'
—Long.

44. **Pie vivere, et Deum et patriam diligere**   *Latin* 'To live piously, and to love (both) God and our country'
—Redmond.

45. **Preux quoique pieux**   *French* 'Valiant though pious'
—Long.

46. **Pro Rege pio**   *Latin* 'For a pious king'
—Thornton.

47. **P. T. V. (Pietas tutissima virtus)**   *Latin* 'Piety is the safest virtue'
—Ernst, Margrave of Brandenburg (1583–1613).

48. **Sapienter et pie**   *Latin* 'Wisely and piously'
—Park.

49. **Scientia et pietas**   *Latin* 'Knowledge and piety'
—Wesleyan College, Macon, Georgia.

50. **Sis pius in primis**   *Latin* 'Be pious among the first'
—Barlow (Bt.).

51. **Sobrie, pie, juste**   *Latin* 'Soberly, piously, righteously'
—Middleton.

52. **Valet pietas**   *Latin* 'Piety is strong'
—Valpy.

POSSESSION

1. **Avec ce qui je tienne je suis**   *French* 'With what I hold I am'
—Bradshaw.

2. **Ceidw Owain a gafodd**   *Welsh* 'Let Owen hold what he obtained'
—Bulkeley-Owen (of Tedmore Hall, Shrewsbury).

3. **Clamabunt omnes te, liber, esse meum**   *Latin* 'All will cry, O book, that thou art mine'
—Desbrisay.

4. **Ea nostra voco**   *Latin* 'I call these things our own'
—Pechell (Bt.).

5. **Enough in my hand**

—Cunninghame.

6. **Et teneo et teneor** *Latin* 'I both hold and am held'

—Holden.

7. **Habet et suam** *Latin* 'He has also his own'

—Seton Viscount Kingstoun.

8. **Huic habeo non tibi** *Latin* 'I hold it for him, not for thee'

—Burroughs, Ellis, Newton.

9. **Integra mens augustissima possessio** *Latin* 'An honest mind is the most glorious possession'

—Blayney (B.).

10. **Je le tiens** *French* 'I hold it'

—Audley (B.), Touchet.

11. **Let Curzon hold what Curzon held**

—Curson, Howe (E.).

12. **Libertas res inaestimabilis** *Latin* 'Freedom is a priceless possession'

—Ernst VI, Count of Mansfeld (1561–1609).

13. **Meum et tuum** *Latin* 'Mine and yours'

—Payson (U.S.).

14. **Mihi et meae** *Latin* 'For me and for mine'

—Anne Boleyn, Queen of Henry VIII.

15. **Mihi terraque lacusque** *Latin* 'Mine are the land and the pools'

—Fullarton.

16. **Nec habeo, nec careo, nec curo** *Latin* 'I have neither property, want, nor care'

—Bowstring-Makers' Company, Withers.

17. **Nil tibi** *Latin* 'Nothing for you'

—Campbell.

18. **Of old I hold**

—Levy.

19. **Omne meum, nihil meum** *Latin* 'Everything mine, nothing mine'

—Graham.

20. **Per ferrum obtinui** *Latin* 'I have got possession by my sword'

—Hillas.

21. **Quae habet manus tenebit** *Latin* 'My hand will hold fast what it has'

—Templeman.

22. **Qui potest capere, capiat**   *Latin* 'Let him take who can take'
— Glegg.

23. **Quod tuum tene**   *Latin* 'Keep what is your own'
— Cheetham, Chetham.

24. **Teneo**   *Latin* 'I retain'
— Staples.

25. **Teneo et credo**   *Latin* 'I hold and believe'
— Carson.

26. **Teneo tenuere majores**   *Latin* 'I hold (what) my ancestors held'
— Twenlow.

27. **Tenuimus**   *Latin* 'We have held'
— Lockett.

28. **Tuum est**   *Latin* 'It is thine'
— Cowper (E.), Cooper (of Toddington).

29. **Tyrii tenuere coloni**   *Latin* 'Tyrian husbandmen possessed it'
— McLaurin (of Dreghorn).

30. **Virtute nulla possessio major**   *Latin* 'No possession is greater than virtue'
— Cawarden.

31. **Vix ea nostra voco**   *Latin* 'I scarce call these things our own'
— [Ovid, *Met.* xiii. 140.] Argyll (D.), Brooke and Warwick (E.), Fountain (of Narford and Southacre, Co. Norfolk), Grenville, Hussey, Campbell (of Weasenham, Cockley Cley, and Fakenham, Co. Norfolk), Hussey (Co. Sussex).

POSSIBILITY (*See also* FUTURE, THE.)
1. **Es mag noch wohl gerathen**   *German* 'It may still happen'
— Wolfgang, Count of the Palatinate of Neumark (1494–1558).

2. **Fal y gallo**   *Welsh* 'As I can'
— Greenly (of Titley Court, Co. Hereford).

3. **Fortasse**   *Latin* 'Perhaps'
— Fogg (U.S.).

4. **If I can**
— Campbell Colquhon (of Killermont).

5. **Je ne puis**   *French* 'I cannot'
— Delves (of Cheshire and Lancashire).

6. **Nil impossibile** *Latin* 'Nothing is impossible'
—Du Bisson.

7. **Peradventure**
—Elliot (Bt.), Cockburn (of Kenderland).

8. **Si je pouvois** *French* 'If I could'
—Cleland.

9. **Si je puis** *French* 'If I can'
—Colquhoun (of Rossdhu, Bt.), Colquhon, Cahun, Eyre, Radcliffe.

10. **Si possem** *Latin* 'If I could'
—Livingstone (of Miltoun, etc.).

11. **Tant que je puis** *French* 'As much as I can'
—De Cardonnell, Hilton, Jolliffe (Bt.), Lawson (of Cramlington).

12. **Tantum quantum possum** *Latin* 'As much as I can' *or* 'As far as I am able'
—Friedrich the Wise, Elector of Saxony (1463–1525).

13. **Ut possim** *Latin* 'As I can'
—Livingston (of Glentarran).

POWER (*See also* ABILITY; FORCE; STRENGTH.)

1. **A ma puissance** *French* 'According to my power'
—Hale U. D. C., U.K.; Stamford (E.), Grey.

2. **An tu tonitru?** *Latin* 'Wilt thou with thy thunder?'
—Cox (of Charton).

3. **Armis potentius aequum** *Latin* 'Justice is more powerful than arms'
—Falconer (of Newton, Scotland).

4. **Ciall agos neart** *Gaelic* 'Reason and power'
—O'Connell (of Derrynane Abbey, Co. Kerry).

5. **Clementia in potentia** *Latin* 'Clemency in power'
—Compton.

6. **Consilio et vi** *Latin* 'By wisdom and might'
—Perrier.

7. **En bon et poyer** *Old French* 'In right and might'
—Cockayne.

8. **Juncti valemus** *Latin* 'Being joined we are powerful'
—Walker.

9. **Knowledge is power**
—Sharpe.

10. **L'Union fait la force** *French* 'Union constitutes power'
—Order of Leopold (Belgium).

11. **Mihi res subjungere conor** *Latin* 'My aim is to subject things to myself'
—Crackanthorpe.

12. **More light, more power**
—Shoreditch B. C., U.K.

13. **Nec viribus nec numero** *Latin* 'Neither by power nor numbers'
—Wemyss.

14. **Nell' armi e nelle lettere consiste la virtu** *Italian* 'Power consists in weapons and in knowledge'
—Franz, Duke of Braunschweig-Lüneburg (1572–1601).

15. **Omnis a deo potestas** *Latin* 'All power is from God'
—Griffith (U.S.).

16. **Peace with power**
—Edwards (of Roby).

17. **Por la razon o la fuerza** *Spanish* 'By right or might'
—Republic of Chile.

18. **Prudentia et vi** *Latin* 'By prudence and might'
—Innes.

19. **Resolve is power**
—Stewart.

20. **Savoir pouvoir** *French* 'Knowledge is power'
—Hodge.

21. **Scientia est potentia** *Latin* 'Knowledge is power'
—Miami-Dade Community College, Miami, Florida; Tylden (U.S.).

22. **Sine stet viribus** *Latin* 'Let him stand with power'
—Abinger.

23. **Terra marique potens** *Latin* 'Powerful by land and sea'
—O'Malley (Bt.).

24. **Vim promovet insitam** *Latin* 'It extends an ingrafted power'
—University of Bristol, Bristol, U.K.

25. **Vires animat virtus** *Latin* 'Virtue animates our powers'
—Campbell, Garden, Gairden.

26. **Vires veritas** *Latin* 'Truth gives power'
—Kennedy (of Clowburn).

27. **Virtus incendit vires** *Latin* 'Virtue excites our powers'
—Strangford (V.).

28. **Y cadarn a'r cyfrwys** *Welsh* 'The mighty and the cunning'
—Williams, Wynn-Williams.

PRAISE (*See also* ADMIRATION; HONOR; MILITARY DISTINCTION.)

1. **Alleluiah**
—Tuite (Bt.).

2. **Candoris praemium honos** *Latin* 'Praise is the reward of sincerity'
—Dunbar.

3. **Hinc laus et honos** *Latin* 'Hence praise and honor'
—Rae.

4. **Laudans invocabo Dominum** *Latin* 'I will call upon the Lord with praise'
—Palgrave.

5. **Laudari a laudato** *Latin* 'To be praised by one praised already'
—Hammick (Bt.).

6. **Laudes cano heroum** *Latin* 'I sing the praise of heroes'
—Dailie.

7. **Laudo manentem** *Latin* 'I praise him that waits'
—Onslow, Stanhope.

8. **Laus Deo** *Latin* 'Praise be to God'
—Arbuthnott (V.).

9. **Laus recti diuturna beat** *Latin* 'Enduring praise of righteousness blesses'
—Ludwig Rudolf, Duke of Braunschweig in Blandenburg (1671–1735).

10. **La vita al fin e'l di loda la sera** *Italian* 'Praise life when it is at an end, and the day when it is night'
—Le Couteur.

11. **Postera crescam laude** *Latin* 'I will flourish in the praise of my descendants'
—University of Melbourne, Melbourne, Australia.

12. **Sit laus Deo** *Latin* 'Praise be to God'
—Arbuthnot (of Catherlan).

13. **Sunt sua praemia laudi** *Latin* 'His rewards are his praise'
—Barberrie, Brown, Pemberton.

14. **Te Deum laudamus**　*Latin* 'We praise thee, O God'
—Harper, McWhirter.

15. **Virtutis praemium laus**　*Latin* 'Praise is the prize of virtue'
—Jervoise (Bt.).

16. **Vivam te laudare**　*Latin* 'Let me live to praise you'
—Chambers.

PREPAREDNESS (*See also* FORESIGHT.)

1. **Ad arma paratus**　*Latin* 'Prepared for arms'
—Johnstone (of Corehead).

2. **Agitatione paratus**　*Latin* 'Prepared by activity'
—Russell.

3. **Always ready**
—Glanford Brigg R. D. C., U.K.; Hall.

4. **Animis opibusque parati**　*Latin* 'Prepared in mind and resources'
—State of South Carolina.

5. **Arma parata fero**　*Latin* 'I carry arms in readiness'
—Campbell, Macguffe.

6. **Audax et promptus**　*Latin* 'Bold and ready'
—Douglas (Bt.).

7. **Aye ready**
—Newlands (B.).

8. **Bello ac pace paratus**　*Latin* 'In war and peace prepared'
—Brackenridge (Co. Somerset).

9. **Bene praeparatum pectus**　*Latin* 'A heart well prepared'
—[Horace, *Car.* ii. 10, 12.] Jex-Blake.

10. **Be prepared**
—Boy Scouts of America; Girl Scouts of America.

11. **Be ready**
—Lawrence (Bt.).

12. **Cave, paratus**　*Latin* 'Prepared, be cautious'
—Johnston.

13. **Consulit et ornat**　*Latin* 'He deliberates and prepares'
—Dunbar.

14. **Custos et pugnax**　*Latin* 'A vigilant watch and prepared to fight'
—Marjoribanks.

15. **Estote semper parati**　*Latin* 'Be always prepared'
—Fraser.

16. **Ever ready**

—Bryson, Burn.

17. **Ferré va ferme** *French* 'The shod horse goes surely'

—Farrer.

18. **Fidelis et paratus** *Latin* 'Faithful and ready'

—Soote.

19. **Firmior quo paratior** *Latin* 'The more prepared, the stronger'

—Dunbar, Selkirk (E.).

20. **Fortior quo paratior** *Latin* 'The better prepared, the stronger'

—Hornsey B. C., U.K.

21. **Generosus et paratus** *Latin* 'Generous and prepared'

—Harwood.

22. **I am ever prepared**

—MacBreid, McLevrard.

23. **I am readie**

—Frasier (of Pitcallain).

24. **I am ready**

—Fairley, Frazer, Maxwell (Bt.), Scot (of Hundilshope).

25. **Impromptu** *Latin* 'In readiness'

—Dunbar (of Mochrun).

26. **In omnia paratus** *Latin* 'Ready for all things'

—Dunally (B.), Reay.

27. **In omnia promptus** *Latin* 'Ready for everything'

—Rae (Bt.).

28. **In promptu** *Latin* 'In readiness'

—Dunbar (Bt.), Trotter.

29. **Integer audax promptus** *Latin* 'Sound, bold, ready'

—Williams (U.S.).

30. **In utroque paratus** *Latin* 'Prepared in either case'

—Deacon, Blome, Elphinston, Mackenzie, Murray (of Clarendon), Akroyd.

31. **In utrumque paratus** *Latin* 'Prepared for either'

—Mackenzie (of Delvin, Bt.), Caldecott (of Rugby Lodge), Lawford.

32. **In utrumque utroque paratus** *Latin* 'Prepared for both and in both'

—Deacon, Elphingston, Mackenzie, Murray.

33. **Je suis prest** *Old French* 'I am ready'

—Fraser (B.), Tytler.

34. **Je suis prêt**   *French* 'I am ready'
—Farnham (B.), Fraser, Lovat, Maxwell, Simpson.

35. **Juste rem para**   *Latin* 'Prepare the matter properly'
—Apthorp (U.S.).

36. **Listo**   *Spanish* 'Ready'
—Mason (U.S.).

37. **Nec abest jugum**   *Latin* 'Nor is a yoke wanting'
—Hay (of Leith).

38. **Never unprepared**
—Stewart.

39. **Nocet differre paratis**   *Latin* 'For those ready it is injurious to delay'
—Elliot.

40. **Noctes diesque praesto**   *Latin* 'Ready by night or day'
—Murray.

41. **Nunquam non paratus**   *Latin* 'Never unprepared'
—Gibbs, Johnson (of Newcastle), Johnstone (of Westhall, Bt.), Johnstone (of Alva, Galabank, Gratney, etc.), Knight, Kerrick (of Gelderston), Betton, Skinner, Kemper Military School and College, Boonville, Missouri.

42. **Omnis fortunae paratus**   *Latin* 'Prepared for any event'
—Forbes (U.S.).

43. **Pace et bello paratus**   *Latin* 'In peace and war prepared'
—Frazer.

44. **Parat et curat**   *Latin* 'He prepares and is cautious'
—Stewart (of Blacaskie).

45. **Paratus**   *Latin* 'Ready'
—Sword.

46. **Paratus ad arma**   *Latin* 'Prepared for war'
—Johnson (Co. Berks, Bt.).

47. **Paratus et fidelis**   *Latin* 'Ready and faithful'
—Carruthers, Hamond (Bt.), Walford.

48. **Paratus sum**   *Latin* 'I am prepared'
—Campbell (Bt.), Fairlie, McLure.

49. **Parat usum**   *Latin* 'It prepares to use it'
—Hart.

50. **Praemonitus praemunitus**   *Latin* 'Forewarned, forearmed'
—Rickart.

51. **Praestò et praestò** *Latin* 'Ready and ready'

—Hawkins.

52. **Praestò pro patriâ** *Latin* 'Ready for my country'

—Neilson.

53. **Prest** *Old French* 'Ready'

—Sheffield.

54. **Prest, et, prest** *Old French* 'Ready, ay, ready'

—Hamilton.

55. **Prest a faire** *Old French* 'Ready to act'

—Fareham U. D. C., U.K.

56. **Prest d'accomplier** *Old French* 'Ready to accomplish'

—Heber (Co. York), Shrewsbury (E.), Talbot.

57. **Prest pour mon pays** *Old French* 'Ready for my country'

—Monson (B.).

58. **Pret** *French* 'Ready'

—Aston.

59. **Prêt d'accomplir** *French* 'Ready to achieve'

—Nuneaton B. C., U.K.

60. **Pret d'accomplir** *French* 'Ready to accomplish'

—Aston (Co. Chester).

61. **Promptus** *Latin* 'Ready'

—Donaldson, Kempt, Russel, Selby.

62. **Promptus ad certamen** *Latin* 'Ready for the contest'

—Sinclair.

63. **Promptus et fidelis** *Latin* 'Ready and faithful'

—Carruthers, Crondace.

64. **Quo paratior** *Latin* 'The readier we are'

—Coats.

65. **Ready**

—Archever, Fraser (of Farralane).

66. **Ready, aye, ready**

—Napier (B.), Nicolson, Scott (of Thirlestane).

67. **Ready and faithful**

—Gorham, Walker.

68. **Reddie aye reddie**

—Reddie.

69. **Securior qui paratior** *Latin* 'The better prepared the more secure'

—Johnston (of Gormach), Johnson.

70. **Semper apparatus** *Latin* 'Always prepared'
—Stuart.

71. **Semper parati** *Latin* 'Always prepared'
—Fraser, Frazer.

72. **Semper paratus** *Latin* 'Always prepared'
—Clifford (B.), Clifford, Constable (Bt.), Dallas, Johnstone (of Stratton), Knowles (Bt.), Leckey (of Londonderry), Mounsey, Phillpotts, Roydes, Stewart (of Inchbrock), Usticke, Upton (of Ingmire), Wells (of Grebly Hall), Welles; United States Coast Guard.

73. **Semper praecinctus** *Latin* 'Ever ready', *lit.*, 'girt up'
—Mulholland.

74. **Semper pugnare paratus** *Latin* 'Always ready to fight'
—Litchfield.

75. **Sic paratior** *Latin* 'Thus the better prepared'
—Johnston (of Poulton).

76. **Si monent tubae, paratus** *Latin* 'Prepared when the trumpets warn'
—Sissons.

77. **Si sonent tubae paratus** *Latin* 'If the trumpets sound, I am ready'
—Sisson.

78. **Toujours pret (*or* prest)** French
—Anstruther (of Elie House, Bt.), Abbott, Clanwilliam (E.), Carmichael (Bt.), Crawfurd, Daniel, Dayman, Dease, Donald, Gibon, Hawkins, Knight, Meade, McConnell, Macdonell, Ogilvie, Petty, Phelps, Sutton (Bt.), Smyth (Bt.), Tyssen (of Hackney and Didlington).

79. **Toute foys preste** *Old French* 'Always ready'
—Pigott.

80. **Tout jours prest** *Old French* 'Always ready'
—Sutton (Bt.).

81. **Tout prest** *Old French* 'Quite ready'
—Murray.

82. **Ubique paratus** *Latin* 'Everywhere prepared'
—Frazer (of Fingask).

83. **Ut quocumque paratus**   *Latin* 'That I may be prepared on every side'

—Cavan (E.), Lambert (Co. Meath), Lambart (Co. Mayo).

84. **Utrinque paratus**   *Latin* 'Prepared on all sides'

—Cottingham.

85. **Ut sim paratior**   *Latin* 'That I may be the better prepared'

—Clepham.

PRESENT, THE   (*See also* TIME.)

1. **Aut nunc aut nunquam**   *Latin* 'Either now or never'

—Lee.

2. **Hodie mihi cras tibi**   *Latin* 'Today for me, tomorrow for thee'
—Johann Christian, Duke of Brieg (1591–1639).

3. **Hodie non cras**   *Latin* 'Today, not tomorrow'
—Mostyn, Vaux (B.), Bowyer-Vaux (Great Yarmouth).

4. **Jam jam**   *Latin* 'Now now', i.e., 'forthwith'

—Buxton.

5. **Laetus in praesens animus**   *Latin* 'A happy spirit in the present'

—Powell (U.S.).

6. **Maintenant ou jamais**   *French* 'Now or never'

—Barnard.

7. **Nunc aut nunquam**   *Latin* 'Now or never'
—Hampson (Bt.), Kilmorey (E.), Needham.

8. **Nunc et semper**   *Latin* 'Now and ever'

—Whorwood.

9. **Nunc ut olim**   *Latin* 'Now as formerly'

—Longcroft.

10. **Pride in our past, faith in our future**

—Hertford B. C., U.K.

11. **Pride in the past/ Faith in the future**

—Hastings College, Hastings, Nebraska.

12. **Quod adest**   *Latin* 'That which is present'

—Marsham (of Norfolk).

PRIDE   (*See also* BOASTFULNESS.)

1. **A falcon towering in his pride of place**

—Cowie.

2. **Fier et fort**   *French* 'Proud and strong'
          —Shelton.

3. **Fier et sage**   *French* 'Proud and wise'
          —Sir Thomas Bradford, G. C. B.

4. **Fier mais sensible**   *French* 'Proud but sympathetic'
          —Burt (U.S.).

5. **Fier sans tache**   *French* 'Proud, without blemish'
          —Goff.

6. **In his pride of place**
          —Cowie.

7. **Nulli praeda**   *Latin* 'A prey to no one'
          —McCabin, McCalle, Arundel.

8. **Nulli praeda sumus**   *Latin* 'We are a prey to no one'
          —Marley.

9. **Pride and industry**
          —Barbados.

10. **Pride in our past, faith in our future**
          —Hertford B. C., U.K.

11. **Pride in the past/ Faith in the future**
          —Hastings College, Hastings, Nebraska.

12. **Resistit Deus superbis**   *Latin* 'God resisteth the proud'
          —[1 Peter, v. 5.] Philipp, Landgrave of Hesse-Butzbach (1581–1643).

13. **Stolz und treu**   *German* 'Proud and true'
          —Cram (U.S.).

14. **Sume superbiam quaesitam mentis**   *Latin* 'Assume the pride of mind which you have acquired'
          —Seaver.

15. **Tantum in superbos**   *Latin* 'Only against the proud'
          —Jacob.

16. **Vif, courageux, fier**   *French* 'Spirited, courageous, proud'
          —Falcon.

17. **Vite, courageux, fier**   *French* 'Swift, courageous, proud'
          —Harrison.

18. **We stoop not**
          —Anderton (of Euxton).

PRIMACY

1. **Ante omnia erit** *Latin* 'It will be before all things'
   —Dunch.

2. **Devant si je puis** *French* 'Foremost if I can'
   —Mainwaring (Bt.), Mainwaring, Scrope, Jackson, Grindley.

3. **Inter primos** *Latin* 'Among the first'
   —Hopkins.

4. **Labore et virtute** *Latin* 'By industry and virtue'
   —Gardner, Pigott.

5. **Optimum quod primum** *Latin* 'That is best that is first'
   —Kirk (of Aberfoil).

6. **Primus** *Latin* 'First'
   —Ellis.

7. **Primus in Indis** *Latin* 'First in India'
   —39th Foot (Dorsetshire) Regiment.

8. **Primus inter pares** *Latin* 'First among equals'
   —Columbus College, Columbus, Georgia.

9. **Primus tametsi virilis** *Latin* 'First yet manly'
   —Primerose.

10. **Second to none**
    —2nd Dragoons (Royal Scots Greys).

PRINCELINESS (*See also* CROWN; NOBILITY; ROYALTY.)

1. **Armet nos ultio regum** *Latin* 'Let vengeance for princes arm us'
   —Portal.

2. **Camera principis** *Latin* 'Chamber (court) of the Prince'
   —Coventry City and C. B. C., U.K.

3. **Deo et principe** *Latin* 'With God and the prince'
   —Lamb (Bt.).

4. **Deo et principi** *Latin* 'For God and the prince'
   —Montolien.

5. **Gronwi hil Gwernimon** *Welsh* 'Gronow's of the race of princes'
   —Gronow.

6. **My prince and my country**
   —Harris (B.).

7. **Obsta principiis** *Latin* 'Block the princes'
   —Hancock (U.S.).

8. **Princeps patriae pater** *Latin* 'The prince is the father of his country'

     —Bogislaus IV, Duke of Pomerania (1580–1637).

PRINCIPLES (*See also* LAW; RECTITUDE.)
1. **Praecepta non homines** *Latin* 'Principles, not men'
     —Newport Pagnell U. D. C., U.K.

2. **Principia non homines** *Latin* 'Principles, not men'
     —Webb (U.S.).

PROFANITY
1. **Nulla temerata nube** *Latin* 'No profane thing under a cloud'
     —Howison.

2. **Odi profanum** *Latin* 'I hate whatever is profane'
     —[Horace, *Odes* iii. 1.] Hare, Listowel (E.).

PROPER NAMES (*See also* NAME.)
1. **Acre**
     —Cameron (Bt.).

2. **Agincourt**
     —Lenthall (of Oxon), Waller (Bt.), Wodehouse (B.), Walker (Bt.).

3. **Alba de Tormes**
     —Hamilton (of Woodbrook, Bt.).

4. **Albuera**
     —Lumley.

5. **Algiers**
     —Exmouth (V.), Pellew.

6. **Arolla**
     —Macdonald (of Dalchosnie, Co. Perth).

7. **Arriverette**
     —Cameron (of Fassiefern, Bt.).

8. **Atalanta**
     —Hardinge (Bt.).

9. **Azincourt**
     —Billam, Waller (Bt.), Lenthall (of Oxon).

10. **Baroach**

—Nicholson.

11. **Barrosa**

—Gough (V.).

12. **Boulogne et Cadiz**

—Heygate (Bt.).

13. **Cabool**

—Burnes (of Montrose and Ladbroke Square, London).

14. **Caen, Cressie, Calais**

—Radcliffe (of Fox-Denton and Ordshall).

15. **Caffraria**

—Willshire (Bt.).

16. **Canada**

—Prevost (Bt.), Smith.

17. **Caradoc**

—Howden (B.).

18. **China**

—Gough (V.).

19. **Chounda**

—Littler.

20. **Coloony**

—Gort (V.).

21. **Ghuznee**

—Keane (B.).

22. **Goojerat**

—Gough (V.).

23. **Hindostan**

—Hussey (of Wood Walton, Co. Huntingdon).

24. **Kars**

—Williams (Bt.).

25. **Khelat**

—Willshire (Bt.).

26. **Kymmer-yn Lydeirnon**

—Hughes.

27. **Lissa**

—Hoste (Bt.).

28. **Lybia**

—Doyle (Bt.).

29. **Madripore**
—Hislop (Bt.).

30. **Maharajpore**
—Littler.

31. **Maya**
—Cameron (Bt.).

32. **Minorca**
—Duckworth (Bt.).

33. **Mouguerre**
—Byng, Strafford (B.).

34. **Moveo et proficior** *Latin* 'I proceed and prosper'
—Ranfurly (E.).

35. **Nagpore**
—Jenkins.

36. **Navarin**
—Codrington.

37. **Netherlands**
—Jones (of Cranmer Hall, Co. Norfolk, Bt.).

38. **Nile**
—Thompson (Bt.).

39. **Orthes**
—Walker (Bt.), Harvey (of Thorpe).

40. **Pelasgi**
—Starke.

41. **Pennsylvania**
—Penn (of Stoke Pogis, Co. Bucks).

42. **Piedmontaise**
—Hardinge.

43. **Pilot**
—Nicolas (of Cornwall).

44. **Salamanca**
—Combermere (V.).

45. **San Josef**
—Nelson (E.).

46. **Sherwoode**
—Hood.

47. **Spartan**
—Brenton (Bt.).

48. **Spurs, 1513**

—Clarke (of Kensington).

49. **St. Domingo**

—Louis (Bt.), Duckworth (Bt.).

50. **St. Sebastian**

—Collier (Bt.).

51. **St. Vincent**

—Radstock (B.).

52. **Ternate**

—Burr.

53. **Towton**

—Mathew.

54. **Trafalgar**
—Nelson (E.), Northesk (E.), Codrington, Harvey, Tyler.

55. **Waterloo**

—Nicholson.

56. **West Indies**
—Prevost (of Belmont, Co. Hants, Bt.).

PROSPERITY (*See also* FLOURISHING; INCREASE; SUCCESS.)

1. **Adversis major, par secundis** *Latin* 'Greater than adversity, a match for prosperity'

—Bulwer, Forbes.

2. **Amser yw'n golud** *Welsh* 'Time is our wealth'
—Ystradgynlais R. D. C., U.K.

3. **By industry we prosper**

—Gavin (of Lanton).

4. **Contranando incrementum** *Latin* 'Prosperity by swimming against the stream'

—Town of Peebles.

5. **Copiosè et opportunê** *Latin* 'Plentifully and opportunely'
—Bunting.

6. **Cressa ne careat** *Latin* 'Let not Cressa (Cresswell) want'
—Cresswell.

7. **Dum sedulo prospero** *Latin* 'While engaged industriously I prosper'

—Swinton.

8. **E tellure effodiuntur opes** *Latin* 'Our wealth is dug out of the earth'
                                                    —Aston (of Bescot).

9. **E terra divitiae** *Latin* 'From the earth, riches'
                                                    —Swadlincote U. D. C., U.K.

10. **Floret qui laborat** *Latin* 'He who labors prospers'
                                —Mossley B. C., Rawtenstall B. C., U.K., Ross.

11. **Floret qui vigilat** *Latin* 'He is prosperous who is vigilant'
                                                    —Smith.

12. **Geld verbindet, sucht und findet** *German* 'Money binds, seeks and finds'
                                —Ludwig VIII, Landgrave of Hesse-Darmstadt
                                                    (1691–1768).

13. **Golud gwlad rhyddid** *Welsh* 'The wealth of the land is freedom'
                                                    —Cardiganshire C. C., U.K.

14. **Happiness and prosperity through unity** *(from Burmese)*
                                                    —Union of Burma.

15. **Hoc fonte derivata copia** *Latin* 'Wealth, drawn from this spring'
                                                    —Wells City Council, U.K.

16. **Honesta bona** *Latin* 'Wealth honorably got'
                                                    —Edgell, Wyatt-Edgell.

17. **Hwy peri clod na golud** *Welsh* 'Fame lasts longer than riches'
                                                    —Lloyd (of Rosindale and Aston).

18. **Indocilis pauperiem pati** *Latin* 'Untaught to suffer poverty'
                                                    —Merchants of Bristol.

19. **Inopem me copia fecit** *Latin* 'Plenty has made me poor'
                                                    —Bell.

20. **In prosperis time, in adversis spera** *Latin* 'In prosperity, fear, in adversity, hope'
                                                    —Gabriel.

21. **Le bon temps viendra** *French* 'The prosperous time will come'
                                —Griffith (of Llwynduris), Farrington, Harcourt (of
                                                    Aukerwycke), Wrey (Bt.).

22. **Liberty and prosperity**
                                                    —State of New Jersey.

23. **Macte virtute esto** *Latin* 'Go on and prosper'
                                                    —Dixon, Lowndes.

24. **Melius est nomen bonum quam divitiae multae** *Latin* 'A good name is rather to be chosen than great riches'
—[Prov. xxii. 1.] Alexander, Duke of Schleswig-Holstein (1573–1627).

25. **Metuo secundis** *Latin* 'I am fearful in prosperity'
—Hodgeson, Uppleby (of Wootton).

26. **Mihi lucra** *Latin* 'My gains'
—Scott.

27. **Mon tresor** *French* 'My treasure'
—Montresor.

28. **Moveo et proficior** *Latin* 'I proceed and prosper'
—Ranfurly (E.).

29. **Nid cyfoeth ond boddlonrwydd** *Welsh* 'No wealth without contentment'
—Garnons (Co. Denbigh and Co. Herts.).

30. **Non opes, sed ingenium** *Latin* 'Not wealth, but mind'
—Ross.

31. **Omni secundo** *Latin* 'Everything prosperous'
—Murdock.

32. **Opes consilium parit** *Latin* 'Wisdom begets wealth'
—Bridgwater B. C., U.K.

33. **Opes industria parit** *Latin* 'Industry produces riches'
—Tomlin.

34. **Opes parit industria** *Latin* 'Industry begets plenty' *or* 'Industry produces riches'
—Bingley U. D. C., U.K.; Benson.

35. **Opes regum, corda subditorum** *Latin* 'The riches of kings are the hearts of their subjects'
—Order of Leopold (Austria).

36. **Opima spolia** *Latin* 'The richest of the spoil'
—O'Meara.

37. **Oro y plata** *Spanish* 'Gold and silver'
—State of Montana.

38. **Pax, copia, sapientia** *Latin* 'Peace, plenty, wisdom'
—Fleming (Bt.), Fleming (of Manchester), West.

39. **Pax, copia, virtus** *Latin* 'Peace, plenty, virtue'
—McAdam, Stewart.

40. **Pax copia** *Latin* 'Peace, plenty'
—Read.

41. **Pax et copia**   *Latin* 'Peace and plenty'
—Chandlee, David.

42. **Peace and plenty**
—Barnes.

43. **Praedae memor**   *Latin* 'Mindful of gain'
—Graham.

44. **Prestat opes sapientia**   *Latin* 'Wisdom is preferable to riches'
—Livingston (U.S.); Upcher.

45. **Progress, peace, prosperity**
—The Gambia.

46. **Prospere qui sedulo**   *Latin* '(He does) prosperously (who does) industriously'
—Cunninghame.

47. **Prospere si propere**   *Latin* 'Prosperously if promptly'
—Peat.

48. **Qui uti scit ei bona**   *Latin* 'Be wealth to him who knows how to use it'
—Berwick (B.), Hill.

49. **Rhyddid hedd a llwyddiant**   *Welsh* 'Freedom, peace, and prosperity'
—Carmarthen B. C., U.K.

50. **Secundis dubiisque rectus**   *Latin* 'Upright both in prosperity and in perils'
—[after Horace, *Car.* iv. 9, 35.] Camperdown (E.), Cleveland (D.), Lippincott.

51. **Secundo, curo**   *Latin* 'I prosper and am cautious'
—Buchanan.

52. **Sedule et prospere**   *Latin* 'Diligently and prosperously'
—White.

53. **Sedule et secunde**   *Latin* 'Diligently and prosperously'
—Lookyer.

54. **Sioth chain agus fairsinge**   *Gaelic* 'Peace and plenty'
—Kavanagh.

55. **Spero infestis, metuo secundis**   *Latin* 'I hope in adversity, I fear in prosperity'
—Ellerton, Ludlow (E.), Stewart.

56. **Spero procedere**   *Latin* 'I hope to prosper'
—Hopkirk.

57. **Sub pace copia**   *Latin* 'Under peace, plenty'
—France, Franco.

58. **Undeb hedd llwyddiant**   *Welsh* 'Unity, peace, prosperity'
—Breconshire C. C., U.K.

59. **Ut prosim aliis prosim**   *Latin* 'Let me prosper that I may benefit others'
—Ferguson.

60. **Vertu surpasse richesse**   *French* 'Virtue excels riches'
—Johann, Duke of Holstein-Gottorp (1606–55).

61. **Wisdom above riches**
—Nuthoobhoy.

PROTECTION (*See also* DEFENSE; SUPPORT.)

1. **Ad arma paratus**   *Latin* 'Prepared for arms'
—Johnstone (of Corehead).

2. **Aegis fortissima virtus**   *Latin* 'Virtue is the strongest shield'
—Aspinall.

3. **Better a wee bush than nae bield**   *Scots dial.* 'Better a wee bush than no shelter'
—Burns.

4. **Cassis tutissima virtus**   *Latin* 'Virtue is the safest helmet'
—Armour, Charrington, Cholmondeley (M.), Delamere (B.), Helme.

5. **Clypeus omnibus in te sperantibus**   *Latin* 'Thou art a shield to all who place their hope in thee'
—[after Prov. xxx. 5.] Maximilian, Prince-Elector of Bavaria (1573–1651); Maximilian Emanuel, Elector of Bavaria (1662–1726).

6. **Crux auctrix et tutrix**   *Latin* 'The Cross my help and protection'
—Friedrich II, Duke of Saxony-Gotha and Altenburg (1676–1732).

7. **Dea providentia nostra est haereditas**   *Latin* 'The goddess providence is our inheritance'
—Turner (U.S.).

8. **Decus et tutamen**   *Latin* 'An honor and a protection'
—Gravesend B. C., U.K.

9. **Dirigo et defendo**   *Latin* 'I direct and protect'
—Sheppard.

10. **Forte escu** *French* 'Strong shield'
—Fortescue.

11. **Forte scutum salus ducum** *Latin* 'A strong shield is the safety of generals'
—Fortescue (E.), Fortescue, Clermont (B.).

12. **Garde le droit** *French* 'Protect the right'
—Wright (U.S.).

13. **Garde le roy** *Old French* 'Defend the king'
—Lane (of King's Bromley).

14. **Garde ta bien aimée** *French* 'Protect thy well-beloved'
—Maze.

15. **God's providence is my inheritance**
—House in Inverkeithing, Scotland.

16. **Gorau tarian cyfiawnder** *Welsh* 'The best shield is justice'
—Flintshire C. C., U.K.

17. **Hic regit, ille tuetur** *Latin* 'This governs, that protects'
—Philipp II, Duke of Pomerania (1573–1618).

18. **Hinc decus inde tegmen** *Latin* 'From this quarter honor, from that protection'
—Graham.

19. **Industria murus** *Latin* 'Industry is a protection'
—Thomson.

20. **Monemus et munimus** *Latin* 'We counsel and protect'
—Monmouth B. C., U.K.

21. **Natos et nostra tuemur** *Latin* 'We protect our sons and our property'
—Anne of Austria, wife of Louis XIII (1601–66).

22. **Navem tuam Christe tuere** *Latin* 'Protect Thy ship, O Christ!'
—Friedrich II, the Wise, Elector of the Palatinate of Rhein (1483–1556).

23. **Pietas praesidium firmissimum** *Latin* 'Piety is the surest protection'
—Ernst, Margrave of Brandenburg (1583–1613).

24. **Pro arae et regni custodia** *Latin* 'For the guardianship of the altar and the kingdom'
—Queen Mary of England.

25. **Qui distulit non abstulit ipse me protegat**   *Latin* 'He who has removed it has not taken it away: may he himself protect me'
—Edward Fortunatus, Margrave of Baden (referring to his aversion to the Roman Church).

26. **Scuto magis quam gladio**   *Latin* 'With the shield more than the sword'
—Shield.

27. **Sedulo et honeste tutela**   *Latin* 'Guardianship with honor and diligence'
—Lyell.

28. **Statio bene fida carinis**   *Latin* 'A trustworthy harbor for vessels'
—Queenstown Harbour, Cork, Ireland.

29. **Sub tuum praesidium**   *Latin* 'Under thy protection'
—Order of St. Anna.

30. **Turris prudentia custos**   *Latin* 'Prudence is the safeguard of the tower'
—Lauder.

31. **Vérité soyez ma garde**   *French* 'Truth be my protection'
—Brewster.

32. **Virtus tutissima cassis**   *Latin* 'Virtue is the safest helmet'
—Barker, Bellairs, Finch, Hatton, Stephenson, Williams.

33. **Ysgwyd**   *Welsh* 'A shield'
—Hughes.

PROVIDENCE (*See also* DIVINE GIFTS; DIVINE GUIDANCE; DIVINITY; SALVATION.)

1. **Benigno Numine**   *Latin* 'By benign Providence'
—Bently, Chatham (E.), Davies, Copeland, Grenville, Hicks, Meigh, Pitt, Smith (of Dorchester).

2. **By the providence of God**
—Atkyns, MacSween.

3. **Confido in providentia**   *Latin* 'I trust in providence'
—Richardson.

4. **Dea providentia nostra est haereditas**   *Latin* 'The goddess providence is our inheritance'
—Turner (U.S.).

5. **Dei Providentia juvat**   *Latin* 'The providence of God is our help'
—Welman (of Poundsford Park).

6. **Deo non fortunâ** *Latin* 'By Providence, not by fortune'
—Digby (E.), Harrison.

7. **Deo non fortunae** *Latin* 'To God not fortune'
—Gardiners.

8. **Favente Numine** *Latin* 'By the favor of Providence'
—Dyce-Sombre, Micklethwayt, Peckham.

9. **Goddes vorsehen wirt geschen** *German* 'God's providence will happen'
—Julius, Duke of Braunschweig-Wolfenbüttel (1529–89).

10. **God's providence is my inheritance**
—House in Inverkeithing, Scotland.

11. **Numen et omnia** *Latin* 'Providence and all things'
—Graham.

12. **Omnia Providentiae committo** *Latin* 'I commit all things to Providence'
—Devenish, Meares.

13. **Provide**
—Stewart (of Grandtully, Bt.).

14. **Providence**
—Craick.

15. **Providence and perseverance**
—Furnaval.

16. **Providence with adventure**
—Hawkins.

17. **Providentiâ** *Latin* 'By providence'
—Anderson.

18. **Providentia Domini sufficientia mihi** *Latin* 'God's providence suffices for me'
—Johanne Magdalene, Duchess of Saxony-Weissenfels (1656–86).

19. **Providentiae fido** *Latin* 'I trust to Providence'
—Stewart (of Fornese).

20. **Providentiae haec divinae obnoxia** *Latin* 'This stands under divine providence'
—Friedrich Wilhelm, Elector of Brandenburg (1620–88).

21. **Providentiae me committo** *Latin* 'I commit myself to Providence'
—Kyle, Park (of Fulfordlies).

22. **Providentia et industria** *Latin* 'By providence and industry'
—Anderson.

23. **Providentiâ et virtute** *Latin* 'By providence and virtue'
—Rankin.

24. **Providentia sumus** *Latin* 'We are with providence'
—Blatchford (U.S.).

25. **Providentia tutamen** *Latin* 'Providence is my safeguard'
—Thomson.

26. **Providentiâ tutamur** *Latin* 'We are protected by Providence'
—Kenyon, Norden.

27. **Provyd**
—Stewart.

28. **Sustentatus providentiâ** *Latin* 'Sustained by providence'
—Rolland.

29. **Totum est providentia** *Latin* 'Everything is by providence'
—Judge.

30. **Virtute et numine** *Latin* 'By virtue and providence'
—Cloncurry (B.), Creagh, Lawless.

PROVOCATION
1. **Audi consilium** *Latin* 'Heed counsel'
—West Riding C. C., U.K.

2. **Nemo me impune lacessit** *Latin* 'No one provokes me with impunity'
—Irwin (Co. Sligo), Nettles (of Nettleville, Co. Cork);
Order of St. Andrew of Scotland.

3. **Noli irritare leonem** *Latin* 'Irritate not the lion'
—Abbs, Underwood.

4. **Noli irritare leones** *Latin* 'Do not exasperate the lions'
—Lyons (B.), Lyons (of Ledestown).

PRUDENCE (*See also* CAUTION; DISCRETION; FORESIGHT; MODERATION; WISDOM.)
1. **Adest prudenti animus** *Latin* 'Courage belongs to the prudent'
—Hamilton (of Mount Hamilton).

2. **Agendo gnaviter** *Latin* 'By acting prudently'
—Leeke (Co. Salop), Rowe, Whitworth.

3. **Amore et prudentia** *Latin* 'By love and by prudence'
   —Friedrich II, Duke of Saxony-Gotha and Altenburg
   (1676–1732).

4. **Animo et prudentia** *Latin* 'By courage and prudence'
   —Howett, Jowett, Lyon, Mellor.

5. **Animum prudentia firmat** *Latin* 'Prudence strengthens courage'
   —Brisbane (of Scotland).

6. **A tout pourvoir** *French* 'To provide for everything'
   —Oliphant (Co. Perth).

7. **Auriga virtutum prudentia** *Latin* 'Prudence is the directress of
   the virtues'
   —Mawbey (of Surrey).

8. **Ayez prudence** *French* 'Have prudence'
   —Biss (of Durham).

9. **Consilio ac virtute** *Latin* 'By prudence and valor'
   —Lewin.

10. **Consilio et prudentia** *Latin* 'By wisdom and prudence'
    —Clancarty (E.), Le-Poer Trench.

11. **Constans et prudens** *Latin* 'Constant and prudent'
    —Campbell (of Skerrington).

12. **Constanter et prudentia** *Latin* 'Firmly and prudently'
    —Campbell (of Sombey), Cessnock (of Treesbank and
    Fairfield).

13. **Consulto et audaciter** *Latin* 'With prudence and daring'
    —Plummer.

14. **Cruce non prudentia** *Latin* 'By the cross, not by prudence'
    —Topham.

15. **Cum prudentia sedulus** *Latin* 'Diligent with prudence'
    —Beatson, Betson.

16. **Cura et candore** *Latin* 'With care and sincerity'
    —Cunningham (Bt.), Forbes (of Ardo).

17. **D. F. D. H. I. D. W. A. (Die Furcht des Herrn ist der Weisheit
    Anfang)** *German* 'Fear of the Lord is the beginning of wis-
    dom'
    —[Ps., cxi. 10.] Dorothee Hedwig, Princess of Anhalt
    (1587–1608); Johann Sigismund, Elector of
    Brandenburg (1572–1619).

18. **Die Furcht des Herrn ist die Krone der Weisheit** *German* 'Fear of the Lord is the crown of wisdom'
—Bernhard VII, Prince of Anhalt (1540–70).

19. **Estote prudentes** *Latin* 'Be ye prudent'
—Wilkins.

20. **Fato prudentia major** *Latin* 'Prudence is greater than fate'
—[Vergil, *Geor.* i. 416.] Cheney, Lomax (of Clayton); Catherine de Medicis (1519–89).

21. **Fortis qui prudens** *Latin* 'He is brave who is prudent'
—Ormsby.

22. **Fortitudine et prudentiâ** *Latin* 'By fortitude and prudence'
—Hargreaves, Herbert, Hacket, Lighton (Bt.), O'Reilly (of Knock Abbey), Powis (E.), Younge (of Bassingbourn).

23. **Fortitudo et prudentia** *Latin* 'Fortitude and prudence'
—Egan.

24. **Industry and prudence conquer**
—Accrington B. C., U.K.

25. **In prudentia & simplicitate** *Latin* 'In prudence and simplicity'
—Vaughan (U.S.).

26. **Labore et prudentia** *Latin* 'By labor and prudence'
—Bartolozzi, Brighouse B. C., U.K.

27. **Nec cunctando nec temere agendo** *Latin* 'Neither by delaying nor by acting rashly'
—Twemlow.

28. **Nec improvidus** *Latin* 'Not improvident'
—Danskine.

29. **Nec temere nec lente** *Latin* 'Neither rashly nor slowly'
—Joynt.

30. **Nil nisi prudenter** *Latin* 'Only prudently'
—Bernhard, Duke of Saxony-Meiningen (1649–1706).

31. **Nil temere** *Latin* 'Nothing rashly'
—Balfour, Tennyson, Tennyson-D'Encourt.

32. **Nil temere, neque timore** *Latin* 'Nothing rashly, nor with fear'
—Berney (Bt.).

33. **Nil temerè tenta, nil timidè** *Latin* 'Attempt nothing either rashly or timidly'
—Buckle (Co. Sussex).

34. **Non temere** *Latin* 'Not rashly'
—Balfour, Forbes (of Edinglassie, Bt.).

35. **Not rashly, nor with fear**
                    —Harrison.

36. **Ornat fortem prudentia**   *Latin* 'Prudence adorns the brave'
                    —Dunbar.

37. **Pie et prudenter**   *Latin* 'With piety and prudence'
                    —Heinrich X, Count Reuss (1662–1711).

38. **Pietate, legibus, justitia**   *Latin* 'By piety, by prudence and by justice'
                    —Friedrich I, Duke of Saxony-Gotha and Altenburg (1646–91).

39. **Pietate et prudentia**   *Latin* 'By piety and prudence'
                    —August, Duke of Saxony-Zörbig (1655–1715).

40. **Pietatem prudentiae praefer**   *Latin* 'Prefer piety to prudence'
                    —Otto, Landgrave of Hesse (1594–1617).

41. **Praetis prudentia praestat**   *Latin* 'Prudence is preferable to money'
                    —Morison (U.S.).

42. **Pretio prudentia**   *Latin* 'Prudence rather than money'
                    —Richardson (U.S.).

43. **Pretio prudentia praestat**   *Latin* 'Prudence is better than profit'
                    —Morison.

44. **Provide et constanter**   *Latin* 'Prudently and steadfastly'
                    —Friedrich Wilhelm, Duke of Mecklenburg-Schwerin (1675–1713).

45. **Provide et fortiter**   *Latin* 'With prudence and with courage'
                    —Johann Georg I, Elector of Saxony (1585–1656).

46. **Providus esto**   *Latin* 'Be thou circumspect'
                    —Maxtone.

47. **Prudens, fidelis, et audax**   *Latin* 'Prudent, faithful, and bold'
                    —Leigh.

48. **Prudens et innocuus**   *Latin* 'Prudent and harmless'
                    —Kingsbury.

49. **Prudens futuri**   *Latin* 'Prudent for the future'
                    —Letchworth U. D. C., U.K.

50. **Prudens qui patiens**   *Latin* 'He is prudent who is patient'
                    —Coke, Leicester (E.), Lushington (of Pool and Kent).

51. **Prudens simplicitas beat**   *Latin* 'Prudent simplicity blesses'
                    —Frederick.

52. **Prudent comme le serpent** *French* 'Prudent as the serpent'
—Taylor.

53. **Prudenter et constanter** *Latin* 'Prudently and steadfastly'
—Johann Ernst II, Duke of Saxony-Weimar (1627–83).

54. **Prudenter et simpliciter** *Latin* 'Prudently and simply'
—Vaughan (U.S.).

55. **Prudenter qui sedulo** *Latin* '(He does) prudently who (does) industriously'
—Milne.

56. **Prudenter vigilo** *Latin* 'I watch prudently'
—Donaldson.

57. **Prudentia** *Latin* 'With prudence'
—Young, Jaggard.

58. **Prudentia, fraudis nescia** *Latin* 'Prudence, which knows not deceit'
—Elphinston.

59. **Prudentia decus innocentia** *Latin* 'Prudence, grace, innocence'
—Ramsay.

60. **Prudentiâ et animis** *Latin* 'By prudence and courage'
—Steel.

61. **Prudentiâ et animo** *Latin* 'By prudence and courage'
—Antram, Ochterlony (Bt.).

62. **Prudentiâ et constantiâ** *Latin* 'With prudence and constancy'
—Denman (B.).

63. **Prudentia et honor** *Latin* 'Prudence and honor'
—McKinna.

64. **Prudentia et justitia** *Latin* 'With prudence and justice'
—Kaye-Shuttleworth.

65. **Prudentia et marte** *Latin* 'With prudence and courage'
—Mylne.

66. **Prudentiâ et simplicitate** *Latin* 'With prudence and simplicity'
—Lant.

67. **Prudentia et vi** *Latin* 'By prudence and might'
—Innes.

68. **Prudentia et vigilantia** *Latin* 'By prudence and watchfulness'
—Purchon.

69. **Prudentia et virtute** *Latin* 'By prudence and valor'
—Rankin.

70. **Prudentia gloriam acquirit**   *Latin* 'Prudence obtains glory'
—Litton.

71. **Prudentia in adversos**   *Latin* 'Prudence in adversity'
—Tollet (of Betley), Wickstead.

72. **Prudentia me sustinet**   *Latin* 'Prudence upholds me'
—Boyd.

73. **Prudentia praestat**   *Latin* 'Prudence excels'
—Morison.

74. **Prudentiâ simplicitate**   *Latin* 'With prudence and simplicity'
—Wyrley-Birch (of Wretham, Co. Norfolk).

75. **Prudentia tutus**   *Latin* 'Safe by prudence'
—Brodigan.

76. **Prudhomme et loyale**   *French* 'Prudent and loyal'
—Prudham.

77. **Resolutio cauta**   *Latin* 'A prudent resolution'
—Bethune.

78. **Robori prudentia praestat**   *Latin* 'Prudence excels strength'
—Young.

79. **Sapientia/ caritas/ prudentia**   *Latin* 'Wisdom/ charity/ prudence'
—Saint Mary of the Plains College, Dodge City, Kansas.

80. **Secura quae prudentes**   *Latin* 'What prudent people do is secure'
—Gray.

81. **Si sit prudentia**   *Latin* 'If there be prudence'
—[Juvenal, *Sat.* vii. 20.] Auckland (B.), Brown, Eden (Bt.), Henley (B.).

82. **Solertia ditat**   *Latin* 'Prudence enriches'
—Whitelaw.

83. **Turris prudentia custos**   *Latin* 'Prudence is the safeguard of the tower'
—Lauder.

84. **Victrix prudentia**   *Latin* 'Prudence is conqueror'
—Gordon.

85. **Virtute et prudentiâ**   *Latin* 'By virtue and prudence'
—Dames, Hepburn.

86. **Voor moed, beleid, trouw**   *Dutch* 'For courage, prudence, and fidelity'
—Order of Wilhelm (Netherlands).

PURITY (*See also* INNOCENCE; INTEGRITY; RECTITUDE; VIRTUE.)

1. **Absque dedecore** *Latin* 'Without stain'
    —Napier (of Falside).

2. **Agitatione purgatur** *Latin* 'It is purified by agitation'
    —Russell (Bt.).

3. **Beati mundi corde** *Latin* 'Blessed are the pure in heart'
    —[Matt., v. 8.] Lancing College, U.K.

4. **Candidiora pectora** *Latin* 'Purer (whiter) hearts'
    —Whytt.

5. **Candidus cantabit moriens** *Latin* 'The pure man will die cheerfully'
    —Cawdor (E.).

6. **Caste et pie** *Latin* 'Purely and piously'
    —Johann Georg II, Elector of Saxony (1613–80).

7. **Cor mundum crea in me Deus** *Latin* 'Create in me a clean heart, O God'
    —O'Crean, Lynch.

8. **Fides puritas** *Latin* 'Faith, purity'
    —Webster.

9. **Fonte puro** *Latin* 'From a pure fountain'
    —Lake.

10. **Hauri ex puro** *Latin* 'To be drawn from the pure fountain'
    —Pemberton.

11. **Immaculata gens** *Latin* 'An unspotted race'
    —Vaughan.

12. **Non eget integer** *Latin* 'The pure of life wants not'
    —Espinasse.

13. **Pectore puro** *Latin* 'With a clean breast'
    —Royall (U.S.).

14. **Pura sequi** *Latin* 'To follow pure things'
    —Milward (Co. Worcester).

15. **Pure de fonte** *French* 'From a clear spring'
    —Spring, Casborne.

16. **Pure et loyale** *French* 'Pure and loyal'
    —Amalie Elisabeth, Landgravine of Hesse-Cassel (1619–51).

17. **Pur et seincere** *Old French* 'Pure and sincere'
    —Luise Juliane, daughter of Prince of Orange (B. 1576).

18. **Pur sans peur**   *French* 'Pure without fear'
—White.

19. **Sans tache**   *French* 'Without stain'
—Gormanston (V.), Le Blanc, Martin (of Abercairny), Martin (of Colston-Basset), Michell, Moray, Napair (of Milliken, Bt.), Napier (of Blackstone), Preston, Hurry, Ure, Urie.

20. **Sine labe lucebit**   *Latin* 'He shall shine unblemished'
—Crawford.

21. **Sine labe nota**   *Latin* 'Known to be without a stain'
—Crawfurd (of Kilburney), McKenzie.

22. **Sine macula**   *Latin* 'Without spot'
—Cary, McCulloch, McKenzie, Synnot, Norcliffe.

23. **Sine macula macla**   *Latin* 'Stained without stain'
—Clough.

24. **Sit sine labe**   *Latin* 'Let it be without stain'
—Scott.

25. **Toujours sans tache**   *French* 'Always without a stain'
—Tabutean.

26. **Veritas, puritas**   *Latin* 'Truth and purity'
—Webster.

27. **Virgini immaculatae Bavaria immaculata (V. I. B. I.)**   *Latin* 'To the Immaculate Virgin Immaculate Bavaria'
—Order of St. George of Bavaria.

28. **Virginitas et unitas nostra fraternitas**   *Latin* 'Chastity and unity form our brotherhood'
—Pin-makers' Company.

29. **Vita et pectore puro**   *Latin* 'With pure life and heart'
—Beloe.

PURPOSE (*See also* DIRECTION; INTENTION.)

1. **Ad escam et usum**   *Latin* 'For food and use'
—Graden.

2. **Alta sententia**   *Latin* 'With high purpose'
—Arnold U. D. C., U.K.

3. **Avise la fin**   *French* 'Consider the end'
—Ailsa (M.), Kennedy.

4. **Avis la fin**   *French* 'Consider the end'
—Keydon.

5. **By aim and by effort**
                                        —Higginbotham.

6. **Consider thy purpose**
                        —Stevenage Development Corp., U.K.

7. **Honor, purpose, wisdom**
                        —Palo Verde College, Blythe, California.

8. **Justitiae propositique tenax** *Latin* 'Tenacious of justice and of purpose'
                                        —Stuart (Bt.).

9. **Justum et tenacem** *Latin* 'Just and firm of purpose'
                        —Colthurst (Bt.), Macknight or McKnight.

10. **Justum et tenacem propositi** *Latin* 'Just and firm of purpose'
                                        —Holmes.

11. **Justus ac tenax propositi** *Latin* 'Just and firm to my purpose'
                                        —Jones.

12. **Justus et propositi tenax** *Latin* 'Just and firm of purpose'
                        —Chedworth, How, Penrice (of Gt. Yarmouth).

13. **Justus propositi tenax** *Latin* 'The just is firm of purpose'
                                        —Ferrand.

14. **Meditari et agere** *Latin* 'To plan and to do'
                                        —Gross (U.S.).

15. **Non frustra** *Latin* 'Not without a purpose'
                                        —Barrow.

16. **Not in vain**
                        —Aylet (Co. Essex), Branfill, Brandon.

17. **Producing people with purpose**
                        —Miami Christian College, Miami, Florida.

18. **Propositi tenax** *Latin* 'Firm of purpose'
                                        —Bunny, Strutt, Smith.

PURSUIT (*See also* FOLLOWING; HUNTING; SEARCH and DISCOVERY.)

1. **Ardenter prosequor alis** *Latin* 'Eagerly do I pursue in my winged course'
                                        —Graeme.

2. **Chase**
                                        —Geary (Bt.).

3. **Digna sequens** *Latin* 'Pursuing worthy aims'
                                        —Botsford.

4. **Faint yet pursuing**
—Dickinson.

5. **Nigarum vestigia premo** *Latin* 'I track the footprints of the dark ones'
—Seton.

6. **Non inferiora** *Latin* 'Not mean pursuits'
—Monro (of Bearcroft).

7. **Non inferiora secutus** *Latin* 'Not having followed mean pursuits'
—Buchan (of Kelly), Count St. Aldergoude, Bromley, Grant, Montford (B.).

8. **Quae recta sequor** *Latin* 'I pursue things honorable'
—Campbell.

9. **So run that you may obtain**
—[1 Cor. ix. 24.] Baker.

REASON (*See also* MIND; THOUGHT.)

1. **Alles mit Gott, nichts ohn Ursach** *German* 'Everything with God: nothing without reason'
—Elisabeth, Duchess of Saxony (1593–1650).

2. **Appetitus rationi pareat** *Latin* 'Let your desires obey your reason'
—[Cicero, de Off. I. 39. 10.] Custance (of Weston, Co. Norfolk).

3. **Ciall agos neart** *Gaelic* 'Reason and power'
—O'Connell (of Derrynane Abbey, Co. Kerry).

4. **Come now, and let us reason together**
—[from Isaiah iv. 18.] Lyndon B. Johnson.

5. **Dux vitae ratio** *Latin* 'Reason is the guide of life'
—Bennett, Boulton, West.

6. **Dux vitae ratio in cruce victoria** *Latin* 'Reason the guide of life, victory in the cross'
—Fanshaw.

7. **Follow reason**
—Spooner (U.S.).

8. **For right and reason**
—Graham, King.

9. **Lege et ratione** *Latin* 'By law and reason'
—Crookshank (U.S.).

10. **Lex ratio summa or Lex summa ratio** *Latin* 'Law is the highest reason'

   —Law.

11. **Moriendo vivo** *Latin* 'In dying I live'

   —Yaldwyn.

12. **Mors janua vitae** *Latin* 'Death is the gate of life'

   —Brograve.

13. **Mors mihi vita est** *Latin* 'Death is life to me'

   —Wolseley, Wolseley (Bt.).

14. **Per funera vitam** *Latin* 'Through death, life'

   —Scots Guards, U.K.

15. **Perit ut vivat** *Latin* 'He dies that he may live'

   —Fenwick, Phin.

16. **Quorsum vivere mori? Mori vita** *Latin* 'Wherefore live to die? To die is life'

   —Blencowe.

17. **Raison pour guide** *French* 'Reason for guide'

   —Gascoyne.

18. **Ratione, non irâ** *Latin* 'By reason, not by rage'

   —Small (of Curriehill).

19. **Ratione, non vi** *Latin* 'By reason, not by force'

   —McTaggart (Bt.).

20. **Reason contents me**

   —Graham (of Esk and Netherby, Bt.).

21. **Right and reason**

   —Graham (of Leitchtown).

22. **Rycht and reason**

   —Graham.

23. **Suivez la raison** *French* 'Follow reason'

   —Armistead.

24. **Suivez raison** *French* 'Follow reason'

   —Browne (of Elsing Hall, Co. Norfolk), Browne, Barberrie, Dixon (of Unthank Hall), Hillasdon, Kilmaine (B.), Montague (V.), Sligo (M.), Wyatt.

REBIRTH (*See also* BIRTH; DEATH; LIFE; PARADISE; SALVATION.)

1. **Aqua cadit resurgere** *Latin* 'Water falls to rise again'

   —Waterfall.

2. **Aucto splendore resurgo**   *Latin* 'I rise again with increased glory'
—85th Foot (Shropshire Light Infantry).

3. **Depressa resurgo**   *Latin* 'Although laid low, I rise again'
—Pintard (U.S.).

4. **Disce mori ut vivas**   *Latin* 'Learn to die that thou mayest live'
—Unett.

5. **Domum antiquam redintegrare**   *Latin* 'To resuscitate an ancient house'
—Hepburn (of Smeaton, Bt.).

6. **Ero quod eram**   *Latin* 'I will again be what I was'
—Landen, Scrogie.

7. **Et mortua virescunt**   *Latin* 'Even dead things begin to flourish'
—Lindsay.

8. **Ex seipso renascens**   *Latin* 'Born again from its own ashes'
—Fraser.

9. **Extinctus orior**   *Latin* 'I rise when dead'
—Douglas.

10. **Ex urna resurgam**   *Latin* 'I shall rise again from the urn (i.e., the tomb)'
—Blandy.

11. **Inclinata resurgo**   *Latin* 'Though bowed down, I rise again'
—Johann Adolf, Duke of Schleswig-Holstein-Sonderburg-
Plön (1634–1704), Cooper.

12. **Instaurator ruinae**   *Latin* 'A repairer of ruin'
—Forsyth.

13. **I renew my age**
—Garshore.

14. **Lauro resurgo**   *Latin* 'I rise again with the laurel'
—Lorain.

15. **Mortua vivescunt**   *Latin* 'The dead revive'
—Lindsay (of Blackholm).

16. **Percussa resurgo**   *Latin* 'Being struck down I rise again'
—Jordan.

17. **Percussus elevor**   *Latin* 'Smitten down I am lifted up'
—Dovaston.

18. **Raised again**
—Hunter.

19. **Recuperatus**   *Latin* 'Recovered'
—MacWilliams (U.S.).

20. **Redeunt Saturnia regna** *Latin* 'The golden age is returning'
—[Vergil, *Ecl.* iv. 6.] Friedrich August II, Elector of Saxony (1696–1763).

21. **Renascentur** *Latin* 'They will rise again'
—Avonmore (V.), Skiffington.

22. **Renovabitur ut aquilae juventus tua** *Latin* 'Thy youth shall be renewed as the eagles'
—Barlow.

23. **Renovate animos** *Latin* 'Renew your courage'
—Hay, Drummond, Kinnoul (E.).

24. **Renovato nomine** *Latin* 'With renewed name'
—Lyttelton, Westcote.

25. **Renovatur aetas ejus sicut aquilae** *Latin* 'His age is renewed like the eagle's'
—Raymond.

26. **Reparabit cornua Phoebe** *Latin* 'The moon will replenish her horns'
—Polwarth (B.), Scott (of Abbotsford (Bt.), Scott (of Raeburn and Harden).

27. **Restitutor** *Latin* 'A restorer'
—Order of Danebrog (Denmark).

28. **Resurgam** *Latin* 'I shall rise again'
—Crosby, Stewart (of Newhall).

29. **Resurgere tento** *Latin* 'I strive to rise again'
—Straiton.

30. **Resurgo** *Latin* 'I rise again'
—Cooper, Haxton, McFall.

31. **Revirescam** *Latin* 'I shall flourish again'
—Dalgleish.

32. **Revirescat** *Latin* 'May it flourish again'
—Gould, Maxwell.

33. **Reviresco** *Latin* 'I grow green again'
—Rishton U. D. C., U.K.

34. **Rinasco piu glorioso** *Italian* 'I rise again more glorious'
—St. Clair, St. Clair-Erskine (Earl of Rosslyn).

35. **Ut reficiar** *Latin* 'That I may be replenished'
—Archbald, Archibald.

36. **Ut resurgam** *Latin* 'That I may rise again'
—Pennycock (of Newhall).

37. **Viresco vulnere** *Latin* 'I revive by my wounds'
—Oldfield.

38. **Vive revicturus** *Latin* 'Live (as if) about to live again'
—Vivian.

RECTITUDE (*See also* FAIRNESS; HONESTY; HONOR; INTEGRITY;
PRINCIPLES; PURITY; RIGHTEOUSNESS; RIGHTS; TRUSTWORTHINESS;
VIRTUE; WORTHINESS.)

1. **A bon droit** *French* 'Rightfully'
—Slade (Bt.).

2. **Ad amussim** *Latin* 'By the plumb-line'
—Cunyngham (Bt.).

3. **Agissez honnêtement** *French* 'Act uprightly'
—Cardwell.

4. **Always do right. This will gratify some people and astonish the rest.**
—(from Mark Twain) Wilbur Lucius Cross.

5. **Assist the right**
—Korda.

6. **Audax in recto** *Latin* 'Bold in the right'
—Stewart.

7. **Aufrichtig, beständig, so lang ich lebendig** *German* 'Upright and
steadfast so long as I live'
—Ludwig VIII, Landgrave of Hesse-Darmstadt
(1691–1768).

8. **Benefac, Domine, bonis et rectis corde** *Latin* 'Do good, O Lord,
unto those that be good, and to them that are upright in their
hearts'
—[Ps. cxxv. 4.] Wilhelm V, Duke of Bavaria (1548–1626).

9. **Be sure you're right, then go ahead**
—Davy Crockett.

10. **Bonus justus et utilis** *Latin* 'Good, just, and useful'
—Lerrier.

11. **Claritate dextra** *Latin* 'With a bright light on the right'
—Brady, Geale-Brady.

12. **Corde recto elati omnes** *Latin* 'All are elevated by a right heart'
—Playing-card Makers' Company.

13. **Desire the right**
—Falkland Islands.

14. **Droit**   *French* 'Right'
>> —Tunstall (of Durham Hartley).

15. **Droyt et devaunt**   *Old French* 'Right and forward'
>> —Drury.

16. **Dum clarum rectum teneam**   *Latin* 'May I keep the line of right as well as of glory'
>> —Penn (of Stoke Park).

17. **En bon et poyer**   *Old French* 'In right and might'
>> —Cockayne.

18. **En droyt devant**   *Old French* 'Foremost in right'
>> —Molineux.

19. **Et decus et pretium recti**   *Latin* 'Both the honor and the reward of rectitude'
>> —Fitz-Roy, Grafton (D.), Southampton (B.), Disney.

20. **Fac recte et nil time**   *Latin* 'Do right and fear nothing'
>> —Jeffries, Hill.

21. **Fac recte nil time**   *Latin* 'Do right, fear nothing'
>> —Ashworth.

22. **Fas ducit**   *Latin* 'Right leads'
>> —Rasch (Bt.).

23. **For right**
>> —Stirling (of Denchray).

24. **For right and reason**
>> —Graham, King.

25. **Fortis si jure fortis**   *Latin* 'Strong if strong in right'
>> —Stockenstrom (Bt.).

26. **Fortiter et recte**   *Latin* 'Boldly and justly'
>> —Crayford U. D. C., U.K., Drake (Bt.), Rankin, Anderson.

27. **Garde le droit**   *French* 'Protect the right'
>> —Wright (U.S.).

28. **Habeo pro jus fasque**   *Latin* 'I stay on the side of law and right'
>> —Cushman (U.S.).

29. **In dubiis rectus**   *Latin* 'Upright in doubtful affairs'
>> —Lees.

30. **Industria et probitate**   *Latin* 'By industry and probity'
>> —Hives, Washbourne, Browne (of Ebbw Vale, Co. Monmouth).

31. **In recto fides** *Latin* 'Faith in rectitude'
   —Dixon.

32. **Integer vitae** *Latin* 'Upright in life'
   —[from Horace, *Odes* I. xxii. 1.] Beynon, Christie, Egginton.

33. **Intus si recte, ne labora** *Latin* 'If right within, trouble not'
   —Shrewsbury School, U.K.

34. **In uprightness God will support us**
   —Barrett.

35. **Je maintien devrai** *French* 'I maintain the right'
   —Nesbitt.

36. **Je voil droit avoir** *Old French* 'I will have right'
   —Huntley.

37. **Jure, non dono** *Latin* 'By right, not by gift'
   —Foulkes, Lloyd.

38. **Jus floruit** *Latin* 'Right has flourished'
   —Taylor.

39. **Kia kaha ki te mahi tika** *Maori?* 'Be strong to do that which is right'
   —Ward.

40. **Law and Right**
   —Allen.

41. **Maintien le droit** *French* 'Support the right'
   —Brydges (of Denton Court, Bt.), Bridges, Leatham.

42. **May the right prevail** *(from Greek)*
   —[Aeschylus, *Agamemnon*, 1. 121.] Brighton College, U.K.

43. **Mens conscia recti** *Latin* 'A mind conscious of rectitude'
   —Ashbrook (V.), Boulton, Collis, Crisp, Chrisop, Flower, Jary (of Burlingham), Kirsop, Nightingale, Phillips, Macartney (Bt.), Sillifant, Wright, Westmore, Watlington.

44. **Mens sibi conscia recti** *Latin* 'A mind conscious to itself of rectitude'
   —Crespyny, Wright (Bt.).

45. **Mentes consciae recti** *Latin* 'Minds conscious of their rectitude'
   —Wylie.

46. **Mon droit** *French* 'My right'
   —Ingilby (Bt.).

47. **Murus aeneus mens conscia recti**   *Latin* 'A mind conscious of rectitude is a brazen wall'

—Field.

48. **Nil nisi de jure**   *Latin* 'Nothing unless by right'

—Lomax.

49. **On in the right**

—Cawardine.

50. **Optima sapientia probitas**   *Latin* 'Probity is the best wisdom'

—Salmond.

51. **Per saxa per ignes fortiter et recte**   *Latin* 'Through rocks, through fires, bravely and rightly'

—Elliot (U.S.).

52. **Per vias rectas**   *Latin* 'By right ways'

—Blackwood (Bt.), Dufferin (B.).

53. **Pervicax recte**   *Latin* 'Steadfast in the right'

—McEwen.

54. **Por la razon o la fuerza**   *Spanish* 'By right or might'

—Republic of Chile.

55. **Quid leges sine moribus?**   *Latin* 'What are laws without morals?'

—Edwards (of Ashill, co. Norfolk).

56. **Recta pete**   *Latin* 'Seek for right things'

—Fletcher.

57. **Recta sequor**   *Latin* 'I follow uprightly'

—Keith.

58. **Recta vel ardua**   *Latin* 'Upright even (when) difficult'

—Evelick, Lindsay.

59. **Recte agens confido**   *Latin* 'While acting uprightly I am confident'

—Perry (of Avon Dasset).

60. **Recte et fideliter**   *Latin* 'Rightly and faithfully'

—Gibson, Spode.

61. **Recte et sapienter**   *Latin* 'Rightly and wisely'

—Heard.

62. **Rectitudine sto**   *Latin* 'I stand with the right'

—Du Pont (U.S.).

63. **Rectus in curvo**   *Latin* 'I keep upright in a curve (i.e., in a crooked path)'

—Symonds (of Great Ormesby).

64. **Right and reason**
                                        —Graham (of Leitchtown).

65. **Right can never die**
                                        —Toler.

66. **Right revere, and persevere**
                                        —Berry.

67. **Rycht and reason**
                                        —Graham.

68. **Scientia et industria cum probitate**   *Latin* 'Knowledge and dili-
    gence with uprightness'
                     —Lincoln College, Canterbury, New Zealand.

69. **Secundis dubiisque rectus**   *Latin* 'Upright both in prosperity and
    in perils'
                     —[after Horace, *Car.* iv. 9, 35.] Camperdown (E.),
                                        Cleveland (D.), Lippincott.

70. **Senzillo y leal**   *Spanish* 'Upright and loyal'
                     —Wilhelm, Prince of Anhalt-Bernburg-Harzgerode
                                        (1643–1709).

71. **Si recte facies**   *Latin* 'If you will do rightly'
                                        —Drummond.

72. **Soit droit fait**   *French* 'Let right be done'
                     —Queen's University, Kingston, Ontario, Canada.

73. **Sto ne per vim sed per jus**   *Latin* 'I stand not by strength, but by
    right'
                                        —Stone.

74. **Studiis et rebus honestis**   *Latin* 'Through studies and upright
    affairs'
                     —University of Vermont, Burlington, Vermont.

75. **Tenez le droit**   *French* 'Keep the right'
                                        —Clifton (Bt.), Wilkinson.

76. **Thue Recht scheu Nimant**   *German* 'Do right and fear nobody'
                     —Johann Friedrich III, Duke of Saxony (1538–65); Julius
                                Franz, Duke of Saxony-Lauenburg (1641–89).

77. **Tiens le droit**   *French* 'Hold (or clench) the right'
                                        —Clench (of Horstead).

78. **Tue Recht und Scheiwe niemand**   *German* 'Do right, and fear no
    man'
                     —Karl, Margrave of Baden (1598–1625).

79. **Verum atque decus** *Latin* 'The truth and rectitude'
—Brown, Lee.

RELIGION (*See also* CHRIST, JESUS; CROSS, THE; DIVINITY; FAITH;
GRACE; SALVATION.)

1. **All for religion**
—Langton.

2. **All worship be to God only**
—[Matt. iv. 10.] Fishmongers' Company, London.

3. **Ama Deum et serva mandata** *Latin* 'Love God and keep his commandments'
—Synnot.

4. **Civil and religious liberty**
—Wood (of Singleton Lodge).

5. **Dieu et la réligion** *French* 'God and religion'
—Bondier.

6. **Ecclesiae et litteris** *Latin* 'For the church and literature'
—King College, Bristol, Tennessee.

7. **Ecclesiae filii** *Latin* 'Sons of the church'
—St. Edmund's School, Canterbury, U.K.

8. **Felicem reddet religio** *Latin* 'Religion will render happy'
—Millar.

9. **Floreat Ecclesia Anglicana** *Latin* 'May the Church of England flourish'
—Glastonbury B. C., U.K.

10. **In Papam cornua tendo** *Latin* 'I stretch my horns against the Pope'
—Aston.

11. **In veritate religionis confido** *Latin* 'I trust in the truth of religion'
—25th Foot (King's Own Scottish Borderers).

12. **Le roy et l'église** *Old French* 'The king and the church'
—Rogers.

13. **Missionary/ Biblical/ Evangelistic**
—Arlington Baptist College, Arlington, Texas.

14. **Patriae et religioni fidelis** *Latin* 'Faithful to country and religion'
—Teevan.

15. **Per ecclesiam ad coelum** *Latin* 'Through the church to heaven'
—Eccles.

16. **Pour l'église** *French* 'For the church'
—Wandesford.

17. **Preparing evangels of our heritage**
—Gulf-Coast Bible College, Houston, Texas.

18. **Pro aris** *Latin* 'For our altars'
—Harris.

19. **Pro aris et focis** *Latin* 'For our altars and our homes'
—Blomfield, Campbell (of Shirven), Hazlerigge (Bt.), Kirkland, McNaught, Purdon, Phelips, Snell, Wait, Woodford.

20. **Pro ecclesia** *Latin* 'For the church'
—Whittingham (U.S.).

21. **Pro ecclesia, pro Texana** *Latin* 'For the church, for Texas'
—Baylor University, Waco, Texas.

22. **Pro ecclesia Dei** *Latin* 'For the church of God'
—Swainson.

23. **Pro ecclesia et patria** *Latin* 'For church and country'
—Trinity College, Hartford, Connecticut.

24. **Pro patria et religione** *Latin* 'For country and religion'
—Shanly.

25. **Religio, libertas et scientia** *Latin* 'Religion, liberty, and knowledge'
—Cedar Crest College, Allentown, Pennsylvania.

26. **Religioni et bonis artibus** *Latin* 'For religion and the liberal arts'
—St. Louis University, St. Louis, Missouri.

27. **Religioni reipublicae** *Latin* 'For religion and the state'
—King Henry VIII School, Coventry, U.K.

28. **Scientiis/ artibus/ religioni** *Latin* 'By knowledge, by art, by religion'
—Mercer University, Macon, Georgia.

29. **Sicut oliva virens laetor in aede Dei** *Latin* 'As the flourishing olive, I rejoice in the house of God'
—[after Ps., lii. 8.] Oliver.

30. **Stat religione parentum** *Latin* 'He continues in the religion of his forefathers'
—De Grey, Lucas (of Castle Thane).

31. **Tam aris quam aratris** *Latin* 'As well by altars as by ploughs'
—Oxley.

32. **Tout pour l'église** *French* 'All for the church'
—Wandesford.

33. **Usque ad aras** *Latin* 'Even to the altars'
—Herne, Burchell.

REPUTATION (*See also* FAME; INTEGRITY; PURITY.)

1. **Agnoscar eventu** *Latin* 'I shall be known by the results'
—Ross (of Auchlossen).

2. **A good name endureth**
—Hornchurch U. D. C., U.K.

3. **Fama praestante praestantior virtus** *Latin* 'Virtue is more outstanding along with an outstanding reputation'
—Morgan (U.S.).

4. **Fama proclamat honorem** *Latin* 'Reputation proclaims honor'
—Perot (U.S.).

5. **Melius est nomen bonum quam divitiae multae** *Latin* 'A good name is rather to be chosen than great riches'
—[Prov. xxii. 1.] Alexander, Duke of Schleswig-Holstein (1573–1627).

6. **Nec male notus eques** *Latin* 'A knight not badly known'
—Southwell (V.), Southwell.

7. **Omnia si perdas, famam servare memento** *Latin* 'If all else thou hast lost, remember to preserve thy fair name'
—Ulrich, Duke of Mecklenburg (1528–1603).

8. **Postera crescam laude** *Latin* 'I shall grow in the esteem of posterity'
—[Horace, *Odes*, III. xxx. 7–8.] Melbourne.

9. **Retinens vestigia famae** *Latin* 'Keeping in the footsteps of good report'
—Lloyd (of Seaton), Lyster.

10. **Virtute et claritate** *Latin* 'By virtue and high repute'
—Hara, O'Hara.

11. **Wrth ein ffrwythau ein hadnabyddir** *Welsh* 'Let us be known by our actions'
—Ellis (of Merinoth).

12. **Wrth ein ffrwyth yr adnabyddir** *Welsh* 'We are known by our actions'
—Ellis.

REST

1. **At secura quies**   *Latin* 'But in repose is safety'
—Huskisson.

2. **Crux mihi grata quies**   *Latin* 'The cross is my pleasing rest'
—Adam, Edie, McAdam.

3. **Cura quietem**   *Latin* 'Seek repose'
—Hall (Bt.).

4. **Desier na repos**   *French* 'Desire not rest'
—Howard.

5. **Grata quies**   *Latin* 'Rest is grateful'
—Bexley.

6. **Here we rest**
—State of Alabama, 1868–1939.

7. **In caelo quies**   *Latin* 'There is rest in heaven'
—Bewicke, Boscawen, Coldham, Dolphin (of Eyford), Horlock.

8. **In labore quies**   *Latin* 'In labor is rest'
—Helyer.

9. **I rest to rise**
—Blayney.

10. **Labour to rest**
—Kempe (U.S.).

11. **Lauro redimita quiescam**   *Latin* 'I will rest crowned with laurels'
—Lyon.

12. **Mon repos est au ciel**   *French* 'My rest is in heaven'
—Elisabeth Charlotte, Consort of Georg Wilhelm, Elector of Brandenburg (1597–1660).

13. **Mors aerumnarum requies**   *Latin* 'Death is rest from afflictions'
—Rumney.

14. **Nunc mihi grata quies**   *Latin* 'Now is there pleasant repose for me'
—Gordon.

15. **Otium cum dignitate**   *Latin* 'Repose with dignity'
—Kelso, Montagu.

16. **Otium ex labore**   *Latin* 'Rest from labor'
—Remsen (U.S.).

17. **Parta labore quies**   *Latin* 'Rest attained by labor'
—Fulton.

18. **Pax tua, Domine, est requies mea** *Latin* 'Thy peace, O Lord! is my rest'
—Umphray.

19. **Perseverantia et cura quies** *Latin* 'Rest by perseverance and care'
—Hall.

20. **Quiescam** *Latin* 'I shall have rest'
—Stebbing (of Woodrising).

21. **Quiescens et vigilans** *Latin* 'Resting and waking'
—Fairnie, Fernie.

22. **Quieta non movere** *Latin* 'Not to disturb things at rest'
—Sketchley.

23. **Recreation**
—Forrester.

24. **Requiesco a laboribus meis** *Latin* 'I rest from my labors'
—[after Rev. xiv. 13.] Heinrich Julius, Duke of
Braunschweig-Wolfenbüttel (1564–1613).

25. **Requiesco sub umbra** *Latin* 'I rest under the shade'
—Hamilton (of Dalziel).

26. **Saturet quies** *Latin* 'Let rest suffice'
—Salter.

27. **Semper otium rogo divos** *Latin* 'I always ask leisure from the gods'
—Everest.

28. **Sub libertate quietem** *Latin* 'Rest under liberty'
—Burrell, Cay, Carter, Hoblyn, Kay, Keay (of Scotland),
Peter, Parker, Walsham (Bt.).

29. **Sub umbra quies** *Latin* 'Rest under the shade'
—Sharpe.

30. **Sub umbra quiescam** *Latin* 'I will rest under the shadow'
—Fairn.

31. **Tu mihi curarum requies** *Latin* 'You are for me a relief from care'
—Goldsmith (U.S.).

32. **Ut quiescas labora** *Latin* 'Work so you may rest'
—Gallandet (U.S.).

33. **Ut secura quies** *Latin* 'That the rest (may be) safe'
—Huskisson.

34. **Volabo ut requiescam** *Latin* 'I will fly (away) to be at rest'
—[Ps. lv. 6.] Collens or Collins (of Offwell, Co. Dorset).

RESTRAINT

1. **Perseverantia vincit** *Latin* 'Perseverance succeeds'
   —Kesteven C. C., U.K.; Burnes

RESULTS

1. **Exitus acta probat** *Latin* 'The end proves the deed'
   —Biset, Nisbet, Nivison, Stanhope.

2. **Quocunque jeceris stabit** *Latin* 'Wherever you may cast it, it will stand'
   —Isle of Man; McLeod (of Cadboll, etc.).

3. **Quod severis metes** *Latin* 'Thou shalt reap what thou hast sown'
   —Bliss.

4. **Sicut serimus sic metimus** *Latin* 'Just as we sow we reap'
   —Wood.

5. **Ut sementem feceris ita et metes** *Latin* 'As you sow you shall reap'
   —Wilson.

REVERENCE (*See also* DEVOTION; PIETY.)

1. **Ante et post cole Deum** *Latin* 'Before and after (sunset), worship God'
   —Gotobed.

2. **Cui debetur reverentia** *Latin* 'Reverence to whom it is due'
   —Tulloh.

3. **La culte en difficulté** *French* 'Worship in hardship'
   —Harrison.

REWARD (*See also* MILITARY DISTINCTION.)

1. **A la constancia militar premio** *Spanish* 'Reward of military fortitude'
   —Order of St. Herminigilde (Spain).

2. **Altera merces** *Latin* 'Another reward'
   —McLean (of Ardgour), Maclaine.

3. **Assez gaigne qui malheur perd** *French* 'He gains enough who loses misfortune'
   —Ernestine Sophie, Margravine of Baden (1612–58).

4. **Campi fero praemia belli** *Latin* 'I bear the rewards of the battle-field'

   —Campbell (of Skerrington).

5. **Eruditio et meritum pro omnibus** *Latin* 'Learning and reward for all'

   —Isothermal Community College, Spindale, North Carolina.

6. **Et decus et pretium recti** *Latin* 'Both the honor and the reward of rectitude'

   —Fitz-Roy, Grafton (D.), Southampton (B.), Disney.

7. **Extant rectè factis praemia** *Latin* 'The rewards of good deeds endure'

   —Coffin (Bt.).

8. **Hac virtus mercede digna** *Latin* 'Virtue is worthy of this reward'

   —Robertson.

9. **Honor fidelitatis praemium** *Latin* 'Honor is the reward of fidelity'

   —Boston (B.), Irby.

10. **Honor praemium virtutis est** *Latin* 'Honor is the reward of virtue'

    —Flynn.

11. **Honor virtutis praemium** *Latin* 'Honor is the reward of virtue'
    —Bell, Boyle, Cork and Orrery (E.), Hawtin, Hawtyn, Hole, Ferrers (E.), Fielding, Shirley.

12. **Honor virtutis pretium** *Latin* 'Honor is the reward of virtue'

    —Mills.

13. **Honos fidelitatis praemium** *Latin* 'Honor the reward of fidelity'
    —Irby.

14. **Honos industriae praemium** *Latin* 'Honor the reward of industry'

    —King (of Campsie, bt.).

15. **Industriae praemium** *Latin* 'The reward of industry'

    —Heath (Bt.).

16. **In pretium persevero** *Latin* 'I persevere for my reward'

    —Jenner.

17. **Laboranti palma** *Latin* 'The palm to him who strives for it'

    —Hay.

18. **Merces haec certa laborum** *Latin* 'This is the sure reward of industry'

    —Seton (Bt.).

19. **Munus et monumentum victoriae Spures, 1513** *Latin* 'A reward and remembrance of the victory of Spurs, 1513'
> —Longeville-Clarke.

20. **Nec prece, nec pretio** *Latin* 'Neither by entreaty nor reward'
> —Bateman (B.), Hanbury.

21. **Nec pretio, nec prece** *Latin* 'Neither by bribery nor prayer'
> —Bateman.

22. **Non sine praeda** *Latin* 'Not without booty'
> —Echlin.

23. **Non sine pulvere palma** *Latin* 'A reward not without labor'
> —Peirse.

24. **Palma non sine pulvere** *Latin* 'The palm is not obtained without labor'
> —Archbald, Doughty, Lamb, Liverpool (E.).

25. **Palma virtuti** *Latin* 'The palm to virtue'
> —Palmer (of Wingham, Bt.), Palmer (of Fairfield, Bt.), Palmer.

26. **Perseverantia palmam obtinebit** *Latin* 'Perseverance will obtain the reward'
> —Tooth.

27. **Portanti spolia palma** *Latin* 'The spoils are the palm (i.e., reward) for the one who carries them off'
> —Feltham.

28. **Post spinas palma** *Latin* 'After thorns the palm' *or* 'After difficulties a reward'
> —Godfrey, Paget.

29. **Praemiando incitat** *Latin* 'It incites by rewarding'
> —Order of St. Stanislaus (Russia).

30. **Praemium, virtus, gloria** *Latin* 'Reward, virtue, glory'
> —Crosane.

31. **Praemium, virtus, honor** *Latin* 'Reward, virtue, honor'
> —Brown (of Blackburn), Cox.

32. **Praemium honor** *Latin* 'The reward is honor'
> —Foster.

33. **Praemium virtutis** *Latin* 'The reward of virtue'
> —Pringle.

34. **Praemium virtutis honor** *Latin* 'Honor is the reward of virtue'
> —Cheere, Lovelace, Tetlow (of Haughton).

35. **Pretium et causa laboris** *Latin* 'The reward and cause of labor'
—Frederick.

36. **Pretium non vile laborum** *Latin* 'No mean reward of our labor'
—Order of the Golden Fleece (Austria and Spain).

37. **Pretium victoribus corona** *Latin* 'The reward to the conquerors is a crown'
—Knapton.

38. **Pretium virtutis** *Latin* 'The prize of bravery'
—Welsh.

39. **Prix de vertu** *French* 'The reward of virtue'
—National Order of France.

40. **Publica salus mea merces** *Latin* 'The public security is my reward'
—Dick.

41. **Publicum meritorum praemium** *Latin* 'The public reward of meritorious services'
—Order of St. Stephen (Austria).

42. **Sic bene merenti palma** *Latin* 'The palm to him who so well merits it'
—Palmer.

43. **Sic itur ad astra. Optime de patria meruit** *Latin* 'Thus he goes to the heavens. He deserved well from his homeland'
—Pease (U.S.).

44. **Sua praemia virtus** *Latin* 'Virtue is its own reward'
—McCartney.

45. **Subimet merces industria** *Latin* 'Industry is its own reward'
—Miller.

46. **Sui ipsius praemium** *Latin* 'His own reward'
—Preston.

47. **Sunt sua praemia laudi** *Latin* 'His rewards are his praise'
—Barberrie, Brown, Pemberton.

48. **The reward of valor**
—Moodie.

49. **Thournib' creve'th** *Gaelic* 'I give you the palm of victory (i.e., the laurel)'
—Creagh.

50. **Tot praemia vitae** *Latin* 'So many are the rewards of life'
—Sullivan.

51. **Victoria gloria merces**　*Latin* 'Victory, glory, reward'
　　　　　　　　　　　—Berwick-upon-Tweed B. C., U.K.

52. **Vincenti dabitur laurea**　*Latin* 'The laurel is given to the conqueror'
　　　　　　　　　　　—Vincent (U.S.).

53. **Virtus sibimet merces**　*Latin* 'Virtue is its own reward'
　　　　　　　　　　　—Mackellar.

54. **Virtus sibi munus**　*Latin* 'Virtue, a reward in itself'
　　　　　　　　　　　—Van Cortlandt (U.S.).

55. **Virtus sibi praemium**　*Latin* 'Virtue is its own reward'
　　　　　　　　　　　—Calderwood, Wilson (Co. Lanark).

56. **Virtus virtutis praemium**　*Latin* 'Virtue is its own reward'
　　　　　　　　　　　—MacMoran.

57. **Virtute sibi praemium**　*Latin* 'By virtue he gains reward for himself'
　　　　　　　　　　　—Fenwick.

58. **Virtutibus praemium honor**　*Latin* 'Honor the reward of virtues'
　　　　　　　　　　　—Ffeilden (of Witton).

59. **Virtutis praemium**　*Latin* 'The reward of virtue'
　　　　　　　　　　　—Stewart (of Overton).

60. **Virtutis praemium felicitas**　*Latin* 'Happiness the reward of virtue'
　　　　　　　　　　　—Jones.

61. **Virtutis praemium honor**　*Latin* 'Honor is the reward of virtue'
　　　　　　　　　　　—Denbigh (E.), Fielden, Feniscowles, Millington.

62. **Virtutis regia merces**　*Latin* 'Royal is the reward of virtue'
　　　　　　　　　　　—Alpin, MacGregor, Peter, Skene (of Skene).

RIGHTEOUSNESS (*See also* FAIRNESS; GOODNESS; HONESTY;
　　INTEGRITY; NOBILITY; PURITY; RECTITUDE.)

1. **Bonne espérance et droit en avant**　*French* 'Forward, good hope and right!'
　　　　　　　　　　　—Nugent.

2. **Byddwch gyfiawn ac nag ofnwch**　*Welsh* 'Be righteous, and fear not'
　　　　　　　　　　　—Lewis (of Gilfach).

3. **Diligite justitiam qui judicatis terram**　*Latin* 'Love righteousness, ye that be judges of the earth'
　　　　　　　　　　　—Jacob, Margrave of Baden-Hochberg (1562–90).

4. **Justitia exaltat gentem**   *Latin* 'Righteousness exalteth a nation'
—[Prov. xiv. 34.] Karl, Count of the Palatinate of
Birkenfeld (1560–1600).

5. **Justi ut sidera fulgent**   *Latin* 'The righteous shine as the stars'
—McColl, Sandilands.

6. **Justus non derelinquetur**   *Latin* 'The righteous shall not be forsaken'
—[after Ps. xxxvii. 25.] Albert IV, Duke of Bavaria
(1447–1508); Heinrich II, the Younger, Duke of
Braunschweig-Wolfenbüttel (1489–1568).

7. **Justus ut palma**   *Latin* 'The righteous man is as the palm tree'
—Palmes.

8. **Justus ut palma florebit**   *Latin* 'The righteous shall flourish as the
palm tree'
—Friedrich, Margrave of Brandenburg (1588–1611),
Order of St. George (Bavaria).

9. **Laus recti diuturna beat**   *Latin* 'Enduring praise of righteousness
blesses'
—Ludwig Rudolf, Duke of Braunschweig in Blandenburg
(1671–1735).

10. **Lex justo non est posita**   *Latin* 'Law is not made for the righteous'
—Moritz, Landgrave of Hesse-Cassel (1572–1632).

11. **Non vidi justum derelictum**   *Latin* 'I have not seen the righteous
forsaken'
—[Ps. xxxvii. 25.] Heinrich II, the Younger, Duke of
Braunschweig-Wolfenbüttel (1489–1568).

12. **Omnia recte**   *Latin* 'All things rightly'
—McCracken.

13. **Pietas ad omnia utilis**   *Latin* 'Righteousness is useful for all
things'
—Heinrich Posthumus (1572–1635); Georg, Duke of
Braunschweig-Lüneburg (1582–1641); Johann,
Duke of Braunschweig-Lüneburg (1583–1628);
Friedrich Wilhelm II, Duke of Saxony-Altenburg
(1603–69); Christian Ernst, Margrave of
Brandenburg-Baireuth (1644–1712); Johann
Adolf II, Duke of Saxony-Weissenfels
(1685–1746).

14. **Sanctitas**   *Latin* 'Sanctity'
—Cowan.

15. **Sobrie, pie, juste** *Latin* 'Soberly, piously, righteously'
—Middleton.

16. **The righteous are bold as a lion**
—McBrayne.

17. **Ua mau ke ea o ka aina i ka pono** *Hawaiian* 'The life of the land is preserved in righteousness'
—State of Hawaii.

18. **Ut palma justus** *Latin* 'The righteous is like the palm'
—Palmes.

19. **Walk the straight way**
—Balli.

20. **Y cyfiawn sydd hy megis llew** *Welsh* 'The righteous is bold like a lion'
—Hughes (of Alltwyd).

RIGHTS

1. **Au bon droit** *French* 'With good right'
—Dalling (Bt.), Egremont (E.)., Windham.

2. **Droit à chacun** *French* 'To each his right'
—Dodede.

3. **Foi, roi, droit** *French* 'Faith, king, right'
—Lynes.

4. **Haud facile emergunt** *Latin* 'They do easily rise up'
—Bennett.

5. **Jus meum tuebor** *Latin* 'I will defend my right'
—Reynolds.

6. **Lauro resurgo** *Latin* 'I rise again with the laurel'
—Lorain.

7. **Non jure deficit** *Latin* 'He is not wanting in right'
—Foulis (Bt.).

8. **Non sanz droict** *Old French* 'Not without right'
—Shakespear; Warwickshire C. C., U.K.

9. **Non sine jure** *Latin* 'Not without right'
—Charter.

10. **Our liberties we prize and our rights we will maintain**
—State of Iowa.

11. **Per lucem ac tenebras mea sidera sanguine surgent** *Latin* 'Through light and darkness my star will arise in blood'
—Cayley.

12. **Regardez mon droit** *French* 'Respect my right'
—Middleton (Bt.).

13. **Richt do and fear na**
—King.

14. **Sic nos, sic sacra tuemur** *Latin* 'Thus we defend ourselves and sacred rights'
—McMahon (Bt.).

RISING

1. **Ad summum emergunt** *Latin* 'They rise to the top'
—Fullarton.

2. **Clausus mox excelsior** *Latin* 'Though shut in, by and by higher'
—Close.

3. **Concussus surgo** *Latin* 'Though shaken, I rise'
—Garriock, Garrow, Count-Jarnac.

4. **Haud facile emergunt** *Latin* 'They do easily rise up'
—Bennett.

5. **Hinc orior** *Latin* 'Hence I rise'
—Cameron, Hervie, Howie, Paterson, Stewart (of Dalguise).

6. **I rise with the morning**
—Cockburn.

7. **Lauro scutoque resurgo** *Latin* 'I rise again with laurel and shield'
—Loraine (Bt.).

8. **Leve et reluis** *French* 'Rise and shine'
—Lawson (Co. York, bt.), Lawson.

9. **Où ne monterai-je pas?** *French* 'Whither shall I not climb?'
—Nicolas Fouquet.

10. **Per ardua surgo** *Latin* 'I rise through difficulties'
—Fenton, Mahon.

11. **Rise and shine**
—Lawson.

12. **Scandit sublimia** *Latin* 'He scales great heights'
—Crumpe.

13. **Sine pondere sursum**   *Latin* 'Upwards without weight'
—Panton.

14. **Surgam**   *Latin* 'I shall rise'
—Hutchison.

15. **Surgamus ergo strenue**   *Latin* 'Let us therefore arise with vigor'
—Baildon U. D. C., U.K.

16. **Surge illuminare**   *Latin* 'Rise to shine'
—Scott.

17. **Surgere tento**   *Latin* 'I try to rise'
—Straton.

18. **Surgimus**   *Latin* 'We rise'
—Saltburn and Maske-by-the-Sea U. D. C., U.K.

19. **Surgite, lumen adest**   *Latin* 'Arise, the light is near'
—Glover.

20. **Surgo, lumen adest**   *Latin* 'I arise, light is near'
—Lawson.

21. **Sursum prorsusque**   *Latin* 'Upward and onward'
—Gill.

22. **Upward**
—Lorimer, Simons.

23. **Ut sursum desuper**   *Latin* 'I swoop down to soar again'
—Rumbold.

24. **Viresco et surgo**   *Latin* 'I flourish and rise'
—Maxwell.

25. **We rise**
—Martinson (of Newcastle-on-Tyne).

RISK

1. **Ehe wiegs dann wags**   *German* 'Rather weigh than venture'
—Bogislaus XIII, Duke of Pomerania zu Barth
(1544–1606).

2. **Ich habs gewagt**   *German* 'I chanced it'
—Hugel (U.S.).

3. **I gain by hazard**
—Hamilton (of Edinburgh).

4. **Il y a de ma vie**   *French* 'My life is at stake'
—Lievre.

5. Live, love, think, pray, dare
>—United Daughters of the Confederacy.

6. Nothing hazard, nothing have
>—Suttie (Bt.).

7. Nothing venture, nothing have
>—Boswell.

8. **Regis ad exemplum totus componitur orbis** *Latin* 'After the pattern of the king is the whole country modelled'
>—[Claudianus, *Panegyris de Quarto Consulatu Honorii*, vers. 300.] Philipp, Duke of Saxony (1578–1605).

9. Venture and gain
>—Hay, Wilson (of Fraserburgh).

10. Venture forward
>—Bruce (of Garvet).

11. We'll put it to a venture
>—Halcrow.

ROYALTY (*See also* CROWN; LEADERSHIP; PRINCELINESS.)

1. **A Deo et rege** *Latin* 'From God and the king'
>—Chesterfield (E.), Fawkes, Hampton, Harrington (E.), Lewis, Scudmore (Bt.), Stanhope (E.), Strachy (Bt.).

2. **A rege et victoria** *Latin* 'From the king and by conquest'
>—Barry, Ligonier, Thatchell.

3. **A regibus amicis** *Latin* 'From friendly kings'
>—Ruck, Keene.

4. **Au roy donne devoir** *Old French* 'Give duty to the king'
>—Royden (Bt.).

5. **Aut Caesar aut nihil** *Latin* 'Either Caesar or no one'
>—Wall.

6. **Bhear na righ gan** *Gaelic* 'May the king live forever'
>—Fleming.

7. **Colens Deum et regem** *Latin* 'Honouring God and the King'
>—Collins.

8. **Cor regis in manu Domini est** *Latin* 'The heart of the king is in the hand of the Lord'
>—[Prov. xxi. 1.] Ferdinand I, Emperor of Germany (1503–64).

9. **Cuidich an righ** *Scots Gaelic* 'Assist the king'
>—McDonnel, Seaforth Highlanders, U.K.

10. **Deo, patriae, regi** *Latin* 'For God, my country and my king'
—Cooper.

11. **Deo, regi, et patriae** *Latin* 'To God, my king, and my country'
—Irvine.

12. **Deo, regi, patriae** *Latin* 'To God, my king, my country'
—Duncombe (of Cassgrove), Feversham (B.), Irvine (of Kinconssie).

13. **Deo, regi, vicino** *Latin* 'To God, my king, my neighbor'
—Bromsgrove Grammar School, Cookes, Worcester Coll. Oxon.

14. **Deo, regi fidelis** *Latin* 'Faithful to God and the king'
—Atkinson, O'Daly.

15. **Deo et regi** *Latin* 'For God and the king'
—Stanhope.

16. **Deo et regi asto** *Latin* 'I stand by God and the king'
—Deacon.

17. **Deo et regi fidelis** *Latin* 'Faithful to God and the king'
—Daly.

18. **Deo fidelis et regi** *Latin* 'Faithful to God and king'
—Dunsandle (B.).

19. **Deo inspirante, rege favente** *Latin* 'By the inspiration of God and the king's favor'
—Stahlschmidt.

20. **Deo regique debeo** *Latin* 'I owe duty to God and the king'
—Johnson.

21. **Deum cole, regem serva** *Latin* 'Worship God, revere the king'
—Cole (Earl of Enniskillen), Cole (of Twickenham), Townshend (co. Cork), Coleridge, Jones.

22. **Deum et regem** *Latin* 'God and king'
—Collins.

23. **Deum time, Caesarem honora** *Latin* 'Fear God, honor the king'
—[1 Peter, ii. 17.] Christian II, Elector of Saxony (1583–1611).

24. **Deum time, regem honora** *Latin* 'Fear God, honor the king'
—[1 Peter, ii. 17.] Otto Heinrich, Count of the Palatinate of Sulzbach (1556–1604); Armstrong (B.).

25. **Deus, patria, rex** *Latin* 'God, native land, and king'
—Phillipps, Phillips, Tarlton.

26. **Dieu, un roi, une foi**   *French* 'God, one king, one faith'
—Rush.

27. **Dieu et mon roi**   *French* 'God and my king'
—Rawlinson.

28. **Dii rexque secundent**   *Latin* 'The Gods and the king will favor us'
—Soapmakers' Company.

29. **El rey y la patria**   *Spanish* 'King and country'
—Order of St. Ferdinand.

30. **En Dieu et mon roy**   *Old French* 'In God and my king'
—Churchyard.

31. **E rege et victoria**   *Latin* 'From the king and by victory'
—Bulen.

32. **Et regem defendere victum**   *Latin* 'To defend the king even in his defeat'
—Whitgreave (of Moseley Court).

33. **Favente Numine regina servatur**   *Latin* 'By the favor of the Deity the Queen is preserved'
—Micklethwait (Bt.).

34. **Fear God, honor the king**
—Wrexham B. C., U.K.; Bromley-Davenport, Davenport, Porter.

35. **Fidelitas regi et justitia mihi**   *Latin* 'Fidelity to the king and justice to myself'
—Dawson.

36. **Fidelitas urbis salus regis**   *Latin* 'The faithfulness of the city is the safety of the king'
—Bridgnorth B. C., U.K.

37. **Fidus Deo et Regi**   *Latin* 'Faithful to God and the King'
—De Bary.

38. **Floreat majestas**   *Latin* 'Let majesty flourish'
—Brown (Bt.).

39. **Foi, roi, droit**   *French* 'Faith, king, right'
—Lynes.

40. **For God, Queen, and country**
—Harleyford, Buckinghamshire, England.

41. **Foy, roi, droit**   *Old French* 'Faith, king, duty'
—Lynes (of Tooley Park).

42. **Garde le roy**   *Old French* 'Defend the king'
—Lane (of King's Bromley).

43. **Gratior est a rege pio**   *Latin* 'It is more agreeable coming from a pious king'
          —Gibbons (Bt.).

44. **Gud og Kongen**   *Danish* 'God and the king'
          —Order of the Danebrog (Denmark).

45. **Habent sua sidera reges**   *Latin* 'Kings have their stars'
          —De Vahl-Samuel, Samuel.

46. **J'aime mon Dieu, mon roi, et ma patrie**   *French* 'I love my God, my king, and my country'
          —Kirvin.

47. **Legi regi fidelis**   *Latin* 'Faithful to the king and law'
          —Barry, Sautry.

48. **Le roy, la loy**   *Old French* 'The king, the law'
          —Larcom (Bt.).

49. **Le roy, la loy, la foy**   *Old French* 'King, law, faith'
          —Grover.

50. **Le roy et l'église**   *Old French* 'The king and the church'
          —Rogers.

51. **Le roy et l'estat**   *Old French* 'The king and the state'
          —Ashburnham (E.), Sherard.

52. **Le roy le veut**   *Old French* 'It is the king's pleasure'
          —De Clifford.

53. **Mon Dieu, mon roi, et ma patrie**   *French* 'My god, my king, and my country'
          —Kerwan (Co. Galway).

54. **My king and country**
          —Tyler.

55. **Nec rege, nec populo, sed utroque**   *Latin* 'Neither for king nor people, but for both'
          —Rolle (B.), Wilkinson.

56. **Non mihi, sed Deo et regi**   *Latin* 'Not for myself, but for god and the king'
          —Booth (of Salford).

57. **Nostre roy et nostre foy**   *Old French* 'Our king and our faith'
          —Neel.

58. **One faith, one king, one law**
          —Bourk.

59. **Pour Dieu et mon Roi**   *French* 'For God and my King'
          —Bagot.

60. **Pour le roi et la patrie** *French* 'For the king and the country'
—Lynde (U.S.).

61. **Pour le roy** *Old French* 'For the king'
—Macaul, Peaterson.

62. **Pour mon Roy** *Old French* 'For my King'
—Janvim.

63. **Pro Deo, patriâ, et rege** *Latin* 'For God, my country, and my king'
—Blades (of High Paull), Beugo, James (of Dublin, Bt.).

64. **Pro Deo, pro Rege, pro patria, et lege** *Latin* 'For God, for the King, for the country, and the law'
—Blakemore.

65. **Pro Deo, rege, et patriâ** *Latin* 'For God, my king, and my country'
—Blaydes (of Rawby), McDowall.

66. **Pro Deo et Caesare** *Latin* 'For God and the emperor'
—Franz Ludwig, Count of the Palatinate (b. 1664); Johann Ernst, Duke of Saxony-Saalfeld (1658–1729).

67. **Pro Deo et rege** *Latin* 'For God and the king'
—Bickerton, Blacker, Golding, Hawkins, Masterton, Rosse (E.).

68. **Pro fide, lege, et rege** *Latin* 'For faith, laws, and king'
—Order of the White Eagle (Polish).

69. **Pro fide rege et patria pugno** *Latin* 'I fight for the faith, king, and country'
—Lentaigne, O'Neill.

70. **Pro lege, senatuque rege** *Latin* 'For law, senate, and sovereign'
—Dodsworth (Bt.).

71. **Pro legibus et regibus** *Latin* 'For laws and kings'
—Wilson (Bt.).

72. **Pro patriâ et rege** *Latin* 'For country and king'
—Jones, Thomas.

73. **Pro rege** *Latin* 'For the king'
—Burnaby (Bt.), Christie, Graham, McPhie, Porcher (of Clyffe), Mackie.

74. **Pro rege, lege, grege** *Latin* 'For the king, the law, and the people'
—Bessborough (E.), Brougham (B.), Ponsonby (B.), Whither.

75. **Pro rege, pro lege, pro grege** *Latin* 'For king, for law, for the common people'
—Damon (U.S.).

76. **Pro rege, pro lege, pro patriae conamur** *Latin* 'We strive for king, for law, and for country'
—18th Hussars, U.K.

77. **Pro rege dimico** *Latin* 'I do battle for the king'
—Dymoke (Bt.).

78. **Pro rege et grege** *Latin* 'For king and people'
—Grieve, Paterson.

79. **Pro rege et lege** *Latin* 'For king and law'
—Leeds City and C. B. C., U.K.; Horton (of Howroyde); Kidson; Mandit; Stewart (of Fincastle).

80. **Pro rege et limite** *Latin* 'For our king and the border'
—Elliot.

81. **Pro rege et patriâ** *Latin* 'For my king and country'
—Ainslie (Bt.), Aberherdour, Bell, Carr, Cameron (of Lochiel), De Tabley (B.), Franklyn, Hamond (of St. Albans Court), Leven (E.), Leicester, Leslie, Lyon, McCubbin, Pode, Smith (of Preston, Bt.), Stewart, Wheatley.

82. **Pro rege et patriâ pugnans** *Latin* 'Fighting for my king and country'
—Pasley (Bt.), Smith.

83. **Pro rege et populo** *Latin* 'For king and people'
—Barrow (Bt.), Basset (B.).

84. **Pro rege et pro patriâ semper** *Latin* 'Always for my king and my country'
—Lawrence.

85. **Pro rege et religione** *Latin* 'For my king and faith'
—Boycott (Co. Salop).

86. **Pro rege et republica** *Latin* 'For king and state'
—Paul (Bt.).

87. **Pro rege in tyrannos** *Latin* 'For the king against tyrants'
—Johnston, Macdonald, McDowall (of Logan).

88. **Pro Rege pio** *Latin* 'For a pious king'
—Thornton.

89. **Pro rege saepe** *Latin* 'For the king often'
—Wright.

90. **Pro rege saepe, pro patriâ semper**   *Latin* 'For the king often, for my country always'
—Eyre, Redington.

91. **Pro rege saepe, pro republica semper**   *Latin* 'For the king often, for the commonwealth always'
—Gibson.

92. **Pro rege semper**   *Latin* 'For the king always'
—Morris, Thoyts.

93. **Rege et patriâ**   *Latin* 'By my king and country'
—Bower.

94. **Regem defendere victum**   *Latin* 'To defend the conquered king'
—Whitgreave.

95. **Reges creantur regibus**   *Latin* 'Kings are born of kings'
—Friedrich August I, Elector of Saxony (1670–1733).

96. **Regi et patriae fidelis**   *Latin* 'Faithful to king and country'
—Norbury (B.).

97. **Regi fidelis**   *Latin* 'Faithful to the king'
—Moulson.

98. **Regi legi fidelis**   *Latin* 'Faithful to king and law'
—Barry.

99. **Regi patriaeque**   *Latin* 'To the king and country'
—Leeper.

100. **Regi patriaeque fidelis**   *Latin* 'Faithful to my king and country'
—Scott (of Great Barr, bt.).

101. **Regi regnoque fidelis**   *Latin* 'Faithful to king and kingdom'
—Pocock (Bt.), Simpson.

102. **Regis ad exemplum totus componitur orbis**   *Latin* 'After the pattern of the king is the whole country modelled'
—[Claudianus, *Panegyris de Quarto Consulatu Honorii*, vers. 300.] Philipp, Duke of Saxony (1578–1605).

103. **Regis donum gratum bonum**   *Latin* 'A king's gift is pleasant and good'
—Kingdon.

104. **Regi semper fidelis**   *Latin* 'Ever faithful to the king'
—Smythe (Bt.).

105. **Regium est, omnibus benefacere**   *Latin* 'To benefit all is a king's part'
—Joachim II, Elector of Brandenburg (1505–71).

106. **Rere Vaka Na Kaloo Ka Doka Na Tui**   *Fijian* 'Fear God, honor the king'
>>> —Fiji.

107. **Rex Deus quisquam humanus est**   *Latin* 'The king is a kind of human God'
>>> —George III, son of Bogislaus XIII, Duke of Pomerania (1582–1617).

108. **Rex et nostra jura**   *Latin* 'The king and our laws'
>>> —Great Yarmouth C. B. C., U.K.

109. **Rex mundi**   *Latin* 'King of the world'
>>> —Raymond (U.S.).

110. **Rex non verba**   *Latin* 'The king, not words'
>>> —Wilson.

111. **Rex spicula nescit**   *Latin* 'The king knows not the arrow'
>>> —Louis XII.

112. **Ruinam salutarunt pro rege**   *Latin* 'They have hailed ruin in the cause of the king'
>>> —Burnes.

113. **Sacrarium regis cunabula legis**   *Latin* 'The shrine of the king and the cradle of the law'
>>> —Bury St. Edmunds B. C., U.K.

114. **Saepe pro rege, semper pro republica**   *Latin* 'Often for the king, always for the commonwealth'
>>> —Vassall (of Milford).

115. **Saepe pro rege semper pro patria**   *Latin* 'Often for the king, always for the country'
>>> —Clarke (U.S.).

116. **Stans cum rege**   *Latin* 'Standing with the king'
>>> —Chadwick.

117. **Subditus fidelis regis est salus regni**   *Latin* 'A faithful subject of the king is a preserver of the monarchy'
>>> —Hopper (of Belmont).

118. **Time Deum, honora Caesarem**   *Latin* 'Fear God; honor the emperor'
>>> —[after 1 Peter, ii. 17.] Julius Ernst, Duke of Braunschweig-Lüneberg-Danneburg (1571–1636); August, Duke of Saxony (1589–1615).

119. **Tota gloriosa filia regis intrinsecus** *Latin* 'The daughter of the king is all glorious within'

—Jewell.

120. **Un Dieu, un roi** *French* 'One God, one king'

—D'Arcy, Lyttleton.

121. **Un Dieu, un roy, un coeur** *Old French* 'One God, one king, one heart'

—Lake (Bt.).

122. **Un Dieu, un roy, un foy** *Old French* 'One God, one king, one faith'

—Curle, Rush.

123. **Un Dieu et un Roi** *French* 'One God and one king'

—De Jersey.

124. **Ung Dieu, ung roy, une loy** *Old French* 'One God, one king, one law'

—Town of Lyons, France.

125. **Ung Dieu et ung roy** *Old French* 'One God and one king'

—Daray, Hatherton (B.).

126. **Ung roy, ung foy, ung loy** *Old French* 'One king, one faith, one law'

—Burke (of Marble Hill, Bt.), Burke (of Kilcoran, Owen, and Clongowna), Clanricarde (M.), De Burgo (Bt.), Rush.

127. **Un roy, une foy, une loy** *Old French* 'One king, one faith, one law'

—De Burgh.

128. **Vivat rex** *Latin* 'Long live the king'

—McCorquodill, McCorgusdell.

129. **Vive le roy** *French* 'Long live the king'

—Gairden (of Barrowfield).

RUNNING

1. **Currendo** *Latin* 'By running'

—Hollist.

2. **Curre ut vincas** *Latin* 'Run that you may conquer'

—Warren.

3. **Currit qui curat** *Latin* 'He runs who takes care'

—Fuller.

4. **Cursum perficio**   *Latin* 'I accomplish the race'
—Hunter.

5. **Sic curre ut capias**   *Latin* 'Run so you may catch'
—Currey (U.S.), Curry (U.S.).

6. **Sic curre ut comprendas**   *Latin* 'Run so that you may obtain'
—Stevenson.

SACRIFICE

1. **Et vitam impendere vero**   *Latin* 'To sacrifice even life to truth'
—[Juvenal, *Sat.* vi. 91.] Holland (B.), Rousseau.

2. **Fideli distillant sanguine corde**   *Latin* 'Their heart bleeds drop by drop for the faithful'
—Fayting.

3. **Je meurs pour ceux que j'aime**   *French* 'I die for those whom I love'
—Paterson, Wallace.

4. **Proprio vos sanguine pasco**   *Latin* 'I feed you with my own blood'
—Cantrell (Co. Lancaster).

5. **Sacrifice or service**
—Dakota Wesleyan University, Mitchell, South Dakota.

6. **Sanguine Christe tuo**   *Latin* 'By thy blood, O Christ'
—Bramhall.

7. **Sustento sanguine signa**   *Latin* 'I support the standard with my blood'
—Seton.

8. **Victima Deo**   *Latin* 'A sacrifice to God'
—Veale.

9. **Vitam impendere vero**   *Latin* 'To pay your life for truth'
—[Juvenal *Sat.* iv. 93.] Jean Jacques Rousseau (1712–1778); Arthur Schopenhauer (1788–1860).

10. **Vivo et morior pro quibus amo**   *Latin* 'I live and die for those whom I love'
—Chandler (U.S.).

SADNESS (*See also* DESPAIR; SUFFERING.)

1. **Amat victoria curam**   *Latin* 'Victory loves sorrow', i.e., 'No victory without sorrow'
—Matthias, Emperor of Germany (1557–1619).

2. **Amat victoria curam** *Latin* 'Victory and care are close friends'
   (*lit.* 'Victory loves care')
   —Clark (Bt.), Clerk (of Penicuik, Co. Edinburgh, Bt.),
   Clerk (of Norwich).

3. **France et sans dol** *French* 'For France and without sorrow'
   —Cartier.

4. **Kein Freud ohne Leid** *German* 'No joy without sorrow'
   —Albert Friedrich, Margrave of Brandenburg (1582–1600).

5. **Moeret qui laborat** *Latin* 'He is sad who labors'
   —Storie.

6. **Nec triste, nec trepidum** *Latin* 'Neither sad nor fearful'
   —Trist.

7. **Nihil hoc triste recepto** *Latin* 'This being received, sorrow is at
   an end'
   —Order of our Redeemer.

8. **Tristis et fidelis** *Latin* 'Sad and faithful'
   —D'Alton.

9. **Victo dolore** *Latin* 'Grief overcome'
   —Simpson.

SALVATION (*See also* CHRIST, JESUS; CROSS, THE; GRACE; PROVIDENCE;
RELIGION.)

1. **A. B. C. D. E. F. (Allein bei Christo die ewige Freude)**
   German 'With Christ alone is eternal joy'
   —Albrecht Günther, Count Schwarzburg (1582–1634).

2. **A cruce salus** *Latin* 'Salvation from the cross'
   —Burgh, Bourke, De Burgho, Downes (B.), Jefferson (Co.
   York), Mayo (E.).

3. **Agnus Dei mihi salus** *Latin* 'The Lamb of God is my salvation'
   —Lammin.

4. **Agnus Dei salvator meus** *Latin* 'The Lamb of God, my savior'
   —Haslam.

5. **Certa cruce salus** *Latin* 'Sure salvation through the cross'
   —Garritte, Kinnaird (B.).

6. **Christi pennatus sidera morte peto** *Latin* 'Furnished with wings
   (feathers), by the death of Christ I seek the stars'
   —Fetherston.

7. **Creta cruce salus** *Latin* 'Salvation born from the cross'
   —Kinnaird (B.), Waterhouse.

8. **Cruce salus** *Latin* 'Through the cross salvation'
—Shee.

9. **Crux Christi mea salus** *Latin* 'The Cross of Christ is my salvation'
—Johann Georg, Duke of Saxony-Weissenfels (1677–1712).

10. **Crux Christi nostra salus** *Latin* 'The Cross of Christ is our salvation'
—Friedrich the Wise, Elector of Saxony (1463–1525).

11. **Crux Christi salus mea** *Latin* 'My salvation is the cross of Christ'
—Peck.

12. **Crux dat salutem** *Latin* 'The cross gives salvation'
—Sinclair.

13. **Crux salutem confert** *Latin* 'The cross confers salvation'
—Barclay.

14. **Cum cruce salus** *Latin* 'Salvation with the cross'
—Mountain.

15. **Cum Deo salus** *Latin* 'With God salvation'
—Christian, Duke of Saxony-Weissenfels (1682–1736).

16. **Deus salutem disponit** *Latin* 'God orders salvation'
—Archer.

17. **Deus scutum et cornu salutis** *Latin* 'God my shield and the horn of my salvation'
—Thoroton.

18. **Ex Oriente salus** *Latin* 'Salvation from the East'
—Eastbourne College, U.K.

19. **Galea spes salutis** *Latin* 'Hope is the helmet of salvation'
—Cassels, Dudley.

20. **Hinc mihi salus** *Latin* 'Hence comes salvation to me'
—Peverell (of Hants), Maberly, Spalding.

21. **Horae semper sola salus servire deo** *Latin* 'At all times the only salvation is to serve God'
—Jarvis (U.S.).

22. **I. D. H. I. D. H. (In dem Herrn ist das Heil)** *German* 'In the Lord is salvation'
—Dorothee, Princess of Anhalt (1580–1618).

23. **In Christo salus** *Latin* 'Salvation is in Christ'
—Abernethy.

24. **In coelo salus** *Latin* 'In heaven salvation'
—Seale (Bt.).

25. **In cruce salus**   *Latin* 'In the cross is salvation'
         —Aiken, Abercromby, Brigham, Bourke, Langholme,
               Mountem, Marr, Lawrence, Tailour, Tailyour.

26. **In Deo salus mea et gloria mea**   *Latin* 'In God my salvation and
    my glory'
         —Johann Adolf I, Duke of Saxony-Weissenfels (1649–97).

27. **In Deo salutem**   *Latin* 'Salvation in God'
                                                  —Scobell.

28. **In Deo sola salus**   *Latin* 'The only salvation is in God'
                                                  —Grundy.

29. **In Deo solo salus est**   *Latin* 'Salvation is in God alone'
                                                  —Sparrow.

30. **In manibus Domini sorsque salusque mea**   *Latin* 'In the hands of
    the Lord are my fate and salvation'
         —Marie Elisabeth, Countess of Oldenburg (1581–1619);
               Anton Günther, last Count of Oldenburg and
                         Delmenhorst (1583–1667).

31. **In solo Deo salus**   *Latin* 'Salvation is in God alone'
                                                  —Harewood (E.).

32. **I saved the king**
                                                  —Torrance.

33. **L'esperance du salut**   *French* 'The hope of salvation'
                                                  —Grabham.

34. **Monachus salvabor**   *Latin* 'I a monk shall be saved'
                                —Monkhouse (of Newcastle-on-Tyne).

35. **Naufragus in portum**   *Latin* 'Shipwrecked I got into haven'
                                                  —Heard.

36. **Salus et decus**   *Latin* 'Salvation and glory'
                                                  —Lloyd (U.S.).

37. **Salus et gloria**   *Latin* 'Our salvation and our glory'
                         —Order of the Star of the Cross (Austria).

38. **Salus in fide**   *Latin* 'Salvation through faith'
                                                  —Magrath.

39. **Salus mea Christus**   *Latin* 'Christ is my salvation'
                                                  —Forbes.

40. **Salus per Christum**   *Latin* 'Salvation through Christ'
         —Abernethy, Christian, Forbes (of Culloden), Hare (of
               Docking, Co. Norfolk), Gordon, Leith (of
                                        Whitehaugh).

41. **Salus per Christum Redemptorem** *Latin* 'Salvation through Christ the Redeemer'
—Moray (E.), Stewart, Stuart (of Duncarn).

42. **Salutem disponit Deus** *Latin* 'God dispenses salvation'
—Edgar.

43. **Sola cruce salus** *Latin* 'The only salvation is through the cross'
—Barclay, Brookbank.

44. **Sola Deo salus** *Latin* 'The only salvation is in God'
—Robinson.

45. **Sola Deus salus** *Latin* 'God the only salvation'
—Archer.

46. **Solo Deo salus** *Latin* 'Salvation through God only'
—Montagu.

47. **Sub cruce salus** *Latin* 'Salvation under the cross'
—Fletcher (Co. Stafford), Bangor (V.), Ward (of Willey), Capron.

48. **Tollit peccata mundi** *Latin* 'He taketh away the sins of the world'
—[John, i. 29.] Farley.

49. **Tu certa salutis anchora** *Latin* 'Thou a sure anchor of salvation'
—Gillespie.

SATISFACTION

1. **Art, industry, contentment**
—Basildon Development Corp.

2. **Il suffit** *French* 'It suffices'
—Darker.

3. **Nec careo, nec curo** *Latin* 'I have neither want nor care'
—Craw.

4. **No mas** *Spanish* 'No more'
—Roderich, Duke of Württemberg (1618–51).

5. **Non sine** *Latin* 'Not without'
—Oliver.

6. **Non sufficit orbis** *Latin* 'The world does not suffice'
—Philip II of Spain.

7. **Parum sufficit** *Latin* 'Little suffices'
—Browne (Bt.).

8. **Satis est prostrasse leoni**   *Latin* 'It is enough to a lion to have laid low'

   —Salusbury (Bt.).

9. **Tout droit**   *French* 'All right'

   —Carre, Carr, Carling, Ker.

SCHOOL MOTTOES

1. **Academic—Vocational—Cultural—Patriotic—Spiritual**
   —The School of the Ozarks, Point Lookout, Missouri.

2. **Achievement/Citizenship**
   —Norfolk State University, Norfolk, Virginia.

3. **Ad astra per aspera**   *Latin* 'Through adversity to the stars'
   —Campbell University, Buies Creek, North Carolina.

4. **Ad summum**   *Latin* 'To the highest'
   —University of Alaska, Fairbanks, Alaska.

5. **Ad virtutem per sapientiam**   *Latin* 'To virtue through wisdom'
   —Castle Jr. College, Windham, New Hampshire.

6. **A friend to youth**
   —Florida College, Temple Terrace, Florida.

7. **A full and abundant life in a contemporary society**
   —Abraham Baldwin Agricultural College, Tifton, Georgia.

8. **Alabama's best little public university**
   —University of Montevallo, Montevallo, Alabama.

9. **Alenda lux ubi orta libertas**   *Latin* 'Where light has arisen there liberty should be sustained'
   —Davidson College, Davidson, North Carolina;
   Community College of Beaver County,
   Monaca, Pennsylvania.

10. **Aletheuontes de en Agape**   *(transliterated from Greek)* 'Speaking the truth in love'
    —Brandon University, Brandon, Manitoba, Canada.

11. **Altiora in votis**   *Latin* 'I pray for the higher things'
    —Highgate School, U.K.

12. **Altiora petamus**   *Latin* 'Let us strive for loftier things'
    —University of Salford, Salford, U.K.

13. **Altiora peto**   *Latin* 'I seek higher things'
    —Oliphant (of Newton, co. Perth), Warwick School, U.K.

14. **And the bush was not consumed**
> —Jewish Theological Seminary of America, New York City, New York.

15. **'And the glow from that fire can truly light the world'**
> —John F. Kennedy University, Orinda, California.

16. **Animo et fide** *Latin* 'Through soul and faith'
> —Pensacola Jr. College, Pensacola, Florida.

17. **An open way to new worlds**
> —Flaming Rainbow University, Stilwell, Oklahoma.

18. **An uncommon experience that lasts a lifetime**
> —University of Redlands, Redlands, California.

19. **'A place to grow'**
> —Los Angeles Baptist College, Newhall, California.

20. **A private university in the public service**
> —New York University, New York City, New York.

21. **Arduus ad solem** *Latin* 'Lifted up to the sun'
> —University of Manchester, Manchester, U.K.

22. **Armed with the Word, empowered by the spirit**
> —Western Evangelical Seminary, Portland, Oregon.

23. **Ars mercede viget** *Latin* 'Art flourishes by patronage'
> —Reading School, U.K.

24. **Artes/scientias/humanitates** *Latin* 'Arts/sciences/humanities'
> —New Mexico Highlands University, Las Vegas, New Mexico.

25. **Assiduitate, non desidia** *Latin* 'By industry, not sloth'
> —King William's College, Isle of Man, U.K.

26. **Assiduitate non desidiâ** *Latin* 'By assiduity, not by sloth'
> —Loch (of Drylaw and Rachan).

27. **A tradition of excellence**
> —New York State University College at Potsdam, New York.

28. **A university for all the Americas**
> —Pan American University, Edinburg, Texas.

29. **Beati mundi corde** *Latin* 'Blessed are the pure in heart'
> —[Matt., v. 8.] Lancing College, U.K.

30. **Benedictus es, O Domine: doce me Statuta Tua** *Latin* 'Blessed art thou, O Lord: teach me Thy statutes'
> —Bradfield College, U.K.

31. **Bind up the testimony and seal the law**
    —Westminster College, New Wilmington, Pennsylvania.

32. **Bonitas/veritas/pulchritas** *Latin* 'Goodness/truth/beauty'
    —Marycrest College, Davenport, Iowa.

33. **Bonitatem et disciplinam et scientiam doce me** *Latin* 'Teach me
    goodness and discipline and knowledge'
    —College of Mount Saint Vincent, Riverdale, New York.

34. **Building Christian character**
    —Southwestern Christian College, Terrell, Texas.

35. **Caritas** *Latin* 'Love'
    —Briar Cliff College, Sioux City, Iowa.

36. **Certa bonum certamen** *Latin* 'Fight the good fight'
    —Iona College, New Rochelle, New York.

37. **Christ above all**
    —William Jennings Bryan College, Dayton, Tennessee.

38. **Christ for the world**
    —Yankton College, Yankton, South Dakota.

39. **Christianity and culture**
    —Franklin College, Franklin, Indiana.

40. **Christian service/ character/ culture**
    —Coker College, Hartsville, South Carolina.

41. **Christo et humanitati** *Latin* 'For Christ and humanity'
    —Blackburn College, Carlinville, Illinois.

42. **Christ preeminent**
    —Messiah College, Grantham, Pennsylvania.

43. **Christus primatum tenens** *Latin* 'Christ holding the first place'
    —Westmont College, Santa Barbara, California.

44. **Clavis ad futura** *Latin* 'Key to the future'
    —Greenville Technical College, Greenville, South
    Carolina.

45. **Coadyuvando el presente, formando el porvenir** *Old Spanish*
    'Guide to the present, moulder of the future'
    —University of Toledo, Toledo, Ohio.

46. **Cogito ergo sum. Deo gratias** *Latin* 'I think therefore I am.
    Thanks be to God'
    —Shorter College, North Little Rock, Arkansas.

47. **Commitment to excellence**
    —U.S. Air Force Academy, Colorado Springs, Colorado.

48. **Communicating the Word**
—Denver Baptist Bible College, Denver, Colorado.

49. **Consagracion/ educacion** *Spanish* 'Consecration/ education'
—Antillian Coll., Mayagüez, Puerto Rico.

50. **Constitution/ Wisdom/ Justice/ Moderation**
—University System of Georgia.

51. **Cor ad cor loquitur** *Latin* 'Heart speaks to heart'
—Cardinal Newman College, St. Louis, Missouri.

52. **Cor meum tibi offero Domine** *Latin* 'I offer my heart to you, Lord'
—Calvin Theological Seminary, Grand Rapids, Michigan.

53. **Culture for service**
—Clark College, Atlanta, Georgia.

54. **Dat Deus incrementum** *Latin* 'God giveth the increase'
—Westminster School, U.K.

55. **Date eleemosynam et ecce omnia munda sunt vobis** *Latin* 'Give alms and lo! all pure things are yours'
—Wyggesden School, Leicester, U.K.

56. **Decus et veritas** *Latin* 'Glory and truth'
—Rockford College, Rockford, Illinois.

57. **Dedicated to training hand, mind, heart**
—Snead State Junior College, Boaz, Alabama.

58. **Dei sub numine viget** *Latin* 'He grows strong in the presence of God'
—Princeton University, Princeton, New Jersey.

59. **Deo, regi, vicino** *Latin* 'To God, my king, my neighbor'
—Bromsgrove Grammar School, Cookes, Worcester Coll.
Oxon.

60. **Deo ac veritati** *Latin* 'For God and truth'
—Colgate University, Hamilton, New York.

61. **Deo fisus labora** *Latin* 'Work while trusting in God'
—William Jewell College, Liberty, Missouri.

62. **Deo patriae, scientiis, artibus** *Latin* 'For God and country through sciences and arts'
—Gonzaga University School of Law, Spokane,
Washington.

63. **Deus providebit** *Latin* 'God will provide'
—Berton (Bt.), Bolger (of Wexford), Brummind (of Blair), Lesly (of Aberdden), Marshall, Matherm Mein, Mundy, Prideaux (Bt.), Dominican School of Philosophy and Theology, California.

64. **Developing human and natural resources**
—Coahoma Junior College, Clarksdale, Mississippi.

65. **Dieu et mon droit** *French* 'God and my right'
—Sovereigns of Great Britain (since Henry VI); United Kingdom of Great Britain and Northern Ireland; Georg Wilhelm, Elector of Brandenburg (1595–1640); Sherborne School, U.K. (founded 1550).

66. **Diligence/ Discipline/ Integrity**
—Steed College, Johnson City, Tennessee.

67. **Diligence/ Integrity/ Knowledge**
—McNeese State University, Lake Charles, Louisiana.

68. **Disciplina praesidium civitatis** *Latin* 'Discipline, the guardian of the state'
—University of Texas, Austin, Texas.

69. **Distinctively Christian**
—Tennessee Temple University, Chattanooga, Tennessee.

70. **Docendum et discendum** *Latin* 'To be taught and to be learnt'
—Blackheath Proprietary School, U.K.

71. **Dominus illuminatio mea** *Latin* 'The Lord is my light'
—University of Oxford, Leycester (of White Place).

72. **Dominus illuminatio mea** *Latin* 'The Lord, my illumination'
—Oxford University, Oxford, U.K.

73. **Duty, honor, country**
—West Point U.S. Military Academy, West Point, New York.

74. **Duw a Digon** *Welsh* 'God is enough'
—Denbighshire C. C., U.K.

75. **Ecce quam bonum** *Latin* 'Behold how good'
—The University of the South, Sewanee, Tennessee.

76. **Ecclesiae et litteris** *Latin* 'For the church and literature'
—King College, Bristol, Tennessee.

77. **Ecclesiae filii** *Latin* 'Sons of the church'
—St. Edmund's School, Canterbury, U.K.

78. **Education for a democracy of excellence**
—Dutchess Community College, Poughkeepsie, New York.

79. **Education for excellence**
—Durham Technical Institute, Durham, North Carolina.

80. **Education for greater service**
—Arkansas College, Batesville, Arkansas.

81. **Education for service**
—Boston State College, Boston, Massachusetts.

82. **Education is life**
—Eastern Montana College, Billings, Montana.

83. **Education is the mother of wisdom and of virtue** *from Greek*
—Edinburgh Academy, Edinburgh.

84. **Education is the mother of wisdom of virtue**
—(from Greek) Edinburgh Academy, Edinburgh.

85. **Education/ Service/ Research**
—Indiana University, Division of Allied Health Sciences, Bloomington, Indiana.

86. **Educatio pro omnibus** *Latin* 'Education for all'
—Sampson Technical College, Clinton, North Carolina.

87. **Emollit mores nec sinit esse feros** *Latin* 'It softens one's manners and does not allow them to be crude'
—[Ovid, *Ex Ponto*, II. ix. 47.] University of South Carolina at Aiken, Aiken, South Carolina.

88. **Emphasis excellence**
—Kilgore College, Kilgore, Texas.

89. **En Dieu est tout** *French* 'In God is everything'
—Davies, Chambre, Conolly (of Castletown), Wentworth (co. York), Watson, Watson-Wentworth (of Rockingham, M.); Wentworth Military Academy, Lexington, Missouri.

90. **Engineering/ Technology/ Science**
—South Dakota School of Mines and Technology, Rapid City, South Dakota.

91. **Equality**
—University of Wyoming, Laramie, Wyoming.

92. **Eruditio/ ductus/ societas** *Latin* 'Learning/ leadership/ fellowship'
—Indian River Community College, Ft. Pierce, Florida.

93. **Eruditio et meritum pro omnibus** *Latin* 'Learning and reward for all'
    —Isothermal Community College, Spindale, North Carolina.

94. **Esse quam videri** *Latin* 'To be rather than seem to be'
    —Addenbrooke, Beadon, Crawley-Boevey (Bt.), Bonham, Brownlow, Bunbury, Collett, Couts, Croft (Bt.), Deline, Flinn, Gratten, Hammerton, Hill, Hood, Longley, Lurgan (B.), Maitland, Maris, Mathil, Oakes, Round, Sheriff, St. Paul (Bt.), St. Paul, Swire (of Cononley), Thurston (of Weston, Co. Suffolk), Thurston (of Talgarth), Turner, Turnour (of Swaffham, Co. Norfolk), Winterton (E.), Woodcock (of Coventry); National College of Chiropractic, Lombard, Illinois.

95. **Est cotis vis in acutis** *Latin* 'The use of a whetstone is to sharpen'
    —Somersetshire College, Bath, U.K.

96. **Esto perpetua** *Latin* 'May she exist forever'
    —Royal Naval School, Eltham, U.K.

97. **Et docere et rerum exquirere causas** *Latin* 'To teach and to inquire into the nature of things'
    —University of Georgia, Athens, Georgia.

98. **Exaltum cornu in Deo** *Latin* 'The horn is exalted in God'
    —Truro C. C., U.K.

99. **Excellence**
    —University of Wisconsin, Eau Claire, Wisconsin.

100. **Excellence for Christ**
    —St. Andrews Presbyterian College, Laurinburg, North Carolina.

101. **Excellence through education**
    —Naval Postgraduate School, Monterey, California.

102. **Excellentia** *Latin* 'Excellence'
    —University of Tennessee at Martin, Martin, Tennessee.

103. **Ex Oriente salus** *Latin* 'Salvation from the East'
    —Eastbourne College, U.K.

104. **Ex scientia tridens** *Latin* 'Out of knowledge, a trident'
    —United States Naval Academy, Annapolis, Maryland.

105. **Fiat lux**   *Latin* 'Let there be light'
      —[Genesis, i. 3.] Rollins College, Winter Park, Florida;
      Atlantic Union College, South Lancaster,
      Massachusetts.

106. **Fide et literis**   *Latin* 'By faith and by letters'
      —St. Paul's School, London.

107. **Fidelitas/ veritas/ integritas**   *Latin* 'Fidelity/ truth/ integrity'
      —Salmon P. Chase College of Law of Northern Kentucky
      University, Covington, Kentucky.

108. **Fides lumen praebeat**   *Latin* 'May faith grant light'
      —St. Gregory's College, Shawnee, Oklahoma.

109. **Floreat Etona**   *Latin* 'May Eton flourish'
      —Eton U. D. C., U.K.; Eton College, U. K.

110. **Floreat scientia**   *Latin* 'Let knowledge flourish'
      —Massey University, Palmerston North, New Zealand.

111. **Floreat usque Leo**   *Latin* 'May the Lion ever flourish'
      —St. Mark's School, Windsor, U.K.

112. **Fons vitae sapientia**   *Latin* 'Wisdom is the fountain of life'
      —Trent College, U.K.

113. **For the spiritual and educational guidance of youth**
      —Paul Quinn College, Waco, Texas.

114. **Forward California**
      —Sacramento City College, Sacramento, California.

115. **Freedom with responsibility, equal justice under law**
      —Western State University College of Law, Fullerton and
      San Diego, California.

116. **Freely ye received, freely give**
      —Pepperdine University, Malibu, California.

117. **Gateway to world service**
      —Simpson College, San Francisco, California.

118. **God, Our Father—Christ, Our Redeemer—Man, Our Brother**
      —Morris Brown College, Atlanta, Georgia.

119. **God hath made of one blood all nations of men**
      —Berea College, Berea, Kentucky.

120. **Gratia et veritas**   *Latin* 'Grace and truth'
      —Luther Theological Seminary, St. Paul, Minnesota.

121. **Habebunt lumen vitae**   *Latin* 'They shall have the light of life'
      —Atlantic Christian College, Wilson, North Carolina.

122. **Haec studia oblectant** *Latin* 'These studies give delight'
—Clifton College, U.K.

123. **Head/ Heart/ Hand**
—Bethune-Cookman College, Dayton Beach, Florida.

124. **Heroum filii** *Latin* 'Sons of heroes'
—Wellington College, U.K.

125. **Hic et ubique terrarum** *Latin* 'Here, there, and everywhere'
—University of Paris.

126. **High merit, high reward**
—Hymers College, Hull, U.K.

127. **Hinc lucem et pocula sacra** *Latin* 'Hence light and sacred draughts'
—Cambridge University, U.K.

128. **Holding forth the Word of life**
—Great Lakes Bible College, Lansing, Michigan; Boise Bible College, Boise, Idaho.

129. **Honestas et diligentia** *Latin* 'Honesty and diligence'
—Suffolk University Law School, Boston, Massachusetts.

130. **Honor, purpose, wisdom**
—Palo Verde College, Blythe, California.

131. **Honor nourishes the arts**
—International Fine Arts College, Miami, Florida.

132. **In bono vince** *Latin* 'Conquer by the good'
—Ramsgate College, U.K.

133. **In Christo fratres** *Latin* 'Brothers in Christ'
—Tonbridge School, U.K.

134. **In Deo speramus** *Latin* 'We trust in God'
—Brown University, Providence, Rhode Island.

135. **Industria** *Latin* 'By industry'
—Calrow, Crierie, Fettes, Fiddes, Gentle, Keltie, McCrire, Ogilvy, Fettes College, U.K.; Peel (Bt.).

136. **In fide fiducia** *Latin* 'There is trust in faith'
—Leys School, Cambridge, U.K.

137. **In fide vestra virtutem in virtute autem scientiam** *Latin* '(Have) virtue in your faith but knowledge in your virtue'
—Agnes Scott College, Decatur, Georgia.

138. **In lumine tuo videbimus lumen** *Latin* 'In thy light we shall see the light'
>—Columbia University, New York City; College of Great Falls, Great Falls, Montana.

139. **In sapientia modus** *Latin* 'In wisdom a means'
>—The University of New England, Australia.

140. **Intaminatis fulget honoribus** *Latin* 'He shines with spotless honors'
>—Wofford College, Spartanburg, South Carolina.

141. **Integrias/ veritas/ dignitas** *Latin* 'Integrity/ truth/ dignity'
>—Indiana Northern Graduate School of Professional Management.

142. **Integrity/ Quality/ Progress**
>—The Louisville Technical Institute, Louisville, Kentucky.

143. **In time**
>—University of Houston, Houston, Texas; Houston (B.), Houston.

144. **Intus si recte, ne labora** *Latin* 'If right within, trouble not'
>—Shrewsbury School, U.K.

145. **In union strength**
>—Huston-Tillotson College, Austin, Texas.

146. **I will try**
>—Norwich University, Northfield, Vermont.

147. **'I would found an institution where any person can find instruction in any study'**
>—Cornell University, Ithaca, New York.

148. **Je maintiendray** *Old French* 'I shall maintain'
>—Hofstra University School of Law, Hempstead, New York.

149. **Key to the future**
>—University of Wisconsin-Milwaukee, Milwaukee, Wisconsin.

150. **Knowledge, devotion, wisdom, service**
>—Pembroke State University, Pembroke, North Carolina.

151. **Knowledge aflame**
>—Liberty Baptist College, Lynchburg, Virginia.

152. **Knowledge/ Duty/ Honor**
>—South Carolina State College, Orangeburg, South Carolina.

153. **Knowledge for life**
—South Mountain Community College, Arizona.

154. **Knowledge for service**
—Hannibal-LaGrange College, Hannibal, Missouri.

155. **Knowledge is power**
—Sharpe.

156. **Knowledge is structured in consciousness**
—Maharishi International University, Fairfield, Iowa.

157. **Knowledge/ Skill**
—Terra Technical College, Fremont, Ohio.

158. **Knowledge/ Understanding/ Achievement/ Citizenship**
—S. D. Bishop State Junior College, Mobile, Alabama.

159. **Laborare et studere** *Latin* 'Work and study'
—Lincoln University, Jefferson City, Missouri.

160. **Labor et scientia** *Latin* 'Labor and knowledge'
—Rose-Hulman Institute of Technology, Terre Haute,
Indiana.

161. **Labor omnia vincit**
—Ilkeston B. C., Ashton-Under-Lyme B. C., U.K.;
Centenary College of Louisiana, Shreveport,
Louisiana; State of Oklahoma; Bradford City
and C. B. C., U.K.

162. **Language/ Art/ Science**
—Newcomb College, New Orleans, Louisiana.

163. **Learning and labor**
—University of Illinois, Urbana-Champaign, Illinois.

164. **Learning for earning**
—Bryant and Stratton Business Institute, Clarence, New
York.

165. **Learning/ Service/ Integrity**
—Quinsigamond Community College, Worcester,
Massachusetts.

166. **Let knowledge grow from more to more; and so be human life
enriched**
—University of Chicago, Chicago, Illinois.

167. **Let light shine out**
—Northwest College of the Assemblies of God, Kirkland,
Washington.

168. **Lex** *Latin* 'Law'
    —San Francisco Law School, San Francisco, California.

169. **Lex ancilla justitiae** *Latin* 'Law, the servant of justice'
    —The John Marshall Law School, Chicago, Illinois.

170. **Lex pro urbe et orbe** *Latin* 'Law for the city and the world'
    —Vermont Law School, South Royalton, Vermont.

171. **Lex ratio summa or Lex summa ratio** *Latin* 'Law is the highest reason'
    —Law.

172. **Live to the truth**
    —Framingham State College, Framingham, Massachusetts.

173. **Lux** *Latin* 'Light'
    —University of Northern Iowa, Cedar Falls, Iowa.

174. **Lux esto** *Latin* '(Let there) be light'
    —[Genesis, i. 3.] Southwestern College in Kansas, Winfield, Kansas.

175. **Lux et fides** *Latin* 'Light and faith'
    —Taylor University, Upland, Indiana.

176. **Lux et scientia** *Latin* 'Light and knowledge'
    —Andrew College, Cuthbert, Georgia.

177. **Lux et veritas** *Latin* 'Light and truth'
    —Waldorf College, Forest City, Iowa.

178. **Lux et veritas** *Latin* 'Light and truth'
    —Yale University, New Haven, Connecticut.

179. **Lux/ libertas** *Latin* 'Light/ liberty'
    —University of North Carolina School of Nursing, Chapel Hill, North Carolina.

180. **Lux mentis lux orbis** *Latin* 'Light of the mind, light of the world'
    —Sonoma State University, Rohnert Park, California.

181. **Lux mundi** *Latin* 'Light of the world'
    —Thiel College, Greenville, Pennsylvania.

182. **Lux veritas peritia populo nostro** *Latin* 'Light, truth, and skill for our people'
    —Coastal Carolina Community College, Jacksonville, North Carolina.

183. **Manners makyth man**
    —Hood (of Barton Park, Co. Lancaster), Wickham,
        Wykeham (Bishop of Winchester and Lord
        Chancellor of England, founder of New College,
        Oxford, in 1379); New College, Oxford.

184. **May the right prevail** *(from Greek)*
    —[Aeschylus, *Agamemnon*, l. 121.] Brighton College, U.K.

185. **Medicine—To Teach, To Serve, To Search**
    —University of Arkansas for Medical Sciences, Arkansas.

186. **Mens agitat molem** *Latin* 'Mind animates matter'
    —Rossall School, U.K.

187. **Mens/ animus/ corpus** *Latin* 'Mind/ soul/ body'
    —Colby-Sawyer College, New London, New Hampshire.

188. **Mens et manus** *Latin* 'Mind and hand'
    —North Carolina Agricultural and Technical State
        University, Greensboro, North Carolina.

189. **Mente et artificio** *Latin* 'Through mind and skill'
    —Ryerson Polytechnical Institute, Toronto, Ontario,
        Canada.

190. **Mercy**
    —Salve Regina—The Newport College, Newport, Rhode
        Island.

191. **Mihi vivere Christus est** *Latin* 'For me, Christ is life'
    —St. Joseph's Seminary, Yonkers, New York.

192. **Mind/ Body/ Spirit/ Educating the whole man**
    —Oral Roberts University, Tulsa, Oklahoma.

193. **Misericordias Domini in aeternum cantabo** *Latin* 'I will sing the mercies of the Lord forever'
    —[Ps. lxxxix. 1.] Abingdon School, U.K.

194. **Missionary/ Biblical/ Evangelistic**
    —Arlington Baptist College, Arlington, Texas.

195. **Moving people forward**
    —Sampson Technical College, Clinton, North Carolina.

196. **Naturam primum cognoscere rerum** *Latin* 'First to learn the nature of things' or 'Above all to find out the way things are'
    —Australian National University, Canberra, Australia.

197. **Ne incautus futuri** *Latin* 'Not incautious of the future'
    —Hagerstown Business College, Hagerstown Business
        College.

198. **Ne ultra** *Latin* 'Nothing beyond'
—Davidson College, Davidson, North Carolina.

199. **Nil sine magno labore** *Latin* 'Nothing without great labor'
—Brooklyn College (City University of New York),
Brooklyn, New York; Kidd.

200. **Nil sine numine** *Latin* 'Nothing without the Deity'
—State of Colorado; Regis College, Denver, Colorado;
Blundell, Banner, Weld (of Lulworth).

201. **Non ministrari sed ministrare** *Latin* 'Not to be served but to serve'
—Queens College, Charlotte, North Carolina.

202. **Non progredi est regredi** *Latin* 'Not to progress is to regress'
—McCook Community College, McCook, Nebraska.

203. **Non recuso laborem** *Latin* 'I do not refuse work'
—Dover College, U.K.

204. **Non solum ingenii, verum etiam virtutis** *Latin* 'Not only talent, but also virtue'
—Liverpool College, U.K.

205. **Not quantity —but quality**
—Stowe State College, St. Louis, Missouri.

206. **Numen flumenque** *Latin* 'Divinity and the river'
—Marquette University, Milwaukee, Wisconsin.

207. **Nunquam non paratus** *Latin* 'Not unprepared'
—Kemper Military School and College, Boonville,
Missouri.

208. **Obstacles are things to be overcome**
—Samuel Gridley Howe; School for the Instruction of the
Blind, Boston, Mass.

209. **One in Christ Jesus**
—Interdenominational Theological Center, Atlanta,
Georgia.

210. **Opportunity for all**
—Kalamazoo Valley Comunity College, Kalamazoo,
Michigan.

211. **Opportunity through training**
—State Area Vocational-Technical Schools System,
Tennessee.

212. **Orando laborando** *Latin* 'By prayer and by labor'
—Rugby School, U.K.

213. **Our lamb has conquered: Let us follow him**
—Moravian Theological Seminary, Bethlehem,
Pennsylvania.

214. **Ours the task eternal**
—Carleton University, Ottawa, Canada.

215. **Palmam qui meruit ferat** *Latin* 'Let him who has deserved it bear the palm'
—[Jortin, *Lusus Poetici: Ad Ventos*, st. 4.] Royal Naval
School, U.K.

216. **Paratae servire** *Latin* 'Prepared to serve'
—Colby-Sawyer College, New London, New Hampshire.

217. **Paullatim sed firmiter** *Latin* 'Gradually but surely'
—University College School, London.

218. **Peace through law**
—Arizona State University College of Law, Arizona.

219. **Per Jesum Christum** *Latin* 'Through Jesus Christ'
—Luther Theological Seminary, St. Paul, Minnesota.

220. **Per lumen scientiae viam invenient populi** *Latin* 'Through the light of knowledge the people will find a way'
—Texas College, Tyler, Texas.

221. **Per scientiam ad salutem publicam** *Latin* 'Through knowledge to public health'
—Johns Hopkins School of Hygiene and Public Health,
Baltimore, Maryland.

222. **Petimus credimus** *Latin* 'We strive, we believe'
—Bob Jones University, Greenville, South Carolina.

223. **Philosophia pietati ancillans** *Latin* 'Philosophy in service to piety'
—Hanover College, Hanover, Indiana.

224. **Physical/ Mental/ Spiritual/ Social**
—University of Science and Arts of Oklahoma, Chickasha,
Oklahoma.

225. **Physical/ Spiritual/ Social/ Mental**
—Florida College, Temple Terrace, Florida.

226. **Pietas parentum** *Latin* 'Filial affection'
—St. Edward's School, Oxford, U.K.

227. **Plus ultra** *Latin* 'More beyond'
—Shepherd College, Shepherdstown, West Virginia.

228. **Possunt quia posse videntur** *Latin* 'They are able because they seem to be able'
— [Vergil, *Aen.* v. 231.] Bath College, U.K.; Christ College, Brecon, U.K.

229. **Postera crescam laude** *Latin* 'I will flourish in the praise of my descendants'
— University of Melbourne, Melbourne, Australia.

230. **Praesis ut prosis** *Latin* 'Lead that you may serve'
— Lancaster School, U.K.

231. **Preparing evangels of our heritage**
— Gulf-Coast Bible College, Houston, Texas.

232. **Pride in the past/ Faith in the future**
— Hastings College, Hastings, Nebraska.

233. **Primum vir esto** *Latin* 'First, be a man'
— Baker University, Baldwin City, Kansas.

234. **Primus inter pares** *Latin* 'First among equals'
— Columbus College, Columbus, Georgia.

235. **Pro bono humani generis** *Latin* 'For the good of humankind'
— The Rockefeller University, New York, New York.

236. **Pro Christo et humanitate** *Latin* 'For Christ and humanity'
— Olivet College, Olivet, Michigan.

237. **Pro Christo et patria** *Latin* 'For Christ and country'
— Geneva College, Beaver Falls, Pennsylvania; Gilbert, Ker, Verner.

238. **Pro Christo et Republica** *Latin* 'For Christ and the Republic'
— Birmingham-Southern College, Birmingham, Alabama.

239. **Pro corona et foedere Christi** *Latin* 'For the crown and Christ's covenant'
— Cedarville College, Cedarville, Ohio.

240. **Pro Deo et patria** *Latin* 'For God and country'
— University of Dayton School of Law, Dayton, Ohio; Loras College, Dubuque, Iowa.

241. **Pro Deo et patriâ** *Latin* 'For God and our country'
— Maguire.

242. **Producing people with purpose**
— Miami Christian College, Miami, Florida.

243. **Pro ecclesia, pro Texana** *Latin* 'For the church, for Texas'
— Baylor University, Waco, Texas.

244. **Pro ecclesia et patria** *Latin* 'For church and country'
—Trinity College, Hartford, Connecticut.

245. **Pro humanitate** *Latin* 'For humanity'
—Wake Forest University, Winston-Salem, North Carolina.

246. **Prompte et sincere** *Latin* 'Prompt and sincere'
—Calvin Theological Seminary, Grand Rapids, Michigan.

247. **Provenito in altum** *Latin* 'May he appear on high'
—Memorial University of Newfoundland, Canada.

248. **Quant je puis** *French* 'As much as I can'
—Stonyhurst College.

249. **Qui facit per alium facit per se** *Latin* 'He who acts through another acts for himself'
—Perse Grammar School, U.K.

250. **Reach for the stars**
—University of Central Florida, Orlando, Florida.

251. **Religio, libertas et scientia** *Latin* 'Religion, liberty, and knowledge'
—Cedar Crest College, Allentown, Pennsylvania.

252. **Religioni et bonis artibus** *Latin* 'For religion and the liberal arts'
—St. Louis University, St. Louis, Missouri.

253. **Religioni reipublicae** *Latin* 'For religion and the state'
—King Henry VIII School, Coventry, U.K.

254. **Rerum cognoscere causas** *Latin* 'To understand the causes of things'
—The London School of Economics and Political Science.

255. **Research/ Education/ Service**
—Baylor College of Medicine, Houston, Texas.

256. **Research/ Instruction/ Extension: For the advancement of science and arts**
—Auburn University, Auburn, Alabama.

257. **Respice, auspice, prospice** *Latin* 'Look to the past, the present, and the future'
—The City College, City University of New York, New York City, New York.

258. **Sacrifice or service**
—Dakota Wesleyan University, Mitchell, South Dakota.

259. **Sancte et sapienter** *Latin* 'With holiness and wisdom'
—King's College School, London.

260. **Sanitas/ scientia/ sanctitas** *Latin* 'Health/ knowledge/ holiness'
—Gannon University, Erie, Pennsylvania.

261. **Sapiens qui prospicit** *Latin* 'He is wise who looks ahead'
—Malvern College, U.K.

262. **Sapientia aedificavit sibi Domum** *Latin* 'Wisdom has built a Home for itself'
—Rockhurst College, Kansas City, Missouri.

263. **Sapientia/ caritas/ prudentia** *Latin* 'Wisdom/ charity/ prudence'
—Saint Mary of the Plains College, Dodge City, Kansas.

264. **Sapientia Domum aedificavit** *Latin* 'Knowledge has built a Home'
—Crosier Seminary Junior College, Onamia, Minnesota.

265. **Sapientia et doctrina** *Latin* 'Wisdom and teaching'
—Fordham University, New York, New York.

266. **Sapientia felicitas** *Latin* 'Wisdom is happiness'
—University of Oxford.

267. **Sapientia/ virtus/ amicitia** *Latin* 'Knowledge/ virtue/ friendship'
—Central Michigan University, Mt. Pleasant, Michigan.

268. **Scholarship/ Participation/ Service**
—McPherson College, McPherson, Kansas.

269. **Science with practice**
—Queensland Agricultural College, Lawes, Queensland, Australia.

270. **Scientia** *Latin* 'Knowledge'
—Northwestern College of Chiropractic, St. Paul, Minnesota.

271. **Scientiae cedit mare** *Latin* 'The sea yields to knowledge'
—U.S. Coast Guard Academy, New London, Connecticut.

272. **Scientia est potentia** *Latin* 'Knowledge is power'
—Miami-Dade Community College, Miami, Florida; Tylden (U.S.).

273. **Scientia et industria cum probitate** *Latin* 'Knowledge and diligence with uprightness'
—Lincoln College, Canterbury, New Zealand.

274. **Scientia et pietas** *Latin* 'Knowledge and piety'
—Wesleyan College, Macon, Georgia.

275. **Scientia et sapientia**   *Latin* 'Knowledge and wisdom'
                    —Illinois Wesleyan University, Bloomington, Illinois.

276. **Scientia/ integritas**   *Latin* 'Knowledge/ integrity'
                    —Massachusetts Bay Community College, Wellesley Hills,
                                                          Massachusetts.

277. **Scientia/ Pietas que vitalis**   *Latin* 'Learning and devotion are
      vital'
                    —Texas Wesleyan College, Fort Worth, Texas.

278. **Scientia vera cum fide pura**   *Latin* 'True knowledge with pure
      faith'
                    —Beloit College, Beloit, Wisconsin.

279. **Scientiis/ artibus/ religioni**   *Latin* 'By knowledge, by art, by reli-
      gion'
                    —Mercer University, Macon, Georgia.

280. **Sedes sapientiae**   *Latin* 'The seat of wisdom'
                    —Marian College, Indianapolis, Indiana.

281. **Seek the truth**
                    —Northeast Louisiana University, Monroe, Louisiana.

282. **Seek wisdom**
                    —University of Western Australia, Nedlands, Australia.

283. **Semper paratus**   *Latin* 'Always prepared'
                    —Clifford (B.), Clifford, Constable (Bt.), Dallas,
                          Johnstone (of Stratton), Knowles (Bt.), Leckey
                                (of Londonderry), Mounsey, Phillpotts,
                             Roydes, Stewart (of Inchbrock), Usticke,
                             Upton (of Ingmire), Wells (of Grebly Hall),
                                Welles; United States Coast Guard.

284. **Semper veritas**   *Latin* 'Truth always'
                    —Lake City Community College, Lake City, Florida.

285. **Service first**
                    —Minot State College, Minot, North Dakota.

286. **Service is sovereignty**
                    —Alabama A & M University, Alabama.

287. **Service/ Opportunity/ Community/ Learning**
                    —Wayne County Community College, Detroit, Michigan.

288. **Service through education**
                    —Thomas County Community College, Thomasville,
                                                          Georgia.

289. **Serving the King of Kings**
                    —The King's College, Briarcliff Manor, New York.

290. **Sic luceat lux vestra** *Latin* 'May your light thus shine'
—Buxton College, U.K.

291. **Sicut lilium** *Latin* 'Like the lily'
—[after Matt., vi. 28.] Magdalen College School, Oxford,
U.K.

292. **Signum fidei** *Latin* 'The sign of faith'
—Saint Mary's College of California, Moraga, California.

293. **S'intruire pour servir** *French* 'To intrude in order to serve'
—Vincennes University, Vincennes, Indiana.

294. **Sit lux** *Latin* 'Let there be light'
—[Genesis, i. 3.] Tarkio College, Missouri.

295. **Soirbheachadh le Gleann Amuinn** *Gaelic* 'May Glenalmond flourish!'
—Glenalmond College, U.K.

296. **Soit droit fait** *French* 'Let right be done'
—Queen's University, Kingston, Ontario, Canada.

297. **Spanning the world**
—Community College of the Air Force, Alabama.

298. **Spartam nactus es: hanc exorna** *Latin* 'Sparta is thy lot: do her credit'
—[after Euripides, *Fragmenta*, 695.] Loretto School, U.K.

299. **Spes nostra** *Latin* 'Our hope'
—Mount Saint Mary's College, Emmitsburg, Maryland.

300. **Spes unica** *Latin* 'A single hope'
—Our Lady of Holy Cross College, New Orleans,
Louisiana.

301. **Spiritus intus alit** *Latin* 'The spirit nourishes from within'
—[Vergil, *Aen.* vi. 723.] Clifton College, U.K.

302. **Stet fortuna domus** *Latin* 'May the fortunes of the House stand!'
—Harow School, U.K.

303. **Studiis et rebus honestis** *Latin* 'Through studies and upright affairs'
—University of Vermont, Burlington, Vermont.

304. **Studio optimae doctrinae et saluti sanitatis** *Latin* '(Dedicated) to the pursuit of educational excellence and the preservation of health'
—Logan College of Chiropractic, Chesterfield, Missouri.

305. **Succesus per educationem**   *Latin* 'Success through education'
—Thomas Nelson Community College, Hampton, Virginia.

306. **Super antiquas vias**   *Latin* 'Along ancient ways'
—St. Peter's School, York, U.K.

307. **Sursum corda**   *Latin* 'Lift up your hearts'
—Haileybury College, U.K.

308. **Tantum nobis creditum**   *Latin* 'So much has been entrusted to us'
—Erindale College of the University of Toronto, Mississauga, Ontario, Canada.

309. **Teaching/ Research/ Service**
—Arkansas State University, Arkansas.

310. **Tempora mutantur permanet praestantia**   *Latin* 'The times change but excellence prevails'
—Mitchell Community College, Statesville, North Carolina.

311. **Terras irradient**   *Latin* 'They will enlighten (many) lands'
—Amherst College, Amherst, Massachusetts.

312. **Tharros, Dynamis, Philosophia**   *(transliterated from Greek)* 'Courage, strength and love of wisdom'
—Grossmont College, El Cajon, California.

313. **That the people shall know**
—Columbia University Graduate School of Journalism, New York City, New York.

314. **The College Creating the Best**
—Georgia Southwestern College, Americus, Georgia.

315. **The college of the Keys**
—Florida Keys Community College, Key West, Florida.

316. **The college that cares**
—Capital City Junior College, Little Rock, Arkansas.

317. **The college that meets your requirements**
—Metropolitan State College, Denver, Colorado.

318. **The entrance of Thy Word giveth light**
—Mid-South Bible College, Memphis, Tennessee.

319. **The road to knowledge**
—El Camino College, Torrance, California.

320. **The seed is the word**
—Concordia Teachers College, Seward, Nebraska.

321. **The servant of God communicating the Word of God**
    —Bethel Theological Seminary, Arden Hills, Minnesota.

322. **The state, the home, the farm**
    —Abraham Baldwin Agricultural College, Tifton, Georgia.

323. **The torch the staff of knowledge**
    —Merced College, Merced, California.

324. **The truth makes free**
    —Bluffton College, Bluffton, Ohio.

325. **The truth shall make you free**
    —City College of San Francisco, San Francisco, California;
    David Lipscomb College, Nashville, Tennessee.

326. **Think/ Work/ Serve**
    —Tennessee State University, Nashville, Tennessee.

327. **Through truth to freedom**
    —Augsburg College, Minneapolis, Minnesota.

328. **To each his farthest star**
    —Surry Community College, Dobson, North Carolina.

329. **To help people learn**
    —Leeward Community College, Pearl City, Hawaii.

330. **To know Him and to make Him known**
    —Columbia Bible College, Columbia, South Carolina.

331. **To learn/ To search/ To serve**
    —State University of New York.

332. **To live is to learn**
    —Elizabeth City State University, Elizabeth City, North Carolina.

333. **To match job opportunities with job skills**
    —Indiana Vocational Technical College.

334. **To reach out**
    —Golden Valley Lutheran College, Minneapolis, Minnesota.

335. **Tota educatio** *Latin* 'Total education'
    —Lenoir Community College, Kinston, North Carolina.

336. **To travel hopefully**
    —Centennial motto of Western Oregon State College, Monmouth, Oregon.

337. **Tribus unum** *Latin* 'From three, one'
    —Trinity University, San Antonio, Texas.

338. **Truth/ Culture/ Knowledge**
>—Alexander City State Junior College, Alexander City, Alabama; Rochester Community College, Rochester, Minnesota.

339. **Truth even unto its innermost parts**
>—Brandeis University, Waltham, Massachusetts.

340. **Truth/ Knowledge/ Freedom**
>—Harding University, Searcy, Arkansas.

341. **Truth/ Knowledge/ Wisdom/ Education**
>—Independence Community College, Independence, Kansas.

342. **Truth/ Wisdom**
>—University of Southern Florida, Tampa, Florida.

343. **Union, justice and confidence**
>—Northwestern State University, Natchitoches, Louisiana; Alexandria Vocational-Technical Institute, Alexandria, Louisiana.

344. **Union/ confidence/ justice**
>—Louisiana Technical University, Ruston, Louisiana.

345. **Unitas, veritas, caritas** *Latin* 'Unity, truth, charity'
>—Union Theological Seminary, New York, New York.

346. **United we stand, divided we fall**
>—Eastern Kentucky University, Richmond, Kentucky; States of Kentucky and Missouri.

347. **Urbi et orbi** *Latin* 'For the city and the world'
>—Long Island University, Brooklyn, New York.

348. **Ut omnes te cognoscant** *Latin* 'So that all may know you'
>—Niagara University, Niagara Falls, New York.

349. **Ut te cognoscant et vitam habeant** *Latin* 'So that they may know you and have life'
>—Sacred Heart School of Theology, Hales Corners, Wisconsin.

350. **Velut arbor aevo** *Latin* 'May the tree thrive'
>—University of Toronto, Toronto, Ontario, Canada.

351. **Veritas** *Latin* 'Truth'
>—Eiston; Harvard University, Cambridge, Massachusetts; Dominican College of Blauvelt, Orangeburg, New York.

352. **Veritas cum libertate** *Latin* 'Truth with liberty'
>—Winthrop College, Rock Hill, South Carolina.

353. **Veritas et virtus** *Latin* 'Truth and virtue'
—Mississippi College, Clinton, Mississippi.

354. **Veritas liberabit** *Latin* 'The truth will make you free'
—Lafayette College, Easton, Pennsylvania.

355. **Veritas liberabit vos** *Latin* 'The truth will set you free'
—Saint Augustine's College, Raleigh, North Carolina.

356. **Veritas/ libertas** *Latin* 'Truth/ liberty'
—Manatee Jr. College, Bradenton, Florida.

357. **Veritas/ mores/ scientia** *Latin* 'Truth/ morals/ knowledge'
—East Texas Baptist College, Marshall, Texas.

358. **Veritas vincit** *Latin* 'The truth overcomes'
—Southern Missionary College, Collegedale, Tennessee.

359. **Via veritas et vita** *Latin* 'The way, the truth, and the life'
—Felician College, Chicago, Illinois.

360. **Vim promovet insitam** *Latin* 'It extends an ingrafted power'
—University of Bristol, Bristol, U.K.

361. **Vincit omnia veritas** *Latin* 'Truth conquers all things'
—Courcy; Eaton; Goodchild; Kingsale (B.); Laffan (Bt.);
Compton Community College, Compton, California.

362. **Vincit qui patitur** *Latin* 'He conquers who endures'
—Berea College, Berea, Kentucky.

363. **Vires/ artes/ mores** *Latin* 'Strength/ arts/ morals'
—Florida State University, Tallahassee, Florida.

364. **Virtus laudata crescit** *Latin* 'Virtue grows by praise'
—Berkhamsted School, U.K.

365. **Virtutis fortuna comes** *Latin* 'Fortune is the companion of valor'
—Ashtown (B.), Brook, Clancarty (E.), Ferguson (of
Raith), Hughes, Harberton (V.), Trench,
Wellington (D.); Wellington College, U.K.

366. **Vir/veritas/vox** *Latin* 'Man ruth/voice'
—California State Universities and Colleges.

367. **Vir vita terra** *Latin* 'Man, life, earth'
—Delaware Valley College, Doyleston, Pennsyvania.

368. **Vita hominis sine literis mors est** *Latin* 'The life of man without
letters is death'
—Derby School, U.K.

369. **Vocational/ technical/ general**
—Western Wisconsin Technical Institute, Wisconsin.

370. **Vox clamans in deserto**   *Latin* 'A voice crying in the wilderness'
—Dartmouth College, Hanover, New Hampshire.

371. **Where students learn by doing**
—North Dakota State School of Science, Wahpeton, North Dakota.

372. **Where women create their future**
—Barat College, Lake Forest, Illinois.

373. **Wisdom/ Knowledge/ Skill**
—Martin Community College, Williamston, North Carolina.

374. **With the Word to the World**
—Faith Baptist Bible College, Ankeny, Iowa.

375. **Woksape / Woohitika / Wacantognaka / Wowacintanka**
Lakota 'Wisdom/ bravery/ fortitude/ generosity'
—Sinte Gleska College, Rosebud, South Dakota.

376. **Your friendly place to learn**
—Chipola Junior College, Marianna, Florida.

SCRIPTURES (*See also* DIVINE GUIDANCE; RELIGION.)

1. **A gair Duw yn uchaf**   *Welsh* 'The word of God above all'
—Morris.

2. **Armed with the Word, empowered by the spirit**
—Western Evangelical Seminary, Portland, Oregon.

3. **Communicating the Word**
—Denver Baptist Bible College, Denver, Colorado.

4. **Domine, dirige me in verbo tuo**   *Latin* 'Lord, direct me in thy Word!'
—Johann, Duke of Saxony-Weimar (1570–1605).

5. **Fiat secundum Verbum Tuum**   *Latin* 'Let it be done according to Thy Word'
—St. Marylebone B. C., U.K.

6. **Gottes Wort bleibet ewig**   *German* 'God's Word remains forever'
—Dorothee, Duchess of Saxony (1591–1617).

7. **Gottes Wort bleibet in Ewigkeit**   *German* 'God's Word remains to all eternity'
—Johann Ernst, Duke of Saxony-Eisenach (1566–1638).

8. **Gottes Wort mein Hort** *German* 'God's Word is my shield'
> —Ernst VI, Count of Mansfeld (1561–1609); Anna, Electress of Brandenburg (1576–1625); Agnes, Duchess of Saxony (1584–1629); Eva Katharine, Princess of Anhalt (1613–79); Agnes, Margravine of Brandenburg (d. 1629).

9. **Holding forth the Word of life**
> —Great Lakes Bible College, Lansing, Michigan; Boise Bible College, Boise, Idaho.

10. **In nomine tuo Domine laxabo rete meum** *Latin* 'At Thy word, O Lord, will I let down my net'
> —[after Luke, v. 5.] Johann Philipp, Duke of Saxony-Altenburg (1597–1639).

11. **Lehre mich dein Wortt meiner Seelen Hort** *German* 'Teach me thy word, refuge of my soul!'
> —Wilhelm Ludwig, Prince of Anhalt-Köthen (1638–65).

12. **Mare et ferro** *Latin* 'By sea and steel'
> —Redcar B. C., U.K.

13. **Spiritus gladius verbum Dei** *Latin* 'The sword of the spirit is the Word of God'
> —Franks.

14. **The entrance of Thy Word giveth light**
> —Mid-South Bible College, Memphis, Tennessee.

15. **The servant of God communicating the Word of God**
> —Bethel Theological Seminary, Arden Hills, Minnesota.

16. **Verbum Domini manet in aeternum** *Latin* 'The Word of the Lord endureth forever'
> —[1 Peter, i. 25.] Stationers' Company; Friedrich the Wise, Elector of Saxony (1463–1525); Johann, Elector of Saxony (1467–1532); Heinrich the Pious, Duke of Saxony (1473–1541); Friedrich II, Duke of Liegnitz (1480–1547); Johann Friedrich, Elector of Saxony (1503–54); Erich, Duke of Braunschweig-Grubenhagen (1508–32); Johann Ernst, Duke of Saxony-Eisenach (1566–1638); Christian, Duke of Schleswig-Holstein (1570–1633); August, Prince of Anhalt-Plötzkau (1575–1653); Johann II, Count of the Palatinate of Zweibrücken (1584–1635); Johann Georg I, Elector of Saxony (1585–1656); Johann Friedrich, Duke of Saxony (1600–28); Leopold Ludwig, Count of the Palatinate of Veldenz (1625–94).

17. With the Word to the World
  —Faith Baptist Bible College, Ankeny, Iowa.

SEA (*See also* WATER; WAVES.)

  1. **A mari usque ad mare** *Latin* 'From sea to sea'
  —Dominion of Canada.

  2. **Auspice Deo extule mari** *Latin* 'God being my leader, I brought him out of the sea'
  —Phillips-Marshall, Phillips.

  3. **By sea**
  —Runciman (V.).

  4. **By sea and land**
  —Campbell (U.S.).

  5. **Dieu a la mer** *French* 'God owns the sea'
  —Dennis.

  6. **E mare** *Latin* 'From the sea'
  —Hughan.

  7. **E mare ex industria** *Latin* 'From the sea and from industry'
  —West Hartlepool C. B. C., U.K.

  8. **Ex undis aratra** *Latin* 'Ploughs from the waves'
  —Downie (of Edinburgh).

  9. **Immensi tremor Oceani** *Latin* 'The motion of the infinite ocean'
  —Order of St. Michael (France).

  10. **Imperat aequor** *Latin* 'He rules the sea'
  —Monypenny.

  11. **Laidir ise lear Righ** *Gaelic* 'Strong is the king of the sea'
  —O'Learie.

  12. **Mare ditat** *Latin* 'The sea enriches'
  —Waterman (U.S.).

  13. **Mare ditat, rosa decorat** *Latin* 'The sea enriches and the rose adorns'
  —Town of Montrose.

  14. **Mare ditat flores decorant** *Latin* 'The sea enriches and the flowers adorn'
  —Exmouth U. D. C., U.K.

  15. **Mare et ferro** *Latin* 'By sea and steel'
  —Redcar B. C., U.K.

16. **Merses profundo pulchrior evenit** *Latin* 'Sink him in the sea he comes out fairer'
>—Davison (of Lanton, Co. Northumberland).

17. **Mirabile in profundis** *Latin* 'A wonderful object in the deep'
>—Whalley (Co. Somerset and Hants).

18. **Per mare** *Latin* 'By sea'
>—Anderson (of Aberdeen).

19. **Per mare, per terram** *Latin* 'By sea and by land'
>—Royal Marine Forces, U.K.

20. **Per mare, per terras** *Latin* 'By sea and land'
>—Alexander, Caledon (E.), Drummond (of Kildies), Macalester, McAlister, Macdonald (B.), Macdonnell (of Glengarry).

21. **Per mare et per terram** *Latin* 'By sea and land'
>—Boston B. C., U.K.

22. **Per mare per ecclesiam** *Latin* 'By sea and church'
>—Southend-on-Sea C. B. C., U.K.

23. **Per sinum Codanum** *Latin* 'Through the Baltic'
>—Graves.

24. **Pille mise gu muier** *Scots Gaelic* 'I will return to sea'
>—McLaurin.

25. **Porta maris portus salutis** *Latin* 'A gate of the sea and a haven of health'
>—Margate B. C., U.K.

26. **Prae salem notanda** *Latin* 'The well-known place by the sea' *or* 'Famed for salt'
>—Preesall U. D. C., U.K.

27. **Prato et pelago** *Latin* 'By sea and land'
>—Killingworth.

28. **Ro an mor** *Old Cornish* 'Gift of the sea'
>—Newquay U. D. C., U.K.

29. **Scientiae cedit mare** *Latin* 'The sea yields to knowledge'
>—U.S. Coast Guard Academy, New London, Connecticut.

30. **Sea or land**
>—Essington.

31. **Temperat aequor** *Latin* 'He governs the sea'
>—Monypenny.

32. **Terra, mare, fide** *Latin* 'By the earth, sea, and faith'
>—Campbell.

33. **Terra aut mari**   *Latin* 'By land or by sea'
                                        —Parke (U.S.).

34. **Terra marique**   *Latin* 'On land and sea'
                         —Thornton Cleveleys U. D. C., U.K.

35. **Terra marique**   *Latin* 'By land and sea'
                                        —Cuninghame.

36. **Terra marique potens**   *Latin* 'Powerful by land and sea'
                                        —O'Malley (Bt.).

37. **Tra mor tra Meirion**   *Welsh* 'While the sea lasts, so shall Merioneth'
                              —Merioneth C. C., U.K.

SEARCH and DISCOVERY (*See also* EXPLORATION.)

1. **An open way to new worlds**
              —Flaming Rainbow University, Stilwell, Oklahoma.

2. **Cherche et tu trouveras**   *French* 'Seek and thou shalt find'
                                        —Sawyer.

3. **Cherche qui n'a**   *French* 'Let him seek who has not'
                                        —Margary

4. **Comme je trouve**   *French* 'As I find'
       —Butler (Bt.), Kilkenny (E.), Ormonde (M.), Galmoye
                              (V.), Carey, Bowden.

5. **Eureka**   *Greek* 'I have found it'
                         —Robinson, State of California.

6. **In ardua petit**   *Latin* 'He searches after things difficult of attainment'
                              —Malcolm (of Poltalloch).

7. **Je ne serche qu'un**   *Old French* 'I seek but one'
                                        —Compton.

8. **Quaerendo**   *Latin* 'By seeking'
                                        —Smith.

9. **Quaere sic est**   *Latin* 'Seek, so it is'
                                        —Stanhope.

10. **Quaerite et invenietis**   *Latin* 'Seek, and ye shall find'
                              —[Matt. vii. 7.] Langdon.

11. **Si quaeris peninsulam amoenam circumspice**   *Latin* 'If you seek a
    pleasant peninsula, look about you'
                                        —State of Michigan.

12. **Sub sole nihil**   *Latin* '(I seek) nothing beneath the sun'
—Monteith.

13. **Suchet und werdet finden**   *German* 'Seek and ye shall find'
—Finden.

14. **Superna quaerite**   *Latin* 'Seek things above'
—Graves.

15. **Superna quaero**   *Latin* 'I seek heavenly things'
—Greaves.

16. **Suprema quaero**   *Latin* 'I seek the highest'
—Greaves.

17. **To learn/ To search/ To serve**
—State University of New York.

SEASONS (*See also* TIME.)

1. **Hyeme exsuperata**   *Latin* 'When winter (*or* the storm) is over-passed'
—Wrangham.

2. **In season**
—Walkingshaw.

3. **Jam transit hyems**   *Latin* 'Now winter is passing'
—Hague.

4. **Quam non terret hyems**   *Latin* 'Which winter does not nip with cold'
—Caunter.

5. **Quem non torret hyems**   *Latin* 'Which winter does not scorch'
—Kyd.

SECURITY

1. **Altera securitas**   *Latin* 'Another security'
—Henry VIII.

2. **Anchora labentibus undis**   *Latin* 'Amid the drifting currents an anchor'
—Franklin.

3. **Anchora salutis**   *Latin* 'The anchor of safety'
—O'Loghlen (Bt.).

4. **Arx et anchora mihi Deus**   *Latin* 'God is a stronghold and a security for me'
—Rawson.

5. **Deo non arce spes** *Latin* 'My hope is in God, not in my fortress'
—Castell.

6. **Discrimine salus** *Latin* 'Safety in danger'
—Trail.

7. **Dum vigilo tutus** *Latin* 'While I am vigilant I am safe'
—Gordon (of Knockespoch).

8. **Duobus fulcris securius** *Latin* 'Securer with two supports'
—Rudolf August, Duke of Braunschweig-Wolfenbüttel
(1627–1704).

9. **Ferrum equitis salus** *Latin* 'His sword is the safety of the horse-man'
—Smyth.

10. **Firma et stabilis** *Latin* 'Safe and sure'
—Kirkham U. D. C., U.K.

11. **For security**
—Robertoun (of Ernock), Steedman.

12. **God's port our haven**
—Gosport B. C., U.K.

13. **Hic tutus nutrior** *Latin* 'I am nourished safe here'
—Scott.

14. **His securitas** *Latin* 'In these is safety'
—Barton, Barsane.

15. **Hoc securior** *Latin* 'Safer by this'
—Grieson (of Lagg, Bt.), Grier, Grieve, Collison,
Lockhart.

16. **I make sicker** *Scots dialect* 'I make secure'
—Kirkpatrick (Bt.).

17. **I make sure**
—Escotts, Johnstone, Kirkpatrick.

18. **In arce salus** *Latin* 'In the citadel safety'
—Copeman.

19. **In certa salutis anchora** *Latin* 'On a sure anchor of safety'
—Gillespie.

20. **In cornu salutem spero** *Latin* 'I trust in the horn for safety'
—Hunter.

21. **Inde securior** *Latin* 'Hence the safer'
—Murray (of Livingston).

22. **In medio tutissimus** *Latin* 'In the middle path safest'
—Smith (of Lydiate).

23. **In medio tutissimus ibis**   *Latin* 'You will go safest in the middle'
—Harris.

24. **In sale salus**   *Latin* 'In salt safety'
—Salt (Bt.).

25. **In tempestate securitas**   *Latin* 'Safety in the storm'
—Friedrich V, King of Bohemia (1532–96).

26. **In veritate salus**   *Latin* 'There is safety in truth'
—Jeffery (U.S.).

27. **Lux et salus**   *Latin* 'Light and safety'
—Brunton.

28. **Mack all sicker**   *Scots dial.* 'Make all secure'
—Almack.

29. **Make all sure**
—Armourers' and Braziers' Company, London.

30. **Marte suo tutus**   *Latin* 'Safe by his own exertions'
—Byers, Byres.

31. **Medio tutissimus**   *Latin* 'Safest in the middle'
—Langton (of Fransham, Co. Norfolk).

32. **Medio tutissimus ibis**   *Latin* 'The middle course is the safest'
—[Ovid, *Met.* ii. 237.] Heinrich, Count Reuss zu Schleiz (1563–1616).

33. **Medio tutissimus ibis**   *Latin* 'The middle path is safest for you'
—Busfield, Senior.

34. **Medio tutus**   *Latin* 'Safe in the middle'
—McMaster.

35. **Nodo firmo**   *Latin* 'In a firm knot'
—Harrington (Bt.), Harrington.

36. **No sine periculo**   *Latin* 'I swim without danger'
—Walker (of Newcastle-on-Tyne).

37. **Omnia firmat**   *Latin* 'He secures all things'
—Coulquhoun.

38. **Post tot naufragia portum**   *Latin* 'After so many shipwrecks a haven'
—Sandwich (E.), Hine.

39. **Praecipitatus attamen tutus**   *Latin* 'Cast down, yet safe'
—Dunbar.

40. **Praestat tuto quam cito**   *Latin* 'Better safely than quickly'
—Bonar.

41. **Probitas sibi ipsi securitas** *Latin* 'Integrity is its own security'
—Carr.

42. **Pro salute** *Latin* 'For safety'
—Ogilvie (of Edinburgh).

43. **Publica salus mea merces** *Latin* 'The public security is my reward'
—Dick.

44. **Quae amissa salva** *Latin* 'What has been lost is safe'
—Keith, Kintore (E.).

45. **Quae serata secura** *Latin* 'Things locked up are safe'
—Douglas.

46. **Quercus robur salus patriae** *Latin* 'The strength of the oak is the safety of our country'
—Oakes.

47. **Qui plane sane vadit** *Latin* 'Who goes plainly goes safely'
—Taylor.

48. **Recte faciendo securus** *Latin* 'Safe in acting justly'
—Inglis (Bt.).

49. **Salus naufragis salus aegris** *Latin* 'Safety to the shipwrecked, health to the sick'
—Ramsgate B. C., U.K.

50. **Salvus in igne** *Latin* 'Safe in fire'
—Trivett (of Penshurst).

51. **Sapientia tutus** *Latin* 'Safe by wisdom'
—Crewdson.

52. **Secura frugalitas** *Latin* 'Frugality is safe'
—Mitchell (of Filligrige).

53. **Secura quae prudentes** *Latin* 'What prudent people do is secure'
—Gray.

54. **Secure amid perils**
—Henderson.

55. **Secure vivere mors est** *Latin* 'To live without trouble is death'
—Dayrell (of Lillingston).

56. **Securior qui paratior** *Latin* 'The better prepared the more secure'
—Johnston (of Gormach), Johnson.

57. **Securitas regni** *Latin* 'The security of the kingdom'
—Order of Cyprus.

58. **Securitate** *Latin* 'With security'
                                        —Robertstoun (of Bedley).

59. **Securum praesidium** *Latin* 'A secure fortress'
                —Craigie (of Kilgraston), Craigdaillie (of Aberdeen).

60. **Securus** *Latin* 'Secure'
                                                    —Yates.

61. **Sicker** *Scottish* 'Secure'
                                                    —Douglas.

62. **Sic limina tuta** *Latin* 'In this way our homes are safe'
                                                    —Elliott.

63. **Sic tutus** *Latin* 'Thus safe'
                —Gordon (of Park, Bt.), Gordon (of Craig, etc.).

64. **Sub tigno salus** *Latin* 'Safety under the roof-tree'
                                                    —Innes.

65. **Timor Dei summa securitas** *Latin* 'The fear of God is the great-
    est security'
                        —On a building in Louvigny, France.

66. **Tuta timens** *Latin* 'Fearing safe things'
                                                —Leadbetter.

67. **Tute tua tuta** *Latin* 'Your safe things safely'
                                                —Robison.

68. **Tutissima statio** *Latin* 'The safest station'
                                    —Town of Stranrear, U.K.

69. **Tuto, celeriter, et jucunde** *Latin* 'Safely, speedily, and agreea-
    bly'
                                    —Sutton (of Framlingham).

70. **Tuto et celeriter** *Latin* 'Safely and quickly'
                                    —Penrice (of Yarmouth).

71. **Tutum monstrat iter** *Latin* 'He shows the safe way'
                                                    —Cook.

72. **Tutum refugium** *Latin* 'A safe refuge'
                                            —Gillon, Gullon.

73. **Tutum te littore sistam** *Latin* 'I will stop you safely at the shore'
                                                —Murray.

74. **Tutum te robore reddam** *Latin* 'I will make you safe by my
    strength'
                                            —Crawfurd, Hinde.

75. **Tutus in bello** *Latin* 'Safe amid war'
                                                —Dobell.

76. **Tutus in undis**   *Latin* 'Safe on the waves'
—Graham (Bt.).

77. **Tutus prompto animo**   *Latin* 'Safe in an active mind'
—Welsted.

78. **Tutus si fortis**   *Latin* 'Safe if brave'
—Fairborne, Raeburn.

79. **Via trita via tuta**   *Latin* 'The beaten road is a safe road'
—Agar, Laprimandaye, Normanton (E.).

80. **Vigilante salus**   *Latin* 'Safety while he watches'
—Cochran.

81. **Vigilantia securitas**   *Latin* 'Security by watching'
—Phin, Phine.

82. **Vigilanti salus**   *Latin* 'Safety to the watchful'
—Cochran.

83. **Virtus salus ducum**   *Latin* 'Virtue is the safety of leaders'
—Leader.

84. **Virtus secura sequitur**   *Latin* 'Virtue follows in safety'
—Severne.

85. **Virtus tutissima**   *Latin* 'Virtue is safest'
—Conlan.

86. **Virtute securus**   *Latin* 'Safe by virtue'
—Hawarden (V.).

87. **Virtute tutus**   *Latin* 'By virtue safe'
—Blair, Marshall, Phaire.

88. **Vir tutus et fidelis**   *Latin* 'A man safe and faithful'
—Bomford.

89. **Within the ark safe for ever**
—Shipwrights' Company.

SELF-CONTROL   (*See also* DISCIPLINE; MODERATION.)

1. **Abstinete, sustinete**   *Latin* 'Forbear, bear'
—Shirley.

2. **Animum rege**   *Latin* 'Rule thy mind'
—[Horace, *Ep.* i. 2, 62.] Day, Keith (Bt.), Moore (of Grimeshill), Reeves.

3. **Appetitus rationi pareat** *Latin* 'Let your desires obey your reason'

> —[Cicero, de Off. I. 39. 10.] Custance (of Weston, Co. Norfolk).

4. **Bear and forbear**

> —Bear, Bernard, Bircham (of Reepham, Co. Norfolk), Langford (B.), Moreland (Bt.), Rowley (of Lawton).

5. **Beare and forbeare**

> —Beare.

6. **Bis vincit qui se vincit** *Latin* 'He conquers twice who conquers himself'

> —Bysse.

7. **Imperare sibi maximum imperium est** *Latin* 'Self-rule is the greatest rule'

> —[Seneca, *Ep.* cxiii.] Bernhard, Duke of Saxony-Weimar (1604–39).

8. **Indulge not**

> —Edwards.

9. **I pensieri stretti ed il viso sciolto** *Italian* 'Strict thoughts and a calm expression'

> —Ludwell (U.S.).

10. **Son courage dompter c'est la grand [*sic*] victoire** *French* 'To subdue one's valor is the greatest conquest'

> —Heinrich V, Count Reuss (1602–67).

11. **Sui victoria indicat regem** *Latin* 'Victory over self marks the king'

> —Rye.

12. **Ut tu linguae tuae, sic ego mearum aureum dominus sum** *Latin* 'As you of your tongue, so I of my ears, am lord'

> —House in Edinburgh, Scotland.

SELF-DETERMINATION (*See also* LIBERTY; WILL.)

1. **Alis volat propriis** *Latin* 'I fly with my own wings'

> —State of Oregon, 1848–1858.

2. **Alterius non sit qui suus esse potest** *Latin* 'Let no man own a master who is able to be his own'

> —Paracelsus (1493–1541).

3. **Per se**   *Latin* 'Through himself'

—Thompson (U.S.).

4. **Satis imperat qui sibi est imperiosus**   *Latin* 'He commands enough who has dominion over himself'

—Haultain.

SELF-KNOWLEDGE   (*See also* KNOWLEDGE; WISDOM.)

1. **Cognoies toy meme**   *Old French* 'Know thyself'

—Braddyl.

2. **Cognosce te ipsum**   *Latin* 'Learn to know thyself'
—Anton I, Count of Oldenburg (1505–73).

3. **Cognosce teipsum et disce pati**   *Latin* 'Know thyself, and learn to suffer'

—Rawlings (Co. Cornwall).

4. **Connois vous-même**   *French* 'Know yourself'

—Lacon.

5. **Dum memor ipse mei**   *Latin* 'While I am mindful of myself'
—Irvine (Bt.).

6. **Ex aliis se ipsum nosse facundissima virtus**   *Latin* 'To know yourself from observation of others is the most eloquent virtue'
—Moritz, Landgrave of Hesse-Cassel (1572–1632).

7. **Know thyself**

—Burt.

8. **Non parvum est seipsum noscere**   *Latin* 'It is not a little thing to know oneself'

—Cooper.

9. **Nosce teipsum**   *Latin* 'Know thyself'
—Buck, Frazer, James, Murray, Pringle, Pendred, Stanfield (of Esholt and Burley Wood), Tindal, Tregonwell, Walford.

10. **Posce teipsum**   *Latin* 'Ask thyself'

—Hodges.

11. **Syn ar dy hun**   *Welsh* 'Know thyself'

—De Winton, Wilkins.

12. **Teipsum nosce**   *Latin* 'Know thyself'

—Shaw (of Dublin, Bt.).

SELF-RELIANCE

1. **Chacun le sien**   *French* 'Every man his own'

    —Bourke.

2. **Court no friend, dread no foe**

    —Malloch, Peter.

3. **Cuncta mea mecum**   *Latin* 'My all is with me'

    —Stedman.

4. **Do it with thyself**

    —Buxton.

5. **Ex sese**   *Latin* 'From himself'

    —Elkin.

6. **Fy nhy'n unig**   *Welsh* 'My house alone'

    —Powell.

7. **In seipso totus teres**   *Latin* 'Fully furnished in himself'

    —Smith.

8. **In se teres**   *Latin* 'Rounded in himself'

    —St. Aubyn.

9. **Mind your own business**

    —Remnant (of Billericay).

10. **Nec te quaesiveris extra**   *Latin* 'Nor shall you have looked outside yourself'

    —Harison (U.S.), Harrison (U.S.).

11. **Non aliunde pendere**   *Latin* 'Not to rely on others'

    —Coke.

12. **Suis stat viribus**   *Latin* 'He stands by his own powers'

    —Abinger (B.).

SERIOUSNESS

1. **Graves disce mores**   *Latin* 'Learn serious manners' *or* 'Graves learn manners'

    —Graves (Co. Gloucester).

2. **Gravis dum suavis**   *Latin* 'Grave yet gentle'

    —Graves.

3. **Graviter et pié**   *Latin* 'Gravely and piously'

    —Park.

4. **In earnest**

    —Marshall (of Steadingly, Leeds).

5. **Mit Schimpf mit Ernst** *German* 'With abuse, with seriousness'
—Ernst, Margrave of Baden-Durlach (1482–1553).

6. **Scherze nicht mit Ernst** *German* 'Jest not with serious things'
—Ernst, Margrave of Baden-Durlach (1482–1553); Ernst, Margrave of Brandenburg (1583–1613).

7. **Semper serio** *Latin* 'Always in earnest'
—Hatfield R. D. C., U.K.

8. **Sero sed serie** *Latin* 'Late but in earnest'
—Nairn, Salisbury (M.).

SERVICE (*See also* USEFULNESS.)

1. **Aliis inserviendo consumor** *Latin* 'In the service of others I consume myself'
—Julius, Duke of Braunschweig-Wolfenbüttel (1529–89).

2. **Aliis servio, meipsum contero** *Latin* 'I serve others: myself I destroy'
—Ernst, Duke of Braunschweig-Lüneburg-Zelle (1497–1546).

3. **A private college serving the world**
—Selma University, Selma, Alabama.

4. **A private university in the public service**
—New York University, New York City, New York.

5. **Bound to obey and serve**
—Jane Seymour, 3rd wife of Henry VIII.

6. **Christian service/ character/ culture**
—Coker College, Hartsville, South Carolina.

7. **Christi servitus vera libertas** *Latin* 'True liberty in service to Christ'
—Merrick (U.S.), Vaughan (U.S.).

8. **Culture for service**
—Clark College, Atlanta, Georgia.

9. **De bon vouloir servir le roy** *Old French* 'To serve the king with right good will'
—Bennet, Grey (E.), Grey (Bt.), Tankerville (E.).

10. **Deo regique liber** *Latin* 'Free to serve God and the king'
—Johnson (of Twickenham, Bt.).

11. **Deo servire regnare est** *Latin* 'To serve God is to reign'
—Arundell.

12. **Deo servire summa libertas** *Latin* 'The service of God is perfect freedom'
> —Christian II, Prince of Anhalt-Bernburg (1599–1656).

13. **Education for greater service**
> —Arkansas College, Batesville, Arkansas.

14. **Education for service**
> —Boston State College, Boston, Massachusetts.

15. **Education/ Service/ Research**
> —Indiana University, Division of Allied Health Sciences, Bloomington, Indiana.

16. **Emeritus** *Latin* 'I have served my country'
> —Emeris (of Louth, Co. Lincoln).

17. **Fac me unum Domine ex mercenariis tuis** *Latin* 'Make me one of Thy servants, O Lord'
> —Philipp, Count of the Palatinate (1480–1541).

18. **Faith, work, service**
> —Calne B. C., U.K.

19. **Feythfully serve**
> —Norreys, Norris.

20. **Gateway to world service**
> —Simpson College, San Francisco, California.

21. **He serves his party best who serves his country best**
> —Rutherford B. Hayes.

22. **His regi servitium** *Latin* 'With these we render service to the king'
> —Neilson.

23. **Horae semper sola salus servire deo** *Latin* 'At all times the only salvation is to serve God'
> —Jarvis (U.S.).

24. **Ich Dien** *German* 'I serve'
> —Prince of Wales, Norfolk C. C., U.K.

25. **Inservi Deo et laetare** *Latin* 'Serve God and rejoice'
> —Howard (Bt.), Wicklow (E.).

26. **J'ai bien servi** *French* 'I have served well'
> —Prevost.

27. **Knowledge, devotion, wisdom, service**
> —Pembroke State University, Pembroke, North Carolina.

28. **Knowledge for service**
> —Hannibal-LaGrange College, Hannibal, Missouri.

29. **Learning/ Service/ Integrity**
—Quinsigamond Community College, Worcester,
Massachusetts.

30. **Love, serve**
—Cooper, Shaftesbury (E.).

31. **Loyalment je sers** *French* 'I serve loyally'
—Jephson, Norreys.

32. **Ministrando dignitas** *Latin* 'Dignity in service'
—Leyton B. C., U.K.

33. **Naturae minister** *Latin* 'A servant of nature'
—Helham.

34. **Non mihi commodus uni** *Latin* 'Advantageous not to me alone'
—Gordon, Oswald.

35. **Non ministrari sed ministrare** *Latin* 'Not to be served but to
serve'
—Queens College, Charlotte, North Carolina.

36. **Paratae servire** *Latin* 'Prepared to serve'
—Colby-Sawyer College, New London, New Hampshire.

37. **Pour avoir fidèlement servi** *French* 'For having faithfully served'
—Order of Christian Charity.

38. **Praeclarum regi et regno servitium** *Latin* 'Honorable service to
king and country'
—Ogilvie (of Barras, Bt.).

39. **Praesis ut prosis** *Latin* 'Lead that you may serve'
—Lancaster School, U.K.

40. **Prodesse** *Latin* 'To serve'
—Hindley U. D. C., U.K.

41. **Proudly we serve**
—Horsham U. D. C., U.K.

42. **Publicum meritorum praemium** *Latin* 'The public reward of
meritorious services'
—Order of St. Stephen (Austria).

43. **Regnant qui servirent** *Latin* 'They rule who serve'
—Finchley B. C., U.K.

44. **Sacrifice or service**
—Dakota Wesleyan University, Mitchell, South Dakota.

45. **Scholarship/ Participation/ Service**
—McPherson College, McPherson, Kansas.

46. **Semper patriae servire praesto**   *Latin* 'Be always ready to serve your country'
> —MacGeoghegan.

47. **Semper presto servire**   *Latin* 'Always ready to serve'
> —Bostwick (U.S.).

48. **Serva jugum**   *Latin* 'Keep the yoke'
> —Errol (E.), Hay (of Park, bt.), Hay (of Glenluce, bt.), Nuttall.

49. **Serva jugum sub jugo**   *Latin* 'Keep the yoke under the yoke'
> —Hay (of Locheloy).

50. **Serve and obey**
> —Haberdashers' Company (London).

51. **Serve God and be cheerful**
> —Sutton and Cheam B. C., U.K.

52. **Serve the king**
> —Bennett (of Ireland).

53. **Serve with gladness**
> —Romford B. C., U.K.

54. **Service and efficiency**
> —Stretford B. C., U.K.

55. **Service first**
> —Minot State College, Minot, North Dakota.

56. **Service is sovereignty**
> —Alabama A & M University, Alabama.

57. **Service links all**
> —Leatherhead U. D. C., U.K.; Lindsey C. C., U.K.

58. **Service/ Opportunity/ Community/ Learning**
> —Wayne County Community College, Detroit, Michigan.

59. **Service through education**
> —Thomas County Community College, Thomasville, Georgia.

60. **Serviendo**   *Latin* 'By serving'
> —Simeon.

61. **Serviendo guberno**   *Latin* 'By serving I govern'
> —O'Rourke.

62. **Serving the King of Kings**
> —The King's College, Briarcliff Manor, New York.

63. **Servire Deo regnare est**   *Latin* 'To serve God is to rule'
> —Middleton (of Westerham).

64. **Servire Deo sapere**   *Latin* 'To serve God is to be wise'
                                        —Sadlier.

65. **Servitute clarior**   *Latin* 'More illustrious by service'
                                        —Player.

66. **Servus servorum Dei**   *Latin* 'Servant of the servants of God'
                                        —Connell.

67. **S'intruire pour servir**   *French* 'To intrude in order to serve'
                    —Vincennes University, Vincennes, Indiana.

68. **Teaching/ Research/ Service**
                    —Arkansas State University, Arkansas.

69. **Think/ Work/ Serve**
                    —Tennessee State University, Nashville, Tennessee.

70. **To learn/ To search/ To serve**
                    —State University of New York.

71. **Ung je servirai**   *Old French* 'One will I serve.'
                                        —Carnarvon (e.), Herbert.

72. **Ung je serviray**   *Old French* 'One will I serve'
                    —Fitz-Herbert (of Norbury), Buxton-Fitzherbert (of Black
                                        Castle), Pembroke (E.).

73. **Un je servirai**   *French* 'One will I serve'
                                        —Straus (U.S.).

74. **Ut prosimus**   *Latin* 'That we may be of service'
                                        —Flory.

75. **We serve**
                    —Dartford R. D. C., Wandsworth B. C., U.K.

76. **Who most has served is greatest**
                                        —Sayle.

SHADE

1. **Non semper sub umbra**   *Latin* 'Not always under the shade'
                                        —Farquharson.

2. **Nubem eripiam**   *Latin* 'I will dispel the cloud'
                    —[Vergil, *Aen.* ii. 606.] Shippersdon (of Pidding Hall, and
                                        Murton, Co. Durham).

3. **Occurrent nubes**   *Latin* 'Clouds will intervene'
                                        —St. Germains (E.).

4. **Ope solis et umbrae**   *Latin* 'By help of sun and shade'
                                        —Irvine.

5. **Post nubes** *Latin* 'After clouds'
                                         —Stothard.

6. **Post nubes lux** *Latin* 'After clouds light'
                       —Blunstone, Steddert.

7. **Post nubila** *Latin* 'After clouds'
                                          —Jack.

8. **Requiesco sub umbra** *Latin* 'I rest under the shade'
                 —Hamilton (of Dalziel).

9. **Sub sole, sub umbra, virescens** *Latin* 'In sun or in shade, thriving'
                                —Erving (U.S.).

10. **Sub sole, sub umbra virens** *Latin* 'Flourishing both in sunshine and in shade'
     —Irvine, Irving, Irwine, Winter-Irving.

11. **Sub sole sub umbra crescens** *Latin* 'Increasing both in sunshine and in shade'
          —Irvine (of Murthill), Irvine.

12. **Sub umbra** *Latin* 'Under the shade'
                                 —Elphinstone.

13. **Sub umbra alarum tuarum** *Latin* 'Under the shadow of thy wings'
                                 —Lawder.

14. **Sub umbra quies** *Latin* 'Rest under the shade'
                                 —Sharpe.

15. **Sub umbra quiescam** *Latin* 'I will rest under the shadow'
                                 —Fairn.

SHARING

1. **For all**
                         —Southall B. C., U.K.

2. **I hope to share**
                    —Nisbet, Riddell (Bt.).

3. **Non mihi, non tibi, sed nobis** *Latin* 'Not for me, nor for thee, but for us'
                    —Battersea B. C., U.K.

4. **Right to share**
                                  —Riddell.

SHINING (*See also* BRIGHTNESS; SUN.)

1. **Burning I shine**
—Jehangier.

2. **By these we shine, and it is fortified**
—MacConack.

3. **Fulget** *Latin* 'He shines forth'
—Belsches.

4. **Fulget virtus** *Latin* 'Virtue shines bright'
—Bell.

5. **Fulget virtus intaminata** *Latin* 'Unspotted virtue shines bright'
—Belches.

6. **Good deeds shine clear**
—Minshull.

7. **In caligine lucet** *Latin* 'It shines in darkness'
—Baillie (Bt.).

8. **In lumine luce** *Latin* 'Shine in the light'
—Makins (Bt.).

9. **In lumine luceam** *Latin* 'I may shine in the light'
—Thompson.

10. **Intaminatis fulget honoribus** *Latin* 'He shines with spotless honors'
—Wofford College, Spartanburg, South Carolina.

11. **Inter lachrymas micat** *Latin* 'It shines amidst tears'
—Blunt.

12. **Je luis imperceu** *French* 'I shine unseen'
—Ley.

13. **Let light shine out**
—Northwest College of the Assemblies of God, Kirkland, Washington.

14. **Luceat et crescat** *Latin* 'Let it shine and grow'
—Blackwood.

15. **Lucent in tenebris** *Latin* 'In darkness they let their light shine'
—O'Moran.

16. **Luceo boreale** *Latin* 'I shine at the north'
—Selon.

17. **Luceo et terreo** *Latin* 'I shine and terrify'
—Allan.

18. **Luceo non terreo** *Latin* 'I shine, I do not terrify'
—Allan.

19. **Luceo non uro** *Latin* 'I shine, but do not burn'

—Mackenzie (Bt.), McKenzie, McLeod (of Colbeck), Smith.

20. **Lucet** *Latin* 'It shines'

—Scot.

21. **Lux omnibus refulgeat** *Latin* 'Let the light shine for all'

—Smith.

22. **Micat inter omnes** *Latin* 'He shines amongst all'

—Haggard (of Bradenham, Co. Norfolk).

23. **Opera bona effulgent** *Latin* 'Good works shine forth'

—Jacoby.

24. **Quaeque favilla micat** *Latin* 'Every ember shines'

—Robertson.

25. **Qua pote lucet** *Latin* 'He shines whenever possible'

—Smith (Bt.).

26. **Refulget** *Latin* 'It is resplendent'

—Pitcairn.

27. **Sic luceat lux vestra** *Latin* 'May your light thus shine'

—Buxton College, U.K.

28. **Splendeo tritus** *Latin* 'I shine though worn'

—Ferrers (of Baddesley).

29. **Te splendente** *Latin* 'Whilst thou art shining'

—Carstairs (of Kilconquhar), Buchan.

30. **They by permission shine**

—Murray (of Birmingham).

31. **Virtute et valare luceo non uro** *Latin* 'By virtue and valor I shine, but do not burn'

—Mackenzie.

SIGN

1. **Crede signo** *Latin* 'Trust in this sign'

—Rochdale C. B. C., U.K.

2. **In hoc signo** *Latin* 'Under this sign'

—Woodhouse (Co. Stafford).

3. **In hoc signo spes mea** *Latin* 'In this sign is my hope'

—D'Urban, Taaffe (V.).

4. **Mein Siegel ist ein Ziegel** *German* 'My seal is a brick'

—Pennypacker (U.S.).

5. **Par ce signe à Azincourt** *French* 'By this sign at Agincourt'
—Entwisle (of Foxholes).

6. **Signum quaerens in vellere** *Latin* 'Seeking a sign in a fleece'
—Clarke.

7. **Sol tibi signa dabit** *Latin* 'The sun will show signs to thee'
—Stewart.

8. **Sub hoc signo vinces** *Latin* 'Under this sign thou shalt conquer'
—De Vesci (V.).

SILENCE

1. **Audi, vide, sile** *Latin* 'Hear, see, be silent'
—Tillard.

2. **Aut tace aut face** *Latin* 'Either be silent or act'
—Scott (of Comeston).

3. **Consilii taciturnitas nutrix** *Latin* 'Silence is the nurse of counsel'
—Jesson (of Oakwood).

4. **Face aut tace** *Latin* 'Do or be silent'
—Veel.

5. **Far and tacer** *Italian* 'To do and keep silence'
—Wilhelm V, Landgrave of Hesse-Cassel (1602–37).

6. **Ich schweig und gedenck** *German* 'I am silent and think'
—Ernst IV, Count of Mansfeld (1544–1609).

7. **In silentio et spe** *Latin* 'In silence and hope'
—[after Isaiah, xxx. 15.] Ernst the Pious, Duke of Saxony-Gotha (1601–75); Bernhard, Duke of Saxony-Weimar (1602–39); Elisabeth Dorothee, Landgravine of Hesse (1640–1709).

8. **In silentio et spe fortitudo mea** *Latin* 'In silence and in hope is my strength'
—[after Isaiah, xxx. 15.] Johann the Wise, Margrave of Brandenburg-Küstrin (1513–71); Justus II, Count of Mansfeld (1558–1619).

9. **In silentio fortitudo** *Latin* 'Courage in silence'
—Hardress, Thoresby.

10. **In spe et silentio** *Latin* 'In hope and in silence'
—Joachim Ernst, Prince of Anhalt (1536–86); Otto the Younger, Duke of Braunschweig-Lüneburg-Harburg (1528–1603).

11. **I. S. E. S. (In silentio et spe)** *Latin* 'In silence and in hope'
—Bernhard, Prince of Anhalt (1572–96).

12. **Mutus inglorius** *Latin* 'The dumb is without glory'
—Halford.

13. **Mutus inglorius artis** *Latin* 'The dumb in an art is without glory'
—Halford.

14. **Pares cum paribus** *Latin* 'Like with like'
—Pares (of Hopewell, co. Derby), Firth.

15. **Sape et tace** *Latin* 'Be wise and be silent'
—Connellan.

16. **Sapere et tacere** *Latin* 'To be wise and silent'
—Broadhurst.

17. **Silendo et sperando** *Latin* 'In quietness and in confidence'
—[Isa., xxx. 15.] August, Duke of Saxony-Weissenfels
(1614–80).

18. **Silentio et spe** *Latin* 'In silence and in hope'
—Philipp, Count of the Palatinate of Rhein (1627–50),
Brander.

19. **Silenzio ad concordia** *Italian* 'Silence at agreement'
—Baird (U.S.).

20. **Study quiet**
—Head (Bt.), Patrick.

21. **Supera audi et tace** *Latin* 'Hear celestial things and keep silence'
—Hesse.

22. **Tace** *Latin* 'Be silent'
—Abercromby.

23. **Tais en temps** *French* 'Be silent in time'
—Tey (of Essex).

24. **Utile quod taceas** *Latin* 'It is useful to keep quiet'
—Turner.

SIMILARITY

1. **Ales volat propriis** *Latin* 'The bird flies to its kind'
—Tufton (Bt.).

2. **Pares cum paribus** *Latin* 'Like with like'
—Pares (of Hopewell, co. Derby), Firth.

SIMPLICITY

1. **Dictis factisque simplex**   *Latin* 'Simple in words and deeds'
    —Sawrey, Gilpin.

2. **In prudentia & simplicitate**   *Latin* 'In prudence and simplicity'
    —Vaughan (U.S.).

3. **Plane et sane**   *Latin* 'Simply and sensibly'
    —Vaughan.

4. **Prudens simplicitas**   *Latin* 'A wise simplicity'
    —Amicable Life Insurance Society.

5. **Prudens simplicitas beat**   *Latin* 'Prudent simplicity blesses'
    —Frederick.

6. **Prudenter et simpliciter**   *Latin* 'Prudently and simply'
    —Vaughan (U.S.).

7. **Prudentiâ et simplicitate**   *Latin* 'With prudence and simplicity'
    —Lant.

8. **Prudentiâ simplicitate**   *Latin* 'With prudence and simplicity'
    —Wyrley-Birch (of Wretham, Co. Norfolk).

9. **Qui plane sane vadit**   *Latin* 'Who goes plainly goes safely'
    —Taylor.

10. **Simplex munditiis**   *Latin* 'Plain with neatness'
    —[Horace, *Od.* i. 5. 5.] Symonds (of Pilsdon), Philips (Co. Somerset).

11. **Soyez sage et simple**   *French* 'Be wise and simple'
    —Spry.

SINCERITY   (*See also* HONESTY.)

1. **Candide, sincere**   *Latin* 'With candor and sincerity'
    —Grieve.

2. **Candoris praemium honos**   *Latin* 'Praise is the reward of sincerity'
    —Dunbar.

3. **Constanter et sincere**   *Latin* 'With constancy and with sincerity'
    —Johann Casimir, Count of the Palatinate of Lantern (1543–92); Joachim, Margrave of Brandenburg (1583–1600); Johann Casimir, Prince of Anhalt-Dessau (1596–1660); Rupert, Count of the Palatinate of Rhein (1619–82); Johann Ernst, Duke of Saxony-Saalfeld (1658–1729).

4. **Corda sincera principia vera**   *Latin* 'Sincere hearts are true principles'

—Dudley.

5. **Cura et candore**   *Latin* 'With care and sincerity'
—Cunningham (Bt.), Forbes (of Ardo).

6. **En sincerité et fidelité ma vie je finiray**   *Old French* 'In sincerity and fidelity shall I end my life'
—Anna Sophie, Duchess of Braunschweig-Wolfenbüttel (1598–1659).

7. **Ex candore decus**   *Latin* 'Honor from sincerity'
—Keith (of Craig).

8. **Fortiter et sincere**   *Latin* 'Boldly and sincerely'

—Johnson.

9. **Fortiter et strenue**   *Latin* 'Boldly and earnestly'
—Dempster, McLean.

10. **Germana fides candorque**   *Latin* 'Genuine fidelity and sincerity'
—Falconberg.

11. **Prompte et sincere**   *Latin* 'Prompt and sincere'
—Calvin Theological Seminary, Grand Rapids, Michigan.

12. **Pur et seincere**   *Old French* 'Pure and sincere'
—Luise Juliane, daughter of Prince of Orange (B. 1576).

13. **Sapienter si sincere**   *Latin* 'Wisely if sincerely'
—Davidson.

14. **Sincere et constanter**   *Latin* 'With sincerity and constancy'
—Georg Friedrich Karl, Margrave of Brandenburg-Baireuth (1688–1735); Christian Ludwig, Duke of Braunschweig-Lüneburg-Zelle (1622–65); Ernst August, Duke of Saxony-Weimar (1688–1741).

15. **Sincere et constanter**   *Latin* 'Sincerely and steadfastly'
—Order of the Red Eagle (Prussia).

16. **Sinceritas**   *Latin* 'Sincerity'
—Short, Hazard.

17. **Sinceritate**   *Latin* 'By sincerity'
—Francklin.

SIZE

1. **Je suis petite, mais mes picqûres sont profondes** *French* 'I am small, but my sting strikes deep'
   —Order of the Bee (France).

2. **Licet ex multo parvum** *Latin* 'Little though from much'
   —Samuels.

3. **Magnum in parvo** *Latin* 'Much in little'
   —Little, Congilton.

4. **Multa in parvo** *Latin* 'Much in little'
   —Little, Hepburn.

SOLITUDE

1. **I am alone**
   —Lone.

2. **It's good to be loun**
   —Forrester.

3. **Nimand zonder** *Dutch* 'Without anyone'
   —Van Rensselaer (U.S.).

4. **Solus in pluribus** *Latin* 'Alone among many'
   —Forbes (of Sussex).

5. **Solus inter plurimos** *Latin* 'Alone among many'
   —Forbes (of Kingerloch).

6. **Solus minus solus** *Latin* 'Alone, but not alone'
   —Hoskins.

7. **Un tout seul** *French* 'One alone'
   —Verney.

SPEED (*See also* RUNNING.)

1. **Aequo pede propera** *Latin* 'Hasten with steady pace'
   —East (Bt.).

2. **Aequo pede propera** *Latin* 'Hasten steadily'
   —Leigh B. C., U.K.

3. **Audax et celer** *Latin* 'Bold and quick'
   —Pearce (Bt.).

4. **Catius quam citus** *Latin* 'With more shrewdness than dispatch'
   —Roscow.

5. **Celer** *Latin* 'Swift'
   —Miller.

6. **Celer et audax** *Latin* 'Quick and bold'
    —Jackson; 60th (King's Royal) Rifle Corps, U.K.

7. **Celer et vigilans** *Latin* 'Quick and watchful'
    —Douce.

8. **Celeritas** *Latin* 'Quickness'
    —Becquet.

9. **Celeritas et veritas** *Latin* 'Promptitude and truth'
    —Rolls.

10. **Celeritas executionis est anima consilii. Vive ut vivas**
    Latin 'Rapidity of execution is the soul of a resolve. Live
    that thou mayest live'
    —Friedrich, Duke of Saxony (1640–56).

11. **Celeritas virtus fidelitas** *Latin* 'Speed, virtue, and fidelity'
    —Carpenter (U.S.).

12. **Celeritate** *Latin* 'With quickness'
    —Lane (Co. Hereford).

13. **Celeriter** *Latin* 'Quickly'
    —Lane.

14. **Celeriter et jucunde** *Latin* 'Quickly and pleasantly'
    —Rogers.

15. **Celeriter sed certe** *Latin* 'Swiftly but surely'
    —Grieveson.

16. **Cito, non temere** *Latin* 'Quickly, not rashly'
    —Northcote.

17. **Cito fideliterque** *Latin* 'Quickly and faithfully'
    —Gutch.

18. **Cruce vide et festina** *Latin* 'See by the cross and make haste'
    —Trendall.

19. **Depechez** *French* 'Make haste'
    —Govan.

20. **Eil mit Weil** *Germ* 'Hasten slowly'
    —Friedrich, Margrave of Brandenburg (1530–52).

21. **Esto velocior vita** *Latin* 'Be swifter than life'
    —Shuttleworth.

22. **Expedite** *Latin* 'With despatch'
    —Hunter.

23. **Festina lente** *Latin* 'Hasten slowly'
    —Audenshaw U. D. C., U.K.

24. **Fluminis ritu ferimur**   *Latin* 'We rush on like a brook'
— Rushbrooke.

25. **Fortis et celer**   *Latin* 'Strong and swift'
— Cowell.

26. **Fortis et velox**   *Latin* 'Strong and swift'
— Waldron.

27. **Fortis ferox et celer**   *Latin* 'Strong, fierce, and swift'
— McCarthy.

28. **Fortiter et celeriter**   *Latin* 'Boldly and quickly'
— Mather (of Lauton).

29. **Fortitudine et velocitate**   *Latin* 'With courage and celerity'
— Balnaves, Balneaves.

30. **Fulminis instar**   *Latin* 'Like lightning'
— Hogan.

31. **I hope to speed**
— Cathcart (E.), Cathcart.

32. **In via recta celeriter**   *Latin* 'Swiftly in the right way'
— Kay.

33. **Lente sed certe**   *Latin* 'Slowly but surely'
— Slacke.

34. **Mora trahit periculum**   *Latin* 'Delay brings danger'
— Suckling.

35. **Nec celeri nec forti**   *Latin* 'Neither to the swift nor the strong'
— Sheppard (U.S.).

36. **Nec cito, nec tarde**   *Latin* 'Neither swiftly nor slowly'
— Ballantine.

37. **Nec otius [*sic*] nec altius**   *Latin* 'Neither quicker, nor higher'
— Rudolf II, Emperor of Germany (1552–1612).

38. **Non cito nec tarde**   *Latin* 'Neither quickly nor slowly'
— Bannatyne.

39. **Pernicibus alis**   *Latin* 'With swift wings'
— Chermside.

40. **Prompte et consulto**   *Latin* 'Quickly and advisedly'
— Plenderleith.

41. **Prompte et sincere**   *Latin* 'Prompt and sincere'
— Calvin Theological Seminary, Grand Rapids, Michigan.

42. **Propere et provide**   *Latin* 'Quickly and cautiously'
— Robinson.

43. **Propero sed curo**   *Latin* 'I make haste, but am cautious'
—Graham.

44. **Quod cito fit, cito perit**   *Latin* 'What is quickly done, quickly disappears'
—Friedrich II, Duke of Schleswig-Holstein-Gottorp (1568–87).

45. **Sat cito quia bene sat**   *Latin* 'Quickly enough, because well enough'
—Christian, Duke of Saxony-Eisenberg (1653–1707).

46. **Sat cito si sat bene**   *Latin* 'Quick enough if well enough'
—Colman.

47. **Sat cito si sat tuto**   *Latin* 'Quick enough if safe enough'
—Clerk.

48. **Si celeres quatit pennas**   *Latin* 'If he shakes his swift wings'
—Parkinson-Fortescue.

49. **Speed**
—Johnstone, Garnock.

50. **Speed, strength, and truth united**
—Framework Knitters' Company.

51. **Speed well**
—Speid.

52. **Subito**   *Latin* 'Promptly'
—Cringan, Crinan.

53. **Swift and sure**
—Hood.

54. **Swift and true**
—Fust.

55. **Tuto, celeriter, et jucunde**   *Latin* 'Safely, speedily, and agreeably'
—Sutton (of Framlingham).

56. **Tuto et celeriter**   *Latin* 'Safely and quickly'
—Penrice (of Yarmouth).

57. **Velocitate**   *Latin* 'With velocity'
—Carse.

58. **Vigilans et promptus**   *Latin* 'Vigilant and prompt'
—Wyld.

SPIRIT (*See also* MIND.)

1. **Academic—Vocational—Cultural—Patriotic—Spiritual**
   —The School of the Ozarks, Point Lookout, Missouri.

2. **A clean heart and cheerful spirit**
   —Portman (B.).

3. **Animae capaces mortis** *Latin* 'Souls capable of death'
   —Teesdale.

4. **Animo et fide** *Latin* 'Through soul and faith'
   —Pensacola Jr. College, Pensacola, Florida.

5. **Animus est nobilitas** *Latin* 'The soul is the nobility'
   —Cobham.

6. **Animus nisi paret imperat** *Latin* 'Unless it is obeying, the soul rules'
   —Bernard (U.S.).

7. **Armed with the Word, empowered by the spirit**
   —Western Evangelical Seminary, Portland, Oregon.

8. **Cordi dat animus alas** *Latin* 'My spirit gives wings to my heart'
   —Falconer.

9. **Ex animo** *Latin* 'From the soul'
   —Boyes.

10. **Laetus in praesens animus** *Latin* 'A happy spirit in the present'
    —Powell (U.S.).

11. **Make a clean heart and a cheerful spirit**
    —Portman (B.).

12. **Mens/ animus/ corpus** *Latin* 'Mind/ soul/ body'
    —Colby-Sawyer College, New London, New Hampshire.

13. **Mind/ Body/ Spirit/ Educating the whole man**
    —Oral Roberts University, Tulsa, Oklahoma.

14. **Spiritus gladius** *Latin* 'The sword of the spirit'
    —Hutton (of Marske).

15. **Spiritus intus alit** *Latin* 'The spirit nourishes from within'
    —[Vergil, *Aen.* vi. 723.] Clifton College, U.K.

16. **Terra, aqua, ignis, sal, spiritus, sulphur, Sol, Venus, Mercurius** *Latin* 'Land, water, fire, salt, spirit, sulphur, Sun, Venus, Mercury'
    —Irvine.

17. **Visa per invisa firma** *Latin* 'Things seen are established by things unseen'
    —Spence.

SPORT (*See also* HUNTING.)

1. **Floreat Rugbeia**   *Latin* 'May Rugby flourish'
—Rugby B. C., U.K.

2. **For sport**
—Rose-Cleland.

3. **Optima revelatio stella**   *Latin* 'A star the best revelation'
—Reveley (of Bryn y Gwin).

4. **Pro lusu et praedâ**   *Latin* 'For sport and prey'
—MacMoran, or McMoran.

STARS (*See also* BRIGHTNESS.)

1. **Ad astra**   *Latin* 'To the stars'
—Moorson, Bigsby.

2. **Ad astra nitamur semper ad optima**   *Latin* 'To the stars, to the best things, always our aim'
—Bigsby.

3. **Ad astra per ardua**   *Latin* 'To the stars through difficulties'
—Drummond (of Midhope).

4. **Ad astra per aspera**   *Latin* 'To the stars through difficulties'
—State of Kansas.

5. **Ad astra sequor**   *Latin* 'I follow to the stars'
—Tottenham (Co. Wexford).

6. **Ad astra virtus**   *Latin* 'Virtue rises to the stars'
—Saltmarshe (Co. York).

7. **Ad virtus astra**   *Latin* 'Virtue to the stars'
—Crane.

8. **Alis aspicit astra**   *Latin* 'On wing he looks towards the stars'
—Carnegie.

9. **Arcus, artes, astra**   *Latin* 'The bow, arts, and stars'
—Birney (of Salin), Burmey.

10. **Astra castra, numen, lumen munimen**   *Latin* 'The stars are my camp, the Deity is my light and guard'
—Belcarres (E.), Lindsay (Bt.), Lindsey.

11. **Astra et castra**   *Latin* 'The stars (*or* heaven) and the camp'
—Littler.

12. **Christi pennatus sidera morte peto**   *Latin* 'Furnished with wings (feathers), by the death of Christ I seek the stars'
—Fetherston.

13. **Clarior astris** *Latin* 'Brighter than the stars'
—Baillie.

14. **Crux mea stella** *Latin* 'The cross is my star'
—Devlin.

15. **Dum spiro spero** *Latin* 'While I breathe, I hope'
—State of South Carolina.

16. **Ferret ad astra virtus** *Latin* 'Virtue was borne to the stars'
—Kellett (U.S.).

17. **Habent sua sidera reges** *Latin* 'Kings have their stars'
—De Vahl-Samuel, Samuel.

18. **Itur ad astra** *Latin* 'Our way is to the stars'
—Mackenzie, Mulchinock.

19. **Justi ut sidera fulgent** *Latin* 'The righteous shine as the stars'
—McColl, Sandilands.

20. **Justi velut lumen astrarum** *Latin* 'Just men are like the light of the stars'
—Checkley (U.S.).

21. **L'etoile du nord** *French* 'The star of the north'
—State of Minnesota.

22. **Liberty and independence**
—State of Delaware.

23. **Live free or die**
—State of New Hampshire.

24. **Monstrant astra viam** *Latin* 'The stars show the way'
—Oswald.

25. **Monstrant regibus astra viam** *Latin* 'Stars show the way to kings'
—Order of the Star of Sicily.

26. **Nautis stella refulsit** *Latin* 'The star has shone on sailors'
—Seaman.

27. **Nescit occasum** *Latin* 'It knows not setting'
—Order of the Polar Star.

28. **Nil clarius astris** *Latin* 'Nothing is brighter than the stars'
—Baillie.

29. **Optima revelatio stella** *Latin* 'A star the best revelation'
—Reveley (of Bryn y Gwin).

30. **Per castra ad astra** *Latin* 'Through the camp to the stars'
—Nicholson.

31. **Per lucem ac tenebras mea sidera sanguine surgent** *Latin* 'Through light and darkness my star will arise in blood'
—Cayley.

32. **Quid clarius astris?** *Latin* 'What is brighter than the stars?'
—Baillie (of Hoperig).

33. **Raptim ad sidera tollar** *Latin* 'I shall be snatched aloft to the stars'
—Guille.

34. **Reach for the stars**
—University of Central Florida, Orlando, Florida.

35. **Sapiens dominabitur astris** *Latin* 'A wise man will govern the stars'
—Comber, Hutchinson.

36. **Se inserit astris** *Latin* 'He places himself among the stars'
—Crosse.

37. **Sic ad astra** *Latin* 'This way to the stars'
—McBarnet.

38. **Sidus adsit amicum** *Latin* 'Let my propitious star be present'
—Bateman (Co. Derby).

39. **Sol clarior astro** *Latin* 'The sun is brighter than a star'
—Johnson.

40. **Stella Christi duce** *Latin* 'With the star of Christ for guide'
—Sohier.

41. **Stella clavisque Maris Indici** *Latin* 'The star and key of the Indian Ocean'
—Mauritius.

42. **Stella futura micat divino lumine** *Latin* 'The star of the future twinkles with a divine light'
—Taylour.

43. **Stellis aspirate gemellis** *Latin* 'Breathe on us with your twin stars'
—Twining.

44. **Super sidera votum** *Latin* 'My wishes are above the stars'
—Rattray (of Craighill).

45. **Tendit ad astra** *Latin* 'He directs his gaze towards the stars'
—Maxwell.

46. **To each his farthest star**
—Surry Community College, Dobson, North Carolina.

47. **Venit ab astris** *Latin* 'She (truth) came from the stars'
—Keith.

48. **Virtue, liberty and independence**
—State of Pennsylvania; Barton (U.S.).

49. **Virtus ad astra tendit** *Latin* 'Virtue tends to the stars'
—Ross.

50. **Virtus ad sidera tollit** *Latin* 'Virtue raises to the stars'
—Wilson.

51. **Virtus astra petit** *Latin* 'Virtue aims at the stars'
—Vandeleur.

52. **Virtus tollit ad astra** *Latin* 'Virtue exalts to the stars'
—Innes.

STATE MOTTOES

1. **Agriculture and commerce**
—Maidstone B. C., U.K.; State of Tennessee.

2. **Alis volat propriis** *Latin* 'I fly with my own wings'
—State of Oregon, 1848–1858.

3. **Alki** *Chinook Indian* 'By and by'
—State of Washington.

4. **All for our country**
—State of Nevada.

5. **Animis opibusque parati** *Latin* 'Prepared in mind and resources'
—State of South Carolina.

6. **Audemus jura nostra defendere** *Latin* 'We dare defend our rights'
—State of Alabama.

7. **Cedant arma togae** *Latin* 'Let arms yield to the gown'
—[Cicero, *Off.* xxii.] Read (Bt.).; Territorial seal of Wyoming.

8. **Crossroads of America**
—State of Indiana.

9. **Deus nobis pace olim fecit** *Latin* 'God gave us this freedom'
—Seal of Virginia, 1776–1779.

10. **Dirigo** *Latin* 'I guide'
—State of Maine.

11. **Dum spiro spero** *Latin* 'While I have breath I hope'
—Aschmaty, Asscotti, Auchmuty (of Brianstown), Bainbridge, Baker, Bannatyne (of Newhall), Bloxam, Brooke, Bushell, Colquhon, Compton, Cottee, Cotter (Bt.), Davies (of Marrington Hall), Dearden, Deardon, Dillon (V.), Doran, Drummond, Elrick, Glazebrook, Going, Gordon, Gurney, Hoare (Bt.), Hoare, Hunter, Learmouth, Lee, Monk-Mason (of Mason-Brook), Moore, Morice, Morris, Oldfield, O'Reilly, Partridge (of Hockham, Co. Norfolk), Pearson, Price, Roberts (of Beechfield), Rodwell, Sharp, Smith, Stanton, Stretton, Spearman (of Thornley), Spry, Symonds, Tatlock, Thompson (co. Durham), Walker, Westerman.

12. **Ense petit placidam sub libertate quietam** *Latin* 'By the sword we seek peace but peace only under liberty'
—State of Massachusetts.

13. **Equality before the law**
—State of Nebraska.

14. **Equal rights**
—State of Wyoming.

15. **Esse quam videri** *Latin* 'To be rather than to seem'
—State of North Carolina.

16. **Eureka** *Greek* 'I have found it'
—Robinson, State of California.

17. **Fatti maschi, parole femmine** *Italian* 'Deeds are masculine, words feminine'
—Calvert.

18. **Fatti maschii parole femine** *Italian* 'Deeds are masculine, words feminine'
—State of Maryland.

19. **Felicitate restituta** *Latin* 'With happiness restored'
—Order of the Two Sicilies.

20. **Freedom and unity**
—State of Vermont.

21. **Friendship**
—Carr; State of Texas.

22. **Here we rest**
> —State of Alabama, 1868–1939.

23. **Imperium in imperio** *Latin* 'An empire within an empire'
> —Early motto of State of Ohio (1866–1868).

24. **Industry**
> —State of Utah.

25. **In God we trust**
> —State of Florida.

26. **Labor omnia vincit**
> —Ilkeston B. C., Ashton-Under-Lyme B. C., U.K.;
> Centenary College of Louisiana, Shreveport,
> Louisiana; State of Oklahoma; Bradford City
> and C. B. C., U.K.

27. **L'etoile du nord** *French* 'The star of the north'
> —State of Minnesota.

28. **Libertas et fidelitate** *Latin* 'Freedom and loyalty'
> —Seal of State of West Virginia.

29. **Liberty and independence**
> —State of Delaware.

30. **Liberty and prosperity**
> —State of New Jersey.

31. **Liberty and union, now and forever, one and inseparable**
> —State of North Dakota.

32. **Live free or die**
> —State of New Hampshire.

33. **Meliorem lapsa locavit** *Latin* 'He has planted one better than the one fallen'
> —on the Seal of the State of South Carolina; on the Great
> Seal of the Northwest Territory.

34. **Montani semper liberi** *Latin* 'Mountaineers are always free'
> —State of West Virginia.

35. **Nil sine numine** *Latin* 'Nothing without the Deity'
> —State of Colorado; Regis College, Denver, Colorado;
> Blundell, Banner, Weld (of Lulworth).

36. **Non sibi sed aliis** *Latin* 'Not for ourselves, but for others'
> —Colonial seal of Georgia.

37. **North to the future**
> —State of Alaska.

38. **Oro y plata** *Spanish* 'Gold and silver'
 —State of Montana.

39. **Our liberties we prize and our rights we will maintain**
 —State of Iowa.

40. **Perseverando** *Latin* 'By perseverance'
 —Seal of State of Virginia, Brinckman (Bt.), Brooks, Cope
 (Co. Leicester), Dugdale, Ducie (E.), Dendy,
 Frampton (of Moreton), Farnell, Flower (Bt.), Henley,
 Hanrott, Howell, MacGillivray, McKellar,
 Larkworthy, Morton, Roxby, Turnly, Wood (of
 Barnsley, Bt.).

41. **Quis separabit?** *Latin* 'Who shall separate us?'
 —Seal of State of South Carolina.

42. **Qui transtulit sustinet** *Latin* 'He who transplanted still sustains'
 —State of Connecticut.

43. **Quo sursum velo videre** *Latin* 'I want to see what is beyond'
 —Early motto of Minnesota, changed in 1858.

44. **Regnat populus** *Latin* 'The people rule'
 —State of Arkansas.

45. **Remember the Alamo**
 —Seal of State of Texas.

46. **Salus populi suprema lex esto** *Latin* 'The welfare of the people
 shall be the supreme law'
 —State of Missouri.

47. **Scuto bonae voluntatis tuae coronasti nos** *Latin* 'With the shield
 of Thy good-will Thou hast covered us'
 —State of Maryland.

48. **Sic semper tyrannis** *Latin* 'Thus always to tyrants'
 —State of Virginia.

49. **Si quaeris peninsulam amoenam circumspice** *Latin* 'If you seek a
 pleasant peninsula, look about you'
 —State of Michigan.

50. **State sovereignty, national union**
 —State of Illinois.

51. **Strength from the soil**
 —Coat of Arms of State of North Dakota.

52. **Texas one and indivisible**
 —Seal of State of Texas.

53. **The union**

—State of Oregon.

54. **Tuebor** *Latin* 'I will defend'

—Byng, Torrington (V.); Strafford (B.).; State of Michigan.

55. **Ua mau ke ea o ka aina i ka pono** *Hawaiian* 'The life of the land is preserved in righteousness'

—State of Hawaii.

56. **Under God the people rule**

—State of South Dakota.

57. **Union, justice, confidence**

—State of Louisiana.

58. **United we stand, divided we fall**

—Eastern Kentucky University, Richmond, Kentucky; States of Kentucky and Missouri.

59. **Virtue, liberty and independence**

—State of Pennsylvania; Barton (U.S.).

60. **Virtute et armis** *Latin* 'By virtue and arms'

—Ernst Ludwig, Duke of Saxony (1587–1620); State of Mississippi; Minnitt.

61. **Vis unita fortior** *Latin* 'Strength united is stronger'

—1776 seal of New Hampshire; Brook; Flood; Hales; Hosken; Lidwell; Moore; Mountcashel (E.); Crosby B. C., Stoke-on-Trent City and C. B. C., U.K.

62. **Volens et potens** *Latin* 'Willing and able'

—Original State seal of Nevada.

63. **Wisdom, justice, moderation**

—State of Georgia.

64. **With God, all things are possible**

—State of Ohio.

STATUS

1. **Aquila non captat muscas** *Latin* 'The eagle catcheth not flies'

—Bedingfield (Bt.), Bedingfield (of Ditchingham, Co. Norfolk), Buller (of Cornwall), Chinn (of Gloucester), Drake, Graves (B.), Greaves (of Mayfield), Gothard (of Newcastle), Illidge, Steel (Bt.), Trant, Weddeburn, Weston, Wright.

2. **Elatum a Deo non deprimat**　*Latin* 'Let one not depress him who is exalted by God'
—O'Dempsey.

3. **Haud inferiora secutus**　*Latin* 'Not having mean pursuits'
—Gerard.

4. **Jamais arrière**　*French* 'Never behind'
—Douglas (B.), Douglas (Bt.), Douglas (of Whitriggs), Fryer, Hamilton, Selkirk (E.).

5. **Nec ab ordine cedunt**　*Latin* 'Nor do they depart from their rank'
—Buckworth (of Cley, Co. Norfolk, and Spalding, Co. Lincoln).

6. **Not the last**
—Smith-Ryland.

7. **Ny dessux, ny dessoux**　*Old French* 'Neither above nor below'
—Grove (Bt.).

8. **Par negotiis neque supra**　*Latin* 'Equal to our business and not above it'
—Hill.

9. **Quasi summus magister**　*Latin* 'As though the highest master'
—Somaster.

10. **Sane Baro**　*Latin* 'A baron indeed'
—The Lord Prior of St. John of Jerusalem.

11. **Vix distat summus ab imo**　*Latin* 'The loftiest is scarcely removed from the lowest'
—Whittaker.

STEADFASTNESS (*See also* FIDELITY; FORTITUDE; PERMANENCE; PERSEVERANCE.)

1. **Aequo adeste animo**　*Latin* 'Be present with mind unchangeable'
—Cope (Bt.).

2. **A fin**　*French* 'To the end'
—Airlie (E.), Ogilvie.

3. **A jamais**　*French* 'Forever'
—James (of Dublin, Bt.).

4. **Anchor, fast anchor**
—Gray (B.), Gray (of Durham).

5. **Anchor fast**
—Groat.

6. **Animus tamen idem**   *Latin* 'Yet our mind is unchanged'
   —Cuffe (Bt.), Wheeler.

7. **Antes muerto que mutado**   *Spanish* 'Rather dead than changed'
   —Wilhelm V, Landgrave of Hesse-Cassel (1602–37).

8. **Antiqua constans virtute**   *Latin* 'Steadfast in ancient virtue'
   —Arundel B. C., U.K.

9. **Aufrichtig, beständig, so lang ich lebendig**   *German* 'Upright and steadfast so long as I live'
   —Ludwig VIII, Landgrave of Hesse-Darmstadt (1691–1768).

10. **Aut agere aut mori**   *Latin* 'Either to do or die'
    —Barclay.

11. **Be fast**
    —Mexborough (E.), Savile (of Rufford).

12. **Be it fast**
    —Fotheringham (of Lawhill and Powrie, N. B.).

13. **Be steadfast**
    —Carnock, Carvick, Clarbrick.

14. **Bydand**   *Scots dialect* 'Remaining'
    —Gordon (D.), Gordon (Bt.), Gordon.

15. **Bydand to the last**   *Scots dialect* 'Remaining to the last'
    —Gordon (of Farsbank).

16. **Bydd ddiysgog**   *Welsh* 'Be steadfast'
    —Liverpool (E.).

17. **By watchfulness, by steadfastness**
    —Hare.

18. **Cadere non cedere possum**   *Latin* 'I can fall, but not yield'
    —Cottingham.

19. **Constans contraria spernit**   *Latin* 'The resolute man despises difficulties'
    —Edgeworth.

20. **Constante et firme**   *French* 'Constant and firm'
    —Osbaldeston.

21. **Constanter**   *Latin* 'With constancy'
    —Dukes, Hore (of Pole Hore, Harperstown, etc.).

22. **Constanter in ardua**   *Latin* 'With constancy against difficulties'
    —Harland.

23. **Constantia**   *Latin* 'By constancy'
    —Goodall.

24. **Constantia, virtus** *Latin* 'Constancy and valor'
—Fitz-William.

25. **Constantia basis virtutum** *Latin* 'Steadfastness is the foundation of the virtues'
—Andover B. C., U.K.

26. **Constantia et fortitudine** *Latin* 'By constancy and fortitude'
—Herbert.

27. **Constare in sententia** *Latin* 'To continue in my opinion'
—Williamson.

28. **Constaunt an' trew** *Middle English*
—Rose (of Worighton).

29. **Cor immobile** *Latin* 'A steadfast heart'
—Hussey (Co. Dublin), Hyett.

30. **Cunctanter tamen fortiter** *Latin* 'Slowly yet resolutely'
—Hutchinson.

31. **Decrevi** *Latin* 'I have resolved'
—Gadesden, Nugent (Bt.).

32. **Demovres ferme** *French* 'Remain steadfast'
—Liverpool (E.).

33. **Der Nagel hält fest** *German* 'The Nail holds fast'
—Nagel (U.S.).

34. **Dum varior idem** *Latin* 'While I change, I am the same'
—Ramsay.

35. **Fast**
—Gray (of Cartyne).

36. **Fast tho' untied**
—Heneage.

37. **Fast without fraude**
—Brooke (of Norton Priory, Bt.).

38. **Fest** *German* 'Firm'
—De La Field.

39. **Fidèle et constant** *French* 'Faithful and steadfast'
—Ernst Ludwig I, Duke of Saxony-Meiningen (1672–1724).

40. **Fidelis et constans** *Latin* 'Faithful and steadfast'
—Bragge.

41. **Fidens et constans** *Latin* 'Trusting and steadfast'
—O'Kearin.

42. **Firm**

—Dalrymple (Bt.), Dalrymple (of Cranstoun, North Berwick), Dalrimple, Laing (of Lindertis), Stair (E.), Wall (of Wortley Park), Meason, Walsh (Bt.), Reid (Bt.).

43. **Firm and faithful**

—Cassidy.

44. **Firm as a rock**

—Tarpey.

45. **Firmè**   *Latin* 'Resolutely'

—Dalrymple, Elphinstone.

46. **Firmè dum fide**   *Latin* 'Firmly while faithfully'

—Heignie.

47. **Firmè durans**   *Latin* 'Firm to the last'

—Leslie (of Wardes).

48. **Firmiora futura**   *Latin* 'Things to come more steadfast'

—Fuller.

49. **Firmiter et fideliter**   *Latin* 'Steadfastly and faithfully'

—Newman.

50. **Firmiter maneo**   *Latin* 'I last steadily'

—Lindsay (of Culsh).

51. **Firm to my trust**

—Glyn (Bt.).

52. **Firmus et fidelis**   *Latin* 'Steadfast and faithful'

—Marwick.

53. **Firmus in firmis**   *Latin* 'Firm among the firm'

—Richardson.

54. **Firmus maneo**   *Latin* 'I remain steadfast'

—Breek, Lindsay.

55. **Fixus ac solidus**   *Latin* 'Firm and substantial'

—Stewart (of Rosling).

56. **Fixus adversa sperno**   *Latin* 'Firm, I despise adversity'

—Hamerton (of Hellifield).

57. **Fortis et stabilis**   *Latin* 'Brave and steadfast'

—Killikelley.

58. **Fortiter et constanter**   *Latin* 'Boldly and steadfastly'

—Johann Georg III, Count of Mansfield in Eisleben (1640–1710); Johann Wilhelm, Duke of Saxony (1677–1707).

59. **Frangas non flectes**   *Latin* 'You may break, but shall not bend me'
>—Collins, Gower, Granville (E.), Jones, Kimber, Owen, Leveson, Sutherland (D.), Whimper.

60. **Grip fast**
>—Leslie (Bt.), Leslie (Co. Antrim, and Aberdeen), Rothes (E.).

61. **Haud ullis labantia ventis**   *Latin* 'Yielding under no winds'
>—Irwin (of Calder Abbey), Irving.

62. **Hold fast**
>—Ancram, Downie, Frome, Lesly, Macloide, McLeod, Smith.

63. **Hold fast, sit sure**
>—Saddlers' Company.

64. **Hold firm**
>—Fiott.

65. **I'll stand sure**
>—Grant.

66. **Immobile**   *Latin* 'Steadfast'
>—Grant.

67. **In dubiis constans**   *Latin* 'Firm amid dangers'
>—Cockburn.

68. **Inébranlable**   *French* 'Not to be shaken'
>—Acland.

69. **Innocenter patienter constanter**   *Latin* 'Innocently, patiently, steadfastly'
>—Stillé (U.S.).

70. **Intrepide et constanter**   *Latin* 'Fearlessly and with constancy'
>—Karl Wilhelm, Prince of Anhalt-Zerbst (1652–1718).

71. **I will**
>—Davis.

72. **I will not equivocate; I will not excuse; I will not retreat a single inch; and I will be heard**
>—William Lloyd Garrison, abolitionist and editor of The Liberator.

73. **Jamais abattu**   *French* 'Never beaten down'
>—Lindoe.

74. **Jamais chancelant**   *French* 'Never wavering'
>—Le Gallais.

75. **Je ne plie ni ne rompe** *French* 'I neither bend nor break'

—Quain.

76. **Je tiens ferme** *French* 'I hold firm'

—Chamberlain.

77. **Keep fast**

—Lesly (of Burdsbank).

78. **Mallem mori quam mutare** *Latin* 'I prefer to die rather than to change (my faith)'

—Gilbert.

79. **Maneo, non fugio** *Latin* 'I stand firm and do not fly'

—Gordon.

80. **Mens immota manet** *Latin* 'The steadfast mind endures'
—Meldrum, Shaw; [Vergil, *Aen.* iv. 449.] Elizabeth, Daughter of James I (1595–1662).

81. **Mutare vel timere sperno** *Latin* 'I scorn either to change or fear'
—Little Lever U. D. C., U.K.

82. **Nec flectitur nec mutant** *Latin* 'They neither bend nor change'
—O'Hegarty.

83. **Never a backward step**

—Thomson (of Fleet, B.).

84. **Never give in**

—Lawrence (Bt.).

85. **Ne vous importer jamais** *French* 'Never let it matter'

—Downing.

86. **Nil moror ictus** *Latin* 'I heed not blows'
—Money, Kyrle (of Much Marcle), Muney (of Whettam).

87. **Nomine et patriae asto** *Latin* 'I stand by in name and for (my) country'

—Fay (U.S.).

88. **Non desistam** *Latin* 'I will not desist'

—Row.

89. **Non fluctu nec flatu movetur** *Latin* 'He is not moved by either wave or wind'

—Parker (of Browsholme).

90. **Non recedam** *Latin* 'I will not go back'

—Newall.

91. **Non sine anchora** *Latin* 'Not without an anchor'

—Drysdale, Drury.

92. **Nulla deditio** *Latin* 'No giving up'
—Kynsey.

93. **Nulla retrorsum** *Latin* 'None backwards'
—Ferrers.

94. **Nulla vestigia retrorsum** *Latin* 'No steps backward'
—[Horace, *Ep.* i. 1. 74.] Levinge.

95. **Nunquam mutans** *Latin* 'Never changing'
—Bowring.

96. **Nunquam retrorsum** *Latin* 'Never backwards'
—Karl, Duke of Braunschweig-Bevern (1713–80).

97. **Patienter et constanter** *Latin* 'Patiently and steadfastly'
—Christian Günther, the Younger, Count of Schwarzburg
and Hohenstein (1616–66).

98. **Persta et praesta** *Latin* 'Stand fast and step ahead'
—Bramhall.

99. **Persto et spero** *Latin* 'I stand fast and hope'
—Merry.

100. **Pervicax recte** *Latin* 'Steadfast in the right'
—McEwen.

101. **Plustost mourier que changer** *Old French* 'Rather die than change (my faith)'
—Hermann Fortunatus, Margrave of Baden-Rodemachern
(1596–1664); Barbara Agnes, Duchess of
Liegnitz (d. 1631).

102. **Plutot rompe que plie** *French* 'Sooner break than bend'
—De Ponthien.

103. **Prius frangitur quam flectitur** *Latin* 'He is sooner broken than bent'
—Ballantine-Dykes (of Dovenley, Warthole,
or Wardhall, etc.).

104. **Provide et constanter** *Latin* 'Prudently and steadfastly'
—Friedrich Wilhelm, Duke of Mecklenburg-Schwerin
(1675–1713).

105. **Prudenter et constanter** *Latin* 'Prudently and steadfastly'
—Johann Ernst II, Duke of Saxony-Weimar (1627–83).

106. **Quid non resolutio?** *Latin* 'What cannot resolution achieve?'
—Ashton.

107. **Resolute and firm**
—Milbanke (Co. York, Bt.).

108. **Resolutio cauta** *Latin* 'A prudent resolution'
—Bethune.

109. **Resolve is power**
—Stewart.

110. **Resolve well, persevere**
—Coleman (Cos. of Norfolk, Wilts, and Gloucester), Moore.

111. **Sagaciter, fideliter, constanter** *Latin* 'Sagaciously, faithfully, constantly'
—Ward (B.).

112. **Sans recuiller jamais** *French* 'Without ever receding'
—Brackenbury.

113. **Sans varier** *French* 'Unchangeable'
—Anna, Princess of Anhalt (d. 1624).

114. **Sapienter et constanter** *Latin* 'Wisely and steadfastly'
—Ernst Ludwig, Count of Mansfeld (1604–32); Johann Ernst I, Duke of Saxony-Weimar (1594–1626).

115. **Sibi constet** *Latin* 'Let him be firmly resolved'
—Richardson.

116. **Sincere et constanter** *Latin* 'Sincerely and steadfastly'
—Order of the Red Eagle (Prussia).

117. **Stabilis** *Latin* 'Firm'
—Grant.

118. **Stabilitate et victoria** *Latin* 'By steadfastness and victory'
—Simmons.

119. **Stabit** *Latin* 'It shall stand'
—Grant.

120. **Stabit quocumque jeceris** *Latin* 'Whichever way you throw it, it will stand'
—The Isle of Man.

121. **Stabit saxum fluet amnis** *Latin* 'The rock will remain and the river will flow'
—Clitheroe B. C., U.K.

122. **Stabo** *Latin* 'I shall stand'
—Hawthorn, Accorne, Hawthorne, Kinnimond.

123. **Stand fast**
—Grant (of Frenchie), Seafield (E.).

124. **Stand fast, stand firm, stand sure**
—Grant (U.S.).

125. **Stand firm**
—Grant.

126. **Stand on**
—Sykes.

127. **Stand suir** *Middle English* 'Stand sure'
—Glenelg (B.).

128. **Stand sure**
—Anderson (of Fermoy, Bt.), Adson, Airderbeck, Grant (of Burnside and Monymusk), Ponton.

129. **Steadfast**
—Mansfield, Mansel.

130. **Steadfast and faithful**
—Axminster U. D. C., U.K.

131. **Still bydand** *Scots dial.* 'Still remaining'
—Gordon.

132. **Sumus ubi fuimus** *Latin* 'We are where we have been'
—Weare.

133. **Sure and steadfast**
—Martin (of Anstey Pastures).

134. **Tam fidus quam fixus** *Latin* 'Equally faithful as steadfast'
—Stewart.

135. **Temperans et constans** *Latin* 'Temperate and steady'
—Verschoyle.

136. **Tenax et fidelis** *Latin* 'Steadfast and faithful'
—Dartford B. C., U.K.

137. **Tenax propositi** *Latin* 'Firm of purpose'
—Gibbes (Bt.), Gilbert (of Cantley Hall), Gibb, Gibbs, Morley, Poole, Rounder.

138. **Tenebo** *Latin* 'I will hold'
—Gray (of Wheatfield).

139. **There is no difficulty to him that wills**
—Hains (U.S.).

140. **Tiens firme** *French* 'Hold firm'
—Squire.

141. **T. V. B. (Treu und beständig)** *German* 'Faithful and steadfast'
—Johann Georg, Margrave of Brandenburg (1577–1624).

142. **Unwandelbar** *German* 'Unchangeable'
—Johann Georg II, Elector of Saxony (1613–80).

143. **Vestigia nulla retrorsum**   *Latin* 'No backward step'
—[Horace, *Ep.* i. 1. 73.] Baily, Buckinghamshire (C.C.,
U.K.), Coningsby, Hampden, Levinge (Bt.),
John Hampden's (1594–1643) Bucks
regiment in the Civil War, 5th Dragoon Guards.
Buckinghamshire C. C., U.K.

144. **Vigilanter et constanter**   *Latin* 'Vigilantly and steadfastly'
—Johann Wilhelm, Duke of Saxony-Eisenach (1666–1729).

145. **Virtute et constantia**   *Latin* 'By valor and constancy'
—Auld (or Aulde).

STRANGER

1. **Advena in sylvis**   *Latin* 'A stranger in the woods'
—Foster.

2. **Annoso robore quercus**   *Latin* 'An oak in aged strength'
—Aikenhead.

3. **Better kinde frembd than frembd kyen**   *Scots dial.* 'Better a kind
stranger than strange kin'
—Waterton.

4. **Like as the oak**
—Uckfield R. D. C., U.K.

5. **Mihi robore robor**   *Latin* 'My strength is in the oak'
—Cunningham.

6. **Murus aeneus esto**   *Latin* 'Be thou a wall of brass'
—Reynell (Bt.), Macleod.

7. **Murus aheneus**   *Latin* 'A wall of brass'
—McLeod, Nielson.

8. **Nostrum viret robur**   *Latin* 'Our strength is as a green tree' *or*
'Wood Green flourishes'
—Wood Green B. C., U.K.

9. **Quercus robur salus patriae**   *Latin* 'The strength of the oak is the
safety of our country'
—Oakes.

10. **Radicem firmant frondes**   *Latin* 'Branches strengthen the root'
—Grant (of Darlway).

11. **Robor et agilitas**   *Latin* 'Strength and agility'
—Baker (U.S.).

12. **Robur**   *Latin* 'Oaken strength'
—Woods.

13. **Sicut quercus** *Latin* 'As the oak'
—Challoner.

14. **Sunt aliena** *Latin* 'They are foreign'
—Fust.

15. **Terris peregrinus et hospes** *Latin* 'A stranger and pilgrim on the earth'
—Bonnell.

16. **Ut ferrum forte** *Latin* 'Strong as iron'
—Fearon.

17. **Vallum aeneum esto** *Latin* 'Be a rampart of brass'
—Bailey.

STRENGTH (*See also* FORCE; POWER; STEADFASTNESS.)

1. **Addunt robur** *Latin* 'They give strength'
—Hamilton (of Westport).

2. **Addunt robur stirpi** *Latin* 'They add strength to the stock'
—Hamilton.

3. **Adverso fortior** *Latin* 'Stronger than adversity'
—Clifton-Dicconson, Dicconson.

4. **Animo et corpore nitor** *Latin* 'With a strong mind and body'
—Venables.

5. **Annoso robore quercus** *Latin* 'An oak in aged strength'
—Aikenhead.

6. **Be firm**
—Coates (of Glasgow), Ferie, Ferrie.

7. **Bersekutu bertambah mutu** *Malay* 'Unity is strength'
—Malaysia.

8. **Be strong and of good courage**
—Beddington.

9. **Be stronger men**
—Jacob Gimbel (1876–1943), merchant and philanthropist who devoted part of his wealth to the education of talented boys.

10. **Be strong in the Lord**
—Best.

11. **Cadernid Gwynedd** *Welsh* 'The strength of Gwynedd'
—Caernarvonshire C. C., U.K.

12. **Caelitus mihi vires** *Latin* 'My strength from heaven'
—Ranelagh (V.).

13. **Caelitus vires** *Latin* 'Strength from heaven'
—Mallet.

14. **Candor dat viribus alas** *Latin* 'Truth gives wings to strength'
—Hogarth, Rochfort.

15. **Castello fortior concordia** *Latin* 'Concord is stronger than a fortress'
—Northampton C. B. C., U.K.

16. **Concordia vim dat** *Latin* 'Concord gives strength'
—Blumberg.

17. **Conjunctio firmat** *Latin* 'Union gives strength'
—Middleton.

18. **Constanter et prudentia** *Latin* 'Firmly and prudently'
—Campbell (of Sombey), Cessnock (of Treesbank and Fairfield).

19. **Dei sub numine viget** *Latin* 'He grows strong in the presence of God'
—Princeton University, Princeton, New Jersey.

20. **Die virescit** *Latin* 'It attains vigor by time'
—Wood (of Grangehaugh).

21. **Diligentia fortior** *Latin* 'Stronger by diligence'
—Truell.

22. **Dureté** *French* 'Hardness'
—Evelyn (of Wotton).

23. **Durum sed certissimum** *Latin* 'Hard but most sure'
—Gillanders.

24. **Et vi et virtute** *Latin* 'Both by strength and virtue'
—Baird (Bt.), Burrowes (Bt.), Stannus.

25. **Ex forti dulcedo** *Latin* 'Out of the strong, sweetness'
—[Judges, xiv. 14.] Johann Friedrich, Duke of Braunschweig-Lüneburg (1625–79).

26. **Ferme et fidèle** *French* 'Firm and faithful'
—Le Maistre.

27. **Fest** *German* 'Strong'
—Delafield (U.S.).

28. **Fide et bello fortis** *Latin* 'Strong in faith and war'
—Carritt.

29. **Fide et in bello fortis**   *Latin* 'Strong in faith and in war'
—Carrot.

30. **Fiducia et vi**   *Latin* 'By confidence and strength'
—Slough B. C., U.K.

31. **Fier et fort**   *French* 'Proud and strong'
—Shelton.

32. **Firm, vigilant, active**
—Muncaster (B.).

33. **Firma durant**   *Latin* 'Strong things last'
—Lesly (of Finrassie).

34. **Firma et ardua**   *Latin* 'Solid and lofty objects'
—Mackenzie (of Rosehaugh).

35. **Firmando firmior haeret**   *Latin* 'By strengthening, it becomes stronger'
—Cardinal Mazarin (1602–61).

36. **Firme**   *French* 'Firmly'
—Dalrymple, Elphinstone, Hay.

37. **Firmior**   *Latin* 'Stronger'
—Brentford and Chiswick B. C., U.K.

38. **Firmior quo paratior**   *Latin* 'The more prepared, the stronger'
—Dunbar, Selkirk (E.).

39. **Firmitas et sanitas**   *Latin* 'Strength and health'
—Griffith.

40. **Firmiter et durabile**   *Latin* 'Strong and lasting'
—Steel (Bt.).

41. **Fit inde firmior**   *Latin* 'Hence it is made stronger'
—Skirvin.

42. **Force avec vertu**   *French* 'Strength with virtue'
—Leigh (of West Hall).

43. **Force d'en haut**   *French* 'Strength from above'
—Mallet.

44. **Fortem exarmat fortior**   *Latin* 'A stronger than he disarms a strong man'
—[after Luke, xi. 22.] Albrecht Alcibiades, Margrave of Brandenburg-Baireuth (1522–57).

45. **Forti et fidele nihil difficile**   *Latin* 'For the strong and faithful nothing is difficult'
—Allen (U.S.).

46. **Fortior es qui se quam qui fortissima vincit Moenia, nec virtus altius ire potest** *Latin* 'Stronger is he who conquers himself than he who conquers the strongest walls; and virtue can mount no higher'
    —Johann Georg I, Prince of Anhalt-Dessau (1567–1618).

47. **Fortior est qui se?** *Latin* 'Who is stronger than (he who conquers) himself?'
    —Poley.

48. **Fortior leone justus** *Latin* 'The just man is stronger than a lion'
    —Goodricke (of Ribstone Hall).

49. **Fortior qui melior** *Latin* 'He is the stronger, who is the better man'
    —Buchan.

50. **Fortior qui se vincit** *Latin* 'He is strongest who conquers himself'
    —Poley (of Boxted Hall), Madden.

51. **Fortior quo mitior** *Latin* 'The milder the stronger'
    —Buchan.

52. **Fortior quo paratior** *Latin* 'The better prepared, the stronger'
    —Hornsey B. C., U.K.

53. **Fortior quo rectior** *Latin* 'Stronger only as much as one is nobler'
    —Sargent (U.S.).

54. **Fortis agendo** *Latin* 'Strong in action'
    —Pittman (U.S.).

55. **Fortis ceu leo fidus** *Latin* 'Strong as a lion and faithful'
    —McBrayne.

56. **Fortis est veritas** *Latin* 'Truth is strong'
    —Angus; Barton (of Threxton, Co. Norfolk); Hutchon; Oxford City and C. B. C., U.K.; City of Oxford.

57. **Fortis et celer** *Latin* 'Strong and swift'
    —Cowell.

58. **Fortis et velox** *Latin* 'Strong and swift'
    —Waldron.

59. **Fortis ferox et celer** *Latin* 'Strong, fierce, and swift'
    —McCarthy.

60. **Fortis in arduis** *Latin* 'Strong in difficulties'
    —Middleton B. C., U.K.

61. **Fortis in armis** *Latin* 'Strong in arms'
    —Armstrong (B.).

62. **Fortis in procella**   *Latin* 'Strong in the storm'
—Woods.

63. **Fortis que felix**   *Latin* 'Strong and happy'
—Minshull (U.S.), Walter (U.S.).

64. **Fortis qui se vincit**   *French* 'Strong is he who conquers himself'
—Thorneycroft, Thornicroft.

65. **Fortis si jure fortis**   *Latin* 'Strong if strong in right'
—Stockenstrom (Bt.).

66. **Fortissima veritas**   *Latin* 'Truth is most powerful'
—Kirkalie, Kirkaldy.

67. **Forti tene manu**   *Latin* 'Hold with a firm hand'
—Corry.

68. **Fortiter in re, et suaviter in modo**   *Latin* 'Firmly in act and gently in manner'
—Beaufort.

69. **Fortius dum juncta**   *Latin* 'Stronger while united'
—Hay.

70. **Hic fidus et roboreus**   *Latin* 'He is trusty and strong'
—Stirling.

71. **Hinc fortior et clarior**   *Latin* 'Hence the stronger and more illustrious'
—Martin.

72. **Industria, virtus et fortitudo**   *Latin* 'Diligence, courage, and strength'
—Derby C. B. C., U.K.

73. **Inexpugnabilis**   *Latin* 'Impregnable'
—Penman.

74. **In fide, justitia, et fortitudine**   *Latin* 'In faith, justice, and strength'
—Order of St. George (Bavaria).

75. **In fide et in bello fortis**   *Latin* 'Strong both in faith and war'
—Bagwell (of Marlfield), Carroll, or O'Carroll (of Ballymore).

76. **Ingenio et viribus**   *Latin* 'By ability and strength'
—Huddlestone.

77. **In libertate vis**   *Latin* 'Strength in freedom'
—Merton and Morden U. D. C., U.K.

78. **Innixus vero validus**   *Latin* 'He that rests upon the truth is strong'
—Lyon.

79. **In robore decus** *Latin* 'Glory in strength'
                                        —Clerk.

80. **In silentio et spe fortitudo mea** *Latin* 'In silence and in hope is
    my strength'
                    —[after Isaiah, xxx. 15.] Johann the Wise, Margrave of
                        Brandenburg-Küstrin (1513–71); Justus II, Count of
                                            Mansfeld (1558–1619).

81. **Instat vi patriae** *Latin* 'He rushes on with the strength of his
    country'
                                        —Tichburn.

82. **Integer audax promptus** *Latin* 'Sound, bold, ready'
                                        —Williams (U.S.).

83. **Interno robore** *Latin* 'By internal strength'
                                        —Mytton.

84. **In union strength**
                    —Huston-Tillotson College, Austin, Texas.

85. **Leo de Juda est robur nostrum** *Latin* 'The Lion of Judah is our
    strength'
                                        —Borlase, Warren.

86. **L'espoir est ma force** *French* 'Hope is my strength'
                                        —Tupper.

87. **Like as the oak**
                                —Uckfield R. D. C., U.K.

88. **L'union fait la force** *French* 'Unity is strength'
                    —Kingdom of Belgium, Republic of Haiti.

89. **Ma force d'en haut** *French* 'My strength is from above'
                                        —Lanpon, Malet.

90. **Me fortem reddit Deus** *Latin* 'God makes me strong'
                                        —Scott.

91. **Mihi robore robor** *Latin* 'My strength is in the oak'
                                        —Cunningham.

92. **Murus aeneus esto** *Latin* 'Be thou a wall of brass'
                                        —Reynell (Bt.), Macleod.

93. **Murus aheneus** *Latin* 'A wall of brass'
                                        —McLeod, Nielson.

94. **Nec celeri nec forti** *Latin* 'Neither to the swift nor the strong'
                                        —Sheppard (U.S.).

95. **Nostrum viret robur** *Latin* 'Our strength is as a green tree' *or* 'Wood Green flourishes'
—Wood Green B. C., U.K.

96. **Omni violentia major** *Latin* 'Too strong for any violence'
—Donelan.

97. **Par fermesse du quesne** *French* 'By firmness of the cane'
—Du Cane.

98. **Per se valens** *Latin* 'Strong through himself'
—Perceval.

99. **Per stabilitas et per fortitudo** *Latin* 'Through stability and strength'
—Holmes (U.S.).

100. **Per vim et virtutem** *Latin* 'By strength and valor'
—Youl.

101. **Pietas cum robore conjuncta** *Latin* 'Piety combined with strength'
—Albert Friedrich, Margrave of Brandenburg (1582–1600).

102. **Pietate fortior** *Latin* 'Stronger by piety'
—Broade, Stanier-Philip-Broade.

103. **Pour bien fort** *French* 'Strong for good'
—Preston.

104. **Preigne haleine, tirez fort** *French* 'Take breath, pull hard'
—Giffard.

105. **Quae juncta firma** *Latin* 'Union is strength'
—Lesly (of Kinivie).

106. **Quercus robur salus patriae** *Latin* 'The strength of the oak is the safety of our country'
—Oakes.

107. **Radicem firmant frondes** *Latin* 'Branches strengthen the root'
—Grant (of Darlway).

108. **Regulier et vigoreux** *French* 'Regular and strong'
—Scott-Ker.

109. **Robore** *Latin* 'By strength'
—Webb.

110. **Robore et sapientia** *Latin* 'By strength and wisdom'
—Robertson.

111. **Robore et sapore** *Latin* 'With strength and taste'
—Robertson.

112. **Robore et vigilantia**   *Latin* 'By strength and watchfulness'
—Aitken.

113. **Robor et agilitas**   *Latin* 'Strength and agility'
—Baker (U.S.).

114. **Robori prudentia praestat**   *Latin* 'Prudence excels strength'
—Young.

115. **Robur**   *Latin* 'Oaken strength'
—Woods.

116. **Robur atque fides**   *Latin* 'Strength and faith'
—Whitaker.

117. **Robur in cruce**   *Latin* 'Strength in the cross'
—Anketill.

118. **Robur in Deo**   *Latin* 'Strength in God'
—Raeburn.

119. **Robur meum Deus**   *Latin* 'God is my strength'
—Rhodes.

120. **Sicut quercus**   *Latin* 'As the oak'
—Challoner.

121. **Si fractus fortis**   *Latin* 'Strong though broken'
—Foster.

122. **Singula cum valeant sunt meliora simul**   *Latin* 'When they are strong separately they are more so together'
—Stuart.

123. **Sit saxum firmit**   *Latin* 'May the stone be firm'
—Stone U. D. C., U.K.; Saxby.

124. **Siyinqaba**   *si-Swati* 'We are the strength'
—Swaziland.

125. **Soies ferme**   *French* 'Be firm'
—Maxwell.

126. **Soyez ferme**   *French* 'Be firm'
—Carrick (E.), Hyde, Skerrin, Foljambe.

127. **Speed, strength, and truth united**
—Framework Knitters' Company.

128. **Spes decus et robur**   *Latin* 'Hope is honor and strength'
—Eardley-Smith (Bt.).

129. **Sto ne per vim sed per jus**   *Latin* 'I stand not by strength, but by right'
—Stone.

130. **Strength**
—Armstrong.

131. **Strength from the soil**
—Coat of Arms of State of North Dakota.

132. **Strength is from heaven**
—Grubb, Whitson.

133. **Strenue et honeste** *Latin* 'Strenuously and honorably'
—Jackson.

134. **Strong and firm**
—Wolrige.

135. **Sub robore virtus** *Latin* 'Virtue under strength'
—Aikin (of Liverpool), Aikman (of Carnie).

136. **Summis viribus** *Latin* 'With all one's might'
—Harben.

137. **Suo se robore firmat** *Latin* 'He establishes himself by his own strength'
—Grant.

138. **Suo stat robore virtus** *Latin* 'Virtue stands by its own strength'
—Mowbray.

139. **Suprema manus validior** *Latin* 'A hand stronger than the highest'
—Merry.

140. **Tam arte quam Marte** *Latin* 'As much by art as strength'
—McLea, Wright.

141. **Tenax** *Latin* 'Firm'
—Stirling.

142. **Tene fortiter** *Latin* 'Hold firmly'
—Bridger.

143. **The strongest arm uppermost**
—O'Brien, Stafford.

144. **The strongest hand uppermost**
—Kennedy.

145. **Thy right hand, O Lord, hath been glorified in strength** *(from Greek)*
—Emerson-Tennant.

146. **Toujours firme** *French* 'Always firm'
—Heneage (of Hainton).

147. **Toujours fort** *French* 'Always strong'
—Hynes.

148. **Turris fortitudinis** *Latin* 'A tower of strength'
—Mansfield.

149. **Tutum te robore reddam** *Latin* 'I will make you safe by my strength'
—Crawfurd, Hinde.

150. **Ubi fides ibi lux et robur** *Latin* 'Where there is faith there is light and strength'
—Birkenhead C. B. C., U.K.

151. **Ubi fides ibi vires** *Latin* 'Where faith is there is strength'
—Hussey.

152. **Unita fortior** *Latin* 'The stronger being united'
—Rundall; Scots Guards, 2nd Battalion; Woodmongers' Company.

153. **Unitate fortior** *Latin* 'Stronger by union'
—Beck; Heston and Isleworth B. C., U.K.

154. **Uno ictu** *Latin* 'By one blow'
—[Caesar *de Bell. Gall.* 1. 2] Morison.

155. **Ut ferrum forte** *Latin* 'Strong as iron'
—Fearon.

156. **Valet anchora virtus** *Latin* 'Virtue our anchor is strong'
—Gardner (B.), Gardner.

157. **Valet et vulnerat** *Latin* 'It is strong, and it wounds'
—Hay (of London).

158. **Valet pietas** *Latin* 'Piety is strong'
—Valpy.

159. **Validus** *Latin* 'Strong'
—Harte.

160. **Vallum aeneum esto** *Latin* 'Be a rampart of brass'
—Bailey.

161. **Vel arte vel Marte** *Latin* 'Either by art or strength'
—Baines, Deans (of Loeg).

162. **Vi et animo** *Latin* 'By strength and courage'
—Hankinson, McCulloch.

163. **Vi et arte** *Latin* 'By strength and skill'
—Ferguson, Stevens.

164. **Vi et industria** *Latin* 'By strength and industry'
—Falconer.

165. **Vi et virtute** *Latin* 'By strength and valor'
—Baird (Bt.), Baird, Bolton, Barnes, Chisholm, Hurst, McTaggart, Smart, Spoight, White; Farriers' Company.

166. **Vigilantia, robur, voluptas** *Latin* 'Vigilance, strength, pleasure'
—Arundell, Blair (Bt.), Hunter.

167. **Vigore** *Latin* 'With vigor'
—Vickers.

168. **Vigore et virtute** *Latin* 'By vigor and virtue'
—Casey.

169. **Vigueur de dessus** *French* 'Strength is from above'
—O'Brien, O'Bryen, Braidwood, Thomond (M.), Willington.

170. **Vigueur l'amour de croix** *French* 'The love of the cross gives strength'
—Andrews, Darnol.

171. **Vincit sapientia robur (V. S. R.)** *Latin* 'Wisdom overcomes strength'
—Johann Ernst, Duke of Saxony-Eisenach (1566–1638).

172. **Vires agminis unus habet** *Latin* 'One has the strength of an army'
—Grylls (of Helston).

173. **Vires/ artes/ mores** *Latin* 'Strength/ arts/ morals'
—Florida State University, Tallahassee, Florida.

174. **Vires et fides** *Latin* 'Strength and faith'
—Cowan.

175. **Vires in arduis** *Latin* 'Strength in difficulties'
—Mac-bain.

176. **Virtus paret robur** *Latin* 'Virtue begets strength'
—Banbury (Bt.), Richardson.

177. **Virtus unita fortior** *Latin* 'Strength is increased by unity'
—Andorra.

178. **Virtute paret robur** *Latin* 'Strength obeys virtue'
—Richardson.

179. **Virtutis robore robur** *Latin* 'Strong as an oak in virtue's strength'
—Dackcombe (Co. Dorset).

180. **Vis et fides** *Latin* 'Strength and faith'
—Campbell (of Co. Hants and Dunoon, Scotland), Wyndham.

181. **Vis et virtus** *Latin* 'Strength and bravery'

—Chisalme.

182. **Vis fortibus arma** *Latin* 'Strength is arms to the brave'

—Cruikshank.

183. **Vis super hostem** *Latin* 'Strength over the enemy'

—O'Donovan.

184. **Vis unita fortior** *Latin* 'Strength united is stronger'

—1776 seal of New Hampshire; Brook; Flood; Hales; Hosken; Lidwell; Moore; Mountcashel (E.); Crosby B. C., Stoke-on-Trent City and C. B. C., U.K.

185. **Vis viri fragilis** *Latin* 'Weak is the strength of man'

—Lilburne, Ruddiman.

186. **Vive valeque** *Latin* 'Live and be strong'

—Green.

187. **Wisdom and strength**

—Crookes.

188. **With thy might**

—Smith.

SUCCESS *(See also* ACCOMPLISHMENT; FLOURISHING; FORTUNE; GLORY; PROSPERITY; VICTORY.)

1. **Beneficio bene erit** *Latin* 'He will succeed by kindness'

—Raisbeck.

2. **Consequitur quodcunque petit** *Latin* 'He hits whatever he aims at'

—Headfort (M.), Drummond, Taylor (of Pennington).

3. **Consequitur quodcunque petit** *Latin* 'He (she) attains whatsoever he (she) aims at'

—Marquess of Headfort; Diana of Poitiers (1499–1566).

4. **Fideliter, fortiter, feliciter** *Latin* 'Faithfully, bravely, and successfully'

—Scourfield (Bt.).

5. **Fortiter, fideliter, feliciter** *Latin* 'Boldly, faithfully, successfully'

—Hutchinson, Jackson, Monck (V.), Rathdowne (E.).

6. **Je ferai bien** *French* 'I shall do well'

—Butler, Green.

7. **Nunquam tentes aut perfice** *Latin* 'Either never attempt, or accomplish'

—Bennet.

8. **Par sit fortuna labori** *Latin* 'Let the success be equal to the labor'
—Palmer (of Carlton, Bt.), Palmer (of Kilmare), Buchanan (of Drumhead), Lowman.

9. **Perge et valeas** *Latin* 'Proceed and you may succeed'

—Hutchinson (U.S.).

10. **Placeam dum peream** *Latin* 'Let me find favor as long as I live'

—Murray.

11. **Pour parvenir à bonne foy** *Old French* 'To obtain success with credit'

—Cutlers' Company.

12. **Pour parvenir au bout il faut souffrir tout** *French* 'To reach the goal we must suffer all things'
—Wilhelm V, Landgrave of Hesse-Cassel (1602–37).

13. **Praestare et prodesse** *Latin* 'To outstrip and do good'

—Gray.

14. **Presto ut praestem** *Latin* 'I undertake that I may perform'

—Preston.

15. **Spem successus alit** *Latin* 'Success nourishes hope'
—Ross (of Balnagowan, Bt.).

16. **Strenue et prospere** *Latin* 'Earnestly and successfully'

—Eamer.

17. **Successus a Deo est** *Latin* 'Success is from God'

—Roberts.

18. **Succesus per educationem** *Latin* 'Success through education'
—Thomas Nelson Community College, Hampton, Virginia.

SUFFERING (*See also* DESPAIR; ENDURANCE; PATIENCE; PERSECUTION; SADNESS.)

1. **Dolore lenio dolorem** *Latin* 'By suffering I alleviate pain'

—Palmer.

2. **Ex duris gloria** *Latin* 'From suffering ariseth glory'

—Bentham.

3. **Laetamur graviora passi** *Latin* 'We rejoice that we have suffered tribulation'
>   —Heinrich Julius, Duke of Braunschweig-Wolfenbüttel
>   (1564–1613).

4. **Malo pati quam foedari** *Latin* 'I prefer suffering to disgrace'
>   —Duckett.

5. **Optimum pati** *Latin* 'It is best to suffer'
>   —Sheldon.

6. **Patior et spero** *Latin* 'I suffer and hope'
>   —Baillie.

7. **Patitur qui vincit** *Latin* 'He who conquers suffers'
>   —Kennard (B.).

8. **Per damna per caedes** *Latin* 'Through losses, through carnage'
>   —Bosanquet, Boyton.

9. **Pour parvenir au bout il faut souffrir tout** *French* 'To reach the goal we must suffer all things'
>   —Wilhelm V, Landgrave of Hesse-Cassel (1602–37).

10. **Suffer**
>   —Gleneagles, Hadden, Halden.

11. **Sufferings are lessons** *(from Greek)*
>   —[Herodotus, *Hist.* i. 207.] Karl, Count of the Palatinate
>   of Birkenfeld (1560–1600).

12. **Y ddioddefws orfu** *Welsh* 'He who suffered has conquered'
>   —De Avan, Williams.

13. **Y ddioddefws y orfu** *Welsh* 'He who suffered has conquered'
>   —Morgan.

SUN (*See also* BRIGHTNESS; DAY; LIGHT; SHINING.)

1. **Aquila petit solem** *Latin* 'The eagle seeks the sun'
>   —Kendall.

2. **Arduus ad solem** *Latin* 'Lifted up to the sun'
>   —University of Manchester, Manchester, U.K.

3. **Esto sol testis**
>   —Jones (Co. Salop, Bt.).

4. **Exsurgunt nubila Phoebo** *Latin* 'After sunshine mount the clouds'
>   —Friedrich Wilhelm, Elector of Brandenburg (1620–88).

5. **Haud fulsit gratior populis**   *Latin* 'Never has the sun shone more kindly for the people (than in his life)'
—Georg Wilhelm, Duke of Braunschweig-Luneburg-Zelle (1624–1705).

6. **Ope solis et umbrae**   *Latin* 'By help of sun and shade'
—Irvine.

7. **Paradisus in sole**   *Latin* 'Paradise in the sun'
—Hubbard (U.S.).

8. **Patiens pulveris atque solis**   *Latin* 'Patient of dust and sun'
—[Horace, *Od.* i. 8. 4.] Floyd (Bt.).

9. **Phoebo lux**   *Latin* 'Light from the sun'
—Kinnaird (B.).

10. **Post nubila Phoebus**   *Latin* 'After clouds sunshine'
—Ahrends, Cranworth (B.), Jack, Jaffray, Jafrey, Purvis, Rolfe, Robinson, Pinkerton, Tarleton (Bt.), Tarlton (of Collingwood), Shuldham.

11. **Post nubila sol**   *Latin* 'After clouds sunshine'
—Pinkerton.

12. **Sine sole nihil**   *Latin* 'Nothing without the sun'
—Pettigrew.

13. **Sol clarior astro**   *Latin* 'The sun is brighter than a star'
—Johnson.

14. **Solem contemplor, despicio terram**   *Latin* 'I gaze on the sun, and despise the earth'
—Bedingfield.

15. **Solem fero**   *Latin* 'I bear the sun'
—Aubrey (Bt.).

16. **Solem ferre possum**   *Latin* 'I can bear the sun'
—Davies, Sanders.

17. **Sol et salubritas**   *Latin* 'Sun and health'
—Bexhill B. C., U.K.

18. **Sol meus testis**   *Latin* 'The sun my witness'
—Boehm.

19. **Sol tibi signa dabit**   *Latin* 'The sun will show signs to thee'
—Stewart.

20. **Sub sole, sub umbra, virescens**   *Latin* 'In sun or in shade, thriving'
—Erving (U.S.).

21. **Sub sole, sub umbra virens** *Latin* 'Flourishing both in sunshine and in shade'
> —Irvine, Irving, Irwine, Winter-Irving.

22. **Sub sole sub umbra crescens** *Latin* 'Increasing both in sunshine and in shade'
> —Irvine (of Murthill), Irvine.

23. **Sub sole viresco** *Latin* 'I flourish under the sun'
> —Irvine (of Artamford).

24. **Sub solo patebit** *Latin* 'It will expand under the sun'
> —Ellies.

25. **Surgit post nubila Phoebus** *Latin* 'The sun rises after clouds'
> —Coachmakers' Company, Constable (Bt.).

26. **Terra, aqua, ignis, sal, spiritus, sulphur, Sol, Venus, Mercurius** *Latin* 'Land, water, fire, salt, spirit, sulphur, Sun, Venus, Mercury'
> —Irvine.

27. **Umbra non cedit soli** *Latin* 'The shadow does not yield to the sun'
> —Günther, Count Schwarzburg in Arnstadt (1490–1552).

28. **Ung sent ung soleil** *Old French* 'One faith, one sun'
> —Lloyd-Verney, Verney.

29. **Volvitur et ridet** *Latin* 'He (the sun) revolves and smiles'
> —Fairwether.

SUPPORT (*See also* PROVIDENCE.)

1. **Auspice Teucro** *Latin* 'Under the auspices of Teucer'
> —Tucker.

2. **Auspicio regis, senatus Angliae** *Latin* 'Under the auspices of the sovereign and senate of England'
> —East India Company.

3. **Coeptis aspirate meis** *Latin* 'Be favorable to my undertakings'
> —Davies.

4. **Imperatricis auspiciis** *Latin* 'Under the auspices of the Empress'
> —Order of the Indian Empire.

5. **Leniter sustineo** *Latin* 'I support gently'
> —Sheath.

6. **Recipiunt feminae sustentacula nobis** *Latin* 'Women receive support from us'
> —Pattern Makers' Company.

7. **Sic sustentata crescit**   *Latin* 'Thus supported it increases'
—Gervais.

8. **Sustineatur**   *Latin* 'Let it be sustained'
—Cullum (Bt.).

9. **Undique fulsus**   *Latin* 'Supported all round'
—Myrton.

THOUGHT   (*See also* JUDGMENT; MIND; REASON.)

1. **Cave ut comprehendas**   *Latin* 'Take care you understand'
—Drury.

2. **Cogito**   *Latin* 'I reflect'
—Weems.

3. **Cogito ergo sum. Deo gratias**   *Latin* 'I think therefore I am.
Thanks be to God'
—Shorter College, North Little Rock, Arkansas.

4. **Consulit et ornat**   *Latin* 'He deliberates and prepares'
—Dunbar.

5. **Consulto**   *Latin* 'I deliberate'
—Peddie.

6. **Diu delibera cito fac**   *Latin* 'Think long, act fast'
—Davie (U.S.).

7. **Ich schweig und gedenck**   *German* 'I am silent and think'
—Ernst IV, Count of Mansfeld (1544–1609).

8. **Je pense**   *French* 'I think'
—Weymiss (E.).

9. **Je pense à qui pense plus**   *French* 'I think of him who is the most
thoughtful'
—Rose, Cleland.

10. **Je pense plus**   *French* 'I think the more'
—Marr (E.).

11. **Pensa poi fa**   *Italian* 'Consider, then act'
—August, Duke of Braunschweig-Wolfenbüttel
(1579–1666).

12. **Penser avant parler**   *French* 'Think before you speak'
—Carbonell.

13. **Penses comment**   *French* 'Think in what manner'
—Davell, Deyvelle.

14. **Pensez à moi** *French* 'Think of me'
—Giles.

15. **Pensez en bien** *French* 'Think on good'
—Noel, Wentworth.

16. **Pensez forte** *French* 'Think firmly'
—Bromley (Bt.), Paunceforte.

17. **Perspicere quam ulcisci** *Latin* 'To discern rather than to avenge'
—Manigault (U.S.).

18. **Plus penser que dire** *French* 'To think rather than to speak'
—Adolf, Duke of Schleswig-Holstein-Gottorp (1526–86);
Ernst Friedrich, Margrave of Baden-Durlach
(1560–1604); Friedrich, Landgrave of Hesse-
Homburg (1585–1638); Sigismund, Margrave of
Brandenburg (1592–1640); Anton Günther, Prince of
Schwarzburg-Arnstadt (1653–1716).

19. **Prius quam factum considera** *Latin* 'Think before you act'
—Reeves.

20. **Que pensez** *French* 'What think ye?'
—St. Lawrence.

21. **Qui pense?** *French* 'Who thinks?'
—Howth (E.), Lawrence, Walford.

22. **Respice** *Latin* 'Consider'
—Nepean.

23. **Rien sans raison** *French* 'Nothing without reflection'
—Ernst August, Duke of Saxony-Weimar (1688–1741).

24. **Tak a thocht**
—Fairlie.

25. **Tempus omnia revelat** *Latin* 'Time reveals all things'
—Atkinson.

26. **Thincke and thancke**
—Tate (of Burleigh Park).

27. **Think and thank**
—Ailesbury (M.), Montefiore (Bt.).

28. **Think on**
—Maxwell (of Calderwood, Bt.), Macclellan, Ross.

29. **Think well**
—Erskine (of Sheefield).

30. **Think/ Work/ Serve**
—Tennessee State University, Nashville, Tennessee.

TIME (*See also* FUTURE, THE; PAST, THE; PRESENT, THE; SEASONS; TIMELINESS; TRANSIENCE.)

1. **Ad pontes prospicimus** *Latin* 'At the bridges we look forward' i.e., 'From our ancient past we look forward to the future'
—Staines U. D. C., U.K.

2. **À la bonne heure** *French* 'In good time'
—Bonnor.

3. **Alki** *Chinook Indian* 'By and by'
—State of Washington.

4. **Alles mit der Zeit** *German* 'Everything comes in time'
—Franz Erdmann, Duke of Saxony-Lauenburg (1629–66).

5. **Alles mit Gott, und der Zeit** *German* 'Everything is with God and with time'
—Erdmuthe Sophie, Margravine of Brandenburg (1644–70).

6. **Alles steht bei glvck und Zeit** *German* 'Everything comes with luck and with time'
—Ferdinand II, Emperor of Germany (1578–1637); Friedrich Ulrich, Duke of Braunschweig-Wolfenbüttel (1591–1634).

7. **Amser yw'n golud** *Welsh* 'Time is our wealth'
—Ystradgynlais R. D. C., U.K.

8. **Aspice, respice** *Latin* 'Look to the future and the past'
—Wellingborough U. D. C., U.K.

9. **Avise le temps** *French* 'Consider the times'
—Omond.

10. **Carpe diem** *Latin* 'Seize the present opportunity'
—[Horace, *Od.* i. 11.] Clarke, Berns, Paynter, Langford, Webster.

11. **Chacun en son temps** *French* 'Everyone in his time'
—Emperor Maximilian, Austria.

12. **Coadyuvando el presente, formando el porvenir** *Old Spanish* 'Guide to the present, moulder of the future'
—University of Toledo, Toledo, Ohio.

13. **Corrige praeteritum, praesens rege, cerne futurum** *Latin* 'Correct the past, rule the present, see to the future'
—Otto the Younger, Duke of Braunschweig-Lüneburg-Harburg (1528–1603)

14. **Cum Deo et die** *Latin* 'With God and time'
> —Eduard, Count of the Palatinate of Rhein (1625–63);
> Friedrich III, Duke of Saxony-Gotha and Altenburg
> (1699–1772); Christian, Duke of Saxony-Merseburg
> (1615–91); Eberhard Ludwig, Duke of
> Württemberg (1676–1733).

15. **Demum** *Latin* 'At last'
> —White (U.S.).

16. **Dum tempus habemus operemur bonum** *Latin* 'Whilst we have time let us do good'
> —Crisp.

17. **Early and late**
> —Wilkinson.

18. **Et patribus et posteris** *Latin* 'Both for our ancestors and our posterity'
> —Lydall.

19. **For as Tyme doth haste so life doth waste**
> —Sundial dated 'Anno 1560', at Stanwardine Hall near
> Baschurch, Salop, England.

20. **Fugit hora** *Latin* 'The hour flies'
> —Forbes.

21. **Fugit irrevocabile tempus** *Latin* 'Irrevocable time flies'
> —Shadforth.

22. **Fuimus et sub Deo erimus** *Latin* 'We have been, and we shall be under God'
> —Cohan, Holland.

23. **History cannot be destroyed by time**
> —Conroy.

24. **Il tempo passa** *Italian* 'Time flies'
> —Boynton (Bt.).

25. **In dies** *Latin* 'Daily (more)'
> —August, Duke of Braunschweig-Wolfenbüttel
> (1579–1666).

26. **In time**
> —University of Houston, Houston, Texas; Houston (B.),
> Houston.

27. **I number none but sunny hours**
> —Sundial at Paul's Cross, London.

28. **Looking backward, looking forward**
> —Twickenham B. C., U.K.

29. **Mature**   *Latin* 'In good time'
                                                          —Smith.

30. **Memor esto brevis aevi**   *Latin* 'Be mindful that time is short'
                                                          —Milnes.

31. **Mit der Zeit**   *German* 'In good time'
        —Otto Heinrich, Elector of the Palatinate (1502–59).

32. **Mit Gott und mit der Zeit**   *German* 'With God and with time'
                —Philipp, Duke of Saxony-Lauchstädt (1657–90).

33. **Ni diothlaith rightear Seanchus le h-aimsir**   *Gaelic* 'History is not destroyed by time'
                —Conroy (of Llanbrynmair, Montgomeryshire, and of Bettifield, Co. Roscommon, Bt.).

34. **Nil extra numerum**   *Latin* 'Nothing out of time'
                                                          —Randall.

35. **Non credo tempori**   *Latin* 'I do not trust to time'
                                —Order of St. Nicholas (Russia).

36. **Non numero horas nisi serenas**   *Latin* 'I count none but cloudless hours'
                                —Sundial near Venice, Italy.

37. **Omnia cum Deo et tempore**   *Latin* 'Everything with God and with time'
                —Wilhelm Ludwig, Duke of Württemberg (1647–77).

38. **Omnia cum tempore**   *Latin* 'All things come in time'
                —Julius Heinrich, Duke of Saxony-Lauenburg (1586–1665).

39. **Omnia fert aetas**   *Latin* 'Time brings all things'
                                —Cheese, Lucadon.

40. **Ora e sempre**   *Latin* 'Now and always'
                                                          —Farmer.

41. **Per multos annos**   *Latin* 'Through many years'
                                                          —Phillips.

42. **Priora cole meliora sequere**   *Latin* 'Cherish the past but strive for better things in the future'
                                —Enfield U. D. C., U.K.

43. **Redeem the time**
                                                          —Hancocks.

44. **Regit omnia tempus**   *Latin* 'Time rules all things'
                                                          —Boag.

45. **Respice, auspice, prospice**   *Latin* 'Look to the past, the present, and the future'
> —The City College, City University of New York, New York City, New York.

46. **Respice, prospice**   *Latin* 'Look backward and forward'
> —Lloyd (of Gloucester).

47. **Respice aspice prospice**   *Latin* 'Look to the past, the present, and the future'
> —Tettenhall U. D. C., Bootle C. B. C., Halesowen B.C., U.K.

48. **Respice aspice prospice**   *Latin* 'Look back, look around, and look forward'
> —Brooks, Holland.

49. **Respice prospice**   *Latin* 'Look to the past and to the future'
> —Trowbridge U. D. C., Stoke Newington B. C., Ealing B. C., U.K.

50. **Respiciens prospiciens**   *Latin* 'Looking behind, looking before'
> —Tennyson.

51. **Sans heure**   *French* 'Without a time'
> —Arnell.

52. **Semper in tempore**   *Latin* 'Always in time'
> —Randles.

53. **Sic fuit, est, et erit**   *Latin* 'Thus it has been, is, and will be'
> —Stewart (of Burgh).

54. **Start in time**
> —Brooks (U.S.).

55. **Tais en temps**   *French* 'Be silent in time'
> —Tey (of Essex).

56. **Tandem**   *Latin* 'At length'
> —Prince of Anhalt-Dessau (1627–93); August, Duke of Braunschweig-Wolfenbüttel (1579–1666); Karl II, Count of Mansfeld (1543–95); Christian Wilhelm, Prince of Schwarzburg-Sondershausen (1647–1721); Cunningham, Finnie.

57. **Tandem licet sero**   *Latin* 'At length though late'
> —Campbell.

58. **Tempera te tempori**   *Latin* 'Temper thyself to the times'
> —Le Maire.

59. **Tempore utimur**   *Latin* 'We use time'
> —Greenwich B. C., U.K.

60. **Tempus et casus accidit omnibus** *Latin* 'Time and chance happen to all'
> —Wayne.

61. **Tempus et patientia** *Latin* 'Time and patience'
> —Bradbury (Co. Essex).

62. **Tempus meae opes** *Latin* 'Time is my wealth'
> —Spofforth.

63. **Tempus omnia monstrat** *Latin* 'Time shows all things'
> —Lovell.

64. **Tempus omnia revelat** *Latin* 'Time reveals all things'
> —Atkinson.

65. **Tempus rerum imperator** *Latin* 'Time the ruler of all things'
> —Clockmakers' Company.

66. **Time tryeth troth**
> —Trevelyan (Bt.).

67. **Time tryeth tryst**
> —Drake (U.S.).

68. **Tout avec le temps** *French* 'Everything comes in time'
> —Georg Albrecht, Margrave of Brandenburg-Baireuth
> (1619–66); Joachim Karl, Duke of Braunschweig
> (1573–1615); Julius Heinrich, Duke of Saxony-
> Lauenburg (1586–1665); Johann Christian, Duke of
> Brieg (1591–1639); Sylvius Nimrod, Duke of
> Württemberg (1622–64).

69. **Tout en bon heure** *French* 'All in good time'
> —Hicks (Bt.), Hicks (of Watton, Co. Norfolk), Beach (of
> Oakley Hall).

70. **Tyme proveth truth**
> —Adlam.

71. **Venit hora** *Latin* 'The hour comes'
> —Hoare (Bt.), Hoare (of Cork, Dunmanway, Annabella,
> Factory-Hill, etc., all in the county of Cork, Ireland).

72. **Vespere et mane** *Latin* 'In the evening and the morning'
> —Pierre, Pourie, Purie.

73. **Vive memor lethi, fugit hora** *Latin* 'Live mindful of death; time flies'
> —Bailhache.

74. **What was may be**
> —Oliphant (of Bachiltoun).

TIMELINESS (*See also* TIME.)

1. **All Ding ein Weil** *German* 'There is a proper time for all things'
   —Johann Cicero, Margrave of Brandenburg (1486–99).

2. **Alles zu seiner Zeit** *German* 'Everything at its right time'
   —Georg Friedrich, Margrave of Brandenburg-Anspach (1539–1603); Bernhard VII, Prince of Anhalt (1540–70); Philipp II, Duke of Pomerania (1573–1618).

3. **Ante ferit quam flamma micet** *Latin* 'He strikes (it) before the fire sparkles out'
   —Order of the Golden Fleece (Spain).

4. **Appropinquat dies** *Latin* 'The day is at hand'
   —Johnstone (of Clathrie).

5. **Cognosce occasionem** *Latin* 'Know the proper time'
   —Williams (U.S.).

6. **Labile quod opportunum** *Latin* 'That which is opportune is quickly gone'
   —Howman (of Bexwell, Co. Norfolk).

7. **Never behind**
   —Crewe B. C., U.K.

TOUCH

1. **Na bean d'on chat gun lamhainu** *Scots Gaelic* 'Touch not a cat but with a glove'
   —Macpherson (of Cluny).

2. **Noli me tangere** *Latin* 'Touch me not'
   —Graham, Graeme.

3. **Qui me tanget paenitebit** *Latin* 'Whoever touch me will repent'
   —Macpherson.

4. **Touch not the cat bot** (i.e., without) **a glove**
   —Gillies, MacPherson, McGilleray, Grant, Gillespie, McBean, Mackintosh, McIntosh, McCrombie, Macpherson.

TRADES

1. **All worship be to God only**
   —[Matt. iv. 10.] Fishmongers' Company, London.

2. **Amicitiam trahit amor** *Latin* 'Love draws on friendship'
   —Wire-drawers' Company.

3. **Amore sitis uniti** *Latin* 'Be ye united in love'
   —Tin-plate Workers' and Wire-workers' Company.

4. **Amor et obedientia** *Latin* 'Love and obedience'
   —Painters' Company.

5. **Amorque et obedientia** *Latin* 'Both love and obedience'
   —Painters' Company.

6. **Art, industry, contentment**
   —Basildon Development Corp.

7. **Arts and trades united**
   —Fanmakers' Company.

8. **By hammer and hand all arts do stand**
   —Blacksmiths' Company.

9. **Concordiâ parvae res crescunt** *Latin* 'Small things increase by concord'
   —Merchant Taylors' Company.

10. **Corde recto elati omnes** *Latin* 'All are elevated by a right heart'
    —Playing-card Makers' Company.

11. **Da nobis lucem, Domine** *Latin* 'Give us light, O Lord!'
    —Glaziers' Company.

12. **Drop as rain, distil as dew**
    —Distillers' Comp., London.

13. **Factum est** *Latin* 'It is done'
    —Plasterers' Company.

14. **Grind well**
    —Marblers' Company, London.

15. **Hold fast, sit sure**
    —Saddlers' Company.

16. **In the sweat of thy brow shalt thou eat thy bread**
    —[Gen. iii. 19.] Gardeners' Company.

17. **Join truth with trust**
    —Joiners' Company, London.

18. **Let brotherly love continue**
    —Plasterers' Company, Pipe-makers' Company.

19. **Let us love one another**
    —Basketmakers' Company.

20. **Love as brethren**
    —Coopers' Company, London.

21. **Lumen umbra Dei** *Latin* 'Light is the shadow of God'
    —Glaziers' Company.

22. **Make all sure**
>—Armourers' and Braziers' Company, London.

23. **My trust is in God alone**
>—Cloth-workers' Company, London.

24. **Nec habeo, nec careo, nec curo**   *Latin* 'I have neither property, want, nor care'
>—Bowstring-Makers' Company, Withers.

25. **Pour parvenir à bonne foy**   *Old French* 'To obtain success with credit'
>—Cutlers' Company.

26. **Quae arguuntur a lumine manifestantur**   *Latin* 'What things are questioned light clears up'
>—Tallow Chandlers' Company.

27. **Quae prosunt omnibus artes**   *Latin* 'Arts that are beneficial to all'
>—Surgeons' Company.

28. **Qui fugit molam fugit farinam**   *Latin* 'He who shuns the mill, shuns the flour'
>—Coopers' Company, Exeter.

29. **Recipiunt feminae sustentacula nobis**   *Latin* 'Women receive support from us'
>—Pattern Makers' Company.

30. **Scribere scientes**   *Latin* 'Men skilled in writing'
>—Scriveners' Company.

31. **Serve and obey**
>—Haberdashers' Company (London).

32. **Speed, strength, and truth united**
>—Framework Knitters' Company.

33. **Surgit post nubila Phoebus**   *Latin* 'The sun rises after clouds'
>—Coachmakers' Company, Constable (Bt.).

34. **Tempus rerum imperator**   *Latin* 'Time the ruler of all things'
>—Clockmakers' Company.

35. **The axe is laid at the root of the tree**
>—[Matt. iii. 10.] Woodmongers' Company.

36. **Tota mea fiducia est in deo**   *Latin* 'My whole trust is in God'
>—Pewterers' Company.

37. **Tractent fabrilia fabri**   *Latin* 'Let smiths handle smiths' tools'
>—Smiths' Company, Exeter.

38. **Truth is the light**
>—Wax Chandlers' Company (London).

39. **Unita fortior**   *Latin* 'The stronger being united'
—Rundall; Scots Guards, 2nd Battalion; Woodmongers'
Company.

40. **Unitas societatis stabilitas**   *Latin* 'Unity is the support of society'
—Parish Clerks' Company.

41. **Vi et virtute**   *Latin* 'By strength and valor'
—Baird (Bt.), Baird, Bolton, Barnes, Chisholm, Hurst,
McTaggart, Smart, Spoight, White; Farriers'
Company.

42. **Virginitas et unitas nostra fraternitas**   *Latin* 'Chastity and unity
form our brotherhood'
—Pin-makers' Company.

43. **We are one**
—Armourers' and Braziers' Company (London).

44. **Weave truth with truth**
—Weavers' Company (London).

45. **Within the ark safe for ever**
—Shipwrights' Company.

TRADITION   (*See also* ANCESTRY.)

1. **Ad morem villae de Poole**   *Latin* 'According to the custom of the
town of Poole'
—Poole B. C., U.K.

2. **Antiqui mores**   *Latin* 'Ancient manners'
—Morrice.

3. **Pawb yn ôl ei arfer**   *Welsh* 'Everyone after his custom'
—Jones (of Idrial).

4. **Super antiquas vias**   *Latin* 'Along ancient ways'
—St. Peter's School, York, U.K.

5. **Traditum ab antiquis servare**   *Latin* 'To keep that which is
handed down from ancient times'
—Frere (of Roydon).

6. **Usus rectumque**   *Latin* 'Custom and right'
—Micklethwayte.

7. **Vita more fide**   *Latin* 'By hope, custom, and faith'
—Hanercroft.

TRANQUILLITY (*See also* PEACE.)

1. **Attamen tranquillus** *Latin* 'Tranquil notwithstanding'
—Maitland.

2. **Deus haec otia fecit** *Latin* 'God hath given this tranquillity'
—[after Vergil, *Ec.* i. vi.] Williams (Co. Brecon and Herts.).

3. **Deus nobis haec otia fecit** *Latin* 'God hath given us this tranquillity'
—[Vergil, *Ec.* i. vi.] Town of Liverpool, Vergil, *Ec.* i. vi.] Bolger, Burrow, Hide.

4. **Iechyd, harddwch, heddwch** *Welsh* 'Health, beauty and tranquility'
—Colwyn Bay B. C., U.K.

5. **Mediis tranquillus in undis** *Latin* 'Tranquil in the midst of waters'
—Smyth (Co. Perth).

6. **Pax hospita ruris** *Latin* 'Peace, the hostess of the countryside'
—Jones (U.S.).

7. **Quid pure tranquillet** *Latin* 'What purely calms'
—Thomas.

8. **Seek quiet**
—Deacon.

9. **Tandem tranquillus** *Latin* 'At last tranquil'
—Symmer.

TRANSIENCE (*See also* CHANGE; TIME.)

1. **Alle Ding zergänglich** *German* 'All things are fleeting'
—Ludwig VI, Elector of the Palatinate (1539–83).

2. **Cito pede praeterit aetas** *Latin* 'Life marches on at a swift pace'
—Sargeant (U.S.).

3. **Firmum in vita nihil** *Latin* 'Nothing in life is permanent'
—Bunbury (Bt.), Dolphin, Richardson.

4. **Haec omnia transeunt** *Latin* 'All these things pass away'
—Bourne.

5. **Hic hodie cras urna** *Latin* 'Here today, tomorrow the urn'
—Fletcher.

6. **Hoc etiam praeteribit** *Latin* 'This also will pass by'
—Budgett.

7. **Nil solidum**   *Latin* 'There is nothing unchangeable'
                                —Goldie, Williams (Co. Dorset).

8. **Nunc cinis, ante rosa**   *Latin* 'Now ashes, formerly a rose'
                                —August, Count von der Lippe (d. 1701).

9. **Omnia mundana fluxa**   *Latin* 'All earthly things are fleeting'
                                —Ludwig VI, Elector of the Palatinate (1539–83).

10. **Omnia orta occidunt et aucta senescunt**   *Latin* 'All that is passes
    away, and all that grows grows old'
                                —[Sallust, *Bellum Jugurth*, ii.] Casimir, Margrave of
                                Brandenburg-Baireuth (1481–1527).

11. **On things transitory resteth no glory**
                                —Isham (Bt.).

12. **Perenne sub polo nihil**   *Latin* 'There is nothing permanent under
    heaven'
                                —Pont; Christian I, Prince of Anhalt-Bernberg
                                (1568–1630).

13. **Quicquid crescit in cinere perit**   *Latin* 'Whatever grows perishes
    in ashes'
                                —Ashburner (of Cockermouth).

14. **Raptim transeo, sed vestigia longa relinquo**   *Latin* 'Quickly do I
    pass, but lasting footsteps leave behind'
                                —Bernhard, Duke of Saxony-Weimar (1604–39).

15. **Rien est constant si non l'inconstance durable mesme en son
    changement**   *French* 'Nothing is constant save enduring incon-
    stancy in its changes'
                                —Johann Ernst, Duke of Saxony-Weimar (1594–1626).

16. **Sic cuncta caduca**   *Latin* 'All things are thus unstable'
                                —Henderson.

17. **Tutto alfin vola**   *Italian* 'Everything vanishes in the end'
                                —Spickernell.

18. **Ut migraturus habita**   *Latin* 'Dwell here as one about to depart'
                                —Lauder (of Fountainhall, Bt.).

19. **Victor mortalis est**   *Latin* 'The conqueror is mortal'
                                —Clarke.

TRUST (*See also* CONFIDENCE; FAITH; TRUSTWORTHINESS.)

1. **A. G. T. I. (Allein Gott traue ich)**   *German* 'I trust in God alone'
                                —Dorothee, Duchess of Braunschweig-Lüneberg
                                (1546–1617).

2. **Aspire, persevere, trust**

           —Adams (U.S.).

3. **Bonum est confidere in Domino** *Latin* 'It is well to trust in the Lord'

    —[after Ps. cxviii. 8.] Philipp I, Duke of Pomerania zu Wolgast (1515–60).

4. **Confide in Deo** *Latin* 'Trust in God'

           —Rugeley.

5. **Confidence in God**

           —Coleman.

6. **Confidimus** *Latin* 'We will trust'

           —Boyd.

7. **Confido** *Latin* 'I trust'

    —Bell, Boyd (Bt.), Body (of Merton Hall), Boyd (of Middleton Park), Le Bon, Mills, Peters, Winter.

8. **Confido conquiesco** *Latin* 'I trust and am contented'

    —Dysart (E.), Hodgetts, Maroy, Tollemache, Turner.

9. **Confido in Deo** *Latin* 'I trust in God'

       —[Ps. cxli. 8.] Backhouse.

10. **Confido in Domino** *Latin* 'I trust in the Lord'

           —Peterkin.

11. **Confido in probitate** *Latin* 'I trust in my probity'

           —Cadell.

12. **Confido in providentia** *Latin* 'I trust in providence'

           —Richardson.

13. **Confido non confundar** *Latin* 'I trust and shall not be confounded'

        —Tyndale (of Hayling).

14. **Crede Byron** *Latin* 'Trust Byron'

           —Byron (B.).

15. **Crede cornu** *Latin* 'Trust the horn' *or* 'Trust Hornby'

           —Hornby.

16. **Crede Deo** *Latin* 'Trust in God'

           —Atkinson.

17. **Crede signo** *Latin* 'Trust in this sign'

       —Rochdale C. B. C., U.K.

18. **Credo cruci Christi** *Latin* 'I trust in the cross of Christ'

           —Wood.

19. **Credo legi** *Latin* 'I trust in the law'
—Hamilton.

20. **Cruce non leone fides** *Latin* 'My trust is in the cross, not in the lion'
—Matthew (of Coggeshall, Co. Essex).

21. **Cruci dum fido spiro** *Latin* 'While I trust in the cross I live'
—Douw (U.S.).

22. **Cui fides fide** *Latin* 'Place full confidence in whom you trust'
—Peard.

23. **Deo confidimus** *Latin* 'We trust in God'
—West Ham C. B. C., U.K.

24. **Deo credito justitiam colito** *Latin* 'Practice justice, trusting in God'
—Udheraj.

25. **Deo fidens proficio** *Latin* 'Trusting to God I go forward'
—Chadwick.

26. **Deo fisus labora** *Latin* 'Work while trusting in God'
—William Jewell College, Liberty, Missouri.

27. **Deo semper confido** *Latin* 'In God I trust ever'
—James (of Otterburn).

28. **En Dieu est ma fiance** *French* 'In God is my trust'
—Luttrell.

29. **En Dieu gist ma confiance** *French* 'In God lies my trust'
—Johann Georg, Margrave of Brandenburg (1577–1624).

30. **En Dieu seul gist ma confiance** *French* 'In God alone rests my trust'
—Sophie Ursula, Countess of Oldenburg (1601–41).

31. **Fidens et constans** *Latin* 'Trusting and steadfast'
—O'Kearin.

32. **Fidentem nescit deseruisse Deus** *Latin* 'God deserts not him who trusts him'
—Johann Günther, Count of Schwarzburg and Hohenstein (1577–1631).

33. **Fide sed cui vide** *Latin* 'Trust, but be careful whom'
—Wilhelm V, Landgrave of Hesse-Cassel (1602–37);
Dorothee Sophie, Duchess of Saxony (1587–1645).

34. **Fide sed vide** *Latin* 'Trust but take care'
—Petrie, Reynolds.

35. **Fide sed vide**   *Latin* 'Trust, but be careful whom'
—Christian I, Elector of Saxony (1560–91).

36. **Fidite virtuti**   *Latin* 'Trust in virtue'
—Bard (U.S.).

37. **Fido Deo et ipse**   *Latin* 'I myself, too, trust in God'
—Gibbons.

38. **Fido non timeo**   *Latin* 'I trust, I do not fear'
—Hermon.

39. **Firm to my trust**
—Glyn (Bt.).

40. **Fisus et fidus**   *Latin* 'Trusted and faithful'
—Maitland.

41. **Fronti nulla fides**   *Latin* 'There is no trusting a countenance (appearances)'
—Cripps.

42. **Honor et veritas**   *Latin* 'Honor and truth'
—Waller (Bt.).

43. **I. D. F. N. (In Domino fiducia nostra)**   *Latin* 'In the Lord is our trust'
—August, Prince of Anhalt-Plötzkau (1575–1653).

44. **In caelo confidemus**   *Latin* 'We will trust in heaven'
—Hills.

45. **In cruce confido**   *Latin* 'I trust in the cross'
—Thrale.

46. **In cruce spero**   *Latin* 'I trust in the cross'
—Allardic, Barclay.

47. **In Deo confidemus**   *Latin* 'In God is our trust'
—Pryce.

48. **In Deo confido**   *Latin* 'I trust in God'
—Kirkman, Tovy, Lawford, Moore.

49. **In Deo confido, nil desperandum**   *Latin* 'Trust in God, nothing is to be despaired of'
—Kelly.

50. **In Deo est mihi omnis fides**   *Latin* 'In God is my whole trust'
—Palmer (Bt.).

51. **In Deo et in ipso confido**   *Latin* 'In God and in myself I trust'
—Richardson.

52. **In Deo et veritate fido**   *Latin* 'I trust in God and in truth'
—Hooper (U.S.).

53. **In Deo fidemus** *Latin* 'We trust in God'
—Brighton C. B. C., U.K.

54. **In Deo fides** *Latin* 'My trust is in God'
—Chapple.

55. **In Deo fido** *Latin* 'I trust in God'
—Medley.

56. **In Deo manuque fides** *Latin* 'In God and my hand is my trust'
—Mackesy.

57. **In Deo solo confido** *Latin* 'I trust in God alone'
—Converse (U.S.).

58. **In Deo solo speravi** *Latin* 'In God alone have I trusted'
—Allen.

59. **In Deo speramus** *Latin* 'We trust in God'
—Brown University, Providence, Rhode Island.

60. **In Deo speravi** *Latin* 'In God have I trusted'
—Clark (Bt.).

61. **In Domino confido** *Latin* 'I trust in the Lord'
—[Ps., xi. 1.] Asheton, Cargill, Cockburn, Erskin, Erskine, Newdigate, McGill, Williams, Walker, Willyams., Ernst the Pious, Duke of Saxony-Gotha (1601–75); Friedrich Wilhelm, Duke of Saxony (1603–19).

62. **In Domino fiducia nostra** *Latin* 'In the Lord is our trust'
—Karl Wilhelm, Prince of Anhalt-Zerbst (1652–1718).

63. **In God is all my trust**
—Grant; Pewterers' Company.

64. **In God is all our trust**
—Brewers' Company, Bricklayers and Tilers' Company.

65. **In God I trust**
—Frazer, Thompson.

66. **In God we trust**
—Scott (U.S.), on coins of the United States; State of Florida.

67. **In heaven is all my trust**
—Ambrose.

68. **In Jehovah fides mea** *Latin* 'In Jehovah is my trust'
—Brailsford.

69. **In misericordia Dei confido** *Latin* 'I trust in the mercy of God'
—Durand.

70. **Innocent and true**

—Arbuthnot (Bt.).

71. **In te, Domine, speravi** *Latin* 'In Thee, O Lord, have I put my trust'

—Abbs, Greenhill, Haire, Lyon (of Auldabar), Prestwich, Rouse, Strathmore (E.), Vale.

72. **In te fido** *Latin* 'I trust in thee'

—McLarty.

73. **In the Lord is all our trust**

—Masons' Company (London).

74. **I trust in God**

—Richardson, Wheatly.

75. **Je me fie en Dieu** *French* 'I trust in God'

—Blois (Bt.), Plymouth (E.), Windsor.

76. **Join truth with trust**

—Joiners' Company, London.

77. **Jovi praestat fidere quam homine** *Latin* 'It is preferable to trust in Jove rather than in a man'

—Stuyvesant (U.S.).

78. **Keep traist** *Scots dialect*

—Hepburn.

79. **Keep tryst** *Scots dialect*

—Belches, Hepburn (Bt.).

80. **Keep tryst and trust**

—Millar.

81. **Keep tryste** *Scots dialect*

—Sempill, Semple (of Cathcart, etc.), Hepburn (of Colquhalzie).

82. **Leoni non sagittis fido** *Latin* 'I trust to the lion not to my arrows'

—Egerton.

83. **Lippen to God** *Scots dial.* 'Trust God'

—Watson.

84. **Mea fides in sapientia** *Latin* 'My trust is in wisdom'

—Fryer.

85. **Merere et confide** *Latin* 'Deserve and trust'

—Winwood.

86. **M. V. S. Z. G. A. (Mein Vertrauen steht zu Gott allein)** *German* 'My trust is in God alone'

—Johann Adolf II, Duke of Saxony-Weissenfels (1649–97).

87. **My trust is in God alone**
                    —Cloth-workers' Company, London.

88. **My trust is in the Lord**
                                    —Unwin.

89. **Nimium ne crede sereno**   *Latin* 'Put not much trust in fair weather'
                    —[after Vergil, *Aen.* v. 870.] Friedrich Wilhelm, Elector of Brandenburg (1620–88).

90. **Non credo tempori**   *Latin* 'I do not trust to time'
                    —Order of St. Nicholas (Russia).

91. **Our trust is in God**
                    —Sadlers' Company, London.

92. **Sapiente diffidentia**   *Latin* 'With wise distrust'
                    —Adam Wenzel, Duke of Teschen (1574–1617).

93. **Scio cui confido**   *Latin* 'I know in whom I trust'
                                    —Aungier.

94. **Spero in Deo**   *Latin* 'I trust in God'
                                    —Blackie.

95. **Tota mea fiducia est in deo**   *Latin* 'My whole trust is in God'
                    —Pewterers' Company.

96. **Traue Gott, thue recht, scheue niemand**   *German* 'Trust God, do right, fear nobody'
                    —Wilhelm, Duke of Saxony-Weimar (1596–1622).

97. **Trauw, schauw, wem**   *German* 'Trust, but be careful whom'
                    —Franz Julius, Duke of Saxony (1584–1634).

98. **Trust and triumph**
                    —Gainsborough R. D. C., U.K.

99. **Trustie and bydand**   *Scots dial.*
                    —Leith (of Craighill).

100. **Trustie to the end**
                                    —Leith-Hay.

101. **Trust in God**
                    —Davis, Hardness, Husdell.

102. **Trust in God and not in strength**
                                    —Renton.

103. **Trust winneth troth**
                    —Rawdon-Hastings (Marquis of Hastings).

104. **Trusty and true**
                    —Scott (of Hussindene).

105. **Trusty to the end**

—Lumsden.

106. **T. S. W. (Trau, schau, wem)** *German* 'Trust, but be careful whom'

—Christian I, Elector of Saxony (1560–91).

107. **Vertrau Gott, tue Recht, scheu Niemandt** *German* 'Trust in God, do right, fear no man'

—Bernhard, Prince of Anhalt (1572–96).

108. **Vide cui fidas** *Latin* 'Beware whom you trust'

—Ferdinand, Duke of Bavaria (1550–1608).

109. **Virtuti fido** *Latin* 'I trust in virtue'

—Ap-Eynions.

110. **V. S. W. (Vertrau Schau Wem)** *German* 'Trust, but be careful whom'

—Johann Georg, Duke of Wohlau (1552–92).

111. **zV ChrIsto Ist MeIn VerDraVen** *German* 'In Christ is my trust.'
—(The capital letters, rearranged, give the year 1618).
Johann Georg I, Prince of Anhalt-Dessau
(1567–1618, in somewhat modified Roman
numerals: MDCVVVIII).

TRUSTWORTHINESS (*See also* FIDELITY; HONESTY; INTEGRITY; REPUTATION.)

1. **Candide me fides** *Latin* 'You will trust me favorably'

—Hill.

2. **Fortis et fidus** *Latin* 'Brave and trusty'
—Flint, Loughnan, McClauchlan, McLachlan (of Kilchoan), McLauchlan.

3. **Hic fidus et roboreus** *Latin* 'He is trusty and strong'

—Stirling.

4. **Keep trust**

—Polwarth (B.).

5. **My word is my bond**

—Smallman.

6. **Seur et loyal** *French* 'Sure and loyal'

—Colbarne.

7. **Sur et loyal** *French* 'Sure and loyal'

—Wild.

8. **Trusty and kind**
—Law.

9. **Verax atque probus** *Latin* 'Trustworthy and honest'
—Ruttledge.

TRUTH (*See also* FACTUALITY; HONESTY.)

1. **Adorn the truth**
—Waddel.

2. **A la vérité** *French* 'In truth'
—Bremer.

3. **Aletheuontes de en Agape** *(transliterated from Greek)* 'Speaking the truth in love'
—Brandon University, Brandon, Manitoba, Canada.

4. **Amica veritas** *Latin* 'Truth is dear'
—Nesbett.

5. **Bonitas/veritas/pulchritas** *Latin* 'Goodness/truth/beauty'
—Marycrest College, Davenport, Iowa.

6. **By truth and diligence**
—Lucy.

7. **Candor dat viribus alas** *Latin* 'Truth gives wings to strength'
—Hogarth, Rochfort.

8. **Celeritas et veritas** *Latin* 'Promptitude and truth'
—Rolls.

9. **Cherche la vérité** *French* 'Seek the truth'
—De La Rue (Bt.).

10. **Decus et veritas** *Latin* 'Glory and truth'
—Rockford College, Rockford, Illinois.

11. **Demeure par la vérité** *French* 'Stick by the truth'
—Mason.

12. **Deo ac veritati** *Latin* 'For God and truth'
—Colgate University, Hamilton, New York.

13. **Deus veritatem protegit** *Latin* 'God protects the truth'
—Roper.

14. **Deutlich und wahr** *German* 'Distinct and true'
—Schrieber.

15. **De vivis nil nisi verum** *Latin* 'Of the living speak nothing but what is true'
—Hyde.

16. **Dux mihi veritas** *Latin* 'Truth is my guide'
—Haggard.

17. **En suivant la vérité** *French* 'By following truth'
—Portsmouth (E.), Wallop, Williams (Co. Monmouth).

18. **Et juste et vrai** *French* 'Both just and true'
—Ray, Wray.

19. **Et vitam impendere vero** *Latin* 'To sacrifice even life to truth'
—[Juvenal, *Sat.* vi. 91.] Holland (B.), Rousseau.

20. **Ex caligine veritas** *Latin* 'Truth out of darkness'
—Claverly.

21. **Ex libertate veritas** *Latin* 'From liberty, truth'
—Aspland.

22. **Ex vero decus** *Latin* 'Honor from the truth'
—Jones.

23. **Fidei coticula crux** *Latin* 'The cross is the test of truth'
—Chevallier, Clarendon (E.), Baker (Bt.), Jersey (E.),
Villers, Whatton.

24. **Fidelitas et veritas** *Latin* 'Fidelity and truth'
—Peters.

25. **Fidelitas/ veritas/ integritas** *Latin* 'Fidelity/ truth/ integrity'
—Salmon P. Chase College of Law of Northern Kentucky
University, Covington, Kentucky.

26. **Fides nudaque veritas** *Latin* 'Faith and naked truth'
—Lushington.

27. **Fortis est veritas** *Latin* 'Truth is strong'
—Angus; Barton (of Threxton, Co. Norfolk); Hutchon;
Oxford City and C. B. C., U.K.; City of Oxford.

28. **Fortissima veritas** *Latin* 'Truth is most powerful'
—Kirkalie, Kirkaldy.

29. **Gaudet in luce veritas** *Latin* 'Truth rejoices in the light'
—Moilliet.

30. **Gratia et veritas** *Latin* 'Grace and truth'
—Luther Theological Seminary, St. Paul, Minnesota.

31. **Gwir yn erbyn y byd** *Welsh* 'Truth against the world'
—Truscott.

32. **Hold to the truth**
—Braintree and Bocking U. D. C., U.K.

33. **Honestas et veritas** *Latin* 'Honor and truth'
—Kemp.

34. **Honor veritas et justitia** *Latin* 'Honor truth and justice'
—Southam.

35. **Incorrupta fides, nudaque veritas** *Latin* 'Uncorrupted faith and the naked truth'
—Forde, Myers (Bt.), Waskett (of Hingham).

36. **In Deo et veritate fido** *Latin* 'I trust in God and in truth'
—Hooper (U.S.).

37. **Industria veritas et hospitalitas** *Latin* 'Industry, truth, and hospitality'
—Harris.

38. **Innixus vero validus** *Latin* 'He that rests upon the truth is strong'
—Lyon.

39. **In scientia veritas in arte honestas** *Latin* 'Truth in science, honesty in art'
—Wells (Bt.).

40. **In veritate religionis confido** *Latin* 'I trust in the truth of religion'
—25th Foot (King's Own Scottish Borderers).

41. **In veritate salus** *Latin* 'There is safety in truth'
—Jeffery (U.S.).

42. **In veritate triumpho** *Latin* 'I triumph in the truth'
—Biddulph, Greaves, Myddleton.

43. **In veritate victoria** *Latin* 'Victory is in truth'
—Akroyd (of Bankfield), Huntingdon (E.), Hastings (Bt.), Abney, Hastings (of Willesley Hall), Ingham, Loughborough B. C., U.K.

44. **Invicta veritate** *Latin* 'By invincible truth'
—Abell.

45. **Je dis la vérité** *French* 'I tell the truth'
—Pedder (of Ashton Lodge).

46. **Join truth with trust**
—Joiners' Company, London.

47. **Justitia et veritas** *Latin* 'Justice and truth'
—Charles I (1600–49); Lawriston.

48. **Justitia/ veritas** *Latin* 'Justice/ truth'
—Olivet Nazarene College, Kankakee, Illinois.

49. **Labor et veritas** *Latin* 'Industry and truth'
—Elliot (Bt.).

50. **Le beau est le splendeur du vrai** *French* 'Beauty is the splendor of truth'

—Doulton.

51. **Live to the truth**
—Framingham State College, Framingham, Massachusetts.

52. **Lux et veritas** *Latin* 'Light and truth'
—Waldorf College, Forest City, Iowa.

53. **Lux et veritas** *Latin* 'Light and truth'
—Yale University, New Haven, Connecticut.

54. **Lux veritas peritia populo nostro** *Latin* 'Light, truth, and skill for our people'
—Coastal Carolina Community College, Jacksonville, North Carolina.

55. **Magna est veritas** *Latin* 'Great is truth'

—Stillingfleet.

56. **Magna est veritas et prevalebit** *Latin* 'Truth is great and will prevail'

—Roden.

57. **Magna vis veritatis** *Latin* 'Great is the force of truth'

—Taylor.

58. **My lure is truth**

—Hawkshaw.

59. **Ne quid falsi** *Latin* 'Nothing false'
—Wollaston (of Shenton).

60. **Nihil verius** *Latin* 'Nothing more true'

—Weir.

61. **Nil veretur veritas** *Latin* 'Truth fears nothing'

—Napier.

62. **Norma tuta veritas** *Latin* 'Truth is a safe rule'

—Morrall.

63. **Omnia vincit veritas** *Latin* 'Truth conquers all things'
—Munn, Nash.

64. **Onward upward**
—Kentucky State University, Frankfort, Kentucky.

65. **Optima est veritas** *Latin* 'Truth is best'
—Thompson, Thomson.

66. **Orna verum** *Latin* 'Honor the truth'
—Weddell, Waddell.

67. **Patria veritas fides**   *Latin* 'Country, truth, faith'
—Everett (U.S.).

68. **Pellit mendacia verum**   *Latin* 'Truth unmasks falsehood'
—Heinrich Julius, Duke of Braunschweig-Wolfenbüttel (1564–1613).

69. **Pravda vít ezí**   *Slovak* 'Truth prevails'
—Czechoslovakia.

70. **Probitas veritas honos**   *Latin* 'Integrity, truth, and honor'
—Browne.

71. **Pro veritate**   *Latin* 'For truth'
—Keith (of Pittendrum).

72. **Pro veritate suffer fortiter**   *Latin* 'Endure bravely for the truth'
—Sharpless (U.S.).

73. **Quaere verum**   *Latin* 'Seek truth'
—Birchall.

74. **Quarere verum**   *Latin* 'To seek the truth'
—Carleton (V.).

75. **Quid verum atque decens**   *Latin* 'What is true and befitting'
—Ricketts (of Combe), Trevor.

76. **Quid verum atque decens curo et rogo**   *Latin* 'I care for and ask what is true and befitting'
—[Horace, *Ep.* i. 1. 11.] La Touche.

77. **Quod verum atque decens**   *Latin* 'What is true and befitting'
—Dungannon (V.).

78. **Quod verum tutum**   *Latin* 'What is true is safe'
—Courtenay.

79. **Quo veritas?**   *Latin* 'Whither is truth fled?'
—Pulteney.

80. **Re vera**   *Latin* 'In a state of truth'
—Reeve (U.S.).

81. **Sapientia et veritas**   *Latin* 'Wisdom and truth'
—Douglas (of Bads).

82. **Seek the truth**
—Northeast Louisiana University, Monroe, Louisiana.

83. **Semper veritas**   *Latin* 'Truth always'
—Lake City Community College, Lake City, Florida.

84. **Semper verus**   *Latin* 'Always true'
—Howe, Home (of Kames).

85. **Speed, strength, and truth united**
—Framework Knitters' Company.

86. **Speranza é verita** *Italian* 'Hope and truth'
—Pegler.

87. **Stat veritas** *Latin* 'Truth endures'
—Sanderman.

88. **Sto pro veritate** *Latin* 'I stand for the truth'
—Guthrie, Guthry.

89. **Sub cruce veritas** *Latin* 'Truth under the cross'
—Adams, Crosse.

90. **Tenes le vraye** *Old French* 'Hold to the truth'
—Townley.

91. **Tenez le vraye** *Old French* 'Keep (*or* speak) the truth'
—Townley (of Townley).

92. **The truth against the world**
—Byam, Edwards (U.S.).

93. **The truth makes free**
—Bluffton College, Bluffton, Ohio.

94. **The truth shall make you free**
—City College of San Francisco, San Francisco, California;
David Lipscomb College, Nashville, Tennessee.

95. **Through truth to freedom**
—Augsburg College, Minneapolis, Minnesota.

96. **Tiens à la vérité** *French* 'Adhere to truth'
—De Blaquiere (B.), Courtland, Hoffman, Lewthwait.

97. **Time tryeth troth**
—Trevelyan (Bt.).

98. **Truth**
—Leithbridge (Bt.).

99. **Truth, honor, and courtesy**
—Gentleman.

100. **Truth and beauty**
—Eccles (V.).

101. **Truth and freedom** *(from Greek)*
—Wakefield.

102. **Truth and liberty**
—Tylden (of Milsted).

103. **Truth/ Culture/ Knowledge**
>—Alexander City State Junior College, Alexander City, Alabama; Rochester Community College, Rochester, Minnesota.

104. **Truth even unto its innermost parts**
>—Brandeis University, Waltham, Massachusetts.

105. **Truth is the light**
>—Wax Chandlers' Company (London).

106. **Truth/ Knowledge/ Freedom**
>—Harding University, Searcy, Arkansas.

107. **Truth/ Knowledge/ Wisdom/ Education**
>—Independence Community College, Independence, Kansas.

108. **Truth prevails**
>—Gordon.

109. **Truth will prevail**
>—McKenzie (of Ardross).

110. **Truth/ Wisdom**
>—University of Southern Florida, Tampa, Florida.

111. **Tyme proveth truth**
>—Adlam.

112. **Unitas, veritas, caritas** *Latin* 'Unity, truth, charity'
>—Union Theological Seminary, New York, New York.

113. **Venit ab astris** *Latin* 'She (truth) came from the stars'
>—Keith.

114. **Vera sequor** *Latin* 'I follow truth'
>—Hale, Landon.

115. **Veritas** *Latin* 'Truth'
>—Eiston; Harvard University, Cambridge, Massachusetts; Dominican College of Blauvelt, Orangeburg, New York.

116. **Veritas, libertas** *Latin* 'Truth and liberty'
>—Abraham.

117. **Veritas, puritas** *Latin* 'Truth and purity'
>—Webster.

118. **Veritas cum libertate** *Latin* 'Truth with liberty'
>—Winthrop College, Rock Hill, South Carolina.

119. **Veritas et patria** *Latin* 'Truth and my country'
>—Hoadly.

120. **Veritas et virtus** *Latin* 'Truth and virtue'
—Mississippi College, Clinton, Mississippi.

121. **Veritas et virtus vincunt** *Latin* 'Truth and virtue prevail'
—Walsh.

122. **Veritas ingenio** *Latin* 'Truth with wit'
—Gordon.

123. **Veritas liberabit** *Latin* 'The truth will make you free'
—Lafayette College, Easton, Pennsylvania, Bodenham (of Rotherwas).

124. **Veritas liberabit vos** *Latin* 'The truth will set you free'
—Saint Augustine's College, Raleigh, North Carolina.

125. **Veritas liberavit** *Latin* 'Truth has freed me'
—Slingsby.

126. **Veritas/ libertas** *Latin* 'Truth/ liberty'
—Manatee Jr. College, Bradenton, Florida.

127. **Veritas magna est** *Latin* 'Truth is great'
—Jephson (Bt.).

128. **Veritas me dirigit** *Latin* 'Truth directs me'
—Brocklehurst.

129. **Veritas/ mores/ scientia** *Latin* 'Truth/ morals/ knowledge'
—East Texas Baptist College, Marshall, Texas.

130. **Veritas non opprimitur** *Latin* 'There is no crushing the truth'
—Calderwood.

131. **Veritas odit morem** *Latin* 'Truth hates custom'
—Parry.

132. **Veritas odium parit** *Latin* 'Truth breeds hatred'
—Kennedy.

133. **Veritas omnia vincit** *Latin* 'Truth conquers all things'
—Kedslie.

134. **Veritas praevalebit** *Latin* 'Truth shall prevail'
—Paul.

135. **Veritas premitur non opprimitur** *Latin* 'Truth may be oppressed, not suppressed'
—Karl Ludwig, Elector of the Palatinate (1617–80), Calderwood (of Pittedy and Dalkeith).

136. **Veritas quasi rosa resplendet** *Latin* 'The truth shows forth like a rose'
—Trew (U.S.).

137. **Veritas securis**   *Latin* 'Truth has authority'
—Scribner (U.S.).

138. **Veritas sine timore**   *Latin* 'Truth without fear'
—Phelps (U.S.).

139. **Veritas superabit**   *Latin* 'Truth will conquer'
—Hill (of Edinburgh).

140. **Veritas superabit montes**   *Latin* 'Truth shall cross mountains'
—Hill.

141. **Veritas temporis filia**   *Latin* 'Truth is the daughter of time'
—Queen Mary (1516–1558).

142. **Veritas via vitae**   *Latin* 'Truth is the way of life'
—Tyrell.

143. **Veritas victrix**   *Latin* 'Truth is conqueror'
—Wilde.

144. **Veritas vincet**   *Latin* 'Truth will conquer'
—Orpen (of Glancrough).

145. **Veritas vincit**   *Latin* 'The truth conquers'
—Southern Missionary College, Collegedale, Tennessee,
French, Keith, Parker (Co. Cork), Wright.

146. **Veritas vincit omnia**   *Latin* 'Truth conquers all things'
—Heinrich Julius, Duke of Braunschweig-Wolfenbüttel
(1564–1613); Waterhouse.

147. **Veritate et justitiâ**   *Latin* 'With truth and justice'
—Ximenes.

148. **Veritatem**   *Latin* 'Truth'
—Tatham.

149. **Veritatis assertor**   *Latin* 'The asserter of truth'
—Niblett.

150. **Veritatis cultores, fraudis inimici**   *Latin* 'Worshippers of truth,
enemies of falsehood'
—[Cicero, *De Off.* i. 30. 109.] Truth, the London Journal.

151. **Veritatis et aequitatis tenax**   *Latin* 'Persevering in truth and justice'
—Rust.

152. **Vérité sans peur**   *French* 'Truth without fear'
—Bedford, Gunning, Middleton (B.), Willoughby.

153. **Vérité soyez ma garde**   *French* 'Truth be my protection'
—Brewster.

154. **Vérité vient** *French* 'Truth comes'
—Vere.

155. **Vero nihil verius** *Latin* 'Nothing truer than truth'
—De Vere (Bt.), Vere (of Craigie Hall).

156. **Vero pro gratis** *Latin* 'Truly for free'
—Webster (U.S.).

157. **Verum atque decus** *Latin* 'The truth and rectitude'
—Brown, Lee.

158. **Verum dicit** *Latin* 'He speaks the truth'
—Stanford (U.S.).

159. **Verus** *Latin* 'True'
—Peters.

160. **Verus ad finem** *Latin* 'True to the end'
—Deucher Lizars, Peters.

161. **Verus et fidelis** *Latin* 'True and faithful'
—Parkin.

162. **Verus et fidelis semper** *Latin* 'True and faithful ever'
—Aylward.

163. **Verus et sedulus** *Latin* 'True and diligent'
—McCulloch.

164. **Via veritas et vita** *Latin* 'The way, the truth, and the life'
—Felician College, Chicago, Illinois.

165. **Vi et veritate** *Latin* 'By force and by truth'
—Sloan.

166. **Vigilans et verus** *Latin* 'Vigilant and true'
—Wenley.

167. **Vincit omnia veritas** *Latin* 'Truth conquers all things'
—Courcy; Eaton; Goodchild; Kingsale (B.); Laffan (Bt.);
Compton Community College, Compton, California.

168. **Vincit veritas** *Latin* 'Truth conquers'
—Alison (Bt.), Bery, Burn, Coote (Bt.), Dickin, Edwards,
Gort (V.), Galwey, Hastings, Napier, McKenny (Bt.),
Peacocke (Bt.), O'Shee, Shee, Morrison, Webster,
Orpen.

169. **Vires veritas** *Latin* 'Truth gives power'
—Kennedy (of Clowburn).

170. **Virtus impendere vero** *Latin* 'It is virtue to be devoted to truth'
—Brown.

171. **Virtus patientia veritas**   *Latin* 'Virtue, patience, truth'
—Johnson.

172. **Virtus veritas libertas**   *Latin* 'Virtue, truth, and freedom'
—Glossop B. C., U.K.

173. **Virtute et veritate**   *Latin* 'With virtue and truth'
—Blathwayte.

174. **Vir/veritas/vox**   *Latin* 'Man/truth/voice'
—California State Universities and Colleges.

175. **Vis veritatis magna**   *Latin* 'The force of truth is great'
—Hall.

176. **Vitam impendere vero**   *Latin* 'To pay your life for truth'
—[Juvenal *Sat.* iv. 93.] Jean Jacques Rousseau (1712–1778);
Arthur Schopenhauer (1788–1860).

177. **Vitam impendere vero**   *Latin* 'To devote life to the truth'
—Brown, Ramage, Reichel.

178. **Vivat veritas**   *Latin* 'Let truth endure'
—Duncan.

179. **Weave truth with truth**
—Weavers' Company (London).

180. **With truth and diligence**
—Lucy (of Charlecote).

UBIQUITY

1. **Cogi posse negat**   *Latin* 'He says that he cannot be compelled'
—Masterton (U.S.).

2. **Cu re bu (or Cu reubha)**   *Gaelic* 'I have broken my hold'
—O'Farrell.

3. **Hic et ubique terrarum**   *Latin* 'Here, there, and everywhere'
—University of Paris.

4. **J'ai la clef**   *French* 'I have the key'
—Grieve, Grive.

5. **Live, love, think, pray, dare**
—United Daughters of the Confederacy.

6. **Naturae minister**   *Latin* 'A servant of nature'
—Helham.

7. **Non haec sed me**   *Latin* 'Not these things, but me'
—Scrope.

8. **Proprio vos sanguine pasco**   *Latin*   'I feed you with my own blood'
—Cantrell (Co. Lancaster).

9. **Refero**   *Latin*   'I bring back'
—Campbell (of Gargunnock).

10. **Ubique**   *Latin*   'Everywhere'
—Royal Artillery, Royal Engineers.

UNCLASSIFIED

1. **Acu rem tetigit**   *Latin*   'He hit the nail on the head'
—Taylor (U.S.).

2. **Aquilae vitem pocula vitam**   *Latin*   'Let me avoid the cup—the sustenance of the eagle'
—Boteler.

3. **Be not wanting**
—Bazilie.

4. **Betrayed, not conquered**
—Howden (B.).

5. **Creag dhubh chloinn Chatain**   *Scots Gaelic*   'The black rock of clan Chattan'
—Macpherson.

6. **Creag dubh**   *Scots Gaelic*   'A black rock'
—Farquharson.

7. **Cum grano salis**   *Latin*   'With a grain of salt'
—Kerr.

8. **Dakyns, the devil's in the hempe**
—Dakyns

9. **De me praesagia olim**   *Latin*   'Once (there were) prophecies about me'
—Hasell (U.S.).

10. **Dissipatae**   *Latin*   'Dispersed'
—Scrymgeour (of Dundee), Scrimgeour.

11. **Echel Coryg**   *Gaelic*   'The Axle of Corgy'
—White.

12. **En martélant**   *French*   'Through hammering'
—Martin.

13. **E pur si muove!**   *Italian*   'But it does move!'
—[Galileo, speaking before the Inquisition about the revolution of the earth] Williams and Norgate, publishers, London.

14. **Eundo** *Latin* 'By going'

—Russell.

15. **Every point**

—Young.

16. **Fabula sed vera** *Latin* 'A story, but a true one'

—Story.

17. **Fare wel til then**

—Goodricke.

18. **Ferro non gladio** *Latin* 'By iron, not the sword'

—Guest (Bt.).

19. **Fingit premendo** *Latin* 'He shapes by pressing'

—Cutcliffe.

20. **For my Duchas**

—Grant

21. **Française** *French* 'French'

—Harris.

22. **Fugite fures omnes** *Latin* 'Fly all ye thieves'

—Johnson (of Wilmslow).

23. **Gare le pied fort** *French* 'Clear the way for the strong foot'

—Bedford.

24. **Have at all**

—Drummond (of Carlourie).

25. **Have wandered**

—Edwards (U.S.).

26. **Henricus a Henrico** *Latin* 'Henry from Henry'

—Fitz-Henry.

27. **Holden**

—Holden.

28. **I beare the bel**

—Bell (of Rammerscales).

29. **I byde ye fair**

—Maxwell.

30. **I face all weathers**

—Mackenzie, Mackintosh.

31. **Ilias in nuce** *Latin* 'An Iliad in a nutshell'

—Ogden.

32. **Incipe** *Latin* 'Begin'

—Branthwaite.

33. **In multis, in magnis, in bonis** *Latin* 'In many, in great, in good things'

—Bowes (of Bradley).

34. **Interna praestant** *Latin* 'Inward things are best'

—Arbuthnot.

35. **In utroque** *Latin* 'In both'

—Valange, Wallange.

36. **In utrumque** *Latin* 'For both'

—Ranken.

37. **Iterum, iterum, iterumque** *Latin* 'Again, again, and again'

—Foote.

38. **Kynd kynn knawne kepe** *Middle English, dialectal* 'Keep your own kin-kind'

—Kaye (of Denby Grange, bt.).

39. **Light on**

—Lighton (of Ullishaven).

40. **Magnes et adamas** *Latin* 'The magnet and adamant'

—Ross.

41. **Migremus hinc** *Latin* 'We shall migrate hence'

—Willmott.

42. **Mihi tibi** *Latin* 'To me and to you'

—Pope (Co. Shropshire).

43. **Montjoie Saint-Denys** *French*

—[an ancient war-cry of the French kings] Town of St. Denis.

44. **Nec arrogo, nec dubito** *Latin* 'I neither arrogate nor hesitate'

—Assherton.

45. **Nec avarus nec profusus** *Latin* 'Neither greedy nor lavish'

—Bryan.

46. **Nec deficit alter** *Latin* 'Nor is another wanting'

—[Vergil, *Aen.* vi. 143.] Gregory, Roddam (of Roddam), Smith.

47. **Nec momentum sine linea** *Latin* 'No moment without a line'

—[Pliny, *Nat. Hist.* xxxv. 36. 10.] Cardinal Richelieu.

48. **Non nobis Domine** *Latin* 'Not unto us, O Lord'

—Willis.

49. **Non nobis esto [sic] Latin**

—Gould.

50. **Opinionem vincere omnium** *Latin* 'To overcome the opinion of all'

—Antill (U.S.).

51. **Over fork over**

—Conyngham (M.), Cunninghame (Bt.), Cunninghame (of Kilmaurs, Milucray, Corshill, etc.).

52. **Par pari refero** *Latin* 'I return like to like'

—Wall (U.S.).

53. **Perforatus** *Latin* 'Bored'

—Board.

54. **Pour quoy non** *Old French* 'Why not'

—Maundy.

55. **Projeci** *Latin* 'I have thrown'

—Main.

56. **Quis occursabit?** *Latin* 'Who will encounter me?'

—Hamilton.

57. **Sanguine inscribam** *Latin* 'I will inscribe it with blood'

—Buchanan.

58. **Sans venin** *French* 'Without venom'

—Guinand (U.S.).

59. **Secum cuique** *Latin* 'To everyone with himself'

—Thomson.

60. **Set on**

—Seton (of Fordingbridge), Campbell.

61. **Simili frondescit virga metallo** *Latin* 'The bough has leaves of similar metal'

—[Vergil *Aen.* vi. 144.] Calmady.

62. **Standard**

—Kidder.

63. **Te pro te** *Latin* 'Thee for thee'

—Savage.

64. **Tevertite** *Latin* 'Return ye'

—Wardrop, Smollet, Herries.

65. **The entrance to an enchanted world**

—Clapp (U.S.).

66. **The grit poul**

—Mercer.

67. **The right and sleep**

—White (U.S.).

68. **The wicked borroweth and payeth not again**
—Pownall (U.S.).

69. **Thus**
—St. Vincent (V.), Jervis.

70. **Thus far**
—Campbell (of Glenfalloch).

71. **Tout est en haut**   *French* 'All is above'
—Whitford.

72. **Transfigam**   *Latin* 'I will transfix'
—Colt (of Gartsherrie), Coult (of Inveresk).

73. **Tu vincula frange**   *Latin* 'Break the chains'
—Napier.

74. **Tynctus cruore Saraceno**   *Latin* 'Tinged with Saracen's blood'
—Tynte.

75. **Uno avulso, non deficit alter**   *Latin* 'When one is torn away another is not wanting'
—Kingdom of Austria.

76. **Ut apes geometriam**   *Latin* 'As bees geometry'
—Petty.

77. **Vade ad formicam**   *Latin* 'Go to the ant'
—[Prov. v. 6.] Anketel.

78. **Vectis**   *Latin* 'A lever'
—Holmes.

79. **Vir gregis**   *Latin* 'A man of the crowd'
—Clarke.

80. **Watch the temptation**
—Keith.

81. **Ye great pule**
—Mercer.

UNIQUENESS

1. **An uncommon experience that lasts a lifetime**
—University of Redlands, Redlands, California.

2. **Chacun à son goût**   *French* 'To each his own'
—Smith (U.S.).

3. **Chacun le sien**   *French* 'Every man his own'
—Bourke.

4. **None such**
                    —Epsom and Ewell B. C., U.K.

5. **Rara avis in terris** *Latin* 'A rarity on this earth'
                    —Kett.

6. **Ung tout seul** *Old French* 'Only one'
                    —Verney.

7. **Unicus est** *Latin* 'He is the only one'
                    —Uniacke.

UNITY

1. **Amore sitis uniti** *Latin* 'Be ye united in love'
                    —Tin-plate Workers' and Wire-workers' Company.

2. **Be mindful to unite**
                    —Brodie (of Lethen).

3. **Bersekutu bertambah mutu** *Malay* 'Unity is strength'
                    —Malaysia.

4. **Bhinneka tunggal ika** *Malay* 'Unity through diversity'
                    —Republic of Indonesia.

5. **Bon accord** *French* 'Good harmony'
                    —Towers.

6. **By concord and industry**
                    —Droylsden U. D. C., U.K.

7. **Castello fortior concordia** *Latin* 'Concord is stronger than a fortress'
                    —Northampton C. B. C., U.K.

8. **Concordans** *Latin* 'Agreeing'
                    —Order of Concord, Brandenburgh.

9. **Concordia, integretate, industria** *Latin* 'By concord, integrity, and industry'
                    —Baron de Rothschild, Rothschild.

10. **Concordia crescimus** *Latin* 'We increase by concord'
                    —Bromhead.

11. **Concordia ditat** *Latin* 'Union enriches'
                    —Julius Ernst, Duke of Braunschweig-Lüneberg-Danneberg (1571–1636).

12. **Concordia et harmonia** *Latin* 'By concord and harmony'
                    —Gallini.

13. **Concordia et industria** *Latin* 'By concord and industry'
—Dent.

14. **Concordia et sedulitate** *Latin* 'By union and diligence'
—Goldsmid(Bt.).

15. **Concordiâ parvae res crescunt** *Latin* 'Small things increase by concord'
—Merchant Taylors' Company.

16. **Concordia praesto** *Latin* 'With one consent we are ready'
—Forbes (of Ballogie).

17. **Concordia res crescunt** *Latin* 'Things increase by union'
—Bromhead (Bt.).

18. **Concordia res parvae crescunt** *Latin* 'Small things increase by concord'
—The States-General.

19. **Concordia vim dat** *Latin* 'Concord gives strength'
—Blumberg.

20. **Concordia vincit** *Latin* 'Unanimity conquers'
—Cochran (of Aberdeen).

21. **Conjunctio firmat** *Latin* 'Union gives strength'
—Middleton.

22. **Cor et manus concordant** *Latin* 'My heart and my hand are in concord'
—Farrel.

23. **Cor unum** *Latin* 'One heart'
—Soke of Peterborough C. C., U.K.

24. **Cor unum, via una** *Latin* 'One heart, one way'
—Cecil, Exeter (M.), Mountsandford (B.), Sandford, Wills.

25. **Distantia jungit** *Latin* 'It joins things that were apart'
—Case.

26. **Dulce est fratres habitare in unum** *Latin* 'It is pleasant for brothers to dwell together in unity'
—[after Ps. cxxxiii. 1.] Friedrich II, Duke of Saxony-Gotha and Altenburg (1676–1732).

27. **Dulce est fratres inhabitare in unum** *Latin* 'It is pleasant for brothers to dwell together in unity'
—[after Ps. cxxxiii. 1.] Rudolph August, Duke of Braunschweig-Wolfenbüttel (1627–1704).

28. **Ego accedo** *Latin* 'I assent'
—Orr.

29. **E pluribus unum**   *Latin* 'One out of many'
—United States of America.

30. **Ex concordia victoriae spes**   *Latin* 'Hope of victory through union'
—Barnard.

31. **Ex septem unus**   *Latin* 'From seven, one'
—Ketchum (U.S.).

32. **Ex unitate incrementum**   *Latin* 'Increase comes from unity'
—Guthrie, Guthry; Guthry, Guthrie.

33. **Ex unitate vires**   *Latin* 'Strength from unity'
—Pembrokeshire C. C., U.K.; Republic of South Africa.

34. **Ex uno omnia**   *Latin* 'All things are from one'
—Ashmole.

35. **Faith, unity, discipline**   *(from Urdu and Bengali)*
—Republic of Pakistan.

36. **Fecit eos in gentem unam**   *Latin* 'This made them into one people'
—Scots Guards, U.K.

37. **Fortius dum juncta**   *Latin* 'Stronger while united'
—Hay.

38. **Fratres habitent inter se concordes**   *Latin* 'Let brethren dwell together in unity'
—[Ps. cxxxiii.] Joseph.

39. **Freedom and unity**
—State of Vermont.

40. **God grant unity**
—Wheelwrights' Company.

41. **Happiness and prosperity through unity**   *(from Burmese)*
—Union of Burma.

42. **Harambee**   *Swahili* 'Together'
—Republic of Kenya.

43. **Insolubili nexu uniti**   *Latin* 'Joined in an indissoluble bond'
—Rudolf August, Duke of Braunschweig-Wolfenbüttel (1627–1704).

44. **In union strength**
—Huston-Tillotson College, Austin, Texas.

45. **In unity progress**
—Ilford B. C., U.K.

46. **Juncti valemus**   *Latin* 'Being joined we are powerful'
   —Walker.

47. **Jungor ut implear**   *Latin* 'I am joined that I may become full'
   —Meik.

48. **La liaison fait ma valeur, la division me perd**   *French* 'Union makes me valuable, division destroys me'
   —Order of the Fan.

49. **Liberty and union, now and forever, one and inseparable**
   —State of North Dakota.

50. **L'union fait la force**   *French* 'Unity is strength'
   —Kingdom of Belgium, Republic of Haiti.

51. **L'Union fait la force**   *French* 'Union constitutes power'
   —Order of Leopold (Belgium).

52. **Many minds, one heart**
   —Chelmsford B. C., U.K.

53. **One and all**
   —Cornwall C. C., U.K.

54. **One faith, one king, one law**
   —Bourk.

55. **One heart, one way**
   —Stourbridge B. C., U.K.

56. **One people, one nation, one destiny**
   —Cooperative Republic Guyana.

57. **One Zambia, one nation**
   —Republic of Zambia.

58. **Out of many, one people**
   —Jamaica.

59. **Preserved by concord**
   —Grand Sachem of the Tammany Society (Columbian Order) of New York, Sons of Liberty.

60. **Quae juncta firma**   *Latin* 'Union is strength'
   —Lesly (of Kinivie).

61. **Quis separabit?**   *Latin* 'Who shall separate us?'
   —Seal of State of South Carolina.

62. **Quis separabit?**   *Latin* 'Who shall separate (Great Britain from Ireland)?'
   —Order of St. Patrick; 5th (Royal Irish) Lancers; 86th Regiment (Royal Irish Rifles); 88th Connaught Rangers.

63. **Quos amor et virtus sociant sors nulla resolvet** *Latin* 'Those whom love and virtue unite no fate shall divide'
—Johann Georg II, Prince of Anhalt-Dessau (1627–93).

64. **Rosa concordiae signum** *Latin* 'A rose, the emblem of harmony'
—Northamptonshire C. C., U.K.

65. **Singula cum valeant sunt meliora simul** *Latin* 'When they are strong separately they are more so together'
—Stuart.

66. **State sovereignty, national union**
—State of Illinois.

67. **Sunt tria haec unum** *Latin* 'These three are one'
—Morison.

68. **Texas one and indivisible**
—Seal of State of Texas.

69. **That they may all be one**
—United Church of Christ.

70. **The knot unites**
—Staffordshire C. C., U.K.

71. **The land divided, the world united**
—Republic of Panama.

72. **The union**
—State of Oregon.

73. **Together**
—Burrows.

74. **Together we aspire, together we achieve**
—Trinidad and Tobago.

75. **Travail, justice, solidarité** *French* 'Work, justice, solidarity'
—Republic of Guinea.

76. **Tria juncta in uno** *Latin* 'Three joined in one'
—Order of the Bath (Britain).

77. **Tribus unum** *Latin* 'From three, one'
—Trinity University, San Antonio, Texas.

78. **Uhuru na umoja** *Swahili* 'Liberty and unity'
—United Republic of Tanzania.

79. **Undeb hedd llwyddiant** *Welsh* 'Unity, peace, prosperity'
—Breconshire C. C., U.K.

80. **Un Dieu, un roi** *French* 'One God, one king'
—D'Arcy, Lyttleton.

81. **Un Dieu, un roy, un coeur**   *Old French* 'One God, one king, one heart'
    —Lake (Bt.).

82. **Un Dieu, un roy, un foy**   *Old French* 'One God, one king, one faith'
    —Curle, Rush.

83. **Un Dieu et un Roi**   *French* 'One God and one king'
    —De Jersey.

84. **Une foy, une loy**   *Old French* 'One faith, one law'
    —Sorel.

85. **Ung Dieu, ung loy, ung foy**   *Old French* 'One God, one law, one faith'
    —Burke (of St. Cleras).

86. **Ung Dieu, ung roy, une loy**   *Old French* 'One God, one king, one law'
    —Town of Lyons, France.

87. **Ung Dieu et ung roy**   *Old French* 'One God and one king'
    —Daray, Hatherton (B.).

88. **Ung nous servons**   *Old French* 'We serve as one'
    —Pembroke B. C., U.K.

89. **Ung par tout, tout par ung**   *Old French* 'One by everything and everything by one'
    —Wriothesley.

90. **Ung roy, ung foy, ung loy**   *Old French* 'One king, one faith, one law'
    —Burke (of Marble Hill, Bt.), Burke (of Kilcoran, Owen, and Clongowna), Clanricarde (M.), De Burgo (Bt.), Rush.

91. **Ung sent ung soleil**   *Old French* 'One faith, one sun'
    —Lloyd-Verney, Verney.

92. **Unidad, paz, justicia**   *Spanish* 'Unity, peace, justice'
    —Republic of Equatorial Guinea.

93. **Union, justice, confidence**
    —State of Louisiana.

94. **Union, justice and confidence**
    —Northwestern State University, Natchitoches, Louisiana; Alexandria Vocational-Technical Institute, Alexandria, Louisiana.

95. **Union, travail, justice**   *French* 'Union, work, justice'
    —Gabon Republic.

96. **Union/ confidence/ justice**
—Louisiana Technical University, Ruston, Louisiana.

97. **Unione augetur** *Latin* 'It is increased by union'
—Miller.

98. **Unione minima vigent** *Latin* 'The smallest things flourish by union'
—Coghlan.

99. **Unita durant** *Latin* 'Things united endure'
—Heinrich Julius, Duke of Braunschweig-Wolfenbüttel (1564–1613); Friedrich August I, Elector of Saxony (1670–1733).

100. **Unita fortior** *Latin* 'The stronger being united'
—Rundall; Scots Guards, 2nd Battalion; Woodmongers' Company.

101. **Unitas, veritas, caritas** *Latin* 'Unity, truth, charity'
—Union Theological Seminary, New York, New York.

102. **Unitas societatis stabilitas** *Latin* 'Unity is the support of society'
—Parish Clerks' Company.

103. **Unitate fortior** *Latin* 'Stronger by union'
—Beck; Heston and Isleworth B. C., U.K.

104. **Unitate praestans** *Latin* 'Excelling by unity'
—Preston R. D. C., U.K.

105. **Unite**
—Brodie (Bt.), Brodie (of Brodie).

106. **Unité, dignité, travail** *French* 'Unity, dignity, work'
—Central African Republic.

107. **Unité, travail, justice** *French* 'Unity, work, justice'
—Republic of Upper Volta.

108. **Unité, travail, progrès** *French* 'Unity, work, progress'
—Republic of Chad, Kingdom of Burundi, Republic of Congo.

109. **United to serve**
—Southwark B. C., U.K.

110. **United we stand, divided we fall**
—Eastern Kentucky University, Richmond, Kentucky; States of Kentucky and Missouri.

111. **Uniti progrediemur** *Latin* 'United we shall go forward'
—Gabon Republic.

112. **Unity, freedom, justice**
—Sierra Leone.

113. **Unity and faith**
—Federation of Nigeria.

114. **Unity and freedom**
—Malawi.

115. **Unity and loyalty**
—Borough of Chippenham.

116. **Unity and progress**
—Melksham U. D. C., U.K.

117. **Unity in diversity**
—General Federation of Women's Clubs.

118. **Un peuple, un but, une foi**   *French* 'One people, one goal, one faith'
—Republic of Mali, Republic of Senegal.

119. **Un roy, une foy, une loy**   *Old French* 'One king, one faith, one law'
—De Burgh.

120. **Virginitas et unitas nostra fraternitas**   *Latin* 'Chastity and unity form our brotherhood'
—Pin-makers' Company.

121. **Virtus unita fortior**   *Latin* 'Strength is increased by unity'
—Andorra.

122. **Vis unita fortior**   *Latin* 'Strength united is stronger'
—1776 seal of New Hampshire; Brook; Flood; Hales; Hosken; Lidwell; Moore; Mountcashel (E.); Crosby B. C., Stoke-on-Trent City and C. B. C., U.K.

123. **We are one**
—Armourers' and Braziers' Company (London).

124. **Workers of all countries, unite!**
—Union of Soviet Socialist Republics.

UNSELFISHNESS (*See also* GENEROSITY; HUMANITY; KINDNESS.)

1. **Agere pro aliis**   *Latin* 'To act for others'
—Ashton.

2. **Alteri, si tibi**   *Latin* 'To another, as if to thyself'
—Harvey (Co. Norfolk), Saville-Onley.

3. **L'un pour l'autre**   *French* 'One for the other'
        —Yates (U.S.).

4. **Non nobis**   *Latin* 'Not unto us'
        —Woodd.

5. **Non nobis nascimur**   *Latin* 'We are not born for ourselves'
        —Lucy, Webb.

6. **Non nobis nati**   *Latin* 'Born not for ourselves'
        —Frank.

7. **Non nobis sed communitati**   *Latin* 'Not for ourselves but for the community'
        —Bexley B. C., U.K.

8. **Non nobis sed omnibus**   *Latin* 'Not for ourselves, but for all mankind'
        —Ashe (of Ashfield, etc.); North Walsham U. D. C., U.K.

9. **Non nobis solum**   *Latin* 'Not for ourselves only'
        —Blayney, Eardley, Fardell, Jacob, Lawless, Moss, Wilson.

10. **Non nobis solum**   *Latin* 'Not for ourselves alone'
        —Beckenham B. C., U.K.

11. **Non nobis solum, sed toti mundo nati**   *Latin* 'Born not for ourselves only, but for the whole world'
        —Rokeby (B.).

12. **Non nobis solum nati**   *Latin* 'We are not born for ourselves alone'
        —Street (U.S.).

13. **Non nobis solum nati sumus**   *Latin* 'We are not born for ourselves only'
        —[Cicero, *de Off*. i. 7. 5.] Bradshaw.

14. **Non nobis tantum nati**   *Latin* 'Born not only for ourselves'
        —Lee Warner (of Walsingham Abbey), Lee Warner (of East Dereham, Co. Norfolk).

15. **Non sibi**   *Latin* 'Not for himself'
        —Cleland, Connell, Connely, Cullen, Lyde, Sage.

16. **Non sibi, cunctis**   *Latin* 'Not for himself, for all men'
        —Moir.

17. **Non sibi sed aliis**   *Latin* 'Not for ourselves, but for others'
        —Colonial seal of Georgia, Vynne.

18. **Non sibi sed toti**   *Latin* 'Not for self but for all'
        —Hampstead B. C., U.K.

19. **Non sibi solum**   *Latin* 'Not alone for self'

—Devan.

20. **Non tua te moveant, sed publica vota**   *Latin* 'Let not your own, but the public wishes move you'

—Alleyne (Bt.).

21. **Nos non nobis**   *Latin* 'We not for ourselves'

—Wilberforce.

22. **Not for ourselves alone**

—Barnes B. C., U.K.

23. **Pro me ipso et aliis**   *Latin* 'For myself and others'

—Carmichael.

24. **Sic vos non vobis**   *Latin* 'So you are not for yourselves'
—Baldock U. D. C., U.K., Walrond, Franks.

25. **Sui oblitus commodi**   *Latin* 'Regardless of his own interest'

—Asgile.

USEFULNESS (*See also* SERVICE.)

1. **Bonus justus et utilis**   *Latin* 'Good, just, and useful'

—Lerrier.

2. **Dulce quod utile**   *Latin* 'That is agreeable which is useful'
—Strang, Strong (Bt.).

3. **Nihil utile quod non honestum**   *Latin* 'Nothing dishonorable is useful'

—Dovers, Moor, Moore (of Fawley).

4. **Non sine usu**   *Latin* 'Not without use'

—Maxwell.

5. **Omne tulit punctum qui miscuit utile dulci**   *Latin* 'He has gained every point who has mixed the useful with the agreeable'
—Warren (of Shipperton).

6. **Pietas ad omnia utilis**   *Latin* 'Righteousness is useful for all things'
—Heinrich Posthumus (1572–1635); Georg, Duke of
Braunschweig-Lüneburg (1582–1641); Johann,
Duke of Braunschweig-Lüneburg (1583–1628);
Friedrich Wilhelm II, Duke of Saxony-Altenburg
(1603–69); Christian Ernst, Margrave of
Brandenburg-Baireuth (1644–1712); Johann
Adolf II, Duke of Saxony-Weissenfels
(1685–1746).

7. **Portio mea quod utile** *Latin* 'May what is useful be my portion'
—Flack.

8. **Pretiosum quod utile** *Latin* 'What is useful is valuable'
—Affleck (Bt.).

9. **Pretiosum quod utile est** *Latin* 'What is useful is valuable'
—Auchinleck.

10. **Prodesse quam conspici** *Latin* 'To be useful rather than to be seen (as useful)'
—Miami University, Oxford, Ohio.

11. **Pro utilitate** *Latin* 'For utility'
—Tennant.

12. **Quid justum non quod utile** *Latin* 'What is just, not what is useful (expedient)'
—Phillips, Phillips (of Garendon Park).

13. **Quod utile** *Latin* 'That which is useful'
—Goldie, Gouldie.

14. **Utile dulci** *Latin* 'The useful with the agreeable'
—Spedding, Shuttleworth.

15. **Utile et dulce** *Latin* 'The useful and agreeable'
—Riddell (Bt.).

16. **Utilem pete finem** *Latin* 'Seek a useful end'
—Marshall.

17. **Utile primo** *Latin* 'Useful at first'
—Reade.

18. **Ut prosim** *Latin* 'That I may be of use'
—Foley (B.), Grigg.

19. **Ut prosim aliis** *Latin* 'That I may be of use to others'
—Greenwood, Jennings.

UTENSILS

1. **Aut malleus hodie aut incus cras** *Latin* 'Either a hammer today or an anvil tomorrow'
—Underwood (U.S.).

2. **By hammer and hand all arts do stand**
—Blacksmiths' Company.

3. **Den Stauf trage ich** *German* 'I carry the tankard'
—Stauffer (U.S.).

4. **The axe is laid at the root of the tree**
—[Matt. iii. 10.] Woodmongers' Company.

VENGEANCE

1. **Armet nos ultio regum**   *Latin* 'Let vengeance for princes arm us'
—Portal.

2. **Bienfaicia paieray malfaictz vangeray**   *Old French* 'Benefits I will reward, injuries I will avenge'
—Walrond.

3. **Dial gwaed Cymru**   *Welsh* 'Avenge the blood of Wales'
—Lloyd, Mostyn (B.).

4. **Haec dextra vindex principis et patriae**   *Latin* 'This right hand is the avenger of my prince and country'
—Ramsey.

5. **Non morietur inultus**   *Latin* 'He shall not die unavenged'
—[after Vergil, *Aen.* ii. 670.] Chevalier Bayard.

6. **Non revertar inultus**   *Latin* 'I will not return unrevenged'
—Lisburne (E.).

7. **Perspicere quam ulcisci**   *Latin* 'To discern rather than to avenge'
—Manigault (U.S.).

8. **Si j'avance, suivez-moi; si je fuis, tuez-moi; si je meurs, vengez-moi**   *French* 'If I advance, follow me; if I flee, kill me; if I die, avenge me'
—La Roche-Jaquelin.

9. **Thournib' creve'th**   *Gaelic* 'I give you the palm of victory (i.e., the laurel)'
—Creagh.

10. **Triumpho morte tam vitâ**   *Latin* 'I triumph equally in death as in life'
—Allen (V.).

VICTORY   (*See also* CONQUEST; SUCCESS.)

1. **A Deo victoria**   *Latin* 'Victory from God'
—Graham, Graeme.

2. **Amat victoria curam**   *Latin* 'Victory loves sorrow', i.e., 'No victory without sorrow'
—Matthias, Emperor of Germany (1557–1619).

3. **Amat victoria curam** *Latin* 'Victory and care are close friends'
(*lit.* 'Victory loves care')
—Clark (Bt.), Clerk (of Penicuik, Co. Edinburgh, Bt.),
Clerk (of Norwich).

4. **A Nilo victoria** *Latin* 'Victory from the Nile'
—Gould.

5. **Ante victoriam ne cane triumphum** *Latin* 'Before the victory do
not celebrate a triumph'
—Thompson (U.S.).

6. **Aude et prevalebis** *Latin* 'Dare, and thou shalt prevail'
—Frend.

7. **Aut vincam aut peream** *Latin* 'I will either conquer or perish'
—Purcell.

8. **Britannia victrix** *Latin* 'Britannia victorious'
—Northesk (E.).

9. **Buagh** *Scots Gaelic* 'Victory'
—Ternan.

10. **Bua noo bawse** *Gaelic* 'Victory or death'
—O'Hagan.

11. **Cura dat victoriam** *Latin* 'Caution gives victory'
—Denham.

12. **De caelo victoria** *Latin* 'Victory is from heaven'
—Friedrich II, the Wise, Elector of the Palatinate
(1483–1556).

13. **E rege et victoria** *Latin* 'From the king and by victory'
—Bulen.

14. **Essorant victorieux** *French* 'Soaring victorious'
—Nicolle.

15. **Ex campo victoriae** *Latin* 'From the field of victory'
—Campbell.

16. **Ex concordia victoriae spes** *Latin* 'Hope of victory through
union'
—Barnard.

17. **Ex hoc victoria signo** *Latin* 'Victory (is gained) from this sign'
—Rattary (of Scotland).

18. **God giveth the victory**
—Simon.

19. **Had on and win**
—Hadwen.

20. **In cruce victoria** *Latin* 'Victory through the cross'
—Snell.

21. **In veritate victoria** *Latin* 'Victory is in truth'
—Akroyd (of Bankfield), Huntingdon (E.), Hastings (Bt.), Abney, Hastings (of Willesley Hall), Ingham.

22. **In veritate victoria** *Latin* 'Victory is in truth'
—Loughborough B. C., U.K.

23. **I the people am victorious** *(from Greek)*
—Nicolas (of London).

24. **Jussu regis India subacta** *Latin* 'India subdued by the king's command'
—Munro (Bt.).

25. **Laissir ronam aboo** *Gaelic* 'The torch that leads to victory'
—Mahoney.

26. **La mayor victorio de ellas es el bien merecellas** *Spanish* 'The greatest victory is in having deserved it'
—Guevera.

27. **Lamh foistenach abu** *Gaelic* 'The gentle hand defying'
—O'Sullivan.

28. **Manibus victoria dextris** *Latin* 'Victory by our right hands'
—Adair (Bt.).

29. **Manibus victoria dextris** *Latin* 'By our right hands victory'
—Lord Waveney.

30. **Mortem aut triumphum** *Latin* 'Death or victory'
—Clifton (of Lytham and Clyfton).

31. **Non est sine pulvere palma** *Latin* 'The palm is not obtained without toil'
—Yarburgh (of Heslington).

32. **Non praeda, sed victoria** *Latin* 'Not plunder, but victory'
—Chambers.

33. **Non providentia sed victoria** *Latin* 'Not in providence but in victory'
—Coffy.

34. **Obstando supera** *Latin* 'Overcome by resisting'
—Scott.

35. **Patientia victrix** *Latin* 'Patience is victorious'
—Dalton.

36. **Pax una triumphis innumeris potior**   *Latin* 'One peace is better than countless victories'
>>> —Friedrich, Duke of Braunschweig-Lüneburg (1574–1648); Friedrich Wilhelm, Elector of Brandenburg (1620–88).

37. **Perrumpo**   *Latin* 'I break through'
>>> —Ramsay.

38. **Perseverantia victor**   *Latin* 'Victor through perseverance'
>>> —Campbell.

39. **Rapit ense triumphos**   *Latin* 'He gains victories by the sword'
>>> —Smith.

40. **Sequitur victoria fortes**   *Latin* 'Victory follows the brave'
>>> —Campbell.

41. **Sine clade sterno**   *Latin* 'I defeat without destruction'
>>> —Thicknesse.

42. **Sine labore non paritur gloriosa victoria**   *Latin* 'Without labor no glorious victory is won'
>>> —Albrecht, Duke of Saxony-Coburg (1648–99).

43. **Sionnach aboo**   *Gaelic* 'The fox defying'
>>> —Fox.

44. **Sola ubique triumphans**   *Latin* 'Alone triumphant everywhere'
>>> —Carville.

45. **Sola ubique triumphat**   *Latin* 'Alone she triumphs everywhere'
>>> —Order of Ladies Slaves to Virtue.

46. **Soli Deo victoria**   *Latin* 'To God alone the victory'
>>> —Johann Friedrich, Elector of Saxony (1503–54).

47. **Stabilitate et victoria**   *Latin* 'By steadfastness and victory'
>>> —Simmons.

48. **Sui victoria indicat regem**   *Latin* 'Victory over self marks the king'
>>> —Rye.

49. **Tandem bona causa triumphat**   *Latin* 'At length the good cause triumphs'
>>> —Heinrich Julius, Duke of Braunschweig-Wolfenbüttel (1564–1613); Joachim Karl, Duke of Braunschweig (1573–1615); Otto the Younger, Duke of Braunschweig-Lüneburg-Harburg (1528–1603); August, Count of the Palatinate of Sulzbach (1582–1632); August, Elector of Saxony (1526–86); Christian, Duke of Schleswig-Holstein (1570–1633).

50. **Tenebras expellit et hostes** *Latin* 'He drives forth darkness and the foe'
—Smith.

51. **Terra marique victor** *Latin* 'Victorious by land and sea'
—Trigger.

52. **Unser glaub ist der sieg, der die welt überwunden hatt** *German* 'The victory that overcometh the world, even our faith'
—[1 John, v. 4.] August, Prince of Anhalt-Plötzkau (1575–1653).

53. **Valebit** *Latin* 'He will prevail'
—Lysons (of Hemsted).

54. **Vel exuviae triumphant** *Latin* 'Even the spoils triumphant'
—Queen's (Royal W. Surrey) Regiment.

55. **Victoria** *Latin* 'Victory'
—Conqueror, La Beaume, Locock (Bt.).

56. **Victoria, fortitudo, virtus** *Latin* 'Victory, fortitude, and virtue'
—Young.

57. **Victoria a Domino** *Latin* 'Victory from the Lord'
—Webb.

58. **Victoria concordiâ crescit** *Latin* 'Victory increases by concord'
—Amherst (B.), Amherst (of Didlington Hall, Co. Norfolk).

59. **Victoria gloria merces** *Latin* 'Victory, glory, reward'
—Berwick-upon-Tweed B. C., U.K.

60. **Victoriam coronat Christus** *Latin* 'Christ crowns the victory'
—Campbell (of Abernchill, bt.).

61. **Victoria non praeda** *Latin* 'Victory, not booty'
—Durham (of Largo), Sandilands.

62. **Victoria signum** *Latin* 'The emblem of victory'
—Taylor.

63. **Victoria vel mors** *Latin* 'Victory or death'
—Macdonald, McDowall.

64. **Victorious**
—O'Rourke.

65. **Victor sine sanguine** *Latin* 'A victor without blood'
—Smith.

66. **Victory for us** *(from Arabic)*
—Republic of the Sudan.

67. **Victory or death**
>—O'Hagan.

68. **Victrix patientia duris**   *Latin* 'Patience is victorious in hardship'
>—Carter.

69. **Vigilando ascendimus**   *Latin* 'We rise by being vigilant'
>—Order of the White Falcon (Saxe-Weimar); Ernst August,
>Duke of Saxony-Weimar (1688–1741).

70. **Vivere virtute victoria**   *Latin* 'To live in virtue is victory'
>—Ernst, Duke of Braunschweig-Lüneburg (1564–1611).

71. **Who dares wins**
>—Yerburgh.

72. **Will win, well wear**
>—Hort.

VIGILANCE   (*See also* DEFENSE; WAKEFULNESS; WARNING.)

1. **Agros vigilantia servat**   *Latin* 'Vigilance serves the land'
>—Messinger (U.S.).

2. **Alert**
>—Crasdale.

3. **Audax et vigilans**   *Latin* 'Bold and vigilant'
>—Currie.

4. **Beware**
>—Cleborne; Chorley B. C., U.K.

5. **Beware in time**
>—Lumsden, Lumsdaine, White.

6. **Beware my edge**
>—Gibbs (U.S.).

7. **Beware the reaping**
>—Brookfield.

8. **Be watchful**
>—Daroch, Darsch.

9. **By watchfulness, by steadfastness**
>—Hare.

10. **Cave!**   *Latin* 'Beware!'
>—Cave.

11. **Cave! adsum**   *Latin* 'Beware! I am present'
>—Ashmore, Jardine (Bt.), Jardin.

12. **Cave! Deus videt** *Latin* 'Beware! God sees'
—Cave.

13. **Cave et aude** *Latin* 'Beware and dare'
—Darwin.

14. **Cave Leam** *Latin* 'Beware the lioness'
—Lea.

15. **Cave lupum** *Latin* 'Beware the wolf'
—Hubbard.

16. **Celer et vigilans** *Latin* 'Quick and watchful'
—Douce.

17. **Cubo et excubo** *Latin* 'I sleep and watch'
—Graeme.

18. **Cubo sed curo** *Latin* 'I lie down, but am on guard'
—Dickson.

19. **Cura, vigila** *Latin* 'Have a care; keep watch'
—Rudolf II, Emperor of Germany (1552–1612).

20. **Curo dum quiesco** *Latin* 'I am on guard whilst I rest'
—Maxwell.

21. **Custos et pugnax** *Latin* 'A vigilant watch and prepared to fight'
—Marjoribanks.

22. **Dat cura commodum** *Latin* 'Vigilance ensures advantage'
—[Vergil, *Aen.* iv. 5.] Milne.

23. **Dat cura quietem** *Latin* 'Vigilance ensures tranquillity'
—Medlicott (Bt.).

24. **Diligentia et vigilantia** *Latin* 'Diligence and watchfulness'
—Semple.

25. **Ditat virtus** *Latin* 'Virtue enriches'
—Cheap.

26. **Dum vigilo, pareo** *Latin* 'While I watch, I obey'
—Gordon.

27. **Dum vigilo curo** *Latin* 'While I watch, I take care'
—Cranstoun.

28. **Dum vigilo tutus** *Latin* 'While I am vigilant I am safe'
—Gordon (of Knockespoch).

29. **Esto vigilans** *Latin* 'Be vigilant'
—Lloyd (of Dolobran), Okeover.

30. **Ever watchful**
—White (Bt.).

31. **Eviglia [*sic*] qui dormis**   *French* 'Wake up, you who sleep'
—Wakeman.
32. **Fide et vigilantia**   *Latin* 'By faith and vigilance'
—Stepney (Bt.).
33. **Fidel je garderay**   *Old French* 'I shall guard faithfully'
—Castellain.
34. **Firm, vigilant, active**
—Muncaster (B.).
35. **Floret qui vigilat**   *Latin* 'He is prosperous who is vigilant'
—Smith.
36. **Fortis et vigilans**   *Latin* 'Brave and vigilant'
—Orr.
37. **Fortiter et vigilanter**   *Latin* 'Boldly and vigilantly'
—Tyson.
38. **Gang warily**   *Scots dialect*
—Drummond.
39. **Garde**   *French* 'Watch'
—M'Kenzie.
40. **Garde bien**   *French* 'Watch well'
—Carrick, Montgomery.
41. **Garde garde**   *French* 'Guard carefully'
—Edmonstone-Montgomerie.
42. **Gardez**   *French* 'Beware'
—Cave (Bt.).
43. **Gardez bien**   *French* 'Watch well'
—Eglinton (E.), Livere, Montgomery (Co. Donegal, Bt.),
Montgomery (of Stanhope, Bt.).
44. **Gare la bête**   *French* 'Beware of the beast'
—Garbett.
45. **Go on, and take care**
—Thompson (Co. York).
46. **Guardez vous**   *French* 'Guard yourself'
—Lidiard.
47. **Guard yourself**
—Middleton (of Kill Hill).
48. **Hazard warily**
—Seton (of Abercorn, Bt.).
49. **Hinc vigilo**   *Latin* 'Hence I watch'
—Philip II of Spain.

50. **I'll be wary**
—Finlay.

51. **Indefessus vigilando** *Latin* 'Unwearied by watching'
—Read (U.S.).

52. **In vigilia sic vinces** *Latin* 'In watchfulness thus will you conquer'
—Price.

53. **In well beware**
—Wombwell (Bt.).

54. **Je suis veillant à plaire** *French* 'I am watchful to please'
—Saunderson.

55. **Keep watch**
—Bryden (of Berwick).

56. **Per bellum qui providet** *Latin* 'One who is circumspect through war'
—Liddersdale.

57. **Plus vigila** *Latin* 'Watch more'
—White.

58. **Prudentia et vigilantia** *Latin* 'By prudence and watchfulness'
—Purchon.

59. **Quo virtus ducit scando** *Latin* 'I climb where virtue leads'
—Follet.

60. **Robore et vigilantia** *Latin* 'By strength and watchfulness'
—Aitken.

61. **Secundis rebus cave** *Latin* 'In well, beware'
—Wombwell U. D. C., U.K.

62. **Semper caveto** *Latin* 'Always be wary'
—Ball (U.S.).

63. **Semper vigilans** *Latin* 'Always watchful'
—Bourne, England, Todd, Walker, Williams, Wilson (of Edinburgh, Smeaton Castle, etc.), Hughes (of Clapham).

64. **Sobrii este vigilantes** *Latin* 'Be well advised by watching'
—Geekie.

65. **Spem vigilantia firmat** *Latin* 'Vigilance strengthens hope'
—Dunbar.

66. **Toujours en vedette** *French* 'Ever on guard'
—Frederick the Great (1712–1786).

67. **Ut vivas vigila** *Latin* 'Watch that you may live'
—Arnold (of Ashby).

68. **Vaillant et veillant**   *French* 'Valiant and vigilant'
—Cardwell.

69. **Veillant et vaillant**   *French* 'Watchful and valiant'
—Erskine (Bt.).

70. **Veilliez et ne craignez pas**   *French* 'Watch and fear not'
—Gurdlestone.

71. **Vide cui fidas**   *Latin* 'Beware whom you trust'
—Ferdinand, Duke of Bavaria (1550–1608).

72. **Vie vers vertu**   *French* 'Life towards virtue'
—Veevers.

73. **Vigila**   *Latin* 'Be watchful'
—Amderson (U.S.).

74. **Vigila et aude**   *Latin* '(Be) vigilant and dare'
—Campbell (Bt.).

75. **Vigila et ora**   *Latin* 'Watch and pray'
—[Matt., xxvi. 41 and Mark, xiii. 33.] Wake (Bt.), Rogers,
Croxwell.

76. **Vigilance**
—Laing (of Lothian).

77. **Vigilando**   *Latin* 'By watching'
—Campbell (Bt.), McLeod.

78. **Vigilando ascendimus**   *Latin* 'We rise by being vigilant'
—Order of the White Falcon (Saxe-Weimar), Ernst August,
Duke of Saxony-Weimar (1688–1741).

79. **Vigilando munio**   *Latin* 'I defend by being vigilant'
—Kirkaldie.

80. **Vigilando quiesco**   *Latin* 'In watching I rest'
—Tredcroft.

81. **Vigilans**   *Latin* 'Watchful'
—Burton, Kadwell, Johnson, Smith, Taylor.

82. **Vigilans et audax**   *Latin* 'Vigilant and bold'
—Bradley (of Co. Worcester), Corrie, Cockburn (Bt.),
Campbell (Bt.), Dunn.

83. **Vigilans et certus**   *Latin* 'Vigilant and sure'
—Anderson.

84. **Vigilans et fidelis**   *Latin* 'Watchful and faithful'
—Wilson.

85. **Vigilans et promptus**   *Latin* 'Vigilant and prompt'
—Wyld.

86. **Vigilans et verus** *Latin* 'Vigilant and true'
—Wenley.

87. **Vigilans non cadit** *Latin* 'The vigilant man falls not'
—Calder (Bt.).

88. **Vigilant**
—Laing, Newcomen.

89. **Vigilant and resolute**
—Harding (of Petherton, b.).

90. **Vigilante** *Latin* 'Watching'
—Clare.

91. **Vigilanter** *Latin* 'Watchfully'
—Gregory, Stawell, Wegg.

92. **Vigilanter et constanter** *Latin* 'Vigilantly and steadfastly'
—Johann Wilhelm, Duke of Saxony-Eisenach (1666–1729).

93. **Vigilantes** *Latin* 'The vigilant ones'
—Hardinge (U.S.), Cleethorpes B. C., U.K.

94. **Vigilante salus** *Latin* 'Safety while he watches'
—Cochran.

95. **Vigilantia** *Latin* 'Vigilance'
—Aird, Carfrea.

96. **Vigilantia, robur, voluptas** *Latin* 'Vigilance, strength, pleasure'
—Arundell, Blair (Bt.), Hunter.

97. **Vigilantia et virtute** *Latin* 'By vigilance and valor'
—Porter.

98. **Vigilantia non cadet** *Latin* 'Vigilance will not miscarry'
—Cadell.

99. **Vigilantia praestat** *Latin* 'Vigilance is preeminent'
—Coxe (U.S.).

100. **Vigilantibus** *Latin* 'While they watch'
—Acheson, Atchison, Gosford (E.).

101. **Vigilantibus non dormientibus** *Latin* 'For the vigilant not for the sleeping'
—Bristowe.

102. **Vigilate** *Latin* 'Watch'
—Allcock, Leeds (Bt.), Longstaff, Tucker.

103. **Vigilate et orate** *Latin* 'Watch and pray'
—[Matt. xxvi. 41 and Mark, xiii. 33.] Clevedon U. D. C., U.K.; Capron, Castlemaine (V.), Handcock, Shuckburgh.

104. **Vigilat et orat**   *Latin* 'He watches and prays'
—Fennison.

105. **Vigilo**   *Latin* 'I watch'
—Desse, Gregson, Geikie, McHado.

106. **Vigilo et spero**   *Latin* 'I watch and hope'
—Galbraith, Twitoe.

107. **Vincit vigilantia**   *Latin* 'Vigilance conquers'
—Wright.

108. **Virtus patrimonio nobilior**   *Latin* 'Virtue is nobler than inheritance'
—Trelawney.

109. **Virtute et vigilantia**   *Latin* 'By virtue and vigilance'
—Sharp.

110. **Ware the horn**
—Savage.

111. **Watch**
—Forbes (of Cragedar), Gordon (of Haddo).

112. **Watch and pray**
—[Matt. xxvi. 41 and Mark xiii. 33.] Fowler (U.S.); Forbes (of Craigievar Castle, Bt.).

113. **Watchful and bold**
—Coats.

114. **Watch weel**
—Scott (of Abbotsford, Bt.).

115. **Watch well**
—Halyburton (of Pitcur, Newmains, etc.).

116. **Watch wiel**   *Middle English*
—Scott.

117. **We beg you see warily**
—Cornwall (of Bonhard).

VIRTUE (*See also* GOODNESS; HONESTY; INTEGRITY; NOBILITY; PIETY; PURITY; RECTITUDE; WORTHINESS.)

1. **Absque virtute nihil**   *Latin* 'Nothing without virtue'
—Rogers-Harrison.

2. **Ad aethera virtus**   *Latin* 'Virtue to heaven'
—Hemming.

3. **Ad astra virtus** *Latin* 'Virtue rises to the stars'
    —Saltmarshe (Co. York).

4. **Adhaereo virtuti** *Latin* 'I cling to virtue'
    —Kennedy (Bt.).

5. **Adversa virtute repello** *Latin* 'I repel adversity by virtue'
    —Denison, Dennistoun, Londesborough (B.), Medhurst.

6. **Ad virtus astra** *Latin* 'Virtue to the stars'
    —Crane.

7. **Ad virtutem per sapientiam** *Latin* 'To virtue through wisdom'
    —Castle Jr. College, Windham, New Hampshire.

8. **Aegis fortissima virtus** *Latin* 'Virtue is the strongest shield'
    —Aspinall.

9. **Amator de virtus** *Latin* 'Lover of virtue'
    —Case (U.S.).

10. **Amicitia cum virtute** *Latin* 'Friendship with virtue'
    —Bradbury.

11. **Amicitiae virtutisque faedus** *Latin* 'The league of friendship and virtue'
    —Grand Order of Wurtemburg; Hippisley (Bt.), Nelson (of Beeston, co. Norfolk).

12. **Amo honesta** *Latin* 'I love noble deeds'
    —Thomson.

13. **Amo probos** *Latin* 'I love the virtuous'
    —Blair, Scot, Scott, Towle.

14. **Anchora sit virtus** *Latin* 'Let virtue be my anchor'
    —Ford (of Essex).

15. **Antiqua constans virtute** *Latin* 'Steadfast in ancient virtue'
    —Arundel B. C., U.K.

16. **Antiqui colant Antiquum Dierum** *Latin* 'Let men of the ancient virtues worship the Ancient of Days'
    —Chester City and C. B. C., U.K.

17. **Aspera ad virtutem est via** *Latin* 'The road to virtue is rough'
    —Edwardes (of Gileston).

18. **Aspera via ad virtutem** *Latin* 'Rough is the path to virtue'
    —Albrecht, Margrave of Brandenburg-Anspach (1620–67).

19. **Aspera virtus** *Latin* 'Virtue is difficult'
    —Sinclair (Bt.).

20. **Basis virtutum constantia** *Latin* 'Constancy is the foundation of virtue'
—Devereux, Hereford(V.).

21. **Cassis tutissima virtus** *Latin* 'Virtue is the safest helmet'
—Armour, Charrington, Cholmondeley (M.), Delamere (B.), Helme.

22. **Celeritas virtus fidelitas** *Latin* 'Speed, virtue, and fidelity'
—Carpenter (U.S.).

23. **C'est la seule vertu qui donne la noblesse** *French* 'Virtue alone confers nobility'
—Greame (Co. York).

24. **Chi s'arma di virtu, vince ogni forza** *Italian* 'He who arms himself with virtue overcomes all powers'
—Friedrich I, Duke of Saxony-Gotha and Altenburg (1646–91).

25. **Chi semina virtu raccologie fama** *Italian* 'He who sows virtue, reaps glory'
—Johann Friedrich, Duke of Württemberg (1585–1628).

26. **Chi semini vertu racoglia fama** *Italian* 'Who sows virtue gathers fame'
—Coore (of Scruton Hall).

27. **Clarior virtus honoribus** *Latin* 'Virtue is more illustrious than preferments'
—Clay.

28. **Con la virtu e l'arme s'acquista gloria** *Italian* 'With virtue and arms is glory won'
—Johann Wilhelm II, Duke of Saxony (1600–32).

29. **Conquer death by virtue**
—Sherman (U.S.).

30. **Conscientia virtuti satis amplum theatrum est** *Latin* 'A good conscience is a sufficient sphere of activity for virtue'
—Friedrich V, Margrave of Baden-Durlach (1594–1659).

31. **Constantia et virtute** *Latin* 'By constancy and virtue'
—Amherst (E.).

32. **Cordi dat robora virtus** *Latin* 'Virtue gives strength to the heart'
—Porch (of Edgarley).

33. **Crescitque virtute** *Latin* 'And he increases by virtue'
—Mackenzie.

34. **Crescit sub pondere virtus** *Latin* 'Virtue thrives beneath oppression'
—Chapman (Bt.), Chapman (of Whitby), Denbigh (E.), Fielding, Seys, Slatter (of Chesterfield).

35. **Crescit sub pondere virtus ventis secundis** *Latin* 'Virtue, though burdened, increases amid favorable winds'
—Slater (U.S.).

36. **Dat virtus quod forma negat** *Latin* 'Virtue gives what beauty denies'
—Bertrand Du Guesclin (D. 1380).

37. **Decus summum virtus** *Latin* 'Virtue is the highest honor'
—Holburne (Bt.), Hulburn.

38. **Deo et virtuti** *Latin* 'For God and virtue'
—Lackerstein.

39. **De vertu bonheur** *French* 'From virtue fortune'
—Sophie, Electress of Hanover (1630–1714).

40. **Discretio moderatrix virtutum** *Latin* 'Discretion is the moderator of virtues'
—Quincy (U.S.).

41. **Ditat virtus** *Latin* 'Virtue enriches'
—Cheap.

42. **Domat omnia virtus** *Latin* 'Virtue conquers all things'
—Gough (of Perry Hall), Ffarington (of Ffarington).

43. **Donat anima virtus** *Latin* 'The soul gives virtue'
—Gough (U.S.).

44. **Dura pati virtus** *Latin* 'Suffering hardships is a virtue'
—August, Duke of Saxony-Lauenburg (1577–1656).

45. **Duriora virtus** *Latin* 'Virtue tries harder things'
—Wyatt.

46. **Et arma et virtus** *Latin* 'Both arms and virtue'
—Dundas, Hamilton (of Westburn).

47. **Et fide et virtute** *Latin* 'By both faith and virtue'
—Porter.

48. **Et vi et virtute** *Latin* 'Both by strength and virtue'
—Baird (Bt.), Burrowes (Bt.), Stannus.

49. **Ex candore virtus** *Latin* 'Virtue from candor'
—Whyte.

50. **Ex sola virtute honos** *Latin* 'Honor springs from virtue alone'
—Johnston, Johnstone.

51. **Ex virtute honos** *Latin* 'Honor from virtue'
—Jardin.

52. **Fama praestante praestantior virtus** *Latin* 'Virtue is more outstanding along with an outstanding reputation'
—Morgan (U.S.).

53. **Fama sed virtus non moriatur** *Latin* 'Fame perishes, but not virtue'
—Ingersoll (U.S.).

54. **Fato fortior virtus** *Latin* 'Virtue is stronger than fate'
—Hertslet.

55. **Ferret ad astra virtus** *Latin* 'Virtue was borne to the stars'
—Kellet (Bt.), Kellett (U.S.).

56. **Fide, labore, et virtute** *Latin* 'By faith, labor, and virtue'
—Maryott.

57. **Fidei virtutem adde** *Latin* 'Add to your faith virtue'
—Lee.

58. **Fidite virtuti** *Latin* 'Trust in virtue'
—Bard (U.S.).

59. **Florescit vulnere virtus** *Latin* 'Virtue flourishes after a wound'
—Bisson.

60. **Floret virtus vulnerata** *Latin* 'Wounded virtue flourishes'
—Floyer.

61. **Force avec vertu** *French* 'Strength with virtue'
—Leigh (of West Hall).

62. **Forma perit, virtus remanet** *Latin* 'Beauty perishes; virtue remains'
—August, Count von der Lippe (D. 1701).

63. **Fors et virtus** *Latin* 'Fortune and virtue'
—Lotbiniere (U.S.).

64. **Fortior es qui se quam qui fortissima vincit Moenia, nec virtus altius ire potest** *Latin* 'Stronger is he who conquers himself than he who conquers the strongest walls; and virtue can mount no higher'
—Johann Georg I, Prince of Anhalt-Dessau (1567–1618).

65. **Fortunam honestent virtute** *Latin* 'Let them make honorable their fortune by their virtue'
—Brandreth.

66. **Fragrat post funera virtus** *Latin* 'Virtue smells sweet after death'
—Chiesly.

67. **Fulcrum dignitatis virtus** *Latin* 'Virtue is the support of dignity'
—Bull.

68. **Fulget virtus** *Latin* 'Virtue shines bright'
—Bell.

69. **Fulget virtus intaminata** *Latin* 'Unspotted virtue shines bright'
—Belches.

70. **Gaudet tentamine virtus** *Latin* 'Virtue exults in the trial'
—Dartmouth (E.), Legge.

71. **Gottes furcht die schönste Tugend, Gewöhnt das Alter, zeirt die Jugend** *German* 'Fear of God is the fairest virtue; it reconciles old age, and adorns youth'
—Sophie, Princess of Anhalt (1654–1724).

72. **Hac virtus mercede digna** *Latin* 'Virtue is worthy of this reward'
—Robertson.

73. **Hoc virtutis opus** *Latin* 'This is the work of virtue'
—Bulwer-Lytton (Bt.).

74. **Honor, virtus, probitas** *Latin* 'Honor, virtue, and probity'
—Barrett.

75. **Honor et virtus** *Latin* 'Honor and virtue'
—Akins, Grogan (Bt.), Morgan.

76. **Honor praemium virtutis est** *Latin* 'Honor is the reward of virtue'
—Flynn.

77. **Honor virtutem coronat** *Latin* 'Honor crowns virtue'
—Davies.

78. **Honor virtutis** *Latin* 'The honor of virtue'
—Burdon.

79. **Honor virtutis praemium** *Latin* 'Honor is the reward of virtue'
—Bell, Boyle, Cork and Orrery (E.), Hawtin, Hawtyn, Hole, Ferrers (E.), Fielding, Shirley.

80. **Honor virtutis pretium** *Latin* 'Honor is the reward of virtue'
—Mills.

81. **Honos fidelitatis praemium** *Latin* 'Honor the reward of fidelity'
—Irby.

82. **Honos virtutis satelles** *Latin* 'Honor the attendant of virtue'
—Baker.

83. **Immersabilis est vera virtus** *Latin* 'True virtue cannot be overwhelmed'
—Codrington.

84. **Immortalis virtutis et gloriae fama perpetim post fata superstes**
Latin 'The imperishable renown of virtue and glory survive death forever'
—Johann Georg II, Prince of Anhalt-Dessau (1627–93).

85. **In ardua virtus** *Latin* 'Virtue against difficulties'
—Leathes (of Herringfleet), Wolstenholme.

86. **In arduis viget virtus** *Latin* 'Virtue flourishes in adversity'
—Gurdon (of Letton, Cranworth, and Barnham Broom, Co. Norfolk), Gurdon-Rebow, Dorien, Magens.

87. **Inclytus virtute** *Latin* 'Renowned for virtue'
—Kyan.

88. **Inconcussa virtus** *Latin* 'Unshaken virtue'
—Benson, Lane.

89. **Industria, intelligentia, virtus** *Latin* 'Industry, intelligence, virtue'
—Dexter (U.S.).

90. **Industria et virtute** *Latin* 'By industry and virtue'
—Beaver.

91. **In fide vestra virtutem in virtute autem scientiam** *Latin* '(Have) virtue in your faith but knowledge in your virtue'
—Agnes Scott College, Decatur, Georgia.

92. **In iustitia virtutes omnes** *Latin* 'All virtues are in justice'
—Sims (U.S.).

93. **Ino [*sic*] virtus et fata vocant** *Latin* 'Thence virtue and fate call'
—Jones (U.S.).

94. **Invia virtuti via nulla** *Latin* 'No road is inaccessible to virtue'
—Seton.

95. **Invidam virtute vincam** *Latin* 'I will conquer the hostile by virtue'
—Foster (U.S.).

96. **J'aime l'honneur qui vient par la vertu** *French* 'I love the honor which is attained through virtue'
—Order of the Noble Passion.

97. **Je veulx tousiours la vertu svyvre** *Old French* 'I desire always to follow virtue'
—Philipp, Landgrave of Hesse-Butzbach (1581–1643).

98. **Justitia et virtus** *Latin* 'Justice and virtue'
—Charlesworth.

99. **Justitia virtutum regina**   *Latin* 'Justice is the queen of the virtues'
                                                   —Goldsmiths' Company.

100. **Laus virtutis actio**   *Latin* 'The deed commends the virtue'
                                                   —Rawson.

101. **La vertu est la seule noblesse**   *French* 'Virtue is the only nobility'
                                                   —Guildford (E.), North.

102. **La vertu surmonte tout obstacle**   *French* 'Virtue overcomes every
       obstacle'
                                                   —Rowley.

103. **L'honneur est mon tresor, la vertu ma conduite**   *French* 'Honor is
       my treasure, virtue my guide'
                         —Wilhelm VI, Landgrave of Hesse-Cassel (1629–63);
                              Hedwig Sophie, Landgravine of Hesse-Cassel
                                                   (1623–83).

104. **Libertas virtusque**   *Latin* 'Liberty and virtue'
                                                   —Fry.

105. **Libertas virtus sunt summa potestas**   *Latin* 'Liberty and virtue
       are the highest power'
                                                   —Richards.

106. **Libertate extincta nulla virtus**   *Latin* 'There is no virtue when
       liberty is dead'
                                                   —Fletcher.

107. **Lucem amat virtus**   *Latin* 'Virtue loves the light'
                                                   —Strachey.

108. **Major virtus quam splendor**   *Latin* 'Virtue is preferable to splen-
       dor'
                                                   —Auld, Baillie (of Jerviswood).

109. **Mea anchora virtus**   *Latin* 'Virtue is my anchor'
                                                   —Richardson.

110. **Mea dos virtus**   *Latin* 'Virtue is my dower'
                                                   —Meadows (Co. Suffolk).

111. **Mea virtute me involvo**   *Latin* 'I wrap myself in my virtue'
                                                   —Williams (of Clovelly Court, Bt.).

112. **Melior fortunâ virtus**   *Latin* 'Virtue is better than fortune'
                                                   —Mellor.

113. **Murus aeneus virtus**   *Latin* 'Virtue is a wall of brass'
                                                   —Walton (of Clifton, Gloucestershire).

114. **Nach Tugend ich tracht, Alles eiteles veracht** *German* 'I aspire to virtue, and all frivolity despise'
—Sibylle, Margravine of Baden (1620–79).

115. **Nec virtus nec copia desunt** *Latin* 'Neither virtue nor plenty are lacking'
—Macclesfield B. C., U.K.

116. **Nec virtus suprema fefellit** *Latin* 'Supreme virtue has not failed'
—Butler (U.S.).

117. **Nihil quod obstat virtuti** *Latin* 'Nothing which is opposed to virtue'
—Higgins.

118. **Nihil virtuti invium** *Latin* 'Nothing is inaccessible to virtue'
—Coldridge, Coleridge.

119. **Nil intentatum virtus generosa relinquit** *Latin* 'Noble virtue leaves nothing untried'
—Karl Maximilian, Duke of Württemberg (1654–89).

120. **Nil virtuti invisum** *Latin* 'Nothing is hateful to virtue'
—Georg Aribert, Prince of Anhalt (1606–43).

121. **Nisi virtus vilior alga** *Latin* 'Without virtue viler than the seaweed'
—Moises, Algar.

122. **Nobilitas est sola virtus** *Latin* 'Virtue is the only nobility'
—Thackeray.

123. **Nobilitas unica virtus** *Latin* 'Virtue is the only nobility'
—Steward (of Nottingham).

124. **Nobilitatis virtus non stemma character** *Latin* 'Virtue, not pedigree, should characterize nobility'
—Freshfield (of Stoke Newington), Westminster (M.).

125. **Non abest virtuti sors** *Latin* 'Fortune deserts not virtue'
—Nisbet.

126. **Non obest virtute sors** *Latin* 'Our lot is not adverse to our virtue'
—Nisbet.

127. **Non solum ingenii, verum etiam virtutis** *Latin* 'Not only talent, but also virtue'
—Liverpool College, U.K.

128. **Non vi, sed virtute** *Latin* 'Not by violence, but by virtue'
—Elphinstone, Ramsbottom.

129. **Non vi, virtute** *Latin* 'Not by force, but by virtue'
—Borrows (Bt.).

130. **Numine et virtute** *Latin* 'By God's providence and by virtue'
—Yule.

131. **Omnia illi adsunt bona quem penes est virtus** *Latin* 'All good things are with him who possesses virtue'
—[Plautus, *Amphitruo*, ii. 2. 20.] Friedrich I, Duke of Saxony-Gotha and Altenburg (1646–91).

132. **Omnia superat virtus** *Latin* 'Virtue conquers all'
—Gardiner.

133. **Palma virtuti** *Latin* 'The palm to virtue'
—Palmer (of Wingham, Bt.), Palmer (of Fairfield, Bt.), Palmer.

134. **Par viribus virtus** *Latin* 'Our virtue is a match to their strength'
—Pakington.

135. **Patriis virtutibus** *Latin* 'By hereditary virtues'
—Clements, Leitrim (E.).

136. **Pax, copia, virtus** *Latin* 'Peace, plenty, virtue'
—McAdam, Stewart.

137. **Per adversa virtus** *Latin* 'Virtue through misfortunes'
—Lighton.

138. **Per ardua virtus** *Latin* 'Virtue through difficulties'
—Sinclair, Tomlins.

139. **Per aspera virtus** *Latin* 'Virtue through hardships'
—Ross (of Craigie).

140. **Petit ardua virtus** *Latin* 'Virtue seeks difficulties'
—Douglas.

141. **Pietas est optima virtus** *Latin* 'Piety is the chief virtue'
—Heinrich VIII, Count Reuss (1652–1711).

142. **Pietas tutissima virtus** *Latin* 'Piety is the surest virtue'
—Ainslie.

143. **Pietas tutissima virtus** *Latin* 'Piety is the safest virtue'
—Christoph, Duke of Mecklenburg (1537–92); Friedrich Wilhelm I, Duke of Saxony-Weimar (1562–1602); Magnus, Duke of Braunschweig-Lüneburg (1577–1632); August, Duke of Saxony (1589–1615); Friedrich Wilhelm II, Duke of Saxony-Altenburg (1603–69); Georg Friedrich, Margrave of Brandenburg-Anspach (1678–1703).

144. **Plustot mourire que vivere sans vertu**   *Old French* 'Rather die than live without virtue'
—Johann, Margrave of Brandenburg (1597–1628); Friedrich, Duke of Saxony (1599–1625); Elisabeth, Margravine of Baden (1620–96).

145. **Pollet virtus**   *Latin* 'Virtue excels'
—Maryborough (B.), Poole, Pole.

146. **Post funera virtus**   *Latin* 'Virtue survives death'
—Bogislaus XIII, Duke of Pomerania zu Barth (1544–1606); Robertson.

147. **Post mortem virtus virescit**   *Latin* 'Virtue flourishes after death'
—Tyssen-Amherst (of Didlington Hall, Co. Norfolk), Tyssen (of Hackey).

148. **Post virtutem curro**   *Latin* 'I run after virtue'
—Briscoe.

149. **Potior origine virtus**   *Latin* 'Virtue is better than lineage'
—Scot, Scott.

150. **Praemium, virtus, gloria**   *Latin* 'Reward, virtue, glory'
—Crosane.

151. **Praemium, virtus, honor**   *Latin* 'Reward, virtue, honor'
—Brown (of Blackburn), Cox.

152. **Praemium virtutis**   *Latin* 'The reward of virtue'
—Pringle.

153. **Praemium virtutis honor**   *Latin* 'Honor is the reward of virtue'
—Cheere, Lovelace, Tetlow (of Haughton).

154. **Praestat auro virtus**   *Latin* 'Virtue is better than gold'
—Cunningham.

155. **Prevalet virtus**   *Latin* 'Virtue prevails'
—Zouch.

156. **Principis est virtus maxima nosse Deum**   *Latin* 'To know God is the highest virtue in a prince'
—Karl, Duke of Mecklenburg (D. 1610); Franz, Duke of Pomerania (1577–1620); Johann, Duke of Saxony-Weimar (1570–1605).

157. **Principis est virtus se nosse deumque suosque**   *Latin* 'To know God and his own people is the virtue of a prince'
—Christian, Duke of Schleswig-Holstein (1570–1633).

158. **Prisca virtute fideque**   *Latin* 'With ancient virtue and fidelity'
—Johann Adolf, Duke of Schleswig-Holstein-Sonderburg-Plön (1634–1704).

159. **Prix de vertu** *French* 'The reward of virtue'
—National Order of France.

160. **Pro patria et virtute** *Latin* 'For country and virtue'
—Higgins.

161. **Propria virtute audax** *Latin* 'Bold in his own virtue'
—Madden.

162. **Providentiâ et virtute** *Latin* 'By providence and virtue'
—Rankin.

163. **Pro virtute** *Latin* 'For virtue'
—Reid (of Seabank).

164. **P. T. V. (Pietas tutissima virtus)** *Latin* 'Piety is the safest virtue'
—Ernst, Margrave of Brandenburg (1583–1613).

165. **Quos amor et virtus sociant sors nulla resolvet** *Latin* 'Those whom love and virtue unite no fate shall divide'
—Johann Georg II, Prince of Anhalt-Dessau (1627–93).

166. **Quo virtus ducit scando** *Latin* 'I climb where virtue leads'
—Follet.

167. **Quo virtus et fata vocat** *Latin* 'Where virtue and the fates call (me)'
—Ffolliott.

168. **Quo vocat virtus** *Latin* 'Where virtue calls'
—Jauncey (U.S.).

169. **Rather virtue than learning**
—Stith (U.S.).

170. **Resurgit ex virtute vera gloria** *Latin* 'True glory rises from virtue'
—Albert V, Duke of Bavaria (1528–79).

171. **Sal sapit omnia** *Latin* 'Salt savors everything'
—Salters' Company.

172. **Sapientia et virtus** *Latin* 'Wisdom and virtue'
—Douglas.

173. **Sapientia/ virtus/ amicitia** *Latin* 'Knowledge/ virtue/ friendship'
—Central Michigan University, Mt. Pleasant, Michigan.

174. **Scandit sublimia virtus** *Latin* 'Virtue scales great heights'
—Crumpe.

175. **Semper virescit virtus** *Latin* 'Virtue always flourishes'
—Lind, Marishall.

176. **Semper virtuti constans**   *Latin* 'Always constant to virtue'
        —Beavan.

177. **Semper virtuti vivo**   *Latin* 'I always live by virtue'
        —Sideserf.

178. **Sic virescit virtus**   *Latin* 'Thus virtue flourishes'
        —Ronald.

179. **Sic viret virtus**   *Latin* 'So virtue flourishes'
        —Anderson.

180. **Sine virtute vani sunt honores**   *Latin* 'Without virtue honors are empty'
        —Bozman (U.S.).

181. **Societas scientia virtus**   *Latin* 'Fellowship, knowledge, virtue'
        —Milner (U.S.).

182. **Sola et unica virtus**   *Latin* 'Virtue alone and without a peer'
        —Collis, Harris, Hanson, Henley.

183. **Sola juvat virtus**   *Latin* 'Virtue alone delights'
        —Blairtyre (B.), Owen.

184. **Sola nobilitas virtus**   *Latin* 'Virtue is the only nobility'
        —Abercorn (M.), Blake (of Menlo, Bt.), Standish.

185. **Sola nobilitat virtus**   *Latin* 'Virtue alone ennobles'
        —Hamilton (of Silverton), Hill (Bt.), Mowbray.

186. **Sola virtus invicta**   *Latin* 'Virtue alone invincible'
        —Norfolk (D.), Howard (of Greystoke), Howard (of Corby Castle), Haige, Hanson, Harris, Collis.

187. **Sola virtus invicta, 1632**   *Latin* 'Virtue alone unconquered, 1632'
        —Bispham (U.S.), Hansom (U.S.), Reynolds (U.S.).

188. **Sola virtus munimentum**   *Latin* 'Virtue alone is our stronghold'
        —Mason.

189. **Sola virtus nobilitat**   *Latin* 'Virtue alone ennobles'
        —Henderson (Bt.).

190. **Sola virtus reddit nobilem**   *Latin* 'Virtue alone renders noble'
        —Storey.

191. **Sola virtus triumphat**   *Latin* 'Virtue alone triumphs'
        —Carvile.

192. **Spernit pericula virtus**   *Latin* 'Virtue despises danger'
        —Carpenter, Ramsay (of Banff House, Bt.), Forrester.

193. **Stat fortuna domus virtute**   *Latin* 'The fortune of our house endures through virtue'
        —Molyneux (Bt.).

194. **Sua praemia virtus** *Latin* 'Virtue is its own reward'
—McCartney.

195. **Sub robore virtus** *Latin* 'Virtue under strength'
—Aikin (of Liverpool), Aikman (of Carnie).

196. **Suo stat robore virtus** *Latin* 'Virtue stands by its own strength'
—Mowbray.

197. **Superabit omnia virtus** *Latin* 'Virtue shall overcome all things'
—Rabett.

198. **Tachez surpasser en vertue** *French* 'Strive to surpass in virtue'
—Taylor.

199. **Tam genus quam virtus** *Latin* 'As much lineage as virtue'
—Lunden.

200. **Tam virtus quam honos** *Latin* 'As well virtue as honor'
—Hamilton.

201. **Tam virtute quam labore** *Latin* 'As much by virtue as by exertion'
—Hamilton.

202. **Tendens ad aethera virtus** *Latin* 'Virtue aspiring towards heaven'
—Lewthwaite.

203. **Tendit in ardua virtus** *Latin* 'Virtue aims at difficulties'
—Lloyd.

204. **Teneat, luceat, floreat, vi, virtute, et valore** *Latin* 'May it hold, shine, and flourish, by valor, virtue, and worth'
—Kenny (of Kilcloghar and Correndos, Co. Galway),
Kenny (of Ballyflower, Co. Roscommon).

205. **Tugendt macht Edel** *German* 'Virtue confers nobility'
—Friedrich IV, Count of the Palatinate (1594–1610).

206. **Turris tutissima virtus** *Latin* 'Virtue is the safest fortress'
—Carlyon.

207. **Uni aequus virtuti** *Latin* 'Friendly to virtue alone'
—Mansfield (E.).

208. **Unica virtus necessaria** *Latin* 'Only virtue is necessary'
—Colley, Wellesley.

209. **Utere virtute** *Latin* 'Employ virtue'
—Johann, Duke of Holstein-Gottorp (1606–55).

210. **Valet anchora virtus** *Latin* 'Virtue our anchor is strong'
—Gardner (B.), Gardner.

211. **Valore et virtute**   *Latin* 'By valor and virtue'
                                                    —Salle.

212. **Vera virtus immersabilis**   *Latin* 'True virtue is invincible'
                                                    —Codrington.

213. **Veritas et virtus**   *Latin* 'Truth and virtue'
                           —Mississippi College, Clinton, Mississippi.

214. **Veritas et virtus vincunt**   *Latin* 'Truth and virtue prevail'
                                                    —Walsh.

215. **Vertu cherche honneur**   *French* 'Virtue seeks honor'
                                                    —D'Arcy.

216. **Vertu embellit**   *French* 'Virtue beautifies'
               —Kunigunde Juliane, Princess of Anhalt (1608–56);
                           Kunigunde Juliane, Landgravine of Hesse
                                                    (1608–56).

217. **Vertue vaunceth**   *Middle English* 'Virtue advances (men)'
                           —Verney, Willoughby de Broke (B.).

218. **Vertu surpasse richesse**   *French* 'Virtue excels riches'
                           —Johann, Duke of Holstein-Gottorp (1606–55).

219. **Via tuta virtus**   *Latin* 'Virtue is a safe path'
                                                    —Dick.

220. **Vi aut virtute**   *Latin* 'By force or virtue'
                                                    —Chisholm.

221. **Victoria, fortitudo, virtus**   *Latin* 'Victory, fortitude, and virtue'
                                                    —Young.

222. **Videte et cavete ab avaritia**   *Latin* 'Recognize and guard against
         greed'
                           —[after Luke, xii. 15.] Pownall (U.S.).

223. **Vie vers vertu**   *French* 'Life towards virtue'
                                                    —Veevers.

224. **Viget in cinere virtus**   *Latin* 'Virtue flourishes after death'
                                                    —Davidson.

225. **Vigore et virtute**   *Latin* 'By vigor and virtue'
                                                    —Casey.

226. **Vim vincit virtus**   *Latin* 'Virtue prevails over force'
                           —Julius Friedrich, Duke of Württemberg (1588–1635).

227. **Vincet virtute**   *Latin* 'He shall conquer by virtue'
                                                    —Smart.

228. **Vincit omnia pertinax virtus**   *Latin* 'Stubborn virtue conquers all'
                                                    —Stokes.

229. **Vincit omnia virtus** *Latin* 'Virtue conquers everything'
—Vicars.

230. **Vincit pericula virtus** *Latin* 'Virtue overcomes dangers'
—Maine, Thornton.

231. **Vires animat virtus** *Latin* 'Virtue animates our powers'
—Campbell, Garden, Gairden.

232. **Virescit in arduis virtus** *Latin* 'Virtue flourishes in difficulties'
—Keir.

233. **Virescit virtus** *Latin* 'Virtue flourishes'
—Jackson.

234. **Virescit vulnere virtus** *Latin* 'Her virtue flourishes by her wound'
—Galloway (E.), Brownrigg (Bt.), Burnett (Bt.), Green, Ker, Webb, Foot.

235. **Virtue**
—Ferguson.

236. **Virtue, have virtue**
—Ross.

237. **Virtue, liberty and independence**
—State of Pennsylvania; Barton (U.S.).

238. **Virtue is honor**
—Kenrick.

239. **Virtue is my honour**
—McLannahan.

240. **Virtue mine honor**
—Maclean (Bt.), McLean.

241. **Virtue only has claim to honour**
—Rumsey (U.S.).

242. **Virtus** *Latin* 'Virtue'
—Errington.

243. **Virtus, laus, actio** *Latin* 'Virtue, glory, action'
—Frazer.

244. **Virtus, non stemma** *Latin* 'Virtue, not pedigree'
—Ebury (B.), Westminster (M.), Grosvenor.

245. **Virtus acquirit honorem** *Latin* 'Virtue gains honor'
—Spence.

246. **Virtus actione consistit** *Latin* 'Virtue consists of action'
—Craven (U.S.).

247. **Virtus ad aethera tendit** *Latin* 'Virtue reaches to heaven'
—Balfour, Cairns.

248. **Virtus ad astra** *Latin* 'Virtue to the sky'
—Innes, Phillips-Flamank.

249. **Virtus ad astra tendit** *Latin* 'Virtue tends to the stars'
—Ross.

250. **Virtus admixta decori** *Latin* 'Virtue combined with beauty'
—Emanuel Leberecht, Prince of Anhalt-Plötzkau
(1671–1704).

251. **Virtus ad sidera tollit** *Latin* 'Virtue raises to the stars'
—Wilson.

252. **Virtus ariete fortior** *Latin* 'Virtue is stronger than a battering-ram'
—Abingdon (E.), Bertie.

253. **Virtus astra petit** *Latin* 'Virtue aims at the stars'
—Vandeleur.

254. **Virtus auget honorem** *Latin* 'Virtue increases honor'
—Edmounstone (Bt.).

255. **Virtus auget honores** *Latin* 'Virtue increases honors'
—Charles.

256. **Virtus auro praeferenda** *Latin* 'Virtue is to be preferred to gold'
—Allen.

257. **Virtus basis vitae** *Latin* 'Virtue is the basis of life'
—Stafford (B.).

258. **Virtus castellum meum** *Latin* 'Virtue my castle'
—Bence (of Thorington).

259. **Virtus constat in actione** *Latin* 'Virtue consists in action'
—Norgate.

260. **Virtus cura servabit** *Latin* 'Virtue shall preserve by care'
—Browne.

261. **Virtus dedit, cura servabit** *Latin* 'What virtue has given, discretion will preserve'
—Browne.

262. **Virtus depressa resurget** *Latin* 'Virtue, though depressed, shall rise again'
—Kendall.

263. **Virtus difficilia vincit** *Latin* 'Virtue conquers difficulties'
—Whitburn.

264. **Virtus dum patior vincit**   *Latin* 'Provided I bear patiently, virtue conquers'

        —Weems.

265. **Virtus durissima ferret**   *Latin* 'Virtue will bear the greatest hardships'

        —McLean.

266. **Virtus duxit avorum**   *Latin* 'The virtue of our ancestry was our guide'

        —Seton.

267. **Virtus est Dei**   *Latin* 'Virtue is of God'

        —Briggs, Brooke.

268. **Virtus est vitium fugere**   *Latin* 'It is virtue to flee from vice'

        —[Horace, *Ep.* i. 1. 41.] Reynardson.

269. **Virtus et fortitudo invincibilia sunt**   *Latin* 'Virtue and fortitude are invincible'

        —McGuire.

270. **Virtus et honos**   *Latin* 'Virtue and honor'

        —Order of St. Hubert of Loraine and of Bar, Order of Merit of the Bavarian Crown.

271. **Virtus et industria**   *Latin* 'Virtue and industry'

        —Browne (of London).

272. **Virtus et nobilitas**   *Latin* 'Virtue and nobility'

        —Henvill, Llewellin.

273. **Virtus et spes**   *Latin* 'Virtue and hope'

        —Caldwell.

274. **Virtus fides fortitudo**   *Latin* 'Virtue, fidelity, and fortitude'

        —Spens.

275. **Virtus fortunae victrix**   *Latin* 'Virtue conquers fortune'

        —Sandes.

276. **Virtus honoris Janua**   *Latin* 'Virtue, the gateway to honor'

        —Burr (U.S.), Farlow (U.S.).

277. **Virtus impendere vero**   *Latin* 'It is virtue to be devoted to truth'

        —Brown.

278. **Virtus in actione consistit**   *Latin* 'Virtue consists in action'

        —Craven (E.), Clayton (Bt.), Halford, Sier.

279. **Virtus incendit vires**   *Latin* 'Virtue excites our powers'

        —Strangford (V.).

280. **Virtus incumbet honori**   *Latin* 'Virtue will rest upon honor'

        —Williams (of Eltham).

281. **Virtus insignit audentes** *Latin* 'Virtue renders the bold illustrious'
—Beamish.

282. **Virtus intaminatis fulget honoribus** *Latin* 'Virtue shines with unspotted honors'
—[Horace, *Car.* iii. 2. 17.] Truss.

283. **Virtus invicta** *Latin* 'Virtue is invincible'
—Morrogh.

284. **Virtus invicta gloriosa** *Latin* 'Unconquered virtue is glorious'
—Thomas (Bt.), Bentham (of Lincoln's Inn).

285. **Virtus invicta viget** *Latin* 'Unconquered virtue flourishes'
—Penyston.

286. **Virtus invidiae scopus** *Latin* 'Virtue is the mark of envy'
—Methuen (B.).

287. **Virtus labi nescit** *Latin* 'Virtue cannot stumble'
—Ludwig Günther, Count of Schwarzburg-Rudolstadt (1581–1646).

288. **Virtus late dominatur** *Latin* 'Virtue rules far and wide'
—Johann Georg III, Elector of Saxony (1647–91).

289. **Virtus laudanda** *Latin* 'Virtue is praiseworthy'
—Patton.

290. **Virtus laudata crescit** *Latin* 'Virtue grows by praise'
—Berkhamsted School, U.K.

291. **Virtus libertas et patria** *Latin* 'Virtue, liberty, and country'
—Wetmore (U.S.).

292. **Virtus maturat** *Latin* 'Virtue ripens'
—Riddel, Riddell.

293. **Virtus mihi scutum** *Latin* 'Virtue is to me a shield'
—Warren.

294. **Virtus mille scuta** *Latin* 'Virtue equals a thousand shields'
—Clifford (Bt.), Dayrell, Howard (of Effingham, b.), Sadler, Vyse.

295. **Virtus nobilitat** *Latin* 'Virtue ennobles'
—Order of the Belgic Lion for Civil Merit; Gwinnett, Henderson.

296. **Virtus nobilitat honoremque parit** *Latin* 'Virtue ennobles and brings honor'
—Friedrich, Duke of Schleswig-Holstein and Norburg (1581–1658).

297. **Virtus nobilitat omnia** *Latin* 'Virtue ennobles all things'
—Stetson (U.S.).

298. **Virtus non vertitur** *Latin* 'Virtue does not turn'
—Donegan, Sarsfield.

299. **Virtus omnia nobilitat** *Latin* 'Virtue ennobles all things'
—Herrick, Heyrick, Eyrick.

300. **Virtus omnia vincit** *Latin* 'Virtue conquers all things'
—White.

301. **Virtus paret robur** *Latin* 'Virtue begets strength'
—Banbury (Bt.), Richardson.

302. **Virtus patientia veritas** *Latin* 'Virtue, patience, truth'
—Johnson.

303. **Virtus patrimonio nobilior** *Latin* 'Virtue is nobler than inheritance'
—Trelawney.

304. **Virtus plus gladio vera timetur** *Latin* 'True virtue is more feared than the sword'
—Johann, Duke of Braunschweig-Lüneburg-Harburg (1573–1625).

305. **Virtus post facta** *Latin* 'Virtue after exploits'
—Borthwick.

306. **Virtus post fata superstes** *Latin* 'Virtue survives death'
—Johann Casimir, Duke of Saxony-Coburg (1564–1633).

307. **Virtus post funera vivit** *Latin* 'Virtue lives after the tomb'
—Stansfield.

308. **Virtus potentior auro** *Latin* 'Virtue is more powerful than gold'
—Falconer.

309. **Virtus prae numine** *Latin* 'Virtue under the presence of the Divinity'
—Price.

310. **Virtus prae nummis** *Latin* 'Virtue is preferable to money'
—Stuart.

311. **Virtus praestantior auro** *Latin* 'Virtue is more excellent than gold'
—Severne, Whieldon.

312. **Virtus praestat auro** *Latin* 'Virtue is better than gold'
—Cunninghame.

313. **Virtus pretiosior auro** *Latin* 'Virtue is more precious than gold'
—Robinson.

314. **Virtus prevalebit** *Latin* 'Virtue will prevail'
—Ranken.

315. **Virtus probata florebit** *Latin* 'Tried virtue will flourish'
—Bandon (E.), Bernard.

316. **Virtus probata florescit** *Latin* 'Tried virtue flourishes'
—Cologan.

317. **Virtus propter se** *Latin* 'Virtue for its own sake'
—Radcliffe (Bt.), Reppington (of Arnington).

318. **Virtus pyramis** *Latin* 'Virtue is a pyramid'
—Kinchant.

319. **Virtus repulsae nescia sordidae** *Latin* 'Virtue unconscious of base repulse'
—[Horace, *Car*. iii. 2. 17.] Desart (E.), Laurie.

320. **Virtus rosa suavior stella clarior** *Latin* 'Virtue is sweeter than a rose, brighter than a star'
—Lloyd.

321. **Virtus salus ducum** *Latin* 'Virtue is the safety of leaders'
—Leader.

322. **Virtus se coronat** *Latin* 'Virtue crowns itself'
—Woodbridge (U.S.).

323. **Virtus secura sequitur** *Latin* 'Virtue follows in safety'
—Severne.

324. **Virtus semper eadem** *Latin* 'Virtue is always the same'
—Turville.

325. **Virtus semper valet** *Latin* 'Virtue always avails'
—Woodward.

326. **Virtus semper viret** *Latin* 'Virtue always flourishes'
—Woodward.

327. **Virtus semper viridis** *Latin* 'Virtue is ever green'
—Green, Belmore (E.), Corry, France (of Cheshire), Laurie (Bt.), Lowry.

328. **Virtus sibi aureum** *Latin* 'Virtue is worth gold to itself'
—Knight.

329. **Virtus sibimet merces** *Latin* 'Virtue is its own reward'
—Mackellar.

330. **Virtus sibi munus** *Latin* 'Virtue, a reward in itself'
—Van Cortlandt (U.S.).

331. **Virtus sibi praemium** *Latin* 'Virtue is its own reward'
—Calderwood, Wilson (Co. Lanark).

332. **Virtus sine dote**   *Latin* 'Virtue without a dowry'
—Davies.

333. **Virtus sine macula**   *Latin* 'Virtue unspotted'
—Russell.

334. **Virtus sine metu**   *Latin* 'Virtue without fear'
—Howard.

335. **Virtus sola**   *Latin* 'Virtue alone'
—Henderson.

336. **Virtus sola felicitas**   *Latin* 'Virtue is the only happiness'
—Bliss.

337. **Virtus sola invicta**   *Latin* 'Virtue alone is invincible'
—Eyre (of Wilts), Field.

338. **Virtus sola nobilitas**   *Latin* 'Virtue is the only nobility'
—Blake (of Menlo, bt.), Throckmorton (Bt.).

339. **Virtus sola nobilitat**   *Latin* 'Virtue alone ennobles'
—Caddle, Blake (of Furbough), Henrison, Wallscourt (B.),
Watson.

340. **Virtus sub cruce crescit**   *Latin* 'Virtue increases under the cross'
—Bury.

341. **Virtus sub cruce crescit, ad aethera tendens**   *Latin* 'Virtue grows under the cross, and looks to heaven'
—Charleville (E.).

342. **Virtus sub pondere crescit**   *Latin* 'Virtue increases under the burden'
—Feilden, Jephson.

343. **Virtus superat fortunam**   *Latin* 'Virtue prevails over fate'
—Johann Ernst, Prince of Anhalt (1578–1602).

344. **Virtus tollit ad astra**   *Latin* 'Virtue exalts to the stars'
—Innes.

345. **Virtus triumphat**   *Latin* 'Virtue triumphs'
—Church.

346. **Virtus tutamen**   *Latin* 'Virtue is a defense'
—Germon.

347. **Virtus tutissima**   *Latin* 'Virtue is safest'
—Conlan.

348. **Virtus tutissima cassis**   *Latin* 'Virtue is the safest helmet'
—Barker, Bellairs, Finch, Hatton, Stephenson, Williams.

349. **Virtus ubique**   *Latin* 'Virtue everywhere'
—Stevenson, Verst.

350. **Virtus ubique sedem**   *Latin* 'Virtue has its home everywhere'
       —Stevensone.

351. **Virtus vera nobilitas**   *Latin* 'Virtue is true nobility'
       —Henville.

352. **Virtus vera nobilitas est**   *Latin* 'Virtue is true nobility'
       —Mather (U.S.).

353. **Virtus veritas libertas**   *Latin* 'Virtue, truth, and freedom'
       —Glossop B. C., U.K.

354. **Virtus verus honos**   *Latin* 'Virtue is true honor'
       —Burr.

355. **Virtus viget in arduis**   *Latin* 'Virtue flourishes in difficulties'
       —Gurdon.

356. **Virtus vincit invidium**   *Latin* 'Virtue overcometh envy'
       —Cornwallis (E.), Clibborn, Mann.

357. **Virtus virtutis praemium**   *Latin* 'Virtue is its own reward'
       —MacMoran.

358. **Virtus vitium fugere**   *Latin* 'It is virtue to shun vice'
       —Whitby.

359. **Virtus vulnere virescit**   *Latin* 'Virtue gains strength by a wound'
       —Leith.

360. **Virtute**   *Latin* 'By virtue'
       —Karl, Margrave of Baden (1598–1625); Cooper (Bt.),
       Church, Dick, Ferguson, Keane.

361. **Virtute, non viribus**   *Latin* 'By virtue, not by force'
       —Derrick.

362. **Virtute, non viribus vincent**   *Latin* 'They shall conquer by virtue, not by force'
       —Vincent.

363. **Virtute acquiritur**   *Latin* 'It is acquired by virtue'
       —Robertson.

364. **Virtute acquiritur honos**   *Latin* 'Honor is acquired by virtue'
       —Richardson (Bt.), Richardson, Richie, Ritchie, Spence.

365. **Virtute ad astra**   *Latin* 'Through virtue to heaven'
       —Home (of Staines).

366. **Virtute adepta**   *Latin* 'Acquired by virtue'
       —Paton.

367. **Virtute cresco**   *Latin* 'I grow by virtue'
       —Burnet, Forbes, Leask.

368. **Virtute decet non sanguine niti**   *Latin* 'Man should rely on his
virtue and not on his descent'
—Simon VII, Count von der Lippe (1588–1627).

369. **Virtute decoratus**   *Latin* 'Adorned with virtue'
—Glasscott.

370. **Virtute duce**   *Latin* 'With virtue for guide'
—Elder, Shannon, Shand (of the Burn, co. Forfar).

371. **Virtute et amicitia**   *Latin* 'By virtue and friendship'
—Jervis.

372. **Virtute et amore**   *Latin* 'By virtue and love'
—McKenzie.

373. **Virtute et armis**   *Latin* 'By virtue and arms'
—Ernst Ludwig, Duke of Saxony (1587–1620); State of
Mississippi; Minnitt.

374. **Virtute et claritate**   *Latin* 'By virtue and high repute'
—Hara, O'Hara.

375. **Virtute et constantia**   *Latin* 'Through virtue and tenacity'
—Malta.

376. **Virtute et honore**   *Latin* 'With virtue and honor'
—Wells.

377. **Virtute et industria**   *Latin* 'By virtue and industry'
—Bristol City and C. B. C., U.K.; City of Bristol, U.K.

378. **Virtute et ingenio**   *Latin* 'By virtue and ability'
—Master.

379. **Virtute et non vi**   *Latin* 'By virtue and not by violence'
—Bradstreet.

380. **Virtute et numine**   *Latin* 'By virtue and providence'
—Cloncurry (B.), Creagh, Lawless.

381. **Virtute et opera**   *Latin* 'By virtue and energy'
—Bennie, Bernie.

382. **Virtute et opere**   *Latin* 'Through virtue and work'
—Prime (U.S.).

383. **Virtute et probitate**   *Latin* 'By virtue and honesty'
—Magan.

384. **Virtute et prudentiâ**   *Latin* 'By virtue and prudence'
—Dames, Hepburn.

385. **Virtute et robore**   *Latin* 'By virtue and strength'
—Borough (Co. Salop), Pillans (of East Dereham, co.
Norfolk).

386. **Virtute et sapientia** *Latin* 'By virtue and wisdom'
—Brownrigg.

387. **Virtute et valare luceo non uro** *Latin* 'By virtue and valor I shine, but do not burn'
—Mackenzie.

388. **Virtute et valore** *Latin* 'By virtue and valor'
—Stamer (Bt.), Batt, McKenzie, Peppard, Noble, Mackenzie (of Ganloch, co. Ross, Bt.), Waldron.

389. **Virtute et veritate** *Latin* 'With virtue and truth'
—Blathwayte.

390. **Virtute et vigilantia** *Latin* 'By virtue and vigilance'
—Sharp.

391. **Virtute et votis** *Latin* 'By virtue and vows'
—Neilson (of Manwood).

392. **Virtute experiamur** *Latin* 'We will attempt it with virtue'
—Philipp, Duke of Schleswig-Holstein (1584–1663).

393. **Virtute fideque** *Latin* 'By virtue and faith'
—Elibank (B.), Murray, McMurray.

394. **Virtute honor** *Latin* 'Honor through virtue'
—Richardson.

395. **Virtutem ante pono honorem** *Latin* 'I prefer virtue to honor'
—McPherson (U.S.).

396. **Virtutem avorum aemulus** *Latin* 'Rivalling the virtue of the ancestors'
—Mortimer (U.S.).

397. **Virtutem coronat honos** *Latin* 'Honor crowns virtue'
—Drummond.

398. **Virtute me involvo** *Latin* 'I wrap myself in my virtue'
—[Horace, *Car.* iii. 29. 54.] Dereham (or Deerham).

399. **Virtutem extendere factis** *Latin* 'To increase virtue by deeds'
—[Vergil, *Aen.* vi. 806.] Fisher.

400. **Virtutem hilaritate colere** *Latin* 'Nurture virtue with lightheartedness'
—Wynkoop (U.S.).

401. **Virtutem sequitur fama** *Latin* 'Fame follows virtue'
—Dance.

402. **Virtutem sic et culpam** *Latin* 'Virtue thus and blame'
—Maxwell.

403. **Virtute nihil invium**   *Latin* 'No way is impassable to virtue'
—Chamberlayne, Hillary.

404. **Virtute non aliter**   *Latin* 'By virtue not otherwise'
—Moir (of Hilton).

405. **Virtute non armis fido**   *Latin* 'I trust in virtue, not in arms'
—Egerton.

406. **Virtute non sanguine**   *Latin* 'By virtue not by blood'
—Southby.

407. **Virtute non vi**   *Latin* 'By virtue not by force'
—Barneby, Chivas, Shivez, Coppinger, Derrick, Rumsey.

408. **Virtute nulla possessio major**   *Latin* 'No possession is greater than virtue'
—Cawarden.

409. **Virtute orta**   *Latin* 'Sprung from virtue'
—Stewart.

410. **Virtute orta occidunt rarius**   *Latin* 'Things sprung from virtue rarely perish'
—Aiton.

411. **Virtute parata**   *Latin* 'Acquired by virtue'
—Melville, 2Whytt.

412. **Virtute paret robur**   *Latin* 'Strength obeys virtue'
—Richardson.

413. **Virtute parta**   *Latin* 'Acquired by virtue'
—Hallyday, White.

414. **Virtute probitate**   *Latin* 'By virtue and integrity'
—Magan.

415. **Virtute promoveo**   *Latin* 'I advance by virtue'
—Sideserf (of Rochlaw).

416. **Virtute res parvae crescunt**   *Latin* 'Small things increase by virtue'
—Town of Anstruther, U.K.

417. **Virtute securus**   *Latin* 'Safe by virtue'
—Hawarden (V.).

418. **Virtute sibi praemium**   *Latin* 'By virtue he gains reward for himself'
—Fenwick.

419. **Virtute spernit victa**   *Latin* 'Virtuously he spurns the conquered'
—Elliott (U.S.).

420. **Virtute superanda fortuna** *Latin* 'Fortune is to be overcome by virtue'
—Whiteford.

421. **Virtute tutus** *Latin* 'By virtue safe'
—Blair, Marshall, Phaire.

422. **Virtute viget** *Latin* 'He flourishes by virtue'
—Keirie, Paton.

423. **Virtute vinces** *Latin* 'By virtue thou shalt conquer'
—Leatham.

424. **Virtute vincet** *Latin* 'He shall conquer by virtue'
—Cooper.

425. **Virtute vincit invidiam** *Latin* 'He conquers envy by virtue'
—Mann.

426. **Virtute viresco** *Latin* 'I flourish by virtue'
—Paterson.

427. **Virtuti** *Latin* 'To virtue'
—Dick.

428. **Virtuti beneficentia** *Latin* 'Kindness to virtue'
—Order of the Lion of Lembourg.

429. **Virtutibus praemium honor** *Latin* 'Honor the reward of virtues'
—Ffeilden (of Witton).

430. **Virtuti et fidelitati** *Latin* 'For virtue and fidelity'
—Order of the Golden Lion.

431. **Virtuti et fortunae** *Latin* 'To virtue and fortune'
—Gardiner.

432. **Virtuti fido** *Latin* 'I trust in virtue'
—Ap-Eynions.

433. **Virtuti honores soli** *Latin* 'Honors to virtue alone'
—Wrowe-Walton.

434. **Virtuti non armis fido** *Latin* 'I trust to virtue, not to arms'
—Wilton (E.), Egerton (Bt.), Twiss (of Kerry).

435. **Virtuti nulla via invia** *Latin* 'To virtue no way is impassable'
—[Ovid, *Met.* xiv. 113.] Georg Friedrich, Duke of Württemberg (1657–85).

436. **Virtuti omnia parent** *Latin* 'All things obey virtue'
—Butter.

437. **Virtutis** *Latin* 'Of virtue'
—Skeen.

438. **Virtutis amore** *Latin* 'Through love to virtue'
—[Horace, *Ep.* i. 16. 52.] Annesley (E.), Annesley (of Bletchingdon), Mountmorris (E.), Stephens (of Tregenna).

439. **Virtutis gloria crescit** *Latin* 'The glory of virtue increases'
—Tytler.

440. **Virtutis gloria merces** *Latin* 'Glory is the reward of virtue'
—Friedrich III, Duke of Schleswig-Holstein-Gottorp (1597–1659).

441. **Virtutis gloria parta** *Latin* 'The glory of virtue obtained'
—Napier.

442. **Virtuti si vis nobilis esse stude** *Latin* 'If you will be noble strive after virtue'
—Friedrich IV, Count of the Palatinate (1594–1610).

443. **Virtutis laus actio** *Latin* 'The praise of virtue is action'
—Corbet (Bt.), Rumbold (Bt.), Tansley.

444. **Virtutis praemium** *Latin* 'The reward of virtue'
—Stewart (of Overton).

445. **Virtutis praemium felicitas** *Latin* 'Happiness the reward of virtue'
—Jones.

446. **Virtutis praemium honor** *Latin* 'Honor is the reward of virtue'
—Denbigh (E.), Fielden, Feniscowles, Millington.

447. **Virtutis praemium laus** *Latin* 'Praise is the prize of virtue'
—Jervoise (Bt.).

448. **Virtutis regia merces** *Latin* 'Royal is the reward of virtue'
—Alpin, MacGregor, Peter, Skene (of Skene).

449. **Virtutis robore robur** *Latin* 'Strong as an oak in virtue's strength'
—Dackcombe (Co. Dorset).

450. **Virtutis stemmata** *Latin* 'The pedigrees of virtue'
—Cobb.

451. **Vitae via virtus** *Latin* 'Virtue is the way of life'
—Dawson, Portarlington (E.), Rust, Watkins, Weeks.

452. **Vivere virtute victoria** *Latin* 'To live in virtue is victory'
—Ernst, Duke of Braunschweig-Lüneburg (1564–1611).

453. **Vivit post funera virtus** *Latin* 'Virtue survives death'
—Nottingham City and C. B. C., U.K.; Boyle, Craig,
Shannon (E.); Wilhelm IV, Landgrave of Hesse-
Cassel (1532–92); Ernst Friedrich, Margrave of
Baden-Durlach (1560–1604); Johann Adolf, Duke
of Schleswig-Holstein-Gottorp (1575–1616);
Ludwig V, Landgrave of Hesse-Darmstadt
(1577–1626); Ludwig Günther, Count
Schwarzburg-Rudolstadt (1581–1646); Adolf
Friedrich I, Duke of Mecklenburg-Schwerin
(1588–1658).

454. **Wheare vertu lys love never dys**
—Thompson.

VISION

1. **Apparet quod latebat** *Latin* 'What lay hidden appears'
—Edgar.

2. **Circumspice** *Latin* 'Look round you'
—Wise.

3. **Credunt quod vident** *Latin* 'They believe what they see' or
'Because they see'
—Elliott.

4. **Dum sisto vigilo** *Latin* 'Whilst I stand still I watch'
—Gordon (Bt.).

5. **He who looks at Martin's ape, Martin's ape will look at him**
—Martin.

6. **Illaeso lumine solem** *Latin* '(To behold) the sun with sight
unhurt'
—Rosslyn (E.), Wedderburn.

7. **Je voys** *Old French* 'I see'
—Jossey (of Westpans).

8. **Littora specto** *Latin* 'I view the shores'
—Hamilton.

9. **Look and live**
—St. Barbe.

10. **Look through**
—Acklom (U.S.).

11. **Miserrima vidi** *Latin* 'I have seen most miserable things'
—Zephani.

12. **Observe**
> —Achieson, Atcheson.

13. **Prospicio**   *Latin* 'I look out'
> —Scripps (U.S.).

14. **Quo sursum velo videre**   *Latin* 'I want to see what is beyond'
> —Early motto of Minnesota, changed in 1858.

15. **Regarde bien**   *French* 'Look carefully'
> —Napier (Bt.).

16. **Respicit haec populum, respicit illa polum**   *Latin* 'One glances down on the people, the other up to heaven'
> —Ferdinand IV, King of Rome (1633–54).

17. **Sic te non vidimus olim**   *Latin* 'We did not formerly see thee thus'
> —Playfair (of Meigle).

18. **Sursum specto**   *Latin* 'Look upwards'
> —Stronach.

19. **Suspice**   *Latin* 'Look up'
> —Edlin.

WAKEFULNESS (*See also* VIGILANCE.)

1. **Deffro mae'n Ddydd**   *Welsh* 'Awake! It is day'
> —Cardiff City and C. B. C., U.K.

2. **Dinna waken sleeping dogs**
> —Robertson (of Lude).

3. **Excitat**   *Latin* 'He rouses'
> —Ford.

4. **I rise with the morning**
> —Cockburn.

5. **Non dormio**   *Latin* 'I sleep not'
> —Maxwell.

6. **Non dormit custos**   *Latin* 'The guard sleeps not'
> —Friedrich II, Duke of Saxony-Gotha (1676–1732).

7. **Non dormit qui custodit**   *Latin* 'The sentinel sleeps not'
> —Coghill (Bt.), Gulliver, McKellip, McKillop, Myers (Co. Essex), Louthian, Shore (of Norton Hall).

8. **Non omnibus dormio**   *Latin* 'I am not asleep to everybody'
> —Balvaird.

9. **Nunquam dormio**   *Latin* 'I never sleep'
> —Maxwell.

10. **Quiescens et vigilans**   *Latin* 'Resting and waking'
—Fairnie, Fernie.

WALKING

1. **Gänger**   *German* 'A walker'
—Walker.

2. **In lumine ambulo**   *Latin* 'I walk in the light'
—Gilmour.

3. **Mare et ferro**   *Latin* 'By sea and steel'
—Redcar B. C., U.K.

4. **Passibus aequis**   *Latin* 'With measured tread'
—Walker.

5. **Passibus citis sed aequis**   *Latin* 'With rapid but regulated steps'
—Taunton (B.).

6. **Pedetentim**   *Latin* 'Step by step'
—Foote.

7. **Per tela per hostes**   *Latin* 'Through arrows and enemies'
—Brymer.

8. **Si non consilio impetu**   *Latin* 'If not by stratagem, by assault'
—Agnew.

WAR   (*See also* AGGRESSION; CONFLICT; ENEMIES; HOSTILITY; OPPOSITION; PEACE; WEAPONS.)

1. **Agnus in pace, leo in bello**   *Latin* 'A lamb in peace, a lion in war'
—Edmonds.

2. **Arma pacis fulcra**   *Latin* 'Arms are the supporters of peace'
—Artillery Company.

3. **Arma tuentur pacem**   *Latin* 'Arms maintain peace'
—Fowke (Bt.).

4. **Aut manum aut ferrum**   *Latin* 'Either the hand or the sword'
—Wayland.

5. **Aut pax aut bellum**   *Latin* 'Either peace or war'
—Donaldson (of Kinnardie), Gunn, Hall, Heaton, Morris, Tweedie.

6. **Aut suavitate aut vi**   *Latin* 'Either by gentleness or by force'
—Hopkins (Bt.).

7. **Aut vi aut suavitate**   *Latin* 'Either by force or mildness'
—Griffith.

8. **Bella dextra** *Latin* 'Wars with the right hand'
—Ellis.

9. **Bella! Horrida bella!** *Latin* 'Wars! Horrid wars!'
—Lisle (Bt.), Lysaght.

10. **Bello ac pace paratus** *Latin* 'In war and peace prepared'
—Brackenridge (Co. Somerset).

11. **Certa bonum certamen** *Latin* 'Fight the good fight'
—Iona College, New Rochelle, New York.

12. **Certamine summo** *Latin* 'In the battle's height'
—Brisbane (Bt.), McOnoghuy.

13. **Christiana militia** *Latin* 'Christian warfare'
—Order of the Knights of Christ of Portugal, founded 1317.

14. **Civitas in bello in pace fidelis** *Latin* 'In war and in peace a faithful city'
—Worcester City and C. B. C., U.K.

15. **Cogadh na sithe** *Scots Gaelic* 'Peace or war'
—McCrummen.

16. **Cogit in hostem** *Latin* 'He attacks the enemy'
—McGilchrist.

17. **Cominus et eminus** *Latin* 'In close or distant combat'
—Order of the Porcupine (France).

18. **Deo ac bello** *Latin* 'By God and war'
—Chambers.

19. **Ex bello quies** *Latin* 'Peace arises out of war'
—Murray.

20. **Fide et bello fortis** *Latin* 'Strong in faith and war'
—Carritt.

21. **Fide et in bello fortis** *Latin* 'Strong in faith and in war'
—Carrot.

22. **Fidelis et in bello fortis** *Latin* 'Faithful and brave in war'
—Gillespie.

23. **Fight**
—Ashe (of Ashfield), Orkney (E.), Rosslyn (E.), Sinclair (B.), St. Clair.

24. **Fight and faith**
—St. Clair.

25. **Fight on, quoth Fitton**
—Fitton.

26. **Fight the good fight**
—Robertson (of Oakridge (B.).

27. **Firmius ad pugnam** *Latin* 'Stronger for battle'
—Panton.

28. **Fortis in bello** *Latin* 'Brave in war'
—Cantillon de Ballyluge.

29. **Fractus pugnatu** *Latin* 'Broken with fighting'
—Hansard.

30. **Gung ho** *Chinese* 'Work together'
—Carlson's Raiders, U.S. Marine detachment in World War II under General E. F. Carlson.

31. **Haec praestat militia** *Latin* 'This warfare excels'
—Bannerman.

32. **Have at you**
—Grant.

33. **Ils ne passeront pas** *French* 'They shall not pass'
—French forces at Verdun, World War I.

34. **In bello invictus in amore probus** *Latin* 'Unconquered in war, honorable in love'
—Steele, Steele-Graves.

35. **In bello quies** *Latin* 'There is peace in war,' *i.e.,* 'Peace is obtained by war'
—Murray (of Ochtertyre, Bt.).

36. **In fide et in bello fortis** *Latin* 'Strong both in faith and war'
—Bagwell (of Marlfield), Carroll, or O'Carroll (of Ballymore).

37. **Marte et clypeo** *Latin* 'By war and the shield'
—Methen (of Craiglownie).

38. **Marte et ingenio** *Latin* 'By war and wit'
—Smith (Co. Essex, Bt.).

39. **Marte et mari faventibus** *Latin* 'War and wave favoring'
—Morris.

40. **Martis non Cupidinis** *Latin* 'Of Mars not Cupid'
—Fletcher (Bt.).

41. **Mente non Marte** *Latin* 'By the mind, not by war'
—Locke.

42. **Milita bonam militiam retinens fidem et bonam conscientiam**
    Latin 'War a good warfare, holding faith, and a good conscience'
    —[1 Tim., i. 18–19.] Rudolf, Prince of Anhalt-Zerbst (1576–1621); Wilhelm, Duke of Saxony (1596–1622).

43. **Militemus** *Latin* 'Let us fight'
    —Maximilian, Archduke of Austria (1558–1620).

44. **Militia mea multiplex** *Latin* 'My warfare is manifold'
    —Toke (of Godinton), Tooke.

45. **Non arte sed Marte** *Latin* 'Not by science but by war'
    —Nasmyth (Bt.).

46. **Nulla salus bello** *Latin* 'No safety in war'
    —Lorimer.

47. **Pace et bello paratus** *Latin* 'In peace and war prepared'
    —Frazer.

48. **Pace vel bello** *Latin* 'In peace or war'
    —McTurk.

49. **Paratus ad arma** *Latin* 'Prepared for war'
    —Johnson (Co. Berks, Bt.).

50. **Paritur bello** *Latin* 'It is obtained by war'
    —Murray.

51. **Paritur pax bello** *Latin* 'Peace is obtained by war'
    —Blane (Bt.).

52. **Pax aut bellum** *Latin* 'Peace or war'
    —Blane (Bt.), Blain, Thesiger.

53. **Pax finis bello** *Latin* 'Peace the end of war'
    —Ellis.

54. **Pax in bello** *Latin* 'Peace in war'
    —Godolphin (B.), Leeds (D.), Osborne (of Newtown, Bt.), Bernal-Osborne.

55. **Pax potior bello** *Latin* 'Peace preferable to war'
    —Bastard (of Kitley, Co. Devon), Nemehard.

56. **Pax quaeritur bello** *Latin* 'Peace is obtained by war'
    —Cromwell (of Cheshunt Park).

57. **Per acuta belli** *Latin* 'Through the asperities of war'
    —Carpenter, Tyrconnel (E.).

58. **Per aspera belli** *Latin* 'Through the hardships of war'
    —Hopkins, Watson (of Ireland).

59. **Per bellum qui providet** *Latin* 'One who is circumspect through war'
—Liddersdale.

60. **Primi et ultimi in bello** *Latin* 'First and last in war'
—O'Gorman.

61. **Primus ultimusque in acie** *Latin* 'First and last in battle'
—Skerrett.

62. **Pro bello vel pace** *Latin* 'For war or peace'
—Anderson, Anderton.

63. **Pugna pro patriâ** *Latin* 'Fight for your country'
—Doughty, Tichborne (Bt.).

64. **Pugno pro aris** *Latin* 'I fight for our altars'
—Le Vrier.

65. **Pugno pro patriâ** *Latin* 'I fight for my country'
—Ogilvy (of Ragel).

66. **Pugno pugnas pugnavi** *Latin* 'I have fought battles with my fist'
—Despard.

67. **Quaesita marte tuenda arte** *Latin* 'Things obtained by war must be defended by art'
—Luttrell.

68. **Tam marte quam arte** *Latin* 'As much by war as by skill'
—Logie, Milne.

69. **Tam Marti quam Mercurio** *Latin* 'As much devoted to Mars as Mercury'
—Gascoigne.

70. **Tam pace quam proelio** *Latin* 'In peace as well as in war'
—Gordon.

71. **Tum pace quam praelio** *Latin* 'As well in peace as in war'
—Gordon.

72. **Tutus in bello** *Latin* 'Safe amid war'
—Dobell.

73. **Unconditional surrender**
—War goal enunciated by President Franklin D. Roosevelt in 1943 and subsequently sloganized.

74. **Utrumque** *Latin* 'Both (peace and war)'
—King Henry II.

75. **Vel pax, vel bellum** *Latin* 'Either peace or war'
—Frazer (of Eskdale), Gordon (of Rothemay), Gunn.

76. **Vi martiali Deo adjuvante** *Latin* 'By force of war, God helping'
—Marshall.

77. **Virtuti in bello** *Latin* 'To bravery in war'
—Order of St. Henry of Saxony.

78. **Virtutis in bello praemium** *Latin* 'The reward of valor in war'
—Steuart (of Allanton).

79. **Viva la guèrra è l'amor** *Spanish* 'Long live war and love!'
—Franz Albert, Duke of Saxony (1598–1642).

80. **Vive la guerre et l'amor** *French* 'Long live war and love!'
—Rudolf Maximilian, Duke of Saxony (1595–1647).

81. **We are the few, the proud, the Marines**
—United States Marine Corps.

82. **When in doubt, fight**
—General Ulysses S. Grant.

WARNING (*See also* FORESIGHT; VIGILANCE.)

1. **Blow shrill**
—Mercier (of Northumberland).

2. **Craig elachie** *Gaelic* 'The rock of alarm'
—Grant.

3. **Delectando pariterque monendo** *Latin* 'By pleasing as well as by warning'
—McKay (U.S.).

4. **Don't tread on me**
—On the first American flag of the Revolutionary War.

5. **Erit haec quoque cognita monstris** *Latin* 'This, too, shall be learnt from portents'
—Louis XIII (1601–43).

6. **Insult me not**
—McKenzie (of Applecross, Co. Ross).

7. **Monitus, munitus** *Latin* 'Forewarned, forearmed'
—Horn (of Westerhall).

8. **Praemonitus praemunitus** *Latin* 'Forewarned, forearmed'
—Rickart.

WATER (*See also* SEA; WAVES.)

1. **Aqua cadit resurgere** *Latin* 'Water falls to rise again'
—Waterfall.

2. **A rore colorem**   *Latin* 'Its color from the dew'
    —Murray.

3. **Arx celebris fontibus**   *Latin* 'A stronghold famed for its springs'
    —Harrogate B. C., U.K.

4. **Benedicite fontes Domino**   *Latin* 'O all ye springs, bless the Lord'
    —Buxton B. C., U.K.

5. **Drop as rain, distil as dew**
    —Distillers' Comp., London.

6. **Dum defluat amnis**   *Latin* Till the river ceases to flow'
    —Walton and Weybridge U. D. C., U.K.

7. **Et plui super unam civitatem**   *Latin* 'And I caused it to rain upon one city'
    —Metropolitan Water Board, London, U.K.

8. **Ex fonte perenni**   *Latin* 'Out of everlasting waters'
    —Brooke.

9. **Fonte puro**   *Latin* 'From a pure fountain'
    —Lake.

10. **Hauri ex puro**   *Latin* 'To be drawn from the pure fountain'
    —Pemberton.

11. **Ligurio rores**   *Latin* 'I lick up the dew'
    —Shepperson.

12. **Non aqua solum**   *Latin* 'Not water only'
    —Gunson.

13. **Non terra, sed aquis**   *Latin* 'Not by land, but by water'
    —Dunnet.

14. **Pula**   *Tswana* 'Rain'
    —Republic of Botswana.

15. **Pure de fonte**   *French* 'From a clear spring'
    —Spring, Casborne.

16. **Secus rivos aquarum**   *Latin* 'By rivers of water'
    —Rivers (Bt.).

17. **Terra, aqua, ignis, sal, spiritus, sulphur, Sol, Venus, Mercurius**
    Latin 'Land, water, fire, salt, spirit, sulphur, Sun, Venus, Mercury'
    —Irvine.

WAVES (*See also* SEA; WATER.)

1. **Nec flatu, nec fluctu** *Latin* 'Neither by wind nor wave'
—Edward, Udward.

2. **Nec fluctu, nec flatu** *Latin* 'Neither by wave nor wind'
—Burnet (of Dalleladies).

3. **Non fluctu nec flatu movetur** *Latin* 'He is not moved by either wave or wind'
—Parker (of Browsholme).

4. **Par fluctus portui** *Latin* 'The wave is equal to the haven'
—Wilbraham.

5. **Per fluctus ad oram** *Latin* 'Through waves to the shore'
—Burrell.

6. **Per undas, per agros** *Latin* 'Through the waves, through the fields'
—Cambridgeshire C. C., U.K.

WAY (*See also* DIRECTION.)

1. **Faugh a bollagh** *Gaelic* 'Clear the way'
—Gough (V.).

2. **Fit via vi** *Latin* 'A way is made by labor'
—Campbell, Way.

3. **Gradu diverso via una** *Latin* 'The same way by different steps'
—Calthorpe (B.).

4. **Invia virtuti pervia** *Latin* 'Pathless ways may be trodden by valor'
—Hamilton.

5. **Lux tua via mea** *Latin* 'Thy light is my way'
—Blount (Bt.), Blount.

6. **Negata tentat iter via** *Latin* 'He attempts a journey on a neglected road'
—Card (U.S.).

7. **Per lumen scientiae viam invenient populi** *Latin* 'Through the light of knowledge the people will find a way'
—Texas College, Tyler, Texas.

8. **Suffibulatus majores sequor** *Latin* 'Having buckled on my armaments, I follow my ancestors'
—Hathorn, Stewart.

9. **Through the narrow way** (*from Greek*)
—Clarke.

10. **Tramite recta**   *Latin* 'By a direct path'
—Roe (Bt.).

11. **Via veritas et vita**   *Latin* 'The way, the truth, and the life'
—Felician College, Chicago, Illinois.

WEAPONS (*See also* DEFENSE; WAR.)

1. **A cuspide corona**   *Latin* 'By a spear a crown'
—Broderick, Chapman, Midleton (V.).

2. **Arcui meo non confido**   *Latin* 'I trust not to my bow'
—[Ps. xliv. 6.] Wilkes.

3. **Arcus, artes, astra**   *Latin* 'The bow, arts, and stars'
—Birney (of Salin), Burmey.

4. **Arma pacis fulcra**   *Latin* 'Arms are the supporters of peace'
—Artillery Company.

5. **Arma parata fero**   *Latin* 'I carry arms in readiness'
—Campbell, Macguffe.

6. **Arma tuentur pacem**   *Latin* 'Arms maintain peace'
—Fowke (Bt.).

7. **Arma virumque cano**   *Latin* 'Arms and the man I sing'
—[Vergil, *Aeneid* i. 1.] Gabriel.

8. **Armé à tous points**   *French* 'Armed at all points'
—Byrom.

9. **Armis et animis**   *Latin* 'By arms and courage'
—Carnagie, Carnegie, Gilfillan.

10. **Armis et diligentia**   *Latin* 'By arms and diligence'
—Baskin (of Scotland).

11. **Armis et fide**   *Latin* 'By arms and fidelity'
—Campbell (of Auchawilling).

12. **Armis et industria**   *Latin* 'By arms and industry'
—Cochran (of Balbarchan).

13. **Armis frango**   *Latin* 'I break by arms'
—Gib.

14. **Armis potentius aequum**   *Latin* 'Justice is more powerful than arms'
—Falconer (of Newton, Scotland).

15. **Artibus et armis**   *Latin* 'By arts and arms'
—Elton (Bt.).

16. **As an arrow true**
—Nicolls.

17. **A wight 'quick' man never wants a weapon**
—Wightman.

18. **By the sword**
—Atkins (of Fountainville, Co. Cork).

19. **Cedant arma** *Latin* 'Let arms yield'
—Best.

20. **Cedant arma labori** *Latin* 'Let arms give place to labor'
—Stubs.

21. **Cedant arma togae** *Latin* 'Let arms yield to the gown'
—[Cicero, *Off.* xxii.] Read (Bt.).; Territorial seal of Wyoming.

22. **Clamant nostra tela in regis querela** *Latin* 'Our weapons clash in the king's quarrel'
—Woolwich B. C., U.K.

23. **Con la virtu e l'arme s'acquista gloria** *Italian* 'With virtue and arms is glory won'
—Johann Wilhelm II, Duke of Saxony (1600–32).

24. **Consilio et armis** *Latin* 'By wisdom and arms'
—Stephens.

25. **Cuspis fracta causa coronae** *Latin* 'A spear broken in the cause of the crown' or, 'A spear broken is the cause of a crown'
—Rolt (Co. Kent).

26. **Dat tela fidelitas** *Latin* 'Fidelity supplies weapons'
—Tipping.

27. **Deo duce, ferro comitante** *Latin* 'God my guide, and my sword my companion'
—Caulfield, Charlemont (E.).

28. **Deo et gladio** *Latin* 'By God and my sword'
—Crealock, Crealocke.

29. **Deo non armis fido** *Latin* 'I trust in God, not in arms'
—Boycott, Morse, Morse-Boycott.

30. **Dieu et mon espée** *French* 'God and my sword'
—Norton (of Elmham, Co. Norfolk), Rickinghall (Co. Suffolk).

31. **Ense et animo** *Latin* 'With sword and courage'
—Grant (Bt.).

32. **Ense libertatem petit**   *Latin* 'He seeks liberty by his sword'
—Caldwell.

33. **Ense libertatem petit inimico tyrannis**   *Latin* 'He demands liberty from tyrants with a hostile sword'
—Caldwell.

34. **Ense petit placidam sub libertate quietam**   *Latin* 'By the sword we seek peace but peace only under liberty'
—State of Massachusetts.

35. **Et arma et virtus**   *Latin* 'Both arms and virtue'
—Dundas, Hamilton (of Westburn).

36. **Et nos quoque tela sparsimus**   *Latin* 'And we also have hurled our javelins'
—Hastings (M.).

37. **Ferro comite**   *Latin* 'My sword my companion'
—Mordaunt (Bt.), Tolson (of Bridekirk, Co. Cumberland).

38. **Ferro consulto**   *Latin* 'I argue with the sword'
—Tregose.

39. **Ferro mea recupero**   *Latin* 'I recover my own with my sword'
—Bryan.

40. **Ferrum equitis salus**   *Latin* 'His sword is the safety of the horseman'
—Smyth.

41. **Fortis in armis**   *Latin* 'Strong in arms'
—Armstrong (B.).

42. **Fortis valore et armis**   *Latin* 'Strong in courage and arms'
—Hatch.

43. **Fortitudine et ense**   *Latin* 'By valor and the sword'
—Crossdell.

44. **Fractum non abjicio ensem**   *Latin* 'I throw not away the broken sword'
—Armitage.

45. **Gladio et arcu**   *Latin* 'With sword and bow'
—Stubber.

46. **Gladio et virtute**   *Latin* 'By the sword and by valor'
—Garstin.

47. **Gladium musarum nutrix**   *Latin* 'The sword is the nurse of the muses'
—Mill.

48. **Gogoniant y cleddyf** *Welsh* 'The glory of the sword'
—Gwyn, Gwynne.

49. **His fortibus arma** *Latin* 'Arms to these brave men'
—Nisbet.

50. **His Saladinum vicimus armis** *Latin* 'We conquered Saladin with these arms'
—Minshull.

51. **Hoeg dy fwyall** *Welsh* 'Sharpen your battle-axe'
—Price-Williams.

52. **In ferro tutamen** *Latin* 'Defense in the sword'
—Ferrier.

53. **In ferrum libertate ruebant** *Latin* 'Through liberty they rushed to the sword'
—Gardner.

54. **Jaculis nec arcu** *Latin* 'With javelins, not with bow'
—Bowes.

55. **Juncta arma decori** *Latin* 'Arms united to merit'
—McGouan.

56. **Jure et dignitate gladii** *Latin* 'By the right and dignity of the sword'
—Cheshire C. C., U.K.

57. **Leges arma tenent sanctas** *Latin* 'Arms cause laws to be respected'
—Benson.

58. **Legibus et armis** *Latin* 'By laws and arms'
—Gordon (of Gordonbank).

59. **Le nom, les armes, la loyauté** *French* '(My) name, (my) arms, (my) loyalty'
—Newland.

60. **Leoni non sagittis fido** *Latin* 'I trust to the lion not to my arrows'
—Egerton.

61. **Liliae praelucent telis** *Latin* 'Lilies outshine weapons of war'
—Webber.

62. **Literis et armis** *Latin* 'By letters and by arms'
—Wilhelm Ernst, Duke of Saxony-Weimar (1662–1728).

63. **Marte et industria** *Latin* 'By arms and industry'
—Ogilvy.

64. **Marte et labore** *Latin* 'By arms and toil'
—Newgill.

65. **Marte non Arte**   *Latin* 'By arms not art'
—Neasmith.

66. **Nec ferro, nec igne**   *Latin* 'Neither by sword nor fire'
—McKaile.

67. **Nec ferro nec igni**   *Latin* 'Neither by sword nor by fire'
—Appleby B. C., U.K.

68. **Nec gladio, nec arcu**   *Latin* 'Neither by sword, nor bow'
—Dudley (U.S.).

69. **Ne cuiquam serviat ensis**   *Latin* 'Let not your sword be the slave of anyone'
—Peachy.

70. **Nell' armi e nelle lettere consiste la virtu**   *Italian* 'Power consists in weapons and in knowledge'
—Franz, Duke of Braunschweig-Lüneburg (1572–1601).

71. **Non eget arcu**   *Latin* 'He does not need a bow'
—Elliot, Kynymound, Minto (E.).

72. **Non eget jaculis**   *Latin* 'He needs not javelins'
—Clark.

73. **Non eget Mauri jaculis**   *Latin* 'He needs not the Moorish javelins'
—[Horace, *Car.* i. 22. 1.] Miller.

74. **Non eget Mauri jaculis neque arcu**   *Latin* 'He needs neither the javelins of the Moors nor the bow'
—Watts.

75. **Non solum armis**   *Latin* 'Not by arms only'
—Lindsay (of Cairnie).

76. **Numine et arcu**   *Latin* 'By the Deity and my bow'
—Bowman.

77. **Par la grace et par les armes**   *French* 'By grace and by arms'
—Ludwig Friedrich, Duke of Schleswig-Holstein-Sonderburg-Beck (1654–1728).

78. **Pax armis acquiritur**   *Latin* 'Peace is acquired by arms'
—Arrat.

79. **Per Deum et ferrum obtinui**   *Latin* 'By God and my sword have I prevailed'
—Hill.

80. **Per ferrum obtinui**   *Latin* 'I have got possession by my sword'
—Hillas.

81. **Per ignem per gladium**   *Latin* 'By fire and sword'
—Welbey (Bt.).

82. **Pietate, legibus, et armis** *Latin* 'By piety, by law, and by arms'
—Philipp, Landgrave of Hesse-Butzbach (1581–1643).

83. **Quondam his vicimus armis** *Latin* 'We formerly conquered with these arms'
—Carleton, Dorchester (B.).

84. **Rex spicula nescit** *Latin* 'The king knows not the arrow'
—Louis XII.

85. **Rubet ensis sanguine Arabum** *Latin* 'The sword is red with the blood of the Arabs'
—Order of St. James of the Sword.

86. **Saevumque tridentem servamus** *Latin* 'Let us preserve the dread trident'
—Broke, Loraine.

87. **Scuto magis quam gladio** *Latin* 'With the shield more than the sword'
—Shield.

88. **Securis fecit securum** *Latin* 'My axe saved me'
—Luxmore.

89. **Shoot thus**
—Yeoman.

90. **Sica inimicis** *Latin* 'A dagger to his enemies'
—McLoskey.

91. **Spiritus gladius** *Latin* 'The sword of the spirit'
—Hutton (of Marske).

92. **Steel to the back**
—Steel.

93. **Tela spoliis data** *Latin* 'Weapons given by spoils'
—Sharpe.

94. **Tutamen tela coronae** *Latin* 'Our weapons are the defense of the crown'
—Tisdall.

95. **Venabulis vinco** *Latin* 'I conquer with hunting-spears'
—Venables.

96. **Vi et armis** *Latin* 'By force and arms'
—Armstrong.

97. **Vincit cum legibus arma** *Latin* 'He conquers arms by laws'
—Atkyns.

98. **Virtus plus gladio vera timetur**   *Latin* 'True virtue is more feared than the sword'
 —Johann, Duke of Braunschweig-Lüneburg-Harburg (1573–1625).

99. **Virtute et armis**   *Latin* 'By virtue and arms'
 —Ernst Ludwig, Duke of Saxony (1587–1620); State of Mississippi; Minnitt.

100. **Virtute nihil obstat et armis**   *Latin* 'Nothing resists valor and arms'
 —Adlborough (E.).

101. **Virtute non armis fido**   *Latin* 'I trust in virtue, not in arms'
 —Egerton.

102. **Virtuti non armis fido**   *Latin* 'I trust to virtue, not to arms'
 —Wilton (E.), Egerton (Bt.), Twiss (of Kerry).

103. **Vis fortibus arma**   *Latin* 'Strength is arms to the brave'
 —Cruikshank.

104. **Vi vivo et armis**   *Latin* 'I live by force and arms'
 —Hennessy, O'Hennessy.

105. **Weapon forefendeth evil**
 —Mitford.

WILL   (*See also* ACTION; DESIRE; DIVINE GUIDANCE; INTENTION; SELF-DETERMINATION.)

1. **De bon vouloir**   *French* 'With goodwill'
 —Goodwin.

2. **Ma volonté**   *French* 'My will'
 —Charles, Duke of Orleans, father of Louis XII of France.

3. **Omnes benevolentia**   *Latin* 'All men (treat) with good will'
 —Phillips (U.S.).

4. **Remigio altissimi**   *Latin* 'According to the will of the highest'
 —Rudolf August, Duke of Braunschweig-Wolfenbüttel (1627–1704).

5. **There is no difficulty to him that wills**
 —Haines; Hains (U.S.).

6. **Will well**
 —Urquhart (of Craigston).

WILLINGNESS

1. **Fons vitae sapientia** *Latin* 'Wisdom is the fountain of life'
—Trent College, U.K.

2. **Invitum sequitur honos** *Latin* 'Honor follows even the unwilling man'
—Gerard (U.S.).

3. **I will who will not**
—Wilson.

4. **Nec deerit operi dextra** *Latin* 'Nor shall my hand be wanting to the work'
—Brothwick (of Mayshiels).

5. **Nec volenti, nec nolenti** *Latin* 'For one neither willing, nor for one unwilling'
—Westby (of Thornhill).

6. **Nil durum volenti** *Latin* 'Nothing is hard to a willing man'
—Arthur, Crawfurd.

7. **Please God I live, I'll go**
—Lloyd.

8. **Valens et volens** *Latin* 'Able and willing'
—Fetherston (of Bracklyn), Fetherstonhaugh.

9. **Volens et potens** *Latin* 'Willing and able'
—Original State seal of Nevada.

10. **Volens et valens** *Latin* 'Willing and able'
—Fetherston (Bt.).

11. **Volenti nil difficile** *Latin* 'To the willing nothing is difficult'
—Cruch.

12. **Volo non valeo** *Latin* 'I am willing but unable'
—Carlisle (E.), Greystock, Howard.

WISDOM (*See also* KNOWLEDGE; MIND; PRUDENCE; SELF-KNOWLEDGE.)

1. **Ad virtutem per sapientiam** *Latin* 'To virtue through wisdom'
—Castle Jr. College, Windham, New Hampshire.

2. **Be bolde, be wyse**
—Gollop (of Strode).

3. **Bedhoh fyr ha heb drok** *Cornish* 'Be wise and without evil'
—Carthew (of East Dereham).

4. **Be wise as a serpent, harmless as a dove**
—[Matt. x. 16.] Lewis.

5. **Bibe si sapis** *Latin* 'Drink if you are wise'
—Brunner (Bt.).

6. **Callide et honeste** *Latin* 'Wisely and honourably'
—Calley (of Burderop).

7. **Catius quam citus** *Latin* 'With more shrewdness than dispatch'
—Roscow.

8. **Con can an** *Gaelic* 'Wisdom without reproach'
—Concanon.

9. **Consilio et anima** *Latin* 'By wisdom and courage'
—Wanstead and Woodford B. C., U.K.

10. **Consilio et animis** *Latin* 'By wisdom and courage'
—Gibson, Lauderdale (E.), Maitland (Bt.), Ramadge;
Kiveton Park R. D. C., Surbiton B. C., U.K.

11. **Consilio et armis** *Latin* 'By wisdom and arms'
—Stephens.

12. **Consilio et impetu** *Latin* 'By wisdom and energy'
—Agnew (Bt.).

13. **Consilio et prudentia** *Latin* 'By counsel and by wisdom'
—Atherton U. D. C., U.K.

14. **Consilio et prudentia** *Latin* 'By wisdom and prudence'
—Clancarty (E.), Le-Poer Trench.

15. **Consilio et vi** *Latin* 'By wisdom and might'
—Perrier.

16. **Consilio non impetu** *Latin* 'By counsel, not by force'
—Agnew (Bt.), Agnew (of Barnbarroch, Dalreagle, and
Lochryan).

17. **Constitution/ Wisdom/ Justice/ Moderation**
—University System of Georgia.

18. **Cor sapientis quaerit sapientiam** *Latin* 'The heart of the wise man seeks wisdom'
—Anna Sophie, Duchess of Braunschweig-Wolfenbüttel
(1598–1659).

19. **Ein weiser gewinnet die stadt der starcken** *German* 'A wise man scaleth the city of the mighty'
—[Prov. xxi. 22.] Maximilian Emanuel, Elector of Bavaria
(1662–1726).

20. **Entends-toi** *French* 'Understand well'
—St. Clair.

21. **Être sage c'est penser à tout**   *French* 'To be wise is to think of everything (beforehand)'
    —Leopold Ebrehard, Duke of Württemberg-Mümpelgart (1670–1723).

22. **Fier et sage**   *French* 'Proud and wise'
    —Sir Thomas Bradford, G. C. B.

23. **Fons vitae sapientia**   *Latin* 'Wisdom is the fountain of life'
    —Trent College, U.K.

24. **Fortiter ac sapienter**   *Latin* 'Bravely and wisely'
    —Hordern.

25. **Fortiter et sapienter ferre**   *Latin* 'To bear bravely and wisely'
    —Porritt.

26. **Fortitudine, doctrina, sapientia**   *Latin* 'By bravery, by knowledge, by wisdom'
    —Friedrich II, Duke of Saxony-Gotha and Altenburg (1676–1732).

27. **Fortitudine et sapientia**   *Latin* 'With fortitude and wisdom'
    —Fox.

28. **Foys sapience et chevalerie**   *Old French* 'Faith, wisdom, and chivalry'
    —A'Beckett.

29. **Honor, purpose, wisdom**
    —Palo Verde College, Blythe, California.

30. **In concilio consilium**   *Latin* 'In council is wisdom'
    —Lancashire C. C., U.K.

31. **Induce animum sapientem**   *Latin* 'Put on a wise mind'
    —Sundial on the porch of a church in Eyam, England.

32. **Initium sapientiae est timor dei**   *Latin* 'The beginning of wisdom is fear of God'
    —Martin (U.S.).

33. **Initium sapientiae timor Domini** *Latin* 'The fear of the Lord is the beginning of wisdom'
—[Ps., cxi. 10.] Eberhard I, Duke of Württemberg (1445–95); Friedrich, Margrave of Brandenburg (1530–52); Johann August, Count of the Palatinate of Veldenz (1575–1611); Christian II, Elector of Saxony (1583–1611); Joachim, Margrave of Brandenburg (1583–1600); Johann Philipp, Duke of Saxony-Altenburg (1597–1639); Sophie, Princess of Anhalt (1654–1724); Karl Emil, Margrave of Brandenburg (1655–74).

34. **In multis, in magnis, in bonis expertus** *Latin* 'Experienced in many, in great, in good things'
—Bowes.

35. **In pace ut sapiens** *Latin* 'In peace as a wise man'
—Sloper.

36. **In sapientia modus** *Latin* 'In wisdom a means'
—The University of New England, Australia.

37. **Knowledge, devotion, wisdom, service**
—Pembroke State University, Pembroke, North Carolina.

38. **Lege, sapere aude** *Latin* 'Read, dare to be wise'
—Tattershall.

39. **Liber ac sapiens esto** *Latin* 'Be free and wise'
—Bradley (U.S.).

40. **Mea fides in sapientia** *Latin* 'My trust is in wisdom'
—Fryer.

41. **Nemo solus sapit** *Latin* 'No one is wise by himself'
—Sir Jos. Paxton (Knt.).

42. **Ne supra modum sapere** *Latin* 'Be not over wise'
—Newport (Bt.), Nassu.

43. **Noli altum sapere** *Latin* 'Desire not to be overwise'
—Clarke.

44. **Nosse Deum et bene posse mori sapientia summa est** *Latin* 'To know God and to be able to die happily is the highest wisdom'
—Ernst, Duke of Braunschweig-Lüneburg (1564–1611); August, Duke of Braunschweig-Lüneburg (1568–1636).

45. **Opes consilium parit** *Latin* 'Wisdom begets wealth'
—Bridgwater B. C., U.K.

46. **Optima sapientia probitas** *Latin* 'Probity is the best wisdom'
—Salmond.

47. **Pax, copia, sapientia** *Latin* 'Peace, plenty, wisdom'
—Fleming (Bt.), Fleming (of Manchester), West.

48. **Philosophia pietati ancillans** *Latin* 'Philosophy in service to piety'
—Hanover College, Hanover, Indiana.

49. **Prestat opes sapientia** *Latin* 'Wisdom is preferable to riches'
—Livingston (U.S.); Upcher.

50. **Profunda cernit** *Latin* 'He comprehends profound things'
—Gourlay, Simson.

51. **Prudens sicut serpens** *Latin* 'Wise as the serpent'
—Pole.

52. **Prudens simplicitas** *Latin* 'A wise simplicity'
—Amicable Life Insurance Society.

53. **Quanti est sapere** *Latin* 'How great it is to be wise'
—Shardlow R. D. C., U.K.

54. **Quo Minerva ducit, sequor** *Latin* 'Where Minerva leads, I follow'
—Tayloe (U.S.).

55. **Recte et sapienter** *Latin* 'Rightly and wisely'
—Heard.

56. **Rerum sapientia custos** *Latin* 'Wisdom is the guardian of things'
—Affleck, Auchinleck.

57. **Robore et sapientia** *Latin* 'By strength and wisdom'
—Robertson.

58. **Sagaciter, fideliter, constanter** *Latin* 'Sagaciously, faithfully, constantly'
—Ward (B.).

59. **Sagax et audax** *Latin* 'Shrewd and bold'
—O'Naghten.

60. **Sagesse sans tache** *Latin* 'Wisdom without spot'
—Concanon.

61. **Sancte et sapienter** *Latin* 'With holiness and wisdom'
—King's College School, London.

62. **Sape et tace** *Latin* 'Be wise and be silent'
—Connellan.

63. **Sapere aude** *Latin* 'Dare to be wise'
—Amos, Cooper, Wise, Macclesfield (E.), Townley-Parker, Wise (of Ford House); Oxfordshire C. C., Oldham C. B. C., U.K.

64. **Sapere aude, et tace** *Latin* 'Dare to be wise, and hold your tongue'
—Hesse.

65. **Sapere aude, incipe** *Latin* 'Dare to be wise, begin at once'
—Birney.

66. **Sapere et tacere** *Latin* 'To be wise and silent'
—Broadhurst.

67. **Sapiens dominabitur astris** *Latin* 'A wise man will govern the stars'
—Comber, Hutchinson.

68. **Sapiens non eget** *Latin* 'The wise man never wants'
—Dunbar.

69. **Sapiens qui assiduus** *Latin* 'He is wise who is industrious'
—Hansler (of Eastwood), Mitchell (Bt.), Mitchell (of Barry), Sperling.

70. **Sapiens qui prospicit** *Latin* 'He is wise who looks ahead'
—Malvern College, U.K.

71. **Sapiens qui vigilat** *Latin* 'He is wise who watches'
—Bagshot, Fowler.

72. **Sapienter et constanter** *Latin* 'Wisely and steadfastly'
—Ernst Ludwig, Count of Mansfeld (1604–32); Johann Ernst I, Duke of Saxony-Weimar (1594–1626).

73. **Sapienter et fortiter** *Latin* 'Wisely and bravely'
—Ludwig Günther, Count Schwarzburg-Ebeleben (1621–81).

74. **Sapienter et pie** *Latin* 'Wisely and piously'
—Park.

75. **Sapienter si sincere** *Latin* 'Wisely if sincerely'
—Davidson.

76. **Sapientia aedificavit sibi Domum** *Latin* 'Wisdom has built a Home for itself'
—Rockhurst College, Kansas City, Missouri.

77. **Sapientia/ caritas/ prudentia** *Latin* 'Wisdom/ charity/ prudence'
—Saint Mary of the Plains College, Dodge City, Kansas.

78. **Sapientia domus erecta est** *Latin* 'The house is built up by wisdom'

—Clippingdale.

79. **Sapientia donum Dei** *Latin* 'Wisdom is the gift of God'

—Field.

80. **Sapientia et doctrina** *Latin* 'Wisdom and teaching'

—Fordham University, New York, New York.

81. **Sapientia et veritas** *Latin* 'Wisdom and truth'

—Douglas (of Bads).

82. **Sapientia et virtus** *Latin* 'Wisdom and virtue'

—Douglas.

83. **Sapientia felicitas** *Latin* 'Wisdom is happiness'

—University of Oxford.

84. **Sapientia non violentia** *Latin* 'By wisdom, not by force'

—Philipp II, Duke of Pomerania (1573–1618).

85. **Sapientia tutus** *Latin* 'Safe by wisdom'

—Crewdson.

86. **Sapit qui Deo sapit** *Latin* 'He is wise who is wise through God'

—Wiseman.

87. **Sapit qui Deum sapit** *Latin* 'He is a wise man who has the knowledge of God'

—Wiseman.

88. **Sapit qui laborat** *Latin* 'He is wise who exerts himself'

—Dunbar.

89. **Sapit qui reputat** *Latin* 'He is wise who reflects'

—McClellan, McClelland, Macklellan.

90. **Scientia et sapientia** *Latin* 'Knowledge and wisdom'

—Illinois Wesleyan University, Bloomington, Illinois.

91. **Sedes sapientiae** *Latin* 'The seat of wisdom'

—Marian College, Indianapolis, Indiana.

92. **Seek wisdom**

—University of Western Australia, Nedlands, Australia.

93. **Semper sapit suprema** *Latin* 'He is always wise about the highest matters'

—Selby (of Biddleston and Earle).

94. **Serpentes velut et columbae** *Latin* 'As serpents and doves'

—Emys.

95. **Servire Deo sapere** *Latin* 'To serve God is to be wise'

—Sadlier.

96. **Simplices sicut pueri, sagaces sicut serpentes** *Latin* 'Harmless as boys, wise as serpents'

—Vaughan.

97. **Sit dux sapientia** *Latin* 'Wisdom be our guide'

—Woodroffe.

98. **Soyez sage** *French* 'Be wise'

—Eliott.

99. **Soyez sage et simple** *French* 'Be wise and simple'

—Spry.

100. **Timor Domini initium sapientiae (est)** *Latin* 'The fear of the Lord is the beginning of wisdom'

—[Ps., cxi. 10.] Georg Wilhelm, Count of the Palatinate of Birkenfeld (1591–1669); Magdalene Auguste, Duchess of Saxony-Gotha and Altenburg (1679–1740).

101. **Truth/ Knowledge/ Wisdom/ Education**

—Independence Community College, Independence, Kansas.

102. **Truth/ Wisdom**

—University of Southern Florida, Tampa, Florida.

103. **Valde et sapienter** *Latin* 'With force and wisdom'

—Musgrave, Sagar-Musgrave.

104. **Victrix fortunae sapientia** *Latin* 'Wisdom the conqueror of fortune'

—Andrews (Bt.), Calthrop (of Stanhoe Hall, Co. Norfolk).

105. **Victrix fortunae sapientia** *Latin* 'Wisdom overcomes fate'

—Friedrich, Duke of Saxony (1596–1622).

106. **Vincit sapientia robur (V. S. R.)** *Latin* 'Wisdom overcomes strength'

—Johann Ernst, Duke of Saxony-Eisenach (1566–1638).

107. **Virtute et sapientia** *Latin* 'By virtue and wisdom'

—Brownrigg.

108. **Wisdom, justice, moderation**

—State of Georgia.

109. **Wisdom above riches**

—Nuthoobhoy.

110. **Wisdom and strength**

—Crookes.

111. **Wisdom/ Knowledge/ Skill**
>—Martin Community College, Williamston, North Carolina.

112. **Wisdom's beginning is God's fear**
>—Campbell.

113. **Wise and harmless**
>—Grant (of Carron).

114. **With wisdom and courage**
>—St. Pancras B. C., U.K.

115. **Woksape / Woohitika / Wacantognaka / Wowacintanka**
Lakota 'Wisdom/ bravery/ fortitude/ generosity'
>—Sinte Gleska College, Rosebud, South Dakota.

WORDS (*See also* SCRIPTURES.)

1. **Deeds not words**
>—Dawson (of Low Wray), Rickford (of Aylesbury), Sainthill, Pirie, Combs.

2. **Diciendo y haciendo** *Spanish* 'Saying and doing'
>—Paget (Co. Somerset).

3. **Dixi, Dixi** *Latin* 'I have said, I have said'
>—Dixon.

4. **Either discard the word, or becomingly adhere to it** (*from Greek*)
>—Mores.

5. **Eloquentia sagitta** *Latin* 'Eloquence (is) my arrow'
>—Bland.

6. **En parole je vis** *French* 'I live on the word'
>—Legge, Stawell (B.).

7. **Et dixi nunc coepi** *Latin* 'I have said, now I begin'
>—Stubbs.

8. **Et loquor et taceo** *Latin* 'I both speak and hold my tongue'
>—Keith.

9. **Facta non verba** *Latin* 'Deeds not words'
>—Hoyle (Co. York), De Rinzey, De Renzey, Wells (of Sporle, co. Norfolk), Wilson (of Beckenham).

10. **Factis non verbis** *Latin* 'By deeds not words'
>—Dumergue, Money.

11. **Facto non verbo** *Latin* 'By deed not word'
>—Day.

12. **Facundia felix**   *Latin* 'Happy eloquence'
—Scot, Scott.

13. **Fare, fac**   *Latin* 'Say and act'
—Fairfax (B.), Ramsay-Fairfax-Lucy (Bt.).

14. **Fare et age**   *Latin* 'Say and do'
—Say (of Swaffham, Co. Norfolk).

15. **Fare fac**   *Latin* 'Speak, do'
—Fairfax (B.), Fairfax.

16. **Fari aude**   *Latin* 'Dare to speak'
—Child (U.S.).

17. **Fari quae sentias**   *Latin* 'To speak what you think'
—Walpole.

18. **Fari quae sentiat**   *Latin* 'To speak what he may think'
—Barkas, Orford (E.), Walpole.

19. **Fari quae sentient**   *Latin* 'To speak what they think'
—Bretargh, Walpole.

20. **Gesta verbis praeveniunt**   *Latin* 'Their deeds go before their words'
—Eckley, Harcourt, Swanston, Woodcock.

21. **Laissez dire**   *French* 'Let them speak'
—Middleton, Myddleton, Wharton.

22. **Language/ Art/ Science**
—Newcomb College, New Orleans, Louisiana.

23. **Lassez dire**   *Old French* 'Let them say'
—Middleton.

24. **Lesses dire**   *Old French* 'Let speak'
—Middleton, Wharton.

25. **Let them talk**
—Hewetson.

26. **Loquendo placet**   *Latin* 'He pleases when he speaks'
—Fairfowl.

27. **Mot pour mot**   *French* 'Word for word'
—Harries.

28. **Nescit vox missa reverti**   *Latin* 'When a word is once spoken it cannot be recalled'
—Halsey.

29. **Parle bien**   *French* 'Speak well'
—Parlby.

30. **Parle bien ou parle rien** *French* 'Speak well or say nothing'
—Downs.

31. **Parlez bien, ou ne parlez rien** *French* 'Speak well or do not say anything'
—Parlett (of Woodrising, Co. Norfolk).

32. **Prima voce salutat** *Latin* 'He salutes with early voice'
—Boucherett.

33. **Quod dixi, dixi** *Latin* 'What I have said I have said'
—Dixie (Bt.), Dixon (Co. York).

34. **Res non verba quaeso** *Latin* 'I seek deeds, not words'
—Mountford.

35. **Rex non verba** *Latin* 'The king, not words'
—Wilson.

36. **Saie and doe**
—Watkin.

37. **Say and do**
—Everard (of Middleton, Co. Norfolk).

38. **Sermoni consona facta** *Latin* 'Deeds agreeing with words'
—Collins (Co. Devon), Trelawney.

39. **Tace aut fac** *Latin* 'Say nothing or do'
—Burgess, Scott (Bt.), Scott.

40. **The seed is the word**
—Concordia Teachers College, Seward, Nebraska.

41. **Vox clamans in deserto** *Latin* 'A voice crying in the wilderness'
—Dartmouth College, Hanover, New Hampshire.

WORLD (*See also* EARTH.)

1. **Ex vile pretiosa** *Latin* 'Valuable things out of a base one'
—Pattinson.

2. **Lux mentis lux orbis** *Latin* 'Light of the mind, light of the world'
—Sonoma State University, Rohnert Park, California.

3. **Lux mundi** *Latin* 'Light of the world'
—Thiel College, Greenville, Pennsylvania.

4. **With the Word to the World**
—Faith Baptist Bible College, Ankeny, Iowa.

WORTHINESS (*See also* RECTITUDE; VIRTUE.)

1. **Bellement et hardiment** *French* 'Handsomely and hardily'
   —Buck.

2. **Bene** *Latin* 'Well'
   —Binney.

3. **Bene denoto** *Latin* 'I indicate well'
   —Shaw.

4. **Bene merentibus** *Latin* 'To the well-deserving'
   —Order of the Lion of Lembourg, and St. Charles of
   Wurtemberg.

5. **Bien fait** *French* 'Well done'
   —Weldon.

6. **Bien ou rien** *French* 'Well or not at all'
   —Scott.

7. **By worth**
   —Keighley B. C., Farnham U. D. C., U.K.

8. **Emare** *Latin* 'Have your price'
   —Hughan.

9. **En faizant bien** *Old French* 'In doing well'
   —Perchard.

10. **Estimatione nixa** *Latin* 'Relying on my worth'
    —Cheyne.

11. **Est meruisse satis** *Latin* 'It is sufficient to have deserved'
    —Massingberd (Co. Lincoln).

12. **Ex merito** *Latin* 'Through merit'
    —Cheston, Tharrold.

13. **Ex vile pretiosa** *Latin* 'Valuable things out of a base one'
    —Pattinson.

14. **Fert palmam mereat** *Latin* 'He bears the palm, let him deserve
    it'
    —Bates.

15. **Genti aequus utrique** *Latin* 'Worthy of both families'
    —Booth-Gore (Bt.).

16. **High merit, high reward**
    —Hymers College, Hull, U.K.

17. **Illustribus et nobilitati** *Latin* 'For the illustrious and the enno-
    bled'
    —Order of the Lion of Lembourg.

18. **Ingenio et merito**   *Latin* 'By ability and desert'
—Grout.

19. **In te digna sequere**   *Latin* 'Follow what is worthy in yourself'
—Parnell.

20. **Juncta arma decori**   *Latin* 'Arms united to merit'
—McGouan.

21. **Le mieulx que je puis**   *Old French* 'The best that I can'
—Cheney.

22. **Major opima ferat**   *Latin* 'Let the more worthy carry off the honors'
—Moir (of Stonniewood), More.

23. **Meliora supersunt**   *Latin* 'Better things remain'
—Annesley.

24. **Merebimur**   *Latin* 'We shall deserve'
—15th (King's Own) Hussars, U.K.

25. **Mereo et merito**   *Latin* 'I deserve it, and rightly so'
—Merritt (U.S.).

26. **Merere**   *Latin* 'To deserve'
—Currer (of Cliften House), Roundell.

27. **Merere et confide**   *Latin* 'Deserve and trust'
—Winwood.

28. **Meret qui laborat**   *Latin* 'He is deserving who is industrious'
—Storie.

29. **Merite**   *Latin* 'Merit'
—Currier.

30. **Meritez**   *French* 'Deserve'
—Waltham.

31. **Merito**   *Latin* 'Deservedly'
—Dunlop (Bt.), Delap, Delop.

32. **Merui**   *Latin* 'I have deserved'
—Paterson.

33. **Meruisse manu**   *Latin* 'To have merited by the hand'
—Wills.

34. **Ne vile**   *Latin* 'Not vile'
—Nevile.

35. **Ne vile fano**   *Latin* 'Bring nothing base to the temple'
—Fane, Westmoreland (E.), Stapleton.

36. **Ne vile velis** *Latin* 'Wish nothing base'
—Abergavenny (E.), Braybrooke (B.), Nevile (of Thornley), Nevill.

37. **Nil indigne** *Latin* 'Nothing unworthily'
—Wordie.

38. **Nomine digna** *Latin* 'May it be worthy of the name'
—Rhodesia.

39. **Non deficit** *Latin* 'He is not wanting'
—Foulis, Hamilton.

40. **Non deficit alter** *Latin* 'Another is not wanting'
—[Vergil, *Aen.* vi. 143.] Auldjo, Aljoy, Smith (of Berdodc), Stainforth, Walwyn (Co. Herts.).

41. **Non his insignitus** *Latin* 'Distinguished not by these'
—Sydenham.

42. **Non quam diu sed quam bene** *Latin* 'Not how long, but how well'
—Ernst Ludwig I, Duke of Saxony-Meiningen (1672–1724).

43. **Optime merenti** *Latin* 'To the best deserving'
—Witham.

44. **Optime merito de rege** *Latin* 'To him who has best deserved of the king'
—Order of Francis of the Two Sicilies.

45. **Optimum vix satis** *Latin* 'The best is scarcely enough'
—Updike (U.S.).

46. **Optimus est qui optime facit** *Latin* 'The best is he who does the best'
—Best.

47. **Ou bien ou rien** *French* 'Either well or not at all'
—Sotheby.

48. **Palmam qui meruit ferat** *Latin* 'Let him who has deserved it bear the palm'
—[Jortin, *Lusus Poetici: Ad Ventos*, st. 4.] Royal Naval School, U.K.

49. **Palmam qui meruit ferat** *Latin* 'Let him who has earned it bear the palm'
—Nelson (E.).

50. **Por dysserver** *Old French* 'To deserve'
—Carr.

51. **Pour deservir**   *French* 'To deserve'
—Carr.

52. **Pour le merite**   *French* 'For merit'
—Military Order of Merit (France).

53. **Praeclarior, quo propinquior**   *Latin* 'The more illustrious, the nearer'
—Constable.

54. **Quicquid dignum sapiente bonoque est**   *Latin* 'Whatever is worthy of a wise man and a good'
—Peach.

55. **Qui sis non unde**   *Latin* 'What you are, not whence'
—Whatman.

56. **Qui tel?**   *French* 'Who such?'
—Kettle.

57. **Quod merui meum est**   *Latin* 'What I have deserved is mine'
—Noguier.

58. **Re et merito**   *Latin* 'By reality and merit'
—Vassal-Fox, Gildea, Hebden (of Appleton).

59. **Sufficit meruisse**   *Latin* 'It is enough to have deserved well'
—Plumptre.

60. **Tam interna quam externa**   *Latin* 'As well internal as external (qualities)'
—Arbuthnot.

61. **Teneat, luceat, floreat, vi, virtute, et valore**   *Latin* 'May it hold, shine, and flourish, by valor, virtue, and worth'
—Kenny (of Kilcloghar and Correndos, Co. Galway), Kenny (of Ballyflower, Co. Roscommon).

62. **True worth never fails**
—Failsworth U. D. C., U.K.

63. **Virtute et merito**   *Latin* 'By bravery and merit'
—Order of Charles III (Spain).

64. **Whatever is worth doing is worth doing well**
—Andrew Carnegie.

ZEALOUSNESS (*See also* DILIGENCE.)

1. **Ardens**   *Latin* 'Fervent'
—Peat (of Sevenoakes).

2. **Fervor non furor**   *Latin* 'Fervor, not fury'
—Monks.

3. **Tout zèle**   *French* 'All zeal'

—Touzel.

4. **Zeal and honor**

—Blomfield.

5. **Zealous**

—Hood (Bt.).

Index I: Mottoes & Categories

Index I: Mottoes & Categories

This index contains, in one alphabetic order, all of the mottoes and categories listed in the text. Categories appear in **BOLDFACE SMALL CAPITALS** *with reference given to the first page on which the listings for the category begin. All other references are to specific categories by name and mottoes by entry number.*

A

Ab alto speres alteri quod feceris, EXPECTATION: 1
A. B. C. D. E. F. (Allein bei Christo die ewige Freude), CHRIST, JESUS: 1; SALVATION: 1
A. B. D. E. (Anfang bedenk das Ende), FINISH: 1
Abest timor, COURAGE: 1
ABILITY, p. 41
A blessing to the aged, BLESSING: 1
A bon droit, RECTITUDE: 1
A bonis ad meliora, ASPIRATION: 1; IMPROVEMENT: 1; LOCAL GOVERNMENT: 1
Ab origine fidus, FIDELITY: 1
Abscissa virescit, FLOURISHING: 1
Absit fraus, DECEPTION: 1
Absit ut glorier nisi in cruce, CROSS, THE: 1
Absque dedecore, PURITY: 1
Absque Deo nihil, DIVINITY: 1
Absque labore nihil, INDUSTRIOUSNESS: 1
Absque metu, COURAGE: 2
Absque virtute nihil, VIRTUE: 1

Abstinete, sustinete, SELF-CONTROL: 1
Abstulit qui dedit, GIFTS and GIVING: 1
Ab uno ad omnes, GIFTS and GIVING: 2
Academic—Vocational—Cultural—Patriotic—Spiritual, KNOWLEDGE: 1; PATRIOTISM: 1; SCHOOL MOTTOES: 1; SPIRIT: 1
Accendit cartu, INCENTIVE: 1
ACCEPTANCE, p. 43
Accidit in puncto quod non speratur in anno, EXPECTATION: 2
Accipe daque fidem, FAITH: 1
Accipe quantum vis, GENEROSITY: 1
Accipiter praedam sequitur, nos gloriam, BIRDS: 1; GLORY: 1
ACCOMPLISHMENT, p. 43
Acer non effrenus, LIMITATION: 1
Achievement/Citizenship, SCHOOL MOTTOES: 2
A clean heart and cheerful spirit, HAPPINESS: 1; HEART: 1; SPIRIT: 2
A coeur vaillant rien d'impossible, COURAGE: 3
Acquirit qui tuetur, DEFENSE: 1
ACQUISITION, p. 45
Acre, PROPER NAMES: 1

861

A cruce salus, CROSS, THE: 2;
SALVATION: 2
ACTION, p. 45
Action, ACTION: 1; LOCAL
GOVERNMENT: 2
Actio virtutis laus, DEEDS: 1
Acu rem tetigit, UNCLASSIFIED: 1
A cuspide corona, CROWN: 1;
WEAPONS: 1
A cuspide honos, HONOR: 1
Ad aethera virtus, VIRTUE: 2
Ad alta, ASPIRATION: 2
Ad amussim, RECTITUDE: 2
Ad aras usque obsequens,
OBEDIENCE: 1
Ad ardua tendit, ASPIRATION: 3
Ad arma paratus, PREPAREDNESS: 1;
PROTECTION: 1
Ad astra, ASPIRATION: 4; STARS: 1
Ad astra nitamur semper ad optima,
ASPIRATION: 5; STARS: 2
Ad astra per ardua, ADVERSITY: 1;
ASPIRATION: 6; STARS: 3
Ad astra per aspera, SCHOOL
MOTTOES: 3; STARS: 4
Ad astra sequor, ASPIRATION: 9;
STARS: 5
Ad astra virtus, STARS: 6; VIRTUE: 3
Ad coelos volans, ASPIRATION: 10
Ad coelum tendit, ASPIRATION: 11
Adde calcar, INCENTIVE: 2
Addecet honeste vivere, HONOR: 2
Addere legi justitiam decus, JUSTICE: 1;
LAW: 1
Addicunt aves, BIRDS: 2
Ad diem tendo, DESTINATION: 1
A ddioddefws a orfu, ENDURANCE: 1;
LOCAL GOVERNMENT: 3
Addit frena feris, ANIMALS: 1;
LIMITATION: 2
Addunt robur, STRENGTH: 1
Addunt robur stirpi, STRENGTH: 2
A Deo, non fortuna, DIVINE
GUIDANCE: 1; FORTUNE: 1
A Deo data, DIVINE GIFTS: 1
A deo et patre, DIVINE GIFTS: 2
A Deo et rege, DIVINE GIFTS: 3;
DIVINITY: 2; LOCAL GOVERNMENT: 4;
ROYALTY: 1
A deo in Deo, DIVINE GIFTS: 4
A Deo lux nostra, DIVINE GIFTS: 5;
LIGHT: 1

A Deo victoria, DIVINE GUIDANCE: 2;
VICTORY: 1
Ad escam et usum, PURPOSE: 1
Adest prudenti animus, COURAGE: 4;
PRUDENCE: 1
Ad faedera cresco, CONCILIATION: 1
Ad finem fidelis, FIDELITY: 2
Ad finem spero, HOPE: 1
Ad gloriam per spinas, GLORY: 2
Adhaereo, FIDELITY: 3
Adhaereo virtuti, VIRTUE: 4
Adhuc hic hesterna, LOCAL
GOVERNMENT: 5; PAST, THE: 1
Adhuc viresco, FLOURISHING: 2
A Dieu seul la gloire, GLORY: 3
Adjuva, o Virgo, res tua agitur, DIVINE
GUIDANCE: 3
Adjuvante Deo, DIVINE GUIDANCE: 4
Adjuvante Deo, quid timeo?, DIVINE
GUIDANCE: 5
Adjuvante Deo in hostes, DIVINE
GUIDANCE: 6
Ad littora tendit, DESTINATION: 2
Ad littora tendo, DESTINATION: 3
Ad majorem Dei gloriam, DIVINITY: 3
Ad metam, GOALS: 1
ADMIRATION, p. 47
Ad morem villae de Poole, LOCAL
GOVERNMENT: 6; TRADITION: 1
Ad mortem fidelis, FIDELITY: 4
A Domino auxilium meum, DIVINE
GUIDANCE: 7
Adorn the truth, TRUTH: 1
Ad pontes prospicimus, LOCAL
GOVERNMENT: 7; TIME: 1
Ad rem, DIRECTNESS: 1
Adsit Deus, DIVINE GUIDANCE: 8
Adsit Deus non demovebor, DIVINE
GUIDANCE: 9
Ad summa virtus, COURAGE: 5
Ad summum, ASPIRATION: 12; SCHOOL
MOTTOES: 4
Ad summum emergunt, RISING: 1
Ad te, Domine, DIVINITY: 4
ADVANCE, p. 47
Advance, ADVANCE: 1; LOCAL
GOVERNMENT: 8
Advance with courage, ADVANCE: 2;
COURAGE: 6
Advena in sylvis, STRANGER: 1
Adversa virtute repello, ADVERSITY: 3;
VIRTUE: 5

Adversis major, par secundis,
  ADVERSITY: 4; PROSPERITY: 1
ADVERSITY, p. 51
Adverso fortior, ADVERSITY: 5;
  STRENGTH: 3
Ad virtus astra, STARS: 7; VIRTUE: 6
Ad virtutem per sapientiam, SCHOOL
  MOTTOES: 5; VIRTUE: 7; WISDOM: 1
Aegis fortissima virtus, PROTECTION: 2;
  VIRTUE: 8
Aequabiliter et diligenter,
  CONSISTENCY: 1; DILIGENCE: 1
Aequaliter et diligenter, DILIGENCE: 2;
  EQUANIMITY: 1
Aequam servare mentem,
  EQUANIMITY: 2
Aequanimiter, EQUANIMITY: 3
Aequat munia comparis, DUTY: 1
Aequitas actionem regulam,
  FAIRNESS: 1
Aequitas actionum regula, FAIRNESS: 2
Aequitate ac diligentia, DILIGENCE: 3;
  FAIRNESS: 3
Aequo adeste animo, MIND: 1;
  STEADFASTNESS: 1
Aequo animo, EQUANIMITY: 4
Aeternitas, ETERNITY: 1
A falcon towering in his pride of place,
  PRIDE: 1
A favore regis nomen, NAME: 1
Affectat Olympo, ASPIRATION: 13;
  PARADISE: 1
A fin, STEADFASTNESS: 2
A foye, FAITH: 2
A friend to youth, FRIENDSHIP: 1;
  SCHOOL MOTTOES: 6
After darkness comes light,
  DARKNESS: 1; LIGHT: 2
A full and abundant life in a
  contemporary society, LIFE: 1;
  SCHOOL MOTTOES: 7
A fyno Duw a fydd, DIVINE
  GUIDANCE: 10
A Gadibus usque auroram,
  DIRECTION: 1
A gair Duw yn uchaf, SCRIPTURES: 1
AGE, p. 56
Age aut perfice, ACCOMPLISHMENT: 1;
  ACTION: 2
Age in aeternum, ETERNITY: 2
Agendo gnaviter, PRUDENCE: 2
Age officium tuum, DUTY: 2

Age quod agis, ATTENTIVENESS: 1
Agere et pati, ENDURANCE: 2
Agere pro aliis, KINDNESS: 1;
  UNSELFISHNESS: 1
AGGRESSION, p. 57
Agincourt, PROPER NAMES: 2
Agissez honnêtement, RECTITUDE: 3
Agitatione paratus, PREPAREDNESS: 2
Agitatione purgatur, PURITY: 2
Agite pro viribus, ACTION: 3
Agmina ducens, LEADERSHIP: 1
Agnoscar eventu, REPUTATION: 1
Agnus Dei mihi salus, SALVATION: 3
Agnus Dei salvator meus, ANIMALS: 2;
  CHRIST, JESUS: 2; SALVATION: 4
Agnus in pace, leo in bello,
  ANIMALS: 3; WAR: 1
A good conscience is a sure defence,
  CONSCIENCE: 1; DEFENSE: 2
A good name endureth, LOCAL
  GOVERNMENT: 9; REPUTATION: 2
AGRICULTURE, p. 58
Agriculture and commerce,
  AGRICULTURE: 1; COMMERCE: 1;
  LOCAL GOVERNMENT: 10; STATE
  MOTTOES: 1
Agros vigilantia servat, VIGILANCE: 1
A. G. T. I. (Allein Gott traue ich),
  TRUST: 1
A Home! A Home! A Home!, HOME: 1
Aides Dieu!, DIVINE GUIDANCE: 11
Aide toi et le ciel t'aidera, DIVINE
  GUIDANCE: 12
Aime le meilleur, LOVE: 1
Aimer sans crainte, FEAR: 1; LOVE: 2
Aime ton frère, LOVE: 3
Aimez loyaulté, FIDELITY: 5
Aim high, ASPIRATION: 14
Ainsi et peut estre meilleur,
  ASPIRATION: 15
Ainsi il est, FACTUALITY: 1
Ainsi je frappe, AGGRESSION: 1
A jamais, STEADFASTNESS: 3
Alabama's best little public university,
  SCHOOL MOTTOES: 8
À la bonne heure, TIME: 2
A la constancia militar premio,
  MILITARY DISTINCTION: 1; REWARD: 1
A la garde de Dieu, DIVINE
  GUIDANCE: 13
A l'amy fidèle pour jamais,
  FIDELITY: 6; FRIENDSHIP: 2

A la vérité, TRUTH: 2
A la volonté de Dieu, DIVINE
    GUIDANCE: 14
Alba de Tormes, PROPER NAMES: 3
Albuera, PROPER NAMES: 4
Alenda lux ubi orta libertas,
    LIBERTY: 1; LIGHT: 3; SCHOOL
    MOTTOES: 9
Alert, VIGILANCE: 2
Ales volat propriis, BIRDS: 3;
    SIMILARITY: 1
Aletheuontes de en Agape, SCHOOL
    MOTTOES: 10; TRUTH: 3
Algiers, PROPER NAMES: 5
Aliena insania frui optimum,
    BENEFITS: 1
Alienus ambitioni, AMBITION: 1
Aliis inserviendo consumor, SERVICE: 1
Aliis reposita, CONSERVATION: 1
Aliis servio, meipsum contero,
    SERVICE: 2
À l'immortalité, IMMORTALITY: 1
Alis aspicit astra, ASPIRATION: 16;
    STARS: 8
Alis et animo, COURAGE: 7
Alis nutrior, NOURISHMENT: 1
Alis volat propriis, SELF-
    DETERMINATION: 1; STATE
    MOTTOES: 2
Alki, STATE MOTTOES: 3; TIME: 3
Alla corona fidissimo, CROWN: 2;
    FIDELITY: 7
All Ding ein Weil, TIMELINESS: 1
Alle Ding zergänglich, TRANSIENCE: 1
Allein in Gott mein Vertrauen,
    DIVINITY: 5
Alleluiah, PRAISE: 1
Alles in Gottes Gewalt, DIVINITY: 6
Alles mit Bedacht, FORESIGHT: 1
Alles mit der Zeit, TIME: 4
Alles mit Gott, nichts ohn Ursach,
    DIVINITY: 7; REASON: 1
Alles mit Gott, und der Zeit,
    DIVINITY: 8; TIME: 5
Alles Nach Gotes Willen, DIVINE
    GUIDANCE: 15
Alles steht bei glvck und Zeit,
    FORTUNE: 2; TIME: 6
Alles von Gott, DIVINITY: 9
Alles zur Ehre Gottes, DIVINITY: 10
Alles zu seiner Zeit, TIMELINESS: 2
Allezeit mit Hut, CAUTION: 1

All for our country, COUNTRY: 1;
    PATRIOTISM: 2; STATE MOTTOES: 4
All for religion, RELIGION: 1
All is in God, DIVINITY: 11
All my hope is in God, DIVINITY: 12;
    HOPE: 2
Allons, Dieu ayde, DIVINE
    GUIDANCE: 16
All's well, CONFIDENCE: 1; LOCAL
    GOVERNMENT: 11
All things for the glory of God,
    DIVINITY: 13; LOCAL
    GOVERNMENT: 12
All this beauty is of God, BEAUTY: 1;
    DIVINITY: 14; LOCAL
    GOVERNMENT: 13
All worship be to God only,
    RELIGION: 2; TRADES: 1
Alnus semper floreat, FLOURISHING: 3
A lo hecho pecho, ENDURANCE: 3
Alta pete, ASPIRATION: 17
Alta petit, ASPIRATION: 18
Alta peto, ASPIRATION: 19
Alta sententia, LOCAL
    GOVERNMENT: 14; PURPOSE: 2
Alte fert aquila, BIRDS: 4; LOFTINESS: 1
Altera merces, REWARD: 2
Altera securitas, SECURITY: 1
Alteri, si tibi, UNSELFISHNESS: 2
Alteri prosis saeculo, FUTURE, THE: 1
Alterius non sit qui suus esse potest,
    SELF-DETERMINATION: 2
Alterum non laedere, CONCERN: 1
Alte volat, LOFTINESS: 2
Alte volo, LOFTINESS: 3
Altiora in votis, ASPIRATION: 20; DIVINE
    GUIDANCE: 17; SCHOOL MOTTOES: 11
Altiora petamus, ASPIRATION: 21;
    SCHOOL MOTTOES: 12
Altiora pete, ASPIRATION: 22
Altiora petenda, ASPIRATION: 23
Altiora petimus, ASPIRATION: 24;
    LOCAL GOVERNMENT: 15
Altiora peto, ASPIRATION: 25; SCHOOL
    MOTTOES: 13
Altiora sequimur, ASPIRATION: 26
Altiora spero, ASPIRATION: 27
Altiora videnda, ASPIRATION: 28
Altius, LOFTINESS: 4
Altius ibunt qui ad summa nituntur,
    ASPIRATION: 29
Altius tendo, ASPIRATION: 30

Altrincham en avant, LEADERSHIP: 2;
  LOCAL GOVERNMENT: 16
Always, FIDELITY: 8
Always advancing, IMPROVEMENT: 2;
  LOCAL GOVERNMENT: 17
Always do right. This will gratify some
  people and astonish the rest.,
  RECTITUDE: 4
Always faithful, FIDELITY: 9
Always for liberty, LIBERTY: 2
Always helping, ASSISTANCE: 1
Always ready, LOCAL
  GOVERNMENT: 18; PREPAREDNESS: 3
Always the same, CONSISTENCY: 2
Always to excel, ASPIRATION: 31;
  EXCELLENCE: 1
A. M. A. D. (Auxilium meum a Deo),
  DIVINE GUIDANCE: 18
Ama Deum et serva mandata,
  RELIGION: 1
A magnis ad maiora, IMPROVEMENT: 3;
  LOCAL GOVERNMENT: 19
Ama gregem, LOVE: 4
Amantes ardua dumos, FLORA: 1
Amantibus justitiam, pietatem, fidem,
  PIETY: 1
A ma puissance, LOCAL
  GOVERNMENT: 20; POWER: 1
A mari usque ad mare, SEA: 1
Amator de virtus, VIRTUE: 9
A ma vie, FIDELITY: 10
AMBITION, p. 59
Ambition sans envie, AMBITION: 2
Ambo dexter, ABILITY: 1; HANDS: 1
A. M. G. (Alles mit Gott), DIVINITY: 15
Amica veritas, TRUTH: 4
Amice, LOVE: 5
Amicis prodesse, nemini nocere,
  CONCERN: 2
Amicitia cum libertate, FRIENDSHIP: 3;
  LIBERTY: 3
Amicitia cum virtute, FRIENDSHIP: 4;
  VIRTUE: 10
Amicitiae virtutisque faedus,
  FRIENDSHIP: 5; VIRTUE: 11
Amicitiam trahit amor, FRIENDSHIP: 6;
  LOVE: 6; TRADES: 2
Amicitia permanens et incorrupta,
  FRIENDSHIP: 7
Amicitia praesidium firmissimum,
  FRIENDSHIP: 8
Amicitia reddit honores, FRIENDSHIP: 9

Amicitia sine fraude, FRIENDSHIP: 10
Amico fidus ad aras, FIDELITY: 11;
  FRIENDSHIP: 11
Amicos semper amat, FRIENDSHIP: 12
Amicta vitibus ulmo, FLORA: 2
Amicum proba hostem scito,
  FRIENDSHIP: 13
Amicus, FRIENDSHIP: 14
Amicus amico, FRIENDSHIP: 15
Amicus certus, FRIENDSHIP: 16
Amicus vitae solatium, FRIENDSHIP: 17
Amitié, FRIENDSHIP: 18
Amo, LOVE: 7
Amo, inspicio, LOVE: 8
Amoenitas, salubritas, urbanitas,
  ENJOYMENT: 1; HEALING and
  HEALTH: 1
Amoenitas salubritas urbanitas,
  ENJOYMENT: 2; HEALING and
  HEALTH: 2; LOCAL GOVERNMENT: 21
Amo honesta, VIRTUE: 12
Amo pacem, LOVE: 9; PEACE: 1
Amo probos, VIRTUE: 13
Amor Dei et proximi summa
  beatitudo, HAPPINESS: 2; LOVE: 10
Amor distantia jungit, LOVE: 11
Amor dulcis patriae, LOVE: 12;
  PATRIOTISM: 3
Amore et prudentia, LOVE: 13;
  PRUDENCE: 3
Amore floresco, LOVE: 14
Amorem progenerat amor, LOVE: 15
Amore non vi, LOVE: 16
Amore patriae, PATRIOTISM: 4
Amore sitis uniti, LOVE: 17; TRADES: 3;
  UNITY: 1
Amor et obedientia, LOVE: 18;
  OBEDIENCE: 2; TRADES: 4
Amor et pax, LOVE: 19; PEACE: 2
Amore vici, LOVE: 20
Amore vinci, LOVE: 21
Amor patitur moras, LOVE: 22
Amor patriae vincit, COUNTRY: 2;
  LOVE: 23; PATRIOTISM: 5
Amorque et obedientia, LOVE: 26;
  OBEDIENCE: 3; TRADES: 5
Amor sine timore, FEAR: 2; LOVE: 27
Amor vincit omnia, LOVE: 28
Amor vincit patriae, COUNTRY: 3;
  LOVE: 29; PATRIOTISM: 6
Amour avec loyaulté, FIDELITY: 12;
  LOVE: 30

Mottoes & Categories

Amour de la bonté, GOODNESS: 1
Amo ut invenio, LOVE: 31
Amser yw'n golud, LOCAL
  GOVERNMENT: 22; PROSPERITY: 2;
  TIME: 7
ANCESTRY, p. 59
Anchor, fast anchor, STEADFASTNESS: 4
Anchora labentibus undis, SECURITY: 2
Anchora salutis, SECURITY: 3
Anchora sit virtus, VIRTUE: 14
Anchora spei Cereticae est in te,
  Domine, DIVINITY: 16; HOPE: 3;
  LOCAL GOVERNMENT: 23
Anchor fast, STEADFASTNESS: 5
Ancient and loyal, FIDELITY: 13;
  LOCAL GOVERNMENT: 24
And the bush was not consumed,
  FIRE: 1; SCHOOL MOTTOES: 14
'And the glow from that fire can truly
  light the world', ENLIGHTENMENT: 1;
  SCHOOL MOTTOES: 15
Angelis suis praecepit de te, DIVINE
  GUIDANCE: 19
ANGER, p. 62
Angliae cor, FEELINGS: 1; LOCAL
  GOVERNMENT: 25
An Gottes Segen ist alles gelegen,
  BLESSING: 2; DIVINE GUIDANCE: 20
Anguis in herba, ANIMALS: 4
Angusta ad augusta, IMPROVEMENT: 4
A. N. G. W. (Alles nach Gottes
  Willen), DIVINE GUIDANCE: 21
A Nilo victoria, VICTORY: 4
Animae capaces mortis, SPIRIT: 3
Anima in amicis una, FRIENDSHIP: 19
ANIMALS, p. 62
Animi fortitudo, FORTITUDE: 1
Animis et fato, COURAGE: 8;
  FORTUNE: 3
Animis opibusque parati, MIND: 2;
  PREPAREDNESS: 4; STATE MOTTOES: 5
Animo, COURAGE: 9
Animo, non astutia, CLEVERNESS: 1;
  COURAGE: 10
Animo et corpore nitor, MIND: 3;
  STRENGTH: 4
Animo et fide, FAITH: 7; LOCAL
  GOVERNMENT: 26; SCHOOL
  MOTTOES: 16; SPIRIT: 4
Animo et prudentia, COURAGE: 12;
  PRUDENCE: 4

Animo et scientia, COURAGE: 13;
  KNOWLEDGE: 2
Animose certavit, COURAGE: 14;
  FORTUNE: 4
Animum fortuna sequitur,
  COURAGE: 15
Animum ipse parabo, COURAGE: 16
Animum prudentia firmat,
  COURAGE: 17; PRUDENCE: 5
Animum rege, SELF-CONTROL: 2
Animus, non res, MIND: 4
Animus est nobilitas, NOBILITY: 1;
  SPIRIT: 5
Animus et fata, COURAGE: 18;
  FORTUNE: 5
Animus nisi paret imperat, SPIRIT: 6
Animus non deficit aequus,
  EQUANIMITY: 5
Animus tamen idem, STEADFASTNESS: 6
Animus valet, COURAGE: 19
Annique vivesque pariter crescent,
  INCREASE: 1
Annoso robore quercus, STRANGER: 2;
  STRENGTH: 5
Annuit coeptis, DIVINE GUIDANCE: 22
An obedient wife governs her husband,
  OBEDIENCE: 4
An open way to new worlds, SCHOOL
  MOTTOES: 17; SEARCH and
  DISCOVERY: 1
Ante et post cole Deum, REVERENCE: 1
Ante expectatum diem,
  EXPECTATION: 3
Ante ferit quam flamma micet,
  TIMELINESS: 3
Ante honorem humilitas, HUMILITY: 1
Ante omnia erit, PRIMACY: 1
Ante omnia sylvae, FLORA: 3
Antes muerto que mutado, CHANGE: 1;
  DEATH: 1; STEADFASTNESS: 7
Ante victoriam ne cane triumphum,
  VICTORY: 5
Antiqua constans virtute, LOCAL
  GOVERNMENT: 27; STEADFASTNESS: 8;
  VIRTUE: 15
Antiqui colant Antiquum Dierum,
  LOCAL GOVERNMENT: 28; VIRTUE: 16
Antiqui mores, TRADITION: 2
Antiquo decore virens,
  FLOURISHING: 6; GLORY: 4
Antiquum assero decus, HONOR: 3

Antiquum decus floreat,
FLOURISHING: 7; GLORY: 5; LOCAL
GOVERNMENT: 29

Antiquum obtinens (honorem),
HONOR: 4

An tu tonitru?, POWER: 2

An uncommon experience that lasts a
lifetime, SCHOOL MOTTOES: 18;
UNIQUENESS: 1

Aperto vivere voto, DIRECTNESS: 2

'A place to grow', GROWTH: 1; SCHOOL
MOTTOES: 19

A pledge of better times,
DEDICATION: 1

A posse ad esse, ACCOMPLISHMENT: 2

Apparet quod latebat, VISION: 1

Appetitus rationi pareat, DESIRE: 1;
REASON: 2; SELF-CONTROL: 3

Appropinquat dies, TIMELINESS: 4

Après donner in [*sic*] faut prendre,
GIFTS and GIVING: 3

A private college serving the world,
SERVICE: 3

A private university in the public
service, SCHOOL MOTTOES: 20;
SERVICE: 4

Apto cum lare, HOME: 2

Aqua cadit resurgere, REBIRTH: 1;
WATER: 1

Aquilae vitem pocula vitam,
UNCLASSIFIED: 2

Aquila non captat muscas, BIRDS: 5;
STATUS: 1

Aquila petit solem, ASPIRATION: 32;
BIRDS: 6; SUN: 1

Arbor vitae Christus, fructus per fidem
gustamus, CHRIST, JESUS: 3

Archoille, FLORA: 4

Arctaeos Numine fines, DIVINE
GUIDANCE: 23

Arcui meo non confido, WEAPONS: 2

Arcus, artes, astra, ART: 1; STARS: 9;
WEAPONS: 3

Ardens, ZEALOUSNESS: 1

Ardens fide, FAITH: 8; LOCAL
GOVERNMENT: 30

Ardenter amo, LOVE: 32

Ardenter prosequor alis, PURSUIT: 1

Ardentibus votis, DIVINE GUIDANCE: 24

Ardet virtus, non urit, COURAGE: 20

Ardua difficilia ascensu, ADVERSITY: 6

Ardua petit ardea, ASPIRATION: 33;
BIRDS: 7

Ardua tendo, ASPIRATION: 34

Ardua vinco, ACCOMPLISHMENT: 3

Arduis saepe, metu nunquam,
ADVERSITY: 7

Arduus ad solem, LOFTINESS: 5;
SCHOOL MOTTOES: 21; SUN: 2

Ar Duw y gyd, DIVINE GUIDANCE: 25

A rege et victoria, CONQUEST: 1;
ROYALTY: 2

A regibus amicis, ROYALTY: 3

Arma pacis fulcra, WAR: 2; WEAPONS: 4

Arma parata fero, PREPAREDNESS: 5;
WEAPONS: 5

Armat et ornat, DEFENSE: 3

Arma tuentur pacem, WAR: 3;
WEAPONS: 6

Arma virumque cano, WEAPONS: 7

Armé à tous points, WEAPONS: 8

Armé de foi hardi, AUDACITY: 1;
FAITH: 9

Armed with integrity, INTEGRITY: 1

Armed with the Word, empowered by
the spirit, SCHOOL MOTTOES: 22;
SCRIPTURES: 2; SPIRIT: 7

Armet nos ultio regum,
PRINCELINESS: 1; VENGEANCE: 1

Armis et animis, COURAGE: 21;
WEAPONS: 9

Armis et diligentia, DILIGENCE: 4;
WEAPONS: 10

Armis et fide, FIDELITY: 14;
WEAPONS: 11

Armis et industria,
INDUSTRIOUSNESS: 2; WEAPONS: 12

Armis frango, WEAPONS: 13

Armis potentius aequum, JUSTICE: 4;
POWER: 3; WEAPONS: 14

Arolla, PROPER NAMES: 6

A rore colorem, WATER: 2

Arriverette, PROPER NAMES: 7

Ars bona violentia, ART: 2

Ars longa, vita brevis, ART: 3

Ars mercede viget, ART: 4; SCHOOL
MOTTOES: 23

Art, industry, contentment, ART: 5;
HAPPINESS: 3; INDUSTRIOUSNESS: 3;
SATISFACTION: 1; TRADES: 6

ART, p. 66

Arte, Marte, vigore, ABILITY: 2;
COURAGE: 22; LIVELINESS: 1; LOCAL
GOVERNMENT: 31

Arte conservatus, ABILITY: 3

Arte et animo, ABILITY: 4; COURAGE: 23

Arte et industria, ART: 6;
INDUSTRIOUSNESS: 4

Arte et labore, ABILITY: 5; ART: 7;
INDUSTRIOUSNESS: 5; LOCAL
GOVERNMENT: 32

Arte et Marte, ABILITY: 6; COURAGE: 24

Arte faventi nil desperandum,
ABILITY: 7; LOCAL GOVERNMENT: 33

Arte fideque, ART: 8; FAITH: 10

Arte firmus, ART: 9

Arte non impetu, ABILITY: 8

Arte non vi, ABILITY: 9

Artes honorabit, ART: 10

Artes/scientias/humanitates, ART: 11;
SCHOOL MOTTOES: 24

Arte utile facio, ART: 12

Arte vel Marte, ABILITY: 10; ART: 13

Artibus et armis, ABILITY: 11; ART: 14;
WEAPONS: 15

Artis vel Martis, ABILITY: 12;
COURAGE: 25

Arts and trades united, ART: 15;
TRADES: 7

Arx celebris fontibus, LOCAL
GOVERNMENT: 34; WATER: 3

Arx et anchora mihi Deus, DIVINE
GUIDANCE: 26; SECURITY: 4

Arx fortissima nomen Domini,
DIVINITY: 17

As an arrow true, WEAPONS: 16

Ascendam, ASPIRATION: 35

Ascendo, ASPIRATION: 36

As God wills, DIVINE GUIDANCE: 27

As God wills, so be it, DIVINE
GUIDANCE: 28

Asgre lan diogel ei phercen,
CONSCIENCE: 2; DEFENSE: 5

A spe in spem, HOPE: 4

Aspera ad virtutem est via, VIRTUE: 17

Aspera juvant, DANGER: 1

Aspera me juvant, ADVERSITY: 8

Aspera via ad virtutem, VIRTUE: 18

Aspera virtus, VIRTUE: 19

Aspice, respice, LOCAL
GOVERNMENT: 35; TIME: 8

Aspice et imitare, IMITATION: 1

Aspiciunt oculis superi mortalia justis,
DIVINITY: 18

Aspira, ASPIRATION: 37

ASPIRATION, p. 68

Aspire, persevere, and indulge not,
ASPIRATION: 38; PERSEVERANCE: 1

Aspire, persevere, trust,
ASPIRATION: 39; PERSEVERANCE: 2;
TRUST: 2

Aspiro, ASPIRATION: 40

Assaj ben' balla à chi la fortuna suona,
FORTUNE: 6

Assaye, EFFORT: 1

Assez dure, ENDURANCE: 4

Assez gaigne qui malheur perd,
REWARD: 3

Assiduitas, DILIGENCE: 5

Assiduitate, DILIGENCE: 6

Assiduitate, non desidia, DILIGENCE: 7;
SCHOOL MOTTOES: 25

Assiduitate non desidiâ, DILIGENCE: 8;
SCHOOL MOTTOES: 26

ASSISTANCE, p. 73

Assist the right, RECTITUDE: 5

Ast necas tu, DEATH: 2

Astra castra, numen, lumen munimen,
DIVINE GUIDANCE: 29; STARS: 10

Astra et castra, STARS: 11

Atalanta, PROPER NAMES: 8

At all times God me defend, DIVINE
GUIDANCE: 30

A tenir promesse vient de noblesse,
NOBILITY: 2

A te pro te, GIFTS and GIVING: 4

A toujours loyale, FIDELITY: 15

A tout jour loill, FIDELITY: 16

A tout pourvoir, PRUDENCE: 6

A tradition of excellence,
EXCELLENCE: 2; SCHOOL
MOTTOES: 27

A tribulacione, ADVERSITY: 9

At secura quies, REST: 1

At servata fides perfectus amorque
ditabunt, FIDELITY: 17; LOVE: 33

At spes infracta, HOPE: 5

At spes non fracta, HOPE: 6; LOCAL
GOVERNMENT: 36

At spes solamen, HOPE: 7

Attamen tranquillus, TRANQUILLITY: 1

ATTEMPT, p. 75

Attendez, PATIENCE: 1

Attendez vouz, PATIENCE: 2

ATTENTIVENESS, p. 75

At vincet pauperiem virtus,
COURAGE: 26

Au bon droit, RIGHTS: 1

Auch Tulpen darf man lieben,
FLORA: 7

Au coeur vaillant rien impossible,
COURAGE: 27

Auctor, NOURISHMENT: 2

Auctor pretiosa facit, GIFTS and
GIVING: 5

Auctor pretiosa fecit, GIFTS and
GIVING: 6

Aucto splendore resurgo, GLORY: 6;
REBIRTH: 2

Audacem juvant fata, AUDACITY: 2

Audaces fortuna juvat, AUDACITY: 3

Audaces fortuna juvat timidosque
repellit, FORTUNE: 7

Audaces juvat, AUDACITY: 4

Audaces juvo, AUDACITY: 5

Audacia, AUDACITY: 6

Audacia et industria, AUDACITY: 7;
DILIGENCE: 9

Audacia et virtute adepta,
AUDACITY: 8; COURAGE: 28

Audaci favet fortuna, AUDACITY: 9

Audaciter, AUDACITY: 10

AUDACITY, p. 76

Audacter et aperte, AUDACITY: 11

Audacter et sincere, AUDACITY: 12;
LOCAL GOVERNMENT: 37

Audacter et strenue, AUDACITY: 13

Audax, AUDACITY: 14

Audax at cautus, AUDACITY: 15;
CAUTION: 2

Audax bona fide, AUDACITY: 16

Audax ero, AUDACITY: 17

Audax et celer, AUDACITY: 18; SPEED: 3

Audax et justus, AUDACITY: 19;
JUSTICE: 5

Audax et promptus, AUDACITY: 20;
PREPAREDNESS: 6

Audax et vigilans, AUDACITY: 21;
VIGILANCE: 3

Audax ingenii, AUDACITY: 22

Audax in recto, AUDACITY: 23;
RECTITUDE: 6

Audax justum perficere, AUDACITY: 24;
JUSTICE: 6

Audax omnia perpeti, AUDACITY: 25;
ENDURANCE: 5

Audax pro suis, AUDACITY: 26

Audax vincendo, AUDACITY: 27

Aude, incipe, AUDACITY: 28

Aude et prevalebis, AUDACITY: 29;
VICTORY: 6

Aude fieri justum, JUSTICE: 7

Audemus dum cavemus, AUDACITY: 30;
CAUTION: 3; LOCAL GOVERNMENT: 38

Audemus jura nostra defendere,
DEFENSE: 6; STATE MOTTOES: 6

Audentes fortuna juvat, AUDACITY: 31

Audentior, AUDACITY: 32; LOCAL
GOVERNMENT: 39

Audentior ibo, AUDACITY: 33

Audeo, AUDACITY: 34

Audi, vide, sile, DISCRETION: 1;
SILENCE: 1

Audi alteram partem, LISTENING: 1

Audi consilium, GUIDANCE: 1;
PROVOCATION: 1

Au Dieu foy, aux amis foyer,
FAITH: 11; HOME: 3

Audio et juvo, ASSISTANCE: 2;
LISTENING: 2

Audio sed taceo, DISCRETION: 2

Audito et gradito, DISCRETION: 3

Au fait, FACTUALITY: 2

Auf deinen Wegen leit Herr Gott mich
allezeit, DIVINITY: 19

Auf Gott meine Hoffnung,
DIVINITY: 20

Aufrichtig, beständig, so lang ich
lebendig, RECTITUDE: 7;
STEADFASTNESS: 9

Augeo, INCREASE: 2

Augeor dum progredior, INCREASE: 3

A university for all the Americas,
HUMANITY: 1; SCHOOL MOTTOES: 28

Au plaisir fort de Dieu, DIVINE
GUIDANCE: 31

Auriga virtutum prudentia,
HUMANITY: 2; PRUDENCE: 7

Au roy donne devoir, DUTY: 3;
ROYALTY: 4

Ausim et confido, CONFIDENCE: 2;
COURAGE: 29

Auspice Christo, CHRIST, JESUS: 4;
DIVINE GUIDANCE: 32

Auspice Deo, DIVINE GUIDANCE: 33

Auspice Deo extule mari, DIVINE
GUIDANCE: 34; SEA: 2

Auspice Deo vinces, DIVINE
GUIDANCE: 35
Auspice Numine, DIVINE GUIDANCE: 36
Auspice summo Numine, DIVINE
GUIDANCE: 37
Auspice Teucro, SUPPORT: 1
Auspicio regis, senatus Angliae,
SUPPORT: 2
Auspicium melioris aevi,
DEDICATION: 2
Aut agere aut mori, STEADFASTNESS: 10
Aut Caesar aut nihil, ROYALTY: 5
Aut homo aut nullus, HOSTILITY: 1
AUTHORITY, p. 82
Aut liber aut nullus, LIBERTY: 4
Aut malleus hodie aut incus cras,
UTENSILS: 1
Aut manum aut ferrum, WAR: 4
Aut mors aut libertas, DEATH: 3;
LIBERTY: 5
Aut mors aut victoria, DEATH: 4
Aut mors aut vita decora, DEATH: 5;
HONESTY: 1; HONOR: 5
Aut nunc aut nunquam, PRESENT,
THE: 1
Aut nunquam tentes aut perfice,
ACCOMPLISHMENT: 4; ATTEMPT: 1
Aut omnes aut nullus, MEASURE: 1
Aut pax aut bellum, WAR: 5
Autre n'auray, FIDELITY: 18
Aut suavitate aut vi, FORCE: 1;
GENTLENESS: 1; WAR: 6
Aut tace aut face, ACTION: 4;
SILENCE: 2
Aut viam inveniam aut faciam,
PERSEVERANCE: 3
Aut vi aut suavitate, FORCE: 2;
GENTLENESS: 2; WAR: 7
Aut vincam aut peream, DEATH: 6;
VICTORY: 7
Au valeureux coeur rien impossible,
COURAGE: 30
Aux armes vaillant, en amour
constant, COURAGE: 31; LOVE: 34
Auxilia auxiliis, GUIDANCE: 2
Auxiliante resurgo, GUIDANCE: 3
Auxilio ab alto, DIVINE GUIDANCE: 38
Auxilio Dei, DIVINE GUIDANCE: 39
Auxilio Dei supero, DIVINE
GUIDANCE: 40
Auxilio Divino, DIVINE GUIDANCE: 41;
LOCAL GOVERNMENT: 40

Auxilium, ASSISTANCE: 3
Auxilium ab alto, DIVINE GUIDANCE: 42
Auxilium meum ab alto, DIVINE
GUIDANCE: 43
Auxilium meum a Domino, DIVINE
GUIDANCE: 44
Avance!, ADVANCE: 4
Avancez!, ADVANCE: 5
Avant!, ADVANCE: 6
Avant sans peur, ADVANCE: 7;
COURAGE: 32
Avauncez et archez bien, ADVANCE: 8;
EXHORTATION: 1
Avec ce que je tiens, je suis content,
HAPPINESS: 4
Avec ce qui je tienne je suis,
POSSESSION: 1
Ave Maria plena gratia, DIVINE
GUIDANCE: 45
Ave Mater Angliae, LOCAL
GOVERNMENT: 41; PARENTS: 1
Aversos compono animos, et secula
cogo, CONCILIATION: 2
A vino Duw dervid, DIVINE
GUIDANCE: 46
Avi numerantur avorum, ANCESTRY: 1
A virtute orta, COURAGE: 33
Avise la fin, PURPOSE: 3
Avise le temps, TIME: 9
A vision of peace, PEACE: 3
Avis la fin, PURPOSE: 4
Avitae gloriae memor, ANCESTRY: 2
Avita et aucta, HONOR: 6
Avito evehor honore, ANCESTRY: 3
Avito jure, ANCESTRY: 4
Avito non sine honore, ANCESTRY: 5
Avitos juvat honores, ANCESTRY: 6;
HONOR: 7
Avitos novit honores, ANCESTRY: 7
Avito viret honore, ANCESTRY: 8
Aviumque volatus, BIRDS: 8
A vonno Div dervid, DIVINE
GUIDANCE: 47
A vo penn bit pont, LEADERSHIP: 3;
LOCAL GOVERNMENT: 42
Avorum honor, ANCESTRY: 9
Avorum honori, ANCESTRY: 10
A vous entier, FIDELITY: 19
A wight 'quick' man never wants a
weapon, WEAPONS: 17
Ay, forward, ADVANCE: 9
Aye ready, PREPAREDNESS: 7

Ayez prudence, PRUDENCE: 8
Aymez loyaulté, FIDELITY: 20
A youth over his enemies defying,
  DEFIANCE: 1
Azincourt, PROPER NAMES: 9

B

Barn ar agen, JUDGMENT: 1
Barn yn uchaf, JUSTICE: 8
Baroach, PROPER NAMES: 10
Barrosa, PROPER NAMES: 11
Basis virtutum constantia,
  FIDELITY: 21; VIRTUE: 20
Be and not seem, INTEGRITY: 2
Bear and forbear, SELF-CONTROL: 4
Beare and forbeare, SELF-CONTROL: 5
Bear thee well, ENDURANCE: 6
Bear up, ENDURANCE: 7
Be as God will, DIVINE GUIDANCE: 48
Beati misericordes, quoniam ipsis
  misericordia tribuetur, MERCY: 1
Beati mundi corde, PURITY: 3; SCHOOL
  MOTTOES: 29
Beati pacifici, PEACE: 4
Beati qui durant, ENDURANCE: 8
Beatus qui implevit, BLESSING: 3;
  FINISH: 2
Beau don, GIFTS and GIVING: 7; LOCAL
  GOVERNMENT: 43
BEAUTY, p. 82
Beauty and grace, BEAUTY: 2; GRACE: 1
Beauty surrounds, health abounds,
  BEAUTY: 3; HEALING and HEALTH: 3;
  LOCAL GOVERNMENT: 44
Be bolde, be wyse, AUDACITY: 35;
  WISDOM: 2
Bedhoh fyr ha heb drok,
  DECEPTION: 2; WISDOM: 3
Be ever mindful, ATTENTIVENESS: 2
Be faithful, FIDELITY: 22
Be fast, STEADFASTNESS: 11
Befiehl dem Herrn deine Wege,
  DIVINITY: 23
Be firm, STRENGTH: 6
Be hardie, AUDACITY: 36
Be hardy, AUDACITY: 37
BEING, SELF, p. 84
Be in the van, LEADERSHIP: 4
Be it fast, STEADFASTNESS: 12
Be just, and fear not, FEAR: 3;
  JUSTICE: 9; LOCAL GOVERNMENT: 45

Believe in the cross, CROSS, THE: 3
Bella dextra, HANDS: 2; WAR: 8
Bella! Horrida bella!, WAR: 9
Bellement et hardiment,
  WORTHINESS: 1
Bellicae virtutis praemium,
  COURAGE: 34
Bello ac pace paratus,
  PREPAREDNESS: 8; WAR: 10
Bello palmam fero, CONCILIATION: 3
Be mindful, ATTENTIVENESS: 3
Be mindful to unite, UNITY: 2
Bene, WORTHINESS: 2
Bene consulendo, GUIDANCE: 4; LOCAL
  GOVERNMENT: 46
Bene denoto, WORTHINESS: 3
Benedic fontes, Domine, BLESSING: 4
Benedicite fontes Domino, LOCAL
  GOVERNMENT: 47; WATER: 4
Benedicite fontes Dominum,
  BLESSING: 5
Benedic nobis Domine, BLESSING: 6
Benedictio Domini divites facit,
  BLESSING: 7
Benedicto Dei ditat, BLESSING: 8
Benedictus es, O Domine: doce me
  Statuta Tua, DIVINITY: 24; SCHOOL
  MOTTOES: 30
Benedictus qui tollit crucem, CROSS,
  THE: 4
Benefac, Domine, bonis et rectis
  corde, DIVINE GUIDANCE: 49;
  RECTITUDE: 8
Benefacere et laetari,
  ACCOMPLISHMENT: 5
Bene factum, ACCOMPLISHMENT: 6
Beneficii memor, BENEFITS: 2
Beneficio bene erit, KINDNESS: 2;
  SUCCESS: 1
Beneficiorum memor, BENEFITS: 3
BENEFITS, p. 84
Be neither tyrant nor slave, LIBERTY: 6
Bene merentibus, WORTHINESS: 4
Bene paratum dulce, ACQUISITION: 1
Bene praeparatum pectus, HEART: 2;
  PREPAREDNESS: 9
Bene qui pacifice, PEACE: 5
Bene qui sedulo, INDUSTRIOUSNESS: 6
Bene tenax, PERSEVERANCE: 4
Benevolentia et justitia, JUSTICE: 10;
  KINDNESS: 3
Benigno Numine, PROVIDENCE: 1

Benigno numine enisus, DIVINE
GUIDANCE: 50
Be not wanting, UNCLASSIFIED: 3
Ben ti voglio, KINDNESS: 4
Be prepared, PREPAREDNESS: 10
Be ready, PREPAREDNESS: 11
Be right and persist, PERSEVERANCE: 5
Bersekutu bertambah mutu,
STRENGTH: 7; UNITY: 3
Be steadfast, STEADFASTNESS: 13
Be steady, EQUANIMITY: 6
Be strong and of good courage,
COURAGE: 35; STRENGTH: 8
Be stronger men, STRENGTH: 9
Be strong in the Lord, STRENGTH: 10
Be sure, DEPENDABILITY: 1
Be sure you're right, then go ahead,
RECTITUDE: 9
Be traist, FIDELITY: 23
Betrayed, not conquered,
UNCLASSIFIED: 4
Be treist, FIDELITY: 24
Be trewe, FIDELITY: 25
Be true, FIDELITY: 26
Be true and you shall never rue,
FIDELITY: 27
Be trwgh and delygent, DILIGENCE: 10;
FIDELITY: 28
Better a wee bush than nae bield,
PROTECTION: 3
Better deathe than shame, DEATH: 7
Better kinde frembd than frembd
kyen, STRANGER: 3
Better to wear out than to rust out,
PERSEVERANCE: 6
Beware, LOCAL GOVERNMENT: 48;
VIGILANCE: 4
Beware in time, VIGILANCE: 5
Beware my edge, VIGILANCE: 6
Beware the reaping, VIGILANCE: 7
Be watchful, VIGILANCE: 8
Be wise as a serpent, harmless as a
dove, ANIMALS: 5; BIRDS: 9;
HARMLESSNESS: 1; WISDOM: 4
Bhear na righ gan, ROYALTY: 6
Bhinneka tunggal ika, NATIONAL
MOTTOES: 1; UNITY: 4
Bibe si sapis, WISDOM: 5
Bide your time, PATIENCE: 3
Bien est qui bien fait, DEEDS: 2
Bienfaicia paieray malfaictz vangeray,
VENGEANCE: 2

Bien faire et ne rien dire, DEEDS: 3
Bien fait, WORTHINESS: 5
Bien ou rien, WORTHINESS: 6
Bien sûr, CERTAINTY: 1
Bind up the testimony and seal the
law, LAW: 2; SCHOOL MOTTOES: 31
BIRDS, p. 85
BIRTH, p. 87
Bis dat qui cito dat, GENEROSITY: 2
Bi'se mac na slaurie, OFFSPRING: 1
Bis vincit qui se vincit, CONQUEST: 2;
SELF-CONTROL: 6
Bis vivit qui bene, LIFE: 2
BLESSING, p. 87
Blow, hunter, thy horn, HUNTING: 1
Blow shrill, WARNING: 1
BOASTFULNESS, p. 88
Body, mind, spirit, HEALING and
HEALTH: 4
Bold, AUDACITY: 38
Bona benemerenti benedictio,
BLESSING: 9
Bona bonis, GOODNESS: 2
Bon accord, FELLOWSHIP: 1; UNITY: 5
Bonae virtutis amore, COURAGE: 36
Bona fide sine fraude, HONESTY: 2
Bona quae honesta, HONESTY: 3
Bon fin, FINISH: 3
Bon fortune, FORTUNE: 8
Bonis omnia bona, GOODNESS: 3
Bonitas/veritas/pulchritas, BEAUTY: 4;
GOODNESS: 4; SCHOOL MOTTOES: 32;
TRUTH: 5
Bonitatem et disciplinam et scientiam
doce me, DISCIPLINE: 1;
GOODNESS: 5; KNOWLEDGE: 3;
SCHOOL MOTTOES: 33
Bonne espérance et droit en avant,
ADVANCE: 10; HOPE: 8;
RIGHTEOUSNESS: 1
Bonne et belle assez, GOODNESS: 6
Bono animo esto, COURAGE: 37
Bono vince malum, GOODNESS: 7
Bon temps viendra, HOPE: 9
Bonum est confidere in Domino,
TRUST: 3
Bonus justus et utilis, GOODNESS: 8;
RECTITUDE: 10; USEFULNESS: 1
Books unlike universities are open to
all who would read, KNOWLEDGE: 4
Boulogne et Cadiz, PROPER NAMES: 12

Bound to obey and serve,
OBEDIENCE: 5; SERVICE: 5
Boutez en avant, ADVANCE: 11
BRIGHTNESS, p. 88
Britannia victrix, VICTORY: 8
Buagh, VICTORY: 9
Bualim se, AGGRESSION: 2
Bua noo bawse, DEATH: 8; VICTORY: 10
Building Christian character, CHRIST,
JESUS: 5; SCHOOL MOTTOES: 34
Build sure, DEPENDABILITY: 2
Burning I shine, SHINING: 1
Butleirach abú, DEFIANCE: 2
By aim and by effort, PURPOSE: 5
By assiduity, DILIGENCE: 11
By command of our superiors,
OBEDIENCE: 6
By concord and industry,
INDUSTRIOUSNESS: 7; LOCAL
GOVERNMENT: 49; UNITY: 6
By courage and faith, COURAGE: 38;
FAITH: 12; LOCAL GOVERNMENT: 50
By cunning not by craft,
CLEVERNESS: 2
Bydand, STEADFASTNESS: 14
Bydand to the last, STEADFASTNESS: 15
Bydd ddiysgog, STEADFASTNESS: 16
Byddwch gyfiawn ac nag ofnwch,
FEAR: 4; RIGHTEOUSNESS: 2
Byde, ENDURANCE: 9
Byde be, ENDURANCE: 10
By degrees, GRADUALNESS: 1
By design and endeavour, EFFORT: 2
Byde together, ENDURANCE: 11
Byde tyme, ENDURANCE: 12
By faith I obtain, FAITH: 13
By faith we are saved, FAITH: 14
By hammer and hand all arts do stand,
HANDS: 3; INDUSTRIOUSNESS: 8;
TRADES: 8; UTENSILS: 2
By industry and honor, HONOR: 8;
INDUSTRIOUSNESS: 9
By industry and integrity,
INDUSTRIOUSNESS: 10; INTEGRITY: 3;
LOCAL GOVERNMENT: 51
By industry we prosper,
INDUSTRIOUSNESS: 11; PROSPERITY: 3
By perseverance, PERSEVERANCE: 7
By sea, SEA: 3
By sea and land, SEA: 4
By the grace of God, DIVINE
GUIDANCE: 51; GRACE: 2

By the providence of God,
PROVIDENCE: 2
By these we shine, and it is fortified,
SHINING: 2
By the sword, WEAPONS: 18
By truth and diligence, DILIGENCE: 12;
TRUTH: 6
By valour, COURAGE: 39
By watchfulness, by steadfastness,
STEADFASTNESS: 17; VIGILANCE: 9
By worth, LOCAL GOVERNMENT: 52;
WORTHINESS: 7
By wounding I cure, HEALING and
HEALTH: 5

C

Cabar feidh, ANIMALS: 6
Cabool, PROPER NAMES: 13
Cada uno es hijo de sus obras,
DILIGENCE: 13
Cadenti porrigo dextram,
ASSISTANCE: 4
Cadere non cedere possum,
STEADFASTNESS: 18
Cadernid, cyfiawnder, cynnydd,
ADVANCE: 12; JUSTICE: 11; LOCAL
GOVERNMENT: 53; ORDER: 1
Cadernid Gwynedd, LOCAL
GOVERNMENT: 54; STRENGTH: 11
Caelestem spero coronam, CROWN: 3;
HOPE: 10; PARADISE: 2
Caelestes pandite portae, PARADISE: 3
Caelestia canimus, PARADISE: 4
Caelestia sequor, ASPIRATION: 41;
FOLLOWING: 1; PARADISE: 5
Caelis exploratis, EXPLORATION: 1
Caelitus datum, DIVINE GIFTS: 6
Caelitus mihi vires, PARADISE: 6;
STRENGTH: 12
Caelitus vires, PARADISE: 7;
STRENGTH: 13
Caelum, non animum, MIND: 5
Caelum, non solum, PARADISE: 8
Caelum non animum, CHANGE: 2
Caelum quod quaerimus ultra,
PARADISE: 9
Caelum versus, PARADISE: 10
Caen, Cressie, Calais, PROPER
NAMES: 14
Caesar aut nullus, FIDELITY: 29

C(a)eteris major qui melior,
GOODNESS: 9
Caffraria, PROPER NAMES: 15
Calcar honeste, HONOR: 9
Calco sub pedibus, CONTEMPT: 1
Callide et honeste, HONOR: 10;
WISDOM: 6
Calm, EQUANIMITY: 7
Calton wrth calton Duw a digon,
DIVINITY: 25
Cambray, cité de paix, LOCAL
GOVERNMENT: 55; PEACE: 6
Camera principis, LOCAL
GOVERNMENT: 56; PRINCELINESS: 2
Campi fero praemia belli, MILITARY
DISTINCTION: 2; REWARD: 4
Canada, PROPER NAMES: 16
Candide, DIRECTNESS: 3
Candide, sed caute, CAUTION: 4;
DIRECTNESS: 4
Candide, sincere, DIRECTNESS: 5;
SINCERITY: 1
Candide comme la fleur, BEAUTY: 5;
FLORA: 8
Candide et caute, CAUTION: 5;
DIRECTNESS: 6
Candide et constanter, FAIRNESS: 4
Candide et secure, DIRECTNESS: 7
Candide me fides,
TRUSTWORTHINESS: 1
Candider et constanter, DIRECTNESS: 8
Candidior, LOVE: 35
Candidiora pectora, PURITY: 4
Candidus cantabit moriens, DEATH: 9;
PURITY: 5
Candor dat viribus alas, STRENGTH: 14;
TRUTH: 7
Candore, DIRECTNESS: 9
Candoris praemium honos, PRAISE: 2;
SINCERITY: 2
Capta majora, ASPIRATION: 42
Caput inter nubila condit,
LOFTINESS: 6
Caradoc, PROPER NAMES: 17
Caraid'an am feym, FRIENDSHIP: 20
Cara patria carior libertas,
COUNTRY: 4; LIBERTY: 7;
PATRIOTISM: 7
Cara vita, carior patria, carissima
libertas, COUNTRY: 5; LIBERTY: 8;
LIFE: 3
Cari Deo nihilo carent, DIVINITY: 26

Caritas, LOVE: 36; SCHOOL
MOTTOES: 35
Caritas fructum habet, KINDNESS: 5
Carn na cuimhne, MEMORY: 1
Carpe diem, OPPORTUNITY: 1; TIME: 10
Carpe diem postero ne crede, FUTURE,
THE: 2; OPPORTUNITY: 2
Cassis tutissima virtus, PROTECTION: 4;
VIRTUE: 21
Caste et pie, PIETY: 2; PURITY: 6
Castello fortior concordia, LOCAL
GOVERNMENT: 57; STRENGTH: 15;
UNITY: 7
Castra et nemus Strivilense,
FORTIFICATIONS: 1
Cate at caute, CAUTION: 6
Catius quam citus, SPEED: 4;
WISDOM: 7
Catus [sic] semper viret, CAUTION: 7
CAUSATION, p. 89
Cause caused it, CAUSATION: 1
Caute, sed impavide, CAUTION: 8
Caute et sedulo, CLEVERNESS: 3
Caute nec timide, CAUTION: 9
Caute non astute, CAUTION: 10
Caute sed intrepide, CAUTION: 11
CAUTION, p. 90
Cautus a futuro, CAUTION: 12; FUTURE,
THE: 3
Cautus in consiliis, in facto audax,
AUDACITY: 39; CAUTION: 13
Cautus metuit foveam lupus,
ANIMALS: 7; CAUTION: 14
Cautus sed strenue, CAUTION: 15
Cave!, VIGILANCE: 10
Cave, paratus, CAUTION: 16;
PREPAREDNESS: 12
Cave! adsum, VIGILANCE: 11
Cave cervum, ANIMALS: 8
Cave! Deus videt, VIGILANCE: 12
Cave et aude, VIGILANCE: 13
Cave Leam, ANIMALS: 9; VIGILANCE: 14
Cave lupum, ANIMALS: 10;
VIGILANCE: 15
Cavendo, CAUTION: 17
Cavendo tutus, CAUTION: 18
Cave ut comprehendas, THOUGHT: 1
Cedamus amori, LOVE: 37
Cedant arma, WEAPONS: 19
Cedant arma labori,
INDUSTRIOUSNESS: 12; WEAPONS: 20

Cedant arma togae, STATE MOTTOES: 7;
  WEAPONS: 21
Ceidw Owain a gafodd, POSSESSION: 2
Celer, SPEED: 5
Celer atque fidelis, ACTION: 5;
  FIDELITY: 30
Celer et audax, AUDACITY: 40; SPEED: 6
Celer et vigilans, SPEED: 7;
  VIGILANCE: 16
Celeritas, SPEED: 8
Celeritas et veritas, SPEED: 9; TRUTH: 8
Celeritas executionis est anima consilii.
  Vive ut vivas, SPEED: 10
Celeritas virtus fidelitas, FIDELITY: 31;
  SPEED: 11; VIRTUE: 22
Celeritate, SPEED: 12
Celeriter, SPEED: 13
Celeriter et jucunde, SPEED: 14
Celeriter nil crede, FAITH: 15
Celeriter sed certe, SPEED: 15
Ce m'est égal, EQUALITY: 1
Certa bonum certamen, SCHOOL
  MOTTOES: 36; WAR: 11
Certa cruce salus, CROSS, THE: 5;
  SALVATION: 5
CERTAINTY, p. 92
Certamine parata, ACQUISITION: 2
Certamine summo, WAR: 12
Certanti dabitur, EFFORT: 3
Certavi et vici, CONQUEST: 3
Certior dum cerno, CONFIDENCE: 3
Certior in caelo domus, HOME: 4;
  PARADISE: 11
Certo dirigo ictu, AGGRESSION: 3
Certum pete finem, GOALS: 2
Cervus non servus, ANIMALS: 11;
  LIBERTY: 9
C'est la seule vertu qui donne la
  noblesse, NOBILITY: 3; VIRTUE: 23
C'est mon plaisir, ENJOYMENT: 3
Chacun à son goût, UNIQUENESS: 2
Chacun en son temps, TIME: 11
Chacun le sien, SELF-RELIANCE: 1;
  UNIQUENESS: 3
Chacun sa part, FAIRNESS: 5
CHANGE, p. 92
Chase, PURSUIT: 2
Chassé pour foi, FAITH: 16;
  PERSECUTION: 1
Cherche et tu trouveras, SEARCH and
  DISCOVERY: 2
Cherche la vérité, TRUTH: 9

Cherche qui n'a, SEARCH and
  DISCOVERY: 3
Chéris l'espoir, HOPE: 11
Che sarà sarà, ACCEPTANCE: 1; FATE: 1
Chescun son devoir, DUTY: 4
Ches moy, HOME: 5
Chi dura vince, ENDURANCE: 13
Chi la fa l'aspetti, DEEDS: 4
Chi legge regge, KNOWLEDGE: 5
China, PROPER NAMES: 18
Chi s'arma di virtu, vince ogni forza,
  VIRTUE: 24
Chi semina virtu raccologie fama,
  GLORY: 7; VIRTUE: 25
Chi semini vertu racoglia fama,
  FAME: 1; VIRTUE: 26
Chounda, PROPER NAMES: 19
CHRIST, JESUS, p. 94
Christ above all, CHRIST, JESUS: 6;
  SCHOOL MOTTOES: 37
Christ for the world, CHRIST, JESUS: 7;
  SCHOOL MOTTOES: 38
Christiana militia, WAR: 13
Christianity and culture, CHRIST,
  JESUS: 8; SCHOOL MOTTOES: 39
Christian service/ character/ culture,
  SCHOOL MOTTOES: 40; SERVICE: 6
Christi crux est mea lux, CROSS, THE: 6;
  LIGHT: 4
Christi pennatus sidera morte peto,
  CHRIST, JESUS: 9; SALVATION: 6;
  STARS: 12
Christi servitus vera libertas,
  LIBERTY: 10; SERVICE: 7
Christo duce, CHRIST, JESUS: 10
Christo duce feliciter, CHRIST,
  JESUS: 11; DIVINE GUIDANCE: 52
Christo et humanitati, CHRIST,
  JESUS: 12; MANLINESS: 1; SCHOOL
  MOTTOES: 41
Christo suavis odor, CHRIST, JESUS: 13
Christ preeminent, CHRIST, JESUS: 14;
  SCHOOL MOTTOES: 42
Christum diligere melius est omnibus
  scire, CHRIST, JESUS: 15
Christus dux solus, CHRIST, JESUS: 16;
  DIVINE GUIDANCE: 53
Christus meine Hoffnung, CHRIST,
  JESUS: 17; HOPE: 12
Christus meum asylum, CHRIST,
  JESUS: 18

Christus mihi lucrum, CHRIST,
JESUS: 19
Christus mihi vita, CHRIST, JESUS: 20
Christus mihi vita, mors lucrum,
CHRIST, JESUS: 21
Christus nobiscum, state!, CHRIST,
JESUS: 22
Christus omnia, mundus nihil, CHRIST,
JESUS: 23
Christus pelicano, BIRDS: 10; CHRIST,
JESUS: 24
Christus pelicanus et agnus,
ANIMALS: 12; BIRDS: 11; CHRIST,
JESUS: 25
Christus primatum tenens, CHRIST,
JESUS: 26; SCHOOL MOTTOES: 43
Christus providebit, CHRIST, JESUS: 27
Christus servatus vera libertas, CHRIST,
JESUS: 28; LIBERTY: 11
Christus sit regula vitae, CHRIST,
JESUS: 29
Ciall agos neart, POWER: 4; REASON: 3
Cio che Dio vuole, io voglio, DIVINE
GUIDANCE: 54
Circumspice, VISION: 2
Cito, non temere, SPEED: 16
Cito fideliterque, FIDELITY: 32;
SPEED: 17
Cito pede praeterit aetas,
TRANSIENCE: 2
Civil and religious liberty,
LIBERTY: 12; RELIGION: 4
Civitas in bello in pace fidelis,
FIDELITY: 33; LOCAL
GOVERNMENT: 58; WAR: 14
Civitatis fortuna cives, FORTUNE: 9;
LOCAL GOVERNMENT: 59; PEOPLE: 1
Clamabunt omnes te, liber, esse
meum, POSSESSION: 3
Clamamus, Abba, Pater, DIVINITY: 27
Clamant nostra tela in regis querela,
LOCAL GOVERNMENT: 60;
WEAPONS: 22
Clareo foveoque, BRIGHTNESS: 1
Clarescam, BRIGHTNESS: 2
Clarior alter, CLARITY: 1
Clariora sequor, BRIGHTNESS: 3
Clarior astris, BRIGHTNESS: 4; STARS: 13
Clarior e flammis, BRIGHTNESS: 5
Clariores e tenebris, BRIGHTNESS: 6
Clarior e tenebris, BRIGHTNESS: 7
Clarior ex obscuro, BRIGHTNESS: 8

Clarior hinc honos, HONOR: 11
Clarior virtus honoribus, VIRTUE: 27
Claris dextra factis, DEEDS: 5
Claritate dextra, BRIGHTNESS: 9;
RECTITUDE: 11
CLARITY, p. 99
Clarum reddit industria,
INDUSTRIOUSNESS: 13
Clausus mox excelsior, RISING: 2
Clavis ad futura, FUTURE, THE: 4;
SCHOOL MOTTOES: 44
Clementia et animis, COURAGE: 40;
MERCY: 2
Clementia in potentia, MERCY: 3;
POWER: 5
Clementia tecta rigore, MERCY: 4
CLEVERNESS, p. 100
Clypeus omnibus in te sperantibus,
HOPE: 13; PROTECTION: 5
Coadyuvando el presente, formando el
porvenir, SCHOOL MOTTOES: 45;
TIME: 12
Coeli favore, PARADISE: 12
Coelum ipsum petimus, PARADISE: 13
Coelum non animum mutat,
CHANGE: 3; MIND: 6
Coelumque tueri, PARADISE: 14
Coelum tueri, PARADISE: 15
Coeptis aspirate meis, SUPPORT: 3
Coeur content grande talent,
HAPPINESS: 5; HEART: 3
Coeur Fidèle, FIDELITY: 34
Cogadh na sithe, WAR: 15
Cogi posse negat, UBIQUITY: 1
Cogi qui potest nescit mori, FORCE: 3
Cogit amor, LOVE: 38
Cogit in hostem, WAR: 16
Cogito, THOUGHT: 2
Cogito ergo sum. Deo gratias, SCHOOL
MOTTOES: 46; THOUGHT: 3
Cognoies toy meme, SELF-
KNOWLEDGE: 1
Cognosce occasionem, TIMELINESS: 5
Cognosce te ipsum, SELF-
KNOWLEDGE: 2
Cognosce teipsum et disce pati, SELF-
KNOWLEDGE: 3
Cole credeque Deum, DIVINITY: 28
Cole Deum, DIVINITY: 29
Colens Deum et regem, DIVINITY: 30;
ROYALTY: 7

Mottoes & Categories

Conquer death by virtue, DEATH: 10;
VIRTUE: 29
Conquer or die, CONQUEST: 4;
DEATH: 11
CONQUEST, p. 103
Conquiesco, HAPPINESS: 7
Consagracion/ educacion,
DEDICATION: 3; SCHOOL MOTTOES: 49
CONSCIENCE, p. 108
Conscientia virtuti satis amplum
theatrum est, CONSCIENCE: 3;
VIRTUE: 30
Conservabo ad mortem,
CONSERVATION: 3
Conserva me, Domine, DIVINE
GUIDANCE: 55
Conserva nos Domina, DIVINE
GUIDANCE: 56
Conservata fides perfectus amorque
ditabunt, FIDELITY: 35; LOVE: 39
CONSERVATION, p. 109
Consider the end, FINISH: 5
Consider thy purpose, PURPOSE: 6
Consilii taciturnitas nutrix, SILENCE: 3
Consilio absit discordia, CONFLICT: 1;
LOCAL GOVERNMENT: 63
Consilio ac virtute, COURAGE: 42;
PRUDENCE: 9
Consilio et anima, COURAGE: 43;
LOCAL GOVERNMENT: 64; WISDOM: 9
Consilio et animis, COURAGE: 44;
LOCAL GOVERNMENT: 65; WISDOM: 10
Consilio et armis, WEAPONS: 24;
WISDOM: 11
Consilio et impetu, WISDOM: 12
Consilio et vi, POWER: 6; WISDOM: 15
Consilio non impetu, FORCE: 5;
WISDOM: 16
CONSISTENCY, p. 109
Constancy, FIDELITY: 36
Constans contraria spernit,
STEADFASTNESS: 19
Constans et fidelis, FIDELITY: 37
Constans et fidelitate, FIDELITY: 38
Constans et prudens, FIDELITY: 39;
PRUDENCE: 11
Constans fidei, FAITH: 18; FIDELITY: 40
Constans fides et integritas, FAITH: 19;
INTEGRITY: 5
Constans justitiam moniti, JUSTICE: 14;
MODERATION: 1
Constant, FIDELITY: 41

Constant and faithful, FIDELITY: 42
Constant and true, FIDELITY: 43
Constant be, FIDELITY: 44; LOCAL
GOVERNMENT: 67
Constante et firme, STEADFASTNESS: 20
Constant en tout, FIDELITY: 45
Constanter, FIDELITY: 46;
STEADFASTNESS: 21
Constanter ac non timide, FIDELITY: 47
Constanter et pie, FIDELITY: 48;
PIETY: 3
Constanter et prudentia,
PRUDENCE: 12; STRENGTH: 18
Constanter et sincere, FIDELITY: 49;
SINCERITY: 3
Constanter in ardua,
STEADFASTNESS: 22
Constant et discret et ang amour
secret, DISCRETION: 4; FIDELITY: 50;
LOVE: 40
Constantia, FIDELITY: 51;
STEADFASTNESS: 23
Constantia, virtus, COURAGE: 45;
STEADFASTNESS: 24
Constantia basis virtutum, LOCAL
GOVERNMENT: 68; STEADFASTNESS: 25
Constantia et diligentia,
DILIGENCE: 15; PERSEVERANCE: 9
Constantia et fidelitate, FIDELITY: 52
Constantia et fortitudine,
FORTITUDE: 2; STEADFASTNESS: 26
Constantia et labore,
INDUSTRIOUSNESS: 17
Constantia et virtute, FIDELITY: 53;
VIRTUE: 31
Constantia in ardua, ADVERSITY: 10;
PERSEVERANCE: 10
Constare in sententia,
STEADFASTNESS: 27
Constaunt an' trew, STEADFASTNESS: 28
Constitution/ Wisdom/ Justice/
Moderation, GOVERNMENT: 1;
JUSTICE: 15; MODERATION: 2; SCHOOL
MOTTOES: 50; WISDOM: 17
Consulit et ornat, PREPAREDNESS: 13;
THOUGHT: 4
Consulto, THOUGHT: 5
Consulto et audaciter, AUDACITY: 41;
PRUDENCE: 13
CONTEMPT, p. 110
Contentement passe richesse,
HAPPINESS: 8

Contentus paucis, HAPPINESS: 9

Contra audentior, AUDACITY: 42;
OPPOSITION: 1

Contra fortuna bon coeur,
FORTUNE: 11

Contranando incrementum, LOCAL
GOVERNMENT: 69; PROSPERITY: 4

Contre fortune bon coeur,
FORTUNE: 12

Contre fortune bon coeur, Dieu tourne
tout en bonheur, DIVINE
GUIDANCE: 57; FORTUNE: 13

CONVENIENCE, p. 111

Copia ex industria,
INDUSTRIOUSNESS: 18

Copiosè et opportunê, OPPORTUNITY: 3;
PROSPERITY: 5

Cor ad cor loquitur, FEELINGS: 2;
SCHOOL MOTTOES: 51

Corda serata fero, FEELINGS: 3

Corda serata pando, FEELINGS: 4

Corda sincera principia vera,
SINCERITY: 4

Corde et manu, HANDS: 4

Corde fixam, FEELINGS: 7

Corde manuque, FEELINGS: 8;
HANDS: 5

Corde mente manu, FEELINGS: 9;
HANDS: 6; MIND: 7

Corde recto elati omnes,
RECTITUDE: 12; TRADES: 10

Cordi dat animus alas, HAPPINESS: 10;
HEART: 4; SPIRIT: 8

Cordi dat robora virtus, VIRTUE: 32

Cor et manus, FEELINGS: 10; HANDS: 7

Cor et manus concordant, UNITY: 22

Cor forte calcar non requirit,
INCENTIVE: 3

Cor forte suum calcar est,
INCENTIVE: 4

Cor immobile, STEADFASTNESS: 29

Cor meum tibi offero Domine,
DEDICATION: 4; SCHOOL MOTTOES: 52

Cor mundum crea in me Deus,
PURITY: 7

Cor nobyle, cor immobyle, MIND: 8;
NOBILITY: 4

Cornu exaltabitur honore, HOME: 6;
HONOR: 12

Coronabitur legitime certans,
CROWN: 4

Corona mea Christus, CHRIST,
JESUS: 30; CROWN: 5

Coronat fides, FAITH: 20

Cor regis in manu Domini est,
ROYALTY: 8

Corrige praeteritum, praesens rege,
cerne futurum, TIME: 13

Cor sapientis quaerit sapientiam,
WISDOM: 18

Cor unum, HEART: 5; LOCAL
GOVERNMENT: 70; UNITY: 23

Cor unum, via una, HEART: 6;
UNITY: 24

Cor unum et anima una, FIDELITY: 54

Cor vulneratum, FEELINGS: 11

COUNTENANCE, p. 111

COUNTRY, p. 112

COUNTRYSIDE, p. 121

Couper fait grandir, GROWTH: 2

COURAGE, p. 121

Courage!, COURAGE: 46

Courage, humanity, commerce,
COMMERCE: 2; COURAGE: 47; LOCAL
GOVERNMENT: 71

Courage à la mort, COURAGE: 48

Courage à l'Ecosse, COURAGE: 49

Courage avance le homme,
COURAGE: 50

Courage et esperance, COURAGE: 51;
HOPE: 15

Courage sans peur, COURAGE: 52

Courageux, COURAGE: 53

COURTESY, p. 138

Court hope, HOPE: 16

Court no friend, dread no foe, SELF-
RELIANCE: 2

Courtoisie, bonne aventure,
COURTESY: 2

Craggan phithich, BIRDS: 12

Craig elachie, WARNING: 2

Craignez honte, DISGRACE: 1

Crains Dieu tant que tu viveras,
DIVINITY: 33

Crainte refrainte, FEAR: 5

Cras mihi, FUTURE, THE: 5

Creag dhubh chloinn Chatain,
UNCLASSIFIED: 5

Creag dubh, UNCLASSIFIED: 6

Crede Byron, TRUST: 14

Crede cornu, TRUST: 15

Crede cruci, CROSS, THE: 7

Crede Deo, DIVINITY: 34; TRUST: 16

Crede et vince, FAITH: 21
Crede mihi, FAITH: 22
Crede signo, LOCAL GOVERNMENT: 72;
SIGN: 1; TRUST: 17
Credo, FAITH: 23
Credo, amo et regno, FAITH: 24;
LOVE: 41
Credo Christi cruce, CHRIST, JESUS: 31
Credo cruci Christi, CROSS, THE: 8;
TRUST: 18
Credo Deo, FAITH: 25
Credo et amo, FAITH: 26; LOVE: 42
Credo et videbo, FAITH: 27
Credo legi, LAW: 4; TRUST: 19
Credunt quod vident, VISION: 3
Crescamus, INCREASE: 4
Crescam ut prosim, GOODNESS: 10;
INCREASE: 5
Crescat amicitia, FRIENDSHIP: 21
Crescendo prosim, INCREASE: 6
Crescent, INCREASE: 7
Crescit eundo, GROWTH: 3
Crescitque virtute, VIRTUE: 33
Crescit sub pondere virtus,
OPPRESSION: 1; VIRTUE: 34
Crescit sub pondere virtus ventis
secundis, VIRTUE: 35
Crescitur cultu, FLOURISHING: 8
Cresco, INCREASE: 8
Cresco crescendo, INCREASE: 9
Cresco et spero, HOPE: 17;
INCREASE: 10
Cresco per crucem, CROSS, THE: 9;
INCREASE: 11
Cresco sub jugo, GROWTH: 4
Cressa ne careat, PROSPERITY: 6
Creta cruce salus, CROSS, THE: 10;
SALVATION: 7
Crom abú, DEFIANCE: 3
CROSS, THE, p. 139
Crossroads of America, LOCATION: 1;
STATE MOTTOES: 8
CROWN, p. 145
Crow not, croke not, BOASTFULNESS: 1
Cruce delector, CROSS, THE: 11
Cruce duce, CROSS, THE: 12; DIVINE
GUIDANCE: 58
Cruce dum spiro spero, CROSS, THE: 13;
HOPE: 18
Cruce glorior, CROSS, THE: 14;
GLORY: 9
Cruce insignis, CROSS, THE: 15

Crucem ferre dignum, CROSS, THE: 16
Cruce non hasta, CROSS, THE: 17
Cruce non leone fides, ANIMALS: 13;
CROSS, THE: 18; TRUST: 20
Cruce non prudentia, CROSS, THE: 19;
PRUDENCE: 14
Cruce salus, CROSS, THE: 20;
SALVATION: 8
Cruce spes mea, CROSS, THE: 21;
HOPE: 19
Cruce vide et festina, CROSS, THE: 22;
SPEED: 18
Cruce vincimus, CROSS, THE: 23
Cruciata cruce junguntur, CROSS,
THE: 24
Cruci dum fido spiro, CROSS, THE: 25;
TRUST: 21
Cruci dum spiro fido, CROSS, THE: 26
Cruci dum spiro spero, CROSS, THE: 27;
HOPE: 20
Crucifixa gloria mea, CROSS, THE: 28;
GLORY: 10
Crux auctrix et tutrix, CROSS, THE: 29;
PROTECTION: 6
Crux Christi lux caeli, CROSS, THE: 30
Crux Christi mea salus, CROSS,
THE: 31; SALVATION: 9
Crux Christi nostra corona, CROSS,
THE: 32; CROWN: 6
Crux Christi nostra salus, CROSS,
THE: 33; SALVATION: 10
Crux Christi salus mea, CROSS,
THE: 34; SALVATION: 11
Crux Christi solamen offert, CROSS,
THE: 35
Crux dat salutem, CROSS, THE: 36;
SALVATION: 12
Crux et praesidium et decus, CROSS,
THE: 37; DEFENSE: 7; HONOR: 13
Crux fidei calcar, CROSS, THE: 38;
FAITH: 28
Crux mea lux, CROSS, THE: 39; LIGHT: 5
Crux mea stella, CROSS, THE: 40;
STARS: 14
Crux mihi anchora, CROSS, THE: 41
Crux mihi grata quies, CROSS, THE: 42;
REST: 2
Crux nostra corona, CROSS, THE: 43;
CROWN: 7
Crux praesidium et decus, CROSS,
THE: 44; DEFENSE: 8; HONOR: 14

Crux salutem confert, CROSS, THE: 45;
SALVATION: 13
Crux scutum, CROSS, THE: 46;
DEFENSE: 9
Crux spes unica, CROSS, THE: 47;
HOPE: 21
Cubo et excubo, VIGILANCE: 17
Cubo sed curo, VIGILANCE: 18
Cui debeo fidus, FIDELITY: 55
Cui debetur reverentia, REVERENCE: 2
Cuidich an righ, ASSISTANCE: 5;
ROYALTY: 9
Cui fides fide, CONFIDENCE: 7;
TRUST: 22
Cuimhnich bas Alpin, DEATH: 12
Cuislean mo cridhe, FEELINGS: 12
Cuivis dolori remedium est patientia,
PATIENCE: 4
Culpari metuit fides, FAITH: 29
Cultui avorum fidelis, ANCESTRY: 11
Culture for service, SCHOOL
MOTTOES: 53; SERVICE: 8
Cultus animi quasi humanitatis
quidam cibus, HUMANITY: 3; MIND: 9
Cum corde, FEELINGS: 13
Cum cruce salus, CROSS, THE: 48;
SALVATION: 14
Cum Deo bene faciendo bene faciet,
DIVINITY: 35
Cum Deo et die, DIVINITY: 36; TIME: 14
Cum Deo salus, DIVINITY: 37;
SALVATION: 15
Cum grano salis, UNCLASSIFIED: 7
Cum magnis vixisse, GREATNESS: 1
Cum periculo lucrum, DANGER: 2
Cum plena magis, FULLNESS: 1
Cum prima luce, DAY: 1
Cum principibus, LEADERSHIP: 6
Cum progressu cantus, ADVANCE: 13;
MUSIC: 1
Cum prudentia sedulus,
DILIGENCE: 16; PRUDENCE: 15
Cum secundo flumine, FORTUNE: 14
Cum toga honoris, HONOR: 15
Cuncta mea mecum, SELF-RELIANCE: 3
Cunctanter tamen fortiter,
STEADFASTNESS: 30
Cupio, credo, habeo, DESIRE: 2
Cupio meliora, ASPIRATION: 43
Cupressus honores peperit,
HONESTY: 5; HONOR: 16
Cura, vigila, VIGILANCE: 19

Cura atque industria,
INDUSTRIOUSNESS: 19
Cura dat victoriam, CAUTION: 19;
VICTORY: 11
Curae cedit fatum, CAUTION: 20;
FATE: 3
Cura et candore, PRUDENCE: 16;
SINCERITY: 5
Cura et constantia, FIDELITY: 56
Curae testimonium, CAUTION: 21
Cura et industria, INDUSTRIOUSNESS: 20
Curandum est ut sit mens sana in
corpore sano, HEALING and HEALTH: 6
Curandum omnium bonum,
CONCERN: 3; LOCAL GOVERNMENT: 73
Cura pii diis sunt, PIETY: 4
Cura quietem, REST: 3
Cu re bu (or Cu reubha), UBIQUITY: 2
Cur me persequeris, PERSECUTION: 2
Curo dum quiesco, VIGILANCE: 20
Currendo, RUNNING: 1
Curre ut vincas, CONQUEST: 5;
RUNNING: 2
Currit qui curat, RUNNING: 3
Cur senio praelata juventus', AGE: 1
Cursum perficio, ACCOMPLISHMENT: 7;
RUNNING: 4
Cuspis fracta causa coronae,
CROWN: 8; WEAPONS: 25
Custodi civitatem Domine, DIVINE
GUIDANCE: 59; LOCAL
GOVERNMENT: 74
Custos et pugnax, PREPAREDNESS: 14;
VIGILANCE: 21
Cynghori er llesiant, IMPROVEMENT: 5;
LOCAL GOVERNMENT: 75

D

Dabit Deus his quoque finem, DIVINE
GUIDANCE: 60
Dabit Deus vela, DIVINE GUIDANCE: 61
Dabit otia Deus, DIVINE GIFTS: 8
Dabit qui dedit, GIFTS and GIVING: 8
Dabunt aspera rosas, ADVERSITY: 11;
FLORA: 9
Da gloriam Deo, DIVINITY: 38
Dakyns, the devil's in the hempe,
UNCLASSIFIED: 8
Dando conservat, GIFTS and GIVING: 9
DANGER, p. 148
Danger I court, DANGER: 3

Mottoes & Categories

Da nobis lucem, Domine, DIVINE
GUIDANCE: 62; LIGHT: 6; TRADES: 11
Dant Deo, GIFTS and GIVING: 10
Dante Deo, DIVINE GIFTS: 9
Dante Deo reddam, DIVINE
GUIDANCE: 63
Dant lucem crescentibus orti, LIGHT: 7
Dant priscae decorum, DEEDS: 7;
FAME: 2
Dant vulnera vitam, LIFE: 4
Da pacem domine, PEACE: 8
Dare, AUDACITY: 43
Dare quam accipere, GIFTS and
GIVING: 11
DARKNESS, p. 149
Das Weib so fürchtet Gott, nicht
werden kan zu spot, FEAR: 6
Data fata secutus, FATE: 4
Dat cura commodum, VIGILANCE: 22
Dat cura quietem, VIGILANCE: 23
Dat decus origini, ANCESTRY: 12
Dat Deus incrementum, DIVINE
GIFTS: 10; SCHOOL MOTTOES: 54
Dat Deus originem, DIVINE GIFTS: 11
Date eleemosynam et ecce omnia
munda sunt vobis, GIFTS and
GIVING: 12; SCHOOL MOTTOES: 55
Dat et sumit Deus, DIVINE GIFTS: 12
Dat gloria vires, GLORY: 11
Dat incrementum, INCREASE: 12
Dat tela fidelitas, FIDELITY: 57;
WEAPONS: 26
Dat virtus quod forma negat,
BEAUTY: 6; VIRTUE: 36
DAY, p. 150
Dea providentia nostra est haereditas,
PROTECTION: 7; PROVIDENCE: 4
DEATH, p. 151
De bon cuer, FEELINGS: 14; LOCAL
GOVERNMENT: 76
Debonnaire, GRACEFULNESS: 1
De bon vouloir, WILL: 1
De bon vouloir servir le roy, CROWN: 9;
SERVICE: 9
De caelo victoria, VICTORY: 12
Decens et honestum, HONOR: 17
DECEPTION, p. 158
Decerptae dabunt odorem,
FRAGRANCE: 1
Decide, DECISION: 1
Decide and dare, AUDACITY: 44;
DECISION: 2

DECISION, p. 159
DECORATION, p. 159
Decore, GRACEFULNESS: 2
Decori decus addit avito,
ANCESTRY: 13; HONOR: 18
Decor integer, BEAUTY: 7
Decorum pro patria mori, COUNTRY: 6;
DEATH: 13; PATRIOTISM: 8
Decrevi, STEADFASTNESS: 31
Decus et tutamen, HONOR: 19;
PROTECTION: 8
Decus et veritas, GLORY: 12; SCHOOL
MOTTOES: 56; TRUTH: 10
Decus recte peto, HONOR: 20
Decus summum virtus, HONOR: 21;
VIRTUE: 37
Dedicated to training hand, mind,
heart, HANDS: 8; HEART: 7;
KNOWLEDGE: 6; MIND: 10; SCHOOL
MOTTOES: 57
DEDICATION, p. 159
De Dieu est tout, DIVINE GIFTS: 13
De Dieu tout, DIVINE GIFTS: 14
Dedit meliora dabitque, GIFTS and
GIVING: 13
DEEDS, p. 160
Deeds not words, DEEDS: 8; WORDS: 1
Deeds shaw, DEEDS: 9
Deeds show, DEEDS: 10
Defend, DEFENSE: 10
Defendamus, DEFENSE: 11; LOCAL
GOVERNMENT: 77
Defend and spare not, DEFENSE: 12
Defendendo vinco, DEFENSE: 13
Defend the fold, DEFENSE: 14
DEFENSE, p. 167
Defensio non offensio, DEFENSE: 15
Deffro mae'n Ddydd, LOCAL
GOVERNMENT: 78; WAKEFULNESS: 1
DEFIANCE, p. 170
Deficiam aut efficiam, FAILURE: 1
Defying ye field, OPPOSITION: 2
Degeneranti, genus opprobrium,
DISGRACE: 2
De hirundine, BIRDS: 13
Dei beneficio sum quod sum, DIVINE
GUIDANCE: 64; GRACE: 3
Dei dono sum quod sum, DIVINE
GIFTS: 15
Dei donum, DIVINE GIFTS: 16
Dei gratia, DIVINE GUIDANCE: 65;
GRACE: 4

Dei gratia grata, DIVINITY: 39;
GRACE: 5
Dei gratia sumus quod sumus, DIVINE
GUIDANCE: 66; GRACE: 6; LOCAL
GOVERNMENT: 79
Dei memor, gratus amicis,
DIVINITY: 40
Dei omnia plena, DIVINITY: 41
Dei Providentia juvat, DIVINE
GUIDANCE: 67; PROVIDENCE: 5
Dei sub numine viget, SCHOOL
MOTTOES: 58; STRENGTH: 19
Delectando pariterque monendo,
ENJOYMENT: 4; WARNING: 3
Delectant domi non impediunt foris,
ENJOYMENT: 5
Delectare in Domino, DIVINITY: 42
Delectat amor patriae, COUNTRY: 7
Delectat et ornat, ENJOYMENT: 6
Delectatio, ENJOYMENT: 7
Delectatio mea, ENJOYMENT: 8
Deliciae mei, ENJOYMENT: 9
De marisco, FLORA: 10
De me praesagia olim, UNCLASSIFIED: 9
Demeure par la vérité, TRUTH: 11
De mieux je pense en mieux,
ASPIRATION: 44
De monte alto, LOFTINESS: 7
Demovres ferme, STEADFASTNESS: 32
Demum, TIME: 15
D'en haut, DIVINE GIFTS: 17
Denique caelo fruar, PARADISE: 17
Denique caelum, PARADISE: 18
Denique decus, HONOR: 22
Denique sursum, PARADISE: 19
Den Stauf trage ich, UTENSILS: 3
Denuo fortasse lucescat, CLARITY: 2
Deo, non sagittis fido, DIVINITY: 43
Deo, patriae, amicis, COUNTRY: 8;
DIVINITY: 44; FRIENDSHIP: 22
Deo, patriae, proximo, COUNTRY: 9;
DIVINITY: 45
Deo, patriae, regi, COUNTRY: 10;
DIVINITY: 46; ROYALTY: 10
Deo, patriae, tibi, COUNTRY: 11;
DIVINITY: 47
Deo, regi, et patriae, COUNTRY: 12;
DIVINITY: 48; ROYALTY: 11
Deo, regi, patriae, COUNTRY: 13;
DIVINITY: 49; ROYALTY: 12
Deo, regi, vicino, DIVINITY: 50;
ROYALTY: 13; SCHOOL MOTTOES: 59

Deo, regi fidelis, DIVINITY: 51;
FIDELITY: 58; ROYALTY: 14
Deo, reipublicae, et amicis,
COUNTRY: 14; DIVINITY: 52;
FRIENDSHIP: 23
Deo ac bello, DIVINE GUIDANCE: 68;
WAR: 18
Deo ac veritati, DIVINITY: 53; SCHOOL
MOTTOES: 60; TRUTH: 12
Deo adjuvante, LOCAL
GOVERNMENT: 80
Deo adjuvante, fortuna sequatur,
DIVINE GUIDANCE: 71; FORTUNE: 15
Deo adjuvante arte et industria floret,
ART: 16; DIVINE GUIDANCE: 72;
INDUSTRIOUSNESS: 21; LOCAL
GOVERNMENT: 81
Deo adjuvante labor proficit, DIVINE
GUIDANCE: 73; INDUSTRIOUSNESS: 22;
LOCAL GOVERNMENT: 82
Deo adjuvante non timendum, DIVINE
GUIDANCE: 74
Deo adjuvante vincam, DIVINE
GUIDANCE: 75
Deo adverso, leo vincitur, ANIMALS: 14;
DIVINE GUIDANCE: 76
Deo aspirante virescit, DIVINE
GUIDANCE: 77; FLOURISHING: 9
Deo cari nihilo carent, DIVINITY: 54
Deo confide, DIVINITY: 55
Deo confidimus, DIVINITY: 56; LOCAL
GOVERNMENT: 83; TRUST: 23
Deo confido, DIVINITY: 57
Deo credito justitiam colito,
JUSTICE: 16; TRUST: 24
Deo date, DIVINITY: 58
Deo dirigente, DIVINE GUIDANCE: 78
Deo dirigente crescendum est, DIVINE
GUIDANCE: 79
Deo (Domino) optimo maximo (D. O.
M.), DIVINITY: 59
Deo donum, DIVINE GIFTS: 18
Deo duce, DIVINE GUIDANCE: 80;
LOCAL GOVERNMENT: 84
Deo duce, comite industria, DIVINE
GUIDANCE: 81; INDUSTRIOUSNESS: 23
Deo duce, ferro comitante, DIVINE
GUIDANCE: 82; WEAPONS: 27
Deo duce, fortunâ comitante, DIVINE
GUIDANCE: 83; FORTUNE: 16
Deo duce, sequor, DIVINE
GUIDANCE: 84

Deo duce Christo luce, CHRIST,
JESUS: 32; DIVINE GUIDANCE: 85;
LIGHT: 8

Deo duce comite fortuna, DIVINE
GUIDANCE: 86; FORTUNE: 17

Deo duce decrevi, DIVINE
GUIDANCE: 87

Deo ducente, nil nocet, DIVINE
GUIDANCE: 88

Deo ducente nil nocet, DIVINE
GUIDANCE: 89

Deo duce perseverandum, DIVINE
GUIDANCE: 90; PERSEVERANCE: 11

Deo et amicitiae, DIVINITY: 60;
FRIENDSHIP: 24

Deo et gladio, DIVINE GUIDANCE: 91;
WEAPONS: 28

Deo et labore, DIVINE GUIDANCE: 92;
INDUSTRIOUSNESS: 24

Deo et patriae, COUNTRY: 15;
DIVINITY: 61

Deo et patriae fidelis, COUNTRY: 16;
DIVINITY: 62; FIDELITY: 59

Deo et principe, DIVINITY: 63;
PRINCELINESS: 3

Deo et principi, DIVINITY: 64;
PRINCELINESS: 4

Deo et regi, DIVINITY: 65; ROYALTY: 15

Deo et regi asto, DIVINITY: 66;
FIDELITY: 60; ROYALTY: 16

Deo et regi fidelis, DIVINITY: 67;
FIDELITY: 61; ROYALTY: 17

Deo et virtuti, DIVINITY: 68; VIRTUE: 38

Deo favente, DIVINE GUIDANCE: 93

Deo favente cresco, DIVINE
GUIDANCE: 94

Deo favente florebo, DIVINE
GUIDANCE: 95

Deo favente progredior, DIVINE
GUIDANCE: 96

Deo favente supero, DIVINE
GUIDANCE: 97

Deo fidelis et regi, DIVINITY: 69;
FIDELITY: 62; ROYALTY: 18

Deo fidens, DIVINITY: 70

Deo fidens persistas, DIVINITY: 71;
PERSEVERANCE: 12

Deo fidens proficio, DIVINITY: 72;
TRUST: 25

Deo fisus labora, DIVINITY: 73;
INDUSTRIOUSNESS: 25; SCHOOL
MOTTOES: 61; TRUST: 26

Deo fretus erumpe, DIVINITY: 74;
LOCAL GOVERNMENT: 85

Deo gloria, DIVINITY: 75

Deo gratias, DIVINITY: 76;
GRATITUDE: 1

Deo honor et gloria, DIVINITY: 77;
GLORY: 13; HONOR: 23

Deo inspirante, rege favente, DIVINE
GUIDANCE: 98; ROYALTY: 19

Deo juvante, DIVINE GUIDANCE: 99;
LOCAL GOVERNMENT: 86

Deo juvante consilio et armis, DIVINE
GUIDANCE: 100

Deo juvante gero, DIVINE
GUIDANCE: 101

Deo juvante vinco, DIVINE
GUIDANCE: 102

Deo lux nostra, DIVINITY: 78; LIGHT: 9

Deo non arce spes, DIVINITY: 79;
HOPE: 22; SECURITY: 5

Deo non armis fido, DIVINITY: 80;
WEAPONS: 29

Deo non fortunâ, PROVIDENCE: 6

Deo non fortunae, FORTUNE: 18;
PROVIDENCE: 7

Deo omnia, DIVINITY: 81

Deo omnia plena, DIVINITY: 82

Deo pagit, DIVINITY: 83

Deo parere libertas, LIBERTY: 13;
OBEDIENCE: 7

Deo patriae, scientiis, artibus,
COUNTRY: 17; DIVINITY: 84; SCHOOL
MOTTOES: 62

Deo patriaeque fidelis, COUNTRY: 18;
DIVINITY: 85; FIDELITY: 63

Deo protectori meo, DIVINE
GUIDANCE: 103

Deo regique debeo, DUTY: 5;
ROYALTY: 20

Deo regique liber, CROWN: 10;
SERVICE: 10

Deo regnat, DIVINE GUIDANCE: 104

Deo Reipublicae et amicis esto semper
fidelis, COUNTRY: 19; DIVINITY: 86;
FIDELITY: 64; FRIENDSHIP: 25

Deo semper confido, DIVINITY: 87;
TRUST: 27

Deo servire regnare est, SERVICE: 11

Deo servire summa libertas,
LIBERTY: 14; SERVICE: 12

Deo spes mea, DIVINITY: 88; HOPE: 23

Deo spes meo, DIVINITY: 89; HOPE: 24

Mottoes & Categories

Devouement sans bornes, DEVOTION: 3

De vultu tuo Domine meum prodeat judicium, DIVINE GUIDANCE: 165; JUSTICE: 17

Dextra cruce vincit, CROSS, THE: 49

Dextra fideque, FIDELITY: 66; HANDS: 9

D. F. D. H. I. D. W. A. (Die Furcht des Herrn ist der Weisheit Anfang), FEAR: 8; PRUDENCE: 17

Dhandeon co heiragh ali, OPPOSITION: 3

Dial gwaed Cymru, VENGEANCE: 3

Diciendo y haciendo, WORDS: 2

Dictis factisque simplex, DEEDS: 11; SIMPLICITY: 1

Die da treu sindt in der Liebe Gottes die list ihr [*sic*] ihm nicht nehmen, FIDELITY: 67

Die den Herrn suchen, haben keinen mangell an irgend einem gutt, DIVINITY: 122

Die Furcht des Herrn ist die Krone der Weisheit, FEAR: 9; PRUDENCE: 18

Die Gnad Gottes weirt ewig, DIVINE GUIDANCE: 166; GRACE: 8

Die Lieb der Freund macht Furcht dem Feind, FRIENDSHIP: 28

Dieu, un roi, une foi, DIVINITY: 123; FAITH: 30; ROYALTY: 26

Dieu aidant, DIVINE GUIDANCE: 167

Dieu aide au premier Chrestien, DIVINE GUIDANCE: 168

Dieu aide au premier Chretien (Chrestien) et baron de France, DIVINE GUIDANCE: 169

Dieu a la mer, DIVINITY: 124; SEA: 5

Dieu avec nous, DIVINE GUIDANCE: 170

Dieu ayde, DIVINE GUIDANCE: 171

Dieu defend le droit, DIVINE GUIDANCE: 172

Dieu donne, DIVINE GIFTS: 27

Dieu en soit garde, DIVINE GUIDANCE: 173; LOCAL GOVERNMENT: 93

Dieu est ma roche, DIVINE GUIDANCE: 174

Dieu est mon aide, DIVINE GUIDANCE: 175

Dieu est mon espoir, DIVINITY: 125; HOPE: 30

Dieu est tout, DIVINITY: 126

Dieu et la réligion, DIVINITY: 127; RELIGION: 5

Dieu et ma fiancée, DIVINITY: 128

Dieu et ma foi, DIVINITY: 129; FAITH: 31

Dieu et ma main droite, DIVINE GUIDANCE: 176

Dieu et ma patrie, COUNTRY: 22; DEVOTION: 5; DIVINITY: 130

Dieu et mon devoir, DIVINITY: 131; DUTY: 7

Dieu et mon droit, DIVINITY: 132; NATIONAL MOTTOES: 3; SCHOOL MOTTOES: 65

Dieu et mon espée, WEAPONS: 30

Dieu et mon espée [*sic*], DIVINITY: 133

Dieu et mon pays, COUNTRY: 23; DEVOTION: 6; DIVINITY: 134

Dieu et mon roi, COUNTRY: 24; DEVOTION: 7; ROYALTY: 27

Dieu garda Le Moyle, DIVINE GUIDANCE: 177

Dieu gouverne ma vie, DIVINE GUIDANCE: 178

Dieu le veut, DIVINE GUIDANCE: 179

Dieu m'a fait fort, DIVINE GUIDANCE: 180

Dieu me conduise, DIVINE GUIDANCE: 181

Dieu me garde, DIVINE GUIDANCE: 182

Dieu mon appui, DIVINE GUIDANCE: 183

Dieu nous aventure donne bonne, DIVINE GUIDANCE: 184

Dieu pour la Tranchée, qui contre?, DIVINE GUIDANCE: 185

Dieu pour nous, DIVINE GUIDANCE: 186

Dieu sait tout, DIVINITY: 135

Dieu te garde et regarde, DIVINE GUIDANCE: 187

Die virescit, STRENGTH: 20

Difficiles sed fructuosae, ADVERSITY: 12

Difficilia quae pulchra, ADVERSITY: 13; BEAUTY: 8

Digna sequens, PURSUIT: 3

Dignitas et libertas a Deo et Caesare, HONOR: 24

Dii facientes adjuvant, DIVINE GUIDANCE: 188

Dii moresque dabunt, DIVINE GIFTS: 28

Dii rexque secundent, DIVINE GUIDANCE: 189; ROYALTY: 28

Diis bene juvantibus, DIVINE
GUIDANCE: 190
DILIGENCE, p. 176
Diligence/ Discipline/ Integrity,
DILIGENCE: 17; DISCIPLINE: 2;
INTEGRITY: 6; SCHOOL MOTTOES: 66
Diligence/ Integrity/ Knowledge,
DILIGENCE: 18; INTEGRITY: 7;
KNOWLEDGE: 7; SCHOOL
MOTTOES: 67
Diligenter, DILIGENCE: 19
Diligenter et fideliter, DILIGENCE: 20;
FIDELITY: 68
Diligentes Deus ipse juvat,
DILIGENCE: 21; DIVINE
GUIDANCE: 191
Diligentia, DILIGENCE: 22
Diligentia cresco, DILIGENCE: 23
Diligentia ditat, DILIGENCE: 24
Diligentia et candore, DILIGENCE: 25;
FAIRNESS: 6
Diligentia et honeste, DILIGENCE: 26;
HONESTY: 6
Diligentia et honore, DILIGENCE: 27;
HONOR: 25
Diligentia et vigilantia, DILIGENCE: 28;
VIGILANCE: 24
Diligentia fit ubertas, DILIGENCE: 29
Diligentia fortior, DILIGENCE: 30;
STRENGTH: 21
Diligentia fortunae mater,
DILIGENCE: 31; FORTUNE: 20
Dilige pacem, LOVE: 43; PEACE: 10
Diligite justitiam qui judicatis terram,
RIGHTEOUSNESS: 3
Dinna waken sleeping dogs,
ANIMALS: 15; WAKEFULNESS: 2
Diofn diymffrost, COURAGE: 55
Dios, patria, libertad, COUNTRY: 25;
DIVINITY: 136; LIBERTY: 17;
NATIONAL MOTTOES: 4
Dios mi amparo y esperanza, DIVINE
GUIDANCE: 192
Dios union y libertad, DIVINITY: 137;
LIBERTY: 18; NATIONAL MOTTOES: 5
Diovolendo lo faro, DIVINE
GUIDANCE: 193
DIRECTION, p. 179
DIRECTNESS, p. 180
Dirigat Deus, DIVINE GUIDANCE: 194
Dirige, GUIDANCE: 7
Diriget Deus, DIVINE GUIDANCE: 195

Dirigo, GUIDANCE: 8; STATE
MOTTOES: 10
Dirigo et defendo, GUIDANCE: 9;
PROTECTION: 9
Disce et labora, INDUSTRIOUSNESS: 27;
KNOWLEDGE: 8
Disce ferenda pati, ENDURANCE: 14
Disce mori et vivere Christo, CHRIST,
JESUS: 33; DEATH: 14
Disce mori mundo, DEATH: 15
Disce mori ut vivas, REBIRTH: 4
Disce pati, ENDURANCE: 15
Disciplina, fide, perseverantia,
DISCIPLINE: 3; FIDELITY: 69;
PERSEVERANCE: 13
Disciplina praesidium civitatis,
DISCIPLINE: 4; SCHOOL MOTTOES: 68
DISCIPLINE, p. 181
Discite justitiam, JUSTICE: 18
Discite justitiam moniti, JUSTICE: 19
Discordiae fomes injuria, CONFLICT: 2
Discordia frangimur, CONFLICT: 3
Discordia maxima dilabuntur,
CONFLICT: 4
Discordia praecursor ruinae,
CONFLICT: 5
Discretio moderatrix virtutum,
DISCRETION: 5; VIRTUE: 40
DISCRETION, p. 181
Discrimine salus, DANGER: 4;
SECURITY: 6
DISGRACE, p. 182
Disponendo me, non mutando me,
CHANGE: 4
Dissipatae, UNCLASSIFIED: 10
Distantia jungit, UNITY: 25
Distinctively Christian, CHRIST,
JESUS: 34; SCHOOL MOTTOES: 69
Ditat Deus, DIVINE GIFTS: 29; DIVINE
GUIDANCE: 196
Ditat et alit, IMPROVEMENT: 7
Ditat servata fides, FIDELITY: 70
Ditat virtus, VIGILANCE: 25; VIRTUE: 41
Diu delibera cito fac, ACTION: 6;
THOUGHT: 6
Diuturnitate fragrantior,
FRAGRANCE: 2
Diu virescit, FLOURISHING: 10
Divide et impera, LAW: 5
Divina sibi canit, MUSIC: 2
DIVINE GIFTS, p. 183
DIVINE GUIDANCE, p. 186

Divini gloria ruris, PARADISE: 20
DIVINITY, p. 217
Divino robore, DIVINE GUIDANCE: 197
Divinum auxilium maneat nobiscum,
   DIVINE GUIDANCE: 198
Divisa conjungo, CONCILIATION: 4
Dixi, Dixi, WORDS: 3
Do a good turn (deed) daily, DEEDS: 12
Doce me, Domine, statuta tua, DIVINE
   GUIDANCE: 199
Docendo disce, KNOWLEDGE: 9
Docendum et discendum,
   KNOWLEDGE: 10; SCHOOL
   MOTTOES: 70
Doctrina ferro perennior,
   KNOWLEDGE: 11
Do ever good, DEEDS: 13
Do good, DEEDS: 14
Do it better yet, IMPROVEMENT: 8
Do it with thy might, DEEDS: 15
Do it with thyself, SELF-RELIANCE: 4
Dolce nella memoria, MEMORY: 2
Dolore lenio dolorem, SUFFERING: 1
Doluere dente lacessiti, INJURY: 2
Domat omnia virtus, VIRTUE: 42
Domi ac foris, HOME: 7
Domine, dirige me in verbo tuo,
   DIVINE GUIDANCE: 200; SCRIPTURES: 4
Domine, dirige nos, DIVINE
   GUIDANCE: 201; LOCAL
   GOVERNMENT: 94
Domine, speravi, DIVINITY: 138;
   HOPE: 31
Domine in virtute tua, DIVINITY: 139
Domini est dirigere, DIVINE
   GUIDANCE: 202; LOCAL
   GOVERNMENT: 95
Domini factum, DIVINITY: 140
Domini factum est, DIVINE
   GUIDANCE: 203
Domino fides immobilis, FAITH: 32
Domino quid
   reddam?, DIVINITY: 141
Dominus a dextris, DIVINE
   GUIDANCE: 204
Dominus adjutor meus, DIVINE
   GUIDANCE: 205
Dominus bonus propitiabitur, DIVINE
   GUIDANCE: 206
Dominus dedit, DIVINE GIFTS: 30
Dominus dux noster, DIVINE
   GUIDANCE: 207

Dominus exultatio mea, DIVINITY: 142
Dominus fecit, DIVINE GUIDANCE: 208
Dominus fortissima turris, DIVINE
   GUIDANCE: 209
Dominus ipse faciet, DIVINE
   GUIDANCE: 211
Dominus mihi adiutor, DIVINE
   GUIDANCE: 212; NATIONAL
   MOTTOES: 6
Dominus mihi adjutor, quem
   timebo?, DIVINE
   GUIDANCE: 213
Dominus nobis solet scutum, DIVINE
   GUIDANCE: 214; LOCAL
   GOVERNMENT: 96
Dominus petra mea, DIVINE
   GUIDANCE: 215
Dominus protector meus, DIVINE
   GUIDANCE: 216
Dominus providebit, DIVINE
   GUIDANCE: 217
Dominus salus mea, DIVINE
   GUIDANCE: 218
Dominus virtutum meum scutum,
   DIVINE GUIDANCE: 219
Domum antiquam redintegrare,
   REBIRTH: 5
Domus grata, HOME: 8
Dona dantur desuper, DIVINE GIFTS: 31
Donat anima virtus, VIRTUE: 43
Donec impleat orbem, FULLNESS: 2
Donec rursus impleat orbem,
   FULLNESS: 3
Donec totum impleat orbem,
   FULLNESS: 4
Donner et pardonner, GIFTS and
   GIVING: 14
Do not for to repent, DEEDS: 16
Do no ylle, quoth D'Oylle, DEEDS: 17
Don't tread on me, WARNING: 4
Do or die, DEEDS: 18
Do that ye come fore, DEEDS: 19
Do the day's work,
   INDUSTRIOUSNESS: 28
Doucement, mais fermement,
   MANNER: 1
Dove andate?, DESTINATION: 4
Do well, doubt not, DEEDS: 20
Do well, doubt nought, DEEDS: 21
Do well and doubt not, DEEDS: 22;
   LOCAL GOVERNMENT: 97
Do well and let them say, DEEDS: 23

Mottoes & Categories

Do ye next thyng, DEEDS: 24
Do your duty and leave the rest to
  Providence, DUTY: 8
Dread God, DIVINITY: 144
Dread shame, DISGRACE: 3
Drede God and honour the king,
  FEAR: 10
Drogo nomen, et virtus arma dedit,
  COURAGE: 56; NAME: 3
Droit, RECTITUDE: 14
Droit à chacun, RIGHTS: 2
Droit comme ma flêche,
  DIRECTNESS: 10
Droit et avant, JUSTICE: 20
Droit et loyal, JUSTICE: 21
Droit et loyalté, JUSTICE: 22
Drop as rain, distil as dew,
  TRADES: 12; WATER: 5
Droyt et devaunt, ADVANCE: 14;
  RECTITUDE: 15
Drwy rynwedd gwaed, ANCESTRY: 14
Ducat amor Dei, DIVINITY: 145
Duce Deo, DIVINE GUIDANCE: 220
Duce et auspice, GUIDANCE: 10
Duce natura sequor, FOLLOWING: 2
Ducente Deo, DIVINE GUIDANCE: 221
Duci et non trahi, LEADERSHIP: 7
Ducit amor oppidi, LOCAL
  GOVERNMENT: 98; LOVE: 44
Ducit amor patriae, PATRIOTISM: 9
Ducit Dominus, DIVINE GUIDANCE: 222
Ducitur, non trahitur, LEADERSHIP: 8
Ducitur hinc honos, HONOR: 26
Duc me, sequar, FOLLOWING: 3;
  LEADERSHIP: 9
Ductore Deo, DIVINE GUIDANCE: 223
Ductus, non coactus, LEADERSHIP: 10
DUE, p. 245
Dulce amarum patientia, PATIENCE: 5
Dulcedine capior, ENJOYMENT: 10
Dulce est fratres habitare in unum,
  UNITY: 26
Dulce est fratres inhabitare in unum,
  UNITY: 27
Dulce est pro patria mori,
  COUNTRY: 26; DEATH: 16;
  PATRIOTISM: 10
Dulce meum terra tegit, DEATH: 17
Dulce periculum, DANGER: 5
Dulce pro patriâ periculum,
  COUNTRY: 27; DANGER: 6
Dulce quod utile, USEFULNESS: 2

Dulces ante omnia Musae,
  ENJOYMENT: 11
Dulcidine, GENTLENESS: 3
Dulcis amor patriae, COUNTRY: 28;
  LOVE: 45; PATRIOTISM: 11
Dulcis pro patria labor, COUNTRY: 29;
  INDUSTRIOUSNESS: 29
Dulcius ex asperis, ADVERSITY: 14
Dum clarum rectum teneam,
  RECTITUDE: 16
Dum cresco spero, GROWTH: 5;
  HOPE: 32; INCREASE: 14; LOCAL
  GOVERNMENT: 99
Dum defluat amnis, LOCAL
  GOVERNMENT: 100; WATER: 6
Dum exspiro spero, DEATH: 18;
  HOPE: 33
Dum in arborem, FLORA: 11;
  GROWTH: 6
Dum memor ipse mei, SELF-
  KNOWLEDGE: 5
Dum sedulo prospero,
  INDUSTRIOUSNESS: 30; PROSPERITY: 7
Dum sisto vigilo, VISION: 4
Dum spiro caelestia spero, HOPE: 34;
  ORIGIN: 1
Dum spiro spero, HONOR: 27; HOPE: 35;
  STARS: 15; STATE MOTTOES: 11
Dum tempus habemus operemur
  bonum, DEEDS: 25; TIME: 16
Dum varior, CHANGE: 5
Dum varior idem, STEADFASTNESS: 34
Dum vigilo, pareo, VIGILANCE: 26
Dum vigilo curo, VIGILANCE: 27
Dum vigilo tutus, SECURITY: 7;
  VIGILANCE: 28
Dum vivimus, vivamus, LIFE: 5
Dum vivo, spero, HONOR: 28; HOPE: 36
Dum vivo, vireo, FLOURISHING: 11;
  LIFE: 6
Dum vivo cano, LIFE: 7; MUSIC: 3
Duobus fulcris securius, SECURITY: 8
Dura pati virtus, ADVERSITY: 15;
  VIRTUE: 44
Dura placent fortibus, ADVERSITY: 16
Durat, ditat, placet, ENDURANCE: 16
Durch Gottes Segen, BLESSING: 10
Dureté, STRENGTH: 22
Duriora virtus, VIRTUE: 45
Duris non frangor, ADVERSITY: 17
Durum contra stimulum calcitrare,
  OPPOSITION: 4

Mottoes & Categories

Either discard the word, or
  becomingly adhere to it (*from
  Greek*), WORDS: 4
Either forever, FIDELITY: 71
E labore dulcedo, ENJOYMENT: 12;
  INDUSTRIOUSNESS: 31
Elatum a Deo non deprimat, STATUS: 2
El hombre propone, Dios dispone,
  DIVINE GUIDANCE: 228
El honor es mi guia, GUIDANCE: 12;
  HONOR: 31
Eloquentia sagitta, WORDS: 5
El rey y la patria, PATRIOTISM: 12;
  ROYALTY: 29
Elvenaca floreat vitis, FLOURISHING: 15
E mare, SEA: 6; WORTHINESS: 8
E mare ex industria,
  INDUSTRIOUSNESS: 32; LOCAL
  GOVERNMENT: 101; SEA: 7
E medio ad mediatorem,
  MODERATION: 3
EMERGENCE, p. 251
Emergo, EMERGENCE: 1
Emeritus, PATRIOTISM: 13; SERVICE: 16
Emollit mores nec sinit esse feros,
  MANNERS: 1; SCHOOL MOTTOES: 87
Emphasis excellence, EXCELLENCE: 5;
  SCHOOL MOTTOES: 88
En attendant patience, PATIENCE: 9
En avant, ADVANCE: 15
En avant si je puis, ADVANCE: 16
En bon espoir, HOPE: 37
En bon espoyr, HOPE: 38
En bon et poyer, POWER: 7;
  RECTITUDE: 17
En bon foy, FAITH: 34
En! dat Virginia quartum, MEASURE: 2
Endeavour, EFFORT: 9; LOCAL
  GOVERNMENT: 102
En Dieu affie, DIVINITY: 150
En Dieu est ma fiance, DIVINITY: 151;
  TRUST: 28
En Dieu est ma foy, FAITH: 35
En Dieu est mon esperance,
  DIVINITY: 152; HOPE: 39; LOCAL
  GOVERNMENT: 103
En Dieu est mon espoir, DIVINITY: 153;
  HOPE: 40
En Dieu est tout, DIVINITY: 154;
  SCHOOL MOTTOES: 89
En Dieu et mon roy, DIVINITY: 155;
  ROYALTY: 30

En Dieu gist ma confiance,
  DIVINITY: 156; TRUST: 29
En Dieu ma foi, FAITH: 36
En Dieu ma foy, FAITH: 37
En Dieu ma joye, HAPPINESS: 11
En Dieu mon esperance,
  DIVINITY: 157; HOPE: 41
En Dieu mon esperance et l'espee
  [*sic*]pour ma defense, DEFENSE: 17;
  DIVINITY: 158; HOPE: 42
En Dieu se fie, DIVINITY: 159
En Dieu seul gist ma confiance,
  DIVINITY: 160; TRUST: 30
En Dieu sont nos espèrances,
  DIVINITY: 161
En droyt devant, RECTITUDE: 18
ENDURANCE, p. 252
Endure and hope, ENDURANCE: 17;
  HOPE: 43
Endure fort, ENDURANCE: 18
Endurer faiet durer, ENDURANCE: 19
ENEMIES, p. 255
En espérance je vis, HONOR: 32;
  HOPE: 44
En esperanza, HOPE: 45
En espoir je vive attendant grace,
  GRACE: 9; HOPE: 46
En faizant bien, WORTHINESS: 9
Enfans du roy, OFFSPRING: 2
En! Ferus hostis, HOSTILITY: 2
En foi prest, FAITH: 38
Engineering/ Technology/ Science,
  SCHOOL MOTTOES: 90
En grace affie, GRACE: 10
ENJOYMENT, p. 255
En la rose je fleurie, FLORA: 13;
  FLOURISHING: 16
ENLIGHTENMENT, p. 257
En martélant, UNCLASSIFIED: 12
Enough in my hand, POSSESSION: 5
En parole je vis, WORDS: 6
En pure foi, FAITH: 39
Ense animus major, MIND: 11
Ense et animo, COURAGE: 57;
  WEAPONS: 31
Ense libertatem petit, LIBERTY: 19;
  WEAPONS: 32
Ense libertatem petit inimico tyrannis,
  LIBERTY: 20; WEAPONS: 33
Ense petit placidam sub libertate
  quietam, LIBERTY: 21; PEACE: 11;
  STATE MOTTOES: 12; WEAPONS: 34

En sincerité et fidelité ma vie je
    finiray, FIDELITY: 72; SINCERITY: 6
En suivant la vérité, TRUTH: 17
Entends-toi, WISDOM: 20
En tout fidèle, FIDELITY: 73
En tout loyale, FIDELITY: 74
En tout parfait, PERFECTION: 1
ENTRAPMENT, p. 258
En vain espère, qui ne craint Dieu,
    DIVINITY: 162; HOPE: 47
ENVY, p. 258
Eo altius quo profundius, LOFTINESS: 8
E perseverantia honor, HONOR: 33;
    PERSEVERANCE: 14
E pluribus unum, UNITY: 29
E pur si muove! Italian,
    UNCLASSIFIED: 13
EQUALITY, p. 259
Equality, EQUALITY: 2; SCHOOL
    MOTTOES: 91
Equality before the law, EQUALITY: 3;
    STATE MOTTOES: 13
Equal rights, EQUALITY: 4; STATE
    MOTTOES: 14
Equanimiter, EQUANIMITY: 8
EQUANIMITY, p. 260
Eques sit semper aequus, JUSTICE: 23
Equity, FAIRNESS: 7
Er codiad y caer, FORTIFICATIONS: 2
Erectus, non elatus, EXALTATION: 2
E rege et victoria, ROYALTY: 31;
    VICTORY: 13
Erimus, FUTURE, THE: 7; LOCAL
    GOVERNMENT: 104
Erit haec quoque cognita monstris,
    KNOWLEDGE: 19; WARNING: 5
Ero quod eram, REBIRTH: 6
Errantia lumina fallunt, DECEPTION: 3
Eruditio/ ductus/ societas,
    FELLOWSHIP: 2; KNOWLEDGE: 20;
    LEADERSHIP: 11; SCHOOL
    MOTTOES: 92
Eruditio et meritum pro omnibus,
    KNOWLEDGE: 21; REWARD: 5;
    SCHOOL MOTTOES: 93
Eryr eryrod Eryri, BIRDS: 16
Es mag noch wohl gerathen,
    POSSIBILITY: 1
Esperance, HOPE: 48
Esperance en Dieu, DIVINITY: 163;
    HOPE: 49
Espérance sans peur, HOPE: 50

Espère en Dieu, DIVINITY: 164
Espère et persévère, HOPE: 51;
    PERSEVERANCE: 15
Espère mieux, HOPE: 52
Esperez en Dieu, HOPE: 53
E spinis, ADVERSITY: 18
Espoir me comfort, HOPE: 54
Espoir me conforte, HOPE: 55
Essayez, EFFORT: 10
Essayez hardiment, EFFORT: 11
Esse et videri, INTEGRITY: 8
Esse potius quam haberi, INTEGRITY: 9
Esse quam videri, SCHOOL
    MOTTOES: 94; STATE MOTTOES: 15
Essorant victorieux, VICTORY: 14
Es stehet Alles in Gottes Händen,
    DIVINITY: 165
Est concordia fratrum, PEACE: 12
Est cotis vis in acutis, SCHOOL
    MOTTOES: 95
Est Deo gratia, DIVINITY: 166;
    GRATITUDE: 2
Estimatione nixa, WORTHINESS: 10
Est meruisse satis, WORTHINESS: 11
Est modus, MODERATION: 4
Est modus in rebus, MEASURE: 3
Est nec astu, CLEVERNESS: 4
Est nobilis ira leonis, ANGER: 1;
    ANIMALS: 17; NOBILITY: 5
Est nulla fallacia, DECEPTION: 4
Esto, ACCEPTANCE: 3
Esto bonus et pius ne sit leo te magis
    impavidus, ANIMALS: 18;
    GOODNESS: 12; PIETY: 6
Esto fidelis, FIDELITY: 75
Esto fidelis usque ad finem,
    FIDELITY: 76
Esto fidelis usque ad mortem,
    FIDELITY: 77
Esto memor, ATTENTIVENESS: 4
Esto miles fidelis, FIDELITY: 78
Esto perpetua, ENDURANCE: 22;
    SCHOOL MOTTOES: 96
Esto quod audes, ASPIRATION: 45
Esto quod esse videris, INTEGRITY: 12
Esto semper fidelis, FIDELITY: 79
Esto sol testis, SUN: 3
Estote fideles, FIDELITY: 80
Estote prudentes, PRUDENCE: 19
Estote semper parati,
    PREPAREDNESS: 15
Esto velocior vita, SPEED: 21

Esto vigilans, VIGILANCE: 29
Est pii Deum et patriam diligere,
LOVE: 46; PIETY: 7
Est voluntas Dei, DIVINE
GUIDANCE: 229
Et agere et pati fortiter, Romanum est,
COURAGE: 58
Et arma et virtus, VIRTUE: 46;
WEAPONS: 35
Et arte et Marte, ABILITY: 13;
COURAGE: 59
Et custos et pugnax, CONSERVATION: 4
Et decerptae dabunt odorem,
FRAGRANCE: 3
Et decus et pretium recti, HONOR: 34;
RECTITUDE: 19; REWARD: 6
Et Dieu mon appui, DIVINE
GUIDANCE: 230
Et dixi nunc coepi, WORDS: 7
Et docere et rerum exquirere causas,
KNOWLEDGE: 22; SCHOOL
MOTTOES: 97
Et domi et foris, HOME: 9
E tellure effodiuntur opes, EARTH: 3;
PROSPERITY: 8
E tenebris lux, DARKNESS: 2; LIGHT: 11
Eternitatem cogita, ETERNITY: 3
ETERNITY, p. 261
E terra ad coelum, PARADISE: 22
E terra divitiae, EARTH: 4; LOCAL
GOVERNMENT: 105; PROSPERITY: 9
E terra germino ad coelum expando,
EARTH: 5; GROWTH: 7; INCREASE: 15
Et fide et virtute, FAITH: 40;
VIRTUE: 47
Et finem spero, HOPE: 56
Et juste et vrai, JUSTICE: 24; TRUTH: 18
Et loquor et taceo, WORDS: 8
Et manu et corde, HANDS: 10; HEART: 8
Et Marte et arte, COURAGE: 60
Et mea messis erit, HARVEST: 1
Et mortua virescunt, REBIRTH: 7
Et neglecta virescit, FLOURISHING: 17
Et nos quoque tela sparsimus,
WEAPONS: 36
Et patribus et posteris, TIME: 18
Et patribus et posteritati,
ANCESTRY: 15; LOCAL
GOVERNMENT: 106
Et plui super unam civitatem,
WATER: 7

Et regem defendere victum,
DEFENSE: 18; ROYALTY: 32
Être sage c'est penser à tout,
WISDOM: 21
Et servata fides perfectus amorque
ditabunt, FAITH: 41; LOVE: 47
Et si ostendo non jacto,
BOASTFULNESS: 2
Et suavis et fortis, COURAGE: 61;
ENJOYMENT: 13
Et suivez moi, FOLLOWING: 4
Et teneo et teneor, POSSESSION: 6
Ettle weel, GOALS: 3
Et vi et virtute, STRENGTH: 24;
VIRTUE: 48
Et vitam impendere vero,
SACRIFICE: 1; TRUTH: 19
Eundo, UNCLASSIFIED: 14
Eureka, SEARCH and DISCOVERY: 5;
STATE MOTTOES: 16
Ever faithful, FIDELITY: 81
Ever forward, IMPROVEMENT: 9; LOCAL
GOVERNMENT: 107
Ever ready, PREPAREDNESS: 16
Evertendo faecundat, AGRICULTURE: 2
Ever watchful, VIGILANCE: 30
Every bullet has its billet, FATE: 5
Every day in every way, I am getting
better and better, IMPROVEMENT: 10
Every point, UNCLASSIFIED: 15
Eviglia [*sic*] qui dormis, VIGILANCE: 31
EVIL, p. 262
Ewch ymlaen, IMPROVEMENT: 11
Ewch yn uchaf, ASPIRATION: 46
Ewch yn uwch, ASPIRATION: 47; LOCAL
GOVERNMENT: 108
Ex adverso decus, GLORY: 14
Ex aliis se ipsum nosse facundissima
virtus, SELF-KNOWLEDGE: 6
Exaltabit honore, HONOR: 35
Exaltat humiles, HUMILITY: 2
Exaltatio mea, HAPPINESS: 12
EXALTATION, p. 263
Exaltavit humiles, EXALTATION: 3;
HUMILITY: 3
Exaltum cornu in Deo, DIVINITY: 167;
SCHOOL MOTTOES: 98
Ex animo, SPIRIT: 9
Ex arduis perpetuum nomen, NAME: 4
Ex armis honos, HONOR: 36
Ex bello quies, WAR: 19

Ex caligine veritas, DARKNESS: 3;
  TRUTH: 20
Ex campo victoriae, VICTORY: 15
Ex candore decus, HONOR: 37;
  SINCERITY: 7
Ex candore virtus, VIRTUE: 49
EXCELLENCE, p. 263
Excellence, EXCELLENCE: 6; SCHOOL
  MOTTOES: 99
Excellence for Christ, CHRIST,
  JESUS: 37; EXCELLENCE: 7; SCHOOL
  MOTTOES: 100
Excellence through education,
  EXCELLENCE: 8; SCHOOL
  MOTTOES: 101
Excellentia, EXCELLENCE: 9; SCHOOL
  MOTTOES: 102
Excelsior, ASPIRATION: 48
Except in the cross, CROSS, THE: 51
Except the Lord keep the city, DIVINE
  GUIDANCE: 231; LOCAL
  GOVERNMENT: 109
Excidit amor nunquam, LOVE: 48
Excisa viresco, FLOURISHING: 18
Excitari non hebescere, LIVELINESS: 2
Excitat, WAKEFULNESS: 3
Ex concordia victoriae spes, UNITY: 30;
  VICTORY: 16
Ex corde charitas, KINDNESS: 6
Ex cruce leo, ANIMALS: 19; CROSS,
  THE: 52
Excutit inde canit, MUSIC: 4
Ex duris gloria, SUFFERING: 2
Exegi, ACCOMPLISHMENT: 8
Exempla suorum, ANCESTRY: 16
Exemple brave et louable,
  COURAGE: 62
Exemplum adest ipse homo,
  HOSTILITY: 3
Ex fide fortis, FAITH: 42
Ex flamma lux, LIGHT: 12
Ex fonte perenni, WATER: 8
Ex forti dulcedo, STRENGTH: 25
Ex glande quercus, GROWTH: 8; LOCAL
  GOVERNMENT: 110
Ex hoc victoria signo, VICTORY: 17
Ex hoc vivo, LIFE: 8
EXHORTATION, p. 264
Ex industria, INDUSTRIOUSNESS: 33
Exitus acta probat, RESULTS: 1
Ex libertate veritas, LIBERTY: 22;
  TRUTH: 21

Ex lumine lucrum, LIGHT: 13
Ex malo bonum, GOODNESS: 13
Ex merito, WORTHINESS: 12
Ex monte alto, LOFTINESS: 9
Ex Oriente salus, SALVATION: 18;
  SCHOOL MOTTOES: 103
Expecta cuncta supernè,
  EXPECTATION: 4
EXPECTATION, p. 264
Expectes et sustineas, ENDURANCE: 23;
  HOPE: 57
Expecto, EXPECTATION: 5
Expedite, SPEED: 22
Expende primo, CAUTION: 23
Expertus fidelem, FIDELITY: 82
Expertus fidelem Jupiter, FIDELITY: 83
EXPLORATION, p. 265
Expugnare, CONQUEST: 6
Expugnavi, CONQUEST: 7
Ex recto decus, HONOR: 38
Ex scientia tridens, KNOWLEDGE: 23;
  SCHOOL MOTTOES: 104
Ex seipso renascens, REBIRTH: 8
Ex septem unus, UNITY: 31
Ex sese, SELF-RELIANCE: 5
Ex sola virtute honos, HONOR: 39;
  VIRTUE: 50
Ex sudore voluptas, ENJOYMENT: 14;
  INDUSTRIOUSNESS: 34
Ex sudore vultus, INDUSTRIOUSNESS: 35
Exsurge, domine, judica causam tuam,
  JUDGMENT: 3
Exsurgunt nubila Phoebo, SUN: 4
Extant rectè factis praemia, DEEDS: 32;
  REWARD: 7
Extermination, DESTRUCTION: 2
Ex terra copiam e mari salutem,
  EARTH: 6; FULLNESS: 5; HEALING and
  HEALTH: 7; LOCAL GOVERNMENT: 111
Ex terra lucem, LIGHT: 14; LOCAL
  GOVERNMENT: 112
Extinctus orior, REBIRTH: 9
Extremos pudeat rediisse, DISGRACE: 4
Ex undis aratra, SEA: 8
Ex unguibus leonis, ANIMALS: 20;
  DANGER: 7
Ex unitate incrementum,
  INCREASE: 16; UNITY: 32
Ex unitate vires, UNITY: 33
Ex uno omnia, UNITY: 34
Ex urna resurgam, REBIRTH: 10

Mottoes & Categories

Ex usu commodum, CONVENIENCE: 2;
ENJOYMENT: 15
Ex vero decus, HONOR: 40; TRUTH: 22
Ex vile pretiosa, WORLD: 1;
WORTHINESS: 13
Ex virtute honos, HONOR: 41;
VIRTUE: 51
Ex vulnere salus, HEALING and
HEALTH: 8

F

Fabula sed vera, UNCLASSIFIED: 16
Fac alteri ut tibi vis, DEEDS: 33
Face aut tace, DEEDS: 34; SILENCE: 4
Face the dawn, DAY: 2; LOCAL
GOVERNMENT: 113
Fac et spera, DEEDS: 35; HOPE: 58
Facies qualis mens talis,
COUNTENANCE: 1; MIND: 12
Facie tenus, COUNTENANCE: 2
Fac justa, ACTION: 7
Fac me unum Domine ex mercenariis
tuis, SERVICE: 17
Fac recte et nil time, FEAR: 11;
RECTITUDE: 20
Fac recte nil time, FEAR: 12;
RECTITUDE: 21
Fac simile, DEEDS: 36
Fac similiter, DEEDS: 37
Facta non verba, DEEDS: 38; WORDS: 9
Facta probant, DEEDS: 39
Factis non verbis, DEEDS: 40;
WORDS: 10
Facto non verbo, DEEDS: 41;
WORDS: 11
FACTUALITY, p. 265
Factum est, DEEDS: 42; TRADES: 13
Facundia felix, WORDS: 12
Faded, but not destroyed,
PERSECUTION: 3
FAILURE, p. 265
Faint yet pursuing, PURSUIT: 4
Faire mon devoir, DUTY: 11
Faire sans dire, DEEDS: 43
Faire son devoir, DUTY: 12
FAIRNESS, p. 266
Fais bien, crains rien, DEEDS: 44
Fais qui doit, arrive qui pourra,
DUTY: 13
FAITH, p. 267

Faith, FAITH: 43; LOCAL
GOVERNMENT: 114
Faith, Hope, Charity, FAITH: 44;
HOPE: 59; KINDNESS: 7
Faith, unity, discipline, DISCIPLINE: 5;
FAITH: 45; UNITY: 35
Faith, work, service, FAITH: 46; LOCAL
GOVERNMENT: 115; SERVICE: 18
Faith and hope, FAITH: 47; HOPE: 60
Faith and works, FAITH: 48
Faithful, FIDELITY: 84
Faithful and brave, AUDACITY: 45;
FIDELITY: 85
Faithful and true, FIDELITY: 86
Faithful in adversity, FIDELITY: 87
Faithful to my unhappy country,
COUNTRY: 31; FIDELITY: 88
Faith in industry, FAITH: 49;
INDUSTRIOUSNESS: 36; LOCAL
GOVERNMENT: 116
Faitz proverount, DEEDS: 45
Fal y gallo, POSSIBILITY: 2
Fama candidâ rosâ dulcior, FAME: 3;
FLORA: 14
Famae studiosus honestae, FAME: 4
Famae venientis amore, FAME: 5
Famae vestigia retinens, FAME: 6
Famam extendere factis, DEEDS: 46;
FAME: 7
Famam extendimus factis, FAME: 8
Fama perennis erit, FAME: 9
Fama praestante praestantior virtus,
REPUTATION: 3; VIRTUE: 52
Fama proclamat honorem, HONOR: 42;
REPUTATION: 4
Fama sed virtus non moriatur,
FAME: 10; VIRTUE: 53
Fama semper vivet, FAME: 11
Fama semper vivit, FAME: 12
Fama volat, FAME: 13; LOCAL
GOVERNMENT: 117
FAME, p. 267
Familias firmat pietas,
PERSEVERANCE: 16; PIETY: 8
Far and sure, CONFIDENCE: 8
Far and tacer, DEEDS: 47; SILENCE: 5
Fare, fac, WORDS: 13
Fare et age, WORDS: 14
Fare fac, WORDS: 15
Fare wel til then, UNCLASSIFIED: 17
Fari aude, WORDS: 16
Fari quae sentias, WORDS: 17

Fari quae sentiat, WORDS: 18
Fari quae sentient, WORDS: 19
Fas ducit, RECTITUDE: 22
Fas est ab hoste doceri,
  KNOWLEDGE: 24
Fast, STEADFASTNESS: 35
Fast tho' untied, STEADFASTNESS: 36
Fast without fraude,
  STEADFASTNESS: 37
Fata consiliis potiora, FATE: 6
Fata sequar, FATE: 7
Fata vim invenient, FATE: 10
FATE, p. 283
Fato, nec fraude, nec astu, FATE: 11
Fato fortior virtus, FATE: 12;
  VIRTUE: 54
Fato non merito, FATE: 13
Fato prudentia major, FATE: 14;
  PRUDENCE: 20
Fatti maschi, parole femmine,
  DEEDS: 48; STATE MOTTOES: 17
Fatti maschii parole femine,
  DEEDS: 49; STATE MOTTOES: 18
Faugh a bollagh, WAY: 1
Faut être, NECESSITY: 1
Faveat fortuna, FORTUNE: 22
Favente Deo, DIVINE GUIDANCE: 232
Favente Deo et sedulitate,
  DILIGENCE: 32; DIVINE
  GUIDANCE: 233
Favente Deo supero, DIVINE
  GUIDANCE: 234
Favente des supero, GIFTS and
  GIVING: 15
Favente Numine, PROVIDENCE: 8
Favente Numine regina servatur,
  DIVINE GUIDANCE: 235; ROYALTY: 33
Faventibus auris, FORTUNE: 23
Favet fortuna labori, FORTUNE: 24;
  INDUSTRIOUSNESS: 37
Favore Altissimi, DIVINE
  GUIDANCE: 236; GRACE: 11
Fax mentis honestae gloria, GLORY: 17
Fax mentis incendium gloriae,
  GLORY: 18
Fay bien, crain rien, DEEDS: 50
Fay ce que doy advienne que pourra,
  DEEDS: 51
Fayth hathe no feare, FAITH: 50
Feal pero desdecado, FIDELITY: 89
FEAR, p. 285
Fear God, DIVINITY: 168

Fear God, fear nought, DIVINITY: 169
Fear God, honor the king,
  DIVINITY: 170; LOCAL
  GOVERNMENT: 118; ROYALTY: 34
Fear God and dread nought,
  DIVINITY: 171
Fear God and fight, DIVINITY: 172
Fear God and live, DIVINITY: 173
Fear God and spare nought,
  DIVINITY: 174
Fear God in life, DIVINITY: 175
Fear God in love, DIVINITY: 176
Fear God only, DIVINITY: 177
Fear not, FEAR: 13
Fear not friendship, FRIENDSHIP: 29
Fear nought, FEAR: 14
Fear one, FEAR: 15
Fear to transgress, FEAR: 16
Fecit eos in gentem unam, UNITY: 36
Fecunditate, FLOURISHING: 19
Fecunditate afficior, FLOURISHING: 20
Feed ye my sheep, ANIMALS: 21;
  NOURISHMENT: 3
FEELINGS, p. 291
Felice che puo, HAPPINESS: 13
Felicem reddet religio, HAPPINESS: 14;
  RELIGION: 8
Felici numine crescat, DIVINE
  GUIDANCE: 237; GROWTH: 9
Felicior quo certior, FORTUNE: 25
Felicitate restituta, HAPPINESS: 15;
  STATE MOTTOES: 19
Feliciter floret, FLOURISHING: 21
Felis demulcta mitis, GENTLENESS: 4
Felix qui pacificus, HAPPINESS: 16;
  PEACE: 13
Felix qui prudens, HAPPINESS: 17
FELLOWSHIP, p. 292
Fellowship is life, FELLOWSHIP: 3;
  LOCAL GOVERNMENT: 119
Fe med'um buen hidalgo, FAITH: 51
Ferant mea serta columbae, BIRDS: 17;
  PEACE: 14
Ferar unus et idem, IDENTITY: 1
Ferendo et feriendo, ENDURANCE: 24
Ferendo feres, ENDURANCE: 25
Ferendo non feriendo, ENDURANCE: 26
Ferendum et sperandum,
  ENDURANCE: 27; HOPE: 61
Fer et perfer, ENDURANCE: 28
Fer fortiter, ENDURANCE: 29
Ferio, AGGRESSION: 4

Ferio, tego, DEFENSE: 19
Ferio sed sano, AGGRESSION: 5
Ferme en foy, FAITH: 52
Ferme et fidèle, FIDELITY: 90;
  STRENGTH: 26
Feroci fortior, ANIMALS: 22;
  AUDACITY: 46; FIERCENESS: 1
Feror unus et idem, CONSISTENCY: 3
Feros ferio, AGGRESSION: 6
Ferox inimicis, FIERCENESS: 2
Ferre non ferto, ENDURANCE: 30
Ferret ad astra virtus, STARS: 16;
  VIRTUE: 55
Ferré va ferme, PREPAREDNESS: 17
Ferro comite, WEAPONS: 37
Ferro consulto, WEAPONS: 38
Ferro mea recupero, WEAPONS: 39
Ferro non gladio, UNCLASSIFIED: 18
Ferrum equitis salus, SECURITY: 9;
  WEAPONS: 40
Ferte cito flammas, FIRE: 2
Fert lauream fides, FAITH: 53
Fert palmam mereat, WORTHINESS: 14
Fertur discrimine fructus, DANGER: 8
Fervet opus, INDUSTRIOUSNESS: 38
Fervor non furor, ZEALOUSNESS: 2
Fest, STEADFASTNESS: 38; STRENGTH: 27
Festina lente, CAUTION: 24; LOCAL
  GOVERNMENT: 120; SPEED: 23
Feu sert et sauve, FIRE: 3
Fey e fidalgia, FAITH: 54; FIDELITY: 91
Feythfully serve, SERVICE: 19
Ffyddlawn beunydol, FIDELITY: 92
Ffyddlon at y gorfen, FIDELITY: 93
Fiat Dei voluntas, DIVINE
  GUIDANCE: 238
Fiat divina voluntas, DIVINE
  GUIDANCE: 239
Fiat iustitia, JUSTICE: 25; LOCAL
  GOVERNMENT: 121
Fiat justitia, JUSTICE: 26
Fiat justitia, ruat coelum, JUSTICE: 27
Fiat justitia et pereat mundus,
  JUSTICE: 28
Fiat lux, LIGHT: 15; SCHOOL
  MOTTOES: 105
Fiat pax fiat justitia, JUSTICE: 29;
  PEACE: 15
Fiat secundum Verbum Tuum, DIVINE
  GUIDANCE: 240; LOCAL
  GOVERNMENT: 122; SCRIPTURES: 5

Fiat voluntas Dei, DIVINE
  GUIDANCE: 241
Fiat voluntas Domini, DIVINE
  GUIDANCE: 242
Fiat voluntas tua, Domine, DIVINE
  GUIDANCE: 243
Fida clavo, CONFIDENCE: 9
Fide, labore, et virtute, FAITH: 55;
  INDUSTRIOUSNESS: 39; VIRTUE: 56
Fide, sed cui vide, DIVINITY: 178
Fide et amore, FIDELITY: 94; LOVE: 49
Fide et animus, COURAGE: 63;
  FAITH: 56
Fide et armis, FIDELITY: 95
Fide et bello fortis, FAITH: 57;
  STRENGTH: 28; WAR: 20
Fide et caritate laboro, FAITH: 58;
  INDUSTRIOUSNESS: 40; KINDNESS: 8
Fide et clementia, FAITH: 59
Fide et constantia, FIDELITY: 96
Fide et diligentia, DILIGENCE: 33;
  FAITH: 60; FIDELITY: 97; LOCAL
  GOVERNMENT: 123
Fide et fiducia, CONFIDENCE: 10;
  FIDELITY: 98
Fide et firme, FIDELITY: 99
Fide et fortitudine, FORTITUDE: 3;
  LOCAL GOVERNMENT: 124
Fide et in bello fortis, FAITH: 63;
  STRENGTH: 29; WAR: 21
Fide et industria, FAITH: 64;
  INDUSTRIOUSNESS: 41
Fide et integritate, FIDELITY: 100;
  INTEGRITY: 13
Fide et labore, FAITH: 65;
  INDUSTRIOUSNESS: 42; LOCAL
  GOVERNMENT: 125
Fide et literis, FAITH: 66; SCHOOL
  MOTTOES: 106
Fide et Marte, FIDELITY: 101
Fide et opera, FAITH: 67;
  INDUSTRIOUSNESS: 43
Fide et perseverantia, FAITH: 68;
  PERSEVERANCE: 17
Fide et sedulitate, DILIGENCE: 34;
  FAITH: 69
Fide et spe, FAITH: 70; HOPE: 62
Fide et vigilantia, FAITH: 71;
  VIGILANCE: 32
Fide et virtute, COURAGE: 64;
  FIDELITY: 102
Fidei constans, FAITH: 72

Fidei coticula crux, CROSS, THE: 53;
   TRUTH: 23
Fidei signum, FAITH: 73
Fidei tenax, FAITH: 74
Fidei virtutem adde, FAITH: 75;
   VIRTUE: 57
Fide laboro, FAITH: 76;
   INDUSTRIOUSNESS: 44
Fidele, FIDELITY: 103
Fidèle et constant, FIDELITY: 104;
   STEADFASTNESS: 39
Fidèle pour toujours, FIDELITY: 105
Fideli certa merces, FIDELITY: 106
Fideli certe merces, FIDELITY: 107
Fideli distillant sanguine corde,
   FIDELITY: 108; SACRIFICE: 2
Fideli quod obstat?, FIDELITY: 109
Fidelis, FIDELITY: 110
Fidelis ad mortem, FIDELITY: 111
Fidelis ad urnam, FIDELITY: 112
Fidelis esto, FIDELITY: 113
Fidelis et audax, AUDACITY: 47;
   FIDELITY: 114
Fidelis et constans, FIDELITY: 115;
   STEADFASTNESS: 40
Fidelis et generosus, FIDELITY: 116;
   GENEROSITY: 3
Fidelis et in bello fortis, AUDACITY: 48;
   FIDELITY: 117; WAR: 22
Fidelis et paratus, FIDELITY: 118;
   PREPAREDNESS: 18
Fidelis et suavis, FIDELITY: 119;
   GENTLENESS: 5
Fidelis exsulatae, FAITH: 77
Fidelis in adversis, ADVERSITY: 19;
   FIDELITY: 120
Fidelis in omnibus, FIDELITY: 121
Fidelis inter perfidos, FIDELITY: 122
Fidelis morte, FIDELITY: 123
Fidelisque ad mortem, FIDELITY: 124
Fidelissimus semper, FIDELITY: 125
Fidelis usque ad mortem,
   FIDELITY: 126
Fidelitas, FIDELITY: 127
Fidelitas et veritas, FIDELITY: 128;
   TRUTH: 24
Fidelitas in adversis, ADVERSITY: 20;
   FIDELITY: 129
Fidelitas regi et justitia mihi,
   FIDELITY: 130; JUSTICE: 30;
   ROYALTY: 35

Fidelitas urbis salus regis,
   FIDELITY: 131; LOCAL
   GOVERNMENT: 126; ROYALTY: 36
Fidelitas/ veritas/ integritas,
   FIDELITY: 132; INTEGRITY: 14;
   SCHOOL MOTTOES: 107; TRUTH: 25
Fidelitas vincit, FIDELITY: 133
Fidelitate, FIDELITY: 134
Fidelitate et amore, FIDELITY: 135;
   LOVE: 50
Fidelitate et industria stat Bilstonia,
   FAITH: 78; INDUSTRIOUSNESS: 45;
   LOCAL GOVERNMENT: 127
Fidélité est de Dieu, FIDELITY: 136
Fideliter, FIDELITY: 137
Fideliter, fortiter, feliciter,
   AUDACITY: 49; FIDELITY: 138;
   SUCCESS: 4
Fideliter amo, FIDELITY: 139; LOVE: 51
Fideliter et alacriter, FIDELITY: 140
Fideliter et constanter, FIDELITY: 141
Fideliter et diligenter, DILIGENCE: 35;
   FIDELITY: 142
Fideliter et recte, FIDELITY: 143
Fideliter serva, FIDELITY: 144
Fideli tuta merces, FIDELITY: 145
FIDELITY, p. 293
Fidel je garderay, VIGILANCE: 33
Fidem libertatem amicitiam retinebis,
   FAITH: 79; FRIENDSHIP: 30;
   LIBERTY: 23
Fidem meam observabo, FIDELITY: 146
Fidem meam servabo, FAITH: 80
Fidem parit integritas, INTEGRITY: 15
Fidem rectam qui colendo, FAITH: 81
Fidem respice, FAITH: 82
Fidem servabo, FAITH: 83
Fidem servabo genusque, FAITH: 84
Fidem servare, FAITH: 85
Fidem servat, vinculaque solvit,
   FAITH: 86
Fidem servo, FAITH: 87
Fidem tene, FAITH: 88
Fide non armis, FAITH: 89
Fidens et constans, STEADFASTNESS: 41;
   TRUST: 31
Fidentem nescit deseruisse Deus,
   TRUST: 32
Fide parta, fide aucta, FAITH: 90
Fide patientia labore, FAITH: 91;
   INDUSTRIOUSNESS: 46; PATIENCE: 10

Fideque perennant, ENDURANCE: 31;
FAITH: 92
Fides, FAITH: 93
Fides amicitiae periculosa libertas,
FRIENDSHIP: 31; LIBERTY: 24
Fides culpari metuens, FIDELITY: 147
Fides cum officio, DUTY: 14; FAITH: 94
Fide sed cui vide, TRUST: 33
Fides et amor, FAITH: 95; LOVE: 52
Fides et fortitudo, FAITH: 96;
FORTITUDE: 4
Fides et honor, FAITH: 97; HONOR: 43
Fides et justitia, FAITH: 98; JUSTICE: 31;
LOCAL GOVERNMENT: 128
Fides fortuna fortior, FIDELITY: 148;
FORTUNE: 26
Fides in adversis, ADVERSITY: 21;
FAITH: 99
Fides leone fortior, ANIMALS: 23;
FAITH: 101
Fides lumen praebeat, FAITH: 102;
LIGHT: 16; SCHOOL MOTTOES: 108
Fides mihi panoplia, FAITH: 103
Fides montium Deo, FAITH: 104
Fides non timet, FAITH: 105
Fides nudaque veritas, FAITH: 106;
TRUTH: 26
Fides praestantior auro, FAITH: 107
Fides praevalebit, FAITH: 108
Fides probata coronat, FAITH: 109
Fides puritas, FAITH: 110; PURITY: 8
Fides scutum, FAITH: 111
Fides servata ditat, FIDELITY: 150
Fides servata secundat, FIDELITY: 151
Fides Stephani, FAITH: 112
Fides sufficit, FAITH: 113
Fides unit, FAITH: 114
Fides vincit et veritas custodit,
FAITH: 115
Fide tenes anchoram, FAITH: 116
Fidite virtuti, TRUST: 36; VIRTUE: 58
Fido Deo et ipse, DIVINITY: 179;
TRUST: 37
Fido non timeo, FEAR: 17; TRUST: 38
Fiducia creat fidem, CONFIDENCE: 11;
FIDELITY: 152
Fiducia et labore, CONFIDENCE: 12;
DILIGENCE: 36
Fiducia et vi, CONFIDENCE: 13; LOCAL
GOVERNMENT: 131; STRENGTH: 30
Fidus ad extremum, FIDELITY: 153
Fidus ad finem, FIDELITY:.154

Fidus amicus, FRIENDSHIP: 32
Fidus confido, FIDELITY: 155
Fidus Deo et Regi, DIVINITY: 180;
FIDELITY: 156; ROYALTY: 37
Fidus et audax, AUDACITY: 50;
FIDELITY: 157
Fidus et fortit, COURAGE: 65;
FIDELITY: 158
Fidus et suavis, FIDELITY: 159
Fidus in arcanis, FIDELITY: 160
Fidus in arcanum, FIDELITY: 161
Fiel pero desdichado, FIDELITY: 162
FIERCENESS, p. 313
Fier et fort, PRIDE: 2; STRENGTH: 31
Fier et sage, PRIDE: 3; WISDOM: 22
Fier mais sensible, PRIDE: 4
Fier sans tache, PRIDE: 5
Fight, WAR: 23
Fight and faith, FAITH: 117; WAR: 24
Fight on, quoth Fitton, WAR: 25
Fight the good fight, WAR: 26
Filey et felicitas, HAPPINESS: 18; LOCAL
GOVERNMENT: 132
Finem prospiciens, FINISH: 6
Finem respice, FINISH: 7
Fingit premendo, UNCLASSIFIED: 19
Finis coronat opus, FINISH: 8
Finis dat esse, DEATH: 19
FINISH, p. 314
FIRE, p. 315
Firinneach gus a chrich, FIDELITY: 163
Firm, STEADFASTNESS: 42
Firm, vigilant, active, ACTION: 8;
STRENGTH: 32; VIGILANCE: 34
Firma durant, STRENGTH: 33
Firma et ardua, STRENGTH: 34
Firma et stabilis, LOCAL
GOVERNMENT: 133; SECURITY: 10
Firm and faithful, FIDELITY: 164;
STEADFASTNESS: 43
Firmando firmior haeret,
STRENGTH: 35
Firma nobis fides, FAITH: 118
Firm as a rock, STEADFASTNESS: 44
Firma spe, HOPE: 63
Firma spes, HOPE: 64
Firmè, STEADFASTNESS: 45;
STRENGTH: 36
Firmè dum fide, FIDELITY: 165;
STEADFASTNESS: 46
Firmè durans, STEADFASTNESS: 47
Firm en foi, FAITH: 119

Firmior, LOCAL GOVERNMENT: 134;
STRENGTH: 37
Firmiora futura, STEADFASTNESS: 48
Firmior quo paratior,
PREPAREDNESS: 19; STRENGTH: 38
Firmitas et sanitas, HEALING and
HEALTH: 9; STRENGTH: 39
Firmitas in caelo, PARADISE: 23
Firmitas in caelo, stabilitas in terra,
PARADISE: 24
Firmiter et durabile, STRENGTH: 40
Firmiter et fideliter, FIDELITY: 166;
STEADFASTNESS: 49
Firmiter maneo, STEADFASTNESS: 50
Firmius ad pugnam, WAR: 27
Firmor ad fidem, FAITH: 120
Firm to my trust, STEADFASTNESS: 51;
TRUST: 39
Firmum in vita nihil, TRANSIENCE: 3
Firmus et fidelis, FIDELITY: 167;
STEADFASTNESS: 52
Firmus in Christo, CHRIST, JESUS: 38
Firmus in firmis, STEADFASTNESS: 53
Firmus maneo, STEADFASTNESS: 54
Fisus et fidus, TRUST: 40
Fit inde firmior, STRENGTH: 41
Fit manus aliena sua, HANDS: 11
Fit via vi, INDUSTRIOUSNESS: 47; WAY: 2
Fixus ac solidus, STEADFASTNESS: 55
Fixus adversa sperno, ADVERSITY: 22;
STEADFASTNESS: 56
Flagror non consumor, FIRE: 4
Flectar non frangar, FLEXIBILITY: 1
Flectas non frangas, FLEXIBILITY: 2
Flecti non frangi, FLEXIBILITY: 3
FLEXIBILITY, p. 316
FLORA, p. 316
Floreant lauri, FLOURISHING: 22
Floreat, FLOURISHING: 23; LOCAL
GOVERNMENT: 135
Floreat Actona, FLOURISHING: 24;
LOCAL GOVERNMENT: 136
Floreat Ailesburia, FLOURISHING: 25;
LOCAL GOVERNMENT: 137
Floreat Bathon, FLOURISHING: 26;
LOCAL GOVERNMENT: 138
Floreat crux, CROSS, THE: 54;
FLOURISHING: 27
Floreat Ecclesia Anglicana,
FLOURISHING: 28; LOCAL
GOVERNMENT: 139; RELIGION: 9

Floreat Etona, FLOURISHING: 29;
LOCAL GOVERNMENT: 140; SCHOOL
MOTTOES: 109
Floreat Hova, FLOURISHING: 30; LOCAL
GOVERNMENT: 141
Floreat imperii portus,
FLOURISHING: 31; LOCAL
GOVERNMENT: 142
Floreat industria, FLOURISHING: 32;
INDUSTRIOUSNESS: 48; LOCAL
GOVERNMENT: 143
Floreat majestas, FLOURISHING: 33;
ROYALTY: 38
Floreat Rugbeia, FLOURISHING: 34;
LOCAL GOVERNMENT: 144; SPORT: 1
Floreat Salopia, FLOURISHING: 35;
LOCAL GOVERNMENT: 145
Floreat scientia, KNOWLEDGE: 25;
SCHOOL MOTTOES: 110
Floreat semper fidelis civitas,
FIDELITY: 168; FLOURISHING: 36;
LOCAL GOVERNMENT: 146
Floreat Swansea, FLOURISHING: 37;
LOCAL GOVERNMENT: 147
Floreat usque Leo, FLOURISHING: 38;
LOCAL GOVERNMENT: 148; SCHOOL
MOTTOES: 111
Florens suo orbe monet,
FLOURISHING: 39
Floreo in ungue leonis, ANIMALS: 24;
FLOURISHING: 40
Florescit, FLOURISHING: 41
Florescit vulnere virtus, VIRTUE: 59
Floresco favente Deo, DIVINE
GUIDANCE: 244
Flores curat Deus, FLORA: 15
Floret qui laborat, LOCAL
GOVERNMENT: 149; PROSPERITY: 10
Floret qui vigilat, PROSPERITY: 11;
VIGILANCE: 35
Floret virtus vulnerata, VIRTUE: 60
Floriferis ut apes in saltibus, FLORA: 16
Floruit floreat, FLOURISHING: 42;
LOCAL GOVERNMENT: 150
Floruit fraxinus [*sic*] Latin, FLORA: 17
Flourish, FLOURISHING: 43
Flourish in all weathers,
FLOURISHING: 44
FLOURISHING, p. 319
Fluctuo sed affluo, CHANGE: 6;
PERSEVERANCE: 18
Fluctus fluctu, PERSEVERANCE: 19

Fluminis ritu ferimur, SPEED: 24
Fodina revirescens, FLOURISHING: 45
Foedere non vi, PEACE: 16
Foi, roi, droit, FAITH: 121; RIGHTS: 3;
 ROYALTY: 39
Foi en loyalté, FAITH: 122;
 FIDELITY: 169
Foi est tout, FAITH: 123
FOLLOWING, p. 325
Follow me, FOLLOWING: 5;
 LEADERSHIP: 12
Follow reason, REASON: 7
Fons et origo, ORIGIN: 2
Fons vitae sapientia, SCHOOL
 MOTTOES: 112; WILLINGNESS: 1;
 WISDOM: 23
Fonte puro, PURITY: 9; WATER: 9
For all, LOCAL GOVERNMENT: 151;
 SHARING: 1
For'ard, for'ard, IMPROVEMENT: 12;
 LOCAL GOVERNMENT: 152
For as Tyme doth haste so life doth
 waste, TIME: 19
FORCE, p. 327
Force avec vertu, STRENGTH: 42;
 VIRTUE: 61
Force d'en haut, STRENGTH: 43
FORESIGHT, p. 330
Foresight, FORESIGHT: 2
Foresight is all, FORESIGHT: 3
Forget me not, MEMORY: 3
Forget not, MEMORY: 4
FORGETTING, p. 330
For God, Queen, and country,
 COUNTRY: 32; DIVINITY: 181;
 ROYALTY: 40
For God and my country,
 COUNTRY: 33; DIVINITY: 182
For liberty, LIBERTY: 25
Forma flos, fama flatus, BEAUTY: 9;
 FAME: 14; FLORA: 18
Forma perit, virtus remanet,
 BEAUTY: 10; VIRTUE: 62
Formosa quae honesta, BEAUTY: 11;
 HONOR: 44
For my country, COUNTRY: 34;
 PATRIOTISM: 14
For my Duchas, UNCLASSIFIED: 20
For right, RECTITUDE: 23
For right and reason, REASON: 8;
 RECTITUDE: 24
For security, SECURITY: 11

Fors et virtus, FORTUNE: 27; VIRTUE: 63
Fors non mutat genus, FORTUNE: 28
For sport, SPORT: 2
Fortasse, POSSIBILITY: 3
Forte, FORTUNE: 29
Forte escu, PROTECTION: 10
Fortem exarmat fortior, STRENGTH: 44
Fortem fors juvat, FORTUNE: 30
Fortem posce animum, MIND: 13
Fortem post animum, MIND: 14
Fort en loyalté, FIDELITY: 170
Forte non ignave, COURAGE: 66
Fortes adjuvat ipse Deus,
 AUDACITY: 51; DIVINE GUIDANCE: 245
Forte scutum salus ducum,
 PROTECTION: 11
Fortes fideles, COURAGE: 67;
 FIDELITY: 171
Fortes fortuna adjuvat, FORTUNE: 31
Fortes fortuna juvat, FORTUNE: 32
Fortes semper monstrant
 misericordiam, COURAGE: 68;
 MERCY: 5
Fort et fidèle, AUDACITY: 52;
 FIDELITY: 172
Fort et loyal, AUDACITY: 53;
 FIDELITY: 173
Fortfahren und verharren,
 PERSEVERANCE: 20
For the spiritual and educational
 guidance of youth, GUIDANCE: 13;
 SCHOOL MOTTOES: 113
Forti et fidele nihil difficile,
 ADVERSITY: 23; FIDELITY: 174;
 STRENGTH: 45
Forti et fideli nihil difficile,
 COURAGE: 69; FIDELITY: 175
Forti favet caelum, COURAGE: 70;
 PARADISE: 25
FORTIFICATIONS, p. 332
Forti fors bona, FORTUNE: 33
Forti nihil difficile, COURAGE: 71
Forti non ignavo, COURAGE: 72
Fortior es qui se quam qui fortissima
 vincit Moenia, nec virtus altius ire
 potest, STRENGTH: 46; VIRTUE: 64
Fortior est qui se?, STRENGTH: 47
Fortior leone justus, ANIMALS: 25;
 JUSTICE: 32; STRENGTH: 48
Fortior qui melior, STRENGTH: 49
Fortior qui se vincit, STRENGTH: 50
Fortior quo mitior, STRENGTH: 51

Fortior quo paratior, LOCAL GOVERNMENT: 153; PREPAREDNESS: 20; STRENGTH: 52

Fortior quo rectior, NOBILITY: 6; STRENGTH: 53

Fortiorum fortia facta, COURAGE: 73

Fortis agendo, ACTION: 9; STRENGTH: 54

Fortis atque fidelis, COURAGE: 74; FIDELITY: 176

Fortis cadere, cedere non potest, COURAGE: 75

Fortis cadere, non cedere potest, COURAGE: 76

Fortis ceu leo fidus, ANIMALS: 26; FIDELITY: 177; STRENGTH: 55

Fortis esto, non ferox, COURAGE: 77; FIERCENESS: 3

Fortis est qui se vincit, COURAGE: 78

Fortis est veritas, LOCAL GOVERNMENT: 154; STRENGTH: 56; TRUTH: 27

Fortis et aequus, COURAGE: 79; JUSTICE: 33

Fortis et astutus, AUDACITY: 54

Fortis et celer, SPEED: 25; STRENGTH: 57

Fortis et egregius, AUDACITY: 55; EXCELLENCE: 10

Fortis et fide, COURAGE: 80; FIDELITY: 178

Fortis et fidelis, COURAGE: 81; FIDELITY: 179

Fortis et fidus, COURAGE: 82; TRUSTWORTHINESS: 2

Fortis et hospitalis, COURAGE: 83; HOSPITALITY: 3

Fortis et lenis, COURAGE: 84; GENTLENESS: 6

Fortis et placabilis, COURAGE: 85

Fortis et stabilis, COURAGE: 86; STEADFASTNESS: 57

Fortis et velox, SPEED: 26; STRENGTH: 58

Fortis et vigilans, COURAGE: 87; VIGILANCE: 36

Fortis ferox et celer, FIERCENESS: 4; SPEED: 27; STRENGTH: 59

Fortis fidelis, COURAGE: 88; FIDELITY: 180

Fortis in arduis, ADVERSITY: 24; COURAGE: 89; LOCAL GOVERNMENT: 155; STRENGTH: 60

Fortis in armis, STRENGTH: 61; WEAPONS: 41

Fortis in bello, COURAGE: 90; WAR: 28

Fortis in procella, STRENGTH: 62

Fortis in teipso, COURAGE: 91

Fortis non ferox, COURAGE: 92; FIERCENESS: 5

Fortis que felix, HAPPINESS: 19; STRENGTH: 63

Fortis qui prudens, COURAGE: 93; PRUDENCE: 21

Fortis qui se vincit, STRENGTH: 64

Fortis si jure fortis, RECTITUDE: 25; STRENGTH: 65

Fortissima veritas, STRENGTH: 66; TRUTH: 28

Fortissimus clypeus Dominus, DIVINE GUIDANCE: 246

Fortis sub forte, COURAGE: 94

Fortis sub forte fatiscet, COURAGE: 95

Fortis turris mihi Deus, DIVINE GUIDANCE: 247

Fortis valore et armis, COURAGE: 96; WEAPONS: 42

Forti tene manu, HANDS: 12; STRENGTH: 67

Fortiter, COURAGE: 97

Fortiter, fideliter, feliciter, AUDACITY: 56; FIDELITY: 181; SUCCESS: 5

Fortiter, sed apte, AUDACITY: 57; COURAGE: 98

Fortiter ac sapienter, COURAGE: 99; WISDOM: 24

Fortiter agendo, COURAGE: 100

Fortiter! Ascende!, COURAGE: 101

Fortiter defendit, COURAGE: 102

Fortiter defendit, triumphans, DEFENSE: 20; LOCAL GOVERNMENT: 156

Fortiter defendit triumphans, DEFENSE: 21

Fortiter Deo juvante, DIVINE GUIDANCE: 248

Fortiter et aperte, COURAGE: 103

Fortiter et celeriter, AUDACITY: 58; SPEED: 28

Fortiter et constanter, AUDACITY: 59; STEADFASTNESS: 58

Fortuna rotunda, FORTUNE: 50
Fortuna sequatur, FORTUNE: 51
Fortuna sequitur, FORTUNE: 52
Fortuna ut Luna, FORTUNE: 53
Fortuna vectem [sic] **sequitur,**
　EFFORT: 14; FORTUNE: 54
Fortuna viam ducit, FORTUNE: 55
Fortuna virtuti comes, COURAGE: 118;
　FORTUNE: 56
FORTUNE, p. 334
Fortune, infortune, une fort une,
　FORTUNE: 57
Fortune and opportunity forever,
　FORTUNE: 58; OPPORTUNITY: 4
Fortune de guerre, FORTUNE: 59
Fortune helps the forward,
　FORTUNE: 60
Fortune infortune fort une,
　FORTUNE: 61
Fortune le veut, FORTUNE: 62
For valor, COURAGE: 119
Forward, ADVANCE: 19;
　IMPROVEMENT: 13; LOCAL
　GOVERNMENT: 160
Forward, kind heart, ADVANCE: 20
Forward, non temere, ADVANCE: 21
Forward California,
　IMPROVEMENT: 14; SCHOOL
　MOTTOES: 114
Forward in the name of God,
　ADVANCE: 22
Forward ours, ADVANCE: 23
Forward with God, DIVINITY: 183
Forward without fear, ADVANCE: 24
Fovendo foveo, LOVE: 53
Foy, FAITH: 125
Foy, roi, droit, DUTY: 15; FAITH: 126;
　ROYALTY: 41
Foy en tout, FAITH: 127
Foy est tout, FAITH: 128
Foy pour devoir, DUTY: 16; FAITH: 129
Foys sapience et chevalerie,
　FAITH: 130; WISDOM: 28
Fractum non abjicio ensem,
　WEAPONS: 44
Fractus pugnatu, WAR: 29
FRAGRANCE, p. 341
Fragrat, delectat, et sanat,
　FRAGRANCE: 4; HEALING and
　HEALTH: 10
Fragrat post funera virtus, DEATH: 20;
　VIRTUE: 66

Française, UNCLASSIFIED: 21
France et sans dol, COUNTRY: 35;
　SADNESS: 3
Franche, leal, et oyé, FIDELITY: 187;
　LIBERTY: 27
Franco leale toge, FIDELITY: 188;
　LIBERTY: 28
Frangas non flectes, STEADFASTNESS: 59
Frango, DESTRUCTION: 3
Frango dura patientia,
　PERSEVERANCE: 21
Frappe fort, AGGRESSION: 7
Frapper au but, GOALS: 4
Frappez avec raison, AGGRESSION: 8
Frappez fort, AGGRESSION: 9
Fraternité, justice, travail,
　FELLOWSHIP: 4;
　INDUSTRIOUSNESS: 51; JUSTICE: 36
Fratres habitent inter se concordes,
　UNITY: 38
Free, LIBERTY: 29
Freedom and justice, JUSTICE: 37;
　LIBERTY: 30; NATIONAL MOTTOES: 7
Freedom and unity, LIBERTY: 31;
　STATE MOTTOES: 20; UNITY: 39
Freedom our rock, LIBERTY: 32
Freedom with responsibility, equal
　justice under law, JUSTICE: 38;
　LAW: 6; LIBERTY: 33; SCHOOL
　MOTTOES: 115
Free for a blast, LIBERTY: 34
Freely ye received, freely give, GIFTS
　and GIVING: 16; SCHOOL
　MOTTOES: 116
Frere ayme frere, LOVE: 54
Freund in der Noth gehen wenig auf
　ein Loth, FRIENDSHIP: 33
Fried ernehrt Unfried verzehrt,
　DESTRUCTION: 4; PEACE: 17
FRIENDSHIP, p. 342
Friendship, FRIENDSHIP: 34; STATE
　MOTTOES: 21
Frisch gewagedt ist halb gewonnen,
　ATTEMPT: 2; BIRDS: 18
Frisch gewagt und treu gemeint,
　ATTEMPT: 3; DEATH: 21
From henceforth, FUTURE, THE: 8
Fronti nulla fides, TRUST: 41
Fructu arbor cognoscitur, FRUIT: 2
Fructum habet charitas, KINDNESS: 9
Fructu non foliis, FRUIT: 3
Fructu noscitur, FRUIT: 4

Fructus per fidem, FAITH: 131
Fruges ecce paludis, FRUIT: 5; LOCAL
  GOVERNMENT: 161
FRUIT, p. 345
Fugiendo vincimus, CONQUEST: 8
Fugite fures omnes, UNCLASSIFIED: 22
Fugit hora, TIME: 20
Fugit irrevocabile tempus, TIME: 21
Fuimus, PAST, THE: 3
Fuimus et sub Deo erimus, TIME: 22
Fuimus et sumus, LOCAL
  GOVERNMENT: 162; PAST, THE: 4
Fulcrum dignitatis virtus, VIRTUE: 67
Fulget, SHINING: 3
Fulget virtus, SHINING: 4; VIRTUE: 68
Fulget virtus intaminata, SHINING: 5;
  VIRTUE: 69
FULLNESS, p. 346
Fulminis instar, SPEED: 30
Functa virtute fides, COURAGE: 120;
  FAITH: 132
Fundamentum gloriae humilitas,
  HUMILITY: 4
Fungor fruor, CONVENIENCE: 3
Furor arma ministrat, ANGER: 2
Furth and fear nocht, COURAGE: 121
Furth fortune, FORTUNE: 63
Furth fortune, and fill the fetters,
  FORTUNE: 64
FUTURE, THE, p. 347
Futuri cautus, FUTURE, THE: 9
Futurum invisibile, FUTURE, THE: 10
Fy ngobaith sydd yn Nuw, HOPE: 66
Fy nhy'n unig, SELF-RELIANCE: 6
Fy Nuw a Chymru, COUNTRY: 36;
  DIVINITY: 184

G

Galea spes salutis, HOPE: 67;
  SALVATION: 19
Gänger, WALKING: 1
Gang forrit, ADVANCE: 25
Gang forward, ADVANCE: 26
Gang through, ADVANCE: 27
Gang warily, VIGILANCE: 38
Garde, VIGILANCE: 39
Garde bien, VIGILANCE: 40
Garde garde, VIGILANCE: 41
Garde la foi, FAITH: 133
Garde la foy, FAITH: 134
Garde la loi, LAW: 7

Garde le droit, PROTECTION: 12;
  RECTITUDE: 27
Garde le roy, PROTECTION: 13;
  ROYALTY: 42
Garde ta bien aimée, PROTECTION: 14
Garde ta foy, FAITH: 135
Gardez, VIGILANCE: 42
Gardez bien, VIGILANCE: 43
Gardez la croix, CROSS, THE: 56
Gardez la foy, FAITH: 136
Gardez le capron, CONSERVATION: 5
Gardez l'honneur, HONOR: 46
Gare la bête, VIGILANCE: 44
Gare le pied fort, UNCLASSIFIED: 23
Gateway to world service, SCHOOL
  MOTTOES: 117; SERVICE: 20
Gaude, Maria Virgo!, HAPPINESS: 21
Gaudebunt campi, et omnia quae in iis
  sunt, HAPPINESS: 22
Gaudeo, HAPPINESS: 23
Gaudere et epulari oportet,
  HAPPINESS: 24
Gaudet in luce veritas, LIGHT: 17;
  TRUTH: 29
Gaudet luce, LIGHT: 18
Gaudet patientia duris, PATIENCE: 11
Gaudet tentamine virtus, VIRTUE: 70
Gaudia magna nuncio or Gaudia
  nuncio magna, HAPPINESS: 25
Gaudium adfero, GOOD NEWS: 1
Geld verbindet, sucht und findet,
  PROSPERITY: 12
Generosa virtus nihil timet,
  COURAGE: 122
Generositate, GENEROSITY: 4
GENEROSITY, p. 348
Generosity with justice, GENEROSITY: 5
Generosus et animosus, COURAGE: 123;
  GENEROSITY: 6
Generosus et paratus, GENEROSITY: 7;
  PREPAREDNESS: 21
Generosus nascitur non fit, MANNERS: 2
Genitum se credere mundo, BIRTH: 1
GENIUS, p. 349
Genti aequus utrique, WORTHINESS: 15
Gentle birth and virtue, GENTLENESS: 9
GENTLENESS, p. 350
Germana fides candorque,
  FIDELITY: 189; SINCERITY: 10
Gesta verbis praeveniunt, DEEDS: 52;
  WORDS: 20
Get understanding, KNOWLEDGE: 27

G. H. M. E. (Gott hilf mir Elenden),
DIVINE GUIDANCE: 251

Ghuznee, PROPER NAMES: 21

GIFTS and GIVING, p. 351

G. I. M. T. (Gott ist mein Teil),
DIVINITY: 185

G. I. M. T. (Gott ist mein Trost),
DIVINITY: 186

Give a hand up—not a hand out,
KINDNESS: 10

Give and forgive, GIFTS and GIVING: 17

Give the thankys that are due,
GRATITUDE: 3

Giving and forgiving, GIFTS and
GIVING: 18

Gladio et arcu, WEAPONS: 45

Gladio et virtute, COURAGE: 124;
WEAPONS: 46

Gladium musarum nutrix,
WEAPONS: 47

Gloria calcar habet, GLORY: 19

Gloria Deo!, DIVINITY: 187

Gloria Deo in excelsis, DIVINITY: 188

Gloria Deo in profundis, DIVINITY: 189

Gloria finis, GLORY: 20

Gloria in excelsis Deo, DIVINITY: 190

Gloria non praeda, GLORY: 21

Gloria Patri, DIVINITY: 191

Gloria principum felicitas seculi,
FAME: 15

Gloria sat Deus unus, DIVINITY: 192;
GLORY: 22

Gloria soli Deo, DIVINITY: 193

Gloria virtutis merces, GLORY: 23

Gloria virtutis umbra, GLORY: 24

Glorior in cruci Christi, CROSS,
THE: 57; GLORY: 25

GLORY, p. 353

G. M. G. (Gott mein Gut),
DIVINITY: 194

Gnaviter, ABILITY: 14

Go, and do thou likewise, DEEDS: 53

GOALS, p. 357

God, Our Father—Christ, Our
Redeemer—Man, Our Brother,
DIVINITY: 195; SCHOOL MOTTOES: 118

God and my conscience,
CONSCIENCE: 4; DIVINITY: 196

God be guide, DIVINE GUIDANCE: 252

God be my bede, DIVINE
GUIDANCE: 253

God be my guide, DIVINE
GUIDANCE: 254

God be our friend, DIVINE
GUIDANCE: 255

God be our good guide, DIVINE
GUIDANCE: 256

God can raise to Abraham children of
stones, DIVINITY: 197

God careth for us, DIVINE
GUIDANCE: 257

God caryth for us, DIVINE
GUIDANCE: 258

Goddes grace governe Garneys, DIVINE
GUIDANCE: 259

Goddes vorsehen wirt geschen,
PROVIDENCE: 9

God feedeth ye land, DIVINE
GUIDANCE: 260

God feeds the crows, BIRDS: 19; DIVINE
GUIDANCE: 261

God for us, DIVINE GUIDANCE: 262

God fried (Gott-friede) German,
DIVINE GUIDANCE: 263

God give grace, DIVINE GIFTS: 32;
GRACE: 12

God gives increase, DIVINE GIFTS: 33;
INCREASE: 17

God giveth all, DIVINE GIFTS: 34

God giveth the victory, DIVINE
GIFTS: 35; VICTORY: 18

God grant grace, DIVINE GIFTS: 36;
GRACE: 13

God grant unity, DIVINE GIFTS: 37;
UNITY: 40

God guide all, DIVINE GUIDANCE: 264

God hath made of one blood all
nations of men, INTER-
RELATEDNESS: 1; SCHOOL
MOTTOES: 119

God in his least creatures,
DIVINITY: 198

God is all, DIVINITY: 199

God is love, DIVINITY: 200

God is my defender, DIVINE
GUIDANCE: 265

God is my health, DIVINE
GUIDANCE: 266

God is my help, DIVINE GUIDANCE: 267

God is my safety, DIVINE
GUIDANCE: 268

God is my shield, DIVINE
GUIDANCE: 269

Mottoes & Categories

Gradatim plena, GRADUALNESS: 3
Gradatim vincimus, CONQUEST: 9
GRADUALNESS, p. 363
Gradu diverso via una, WAY: 3
Grandescunt aucta labore,
INDUSTRIOUSNESS: 52
Grand venteurs petits faiseurs,
ACTION: 10; BOASTFULNESS: 3
Grassagh abú, DEFIANCE: 4
Gratâ manu, GRATITUDE: 4
Grata quies, GRATITUDE: 5; REST: 5
Grata sume manu, GRATITUDE: 6
Gratia Dei cibus animae, DIVINE
GUIDANCE: 296; GRACE: 19
Gratia Dei servatus, DIVINE
GUIDANCE: 297
Gratia et veritas, GRACE: 20; SCHOOL
MOTTOES: 120; TRUTH: 30
Gratia naturam vincit, GRACE: 21
Gratias Deo agere, DIVINITY: 211;
GRATITUDE: 7
Gratior est a rege pio, PIETY: 9;
ROYALTY: 43
Gratis a Deo data, DIVINE GIFTS: 40
GRATITUDE, p. 364
Gratitude, GRATITUDE: 8
Gratitude and loyalty, FIDELITY: 190;
GRATITUDE: 9
Grato animo, GRATITUDE: 10
Graves disce mores, MANNERS: 3;
SERIOUSNESS: 1
Gravis dum suavis, SERIOUSNESS: 2
Graviter et pié, SERIOUSNESS: 3
GREATNESS, p. 365
Grind well, INDUSTRIOUSNESS: 53;
TRADES: 14
Grip fast, STEADFASTNESS: 60
Gronwi hil Gwernimon, ANCESTRY: 17;
PRINCELINESS: 5
Grossos qui rodit roditur,
AGGRESSION: 10
Growing, GROWTH: 10
GROWTH, p. 365
Guage and measure, MEASURE: 4
Guarde la foy, FAITH: 137
Guardez vous, VIGILANCE: 46
Guard yourself, VIGILANCE: 47
Gubernat navem Deus, DIVINE
GUIDANCE: 298
Gud og Kongen, DIVINITY: 212;
ROYALTY: 44
GUIDANCE, p. 367

GUILT, p. 369
Gung ho, WAR: 30
G. V. D. S. N. (Gott verläszt die
Sienen nicht), DIVINITY: 213
G. W. A. Z. B. (Gott wende Alles zum
Besten), DIVINITY: 214
Gwell angau na chywilydd,
DEATH: 22; DISGRACE: 5
Gwell angau na gwarth, DEATH: 23;
DISGRACE: 6
Gwell angeu na chwylydd, DEATH: 24
Gwell marw, DEATH: 25
G. W. G. (Gottes Wille Geschehe),
DIVINE GUIDANCE: 299
Gwir yn erbyn y byd, TRUTH: 31
Gwna a ddylit doed a ddel, DUTY: 17
G. W. W. S. (Gott wirds wohl
schaffen), DIVINITY: 215

H

Habebunt lumen vitae, LIGHT: 19;
SCHOOL MOTTOES: 121
Habent sua sidera reges, ROYALTY: 45;
STARS: 17
Habeo non habeor, LIBERTY: 36
Habeo pro jus fasque, LAW: 8;
RECTITUDE: 28
Habere et dispertire, GENEROSITY: 8
Habet et suam, POSSESSION: 7
Hab Gott vor Augen, DIVINITY: 216
Hac Iter Elysium nobis, PARADISE: 26
Hâc ornant, DECORATION: 1
Hactenus invictus, CONQUEST: 10
Hac virtus mercede digna, REWARD: 8;
VIRTUE: 72
Had on and win, VICTORY: 19
Haec aspera terrent, ADVERSITY: 25
Haec dextra vindex principis et
patriae, VENGEANCE: 4
Haec fructus virtutis, COURAGE: 125
Haec generi incrementa fides,
FIDELITY: 191
Haec inimica tyrannis, OPPOSITION: 5
Haec lucra laborum,
INDUSTRIOUSNESS: 54
Haec manus inimica tyrannis,
HOSTILITY: 4
Haec manus ob patriam, COUNTRY: 38;
HANDS: 13; PATRIOTISM: 15

Haec manus pro patriae pugnando vulnera passa, DEFENSE: 22; INJURY: 3

Haec olim meminisse juvabit, MEMORY: 5

Haec omnia transeunt, TRANSIENCE: 4

Haec origo, ORIGIN: 3

Haec ornant, DECORATION: 2

Haec praestat militia, WAR: 31

Haec studia oblectant, KNOWLEDGE: 28; SCHOOL MOTTOES: 122

Half is more than the whole, MEASURE: 5

Hallelujah, HAPPINESS: 26

Hallelujah! Hallelujah! Hallelujah!, HAPPINESS: 27

HANDS, p. 369

Halt Mas in allem Ding, MODERATION: 6

Hanfod tref trefn, LOCAL GOVERNMENT: 167; ORDER: 2

Ha persa la fide, ha perso l'honore, FAITH: 138

HAPPINESS, p. 371

Happiness and prosperity through unity, HAPPINESS: 28; NATIONAL MOTTOES: 8; PROSPERITY: 14; UNITY: 41

Harambee, NATIONAL MOTTOES: 9; UNITY: 42

Hardiment et bellement, AUDACITY: 70

HARMLESSNESS, p. 375

HARVEST, p. 376

Haud facile emergunt, RIGHTS: 4; RISING: 4

Haud fulsit gratior populis, PEOPLE: 2; SUN: 5

Haud inferiora secutus, STATUS: 3

Haud lege peritior, LAW: 9

Haud muto factum, CHANGE: 7

Haud nomine tantum, NAME: 5

Haud timet mortem qui vitam sperat, DEATH: 26

Haud ullis labantia ventis, STEADFASTNESS: 61

Haulte emprise, ASPIRATION: 49; LOCAL GOVERNMENT: 168

Hauri ex puro, PURITY: 10; WATER: 10

Haut et bon, LOFTINESS: 10

Have at all, UNCLASSIFIED: 24

Have at you, WAR: 32

Have faith in Christ, CHRIST, JESUS: 39; FAITH: 139

Have mercy on us, good Lord!, MERCY: 6

Have patience and endure, ENDURANCE: 33; PATIENCE: 12

Have wandered, UNCLASSIFIED: 25

Hazard, zet (yet) forward, ADVANCE: 31

Hazard warily, VIGILANCE: 48

H. D. H. D. (Hilf du heilige Dreifaltigkeit), DIVINE GUIDANCE: 300

Head/ Heart/ Hand, HANDS: 14; MIND: 15; SCHOOL MOTTOES: 123

HEALING and HEALTH, p. 376

Health and happiness, HAPPINESS: 29; HEALING and HEALTH: 11

HEART, p. 379

Heart and hand, FEELINGS: 15; HANDS: 15

Heart of oak, FEELINGS: 16

Heaven's light our guide, GUIDANCE: 14; LOCAL GOVERNMENT: 169; PARADISE: 27

Heb Dduw heb ddim, DIVINITY: 217

Heb Dduw heb ddim, Duw a digon, DIVINITY: 218

Heb nefol nerth, nid sicr saeth, DIVINE GUIDANCE: 301

He conquers who endures, ENDURANCE: 34

Heddwch, PEACE: 18

Help, ASSISTANCE: 6

Help at hand, brother, ASSISTANCE: 7

Help only those who help themselves, ASSISTANCE: 8

Henricus a Henrico, UNCLASSIFIED: 26

Here we rest, REST: 6; STATE MOTTOES: 22

Heroum filii, ANCESTRY: 18; SCHOOL MOTTOES: 124

He seeks high deeds, ASPIRATION: 50; DEEDS: 55

He serves his party best who serves his country best, PATRIOTISM: 16; SERVICE: 21

He who looks at Martin's ape, Martin's ape will look at him, VISION: 5

He yt tholis overcumms, ENDURANCE: 35

H. G. H. G. H. G. (Hilf Gott, hilf
Gott, hilf Gott), DIVINE
GUIDANCE: 302
H. G. Z. G. (Hilf Gott zu Glück),
DIVINE GUIDANCE: 303
H. H. H. H. H. (Hilf, himmlischer
Herr, höchster Hort), DIVINE
GUIDANCE: 304
Hic et ubique terrarum, SCHOOL
MOTTOES: 125; UBIQUITY: 3
Hic fidus et roboreus, STRENGTH: 70;
TRUSTWORTHINESS: 3
Hic fructus virtutis, COURAGE: 126
Hic habitat felicitas, HAPPINESS: 30
Hic hodie cras urna, TRANSIENCE: 5
Hic labor, ADVERSITY: 26
Hic labor, hoc opus, ADVERSITY: 27
Hic murus aheneus, FORTIFICATIONS: 3
Hic regit, ille tuetur, GOVERNMENT: 2;
PROTECTION: 17
Hic tutus nutrior, SECURITY: 13
Hic vastat telis moenia facta suis,
DESTRUCTION: 5
Higher, ASPIRATION: 51
High merit, high reward, SCHOOL
MOTTOES: 126; WORTHINESS: 16
Hinc decus inde tegmen, HONOR: 47;
PROTECTION: 18
Hinc delectatio, ENJOYMENT: 16
Hinc ducitur honos, HONOR: 48
Hinc fortior et clarior, STRENGTH: 71
Hinc garbae nostrae, HARVEST: 2
Hinc honor et opes, HONOR: 49
Hinc honor et salus, HONOR: 50
Hinc illuminabimur,
ENLIGHTENMENT: 2
Hinc incrementum, INCREASE: 18
Hinc laus et honos, HONOR: 51;
PRAISE: 3
Hinc lucem et pocula sacra, LIGHT: 20;
SCHOOL MOTTOES: 127
Hinc mihi salus, SALVATION: 20
Hinc odor et sanitas, FRAGRANCE: 5;
HEALING and HEALTH: 12
Hinc ordo, hinc copia rerum, ORDER: 3
Hinc origo, ORIGIN: 4
Hinc orior, RISING: 5
Hinc spes affulget, HOPE: 68
Hinc spes effulget, HOPE: 69
Hinc usque superna venabor,
PARADISE: 28
Hinc vigilo, VIGILANCE: 49

Hindostan, PROPER NAMES: 23
Hirbarhad, PERSEVERANCE: 23
His calcabo gentes, AGGRESSION: 11
His fortibus arma, WEAPONS: 49
His gloria reddit honores, GLORY: 26
His nitimur et munimur, ASSISTANCE: 9
His parva crescunt, GROWTH: 11
His regi servitium, CROWN: 11;
SERVICE: 22
His Saladinum vicimus armis,
WEAPONS: 50
His securitas, SECURITY: 14
History cannot be destroyed by time,
TIME: 23
His utere mecum, CONVENIENCE: 4
His vinces, CONQUEST: 11
Hoc age, DEEDS: 56
Hoc ardua vincere docet,
ADVERSITY: 28
Hoc duce sub cruce non sine luce,
DIVINE GUIDANCE: 305
Hoc etiam praeteribit, TRANSIENCE: 6
Hoc fonte derivata copia, LOCAL
GOVERNMENT: 170; PROSPERITY: 15
Hoc in loco Deus rupes, DIVINITY: 219
Hoc majorum opus, ANCESTRY: 19
Hoc majorum virtus, ANCESTRY: 20
Hoc opus, INDUSTRIOUSNESS: 55
Hoc securior, SECURITY: 15
Hoc signum non onus, sed honor,
HONOR: 52
Hoc vinco, CONQUEST: 12
Hoc virtutis opus, VIRTUE: 73
Hodie mihi cras tibi, PRESENT, THE: 2
Hodie non cras, PRESENT, THE: 3
Hoeg dy fwyall, WEAPONS: 51
Holden, UNCLASSIFIED: 27
Hold fast, STEADFASTNESS: 62
Hold fast, sit sure, STEADFASTNESS: 63;
TRADES: 15
Hold firm, STEADFASTNESS: 64
Holding forth the Word of life,
SCHOOL MOTTOES: 128;
SCRIPTURES: 9
Hold to the Most High, FIDELITY: 192
Hold to the truth, LOCAL
GOVERNMENT: 171; TRUTH: 32
Holme semper viret, FLOURISHING: 46
HOME, p. 380
Home, HOME: 10
Home, industry, leisure, HOME: 11;
LOCAL GOVERNMENT: 172

Mottoes & Categories

Home and country, COUNTRY: 39;
  HOME: 12
Hominem te esse memento,
  HOSTILITY: 5
Homo homini vulpes, ANIMALS: 27;
  HOSTILITY: 6
Homo proponit, Deus disponit, DIVINE
  GUIDANCE: 306
Homo sum, BEING, SELF: 1;
  HOSTILITY: 7
Honesta bona, PROSPERITY: 16
Honestae gloria fax mentis, GLORY: 27
Honesta libertate, LIBERTY: 37
Honest and fast, HONESTY: 9
Honesta peto, HONOR: 53
Honesta quam magna, HONOR: 54
Honesta quam splendida, HONOR: 55
Honestas, HONESTY: 10
Honestas et diligentia, DILIGENCE: 37;
  SCHOOL MOTTOES: 129
Honestas et fortitudo, COURAGE: 127;
  HONOR: 56
Honestas et veritas, HONOR: 57;
  TRUTH: 33
Honestas optima politia, HONESTY: 11
Honestas quam splendida, HONOR: 58
Honestate vetustas stat, ANCESTRY: 21;
  HONOR: 59
Honeste, HONESTY: 12
Honeste, fortiter, HONOR: 60
Honeste audax, AUDACITY: 71
Honeste et constanter, HONOR: 61
Honeste parata, ACQUISITION: 3
Honeste progrediemur conando,
  EFFORT: 15; IMPROVEMENT: 16;
  LOCAL GOVERNMENT: 173
Honestè vivo, HONESTY: 13
Honestie is good policie, HONESTY: 14
Honesto vivo, HONESTY: 15
Honestum praeferre utili, HONESTY: 16
Honestum praetulit utili, HONOR: 62
Honestum pro patria, JUSTICE: 40
Honestum utili patria, HONOR: 65
Honestum utili praefer, HONOR: 66
Honestum utili prefero, HONOR: 67
HONESTY, p. 381
Honesty is better than riches,
  HONESTY: 17
Honesty is good policy, HONESTY: 18
Honesty is the best policy, HONESTY: 19
Honesty without fear, HONESTY: 20
Honi soit qui mal y pense, DISGRACE: 7

Honneur et patrie, COUNTRY: 42;
  HONOR: 68
Honneur me guide, GUIDANCE: 15;
  HONOR: 69
Honneur pour objet, HONOR: 70
Honneur sans repos, HONOR: 71
HONOR, p. 384
Honor, HONOR: 72
Honor, pietas, HONOR: 73; PIETY: 10
Honor, purpose, wisdom, HONOR: 74;
  PURPOSE: 7; SCHOOL MOTTOES: 130;
  WISDOM: 29
Honor, virtus, probitas, HONOR: 75;
  VIRTUE: 74
Honor alit artes, ART: 17; HONOR: 76;
  LOCAL GOVERNMENT: 174
Honorantes me honorabo, HONOR: 77
Honorate, diligite, timete, FEAR: 20;
  HONOR: 78; LOVE: 55
Honorat mors, DEATH: 27; HONOR: 79
Honor Deo, HONOR: 80
Honore et amore, HONOR: 81; LOVE: 56
Honore et armis, HONOR: 82
Honore et justitia, HONOR: 83;
  JUSTICE: 41
Honore et labore, HONOR: 84;
  INDUSTRIOUSNESS: 56
Honore et virtute, HONOR: 85
Honore integro contemno fortunam,
  HONOR: 86
Honore pietas, HONOR: 87; PIETY: 11
Honores praefero, HONOR: 88
Honor et amor, HONOR: 89; LOVE: 57
Honor et fides, FAITH: 140; HONOR: 90
Honor et honestas, HONESTY: 21;
  HONOR: 91
Honore timore, FEAR: 21; HONOR: 92
Honor et industria, HONOR: 93;
  INDUSTRIOUSNESS: 57; LOCAL
  GOVERNMENT: 175
Honor et justitia, HONOR: 94;
  JUSTICE: 42
Honor et justitia manet amicitia
  florebit semper que, FRIENDSHIP: 36;
  HONOR: 95; JUSTICE: 43
Honor et veritas, HONOR: 96; TRUST: 42
Honor et virtus, HONOR: 97; VIRTUE: 75
Honor fidelitatis praemium,
  FIDELITY: 193; HONOR: 98;
  REWARD: 9
Honor me guide, GUIDANCE: 16;
  HONOR: 99

Honor nourishes the arts, ART: 18;
HONOR: 100; SCHOOL MOTTOES: 131
Honor post funera vivit, DEATH: 28;
HONOR: 101
Honor potestate honorantis,
HONOR: 102
Honor praemium virtutis est,
HONOR: 103; REWARD: 10; VIRTUE: 76
Honor probataque virtus, HONOR: 104
Honor rewards industry, HONOR: 105;
INDUSTRIOUSNESS: 58
Honor sequitur fugientem, HONOR: 106
Honor veritas et justitia, HONOR: 107;
JUSTICE: 44; TRUTH: 34
Honor virtutem coronat, HONOR: 108;
VIRTUE: 77
Honor virtutis, VIRTUE: 78
Honor virtutis praemium, HONOR: 109;
REWARD: 11; VIRTUE: 79
Honor virtutis pretium, HONOR: 110;
REWARD: 12; VIRTUE: 80
Honos alit artes, ART: 19; HONOR: 111
Honos cui honos, HONOR: 112
Honos fidelitatis praemium,
HONOR: 113; REWARD: 13; VIRTUE: 81
Honos industriae praemium,
HONOR: 114; INDUSTRIOUSNESS: 59;
REWARD: 14
Honos virtutis satelles, HONOR: 115;
VIRTUE: 82
Honos vitâ clarior, HONESTY: 22;
HONOR: 116
Honour God, DIVINITY: 220
HOPE, p. 397
Hope, HOPE: 70
Hope and not rue, HOPE: 71
Hope for the best, HOPE: 72
Hope in God, DIVINITY: 221; HOPE: 73
Hope me encourageth, HOPE: 74
Hope to come, HOPE: 75
Hope to share, HOPE: 76
Hope well and have well, HOPE: 77
Hope well and love all well, HOPE: 78;
LOVE: 58
Horae semper sola salus servire deo,
SALVATION: 21; SERVICE: 23
Hora è sempre, FIDELITY: 194
Horror ubique, FEAR: 22
HOSPITALITY, p. 416
Hostes nunc amici, CONCILIATION: 5;
LOCAL GOVERNMENT: 176
HOSTILITY, p. 416

Hostis honori invidia, ENVY: 1;
HONOR: 117; LOCAL
GOVERNMENT: 177
H. R. M. D. D. H. G. (Herr, regiere
mich durch deinen heiligen Geist),
DIVINE GUIDANCE: 307
Huc tendimus omnes, DESTINATION: 5
Huic generi incrementa fides,
FIDELITY: 195
Huic habeo non tibi, POSSESSION: 8
Humani nihil alienum, HOSTILITY: 8
Humani nihil alienum mihi,
HUMANITY: 4; MANLINESS: 2
HUMANITY, p. 417
Humilitate, HUMILITY: 5
HUMILITY, p. 418
Hunter, blow the horn, HUNTING: 2
HUNTING, p. 419
Hwy peri clod na golud, FAME: 16;
PROSPERITY: 17
Hyeme exsuperata, SEASONS: 1
Hyeme viresco, FLOURISHING: 47

I

I abide my time, PATIENCE: 13
I am, I am, BEING, SELF: 2
I am alone, SOLITUDE: 1
I am ever prepared, PREPAREDNESS: 22
I am readie, PREPAREDNESS: 23
I am ready, PREPAREDNESS: 24
I. B. A. G. (Ich bau auf Gott),
DIVINITY: 222
I beare in minde, MEMORY: 6
I beare the bel, UNCLASSIFIED: 28
I burn weil, I see, FIRE: 5
I byde, PATIENCE: 14
I byde it, PATIENCE: 15
I byde my time, PATIENCE: 16
I byde ye fair, UNCLASSIFIED: 29
Ich dien, LOCAL GOVERNMENT: 178;
SERVICE: 24
Ich fürchte and traue Gott in allen
Dingen, FEAR: 23
Ich habs gewagt, RISK: 2
Ich lasz mich genügen am göttlichen
Fügen, HAPPINESS: 31
Ich schweig und gedenck, SILENCE: 6;
THOUGHT: 7
Ich trawe Gott in aller noht,
DIVINITY: 223

Mottoes & Categories

Ich wags, Gott walts, DIVINE
   GUIDANCE: 308
Ich wags mit Gott, DIVINE
   GUIDANCE: 309
Ich weis das mein Erlöser lebt,
   FAITH: 141
I conquer by the wound,
   CONQUEST: 13
I conquer or die, CONQUEST: 14;
   DEATH: 29
Ictus non victus, AGGRESSION: 12
I dare, AUDACITY: 72
I Dduw bo'r diolch, DIVINITY: 224
IDENTITY, p. 419
I desire not to want, DESIRE: 3
I. D. F. N. (In Domino fiducia
   nostra), DIVINITY: 225; TRUST: 43
I. D. F. V. (In Deo faciemus
   virtutem), DIVINITY: 226
I. D. H. I. D. H. (In dem Herrn ist das
   Heil), SALVATION: 22
I die for those I love, DEATH: 30
IDLENESS, p. 419
Iechyd, harddwch, heddwch,
   BEAUTY: 12; HEALING and HEALTH: 13;
   LOCAL GOVERNMENT: 179;
   TRANQUILLITY: 4
I face all weathers, UNCLASSIFIED: 30
If God will, DIVINE GUIDANCE: 310
If I can, POSSIBILITY: 4
I force no friend, I fear no foe,
   FEAR: 24; FORCE: 6
I forget not, FORGETTING: 1
If you aid God, he will aid you, DIVINE
   GUIDANCE: 311; NATIONAL
   MOTTOES: 10
I gain by hazard, RISK: 3
Ignavis nunquam, IDLENESS: 1
Igne constricto, vita secura, FIRE: 6
Igne et ferris vicimus, CONQUEST: 15
Igne et ferro, FIRE: 7
I grow and wither both together,
   GROWTH: 12
I have lived today, LIFE: 9
I hope, HOPE: 79
I hope for better, HOPE: 80
I hope in God, DIVINITY: 227; HOPE: 81
I hope to share, HOPE: 82; SHARING: 2
I hope to speed, HOPE: 83; SPEED: 31
I increase, INCREASE: 19
I keep traist, FIDELITY: 196
Il buon tempo verra, FUTURE, THE: 11

Ilias in nuce, UNCLASSIFIED: 31
I live and die for those I love,
   LOFTINESS: 11; LOVE: 59
I live in hope, HOPE: 84
Illaeso lumine solem, VISION: 6
I'll be wary, VIGILANCE: 50
I'll bide, PATIENCE: 17
I'll deceive no man, DECEPTION: 5
I'll defend, DEFENSE: 23
Illegitimi non carborundum,
   PERSEVERANCE: 24
Ille vincit ego mereo, CONQUEST: 16
I'll hope and not rue, HOPE: 85
Illis honos venit, HONOR: 118
I'll stand sure, STEADFASTNESS: 65
I'll try, EFFORT: 16
Illumino, ENLIGHTENMENT: 3
Illustrans commoda vitae,
   CONVENIENCE: 5
Illustribus et nobilitati, NOBILITY: 7;
   WORTHINESS: 17
Il n'est si ferré qui ne glisse,
   FAILURE: 2; HUMILITY: 6
Il n'y a rien, que soit plus difficile aux
   hommes, que d'estre tyrannisé en
   leur croyance, OPPRESSION: 2
Il n'y a rien si precieux que la liberté,
   LIBERTY: 38
Il principio e il fine mio stà nelle mani
   di Dio, DIVINITY: 228
Ils ne passeront pas, WAR: 33
Il suffit, SATISFACTION: 2
Il tempo passa, TIME: 24
Il vant [sic] mieux mourir que vivre
   sans honeur, DEATH: 31;
   HONESTY: 23; HONOR: 119
Il y a de ma vie, RISK: 4
I make sicker, SECURITY: 16
I make sure, SECURITY: 17
I. M. C. M. (In medio currere metuo),
   FEAR: 25
I mean no harm, INTENTION: 1
I mean well, INTENTION: 2
Imitari quam invidere, IMITATION: 2
IMITATION, p. 420
Immaculata gens, PURITY: 11
Immensi tremor Oceani, SEA: 9
Immer frey [sic], LIBERTY: 39
Immeritas temnere minas,
   CONTEMPT: 3
Immersabilis, ENDURANCE: 36

Immersabilis est vera virtus,
 VIRTUE: 83
Immobile, STEADFASTNESS: 66
Immobilis innocentia, INNOCENCE: 1
Immortalia spero, HOPE: 86;
 IMMORTALITY: 2
Immortalis virtutis et gloriae fama
 perpetim post fata superstes,
 GLORY: 28; VIRTUE: 84
IMMORTALITY, p. 420
Immota fides, FAITH: 142
Immota triumphans, PERMANENCE: 1
Immotus, PERMANENCE: 2
Immutabile, durabile, PERMANENCE: 3
Impavide, COURAGE: 128
Impavido pectore, COURAGE: 129
Impavidum ferient ruinae,
 COURAGE: 130
Impegerit fidus, FIDELITY: 197
Impelle obstantia, ADVERSITY: 29
Imperare sibi maximum imperium est,
 SELF-CONTROL: 7
Imperat aequor, SEA: 10
Imperatricis auspiciis, SUPPORT: 4
Imperio, AUTHORITY: 1
Imperio regit unus aequo,
 AUTHORITY: 2
Imperium in imperio, GOVERNMENT: 3;
 OBSCURITY: 1; STATE MOTTOES: 23
Impero, AUTHORITY: 3
Impetueux, ACTION: 11
Impiger et fidus, FIDELITY: 198;
 LIVELINESS: 3
Impromptu, PREPAREDNESS: 25
IMPROVEMENT, p. 421
In adversis etiam fide, FAITH: 143
In adversis idem, ADVERSITY: 30;
 CONSISTENCY: 4
In alta tende, ASPIRATION: 52
In altum, PARADISE: 29
In arce salus, SECURITY: 18
In ardua, LOFTINESS: 12
In ardua nitor, ADVERSITY: 31
In ardua petit, ACCOMPLISHMENT: 9;
 ADVERSITY: 32; SEARCH and
 DISCOVERY: 6
In ardua tendit, ADVERSITY: 33
In ardua virtus, ADVERSITY: 34;
 VIRTUE: 85
In arduis fidelis, FIDELITY: 199
In arduis fortis, ADVERSITY: 35
In arduis fortitudo, FORTITUDE: 22

In arduis viget virtus, ADVERSITY: 36;
 VIRTUE: 86
In bello invictus in amore probus,
 LOVE: 60; WAR: 34
In bello quies, WAR: 35
In bivio dextra, DECISION: 3
In bono vince, CONQUEST: 17; SCHOOL
 MOTTOES: 132
In caelo confidemus, PARADISE: 30;
 TRUST: 44
In caelo quies, PARADISE: 31; REST: 7
In caelo spes mea est, HOPE: 87;
 PARADISE: 32
In caligine lucet, DARKNESS: 4;
 SHINING: 7
In candore decus, DIRECTNESS: 12;
 HONOR: 120
INCENTIVE, p. 424
Incepta persequor, PERSEVERANCE: 25
In certa salutis anchora, SECURITY: 19
In Christo fratres, CHRIST, JESUS: 40;
 SCHOOL MOTTOES: 133
In Christo omnia, CHRIST, JESUS: 41
In Christo salus, CHRIST, JESUS: 42;
 SALVATION: 23
In Christo speravi, CHRIST, JESUS: 43;
 HOPE: 88
Incidendo sano, HEALING and
 HEALTH: 14
Incipe, UNCLASSIFIED: 32
Inclinata resurgo, REBIRTH: 11
Inclytus perditae recuperator coronae,
 CROWN: 12
Inclytus virtute, VIRTUE: 87
Incoctum pectus honesto, HONOR: 121
In coelo salus, SALVATION: 24
In coelo spero, HOPE: 89; PARADISE: 33
In concilio consilium, GUIDANCE: 17;
 LOCAL GOVERNMENT: 180;
 WISDOM: 30
Inconcussa virtus, VIRTUE: 88
In constantia decus, FIDELITY: 200;
 HONOR: 122
In copia cautus, CAUTION: 26
In corda inimicorum Regis,
 HOSTILITY: 9
In cornu salutem spero, SECURITY: 20
Incorrupta fides, FAITH: 144
Incorrupta fides, nudaque veritas,
 FAITH: 145; TRUTH: 35
INCREASE, p. 424

Incrementum dat Deus, DIVINE
GIFTS: 41; INCREASE: 20

In cruce confido, CROSS, THE: 58;
TRUST: 45

In cruce et lachrymis spes est, CROSS,
THE: 59; HOPE: 90

In cruce fides, CROSS, THE: 60;
FAITH: 146

In cruce glorior, CROSS, THE: 61;
GLORY: 29

In cruce mea fides, CROSS, THE: 62;
FAITH: 147

In cruce mea spes, CROSS, THE: 63;
HOPE: 91

In cruce non in leone fides,
ANIMALS: 28; CROSS, THE: 64;
FAITH: 148

In cruce salus, CROSS, THE: 65;
SALVATION: 25

In cruce spero, CROSS, THE: 66;
TRUST: 46

In cruce spes mea, CROSS, THE: 67;
HOPE: 92

In cruce triumphans, CROSS, THE: 68

In cruce victoria, CROSS, THE: 69;
VICTORY: 20

In cruce vincam, CROSS, THE: 70

In cruce vinco, CROSS, THE: 71

In crucifixa gloria mea, CROSS,
THE: 72; GLORY: 30

In defence, DEFENSE: 24

In defence of the distressed,
DEFENSE: 25

Indefessus vigilando, VIGILANCE: 51

In defiance, DEFIANCE: 5

In Deo confidemus, DIVINITY: 229;
TRUST: 47

In Deo confido, DIVINITY: 230;
TRUST: 48

In Deo confido, nil desperandum,
DIVINITY: 231; TRUST: 49

In Deo confiteor, DIVINITY: 232

In Deo est mihi omnis fides,
DIVINITY: 233; TRUST: 50

In Deo et in ipso confido,
DIVINITY: 234; TRUST: 51

In Deo et veritate fido, DIVINITY: 235;
TRUST: 52; TRUTH: 36

In Deo faciemus virtutem, DIVINE
GUIDANCE: 312

In Deo fidemus, DIVINITY:·236; LOCAL
GOVERNMENT: 181; TRUST: 53

In Deo fides, DIVINITY: 237; TRUST: 54

In Deo fides, lux in tenebris,
DIVINITY: 238

In Deo fido, DIVINITY: 239; TRUST: 55

In Deo manuque fides, DIVINITY: 240;
TRUST: 56

In Deo mea consolatio, DIVINITY: 241

In Deo mea spes, DIVINITY: 242

In Deo non armis fido, DIVINITY: 243

In Deo nostra spes est, DIVINITY: 244;
HOPE: 93

In Deo omnia, DIVINITY: 245

In Deo robur meum, DIVINE
GUIDANCE: 313

In Deo salus mea et gloria mea,
GLORY: 31; SALVATION: 26

In Deo salutem, SALVATION: 27

In Deo sola salus, SALVATION: 28

In Deo solo confido, DIVINITY: 246;
TRUST: 57

In Deo solo salus est, SALVATION: 29

In Deo solo speravi, DIVINITY: 247;
TRUST: 58

In Deo solo spes mea, DIVINITY: 248;
HOPE: 94

In Deo solum (or solo) robur, DIVINE
GUIDANCE: 314

In Deo speramus, DIVINITY: 249;
SCHOOL MOTTOES: 134; TRUST: 59

In Deo speravi, DIVINITY: 250;
HOPE: 95; TRUST: 60

In Deo spero, DIVINITY: 251; HOPE: 96

In Deo spes, DIVINITY: 252; HOPE: 97

In Deo spes est, DIVINITY: 253;
HOPE: 98

In Deo spes mea, DIVINITY: 254;
HOPE: 99

In Deo tutamen, DIVINE
GUIDANCE: 315

Inde securior, SECURITY: 21

Inde spes, HOPE: 100

In dies, TIME: 25

Indignante invidia florebit justus,
ENVY: 2; FLOURISHING: 48

Indocilis pauperiem pati,
PROSPERITY: 18

In Domino confido, DIVINITY: 255;
TRUST: 61

In Domino et non in arcu meo
sperabo, DIVINITY: 256; HOPE: 101

In Domino fiducia nostra,
DIVINITY: 257; TRUST: 62

In dubiis constans, DANGER: 9;
STEADFASTNESS: 67
In dubiis rectus, RECTITUDE: 29
Indubitata fides, FAITH: 149
Induce animum sapientem, MIND: 16;
WISDOM: 31
Indulge fortune, FORTUNE: 65
Indulge not, SELF-CONTROL: 8
Indure but Hope, ENDURANCE: 37;
HOPE: 102
Indure furth, ENDURANCE: 38
Industria, INDUSTRIOUSNESS: 60;
SCHOOL MOTTOES: 135
Industria, intelligentia, virtus,
INDUSTRIOUSNESS: 61; VIRTUE: 89
Industria, virtus, et fortitudo,
COURAGE: 131; FORTITUDE: 23;
INDUSTRIOUSNESS: 62
Industria, virtus et fortitudo,
DILIGENCE: 38; LOCAL
GOVERNMENT: 182; STRENGTH: 72
Industriâ atque fortunâ, FORTUNE: 66;
INDUSTRIOUSNESS: 63
Industria ditat, INDUSTRIOUSNESS: 64;
LOCAL GOVERNMENT: 183
Industriae munus, GIFTS and
GIVING: 19; INDUSTRIOUSNESS: 65
Industriae praemium,
INDUSTRIOUSNESS: 66; REWARD: 15
Industria et frugalitas,
INDUSTRIOUSNESS: 67
Industria et labore,
INDUSTRIOUSNESS: 68
Industria et perseverantia,
INDUSTRIOUSNESS: 69;
PERSEVERANCE: 26
Industria et probitate,
INDUSTRIOUSNESS: 70; RECTITUDE: 30
Industria et spe, HOPE: 103;
INDUSTRIOUSNESS: 71; LOCAL
GOVERNMENT: 184
Industria et virtute,
INDUSTRIOUSNESS: 72; VIRTUE: 90
Industria evehit, EXALTATION: 4;
INDUSTRIOUSNESS: 73
Industria murus, INDUSTRIOUSNESS: 74;
PROTECTION: 19
Industria omnia vincit,
INDUSTRIOUSNESS: 75; LOCAL
GOVERNMENT: 185
Industria permanente,
INDUSTRIOUSNESS: 76

Industria semper crescam,
INDUSTRIOUSNESS: 77
Industria veritas et hospitalitas,
HOSPITALITY: 4;
INDUSTRIOUSNESS: 78; TRUTH: 37
INDUSTRIOUSNESS, p. 425
Industry, INDUSTRIOUSNESS: 79; STATE
MOTTOES: 24
Industry and liberality, GENEROSITY: 9;
INDUSTRIOUSNESS: 80
Industry and prudence conquer,
INDUSTRIOUSNESS: 81; LOCAL
GOVERNMENT: 186; PRUDENCE: 24
Industry enriches,
INDUSTRIOUSNESS: 82; LOCAL
GOVERNMENT: 187
In earnest, SERIOUSNESS: 4
Inébranlable, STEADFASTNESS: 68
In Einem Stehet Vnsere Seligkeit,
BLESSING: 12
Inest clementia forti, COURAGE: 132;
MERCY: 7
Inest jucunditas, HAPPINESS: 32
Inevitabile fatum, FATE: 16
Inexpugnabilis, STRENGTH: 73
In ferro tutamen, DEFENSE: 26;
WEAPONS: 52
In ferrum libertate ruebant,
LIBERTY: 40; WEAPONS: 53
In fide, justitia, et fortitudine,
FAITH: 150; JUSTICE: 45;
STRENGTH: 74
In fide et in bello fortis, FAITH: 151;
STRENGTH: 75; WAR: 36
In fide fiducia, FAITH: 152; SCHOOL
MOTTOES: 136
In fide fortis, FAITH: 153
In fide vestra virtutem in virtute
autem scientiam, FAITH: 154;
KNOWLEDGE: 29; SCHOOL
MOTTOES: 137; VIRTUE: 91
Infirmis opitulare, ASSISTANCE: 10
In futura spector, FUTURE, THE: 12
Ingenio ac labore, ABILITY: 15;
INDUSTRIOUSNESS: 83
Ingenio et merito, ABILITY: 16;
WORTHINESS: 18
Ingenio et viribus, ABILITY: 17;
STRENGTH: 76
Ingenium innumerata labi,
OBSCURITY: 2
Ingenium superat vires, GENIUS: 1

Mottoes & Categories

Innocentia securus, INNOCENCE: 8
Innocue ac provide, HARMLESSNESS: 2
In nomine tuo Domine laxabo rete
  meum, DIVINE GUIDANCE: 320;
  SCRIPTURES: 10
In officio impavidus, COURAGE: 134;
  OFFICE: 1
In omnes casus, FORTUNE: 67
In omnia paratus, PREPAREDNESS: 26
In omnia promptus, PREPAREDNESS: 27
In omnibus caritas, KINDNESS: 11
Inopem me copia fecit, PROSPERITY: 19
Inopinum sed gratum, EXPECTATION: 6
In order to excel, EXCELLENCE: 11
Ino [*sic*] virtus et fata vocant,
  FATE: 20; VIRTUE: 93
In pace ut sapiens, PEACE: 20;
  WISDOM: 35
In Papam cornua tendo, RELIGION: 10
In pede fausto, FORTUNE: 68
In periculis audax, AUDACITY: 73;
  DANGER: 10
In potentatibus salus dextera Domini,
  DIVINE GUIDANCE: 321
In pretium persevero,
  PERSEVERANCE: 27; REWARD: 16
In promptu, PREPAREDNESS: 28
In prosperis time, in adversis spera,
  ADVERSITY: 37; FEAR: 27; HOPE: 111;
  PROSPERITY: 20
In prudentia & simplicitate,
  PRUDENCE: 25; SIMPLICITY: 2
In rebus arctis, ADVERSITY: 38
In recto decus, ACTION: 13; HONOR: 123
In recto fides, FIDELITY: 202;
  RECTITUDE: 31
In robore decus, GLORY: 33;
  STRENGTH: 79
In sale salus, SECURITY: 24
In sanguine foedus, DEVOTION: 8
In sanguine vita, LIFE: 10
In sapientia modus, SCHOOL
  MOTTOES: 139; WISDOM: 36
In scientia veritas in arte honestas,
  ART: 20; HONESTY: 24; TRUTH: 39
In season, SEASONS: 2
In seipso totus teres, SELF-RELIANCE: 7
Inservi Deo et laetare, SERVICE: 25
In se teres, SELF-RELIANCE: 8
Insignia fortuna paria, DESIRE: 4
INSIGNIFICANCE, p. 440

In silentio et spe, HOPE: 112;
  SILENCE: 7
In silentio et spe fortitudo mea,
  HOPE: 113; SILENCE: 8; STRENGTH: 80
In silentio fortitudo, COURAGE: 135;
  SILENCE: 9
Insiste firmiter, PERSEVERANCE: 28
In solo Deo salus, SALVATION: 31
In solo regit qui degit in coelo,
  PARADISE: 37
Insolubili nexu uniti, UNITY: 43
Insontes ut columbae, BIRDS: 20;
  INNOCENCE: 9
In spe et labore transigo vitam,
  HOPE: 114
In spe et silentio, HOPE: 115;
  SILENCE: 10
Insperata floruit, FLOURISHING: 49
In spe resto, HOPE: 116
In spe spiro, HOPE: 117
Inspice, EXPLORATION: 2
Instat vi patriae, COUNTRY: 43;
  STRENGTH: 81
Instaurator ruinae, REBIRTH: 12
Institutae tenax, DEDICATION: 5
In sublime, ASPIRATION: 53
Insult me not, WARNING: 6
Intaminata fide, FAITH: 155
Intaminatis fulget honoribus,
  HONOR: 124; SCHOOL MOTTOES: 140;
  SHINING: 10
Intaminatis honoribus, HONOR: 125
In te, Domine, confido, DIVINITY: 268
In te, Domine, speravi, DIVINITY: 269;
  TRUST: 71
In te, Domine, spes nostra,
  DIVINITY: 270; HOPE: 118
In te Deus speravi, DIVINITY: 271;
  HOPE: 119
In te digna sequere, WORTHINESS: 19
In te fido, TRUST: 72
Integer audax promptus,
  AUDACITY: 74; PREPAREDNESS: 29;
  STRENGTH: 82
Integer vitae, RECTITUDE: 32
Integra mens augustissima possessio,
  HONESTY: 25; MIND: 18; POSSESSION: 9
Integrias/ veritas/ dignitas,
  INTEGRITY: 16; SCHOOL
  MOTTOES: 141
Integritas semper tutamen,
  INTEGRITY: 17

Mottoes & Categories

Invictae fidelitatis praemium,
  FIDELITY: 205; LOCAL
  GOVERNMENT: 197
Invicta fidelitas praemium,
  FIDELITY: 206
Invicta labore, INDUSTRIOUSNESS: 87
Invicta veritate, TRUTH: 44
In victos, CONQUEST: 21
Invictus, MERCY: 10
Invictus maneo, MERCY: 11
Invictus manes, MERCY: 12
Invidam virtute vincam, VIRTUE: 95
Invidere sperno, ENVY: 3
Invidia assecla integritatis, ENVY: 4;
  INTEGRITY: 26
Invidiae claudor, pateo sed semper
  amico, ENVY: 5; FRIENDSHIP: 37
Invidia major, ENVY: 6
Invigila sic vinces, CONQUEST: 22
In vigilia sic vinces, CONQUEST: 23;
  VIGILANCE: 52
In virtute et fortuna, COURAGE: 141;
  FORTUNE: 70
Invita fortuna, FORTUNE: 71
Invita sortem fortuna, FATE: 21;
  FORTUNE: 72
Invitis ventis, FATE: 22
Invitum sequitur honor, DESIRE: 5;
  HONOR: 126
Invitum sequitur honos, HONOR: 127;
  WILLINGNESS: 2
In vulneribus Christi triumpho,
  CHRIST, JESUS: 44
In vulneribus Jesu meum auxilium,
  CHRIST, JESUS: 45
In well beware, VIGILANCE: 53
I pensieri stretti ed il viso sciolto, SELF-
  CONTROL: 9
I press forward, ADVANCE: 32
Ipse amicus, FRIENDSHIP: 38
Ipse fecit nos, ORIGIN: 5
Ira leonis nobilis, ANGER: 3;
  ANIMALS: 29; NOBILITY: 8
Iram leonis nole timere, ANGER: 4;
  ANIMALS: 30
Ire in adversa, ADVANCE: 33;
  ADVERSITY: 39
I renew my age, REBIRTH: 13
I rest to rise, REST: 9
I rise by industry, INDUSTRIOUSNESS: 88
I rise with the morning, RISING: 6;
  WAKEFULNESS: 4

IRONY, p. 444
Irreparabilium felix oblivio rerum,
  FORGETTING: 2
Irrevocabile, PERMANENCE: 4
Irrideo tempestatem, COURAGE: 142
Irrupta copula, FIDELITY: 207
I saved the king, SALVATION: 32
I. S. E. S. (In silentio et spe),
  HOPE: 120; SILENCE: 11
I show not boast, BOASTFULNESS: 4
I soar, LOFTINESS: 13
Ita, MANNER: 4
Iterum, iterum, iterumque,
  UNCLASSIFIED: 37
Iterum virescit, GROWTH: 14
I the people am victorious,
  VICTORY: 23
It is fortified, FORTIFICATIONS: 4
Ito tu et fac similiter, DEEDS: 57
I trow aright, FAITH: 157
I trow aught, FAITH: 158
I trust in God, DIVINITY: 275;
  TRUST: 74
It's good to be loun, SOLITUDE: 2
It shall flourish, FLOURISHING: 51
Itur ad astra, ASPIRATION: 54; STARS: 18
I wait my time, EXPECTATION: 7
I will, STEADFASTNESS: 71
I will defend, DEFENSE: 29
I will follow, FOLLOWING: 6
I will never quit, PERSEVERANCE: 31
I will not equivocate; I will not excuse;
  I will not retreat a single inch; and I
  will be heard, STEADFASTNESS: 72
I will not forget, MEMORY: 8
I will secure him, ENTRAPMENT: 1
I will try, EFFORT: 20; SCHOOL
  MOTTOES: 146
I will who will not, WILLINGNESS: 3
'I would found an institution where
  any person can find instruction in
  any study', KNOWLEDGE: 30; SCHOOL
  MOTTOES: 147

J

Jaculis nec arcu, WEAPONS: 54
J'ai bien servi, SERVICE: 26
J'ai bonne cause, CAUSATION: 2
J'ai bonne esperance, HOPE: 121
J'ai espoir mieux avoir, HOPE: 122
J'ai la clef, UBIQUITY: 4

J'aime à jamais, LOVE: 62
J'aime la liberté, LIBERTY: 43
J'aime le meilleur, LOVE: 63
J'aime l'honneur qui vient par la vertu, HONOR: 128; VIRTUE: 96
J'aime mon Dieu, mon roi, et ma patrie, COUNTRY: 44; DIVINITY: 276; ROYALTY: 46
J'aime qui m'aime, LOVE: 64
Jamais abattu, STEADFASTNESS: 73
Jamais arrière, STATUS: 4
Jamais chancelant, STEADFASTNESS: 74
Jamais sans espérance, HOPE: 123
Jam jam, PRESENT, THE: 4
Jam transit hyems, SEASONS: 3
J'aspire, CONFLICT: 6
J'avance, ADVANCE: 34
J'avance. Foy en Dieu, ADVANCE: 35; FAITH: 159
J'ay bonne cause, CAUSATION: 3
J'ay ma foi tenu à ma puissance, FAITH: 160
J'ayme à jamais, LOVE: 65
J'ayme porter secours, ASSISTANCE: 11; LOVE: 66
Je ayme, LOVE: 67
Je conduis, LEADERSHIP: 13
Je crains Dieu, DIVINITY: 277
Je defie fortune, FORTUNE: 73
Je dis la vérité, TRUTH: 45
Je ferai bien, SUCCESS: 6
Je feray ce que je diray, DEEDS: 58
Je gagne, INCREASE: 22
Je garde ma foi, FAITH: 161
Je garderay, DEFENSE: 30
Je gardye bien, CAUTION: 27
Jehovah, DIVINITY: 278
Jehovah-Jireh, DIVINE GUIDANCE: 322
Jehova portio mea, DIVINITY: 279
Jehova vexillum meum, DIVINITY: 280
Je le feray durant ma vie, DEEDS: 59
Je les maintiendrai, MAINTENANCE: 1
Je le tiens, POSSESSION: 10
Je le vueil, DESIRE: 6
Je loue Dieu grace attendant, MERCY: 13
Je luis imperceu, SHINING: 12
Je maintien devrai, RECTITUDE: 35
Je maintiendrai, MAINTENANCE: 2
Je maintiendray, MAINTENANCE: 3; SCHOOL MOTTOES: 148
Je me contente, HAPPINESS: 33

Je me fie en Dieu, DIVINITY: 281; TRUST: 75
Je m'en souvien-dray, MEMORY: 9
Je me souviendrai, MEMORY: 10
Je me tourne vers l'occident, DIRECTION: 2
Je meurs ou je m'attache, DEATH: 33
Je meurs pour ceux que j'aime, LOVE: 68; SACRIFICE: 3
Je mourrai pour ceux que j'aime, DEATH: 34
Je m'y oblige, DEDICATION: 6
Je ne change qu'en mourant, CHANGE: 8
Je ne cherche qu'un, EXPLORATION: 3
Je ne l'oublierai jamais, MEMORY: 11
Je ne plie ni ne rompe, STEADFASTNESS: 75
Je ne puis, POSSIBILITY: 5
Je ne serche qu'un, SEARCH and DISCOVERY: 7
Je n'oublierai jamais, MEMORY: 12
Je n'oublierai pas, MEMORY: 13
Je pense, THOUGHT: 8
Je pense à qui pense plus, THOUGHT: 9
Je pense plus, THOUGHT: 10
Je reçois pour donner, GIFTS and GIVING: 20
J'espère, HOPE: 124
J'espère bien, HOPE: 125
J'espère en Dieu, DIVINITY: 282; HOPE: 126
Jesu, esto mihi Jesus, CHRIST, JESUS: 46
Jesu est prêt, CHRIST, JESUS: 47
Je suis petite, mais mes picqûres sont profondes, SIZE: 1
Je suis prest, PREPAREDNESS: 33
Je suis prêt, PREPAREDNESS: 34
Je suis veillant à plaire, VIGILANCE: 54
Jesus, CHRIST, JESUS: 48
Jesus Hominum Salvator, CHRIST, JESUS: 49
Jesus meine Zuversicht, CHRIST, JESUS: 50
Jesus seul bon et bel, CHRIST, JESUS: 51
Je tans grace, MERCY: 14
Je tiendray ma puissance par ma foi, FAITH: 162
Je tiens ferme, STEADFASTNESS: 76
Je tiens foi, FAITH: 163
Je tourne vers l'occident, DIRECTION: 3

Je veulx tousiours la vertu svyvre,
VIRTUE: 97

Je veux bonne guerre, FAIRNESS: 8

Je veux de bonne guerre, FAIRNESS: 9

Je veux le droict, DESIRE: 7; JUSTICE: 47

Je veux le droit, DESIRE: 8; JUSTICE: 48

Je vive en esperance, HOPE: 127

Je vive en espoir, HOPE: 128

Je voil droit avoir, RECTITUDE: 36

Je voil droyt avoyre, JUSTICE: 49

Je voys, VISION: 7

Jewel of the Thames, BEAUTY: 13;
LOCAL GOVERNMENT: 198

Joannes est nomen ejus, NAME: 6;
NATIONAL MOTTOES: 11

Join truth with trust, TRADES: 17;
TRUST: 76; TRUTH: 46

Jouir en bien, ENJOYMENT: 17

Jour de ma vie, DAY: 3

Jovi confido, DIVINITY: 283

Jovi praestat fidere quam homine,
DIVINITY: 284; TRUST: 77

Jovis omnia plena, DIVINITY: 285

Joy sans fin, HAPPINESS: 34

Jubilee, HAPPINESS: 35

Jucunda oblivia vitae, FORGETTING: 3

Jucundi acti labores,
INDUSTRIOUSNESS: 89

Jucunditate afficior, ENJOYMENT: 18

Judge, JUDGMENT: 4

Judge and avenge my cause, O Lord,
JUDGMENT: 5

Judge not, JUDGMENT: 6

Judge nought, JUDGMENT: 7

Judge us by our deeds, DEEDS: 60;
LOCAL GOVERNMENT: 199

JUDGMENT, p. 444

Judicemur agendo, JUDGMENT: 8

Judicio et justitia, JUDGMENT: 9

Judicium parium, aut leges terrae,
JUDGMENT: 10

Juncta arma decori, WEAPONS: 55;
WORTHINESS: 20

Juncta virtuti fides, COURAGE: 143;
FIDELITY: 208

Juncti valemus, POWER: 8; UNITY: 46

Jungor ut implear, UNITY: 47

Junxit amicos amor, FRIENDSHIP: 39;
LOVE: 69

Juravi et adjuravi, DEDICATION: 7

Jure, non dono, RECTITUDE: 37

Jure et dignitate gladii, LOCAL
GOVERNMENT: 200; WEAPONS: 56

Jus dicere decus, JUSTICE: 50

Jus floruit, FLOURISHING: 52;
RECTITUDE: 38

Jus meum tuebor, RIGHTS: 5

Jussu regis India subacta, VICTORY: 24

Jus suum cuique, DUE: 1

Justam perficito nihil timeto, FEAR: 28;
JUSTICE: 51

Justa sequor, HONOR: 129

Juste et clementer, JUSTICE: 52;
MERCY: 15

Juste et droit, HONESTY: 26; JUSTICE: 53

Juste et fortiter, COURAGE: 144;
JUSTICE: 54

Juste et vray, JUSTICE: 55

Juste nec timide, FEAR: 29; JUSTICE: 56;
LOCAL GOVERNMENT: 201

Juste rem para, PREPAREDNESS: 35

JUSTICE, p. 445

Justice, paix, travail,
INDUSTRIOUSNESS: 90; JUSTICE: 57;
PEACE: 21

Justice to all, JUSTICE: 58

Justicia omnibus, JUSTICE: 59

Justi germinabunt, JUSTICE: 60

Justi terram incolant, JUSTICE: 61

Justitia, JUSTICE: 62

Justitiae comes magnanimitas,
GENEROSITY: 10; JUSTICE: 63; LOCAL
GOVERNMENT: 202

Justitiae propositique tenax,
JUSTICE: 64; PERSEVERANCE: 32;
PURPOSE: 8

Justitiae soror fides, FAITH: 164;
JUSTICE: 65

Justitia et clementia, JUSTICE: 66;
MERCY: 16

Justitia et concordia, JUSTICE: 67

Justitiae tenax, JUSTICE: 68;
PERSEVERANCE: 33

Justitia et fortitudo invincibilia sunt,
FORTITUDE: 24; JUSTICE: 69

Justitia et pax, JUSTICE: 70; PEACE: 22

Justitia et veritas, JUSTICE: 71;
TRUTH: 47

Justitia et virtus, JUSTICE: 72;
VIRTUE: 98

Justitia exaltat gentem,
RIGHTEOUSNESS: 4

Mottoes & Categories

Justitia stabilitur thronus, CROWN: 14;
JUSTICE: 73
Justitia turris nostra, JUSTICE: 74;
LOCAL GOVERNMENT: 203
Justitia/ veritas, JUSTICE: 75;
TRUTH: 48
Justitia virtutum regina, JUSTICE: 76;
VIRTUE: 99
Justi ut sidera fulgent,
RIGHTEOUSNESS: 5; STARS: 19
Justi velut lumen astrarum,
JUSTICE: 77; LIGHT: 28; STARS: 20
Justum et decorum, HONOR: 130;
JUSTICE: 78
Justum et tenacem, JUSTICE: 79;
PURPOSE: 9
Justum et tenacem propositi,
JUSTICE: 80; PURPOSE: 10
Justum perficito, nihil timeto,
FEAR: 30; JUSTICE: 81
Justus ac tenax, JUSTICE: 82
Justus ac tenax propositi, JUSTICE: 83;
PURPOSE: 11
Justus esto, et non metue, FEAR: 31;
JUSTICE: 84
Justus et fidelis, FIDELITY: 209;
JUSTICE: 85
Justus et propositi tenax, JUSTICE: 86;
PURPOSE: 12
Justus et tenax, JUSTICE: 87
Justus ex fide vivit, FAITH: 165
Justus nec timidus, JUSTICE: 88
Justus non derelinquetur,
RIGHTEOUSNESS: 6
Justus propositi tenax, JUSTICE: 89;
PURPOSE: 13
Justus ut palma, RIGHTEOUSNESS: 7
Justus ut palma florebit,
FLOURISHING: 53; RIGHTEOUSNESS: 8
Juvabitur audax, AUDACITY: 75
Juvant arva parentum, ENJOYMENT: 19
Juvant aspera fortes, ADVERSITY: 40;
COURAGE: 145
Juvant aspera probum, ADVERSITY: 41;
FORTUNE: 74
Juvant Deus impigros, DILIGENCE: 39;
DIVINE GUIDANCE: 323
Juvante Deo, DIVINE GUIDANCE: 324
Juvat dum lacerat, ASSISTANCE: 12
Juvat impigros Deus, DILIGENCE: 40;
DIVINE GUIDANCE: 325;·LOCAL
GOVERNMENT: 204

Juvat lacerat, ASSISTANCE: 13
Juvo audaces clarior hinc honos,
ASSISTANCE: 14
Juxta Salopiam, LOCATION: 3

K

Karanza wheelas karanza, LOVE: 70
Kar Duw, res pub. tia, DIVINITY: 286
Kars, PROPER NAMES: 24
Keep clean the game, HONESTY: 27
Keep faith, FAITH: 166; LOCAL
GOVERNMENT: 205
Keep fast, STEADFASTNESS: 77
Keep firm in the faith, FAITH: 167
Keep traist, TRUST: 78
Keep trust, TRUSTWORTHINESS: 4
Keep tryst, TRUST: 79
Keep tryst and trust, TRUST: 80
Keep tryste, TRUST: 81
Keep watch, VIGILANCE: 55
Kein Freud ohne Leid, HAPPINESS: 36;
SADNESS: 4
Ke ne dune Ke ne tiens ne pret Ke
desire, GIFTS and GIVING: 21
Kensol tra Tonkein ouna Diu mathern
yn, DIVINITY: 287
Key to the future, FUTURE, THE: 13;
SCHOOL MOTTOES: 149
Khelat, PROPER NAMES: 25
Khotso, pula, nala, PEACE: 23
Kia kaha ki te mahi tika,
RECTITUDE: 39
Kind heart, KINDNESS: 12
KINDNESS, p. 454
Knowledge, devotion, wisdom,
service, DEVOTION: 9;
KNOWLEDGE: 31; SCHOOL
MOTTOES: 150; SERVICE: 27;
WISDOM: 37
KNOWLEDGE, p. 455
KNOWLEDGE, p. 455
Knowledge aflame, KNOWLEDGE: 32;
SCHOOL MOTTOES: 151
Knowledge/ Duty/ Honor, DUTY: 18;
HONOR: 131; KNOWLEDGE: 33;
SCHOOL MOTTOES: 152
Knowledge for life, KNOWLEDGE: 34;
LIFE: 11; SCHOOL MOTTOES: 153
Knowledge for service,
KNOWLEDGE: 35; SCHOOL
MOTTOES: 154; SERVICE: 28

Knowledge is power, KNOWLEDGE: 36; POWER: 9; SCHOOL MOTTOES: 155

Knowledge is structured in consciousness, KNOWLEDGE: 37; SCHOOL MOTTOES: 156

Knowledge/ Skill, ABILITY: 18; KNOWLEDGE: 38; SCHOOL MOTTOES: 157

Knowledge/ Understanding/ Achievement/ Citizenship, ACCOMPLISHMENT: 10; KNOWLEDGE: 39; SCHOOL MOTTOES: 158

Known by their fruits, FRUIT: 7; LOCAL GOVERNMENT: 206

Know thyself, SELF-KNOWLEDGE: 7

Kunst, Macht, Kunst, ART: 21

Kymmer-yn Lydeirnon, PROPER NAMES: 26

Kynd kynn knawne kepe, UNCLASSIFIED: 38

L

Labes pejor morte, DEATH: 35; DISGRACE: 8

Labile quod opportunum, TIMELINESS: 6

Labitur et labetur, PERSEVERANCE: 34

La bondad para la medra, GOODNESS: 14

La bonté de Dieu, DIVINITY: 288; GOODNESS: 15

Labora, INDUSTRIOUSNESS: 91

Laboranti numen adest, DIVINE GUIDANCE: 326

Laboranti palma, REWARD: 17

Laborare est orare, INDUSTRIOUSNESS: 92

Laborare et studere, INDUSTRIOUSNESS: 93; SCHOOL MOTTOES: 159

Labora ut in aeternum vivas, IMMORTALITY: 3

Labore, INDUSTRIOUSNESS: 94

Labore et amore, INDUSTRIOUSNESS: 95; LOVE: 71

Labore et diligentia, DILIGENCE: 41; INDUSTRIOUSNESS: 96

Labore et fide, FIDELITY: 210; INDUSTRIOUSNESS: 97

Labore et fiducia, CONFIDENCE: 14; INDUSTRIOUSNESS: 98

Labore et honore, HONOR: 132; INDUSTRIOUSNESS: 99

Labore et ingenio, INDUSTRIOUSNESS: 100; LOCAL GOVERNMENT: 207

Labore et perseverantia, INDUSTRIOUSNESS: 101; PERSEVERANCE: 35

Labore et prudentia, INDUSTRIOUSNESS: 102; LOCAL GOVERNMENT: 208; PRUDENCE: 26

Labore et scientia, INDUSTRIOUSNESS: 103; LOCAL GOVERNMENT: 209

Labore et virtute, INDUSTRIOUSNESS: 104; PRIMACY: 4

Labore et vivere, INDUSTRIOUSNESS: 105

Labore omnia florent, FLOURISHING: 54; INDUSTRIOUSNESS: 106; LOCAL GOVERNMENT: 210

Labore parta, ACQUISITION: 4; INDUSTRIOUSNESS: 107

Labore quaeritur gloria, GLORY: 34

Labor et industria, INDUSTRIOUSNESS: 108

Labor et scientia, INDUSTRIOUSNESS: 109; KNOWLEDGE: 40; SCHOOL MOTTOES: 160

Labor et veritas, INDUSTRIOUSNESS: 110; TRUTH: 49

Labore vinces, INDUSTRIOUSNESS: 111

Labor improbus omnia vincit, INDUSTRIOUSNESS: 112

Labor in venatu, HUNTING: 3; INDUSTRIOUSNESS: 113

Labor ipse voluptas, INDUSTRIOUSNESS: 114

Laboro fide, EFFORT: 21

Labor omnia superat, INDUSTRIOUSNESS: 115

Labor omnia vincit, ADVERSITY: 42; INDUSTRIOUSNESS: 116; LOCAL GOVERNMENT: 211; PERSEVERANCE: 36; SCHOOL MOTTOES: 161; STATE MOTTOES: 26

Labor omnia vincit improbus, INDUSTRIOUSNESS: 117

Labor overcomes all things,
INDUSTRIOUSNESS: 118; LOCAL
GOVERNMENT: 212
Labor vincit omnia,
INDUSTRIOUSNESS: 119
Labour brings plenty,
INDUSTRIOUSNESS: 120; LOCAL
GOVERNMENT: 213
Labour to rest, INDUSTRIOUSNESS: 121;
REST: 10
La culte en difficulté, REVERENCE: 3
Laedere noli, INJURY: 4
Laetamur graviora passi, SUFFERING: 3
Laetavi, HAPPINESS: 37
Laeti acie florent, FLOURISHING: 55
Laetitia et spe immortalitatis,
HAPPINESS: 38; IMMORTALITY: 4
Laetitia per mortem, DEATH: 36;
HAPPINESS: 39
Laeto aere florent, FLOURISHING: 56
Laetus in praesens animus,
HAPPINESS: 40; PRESENT, THE: 5;
SPIRIT: 10
Laetus sorte mea, HAPPINESS: 41
Laetus sorte vives sapienter,
HAPPINESS: 42
La fin couronne les oeuvres, FINISH: 9
La foi me guide, FAITH: 168
La fortune passe par tout, FORTUNE: 75
La générosité, GENEROSITY: 11
Laidir ise lear Righ, CROWN: 15;
SEA: 11
Laissez dire, WORDS: 21
Laissir ronam aboo, VICTORY: 25
La liaison fait ma valeur, la division
me perd, UNITY: 48
La liberté, LIBERTY: 44
La loi le veut, et moi ni mot, LAW: 10
La mayor victorio de ellas es el bien
merecellas, VICTORY: 26
La merle aime la liberté, BIRDS: 21;
LIBERTY: 45
Lamh dearg Eirinn abú, DEFIANCE: 6;
HANDS: 16
Lamh derg aboo, DEFIANCE: 7;
HANDS: 17
Lamh foistenach abu, DEFIANCE: 8;
HANDS: 18; VICTORY: 27
Lamh laider an nachter, DEFIANCE: 9;
HANDS: 19
La mort me suit, DEATH: 37

L'amour de Dieu est pacifique,
LOVE: 72; PEACE: 24
L'amour et l'amitié, FRIENDSHIP: 40;
LOVE: 73
L'amour et loyauté, FIDELITY: 211;
LOVE: 74
Lampada tradam, FIRE: 8
Language/ Art/ Science, ART: 22;
SCHOOL MOTTOES: 162; WORDS: 22
L'anticho valor non è anchor morto,
COURAGE: 146
L'antiquité ne peut pas l'abolir, AGE: 3
Là ou ailleurs, LOCATION: 4
La paix, PEACE: 25
La promesse du futur, FUTURE, THE: 14
Lassez dire, WORDS: 23
Lasz Gott walten, DIVINE
GUIDANCE: 327
Lateat scintillula forsan, OBSCURITY: 3
Latet anguis in herba, ANIMALS: 31;
OBSCURITY: 4
La tête plus que l'argent, LIFE: 12
Laudans invocabo Dominum,
DIVINITY: 289; PRAISE: 4
Laudari a laudato, PRAISE: 5
Laudes cano heroum, PRAISE: 6
Laudo manentem, PRAISE: 7
Laugh lader an aughter,
HAPPINESS: 43; LAUGHTER: 1
LAUGHTER, p. 462
Lauro redimita quiescam, HONOR: 133;
REST: 11
Lauro resurgo, FLORA: 19;
REBIRTH: 14; RIGHTS: 6
Lauro scutoque resurgo, RISING: 7
Laurus crescit in arduis, FLORA: 20
Laus Deo, DIVINITY: 290; PRAISE: 8
Laus recti diuturna beat, PRAISE: 9;
RIGHTEOUSNESS: 9
Laus virtutis actio, DEEDS: 61;
VIRTUE: 100
La vertu est la seule noblesse,
NOBILITY: 9; VIRTUE: 101
La vertu surmonte tout obstacle,
VIRTUE: 102
La vie durante, LIFE: 13
La vita al fin e'l di loda la sera, DAY: 4;
FORTUNE: 76; PRAISE: 10
LAW, p. 462
Law, LAW: 11
Law and Right, LAW: 12;
RECTITUDE: 40

Mottoes & Categories

LISTENING, p. 486
Listo, PREPAREDNESS: 36
Literis et armis, KNOWLEDGE: 48;
WEAPONS: 62
Litteras ne despice, KNOWLEDGE: 49
Littora specto, VISION: 8
Littore sistam, DEFENSE: 31
Live, love, think, pray, dare, LIFE: 14;
LOVE: 78; RISK: 5; UBIQUITY: 5
Live but dread, LIFE: 15
Live free or die, LIBERTY: 76;
STARS: 23; STATE MOTTOES: 32
Live in hope, HOPE: 135; LIFE: 16
LIVELINESS, p. 487
Live to live, LIFE: 17
Live to the truth, SCHOOL
MOTTOES: 172; TRUTH: 51
Live while green, LIFE: 18
LOCAL GOVERNMENT, p. 487
LOCAL GOVERNMENT, p. 487
LOCATION, p. 512
Lock sick, CERTAINTY: 2
Lock sicker, CERTAINTY: 3
LOFTINESS, p. 513
Loisgim agus soilleirghim,
ENLIGHTENMENT: 4
Longo splendescit in usu,
BRIGHTNESS: 10
Look and live, LIFE: 19; VISION: 9
Looking backward, looking forward,
LOCAL GOVERNMENT: 217; TIME: 28
Look through, VISION: 10
Look to the end, saith Kennedy,
FINISH: 10
Look to the past, PAST, THE: 5
Look up and not down, look forward
and not back, look out and not in,
and lend a hand, HUMANITY: 5
Loquendo placet, WORDS: 26
Lord, have mercy!, DIVINITY: 292
Lord, let Glasgow flourish,
FLOURISHING: 58; LOCAL
GOVERNMENT: 218
Lothim agus marbhaim, INJURY: 5
LOVE, p. 515
LOVE, p. 515
Love, LOVE: 79
Love, but dread, LOVE: 80
Love, serve, LOVE: 81; SERVICE: 30
Love and dread, LOVE: 82
Love and loyalty, FIDELITY: 216;
LOVE: 83

Love as brethren, LOVE: 84;
TRADES: 20
Love as you find, LOVE: 85
Love every man, fear no man,
FEAR: 32; LOVE: 86
Loyal, confidential, FIDELITY: 217
Loyal à la mort, FIDELITY: 218
Loyal and industrious, FIDELITY: 219;
INDUSTRIOUSNESS: 124; LOCAL
GOVERNMENT: 219
Loyal and true, FIDELITY: 220; LOCAL
GOVERNMENT: 220
Loyal au mort, FIDELITY: 221
Loyal devoir, DUTY: 20
Loyal en tout, FIDELITY: 222
Loyal in adversity, FIDELITY: 223
Loyal je serai durant ma vie,
FIDELITY: 224
Loyalle suys, FIDELITY: 225
Loyalment je sers, FIDELITY: 226;
SERVICE: 31
Loyal suis je, FIDELITY: 227
Loyalté me lie, FIDELITY: 228
Loyal until death, FIDELITY: 229
Loyaulte n'a honte, FIDELITY: 230
Loyauté me oblige, FIDELITY: 231
Loyauté m'oblige, FIDELITY: 232
Loyauté mon honneur, FIDELITY: 233
Loyauté sans tache, FIDELITY: 234
Loywf as thow fynds, FIDELITY: 235
Luce, LIGHT: 30
Luceat et crescat, GROWTH: 15;
SHINING: 14
Lucem amat virtus, LIGHT: 31;
VIRTUE: 107
Lucem spero, HOPE: 136; LIGHT: 32
Lucem spero clariorem, HOPE: 137;
LIGHT: 33
Lucent in tenebris, DARKNESS: 7;
LIGHT: 34; SHINING: 15
Luceo boreale, SHINING: 16
Luceo et terreo, FIERCENESS: 6;
SHINING: 17
Luceo non terreo, SHINING: 18
Luceo non uro, SHINING: 19
Lucerna pedibus meis, LIGHT: 35
Lucet, SHINING: 20
Luck to Loyne, FORTUNE: 77; LOCAL
GOVERNMENT: 221
Lucrum Christi mihi, CHRIST, JESUS: 52
Luctor, at emergam, ADVERSITY: 43
Luctor, non mergor, ADVERSITY: 44

Lufe God abufe al: and yi nichtbors as yi self, LOVE: 87

Lumen accipe et imperti, LIGHT: 36

Lumen coeleste sequamur, FOLLOWING: 7; PARADISE: 38

Lumen sevimus antique, LIGHT: 37

Lumen umbra Dei, LIGHT: 38; TRADES: 21

L'un pour l'autre, UNSELFISHNESS: 3

Lux, LIGHT: 39; SCHOOL MOTTOES: 173

Lux, salubritas, felicitas, HAPPINESS: 45; HEALING and HEALTH: 15; LIGHT: 40; LOCAL GOVERNMENT: 222

Lux anglis, crux Francis, LIGHT: 41

Lux Dei ibi salus, DIVINITY: 293

Lux esto, LIGHT: 42; SCHOOL MOTTOES: 174

Lux et fides, FAITH: 171; LIGHT: 43; SCHOOL MOTTOES: 175

Lux et humanitas, HUMANITY: 6; LIGHT: 44

Lux et salus, LIGHT: 45; SECURITY: 27

Lux et scientia, KNOWLEDGE: 50; LIGHT: 46; SCHOOL MOTTOES: 176

Lux in tenebris, DARKNESS: 8; LIGHT: 48

Lux/ libertas, LIBERTY: 77; LIGHT: 49; SCHOOL MOTTOES: 179

Lux mea Christus, CHRIST, JESUS: 53; LIGHT: 50

Lux mentis lux orbis, LIGHT: 51; MIND: 21; SCHOOL MOTTOES: 180; WORLD: 2

Lux mihi Deus, DIVINITY: 294

Lux mihi laurus, FLORA: 23; LIGHT: 52

Lux mundi, LIGHT: 53; SCHOOL MOTTOES: 181; WORLD: 3

Lux mundi justitia, JUSTICE: 92; LIGHT: 54

Lux omnibus refulgeat, LIGHT: 55; SHINING: 21

Lux tua via mea, LIGHT: 56; WAY: 5

Lux tua vita mea, LIFE: 20; LIGHT: 57

Lux venit ab alto, LIGHT: 58

Lux veritas peritia populo nostro, ABILITY: 19; LIGHT: 59; SCHOOL MOTTOES: 182; TRUTH: 54

Lux vitae, LIFE: 21; LIGHT: 60

Lybba bu te bu Lybbe, LIFE: 22

Lybia, PROPER NAMES: 28

Lyrae nervos aptavi, MUSIC: 5

M

Mack all sicker, SECURITY: 28

Macte, EXHORTATION: 2

Macte virtute, COURAGE: 147

Macte virtute esto, PROSPERITY: 23

Macte virtute patrum, ANCESTRY: 22; COURAGE: 148

Madripore, PROPER NAMES: 29

Ma force d'en haut, STRENGTH: 89

Magistratus indicat virum, OFFICE: 2

Magna est veritas, TRUTH: 55

Magna est veritas et prevalebit, TRUTH: 56

Magnanimiter crucem sustine, CROSS, THE: 76

Magnanimus esto, GREATNESS: 2

Magna vis fidelitatis, FIDELITY: 236

Magna vis veritatis, TRUTH: 57

Magnes et adamas, UNCLASSIFIED: 40

Magni animi pretium, GREATNESS: 3

Magnum in parvo, SIZE: 3

Magnus et animus, MIND: 22

Magnus Hippocrates; tu nobis major!, GREATNESS: 4

Maharajpore, PROPER NAMES: 30

Maigre l'injustice, INJURY: 6

MAINTENANCE, p. 522

Maintenant ou jamais, PRESENT, THE: 6

Maintien le droit, RECTITUDE: 41

Majora, uberiora, pulchriora, GREATNESS: 5

Majora sequor, ASPIRATION: 56

Majora tenta praesentibus aequus, ASPIRATION: 57

Majores sequor, ANCESTRY: 23

Major opima ferat, WORTHINESS: 22

Majorum vestigia premo, ANCESTRY: 24

Major virtus quam splendor, VIRTUE: 108

Ma joye en Dieu seulement, HAPPINESS: 46

Majulah Singapura, IMPROVEMENT: 18

Make a clean heart and a cheerful spirit, HAPPINESS: 47; HEART: 9; SPIRIT: 11

Make all sure, SECURITY: 29; TRADES: 22

Mala praevisa pereunt, EVIL: 1

Mal au tour, ADVERSITY: 45

Malgré l'envie, ENVY: 7

Malgré le tort, INJURY: 7

Malim esse probus quam haberi,
HONESTY: 28

Malim esse quam videri, INTEGRITY: 28

Malis fortiter obsta, EVIL: 2

Malis obsta, ADVERSITY: 46

Malle debemus Principes esse quam
videri, INTEGRITY: 29

Mallem mori quam foedari,
DEATH: 39; DISGRACE: 9

Mallem mori quam mutare,
STEADFASTNESS: 78

Malo mori quam foedari, DEATH: 40;
DISGRACE: 10

Malo pati quam foedari, DISGRACE: 11;
SUFFERING: 4

Malum bono vince, EVIL: 3

Man do it, DEEDS: 63

Mane diem, DAY: 6

Manent optima coelo, PARADISE: 39

Maneo, PERSEVERANCE: 37

Maneo, non fugio, STEADFASTNESS: 79

Maneo et munio, DEFENSE: 32

Maneo qualis manebam,
CONSISTENCY: 5

Mane proedam, vespere spolium,
HUNTING: 4

Manes non fugio, DEATH: 41

Manet alta mente repostum,
OBSCURITY: 5

Manet amicitia florebitque semper,
FRIENDSHIP: 43

Manet in aeternum, ENDURANCE: 39

MANLINESS, p. 522

MANNER, p. 523

MANNERS, p. 524

Manners makyth man, MANNERS: 5;
SCHOOL MOTTOES: 183

Manu et corde, FEELINGS: 17;
HANDS: 20

Manu forti, HANDS: 21

Manuque, HANDS: 22

Manus haec inimica tyrannis,
HANDS: 23; HOSTILITY: 13

Manus justa nardus, HANDS: 24

Many minds, one heart, LOCAL
GOVERNMENT: 223; UNITY: 52

Marbu mhiann leinn, DESIRE: 9

Mare ditat, SEA: 12

Mare ditat, rosa decorat, FLORA: 24;
LOCAL GOVERNMENT: 224; SEA: 13

Mare ditat flores decorant, FLORA: 25;
LOCAL GOVERNMENT: 225; SEA: 14

Mare et ferro, LOCAL
GOVERNMENT: 226; SCRIPTURES: 12;
SEA: 15; WALKING: 3

Mars denique victor es, CONQUEST: 24

Marte et arte, ART: 23; COURAGE: 149

Marte et clypeo, WAR: 37

Marte et industria,
INDUSTRIOUSNESS: 125; WEAPONS: 63

Marte et ingenio, CLEVERNESS: 5;
WAR: 38

Marte et labore,
INDUSTRIOUSNESS: 126; WEAPONS: 64

Marte et mari faventibus, WAR: 39

Marte non Arte, ART: 24; WEAPONS: 65

Marte suo tutus, SECURITY: 30

Marte vel arte, ART: 25; FORCE: 8

Martis non Cupidinis, LOVE: 88;
WAR: 40

Mature, TIME: 29

Maturity, AGE: 4

Maturus coelo non cadit ante diem,
PARADISE: 40

Mauvais chiens, ANIMALS: 35

Ma volonté, WILL: 2

Maximum proeli impetum et sustinere,
DEFENSE: 33

Maya, PROPER NAMES: 31

May the right prevail, RECTITUDE: 42;
SCHOOL MOTTOES: 184

Mea anchora Christus, CHRIST,
JESUS: 54

Mea anchora virtus, VIRTUE: 109

Mea culpa fides, FIDELITY: 237

Mea Deus gloria, DIVINITY: 295

Mea dos virtus, VIRTUE: 110

Meae memor originis, ORIGIN: 6

Mea fides in sapientia, TRUST: 84;
WISDOM: 40

Mea gloria crux, CROSS, THE: 77;
GLORY: 35

Mea gloria fides, FAITH: 172;
GLORY: 36

Mean, speak, and doe well,
INTENTION: 3

Mean, speak, and do well,
INTENTION: 4

Mea spes est in Deo, DIVINITY: 296;
HOPE: 138

MEASURE, p. 524

Mea virtute me involvo, VIRTUE: 111

Me certum mors certa facit, DEATH: 42
Mecum habita, FELLOWSHIP: 5
Medicine—To Teach, To Serve, To Search, HEALING and HEALTH: 16; SCHOOL MOTTOES: 185
Mediis tranquillus in undis, TRANQUILLITY: 5
Mediocria firma, MODERATION: 12
Mediocria maxima, MODERATION: 13
Mediocriter, MODERATION: 14
Medio tutissimus, MODERATION: 15; SECURITY: 31
Medio tutus, MODERATION: 17; SECURITY: 34
Meditare, DIVINE GUIDANCE: 330
Meditari et agere, PURPOSE: 14
Meditatio mortis optima philosophia, DEATH: 43
Me duce, LEADERSHIP: 16
Me duce carpe viam, LEADERSHIP: 17
Me fortem reddit Deus, DIVINE GUIDANCE: 331; STRENGTH: 90
Mein Anfang und Ende steht in Gottes händen, DIVINE GUIDANCE: 332
Mein End und Leben ist Gott ergeben, DIVINITY: 297
Mein Gott, füg es zum Besten (M. G. F. Z. B.), DIVINE GUIDANCE: 333
Mein Liebe is gekreuziget, LOVE: 89
Mein Siegel ist ein Ziegel, SIGN: 4
Mein Thun und Leben ist Gott ergeben, DIVINITY: 298
Me juvat ire per altum, CONCILIATION: 6
Meliora sequentur, ASPIRATION: 58
Meliora sequimur, FOLLOWING: 8; LOCAL GOVERNMENT: 227
Meliora speranda, EXPECTATION: 9; FORTUNE: 78; HOPE: 139
Meliora sperando, HOPE: 140; IMPROVEMENT: 19
Meliora spero, HOPE: 141; IMPROVEMENT: 20
Meliora spero sequorque, HOPE: 142; IMPROVEMENT: 21
Meliora supersunt, WORTHINESS: 23
Meliore fide quam fortuna, FIDELITY: 238
Meliorem lapsa locavit, IMPROVEMENT: 22; STATE MOTTOES: 33

Melior fortunâ virtus, FORTUNE: 79; VIRTUE: 112
Melitae amor, LOVE: 90
Melius est nomen bonum quam divitiae multae, PROSPERITY: 24; REPUTATION: 5
Members one of another, INTER-RELATEDNESS: 2
Me meliora manent, FORTUNE: 80
Memento Creatorem, MEMORY: 14
Memento mei, MEMORY: 15
Memento mori, DEATH: 44; MEMORY: 16
Me Minerva lucet, ENLIGHTENMENT: 5
Memini, MEMORY: 17
Meminisse juvabit, MEMORY: 18
Memor, ATTENTIVENESS: 5
Memor amici, FRIENDSHIP: 44
Memorare novissima, DEATH: 45; MEMORY: 19
Memores fecere merendo, MEMORY: 20
Memor esto, ATTENTIVENESS: 6
Memor esto brevis aevi, TIME: 30
Memor et fidelis, ATTENTIVENESS: 7; FIDELITY: 239
Memor et gratus, GRATITUDE: 12
Memoria pii aeterna, MEMORY: 21; PIETY: 12
Memor virtutis avitae, ANCESTRY: 25
MEMORY, p. 525
Mens aequa rebus in arduis, EQUANIMITY: 11
Mens agitat molem, MIND: 23; SCHOOL MOTTOES: 186
Mens/ animus/ corpus, MIND: 24; SCHOOL MOTTOES: 187; SPIRIT: 12
Mens conscia recti, MIND: 25; RECTITUDE: 43
Mens cujusque is est quisque, MIND: 26
Mens et manus, FEELINGS: 18; HANDS: 25; MIND: 27; SCHOOL MOTTOES: 188
Mens flecti nescia, MIND: 28
Mens immota, MIND: 29
Mens immota manet, ENDURANCE: 40; STEADFASTNESS: 80
Mens in arduis aequa, EQUANIMITY: 12
Mens pristina mansit, MIND: 30
Mens sana in corpore sano, HEALING and HEALTH: 17
Mens sibi conscia recti, MIND: 31; RECTITUDE: 44

Mente et artificio, MIND: 32; SCHOOL
  MOTTOES: 189
Mente et labore,
  INDUSTRIOUSNESS: 127; MIND: 33
Mente et manu, FEELINGS: 19;
  HANDS: 26
Mente manuque, FEELINGS: 20;
  HANDS: 27
Mente manuque praesto, FEELINGS: 21;
  HANDS: 28
Mente non Marte, MIND: 34; WAR: 41
Mentes consciae recti, MIND: 35;
  RECTITUDE: 45
Mentis honestae gloria, HONESTY: 29;
  MIND: 36
Meor ras tha Dew, DIVINE
  GUIDANCE: 334; GRACE: 22
Merces haec certa laborum,
  INDUSTRIOUSNESS: 128; REWARD: 18
Merci, fortune, FORTUNE: 81
Mercie, MERCY: 17
Mercie is my desire, DESIRE: 10;
  MERCY: 18
MERCY, p. 527
Mercy, MERCY: 19; SCHOOL
  MOTTOES: 190
Mercy is my desire, DESIRE: 11;
  MERCY: 20
Merebimur, WORTHINESS: 24
Mereo et merito, WORTHINESS: 25
Merere, WORTHINESS: 26
Merere et confide, TRUST: 85;
  WORTHINESS: 27
Meret qui laborat,
  INDUSTRIOUSNESS: 129;
  WORTHINESS: 28
Meritas augentur honores, HONOR: 137
Merite, WORTHINESS: 29
Meritez, WORTHINESS: 30
Merito, WORTHINESS: 31
Merses profundo pulchrior evenit,
  SEA: 16
Merui, WORTHINESS: 32
Merui candore favorem, HONESTY: 30
Meruisse manu, WORTHINESS: 33
Messis ab altis, HARVEST: 3; LOCAL
  GOVERNMENT: 228
Messis ab alto, HARVEST: 4
Me stante virebunt, FLOURISHING: 59
Metuenda corolla draconis, FEAR: 33
Metuo secundis, FEAR: 34;
  PROSPERITY: 25

Meum et tuum, POSSESSION: 13
Me vincit, ego mereo, CONQUEST: 25
Mi camokah baalim Yehowah,
  DIVINITY: 299
Micat inter omnes, SHINING: 22
Mieulx serra, IMPROVEMENT: 23
Mieux être que paraître, INTEGRITY: 30
Mieux je sera, IMPROVEMENT: 24
Migremus hinc, UNCLASSIFIED: 41
Migro et respicio, EMERGENCE: 2
Mihi coelum portus, PARADISE: 41
Mihi consulit Deus, DIVINITY: 300
Mihi cura futuri, FUTURE, THE: 16
Mihi et meae, POSSESSION: 14
Mihi gloria sursum, GLORY: 37
Mihi gravato Deus, DIVINITY: 301
Mihi jussa capessere, AUTHORITY: 4
Mihi lucra, PROSPERITY: 26
Mihi lucra pericula, DANGER: 12
Mihi parta tueri, DEFENSE: 34
Mihi res subjungere conor, POWER: 11
Mihi robore robor, STRANGER: 5;
  STRENGTH: 91
Mihi solicitudo futuri, FUTURE, THE: 17
Mihi terraque lacusque, POSSESSION: 15
Mihi tibi, UNCLASSIFIED: 42
Mihi vita Christus, CHRIST, JESUS: 55
Mihi vivere Christus est, CHRIST,
  JESUS: 56; SCHOOL MOTTOES: 191
Miles et fortis, COURAGE: 150;
  MILITARY DISTINCTION: 3
Milita bonam militiam retinens fidem
  et bonam conscientiam,
  CONSCIENCE: 6; FAITH: 173; WAR: 42
MILITARY DISTINCTION, p. 529
Militemus, WAR: 43
Militia mea multiplex, WAR: 44
Minatur, HOSTILITY: 14
MIND, p. 529
Mind/ Body/ Spirit/ Educating the
  whole man, MIND: 37; SCHOOL
  MOTTOES: 192; SPIRIT: 13
Mind your own business, SELF-
  RELIANCE: 9
Ministrando dignitas, LOCAL
  GOVERNMENT: 229; SERVICE: 32
Minorca, PROPER NAMES: 32
Mirabile in profundis, SEA: 17
Mirior invictus, MERCY: 21
Misenach, COURAGE: 151

Miserere mei, Deus, secundum magnam misericordiam tuam, GOODNESS: 16; MERCY: 22

Miserere mihi Deus, MERCY: 23

Misericordias Domini in aeternum cantabo, MERCY: 24; SCHOOL MOTTOES: 193

Misericordia temperet gladium, MERCY: 25

Miseris auxilium (or) opem fero, ASSISTANCE: 15; KINDNESS: 13

Miseris succurrere, ASSISTANCE: 16; KINDNESS: 14

Miseris succurrere disco, ASSISTANCE: 17; KINDNESS: 15

Miseris succurro, ASSISTANCE: 18; KINDNESS: 16

Miserrima vidi, VISION: 11

Missionary/ Biblical/ Evangelistic, RELIGION: 13; SCHOOL MOTTOES: 194

Mit der Zeit, TIME: 31

Mit Gott und mit der Zeit, DIVINITY: 302; TIME: 32

Mitis et audax, AUDACITY: 77; GENTLENESS: 10

Mitis et fortis, COURAGE: 152; GENTLENESS: 11

Mitis sed fortis, COURAGE: 153; GENTLENESS: 12

Mit Schimpf mit Ernst, SERIOUSNESS: 5

Moderata durant, MODERATION: 18

Moderata manent, MODERATION: 19

MODERATION, p. 532

Modeste conabor, MODERATION: 20

Modice augetur modicum, INCREASE: 23

Modico angetur modicum, OBSCURITY: 6

Modicum modice erit magnum, INCREASE: 24

Moenibus crede ligneis, FORTIFICATIONS: 5

Moeret qui laborat, INDUSTRIOUSNESS: 130; SADNESS: 5

Monachus salvabor, SALVATION: 34

Mon devoir fait mon plaisir, DUTY: 21

Mon Dieu, mon roi, et ma patrie, COUNTRY: 50; DIVINITY: 303; ROYALTY: 53

Mon Dieu est ma roche, DIVINITY: 304

Mon droit, RECTITUDE: 46

Monemus et munimus, GUIDANCE: 18; LOCAL GOVERNMENT: 230; PROTECTION: 20

Moneo et munio, DEFENSE: 35; GUIDANCE: 19

Mone sale, GUIDANCE: 20

Mon heur et salut gist en mains de Dieu, DIVINE GUIDANCE: 335; FORTUNE: 82

Moniti meliora sequamur, IMPROVEMENT: 25

Monitus, munitus, WARNING: 7

Mon Mam Cymru, LOCAL GOVERNMENT: 231; PARENTS: 2

Mon privilege et mon devoir, DUTY: 22

Mon repos est au ciel, PARADISE: 42; REST: 12

Monstrant astra viam, STARS: 24

Monstrant regibus astra viam, STARS: 25

Montani semper liberi, LIBERTY: 78; STATE MOTTOES: 34

Monte alto, LOFTINESS: 14

Monte de alto, LOFTINESS: 15

Monte dessus, ASPIRATION: 59

Montes unde auxilium meum, GUIDANCE: 21; LOCAL GOVERNMENT: 232

Montez toujours, ASPIRATION: 60

Montjoie Saint-Denys, UNCLASSIFIED: 43

Mon tresor, PROSPERITY: 27

Mora trahit periculum, SPEED: 34

More light, more power, LIGHT: 61; LOCAL GOVERNMENT: 233; POWER: 12

Mores fingunt fortunam, FORTUNE: 83; MANNERS: 6

Mores hoc mutato, MANNERS: 7

Mores meliore metallo, MANNERS: 8

Moribus antiquis, MANNERS: 9

Moriendo modulor, DEATH: 46

Moriendo vivam, DEATH: 47; LIFE: 23

Moriendo vivo, DEATH: 48; REASON: 11

Moriendum, DEATH: 49

Moriens, sed invictus, DEATH: 50

Moriens cano, DEATH: 51

Mori quam faedari, DEATH: 52

Mors, aut honorabilis vita, DEATH: 53; HONOR: 138

Mors aerumnarum requies, DEATH: 54; REST: 13

Mors aut vita decora, DEATH: 55

Mors Christi mors mortis mihi, CHRIST, JESUS: 57

Mors crucis mea salus, CROSS, THE: 78

Mors in vita, DEATH: 56; LIBERTY: 79

Mors janua vitae, DEATH: 57; REASON: 12

Mors lupi agnis vita, ANIMALS: 36; DEATH: 58

Mors meta laborum, DEATH: 59

Mors mihi lucrum, DEATH: 60; FAITH: 174

Mors mihi vitae fide, DEATH: 61; FAITH: 175

Mors mihi vita est, DEATH: 62; REASON: 13

Mors non timenda est, DEATH: 63

Mors omnibus communis, DEATH: 64

Mors potior macula, DEATH: 65

Mortale non opto, IMMORTALITY: 5

Mort dessus, DEATH: 66

Morte leonis vita, ANIMALS: 37; LIFE: 24

Mortem aut triumphum, DEATH: 67; VICTORY: 30

Mort en droit, DEATH: 68

Morte triumpho, DEATH: 69

Mortua vivescunt, REBIRTH: 15

Mos legem regit, LAW: 33

Mot pour mot, WORDS: 27

Mouguerre, PROPER NAMES: 33

Moveo et proficior, IMPROVEMENT: 26; PROPER NAMES: 34; PROSPERITY: 28

Moveo et propitior, ACTION: 14; CONCILIATION: 7

Moving people forward, IMPROVEMENT: 27; SCHOOL MOTTOES: 195

Mox sese attolit in auris, LOFTINESS: 16

Mox virtute se tollit ad auras, COURAGE: 154; LOFTINESS: 17

M. R. E. A. C. (Mon repos est au ciel), PARADISE: 43

Mullac aboo, DEFIANCE: 10

Multa in parvo, SIZE: 4

Multa tuli fecique, ENDURANCE: 41

Multa virum durando saecula vincit, ANCESTRY: 26; ENDURANCE: 42

Multi pertransibunt et augebitur scientia, KNOWLEDGE: 51; LOCAL GOVERNMENT: 234

Multum in parvo, MEASURE: 7

Munifice et fortiter, COURAGE: 155; GENEROSITY: 13

Munit haec et altera vincit, DEFENSE: 36

Munus et monumentum victoriae Spures, 1513, MILITARY DISTINCTION: 4; REWARD: 19

Murus aeneus, conscientia sana, CONSCIENCE: 7

Murus aeneus esto, STRANGER: 6; STRENGTH: 92

Murus aeneus mens conscia recti, MIND: 38; RECTITUDE: 47

Murus aeneus virtus, VIRTUE: 113

Murus aheneus, STRANGER: 7; STRENGTH: 93

MUSIC, p. 535

Mutabimur, CHANGE: 9

Mutare fidem nescio, FIDELITY: 240

Mutare non est meum, CHANGE: 10

Mutare sperno, CHANGE: 11

Mutare vel timere sperno, CHANGE: 12; FEAR: 35; LOCAL GOVERNMENT: 235; STEADFASTNESS: 81

Mutas inglorius artes, HUMILITY: 7

Muthig vorwartz, ADVANCE: 36; COURAGE: 156

Mutuo amore cresco, GROWTH: 16; LOVE: 91

Mutus inglorius, GLORY: 38; SILENCE: 12

Mutus inglorius artis, GLORY: 39; SILENCE: 13

M. V. S. Z. G. A. (Mein Vertrauen steht zu Gott allein), DIVINITY: 305; TRUST: 86

M. V. Z. G. (Mein Verlangen zu Gott), DESIRE: 12

My defense, DEFENSE: 37

My hope is constant, HOPE: 143

My hope is constant in thee, HOPE: 144

My hope is in God, DIVINITY: 306; HOPE: 145

My hope on high, HOPE: 146

My king and country, PATRIOTISM: 18; ROYALTY: 54

My lure is truth, TRUTH: 58

My might makes my right, FORCE: 9

My prince and my country, PATRIOTISM: 19; PRINCELINESS: 6

My trust is in God alone, DIVINITY: 307; TRADES: 23; TRUST: 87

Mottoes & Categories

My trust is in the Lord, DIVINITY: 308;
TRUST: 88
My word is my bond, HONOR: 139;
TRUSTWORTHINESS: 5

N

Na bean d'on chat gun lamhainu,
ANIMALS: 38; TOUCH: 1
Nach Tugend ich tracht, Alles eiteles
veracht, VIRTUE: 114
Na fyno Duw na fyd, DIVINE
GUIDANCE: 336
Nagpore, PROPER NAMES: 35
NAME, p. 535
Natale solum dulce, COUNTRY: 51;
PATRIOTISM: 20
NATIONAL MOTTOES, p. 536
Nativum retinet decus, HONOR: 140
Natos et nostra tuemur,
PROTECTION: 21
Naturae donum, GIFTS and GIVING: 22
Naturae minister, SERVICE: 33;
UBIQUITY: 6
Naturam primum cognoscere rerum,
FACTUALITY: 3; SCHOOL
MOTTOES: 196
Naufragus in portum, SALVATION: 35
Nautae fida, FIDELITY: 241
Nautis stella refulsit, STARS: 26
Navarin, PROPER NAMES: 36
Navem tuam Christe tuere, CHRIST,
JESUS: 58; PROTECTION: 22
NAVIGATION, p. 539
Nec abest jugum, PREPAREDNESS: 37
Nec ab ordine cedunt, STATUS: 5
Nec ab oriente, nec ab occidente,
DIRECTION: 4
Ne cadam insidiis, ENTRAPMENT: 2
Nec arrogo, nec dubito,
UNCLASSIFIED: 44
Nec avarus nec profusus,
MODERATION: 21; UNCLASSIFIED: 45
Nec beneficii immemor injuriae,
FORGETTING: 5
Nec careo, nec curo, SATISFACTION: 3
Nec celeri nec forti, SPEED: 35;
STRENGTH: 94
Nec cito, nec tarde, MODERATION: 22;
SPEED: 36
Nec cunctando nec temere agendo,
PRUDENCE: 27

Nec cupias, nec metuas, DESIRE: 13;
FEAR: 36; MODERATION: 23
Nec deerit operi dextra,
WILLINGNESS: 4
Nec deficit alter, UNCLASSIFIED: 46
Nec deficit animus, COURAGE: 157
Nec degenero, GOODNESS: 17
Nec desit virtus, COURAGE: 158
Nec devius unquam, CONSISTENCY: 6
Ne cede arduis, ADVERSITY: 49;
PERSEVERANCE: 38
Ne cede malis, ADVERSITY: 50; LOCAL
GOVERNMENT: 236
Ne cede malis; sed contra,
ADVERSITY: 51
Nec elata, nec dejecta, EQUANIMITY: 13
NECESSITY, p. 539
Nec ferro, nec igne, FIRE: 9;
WEAPONS: 66
Nec ferro nec igni, FIRE: 10; LOCAL
GOVERNMENT: 237; WEAPONS: 67
Nec flatu, nec fluctu, WAVES: 1
Nec flectitur nec mutant,
STEADFASTNESS: 82
Nec fluctu, nec flatu, WAVES: 2
Nec gladio, nec arcu, WEAPONS: 68
Nec habeo, nec careo, nec curo,
POSSESSION: 16; TRADES: 24
Nec improvidus, PRUDENCE: 28
Nec invideo, nec despicio, ENVY: 8
Nec lusisse pudet, sed non incidere
lusum, DISGRACE: 12
Nec male notus eques, REPUTATION: 6
Nec me meminisse pigebit, MEMORY: 22
Nec me qui caetera vincit,
CONQUEST: 26
Nec metuas, nec optes, DESIRE: 14;
FEAR: 37
Nec minus fortiter, COURAGE: 159
Nec mireris homines mirabiliores,
GOODNESS: 18
Nec momentum sine linea,
UNCLASSIFIED: 47
Nec mons, nec subtrahit aer,
PERSEVERANCE: 39
Nec mutandus, nec metus,
CHANGE: 13; FEAR: 38
Nec obscura, nec ima, OBSCURITY: 7
Nec opprimere, nec opprimi,
OPPRESSION: 4
Nec otius [*sic*] nec altius, SPEED: 37
Nec parvis sisto, OBSCURITY: 8

Nec placida contenta quiete est, HAPPINESS: 48

Nec pluribus impar, EQUALITY: 6

Nec prece, nec pretio, REWARD: 20

Nec pretio, nec prece, REWARD: 21

Nec quaerere, nec spernere honorem, HONOR: 141

Nec quaerere honorem nec spernere, HONOR: 142

Nec rege, nec populo, sed utroque, PEOPLE: 3; ROYALTY: 55

Nec sinit esse feros, KNOWLEDGE: 52

Nec sorte, nec fato, FORTUNE: 84

Nec spe, nec metu, FEAR: 39; HOPE: 147

Nec spe nec metu, FEAR: 40; HOPE: 148

Nec sperno, nec timeo, FEAR: 41

Nec temere, nec timide, MODERATION: 24

Nec temere nec lente, PRUDENCE: 29

Nec tempore, nec fato, FORTUNE: 85

Nec te quaesiveris extra, SELF-RELIANCE: 10

Nec timeo, nec sperno, FEAR: 42

Nec timet, nec tumet, FEAR: 43

Nec timidè, nec temerè, FEAR: 44

Nec timidus, nec ferus, FEAR: 45; FIERCENESS: 7

Nec timidus nec ferus, FEAR: 46; FIERCENESS: 8

Nec triste, nec trepidum, FEAR: 47; SADNESS: 6

Nec tumidus, nec timidus, FEAR: 48

Ne cuiquam serviat ensis, WEAPONS: 69

Nec vi, nec astutia, FORCE: 10

Nec viribus nec numero, POWER: 13

Nec virtus nec copia desunt, LOCAL GOVERNMENT: 238; VIRTUE: 115

Nec virtus suprema fefellit, VIRTUE: 116

Nec vi standum, nec metu, FEAR: 49; FORCE: 11

Nec volenti, nec nolenti, WILLINGNESS: 5

Ne doubtero, FAITH: 176

Negata tentat iter via, WAY: 6

Ne incautus futuri, FUTURE, THE: 18; SCHOOL MOTTOES: 197

Ne jugu libron je la kovrilo, JUDGMENT: 12

Nell' armi e nelle lettere consiste la virtu, KNOWLEDGE: 53; POWER: 14; WEAPONS: 70

Neminem metue innocens, INNOCENCE: 11

Nemo me impune lacessit, PROVOCATION: 2

Nemo nisi Christus, CHRIST, JESUS: 59

Nemo sibi nascitur, INTER-RELATEDNESS: 3

Nemo sine crimine vivit, GUILT: 1

Nemo sine cruce beatus, CROSS, THE: 79; HAPPINESS: 49

Nemo solus sapit, WISDOM: 41

Ne m'oubliez, FORGETTING: 6

N. E. M. Q. O. (Non est mortale quod opto), DESIRE: 15

Ne nimis altus, LOFTINESS: 18

Ne nimium, MODERATION: 25

Ne obliviscaris, FORGETTING: 7

Ne oubliez, FORGETTING: 8

Ne parcas nec spernas, FAIRNESS: 10

Ne quid falsi, TRUTH: 59

Nescit abolere vetustas, PAST, THE: 6

Nescit amor fines, LOVE: 92

Nescit occasum, STARS: 27

Nescitur Christo, CHRIST, JESUS: 60

Nescit vox missa reverti, WORDS: 28

Ne supra, LIMITATION: 4

Ne supra modum sapere, MODERATION: 28; WISDOM: 42

Ne tenta vel perfice, ACCOMPLISHMENT: 11

Ne tentes aut perfice, ACCOMPLISHMENT: 12

Ne te quaesiveris extra, LIMITATION: 5

Netherlands, PROPER NAMES: 37

Ne timeas recte faciendo, FEAR: 50

Ne traverse pas le pont, LIMITATION: 6

Ne ultra, LIMITATION: 7; SCHOOL MOTTOES: 198

Never a backward step, STEADFASTNESS: 83

Never behind, LOCAL GOVERNMENT: 239; TIMELINESS: 7

Never check, LIMITATION: 8

Never despair, DESPAIR: 2

Never elated never dejected, EQUANIMITY: 14

Never fear, FEAR: 51

Never give in, PERSEVERANCE: 40; STEADFASTNESS: 84

Mottoes & Categories

Nil sine magno labore,
INDUSTRIOUSNESS: 136; SCHOOL
MOTTOES: 199

Nil sine numine, DIVINITY: 312;
SCHOOL MOTTOES: 200; STATE
MOTTOES: 35

Nil sistere contra, OPPOSITION: 7

Nil solidum, TRANSIENCE: 7

Nil temere, PRUDENCE: 31

Nil temere, neque timore, FEAR: 52;
PRUDENCE: 32

Nil temerè tenta, nil timidè,
PRUDENCE: 33

Nil tibi, POSSESSION: 17

Nil time, COURAGE: 161

Nil timeo, COURAGE: 162

Nil timere nec temere, COURAGE: 163

Nil veretur veritas, TRUTH: 61

Nil virtuti invisum, VIRTUE: 120

Nimand zonder, SOLITUDE: 3

Nimium ne crede sereno, TRUST: 89

Ni plus, ni moins, MODERATION: 29

Nisi Christus nemo, CHRIST, JESUS: 61

Nisi Dominus, DIVINITY: 313

Nisi paret imperat, AUTHORITY: 5;
OBEDIENCE: 8

Nisi per te, DIVINE GUIDANCE: 340

Nisi virtus vilior alga, VIRTUE: 121

Nitamur semper ad optima,
EFFORT: 22

Niti facere, experiri, EFFORT: 23

Nitimur et munitur, EFFORT: 24

Nitor donec supero, EFFORT: 25

Nitor in adversum, ADVERSITY: 55

Nobilis est ira leonis, ANGER: 5;
ANIMALS: 39; NOBILITY: 10

Nobilis ira, ANGER: 6; NOBILITY: 11

Nobilis ira leonis, ANGER: 7;
ANIMALS: 40; NOBILITY: 12

Nobilitas est sola virtus, NOBILITY: 13;
VIRTUE: 122

Nobilitas unica virtus, NOBILITY: 14;
VIRTUE: 123

Nobilitat, NOBILITY: 15

Nobilitatis virtus non stemma
character, NOBILITY: 16; VIRTUE: 124

NOBILITY, p. 540

Nobis habitatio felix, HOME: 13; LOCAL
GOVERNMENT: 244

Noblesse oblige, NOBILITY: 17

Nocentes prosequor, EVIL: 4

Nocet differre paratis,
PREPAREDNESS: 39

No country, no fatherland that does
not keep faith, COUNTRY: 53;
FIDELITY: 242

Noctes diesque, DARKNESS: 9; DAY: 7

Noctes diesque praesto, DAY: 8;
PREPAREDNESS: 40

Nocte volamus, DARKNESS: 10

Nodo firmo, SECURITY: 35

No force alters their fashion, FORCE: 12

No heart more true, FIDELITY: 243

Noli altum sapere, WISDOM: 43

Noli irritare leonem, ANIMALS: 41;
PROVOCATION: 3

Noli irritare leones, ANIMALS: 42;
PROVOCATION: 4

Noli mentiri, DECEPTION: 7

Noli me tangere, TOUCH: 2

Nolite cor opponere, FEELINGS: 22

Nolo servile capistrum, LEADERSHIP: 18

No mas, SATISFACTION: 4

Nomen extendere factis, DEEDS: 65;
NAME: 8

Nomine digna, NATIONAL MOTTOES: 16;
WORTHINESS: 38

Nomine et patriae asto,
PATRIOTISM: 22; STEADFASTNESS: 87

Non abest virtuti sors, FORTUNE: 87;
VIRTUE: 125

Non ad perniciem, DESTRUCTION: 6

Non alio libertas conservanda modo,
LIBERTY: 80

Non aliunde pendere, SELF-
RELIANCE: 11

Non aqua solum, WATER: 12

Non arbitrio popularis aurae, FAME: 17

Non arte sed Marte, WAR: 45

Non aspera juvant, ENJOYMENT: 21

Non astutia, CLEVERNESS: 6

Non cantu sed actu, ACTION: 15

Non cate sed caute, CAUTION: 28

Non cito nec tarde, SPEED: 38

Non civium ardor, PEOPLE: 4

Non credo tempori, TIME: 35;
TRUST: 90

Non crux, sed lux, CROSS, THE: 85;
LIGHT: 62

Non deerit alter aureus, FRUIT: 8

Non deest spes, HOPE: 149

Non deficit, WORTHINESS: 39

Non deficit alter, WORTHINESS: 40

Non degener, GOODNESS: 22
Non deludere, DECEPTION: 8
Non desistam, PERSEVERANCE: 41;
   STEADFASTNESS: 88
Non domo dominus, sed domino
   domus, HOME: 14
Non dormio, WAKEFULNESS: 5
Non dormit custos, WAKEFULNESS: 6
Non dormit qui custodit,
   WAKEFULNESS: 7
Non eget arcu, WEAPONS: 71
Non eget integer, PURITY: 12
Non eget jaculis, WEAPONS: 72
Non eget Mauri jaculis, WEAPONS: 73
Non eget Mauri jaculis neque arcu,
   WEAPONS: 74
Non ego sed gratia Dei, DIVINE
   GUIDANCE: 341; GRACE: 23
None is truly great but he that is truly
   good, GOODNESS: 23; GREATNESS: 7
Non est mortale quod opto, DESIRE: 16;
   IMMORTALITY: 6
Non est sine pulvere palma,
   VICTORY: 31
Non est vivere sed valere vita, HEALING
   and HEALTH: 19
None such, LOCAL GOVERNMENT: 245;
   UNIQUENESS: 4
Non extinguar, ENDURANCE: 43
Non fallor, DECEPTION: 9
Non fecimus ipsi, DEEDS: 66
Non fluctu nec flatu movetur,
   STEADFASTNESS: 89; WAVES: 3
Non fraude sed laude, HONOR: 145
Non frustra, PURPOSE: 15
Non generant aquilae columbas,
   BIRDS: 24; OFFSPRING: 3
Non gladio, sed gratia, KINDNESS: 17
Non haec sed me, UBIQUITY: 7
Non haec sine numine, DIVINITY: 315
Non his insignitus, WORTHINESS: 41
Non ignarus mali miseris succurrere
   disco, ASSISTANCE: 19; KINDNESS: 18
Non immemor beneficii,
   GRATITUDE: 13
Non inferiora, PURSUIT: 6
Non inferiora secutus, PURSUIT: 7
Non inferiora sequenda,
   ASPIRATION: 61
Non invita, FORCE: 13; LIFE: 25
Non invita Minerva, GENIUS: 4
Non jure deficit, RIGHTS: 7

Non leoni sed Deo, ANIMALS: 43;
   DIVINITY: 316
Non lumen effugio, LIGHT: 63
Non major alio non minor,
   EQUALITY: 7
Non melior patribus, ANCESTRY: 27
Non metuo, COURAGE: 164
Non mihi, non tibi, sed nobis, LOCAL
   GOVERNMENT: 246; SHARING: 3
Non mihi, sed Deo et regi,
   DIVINITY: 317; ROYALTY: 56
Non mihi commodus uni, SERVICE: 34
Non mihi Domine sed nomini tuo da
   gloriam, DIVINITY: 318
Non mihi sed patriae, COUNTRY: 54;
   PATRIOTISM: 23
Non mihi sed tibi gloria, GLORY: 40
Non minima sed magna prosequor,
   FOLLOWING: 9
Non ministrari sed ministrare, SCHOOL
   MOTTOES: 201; SERVICE: 35
Non minor est virtus quam quaerere,
   arte tueri, ART: 26; COURAGE: 165
Non minor est virtus quam quaerere
   parta tueri, COURAGE: 166;
   DEFENSE: 38
Non modo sed quomodo, MANNER: 5
Non morietur inultus, VENGEANCE: 5
Non moritur cujus fama vivit,
   DEATH: 70; FAME: 18
Non mortale quod opto,
   IMMORTALITY: 7
Non multa sed multum, MEASURE: 9
Non mutat fortuna genus, FORTUNE: 88
Non mutat genus solum, COUNTRY: 55
Non nisi bonis placere cupio,
   GOODNESS: 24
Non nobis, UNSELFISHNESS: 4
Non nobis, Domine, non nobis, sed
   nomini tuo da gloriam,
   DIVINITY: 319
Non nobis Domine, UNCLASSIFIED: 48
Non nobis esto [sic] Latin,
   UNCLASSIFIED: 49
Non nobis nascimur, UNSELFISHNESS: 5
Non nobis nati, UNSELFISHNESS: 6
Non nobis sed communitati, LOCAL
   GOVERNMENT: 247; UNSELFISHNESS: 7
Non nobis sed omnibus, LOCAL
   GOVERNMENT: 248; UNSELFISHNESS: 8
Non nobis solum, sed toti mundo nati,
   UNSELFISHNESS: 11

Non nobis solum nati,
UNSELFISHNESS: 12
Non nobis solum nati sumus,
UNSELFISHNESS: 13
Non nobis tantum nati,
UNSELFISHNESS: 14
Non nostraque Deo, DIVINITY: 320
Non numero horas nisi serenas,
TIME: 36
Non obest virtute sors, VIRTUE: 126
Non oblitus, FORGETTING: 9
Non obliviscar, FORGETTING: 10
Non obscura nec ima, OBSCURITY: 9
Non obstante Deo, DIVINE
GUIDANCE: 342
Non omnia possumus omnes,
ABILITY: 20; LIMITATION: 9
Non omnibus dormio, WAKEFULNESS: 8
Non omnibus nati, BIRTH: 2
Non omnis fert omnia tellus,
AGRICULTURE: 3
Non omnis frangar, DESTRUCTION: 7
Non omnis moriar, DEATH: 71;
IMMORTALITY: 8
Non opes, sed ingenium, MIND: 39;
PROSPERITY: 30
Non ostento, sed ostendo,
BOASTFULNESS: 5
Non parvum est seipsum noscere, SELF-
KNOWLEDGE: 8
Non pas l'ouvrage, mais l'ouvrier,
INDUSTRIOUSNESS: 137; PEOPLE: 5
Non praeda, sed victoria, VICTORY: 32
Non progredi est regredi,
IMPROVEMENT: 28; LOCAL
GOVERNMENT: 250; SCHOOL
MOTTOES: 202
Non providentia sed victoria,
VICTORY: 33
Non quam diu sed quam bene,
WORTHINESS: 42
Non quo, sed quo modo, MANNER: 6
Non rapui, sed recepi, GIFTS and
GIVING: 23
Non recedam, STEADFASTNESS: 90
Non recedet malum a domo ingrati et
seditiosi, EVIL: 5
Non recuso laborem,
INDUSTRIOUSNESS: 138; SCHOOL
MOTTOES: 203
Non revertar inultus, VENGEANCE: 6
Non robore, sed spe, HOPE: 150

Non robore, sed vi, FORCE: 14
Non sanz droict, LOCAL
GOVERNMENT: 251; RIGHTS: 8
Non semper sub umbra, SHADE: 1
Non semper viret, FLOURISHING: 60
Non servit sed laborat,
INDUSTRIOUSNESS: 139
Non sibi, UNSELFISHNESS: 15
Non sibi, cunctis, UNSELFISHNESS: 16
Non sibi, patriae, COUNTRY: 56;
PATRIOTISM: 24
Non sibi, sed patriae, COUNTRY: 57;
PATRIOTISM: 25
Non sibi, sed patriae natus,
COUNTRY: 58; PATRIOTISM: 26
Non sibi sed aliis, STATE MOTTOES: 36;
UNSELFISHNESS: 17
Non sibi sed toti, LOCAL
GOVERNMENT: 252;
UNSELFISHNESS: 18
Non sibi solum, UNSELFISHNESS: 19
Non sine, SATISFACTION: 5
Non sine anchora, STEADFASTNESS: 91
Non sine causa, CAUSATION: 5
Non sine Deo, DIVINITY: 321
Non sine industria,
INDUSTRIOUSNESS: 140
Non sine jure, RIGHTS: 9
Non sine labore, INDUSTRIOUSNESS: 141
Non sine numine, DIVINITY: 322
Non sine periculo, DANGER: 13
Non sine praeda, REWARD: 22
Non sine pulvere palma,
INDUSTRIOUSNESS: 142; REWARD: 23
Non sine sente rosa, IRONY: 1
Non sine usu, USEFULNESS: 4
Non sino, sed dono, GIFTS and
GIVING: 24
Non sola mortali luce gradior, DIVINE
GUIDANCE: 343
Non solum armis, WEAPONS: 75
Non solum ingenii, verum etiam
virtutis, ABILITY: 21; LOCAL
GOVERNMENT: 253; SCHOOL
MOTTOES: 204; VIRTUE: 127
Non solum pane, NOURISHMENT: 4
Non sufficit orbis, EARTH: 8;
SATISFACTION: 6
Non temere, PRUDENCE: 34
Non temere, sed fortiter, AUDACITY: 78
Non terra, sed aquis, WATER: 13
Non timeo, sed caveo, CAUTION: 29

Mottoes & Categories

Non timere sed fortiter, AUDACITY: 79

Non tua te moveant, sed publica vota,
UNSELFISHNESS: 20

Non vi, sed virtute, VIRTUE: 128

Non vi, sed voluntate, FORCE: 15

Non vi, virtute, VIRTUE: 129

Non videri, sed esse, INTEGRITY: 31

Non vidi justum derelictum,
RIGHTEOUSNESS: 11

Non vi sed mente, FORCE: 16; MIND: 40

Non vox, sed votum, DESIRE: 17

Norma tuta veritas, TRUTH: 62

North to the future, FUTURE, THE: 19;
STATE MOTTOES: 37

Nos aspera juvant, ADVERSITY: 56

Nosce teipsum, SELF-KNOWLEDGE: 9

No sine periculo, SECURITY: 36

Nos non nobis, UNSELFISHNESS: 21

Nos nostraque Deo, DIVINITY: 323

Nos pascit Deus, DIVINE GUIDANCE: 344

Nosse Deum et bene posse mori
sapientia summa est, DEATH: 72;
DIVINITY: 324; WISDOM: 44

Nostra quae fecimus,
ACCOMPLISHMENT: 13

Nostre roy et nostre foy, FAITH: 177;
ROYALTY: 57

Nostrum viret robur, LOCAL
GOVERNMENT: 254; STRANGER: 8;
STRENGTH: 95

Not always so, CHANGE: 14

Notandi sunt tibi mores, MANNERS: 10

Not for ourselves alone, LOCAL
GOVERNMENT: 255;
UNSELFISHNESS: 22

Nothing hazard, nothing have, RISK: 6

Nothing venture, nothing have, RISK: 7

Nothing without labor,
INDUSTRIOUSNESS: 143; LOCAL
GOVERNMENT: 256

Not in vain, PURPOSE: 16

Not laws of man but laws of God,
DIVINE GUIDANCE: 345; LAW: 34

Not quantity —but quality,
EXCELLENCE: 12; SCHOOL
MOTTOES: 205

Not rashly, nor with fear, FEAR: 53;
PRUDENCE: 35

Not the last, STATUS: 6

Not too much, MEASURE: 10

N'oublie, FORGETTING: 11

N'oublies, FORGETTING: 12

N'oubliez, FORGETTING: 13

NOURISHMENT, p. 542

Nourissez l'espèrance, HOPE: 151

Nous maintiendrons, MAINTENANCE: 4

Nous travaillerons en esperance,
HOPE: 152; INDUSTRIOUSNESS: 144

Novus ordo seclorum, NATIONAL
MOTTOES: 17; ORDER: 5

Now thus!, MANNER: 7

Now thus, now thus, MANNER: 8

Nox nulla secuta est, DARKNESS: 11

N. R. M. A. D. I. (Non recedet malum
a domo ingrati), EVIL: 6

Nubem eripiam, SHADE: 2

Nul chef-d'oeuvre sans travail,
INDUSTRIOUSNESS: 145

Nulla deditio, PERSEVERANCE: 42;
STEADFASTNESS: 92

Nulla dies sine linea,
INDUSTRIOUSNESS: 146

Nulla fraus tuta latebris,
DECEPTION: 10

Nulla inimicus ero, HOSTILITY: 15

Nulla pallescere culpa, INNOCENCE: 14

Nulla retrorsum, STEADFASTNESS: 93

Nulla rosa sine spinis, FLORA: 26;
IRONY: 2

Nulla salus bello, WAR: 46

Nulla temerata nube, PROFANITY: 1

Nulla vestigia retrorsum,
STEADFASTNESS: 94

Nulli praeda, PRIDE: 7

Nulli praeda sumus, PRIDE: 8

Nullis inimica ero, HOSTILITY: 16

Nullius addictus jurare in verba
magistri, LIBERTY: 81

Nullius in verba, LIBERTY: 82

Nullius in verba magistri, LIBERTY: 83

Numen et lumen effugio,
DIVINITY: 325; LIGHT: 64

Numen et omnia, PROVIDENCE: 11

Numen flumenque, DIVINITY: 326;
SCHOOL MOTTOES: 206

Numero, pondere, et mensura,
MEASURE: 11

Numine, DIVINITY: 327

Numine et arcu, DIVINE
GUIDANCE: 346; WEAPONS: 76

Numine et virtute, DIVINE
GUIDANCE: 347; VIRTUE: 130

Numini et patriae asto, COUNTRY: 59;
DIVINITY: 328

Nunc aut nunquam, PRESENT, THE: 7
Nunc cinis, ante rosa, FLORA: 27;
 TRANSIENCE: 8
Nunc et semper, PRESENT, THE: 8
Nuncia pacis, PEACE: 27
Nuncia pacis oliva, PEACE: 28
Nunc mihi grata quies, REST: 14
Nunc mihi nunc alii, DEDICATION: 8
Nunc ut olim, PRESENT, THE: 9
Nunquam deorsum, FATE: 24
Nunquam dormio, WAKEFULNESS: 9
Nunquam fallentis termes olivae,
 FLORA: 28
Nunquam ingratus, GRATITUDE: 14
Nunquam libertas gratior, LIBERTY: 84
Nunquam mutans, STEADFASTNESS: 95
Nunquam nisi honorificentissimè,
 HONOR: 146
Nunquam non fidelis, FIDELITY: 244
Nunquam non paratus,
 PREPAREDNESS: 41; SCHOOL
 MOTTOES: 207
Nunquam obliviscar, FORGETTING: 14
Nunquam praeponens, FAIRNESS: 11
Nunquam retrorsum,
 STEADFASTNESS: 96
Nunquam senescit, AGE: 5
Nunquam tentes aut perfice,
 ACCOMPLISHMENT: 14; ATTEMPT: 4;
 SUCCESS: 7
Nunquam victus, MERCY: 27
Ny dessux, ny dessoux, STATUS: 7

O

Ob ducem, ob patriam, COUNTRY: 60;
 LEADERSHIP: 19
Obdurum adversus urgentia,
 OPPRESSION: 5
OBEDIENCE, p. 542
Obey and rule, OBEDIENCE: 9
Oblier ne puis, FORGETTING: 15
Obligatam redde Jove, DIVINITY: 329
Obliviscar, FORGETTING: 16
Obliviscaris, FORGETTING: 17
Ob patriam vulnera passi,
 COUNTRY: 61; PATRIOTISM: 27
OBSCURITY, p. 543
Obsequens non servilis, COURTESY: 3
Obsequio non viribus, COURTESY: 4;
 FORCE: 17
Observe, VISION: 12

Obstacles are things to be overcome,
 SCHOOL MOTTOES: 208
Obstando supera, VICTORY: 34
Obsta principiis, PRINCELINESS: 7
Occasionem cognosce, OPPORTUNITY: 5
Occultus non extinctus, OBSCURITY: 10
Occurrent nubes, SHADE: 3
Oculi mei semper respiciunt ad
 Dominum, DIVINITY: 330
Oculis in coelum, LOCAL
 GOVERNMENT: 257; PARADISE: 44
Odi profanum, PROFANITY: 2
Odor vitae, LIFE: 26
OFFICE, p. 544
Officio et fide, DUTY: 23; FIDELITY: 245
Officium praesto, DUTY: 24
OFFSPRING, p. 544
Ofner na ofno angau, FEAR: 54
Of old I hold, POSSESSION: 18
Ofwn yr arglwydd, DIVINITY: 331
O Gott gewähr was ich begehr, DIVINE
 GIFTS: 42
Ohne Furcht, COURAGE: 167
Ohne Hast, aber ohne Rast,
 PERSEVERANCE: 43
Ohne Rast zum Ziel,
 PERSEVERANCE: 44
Ohn Gottes Gunst Alles umsonst,
 DIVINE GUIDANCE: 348; GRACE: 24
Old age is a virtue, AGE: 6
O lector salve celi pateant tibi valve,
 LOCAL GOVERNMENT: 258;
 PARADISE: 45
Olet et sanat, FRAGRANCE: 6; HEALING
 and HEALTH: 20
Olim fecimus, PAST, THE: 8
Olim florebat, FLOURISHING: 61
Olim sic erat, PAST, THE: 9
O Maria, ora pro nobis, DIVINE
 GUIDANCE: 349
Omine secundo, FORTUNE: 89
Omne bene, HAPPINESS: 51
Omne bonum ab alto, GOODNESS: 25
Omne bonum Dei donum, DIVINE
 GIFTS: 43
Omne bonum desuper, DIVINE
 GIFTS: 44
Omne bonum superne, GOODNESS: 26
Omne meum, nihil meum,
 POSSESSION: 19
Omnes arbusta juvant, ENJOYMENT: 22
Omnes benevolentia, WILL: 3

Mottoes & Categories

Omnes fremant licet dicam quod
sentio, DIRECTNESS: 13

Omne solum forti patria, COUNTRY: 62;
COURAGE: 168

Omne solum patria, COUNTRY: 63

Omne solum viro patria est,
COUNTRY: 64; HOME: 15

Omne tulit punctum qui miscuit utile
dulci, USEFULNESS: 5

Omnia bene, HAPPINESS: 52

Omnia bona bonis, GOODNESS: 27;
LOCAL GOVERNMENT: 259

Omnia bona desuper, DIVINE GIFTS: 45

Omnia certa fac, CERTAINTY: 4

Omnia conando docilis solertia vincit,
ABILITY: 22

Omnia cum Deo, DIVINITY: 332

Omnia cum Deo et nihil sine eo,
DIVINITY: 333

Omnia cum Deo et tempore,
DIVINITY: 334; TIME: 37

Omnia cum tempore, TIME: 38

Omnia debeo Deo, DIVINE
GUIDANCE: 350

Omnia Deo confido, DIVINITY: 335

Omnia Deo juvante, DIVINE
GUIDANCE: 351

Omnia Deo pendent, DIVINE
GUIDANCE: 352

Omnia desuper, DIVINE GIFTS: 46

Omnia ex voluntate Dei, DIVINE
GUIDANCE: 353

Omnia fert aetas, TIME: 39

Omnia firmat, SECURITY: 37

Omnia fortitudine vincit,
COURAGE: 169

Omnia fortunae committo,
FORTUNE: 90

Omnia illi adsunt bona quem penes est
virtus, VIRTUE: 131

Omnia in Christo, CHRIST, JESUS: 62

Omnia in nihil, INSIGNIFICANCE: 1

Omnia mei dona Dei, DIVINE GIFTS: 47

Omnia mihi Christus, CHRIST, JESUS: 63

Omnia mundana fluxa, EARTH: 9;
TRANSIENCE: 9

Omnia mundana turbida, EARTH: 10

Omnia orta occidunt et aucta
senescunt, AGE: 7; TRANSIENCE: 10

Omnia probate, quod bonum est
tenete, GOODNESS: 28

Omnia pro bono, GOODNESS: 29

Omnia providentia Dei, DIVINE
GUIDANCE: 354

Omnia Providentiae committo,
PROVIDENCE: 12

Omnia recte, RIGHTEOUSNESS: 12

Omnia relinquit servare rempublicam,
COUNTRY: 65; PATRIOTISM: 28

Omnia si perdas, famam servare
memento, REPUTATION: 7

Omnia subjecisti sub pedibus—oves et
boves, ANIMALS: 44

Omnia superat diligentia,
DILIGENCE: 46

Omnia superat virtus, VIRTUE: 132

Omnia vanitas, INSIGNIFICANCE: 2

Omnia vincit amor, LOVE: 95

Omnia vincit labor,
INDUSTRIOUSNESS: 147

Omnia vincit veritas, TRUTH: 63

Omnibus amicus, FRIENDSHIP: 45

Omnibus optimus, GOODNESS: 30

Omni liber metu, COURAGE: 170

Omnis a deo potestas, DIVINE
GUIDANCE: 355; POWER: 15

Omni secundo, PROSPERITY: 31

Omnis fortunae paratus,
PREPAREDNESS: 42

Omnium rerum vicissitudo,
CHANGE: 15

Omni violentia major, STRENGTH: 96

One and all, LOCAL GOVERNMENT: 260;
UNITY: 53

One faith, one king, one law,
FAITH: 178; LAW: 35; ROYALTY: 58;
UNITY: 54

One heart, one way, HEART: 10; LOCAL
GOVERNMENT: 261; UNITY: 55

One in Christ Jesus, CHRIST, JESUS: 64;
SCHOOL MOTTOES: 209

One on God's side is a majority,
PIETY: 13

One people, one nation, one destiny,
NATIONAL MOTTOES: 18; UNITY: 56

One Zambia, one nation, NATIONAL
MOTTOES: 19; UNITY: 57

Oni heuir ni fedir, AGRICULTURE: 4;
LOCAL GOVERNMENT: 262

On in the right, RECTITUDE: 49

On things transitory resteth no glory,
GLORY: 41; TRANSIENCE: 11

Onus sub honore, HONOR: 147

Onward, ADVANCE: 37;
  IMPROVEMENT: 29; LOCAL
  GOVERNMENT: 263
Onward ever, ADVANCE: 38
Onwards, upwards, ASPIRATION: 62
Onward upward, ASPIRATION: 63;
  TRUTH: 64
On with you, ADVANCE: 39
Opera bona effulgent, DEEDS: 67;
  SHINING: 23
Opera Dei mirifica, DIVINITY: 336
Opera mundi, INDUSTRIOUSNESS: 148
Opes consilium parit, LOCAL
  GOVERNMENT: 264; PROSPERITY: 32;
  WISDOM: 45
Opes industria parit,
  INDUSTRIOUSNESS: 149;
  PROSPERITY: 33
Ope solis et umbrae, SHADE: 4; SUN: 6
Opes parit industria, DILIGENCE: 47;
  LOCAL GOVERNMENT: 265;
  PROSPERITY: 34
Opes regum, corda subditorum,
  CROWN: 17; PROSPERITY: 35
Opiferque per orbem dicor,
  ASSISTANCE: 20
Opima spolia, PROSPERITY: 36
Opinionem vincere omnium,
  UNCLASSIFIED: 50
Opitulante Deo, DIVINE GUIDANCE: 356
O. P. N. J. C. (Ora pro nobis Jesu
  Christe), DIVINE GUIDANCE: 357
Oportet vivere, LIFE: 27
OPPORTUNITY, p. 545
Opportunity for all, OPPORTUNITY: 6;
  SCHOOL MOTTOES: 210
Opportunity through training,
  OPPORTUNITY: 7; SCHOOL
  MOTTOES: 211
OPPOSITION, p. 546
OPPRESSION, p. 547
Optima est veritas, TRUTH: 65
Optima quae que honesto, HONOR: 148
Optima revelatio stella, SPORT: 3;
  STARS: 29
Optima sapientia probitas,
  RECTITUDE: 50; WISDOM: 46
Optima sperando spiro, HOPE: 153
Optime merenti, WORTHINESS: 43
Optime merito de rege,
  WORTHINESS: 44

Optime quod opportune,
  OPPORTUNITY: 8
Optimum est aliena frui insania,
  IMPROVEMENT: 30
Optimum pati, SUFFERING: 5
Optimum quod evenit, GOODNESS: 31
Optimum quod primum, PRIMACY: 5
Optimum vix satis, WORTHINESS: 45
Optimus est qui optime facit,
  WORTHINESS: 46
Optivo cognomine crescit,
  FLOURISHING: 62; NAME: 9
Opus nostrum dirige, GUIDANCE: 22;
  LOCAL GOVERNMENT: 266
Ora e sempre, TIME: 40
Ora et ara, DIVINE GUIDANCE: 358;
  LOCAL GOVERNMENT: 267
Ora et labora, DIVINE GUIDANCE: 359;
  INDUSTRIOUSNESS: 150
Orando laborando, DIVINE
  GUIDANCE: 360;
  INDUSTRIOUSNESS: 151; SCHOOL
  MOTTOES: 212
Orando te aspiciam, DIVINE
  GUIDANCE: 361
Orate et vigilate, DIVINE
  GUIDANCE: 362
Orbe circum cincto, EARTH: 11
Order, freedom, justice, JUSTICE: 93;
  LIBERTY: 85; NATIONAL MOTTOES: 20;
  ORDER: 6
ORDER, p. 547
Ore lego, corde credo, FAITH: 179
'Or glory', GLORY: 42
Oriens sylva, FLORA: 29
ORIGIN, p. 548
Ornat fortem prudentia,
  COURAGE: 171; PRUDENCE: 36
Ornatur radix fronde, DECORATION: 3
Orna verum, TRUTH: 66
Oro y plata, PROSPERITY: 37; STATE
  MOTTOES: 38
Orthes, PROPER NAMES: 39
Ostendo non ostento, BOASTFULNESS: 6
Otium cum dignitate, REST: 15
Otium ex labore,
  INDUSTRIOUSNESS: 152; REST: 16
Ou bien ou rien, WORTHINESS: 47
Oublier ne puis, FORGETTING: 18
Ou le sort appelle, FATE: 25
Où ne monterai-je pas?, RISING: 9

Our country is the world—our
  countrymen are all mankind,
  HUMANITY: 9; MANLINESS: 4
Our hope is on high, HOPE: 154
Our lamb has conquered: Let us
  follow him, FOLLOWING: 10; SCHOOL
  MOTTOES: 213
Our liberties we prize and our rights
  we will maintain, LIBERTY: 86;
  RIGHTS: 10; STATE MOTTOES: 39
Ours the task eternal,
  INDUSTRIOUSNESS: 153; SCHOOL
  MOTTOES: 214
Our trust is in God, DIVINITY: 337;
  TRUST: 91
Out of darkness cometh light,
  DARKNESS: 12; LIGHT: 65; LOCAL
  GOVERNMENT: 268
Out of many, one people, NATIONAL
  MOTTOES: 21; UNITY: 58
Over fork over, UNCLASSIFIED: 51

P

Pace et bello paratus,
  PREPAREDNESS: 43; WAR: 47
Pacem, sed coronatam pacem,
  CROWN: 18; PEACE: 29
Pacem amo, LOVE: 96; PEACE: 30
Pace vel bello, WAR: 48
Pacificum fert conjugium
  praenuncium pacis, PEACE: 31
Pacis, PEACE: 32
Pacis nuncia, PEACE: 33
Paix, travail, patrie,
  INDUSTRIOUSNESS: 154; NATIONAL
  MOTTOES: 22; PATRIOTISM: 29;
  PEACE: 34
Paix et peu, PEACE: 35
Palladia fama, FAME: 19
Palma non sine pulvere,
  INDUSTRIOUSNESS: 155; REWARD: 24
Palma virtuti, REWARD: 25;
  VIRTUE: 133
Pandite, EMERGENCE: 3
Pandite, coelestes portae, PARADISE: 46
Pannus mihi panis, COMMERCE: 3;
  LOCAL GOVERNMENT: 269
P. A. O. V. E. (Pietas ad omnia utilis
  est), PIETY: 14
PARADISE, p. 548
Paradisus in sole, PARADISE: 47; SUN: 7

Par ardua liberi, ADVERSITY: 57;
  LIBERTY: 87
Paratae servire, SCHOOL MOTTOES: 216;
  SERVICE: 36
Parat et curat, CAUTION: 30;
  PREPAREDNESS: 44
Paratus, PREPAREDNESS: 45
Paratus ad aethera, PARADISE: 48
Paratus ad arma, PREPAREDNESS: 46;
  WAR: 49
Paratus et fidelis, FIDELITY: 246;
  PREPAREDNESS: 47
Paratus sum, PREPAREDNESS: 48
Parat usum, PREPAREDNESS: 49
Parce qu'il me plaît, ENJOYMENT: 23
Parcere prostratis, MERCY: 28
Parcere subjectis, MERCY: 29
Parcere subjectis et debellare superbos,
  MERCY: 30
Par ce signe à Azincourt, SIGN: 5
Par commerce, COMMERCE: 4
Par Dieu est mon tout, DIVINE
  GUIDANCE: 363
Pareo, non servo, OBEDIENCE: 10
PARENTS, p. 552
Parere subjectus, OBEDIENCE: 11
Pares cum paribus, SILENCE: 14;
  SIMILARITY: 2
Par fermesse du quesne, STRENGTH: 97
Par fluctus portui, WAVES: 4
Pari animo, EQUANIMITY: 15
Paritur bello, WAR: 50
Paritur pax bello, PEACE: 36; WAR: 51
Par la grace et par les armes,
  GRACE: 25; WEAPONS: 77
Par l'amour et la fidélité envers la
  patrie, COUNTRY: 66; FIDELITY: 247;
  LOVE: 97; PATRIOTISM: 30
Par la volonté de Dieu, DIVINE
  GUIDANCE: 364
Parle bien, WORDS: 29
Parle bien ou parle rien, WORDS: 30
Parlez bien, ou ne parlez rien,
  WORDS: 31
Par loi et droit, LAW: 36
Par negotiis neque supra, STATUS: 8
Par pari, EQUALITY: 8
Par pari refero, UNCLASSIFIED: 52
Par sit fortuna labori,
  INDUSTRIOUSNESS: 156; SUCCESS: 8
Parta labore quies,
  INDUSTRIOUSNESS: 157; REST: 17

Parta tueri, ACQUISITION: 5;
 DEFENSE: 39
Par ternis suppar, MEASURE: 12
Parum sufficit, SATISFACTION: 7
Parva contemnimus, CONTEMPT: 5
Par valeur, COURAGE: 172
Parva seges satis est, HARVEST: 5
Par viribus virtus, VIRTUE: 134
Passant cressant en honneur,
 HONOR: 149
Passez avant, ADVANCE: 40
Pass forward, ADVANCE: 41
Passibus aequis, WALKING: 4
Passibus citis sed aequis, WALKING: 5
Passus rege meos, GUIDANCE: 23
PAST, THE, p. 553
Paterni nominis patrimonium,
 ANCESTRY: 28
Paternis suppar, ANCESTRY: 29
Paterno robore tutus, ANCESTRY: 30
Patet ingeniis campus, ABILITY: 23;
 OPPORTUNITY: 9
PATIENCE, p. 554
Patience, PATIENCE: 20
Patience and resolution, PATIENCE: 21
Patience makes everything light,
 PATIENCE: 22
Patience passe par tout, PATIENCE: 23
Patience passe science,
 KNOWLEDGE: 54; PATIENCE: 24
Patiens, PATIENCE: 25
Patiens pulveris atque solis,
 PATIENCE: 26; SUN: 8
Patienter, PATIENCE: 27
Patienter et constanter, PATIENCE: 28;
 STEADFASTNESS: 97
Patientia casus exsuperat omnes,
 PATIENCE: 29
Patientia et magnanimitas,
 COURAGE: 173; PATIENCE: 30
Patientia et perseverantia,
 PATIENCE: 31; PERSEVERANCE: 45
Patientia et perseverantia cum
 magnanimitate, PATIENCE: 32;
 PERSEVERANCE: 46
Patientia et spe, HOPE: 155;
 PATIENCE: 33
Patientia victrix, PATIENCE: 34;
 VICTORY: 35
Patientiâ vinces, PATIENCE: 35
Patientia vincit, PATIENCE: 36
Patientia vincit omnes, PATIENCE: 37

Patientia vincit omnia, PATIENCE: 38
Patientia vinco, PATIENCE: 39
Patiently persevere, PERSEVERANCE: 47
Patior, potior, ENDURANCE: 44;
 ENJOYMENT: 24
Patior et spero, HOPE: 156;
 SUFFERING: 6
Patior ut potior, ENDURANCE: 45;
 ENJOYMENT: 25
Patitur qui vincit, SUFFERING: 7
Patria cara, carior fides, COUNTRY: 67;
 FAITH: 180
Patria cara, carior libertas,
 COUNTRY: 68; LIBERTY: 88
Patriae et Deo sursum deorsum,
 COUNTRY: 69; PATRIOTISM: 31
Patriae et religioni fidelis,
 COUNTRY: 70; FIDELITY: 248;
 RELIGION: 14
Patriae fidelis, COUNTRY: 71;
 FIDELITY: 249; PATRIOTISM: 32
Patriae fidus, COUNTRY: 72;
 FIDELITY: 250; PATRIOTISM: 33
Patriae infelici fidelis, COUNTRY: 73;
 FIDELITY: 251; PATRIOTISM: 34
Patriae non sibi, COUNTRY: 74;
 PATRIOTISM: 35
Patria fidelis, COUNTRY: 75
Patriam amo, COUNTRY: 76; LOVE: 98;
 PATRIOTISM: 36
Patriam hinc sustinet, COUNTRY: 77;
 PATRIOTISM: 37
Patria veritas fides, COUNTRY: 78;
 FAITH: 181; PATRIOTISM: 38;
 TRUTH: 67
Patrie est où bien on est, COUNTRY: 79
Patriis virtutibus, VIRTUE: 135
PATRIOTISM, p. 556
Pauca suspexi, pauciora despexi,
 ADMIRATION: 2
Paulatim, MEASURE: 13
Paullatim sed firmiter,
 GRADUALNESS: 4; SCHOOL
 MOTTOES: 217
Pauper non in spe, HOPE: 157
Pauper sed non in spe, HOPE: 158
Pauperum solatio, ASSISTANCE: 21;
 KINDNESS: 19
Pawb yn ôl ei arfer, TRADITION: 3
Pax, PEACE: 37
Pax, copia, sapientia, PEACE: 38;
 PROSPERITY: 38; WISDOM: 47

Per coeli favorem, PARADISE: 49

Per constanza et speranza,
FIDELITY: 253; HOPE: 160

Per crucem ad castra, CROSS, THE: 87;
PARADISE: 50

Per crucem ad coelum, CROSS, THE: 88

Per crucem ad coronam, CROSS,
THE: 89; CROWN: 19

Per crucem ad lucem, CROSS, THE: 90;
LIGHT: 66

Per crucem ad stellas, CROSS, THE: 91;
PARADISE: 51

Per crucem confido, CONFIDENCE: 15;
CROSS, THE: 92

Percussa resurgo, REBIRTH: 16

Percussus elevor, REBIRTH: 17

Per damna per caedes, ADVERSITY: 67;
SUFFERING: 8

Per Dei providentiam, DIVINE
GUIDANCE: 367

Per Deum et ferrum obtinui, DIVINE
GUIDANCE: 368; WEAPONS: 79

Per Deum meum transilio murum,
DIVINE GUIDANCE: 369

Perduret probitas, HONESTY: 32

Per ecclesiam ad coelum, PARADISE: 52;
RELIGION: 15

Perenne sub polo nihil, TRANSIENCE: 12

PERFECTION, p. 570

Perfero, LOCAL GOVERNMENT: 270;
PERSEVERANCE: 48

Per ferrum obtinui, POSSESSION: 20;
WEAPONS: 80

Per fidem et constantiam, FAITH: 182

Per fidem et patientiam, FAITH: 183

Per fidem omnia, FAITH: 184

Per fidem vinco, FAITH: 185

Per fluctus ad oram, WAVES: 5

Perforatus, UNCLASSIFIED: 53

Per funera vitam, DEATH: 74;
REASON: 14

Perge coepisti, ACTION: 17;
ADVANCE: 43

Perge et valeas, ADVANCE: 44;
SUCCESS: 9

Perge sed caute, ADVANCE: 45

Pergo sursum, ADVANCE: 46

Periculum fortitudine evasi,
FORTITUDE: 25

Per ignem ferris vicimus,
CONQUEST: 27

Per ignem per gladium, FIRE: 11;
WEAPONS: 81

Periissem, ni per-issem,
PERSEVERANCE: 49

Periissemus, nisi perstitissemus,
PERSEVERANCE: 50

Periissemus nisi per-iissemus,
PERSEVERANCE: 51

Per il suo contrario, OPPOSITION: 8

Perimus licitis, DEATH: 75; LAW: 38

Per incerta certus amor, LOVE: 100

Per industriam, INDUSTRIOUSNESS: 158

Perit ut vivat, DEATH: 76; REASON: 15

Per Jesum Christum, CHRIST, JESUS: 65;
SCHOOL MOTTOES: 219

Per juga, per fluvios, ADVERSITY: 68

Per lucem ac tenebras mea sidera
sanguine surgent, DARKNESS: 13;
LIGHT: 67; RIGHTS: 11; STARS: 31

Per lumen scientiae viam invenient
populi, KNOWLEDGE: 55; SCHOOL
MOTTOES: 220; WAY: 7

PERMANENCE, p. 570

Per mare, SEA: 18

Per mare, per terram, SEA: 19

Per mare, per terras, SEA: 20

Per mare et per terram, LOCAL
GOVERNMENT: 271; SEA: 21

Per mare per ecclesiam, LOCAL
GOVERNMENT: 272; SEA: 22

Per mille ardua, ADVERSITY: 69

Permitte caetera divis, DIVINITY: 338

Per mortem vinco, DEATH: 77

Per multos annos, TIME: 41

Pernicibus alis, SPEED: 39

Per orbem, EARTH: 12

Per pericula ad decus ire juvat,
ADVERSITY: 70; GLORY: 44; LOCAL
GOVERNMENT: 273

Perrumpo, VICTORY: 37

Per saxa per ignes, FIRE: 12

Per saxa per ignes fortiter et recte,
COURAGE: 174; FIRE: 13;
RECTITUDE: 51

Per scientiam ad salutem publicam,
HEALING and HEALTH: 21; SCHOOL
MOTTOES: 221

PERSECUTION, p. 570

Per se, SELF-DETERMINATION: 3

Per se valens, STRENGTH: 98

Persevera, PERSEVERANCE: 52

Mottoes & Categories

Persevera Deoque confido, FAITH: 186;
  PERSEVERANCE: 53
PERSEVERANCE, p. 570
Persevera et vince, CONQUEST: 28;
  PERSEVERANCE: 54
Perseverance, PERSEVERANCE: 55
Perseverando, PERSEVERANCE: 56;
  STATE MOTTOES: 40
Perseverando et cavendo, CAUTION: 31;
  PERSEVERANCE: 57
Perseverantia, PERSEVERANCE: 58
Perseverantia ad finem optatum,
  PERSEVERANCE: 59
Perseverantia dabitur,
  PERSEVERANCE: 60
Perseverantia et cura quies,
  DILIGENCE: 48; PERSEVERANCE: 61;
  REST: 19
Perseverantia et labore,
  INDUSTRIOUSNESS: 159;
  PERSEVERANCE: 62
Perseverantia industria et fidelitas,
  FIDELITY: 254;
  INDUSTRIOUSNESS: 160;
  PERSEVERANCE: 63
Perseverantia omnia vincit,
  CONQUEST: 29; PERSEVERANCE: 64
Perseverantia palma,
  PERSEVERANCE: 65
Perseverantia palmam obtinebit,
  PERSEVERANCE: 66; REWARD: 26
Perseverantia victor,
  PERSEVERANCE: 67; VICTORY: 38
Perseverantia vincit, CONQUEST: 30;
  LOCAL GOVERNMENT: 274;
  PERSEVERANCE: 68; RESTRAINT: 1
Perseveranti dabitur,
  PERSEVERANCE: 69
Persevere, LOCAL GOVERNMENT: 275;
  PERSEVERANCE: 70
Persevere in hope, HOPE: 161;
  PERSEVERANCE: 71
Persevero, PERSEVERANCE: 72
Per sinum Codanum, SEA: 23
Persist, PERSEVERANCE: 73
Perspicax, audax, AUDACITY: 80;
  LIVELINESS: 4
Perspicere quam ulcisci, THOUGHT: 17;
  VENGEANCE: 7
Per stabilitas et per fortitudo,
  ORDER: 7; STRENGTH: 99
Persta et praesta, STEADFASTNESS: 98

Perstando praesto, IMPROVEMENT: 31
Persto et spero, HOPE: 162;
  STEADFASTNESS: 99
Per tela per hostes, ADVERSITY: 71;
  OPPOSITION: 9; WALKING: 7
Per tela per hostes impavidi,
  COURAGE: 175
Per tot discrimina, ADVERSITY: 72
Per tot discrimina rerum,
  PERSEVERANCE: 74
Per undas, per agros, LOCAL
  GOVERNMENT: 276; WAVES: 6
Per undas et ignes fluctuat nec
  mergitur, ENDURANCE: 46
Per varios casus, FORTUNE: 91
Per vias rectas, RECTITUDE: 52
Pervicax recte, RECTITUDE: 53;
  STEADFASTNESS: 100
Per vim et virtutem, COURAGE: 176;
  STRENGTH: 100
Per virtutem scientiamque,
  COURAGE: 177; KNOWLEDGE: 56
Pestis patriae pigrities, IDLENESS: 2
Petimus altiora, ASPIRATION: 68
Petimus credimus, EFFORT: 27; SCHOOL
  MOTTOES: 222
Petit alta, ASPIRATION: 69
Petit ardua virtus, VIRTUE: 140
Peu a peu, GRADUALNESS: 5
Philosophia pietati ancillans, PIETY: 15;
  SCHOOL MOTTOES: 223; WISDOM: 48
Phoebo lux, LIGHT: 68; SUN: 9
Phoebus, lux in tenebris, DARKNESS: 14;
  LIGHT: 69
Physical/ Mental/ Spiritual/ Social,
  HEALING and HEALTH: 22; SCHOOL
  MOTTOES: 224
Physical/ Spiritual/ Social/ Mental,
  HEALING and HEALTH: 23; SCHOOL
  MOTTOES: 225
Pie, juste, temperanter, JUSTICE: 95;
  MODERATION: 30; PIETY: 16
Pie at juste, JUSTICE: 96; PIETY: 17
Piedmontaise, PROPER NAMES: 42
Pie et fortiter, COURAGE: 178; PIETY: 18
Pie et prudenter, PIETY: 19;
  PRUDENCE: 37
Pie repone te, CONFIDENCE: 16
Pietas ad omnia utilis,
  RIGHTEOUSNESS: 13; USEFULNESS: 6
Pietas cum robore conjuncta,
  PIETY: 20; STRENGTH: 101

Pietas est optima virtus, PIETY: 21;
  VIRTUE: 141
Pietas est pax, PEACE: 70; PIETY: 22
Pietas et frugalitas, PIETY: 23
Pietas et justitia principatus columnae,
  GOVERNMENT: 5; JUSTICE: 97;
  PIETY: 24
Pietas parentum, PARENTS: 3; SCHOOL
  MOTTOES: 226
Pietas praesidium firmissimum,
  PIETY: 25; PROTECTION: 23
Pietas summa est scientia, PIETY: 26
Pietate, PIETY: 29
Pietate, fide, et justicia, FIDELITY: 255;
  JUSTICE: 98; PIETY: 30
Pietate, legibus, et armis, LAW: 39;
  PIETY: 31; WEAPONS: 82
Pietate, legibus, justitia, JUSTICE: 99;
  PIETY: 32; PRUDENCE: 38
Pietate et bellica virtute,
  COURAGE: 179; PIETY: 33
Pietate et justicia, JUSTICE: 100;
  PIETY: 34
Pietate et justitia principes dii sunt,
  JUSTICE: 101; PIETY: 35
Pietate et probitate, HONESTY: 33;
  PIETY: 36
Pietate et prudentia, PIETY: 37;
  PRUDENCE: 39
Pietate fortior, PIETY: 38;
  STRENGTH: 102
Pietatem prudentiae praefer,
  PIETY: 39; PRUDENCE: 40
Pietate parentum, ANCESTRY: 31;
  PIETY: 40
Pietatis causa, PIETY: 41
PIETY, p. 576
POSSESSION, p. 579
POSSIBILITY, p. 581
POWER, p. 582
Piety in peace, PEACE: 71; PIETY: 42
Pieux quoique preux, PIETY: 43
Pie vivere, et Deum et patriam
  diligere, COUNTRY: 80; PIETY: 44
Pignus amoris, LOVE: 101
Pille mise gu muier, SEA: 24
Pilot, PROPER NAMES: 43
Placeam, ENJOYMENT: 26
Placeam dum peream, FORTUNE: 92;
  SUCCESS: 10
Placeat nobis quod Deo placet,
  ENJOYMENT: 27

Placidus semper timidus nunquam,
  EQUANIMITY: 16
Plane et sane, SIMPLICITY: 3
Playsyr vaut Payn, ENJOYMENT: 28
Please God I live, I'll go,
  WILLINGNESS: 7
Plena dabit Deus vela, DIVINE
  GUIDANCE: 370
Plena refulget, FULLNESS: 6
Plures labore, dulcibus quidam otiis,
  INDUSTRIOUSNESS: 161
Plus d'effet que de bruit,
  ACCOMPLISHMENT: 16; ACTION: 18
Plus ne m'est rien, rien ne m'est plus,
  INSIGNIFICANCE: 3
Plus penser que dire, THOUGHT: 18
Plus spinis quam ferro, ADVERSITY: 73;
  OPPOSITION: 10
Plustost mourier que changer,
  DEATH: 78; STEADFASTNESS: 101
Plustot mourire que vivere sans vertu,
  DEATH: 79; VIRTUE: 144
Plus ultra, IMPROVEMENT: 32; SCHOOL
  MOTTOES: 227
Plus vigila, VIGILANCE: 57
Plutot rompe que plie,
  STEADFASTNESS: 102
Poco a poco, MEASURE: 15
Point de couronne sans peine,
  CROWN: 20; EFFORT: 28
Point du jour, DAY: 9; LOCAL
  GOVERNMENT: 277
Pollet virtus, VIRTUE: 145
Por dysserver, WORTHINESS: 50
Por la razon o la fuerza, POWER: 17;
  RECTITUDE: 54
Porro unum est necessarium,
  NECESSITY: 2
Porta maris portus salutis, HEALING and
  HEALTH: 24; LOCAL
  GOVERNMENT: 278; SEA: 25
Portanti spolia palma, REWARD: 27
Portio mea Dominus, DIVINITY: 339
Portio mea quod utile, USEFULNESS: 7
Posce teipsum, SELF-KNOWLEDGE: 10
Positis meliora caducis,
  IMPROVEMENT: 33
Posse nolle nobile, NOBILITY: 18
POSSESSION, p. 579
POSSIBILITY, p. 581
Possunt quia posse videntur,
  ABILITY: 24; SCHOOL MOTTOES: 228

Postera crescam laude, OFFSPRING: 4; PRAISE: 11; REPUTATION: 8; SCHOOL MOTTOES: 229

Postera laude recens, ADMIRATION: 3

Post est occasio calva, OPPORTUNITY: 10

Post funera faenus, DEATH: 80

Post funera virtus, DEATH: 81; VIRTUE: 146

Post hominem animus durat, COURAGE: 180

Post mortem triumpho, et morte vici; multis despectus magna feci, DEATH: 82

Post mortem virtus virescit, DEATH: 83; VIRTUE: 147

Post nubes, SHADE: 5

Post nubes lux, LIGHT: 70; SHADE: 6

Post nubila, SHADE: 7

Post nubila Phoebus, SUN: 10

Post nubila sol, SUN: 11

Post proelia praemia, HONOR: 150

Post spinas palma, REWARD: 28

Post tenebras lucem, DARKNESS: 15; LIGHT: 71

Post tenebras lux, DARKNESS: 16; LIGHT: 72

Post tenebris speramus lumen de lumine, DARKNESS: 17; HOPE: 163; LIGHT: 73

Post tot naufragia portum, SECURITY: 38

Post virtutem curro, VIRTUE: 148

Potior origine virtus, VIRTUE: 149

Potius ingenio quam vi, ABILITY: 25

Potius mori quam foedari, DEATH: 84; DISGRACE: 14

Pour appendre oublier ne puis, FORGETTING: 19

Pour avoir fidèlement servi, SERVICE: 37

Pour bien désirer, KINDNESS: 20

Pour bien fort, STRENGTH: 103

Pour deservir, WORTHINESS: 51

Pour Dieu, pour terre, DIVINITY: 340; EARTH: 13

Pour Dieu et mon pays, COUNTRY: 81; DIVINITY: 341

Pour Dieu et mon Roi, DIVINITY: 342; ROYALTY: 59

Pour jamais, ETERNITY: 6

Pour l'advenir, FUTURE, THE: 20

Pour la foi, FAITH: 187

Pour l'église, RELIGION: 16

Pour le merite, WORTHINESS: 52

Pour le roi et la patrie, PATRIOTISM: 39; ROYALTY: 60

Pour le roy, ROYALTY: 61

Pour loyaulté maintenir, FIDELITY: 256

Pour ma libertay pour ma patree, COUNTRY: 82; LIBERTY: 90

Pour ma patrie, COUNTRY: 83

Pour mon Dieu, DIVINITY: 343

Pour mon Roy, ROYALTY: 62

Pour parvenir à bonne foy, SUCCESS: 11; TRADES: 25

Pour parvenir au bout il faut souffrir tout, GOALS: 5; SUCCESS: 12; SUFFERING: 9

Pour qui sait attendre, PATIENCE: 40

Pour quoy non, UNCLASSIFIED: 54

Pour trois, MEASURE: 16

Pour y parvenir, ACCOMPLISHMENT: 17

Poussez en avant, ADVANCE: 47

POWER, p. 582

Powys Paradwys Cymru, LOCAL GOVERNMENT: 279; PARADISE: 53

Practise no fraud, DECEPTION: 11

Praecedentibus insta, FOLLOWING: 11

Praecepta non homines, LOCAL GOVERNMENT: 280; PRINCIPLES: 1

Praecipitatus attamen tutus, SECURITY: 39

Praeclarior, quo propinquior, WORTHINESS: 53

Praeclarius quo difficilius, ADVERSITY: 74

Praeclarum regi et regno servitium, CROWN: 21; PATRIOTISM: 40; SERVICE: 38

Praedae memor, PROSPERITY: 43

Praemiando incitat, REWARD: 29

Praemium, virtus, gloria, GLORY: 45; REWARD: 30; VIRTUE: 150

Praemium, virtus, honor, HONOR: 151; REWARD: 31; VIRTUE: 151

Praemium honor, HONOR: 152; REWARD: 32

Praemium virtutis, REWARD: 33; VIRTUE: 152

Praemium virtutis honor, HONOR: 153; REWARD: 34; VIRTUE: 153

Praemonitus praemunitus, PREPAREDNESS: 50; WARNING: 8

Praenuntia pacis, PEACE: 72

Prae salem notanda, LOCAL
  GOVERNMENT: 281; SEA: 26
Praesis ut prosis, LEADERSHIP: 20;
  SCHOOL MOTTOES: 230; SERVICE: 39
Praesta et persta, DEDICATION: 9
Praestando praesto, DEDICATION: 10
Praestant aeterna caducis, ETERNITY: 7
Praestare et prodesse, SUCCESS: 13
Praestat auro virtus, VIRTUE: 154
Praestat tuto quam cito, SECURITY: 40
Praesto et persisto, PERSEVERANCE: 75
Praesto et persto, PERSEVERANCE: 76
Praestò et praestò, PREPAREDNESS: 51
Praestò pro patriâ, PATRIOTISM: 41;
  PREPAREDNESS: 52
Praesto ut praestem, DEDICATION: 11
Praetis prudentia praestat,
  PRUDENCE: 41
Praevide, ne praeveniare,
  FORESIGHT: 4
Praevisa mala pereunt, FORESIGHT: 5
PRAISE, p. 584
Praise God, DIVINITY: 344
Praise God for all, DIVINITY: 345
Prato et pelago, SEA: 27
Pravda vít ezí, TRUTH: 69
Prece et labore, DIVINE GUIDANCE: 371;
  INDUSTRIOUSNESS: 162
Preigne haleine, tirez fort,
  STRENGTH: 104
Premi, non opprimi, OPPRESSION: 6
Prend moi tel que je suis,
  ACCEPTANCE: 4
Prenez en gré, ACCEPTANCE: 5
Prenez en ire, ANGER: 8
Prenez garde, CAUTION: 32
PREPAREDNESS, p. 585
Preparing evangels of our heritage,
  RELIGION: 17; SCHOOL MOTTOES: 231
PRESENT, THE, p. 590
Preserved by concord, UNITY: 59
Press forward, ADVANCE: 48
Press through, ADVANCE: 49
Prest, PREPAREDNESS: 53
Prest, et, prest, PREPAREDNESS: 54
Prest a faire, PREPAREDNESS: 55
Prestat opes sapientia, PROSPERITY: 44;
  WISDOM: 49
Prest d'accomplier, PREPAREDNESS: 56
Presto et persto, PERSEVERANCE: 77
Presto et spero, DEEDS: 68; HOPE: 164
Presto ut praestem, SUCCESS: 14

Prest pour mon pays, PATRIOTISM: 42;
  PREPAREDNESS: 57
Pret, PREPAREDNESS: 58
Pretio prudentia, PRUDENCE: 42
Pretio prudentia praestat,
  PRUDENCE: 43
Pretiosum quod utile, USEFULNESS: 8
Pretiosum quod utile est,
  USEFULNESS: 9
Pretium et causa laboris,
  INDUSTRIOUSNESS: 163; REWARD: 35
Pretium non vile laborum,
  INDUSTRIOUSNESS: 164; REWARD: 36
Pretiumque et causa laboris,
  INDUSTRIOUSNESS: 165; LOCAL
  GOVERNMENT: 283
Pretium victoribus corona, CROWN: 22;
  REWARD: 37
Pretium virtutis, COURAGE: 181;
  REWARD: 38
Preux quoique pieux, COURAGE: 182;
  PIETY: 45
Prevalet virtus, VIRTUE: 155
PRIDE, p. 590
Pride and industry,
  INDUSTRIOUSNESS: 166; PRIDE: 9
Pride in our past, faith in our future,
  FAITH: 188; FUTURE, THE: 21; LOCAL
  GOVERNMENT: 284; PRESENT,
  THE: 10; PRIDE: 10
Pride in the past/ Faith in the future,
  FAITH: 189; FUTURE, THE: 22;
  PRESENT, THE: 11; PRIDE: 11; SCHOOL
  MOTTOES: 232
PRIMACY, p. 592
Prima voce salutat, WORDS: 32
Primi et ultimi in bello, WAR: 60
Primum tutare domum, DEFENSE: 41;
  HOME: 16
Primum vir esto, MAINTENANCE: 5;
  SCHOOL MOTTOES: 233
Primus, PRIMACY: 6
Primus e stirpe, ORIGIN: 7
Primus in Indis, PRIMACY: 7
Primus inter pares, EQUALITY: 9;
  PRIMACY: 8; SCHOOL MOTTOES: 234
Primus tametsi virilis, PRIMACY: 9
Primus ultimusque in acie, WAR: 61
PRINCELINESS, p. 592
Princeps patriae pater, PRINCELINESS: 8
Principia non homines, PRINCIPLES: 2
Principiis obsta, DANGER: 15

Principis est virtus maxima nosse
Deum, VIRTUE: 156
Principis est virtus se nosse deumque
suosque, VIRTUE: 157
PRINCIPLES, p. 593
Priora cole meliora sequere, LOCAL
GOVERNMENT: 285; TIME: 42
Prisca constantia, FIDELITY: 257;
LOCAL GOVERNMENT: 286
Prisca fides, FAITH: 190
Prisca virtute fideque, FIDELITY: 258;
VIRTUE: 158
Prisco stirpe Hibernico, ANCESTRY: 32
Prist en foyt, FAITH: 191
Pristinae virtutis memores,
COURAGE: 183
Pristinum spero lumen,
BRIGHTNESS: 11; HOPE: 165
Prius frangitur quam flectitur,
STEADFASTNESS: 103
Prius mori quam fidem fallere,
DEATH: 85; FAITH: 192;
FIDELITY: 259
Prius quam factum considera,
ACTION: 19; THOUGHT: 19
Prix de vertu, REWARD: 39;
VIRTUE: 159
Pro amore patriae, COUNTRY: 84;
LOVE: 102; PATRIOTISM: 43
Pro arae et regni custodia,
PROTECTION: 24
Pro ara et focis, HOME: 17
Pro aris, RELIGION: 18
Pro aris et focis, RELIGION: 19
Pro arte non marte, ART: 27
Pro avitâ fide, FAITH: 193
Proba conscientia, CONSCIENCE: 9
Probando et approbando, EFFORT: 29;
MANNER: 9
Pro bello vel pace, WAR: 62
Probis, non pravis, GOODNESS: 33
Probitas cum fortitudine,
FORTITUDE: 26; HONESTY: 34
Probitas et firmitas, HONESTY: 35
Probitas fons honoris, HONOR: 154;
INTEGRITY: 32
Probitas laudatur et alget, HONESTY: 36
Probitas optimum est consilium,
HONESTY: 37
Probitas sibi ipsi securitas,
INTEGRITY: 33; SECURITY: 41
Probitas solo nobilitas, INTEGRITY: 34

Probitas veritas honos, HONOR: 155;
INTEGRITY: 35; TRUTH: 70
Probitas verus honos, HONESTY: 38;
HONOR: 156
Probitate, HONESTY: 39
Probitate ac virtute, INTEGRITY: 36
Probitate consilium perficitur,
INTEGRITY: 37
Probitate et industria, HONESTY: 40;
INDUSTRIOUSNESS: 167
Probitate et labore, HONESTY: 41;
INDUSTRIOUSNESS: 168
Probitate et virtute, HONESTY: 42
Probitatem quam divitias, HONESTY: 43
Pro bona ad meliora,
IMPROVEMENT: 34
Pro bono humani generis,
HUMANITY: 10; SCHOOL
MOTTOES: 235
Pro bono oppido, LOCAL
GOVERNMENT: 287
Probum non paenitet, HONESTY: 44
Procedamus in pace, PATRIOTISM: 44;
PEACE: 73
Pro Christo et humanitate, CHRIST,
JESUS: 66; SCHOOL MOTTOES: 236
Pro Christo et patria, COUNTRY: 85;
SCHOOL MOTTOES: 237
Pro Christo et patria dulce periculum,
CHRIST, JESUS: 67; COUNTRY: 86
Pro Christo et Republica, CHRIST,
JESUS: 68; COUNTRY: 87; SCHOOL
MOTTOES: 238
Pro civibus et civitate, LOCAL
GOVERNMENT: 288; PEOPLE: 6
Proclaim liberty throughout all the
land unto all the inhabitants thereof,
LIBERTY: 91
Pro corona et foedere Christi,
CROWN: 23; SCHOOL MOTTOES: 239
Pro cruce audax, AUDACITY: 81; CROSS,
THE: 93
Procurata industria, DILIGENCE: 49
Pro Deo, patriâ, et rege, COUNTRY: 88;
DIVINITY: 346; ROYALTY: 63
Pro Deo, pro Rege, pro patria, et lege,
COUNTRY: 89; DIVINITY: 347;
LAW: 40; ROYALTY: 64
Pro Deo, rege, et patriâ, COUNTRY: 90;
DIVINITY: 348; ROYALTY: 65
Pro Deo certo, DIVINITY: 349

Pro Deo et Caesare, DIVINITY: 350;
ROYALTY: 66
Pro Deo et catholica fide,
DIVINITY: 351
Pro Deo et ecclesia, DIVINITY: 352
Pro Deo et grege, DIVINITY: 353
Pro Deo et libertate, DIVINITY: 354;
LIBERTY: 92
Pro Deo et meo, DIVINITY: 355
Pro Deo et nobilissima patria
Batavorum, COUNTRY: 91;
DIVINITY: 356
Pro Deo et populo, DIVINITY: 359;
LOCAL GOVERNMENT: 289; PEOPLE: 7
Pro Deo et pro patria, COUNTRY: 93;
DIVINITY: 360
Pro Deo et rege, DIVINITY: 361;
ROYALTY: 67
Prodesse, LOCAL GOVERNMENT: 290;
SERVICE: 40
Prodesse civibus, GUIDANCE: 24
Prodesse quam conspici,
GOODNESS: 34; USEFULNESS: 10
Prodigiose qui laboriose,
INDUSTRIOUSNESS: 169
Producing people with purpose,
PURPOSE: 17; SCHOOL MOTTOES: 242
Pro ecclesia, RELIGION: 20
Pro ecclesia, pro Texana,
RELIGION: 21; SCHOOL MOTTOES: 243
Pro ecclesia Dei, RELIGION: 22
Pro ecclesia et patria, PATRIOTISM: 45;
RELIGION: 23; SCHOOL MOTTOES: 244
PROFANITY, p. 593
Pro fide, FAITH: 194
Pro fide, lege, et rege, FAITH: 195;
LAW: 41; ROYALTY: 68
Pro fide ablectus, FIDELITY: 260
Pro fide ac patria, COUNTRY: 94;
FAITH: 196
Pro fide et merito, FIDELITY: 261
Pro fide et patria, COUNTRY: 95;
FAITH: 197
Pro fide rege et patria pugno,
COUNTRY: 96; FAITH: 198;
ROYALTY: 69
Profunda cernit, WISDOM: 50
Progredere ne regredere, ADVANCE: 50
Progredi non regredi, ADVANCE: 51
Progredior, ADVANCE: 52
Progress, IMPROVEMENT: 35; LOCAL
GOVERNMENT: 291

Progress, peace, prosperity,
IMPROVEMENT: 36; PEACE: 74;
PROSPERITY: 45
Progressio cum populo,
IMPROVEMENT: 37; LOCAL
GOVERNMENT: 292
Progressio et concordia,
FRIENDSHIP: 47; IMPROVEMENT: 38;
LAW: 42
Progress with prudence,
IMPROVEMENT: 39
Pro humanitate, HUMANITY: 11;
SCHOOL MOTTOES: 245
Projeci, UNCLASSIFIED: 55
Pro lege, Rege, grege, CROWN: 24;
LAW: 43; PEOPLE: 8
Pro lege, Rege (et) grege, CROWN: 25;
LAW: 44; PEOPLE: 9
Pro lege, senatuque rege, LAW: 45;
ROYALTY: 70
Pro lege et grege, LAW: 46; PEOPLE: 10
Pro lege et patria, COUNTRY: 97;
LAW: 47
Pro lege et pro grege, LAW: 48;
PEOPLE: 11
Pro lege et Rege, CROWN: 26; LAW: 49
Pro legibus et regibus, LAW: 50;
ROYALTY: 71
Pro libertate, LIBERTY: 93
Pro libertate et commercio,
COMMERCE: 5; LIBERTY: 94
Pro libertate et patriâ, COUNTRY: 98;
LIBERTY: 95
Pro libertate lege sancta, LAW: 51;
LIBERTY: 96
Pro libertate patriae, COUNTRY: 99;
LIBERTY: 97
Pro lusu et praedâ, SPORT: 4
Pro Magna Charta, GOVERNMENT: 6
Pro me ipso et aliis, UNSELFISHNESS: 23
Pro mitra coronam, CROWN: 27
Prompte et consulto, SPEED: 40
Prompte et sincere, SCHOOL
MOTTOES: 246; SINCERITY: 11;
SPEED: 41
Promptus, PREPAREDNESS: 61
Promptus ad certamen,
PREPAREDNESS: 62
Promptus et fidelis, FIDELITY: 262;
PREPAREDNESS: 63
Pro mundi beneficio, BENEFITS: 4
Pro omnibus laus Deo, DIVINITY: 362

Mottoes & Categories

Pro patria, COUNTRY: 100;
PATRIOTISM: 46
Pro patria auxilio Deo, COUNTRY: 101;
PATRIOTISM: 47
Pro patria consumor, COUNTRY: 102;
PATRIOTISM: 48
Pro patriae amicis, FRIENDSHIP: 48
Pro patriae amore, PATRIOTISM: 49
Pro patriâ ejusque libertate,
COUNTRY: 103; LIBERTY: 98;
PATRIOTISM: 50
Pro patria et gloria, COUNTRY: 104;
HONOR: 157; PATRIOTISM: 51
Pro patria et libertate, COUNTRY: 105;
LIBERTY: 99; PATRIOTISM: 52
Pro patriâ et rege, PATRIOTISM: 53;
ROYALTY: 72
Pro patria et religione, COUNTRY: 106;
PATRIOTISM: 54; RELIGION: 24
Pro patria et virtute, COUNTRY: 107;
PATRIOTISM: 55; VIRTUE: 160
Pro patria invictus, PATRIOTISM: 56
Pro patria mori, COUNTRY: 108;
DEATH: 86; PATRIOTISM: 57
Pro patria non timidus perire,
COUNTRY: 109; DEATH: 87;
PATRIOTISM: 58
Pro patria saepe, pro Rege semper,
COUNTRY: 110; CROWN: 28;
PATRIOTISM: 59
Pro patria sanguis, COUNTRY: 111;
PATRIOTISM: 60
Pro patria semper, COUNTRY: 112;
PATRIOTISM: 61
Pro patria uro, COUNTRY: 113;
PATRIOTISM: 62
Pro patria vivere et mori,
COUNTRY: 114; PATIENCE: 41;
PATRIOTISM: 63
Pro pelle cutem, HUNTING: 5
Propere et provide, CAUTION: 33;
SPEED: 42
PROPER NAMES, p. 593
Propero sed curo, CAUTION: 34;
SPEED: 43
Propitio Deo securus ago, DIVINE
GUIDANCE: 372; GRACE: 27
Propositi tenax, PURPOSE: 18
Propria virtute audax, AUDACITY: 82;
VIRTUE: 161
Proprio vos sanguine pasco,
SACRIFICE: 4; UBIQUITY: 8

Proprium decus et patrium, GLORY: 46
Pro prole semper, OFFSPRING: 5
Propter obedientiam, OBEDIENCE: 12
Pro recto, INTEGRITY: 38
Pro rege, ROYALTY: 73
Pro rege, lege, grege, LAW: 52;
PEOPLE: 12; ROYALTY: 74
Pro rege, pro lege, pro grege, LAW: 53;
PEOPLE: 13; ROYALTY: 75
Pro rege, pro lege, pro patriae
conamur, LAW: 54; PATRIOTISM: 64;
ROYALTY: 76
Pro rege ac fide audax, AUDACITY: 83;
FAITH: 199; LOCAL GOVERNMENT: 293
Pro rege dimico, ROYALTY: 77
Pro rege et grege, PEOPLE: 14;
ROYALTY: 78
Pro rege et lege, LAW: 55; LOCAL
GOVERNMENT: 294; ROYALTY: 79
Pro rege et limite, ROYALTY: 80
Pro rege et patriâ, PATRIOTISM: 65;
ROYALTY: 81
Pro rege et patriâ pugnans,
PATRIOTISM: 66; ROYALTY: 82
Pro rege et populo, PEOPLE: 15;
ROYALTY: 83
Pro rege et pro patriâ semper,
PATRIOTISM: 67; ROYALTY: 84
Pro rege et religione, FAITH: 200;
ROYALTY: 85
Pro rege et republica, PATRIOTISM: 68;
ROYALTY: 86
Pro rege in tyrannos, ROYALTY: 87
Pro Rege pio, PIETY: 46; ROYALTY: 88
Pro rege saepe, ROYALTY: 89
Pro rege saepe, pro patriâ semper,
PATRIOTISM: 69; ROYALTY: 90
Pro rege saepe, pro republica semper,
PATRIOTISM: 70; ROYALTY: 91
Pro rege semper, ROYALTY: 92
Pro republicâ, PATRIOTISM: 71
Pro republicâ semper, PATRIOTISM: 72
Prorsum et sursum, IMPROVEMENT: 40
Prorsum semper, IMPROVEMENT: 41;
LOCAL GOVERNMENT: 295
Pro rure pro patria, COUNTRY: 115;
LOCAL GOVERNMENT: 296
Pro salute, SECURITY: 42
Prosecute or perish, ACTION: 20
Prosequor alis, FOLLOWING: 12

Prospere qui sedulo,
INDUSTRIOUSNESS: 170;
PROSPERITY: 46
Prospere si propere, PROSPERITY: 47
PROSPERITY, p. 596
Prospice, FORESIGHT: 6
Prospice, respice, FORESIGHT: 7
Prospicio, VISION: 13
Prosunt gentibus artes, ART: 28; LOCAL
GOVERNMENT: 297
PROTECTION, p. 600
Proudly we serve, LOCAL
GOVERNMENT: 298; SERVICE: 41
Pro utilitate, USEFULNESS: 11
Provenito in altum, SCHOOL
MOTTOES: 247
Pro veritate, TRUTH: 71
Pro veritate suffer fortiter,
ENDURANCE: 47; TRUTH: 72
Provide, PROVIDENCE: 13
Provide et constanter, PRUDENCE: 44;
STEADFASTNESS: 104
Provide et fortiter, COURAGE: 184;
PRUDENCE: 45
PROVIDENCE, p. 602
Providence, PROVIDENCE: 14
Providence and perseverance,
PERSEVERANCE: 78; PROVIDENCE: 15
Providence with adventure,
PROVIDENCE: 16
Providentiâ, PROVIDENCE: 17
Providentiâ Dei, DIVINE GUIDANCE: 373
Providentia Dei conservet, DIVINE
GUIDANCE: 374
Providentiâ Dei stabiliuntur familiae,
DIVINE GUIDANCE: 375
Providentiâ divinâ, DIVINE
GUIDANCE: 376
Providentia Domini sufficientia mihi,
PROVIDENCE: 18
Providentiae fido, PROVIDENCE: 19
Providentiae haec divinae obnoxia,
PROVIDENCE: 20
Providentiae me committo,
PROVIDENCE: 21
Providentia et industria,
INDUSTRIOUSNESS: 171;
PROVIDENCE: 22
Providentiâ et virtute,
PROVIDENCE: 23; VIRTUE: 162
Providentia in adversis, FORESIGHT: 8
Providentia sumus, PROVIDENCE: 24

Providentia tutamen, PROVIDENCE: 25
Providentiâ tutamur, PROVIDENCE: 26
Provide qui laboriose, CAUTION: 35
Providus esto, PRUDENCE: 46
Pro virtute, VIRTUE: 163
Pro virtute bellica, MILITARY
DISTINCTION: 5
Pro virtute et fidelitate, COURAGE: 185;
FIDELITY: 263
Pro virtute patria, COUNTRY: 116;
COURAGE: 186
PROVOCATION, p. 604
Provyd, PROVIDENCE: 27
PRUDENCE, p. 604
Prudens, fidelis, et audax,
AUDACITY: 84; FIDELITY: 264;
PRUDENCE: 47
Prudens et innocuus, HARMLESSNESS: 3;
PRUDENCE: 48
Prudens futuri, FUTURE, THE: 23;
LOCAL GOVERNMENT: 299;
PRUDENCE: 49
Prudens qui patiens, PATIENCE: 42;
PRUDENCE: 50
Prudens sicut serpens, ANIMALS: 45;
WISDOM: 51
Prudens simplicitas, SIMPLICITY: 4;
WISDOM: 52
Prudens simplicitas beat,
PRUDENCE: 51; SIMPLICITY: 5
Prudent comme le serpent,
PRUDENCE: 52
Prudenter et constanter,
PRUDENCE: 53; STEADFASTNESS: 105
Prudenter et simpliciter,
PRUDENCE: 54; SIMPLICITY: 6
Prudenter qui sedulo,
INDUSTRIOUSNESS: 172; PRUDENCE: 55
Prudenter vigilo, PRUDENCE: 56
Prudentia, PRUDENCE: 57
Prudentia, fraudis nescia,
DECEPTION: 12; PRUDENCE: 58
Prudentia decus innocentia,
GRACE: 28; INNOCENCE: 15;
PRUDENCE: 59
Prudentiâ et animis, COURAGE: 187;
PRUDENCE: 60
Prudentiâ et animo, COURAGE: 188;
PRUDENCE: 61
Prudentiâ et constantiâ, FIDELITY: 265;
PRUDENCE: 62

Mottoes & Categories

Prudentia et honor, HONOR: 158;
PRUDENCE: 63

Prudentia et justitia, JUSTICE: 102;
PRUDENCE: 64

Prudentia et marte, COURAGE: 189;
PRUDENCE: 65

Prudentiâ et simplicitate,
PRUDENCE: 66; SIMPLICITY: 7

Prudentia et vi, POWER: 18;
PRUDENCE: 67

Prudentia et vigilantia, PRUDENCE: 68;
VIGILANCE: 58

Prudentia et virtute, COURAGE: 190;
PRUDENCE: 69

Prudentia gloriam acquirit, GLORY: 47;
PRUDENCE: 70

Prudentia in adversos, ADVERSITY: 75;
PRUDENCE: 71

Prudentia me sustinet, PRUDENCE: 72

Prudentia praestat, PRUDENCE: 73

Prudentiâ simplicitate, PRUDENCE: 74;
SIMPLICITY: 8

Prudentia tutus, PRUDENCE: 75

Prudhomme et loyale, FIDELITY: 266;
PRUDENCE: 76

P. T. V. (Pietas tutissima virtus),
PIETY: 47; VIRTUE: 164

Publica salus mea merces, REWARD: 40;
SECURITY: 43

Publicum meritorum praemium,
REWARD: 41; SERVICE: 42

Pugilem claraverat, NOBILITY: 19

Pugna pro patriâ, PATRIOTISM: 75;
WAR: 63

Pugna pro patria, 1625, COUNTRY: 118;
PATRIOTISM: 76

Pugna pro patria, & (Paul Revere),
COUNTRY: 119; PATRIOTISM: 77

Pugno pro aris, WAR: 64

Pugno pro patriâ, PATRIOTISM: 78;
WAR: 65

Pugno pugnas pugnavi, WAR: 66

Pula, NATIONAL MOTTOES: 23;
WATER: 14

Pulchra terra Dei donum, DIVINE
GIFTS: 48; LOCAL GOVERNMENT: 300

Pulchrior ex arduis, ADVERSITY: 76

Pulchritudo et salubritas, BEAUTY: 15;
HEALING and HEALTH: 25; LOCAL
GOVERNMENT: 301

Pulcra pro libertate, LIBERTY: 100

Pullis corvorum invocantibus eum,
BIRDS: 25

Pungit, sed placet, ENJOYMENT: 29

Pura sequi, PURITY: 14

Pure de fonte, PURITY: 15; WATER: 15

Pure et loyale, FIDELITY: 267;
PURITY: 16

Pure foy ma joye, FAITH: 201

Pur et seincere, PURITY: 17;
SINCERITY: 12

PURITY, p. 610

PURPOSE, p. 611

Pur sans peur, FEAR: 56; PURITY: 18

PURSUIT, p. 612

Purus sceleres [sic], GUILT: 3

Pylkington Polledowne,
AGRICULTURE: 5

Q

Qua duxeris adsum, LEADERSHIP: 21

Quae amissa salva, SECURITY: 44

Quae arguuntur a lumine
manifestantur, LIGHT: 74;
TRADES: 26

Quae Caesaris Caesari, quae Dei Deo,
DUTY: 25

Quae fecimus ipsi, DEEDS: 69

Quae habet manus tenebit, HANDS: 29;
POSSESSION: 21

Quae juncta firma, STRENGTH: 105;
UNITY: 60

Quae moderata firma,
MODERATION: 31

Quae prosunt omnibus artes, ART: 29;
TRADES: 27

Quaeque favilla micat, SHINING: 24

Quae recta sequor, HONOR: 159;
PURSUIT: 8

Quae regio in terris nostri non plena
laboris?, EARTH: 14;
INDUSTRIOUSNESS: 173

Quaerendo, SEARCH and DISCOVERY: 8

Quaere sic est, SEARCH and
DISCOVERY: 9

Quaere verum, TRUTH: 73

Quaerite et invenietis, SEARCH and
DISCOVERY: 10

Quae serata secura, SECURITY: 45

Quaesita marte tuenda arte, ART: 30;
WAR: 67

Quae supra, PARADISE: 54

Quae sursum volo, DESIRE: 18
Quae sursum volo videre, PARADISE: 55
Quae vernant crescent, GROWTH: 17
Quae vult valde vult, DESIRE: 19
Qualis ab incepto, CONSISTENCY: 7
Qualis ero spero, HOPE: 166
Qualis vita finis ita, LIFE: 28
Quam non terret hyems, SEASONS: 4
Quam plurimis prodesse,
    GOODNESS: 35
Quam sibi sortem, FORTUNE: 93
Quand fortune me tourmente,
    L'Espoire en Dieu me contente,
    DIVINITY: 363; FORTUNE: 94;
    HOPE: 167
Quanti est sapere, LOCAL
    GOVERNMENT: 302; WISDOM: 53
Quant je puis, EFFORT: 30;
    MANNER: 10; SCHOOL MOTTOES: 248
Quantum est in rebus inane,
    INSIGNIFICANCE: 4
Quantum in rebus inane,
    INSIGNIFICANCE: 5
Qua panditur orbis, LOCATION: 6
Qua pote lucet, SHINING: 25
Quarere verum, TRUTH: 74
Quarta saluti, HEALING and HEALTH: 26
Quasi summus magister, STATUS: 9
Qua tendis?, DESTINATION: 6
Que je surmonte, EXCELLENCE: 13
Quem non torret hyems, SEASONS: 5
Quem te Deus esse jussit, DIVINE
    GUIDANCE: 377
Que pensez, THOUGHT: 20
Quercus, FLORA: 30
Quercus glandifera amica porcis,
    ANIMALS: 46; FLORA: 31
Quercus robur salus patriae,
    SECURITY: 46; STRANGER: 9;
    STRENGTH: 106
Que sçay-je?, KNOWLEDGE: 57
Qui a Dieu, il a tout, DIVINITY: 364
Quia fidem servasti, FIDELITY: 268
Qui capit capitur, ENTRAPMENT: 3
Qui conducit, LEADERSHIP: 22
Quicquid crescit in cinere perit,
    GROWTH: 18; TRANSIENCE: 13
Quicquid dignum sapiente bonoque
    est, WORTHINESS: 54
Qui craint Dieu, fort du tout, FEAR: 57
Qui croit en Dieu croix, CROSS,
    THE: 94; FAITH: 202

Qui dat pauperibus numquam
    indigebit, KINDNESS: 21
Quid capit, capitur, ENTRAPMENT: 4
Quid clarius astris?, STARS: 32
Quid gens sine mente?, MIND: 41
Qui distulit non abstulit ipse me
    protegat, PROTECTION: 25
Quid justum non quod utile,
    JUSTICE: 103; USEFULNESS: 12
Quid leges sine moribus?, LAW: 56;
    RECTITUDE: 55
Quid leone fortius?, ANIMALS: 47;
    COURAGE: 191
Quidni pro sodali?, FELLOWSHIP: 7
Quidni tandem?, DIVINE
    GUIDANCE: 378
Quid nobis ardui, ADVERSITY: 77;
    LOCAL GOVERNMENT: 303
Quid non cor saepius pro
    Immanueli?, CHRIST, JESUS: 69
Quid non Deo juvante, DIVINE
    GUIDANCE: 379
Quid non pro
    patria?, COUNTRY: 120;
    PATRIOTISM: 79
Quid non
    resolutio?, STEADFASTNESS: 106
Quid prodest?, IMPROVEMENT: 42
Quid pure tranquillet,
    TRANQUILLITY: 7
Quid reddam
    Domino?, DIVINITY: 365
Quid retribuam?, GIFTS and
    GIVING: 25
Quid tibi fieri non vis alteri ne feceris,
    DEEDS: 70
Quid tibi vis fieri facias, DEEDS: 71
Quid verum atque decens, TRUTH: 75
Quid verum atque decens curo et rogo,
    TRUTH: 76
Quiescam, REST: 20
Quiescens et vigilans, REST: 21;
    WAKEFULNESS: 10
Quieta non movere, REST: 22
Qui facit per alium facit per se,
    SCHOOL MOTTOES: 249
Qui fugit molam fugit farinam,
    ORIGIN: 8; TRADES: 28
Quihidder will ye? *or* Quidhidder will
    zie?, DIRECTION: 6
Qui honeste fortiter, HONESTY: 45
Qui invidet minor est, ENVY: 9

Qui me tanget paenitebit, TOUCH: 3
Qui modo scandit corruet statim,
    FAILURE: 3
Qui non ciconia tigris, ANIMALS: 48
Qui non dat quod habet non occupat
    ille quod optat, GIFTS and GIVING: 26
Qui non laborat, non manducet,
    INDUSTRIOUSNESS: 174
Qui non patriam
    amat?, COUNTRY: 121;
    LOVE: 103; PATRIOTISM: 80
Qui nos vincet?, CONQUEST: 31
Qui nucleum vult nucem frangat,
    EFFORT: 31
Qui panse, HEALING and HEALTH: 27
Qui patitur vincit, CONQUEST: 32
Qui pense?, THOUGHT: 21
Qui perde la foye n'a plus de perdre,
    FAITH: 203
Qui plane sane vadit, SECURITY: 47;
    SIMPLICITY: 9
Qui plantavit curabit, AGRICULTURE: 6
Qui potest capere, capiat,
    POSSESSION: 22
Quis accursabit?, AGGRESSION: 13
Quis accusabit?, GUILT: 4
Quis audeat luci aggredi, LIGHT: 75
Quis contra nos?, HOSTILITY: 17
Qui seminant in lachrymis, in
    exultatione metent, HAPPINESS: 53
Qui sera sera, ACCEPTANCE: 6; FATE: 26
Qui s'estime petyt deviendra grand,
    GREATNESS: 8
Qui sis non unde, WORTHINESS: 55
Quis
    occursabit?, UNCLASSIFIED: 56
Qui spinosior fragrantior, IRONY: 3
Quis preparet corvo escam
    suam?, BIRDS: 26; NOURISHMENT: 6
Quis prohibeat sperare
    meliora?, HOPE: 168
Quis similis tui in fortibus,
    Domine?, DIVINITY: 366
Qui stadium currit eniti debet ut
    vincat, EFFORT: 32
Qui stat caveat ne cadat, FAILURE: 4
Quis timet?, FEAR: 58
Quis ut Deus?, DIVINITY: 367
Qui tel?, WORTHINESS: 56
Qui transtulit sustinet,
    ENDURANCE: 48; STATE MOTTOES: 42
Qui uti scit ei bona, PROSPERITY: 48

Qui vit content tient assez,
    HAPPINESS: 54
Qui vult capere capiat,
    ACQUISITION: 6; GENEROSITY: 14
Quocunque ferar, DESTINATION: 7
Quocunque jeceris stabit, RESULTS: 2
Quod adest, PRESENT, THE: 12
Quod agis fortiter, COURAGE: 192
Quod cito fit, cito perit, SPEED: 44
Quodcunque evenerit optimum,
    ACCEPTANCE: 7
Quod Deus vult fiat, DIVINE
    GUIDANCE: 380
Quod Deus vult hoc semper fit, DIVINE
    GUIDANCE: 381
Quod Deus vult volo, DIVINE
    GUIDANCE: 382
Quod dixi, dixi, WORDS: 33
Quod eorum minimi [*sic*] mihi,
    DEEDS: 72
Quod ero spero, FUTURE, THE: 24;
    HOPE: 169
Quo Deus et gloria ducunt,
    DIVINITY: 368; GLORY: 48
Quod facio, valde facio, DEEDS: 73
Quod fieri non vis alter [*sic*] ne feceris,
    DEEDS: 74
Quod honestum est decet, HONESTY: 46
Quod honestum utile, HONESTY: 47
Quod improbum terret probo prodest,
    GOODNESS: 36; OBSCURITY: 11
Quod me mihi reddit amicum,
    HEALING and HEALTH: 28
Quod merui meum est,
    WORTHINESS: 57
Quod non pro
    patria?, COUNTRY: 122;
    PATRIOTISM: 81
Quod petis hic est, GOALS: 6
Quod potui perfeci, DEEDS: 75
Quod pudet hoc pigeat, DISGRACE: 15
Quod severis metes, RESULTS: 3
Quod sis esse velis nilque malis,
    ASPIRATION: 70
Quod sors fert ferimus, FORTUNE: 95
Quod sursum volo videre,
    ASPIRATION: 71
Quod tibi fieri non vis alteri ne feceris,
    DEEDS: 76
Quod tibi hoc alteri, DEEDS: 77
Quod tibi id alii, DEEDS: 78
Quod tibi ne alteri, DEEDS: 79

Quod tibi vis alteri feceris, DEEDS: 80

Quod tibi vis fieri fac alteri, DEEDS: 81

Quod tibi vis fieri facias, DEEDS: 82

Quod transtuli retuli, ACQUISITION: 7

Quod tuum tene, POSSESSION: 23

Quod utile, USEFULNESS: 13

Quo duxeris adsum, FOLLOWING: 13

Quod verum atque decens, TRUTH: 77

Quod verum tutum, TRUTH: 78

Quod volo erit, DESIRE: 20

Quod vult, valde vult, DESIRE: 21

Quo fas et gloria, GLORY: 49; LAW: 57

Quo fas et gloria ducunt, GLORY: 50

Quo fata trahunt, FATE: 27

Quo fata trahunt retrahuntque
sequamur, FATE: 28

Quo fata vocant, FATE: 29

Quo honestior eo tutior, HONOR: 160

Quo major eo utilior, GREATNESS: 9

Quo me cunque vocat patria,
COUNTRY: 123; PATRIOTISM: 82

Quo Minerva ducit, sequor,
FOLLOWING: 14; WISDOM: 54

Quondam his vicimus armis,
WEAPONS: 83

Quo paratior, PREPAREDNESS: 64

Quorsum vivere mori? Mori vita,
LIFE: 29; REASON: 16

Quos amor et virtus sociant sors nulla
resolvet, LOVE: 104; UNITY: 63;
VIRTUE: 165

Quos dedit arcus amor, LOVE: 105

Quo spinosior fragrantior,
FRAGRANCE: 7

Quo sursum velo videre, STATE
MOTTOES: 43; VISION: 14

Quo veritas?, TRUTH: 79

Quo virtus ducit scando,
VIGILANCE: 59; VIRTUE: 166

Quo virtus et fata vocat, FATE: 30;
VIRTUE: 167

Quo virtus vocat, COURAGE: 193

Quo vocat virtus, VIRTUE: 168

R

Radicem firmant frondes,
STRANGER: 10; STRENGTH: 107

Radii omnia lustrant,
ENLIGHTENMENT: 6

Raised again, REBIRTH: 18

Raison pour guide, GUIDANCE: 25;
REASON: 17

Ramis micat radix, ORIGIN: 9

Ramosa cornua cervi, ANIMALS: 49;
LOCAL GOVERNMENT: 304

Rapit ense triumphos, VICTORY: 39

Raptim ad sidera tollar, LOFTINESS: 19;
STARS: 33

Raptim transeo, sed vestigia longa
relinquo, TRANSIENCE: 14

Rara avis in terris, UNIQUENESS: 5

Rara bonitas, GOODNESS: 37

Rather die than be disloyal,
FIDELITY: 269

Rather virtue than learning,
VIRTUE: 169

Ratio mihi sufficit, CAUSATION: 6

Ratione, non irâ, ANGER: 9; REASON: 18

Ratione, non vi, FORCE: 18; REASON: 19

Reach for the stars, ASPIRATION: 72;
SCHOOL MOTTOES: 250; STARS: 34

Ready, PREPAREDNESS: 65

Ready, aye, ready, PREPAREDNESS: 66

Ready and faithful, FIDELITY: 270;
PREPAREDNESS: 67

Re alta spero, HOPE: 170

REASON, p. 613

Reason contents me, REASON: 20

Rebellion to tyrants is obedience to
God, OBEDIENCE: 13; OPPOSITION: 11

REBIRTH, p. 614

Rebus angustis fortis, COURAGE: 194

Rebus in adversis spes mea Christus
erit, ADVERSITY: 78; CHRIST, JESUS: 70

Rebus in arduis constans,
FIDELITY: 271

Rebus justis invigilans, JUSTICE: 104

Recipiunt feminae sustentacula nobis,
SUPPORT: 6; TRADES: 29

Recreat et alit, ENJOYMENT: 30;
NOURISHMENT: 7

Recreation, REST: 23

Recta pete, RECTITUDE: 56

Recta sed ardua, ADVERSITY: 79

Recta sequor, RECTITUDE: 57

Recta sursum, DIRECTION: 7

Recta ubique, CONFIDENCE: 17

Recta vel ardua, RECTITUDE: 58

Recte ad ardua, HONOR: 161

Recte agens confido, CONFIDENCE: 18;
RECTITUDE: 59

Mottoes & Categories

Recte et fideliter, FIDELITY: 272;
  RECTITUDE: 60
Recte et sapienter, RECTITUDE: 61;
  WISDOM: 55
Recte et suaviter, GENTLENESS: 13;
  JUSTICE: 105
Recte faciendo, neminem timeo,
  FEAR: 59; JUSTICE: 106
Recte faciendo audax, AUDACITY: 85;
  JUSTICE: 107
Recte faciendo neminem timeas,
  FEAR: 60; JUSTICE: 108
Recte faciendo securus, JUSTICE: 109;
  SECURITY: 48
Recte fac noli timere, DEEDS: 83;
  LOCAL GOVERNMENT: 305
Recte ferio, AGGRESSION: 14
Recte quod honeste, HONESTY: 48
Rectitudine sto, RECTITUDE: 62
Recto cursu, DIRECTION: 8
Recto gradu, DIRECTNESS: 14
RECTITUDE, p. 617
Rectus in curvo, RECTITUDE: 63
Recuperatus, REBIRTH: 19
Redde diem, DAY: 10
Redde suum cuique, DUE: 3
Reddie aye reddie, PREPAREDNESS: 68
Reddite cuique suum, DUE: 4
Reddite Deo, DIVINITY: 369; LOCAL
  GOVERNMENT: 306
Reddunt aspera fortem, COURAGE: 195;
  DANGER: 16
Reddunt commercia mitem,
  FELLOWSHIP: 8
Redeem the time, TIME: 43
Redeunt Saturnia regna, REBIRTH: 20
Redit expectata diu, EXPECTATION: 10
Redoubtable et Fougueux,
  FIERCENESS: 9
Re et merito, WORTHINESS: 58
Refero, UBIQUITY: 9
Refulgent in tenebris, BRIGHTNESS: 12;
  DARKNESS: 18
Refulget, SHINING: 26
Refulget labores nostros coelum,
  DEEDS: 84; LOCAL GOVERNMENT: 307
Regard bien, ATTENTIVENESS: 8
Regarde à la mort, DEATH: 88
Regarde bien, VISION: 15
Regardez mon droit, RIGHTS: 12
Regardez mort, DEATH: 89
Regard the end, FINISH: 11

Rege et patriâ, PATRIOTISM: 83;
  ROYALTY: 93
Regem defendere victum, DEFENSE: 42;
  ROYALTY: 94
Reges creantur regibus, OFFSPRING: 6;
  ROYALTY: 95
Reget et defendet, GOVERNMENT: 7
Regi et patriae fidelis, COUNTRY: 124;
  FIDELITY: 273; ROYALTY: 96
Regi fidelis, FIDELITY: 274;
  ROYALTY: 97
Regi legi fidelis, FIDELITY: 275;
  LAW: 58; ROYALTY: 98
Regio floret patrocinio commercium
  commercioque regnum,
  COMMERCE: 6
Regi patriaeque, PATRIOTISM: 84;
  ROYALTY: 99
Regi patriaeque fidelis, COUNTRY: 125;
  FIDELITY: 276; ROYALTY: 100
Regi regnoque fidelis, FIDELITY: 277;
  ROYALTY: 101
Regis ad exemplum totus componitur
  orbis, RISK: 8; ROYALTY: 102
Regis donum gratum bonum,
  ROYALTY: 103
Regi semper fidelis, FIDELITY: 278;
  ROYALTY: 104
Regis et patriae tantum valet amor,
  COUNTRY: 126; CROWN: 29;
  PATRIOTISM: 85
Regit omnia tempus, TIME: 44
Regium est, omnibus benefacere,
  ROYALTY: 105
Regnant qui servirent, LOCAL
  GOVERNMENT: 308; SERVICE: 43
Regnat populus, PEOPLE: 16; STATE
  MOTTOES: 44
Regulier et vigoreux, STRENGTH: 108
Religio, libertas et scientia,
  KNOWLEDGE: 58; LIBERTY: 101;
  RELIGION: 25; SCHOOL MOTTOES: 251
RELIGION, p. 622
Religioni et bonis artibus,
  RELIGION: 26; SCHOOL MOTTOES: 252
Religioni reipublicae, COUNTRY: 127;
  RELIGION: 27; SCHOOL MOTTOES: 253
Remember, MEMORY: 23
Remember and forget not, MEMORY: 24
Remember the Alamo, MEMORY: 25;
  STATE MOTTOES: 45

Remember the poore, and god wil bles thee and thy store, KINDNESS: 22

Remember there are two sides to every question. Get both., EXPLORATION: 4

Remember thy end, MEMORY: 26

Remember your oath, MEMORY: 27

Remigio altissimi, WILL: 4

Renascentur, REBIRTH: 21

Renovabitur ut aquilae juventus tua, BIRDS: 27; REBIRTH: 22

Renovate animos, REBIRTH: 23

Renovato nomine, REBIRTH: 24

Renovatur aetas ejus sicut aquilae, BIRDS: 28; REBIRTH: 25

Reparabit cornua Phoebe, REBIRTH: 26

Repetens exempla suorum, ANCESTRY: 33

Republique, GOVERNMENT: 8

Repullulat, GROWTH: 19

REPUTATION, p. 624

Requiesco a laboribus meis, INDUSTRIOUSNESS: 175; REST: 24

Requiesco sub umbra, REST: 25; SHADE: 8

Rere Vaka Na Kaloo Ka Doka Na Tui, DIVINITY: 370; ROYALTY: 106

Rerum cognoscere causas, CAUSATION: 7; SCHOOL MOTTOES: 254

Rerum sapientia custos, WISDOM: 56

Research/ Education/ Service, SCHOOL MOTTOES: 255

Research/ Instruction/ Extension: For the advancement of science and arts, SCHOOL MOTTOES: 256

Resistit Deus superbis, DIVINITY: 371; PRIDE: 12

Resistite usque ad sanguinem, DEFIANCE: 11

Res non verba, FACTUALITY: 4

Res non verba quaeso, DEEDS: 85; WORDS: 34

Resolute and firm, STEADFASTNESS: 107

Resolutio cauta, PRUDENCE: 77; STEADFASTNESS: 108

Resolve is power, POWER: 19; STEADFASTNESS: 109

Resolve well, persevere, STEADFASTNESS: 110

Respice, THOUGHT: 22

Respice, auspice, prospice, SCHOOL MOTTOES: 257; TIME: 45

Respice, prospice, TIME: 46

Respice finem, FINISH: 12; LOCAL GOVERNMENT: 310

Respice fines, FINISH: 13

Respice futurum, FUTURE, THE: 25

Respice prospice, LOCAL GOVERNMENT: 311; TIME: 49

Respiciens prospiciens, TIME: 50

Respicio sine luctu, PAST, THE: 10

Respicit haec populum, respicit illa polum, VISION: 16

REST, p. 625

RESTRAINT, p. 627

Restitutor, REBIRTH: 27

RESULTS, p. 627

Resurgam, REBIRTH: 28

Resurgere tento, REBIRTH: 29

Resurgit ex virtute vera gloria, GLORY: 51; VIRTUE: 170

Resurgo, REBIRTH: 30

Retinens vestigia famae, ANCESTRY: 34; REPUTATION: 9

Re vera, TRUTH: 80

REVERENCE, p. 627

Revirescam, FLOURISHING: 63; REBIRTH: 31

Revirescat, FLOURISHING: 64; REBIRTH: 32

Revirescimus, FLOURISHING: 65

Revirescit, FLOURISHING: 66

Reviresco, FLOURISHING: 67; LOCAL GOVERNMENT: 312; REBIRTH: 33

Revise, CHANGE: 16

Revocate animos, COURAGE: 196

REWARD, p. 627

Rex Deus quisquam humanus est, ROYALTY: 107

Rex et nostra jura, LAW: 59; LOCAL GOVERNMENT: 313; ROYALTY: 108

Rex mundi, ROYALTY: 109

Rex non verba, ROYALTY: 110; WORDS: 35

Rex spicula nescit, ROYALTY: 111; WEAPONS: 84

Rhad Duw a ryddid, DIVINITY: 372; LIBERTY: 102

Rhyddid gwerin ffyniant gwlad, COUNTRY: 128; LIBERTY: 103; LOCAL GOVERNMENT: 314

Rhyddid hedd a llwyddiant, LIBERTY: 104; LOCAL GOVERNMENT: 315; PEACE: 75; PROSPERITY: 49

Mottoes & Categories

Richt do and fear na, FEAR: 61;
RIGHTS: 13
Rident florentia prata, HAPPINESS: 55;
LAUGHTER: 3
Rien est constant si non l'inconstance
durable mesme en son changement,
TRANSIENCE: 15
Rien sans Dieu, DIVINITY: 373
Rien sans peine, ADVERSITY: 80
Rien sans raison, THOUGHT: 23
Right and reason, JUSTICE: 110;
REASON: 21; RECTITUDE: 64
Right can never die, JUSTICE: 111;
RECTITUDE: 65
Right onward, ADVANCE: 53
RIGHTEOUSNESS, p. 631
RIGHTS, p. 633
Right revere, and persevere,
JUSTICE: 112; PERSEVERANCE: 79;
RECTITUDE: 66
Right to share, SHARING: 4
Rinasco piu glorioso, REBIRTH: 34
Ripis rapax, rivis audax, AUDACITY: 86
Rise and shine, RISING: 11
RISING, p. 634
RISK, p. 635
R. M. H. D. D. H. G. (Regiere mich
Herr durch dienen heiligen Geist),
DIVINE GUIDANCE: 385
Ro an mor, LOCAL GOVERNMENT: 316;
SEA: 28
Robore, STRENGTH: 109
Robore et sapientia, STRENGTH: 110;
WISDOM: 57
Robore et sapore, STRENGTH: 111
Robore et vigilantia, STRENGTH: 112;
VIGILANCE: 60
Robor et agilitas, STRANGER: 11;
STRENGTH: 113
Robori prudentia praestat,
PRUDENCE: 78; STRENGTH: 114
Robur, STRANGER: 12; STRENGTH: 115
Robur atque fides, FAITH: 204;
STRENGTH: 116
Robur in cruce, CROSS, THE: 95;
STRENGTH: 117
Robur in Deo, DIVINE GUIDANCE: 386;
STRENGTH: 118
Robur in vita Deus, DIVINITY: 374
Robur meum Deus, DIVINE
GUIDANCE: 387; STRENGTH: 119

Rosa concordiae signum, FLORA: 32;
LOCAL GOVERNMENT: 317; UNITY: 64
Rosae inter spinas nascuntur, IRONY: 4
Rosam ne rode, FLORA: 33
Rosam qui meruit ferat, FLORA: 34
Rosa petit coelum, FLORA: 35
Rosario, FLORA: 36
Rosa sine spina, FLORA: 37
Ros coeli, PARADISE: 56
Rosis coronat spina, FLORA: 38
Row and retake, NAVIGATION: 1
ROYALTY, p. 636
Rubet ensis sanguine Arabum,
WEAPONS: 85
Ruinam salutarunt pro rege,
ROYALTY: 112
Rule be ours, GOVERNMENT: 9
RUNNING, p. 644
Rupes mea Dominus, DIVINE
GUIDANCE: 388
Rupto robore nati, BIRTH: 3
Rura mihi placent, COUNTRYSIDE: 2;
LOCAL GOVERNMENT: 318
Ruris amator, COUNTRYSIDE: 3; LOCAL
GOVERNMENT: 319
Rus gratiis musisque dignum,
COUNTRYSIDE: 4; LOCAL
GOVERNMENT: 320
Rutilans rosa sine spina, FLORA: 39
Rycht and reason, REASON: 22;
RECTITUDE: 67

S

SACRIFICE, p. 645
Sacrarium regis cunabula legis,
LAW: 60; LOCAL GOVERNMENT: 321;
ROYALTY: 113
Sacrifice or service, SACRIFICE: 5;
SCHOOL MOTTOES: 258; SERVICE: 44
Sacrificium Dei cor contritum,
DIVINITY: 375
SADNESS, p. 645
Sae bauld, AUDACITY: 87
Saepe creat pulchras aspera spina
rosas, FLORA: 40; IRONY: 5
Saepe pro rege, semper pro republica,
PATRIOTISM: 86; ROYALTY: 114
Saepe pro rege semper pro patria,
PATRIOTISM: 87; ROYALTY: 115
Saevumque tridentem servamus,
WEAPONS: 86

Sagaciter, fideliter, constanter,
FIDELITY: 279; STEADFASTNESS: 111;
WISDOM: 58

Sagax et audax, AUDACITY: 88;
WISDOM: 59

Sagesse sans tache, WISDOM: 60

Saie and doe, WORDS: 36

Saigeadoir collach a buadh,
COURAGE: 197

Sail through, NAVIGATION: 2

Salamanca, PROPER NAMES: 44

Salix flectitur sed non frangitur,
FLEXIBILITY: 4

Sal sapit omnia, VIRTUE: 171

Salt is life, LIFE: 30; LOCAL
GOVERNMENT: 322

Salubritas et eruditio, HEALING and
HEALTH: 29; KNOWLEDGE: 59; LOCAL
GOVERNMENT: 323

Salubritas et industria, HEALING and
HEALTH: 30; LOCAL
GOVERNMENT: 324

Salus et decus, GLORY: 52;
SALVATION: 36

Salus et felicitas, HAPPINESS: 56;
HEALING and HEALTH: 31; LOCAL
GOVERNMENT: 325

Salus et gloria, GLORY: 53; HEALING and
HEALTH: 32; SALVATION: 37

Salus in fide, FAITH: 205;
SALVATION: 38

Salus mea Christus, CHRIST, JESUS: 71;
SALVATION: 39

Salus naufragis salus aegris, LOCAL
GOVERNMENT: 326; SECURITY: 49

Salus per Christum, CHRIST, JESUS: 72;
SALVATION: 40

Salus per Christum Redemptorem,
CHRIST, JESUS: 73; SALVATION: 41

Salus populi, LOCAL
GOVERNMENT: 327; PEOPLE: 17

Salus populi suprema est lex, LAW: 61;
LOCAL GOVERNMENT: 328;
PEOPLE: 18

Salus populi suprema lex, LAW: 62;
LOCAL GOVERNMENT: 329;
PEOPLE: 19

Salus populi suprema lex esto,
LAW: 63; PEOPLE: 20; STATE
MOTTOES: 46

Salus publica salus mea, PEOPLE: 21

Salutem disponit Deus, DIVINITY: 376;
SALVATION: 42

SALVATION, p. 646

Salve magna parens, LOCAL
GOVERNMENT: 330; PARENTS: 4

Salvet me Deus, DIVINE GUIDANCE: 389

Salvus in igne, FIRE: 14; SECURITY: 50

Samoa Muamua le Atua,
DIVINITY: 377; NATIONAL
MOTTOES: 24

Sancta clavis coeli fides, FAITH: 206;
PARADISE: 57

Sancta trinitas mea haereditas,
DIVINITY: 378

Sancte et sapienter, SCHOOL
MOTTOES: 259; WISDOM: 61

Sanctitas, RIGHTEOUSNESS: 14

Sane Baro, STATUS: 10

Sanguine Christe tuo, CHRIST,
JESUS: 74; SACRIFICE: 6

Sanguine inscribam, UNCLASSIFIED: 57

Sanguis et vulnera, INJURY: 8

Sanitas/ scientia/ sanctitas, HEALING
and HEALTH: 33; KNOWLEDGE: 60;
SCHOOL MOTTOES: 260

Sanitate crescamus, HEALING and
HEALTH: 34; LOCAL
GOVERNMENT: 331

San Josef, PROPER NAMES: 45

Sans cause, CAUSATION: 8

Sans changer, CHANGE: 17

Sans changer ma vérité,
CONSISTENCY: 8

Sans charger, LIMITATION: 10;
MODERATION: 32

Sans crainte, COURAGE: 198

Sans Dieu le ne puis, DIVINE
GUIDANCE: 390

Sans Dieu rien, DIVINITY: 379; LOCAL
GOVERNMENT: 332

Sans espine ne se eveille la rose,
IRONY: 6

Sans heure, TIME: 51

Sans mal, EVIL: 7

Sans mauvais désir, GOODNESS: 38

Sans peur, COURAGE: 199

Sans peur et sans reproche,
COURAGE: 200

Sans recuiller jamais,
STEADFASTNESS: 112

Sans tache, PURITY: 19

Sans variance, et à mon droit,
CHANGE: 18
Sans varier, CHANGE: 19;
STEADFASTNESS: 113
Sans venin, UNCLASSIFIED: 58
Sape et tace, SILENCE: 15; WISDOM: 62
Sapere aude, LOCAL
GOVERNMENT: 333; WISDOM: 63
Sapere aude, et tace, WISDOM: 64
Sapere aude, incipe, WISDOM: 65
Sapere et tacere, SILENCE: 16;
WISDOM: 66
Sapiens dominabitur astris, STARS: 35;
WISDOM: 67
Sapiens non eget, WISDOM: 68
Sapiens qui assiduus,
INDUSTRIOUSNESS: 176; WISDOM: 69
Sapiens qui prospicit, FORESIGHT: 9;
SCHOOL MOTTOES: 261; WISDOM: 70
Sapiens qui vigilat, WISDOM: 71
Sapiente diffidentia, TRUST: 92
Sapienter et constanter,
STEADFASTNESS: 114; WISDOM: 72
Sapienter et fortiter, COURAGE: 201;
WISDOM: 73
Sapienter et pie, PIETY: 48; WISDOM: 74
Sapienter proficiens,
IMPROVEMENT: 43; LOCAL
GOVERNMENT: 334
Sapienter si sincere, SINCERITY: 13;
WISDOM: 75
Sapienter uti bonis, ENJOYMENT: 31
Sapientia aedificavit sibi Domum,
SCHOOL MOTTOES: 262; WISDOM: 76
Sapientia/ caritas/ prudentia,
KINDNESS: 23; PRUDENCE: 79;
SCHOOL MOTTOES: 263; WISDOM: 77
Sapientia Domum aedificavit,
KNOWLEDGE: 61; SCHOOL
MOTTOES: 264
Sapientia domus erecta est,
WISDOM: 78
Sapientia donum Dei, DIVINE
GIFTS: 49; WISDOM: 79
Sapientia et doctrina, SCHOOL
MOTTOES: 265; WISDOM: 80
Sapientia et veritas, TRUTH: 81;
WISDOM: 81
Sapientia et virtus, VIRTUE: 172;
WISDOM: 82
Sapientia felicitas, HAPPINESS: 57;
SCHOOL MOTTOES: 266; WISDOM: 83

Sapientia non violentia, FORCE: 19;
WISDOM: 84
Sapientia tutus, SECURITY: 51;
WISDOM: 85
Sapientia/ virtus/ amicitia,
FRIENDSHIP: 49; KNOWLEDGE: 62;
SCHOOL MOTTOES: 267; VIRTUE: 173
Sapit qui Deo sapit, DIVINE
GUIDANCE: 391; WISDOM: 86
Sapit qui Deum sapit, DIVINITY: 380;
WISDOM: 87
Sapit qui laborat,
INDUSTRIOUSNESS: 177; WISDOM: 88
Sapit qui reputat, WISDOM: 89
Sat amico si mihi felix, FRIENDSHIP: 50
Sat cito quia bene sat, SPEED: 45
Sat cito si sat bene, SPEED: 46
Sat cito si sat tuto, SPEED: 47
SATISFACTION, p. 649
Satis est prostrasse leoni, ANIMALS: 50;
SATISFACTION: 8
Satis imperat qui sibi est imperiosus,
SELF-DETERMINATION: 4
Saturet quies, REST: 26
Save me, Lord!, DIVINE GUIDANCE: 392
Savoir pouvoir, KNOWLEDGE: 63;
POWER: 20
Saw through, PERSEVERANCE: 80
Say and do, WORDS: 37
Scandit sublimia, RISING: 12
Scandit sublimia virtus, VIRTUE: 174
Scherze nicht mit Ernst,
SERIOUSNESS: 6
Scholarship/ Participation/ Service,
KNOWLEDGE: 64; SCHOOL
MOTTOES: 268; SERVICE: 45
SCHOOL MOTTOES, p. 650
Science with practice, SCHOOL
MOTTOES: 269
Scienter utor, ABILITY: 26
Scientia, KNOWLEDGE: 65; SCHOOL
MOTTOES: 270
Scientiae cedit mare, KNOWLEDGE: 66;
SCHOOL MOTTOES: 271; SEA: 29
Scientiae et labori detur,
INDUSTRIOUSNESS: 178;
KNOWLEDGE: 67; LOCAL
GOVERNMENT: 335
Scientiae laborisque memor,
INDUSTRIOUSNESS: 179;
KNOWLEDGE: 68

Sermoni consona facta, DEEDS: 86;
INTEGRITY: 40; WORDS: 38
Sero sed serie, SERIOUSNESS: 8
Serpentes velut et columbae,
WISDOM: 94
Servabit me semper Jehovah, DIVINE
GUIDANCE: 402
Servabo fidem, FAITH: 211
Serva fidem, FAITH: 212
Serva jugum, SERVICE: 48
Serva jugum sub jugo, SERVICE: 49
Servare mentem, MIND: 42
Servare modum, MODERATION: 33
Servare munia vitae, DUTY: 28
Servata fides cineri, DEDICATION: 12
Servate fidem cineri, DEDICATION: 13
Servatum sincere, FIDELITY: 296
Serve and obey, SERVICE: 50;
TRADES: 31
Serve God and be cheerful, LOCAL
GOVERNMENT: 343; SERVICE: 51
Serve the king, SERVICE: 52
Serve with gladness, LOCAL
GOVERNMENT: 344; SERVICE: 53
SERVICE, p. 688
Service and efficiency, LOCAL
GOVERNMENT: 345; SERVICE: 54
Service first, SCHOOL MOTTOES: 285;
SERVICE: 55
Service is sovereignty, SCHOOL
MOTTOES: 286; SERVICE: 56
Service links all, LOCAL
GOVERNMENT: 346; SERVICE: 57
Service/ Opportunity/ Community/
Learning, OPPORTUNITY: 11; SCHOOL
MOTTOES: 287; SERVICE: 58
Service through education, SCHOOL
MOTTOES: 288; SERVICE: 59
Serviendo, SERVICE: 60
Serviendo guberno, GOVERNMENT: 10;
SERVICE: 61
Serving the King of Kings, SCHOOL
MOTTOES: 289; SERVICE: 62
Servire Deo regnare est, SERVICE: 63
Servire Deo sapere, SERVICE: 64;
WISDOM: 95
Servitute clarior, SERVICE: 65
Servus servorum Dei, SERVICE: 66
Set on, UNCLASSIFIED: 60
Seur et loyal, FIDELITY: 297;
TRUSTWORTHINESS: 6

Sfida e commanda, AUTHORITY: 6;
LAW: 64
SHADE, p. 692
SHARING, p. 693
Shanet aboo, DEFIANCE: 12
Shee ec y jerrey, PEACE: 77
Shenichun (Shenachie) Erin, OFFICE: 3
Sherwoode, LOCATION: 7; PROPER
NAMES: 46
SHINING, p. 694
Shoot thus, WEAPONS: 89
Sibi constet, STEADFASTNESS: 115
Sibimet merces industria,
INDUSTRIOUSNESS: 181
Sibi quisque dat, GIFTS and GIVING: 27
Sic ad astra, STARS: 37
Sica inimicis, WEAPONS: 90
Sic bene merenti palma, REWARD: 42
Sic cuncta caduca, TRANSIENCE: 16
Sic cuncta nobilitat, NOBILITY: 20
Sic curre ut capias, RUNNING: 5
Sic curre ut comprendas, RUNNING: 6
Sic donec, FUTURE, THE: 26
Si celeres quatit pennas, SPEED: 48
Sic fidem teneo, FIDELITY: 298
Sic fidus ut robur, FIDELITY: 299
Sic fuit, est, et erit, TIME: 53
Sic his qui diligunt, LOVE: 107
Sic itur ad astra, IMMORTALITY: 9
Sic itur ad astra. Optime de patria
meruit, REWARD: 43
Sic itur in altum, PARADISE: 59
Sicker, SECURITY: 61
Sic limina tuta, SECURITY: 62
Sic luceat lux vestra, LIGHT: 76;
SCHOOL MOTTOES: 290; SHINING: 27
Sic mihi si fueris tu leo qualis ens,
ANIMALS: 51
Sic nos, sic sacra tuemur, DEFENSE: 44;
RIGHTS: 14
Sic oculos, sic ille genas, sic ora
ferebat, BEAUTY: 16
Sic olim, FUTURE, THE: 27
Sic paratior, PREPAREDNESS: 75
Sic parvis magna, GREATNESS: 10
Sic rectius progredior, HONOR: 165
Sic semper tyrannis, OPPRESSION: 7;
STATE MOTTOES: 48
Sic sustentata crescit, SUPPORT: 7
Sic te non vidimus olim, VISION: 17
Sic tutus, SECURITY: 63

Sicut aquilae pennis, BIRDS: 30;
LOFTINESS: 22
Sicut iris florebit, FLOURISHING: 73
Sicut lilium, FLORA: 41; SCHOOL
MOTTOES: 291
Sicut oliva virens laetor in aede Dei,
DIVINITY: 382; HAPPINESS: 58;
RELIGION: 29
Sicut quercus, STRANGER: 13;
STRENGTH: 120
Sicut quercus virescit industria,
FLOURISHING: 74;
INDUSTRIOUSNESS: 182; LOCAL
GOVERNMENT: 347
Sicut serimus sic metimus, RESULTS: 4
Sic virescit industria, FLOURISHING: 75;
INDUSTRIOUSNESS: 183; LOCAL
GOVERNMENT: 348
Sic virescit virtus, VIRTUE: 178
Sic viresco, FLOURISHING: 76
Sic viret virtus, VIRTUE: 179
Sic vita humana, LIFE: 31
Sic vivere vivetis, LIFE: 32;
PARADISE: 60
Sic volvere parcas, FATE: 31
Sic vos non vobis, LOCAL
GOVERNMENT: 349;
UNSELFISHNESS: 24
Si Deus nobiscum, DIVINE
GUIDANCE: 403
Si Deus nobiscum quis contra
nos?, DIVINE GUIDANCE: 404
Si Deus pro nobis quis contra
nos?, DIVINE GUIDANCE: 405
Si Deus quis contra?, DIVINE
GUIDANCE: 406
Si Dieu est pour nous, qui sera contre
nous?, DIVINE GUIDANCE: 407
Si Dieu ne veut, Fortune ne peut,
DIVINE GUIDANCE: 408
Si Dieu veult, DIVINE GUIDANCE: 409
Sidus adsit amicum, STARS: 38
Si fractus fortis, STRENGTH: 121
SIGN, p. 695
Signantur cuncta manu, HANDS: 30
Signum fidei, FAITH: 213; SCHOOL
MOTTOES: 292
Signum pacis amor, LOVE: 108;
PEACE: 78
Signum quaerens in vellere, SIGN: 6

Signum salutis semper, HEALING and
HEALTH: 35; LOCAL
GOVERNMENT: 350
Si j'avance, suivez-moi; si je fuis, tuez-
moi; si je meurs, vengez-moi,
ADVANCE: 54; DEATH: 91;
FOLLOWING: 22; LEADERSHIP: 23;
VENGEANCE: 8
Si je n'estoy, BEING, SELF: 3
Si je pouvois, POSSIBILITY: 8
Si je puis, POSSIBILITY: 9
SILENCE, p. 696
Silendo et sperando, CONFIDENCE: 19;
SILENCE: 17
Silentio et spe, HOPE: 173; SILENCE: 18
Silenzio ad concordia, SILENCE: 19
S'ils te mordent, mords les,
DEFENSE: 45
Simili frondescit virga metallo,
UNCLASSIFIED: 61
SIMILARITY, p. 697
Si monent tubae, paratus,
PREPAREDNESS: 76
Simplex munditiis, SIMPLICITY: 10
Simplex vigilum veri, HONESTY: 50
Simplices sicut pueri, sagaces sicut
serpentes, HARMLESSNESS: 4;
WISDOM: 96
SIMPLICITY, p. 698
Sincera fide agere, FAITH: 214
Sincere et constanter,
STEADFASTNESS: 116
Sinceritas, SINCERITY: 16
Sinceritate, SINCERITY: 17
SINCERITY, p. 698
Sine Cerere et Baccho friget Venus,
LOVE: 109
Sine clade sterno, VICTORY: 41
Sine crimine fiat, EXCELLENCE: 14
Sine cruce sine luce, CROSS, THE: 96;
LIGHT: 77
Sine Deo careo, DIVINITY: 383
Sine Deo frustra, DIVINE
GUIDANCE: 410
Sine Deo nihil, DIVINITY: 384
Sine dolo, DIRECTNESS: 15
Sine fine, FINISH: 14
Sine fraude fides, FAITH: 215
Sine injuria, INJURY: 9
Sine labe decus, HONOR: 166; LOCAL
GOVERNMENT: 351
Sine labe fides, FAITH: 216

Sine labe lucebit, PURITY: 20

Sine labe nota, PURITY: 21

Sine labore nihil floret,
INDUSTRIOUSNESS: 184; LOCAL
GOVERNMENT: 352

Sine labore non paritur gloriosa
victoria, INDUSTRIOUSNESS: 185;
VICTORY: 42

Sine macula, PURITY: 22

Sine macula macla, PURITY: 23

Sine metu, COURAGE: 204

Sine numine nihilum, DIVINITY: 385

Sine pondere sursum, RISING: 13

Sine sanguine victor, CONQUEST: 34

Sine sole nihil, SUN: 12

Sine stet viribus, POWER: 22

Sine timore, COURAGE: 205

Sine virtute vani sunt honores,
HONOR: 167; VIRTUE: 180

Singula cum valeant sunt meliora
simul, STRENGTH: 122; UNITY: 65

Singulariter in spe, HOPE: 174

Sin not, EVIL: 8

Si non consilio impetu, CLEVERNESS: 7;
WALKING: 8

Si non datur ultra, LIMITATION: 11

Si non felix, ENJOYMENT: 33

S'intruire pour servir, SCHOOL
MOTTOES: 293; SERVICE: 67

Sionnach aboo, ANIMALS: 52;
VICTORY: 43

Sioth chain agus fairsinge, PEACE: 79;
PROSPERITY: 54

Si possem, POSSIBILITY: 10

Si quaeris peninsulam amoenam
circumspice, SEARCH and
DISCOVERY: 11; STATE MOTTOES: 49

Si recte facies, RECTITUDE: 71

Sis fortis, COURAGE: 206

Si sit prudentia, PRUDENCE: 81

Sis justus, et ne timeas, FEAR: 64;
JUSTICE: 113

Sis justus nec timeas, FEAR: 65;
JUSTICE: 114

Si sonent tubae paratus,
PREPAREDNESS: 77

Sis pius in primis, PIETY: 50

Sit Deus in studiis, DIVINE
GUIDANCE: 411; KNOWLEDGE: 77

Sit dux sapientia, WISDOM: 97

Sit fors ter felix, FATE: 32;
HAPPINESS: 59

Sitivit in te anima mea, DESIRE: 22

Sit laus Deo, PRAISE: 12

Sit lux, LIGHT: 78; SCHOOL
MOTTOES: 294

Sit lux et lux fuit, LIGHT: 79

Sit mihi libertas, LIBERTY: 107

Sit nomen decus, HONOR: 168;
NAME: 10

Sit ordo in omnibus, ORDER: 8

Sit saxum firmit, LOCAL
GOVERNMENT: 353; STRENGTH: 123

Sit sine labe, PURITY: 24

Sit sine labe decus, HONOR: 169

Sit sine labe fides, FAITH: 217

Sit sine spina, FLORA: 42

Sit Tibi sancta cohors comitum,
DEDICATION: 14; LOCAL
GOVERNMENT: 354

Situ exoritur Segeduni, LOCAL
GOVERNMENT: 355; LOCATION: 8

Sit vita nomini congrua, LIFE: 33;
NAME: 11

Sit vult Deus, DIVINE GUIDANCE: 412

Siyinqaba, STRENGTH: 124

SIZE, p. 700

S. M. D. (Susceptor Meus Dominus),
DIVINE GUIDANCE: 413

Smite on, quoth Smith,
AGGRESSION: 15

Sobrie, pie, juste, PIETY: 51;
RIGHTEOUSNESS: 15

Sobrii este vigilantes, VIGILANCE: 64

Societas scientia virtus, FELLOWSHIP: 9;
KNOWLEDGE: 78; VIRTUE: 181

So fork forward, MANNER: 11

Soies content, HAPPINESS: 60

Soies ferme, STRENGTH: 125

Soirbheachadh le Gleann Amuinn,
FLOURISHING: 77; SCHOOL
MOTTOES: 295

Soit droit fait, RECTITUDE: 72; SCHOOL
MOTTOES: 296

Sol, mi, re, fa, MUSIC: 6

Sola bona quae honesta, HONOR: 170;
LOCAL GOVERNMENT: 356

Sola cruce, CROSS, THE: 97

Sola cruce salus, CROSS, THE: 98;
SALVATION: 43

Sola Deo salus, SALVATION: 44

Sola Deus salus, SALVATION: 45

Sola et unica virtus, VIRTUE: 182

Sola gloriosa quae justa, GLORY: 54;
JUSTICE: 115
Sola in Deo salus, DIVINITY: 386
Sola juvat virtus, VIRTUE: 183
Solamen, GUIDANCE: 26
Sola meus turris Deus, DIVINE
GUIDANCE: 414
Sola nobilitas virtus, NOBILITY: 21;
VIRTUE: 184
Sola nobilitat virtus, NOBILITY: 22;
VIRTUE: 185
Sola salus servire Deo, DIVINITY: 387
Sola ubique triumphans, VICTORY: 44
Sola ubique triumphat, VICTORY: 45
Sola virtus invicta, VIRTUE: 186
Sola virtus invicta, 1632, VIRTUE: 187
Sola virtus munimentum, VIRTUE: 188
Sola virtus nobilitat, NOBILITY: 23;
VIRTUE: 189
Sola virtus reddit nobilem,
NOBILITY: 24; VIRTUE: 190
Sola virtus triumphat, VIRTUE: 191
Sol clarior astro, STARS: 39; SUN: 13
Solem contemplor, despicio terram,
SUN: 14
Solem fero, SUN: 15
Solem ferre possum, SUN: 16
Solertia ditat, PRUDENCE: 82
Sol et pastor Deus, DIVINE
GUIDANCE: 415; LOCAL
GOVERNMENT: 357
Sol et salubritas, HEALING and
HEALTH: 36; LOCAL
GOVERNMENT: 358; SUN: 17
Sol et scutum Deus, DIVINE
GUIDANCE: 416
Soli Deo, DIVINITY: 388
Soli Deo gloria, DIVINITY: 389
Soli Deo gloria et honor, DIVINITY: 390
Soli Deo honor, DIVINITY: 391
Soli Deo honor et gloria, DIVINITY: 392
Soli Deo victoria, DIVINITY: 393;
VICTORY: 46
SOLITUDE, p. 700
Sol meus testis, SUN: 18
Solo Deo gloria, DIVINITY: 394
Solo Deo salus, SALVATION: 46
Sol tibi signa dabit, SIGN: 7; SUN: 19
Solus Christus mea rupes, CHRIST,
JESUS: 76
Solus in pluribus, SOLITUDE: 4
Solus inter plurimos, SOLITUDE: 5

Solus mihi invidus obstat,
OPPOSITION: 12
Solus minus solus, SOLITUDE: 6
Solus per Christum Redemptorem,
CHRIST, JESUS: 77
Solus spes mea Christus, CHRIST,
JESUS: 78; HOPE: 175
Son comfort et liesse, HAPPINESS: 61;
LOCAL GOVERNMENT: 359
Son courage dompter c'est la grand
[*sic*] victoire, COURAGE: 207; SELF-
CONTROL: 10
Sors est contra me, FATE: 33
Sors mea a Domino, FATE: 34
Sors mihi grata cadit, ENJOYMENT: 34
Sors omnia versat, FATE: 35
Sorte contentus, HAPPINESS: 62
Sorte sua contentus, HAPPINESS: 63
So run that you may obtain, PURSUIT: 9
Souvenez, MEMORY: 28
Soyez compatissant soyez courtois,
COURTESY: 5; KINDNESS: 24
Soyez content, HAPPINESS: 64
Soyez courtois, COURTESY: 6
Soyez ferme, STRENGTH: 126
Soyez fiel, FIDELITY: 301
Soyez sage, WISDOM: 98
Soyez sage et simple, SIMPLICITY: 11;
WISDOM: 99
Spanning the world, EARTH: 15;
SCHOOL MOTTOES: 297
Spare not, GENEROSITY: 15
Spare nought, GENEROSITY: 16
Spare when you have nought,
GENEROSITY: 17
Spartam nactus es: hanc exorna,
DUTY: 29; SCHOOL MOTTOES: 298
Spartan, PROPER NAMES: 47
Spe, HOPE: 176
Spe aspera levat, HOPE: 177
Spectemur agendo, ACTION: 21;
DEEDS: 87; JUDGMENT: 13; LOCAL
GOVERNMENT: 360
SPEED, p. 700
Speed, SPEED: 49
Speed, strength, and truth united,
SPEED: 50; STRENGTH: 127;
TRADES: 32; TRUTH: 85
Speed well, SPEED: 51
Spe et amore, HOPE: 178; LOVE: 110
Spe et industria, HOPE: 179;
INDUSTRIOUSNESS: 186

Spe et labore, HOPE: 180
Spe expecto, HOPE: 181
Spe gaudeo, HOPE: 182
Spei bonae atque animi,
    COURAGE: 208; HOPE: 183
Spe labor levis, HOPE: 184
Spe meliore vehor, HOPE: 185
Spe melioris alor, HOPE: 186
Spem et speravi, HOPE: 187
Spem fortuna alit, FORTUNE: 99;
    HOPE: 188
Spem pretio non emam, HOPE: 189
Spem renovant alae, HOPE: 190
Spem renovat, HOPE: 191
Spem renovat anni, HOPE: 192
Spem sequimur, HOPE: 193
Spem successus alit, HOPE: 194;
    SUCCESS: 15
Spem vigilantia firmat, HOPE: 195;
    VIGILANCE: 65
Spe nemo ruet, HOPE: 196; LOCAL
    GOVERNMENT: 361
Spe posteri temporis, HOPE: 197
Spera, HOPE: 198
Sperabo, HOPE: 199
Sperando spiro, HOPE: 200
Sperandum, HOPE: 201
Sperandum est, HOPE: 202
Sperandum est esperance, HOPE: 203
Sperans, HOPE: 204
Sperans pergo, HOPE: 205
Sperantes in Domino non deficient,
    HOPE: 206
Speranza é verita, HOPE: 207;
    TRUTH: 86
Sperare timere est, FEAR: 66; HOPE: 208
Sperate et vivite fortes, COURAGE: 209;
    HONOR: 171; HOPE: 209
Sperate futurum, FUTURE, THE: 28;
    HOPE: 210
Sperat infestis, ADVERSITY: 82;
    HOPE: 211
Speratum et completum, HONOR: 172;
    HOPE: 212
Speravi, HOPE: 213
Speravi in Domino, DIVINITY: 395;
    HOPE: 214
Spernit humum, CONTEMPT: 6
Spernit pericula virtus, DANGER: 19;
    VIRTUE: 192
Sperno, CONTEMPT: 7
Spero, HOPE: 215

Spero dum spiro, HOPE: 216
Spero dum spiro, mea spes est unica
    Christus, HOPE: 217
Spero et captivus nitor, HOPE: 218
Spero et progredior, HONOR: 173;
    HOPE: 219
Spero et vivo, HONOR: 174; HOPE: 220
Spero in Deo, DIVINITY: 396; TRUST: 94
Spero infestis, metuo secundis,
    ADVERSITY: 83; HOPE: 221;
    PROSPERITY: 55
Spero invidiam, ENVY: 10
Spero meliora, HOPE: 222
Spero procedere, HOPE: 223;
    PROSPERITY: 56
Spero suspiro donec, HOPE: 224
Spero ut fidelis, FAITH: 218; HOPE: 225
Spes, HOPE: 226
Spes, salus, decus, HONOR: 175;
    HOPE: 227
Spes alit, HOPE: 228
Spes alit agricolam, HOPE: 229
Spes anchora tuta, HOPE: 230
Spes anchora vitae, HOPE: 231
Spes antiqua domus, HOPE: 232
Spes aspera levat, HOPE: 233
Spes audaces adjuvat, HOPE: 234
Spes dabit auxilium, HOPE: 235
Spes decus et robur, HOPE: 236;
    STRENGTH: 128
Spes durat avorum, HOPE: 237
Spes est in Deo, DIVINITY: 397;
    HOPE: 238
Spes et fides, FAITH: 219; HOPE: 239
Spes et fortitudo, FORTITUDE: 27;
    HOPE: 240
Spes et fortuna, FORTUNE: 100;
    HOPE: 241
Spes firma, HOPE: 242
Spes fovet et melius cras fore semper
    ait, HOPE: 243
Spes in Deo, DIVINITY: 398; HOPE: 244
Spes in Domino, DIVINITY: 399;
    HOPE: 245
Spes in extremum, HOPE: 246
Spes infracta, HOPE: 247
Spes in futuro, HOPE: 248
Spes juvat, HOPE: 249
Spes labor levis, HOPE: 250
Spes lucis aeternae, HOPE: 251
Spes magna in Deo, DIVINITY: 400;
    HOPE: 252

Mottoes & Categories

Stella Christi duce, CHRIST, JESUS: 81;
STARS: 40
Stella clavisque Maris Indici, STARS: 41
Stella futura micat divino lumine,
DIVINITY: 403; STARS: 42
Stellis aspirate gemellis, STARS: 43
Stemmata quid
faciunt?, ANCESTRY: 38
Stet, CONSERVATION: 6
Stet fortuna, FORTUNE: 103
Stet fortuna domus, FORTUNE: 104;
SCHOOL MOTTOES: 302
Stet non timeat, COURAGE: 210
Still bydand, STEADFASTNESS: 131
Still without fear, COURAGE: 211
Stimulat sed ornat, DECORATION: 4
Stire steddie, EQUANIMITY: 19
Sto, mobilis, FLEXIBILITY: 5
Sto cado fide et armis, FAITH: 222
Stolz und treu, FIDELITY: 302;
PRIDE: 13
Sto ne per vim sed per jus,
RECTITUDE: 73; STRENGTH: 129
Sto pro fide, FAITH: 223
Sto pro veritate, TRUTH: 88
STRANGER, p. 722
STRENGTH, p. 723
Strength, STRENGTH: 130
Strength from the soil, STATE
MOTTOES: 51; STRENGTH: 131
Strength is from heaven, PARADISE: 61;
STRENGTH: 132
Strenuè et audacter, AUDACITY: 91
Strenue et honeste, HONOR: 176;
STRENGTH: 133
Strenue et prospere, SUCCESS: 16
Strenue insequor, FOLLOWING: 23
Stricta parata neci, DEATH: 92
Strike, AGGRESSION: 16
Strike alike, AGGRESSION: 17
Strike Dakyns, the devil's in the
hempe, AGGRESSION: 18
Strike for the laws, LAW: 65
Strike sure, AGGRESSION: 19
Stringit amore, LOVE: 111
Strive for the gain of all, EFFORT: 33;
LOCAL GOVERNMENT: 365
Strong and firm, STRENGTH: 134
Struggle, EFFORT: 34
St. Sebastian, PROPER NAMES: 50
Studendo et contemplando indefessus,
KNOWLEDGE: 79

Studiis et rebus honestis,
RECTITUDE: 74; SCHOOL
MOTTOES: 303
Studio optimae doctrinae et saluti
sanitatis, EXCELLENCE: 15; HEALING
and HEALTH: 37; SCHOOL
MOTTOES: 304
Study quiet, KNOWLEDGE: 82;
SILENCE: 20
St. Vincent, PROPER NAMES: 51
Sua gratia parvis, BEAUTY: 17
Sua praemia virtus, REWARD: 44;
VIRTUE: 194
Suaviter, GENTLENESS: 14
Suaviter, fortiter, AUDACITY: 92;
GENTLENESS: 15
Suaviter et fortiter, DISCIPLINE: 6;
GENTLENESS: 16
Suaviter in modo, GENTLENESS: 17
Suaviter in modo, fortiter in re,
DEEDS: 89; MANNER: 12
Suaviter in modo fortiter in re,
DEEDS: 90; MANNER: 13
Suaviter sed fortiter, DISCIPLINE: 7;
GENTLENESS: 18
Sub cruce candida, CROSS, THE: 100
Sub cruce canto, CROSS, THE: 101
Sub cruce copia, CROSS, THE: 102
Sub cruce floreamus, CROSS, THE: 103;
FLOURISHING: 78; LOCAL
GOVERNMENT: 366
Sub cruce glorior, CROSS, THE: 104
Sub cruce lux, CROSS, THE: 105;
LIGHT: 80
Sub cruce salus, CROSS, THE: 106;
SALVATION: 47
Sub cruce semper viridis, CROSS,
THE: 107
Sub cruce veritas, CROSS, THE: 108;
TRUTH: 89
Sub cruce vinces, CROSS, THE: 109
Subditus fidelis regis est salus regni,
ROYALTY: 117
Sub hoc signo vinces, SIGN: 8
Subimet merces industria,
INDUSTRIOUSNESS: 187; REWARD: 45
Subito, SPEED: 52
Sub lege libertas, LAW: 66;
LIBERTY: 108
Sub libertate quietem, LIBERTY: 109;
REST: 28

Mottoes & Categories

Sublime petimus *or* Sublimia petimus,
ASPIRATION: 74

Sublimia cures, CONCERN: 4

Sublimiora petamus, ASPIRATION: 75

Sublimiora peto, ASPIRATION: 76

Sublimiora quaero, ASPIRATION: 77

Sublimiora spectemus, ASPIRATION: 78

Sublimis per ardua tendo,
ASPIRATION: 79

Sub montibus altis, LOCATION: 10

Sub onere crescit, ADVERSITY: 84

Sub pace copia, PEACE: 80;
PROSPERITY: 57

Sub pondere, GROWTH: 20

Sub pondere cresco, GROWTH: 21

Sub pondere sursum, ASPIRATION: 80

Sub robore virtus, STRENGTH: 135;
VIRTUE: 195

Sub sole, sub umbra, virescens,
FLOURISHING: 79; SHADE: 9; SUN: 20

Sub sole, sub umbra virens,
FLOURISHING: 80; SHADE: 10; SUN: 21

Sub sole nihil, SEARCH and
DISCOVERY: 12

Sub sole sub umbra crescens,
INCREASE: 25; SHADE: 11; SUN: 22

Sub sole viresco, FLOURISHING: 81;
SUN: 23

Sub solo patebit, INCREASE: 26; SUN: 24

Sub spe, HOPE: 282

Sub tegmine, OBSCURITY: 12

Sub tegmine fagi, OBSCURITY: 13

Sub tigno salus, SECURITY: 64

Sub tutela Domini, DIVINE
GUIDANCE: 419

Sub tuum praesidium, PROTECTION: 29

Sub umbra, SHADE: 12

Sub umbra alarum tuarum, SHADE: 13

Sub umbra quies, REST: 29; SHADE: 14

Sub umbra quiescam, REST: 30;
SHADE: 15

SUCCESS, p. 734

Successus a Deo est, SUCCESS: 17

Succesus per educationem, SCHOOL
MOTTOES: 305; SUCCESS: 18

Suchet und werdet finden, SEARCH and
DISCOVERY: 13

Such is love, LOVE: 112

Sudore non sopore,
INDUSTRIOUSNESS: 188; LOCAL
GOVERNMENT: 367

Suffer, SUFFERING: 10

SUFFERING, p. 735

Sufferings are lessons, SUFFERING: 11

Suffibulatus majores sequor,
ANCESTRY: 39; WAY: 8

Sufficit meruisse, WORTHINESS: 59

Sui ipsius praemium, REWARD: 46

Sui oblitus commodi,
UNSELFISHNESS: 25

Suis ducibus ubique fidelis,
FIDELITY: 303

Suis stat viribus, SELF-RELIANCE: 12

Suivant St. Pierre, FOLLOWING: 24

Suivez de l'ange, FOLLOWING: 25

Suivez la raison, REASON: 23

Suivez moi, FOLLOWING: 26

Suivez raison, REASON: 24

Sui victoria indicat regem, CROWN: 30;
SELF-CONTROL: 11; VICTORY: 48

Sume superbiam quaesitam mentis,
ACQUISITION: 8; MIND: 43; PRIDE: 14

Summa rerum vestigia sequor,
FOLLOWING: 27

Summis viribus, STRENGTH: 136

Summum nec metuam diem nec
optem, EQUANIMITY: 20

Sum quod sum, BEING, SELF: 4

Sumus, BEING, SELF: 5

Sumus ubi fuimus, STEADFASTNESS: 132

SUN, p. 736

Sunt aliena, STRANGER: 14

Sunt sua praemia laudi, PRAISE: 13;
REWARD: 47

Sunt tria haec unum, UNITY: 67

Suo se robore firmat, STRENGTH: 137

Suo stat robore virtus, STRENGTH: 138;
VIRTUE: 196

Supera alta tenere, ASPIRATION: 81

Supera audi et tace, LISTENING: 3;
SILENCE: 21

Superabit omnia virtus, VIRTUE: 197

Supera Moras, LOCAL
GOVERNMENT: 368; LOCATION: 11

Super antiquas vias, PAST, THE: 11;
SCHOOL MOTTOES: 306; TRADITION: 4

Superba frango, DESTRUCTION: 8

Superiora sequor, ASPIRATION: 82

Superna quaerite, SEARCH and
DISCOVERY: 14

Superna quaero, SEARCH and
DISCOVERY: 15

Superna sequor, FOLLOWING: 28;
PARADISE: 62

Super sidera votum, DESIRE: 23;
STARS: 44
SUPPORT, p. 738
Supra spem spero, HOPE: 283
Suprema manus validior, HANDS: 31;
STRENGTH: 139
Suprema quaero, SEARCH and
DISCOVERY: 16
Sure, DEPENDABILITY: 3
Sure and steadfast, DEPENDABILITY: 4;
STEADFASTNESS: 133
Sur esperance, HOPE: 284
Sur et loyal, FIDELITY: 304;
TRUSTWORTHINESS: 7
Surgam, RISING: 14
Surgamus ergo strenue, LOCAL
GOVERNMENT: 369; RISING: 15
Surge illuminare, RISING: 16
Surgere tento, RISING: 17
Surgimus, LOCAL GOVERNMENT: 370;
RISING: 18
Surgite, lumen adest, LIGHT: 81;
RISING: 19
Surgit post nubila Phoebus, SUN: 25;
TRADES: 33
Surgo, lumen adest, LIGHT: 82;
RISING: 20
Sursum, ASPIRATION: 83
Sursum corda, ASPIRATION: 84;
HAPPINESS: 66; SCHOOL MOTTOES: 307
Sursum deorsum, DIRECTION: 9
Sursum prorsusque, RISING: 21
Sursum specto, VISION: 18
Suscipere et finire,
ACCOMPLISHMENT: 19
Suspice, VISION: 19
Suspice Teucro, ADMIRATION: 4
Sustentante Deo, DIVINE
GUIDANCE: 420
Sustentatus providentiâ,
PROVIDENCE: 28
Sustento sanguine signa,
DEDICATION: 15; SACRIFICE: 7
Sustineatur, SUPPORT: 8
Sustine et abstine, ENDURANCE: 50
Sustineo, ENDURANCE: 51
Sustinere, ENDURANCE: 52
Suum cuique tribue, DUE: 5
Suum cuique tribuens, DUE: 6
Suum cuique tribuere, DUE: 7; LOCAL
GOVERNMENT: 371
Swift and sure, SPEED: 53

Swift and true, FIDELITY: 305;
SPEED: 54
Syn ar dy hun, SELF-KNOWLEDGE: 11

T

Tace, SILENCE: 22
Tace aut fac, WORDS: 39
Tache sans tâche, ASPIRATION: 85
Tachez surpasser en vertue,
VIRTUE: 198
Tais en temps, SILENCE: 23; TIME: 55
Tak a thocht, THOUGHT: 24
Tak tent, ATTENTIVENESS: 9
Tam animo mente sublimis,
LOFTINESS: 23
Tam aris quam aratris, RELIGION: 31
Tam arte quam Marte, ABILITY: 29;
STRENGTH: 140
Tam audax quam fidelis,
COURAGE: 212; FIDELITY: 306
Tam corde quam manu, FEELINGS: 24;
HANDS: 32
Tam fidus quam fixus, FIDELITY: 307;
STEADFASTNESS: 134
Tam genus quam virtus, ANCESTRY: 40;
VIRTUE: 199
Tam in arte quam Marte, ABILITY: 30;
FORCE: 20
Tam interna quam externa,
WORTHINESS: 60
Tam marte quam arte, WAR: 68
Tam Marti quam Mercurio, WAR: 69
Tam pace quam proelio, PEACE: 81;
WAR: 70
Tam virtus quam honos, HONOR: 178;
VIRTUE: 200
Tam virtute quam labore,
DILIGENCE: 58; VIRTUE: 201
Tandem, TIME: 56
Tandem bona causa triumphat,
VICTORY: 49
Tandem exaudisti me, LISTENING: 4
Tandem fit arbor, GROWTH: 22
Tandem fit surculus arbor,
GROWTH: 23
Tandem implebitur, FULLNESS: 7
Tandem justitia, JUSTICE: 117
Tandem licet sero, TIME: 57
Tandem patientia victrix, PATIENCE: 43

T. A. N. D. E. M. (Tibi aderit numen divinum, expecta modo), DIVINE GUIDANCE: 421

Tandem tranquillus, TRANQUILLITY: 9

Tandem vincitur, CONQUEST: 35

Tanquam despicatus sum vinco, CONQUEST: 36

Tanti talem genuere parentes, PARENTS: 5

Tant que je puis, POSSIBILITY: 11

Tantum in superbos, PRIDE: 15

Tantum nobis creditum, DUTY: 30; SCHOOL MOTTOES: 308

Tantum quantum possum, POSSIBILITY: 12

Tarde non fur mai grazie diuine, DIVINE GUIDANCE: 422; GRACE: 29

Taurum cornibus prende, ANIMALS: 53

Teaching/ Research/ Service, KNOWLEDGE: 83; SCHOOL MOTTOES: 309; SERVICE: 68

Te Deum laudamus, PRAISE: 14

Te digna sequere, FOLLOWING: 29

Te duce gloriamur, GUIDANCE: 27

Te duce libertas, LEADERSHIP: 24; LIBERTY: 110

Te duce vincimus, CONQUEST: 37

Te favente virebo, FLOURISHING: 82

Teipsum nosce, SELF-KNOWLEDGE: 12

Tela spoliis data, WEAPONS: 93

Temeraire, AUDACITY: 93

Temere ne sperne, CONTEMPT: 8

Temperans et constans, STEADFASTNESS: 135

Temperat aequor, SEA: 31

Tempera te tempori, TIME: 58

Templa, quam dilecta, LOVE: 113

Tempora mutantur permanet praestantia, EXCELLENCE: 16; SCHOOL MOTTOES: 310

Tempore candidior, BEAUTY: 18

Tempore utimur, LOCAL GOVERNMENT: 372; TIME: 59

Tempori parendum, IMPROVEMENT: 45; LOCAL GOVERNMENT: 373

Tempus et casus accidit omnibus, TIME: 60

Tempus et patientia, PATIENCE: 44; TIME: 61

Tempus meae opes, TIME: 62

Tempus omnia monstrat, TIME: 63

Tempus omnia revelat, THOUGHT: 25; TIME: 64

Tempus rerum imperator, TIME: 65; TRADES: 34

Tenax, STRENGTH: 141

Tenax et fide, FAITH: 224; PERSEVERANCE: 81

Tenax et fidelis, FIDELITY: 308; LOCAL GOVERNMENT: 374; PERSEVERANCE: 82; STEADFASTNESS: 136

Tenax et fidus, FIDELITY: 309; PERSEVERANCE: 83

Tenax in fide, FAITH: 225

Tenax propositi, STEADFASTNESS: 137

Tenax propositi vinco, CONQUEST: 38

Tende bene et alta pete, ASPIRATION: 86

Tendens ad aethera virtus, VIRTUE: 202

Tendimus, ADVANCE: 55

Tendimus ad coelum, PARADISE: 63

Tending to peace, PEACE: 82

Tendit ad astra, ASPIRATION: 87; STARS: 45

Tendit ad astra fides, FAITH: 226

Tendit in ardua virtus, VIRTUE: 203

Teneat, luceat, floreat, vi, virtute, et valore, COURAGE: 213; FLOURISHING: 83; VIRTUE: 204; WORTHINESS: 61

Tenebo, STEADFASTNESS: 138

Tenebras expellit et hostes, VICTORY: 50

Tenebras meas, DARKNESS: 19

Tenebris lux, DARKNESS: 20; LIGHT: 83

Tene fortiter, STRENGTH: 142

Tene mensuram et respice finem, MODERATION: 34

Teneo, POSSESSION: 24

Teneo et credo, POSSESSION: 25

Teneo tenuere majores, POSSESSION: 26

Tenes le vraye, TRUTH: 90

Tenez le droit, RECTITUDE: 75

Tenez le vraye, TRUTH: 91

Tentanda via est, ATTEMPT: 5

Tentando superabis, CONQUEST: 39

Tenuimus, POSSESSION: 27

Te pro te, UNCLASSIFIED: 63

Terar dum prosim, GOODNESS: 41

Ter fidelis, FIDELITY: 310

Ternate, PROPER NAMES: 52

Terra, aqua, ignis, sal, spiritus,
sulphur, Sol, Venus, Mercurius,
EARTH: 16; FIRE: 15; SPIRIT: 16;
SUN: 26; WATER: 17

Terra, mare, fide, EARTH: 17;
FAITH: 227; SEA: 32

Terra aut mari, EARTH: 18; SEA: 33

Terra marique fide, FAITH: 228

Terra marique potens, POWER: 23;
SEA: 36

Terra marique victor, VICTORY: 51

Terras irradient, ENLIGHTENMENT: 7;
SCHOOL MOTTOES: 311

Terrena pericula sperno, DANGER: 20

Terrena per vices sunt aliena,
EARTH: 21

Terrere nolo, timere nescio, FEAR: 67

Terris peregrinus et hospes,
STRANGER: 15

Terrorem affero, FEAR: 68

Te splendente, SHINING: 29

Te stante virebo, ENDURANCE: 53;
FLOURISHING: 84

Tevertite, UNCLASSIFIED: 64

Texas one and indivisible, STATE
MOTTOES: 52; UNITY: 68

Thankful, GRATITUDE: 15

Tharros, Dynamis, Philosophia,
COURAGE: 214; SCHOOL
MOTTOES: 312

That the people shall know,
KNOWLEDGE: 84; PEOPLE: 22;
SCHOOL MOTTOES: 313

That they may all be one, UNITY: 69

The axe is laid at the root of the tree,
TRADES: 35; UTENSILS: 4

The buck stops here, DUTY: 31

The College Creating the Best, SCHOOL
MOTTOES: 314

The college of the Keys, LOCATION: 12;
SCHOOL MOTTOES: 315

The college that cares, CONCERN: 5;
SCHOOL MOTTOES: 316

The college that meets your
requirements, SCHOOL MOTTOES: 317

The cross our stay, CROSS, THE: 110

The day of my life, DAY: 11

The Earth is the Lord's, and the
fulness thereof, EARTH: 22

The entrance of Thy Word giveth
light, SCHOOL MOTTOES: 318;
SCRIPTURES: 14

The entrance to an enchanted world,
UNCLASSIFIED: 65

The Fatherland is worth more than the
Kingdom of Heaven, COUNTRY: 131

The field is the world, COMMERCE: 7

The fruit is as the tree, FRUIT: 9

The grit poul, UNCLASSIFIED: 66

The knot unites, LOCAL
GOVERNMENT: 376; UNITY: 70

The land divided, the world united,
NATIONAL MOTTOES: 25; UNITY: 71

The Lord is my only support, DIVINE
GUIDANCE: 423

The Lord will provide, DIVINE
GUIDANCE: 424

The love of liberty brought us here,
LIBERTY: 111; NATIONAL MOTTOES: 26

The love of the people is my strength,
NATIONAL MOTTOES: 27

The noblest motive is the public good,
NOBILITY: 25

The red hand of Ireland, HANDS: 33

There is no difficulty to him that wills,
ADVERSITY: 85; STEADFASTNESS: 139;
WILL: 5

The reward of integrity, INTEGRITY: 41

The reward of valor, COURAGE: 215;
REWARD: 48

The right and sleep, UNCLASSIFIED: 67

The righteous are bold as a lion,
ANIMALS: 54; AUDACITY: 94;
RIGHTEOUSNESS: 16

The road to knowledge,
KNOWLEDGE: 85; SCHOOL
MOTTOES: 319

The same, CONSISTENCY: 13

The seed is the word, SCHOOL
MOTTOES: 320; WORDS: 40

The servant of God communicating
the Word of God, SCHOOL
MOTTOES: 321; SCRIPTURES: 15

The state, the home, the farm,
GOVERNMENT: 11; HOME: 20; SCHOOL
MOTTOES: 322

The strongest arm uppermost,
STRENGTH: 143

The strongest hand uppermost,
HANDS: 34; STRENGTH: 144

The swarthy stranger defying *or* The
red stranger defying, DEFIANCE: 13

The time will come, FUTURE, THE: 29

The torch the staff of knowledge,
  KNOWLEDGE: 86; SCHOOL
  MOTTOES: 323
The tree drops acorns, FLORA: 43
The truth against the world, TRUTH: 92
The truth makes free, SCHOOL
  MOTTOES: 324; TRUTH: 93
The truth shall make you free, SCHOOL
  MOTTOES: 325; TRUTH: 94
The union, STATE MOTTOES: 53;
  UNITY: 72
The wicked borroweth and payeth not
  again, UNCLASSIFIED: 68
They by permission shine, SHINING: 30
The yellow (haired) man defying,
  DEFIANCE: 14
They ryght defend, DEFENSE: 46;
  LOCAL GOVERNMENT: 377
Thincke and thancke, THOUGHT: 26
Think and thank, THOUGHT: 27
Think on, THOUGHT: 28
Think well, THOUGHT: 29
Think/ Work/ Serve,
  INDUSTRIOUSNESS: 189;
  KNOWLEDGE: 87; SCHOOL
  MOTTOES: 326; SERVICE: 69;
  THOUGHT: 30
This I'll defend, DEFENSE: 47
This is our charter, GOVERNMENT: 12
Thole (Endure) and think on,
  ENDURANCE: 54
Thol (Endure) and think,
  ENDURANCE: 55
THOUGHT, p. 739
Thournib' creve'th, REWARD: 49;
  VENGEANCE: 9
Thou shalt want ere I want,
  DEPRIVATION: 2
Through, ADVANCE: 56
Through God revived, DIVINE
  GUIDANCE: 425
Through the narrow way (*from
  Greek*), WAY: 9
Through truth to freedom, SCHOOL
  MOTTOES: 327; TRUTH: 95
Thrust on, ADVANCE: 57
Thue Recht scheu Nimant, FEAR: 69;
  RECTITUDE: 76
Thure et jure, JUSTICE: 118
Thus, UNCLASSIFIED: 69
Thus far, UNCLASSIFIED: 70

Thus thou must do if thou have it,
  NECESSITY: 3
Thy hand, O Lord, hath been glorified
  in strength, DIVINITY: 404
Thy right hand, O Lord, hath been
  glorified in strength, HANDS: 35;
  STRENGTH: 145
Tibi soli, GIFTS and GIVING: 28
Tiens à la vérité, TRUTH: 96
Tiens firme, STEADFASTNESS: 140
Tiens le droit, RECTITUDE: 77
Tiens ta foy, FAITH: 229
Till then thus, FUTURE, THE: 30
TIME, p. 741
Time Deum, DIVINITY: 405
Time Deum, honora Caesarem,
  FEAR: 70; ROYALTY: 118
Time Deum et ne timeas, FEAR: 71
TIMELINESS, p. 746
Timenti Dominum non deerit ullum
  bonum, FEAR: 72
Timere sperno, COURAGE: 216
Timet pudorem, DISGRACE: 16
Time tryeth troth, TIME: 66; TRUTH: 97
Time tryeth tryst, TIME: 67
Timor Dei nobilitas, FEAR: 73;
  NOBILITY: 26
Timor Dei summa securitas, FEAR: 74;
  SECURITY: 65
Timor Domini fons vitae,
  DIVINITY: 406
Timor Domini initium sapientiae (est),
  FEAR: 75; WISDOM: 100
Timoris nescius, COURAGE: 217
Timor omnis abest, COURAGE: 218
Timor omnis abesto, COURAGE: 219
Tod, DEATH: 93
To each his farthest star,
  ASPIRATION: 88; SCHOOL
  MOTTOES: 328; STARS: 46
Together, UNITY: 73
Together we aspire, together we
  achieve, ASPIRATION: 89; NATIONAL
  MOTTOES: 28; UNITY: 74
To God only be all glory,
  DIVINITY: 407
To help people learn, ASSISTANCE: 22;
  KNOWLEDGE: 88; SCHOOL
  MOTTOES: 329
To know Him and to make Him
  known, DIVINITY: 408; SCHOOL
  MOTTOES: 330

To learn/ To search/ To serve,
KNOWLEDGE: 89; SCHOOL
MOTTOES: 331; SEARCH and
DISCOVERY: 17; SERVICE: 70

Toleranda et speranda,
ENDURANCE: 56; HOPE: 285

To live is to learn, LIFE: 34; SCHOOL
MOTTOES: 332

Tollit peccata mundi, SALVATION: 48

To match job opportunities with job
skills, OPPORTUNITY: 13; SCHOOL
MOTTOES: 333

To reach out, CONCERN: 6; SCHOOL
MOTTOES: 334

To rock the cradle of reposing age,
AGE: 8

Tota educatio, KNOWLEDGE: 90;
SCHOOL MOTTOES: 335

Tota gloriosa filia regis intrinsecus,
ROYALTY: 119

Tota mea fiducia est in deo,
DIVINITY: 409; TRADES: 36; TRUST: 95

Tot capita tot sententiae, MIND: 44

Tot praemia vitae, LIFE: 35;
REWARD: 50

Tot rami quot arbores, FLORA: 44

To travel hopefully, HOPE: 286;
SCHOOL MOTTOES: 336

Totum est providentia,
PROVIDENCE: 29

TOUCH, p. 746

Touch not the cat bot (i.e., without) a
glove, ANIMALS: 55; TOUCH: 4

Toujours, FIDELITY: 311

Toujours en vedette, VIGILANCE: 66

Toujours fidèle, FIDELITY: 312

Toujours firme, STRENGTH: 146

Toujours fort, STRENGTH: 147

Toujours gai, LIVELINESS: 5

Toujours jeune, AGE: 9

Toujours le même, CONSISTENCY: 14

Toujours loyale, FIDELITY: 313

Toujours pret (*or* prest) French,
PREPAREDNESS: 78

Toujours propice, FORTUNE: 105

Toujours sans tache, PURITY: 25

Tourne vers l'occident, DIRECTION: 10

Tous jours loyal, FIDELITY: 314

Tout à la gloire de Dieu, DIVINITY: 410

Tout à la volonté de Dieu, DIVINE
GUIDANCE: 426

Tout avec Dieu, DIVINITY: 411

Tout avec Dieu, rien sans raison,
DIVINITY: 412

Tout avec le temps, TIME: 68

Tout coeur, FEELINGS: 25

Tout d'en haut, DIVINE GIFTS: 50

Toute foys preste, PREPAREDNESS: 79

Tout en bon heure, TIME: 69

Tout en foy, FAITH: 230

Tout en la conduicte de Dieu, DIVINE
GUIDANCE: 427

Tout est de Dieu, DIVINITY: 413

Tout est en haut, UNCLASSIFIED: 71

Tout fin fait, FINISH: 15

Tout hardi, AUDACITY: 95

Tout jour, DEPENDABILITY: 5

Tout jour fidèle, FIDELITY: 315

Tout jours prest, PREPAREDNESS: 80

Tout mon contentement est en Dieu,
HAPPINESS: 67

Tout ou rien, MEASURE: 17

Tout par et pour Dieu, DIVINITY: 414

Tout pour Dieu et ma patrie,
COUNTRY: 132; DIVINITY: 415

Tout pour la belle, laquelle j'aime le
plus, BEAUTY: 19

Tout pour l'église, RELIGION: 32

Tout pour l'empire, GOVERNMENT: 13

Tout prest, PREPAREDNESS: 81

Touts jours fidèle, FIDELITY: 316

Tout un durant ma vie,
CONSISTENCY: 15

Tout vient de Dieu, DIVINITY: 416

Tout zèle, ZEALOUSNESS: 3

Toutz foitz chevalier, OFFICE: 4

Towton, PROPER NAMES: 53

Tractent fabrilia fabri, ABILITY: 31;
TRADES: 37

TRADES, p. 746

Trade and navigation, COMMERCE: 8;
NAVIGATION: 3

Trade and plantations,
AGRICULTURE: 7; COMMERCE: 9

TRADITION, p. 749

Traditum ab antiquis servare,
TRADITION: 5

Traditus, non victus, CONQUEST: 40

Traducere aevum leniter, CHANGE: 20

Trafalgar, PROPER NAMES: 54

Tramite recta, WAY: 10

Tra mor tra Meirion, LOCAL
GOVERNMENT: 378; SEA: 37

Turn nor swerve, DIRECTNESS: 16
Turpi secernere honestum,
  JUDGMENT: 14
Turpiter desperatur, DESPAIR: 8
Turris fortis mihi Deus, DIVINE
  GUIDANCE: 429
Turris fortissima Deus, DIVINE
  GUIDANCE: 430
Turris fortissima est nomen Jehovae,
  DIVINITY: 422; LOCAL
  GOVERNMENT: 381
Turris fortissima nomen Domini,
  DIVINE GUIDANCE: 431
Turris fortitudinis, STRENGTH: 148
Turris mihi Deus, DIVINE
  GUIDANCE: 432
Turris prudentia custos,
  PROTECTION: 30; PRUDENCE: 83
Turris tutissima virtus,
  FORTIFICATIONS: 6; VIRTUE: 206
Tutamen, DEFENSE: 50
Tutamen Deus, DIVINE GUIDANCE: 433
Tutamen pulchris, BEAUTY: 21
Tutamen tela coronae, CROWN: 31;
  WEAPONS: 94
Tuta timens, FEAR: 77; SECURITY: 66
Tutela, DEFENSE: 51
Tutemur, DEFENSE: 52
Tute tua tuta, SECURITY: 67
Tutissima statio, LOCAL
  GOVERNMENT: 382; SECURITY: 68
Tuto, celeriter, et jucunde,
  SECURITY: 69; SPEED: 55
Tuto et celeriter, SECURITY: 70;
  SPEED: 56
Tutto alfin vola, TRANSIENCE: 17
Tutto si fa, ACCOMPLISHMENT: 21
Tutum monstrat iter, SECURITY: 71
Tutum refugium, SECURITY: 72
Tutum te littore sistam, SECURITY: 73
Tutum te robore reddam,
  SECURITY: 74; STRENGTH: 149
Tutus in bello, SECURITY: 75; WAR: 72
Tutus in undis, SECURITY: 76
Tutus prompto animo, SECURITY: 77
Tutus si fortis, COURAGE: 220;
  SECURITY: 78
Tuum est, POSSESSION: 28
Tu vincula frange, UNCLASSIFIED: 73
T. V. B. (Treu und beständig),
  FIDELITY: 325; STEADFASTNESS: 141
Tyde what may, FATE: 36

Tyme proveth truth, TIME: 70;
  TRUTH: 111
Tyme tryeth troth, FIDELITY: 326
Tynctus cruore Saraceno,
  UNCLASSIFIED: 74
Tyrii tenuere coloni, POSSESSION: 29

U

Ua mau ke ea o ka aina i ka pono,
  RIGHTEOUSNESS: 17; STATE
  MOTTOES: 55
Ubi amor ibi fides, FAITH: 232;
  LOVE: 114
Ubi bene ibi patria, COUNTRY: 134
Ubi desint vires hominum ibi incipit
  divinum auxilium, DIVINE
  GUIDANCE: 434
Ubi fides ibi lux et robur, FAITH: 233;
  LIGHT: 85; LOCAL GOVERNMENT: 383;
  STRENGTH: 150
Ubi fides ibi vires, FAITH: 234;
  STRENGTH: 151
Ubi lapsus? Quid feci?, FAILURE: 5
Ubi libertas, LIBERTY: 116
Ubi libertas ibi patria, COUNTRY: 135;
  LIBERTY: 117
Ubi mel ibi fel, IRONY: 7
UBIQUITY, p. 769
Ubique, UBIQUITY: 10
Ubique aut nusquam, LOCATION: 13
Ubique fecundat imber,
  NOURISHMENT: 8
Ubique fidelis, FIDELITY: 327
Ubique paratus, PREPAREDNESS: 82
Ubique patriam reminisci,
  COUNTRY: 136
Ubi solum ibi coelum, EARTH: 23
Uhuru na umoja, LIBERTY: 118;
  NATIONAL MOTTOES: 31; UNITY: 78
U. K. O. (Unverhofft Kommt Oft),
  EXPECTATION: 11
Ulterius, IMPROVEMENT: 46
Ulterius et melius, IMPROVEMENT: 47
Ultra aspicio, FORESIGHT: 10
Ultra fert animus, MIND: 45
Ultra pergere, ADVANCE: 58
Umbra non cedit soli, SUN: 27
Una grande libre, LIBERTY: 119;
  NATIONAL MOTTOES: 32
Unalterable, PERMANENCE: 5

Mottoes & Categories

Un bel mourir toute la vie honore,
DEATH: 95; GLORY: 55
Unconditional surrender, WAR: 73
Undeb hedd llwyddiant, LOCAL
GOVERNMENT: 384; PEACE: 83;
PROSPERITY: 58; UNITY: 79
UNCLASSIFIED, p. 770
Unde derivatur?, ORIGIN: 10
Under God the people rule,
PEOPLE: 23; STATE MOTTOES: 56
Un Dieu, un roi, DIVINITY: 423;
ROYALTY: 120; UNITY: 80
Un Dieu, un roy, un coeur,
DIVINITY: 424; HEART: 11;
ROYALTY: 121; UNITY: 81
Un Dieu, un roy, un foy,
DIVINITY: 425; FAITH: 235;
ROYALTY: 122; UNITY: 82
Un Dieu et un Roi, DIVINITY: 426;
ROYALTY: 123; UNITY: 83
Undique fulsus, SUPPORT: 9
Un durant ma vie, CONSISTENCY: 16
Une foi, FAITH: 236
Une foy, une loy, FAITH: 237; LAW: 67;
UNITY: 84
Une foy mesme, FAITH: 238
Une pure foi, FAITH: 239
Ung Dieu, ung loy, ung foy,
DIVINITY: 427; FAITH: 240; LAW: 68;
UNITY: 85
Ung Dieu, ung roy, une loy,
DIVINITY: 428; LAW: 69;
ROYALTY: 124; UNITY: 86
Ung Dieu et ung roy, DIVINITY: 429;
ROYALTY: 125; UNITY: 87
Ung je servirai, SERVICE: 71
Ung je serviray, SERVICE: 72
Ung nous servons, LOCAL
GOVERNMENT: 385; UNITY: 88
Ung par tout, tout par ung, UNITY: 89
Ung roy, ung foy, ung loy, FAITH: 241;
LAW: 70; ROYALTY: 126; UNITY: 90
Ung sent ung soleil, FAITH: 242;
SUN: 28; UNITY: 91
Ung tout seul, UNIQUENESS: 6
Uni aequus virtuti, VIRTUE: 207
Unica spes mea Christus, CHRIST,
JESUS: 82; HOPE: 288
Unica virtus necessaria, VIRTUE: 208
Unicus est, UNIQUENESS: 7

Unidad, paz, justicia, JUSTICE: 121;
NATIONAL MOTTOES: 33; PEACE: 84;
UNITY: 92
Union, justice, confidence,
CONFIDENCE: 20; JUSTICE: 122; STATE
MOTTOES: 57; UNITY: 93
Union, justice and confidence,
CONFIDENCE: 21; JUSTICE: 123;
SCHOOL MOTTOES: 343; UNITY: 94
Union, travail, justice,
INDUSTRIOUSNESS: 192; JUSTICE: 124;
NATIONAL MOTTOES: 34; UNITY: 95
Union/ confidence/ justice,
CONFIDENCE: 22; JUSTICE: 125;
SCHOOL MOTTOES: 344; UNITY: 96
Unione augetur, UNITY: 97
Unione minima vigent, UNITY: 98
UNIQUENESS, p. 774
Unita durant, ENDURANCE: 57;
UNITY: 99
Unita fortior, STRENGTH: 152;
TRADES: 39; UNITY: 100
Unitas, veritas, caritas, KINDNESS: 26;
SCHOOL MOTTOES: 345; TRUTH: 112;
UNITY: 101
Unitas societatis stabilitas, TRADES: 40;
UNITY: 102
Unitate fortior, LOCAL
GOVERNMENT: 386; STRENGTH: 153;
UNITY: 103
Unitate praestans, EXCELLENCE: 17;
LOCAL GOVERNMENT: 387; UNITY: 104
Unite, UNITY: 105
Unité, dignité, travail,
INDUSTRIOUSNESS: 193; NATIONAL
MOTTOES: 35; UNITY: 106
Unité, travail, justice,
INDUSTRIOUSNESS: 194; JUSTICE: 126;
NATIONAL MOTTOES: 36; UNITY: 107
Unité, travail, progrès,
INDUSTRIOUSNESS: 195; NATIONAL
MOTTOES: 37; UNITY: 108
United to serve, LOCAL
GOVERNMENT: 388; UNITY: 109
United we stand, divided we fall,
SCHOOL MOTTOES: 346; STATE
MOTTOES: 58; UNITY: 110
Uniti progrediemur, NATIONAL
MOTTOES: 38; UNITY: 111
UNITY, p. 775

Unity, freedom, justice, JUSTICE: 127;
LIBERTY: 120; NATIONAL
MOTTOES: 39; UNITY: 112

Unity and faith, FAITH: 243; NATIONAL
MOTTOES: 40; UNITY: 113

Unity and freedom, LIBERTY: 121;
NATIONAL MOTTOES: 41; UNITY: 114

Unity and loyalty, FIDELITY: 328;
LOCAL GOVERNMENT: 389; UNITY: 115

Unity and progress, LOCAL
GOVERNMENT: 390; UNITY: 116

Unity in diversity, UNITY: 117

Un je servirai, SERVICE: 73

Uno avulso, non deficit alter,
NATIONAL MOTTOES: 42;
UNCLASSIFIED: 75

Uno ictu, STRENGTH: 154

Un peuple, un but, une foi,
FAITH: 244; GOALS: 8; NATIONAL
MOTTOES: 43; UNITY: 118

Un roy, une foy, une loy, FAITH: 245;
LAW: 71; ROYALTY: 127; UNITY: 119

UNSELFISHNESS, p. 782

USEFULNESS, p. 784

Unser glaub ist der sieg, der die welt
überwunden hatt, FAITH: 246;
VICTORY: 52

Un [sic] **corpus animo sic domus
corpori,** HOME: 21

Unto God only be honor and glory,
DIVINITY: 430; GLORY: 56;
HONOR: 180

Un tout seul, SOLITUDE: 7

Unus et idem, IDENTITY: 2

Unus et idem ferar, IDENTITY: 3

Unwandelbar, STEADFASTNESS: 142

Upward, RISING: 22

Urbi et orbi, EARTH: 24; SCHOOL
MOTTOES: 347

Urbs in rure, COUNTRYSIDE: 5; LOCAL
GOVERNMENT: 391

Usque ad aras, RELIGION: 33

Usque ad aras amicus, FRIENDSHIP: 51

Usque ad mortem, DEATH: 96

Usque ad mortem fidus, FIDELITY: 329

Usque fac et non parcas, DEEDS: 91

Usque fidelis, FIDELITY: 330

Usurpari nolo, HUMILITY: 8

Usus rectumque, TRADITION: 6

Ut amnis vita labitur, LIFE: 36

Ut apes geometriam, UNCLASSIFIED: 76

Ut aquila versus coelum, ANIMALS: 56;
LOFTINESS: 25

Ut aspirat cervus, ANIMALS: 57

Ut conchas auge nostra metalla Deus,
DIVINE GUIDANCE: 435

Ut crescit clarescit, INCREASE: 27

Ut cunque placuerit Deo,
DIVINITY: 431

Ut deficiar, DEPRIVATION: 3

Ut ducam spero, HOPE: 289

UTENSILS, p. 785

Utere dum potes, ENJOYMENT: 35

Utere loris, LIMITATION: 12

Utere mundo, EARTH: 25

Utere virtute, VIRTUE: 209

Ut ferrum forte, STRANGER: 16;
STRENGTH: 155

Ut fert divina voluntas, DIVINE
GUIDANCE: 436

Ut homines liberi sint, LIBERTY: 122;
LOCAL GOVERNMENT: 392

Utile dulci, USEFULNESS: 14

Utile et dulce, USEFULNESS: 15

Utilem pete finem, USEFULNESS: 16

Utile primo, USEFULNESS: 17

Utile quod taceas, SILENCE: 24

Ut implear, FULLNESS: 8

Utitur ante quaesitis, CONVENIENCE: 6

Ut mens cujusque is est quisque,
MIND: 46

Ut migraturus habita, TRANSIENCE: 18

Ut olim, PAST, THE: 12

Ut omnes te cognoscant,
KNOWLEDGE: 93; SCHOOL
MOTTOES: 348

Ut palma justus, RIGHTEOUSNESS: 18

Ut possim, POSSIBILITY: 13

Ut prosim, USEFULNESS: 18

Ut prosim aliis, USEFULNESS: 19

Ut prosim aliis prosim, BENEFITS: 5;
PROSPERITY: 59

Ut prosimus, SERVICE: 74

Ut quiescas labora,
INDUSTRIOUSNESS: 196; REST: 32

Ut quocumque paratus,
PREPAREDNESS: 83

Utraque fortuna contentus,
HAPPINESS: 68

Ut reficiar, REBIRTH: 35

Ut resurgam, REBIRTH: 36

Utrinque paratus, PREPAREDNESS: 84

Mottoes & Categories

Utrique fidelis, FIDELITY: 331; LOCAL
GOVERNMENT: 393
Utrius auctus auxilio, INCREASE: 28
Utriusque auxilio, ASSISTANCE: 23
Utrumque, WAR: 74
Ut sanem vulnero, HEALING and
HEALTH: 38
Ut secura quies, REST: 33
Ut sementem feceris ita et metes,
RESULTS: 5
Ut sibi sic alteri, DEEDS: 92
Ut sim paratior, PREPAREDNESS: 85
Ut sursum desuper, RISING: 23
Ut te cognoscant et vitam habeant,
LIFE: 37; SCHOOL MOTTOES: 349
Ut tibi sic aliis, DEEDS: 93
Ut tibi sic alteri, DEEDS: 94
Ut tu linguae tuae, sic ego mearum
aureum dominus sum, SELF-
CONTROL: 12
Ut vidi ut vici, CONQUEST: 41
Ut vinclo vir verbo ligitur,
DEDICATION: 16
Ut vivas vigila, VIGILANCE: 67

V

Vade ad formicam, UNCLASSIFIED: 77
Vae duplici cordi, DECEPTION: 13
Vae timido, FEAR: 78
Vae victis, CONQUEST: 42
Vaillant et veillant, COURAGE: 221;
VIGILANCE: 68
Vaillaunce avance le homme,
COURAGE: 222
Valde et sapienter, FORCE: 21;
WISDOM: 103
Valebit, VICTORY: 53
Valens et volens, ABILITY: 32;
WILLINGNESS: 8
Valet anchora virtus, STRENGTH: 156;
VIRTUE: 210
Valet et vulnerat, STRENGTH: 157
Valet pietas, PIETY: 52; STRENGTH: 158
Validus, STRENGTH: 159
Vallum aeneum esto, STRANGER: 17;
STRENGTH: 160
Valore et virtute, COURAGE: 223;
VIRTUE: 211
Valor e lealdad, COURAGE: 224;
FIDELITY: 332

Valor et fortuna, COURAGE: 225;
FORTUNE: 106
Valour and loyalty, COURAGE: 226;
FIDELITY: 333
Vana spes vitae, HOPE: 290
Vanitas vanitatum et omnia vanitas,
INSIGNIFICANCE: 6
Vanus est honor, HONOR: 181
Va outre marque,
ACCOMPLISHMENT: 22;
EXCELLENCE: 18
Varietas est propria fortunae,
CHANGE: 21; FORTUNE: 107
Vectis, UNCLASSIFIED: 78
Veillant et vaillant, COURAGE: 227;
VIGILANCE: 69
Veilliez et ne craignez pas,
VIGILANCE: 70
Vel arte vel Marte, ART: 32;
STRENGTH: 161
Vel exuviae triumphant, VICTORY: 54
Velis et remis, NAVIGATION: 4
Velis id quod possis, DESIRE: 24
Velle bene facere, INTENTION: 7
Vellera fertis oves, ANIMALS: 58
Velle vult quod Deus, DIVINE
GUIDANCE: 437
Velocitate, SPEED: 57
Vel pax, vel bellum, WAR: 75
Velut arbor aevo, FLOURISHING: 85;
SCHOOL MOTTOES: 350
Venabulis vinco, CONQUEST: 43;
WEAPONS: 95
Venale nec auro, ACQUISITION: 9;
INTEGRITY: 42
VENGEANCE, p. 786
Venit ab astris, STARS: 47; TRUTH: 113
Venit hora, TIME: 71
Ventis secundis, FORTUNE: 108
Venture and gain, RISK: 9
Venture forward, RISK: 10
Vera sequor, TRUTH: 114
Vera trophaea fides, FAITH: 247
Vera virtus immersabilis, VIRTUE: 212
Verax atque probus, HONESTY: 51;
TRUSTWORTHINESS: 9
Verax et fidelis, FIDELITY: 334
Verbum Domini manet in aeternum,
SCRIPTURES: 16
Veritas, SCHOOL MOTTOES: 351;
TRUTH: 115

Veritas, libertas, LIBERTY: 123;
TRUTH: 116

Veritas, puritas, PURITY: 26;
TRUTH: 117

Veritas cum libertate, SCHOOL
MOTTOES: 352; TRUTH: 118

Veritas et amicitia, LIBERTY: 124

Veritas et patria, COUNTRY: 137;
TRUTH: 119

Veritas et virtus, SCHOOL
MOTTOES: 353; TRUTH: 120;
VIRTUE: 213

Veritas et virtus vincunt, TRUTH: 121;
VIRTUE: 214

Veritas ingenio, TRUTH: 122

Veritas liberabit, LIBERTY: 125;
SCHOOL MOTTOES: 354; TRUTH: 123

Veritas liberabit vos, LIBERTY: 126;
SCHOOL MOTTOES: 355; TRUTH: 124

Veritas liberavit, LIBERTY: 127;
TRUTH: 125

Veritas/ libertas, LIBERTY: 128;
SCHOOL MOTTOES: 356; TRUTH: 126

Veritas magna est, TRUTH: 127

Veritas me dirigit, TRUTH: 128

Veritas/ mores/ scientia,
KNOWLEDGE: 94; SCHOOL
MOTTOES: 357; TRUTH: 129

Veritas non opprimitur, TRUTH: 130

Veritas odit morem, TRUTH: 131

Veritas odium parit, TRUTH: 132

Veritas omnia vincit, TRUTH: 133

Veritas praevalebit, TRUTH: 134

Veritas premitur non opprimitur,
TRUTH: 135

Veritas quasi rosa resplendet,
FLORA: 45; TRUTH: 136

Veritas securis, AUTHORITY: 7;
TRUTH: 137

Veritas sine timore, FEAR: 79;
TRUTH: 138

Veritas superabit, TRUTH: 139

Veritas superabit montes, TRUTH: 140

Veritas temporis filia, TRUTH: 141

Veritas via vitae, TRUTH: 142

Veritas victrix, TRUTH: 143

Veritas vincet, TRUTH: 144

Veritas vincit, SCHOOL MOTTOES: 358;
TRUTH: 145

Veritas vincit omnia, TRUTH: 146

Veritate et justitiâ, JUSTICE: 128;
TRUTH: 147

Veritatem, TRUTH: 148

Veritatis assertor, TRUTH: 149

Veritatis cultores, fraudis inimici,
TRUTH: 150

Veritatis et aequitatis tenax,
JUSTICE: 129; TRUTH: 151

Vérité sans peur, FEAR: 80; TRUTH: 152

Vérité soyez ma garde,
PROTECTION: 31; TRUTH: 153

Vérité vient, TRUTH: 154

Vernon serper viret, FLOURISHING: 86

Vero nihil verius, TRUTH: 155

Vero pro gratis, TRUTH: 156

Versus, DIRECTION: 11

Vertitur in diem, CHANGE: 22; DAY: 12

Vertitur in lucem, CHANGE: 23;
LIGHT: 86

Vertrau Gott, tue Recht, scheu
Niemandt, DIVINITY: 432; TRUST: 107

Vertu cherche honneur, HONOR: 182;
VIRTUE: 215

Vertu embellit, BEAUTY: 22;
VIRTUE: 216

Vertue vaunceth, VIRTUE: 217

Vertu surpasse richesse,
PROSPERITY: 60; VIRTUE: 218

Verum atque decus, RECTITUDE: 79;
TRUTH: 157

Verum dicit, TRUTH: 158

Verus, TRUTH: 159

Verus ad finem, TRUTH: 160

Verus amor patriae, COUNTRY: 138;
LOVE: 115; PATRIOTISM: 91

Verus et fidelis, FIDELITY: 335;
TRUTH: 161

Verus et fidelis semper, FIDELITY: 336;
TRUTH: 162

Verus et sedulus, DILIGENCE: 59;
TRUTH: 163

Verus honor honestas, HONESTY: 52;
HONOR: 183

Vescitur Christo, CHRIST, JESUS: 83

Vespera iam venit; nobiscum Christe
maneto, Extingui lucem nec patiare
tuam, CHRIST, JESUS: 84;
DARKNESS: 21

Vespere et mane, TIME: 72

Vespertilionis, BIRDS: 31

Vestigia nulla retrorsum, LOCAL
GOVERNMENT: 394;
STEADFASTNESS: 143

Vestigia premo majorum,
ANCESTRY: 41
Veteri frondescit honore, GROWTH: 24;
HONESTY: 53; HONOR: 184
Vetustas dignitatem generat, AGE: 10;
LOCAL GOVERNMENT: 395
Veuille bien, INTENTION: 8
Via crucis via lucis, CROSS, THE: 111
Via trita via tuta, SECURITY: 79
Vi at tamen honore, FORCE: 22;
HONOR: 185
Via tuta virtus, VIRTUE: 219
Via una cor unum, FIDELITY: 337
Vi aut virtute, FORCE: 23; VIRTUE: 220
Via veritas et vita, SCHOOL
MOTTOES: 359; TRUTH: 164; WAY: 11
Via vi, FORCE: 24
Vici, CONQUEST: 44
Vicimus, CONQUEST: 45
Vicinas urbes alit, GUIDANCE: 28;
LOCAL GOVERNMENT: 396
Vicisti et vivimus, CONQUEST: 46
Vicit, pepercit, CONQUEST: 47
Vicit amor patriae, COUNTRY: 139;
LOVE: 116; PATRIOTISM: 92
Vi corporis et animi, FORCE: 25
Victima Deo, SACRIFICE: 8
Victo dolore, SADNESS: 9
Victor, CONQUEST: 48
Victoria, VICTORY: 55
Victoria, fortitudo, virtus,
FORTITUDE: 28; VICTORY: 56;
VIRTUE: 221
Victoria a Domino, VICTORY: 57
Victoria concordiâ crescit, VICTORY: 58
Victoria gloria merces, GLORY: 57;
REWARD: 51; VICTORY: 59
Victoriam coronat Christus, CHRIST,
JESUS: 85; VICTORY: 60
Victoria non praeda, VICTORY: 61
Victoria signum, VICTORY: 62
Victoria vel mors, DEATH: 97;
VICTORY: 63
Victor in arduis, CONQUEST: 49
Victorious, VICTORY: 64
Victor mortalis est, TRANSIENCE: 19
Victor sine sanguine, VICTORY: 65
VICTORY, p. 786
Victory for us, VICTORY: 66
Victory or death, DEATH: 98;
VICTORY: 67

Victrix fortuna sapientiae,
FORTUNE: 110
Victrix patientia, PATIENCE: 45
Victrix patientia duris, PATIENCE: 46;
VICTORY: 68
Victrix prudentia, CONQUEST: 50;
PRUDENCE: 84
Victus in arduis, CONQUEST: 51
Vide cui fidas, TRUST: 108;
VIGILANCE: 71
Video alta sequorque, ASPIRATION: 90
Video et taceo, DISCRETION: 6
Video meliora, FORESIGHT: 11;
IMPROVEMENT: 48
Video meliora proboque,
FORESIGHT: 12; IMPROVEMENT: 49
Videte et cavete ab avaritia,
VIRTUE: 222
Vidi, vici, CONQUEST: 52
Viditque Deus hanc lucem esse bonam,
GOODNESS: 42; LIGHT: 87
Vi divina, DIVINE GUIDANCE: 438
Vi et animo, COURAGE: 228;
STRENGTH: 162
Vi et armis, FORCE: 26; WEAPONS: 96
Vi et arte, ABILITY: 33; STRENGTH: 163
Vi et consiliis, FORCE: 27
Vi et fide, FAITH: 248; FORCE: 28
Vi et fide vivo, FAITH: 249; FORCE: 29
Vi et industria, INDUSTRIOUSNESS: 197;
STRENGTH: 164
Vi et libertate, FORCE: 30;
LIBERTY: 129
Vi et veritate, FORCE: 31; TRUTH: 165
Vi et virtute, COURAGE: 229;
STRENGTH: 165; TRADES: 41
Vie vers vertu, VIGILANCE: 72;
VIRTUE: 223
Vif, courageux, fier, COURAGE: 230;
LIVELINESS: 6; PRIDE: 16
Viget in cinere virtus, DEATH: 99;
VIRTUE: 224
Viget sub cruce, CROSS, THE: 112;
FLOURISHING: 87
Vigila, VIGILANCE: 73
Vigila et aude, AUDACITY: 98;
VIGILANCE: 74
Vigila et ora, VIGILANCE: 75
VIGILANCE, p. 791
Vigilance, VIGILANCE: 76
Vigilando, VIGILANCE: 77

Vigilando ascendimus, VICTORY: 69;
VIGILANCE: 78
Vigilando munio, DEFENSE: 53;
VIGILANCE: 79
Vigilando quiesco, VIGILANCE: 80
Vigilans, VIGILANCE: 81
Vigilans et audax, AUDACITY: 99;
VIGILANCE: 82
Vigilans et certus, VIGILANCE: 83
Vigilans et fidelis, FIDELITY: 338;
VIGILANCE: 84
Vigilans et promptus, SPEED: 58;
VIGILANCE: 85
Vigilans et verus, TRUTH: 166;
VIGILANCE: 86
Vigilans non cadit, VIGILANCE: 87
Vigilant, VIGILANCE: 88
Vigilant and resolute, VIGILANCE: 89
Vigilante, VIGILANCE: 90
Vigilanter, VIGILANCE: 91
Vigilanter et constanter,
STEADFASTNESS: 144; VIGILANCE: 92
Vigilantes, VIGILANCE: 93
Vigilante salus, SECURITY: 80;
VIGILANCE: 94
Vigilantia, VIGILANCE: 95
Vigilantia, robur, voluptas,
ENJOYMENT: 36; STRENGTH: 166;
VIGILANCE: 96
Vigilantia et virtute, COURAGE: 231;
VIGILANCE: 97
Vigilantia non cadet, VIGILANCE: 98
Vigilantia praestat, VIGILANCE: 99
Vigilantia securitas, SECURITY: 81
Vigilantibus, VIGILANCE: 100
Vigilantibus non dormientibus,
VIGILANCE: 101
Vigilanti salus, SECURITY: 82
Vigilate, VIGILANCE: 102
Vigilate et orate, LOCAL
GOVERNMENT: 397; VIGILANCE: 103
Vigilat et orat, VIGILANCE: 104
Vigilo, VIGILANCE: 105
Vigilo et spero, HOPE: 291;
VIGILANCE: 106
Vigore, LIVELINESS: 7; STRENGTH: 167
Vigore et virtute, LIVELINESS: 8;
STRENGTH: 168; VIRTUE: 225
Vigueur de dessus, STRENGTH: 169
Vigueur l'amour de croix, CROSS,
THE: 113; STRENGTH: 170
Vill God I sall, DIVINE GUIDANCE: 439

Vi martiali Deo adjuvante, DIVINE
GUIDANCE: 440; WAR: 76
Vim da vi honestae, FORCE: 32
Vim promovet insitam, POWER: 24;
SCHOOL MOTTOES: 360
Vim vincit virtus, FORCE: 33;
VIRTUE: 226
Vim vi repellere licet, FORCE: 34
Vim vi repello, FORCE: 35
Vincam, CONQUEST: 53
Vincam malum bono, GOODNESS: 43
Vincam vel moriar, CONQUEST: 54;
DEATH: 100
Vince fide, FAITH: 250
Vince malum bono, GOODNESS: 44
Vince malum patientia, EVIL: 9;
PATIENCE: 47
Vincendo victus, CONQUEST: 55
Vincenti dabitur, CONQUEST: 56
Vincenti dabitur laurea,
CONQUEST: 57; REWARD: 52
Vincent qui se vincent, CONQUEST: 58
Vincere, CONQUEST: 59
Vincere aut mori, CONQUEST: 60;
DEATH: 101
Vincere est vivere, CONQUEST: 61
Vincere vel mori, CONQUEST: 62;
DEATH: 102
Vincet vel mori, CONQUEST: 63;
DEATH: 103
Vincet virtute, CONQUEST: 64;
VIRTUE: 227
Vincit cum legibus arma, LAW: 72;
WEAPONS: 97
Vincit labor, EFFORT: 37;
INDUSTRIOUSNESS: 198
Vincit liberavit, CONQUEST: 65;
LIBERTY: 130
Vincit omnia, CONQUEST: 66
Vincit omnia industria,
INDUSTRIOUSNESS: 199; LOCAL
GOVERNMENT: 398
Vincit omnia pertinax virtus,
VIRTUE: 228
Vincit omnia veritas, SCHOOL
MOTTOES: 361; TRUTH: 167
Vincit omnia virtus, VIRTUE: 229
Vincit pericula virtus, DANGER: 21;
VIRTUE: 230
Vincit qui curat, CAUTION: 37
Vincit qui devincit, CONQUEST: 67

Mottoes & Categories

Virtus dedit, cura servabit,
DISCRETION: 7; VIRTUE: 261
Virtus depressa resurget, VIRTUE: 262
Virtus difficilia vincit, VIRTUE: 263
Virtus dum patior vincit, VIRTUE: 264
Virtus durat avorum, ANCESTRY: 42
Virtus durissima ferret, VIRTUE: 265
Virtus duxit avorum, GUIDANCE: 29;
VIRTUE: 266
Virtus est Dei, VIRTUE: 267
Virtus est vitium fugere, VIRTUE: 268
Virtus et fortitudo invincibilia sunt,
FORTITUDE: 29; VIRTUE: 269
Virtus et honos, HONOR: 193;
VIRTUE: 270
Virtus et industria,
INDUSTRIOUSNESS: 200; VIRTUE: 271
Virtus et nobilitas, NOBILITY: 28;
VIRTUE: 272
Virtus et spes, HOPE: 292; VIRTUE: 273
Virtus fides fortitudo, FIDELITY: 339;
FORTITUDE: 30; VIRTUE: 274
Virtus fortunae victrix, FORTUNE: 111;
VIRTUE: 275
Virtus honoris Janua, HONOR: 194;
VIRTUE: 276
Virtus impendere vero, TRUTH: 170;
VIRTUE: 277
Virtus in actione consistit, ACTION: 25;
VIRTUE: 278
Virtus in ardua, COURAGE: 235
Virtus in arduis, COURAGE: 236
Virtus in arduo, COURAGE: 237
Virtus in caducis, COURAGE: 238
Virtus incendit vires, POWER: 27;
VIRTUE: 279
Virtus incumbet honori, HONOR: 195;
VIRTUE: 280
Virtus insignit audentes,
AUDACITY: 100; VIRTUE: 281
Virtus intaminatis fulget honoribus,
HONOR: 196; VIRTUE: 282
Virtus invicta, VIRTUE: 283
Virtus invicta gloriosa, GLORY: 59;
VIRTUE: 284
Virtus invicta viget, VIRTUE: 285
Virtus invidiae scopus, ENVY: 11;
VIRTUE: 286
Virtus labi nescit, VIRTUE: 287
Virtus late dominatur, VIRTUE: 288
Virtus laudanda, VIRTUE: 289

Virtus laudata crescit, SCHOOL
MOTTOES: 364; VIRTUE: 290
Virtus libertas et patria,
COUNTRY: 142; LIBERTY: 132;
VIRTUE: 291
Virtus maturat, VIRTUE: 292
Virtus mihi scutum, VIRTUE: 293
Virtus mille scuta, VIRTUE: 294
Virtus nihil inexpertum omittit,
COURAGE: 239
Virtus nobilitat, NOBILITY: 29;
VIRTUE: 295
Virtus nobilitat honoremque parit,
HONOR: 197; NOBILITY: 30;
VIRTUE: 296
Virtus nobilitat omnia, NOBILITY: 31;
VIRTUE: 297
Virtus non vertitur, VIRTUE: 298
Virtus omnia nobilitat, NOBILITY: 32;
VIRTUE: 299
Virtus omnia vincit, VIRTUE: 300
Virtus paret robur, STRENGTH: 176;
VIRTUE: 301
Virtus patientia veritas, PATIENCE: 48;
TRUTH: 171; VIRTUE: 302
Virtus patrimonio nobilior,
VIGILANCE: 108; VIRTUE: 303
Virtus plus gladio vera timetur,
VIRTUE: 304; WEAPONS: 98
Virtus post facta, VIRTUE: 305
Virtus post fata superstes, DEATH: 104;
VIRTUE: 306
Virtus post funera vivit, DEATH: 105;
VIRTUE: 307
Virtus potentior auro, VIRTUE: 308
Virtus prae numine, DIVINITY: 433;
VIRTUE: 309
Virtus prae nummis, VIRTUE: 310
Virtus praestantior auro, VIRTUE: 311
Virtus praestat auro, VIRTUE: 312
Virtus pretiosior auro, VIRTUE: 313
Virtus prevalebit, VIRTUE: 314
Virtus probata florebit, VIRTUE: 315
Virtus probata florescit, VIRTUE: 316
Virtus propter se, VIRTUE: 317
Virtus pyramis, VIRTUE: 318
Virtus repulsae nescia sordidae,
VIRTUE: 319
Virtus rosa suavior stella clarior,
VIRTUE: 320
Virtus salus ducum, SECURITY: 83;
VIRTUE: 321

Virtus se coronat, VIRTUE: 322
Virtus secura sequitur, SECURITY: 84;
    VIRTUE: 323
Virtus semper eadem, VIRTUE: 324
Virtus semper valet, VIRTUE: 325
Virtus semper viret, VIRTUE: 326
Virtus semper viridis, VIRTUE: 327
Virtus sibi aureum, VIRTUE: 328
Virtus sibimet merces, REWARD: 53;
    VIRTUE: 329
Virtus sibi munus, REWARD: 54;
    VIRTUE: 330
Virtus sibi praemium, REWARD: 55;
    VIRTUE: 331
Virtus sine dote, VIRTUE: 332
Virtus sine macula, VIRTUE: 333
Virtus sine metu, FEAR: 81;
    VIRTUE: 334
Virtus sola, VIRTUE: 335
Virtus sola felicitas, HAPPINESS: 70;
    VIRTUE: 336
Virtus sola invicta, VIRTUE: 337
Virtus sola nobilitas, NOBILITY: 33;
    VIRTUE: 338
Virtus sola nobilitat, NOBILITY: 34;
    VIRTUE: 339
Virtus sub cruce crescit, CROSS,
    THE: 114; VIRTUE: 340
Virtus sub cruce crescit, ad aethera
    tendens, CROSS, THE: 115;
    VIRTUE: 341
Virtus sub pondere crescit, VIRTUE: 342
Virtus superat fortunam, FATE: 38;
    VIRTUE: 343
Virtus tollit ad astra, STARS: 52;
    VIRTUE: 344
Virtus triumphat, VIRTUE: 345
Virtus tutamen, DEFENSE: 54;
    VIRTUE: 346
Virtus tutissima, SECURITY: 85;
    VIRTUE: 347
Virtus tutissima cassis,
    PROTECTION: 32; VIRTUE: 348
Virtus ubique, VIRTUE: 349
Virtus ubique sedem, VIRTUE: 350
Virtus unita fortior, STRENGTH: 177;
    UNITY: 121
Virtus vera nobilitas, NOBILITY: 35;
    VIRTUE: 351
Virtus vera nobilitas est, NOBILITY: 36;
    VIRTUE: 352

Virtus veritas libertas, LIBERTY: 133;
    LOCAL GOVERNMENT: 399;
    TRUTH: 172; VIRTUE: 353
Virtus verus honos, HONOR: 198;
    VIRTUE: 354
Virtus viget in arduis, ADVERSITY: 90;
    VIRTUE: 355
Virtus vincit invidium, ENVY: 12;
    VIRTUE: 356
Virtus virtutis praemium, REWARD: 56;
    VIRTUE: 357
Virtus vitium fugere, VIRTUE: 358
Virtus vulnere virescit, VIRTUE: 359
Virtute, VIRTUE: 360
Virtute, non viribus, FORCE: 38;
    VIRTUE: 361
Virtute, non viribus vincent,
    FORCE: 39; VIRTUE: 362
Virtute acquiritur, VIRTUE: 363
Virtute acquiritur honos, HONOR: 199;
    VIRTUE: 364
Virtute ad astra, VIRTUE: 365
Virtute adepta, VIRTUE: 366
Virtute avorum, ANCESTRY: 43
Virtute cresco, VIRTUE: 367
Virtute damnosa quies, IDLENESS: 3
Virtute decet non sanguine niti,
    VIRTUE: 368
Virtute decoratus, VIRTUE: 369
Virtute dignus avorum, ANCESTRY: 44
Virtute doloque, CLEVERNESS: 8;
    COURAGE: 240
Virtute duce, GUIDANCE: 30;
    VIRTUE: 370
Virtute duce, comite fortunâ,
    COURAGE: 241; FORTUNE: 112
Virtute et amicitia, FRIENDSHIP: 52;
    VIRTUE: 371
Virtute et amore, LOVE: 119;
    VIRTUE: 372
Virtute et armis, STATE MOTTOES: 60;
    VIRTUE: 373; WEAPONS: 99
Virtute et claritate, REPUTATION: 10;
    VIRTUE: 374
Virtute et constantia, COURAGE: 242;
    PERSEVERANCE: 84;
    STEADFASTNESS: 145; VIRTUE: 375
Virtute et fide, COURAGE: 243;
    FAITH: 252
Virtute et fidelitate, COURAGE: 244;
    FIDELITY: 340
Virtute et fide vinco, CONQUEST: 70

Virtute et fortitudine, COURAGE: 245;
  FORTITUDE: 31
Virtute et fortuna, COURAGE: 246;
  FORTUNE: 113
Virtute et honore, HONOR: 200;
  VIRTUE: 376
Virtute et industria, LOCAL
  GOVERNMENT: 400; VIRTUE: 377
Virtute et ingenio, ABILITY: 34;
  VIRTUE: 378
Virtute et labore, COURAGE: 247
Virtute et labore verum amicum cole,
  FRIENDSHIP: 53
Virtute et merito, COURAGE: 248;
  WORTHINESS: 63
Virtute et non vi, VIRTUE: 379
Virtute et numine, PROVIDENCE: 30;
  VIRTUE: 380
Virtute et opera,
  INDUSTRIOUSNESS: 201; VIRTUE: 381
Virtute et opere,
  INDUSTRIOUSNESS: 202; VIRTUE: 382
Virtute et probitatè, HONESTY: 54;
  VIRTUE: 383
Virtute et prudentiâ, PRUDENCE: 85;
  VIRTUE: 384
Virtute et robore, OFFSPRING: 7;
  VIRTUE: 385
Virtute et sapientia, VIRTUE: 386;
  WISDOM: 107
Virtute et valare luceo non uro,
  COURAGE: 249; SHINING: 31;
  VIRTUE: 387
Virtute et valore, COURAGE: 250;
  VIRTUE: 388
Virtute et veritate, TRUTH: 173;
  VIRTUE: 389
Virtute et vigilantia, VIGILANCE: 109;
  VIRTUE: 390
Virtute et votis, VIRTUE: 391
Virtute excerptae, COURAGE: 251
Virtute experiamur, ATTEMPT: 6;
  VIRTUE: 392
Virtute fideque, FAITH: 253;
  VIRTUE: 393
Virtute gloria parta, COURAGE: 252;
  GLORY: 60
Virtute honor, HONOR: 201;
  VIRTUE: 394
Virtute invidiam vincas, ENVY: 13
Virtute maenia cedant, COURAGE: 253

Virtutem ante pono honorem,
  HONOR: 202; VIRTUE: 395
Virtutem avorum aemulus,
  ANCESTRY: 45; VIRTUE: 396
Virtutem coronat honos, HONOR: 203;
  VIRTUE: 397
Virtutem coronat opus,
  INDUSTRIOUSNESS: 203
Virtute me involvo, VIRTUE: 398
Virtutem extendere factis, DEEDS: 95;
  VIRTUE: 399
Virtutem hilaritate colere, VIRTUE: 400
Virtutem sequitur fama, FAME: 21;
  VIRTUE: 401
Virtutem sic et culpam, VIRTUE: 402
Virtute nihil invium, VIRTUE: 403
Virtute nihil obstat et armis,
  COURAGE: 254; WEAPONS: 100
Virtute non aliter, VIRTUE: 404
Virtute non armis fido, VIRTUE: 405;
  WEAPONS: 101
Virtute non astutia, COURAGE: 255
Virtute non ferocia, COURAGE: 256
Virtute non sanguine, VIRTUE: 406
Virtute non verbis, COURAGE: 257
Virtute non vi, FORCE: 40; VIRTUE: 407
Virtute nulla possessio major,
  POSSESSION: 30; VIRTUE: 408
Virtute orta, VIRTUE: 409
Virtute orta occidunt rarius,
  VIRTUE: 410
Virtute parata, VIRTUE: 411
Virtute paret robur, STRENGTH: 178;
  VIRTUE: 412
Virtute parta, VIRTUE: 413
Virtute parta tuemini, COURAGE: 258;
  DEFENSE: 55
Virtute probitate, INTEGRITY: 43;
  VIRTUE: 414
Virtute promoveo, ADVANCE: 59;
  VIRTUE: 415
Virtute quies, COURAGE: 259
Virtute res parvae crescunt, LOCAL
  GOVERNMENT: 401; VIRTUE: 416
Virtute securus, SECURITY: 86;
  VIRTUE: 417
Virtute sibi praemium, REWARD: 57;
  VIRTUE: 418
Virtute spernit victa, VIRTUE: 419
Virtute superanda fortuna,
  FORTUNE: 114; VIRTUE: 420

Mottoes & Categories

Virtute tutus, SECURITY: 87;
VIRTUE: 421
Virtute vici, COURAGE: 260
Virtute viget, FLOURISHING: 98;
VIRTUE: 422
Virtute vinces, VIRTUE: 423
Virtute vincet, VIRTUE: 424
Virtute vincit invidiam, ENVY: 14;
VIRTUE: 425
Virtute viresco, FLOURISHING: 99;
VIRTUE: 426
Virtuti, VIRTUE: 427
Virtuti beneficentia, VIRTUE: 428
Virtutibus praemium honor,
HONOR: 204; REWARD: 58;
VIRTUE: 429
Virtuti comes invidia, ENVY: 15
Virtuti damnosa quies, IDLENESS: 4
Virtuti et fidelitati, FIDELITY: 341;
VIRTUE: 430
Virtuti et fortunae, FORTUNE: 115;
VIRTUE: 431
Virtuti fido, TRUST: 109; VIRTUE: 432
Virtuti fortuna comes, COURAGE: 261;
FORTUNE: 116
Virtuti honores soli, VIRTUE: 433
Virtuti in bello, COURAGE: 262;
WAR: 77
Virtuti inimica quies, IDLENESS: 5
Virtuti nihil invium, COURAGE: 263
Virtuti non armis fido, VIRTUE: 434;
WEAPONS: 102
Virtuti nulla via invia, VIRTUE: 435
Virtuti omnia parent, VIRTUE: 436
Virtuti pro patria, COUNTRY: 143;
COURAGE: 264
Virtutis, VIRTUE: 437
Virtutis alimentum honos, HONOR: 205
Virtutis amore, LOVE: 120; VIRTUE: 438
Virtutis avorum praemium,
ANCESTRY: 46
Virtutis comes invidia, ENVY: 16
Virtutis fortuna comes, COURAGE: 265;
FORTUNE: 117; SCHOOL
MOTTOES: 365
Virtutis gloria crescit, VIRTUE: 439
Virtutis gloria merces, COURAGE: 266;
GLORY: 61; VIRTUE: 440
Virtutis gloria parta, VIRTUE: 441
Virtutis honor praemium, HONOR: 206
Virtutis in bello praemium,
COURAGE: 267; WAR: 78

Virtuti si vis nobilis esse stude,
NOBILITY: 37; VIRTUE: 442
Virtutis laus actio, ACTION: 26;
VIRTUE: 443
Virtutis Namurcensis praemium,
COURAGE: 268
Virtutis praemium, REWARD: 59;
VIRTUE: 444
Virtutis praemium felicitas,
HAPPINESS: 71; REWARD: 60;
VIRTUE: 445
Virtutis praemium honor, HONOR: 207;
REWARD: 61; VIRTUE: 446
Virtutis praemium laus, PRAISE: 15;
VIRTUE: 447
Virtutis regia merces, REWARD: 62;
VIRTUE: 448
Virtutis regio merces, COURAGE: 269
Virtutis robore robur, STRENGTH: 179;
VIRTUE: 449
Virtutis stemmata, VIRTUE: 450
Vir tutus et fidelis, FIDELITY: 342;
SECURITY: 88
Vir/veritas/vox, MANLINESS: 5; SCHOOL
MOTTOES: 366; TRUTH: 174
Vir vita terra, EARTH: 26; LIFE: 38;
MANLINESS: 6; SCHOOL MOTTOES: 367
Visa per invisa firma, SPIRIT: 17
Vise à la fin, FINISH: 16
Vise en espoir, HOPE: 293
Vis et fides, FAITH: 254; STRENGTH: 180
Vis et virtus, COURAGE: 270;
STRENGTH: 181
Vis fortibus arma, COURAGE: 271;
STRENGTH: 182; WEAPONS: 103
VISION, p. 825
Vi si non consilio, FORCE: 41
Vis in vita Deus, DIVINITY: 434
Vis super hostem, STRENGTH: 183
Vis unita fortior, LOCAL
GOVERNMENT: 402; STATE
MOTTOES: 61; STRENGTH: 184;
UNITY: 122
Vis veritatis magna, FORCE: 42;
TRUTH: 175
Vis viri fragilis, STRENGTH: 185
Vita brevis gloria aeterna, GLORY: 62;
LIFE: 39
Vitae faciendo nemini timeas,
COURAGE: 272; DUTY: 32
Vita et pectore puro, HEART: 12;
PURITY: 29

Mottoes & Categories

Vulneratur, non vincitur, INJURY: 14
Vulneratus non victus, INJURY: 15
Vulnere sano, HEALING and HEALTH: 39
Vulnere viresco, FLOURISHING: 102;
  INJURY: 16
Vulneror non vincor, INJURY: 17
Vulnus opemque fero, INJURY: 18
Vultus in hostem, HOSTILITY: 19

W

WAKEFULNESS, p. 826
WALKING, p. 827
Walk in the fear of God, FEAR: 82
Walk in the way of God, DIVINITY: 437
Walk the straight way,
  RIGHTEOUSNESS: 19
WAR, p. 827
Ware the horn, VIGILANCE: 110
WARNING, p. 832
Was Gott beschertt, Bleibt vnerwehrtt,
  DIVINE GIFTS: 51
Was Gott bewahrt ist wohl verwahrt,
  DIVINE GUIDANCE: 444
Was Gott erquickt kein neyd erstickt,
  DIVINITY: 438
Was Gott will Ist mein Ziel, DIVINE
  GUIDANCE: 445
Waste not, CONSERVATION: 7
WATER, p. 832
Watch, VIGILANCE: 111
Watch and pray, VIGILANCE: 112
Watchful and bold, AUDACITY: 101;
  VIGILANCE: 113
Watch the temptation,
  UNCLASSIFIED: 80
Watch weel, VIGILANCE: 114
Watch well, VIGILANCE: 115
Watch wiel, VIGILANCE: 116
Waterloo, PROPER NAMES: 55
WAVES, p. 834
WAY, p. 834
Weapon forefendeth evil, EVIL: 10;
  WEAPONS: 105
WEAPONS, p. 835
We are one, TRADES: 43; UNITY: 123
We are the few, the proud, the
  Marines, WAR: 81
Weave truth with truth, TRADES: 44;
  TRUTH: 179
We beg you see warily, VIGILANCE: 117

We build, we fight,
  INDUSTRIOUSNESS: 204
We grow by industry, GROWTH: 25;
  INDUSTRIOUSNESS: 205; LOCAL
  GOVERNMENT: 404
Weigh well, MEASURE: 18
Welcome the coming, speed the
  parting guest, HOSPITALITY: 6
We live in hope, HOPE: 298
We'll put it to a venture, RISK: 11
We long endure, ENDURANCE: 59;
  LOCAL GOVERNMENT: 405
Wer auf Gott vertraut, der hat auf
  einen Fels gebaut, DIVINE
  GUIDANCE: 446
Wer gutes u boses nit kan ertragan
  wirt kein grose chre erjagen,
  EVIL: 11; GOODNESS: 45; HONOR: 208
We rise, RISING: 25
Wer sich verleszet auf Gott, Der kan
  nicht werden zu spott, DIVINITY: 439
Wer will uns scheiden von der Liebe
  Gottes?, DIVINITY: 440
We serve, LOCAL GOVERNMENT: 406;
  SERVICE: 75
We shall die all, DEATH: 109
West Indies, PROPER NAMES: 56
We stoop not, PRIDE: 18
Whatever is worth doing is worth
  doing well, WORTHINESS: 64
Whatsoever thy hand findeth to do, do
  it with thy might, DEEDS: 96
What was may be, TIME: 74
Wheare vertu lys love never dys,
  LOVE: 124; VIRTUE: 454
When friends meet, hearts warm,
  FRIENDSHIP: 54
When in doubt, fight, WAR: 82
Where liberty is, there is my country,
  LIBERTY: 136
Where students learn by doing,
  KNOWLEDGE: 98; SCHOOL
  MOTTOES: 371
Where women create their future,
  FUTURE, THE: 31; SCHOOL
  MOTTOES: 372
Whither will ye, DESTINATION: 8
Who dares wins, AUDACITY: 102;
  VICTORY: 71
Who most has served is greatest,
  SERVICE: 76

Y

998

Z

Index II: Source Information

Index II: Source Information

This index contains, in one alphabetic order, all source information—individual and institutional names—listed in the text. All items are indexed by first significant word or (where applicable) surname. References are to specific categories by name and mottoes by entry number.

A

Abbey, HOPE: 256

Abbot, INDUSTRIOUSNESS: 94

Abbott, DIVINITY: 27; PREPAREDNESS: 78

Abbott (of Darlington, formerly of Suffolk and East Dereham, Norfolk), DUTY: 2

Abbs, ANIMALS: 41; DIVINITY: 269; PROVOCATION: 3; TRUST: 71

Abdy (Bt.), FIDELITY: 308; PERSEVERANCE: 82

A'Beckett, FAITH: 130; WISDOM: 28

Abel, PERSEVERANCE: 44

Abell, TRUTH: 44

Abercorn (M.), ADVANCE: 56; NOBILITY: 21; VIRTUE: 184

Abercrombie, DESIRE: 10, 11; MERCY: 18, 20

Abercrombie (Bt.), ASPIRATION: 69

Abercrombie (U.S.), EQUANIMITY: 12

Abercromby, CROSS, THE: 65; LIFE: 41; SALVATION: 25; SILENCE: 22

Abercromby (B.), LIFE: 49

Abercromby (of Birkenbog, bt.), LIFE: 49

Aberdeen, FAITH: 156

Aberdeen (E.), FORTUNE: 51; MODERATION: 25

Aberdour, HOPE: 69

Abergavenny B. C., U.K., CONCILIATION: 5; LOCAL GOVERNMENT: 176

Abergavenny (E.), WORTHINESS: 36

Aberherdour, PATRIOTISM: 65; ROYALTY: 81

Abernethy, CHRIST, JESUS: 42, 72; SALVATION: 23, 40

Abingdon (E.), VIRTUE: 252

Abingdon School, U.K., MERCY: 24; SCHOOL MOTTOES: 193

Abinger, POWER: 22

Abinger (B.), SELF-RELIANCE: 12

Ablett, FIDELITY: 260

Abney, AUDACITY: 63; HONESTY: 7

Abney-Hastings, DARKNESS: 19

Abraham, LIBERTY: 123; TRUTH: 116

Abraham Baldwin Agricultural College, Tifton, Georgia, GOVERNMENT: 11; HOME: 20; LIFE: 1; SCHOOL MOTTOES: 7, 322

Académie Française, IMMORTALITY: 1

Academy of the Muses, GENIUS: 2

Accorne, STEADFASTNESS: 122

Accrington B. C., U.K.,
INDUSTRIOUSNESS: 81; LOCAL
GOVERNMENT: 186; PRUDENCE: 24

Achany, ADVERSITY: 60; ASPIRATION: 64

Acheson, VIGILANCE: 100

Achieson, VISION: 12

Ackers, LIBERTY: 44

Acklom (U.S.), VISION: 10

Ackworth, ENDURANCE: 58

Acland, STEADFASTNESS: 68

A'Court, INDUSTRIOUSNESS: 52

Acton, ANCESTRY: 2

Acton B. C., U.K., FLOURISHING: 24;
LOCAL GOVERNMENT: 136

Acton (Co. Worcester), COURAGE: 222

Adair, AUDACITY: 72; FIDELITY: 218

Adair (Bt.), FIDELITY: 221;
VICTORY: 28

Adam, ASPIRATION: 38; CROSS, THE: 42;
DIVINE GUIDANCE: 211;
PERSEVERANCE: 1; REST: 2

Adam Wenzel, Duke of Teschen
(1574–1617), TRUST: 92

Adams, CROSS, THE: 12, 108; DIVINE
GUIDANCE: 58; GENIUS: 1; HOME: 4;
MEASURE: 17; PARADISE: 11;
TRUTH: 89

Adams (of Bowden), COUNTRY: 47;
LIBERTY: 56

Adams (U.S.), ASPIRATION: 39;
FAITH: 79; FRIENDSHIP: 30;
LIBERTY: 23; PERSEVERANCE: 2;
TRUST: 2

Addenbrooke, ENDURANCE: 58;
INTEGRITY: 10; SCHOOL MOTTOES: 94

Addington, CROWN: 16; LIBERTY: 62

Addison, DEEDS: 62; HONOR: 2

Addison (U.S.), INJURY: 18

Adlam, TIME: 70; TRUTH: 111

Adlborough (E.), COURAGE: 254;
WEAPONS: 100

Adlington, GOVERNMENT: 4

Adml. Sir G. Eden-Hamond (Bt.
G.C.B.), FLOURISHING: 72

Adnew, Vans, FIDELITY: 22

Adolf, Duke of Schleswig-Holstein-
Gottorp (1526–86), THOUGHT: 18

Adolf Friedrich I, Duke of
Mecklenburg-Schwerin (1588–1658),
FORTUNE: 61; GOVERNMENT: 5;
JUSTICE: 97; LOCAL
GOVERNMENT: 403; PIETY: 24;
VIRTUE: 453

Adolf Friedrich IV, Duke of
Mecklenburg-Strelitz (1738–94),
PEOPLE: 21

Adolf Wilhelm, Duke of Saxony-
Eisenach (1632–68), DIVINITY: 61

Adolf Wilhelm, Duke of Saxony-Jena
(1632–68), DIVINE GUIDANCE: 353;
IRONY: 7

Adson, STEADFASTNESS: 128

Affleck, WISDOM: 56

Affleck (Bt.), USEFULNESS: 8

African Company, COMMERCE: 6

(after Sherwood Forest, the domain of
Robin Hood) Hood, LOCATION: 7

Agar, ACTION: 21; SECURITY: 79

Agardes, DIVINE GUIDANCE: 182

Agnes, Duchess of Saxony
(1584–1629), DIVINE GUIDANCE: 288;
SCRIPTURES: 8

Agnes, Margravine of Brandenburg (d.
1629), DIVINE GUIDANCE: 288;
SCRIPTURES: 8

Agnes Scott College, Decatur,
Georgia, FAITH: 154;
KNOWLEDGE: 29; SCHOOL
MOTTOES: 137; VIRTUE: 91

Agnew, CLEVERNESS: 7; WALKING: 8

Agnew (Bt.), FORCE: 5; WISDOM: 12, 16

Agnew (of Barnbarroch, Dalreagle,
and Lochryan), FORCE: 5;
WISDOM: 16

Ahrends, SUN: 10

Aiken, CROSS, THE: 65; SALVATION: 25

Aikenhead, BIRTH: 3; STRANGER: 2;
STRENGTH: 5

Aikin (of Liverpool), STRENGTH: 135;
VIRTUE: 195

Aikman (of Carnie), STRENGTH: 135;
VIRTUE: 195

Ailesbury (M.), PAST, THE: 3;
THOUGHT: 27

Ailsa (M.), PURPOSE: 3

Ainslie, COUNTRY: 110; CROWN: 28;
PATRIOTISM: 59; PIETY: 27;
VIRTUE: 142

Ainslie (Bt.), PATRIOTISM: 65;
ROYALTY: 81

Aird, VIGILANCE: 95

Airderbeck, STEADFASTNESS: 128

Airlie (E.), STEADFASTNESS: 2

Aiscough, CONQUEST: 19

Aitken, STRENGTH: 112; VIGILANCE: 60

Aiton, FRAGRANCE: 1; VIRTUE: 410

Aiton (of Kippo), FRAGRANCE: 3

Akers, HOPE: 127

Akins, HONOR: 97; VIRTUE: 75

Akroyd, PREPAREDNESS: 30

Akroyd (of Bankfield), Huntingdon
(E.), Hastings (Bt.), Abney,
Hastings (of Willesley Hall),
Ingham, TRUTH: 43; VICTORY: 21

Alabama A & M University, Alabama,
SCHOOL MOTTOES: 286; SERVICE: 56

Albemarle (E.), ADVERSITY: 50; LOCAL
GOVERNMENT: 236

Albert, Archduke of Austria
(1559–1621), FATE: 27

Albert, Count of Nassau-Weilburg
(1537–93), DIVINE GUIDANCE: 15

Albert, Count of Schwarzburg-
Rudolstadt (1527–1605), MERCY: 26

Albert, Margrave of Brandenburg
(1490–1545), BEAUTY: 16; DIVINE
GUIDANCE: 213, 321

Albert Friedrich, Margrave of
Brandenburg (1582–1600),
HAPPINESS: 36; PIETY: 20; SADNESS: 4;
STRENGTH: 101

Albert IV, Duke of Bavaria
(1447–1508), RIGHTEOUSNESS: 6

Albert V, Duke of Bavaria (1528–79),
DIVINITY: 319, 421; GLORY: 51;
VIRTUE: 170

Albrecht, Duke of Saxony-Coburg
(1648–99), CROWN: 20; EFFORT: 28;
INDUSTRIOUSNESS: 185; VICTORY: 42

Albrecht, Duke of Saxony-Eisenach
(1599–1644), CONSCIENCE: 5;
COUNTRY: 37; DIVINE GUIDANCE: 436;
DIVINITY: 205

Albrecht, Margrave of Brandenburg
(1490–1568), DIVINE GUIDANCE: 3,
286, 365; FAITH: 165; GRACE: 17;
PEACE: 56

Albrecht, Margrave of Brandenburg-
Anspach (1620–67), DIVINE
GUIDANCE: 408; FATE: 9; VIRTUE: 18

Albrecht Alcibiades, Margrave of
Brandenburg-Baireuth (1522–51),
DIVINE GUIDANCE: 405;
STRENGTH: 44

Albrecht Günther, Count
Schwarzburg (1582–1634), CHRIST,
JESUS: 1; SALVATION: 1

Alcock, CONTEMPT: 1

Aldersey, FLOURISHING: 3

Aldershot B. C., U.K., COUNTRY: 117;
PATRIOTISM: 74

Aldrige, GUIDANCE: 7

Aldworth, MODERATION: 24

Alexander, LEADERSHIP: 8; MIND: 17;
SEA: 20

Alexander, Duke of Schleswig-Holstein
(1573–1627), PROSPERITY: 24;
REPUTATION: 5

Alexander City State Junior College,
Alexander City, Alabama, SCHOOL
MOTTOES: 338; TRUTH: 103

Alexander Hamilton, IMPROVEMENT: 8

Alexander Heinrich, Duke of
Schleswig-Holstein (1608–67),
FORTUNE: 53

Alexander (of Auchmull), DEEDS: 79

Alexander (of Boghall), FAITH: 87

Alexandria Vocational-Technical
Institute, Alexandria, Louisiana,
CONFIDENCE: 21; JUSTICE: 123;
SCHOOL MOTTOES: 343; UNITY: 94

Algar, VIRTUE: 121

Alison (Bt.), TRUTH: 168

Aljoy, WORTHINESS: 40

Allan, COURAGE: 247; CROSS, THE: 55;
FIERCENESS: 6; FOLLOWING: 27;
SHINING: 17, 18

Allardic, CROSS, THE: 66; TRUST: 46

Allardice, DEFENSE: 25, 37

Allardice (of Dunotter), DEFENSE: 24

Allar-dyce, PEACE: 5

Allcard, FIDELITY: 282

Allcock, VIGILANCE: 102

Ann, Margravine of Brandenburg
(1575–1612), DIVINE GUIDANCE: 385

Anna, Archduchess of Austria
(1573–98), LOVE: 11

Anna, Countess of Oldenburg (b.
1605), DIVINITY: 157; HOPE: 41

Anna, Countess of Schwarzburg
(1584–1652), DIVINITY: 228

Anna, Duchess of Pomerania
(1590–1660), DIVINITY: 389

Anna, Duchess of Wohlau
(1561–1616), DIVINITY: 186

Anna, Electress of Brandenburg
(1576–1625), DIVINE GUIDANCE: 288;
SCRIPTURES: 8

Anna, Margravine of Baden (D. 1621),
DIVINE GUIDANCE: 294

Anna, Princess of Anhalt (d. 1624),
DIVINITY: 204; STEADFASTNESS: 113

Anna Auguste, Princess of Nassau-
Dillenburg (1612–56), ACTION: 10;
BOASTFULNESS: 3

Anna Dorothee, Duchess of Saxony
(1657–1704), ADVERSITY: 6

Anna Marie, Duchess of Saxony
(1589–1626), DIVINITY: 207

Anna Marie, Duchess of Saxony-
Weimar (1575–1643), DIVINITY: 265;
HOPE: 105

Anna Marie, Duchess of Saxony-
Weissenfels (1627–69),
DIVINITY: 157; HOPE: 41

Anna Marie, Margravine of
Brandenburg (1609–80), DESIRE: 12

Anna Sophie, Duchess of
Braunschweig-Wolfenbüttel
(1598–1659), FIDELITY: 72;
SINCERITY: 6; WISDOM: 18

Anna Sophie, Landgravine of Hesse
(1638–83), PATIENCE: 38

Anna Sophie, Princess of Anhalt
(1584–1652), DIVINE GUIDANCE: 332

Anna Sophie, Princess of Anhalt (D.
1704), LOVE: 89

Annand, HOPE: 199, 215

Annand (of Annandale), HONESTY: 47

Anne Boleyn, Queen of Henry VIII.,
POSSESSION: 14

Anne of Austria, wife of Louis XIII
(1601–66), PROTECTION: 21

Anne of Cleves, fourth wife of Henry
VIII., DIVINE GUIDANCE: 272

Annesley, WORTHINESS: 23

Annesley (E.), LOVE: 120; VIRTUE: 438

Annesley (of Bletchingdon), LOVE: 120;
VIRTUE: 438

Anson, DESPAIR: 5

Anson (Bt.), DESPAIR: 5

Anstruthe, PREPAREDNESS: 78

Anstruther, PERSEVERANCE: 50

Anstruther (Bt.), PERSEVERANCE: 49

Answorth, HOPE: 222

Antill (U.S.), HONESTY: 36; HONOR: 94;
JUSTICE: 42; UNCLASSIFIED: 50

Antillian Coll., Mayagüez, Puerto
Rico, DEDICATION: 3; SCHOOL
MOTTOES: 49

The Antiquarian Society, London,
ENDURANCE: 43

Anton Günther, Count of
Schwarzburg-Sondershausen
(1620–66), HOME: 18

Anton Günther, Prince of
Schwarzburg-Arnstadt (1653–1716),
THOUGHT: 18

Anton Heinrich, Count Schwarzburg
(1571–1638), CHRIST, JESUS: 79;
HOPE: 254

Anton I, Count of Oldenburg
(1505–73), SELF-KNOWLEDGE: 2

Anton Ulrich, Duke of Braunschweig-
Wolfenbüttel (1633–1714), DIVINE
GUIDANCE: 24; FIDELITY: 46

Anton Ulrich, Duke of Braunschweig-
Wolfenbüttel (1633–1714); Garfit,
CONSISTENCY: 10

Antram, COURAGE: 188; PRUDENCE: 61

Antrobus (Bt.), DIVINITY: 40

Ap-Eynions, TRUST: 109; VIRTUE: 432

Apothecaries' Company,
ASSISTANCE: 20

Appleby B. C., U.K., FIRE: 10; LOCAL
GOVERNMENT: 237; WEAPONS: 67

Appleton (U.S.), ADVERSITY: 12;
EVIL: 2; GOODNESS: 13

Apreece (Bt.), IMMORTALITY: 3

Apthorp (U.S.), CHRIST, JESUS: 59;
PREPAREDNESS: 35

Arbuthnot, CHANGE: 6; DIVINE
GUIDANCE: 135; PERSEVERANCE: 18;
UNCLASSIFIED: 34; WORTHINESS: 60

Arbuthnot (Bt.), INNOCENCE: 4;
TRUST: 70

Arbuthnot (of Catherlan), PRAISE: 12

Ashton, KINDNESS: 1;
STEADFASTNESS: 106;
UNSELFISHNESS: 1

Ashton-in-Makerfield U. D. C., U.K.,
DIVINITY: 152; HOPE: 39; LOCAL
GOVERNMENT: 103

Ashton-Under-Lyme B. C., U.K.,
INDUSTRIOUSNESS: 116; LOCAL
GOVERNMENT: 211; SCHOOL
MOTTOES: 161; STATE MOTTOES: 26

Ashtown (B.), COURAGE: 265;
FORTUNE: 117

Ashtown (B.), Brook, Clancarty (E.),
Ferguson (of Raith), Hughes,
Harberton (V.), Trench, Wellington
(D.); Wellington College, U.K.,
SCHOOL MOTTOES: 365

Ashurst, DISGRACE: 2; ENDURANCE: 58

Ashworth, FEAR: 12; MIND: 5;
RECTITUDE: 21

Askew, DEEDS: 35; HOPE: 58;
PATIENCE: 29

Askwith, HONOR: 58

Aspinall, PROTECTION: 2; VIRTUE: 8

Aspland, LIBERTY: 22; TRUTH: 21

Asscotti, HONOR: 27; HOPE: 35; STATE
MOTTOES: 11

Assherton, UNCLASSIFIED: 44

Astell, CROSS, THE: 104; DIVINITY: 178

Astley, DEDICATION: 5; JUSTICE: 68;
PERSEVERANCE: 33

Astley (Bt.), DIVINITY: 178

Astley (of Everleigh), DIVINITY: 178

Aston, PREPAREDNESS: 58; RELIGION: 10

Aston (B.), COUNTRY: 59; DIVINITY: 328

Aston (Co. Chester),
ACCOMPLISHMENT: 18;
PREPAREDNESS: 60

Aston (of Bescot), EARTH: 3;
PROSPERITY: 8

Atcherley, HOPE: 197

Atcheson, VISION: 12

Atchison, VIGILANCE: 100

Atherton, ADVANCE: 37

Atherton U. D. C., U.K.,
GUIDANCE: 6; LOCAL
GOVERNMENT: 66; WISDOM: 13

Athlone (E.), DEATH: 40; DISGRACE: 10

Athlumney (B.), DIVINITY: 33

Athol (D.), FORTUNE: 64

Athy, LEADERSHIP: 7

Atkins, CLEVERNESS: 3; FEAR: 3;
JUSTICE: 9; LOCAL GOVERNMENT: 45

Atkins (of Fountainville, Co. Cork),
WEAPONS: 18

Atkinson, COUNTRY: 16; DIVINITY: 34,
51, 62; FAITH: 25; FIDELITY: 58, 59;
HOSTILITY: 1; INDUSTRIOUSNESS: 135;
LOVE: 46; PIETY: 7; ROYALTY: 14;
THOUGHT: 25; TIME: 64; TRUST: 16

Atkinson (U.S.), DIVINE
GUIDANCE: 339; LIFE: 42

Atkyns, LAW: 72; PROVIDENCE: 2;
WEAPONS: 97

Atlantic Christian College, Wilson,
North Carolina, LIGHT: 19; SCHOOL
MOTTOES: 121

Atlantic Union College, South
Lancaster, Massachusetts,
LIGHT: 15; SCHOOL MOTTOES: 105

Atterbury (Bt.), FIDELITY: 221

Atthill, LOFTINESS: 15

Atthill, (Co. Norfolk), HONOR: 77

Attwood, CONQUEST: 72

Atty, FORTUNE: 21

Aubert, DIVINE GUIDANCE: 11;
FAITH: 61; FORTITUDE: 3

Aubertin, FIDELITY: 75

Aubrey (Bt.), SUN: 15

Aubrey (co. Hereford), FAITH: 232;
LOVE: 114

Auburn University, Auburn, Alabama,
SCHOOL MOTTOES: 256

Auchinleck, DEPRIVATION: 3;
USEFULNESS: 9; WISDOM: 56

Auchmuty (of Brianstown),
HONOR: 27; HOPE: 35; STATE
MOTTOES: 11

Auckland (B.), PRUDENCE: 81

Audenshaw U. D. C., U.K., LOCAL
GOVERNMENT: 120; SPEED: 23

Audley (B.), POSSESSION: 10

Aufrere, INTEGRITY: 12

Augsburg College, Minneapolis,
Minnesota, SCHOOL MOTTOES: 327;
TRUTH: 95

August, Count of the Palatinate of
Sulzbach (1582–1632), VICTORY: 49

August, Count von der Lippe (d.
1701), ADVERSITY: 66;
ASPIRATION: 66; BEAUTY: 10;
BLESSING: 10; DIVINITY: 102;
FLORA: 27; TRANSIENCE: 8;
VIRTUE: 62
August, Duke of Braunschweig-
Lüneburg (1568–1636), DEATH: 72;
DIVINE GUIDANCE: 239;
DIVINITY: 324; WISDOM: 44
August, Duke of Braunschweig-
Wolfenbüttel (1579–1666),
ACTION: 16; AGRICULTURE: 3;
CAUTION: 23; CHANGE: 15;
DIVINITY: 186; FORESIGHT: 1;
INTEGRITY: 29; PATIENCE: 43;
THOUGHT: 11; TIME: 25, 56
August, Duke of Saxony (1589–1615),
CHRIST, JESUS: 41; FEAR: 70;
PIETY: 28; ROYALTY: 118; VIRTUE: 143
August, Duke of Saxony-Lauenburg
(1577–1656), ADVERSITY: 15;
DIVINITY: 186; VIRTUE: 44
August, Duke of Saxony-Weissenfels
(1614–80), CONFIDENCE: 19;
DIVINITY: 98, 364, 378; SILENCE: 17
August, Duke of Saxony-Zörbig
(1655–1715), PIETY: 37;
PRUDENCE: 39
August, Duke of Schleswig-Holstein-
Sonderburg-Norburg (1635–99),
DIVINE GUIDANCE: 340
August, Elector of Saxony (1526–86),
DIVINE GUIDANCE: 365; PEACE: 56;
VICTORY: 49
August, Margrave of Brandenburg
(1580–1601), CHRIST, JESUS: 75;
GOALS: 7
August, Prince of Anhalt-Plötzkau
(1575–1653), CHRIST, JESUS: 62;
DIVINITY: 225, 226; FAITH: 246;
INSIGNIFICANCE: 1; SCRIPTURES: 16;
TRUST: 43; VICTORY: 52
August Friedrich, Duke of Schleswig-
Holstein-Gottorp (1646–1705),
JUSTICE: 96; PIETY: 17
August Ludwig, Prince of Anhalt-
Plötzkau (1697–1755),
DIRECTNESS: 14
August Wilhelm, Duke of
Braunschweig-Wolfenbüttel
(1662–1731), DEFENSE: 39

Auld, VIRTUE: 108
Auld (or Aulde), COURAGE: 242;
STEADFASTNESS: 145
Auldjo, WORTHINESS: 40
Aungier, TRUST: 93
Austen (of Shalford), MODERATION: 27
Austen-Cartmell, LIBERTY: 39
Austin, CROSS, THE: 43; CROWN: 7
Australian National University,
Canberra, Australia, FACTUALITY: 3;
SCHOOL MOTTOES: 196
Aveland (B.), DIVINE GUIDANCE: 151;
GENEROSITY: 8
Aveling, GOODNESS: 30
Averquerque, MEMORY: 9
Avonmore (V.), REBIRTH: 21
Axminster U. D. C., U.K.,
STEADFASTNESS: 130
Aylesbury B. C., U.K.,
FLOURISHING: 25; LOCAL
GOVERNMENT: 137
Aylesford (E.), DIRECTNESS: 2
Aylet (Co. Essex), PURPOSE: 16
Aylmer (B.), EQUANIMITY: 17
Aylmer (Bt.), HAPPINESS: 26
Aylmer (of Lyons, Co. Kildare),
HAPPINESS: 26
Ayloffe (Bt.), LIFE: 22
Aylward, FIDELITY: 336; TRUTH: 162
Aymand, LIFE: 13
Aynesworth, COURAGE: 52
Ayre, FLOURISHING: 56; MEASURE: 6
Ayscough, DEEDS: 35; HOPE: 58

B

B. Bond-Cabbell, COURAGE: 128
Babington, EFFORT: 17, 18; FAITH: 128
Backhouse, TRUST: 9
Backie, CONVENIENCE: 1; INJURY: 1
Bacon, CONSCIENCE: 9
Bacon (Bt.), MODERATION: 12
Bacup B. C., U.K., HONOR: 93;
INDUSTRIOUSNESS: 57; LOCAL
GOVERNMENT: 175
Baddeley, FEAR: 7
Baggalay, ANCESTRY: 38
Bagge (of Stradsett), DIVINITY: 397;
HOPE: 238
Bagot, DIVINITY: 342; ROYALTY: 59
Bagot (B.), HONOR: 4

Barrow-in-Furness C. B. C., U.K.,
ASPIRATION: 73; LOCAL
GOVERNMENT: 342

Barry, ADVANCE: 47; CONQUEST: 1;
FAITH: 32; FIDELITY: 212, 275;
FORTITUDE: 6; LAW: 22, 58;
ROYALTY: 2, 47, 98

Barry B. C., U.K., ADVANCE: 12;
JUSTICE: 11; LOCAL
GOVERNMENT: 53; ORDER: 1

Barry (Co. Chester), ADVANCE: 11

Barrymore (E.), ADVANCE: 11

Barsane, SECURITY: 14

Bartholomew, CONQUEST: 13

Bartlett, DIVINE GUIDANCE: 94

Bartlett (U.S.), AGE: 4

Bartolozzi, INDUSTRIOUSNESS: 102;
PRUDENCE: 26

Barton, SECURITY: 14

Barton (of Grove and Clonelly),
FUTURE, THE: 24; HOPE: 169

Barton (of Swinton and Stapleton
Park), FLOURISHING: 8

Barton (of Threxton, Co. Norfolk),
LOCAL GOVERNMENT: 154;
STRENGTH: 56; TRUTH: 27

Barton (U.S.), LIBERTY: 131; STARS: 48;
STATE MOTTOES: 59; VIRTUE: 237

Bartram, ADVANCE: 34

Bartram (U.S.), ADVANCE: 35;
FAITH: 159

Barwell, FIDELITY: 221

Basildon Development Corp, ART: 5;
HAPPINESS: 3; INDUSTRIOUSNESS: 3;
SATISFACTION: 1; TRADES: 6

Baskerville, FAITH: 218; HOPE: 225

Basketmakers' Company, LOVE: 76;
TRADES: 19

Baskin (of Scotland), DILIGENCE: 4;
WEAPONS: 10

Basset (B.), PEOPLE: 15; ROYALTY: 83

Bastable, DEATH: 89

Bastard (of Kitley, Co. Devon),
PEACE: 58; WAR: 55

Bate, DIVINE GUIDANCE: 176

Bateman, REWARD: 21

Bateman (B.), REWARD: 20

Bateman (Co. Derby), FORTUNE: 97,
98; STARS: 38

Bates, HANDS: 10; HEART: 8;
WORTHINESS: 14

Bates (of Denton), FEELINGS: 17;
HANDS: 20

Bateson, DARKNESS: 10

Bateson (Bt.), HONESTY: 38;
HONOR: 156

Bath, ENDURANCE: 34

Bath City and C. B. C., U.K.,
FLOURISHING: 26; LOCAL
GOVERNMENT: 138

Bath College, U.K., SCHOOL
MOTTOES: 228

Bath (M.), CAUSATION: 2

Bathavon R. D. C., U.K.,
COUNTRYSIDE: 4; LOCAL
GOVERNMENT: 320

Bathgate, LIFE: 49

Bathurst (E.),, FAITH: 229

Bathurst (U.S.), DEEDS: 80

Batley B. C., FLOURISHING: 32;
INDUSTRIOUSNESS: 48; LOCAL
GOVERNMENT: 143

Batson, BIRDS: 31

Batt, COURAGE: 250; DIVINE
GUIDANCE: 204; VIRTUE: 388

Battersby, HUMILITY: 1

Battersea B. C., U.K., LOCAL
GOVERNMENT: 246; SHARING: 3

Battye, DIVINITY: 145

Baxter, COURAGE: 257

Bayard (U.S.), FRIENDSHIP: 36;
HONOR: 95; JUSTICE: 43

Bayle, FINISH: 8

Baylor College of Medicine, Houston,
Texas, SCHOOL MOTTOES: 255

Baylor University, Waco, Texas,
RELIGION: 21; SCHOOL MOTTOES: 243

Bayn, COURAGE: 60

Baynard, COURAGE: 200

Bayne, COURAGE: 60

Baynes, ART: 6; INDUSTRIOUSNESS: 4

Baynes (Bt.), ANGER: 2

Bayning (B.), ANCESTRY: 36

Bazilie, UNCLASSIFIED: 3

Beach (of Oakley Hall), TIME: 69

Beadon, INTEGRITY: 10; SCHOOL
MOTTOES: 94

Beale, DEATH: 40; DISGRACE: 10

Beamish, AUDACITY: 100; VIRTUE: 281

Bear, SELF-CONTROL: 4

Beare, SELF-CONTROL: 5

Beath, COURAGE: 117; FORTUNE: 34

Beatie, FOLLOWING: 7; PARADISE: 38

Beaton, COURAGE: 89
Beatson, DILIGENCE: 16; PRUDENCE: 15
Beauchamp, FIDELITY: 312
Beauchamp (E.), FATE: 15
Beauchamp (E.), Lygon, Pindar,
    FAITH: 42
Beaufort, GENTLENESS: 7; MANNER: 3;
    STRENGTH: 68
Beaufort (D.), CHANGE: 12; FEAR: 35
Beaufoy, OBSCURITY: 13
Beauman (of Wexford), COURAGE: 97
Beaumont, HONOR: 4;
    IMPROVEMENT: 24
Beaumont (Bt.), EXALTATION: 2
Beaumont (of Barrow), EXALTATION: 2
Beaumont (of Whitley), DIVINITY: 178
Beauvale (B.), COURAGE: 243
Beavan, VIRTUE: 176
Beaver, INDUSTRIOUSNESS: 72;
    VIRTUE: 90
Bebington B. C., U.K., FORTUNE: 9;
    LOCAL GOVERNMENT: 59; PEOPLE: 1
Becher (Bt.), LIFE: 2
Beck, CROSS, THE: 15; HOPE: 189;
    LOCAL GOVERNMENT: 386;
    STRENGTH: 153; UNITY: 103
Beck, Quayles, DILIGENCE: 5
Beckenham B. C., U.K., LOCAL
    GOVERNMENT: 249;
    UNSELFISHNESS: 10
Beckett (Co. York), GUIDANCE: 24
Beckford, DIVINE GIFTS: 14
Beckwith (of Thurcroft),
    ENJOYMENT: 17
Becquet, SPEED: 8
Beddington, COURAGE: 35;
    STRENGTH: 8
Beddington and Wallington B. C.,
    U.K., ADVERSITY: 61; ASPIRATION: 65
Bedell-Sivright, AGGRESSION: 14
Bedford, FEAR: 80; TRUTH: 152;
    UNCLASSIFIED: 23
Bedford (Co. Warwick), COURAGE: 15
Bedford (D.), ACCEPTANCE: 1; FATE: 1
Bedfordshire C. C., U.K.,
    FIDELITY: 44; LOCAL
    GOVERNMENT: 67
Bedingfield, SUN: 14
Bedingfield (Bt.), BIRDS: 5; EARTH: 2;
    STATUS: 1
Bedingfield (of Ditchingham),
    EARTH: 1

Bedingfield (of Ditchingham, Co.
    Norfolk), BIRDS: 5; STATUS: 1
Bedlow (U.S.), HOPE: 146
Bedwell, CONSISTENCY: 11
Bedworth U. D. C., U.K.,
    GROWTH: 25; INDUSTRIOUSNESS: 205;
    LOCAL GOVERNMENT: 404
Beebee (of Willey Court), DEFENSE: 43
Beech, OBSCURITY: 13
Beith, COURAGE: 117; FORTUNE: 34
Belcarres (E.), DIVINE GUIDANCE: 29;
    STARS: 10
Belches, FLOURISHING: 66; SHINING: 5;
    TRUST: 79; VIRTUE: 69
Beley, DIVINE GUIDANCE: 35
Belgrave, ASPIRATION: 31;
    EXCELLENCE: 1
Bell, ACCEPTANCE: 4; ADVANCE: 20;
    ASPIRATION: 13; CONCILIATION: 3;
    FIDELITY: 66; HANDS: 9; HONOR: 109;
    INDUSTRIOUSNESS: 123; LAW: 13;
    LOVE: 108; PARADISE: 1;
    PATRIOTISM: 65; PEACE: 72, 78;
    PERSEVERANCE: 58; PROSPERITY: 19;
    REWARD: 11; ROYALTY: 81;
    SHINING: 4; TRUST: 7; VIRTUE: 68
Bell, Boyle, Cork and Orrery (E.),
    Hawtin, Hawtyn, Hole, Ferrers
    (E.), Fielding, Shirley, VIRTUE: 79
Bell (of Rammerscales),
    UNCLASSIFIED: 28
Bell (U.S.), HONOR: 142
Bellairs, PROTECTION: 32; VIRTUE: 348
Bellasyse, GOODNESS: 6
Bellew (Bt.), Bellew, DIVINE GIFTS: 50
Bellingham, FRIENDSHIP: 15
Bellingham (Bt.), FACTUALITY: 1
Bellwood, PATIENCE: 3
Belmore (E.), VIRTUE: 327
Beloe, HEART: 12; PURITY: 29
Beloit College, Beloit, Wisconsin,
    FAITH: 207; KNOWLEDGE: 75;
    SCHOOL MOTTOES: 278
Belsches, SHINING: 3
Belsher, FIDELITY: 221
Belshes (of Invernay), FLOURISHING: 66
Bence (of Thorington), VIRTUE: 258

Bennet, ACCOMPLISHMENT: 4, 14;
ATTEMPT: 1, 4; COURAGE: 178;
CROSS, THE: 4; CROWN: 9;
GOODNESS: 37; OPPRESSION: 6;
PERSEVERANCE: 4; PIETY: 18;
SERVICE: 9; SUCCESS: 7
Bennett, DIVINITY: 300;
PERMANENCE: 4; REASON: 5;
RIGHTS: 4; RISING: 4
Bennett (of Ireland), SERVICE: 52
Bennie, INDUSTRIOUSNESS: 201;
VIRTUE: 381
Benshaw, FEELINGS: 20; HANDS: 27
Benson, DEEDS: 50; DILIGENCE: 47;
LAW: 15; LOCAL GOVERNMENT: 265;
PROSPERITY: 34; VIRTUE: 88;
WEAPONS: 57
Benson (of Parkside), DIVINE
GUIDANCE: 406
Bent, DIVINE GUIDANCE: 433;
MODERATION: 24
Bentham, GLORY: 16; SUFFERING: 2
Bentham (of Lincoln's Inn),
GLORY: 59; VIRTUE: 284
Bentinck, DISGRACE: 1
Bently, PROVIDENCE: 1
Benwick-Clennell, FIDELITY: 314
Berea College, Berea, Kentucky,
CONQUEST: 68; INTER-
RELATEDNESS: 1; SCHOOL
MOTTOES: 119, 362
Berens, DIVINE GUIDANCE: 152
Beresford, CROSS, THE: 81; GROWTH: 23
Beresford (Bt.), CROSS, THE: 83
Beresford (V.), CROSS, THE: 83
Berkeley, ADMIRATION: 2
Berkeley (E.), DIVINE GUIDANCE: 170
Berkeley (of Spetchley), DIVINE
GUIDANCE: 170
Berkhamsted School, U.K., SCHOOL
MOTTOES: 364; VIRTUE: 290
Bermondsey B. C., U.K., ART: 28;
LOCAL GOVERNMENT: 297
Bermudas Company,
PERSEVERANCE: 51
Bernal-Osborne, PEACE: 53; WAR: 54
Bernard, AUTHORITY: 5; OBEDIENCE: 8;
SELF-CONTROL: 4; VIRTUE: 315
Bernard (U.S.), SPIRIT: 6
Berney (Bt.), FEAR: 52; PRUDENCE: 32

Bernhard, Duke of Saxony-Meiningen
(1649–1706), CHRIST, JESUS: 44;
DESIRE: 16; DIVINE GUIDANCE: 431;
PRUDENCE: 30
Bernhard, Duke of Saxony-Weimar
(1604–39), DISCRETION: 4; DIVINE
GUIDANCE: 381; DIVINITY: 295;
FIDELITY: 50; FORTUNE: 11;
HOPE: 112; LOVE: 40; SELF-
CONTROL: 7; SILENCE: 7;
TRANSIENCE: 14
Bernhard, Prince of Anhalt (1572–96),
ADVERSITY: 78; CHRIST, JESUS: 70;
DIVINITY: 432; FATE: 28; HOPE: 120;
SILENCE: 11; TRUST: 107
Bernhard VII, Prince of Anhalt
(1540–70), FEAR: 9; PRUDENCE: 18;
TIMELINESS: 2
Bernie, INDUSTRIOUSNESS: 201;
VIRTUE: 381
Bernon (U.S.), DIVINE GUIDANCE: 187
Berns, OPPORTUNITY: 1; TIME: 10
Berrie, CONQUEST: 19
Berry, INDUSTRIOUSNESS: 134;
JUSTICE: 112; PERSEVERANCE: 79;
RECTITUDE: 66
Berry (Bt.), ADVERSITY: 59
Bertie, FIDELITY: 232; VIRTUE: 252
Berton (Bt.), DIVINE GUIDANCE: 154;
SCHOOL MOTTOES: 63
Bertrand Du Guesclin (D. 1380),
BEAUTY: 6; VIRTUE: 36
Berwick (B.), PROSPERITY: 48
Berwick-upon-Tweed B. C., U.K.,
GLORY: 57; REWARD: 51; VICTORY: 59
Bery, TRUTH: 168
Bessborough (E.), LAW: 52;
PEOPLE: 12; ROYALTY: 74
Bessemer, ADVANCE: 38
Best, CROSS, THE: 97; LAW: 32;
LIBERTY: 59; NAME: 5; STRENGTH: 10;
WEAPONS: 19; WORTHINESS: 46
Beste, DIVINITY: 394
Beswicke, PARADISE: 18
Bethel Theological Seminary, Arden
Hills, Minnesota, SCHOOL
MOTTOES: 321; SCRIPTURES: 15
Bethune, GRACEFULNESS: 1;
PRUDENCE: 77; STEADFASTNESS: 108
Bethune (Bt.), GRACEFULNESS: 1

Bethune-Cookman College, Dayton
Beach, Florida, HANDS: 14;
MIND: 15; SCHOOL MOTTOES: 123
Beton, COURAGE: 81; FIDELITY: 179
Betson, COUNTRY: 100; DILIGENCE: 16;
PATRIOTISM: 46; PRUDENCE: 15
Betteason (of Seven Oakes),
ACCEPTANCE: 6; FATE: 26
Bettescombe, IMMORTALITY: 8
Betton, PREPAREDNESS: 41
Betts, BOASTFULNESS: 6
Betune, COURAGE: 89
Beugo, CONQUEST: 31; COUNTRY: 88;
DIVINITY: 346; ROYALTY: 63
Bevan, DEFENSE: 16; DIVINE
GUIDANCE: 150;
INDUSTRIOUSNESS: 140;
LEADERSHIP: 4
Beverley, COUNTRY: 135; LIBERTY: 117
Beverly (E.), DIVINITY: 163; HOPE: 49
Bevers, HOPE: 56
Beville, FUTURE, THE: 10
Bewicke, PARADISE: 31; REST: 7
Bexhill B. C., U.K., HEALING and
HEALTH: 36; LOCAL
GOVERNMENT: 358; SUN: 17
Bexley, GRATITUDE: 5; REST: 5
Bexley B. C., U.K., LOCAL
GOVERNMENT: 247; UNSELFISHNESS: 7
Beynon, RECTITUDE: 32
Bickerton, DIVINITY: 361; ROYALTY: 67
Biddle, DIVINE GUIDANCE: 117
Biddulph, Greaves, Myddleton,
TRUTH: 42
Biddulph (Bt.), ASPIRATION: 75
Biddulph (of Ledbury, Amroth Castle,
Barton, etc.), ASPIRATION: 75
Bideford B. C., U.K., AUDACITY: 83;
FAITH: 199; LOCAL GOVERNMENT: 293
Bigg, CHRIST, JESUS: 20
Biggar (of Wolmet), GIFTS and
GIVING: 18
Bigland, HOPE: 250
Bigland (Co. Lancaster), GRATITUDE: 8
Bigsby, ASPIRATION: 4, 5; EFFORT: 22;
STARS: 1, 2
Bill, COUNTRY: 63
Billairs, CROSS, THE: 62; FAITH: 147
Billam, PROPER NAMES: 9
Billingham U. D. C., U.K., FAITH: 43;
LOCAL GOVERNMENT: 114

Bilston B. C., U.K., FAITH: 78;
INDUSTRIOUSNESS: 45; LOCAL
GOVERNMENT: 127
Bindlosse, ADVANCE: 42
Bindon, COURAGE: 210
Binet, DESIRE: 6
Bingham (of Melcombe), CHRIST,
JESUS: 79; HOPE: 254
Bingley, BLESSING: 3; FINISH: 2
Bingley U. D. C., U.K.,
DILIGENCE: 47; LOCAL
GOVERNMENT: 265; PROSPERITY: 34
Binney, WORTHINESS: 2
Binning, CHRIST, JESUS: 11;
CLEVERNESS: 8; COURAGE: 240;
DIVINE GUIDANCE: 52; FIDELITY: 322
Binns, DILIGENCE: 41;
INDUSTRIOUSNESS: 96
Birch, FAITH: 214
Birch (Bt.), LIBERTY: 53
Birchall, TRUTH: 73
Bircham (of Reepham, Co. Norfolk),
SELF-CONTROL: 4
Bird, CROSS, THE: 21; HOPE: 19
Birkbeck, DIVINITY: 178
Birkenhead C. B. C., U.K.,
FAITH: 233; LIGHT: 85; LOCAL
GOVERNMENT: 383; STRENGTH: 150
Birley, COURAGE: 170
Birmingham City and C. B. C., U.K.,
IMPROVEMENT: 13; LOCAL
GOVERNMENT: 160
Birmingham University, U.K.,
ADVERSITY: 60; ASPIRATION: 64
Birmingham-Southern College,
Birmingham, Alabama, CHRIST,
JESUS: 68; COUNTRY: 87; SCHOOL
MOTTOES: 238
Birney, WISDOM: 65
Birney (of Salin), ART: 1; STARS: 9;
WEAPONS: 3
Birt, Gwynne, EFFORT: 4
Biset, RESULTS: 1
Bishop, BEING, SELF: 5
Bishop Auckland U. D. C., U.K.,
IMPROVEMENT: 45; LOCAL
GOVERNMENT: 373
Bishop's Stortford U. D. C., U.K.,
DIVINITY: 359; LOCAL
GOVERNMENT: 289; PEOPLE: 7
Bispham (U.S.), VIRTUE: 187

Biss, CONSCIENCE: 8; GUILT: 2;
INNOCENCE: 12; MAINTENANCE: 1
Biss (of Durham), PRUDENCE: 8
Bisset, FLOURISHING: 1; GROWTH: 14,
19
Bissland, GOALS: 2
Bisson, GENEROSITY: 2; VIRTUE: 59
Blaauw, CAUTION: 24
Black, CROSS, THE: 85; LIGHT: 62
Black (U.S.), DIVINITY: 119
Blackadder, COURAGE: 269
Blackburn C. B. C., U.K., ABILITY: 5;
INDUSTRIOUSNESS: 5; LOCAL
GOVERNMENT: 32
Blackburn College, Carlinville,
Illinois, CHRIST, JESUS: 12;
MANLINESS: 1; SCHOOL MOTTOES: 41
Blacker, DIVINITY: 361; ROYALTY: 67
Blackett (Bt.), HOPE: 152;
INDUSTRIOUSNESS: 144
Blackett (of Wylan, Matson, etc.),
HOPE: 152; INDUSTRIOUSNESS: 144
Blackheath Proprietary School, U.K.,
KNOWLEDGE: 10; SCHOOL
MOTTOES: 70
Blackie, DIVINITY: 396; TRUST: 94
Blackly (U.S.), EARTH: 25
Blackman, CONFIDENCE: 10;
FIDELITY: 98
Blackpool C. B. C., U.K.,
IMPROVEMENT: 35; LOCAL
GOVERNMENT: 291
Blacksmiths' Company, HANDS: 3;
INDUSTRIOUSNESS: 8; TRADES: 8;
UTENSILS: 2
Blacksmiths' Company, London,
DIVINE GUIDANCE: 28
Blackwell R. D. C., U.K.,
HUMANITY: 6; LIGHT: 44
Blackwood, COURAGE: 258;
DEFENSE: 55; GROWTH: 15;
SHINING: 14
Blackwood (Bt.), RECTITUDE: 52
Bladen, FIDELITY: 312
Blades, PATRIOTISM: 9
Blades (of High Paull), COUNTRY: 88;
DIVINITY: 346; ROYALTY: 63
Blaenavon U. D. C., U.K., HOPE: 6;
LOCAL GOVERNMENT: 36
Blagrave, ART: 27
Blaikie, COURAGE: 244; FIDELITY: 340
Blain, PEACE: 42; WAR: 52

Blair, CROSS, THE: 85; DIVINE
GUIDANCE: 254; LIGHT: 62;
MODERATION: 24; SECURITY: 87;
VIRTUE: 13, 421
Blair (Bt.), ENJOYMENT: 36;
STRENGTH: 166; VIGILANCE: 96
Blair (of Balmill), COUNTENANCE: 1;
MIND: 12
Blairtyre (B.), VIRTUE: 183
Blake (of Furbough), NOBILITY: 34;
VIRTUE: 339
Blake (of Menlo, Bt.), NOBILITY: 21,
33; VIRTUE: 184, 338
Blake-Humfrey, CROWN: 3; HOPE: 10;
PARADISE: 2
Blakely, DIVINE GUIDANCE: 16
Blakemore, COUNTRY: 89;
DIVINITY: 347; LAW: 40; ROYALTY: 64
Blakeney, DIVINE GUIDANCE: 43
Blakeston (Bt.), DEEDS: 22; LOCAL
GOVERNMENT: 97
Bland, FATE: 29; WORDS: 5
Bland (of Kippax Park),
COURAGE: 209; HONOR: 171;
HOPE: 209
Blandy, REBIRTH: 10
Blane (Bt.), PEACE: 36, 42; WAR: 51, 52
Blatchford (U.S.), PROVIDENCE: 24
Blathwayte, TRUTH: 173; VIRTUE: 389
Blaxland, COURAGE: 144; JUSTICE: 54
Blaydes (of Rawby), COUNTRY: 90;
DIVINITY: 348; ROYALTY: 65
Blayds, GRATITUDE: 10
Blayney, REST: 9; UNSELFISHNESS: 9
Blayney (B.), HONESTY: 25; MIND: 18;
POSSESSION: 9
Blencowe, LIFE: 29; REASON: 16
Blenkinsop, DIVINE GUIDANCE: 172
Blenkinsopp, DEATH: 34
Blennerhasset (Bt.), FORTUNE: 32
Blenshell, DIVINE GUIDANCE: 95
Bligh, FINISH: 7
Bliss, HAPPINESS: 70; PARADISE: 40;
RESULTS: 3; VIRTUE: 336
Blofield, DIVINITY: 141
Blois (Bt.), DIVINITY: 281; TRUST: 75
Blome, PREPAREDNESS: 30
Blomfield, HOME: 19; RELIGION: 19;
ZEALOUSNESS: 4
Bloomfield (B.), FORTUNE: 32
Blosse, MODERATION: 24
Blount, LIGHT: 56; WAY: 5

Blount (Bt.), LIGHT: 56; WAY: 5
Blount (of Maple Durham), LIFE: 20;
LIGHT: 57
Blount (of Orletory), CROSS, THE: 78
Bloxam, HONOR: 27; HOPE: 35; STATE
MOTTOES: 11
Bloxham, AUDACITY: 3
Bloxholme, ORIGIN: 10
Bloxsome, AUDACITY: 78, 79
Bluett, DIVINITY: 245
Bluffton College, Bluffton, Ohio,
SCHOOL MOTTOES: 324; TRUTH: 93
Blumberg, STRENGTH: 16; UNITY: 19
Blundeel, IDENTITY: 3
Blundell, DIVINITY: 312; SCHOOL
MOTTOES: 200; STATE MOTTOES: 35
Blunden (Bt.), LOVE: 37
Blunstone, LIGHT: 70; SHADE: 6
Blunt, SHINING: 11
Blyth, Pollock (Bt.), AUDACITY: 13
Blyth B. C., GROWTH: 25;
INDUSTRIOUSNESS: 205; LOCAL
GOVERNMENT: 404
Boag, TIME: 44
Board, UNCLASSIFIED: 53
Bob Jones University, Greenville,
South Carolina, EFFORT: 27; SCHOOL
MOTTOES: 222
Bockenham, FAITH: 51
Boddy, FORCE: 25
Bodenham (of Rotherwas),
LIBERTY: 125; TRUTH: 123
Body (of Merton Hall), TRUST: 7
Boehm, SUN: 18
Bogart (U.S.), FAITH: 124;
FORTITUDE: 14
Bogie, or Boggie, DIVINE
GUIDANCE: 149
Bogislaus IV, Duke of Pomerania
(1580–1637), PRINCELINESS: 8
Bogislaus X, Duke of Pomerania
(1454–1523), DIVINE GUIDANCE: 56
Bogislaus XIII, Duke of Pomerania zu
Barth (1544–1606), CAUTION: 22;
DEATH: 81; LAW: 46; PEOPLE: 10;
RISK: 1; VIRTUE: 146
Bogislaus XIV, Duke of Pomerania
(1580–1637), DIVINE GUIDANCE: 78,
112, 126
Bogle, GENTLENESS: 3; HOPE: 185
Bognor Regis U. D. C., U.K.,
ACTION: 1; LOCAL GOVERNMENT: 2

Boileau (Bt.), FIDELITY: 65
Boise Bible College, Boise, Idaho,
SCHOOL MOTTOES: 128;
SCRIPTURES: 9
Boker (U.S.), IMPROVEMENT: 40
Bolckow, ACCOMPLISHMENT: 19
Bolden, ETERNITY: 6; KINDNESS: 20
Boldero, AUDACITY: 17
Bolger, DIVINE GIFTS: 26
Bolger (of Wexford), DIVINE
GUIDANCE: 154; SCHOOL
MOTTOES: 63
Bolingbroke, ADMIRATION: 1;
CONTEMPT: 4
Bolingbroke (V.), HONOR: 141
Bolton, ASPIRATION: 40; COURAGE: 229;
DEATH: 37; STRENGTH: 165;
TRADES: 41
Bolton (B.), FIDELITY: 5
Bolton (B.), Cowan, Paulett, Stratton,
Winchester (M.), FIDELITY: 20
Bolton C. B. C., U.K., LOCAL
GOVERNMENT: 368; LOCATION: 11
Bolton (U.S.), INDUSTRIOUSNESS: 146
Bomford, FIDELITY: 209, 342;
JUSTICE: 85; SECURITY: 88
Bonar, PARADISE: 18; SECURITY: 40
Bond, DISGRACE: 12; EARTH: 8
Bondier, DIVINITY: 127; RELIGION: 5
Bonham, INTEGRITY: 10; SCHOOL
MOTTOES: 94
Bonnell, STRANGER: 15
Bonner, FIDELITY: 289
Bonnor, TIME: 2
Bonsall, COUNTRY: 100; PATRIOTISM: 46
Bonteine, DIVINITY: 389
Bontine, DIVINE GUIDANCE: 370
Bonus, DIVINE GUIDANCE: 206
Booker, ASPIRATION: 11
Booth, FUTURE, THE: 24; HOPE: 169;
LIBERTY: 36
Booth (Bt.), CONQUEST: 19; DIVINE
GUIDANCE: 114; FUTURE, THE: 24;
HOPE: 169
Booth (of Salford), DIVINITY: 317;
ROYALTY: 56
Boothby (Bt.), CHRIST, JESUS: 57
Booth-Gore (Bt.), WORTHINESS: 15
Bootle C. B. C., LOCAL
GOVERNMENT: 309; TIME: 47
Bor, FLOURISHING: 73
Borelands, ADVANCE: 49

Borlase, ANIMALS: 32; FOLLOWING: 29;
STRENGTH: 85
Borough (Co. Salop), OFFSPRING: 7;
VIRTUE: 385
Borough of Chippenham,
FIDELITY: 328; LOCAL
GOVERNMENT: 389; UNITY: 115
Borough of Glasgow, FLOURISHING: 57;
LOCAL GOVERNMENT: 214
Borron, COURAGE: 175
Borrows (Bt.), VIRTUE: 129
Borthwick, DIVINE GIFTS: 6; FAITH: 70;
HEALING and HEALTH: 8; HOPE: 62;
LEADERSHIP: 22; VIRTUE: 305
Borthwick (of Stow), FEELINGS: 20;
HANDS: 27
Bosanquet, ADVERSITY: 67;
SUFFERING: 8
Boscawen, KNOWLEDGE: 54;
PARADISE: 31; PATIENCE: 24; REST: 7
Boss, DILIGENCE: 13
Boston (B.), FIDELITY: 193; HONOR: 98;
REWARD: 9
Boston B. C., U.K., LOCAL
GOVERNMENT: 271; SEA: 21
Boston State College, Boston,
Massachusetts, SCHOOL
MOTTOES: 81; SERVICE: 14
Bostwick (U.S.), SERVICE: 47
Bosvile, DIVINITY: 272
Boswell, COURAGE: 97; RISK: 7
Boswell (Bt.), FAITH: 256
Boswell (of Dowen), HOPE: 80
Bosworth, COURAGE: 19
Boteler, DEEDS: 16; UNCLASSIFIED: 2
Botesham, Jermyn, DIRECTION: 4
Botfield, CAUSATION: 3; DIVINE
GUIDANCE: 424
Bothwell (B.), OPPRESSION: 5
Bothwell (of Gleneorse), OPPRESSION: 5
Botsford, PURSUIT: 3
Bottomley, FIDELITY: 106
Bottomly, FIDELITY: 106
Boucher, DEATH: 40; DISGRACE: 10;
FORCE: 15
Boucher (U.S.), EARTH: 7
Boucherett, WORDS: 32
Boudinot, DIVINITY: 390
Boughey (Bt.), HONOR: 141
Boughton (Bt.), DIVINE GIFTS: 43
Boultbee, DIVINITY: 398; HOPE: 244

Boulton, DUTY: 12; MIND: 25;
REASON: 5; RECTITUDE: 43
Boulton (Bt.), PERSEVERANCE: 31
Bourk, FAITH: 178; LAW: 35;
ROYALTY: 58; UNITY: 54
Bourke, CROSS, THE: 2, 65;
SALVATION: 2, 25; SELF-RELIANCE: 1;
UNIQUENESS: 3
Bourne, TRANSIENCE: 4; VIGILANCE: 63
Bournemouth C. B. C., U.K.,
BEAUTY: 15; HEALING and HEALTH: 25;
LOCAL GOVERNMENT: 301
Bouverie, COUNTRY: 68; LIBERTY: 88
Bover, FORTUNE: 65
Bovier, FAITH: 58, 76;
INDUSTRIOUSNESS: 40, 44;
KINDNESS: 8
Bowden, HONOR: 132, 181;
INDUSTRIOUSNESS: 99; SEARCH and
DISCOVERY: 4
Bowdoin (U.S.), ANIMALS: 56;
LOFTINESS: 25
Bowdon U. D. C., U.K., GIFTS and
GIVING: 7; LOCAL GOVERNMENT: 43
Bowen, CAUTION: 12; FUTURE, THE: 3;
LAW: 11
Bower, GOALS: 1; HOPE: 77, 78;
LOVE: 58; PATRIOTISM: 83;
ROYALTY: 93
Bowes, CHANGE: 18; WEAPONS: 54;
WISDOM: 34
Bowes (of Bradley), UNCLASSIFIED: 33
Bowhie, COUNTRY: 122; PATRIOTISM: 81
Bowie, COUNTRY: 122; PATRIOTISM: 81
Bowie (U.S.), DIVINITY: 327
Bowles, DEEDS: 94
Bowman, CONCERN: 4; DIVINE
GUIDANCE: 346; WEAPONS: 76
Bowring, ADVANCE: 37;
STEADFASTNESS: 95
Bowstring-Makers' Company,
POSSESSION: 16; TRADES: 24
Bowyer (Bt.), HAPPINESS: 8
Bowyer-Vaux (Great Yarmouth),
PRESENT, THE: 3
Boy Scouts of America, DEEDS: 12;
PREPAREDNESS: 10
Boycott, DIVINITY: 80; WEAPONS: 29
Boycott (Co. Salop), FAITH: 200;
ROYALTY: 85
Boyd, HANDS: 21; HOPE: 258;
PRUDENCE: 72; TRUST: 6

Boyd (Bt.), TRUST: 7
Boyd (of Middleton Park), TRUST: 7
Boyd (of Trochrig), ETERNITY: 3
Boyes, PATIENCE: 2; SPIRIT: 9
Boyes (of Scotland), PATIENCE: 1
Boyle, DEEDS: 76; DIVINE
    GUIDANCE: 217, 275; ENJOYMENT: 12;
    HONOR: 109; INDUSTRIOUSNESS: 31;
    LOCAL GOVERNMENT: 403;
    REWARD: 11; VIRTUE: 453
Boylston (U.S.), FAITH: 170;
    FRIENDSHIP: 42; LIBERTY: 66
Boyne (V.), FEAR: 42
Boynton (Bt.), TIME: 24
Boys, PATIENCE: 2
Boyton, ADVERSITY: 67; SUFFERING: 8
Bozman (U.S.), HONOR: 167;
    VIRTUE: 180
Brabazon (Bt.), DIVINE GUIDANCE: 443
Bracebridge (Co. Warwick), DIVINE
    GUIDANCE: 48
Bracebridge (of Atherstone), DIVINE
    GUIDANCE: 48
Brackenbury, STEADFASTNESS: 112
Brackenridge (Co. Somerset),
    PREPAREDNESS: 8; WAR: 10
Bracknell Development Corp., U.K.,
    HOME: 11; LOCAL GOVERNMENT: 172
Bradbury, FAIRNESS: 2; FRIENDSHIP: 4;
    VIRTUE: 10
Bradbury (Co. Essex), PATIENCE: 44;
    TIME: 61
Braddyl, SELF-KNOWLEDGE: 1
Bradfield College, U.K., DIVINITY: 24;
    SCHOOL MOTTOES: 30
Bradford City and C. B. C., U.K.,
    INDUSTRIOUSNESS: 116; LOCAL
    GOVERNMENT: 211; SCHOOL
    MOTTOES: 161; STATE MOTTOES: 26
Bradford (E.), MODERATION: 24
Bradley (of Co. Worcester),
    AUDACITY: 99; VIGILANCE: 82
Bradley (U.S.), LIBERTY: 46;
    WISDOM: 39
Bradshaigh, HAPPINESS: 54
Bradshaw, BLESSING: 9; DIVINE
    GUIDANCE: 141; DIVINITY: 131;
    DUTY: 7; HAPPINESS: 4; HOPE: 27;
    POSSESSION: 1; UNSELFISHNESS: 13
Bradshaw (of Barton), HAPPINESS: 54
Bradstreet, VIRTUE: 379
Brady, BRIGHTNESS: 9; RECTITUDE: 11

Bragge, DEATH: 27; FIDELITY: 115;
    HONOR: 79; STEADFASTNESS: 40
Braidwood, STRENGTH: 169
Brailsford, DIVINITY: 267; TRUST: 68
Braintree and Bocking U. D. C., U.K.,
    LOCAL GOVERNMENT: 171; TRUTH: 32
Bramble, CONTEMPT: 8
Bramhall, CHRIST, JESUS: 74;
    SACRIFICE: 6; STEADFASTNESS: 98
Bramwell (Bt.), DILIGENCE: 19
Brand, ADVANCE: 1; LOCAL
    GOVERNMENT: 8
Brand (of Baberton), ADVANCE: 9
Brandeis University, Waltham,
    Massachusetts, SCHOOL
    MOTTOES: 339; TRUTH: 104
Brandenburgh, UNITY: 8
Brander, HOPE: 173; SILENCE: 18
Brander (Co. Hants), EVIL: 11;
    GOODNESS: 45; HONOR: 208
Brandling, COURAGE: 64; FIDELITY: 102
Brandon, PURPOSE: 16
Brandon University, Brandon,
    Manitoba, Canada, SCHOOL
    MOTTOES: 10; TRUTH: 3
Brandreth, FORTUNE: 47; VIRTUE: 65
Branfill, PURPOSE: 16
Branthwaite, UNCLASSIFIED: 32
Brassey (B.), ADVERSITY: 7
Braybrooke (B.), WORTHINESS: 36
Breadalbane (M.), FOLLOWING: 5;
    LEADERSHIP: 12
Breame, DIVINE GUIDANCE: 265
Breary, CHRIST, JESUS: 51
Breconshire C. C., U.K., LOCAL
    GOVERNMENT: 384; PEACE: 83;
    PROSPERITY: 58; UNITY: 79
Breek, STEADFASTNESS: 54
Bremer, TRUTH: 2
Brentford and Chiswick B. C., U.K.,
    LOCAL GOVERNMENT: 134;
    STRENGTH: 37
Brenton (Bt.), ADVANCE: 30; PROPER
    NAMES: 47
Brentwood U. D. C., U.K., FAITH: 8;
    LOCAL GOVERNMENT: 30
Brereton (Co. Norfolk), DIVINE
    GUIDANCE: 356
Bretargh, WORDS: 19
Bretherton, CROSS, THE: 86
Brett, CONQUEST: 45; DESIRE: 24
Brettell, DIVINE GUIDANCE: 400

Brewers' Company, DIVINITY: 261;
TRUST: 64

Brewster, FORTITUDE: 26;
HONESTY: 34; PROTECTION: 31;
TRUTH: 153

Brewster (U.S.), FORTUNE: 57;
LIBERTY: 71

Brey, COURAGE: 26; GRADUALNESS: 1

Briar Cliff College, Sioux City, Iowa,
LOVE: 36; SCHOOL MOTTOES: 35

Brickdale, FAITH: 61; FORTITUDE: 3

Bricklayers and Tilers' Company,
DIVINITY: 261; TRUST: 64

Bridge, CONCILIATION: 6;
COURAGE: 180

Bridgeman, MODERATION: 24

Bridgen (U.S.), HONESTY: 40;
INDUSTRIOUSNESS: 167

Bridgend U. D. C., U.K.,
LEADERSHIP: 3; LOCAL
GOVERNMENT: 42

Bridger, STRENGTH: 142

Bridges, DEFENSE: 30; RECTITUDE: 41

Bridgewater (E.), FUTURE, THE: 26

Bridgman, DIVINE GUIDANCE: 5

Bridgnorth B. C., U.K.,
FIDELITY: 131; LOCAL
GOVERNMENT: 126; ROYALTY: 36

Bridgwater B. C., U.K., LOCAL
GOVERNMENT: 264; PROSPERITY: 32;
WISDOM: 45

Bridlington B. C., U.K., HEALING and
HEALTH: 35; LOCAL
GOVERNMENT: 350

Bridport (B.), EQUANIMITY: 17

Brierley Hill U. D. C., U.K.,
INDUSTRIOUSNESS: 184; LOCAL
GOVERNMENT: 352

Briggs, AUDACITY: 62; FIDELITY: 183;
LIMITATION: 6; VIRTUE: 267

Brigham, CROSS, THE: 65;
SALVATION: 25

Brighouse B. C., U.K.,
INDUSTRIOUSNESS: 102; LOCAL
GOVERNMENT: 208; PRUDENCE: 26

Bright, BRIGHTNESS: 7; DARKNESS: 15;
LIGHT: 71

Brighton C. B. C., U.K.,
DIVINITY: 236; LOCAL
GOVERNMENT: 181; TRUST: 53

Brighton College, U.K.,
RECTITUDE: 42; SCHOOL
MOTTOES: 184

Brinckerhoff (U.S.), FAITH: 19;
INTEGRITY: 5

Brinckman (Bt.), PERSEVERANCE: 56;
STATE MOTTOES: 40

Brinkley, CHANGE: 9

Brisbane, DIVINE GIFTS: 8; IDLENESS: 3,
4

Brisbane (Bt.), DIVINITY: 168;
GENEROSITY: 16; WAR: 12

Brisbane (of Scotland), COURAGE: 17;
PRUDENCE: 5

Brisbane-McDougall, DIVINE GIFTS: 8

Brisco (of Coghurst), GRATITUDE: 6

Briscoe, HOPE: 215; VIRTUE: 148

Bristol City and C. B. C., U.K.,
LOCAL GOVERNMENT: 400;
VIRTUE: 377

Bristol (M.), MEMORY: 12

Bristowe, VIGILANCE: 101

Broadalbine Maxwell (of Teylling),
PATIENCE: 17

Broade, PIETY: 38; STRENGTH: 102

Broadhead, CONFIDENCE: 5

Broadhurst, SILENCE: 16; WISDOM: 66

Broadley, GRATITUDE: 13

Broadley (Bt.), HONOR: 46

Broadly, DEATH: 28; HONOR: 101

Broadmead, FIDELITY: 289

Broadwood, FLOURISHING: 69

Brock, JUSTICE: 58

Brockett, MERCY: 11

Brockett (U.S.), CROSS, THE: 39;
LIGHT: 5

Brocklehurst, TRUTH: 128

Broderick, CROWN: 1; WEAPONS: 1

Brodie (Bt.), UNITY: 105

Brodie (of Brodie), UNITY: 105

Brodie (of Lethen), UNITY: 2

Brodigan, PRUDENCE: 75

Brograve, DEATH: 19, 57; REASON: 12

Broigg, DEATH: 27; HONOR: 79

Broke, WEAPONS: 86

Bromage, DIVINE GUIDANCE: 121

Brome (of West Malling), DIVINE
GUIDANCE: 201; LOCAL
GOVERNMENT: 94

Bromhead, UNITY: 10

Bromhead (Bt.), UNITY: 17

Bromley, PURSUIT: 7

Bruce (of Mowance), LOVE: 95
Bruce (of Pittarthie), FIDELITY: 319
Bruce (of Wester-Kinloch),
  COURAGE: 5
Brudenel, GRACE: 10
Bruen (U.S.), FAITH: 111
Bruges, PARADISE: 41
Bruges (co. Wilts), COUNTRY: 62;
  COURAGE: 168
Brummind (of Blair), DIVINE
  GUIDANCE: 154; SCHOOL
  MOTTOES: 63
Brunner (Bt.), WISDOM: 5
Bruno II, Count of Mansfeld
  (1545–1615), FINISH: 1
Bruno III, Count of Mansfeld
  (1576–1644), CHRIST, JESUS: 79;
  HOPE: 254
Brunswick and Luenburg, ACTION: 13;
  HONOR: 123
Brunton, LIGHT: 45; SECURITY: 27
Bryan, COURAGE: 81; FIDELITY: 179;
  MODERATION: 21; UNCLASSIFIED: 45;
  WEAPONS: 39
Bryant and Stratton Business Institute,
  Clarence, New York,
  KNOWLEDGE: 42; SCHOOL
  MOTTOES: 164
Bryce, JUSTICE: 26
Bryden (of Berwick), VIGILANCE: 55
Brydges (of Denton Court, Bt.),
  RECTITUDE: 41
Brymer, ADVERSITY: 71; OPPOSITION: 9;
  WALKING: 7
Bryson, DIVINE GUIDANCE: 278;
  PREPAREDNESS: 16
Buccleugh (D.), LOVE: 7
Buchan, SHINING: 29; STRENGTH: 49, 51
Buchan (E.), JUDGMENT: 7
Buchan (of Kelly), PURSUIT: 7
Buchanan, ACTION: 20; AUDACITY: 7,
  75; CAUTION: 36; DILIGENCE: 9;
  FORTUNE: 49; HONOR: 11; MERCY: 27;
  PROSPERITY: 51; UNCLASSIFIED: 57
Buchanan (of Ardock), BRIGHTNESS: 3
Buchanan (of Drumakill), DIVINE
  GUIDANCE: 278
Buchanan (of Drumhead),
  INDUSTRIOUSNESS: 156; SUCCESS: 8
Buchanan (of Miltown), HONOR: 26
Buchanan (U.S.), ASSISTANCE: 14
Buchanan-Hamilton, AUDACITY: 5

Buck, JUSTICE: 8; SELF-KNOWLEDGE: 9;
  WORTHINESS: 1
Buck (of Agecroft), GOODNESS: 34
Buckeley (Bt.), MODERATION: 24
Buckingham (D.), LOVE: 113
Buckinghamshire, COUNTRY: 32;
  DIVINITY: 181; ROYALTY: 40
Buckinghamshire C. C., U.K., LOCAL
  GOVERNMENT: 394;
  STEADFASTNESS: 143
Buckinghamshire (E.), GIFTS and
  GIVING: 5
Buckle (Co. Sussex), PRUDENCE: 33
Buckler (U.S.), FIDELITY: 111
Buckston, KINDNESS: 9
Buckworth (of Cley, Co. Norfolk, and
  Spalding, Co. Lincoln), STATUS: 5
Budge, DEATH: 92
Budgett, TRANSIENCE: 6
The Buffs (East Kent Regiment),
  GROWTH: 24; HONESTY: 53;
  HONOR: 184
The Buffs (East Kent Regt.), U.K.,
  MERCY: 9
Bulen, ROYALTY: 31; VICTORY: 13
Bulkeley-Owen (of Tedmore Hall,
  Shrewsbury), POSSESSION: 2
Bull, VIRTUE: 67
Bull (U.S.), AUDACITY: 16
Buller (of Cornwall), BIRDS: 5;
  STATUS: 1
Bullman, PATIENCE: 27
Bullock, DIVINITY: 163; HOPE: 49
Bullock (of Faulkbourn),
  CONSCIENCE: 8; GUILT: 2;
  INNOCENCE: 12
Bulman, COUNTRY: 100;
  PATRIOTISM: 46
Bulwer, ADVERSITY: 4; HOPE: 269;
  PROSPERITY: 1
Bulwer-Lytton (Bt.), VIRTUE: 73
Bunbury, INTEGRITY: 10; SCHOOL
  MOTTOES: 94
Bunbury (Bt.), TRANSIENCE: 3
Bunce, LIFE: 32; PARADISE: 60
Bundy, GOALS: 2
Bunney, DEATH: 66
Bunny, ASPIRATION: 59; DEATH: 66;
  PURPOSE: 18
Bunten (of Kilbride), AUDACITY: 61;
  FIDELITY: 182

Bunting, OPPORTUNITY: 3; PROSPERITY: 5

Burchell, RELIGION: 33

Burder, ADVERSITY: 42; PERSEVERANCE: 36

Burder (U.S.), CROSS, THE: 57; GLORY: 25

Burdett, LEADERSHIP: 17

Burdon, VIRTUE: 78

Burgess, PATIENCE: 19; WORDS: 39

Burgh, CROSS, THE: 2; SALVATION: 2

Burgh, Byam, DEEDS: 5

Burgrave, DEATH: 19

Burke, ASPIRATION: 23; CONQUEST: 19; DEFIANCE: 13

Burke (of Kilcoran, Owen, and Clongowna), FAITH: 241; LAW: 70; ROYALTY: 126; UNITY: 90

Burke (of Marble Hill, Bt.), FAITH: 241; LAW: 70; ROYALTY: 126; UNITY: 90

Burke (of St. Cleras), DIVINITY: 427; FAITH: 240; LAW: 68; UNITY: 85

Burlington (E.), Devonshire (D.), Cruickshank, Hardwick, Waterpark (B.), Waring, CAUTION: 18

Burmey, ART: 1; STARS: 9; WEAPONS: 3

Burn, PREPAREDNESS: 16; TRUTH: 168

Burnaby (Bt.), ROYALTY: 73

Burne, LOCAL GOVERNMENT: 274; PERSEVERANCE: 68; RESTRAINT: 1

Burnell, KINDNESS: 5

Burnes, ANCESTRY: 3; CONQUEST: 30; FLOURISHING: 65; ROYALTY: 112

Burnes (of Montrose), COUNTRY: 61; PATRIOTISM: 27

Burnes (of Montrose and Ladbroke Square, London), PROPER NAMES: 13

Burnet, FELLOWSHIP: 7; GROWTH: 17, 23; VIRTUE: 367

Burnet (of Dalleladies), WAVES: 2

Burnett, IMMORTALITY: 6

Burnett (Bt.), VIRTUE: 234

Burney, DIVINE GIFTS: 44

Burnham, FEAR: 71

Burnley C. B. C., U.K., INDUSTRIOUSNESS: 165; LOCAL GOVERNMENT: 283

Burns, FAITH: 226; FLORA: 46; PROTECTION: 3

Burnside (of Whitlaw), Gordon, GRADUALNESS: 3

Burr, HONOR: 198; PROPER NAMES: 52; VIRTUE: 354

Burr (U.S.), HONOR: 194; VIRTUE: 276

Burrard (Bt.), PERSEVERANCE: 55

Burrell, EQUANIMITY: 5; FIDELITY: 3; LIBERTY: 109; REST: 28; WAVES: 5

Burrell (of Knepp Castle, Co. Sussex, bt.), HOSTILITY: 4

Burroughes, AUDACITY: 3

Burroughes (of Burlingham and Long Stratton, Co. Norfolk), FAITH: 5

Burroughs, POSSESSION: 8

Burroughs (of Burlingham and Long Stratton, Co. Norfolk), COURAGE: 11; LOCAL GOVERNMENT: 26

Burrow, DIVINE GIFTS: 26; LOCAL GOVERNMENT: 90; TRANQUILLITY: 3

Burrowes (Bt.), STRENGTH: 24; VIRTUE: 48

Burrows, UNITY: 73

Burt, SELF-KNOWLEDGE: 7

Burt (U.S.), PRIDE: 4

Burtee (Bt.), CONQUEST: 19

Burton, FRIENDSHIP: 17; VIGILANCE: 81

Burton (of Burton Hall and Longner), DIVINE GUIDANCE: 217

Burton (of Lindley and Bedworth), LIFE: 21; LIGHT: 60

Burton-upon-Trent C. B. C., U.K., ART: 17; HONOR: 76; LOCAL GOVERNMENT: 174

Bury, CROSS, THE: 114; VIRTUE: 340

Bury C. B. C., U.K., INDUSTRIOUSNESS: 199; LOCAL GOVERNMENT: 398

Bury St. Edmunds B. C., U.K., LAW: 60; LOCAL GOVERNMENT: 321; ROYALTY: 113

Busfield, MODERATION: 16; SECURITY: 33

Bush, GROWTH: 23

Bushby, FRUIT: 3

Bushe, COURAGE: 160; HOPE: 74; MODERATION: 18

Bushell, HONOR: 27; HOPE: 35; STATE MOTTOES: 11

Busk, DISCIPLINE: 7; GENTLENESS: 18

Butcher (U.S.), EQUANIMITY: 6

Butchers' Company, ANIMALS: 44

Bute (M.), ANCESTRY: 8

Butler, ASPIRATION: 61; BENEFITS: 2;
CHRIST, JESUS: 32; DEFIANCE: 2;
DIVINE GUIDANCE: 85, 254;
DIVINITY: 406; ENJOYMENT: 31;
EXALTATION: 1;
INDUSTRIOUSNESS: 117; LIGHT: 8;
SUCCESS: 6
Butler (Bt.), SEARCH and DISCOVERY: 4
Butler (U.S.), VIRTUE: 116
Butler-Danvers, LIBERTY: 70
Butter, DIVINE GUIDANCE: 195;
VIRTUE: 436
Butterworth, DIVINE GUIDANCE: 366
Buxton, DEEDS: 15; PRESENT, THE: 4;
SELF-RELIANCE: 4
Buxton B. C., U.K., LOCAL
GOVERNMENT: 47; WATER: 4
Buxton (Bt.), DEEDS: 96
Buxton College, U.K., LIGHT: 76;
SCHOOL MOTTOES: 290; SHINING: 27
Buxton-Fitzherbert (of Black Castle),
SERVICE: 72
Byam, TRUTH: 92
Byass, DILIGENCE: 11
Byers, SECURITY: 30
Byng, DEFENSE: 48; PROPER NAMES: 33;
STATE MOTTOES: 54
Byres, GOVERNMENT: 9; SECURITY: 30
Byrom, WEAPONS: 8
Byron (B.), TRUST: 14
Bysse, CONQUEST: 2; SELF-CONTROL: 6
Bythesea, CHANGE: 12; FEAR: 35

C

Cabot (U.S.), FEELINGS: 23
Caddle, NOBILITY: 34; VIRTUE: 339
Cadell, HONESTY: 4; TRUST: 11;
VIGILANCE: 98
Cadogan (E.), ENVY: 9
Caernarvonshire C. C., U.K., LOCAL
GOVERNMENT: 54; STRENGTH: 11
Cahun, POSSIBILITY: 9
Cairncross, ACQUISITION: 2; FEAR: 59;
JUSTICE: 106
Cairnie, ASPIRATION: 2
Cairns, HOPE: 282; VIRTUE: 247
Cairns (of Pilmor), FLOURISHING: 14
Caithness (E.), DEVOTION: 1
Calandrine, ASPIRATION: 83
Calcott, DIVINE GUIDANCE: 170
Calcraft, DIVINE GUIDANCE: 170

Caldecott (of Rugby Lodge),
PREPAREDNESS: 31
Calder, ATTENTIVENESS: 3; FINISH: 16
Calder (Bt.), VIGILANCE: 87
Calderwood, HOPE: 215; REWARD: 55;
TRUTH: 130; VIRTUE: 331
Calderwood (of Pittedy and Dalkeith),
TRUTH: 135
Caldwell, DEEDS: 35; HOPE: 58, 292;
LIBERTY: 19, 20; VIRTUE: 273;
WEAPONS: 32, 33
Caldwell (of Lindley Wood),
EFFORT: 23
Caldwell (U.S.), COURAGE: 101
Caledon (E.), SEA: 20
California State Universities and
Colleges, MANLINESS: 5; SCHOOL
MOTTOES: 366; TRUTH: 174
Call (Bt.), GRATITUDE: 4
Callaghan, AUDACITY: 50;
FIDELITY: 157
Callaway (U.S.), DIVINE
GUIDANCE: 418
Callender, INTENTION: 2
Calley (of Burderop), HONOR: 10;
WISDOM: 6
Callow, COUNTRY: 112; PATRIOTISM: 61
Calmady, UNCLASSIFIED: 61
Calne B. C., U.K., FAITH: 46; LOCAL
GOVERNMENT: 115; SERVICE: 18
Calrow, INDUSTRIOUSNESS: 60; SCHOOL
MOTTOES: 135
Calthorpe, DIVINITY: 365
Calthorpe (B.), WAY: 3
Calthrop (of Stanhoe Hall, Co.
Norfolk), FORTUNE: 109;
WISDOM: 104
Calvert, DEEDS: 48; STATE MOTTOES: 17
Calvin Coolidge, INDUSTRIOUSNESS: 28
Calvin Theological Seminary, Grand
Rapids, Michigan, DEDICATION: 4;
SCHOOL MOTTOES: 52, 246;
SINCERITY: 11; SPEED: 41
Camberwell B. C., U.K.,
CONFIDENCE: 1; LOCAL
GOVERNMENT: 11
Cambridge University, U.K.,
LIGHT: 20; SCHOOL MOTTOES: 127
Cambridgeshire C. C., U.K., LOCAL
GOVERNMENT: 276; WAVES: 6
Camden (M.), JUDGMENT: 10

Cameren (Brittany), GIFTS and
GIVING: 3
Cameron, RISING: 5
Cameron (Bt.), PROPER NAMES: 1, 31
Cameron (of Fassiefern, Bt.), PROPER
NAMES: 7
Cameron (of Lochiel), PATRIOTISM: 65;
ROYALTY: 81
Campbell, ACTION: 3; ADVANCE: 19;
ATTENTIVENESS: 6; AUDACITY: 4;
CAUTION: 24; COURAGE: 151; CROSS,
THE: 90; DEEDS: 35; DESIRE: 9;
DILIGENCE: 44; DIVINE
GUIDANCE: 118; EARTH: 17;
FAITH: 227, 248; FOLLOWING: 6, 20;
FORCE: 28; FORGETTING: 1, 17;
GOOD NEWS: 1; HONOR: 82, 159;
HOPE: 58; IMPROVEMENT: 47;
INDUSTRIOUSNESS: 47, 101, 198;
LIGHT: 66; LOCATION: 6; MEMORY: 3,
17; OPPORTUNITY: 8;
PERSEVERANCE: 35, 67;
POSSESSION: 17; POWER: 25;
PREPAREDNESS: 5; PURSUIT: 8;
SEA: 32; TIME: 57; UNCLASSIFIED: 60;
VICTORY: 15, 38, 40; VIRTUE: 231;
WAY: 2; WEAPONS: 5; WISDOM: 112
Campbell (Bt.), ATTENTIVENESS: 3;
AUDACITY: 11, 98, 99;
FOLLOWING: 5; FORGETTING: 7;
LEADERSHIP: 12; PREPAREDNESS: 48;
VIGILANCE: 74, 77, 82
Campbell Colquhon (of Killermont),
POSSIBILITY: 4
Campbell (of Abernchill, bt.), CHRIST,
JESUS: 85; VICTORY: 60
Campbell (of Ardintenny), Billing (co.
Norfolk), FAITH: 228
Campbell (of Auchawilling),
FIDELITY: 14; WEAPONS: 11
Campbell (of Auchinbreck, Bt.),
MEMORY: 4
Campbell (of Auchmannock),
PATIENCE: 16
Campbell (of Ballochyle), MEMORY: 8
Campbell (of Barbreck), MEMORY: 6
Campbell (of Blythswood), EFFORT: 37
Campbell (of Co. Hants and Dunoon,
Scotland), FAITH: 254;
STRENGTH: 180
Campbell (of Gargunnock),
UBIQUITY: 9

Campbell (of Gartsford, bt.),
COURAGE: 276
Campbell (of Glenfalloch),
UNCLASSIFIED: 70
Campbell (of Islay), FRIENDSHIP: 32
Campbell (of Jurd and Achteny),
AUDACITY: 5
Campbell (of Moy), ATTENTIVENESS: 2
Campbell (of Perthshire),
COUNTRY: 120; PATRIOTISM: 79
Campbell (of Powis, Bt.),
FIDELITY: 322
Campbell (of Purvis, bt.), FAITH: 109
Campbell (of Shirven), HOME: 19;
RELIGION: 19
Campbell (of Skerrington),
FIDELITY: 39; MILITARY
DISTINCTION: 2; PRUDENCE: 11;
REWARD: 4
Campbell (of Sombey), PRUDENCE: 12;
STRENGTH: 18
Campbell (of Weasenham, Cockley
Cley, and Fakenham, Co. Norfolk),
POSSESSION: 31
Campbell University, Buies Creek,
North Carolina, ASPIRATION: 7;
SCHOOL MOTTOES: 3
Campbell (U.S.), SEA: 4
Camperdown (E.), DANGER: 17;
ENDURANCE: 15; PROSPERITY: 50;
RECTITUDE: 69
Campi, HAPPINESS: 22
Candler (of Acomb), FIDELITY: 4
Canning (V.), ADVERSITY: 51
Cannock U. D. C., U.K. (a former
Royal Forest and Chase),
HUNTING: 3; INDUSTRIOUSNESS: 113
Cant, CONSERVATION: 1
Canterbury City and C. B. C., U.K.,
LOCAL GOVERNMENT: 41; PARENTS: 1
Canterbury (V.), ACCOMPLISHMENT: 17
Cantillon de Ballyluge, COURAGE: 90;
WAR: 28
Cantrell (Co. Lancaster), SACRIFICE: 4;
UBIQUITY: 8
Capel, FAITH: 61; FORTITUDE: 3;
LIFE: 31
Capital City Junior College, Little
Rock, Arkansas, CONCERN: 5;
SCHOOL MOTTOES: 316

Source Information

Carrington (B.), FIDELITY: 308;
PERSEVERANCE: 82
Carritt, FAITH: 57; STRENGTH: 28;
WAR: 20
Carroll, or O'Carroll (of Ballymore),
FAITH: 151; STRENGTH: 75; WAR: 36
Carrot, FAITH: 63; STRENGTH: 29;
WAR: 21
Carruthers, FIDELITY: 246, 262;
PREPAREDNESS: 47, 63
Carsair, FORGETTING: 6
Carse, FATE: 23; SPEED: 57
Carshalton U. D. C., U.K.,
COURAGE: 11; FAITH: 5; LOCAL
GOVERNMENT: 26
Carson, POSSESSION: 25
Carson (of Scarning, co. Norfolk),
DEATH: 40; DISGRACE: 10
Carstairs (of Kilconquhar), SHINING: 29
Carter, ACCOMPLISHMENT: 2;
ADVANCE: 40; DIVINE GUIDANCE: 145;
LIBERTY: 109; PATIENCE: 46;
REST: 28; VICTORY: 68
Carter (U.S.), GUILT: 3
Carteret (B.), DUTY: 20
Carthew (of East Dereham),
DECEPTION: 2; WISDOM: 3
Cartier, COUNTRY: 35; SADNESS: 3
Cartwright (of co. Notts,
Northampton and Suffolk),
DEFENSE: 14
Carvick, STEADFASTNESS: 13
Carvile, VIRTUE: 191
Carville, VICTORY: 44
Cary, COURAGE: 251; PURITY: 22
Cary (U.S.), DIVINITY: 383
Carysfort (E.), HANDS: 23;
HOSTILITY: 13
Casborne, PURITY: 15; WATER: 15
Case, UNITY: 25
Case (U.S.), VIRTUE: 9
Casey, LIVELINESS: 8; STRENGTH: 168;
VIRTUE: 225
Cashen, FLORA: 33
Casimir, Margrave of Brandenburg-
Baireuth (1481–1527), AGE: 7;
CHRIST, JESUS: 22; TRANSIENCE: 10
Casley, DEATH: 40; DISGRACE: 10
Cass (of East Barnet), COUNTRY: 136
Cassan (Queen's County),
ENJOYMENT: 19
Cassels, HOPE: 67; SALVATION: 19

Cassidy, FIDELITY: 164;
STEADFASTNESS: 43
Castell, DIVINITY: 79; HOPE: 22;
SECURITY: 5
Castellain, VIGILANCE: 33
Castle Jr. College, Windham, New
Hampshire, SCHOOL MOTTOES: 5;
VIRTUE: 7; WISDOM: 1
Castleford U. D. C., U.K.,
AUDACITY: 12; LOCAL
GOVERNMENT: 37
Castlemaine (V.), LOCAL
GOVERNMENT: 397; VIGILANCE: 103
Castleman, DIVINITY: 442
Castle-Steuart (E.), ADVANCE: 19
Caswall, MEASURE: 9
Cathcart, HOPE: 83; SPEED: 31
Cathcart (Bt.), FAITH: 14
Cathcart (E.), HOPE: 83; SPEED: 31
Catherine de Medicis (1519–89),
FATE: 14; PRUDENCE: 20
Catlin (U.S.), EQUANIMITY: 16
Caton, CAUTION: 7; CONQUEST: 54;
DEATH: 100
Caton (of Binbrook), ANIMALS: 7;
CAUTION: 14
Catsznellage, LIMITATION: 4
Cattley, ASPIRATION: 68
Catty, ASPIRATION: 36
Caulfield, DIVINE GUIDANCE: 82;
WEAPONS: 27
Caunter, SEASONS: 4
Cavan, CONQUEST: 19
Cavan (E.), PREPAREDNESS: 83
Cave, VIGILANCE: 10, 12
Cave (Bt.), VIGILANCE: 42
Cavendish, CAUTION: 18
Cawarden, POSSESSION: 30;
VIRTUE: 408
Cawardine, RECTITUDE: 49
Cawdor (E.), ATTENTIVENESS: 3;
DEATH: 9; PURITY: 5
Cawley (Bt.), DESIRE: 2
Cawood, GENTLENESS: 14
Cay, COUNTRY: 68; LIBERTY: 88, 109;
REST: 28
Cay (of Charlton), FLORA: 42
Cayley, DARKNESS: 13; LIGHT: 67;
RIGHTS: 11; STARS: 31
Cayton, ASPIRATION: 10
Cayzer, CAUTION: 8
Cecil, HEART: 6; UNITY: 24

Cedar Crest College, Allentown, Pennsylvania, KNOWLEDGE: 58; LIBERTY: 101; RELIGION: 25; SCHOOL MOTTOES: 251

Cedarville College, Cedarville, Ohio, CROWN: 23; SCHOOL MOTTOES: 239

Centenary College of Louisiana, Shreveport, Louisiana, INDUSTRIOUSNESS: 116; LOCAL GOVERNMENT: 211; SCHOOL MOTTOES: 161; STATE MOTTOES: 26

Centennial motto of Western Oregon State College, Monmouth, Oregon, HOPE: 286; SCHOOL MOTTOES: 336

Central African Republic, EQUALITY: 10; INDUSTRIOUSNESS: 193; NATIONAL MOTTOES: 35, 46; UNITY: 106

Central Michigan University, Mt. Pleasant, Michigan, FRIENDSHIP: 49; KNOWLEDGE: 62; SCHOOL MOTTOES: 267; VIRTUE: 173

Cessnock (of Treesbank and Fairfield), PRUDENCE: 12; STRENGTH: 18

Chaceler (of Shieldhill), EXCELLENCE: 13

Chadwick, DIVINITY: 72; FAITH: 34; LOCATION: 3; ROYALTY: 116; TRUST: 25

Chadwick (of Lynn, Co. Norfolk), FIDELITY: 94; LOVE: 49

Chadwick (of Pudleston Court), DIRECTNESS: 12; HONOR: 120

Challen (of Shermanbury), DIVINITY: 187

Challoner, STRANGER: 13; STRENGTH: 120

Chalmers, FORTUNE: 110

Chalmers (of Blancraig and Auldbar Castle), HOPE: 215

Chalmers (of Culto), ADVANCE: 5

Chalmers (of Gaitgarth), DIVINE GUIDANCE: 379

Chamberlain, STEADFASTNESS: 76

Chamberlain (Bt.), FAITH: 219; HOPE: 239

Chamberlaine, AUDACITY: 3

Chamberlayne, COURAGE: 263; DEATH: 65; GOODNESS: 34; VIRTUE: 403

Chambers, DIVINE GUIDANCE: 68; FAITH: 153; FLORA: 23; HOPE: 216; LIGHT: 52; PRAISE: 16; VICTORY: 32; WAR: 18

Chambers (of Scotland), ADVANCE: 5

Chambre, BEAUTY: 21; DIVINITY: 154

Chamer, DIRECTNESS: 2

Champion (U.S.), ASPIRATION: 70

Champneys (Bt.), COUNTRY: 109; DEATH: 87; PATRIOTISM: 58

Chandlee, PEACE: 47; PROSPERITY: 41

Chandler (U.S.), LOVE: 123; SACRIFICE: 10

Channing (Bt.), DIVINE GUIDANCE: 249

Chapin (U.S.), DIVINE GUIDANCE: 40

Chaplin, ADVERSITY: 42; PERSEVERANCE: 36

Chapman, CROWN: 1; OPPORTUNITY: 10; WEAPONS: 1

Chapman (Bt.), OPPRESSION: 1; VIRTUE: 34

Chapman (of Whitby), OPPRESSION: 1; VIRTUE: 34

Chapple, DIVINITY: 237; TRUST: 54

Chard, DESPAIR: 5

Charlemont (E.), DIVINE GUIDANCE: 82; WEAPONS: 27

Charles, HONOR: 192; VIRTUE: 255

Charles, Duke of Orleans, father of Louis XII of France, WILL: 2

Charles I (1600–49), JUSTICE: 71; TRUTH: 47

Charles the Bold (1433–77), AGGRESSION: 1

Charles (U.S.), DESIRE: 25

Charles V, Emperor of Germany (1500–58), EXPECTATION: 2; IMPROVEMENT: 32

Charlesworth, JUSTICE: 72; VIRTUE: 98

Charleville (E.), CROSS, THE: 115; VIRTUE: 341

Charlotte Dorothee Sophie, Duchess of Saxony-Weimar (1669–1708), DIVINE GUIDANCE: 407

Charlton, CONSCIENCE: 10; JUSTICE: 116

Charlton (of Lea Hall), CHANGE: 19

Charnock, HAPPINESS: 60

Charnocke, HAPPINESS: 64

Charrington, PROTECTION: 4; VIRTUE: 21

Charter, RIGHTS: 9

Charters or Chartres (of Hempsfield and Kingfauns), KINDNESS: 17

Chartres, GOVERNMENT: 12

Chater, INDUSTRIOUSNESS: 89

Chatham B. C., U.K., FIDELITY: 220; LOCAL GOVERNMENT: 220

Chatham (E.), PROVIDENCE: 1

Chatteris, LIBERTY: 53

Chatteris, Birch (Bt.), NATIONAL MOTTOES: 13

Chatterton (Bt.), FIDELITY: 218

Chatto, FRIENDSHIP: 45

Chauncy (U.S.), ASPIRATION: 79

Chawner, DESPAIR: 5

Chaytor (Bt.), FORTUNE: 62

Cheap, VIGILANCE: 25; VIRTUE: 41

Checkley (U.S.), JUSTICE: 77; LIGHT: 28; STARS: 20

Chedworth, JUSTICE: 86; PURPOSE: 12

Cheere, HONOR: 153; REWARD: 34; VIRTUE: 153

Cheese, TIME: 39

Cheetham, POSSESSION: 23

Cheever (U.S.), INDUSTRIOUSNESS: 67

Cheevers, FAITH: 35

Chein or Cheyne, PATIENCE: 36

Chelmsford (B.), FORTUNE: 100; HOPE: 241

Chelmsford B. C., U.K., LOCAL GOVERNMENT: 223; UNITY: 52

Chelsea B. C., U.K., DIVINITY: 314; LOCAL GOVERNMENT: 242

Cheltenham B. C., U.K., HEALING and HEALTH: 29; KNOWLEDGE: 59; LOCAL GOVERNMENT: 323

Cheney, FATE: 14; PRUDENCE: 20; WORTHINESS: 21

Chermside, SPEED: 39

Cherry, HOPE: 11

Cheshire C. C., U.K., LOCAL GOVERNMENT: 200; WEAPONS: 56

Chester City and C. B. C., U.K., LOCAL GOVERNMENT: 28; VIRTUE: 16

Chester (of Royston), ENDURANCE: 58

Chesterfield (E.), DIVINE GIFTS: 3; ROYALTY: 1

Chesterman (of Wilts and Beds), FIDELITY: 289

Cheston, WORTHINESS: 12

Chetham, POSSESSION: 23

Chetham Strode (of South Hill), DEATH: 40; DISGRACE: 10

Chetwode (Bt.), CHRIST, JESUS: 30; CROWN: 5

Chetwynd (Bt.), DIVINE GUIDANCE: 380

Chetwynd (V.), HONESTY: 38; HONOR: 156

Chevalier Bayard, VENGEANCE: 5

Chevallier, CROSS, THE: 53; TRUTH: 23

Cheyne, DIVINITY: 168; WORTHINESS: 10

Chichester, DESIRE: 5; FAITH: 52; HONOR: 126

Chichester (E.), COUNTRY: 140; LOVE: 117; PATRIOTISM: 93

Chichester R. D. C., U.K., LOCAL GOVERNMENT: 5; PAST, THE: 1

Chichester (V.), FAITH: 119

Chiesly, DEATH: 20; VIRTUE: 66

Chigwell U. D. C., U.K., IMPROVEMENT: 28; LOCAL GOVERNMENT: 250

Child (of Dervil), HOPE: 228

Child (of Newfield Hall, Bigelly House, etc.), IMITATION: 2

Child (U.S.), WORDS: 16

Chilton, NOURISHMENT: 5

Chingford B. C., U.K., DIVINITY: 13; LOCAL GOVERNMENT: 12

Chinn (of Gloucester), BIRDS: 5; STATUS: 1

Chinnery (Bt.), MODERATION: 24

Chipman, CHRIST, JESUS: 48

Chipola Junior College, Marianna, Florida, KNOWLEDGE: 100; SCHOOL MOTTOES: 376

Chippendall, FAITH: 120

Chippenham, CHRIST, JESUS: 48

Chisalme, COURAGE: 270; STRENGTH: 181

Chisholm, AGGRESSION: 6; COURAGE: 229; FORCE: 23; STRENGTH: 165; TRADES: 41; VIRTUE: 220

Chivas, FORCE: 40; VIRTUE: 407

Cholmondeley (M.), PROTECTION: 4; VIRTUE: 21

Chorley B. C., U.K., LOCAL GOVERNMENT: 48; VIGILANCE: 4

Chorley R. D. C., DEEDS: 87; LOCAL GOVERNMENT: 360

Chresly, FAITH: 27

Chrisop, MIND: 25; RECTITUDE: 43

Christ College, Brecon, U.K., SCHOOL
MOTTOES: 228

Christall, ADVERSITY: 58

Christian, CHRIST, JESUS: 72;
SALVATION: 40

Christian, Count of the Palatinate of
Bischweiler (1598–1654), DIVINE
GUIDANCE: 217

Christian, Duke of Braunschweig-
Lüneburg (1566–1633),
DIVINITY: 411; JUSTICE: 67;
MODERATION: 26

Christian, Duke of Saxony (1652–89),
DIVINE GUIDANCE: 124; JUSTICE: 100;
PIETY: 34

Christian, Duke of Saxony-Eisenberg
(1653–1707), COUNTRY: 9;
DIVINITY: 45; INSIGNIFICANCE: 2;
SPEED: 45

Christian, Duke of Saxony-Eisenburg
(1653–1707), DIVINE GUIDANCE: 103

Christian, Duke of Saxony-Merseburg
(1615–91), DIVINITY: 36; TIME: 14

Christian, Duke of Saxony-Weissenfels
(1682–1736), DIVINITY: 37;
SALVATION: 15

Christian, Duke of Schleswig-Holstein
(1570–1633), SCRIPTURES: 16;
VICTORY: 49; VIRTUE: 157

Christian, Duke of Wohlau (1618–72),
BLESSING: 2; DIVINE GUIDANCE: 20;
PATIENCE: 38

Christian, Margrave of Brandenburg-
Anspach (1623–43), HOPE: 132

Christian, Margrave of Brandenburg-
Baireuth (1581–1655), DIVINE
GUIDANCE: 18, 21

Christian Albert, Duke of Holstein-
Gottorp (1641–94), ADVERSITY: 66;
ASPIRATION: 66

Christian August, Count of the
Palatinate of Sulzbach (1622–1708),
CHRIST, JESUS: 63

Christian Ernst, Duke of Saxony-
Coburg-Saalfeld (1683–1745),
DESIRE: 16

Christian Ernst, Margrave of
Brandenburg-Baireuth (1644–1712),
BLESSING: 11; DIVINE GUIDANCE: 371;
INDUSTRIOUSNESS: 162; LIBERTY: 80;
RIGHTEOUSNESS: 13; USEFULNESS: 6

Christian Günther, the Younger,
Count of Schwarzburg and
Hohenstein (1616–66), PATIENCE: 28;
STEADFASTNESS: 97

Christian Günther the Elder, Count of
Schwarzburg and Hohenstein
(1578–1642), PATIENCE: 7

Christian I, Elector of Saxony
(1560–91), DEATH: 26; TRUST: 35,
106

Christian I, Prince of Anhalt-Bernberg
(1568–1630), TRANSIENCE: 12

Christian I, Prince of Anhalt-Bernburg
(1568–1630), DIVINE GIFTS: 31;
DIVINE GUIDANCE: 348; GRACE: 24

Christian II, Elector of Saxony
(1583–1611), DIVINITY: 100;
FEAR: 26; ROYALTY: 23; WISDOM: 33

Christian II, Prince of Anhalt-
Bernburg (1599–1656),
DIVINITY: 412; FIDELITY: 48;
HONOR: 24; LIBERTY: 14; PIETY: 3;
SERVICE: 12

Christian Ludwig, Duke of
Braunschweig-Lüneburg-Zelle
(1622–65), FIDELITY: 300;
SINCERITY: 14

Christian Ludwig, Duke of
Mecklenburg-Schwerin (1632–92),
DESIRE: 16; DIVINE GUIDANCE: 405

Christian Ulrich, Duke of
Württemberg-Oels-Bernstadt
(1652–1704), JUSTICE: 101; PIETY: 35

Christian Wilhelm, HOPE: 254

Christian Wilhelm, Margrave of
Brandenburg (1587–1665), CHRIST,
JESUS: 79; CROWN: 25; DIVINE
GUIDANCE: 445; FIDELITY: 259;
LAW: 44, 46; PEOPLE: 9, 10

Christian Wilhelm, Prince of
Schwarzburg-Sondershausen
(1647–1721), TIME: 56

Christiane, Duchess of Saxony-
Eisenberg (1659–79), CHRIST,
JESUS: 16; DIVINE GUIDANCE: 53

Christiane Wilhelmine, Duchess of
Saxony-Weissenfels (D. 1707),
DIVINE GUIDANCE: 426

Christie, LIFE: 33; NAME: 11;
RECTITUDE: 32; ROYALTY: 73

Christie (of Craigtoun),
FLOURISHING: 76

Christison, GUIDANCE: 31
Christoph, Count of the Palatinate of
Simmern (1551–74), DIVINITY: 216
Christoph, Duke of Mecklenburg
(1537–92), PIETY: 28; VIRTUE: 143
Christoph, Margrave of Baden-
Rodemachern (1537–75), HONOR: 30
Christopher, ABILITY: 3
Christy, FLOURISHING: 76
Church, INJURY: 11; VIRTUE: 345, 360
Churchill, FIDELITY: 89
Churchill (B.), DIVINE GUIDANCE: 172
Churchward, GENTLENESS: 17
Churchyard, DIVINITY: 155;
ROYALTY: 30
Churton, ADVANCE: 5
Chute, FORTUNE: 59
The City College, City University of
New York, New York City, New
York, SCHOOL MOTTOES: 257;
TIME: 45
City College of San Francisco, San
Francisco, California, SCHOOL
MOTTOES: 325; TRUTH: 94
City of Bristol, U.K., LOCAL
GOVERNMENT: 400; VIRTUE: 377
City of Edinburgh, DIVINITY: 314;
LOCAL GOVERNMENT: 243
City of Gloucester, FIDELITY: 149;
LOCAL GOVERNMENT: 130
City of London, DIVINE
GUIDANCE: 201; LOCAL
GOVERNMENT: 94
City of Oxford, LOCAL
GOVERNMENT: 154; STRENGTH: 56;
TRUTH: 27
City of Paris, France, ENDURANCE: 46
Clacton U. D. C., U.K.,
HAPPINESS: 45; HEALING and
HEALTH: 15; LIGHT: 40; LOCAL
GOVERNMENT: 222
Clancarty (E.), COURAGE: 265; DIVINE
GUIDANCE: 185; FORTUNE: 117;
PRUDENCE: 10; WISDOM: 14
Clanmorris (B.), CHRIST, JESUS: 79;
HOPE: 254
Clanricarde (M.), FAITH: 241; LAW: 70;
ROYALTY: 126; UNITY: 90
Clanwilliam (E.), PREPAREDNESS: 78
Clapp (U.S.), UNCLASSIFIED: 65
Clapperton, FAITH: 107
Clarbrick, STEADFASTNESS: 13

Clare, BRIGHTNESS: 1; VIGILANCE: 90
Clare (E.), ADMIRATION: 1;
CONTEMPT: 4
Clarendon (E.), CROSS, THE: 53;
TRUTH: 23
Clarina (B.), COUNTRY: 99; LIBERTY: 97
Clark, COURAGE: 13; EFFORT: 36;
EQUALITY: 7; HOPE: 95;
KNOWLEDGE: 2; WEAPONS: 72
Clark (Bt.), DIVINITY: 250; SADNESS: 2;
TRUST: 60; VICTORY: 3
Clark College, Atlanta, Georgia,
SCHOOL MOTTOES: 53; SERVICE: 8
Clark (of Belford and Werk),
FORTITUDE: 15
Clark (of Courie Castle), LIBERTY: 34
Clarke, EXALTATION: 2;
FLOURISHING: 67; FORTIFICATIONS: 5;
FUTURE, THE: 29; JUSTICE: 91;
LAW: 27; OPPORTUNITY: 1; SIGN: 6;
TIME: 10; TRANSIENCE: 19;
UNCLASSIFIED: 79; WAY: 9;
WISDOM: 43
Clarke (of Ardington), CROSS, THE: 1
Clarke (of Ashgate, Co. Derby),
CHANGE: 17
Clarke (of Kensington), PROPER
NAMES: 48
Clarke (of Rossmore, bt.), FIDELITY: 52
Clarke (U.S.), DESIRE: 25;
PATRIOTISM: 87; ROYALTY: 115
Clarkson, ADVERSITY: 59
Clavering, ASPIRATION: 10
Claverly, DARKNESS: 3; TRUTH: 20
Claxton, HOPE: 103;
INDUSTRIOUSNESS: 71; LOCAL
GOVERNMENT: 184
Clay, VIRTUE: 27
Clay (Bt.), EARTH: 12
Claydon, HONESTY: 43
Clayhills, FEELINGS: 5
Clayton (Bt.), ACTION: 25;
ANIMALS: 47; COURAGE: 191;
VIRTUE: 278
Clayton (of Adlington Hall, Bt.),
HONESTY: 43
Clayton (of Enfield), FORTUNE: 95
Cleborne, ENVY: 13; LOCAL
GOVERNMENT: 48; VIGILANCE: 4
Cleethorpes B. C., U.K.,
VIGILANCE: 93

Cockburn (Bt.), AUDACITY: 99;
INCENTIVE: 1; PERSEVERANCE: 3;
VIGILANCE: 82
Cockburn (of Kenderland),
POSSIBILITY: 7
Cocks, GOODNESS: 34
Coddington, DESIRE: 14; FEAR: 37
Codman (U.S.), PEACE: 54
Codrington, HOSTILITY: 19; PROPER
NAMES: 36, 54; VIRTUE: 83, 212
Coffin, FLOURISHING: 50
Coffin (Bt.), DEEDS: 32; REWARD: 7
Coffin (U.S.), DARKNESS: 17;
HOPE: 163; LIGHT: 73
Coffy, VICTORY: 33
Cogan, FAITH: 18; FIDELITY: 40
Coggan, FAITH: 18; FIDELITY: 40
Coghill, LIFE: 7; MUSIC: 3
Coghill (Bt.), WAKEFULNESS: 7
Coghlan, UNITY: 98
Cohan, TIME: 22
Cokain, ADVERSITY: 9
Cokaine, HOPE: 38
Coke, PATIENCE: 42; PRUDENCE: 50;
SELF-RELIANCE: 11
Coker, JUSTICE: 26
Coker College, Hartsville, South
Carolina, SCHOOL MOTTOES: 40;
SERVICE: 6
Colbarne, FIDELITY: 297;
TRUSTWORTHINESS: 6
Colborne, ADVERSITY: 82; HOPE: 211
Colborne (B.), FAITH: 18; FIDELITY: 40
Colby, DESTRUCTION: 7
Colby-Sawyer College, New London,
New Hampshire, MIND: 24; SCHOOL
MOTTOES: 187, 216; SERVICE: 36;
SPIRIT: 12
Colclough, AGGRESSION: 11
Coldham, PARADISE: 31; REST: 7
Coldicott, BEING, SELF: 4
Coldridge, VIRTUE: 118
Coldstream, HOPE: 135; LIFE: 16
Cole (Earl of Enniskillen),
DEVOTION: 2; DIVINITY: 96;
ROYALTY: 21
Cole (of Twickenham), DEVOTION: 2;
DIVINITY: 96; ROYALTY: 21
Cole (U.S.), HARVEST: 5
Colebrooke (Bt.), GOODNESS: 39
Colegrave, FAITH: 72
Colel, INTEGRITY: 12

Coleman, DEATH: 63; FEAR: 3;
JUSTICE: 9; LOCAL GOVERNMENT: 45;
TRUST: 5
Coleman (Cos. of Norfolk, Wilts, and
Gloucester), STEADFASTNESS: 110
Coleridge, DEVOTION: 2; DIVINITY: 96;
ROYALTY: 21; VIRTUE: 118
Coles, INTER-RELATEDNESS: 3
Colgate University, Hamilton, New
York, DIVINITY: 53; SCHOOL
MOTTOES: 60; TRUTH: 12
Collas, CROSS, THE: 47; HOPE: 21
College of Great Falls, Great Falls,
Montana, LIGHT: 25; SCHOOL
MOTTOES: 138
College of Mount Saint Vincent,
Riverdale, New York, DISCIPLINE: 1;
GOODNESS: 5; KNOWLEDGE: 3;
SCHOOL MOTTOES: 33
Collens or Collins (of Offwell, Co.
Dorset), REST: 34
Collett, INTEGRITY: 10; SCHOOL
MOTTOES: 94
Colley, VIRTUE: 208
Collier (Bt.), PROPER NAMES: 50
Collingwood, CONSCIENCE: 8;
GUILT: 2; INNOCENCE: 12
Collingwood, Mitchell,
CONSISTENCY: 3
Collingwood (B.), IDENTITY: 1
Collins, COURAGE: 243; DILIGENCE: 32;
DIVINE GUIDANCE: 233; DIVINITY: 30,
97; FIDELITY: 121; INTEGRITY: 40;
LIFE: 4; ROYALTY: 7, 22;
STEADFASTNESS: 59
Collins, WBeauvale (B.), FAITH: 252
Collins (Co. Devon), DEEDS: 86;
WORDS: 38
Collins (of Betterton), LOCATION: 5
Collis, FINISH: 7; MIND: 25;
RECTITUDE: 43; VIRTUE: 182, 186
Collison, SECURITY: 15
Collmore, CONSISTENCY: 9; LOCAL
GOVERNMENT: 338
Collyer, DIVINE GUIDANCE: 44
Collyr (of Norwich), ADVANCE: 4
Colman, SPEED: 46
Colmore, FORTUNE: 35
Colne B. C., U.K., ENDURANCE: 59;
LOCAL GOVERNMENT: 405
Cologan, VIRTUE: 316

Colonial seal of Georgia, STATE
MOTTOES: 36; UNSELFISHNESS: 17

Colpoys, DIVINE GIFTS: 27

Colquhon, CAUTION: 24; CROSS,
THE: 112; FLOURISHING: 87;
HONOR: 27; HOPE: 35; POSSIBILITY: 9;
STATE MOTTOES: 11

Colquhoun (of Rossdhu, Bt.),
POSSIBILITY: 9

Colston, DEEDS: 53

Colt (Bt.), ENDURANCE: 58

Colt (of Gartsherrie), UNCLASSIFIED: 72

Colthurst (Bt.), JUSTICE: 79; PURPOSE: 9

Colton (U.S.), DESPAIR: 2

Columball (Co. Derby), LOVE: 96;
PEACE: 30

Columbia Bible College, Columbia,
South Carolina, DIVINITY: 408;
SCHOOL MOTTOES: 330

Columbia University, New York City,
LIGHT: 24; SCHOOL MOTTOES: 138

Columbia University Graduate School
of Journalism, New York City, New
York, KNOWLEDGE: 84; PEOPLE: 22;
SCHOOL MOTTOES: 313

Columbus College, Columbus,
Georgia, EQUALITY: 9; PRIMACY: 8;
SCHOOL MOTTOES: 234

Colvell (Co. Essex), DIVINITY: 11

Colvil, FORGETTING: 10, 16, 18

Colvile, DIVINITY: 11; LOCAL
GOVERNMENT: 275;
PERSEVERANCE: 70

Colville, FIDELITY: 2; FORGETTING: 16

Colville (B.), FORGETTING: 18

Colwyn Bay B. C., U.K., BEAUTY: 12;
HEALING and HEALTH: 13; LOCAL
GOVERNMENT: 179; TRANQUILLITY: 4

Combe, COURAGE: 163

Comber, STARS: 35; WISDOM: 67

Combermere (V.), FORTUNE: 69;
PROPER NAMES: 44

Combrey, GOALS: 1

Combs, DEEDS: 8; WORDS: 1

Commissioners of Trade and
Plantations, AGRICULTURE: 7;
COMMERCE: 9

Community Chest, KINDNESS: 10

Community College of Beaver County,
Monaca, Pennsylvania, LIBERTY: 1;
LIGHT: 3; SCHOOL MOTTOES: 9

Community College of the Air Force,
Alabama, EARTH: 15; SCHOOL
MOTTOES: 297

Compton, HONOR: 27; HOPE: 35;
MERCY: 3; POWER: 5; SEARCH and
DISCOVERY: 7; STATE MOTTOES: 11

Compton (Bt.), DIVINITY: 313

Compton Community College,
Compton, California, SCHOOL
MOTTOES: 361; TRUTH: 167

Compton (Northampton, m.),
EXPLORATION: 3

Compton (of Carham), DIVINITY: 313

Comrie, Comrey, Comry, GOALS: 1

Comyn, CHANGE: 2;
INDUSTRIOUSNESS: 18

Conant, EFFORT: 7

Conant (U.S.), EFFORT: 8

Concanon, WISDOM: 8, 60

Concordia Teachers College, Seward,
Nebraska, SCHOOL MOTTOES: 320;
WORDS: 40

Conder, LEADERSHIP: 13

Confederate States of America,
COUNTRY: 53; FIDELITY: 242

Congilton, SIZE: 3

Congleton B. C., U.K.,
DEDICATION: 14; LOCAL
GOVERNMENT: 354

Congleton R. D. C., U.K.,
COUNTRYSIDE: 2; LOCAL
GOVERNMENT: 318

Congreave, DEATH: 70; FAME: 18

Congreave (Bt.), DEATH: 70; FAME: 18

Congreve (Bt.), LOCAL
GOVERNMENT: 275;
PERSEVERANCE: 70

Coningsby, JUSTICE: 61;
STEADFASTNESS: 143

Conlan, SECURITY: 85; VIRTUE: 347

Connell, SERVICE: 66;
UNSELFISHNESS: 15

Connellan, MODERATION: 10;
SILENCE: 15; WISDOM: 62

Connely, UNSELFISHNESS: 15

Conolly (of Castletown), DIVINITY: 154

Conqueror, VICTORY: 55

Conroy, AGE: 3; TIME: 23

Conroy (of Llanbrynmair,
Montgomeryshire, and of Bettifield,
Co. Roscommon, Bt.), PAST, THE: 7;
TIME: 33

Crawfurd, BIRDS: 19; CONQUEST: 6, 10;
DILIGENCE: 33; DIVINE
GUIDANCE: 261, 274, 351;
FIDELITY: 97; FLOURISHING: 21;
PREPAREDNESS: 78; SECURITY: 74;
STRENGTH: 149; WILLINGNESS: 6
Crawfurd (of Cartsburn), DEEDS: 77
Crawfurd (of Kilburney), PURITY: 21
Crawfurd (of Newfield), PATIENCE: 16
Crawhall, PERSEVERANCE: 76
Crawley Development Corp., U.K.,
EFFORT: 2
Crawley-Boevey (Bt.), INTEGRITY: 10;
SCHOOL MOTTOES: 94
Crayford U. D. C., U.K.,
AUDACITY: 64; LOCAL
GOVERNMENT: 157; RECTITUDE: 26
Creagh, PROVIDENCE: 30; REWARD: 49;
VENGEANCE: 9; VIRTUE: 380
Crealock, DIVINE GUIDANCE: 91;
WEAPONS: 28
Crealocke, DIVINE GUIDANCE: 91;
WEAPONS: 28
Cree, ENJOYMENT: 6; INTEGRITY: 41
Cregoe, FORTUNE: 35
Cregol, FORTUNE: 36
Creighton-Stuart, ANGER: 6;
NOBILITY: 11
Cremorne (B.), FORTUNE: 105
Crespyny, MIND: 31; RECTITUDE: 44
Cresswell, PROSPERITY: 6
Creswell, ACCOMPLISHMENT: 4;
ATTEMPT: 1
Crew (of Crew, Crewcombe, etc.),
HOPE: 125
Crewdson, SECURITY: 51; WISDOM: 85
Crewe (B.), FOLLOWING: 21
Crewe B. C., U.K., LOCAL
GOVERNMENT: 239; TIMELINESS: 7
Crewkerne U. D. C., U.K.,
FAITH: 166; LOCAL GOVERNMENT: 205
Crichton, DIVINE GIFTS: 38;
FIDELITY: 110; FINISH: 14; GRACE: 14
Crichton (of Easthill), DIVINE
GUIDANCE: 271
Crickett, FAITH: 1
Crierie, INDUSTRIOUSNESS: 60; SCHOOL
MOTTOES: 135
Crinan, SPEED: 52
Cringan, SPEED: 52
Cripps, TRUST: 41

Crisp, DEEDS: 25; MIND: 25;
RECTITUDE: 43; TIME: 16
Croall, ADVANCE: 32
Crockatt, ATTENTIVENESS: 9
Crockett, BOASTFULNESS: 1
Croft, COURAGE: 224; FIDELITY: 332
Croft (Bt.), INTEGRITY: 10; SCHOOL
MOTTOES: 94
Crofton (B.), DIVINE GIFTS: 10
Crofton (Bt.), DIVINE GIFTS: 10
Crofts, COURAGE: 244; FIDELITY: 340
Croker, FAITH: 160, 162
Croker (of Trevillas), DIVINE
GUIDANCE: 115
Crombie, DIVINITY: 168
Crommelin, DEEDS: 35; HOPE: 58
Crompton, FIDELITY: 216; LOVE: 83
Cromwell, DEATH: 59; FEAR: 62
Cromwell (of Cheshunt Park),
PEACE: 59; WAR: 56
Crondace, FIDELITY: 262;
PREPAREDNESS: 63
Crookes, STRENGTH: 187; WISDOM: 110
Crookshank, ADVERSITY: 59
Crookshank (U.S.), LAW: 14; REASON: 9
Croome, ANGER: 3; ANIMALS: 29;
NOBILITY: 8
Cropper, FEAR: 32; LOVE: 86
Crosane, GLORY: 45; REWARD: 30;
VIRTUE: 150
Crosbie, DESPAIR: 5; ENVY: 2;
FLOURISHING: 48
Crosby, LEADERSHIP: 24; LIBERTY: 110;
REBIRTH: 28
Crosby B. C., LOCAL
GOVERNMENT: 402; STATE
MOTTOES: 61; STRENGTH: 184;
UNITY: 122
Crosby (U.S.), EQUANIMITY: 10
Crosier Seminary Junior College,
Onamia, Minnesota,
KNOWLEDGE: 61; SCHOOL
MOTTOES: 264
Crosley, CONFIDENCE: 15; CROSS,
THE: 92
Cross, CONQUEST: 20; CROSS, THE: 13,
102; HOPE: 18
Cross (V.), CROSS, THE: 7
Crossdell, COURAGE: 114; WEAPONS: 43
Crosse, CROSS, THE: 108; GOALS: 2;
LOFTINESS: 20; STARS: 36; TRUTH: 89
Crossley, GOODNESS: 25

Crossley (of Scaitcliffe), FAITH: 26;
   LOVE: 42
Cross, Wilbur Lucius, RECTITUDE: 4
Crosthwaite, CONQUEST: 4; DEATH: 11;
   FINISH: 8
Crouch, ACCOMPLISHMENT: 4;
   ATTEMPT: 1
Crowfoot (of Beccles), CAUTION: 17
Crown of England, DISGRACE: 7
Croxwell, VIGILANCE: 75
Croydon C. B. C., U.K., HEALING and
   HEALTH: 34; LOCAL
   GOVERNMENT: 331
Cruch, WILLINGNESS: 11
Cruikshank, COURAGE: 271;
   STRENGTH: 182; WEAPONS: 103
Cruikshanks (of London),
   DISCRETION: 3
Crumpe, RISING: 12; VIRTUE: 174
Cuffe (Bt.), STEADFASTNESS: 6
Cullen, COURAGE: 236;
   UNSELFISHNESS: 15
Culley, FRIENDSHIP: 12
Cullingford (of Bayswater),
   FORTUNE: 103
Cullum (Bt.), SUPPORT: 8
Culme, INNOCENCE: 1
Cumberland C.C., U.K., LOCAL
   GOVERNMENT: 270;
   PERSEVERANCE: 48
Cuming (of Reluglas), COURAGE: 46
Cummin, COURAGE: 46
Cummin (of Brunthill), HARVEST: 2
Cumming (of Coulter, bt.),
   COURAGE: 46
Cumming (of Pitully), COURAGE: 46
Cunard (Bt.), PERSEVERANCE: 7
Cuninghame, EARTH: 20; SEA: 35
Cunliffe (Bt.), FIDELITY: 137
Cunningham, DIVINE GUIDANCE: 342;
   FIDELITY: 56; STRANGER: 5;
   STRENGTH: 91; TIME: 56; VIRTUE: 154
Cunningham (Bt.), PRUDENCE: 16;
   SINCERITY: 5
Cunningham (U.S.), FRIENDSHIP: 53
Cunninghame, DIVINITY: 381;
   ENVY: 15; FIDELITY: 56;
   INDUSTRIOUSNESS: 170;
   POSSESSION: 5; PROSPERITY: 46;
   VIRTUE: 312
Cunninghame (Bt.), UNCLASSIFIED: 51

Cunninghame (of Craigends),
   MANNER: 11
Cunninghame (of Kilmaurs, Milucray,
   Corshill, etc.), UNCLASSIFIED: 51
Cunyngham (Bt.), RECTITUDE: 2
Cure (of Blake Hall), DUTY: 13
Curle, DIVINITY: 425; FAITH: 235, 236;
   ROYALTY: 122; UNITY: 82
Currer (of Cliften House),
   WORTHINESS: 26
Currey (U.S.), RUNNING: 5
Currie, AUDACITY: 21; VIGILANCE: 3
Currier, WORTHINESS: 29
Curriers' Company, DIVINITY: 401;
   HOPE: 257
Curry, ASPIRATION: 40; COURAGE: 84;
   GENTLENESS: 6
Curry (U.S.), RUNNING: 5
Curson, POSSESSION: 11
Curteis, INTENTION: 7
Curtin (U.S.), KNOWLEDGE: 4
Curtis, INTENTION: 7
Curtis (Bt.), CONQUEST: 9
Curtis (of Gatcombe, bt.),
   ADVERSITY: 59
Curtoys, COURTESY: 5, 6; KINDNESS: 24
Curwen, BEING, SELF: 3
Curzon, GENTLENESS: 13; JUSTICE: 105
Cusack, DIVINE GUIDANCE: 45;
   DIVINITY: 125; HOPE: 30
Cushman (U.S.), LAW: 8;
   RECTITUDE: 28
Cushney, HOPE: 265
Cust, DEATH: 32; PEACE: 19
Custance (of Weston, Co. Norfolk),
   DESIRE: 1; REASON: 2; SELF-
   CONTROL: 3
Cutbush (U.S.), KNOWLEDGE: 12
Cutcliffe, UNCLASSIFIED: 19
Cuthbert, COURAGE: 159
Cuthbertson, COURAGE: 159
Cutler, ADVERSITY: 42;
   PERSEVERANCE: 36
Cutlers' Company, SUCCESS: 11;
   TRADES: 25
Cutting (U.S.), FUTURE, THE: 2;
   OPPORTUNITY: 2
Cuyler (Bt.), DIVINITY: 43
Czechoslovakia, TRUTH: 69

D

Dackcombe (Co. Dorset),
   STRENGTH: 179; VIRTUE: 449
Dacre (B.), KINDNESS: 20
Dadley, DEFENSE: 28
Daeg, DEATH: 40; DISGRACE: 10
Dagenham B. C., U.K., DEEDS: 60;
   LOCAL GOVERNMENT: 199
Dailie, PRAISE: 6
Dakota Wesleyan University, Mitchell,
   South Dakota, SACRIFICE: 5; SCHOOL
   MOTTOES: 258; SERVICE: 44
Dakyn, UNCLASSIFIED: 8
Dakyns (of Derbyshire),
   AGGRESSION: 18
Dale (of Ashborne), FAME: 17
Dalgairns, COUNTRY: 83
Dalgleish, FLOURISHING: 63;
   REBIRTH: 31
Dalgleish (of Scotscraig), ENJOYMENT: 9
Dalhousie (E.), DIVINE GUIDANCE: 359;
   INDUSTRIOUSNESS: 150
Dall, FAITH: 20
Dallas, PREPAREDNESS: 72; SCHOOL
   MOTTOES: 283
Dallas (Bt.), LIGHT: 58
Dallaway, MANNERS: 10
Dalling (Bt.), RIGHTS: 1
Dalmahoy (of Ravelridge), COURAGE: 2
Dalrimple, STEADFASTNESS: 42
Dalrymple, DEFENSE: 32, 35; DIVINE
   GIFTS: 38; GRACE: 14; GUIDANCE: 19;
   STEADFASTNESS: 45; STRENGTH: 36
Dalrymple (Bt.), STEADFASTNESS: 42
Dalrymple (of Cranstoun, North
   Berwick), STEADFASTNESS: 42
Dalsiel, AUDACITY: 72
D'Alton, COURAGE: 81; CROSS, THE: 73;
   FAITH: 231; FIDELITY: 179;
   PATIENCE: 34; SADNESS: 8;
   VICTORY: 35
Daly, DIVINITY: 67; FIDELITY: 61;
   ROYALTY: 17
Dalyell, AUDACITY: 72
Dalziell, AUDACITY: 72
Damer, ADVERSITY: 87
Dames, PRUDENCE: 85; VIRTUE: 384
Damon (U.S.), LAW: 53; PEOPLE: 13;
   ROYALTY: 75
Dampier, DIVINE GUIDANCE: 215

Dance, FAME: 21; VIRTUE: 401
Dandridge, FAITH: 143
Daniel, COUNTRY: 97; LAW: 47, 66;
   LIBERTY: 108; PREPAREDNESS: 78
Daniel (Co. Stafford), ADVERSITY: 42;
   PERSEVERANCE: 36
Daniell, COUNTRY: 95; FAITH: 197
Danskine, PRUDENCE: 28
D'Anvers, FAITH: 122; FIDELITY: 169,
   170
Daray, DIVINITY: 429; ROYALTY: 125;
   UNITY: 87
Darby, DIVINITY: 431
Darch, COUNTRY: 135; LIBERTY: 117
D'Arcy, DIVINITY: 423; HONOR: 182;
   MERCY: 13; ROYALTY: 120; UNITY: 80;
   VIRTUE: 215
Dare, FIDELITY: 234
Darell, FIDELITY: 318
Darit, CHRIST, JESUS: 31
Darker, SATISFACTION: 2
Darley, ABILITY: 35; AUDACITY: 43
Darling, DIVINE GIFTS: 18
Darlington, CROSS, THE: 13, 27;
   HOPE: 18, 20
Darlington C. B. C., U.K.,
   FLOURISHING: 32;
   INDUSTRIOUSNESS: 48; LOCAL
   GOVERNMENT: 143
Darly, LIMITATION: 12
Darnell, DIVINE GUIDANCE: 143
Darnley (E.), FINISH: 7
Darnol, CROSS, THE: 113;
   STRENGTH: 170
Daroch, VIGILANCE: 8
Darsch, VIGILANCE: 8
Dartford B. C., U.K., FIDELITY: 308;
   LOCAL GOVERNMENT: 374;
   STEADFASTNESS: 136
Dartford R. D. C., LOCAL
   GOVERNMENT: 406; SERVICE: 75
Dartmouth College, Hanover, New
   Hampshire, SCHOOL MOTTOES: 370;
   WORDS: 41
Dartmouth (E.), VIRTUE: 70
Darwen B. C., U.K.,
   INDUSTRIOUSNESS: 1
Darwin, VIGILANCE: 13
Daubeney, DISCIPLINE: 6;
   GENTLENESS: 16
Davell, THOUGHT: 13

De Massue, DIVINE GUIDANCE: 220; FEAR: 1; FIDELITY: 256; LOVE: 2
De Meuron, ADVERSITY: 87
De Montmorency, DIVINE GUIDANCE: 145
De Ponthien, STEADFASTNESS: 102
De Renzey, DEEDS: 38; WORDS: 9
De Rinzey, DEEDS: 38; WORDS: 9
De Salis, FLEXIBILITY: 4
De Saumarez (B.), DIVINITY: 251; HOPE: 96
de Tabley (B.), DIVINITY: 420; PATRIOTISM: 65; ROYALTY: 81
De Teissier, ORDER: 8
De Tuch, CERTAINTY: 1
De Vahl-Samuel, ROYALTY: 45; STARS: 17
De Vere (Bt.), TRUTH: 155
De Vesci (V.), SIGN: 8
De Veulle, INTENTION: 8
De Windt, ANCESTRY: 25
De Winton, FIDELITY: 80; SELF-KNOWLEDGE: 11
De Worms, LIMITATION: 13
Deacon, DIVINITY: 66; FIDELITY: 60; PREPAREDNESS: 30, 32; ROYALTY: 16; TRANQUILLITY: 8
Deane, COURAGE: 69; ENDURANCE: 26; FAITH: 168; FIDELITY: 175
Deans, ABILITY: 10; ART: 13
Deans (of Loeg), ART: 32; STRENGTH: 161
Dearden, HONOR: 27; HOPE: 35; STATE MOTTOES: 11
Deardon, HONOR: 27; HOPE: 35; STATE MOTTOES: 11
Dease, PREPAREDNESS: 78
DeBurgos, DEFIANCE: 13
Decies (Bt.), CROSS, THE: 83
Dee, ADVERSITY: 26
Dee (of Mortlake), INDUSTRIOUSNESS: 55
Delacherois, DEEDS: 35; HOPE: 58
Delafield (U.S.), STRENGTH: 27
Delamere (B.), PROTECTION: 4; VIRTUE: 21
Delap, ADVERSITY: 18; WORTHINESS: 31
Delaval, DIVINE GUIDANCE: 181
Delaware Valley College, Doyleston, Pennsyvania, EARTH: 26; LIFE: 38; MANLINESS: 6; SCHOOL MOTTOES: 367

Deline, INTEGRITY: 10; SCHOOL MOTTOES: 94
Delmege, PERSEVERANCE: 29
Delop, WORTHINESS: 31
Delves, FORTUNE: 73
Delves (of Cheshire and Lancashire), POSSIBILITY: 5
Delway, ASPIRATION: 45
Democratic Republic of the Congo, INDUSTRIOUSNESS: 90; JUSTICE: 57; PEACE: 21
DeMolines, CONQUEST: 72
DeMontmorency, DIVINE GUIDANCE: 171
Dempster, AUDACITY: 66; DEATH: 55; SINCERITY: 9
Denbigh (E.), HONOR: 207; OPPRESSION: 1; REWARD: 61; VIRTUE: 34, 446
Denbighshire C. C., U.K., DIVINITY: 146; SCHOOL MOTTOES: 74
Dendy, ADVERSITY: 64; PAST, THE: 10; PERSEVERANCE: 56; STATE MOTTOES: 40
Denham, CAUTION: 19; VICTORY: 11
Denham (Bt.), ADVERSITY: 41; FORTUNE: 74
Denison, ADVERSITY: 3; GUIDANCE: 24; LAW: 5; VIRTUE: 5
Denison (U.S.), HOME: 8
Denman (B.), FIDELITY: 265; PRUDENCE: 62
Dennett, DIVINE GUIDANCE: 367
Dennis, DISCIPLINE: 7; DIVINITY: 124; GENTLENESS: 18; SEA: 5
Dennistoun, ADVERSITY: 3; VIRTUE: 5
Denny (Bt.), HARVEST: 1
Dent, INDUSTRIOUSNESS: 16; UNITY: 13
Dent (Co. York), PATIENCE: 31; PERSEVERANCE: 45
Denton U. D. C., U.K., LOCAL GOVERNMENT: 275; PERSEVERANCE: 70
Denver Baptist Bible College, Denver, Colorado, SCHOOL MOTTOES: 48; SCRIPTURES: 3
Denys (Bt.), FIDELITY: 194
Der, DIVINE GUIDANCE: 161
Derby C. B. C., U.K., COURAGE: 131; DILIGENCE: 38; LOCAL GOVERNMENT: 182; STRENGTH: 72
Derby (E.), CHANGE: 17

Dod (of Edge), CAUTION: 26
Doddridge, LIFE: 5
Dodede, RIGHTS: 2
Dodsworth (Bt.), LAW: 45;
   ROYALTY: 70
Doe, PERSEVERANCE: 76
Doig, ADVERSITY: 50; LOCAL
   GOVERNMENT: 236
D'Olier, DIVINITY: 288; GOODNESS: 15
Doller, FORTUNE: 32
Dolling (of Magheralin), HOPE: 215
Dolphin, FIDELITY: 188; LIBERTY: 28;
   TRANSIENCE: 3
Dolphin (of Eyford), PARADISE: 31;
   REST: 7
Dominican College of Blauvelt,
   Orangeburg, New York, SCHOOL
   MOTTOES: 351; TRUTH: 115
Dominican Republic, COUNTRY: 25;
   DIVINITY: 136; LIBERTY: 17;
   NATIONAL MOTTOES: 4
Dominican School of Philosophy and
   Theology, California, DIVINE
   GUIDANCE: 154; SCHOOL
   MOTTOES: 63
Dominion of Canada, SEA: 1
Domville, FAILURE: 4
Don (Bt.), FRUIT: 8
Don (of Spittal), DUE: 4
Donald, DEEDS: 35; HOPE: 58;
   PREPAREDNESS: 78
Donaldson, CROSS, THE: 105;
   EQUANIMITY: 18, 19; HOPE: 143;
   HOSTILITY: 15, 16; LIGHT: 80;
   PREPAREDNESS: 61; PRUDENCE: 56
Donaldson (of Kinnardie), WAR: 5
Doncaster C. B. C., U.K.,
   HAPPINESS: 6; LOCAL
   GOVERNMENT: 61
Done, DIVINE GIFTS: 47
Donegal (M.), DESIRE: 5; HONOR: 126
Donegall (M.), HONOR: 106
Donegan, VIRTUE: 298
Donelan, STRENGTH: 96
Doneraile (V.), LOFTINESS: 10
Dongan (U.S.), DIVINE GUIDANCE: 396
Donkin, HOPE: 109, 287
Donkin (of Ripon), ENDURANCE: 15
Donoughmore (E.), CROSS, THE: 55
Donovan, DIVINE GUIDANCE: 6
Donville (of St. Albans, Bt.), PEACE: 40

Doran, HONOR: 27; HOPE: 35; STATE
   MOTTOES: 11
Dorchester (B.), WEAPONS: 83
Dorien, ADVERSITY: 36; VIRTUE: 86
Dormer (B.), DIVINE GUIDANCE: 54
Dorothee, Duchess of Braunschweig-
   Lüneberg (1546–1617), TRUST: 1
Dorothee, Duchess of Braunschweig-
   Wolfenbüttel (1607–34),
   DIVINITY: 213
Dorothee, Duchess of Saxony
   (1601–75), DIVINE GUIDANCE: 448;
   SCRIPTURES: 6
Dorothee, Electress of Brandenburg
   (1636–89), DIVINE GUIDANCE: 293
Dorothee, Electress of Brandenburg
   and Duchess of Braunschweig-
   Lüneburg-Zelle (1636–89),
   GOODNESS: 28
Dorothee, Margravine of Brandenburg
   (1596–1649), DIVINE GUIDANCE: 335;
   DIVINITY: 157; FORTUNE: 82;
   HOPE: 41
Dorothee, Princess of Anhalt
   (1580–1618), SALVATION: 22
Dorothee Auguste, Duchess of
   Braunschweig (1577–1625),
   DIVINITY: 215
Dorothee Hedwig, Princess of Anhalt
   (1587–1608), FEAR: 8; PRUDENCE: 17
Dorothee Sophie, Duchess of Saxony
   (1587–1645), DIVINE GUIDANCE: 57;
   FORTUNE: 13; TRUST: 33
Dorothee Susanne, Duchess of Saxony-
   Weimar (1544–92); WDorothee
   Sophie, Duchess of Saxony
   (1587–1645), FAITH: 141
Dorset C. C., U.K., FEAR: 83; LOCAL
   GOVERNMENT: 407
Dorset (D.), ACCOMPLISHMENT: 4;
   ATTEMPT: 1
Dossey, HANDS: 23; HOSTILITY: 13
Douce, SPEED: 7; VIGILANCE: 16
Doughty, INDUSTRIOUSNESS: 155;
   PATRIOTISM: 75; REWARD: 24;
   WAR: 63

Douglas, ADVANCE: 19; ASPIRATION: 83;
  COUNTRY: 100; COURAGE: 81; DIVINE
  GUIDANCE: 262; FIDELITY: 179;
  FORTUNE: 91; GROWTH: 23;
  HOPE: 140, 222; IMPROVEMENT: 19;
  PATRIOTISM: 46; REBIRTH: 9;
  SECURITY: 45, 61; VIRTUE: 140, 172;
  WISDOM: 82
Douglas (B.), STATUS: 4
Douglas (Bt.), AUDACITY: 20;
  CERTAINTY: 3; PREPAREDNESS: 6;
  STATUS: 4
Douglas (of Bads), TRUTH: 81;
  WISDOM: 81
Douglas (of Carnoustie, Bt.),
  COUNTRY: 100; PATRIOTISM: 46
Douglas (of Cavers), DEEDS: 18
Douglas (of Rosehill), CROSS, THE: 61;
  GLORY: 29
Douglas (of Springwood (Bt.),
  DEEDS: 18
Douglas (of Whitriggs), STATUS: 4
Douglass, DIVINITY: 183;
  EXPECTATION: 9; FORTUNE: 78;
  HOPE: 139
Doulton, BEAUTY: 14; TRUTH: 50
Douw (U.S.), CROSS, THE: 25;
  TRUST: 21
Dovaston, REBIRTH: 17
Dover, DEEDS: 13
Dover College, U.K.,
  INDUSTRIOUSNESS: 138; SCHOOL
  MOTTOES: 203
Dovers, HONESTY: 31; USEFULNESS: 3
Dow, PATIENCE: 20, 25
Dowie, PATIENCE: 20
Dowling, AUDACITY: 55;
  EXCELLENCE: 10
Downe (V.), DISGRACE: 16
Downes (B.), CROSS, THE: 2;
  SALVATION: 2
Downie, STEADFASTNESS: 62
Downie (of Edinburgh), SEA: 8
Downing, STEADFASTNESS: 85
Downs, WORDS: 30
Downshire (M.), ACCOMPLISHMENT: 12
Dowse (U.S.), GLORY: 34
D'Oy (bt.), COUNTRY: 62
Doyle (Bt.), FORTITUDE: 13; PROPER
  NAMES: 28
D'Oyley (Bt.), DEEDS: 17
D'Oyley (co. Norfolk), DEEDS: 17

D'Oyly (bt.), COURAGE: 168
Doyne, DEFIANCE: 10
Dr. John Bull, author of *God Save the
  Queen* (*King*) (temp. Elizabeth I),
  MUSIC: 6
Draghorn, CONVENIENCE: 6
Drago, ENVY: 6
Drake, BIRDS: 5; STATUS: 1
Drake (Bt.), ADVERSITY: 59;
  AUDACITY: 64; DIVINE GUIDANCE: 41;
  GREATNESS: 10; LOCAL
  GOVERNMENT: 40; RECTITUDE: 26
Drake (U.S.), TIME: 67
Dramond, ASSISTANCE: 17;
  KINDNESS: 15
Draper, CONQUEST: 47
Drapers' Company (London),
  DIVINITY: 430; GLORY: 56;
  HONOR: 180
Drax, DEATH: 68
Drayton (U.S.), PARADISE: 26
Drew (descendant of the family of
  Drogo), COURAGE: 56; NAME: 3
Drinkwater, FLOURISHING: 54;
  INDUSTRIOUSNESS: 106; LOCAL
  GOVERNMENT: 210
Drinkwater (of Irwell), Fouler,
  MODERATION: 27
Drisdale, NOURISHMENT: 4
Drogheda (M.), COURAGE: 75
Drought, DEPRIVATION: 1
Droylsden U. D. C., U.K.,
  INDUSTRIOUSNESS: 7; LOCAL
  GOVERNMENT: 49; UNITY: 6
Drummond, CAUTION: 11;
  COURAGE: 162; DIVINITY: 292;
  FLEXIBILITY: 5; GLORY: 26;
  HONOR: 27, 203; HOPE: 35; LIFE: 8;
  REBIRTH: 23; RECTITUDE: 71; STATE
  MOTTOES: 11; SUCCESS: 2;
  VIGILANCE: 38; VIRTUE: 397
Drummond (of Carlourie),
  UNCLASSIFIED: 24
Drummond (of Cultmalundy),
  FEELINGS: 13
Drummond (of Innermay),
  FIDELITY: 221
Drummond (of Kildies), SEA: 20
Drummond (of London), ART: 23;
  COURAGE: 149

Dundas, ABILITY: 10; ART: 13;
   CHANGE: 16; EFFORT: 1, 10; LIFE: 17;
   VIRTUE: 46; WEAPONS: 35
Dundas (Bt.), EFFORT: 10
Dundas (of Keukevil), EFFORT: 11
Dundonald (E.), COURAGE: 247
Dunfermline (E.), FIDELITY: 283
Dungannon (V.), TRUTH: 77
Duniguid, HOPE: 155; PATIENCE: 33
Dunlop (Bt.), WORTHINESS: 31
Dunlop (of Garnkirk), ADVERSITY: 18
Dunmore (E.), FORTUNE: 64
Dunmure, HOPE: 230
Dunn, AUDACITY: 99; VIGILANCE: 82
Dunne, DEFIANCE: 10
Dunnet, WATER: 13
Dunning, HONOR: 177;
   KNOWLEDGE: 81
Dunphy, COURAGE: 122
Dunraven (E.), ASPIRATION: 71;
   PARADISE: 55
Dunsandle (B.), DIVINITY: 69;
   FIDELITY: 62; ROYALTY: 18
Dunsany (B.), CAUTION: 24
Dunscombe, FIDELITY: 133
Duntz (Bt.), FAIRNESS: 11
Duport, FATE: 22
Durand, MERCY: 8; TRUST: 69
Durant, ENDURANCE: 8
D'Urban, CONQUEST: 19; CROSS,
   THE: 26; HOPE: 107; SIGN: 3
Durell, FIDELITY: 116; GENEROSITY: 3
Durham, DIVINITY: 435;
   IMPROVEMENT: 46; INCREASE: 3;
   MIND: 45
Durham (E.), FUTURE, THE: 15
Durham (of Largo), VICTORY: 61
Durham Technical Institute, Durham,
   North Carolina, EXCELLENCE: 4;
   SCHOOL MOTTOES: 79
Durnard, DEFENSE: 47
Durno, HONOR: 38
Durrant (Bt.), DEATH: 35; DISGRACE: 8
Dursley R. D. C., U.K., DIVINITY: 203;
   LOCAL GOVERNMENT: 164
Duryee (U.S.), FUTURE, THE: 14
Dutchess Community College,
   Poughkeepsie, New York,
   KNOWLEDGE: 13; SCHOOL
   MOTTOES: 78
Dutton, FAITH: 211
D'Warris, FORTITUDE: 6

Dyce, AUDACITY: 44; DECISION: 2
Dyce-Sombre, PROVIDENCE: 8
Dyers' Company, DIVINITY: 38
Dymocke, FAITH: 136
Dymoke (Bt.), ROYALTY: 77
Dymond, FIDELITY: 284
Dynevor (B.), AUDACITY: 89;
   HUMANITY: 7
Dysart (E.), TRUST: 8
Dyson, CROSS, THE: 26;
   IMMORTALITY: 5

E

Ealing B. C., U.K., LOCAL
   GOVERNMENT: 311; TIME: 49
Eamer, SUCCESS: 16
Eardley, UNSELFISHNESS: 9
Eardley-Smith (Bt.), HOPE: 236;
   STRENGTH: 128
Earle-Drax, DEATH: 68
Early motto of Minnesota, changed in
   1858, STATE MOTTOES: 43; VISION: 14
Early motto of State of Ohio
   (1866–1868), GOVERNMENT: 3; STATE
   MOTTOES: 23
East, ADVANCE: 34
East (Bt.), ADVANCE: 3; SPEED: 1
East Ham C. B. C., U.K.,
   IMPROVEMENT: 37; LOCAL
   GOVERNMENT: 292
East India Company, DIVINE
   GUIDANCE: 89, 131; SUPPORT: 2
East Land Company, DESPAIR: 1
East Retford B. C., U.K., AGE: 10;
   LOCAL GOVERNMENT: 395
East Suffolk C. C., U.K.,
   GUIDANCE: 22; LOCAL
   GOVERNMENT: 266
East Texas Baptist College, Marshall,
   Texas, KNOWLEDGE: 94; SCHOOL
   MOTTOES: 357; TRUTH: 129
Eastbourne C. B. C., U.K.,
   FOLLOWING: 8; LOCAL
   GOVERNMENT: 227
Eastbourne College, U.K.,
   SALVATION: 18; SCHOOL
   MOTTOES: 103
Eastern Kentucky University,
   Richmond, Kentucky, SCHOOL
   MOTTOES: 346; STATE MOTTOES: 58;
   UNITY: 110

8th Foot (King's Liverpool Regt.),
ADVERSITY: 47
The Eighth Hussars, COURAGE: 183
88th Connaught Rangers, UNITY: 62
85th Foot (Shropshire Light Infantry),
GLORY: 6; REBIRTH: 2
86th Regiment (Royal Irish Rifles),
UNITY: 62
Eiston, SCHOOL MOTTOES: 351;
TRUTH: 115
Ekles, DEFENSE: 43
El Camino College, Torrance,
California, KNOWLEDGE: 85; SCHOOL
MOTTOES: 319
Elder, GUIDANCE: 30; VIRTUE: 370
Eldon (E.), HONOR: 162, 169
Eleonore, daughter of Prince Rudolf of
Anhalt-Zerbst (1608–81), DIVINE
GUIDANCE: 307; DIVINITY: 410
Eleonore, Electress of Brandenburg
(1583–1607), DIVINE GUIDANCE: 251
Eleonore, third consort of Emperor
Ferdinand III (d. 1686), GLORY: 53;
HEALING and HEALTH: 32
Eleonore Dorothee, Duchess of
Saxony-Weimar (1602–64),
PATIENCE: 9
Eleonore Erdmuthe Luise, Margravine
of Brandenburg (1662–96),
DIVINITY: 157; HOPE: 41
Eleonore Sophie, Princess of Anhalt
(1603–75), DIVINE GUIDANCE: 447
11th (Prince Albert's Own) Hussars,
FIDELITY: 317
Elford (Bt.), ADVERSITY: 13; BEAUTY: 8
Elgin (E.), PAST, THE: 3
Elibank (B.), FAITH: 253; VIRTUE: 393
Eliot, ANCESTRY: 19; DIVINITY: 321
Eliot-Lockhart, ANCESTRY: 19
Eliott, WISDOM: 98
Elisabeth, Duchess of Braunschweig
(1553–1617), DIVINE GUIDANCE: 178
Elisabeth, Duchess of Saxony
(1593–1650), DIVINITY: 7;
HAPPINESS: 67; PATIENCE: 23;
REASON: 1
Elisabeth, Duchess of Saxony-Coburg
(1540–94), DIVINE GUIDANCE: 304
Elisabeth, Duchess of Schleswig-
Holstein (1580–1653), DIVINE
GUIDANCE: 21

Elisabeth, Electress of Brandenburg
(1563–1607), DIVINE GUIDANCE: 307
Elisabeth, Margravine of Baden
(1620–96), DEATH: 79; VIRTUE: 144
Elisabeth Charlotte, consort of Georg
Wilhelm, Elector of Brandenburg
(1597–1660), DIVINITY: 440;
PARADISE: 42; REST: 12
Elisabeth Dorothee, Landgravine of
Hesse (1640–1709), HOPE: 112;
SILENCE: 7
Elisabeth Ernestine Antonie, Duchess
of Saxony (1681–1766), DIVINE
GUIDANCE: 421
Elisabeth Henriette, Landgravine of
Hesse (1661–83), DIVINE
GUIDANCE: 329
Elisabeth Sophie, Duchess of Saxony-
Gotha (1619–80), DIVINITY: 330
Elisabeth Sophie, Duchess of Saxony-
Lauenburg (1599–1627), CHRIST,
JESUS: 79; HOPE: 254
Elizabeth, Daughter of James I
(1595–1662), ENDURANCE: 40;
STEADFASTNESS: 80
Elizabeth City State University,
Elizabeth City, North Carolina,
LIFE: 34; SCHOOL MOTTOES: 332
Elizabeth of Austria, wife of Charles
IX of France (1554–92),
DIVINITY: 254; HOPE: 99
Elkin, SELF-RELIANCE: 5
Ellacombe, DECEPTION: 10
Ellames, FEAR: 41
Elleis, CONTEMPT: 7
Ellenborough (E.), DIVINITY: 32;
JUSTICE: 12; LAW: 3
Ellerton, ADVERSITY: 83; HOPE: 221;
PROSPERITY: 55
Ellies, INCREASE: 26; SUN: 24
Elliot, ANCESTRY: 19; ANIMALS: 58;
CAUTION: 5; DIRECTNESS: 6;
HAPPINESS: 32; HOME: 2;
PREPAREDNESS: 39; ROYALTY: 80;
WEAPONS: 71
Elliot (Bt.), INDUSTRIOUSNESS: 110;
POSSIBILITY: 7; TRUTH: 49
Elliot (U.S.), COURAGE: 174; FIRE: 13;
RECTITUDE: 51
Elliott, SECURITY: 62; VISION: 3
Elliott (of Harwood), COURAGE: 97
Elliott (U.S.), VIRTUE: 419

Eton U. D. C., U.K.,
FLOURISHING: 29; LOCAL
GOVERNMENT: 140; SCHOOL
MOTTOES: 109
Eure, ABILITY: 12; COURAGE: 25
Eustace, DIVINITY: 389;
PERSECUTION: 2
Eva Christine, Margravine of
Brandenburg (1590–1657), DIVINE
GUIDANCE: 307
Eva Katharine, Princess of Anhalt
(1613–79), DIVINE GUIDANCE: 288;
SCRIPTURES: 8
Evans, COUNTRY: 99; GOALS: 2;
LIBERTY: 97
Evans (Lyng, co. Norfolk),
LIBERTY: 53; NATIONAL MOTTOES: 13
Evans (of Ash Hall), LIBERTY: 53;
NATIONAL MOTTOES: 13
Evelick, RECTITUDE: 58
Evelyn (of Wotton), STRENGTH: 22
Everard (of Middleton, Co. Norfolk),
WORDS: 37
Everest, REST: 27
Everett, CAUTION: 24
Everett (U.S.), COUNTRY: 78;
DEEDS: 24; FAITH: 181;
PATRIOTISM: 38; TRUTH: 67
Evers, ETERNITY: 6; PAST, THE: 3
Every (Bt.), DUE: 4
Ewart, COURAGE: 1
Ewen (of Craigton), AUDACITY: 10
Ewig Friedrich, Duke of Württemberg
(1657–85), AUDACITY: 39;
CAUTION: 13
Exeter City and C. B. C., U.K.,
FIDELITY: 288; LOCAL
GOVERNMENT: 339
Exeter (M.), HEART: 6; UNITY: 24
Exmouth U. D. C., U.K., FLORA: 25;
LOCAL GOVERNMENT: 225; SEA: 14
Exmouth (V.), PROPER NAMES: 5
Eye B. C., U.K., LOCAL
GOVERNMENT: 257; PARADISE: 44
Eyre, FLOURISHING: 55;
INNOCENCE: 11; PATRIOTISM: 69;
POSSIBILITY: 9; ROYALTY: 90
Eyre (of Wilts), VIRTUE: 337
Eyrick, NOBILITY: 32; VIRTUE: 299
Eyton, DEDICATION: 6

F

Faal, HONESTY: 10
Fagan, COUNTRY: 18; DIVINITY: 85;
FIDELITY: 63
Failsworth U. D. C., U.K., LOCAL
GOVERNMENT: 379; WORTHINESS: 62
Fairbairn, PERSEVERANCE: 38
Fairborne, COURAGE: 220;
SECURITY: 78
Fairburn, CONSISTENCY: 9; LOCAL
GOVERNMENT: 338
Fairfax, WORDS: 15
Fairfax (B.), WORDS: 13, 15
Fairfax (of Gilling Castle), DEEDS: 59
Fairfowl, WORDS: 26
Fairholm, FIDELITY: 99
Fairley, PREPAREDNESS: 24
Fairlie, DIVINE GUIDANCE: 330;
PREPAREDNESS: 48; THOUGHT: 24
Fairlie-Cunninghame (Bt.),
FORTITUDE: 6
Fairn, REST: 30; SHADE: 15
Fairnie, REST: 21; WAKEFULNESS: 10
Fairquhar, FIDELITY: 95
Fairwether, SUN: 29
Faith Baptist Bible College, Ankeny,
Iowa, SCHOOL MOTTOES: 374;
SCRIPTURES: 17; WORLD: 4
Falcon, COURAGE: 230; LIVELINESS: 6;
PRIDE: 16
Falconberg, FIDELITY: 189;
SINCERITY: 10
Falconer, AUDACITY: 57; COURAGE: 98;
HAPPINESS: 10; HEART: 4;
INDUSTRIOUSNESS: 197; PARADISE: 48;
SPIRIT: 8; STRENGTH: 164;
VIRTUE: 308
Falconer (of Halkerton), LIFE: 49
Falconer (of Newton, Scotland),
JUSTICE: 4; POWER: 3; WEAPONS: 14
Falkiner (Bt.), FORTUNE: 41
Falkland Islands, LOCAL
GOVERNMENT: 87; RECTITUDE: 13
Falkland (V.), FIDELITY: 204
Falkner, LIFE: 48
Fallous, AUDACITY: 62; FIDELITY: 183
Falmouth (E.), KNOWLEDGE: 54;
PATIENCE: 24
Falshaw, COURAGE: 134; OFFICE: 1
Fane, WORTHINESS: 35

Fanmakers' Company, ART: 15;
TRADES: 7

Fanshaw, CROSS, THE: 50; REASON: 6

Fardell, UNSELFISHNESS: 9

Fareham U. D. C., U.K.,
PREPAREDNESS: 55

Farie, FEELINGS: 9; HANDS: 6; MIND: 7

Farley, SALVATION: 48

Farlow (U.S.), HONOR: 194;
VIRTUE: 276

Farmer, FIDELITY: 194; TIME: 40

Farnall, LOCAL GOVERNMENT: 275;
PERSEVERANCE: 70

Farnborough U. D. C., U.K.,
FAITH: 98; JUSTICE: 31; LOCAL
GOVERNMENT: 128

Farnell, PERSEVERANCE: 56; STATE
MOTTOES: 40

Farnham (B.), PREPAREDNESS: 34

Farnham U. D. C., U.K., LOCAL
GOVERNMENT: 52; WORTHINESS: 7

Farnworth B. C., U.K., FEAR: 29;
JUSTICE: 56; LOCAL
GOVERNMENT: 201

Farquhar, CHANGE: 22; DAY: 12;
FAITH: 222

Farquhar (Bt.), FEELINGS: 20;
HANDS: 27

Farquharson, FEAR: 24; FORCE: 6;
MEMORY: 1, 7; SHADE: 1;
UNCLASSIFIED: 6

Farquharson (of Houghton),
ENLIGHTENMENT: 3

Farquharson (of Invercauld),
FAITH: 61; FORTITUDE: 3

Farrel, UNITY: 22

Farrer, PREPAREDNESS: 17

Farriers' Company, COURAGE: 229;
STRENGTH: 165; TRADES: 41

Farrington, PROSPERITY: 21

Farside, COURAGE: 121

Faulkner, LIFE: 48

Faunce, ACCOMPLISHMENT: 12

Favil, DIVINITY: 129; FAITH: 31

Favill, FAITH: 36

Fawcett, DUTY: 23; FIDELITY: 245

Fawkes, DIVINE GIFTS: 3; ROYALTY: 1

Fay (U.S.), PATRIOTISM: 22;
STEADFASTNESS: 87

Fayting, FIDELITY: 108; SACRIFICE: 2

Fea, DEEDS: 35; HOPE: 58

Fearon, LOCAL GOVERNMENT: 275;
PERSEVERANCE: 70; STRANGER: 16;
STRENGTH: 155

Fearon (of Hunstanton), CAUTION: 9

Federal Republic of Cameroon,
INDUSTRIOUSNESS: 154; NATIONAL
MOTTOES: 22; PATRIOTISM: 29;
PEACE: 34

Federation of Nigeria, FAITH: 243;
NATIONAL MOTTOES: 40; UNITY: 113

Feilden, VIRTUE: 342

Feld, ASPIRATION: 37

Felician College, Chicago, Illinois,
SCHOOL MOTTOES: 359; TRUTH: 164;
WAY: 11

Fellows, CONFIDENCE: 5; HONOR: 150;
PATIENCE: 32; PERSEVERANCE: 46

Fels (U.S.), FIRE: 3

Feltham, REWARD: 27

Feltham U. D. C., U.K.,
IMPROVEMENT: 17; LOCAL
GOVERNMENT: 193

Feniscowles, HONOR: 207; REWARD: 61;
VIRTUE: 446

Fennison, VIGILANCE: 104

Fenouiler, HOPE: 103;
INDUSTRIOUSNESS: 71; LOCAL
GOVERNMENT: 184

Fenton, ADVERSITY: 65; BEAUTY: 5;
CONQUEST: 70; DEATH: 23;
DISGRACE: 6; FLORA: 8; RISING: 10

Fenwick, DEATH: 76; FIDELITY: 16,
312, 314; REASON: 15; REWARD: 57;
VIRTUE: 418

Fenwick (of Longframlington),
FIDELITY: 15

Fenwicke, FIDELITY: 313

Ferdinand, Duke of Bavaria
(1550–1608), TRUST: 108;
VIGILANCE: 71

Ferdinand Albert, Duke of
Braunschweig-Bevern (1680–1735),
DIVINE GUIDANCE: 236; GRACE: 11

Ferdinand I, Emperor of Germany
(1503–64), JUSTICE: 28; ROYALTY: 8

Ferdinand II, Emperor of Germany
(1578–1637), FORTUNE: 2; TIME: 6

Ferdinand III, Emperor of Germany
(1608–57), JUSTICE: 100; PIETY: 34

Source Information

Fitzgerald, COURAGE: 81; DEFIANCE: 3; FIDELITY: 179; GRATITUDE: 13

Fitzgerald and Vesci (B.), DEFIANCE: 12

Fitzgerald (of Castle Ishen (Bt.), DEFIANCE: 12

Fitzgerald (of Turlough), HONOR: 104

Fitzgerald (the Knight of Glyn and the Knight of Kerry), DEFIANCE: 12

FitzGibbon, HONOR: 86

Fitz-Henry, UNCLASSIFIED: 26

Fitz-Herbert, HONOR: 125

Fitz-Herbert (of Norbury), SERVICE: 72

Fitzhugh, GLORY: 32; MODERATION: 9

Fitz-James, FIDELITY: 287

Fitz-Marmaduke, FAITH: 22

Fitz-Morris, COURAGE: 257

Fitz-Patrick, COURAGE: 94

Fitz-Roy, HONOR: 34; RECTITUDE: 19; REWARD: 6

Fitz-William, COURAGE: 45; STEADFASTNESS: 24

Fitzwilliams, DIVINE GUIDANCE: 74

Fitzwygram (Bt.), COUNTRY: 28; LOVE: 45; PATRIOTISM: 11

Flack, USEFULNESS: 7

Flaming Rainbow University, Stilwell, Oklahoma, SCHOOL MOTTOES: 17; SEARCH and DISCOVERY: 1

Flavel, DIVINE GUIDANCE: 428

Fleetwood B. C., U.K., IMPROVEMENT: 29; LOCAL GOVERNMENT: 263

Fleetwood (Bt.), DEEDS: 77

Fleming, DEEDS: 62; GROWTH: 21; JUDGMENT: 1; ROYALTY: 6

Fleming (Bt.), PEACE: 38; PROSPERITY: 38; WISDOM: 47

Fleming (of Manchester), PEACE: 38; PROSPERITY: 38; WISDOM: 47

Fletcher, ASPIRATION: 17; CAUTION: 24; COURAGE: 81; DANGER: 14; DIRECTNESS: 10; FIDELITY: 179; LIBERTY: 65; RECTITUDE: 56; TRANSIENCE: 5; VIRTUE: 106

Fletcher (Bt.), LOVE: 88; WAR: 40

Fletcher (Co. Stafford), CROSS, THE: 106; SALVATION: 47

Fletcher (of Ashford), DIVINE GUIDANCE: 186

Fletcher (of Kevan), HOPE: 205

Flinn, INTEGRITY: 10; SCHOOL MOTTOES: 94

Flint, COURAGE: 82; TRUSTWORTHINESS: 2

Flintshire C. C., U.K., JUSTICE: 39; LOCAL GOVERNMENT: 166; PROTECTION: 16

Flood, LOCAL GOVERNMENT: 402; STATE MOTTOES: 61; STRENGTH: 184; UNITY: 122

Florida College, Temple Terrace, Florida, FRIENDSHIP: 1; HEALING and HEALTH: 23; SCHOOL MOTTOES: 6, 225

Florida Keys Community College, Key West, Florida, LOCATION: 12; SCHOOL MOTTOES: 315

Florida State University, Tallahassee, Florida, ART: 33; SCHOOL MOTTOES: 363; STRENGTH: 173

Flory, SERVICE: 74

Flower, MIND: 25; RECTITUDE: 43

Flower (Bt.), PERSEVERANCE: 56; STATE MOTTOES: 40

Flowers, FLORA: 15

Floyd (Bt.), PATIENCE: 26; SUN: 8

Floyer, VIRTUE: 60

Flux, PERSEVERANCE: 19

Flynn, HONOR: 103; REWARD: 10; VIRTUE: 76

Fogg (U.S.), POSSIBILITY: 3

Foley (B.), USEFULNESS: 18

Foliot, HOPE: 75

Foliott, HOPE: 75

Foljambe, STRENGTH: 126

Folke, MODERATION: 33

Follet, VIGILANCE: 59; VIRTUE: 166

Folville, LOVE: 53

Foot, VIRTUE: 234

Foote, LOVE: 48; UNCLASSIFIED: 37; WALKING: 6

Footner, DUTY: 6

Forbes, ADVERSITY: 4; CHRIST, JESUS: 71; COURAGE: 256; ENJOYMENT: 16; FEAR: 44; FIDELITY: 196; GLORY: 18; GRACE: 18; HOPE: 181; IDLENESS: 5; INNOCENCE: 14; MODERATION: 24; PROSPERITY: 1; SALVATION: 39; TIME: 20; VIRTUE: 367

Forbes (B.), GRACE: 18

Frewen (of Northiam), CHANGE: 10

Friedrich, Count of the Palatinate of Vohenstrauss (1557–97), CROWN: 14; ENDURANCE: 19; FORTUNE: 6; JUSTICE: 73

Friedrich, Duke of Braunschweig-Lüneberg (1574–1648), DIVINE GUIDANCE: 332

Friedrich, Duke of Braunschweig-Lüneburg (1574–1648), DESTRUCTION: 4; DIVINITY: 9; PEACE: 17, 62; VICTORY: 36

Friedrich, Duke of Saxony (1599–1625), DEATH: 79; DIVINITY: 412; FATE: 37; FORGETTING: 2; SPEED: 10; VIRTUE: 144; WISDOM: 105

Friedrich, Duke of Saxony (D. 1586), COURAGE: 31; LOVE: 34

Friedrich, Duke of Schleswig-Holstein and Norburg (1581–1658), HONOR: 197; NOBILITY: 30; VIRTUE: 296

Friedrich, Duke of Württemberg (1615–82), DEATH: 31; DIVINE GUIDANCE: 116; HONESTY: 23; HONOR: 119

Friedrich, Landgrave of Hesse (1616–82); Bisshopp (Bt.), DIVINITY: 352

Friedrich, Landgrave of Hesse-Homburg (1585–1638), THOUGHT: 18

Friedrich, Margrave of Brandenburg (1588–1611), DIVINE GUIDANCE: 327; FEAR: 26; FLOURISHING: 53; RIGHTEOUSNESS: 8; SPEED: 20; WISDOM: 33

Friedrich, Margrave of Brandenburg-Anspach (1616–34), DIVINE GUIDANCE: 107

Friedrich Achilles, Duke of Württemberg (1591–1630), DIVINE GUIDANCE: 130

Friedrich Adolf, Count von der Lippe (1667–1718), HONOR: 130; JUSTICE: 78

Friedrich August I, Elector of Saxony (1670–1733), ENDURANCE: 57; FEAR: 21; GOVERNMENT: 7; GRATITUDE: 14; HONOR: 92; OFFSPRING: 6; ROYALTY: 95; UNITY: 99

Friedrich August II, Elector of Saxony (1696–1763), REBIRTH: 20

Friedrich Christoph, Count of Mansfeld (1564–1631), EFFORT: 32; PATIENCE: 38

Friedrich Heinrich, Count of the Palatinate (1614–29), DIVINITY: 61

Friedrich Heinrich, Duke of Saxony-Neustadt (1668–1713), JUSTICE: 100; PIETY: 34

Friedrich I, Duke of Saxony-Gotha and Altenburg (1646–91), ACCOMPLISHMENT: 16; ACTION: 18; ADVERSITY: 66; ASPIRATION: 66; FOLLOWING: 3; JUSTICE: 99; LEADERSHIP: 9; PIETY: 32; PRUDENCE: 38; VIRTUE: 24, 131

Friedrich II, Duke of Liegnitz (1480–1547), SCRIPTURES: 16

Friedrich II, Duke of Saxony-Gotha (1676–1732), WAKEFULNESS: 6

Friedrich II, Duke of Saxony-Gotha and Altenburg (1676–1732), COURAGE: 113; CROSS, THE: 29; KNOWLEDGE: 26; LOVE: 13; PROTECTION: 6; PRUDENCE: 3; UNITY: 26; WISDOM: 26

Friedrich II, Duke of Schleswig-Holstein-Gottorp (1568–87), SPEED: 44

Friedrich II, Elector of the Palatinate (1483–1556), DIVINE GUIDANCE: 165; JUSTICE: 17

Friedrich II, the Wise, Elector of the Palatinate (1483–1556), DIVINITY: 318, 401; HOPE: 257; VICTORY: 12

Friedrich II, the Wise, Elector of the Palatinate of Rhein (1483–1556), CHRIST, JESUS: 58; PROTECTION: 22

Friedrich III, Duke of Saxony-Gotha and Altenburg (1699–1772), DIVINITY: 36; JUSTICE: 100; PIETY: 34; TIME: 14

Friedrich III, Duke of Schleswig-Holstein-Gottorp (1597–1659), DESIRE: 15; GLORY: 61; VIRTUE: 440

Friedrich IV, Count of the Palatinate (1594–1610), JUSTICE: 95; MODERATION: 30; NOBILITY: 27, 37; PIETY: 16; VIRTUE: 205, 442

Friedrich IV, Duke of Liegnitz
(1552–96), DIVINITY: 185

Friedrich Karl, Duke of Württemberg
(1652–98), ADVERSITY: 16;
DIVINITY: 118; HOPE: 29

Friedrich Ludwig, Count of the
Palatinate of Landsberg (1619–81),
CHRIST, JESUS: 79; HOPE: 254

Friedrich Magnus, Margrave of Baden-
Durlach (1647–1709), DUTY: 27;
GLORY: 50

Friedrich the Wise, Elector of Saxony
(1463–1525), CROSS, THE: 33;
POSSIBILITY: 12; SALVATION: 10;
SCRIPTURES: 16

Friedrich Ulrich, Duke of
Braunschweig-Wolfenbüttel
(1591–1634), BLESSING: 2; DIVINE
GIFTS: 39; DIVINE GUIDANCE: 20, 427,
435; DIVINITY: 61, 92; FAILURE: 2;
FORTUNE: 2; GRACE: 7; HUMILITY: 6;
TIME: 6

Friedrich Ulrich, Duke of
Braunschweig-Wolfenbüttel
(1591–1634); Johann Georg I,
Elector of Saxony (1613–80);
Friedrich Heinrich, Count of the
Palatinate (1614–29); Adolf
Wilhelm, Duke of Saxony-Eisenach
(1632–68); Outhwaite, COUNTRY: 15

Friedrich V, King of Bohemia
(1532–96), DIVINE GUIDANCE: 217;
SECURITY: 25

Friedrich V, Margrave of Baden-
Durlach (1594–1659),
CONSCIENCE: 3; IRONY: 6; VIRTUE: 30

Friedrich Wilhelm, Duke of
Mecklenberg-Schwerin (1675–1713),
OBEDIENCE: 1

Friedrich Wilhelm, Duke of
Mecklenburg-Schwerin (1675–1713),
DIVINITY: 368; GLORY: 48;
PRUDENCE: 44; STEADFASTNESS: 104

Friedrich Wilhelm, Duke of Saxony
(1603–19), DIVINITY: 255; TRUST: 61

Friedrich Wilhelm, Elector of
Brandenburg (1620–88), DIVINE
GIFTS: 1; DIVINE GUIDANCE: 441;
DIVINITY: 359; FLOURISHING: 89;
GRACE: 30; LAW: 63; LOCAL
GOVERNMENT: 289; PATIENCE: 37;
PEACE: 62; PEOPLE: 7, 20;
PROVIDENCE: 20; SUN: 4; TRUST: 89;
VICTORY: 36

Friedrich Wilhelm, Elector of
Branderburg (1620–88), DIVINE
GUIDANCE: 128

Friedrich Wilhelm I, Duke of Saxony-
Weimar (1562–1602), CHRIST,
JESUS: 33; DEATH: 14; PIETY: 28;
VIRTUE: 143

Friedrich Wilhelm II, Duke of Saxony-
Altenburg (1603–69), PIETY: 28;
RIGHTEOUSNESS: 13; USEFULNESS: 6;
VIRTUE: 143

Friern Barnet U. D. C., U.K.,
COUNTRYSIDE: 3; LOCAL
GOVERNMENT: 319

Frizell (U.S.), CHRIST, JESUS: 47

Frome, STEADFASTNESS: 62

Frost, EARTH: 5; GROWTH: 7;
INCREASE: 15; PARADISE: 22

Fructuozo, FAITH: 131

Fruiterers' Company, CHRIST, JESUS: 3

Fry, LIBERTY: 63; VIRTUE: 104

Frye, ADVERSITY: 38

Fryer, STATUS: 4; TRUST: 84;
WISDOM: 40

Fulford (of Fulford), ENDURANCE: 7

Fulham B. C., U.K., LOCAL
GOVERNMENT: 288; PEOPLE: 6

Fullarton, POSSESSION: 15; RISING: 1

Fuller, ADVERSITY: 20; FIDELITY: 129;
RUNNING: 3; STEADFASTNESS: 48

Fullerton (of Westwood), DARKNESS: 8;
LIGHT: 48

Fulton, DEEDS: 69;
INDUSTRIOUSNESS: 157; REST: 17

Furlong, GENEROSITY: 12

Furnaval, PERSEVERANCE: 78;
PROVIDENCE: 15

Furnival, HONOR: 136

Furse, COURAGE: 158

Fust, EARTH: 21; FIDELITY: 305;
SPEED: 54; STRANGER: 14

Futroye, DEATH: 93

Fydell, FIDELITY: 76

Fyers, COURAGE: 20
Fyffe (of Dron), HONOR: 17
Fynney, MIND: 13
Fyres, COURAGE: 20

G

Gabb, LIBERTY: 82
Gabon Republic,
  INDUSTRIOUSNESS: 192; JUSTICE: 124;
  NATIONAL MOTTOES: 34, 38;
  UNITY: 95, 111
Gabriel, ADVERSITY: 37; FEAR: 27;
  HOPE: 111; PROSPERITY: 20;
  WEAPONS: 7
Gadesden, STEADFASTNESS: 31
Gage, DIVINITY: 413; HOPE: 9
Gage (V.), COURAGE: 52
Gainsborough R. D. C., U.K., LOCAL
  GOVERNMENT: 380; TRUST: 98
Gainsborough U. D. C., U.K.,
  EFFORT: 33; LOCAL
  GOVERNMENT: 365
Gairden, CROSS, THE: 24; POWER: 25;
  VIRTUE: 231
Gairden (of Barrowfield),
  ROYALTY: 129
Gairdner, DIVINITY: 283; INTENTION: 1
Galbraith, HOPE: 291; VIGILANCE: 106
Gale, HOPE: 53
Galiez, DIVINE GUIDANCE: 197
Gall, PATIENCE: 36
Gallandet (U.S.),
  INDUSTRIOUSNESS: 196; REST: 32
Gallightly, CONQUEST: 10
Gallini, UNITY: 12
Galloway, ASPIRATION: 51; DIVINE
  GUIDANCE: 101
Galloway (E.), VIRTUE: 234
Galmoye (V.), SEARCH and
  DISCOVERY: 4
Galton (Co. Warwick), LIGHT: 18
Galway, ENTRAPMENT: 5
Galway (V.), CROSS, THE: 26;
  DEEDS: 46; FAME: 7
Galwey, TRUTH: 168
The Gambia, IMPROVEMENT: 36;
  PEACE: 74; PROSPERITY: 45
Gambier, FAITH: 89
Gammell, DEATH: 50
Gamon, COURAGE: 236

Gandolfi (D.), ANCESTRY: 26;
  ENDURANCE: 42
Gannon University, Erie,
  Pennsylvania, HEALING and
  HEALTH: 33; KNOWLEDGE: 60;
  SCHOOL MOTTOES: 260
Garbett, VIGILANCE: 44
Garden, ENDURANCE: 50; POWER: 25;
  VIRTUE: 231
Gardeners' Company,
  INDUSTRIOUSNESS: 86; TRADES: 16
Gardiner, DESPAIR: 5; FORTUNE: 115;
  HONOR: 105; INDUSTRIOUSNESS: 58;
  LOCAL GOVERNMENT: 275;
  PERSEVERANCE: 70; VIRTUE: 132, 431
Gardiner (of Ely), FIDELITY: 94;
  LOVE: 49
Gardiner (U.S.), COUNTRY: 108;
  DEATH: 86; PATRIOTISM: 57
Gardiners, FORTUNE: 18;
  PROVIDENCE: 7
Gardner, COURAGE: 141; FORTUNE: 70;
  INDUSTRIOUSNESS: 104; LIBERTY: 40;
  PRIMACY: 4; STRENGTH: 156;
  VIRTUE: 210; WEAPONS: 53
Gardner (B.), STRENGTH: 156;
  VIRTUE: 210
Gardyne, CROSS, THE: 24
Garmston, DIVINITY: 336
Garnett, DILIGENCE: 27; HONOR: 25
Garnett-Orme, DILIGENCE: 26;
  HONESTY: 6
Garneys, DIVINE GUIDANCE: 259;
  FLEXIBILITY: 1
Garnock, SPEED: 49
Garnons (Co. Denbigh and Co.
  Herts.), HAPPINESS: 50;
  PROSPERITY: 29
Garratt, FAITH: 232; LOVE: 114
Garrett, COUNTRY: 135; FIDELITY: 289;
  LIBERTY: 117
Garriock, RISING: 3
Garritte, CROSS, THE: 5; SALVATION: 5
Garrow, RISING: 3
Garshore, REBIRTH: 13
Garstang R. D. C., U.K., CONCERN: 3;
  LOCAL GOVERNMENT: 73
Garstin, COURAGE: 124; WEAPONS: 46
Garvagh (B.), ADVERSITY: 51
Garvey, FEAR: 65; JUSTICE: 114;
  MERCY: 21
Gascoigne, WAR: 69

Gascoyne, GUIDANCE: 25; REASON: 17

Gaskell, DIVINITY: 402; HOPE: 198, 226, 260

Gaskell (of York), FAITH: 208

Gason, FAME: 12

Gatty, CAUTION: 6, 28

Gaude de Martainville, ENJOYMENT: 3

Gaury, CONFIDENCE: 17

Gavin, MEMORY: 23

Gavin (of Lanton), INDUSTRIOUSNESS: 11; PROSPERITY: 3

Gay (of Bath), FORTUNE: 101

Gay (of Thurning Hall, co. Norfolk), LIVELINESS: 5

Gealagh, DEFENSE: 22; INJURY: 3

Geale-Brady, BRIGHTNESS: 9; RECTITUDE: 11

Geary (Bt.), PURSUIT: 2

Ged, ENDURANCE: 16

Geddes, or Geddeis, ASPIRATION: 42

Geedham, DIVINE GUIDANCE: 253

Geekie, VIGILANCE: 64

Geer (U.S.), CAUSATION: 8

Geikie, VIGILANCE: 105

Gell, OBEDIENCE: 15; PEACE: 77

Gellatly, CONQUEST: 10

Gellie, DIVINE GUIDANCE: 197

Gen. Sir R. Gardiner, G. C. B., CONFIDENCE: 4

General Dwight D. Eisenhower, DEEDS: 90; MANNER: 13

General Federation of Women's Clubs, UNITY: 117

General George S. Patton, IMPROVEMENT: 15

General Joseph W. ('Vinegar Joe') Stilwell, PERSEVERANCE: 24

General Thomas Jonathan (Stonewall) Jackson, DUTY: 8

General Ulysses S. Grant, WAR: 82

Geneva College, Beaver Falls, Pennsylvania, COUNTRY: 85; SCHOOL MOTTOES: 237

Gennys, DIVINITY: 75

Gent, COURAGE: 132; MERCY: 7

Gentle, INDUSTRIOUSNESS: 60; SCHOOL MOTTOES: 135

Gentleman, COURTESY: 7; HONOR: 179; TRUTH: 99

Georg, Count of the Palatinate of Simmern (1518-69), DIVINITY: 210

Georg, Duke of Braunschweig-Lüneburg (1582-1641), CHRIST, JESUS: 82; COUNTRY: 117; HOPE: 288; PATRIOTISM: 73; RIGHTEOUSNESS: 13; USEFULNESS: 6

Georg Albrecht, Margrave of Brandenburg (1591-1615), DIVINITY: 298; JUSTICE: 13

Georg Albrecht, Margrave of Brandenburg-Baireuth (1619-66), DIVINITY: 15; TIME: 68

Georg Aribert, Prince of Anhalt (1606-43), VIRTUE: 120

Georg Friedrich, Duke of Württemberg (1657-85), VIRTUE: 435

Georg Friedrich, Margrave of Baden-Hochberg (1573-1638), DIVINE GUIDANCE: 413

Georg Friedrich, Margrave of Brandenburg-Anspach (1539-1603), DESTRUCTION: 5; DIVINE GUIDANCE: 237, 405; FAITH: 165; GROWTH: 9; PIETY: 28; TIMELINESS: 2; VIRTUE: 143

Georg Friedrich, Margrave of Brandenburg (1539-1603); Georg III, Duke of Brieg (1611-64), DIVINE GUIDANCE: 15

Georg Friedrich Karl, Margrave of Brandenburg-Baireuth (1688-1735), FIDELITY: 300; SINCERITY: 14

Georg Gustav, Count of the Palatinate of Rhein zu Lautereck (1564-1634), DIVINITY: 389

Georg III, Duke of Brieg (1611-64), DIVINE GUIDANCE: 318; FATE: 19, 34

Georg III, his son (1582-1617), LAW: 46; PEOPLE: 10

Georg III, son of Bogislaus XIII, Duke of Pomerania (1528-1617), DEATH: 95; GLORY: 55

Georg Rudolf, Duke of Liegnitz (1595-1653), DIVINE GUIDANCE: 405

Georg the Pious, Margrave of Brandenburg-Anspach (1484-1543), DIVINE GUIDANCE: 290, 405; FAITH: 33

Georg Wilhelm, Count of the Palatinate of Birkenfeld (1591-1669), FEAR: 75; WISDOM: 100

Georg Wilhelm, Duke of
Braunschweig-Lüneburg-Zelle
(1624–1705), DUTY: 27; GLORY: 50;
JUSTICE: 100; PEOPLE: 2; PIETY: 34;
SUN: 5

Georg Wilhelm, Elector of
Brandenburg (1595–1640),
COURAGE: 27; DIVINITY: 132;
LIBERTY: 13; NATIONAL MOTTOES: 3;
OBEDIENCE: 7; SCHOOL MOTTOES: 65

Georg Wilhelm, Margrave of
Brandenburg-Baireuth (1678–1726),
CONSISTENCY: 14

George III, son of Bogislaus XIII,
Duke of Pomerania (1582–1617),
ROYALTY: 107

Georgia Southwestern College,
Americus, Georgia, SCHOOL
MOTTOES: 314

Geraldine (Co. Kildare), DEFIANCE: 3

Gerard, STATUS: 3

Gerard (Bt.), DIVINITY: 152; HOPE: 39

Gerard (of Prescot), DIVINITY: 152;
HOPE: 39

Gerard (U.S.), HONOR: 127;
WILLINGNESS: 2

Germon, DEFENSE: 54; VIRTUE: 346

Gernon, CONTEMPT: 5

Gerrard, FIDELITY: 223; GOODNESS: 7

Gervais, SUPPORT: 7

Gethin (Bt.), EFFORT: 35

Gib, HOPE: 215; WEAPONS: 13

Gibb, FAITH: 107; STEADFASTNESS: 137

Gibbes (Bt.), STEADFASTNESS: 137

Gibbes (U.S.), COUNTRY: 3; LOVE: 29;
PATRIOTISM: 6

Gibbons, DIVINITY: 179; TRUST: 37

Gibbons (Bt.), PIETY: 9; ROYALTY: 43

Gibbs, DIVINE GUIDANCE: 192;
GOALS: 4; LOCAL GOVERNMENT: 275;
PERSEVERANCE: 70;
PREPAREDNESS: 41;
STEADFASTNESS: 137

Gibbs (U.S.), VIGILANCE: 6

Gibon, PREPAREDNESS: 78

Gibson, COURAGE: 44; EMERGENCE: 3;
FIDELITY: 272; LOCAL
GOVERNMENT: 65; PARADISE: 3;
PATRIOTISM: 70; RECTITUDE: 60;
ROYALTY: 91; WISDOM: 10

Gibson (of Durie), PARADISE: 46

Giffard, GENEROSITY: 15;
STRENGTH: 104

Gifford, DEATH: 84; DISGRACE: 14;
GENEROSITY: 17

Gifford (B.), DIVINITY: 322

Gilbert, COUNTRY: 85; SCHOOL
MOTTOES: 237; STEADFASTNESS: 78

Gilbert (Bt.), DEATH: 39; DISGRACE: 9

Gilbert (of Cantley Hall),
STEADFASTNESS: 137

Gilchrist, CONFIDENCE: 10; FAITH: 172;
FIDELITY: 98; GLORY: 36

Gildea, ENDURANCE: 58;
WORTHINESS: 58

Gildowrie, FAITH: 21

Giles, THOUGHT: 14

Giles (U.S.), COUNTRY: 48, 49;
LIBERTY: 57, 58

Gilfillan, COURAGE: 21; WEAPONS: 9

Gill, DIVINE GUIDANCE: 410;
DIVINITY: 270; HOPE: 118; RISING: 21

Gillanders, STRENGTH: 23

Gillbanks, HONOR: 85

Gillespie, ANIMALS: 55; AUDACITY: 48;
FIDELITY: 117; SALVATION: 49;
SECURITY: 19; TOUCH: 4; WAR: 22

Gillespie-Staunton, MODERATION: 19

Gillies, ANIMALS: 55; TOUCH: 4

Gillingham B. C., U.K., DEFENSE: 56;
HOME: 22; LOCAL GOVERNMENT: 408

Gillman, ACTION: 15

Gillon, SECURITY: 72

Gilmer, DEEDS: 64

Gilmour, LIGHT: 21;
PERSEVERANCE: 69; WALKING: 2

Gilpin, DEEDS: 11; FAITH: 238;
SIMPLICITY: 1

Gilpin (of Bungay, Suffolk),
FAITH: 125

Gilroy, FIDELITY: 2

Gingle, DEATH: 40; DISGRACE: 10

Ginkell, DEATH: 40; DISGRACE: 10

Gipping R. D. C., U.K., DIVINE
GUIDANCE: 202; LOCAL
GOVERNMENT: 95

Girl Scouts of America, DEEDS: 12;
PREPAREDNESS: 10

Girvan, HOME: 10

Gisela Agnes, consort of Prince
Emanuel Leberecht of Anhalt-
Plötzkau (d. 1670), DIVINITY: 438

Gladstone (Bt.), COURAGE: 64;
FIDELITY: 102

Glamorgan C. C., U.K.,
ENDURANCE: 1; LOCAL
GOVERNMENT: 3

Glanford Brigg R. D. C., U.K., LOCAL
GOVERNMENT: 18; PREPAREDNESS: 3

Glanville, CONFIDENCE: 5

Glasbern, CONQUEST: 19

Glasford, FAITH: 190

Glasgow, OBEDIENCE: 11

Glasgow (E.), DIVINE GUIDANCE: 217

Glasham, CONQUEST: 19

Glass, ADVERSITY: 44; EMERGENCE: 1

Glasscott, VIRTUE: 369

Glassford, FEELINGS: 19; HANDS: 26

Glass-sellers' Company, CONFLICT: 3

Glastonbury B. C., U.K.,
FLOURISHING: 28; LOCAL
GOVERNMENT: 139; RELIGION: 9

Glazebrook, HONOR: 27; HOPE: 35;
STATE MOTTOES: 11

Glaziers' Company, DIVINE
GUIDANCE: 62; LIGHT: 6, 38;
TRADES: 11, 21

Glegg, POSSESSION: 22

Gleim (U.S.), FAITH: 111

Glen, ASPIRATION: 17

Glenalmond College, U.K.,
FLOURISHING: 77; SCHOOL
MOTTOES: 295

Glendoning (of Partoun), CHRIST,
JESUS: 39; FAITH: 139

Glendonwyn, CHRIST, JESUS: 39;
FAITH: 139

Gleneagles, SUFFERING: 10

Glenelg (B.), FLOURISHING: 65;
STEADFASTNESS: 127

Glengall (E.), DIVINE GUIDANCE: 254

Glenlyon (B.), FORTUNE: 64

Glennon, COURAGE: 123;
GENEROSITY: 6

Gloag, ACQUISITION: 6; AGE: 5;
GENEROSITY: 14

Glossop B. C., U.K., LIBERTY: 133;
LOCAL GOVERNMENT: 399;
TRUTH: 172; VIRTUE: 353

Gloster, PATIENCE: 19

Gloucester City and C. B. B. C., U.K.,
FAITH: 100; LOCAL GOVERNMENT: 129

Gloucestershire C. C., U.K.,
IMPROVEMENT: 41; LOCAL
GOVERNMENT: 295

Glover, FEAR: 42; LIGHT: 81; RISING: 19

Glovers' and Skinners' Company,
DIVINITY: 389

Glyn, LAW: 51; LIBERTY: 96

Glyn (Bt.), STEADFASTNESS: 51;
TRUST: 39

Goadie, HONESTY: 10

Godalming B. C., U.K.,
FIDELITY: 214; LIBERTY: 47; LOCAL
GOVERNMENT: 215

Goddard (of Swindon), ANIMALS: 11;
LIBERTY: 9

Godden, DIVINITY: 285

Godfray, DIVINITY: 106; PEACE: 9

Godfrey, ANIMALS: 12; BIRDS: 11;
CHRIST, JESUS: 25; FEELINGS: 7;
FRIENDSHIP: 35; REWARD: 28

Godfrey (Bt.), DIVINE GUIDANCE: 263;
DIVINITY: 108; LIBERTY: 15

Godley (Co. Leitrim), DIVINITY: 379;
LOCAL GOVERNMENT: 332

Godma, PARADISE: 9

Godolphin (B.), PEACE: 53; WAR: 54

Goff, HONESTY: 11; PRIDE: 5

Goffdon, FEELINGS: 6; HANDS: 4

Going, HONOR: 27; HOPE: 35; STATE
MOTTOES: 11

Golden Valley Lutheran College,
Minneapolis, Minnesota,
CONCERN: 6; SCHOOL MOTTOES: 334

Goldie, TRANSIENCE: 7; USEFULNESS: 13

Goldie-Scott, FIDELITY: 139; LOVE: 51

Golding, DIVINITY: 361; ROYALTY: 67

Goldmid (Bt.), DIVINITY: 366

Goldsmid, DIVINITY: 299, 366

Goldsmid(Bt.), DILIGENCE: 14;
UNITY: 14

Goldsmith (U.S.), REST: 31

Goldsmiths' Company, DIVINITY: 407;
JUSTICE: 76; VIRTUE: 99

Gollop (of Strode), AUDACITY: 35;
WISDOM: 2

Gomm, FIDELITY: 253; HOPE: 160

Gonzaga University School of Law,
Spokane, Washington, COUNTRY: 17;
DIVINITY: 84; SCHOOL MOTTOES: 62

Gooch, GRATITUDE: 12

Goodale, Goodalle, DIVINE
GUIDANCE: 281

Goodall, FIDELITY: 51;
  STEADFASTNESS: 23
Goodchild, SCHOOL MOTTOES: 361;
  TRUTH: 167
Gooden-Chisholm, AGGRESSION: 6
Goodere, ABILITY: 24
Goodge, AUDACITY: 4
Gooding, ADVERSITY: 55
Goodlake, DIVINE GIFTS: 45
Goodricke, UNCLASSIFIED: 17
Goodricke (of Ribstone Hall),
  ANIMALS: 25; JUSTICE: 32;
  STRENGTH: 48
Goodsir, COURAGE: 244; FIDELITY: 340
Goodwin, COURAGE: 64;
  FIDELITY: 102; FLORA: 21; WILL: 1
Goodwright, ASPIRATION: 1;
  IMPROVEMENT: 34
Googe, AUDACITY: 4
Goold (Bt.), DIVINE GUIDANCE: 140
Goole B. C., U.K., ADVANCE: 1; LOCAL
  GOVERNMENT: 8
Gorden (of Invergordon), FEELINGS: 8;
  HANDS: 5
Gordon, ANCESTRY: 23; CHRIST,
  JESUS: 72; CLEVERNESS: 6;
  CONQUEST: 50; COURAGE: 9;
  DEATH: 41; DECEPTION: 1; DIVINE
  GUIDANCE: 279; DIVINITY: 70, 168;
  FORTUNE: 51; HONOR: 27; HOPE: 35,
  79, 215; LIBERTY: 89;
  MODERATION: 25; OBSCURITY: 12;
  PATIENCE: 45; PEACE: 49, 81;
  PERSEVERANCE: 37; PRUDENCE: 84;
  REST: 14; SALVATION: 40;
  SERVICE: 34; STATE MOTTOES: 11;
  STEADFASTNESS: 14, 79, 131;
  TRUTH: 108, 122; VIGILANCE: 26;
  WAR: 70, 71
Gordon (Bt.), CLEVERNESS: 1;
  COURAGE: 10; STEADFASTNESS: 14;
  VISION: 4
Gordon (Co. Aberdeen and
  Terpersey), HONOR: 145
Gordon (co. Down), CLEVERNESS: 1;
  COURAGE: 10
Gordon (D.), CLEVERNESS: 1;
  COURAGE: 10; STEADFASTNESS: 14
Gordon (of Aberdeenshire), DANGER: 8
Gordon (of Ardmellie), ENDURANCE: 10
Gordon (of Aston and Craighlaw),
  DIVINITY: 144

Gordon (of Auchendown),
  ENDURANCE: 11
Gordon (of Banff), ADVERSITY: 52
Gordon (of Beldorney), HOPE: 108
Gordon (of Carnousie), DEATH: 5;
  HONESTY: 1; HONOR: 5
Gordon (of Cockclarochie),
  ENDURANCE: 9
Gordon (of Craig, etc.), SECURITY: 63
Gordon (of Earlston, Bt.),
  DIVINITY: 144
Gordon (of Edinglassie), DIVINITY: 21,
  22
Gordon (of Embo, bt.), ADVANCE: 24
Gordon (of Farsbank),
  STEADFASTNESS: 15
Gordon (of Glastirim),
  CONCILIATION: 4
Gordon (of Gordonbank), LAW: 20;
  WEAPONS: 58
Gordon (of Haddo), VIGILANCE: 111
Gordon (of Knockespoch),
  SECURITY: 7; VIGILANCE: 28
Gordon (of Park, Bt.), SECURITY: 63
Gordon (of Rothemay), WAR: 75
Gordon (of Tacachie), FIDELITY: 81
Gordon (of Tichmurie), ASPIRATION: 22
Gordon-Cumming, COURAGE: 198
Gore (Bt.), CONQUEST: 19;
  DIVINITY: 387
Gorham, FIDELITY: 270;
  PREPAREDNESS: 67
Gormanston (V.), PURITY: 19
Gort (V.), PROPER NAMES: 20;
  TRUTH: 168
Gosford (E.), VIGILANCE: 100
Gosker, DIVINITY: 402; HOPE: 260
Gosport B. C., U.K., LOCAL
  GOVERNMENT: 163; SECURITY: 12
Gossip, FORESIGHT: 7
Gothard (of Newcastle), BIRDS: 5;
  STATUS: 1
Gotobed, REVERENCE: 1
Goudie, HONESTY: 10
Gough (of Perry Hall), VIRTUE: 42
Gough (U.S.), VIRTUE: 43
Gough (V.), PROPER NAMES: 11, 18, 22;
  WAY: 1
Gould, FLOURISHING: 64; HONESTY: 41;
  INDUSTRIOUSNESS: 168; REBIRTH: 32;
  UNCLASSIFIED: 49; VICTORY: 4
Gouldie, USEFULNESS: 13

Gourgas (U.S.), DIVINITY: 82
Gourlay, Simson, WISDOM: 50
Govan, SPEED: 19
Gow, FRIENDSHIP: 20
Gowans, FUTURE, THE: 24; HOPE: 169
Gower, STEADFASTNESS: 59
Grabham, HOPE: 129; SALVATION: 33
Grace and Geraldines (of Courtstoun),
   DEFIANCE: 4
Grace (Bt.), DEEDS: 6; GRACE: 10;
   NAME: 2
Graden, PURPOSE: 1
Graeme, DIVINE GUIDANCE: 2;
   PURSUIT: 1; TOUCH: 2; VICTORY: 1;
   VIGILANCE: 17
Grafton (D.), HONOR: 34;
   RECTITUDE: 19; REWARD: 6
Graham, ASPIRATION: 73; CAUTION: 34;
   DIRECTNESS: 7; DIVINE GUIDANCE: 2,
   354; FAITH: 95; FINISH: 3;
   FORGETTING: 8, 11, 13; FUTURE,
   THE: 1; GRATITUDE: 13; HONOR: 47;
   LIBERTY: 51; LOCAL
   GOVERNMENT: 342; LOVE: 52;
   MEMORY: 28; MODERATION: 24;
   POSSESSION: 19; PROSPERITY: 43;
   PROTECTION: 18; PROVIDENCE: 11;
   REASON: 8, 22; RECTITUDE: 24, 67;
   ROYALTY: 73; SPEED: 43; TOUCH: 2;
   VICTORY: 1
Graham (Bt.), DILIGENCE: 35;
   FIDELITY: 142; SECURITY: 76
Graham (of Braco), DEFENSE: 13
Graham (of Douglastown), LOVE: 101
Graham (of Drumgoon), CAUSATION: 6
Graham (of Dumblane),
   FOLLOWING: 12
Graham (of Duntroon), DIRECTION: 7
Graham (of Esk and Netherby, Bt.),
   REASON: 20
Graham (of Gartur), GRACE: 26;
   PEACE: 65
Graham (of Killern), ATTENTIVENESS: 6
Graham (of Leitchtown), JUSTICE: 110;
   REASON: 21; RECTITUDE: 64
Graham (of Merickle), GUIDANCE: 3
Graham (of Monargan), FATE: 24
Gran, UNCLASSIFIED: 20
Granard (E.), GLORY: 18
Grand Duchy of Tuscany,
   FIDELITY: 283

Grand Order of Wurtemburg,
   FRIENDSHIP: 5; VIRTUE: 11
Grand Sachem of the Tammany
   Society (Columbian Order) of New
   York, Sons of Liberty, UNITY: 59
Granger, HONESTY: 11
Grant, ANIMALS: 55; CONQUEST: 36;
   COURAGE: 226; DIVINITY: 260;
   FIDELITY: 333; FIRE: 2; PURSUIT: 7;
   STEADFASTNESS: 65, 66, 117, 119,
   125; STRENGTH: 137; TOUCH: 4;
   TRUST: 63; WAR: 32; WARNING: 2
Grant (Bt.), COURAGE: 57; DUE: 4;
   WEAPONS: 31
Grant (of Auchrraine), AUDACITY: 6
Grant (of Burnside and Monymusk),
   STEADFASTNESS: 128
Grant (of Carron), HARMLESSNESS: 5;
   WISDOM: 113
Grant (of Dalvey, bt.),
   FLOURISHING: 82
Grant (of Darlway), STRANGER: 10;
   STRENGTH: 107
Grant (of Frenchie), Seafield (E.),
   STEADFASTNESS: 123
Grant (of Kilgraston), LAW: 16
Grant (of Monymusk), DUE: 4
Grant (of Monymusk, bt.), DIVINE
   GUIDANCE: 322
Grant (U.S.), STEADFASTNESS: 124
Grant-Dalton, CONSCIENCE: 10;
   JUSTICE: 116
Grantham, DIVINE GIFTS: 7
Grantham (of Ketton), HONOR: 81;
   LOVE: 56
Grantley (B.), ANCESTRY: 1
Granville, ANCESTRY: 33;
   FRIENDSHIP: 48
Granville (E.), STEADFASTNESS: 59
Grassick, DIVINITY: 174
Grattan, COUNTRY: 114; PATIENCE: 41;
   PATRIOTISM: 63
Gratten, INTEGRITY: 10; SCHOOL
   MOTTOES: 94
Graver-Browne (of Morley Hall, co.
   Norfolk), HOPE: 284
Graves, SEA: 23; SEARCH and
   DISCOVERY: 14; SERIOUSNESS: 2
Graves (B.), BIRDS: 5; STATUS: 1
Graves (Co. Gloucester), MANNERS: 3;
   SERIOUSNESS: 1

Gravesend B. C., U.K., HONOR: 19;
PROTECTION: 8
Gravine (of Edinburgh), ASSISTANCE: 1
Gray, BRIGHTNESS: 5, 7; FIDELITY: 41;
LEADERSHIP: 26; LIBERTY: 135;
PRUDENCE: 80; SECURITY: 53;
SUCCESS: 13
Gray (B.), STEADFASTNESS: 4
Gray (of Cartyne), STEADFASTNESS: 35
Gray (of Durham), STEADFASTNESS: 4
Gray (of Wheatfield),
STEADFASTNESS: 138
Grazebrook (of Pedmore, Co.
Worcester), KNOWLEDGE: 52
Greame (Co. York), NOBILITY: 3;
VIRTUE: 23
Great Lakes Bible College, Lansing,
Michigan, SCHOOL MOTTOES: 128;
SCRIPTURES: 9
Great Seal of the Confederate States of
America, DIVINE GUIDANCE: 105;
NATIONAL MOTTOES: 2
Great Seal of United States of
America, DIVINE GUIDANCE: 22;
NATIONAL MOTTOES: 17; ORDER: 5
Great Yarmouth C. B. C., U.K.,
LAW: 59; LOCAL GOVERNMENT: 313;
ROYALTY: 108
Greathead, DIVINITY: 163; HOPE: 49
Greatorex, FLOURISHING: 101
Greaves, DIVINE GUIDANCE: 1;
DIVINITY: 402; FORTUNE: 1;
HOPE: 260; SEARCH and
DISCOVERY: 15, 16
Greaves (of Mayfield), BIRDS: 5;
STATUS: 1
Greaves-Banning, DIVINE GUIDANCE: 1;
FORTUNE: 1
Green, CONSERVATION: 7;
FLOURISHING: 71; LIFE: 50;
STRENGTH: 186; SUCCESS: 6;
VIRTUE: 234, 327
Green (Bt.), EQUANIMITY: 2
Green (of Lichfield), FEAR: 42
Greenall, ASPIRATION: 19
Greenfield, GROWTH: 13
Greenhill, ART: 19; DIVINITY: 269;
HONOR: 111; TRUST: 71
Greenhut, FIDELITY: 286
Greenless, FLOURISHING: 92
Greenly, FIDELITY: 235

Greenly (of Titley Court, Co.
Hereford), POSSIBILITY: 2
Green-Price, LIFE: 43
Greensugh, DIVINITY: 178
Greenville Technical College,
Greenville, South Carolina, FUTURE,
THE: 4; SCHOOL MOTTOES: 44
Greenwich B. C., U.K., LOCAL
GOVERNMENT: 372; TIME: 59
Greenwood, USEFULNESS: 19
Gregorson, DEEDS: 31
Gregory, CROSS, THE: 46, 82;
DEFENSE: 9; LIBERTY: 53;
LOFTINESS: 4; NATIONAL
MOTTOES: 13; UNCLASSIFIED: 46;
VIGILANCE: 91
Gregson, VIGILANCE: 105
Grehan, FORGETTING: 12
Greig, AGGRESSION: 19; HANDS: 30;
LOCAL GOVERNMENT: 275;
PERSEVERANCE: 70
Grenehalgh, DIVINE GUIDANCE: 350
Grenfell, DUTY: 20
Grenville, POSSESSION: 31;
PROVIDENCE: 1
Gresley (Bt.), FIDELITY: 238
Grey, HONESTY: 29; LOCAL
GOVERNMENT: 20; MIND: 36;
POWER: 1
Grey (Bt.), CROWN: 9; SERVICE: 9
Grey (E.), CROWN: 9; SERVICE: 9
Greystock, WILLINGNESS: 12
Grier, SECURITY: 15
Grierson, HOPE: 191, 192
Grieson (of Lagg, Bt.), SECURITY: 15
Grieve, CAUTION: 5; DIRECTNESS: 5, 6;
FIDELITY: 268; PEOPLE: 14;
ROYALTY: 78; SECURITY: 15;
SINCERITY: 1; UBIQUITY: 4
Grieveson, SPEED: 15
Griffen, CONQUEST: 53, 67
Griffith, FORCE: 2; GENTLENESS: 2;
HEALING and HEALTH: 9; HOPE: 50;
STRENGTH: 39; WAR: 7
Griffith (of Llwynduris),
PROSPERITY: 21
Griffith (U.S.), DIVINE GUIDANCE: 355;
POWER: 15
Griffiths, CROSS, THE: 85;
FRIENDSHIP: 51; LIGHT: 62
Griffiths (U.S.), JUSTICE: 10;
KINDNESS: 3

Grigg, USEFULNESS: 18
Grimaldi, DIVINE GUIDANCE: 99;
  LOCAL GOVERNMENT: 86
Grimond, PATIENCE: 11
Grimshaw, CONQUEST: 38
Grimston, DEEDS: 45; MODERATION: 12
Grindley, GOODNESS: 22; PRIMACY: 2
Grissell, ADVANCE: 48
Grive, UBIQUITY: 4
Groat, STEADFASTNESS: 5
Grocers' Company, DIVINE GIFTS: 36;
  GRACE: 13
Grogan (Bt.), HONOR: 97; VIRTUE: 75
Gronow, ANCESTRY: 17;
  PRINCELINESS: 5
Groseth, COUNTRY: 100;
  PATRIOTISM: 46
Gross (U.S.), PURPOSE: 14
Grossett (Co. Wilts), COUNTRY: 101;
  PATRIOTISM: 47
Grossmont College, El Cajon,
  California, COURAGE: 214; SCHOOL
  MOTTOES: 312
Grosvenor, VIRTUE: 244
Grote (of Surrey), GOODNESS: 34
Grout, ABILITY: 16; WORTHINESS: 18
Grove, DIRECTION: 5
Grove (Bt.), CHANGE: 17; STATUS: 7
Grover, FAITH: 169; LAW: 24;
  ROYALTY: 49
Growse (of Beldeston, co. Suffolk),
  AGGRESSION: 10
Groze, DIVINE GUIDANCE: 99; LOCAL
  GOVERNMENT: 86
Grubb, PARADISE: 61; STRENGTH: 132
Grundy, AUDACITY: 85; JUSTICE: 107;
  SALVATION: 28
Grylls (of Helston), STRENGTH: 172
Gubbay, HONOR: 154; INTEGRITY: 32
Guerrant (U.S.), FIRE: 4
Guest, MODERATION: 24
Guest (Bt.), UNCLASSIFIED: 18
Guevera, VICTORY: 26
Guidott, PEACE: 57
Guildford (E.), COURAGE: 11; FAITH: 5;
  LOCAL GOVERNMENT: 26;
  NOBILITY: 9; VIRTUE: 101
Guillamore (V.), INJURY: 15
Guille, LOFTINESS: 19; PARADISE: 21;
  STARS: 33
Guinand (U.S.), UNCLASSIFIED: 58
Guiness, DIVINITY: 402; HOPE: 260

Guise, HONOR: 160
Gulf-Coast Bible College, Houston,
  Texas, RELIGION: 17; SCHOOL
  MOTTOES: 231
Gull, DIVINE GUIDANCE: 410
Gulland, INNOCENCE: 2
Gulliver, WAKEFULNESS: 7
Gullon, SECURITY: 72
Gully, CROSS, THE: 83, 84
Gumbleton, DEATH: 44; MEMORY: 16
Gun, COUNTRY: 140; LOVE: 117;
  PATRIOTISM: 93
Gunman, DIVINE GUIDANCE: 364
Gunn, WAR: 5, 75
Gunning, FEAR: 80; TRUTH: 152
Gunning (Bt.), AUTHORITY: 2
Gunson, WATER: 12
Günther, Count Schwarzburg
  (1570–1643), FORTUNE: 53;
  JUSTICE: 100; PIETY: 34
Günther, Count Schwarzburg in
  Arnstadt (1490–1552), SUN: 27
Gurdlestone, VIGILANCE: 70
Gurdon, ADVERSITY: 90; VIRTUE: 355
Gurdon (of Letton, Cranworth, and
  Barnham Broom, Co. Norfolk),
  ADVERSITY: 36; VIRTUE: 86
Gurdon-Rebow, ADVERSITY: 36;
  VIRTUE: 86
Gurney, HONOR: 27; HOPE: 35; STATE
  MOTTOES: 11
Gurwood, ETERNITY: 6; FOLLOWING: 5;
  LEADERSHIP: 12
Gustav Adolf, Margrave of Baden-
  Durlach (1631–77), GROWTH: 20
Gustav Christoph, Margrave of Baden
  (1566–1609), DIVINE GUIDANCE: 316;
  FATE: 17
Gusthart, ANCESTRY: 7
Gutch, FIDELITY: 32; SPEED: 17
Guthrie, FEAR: 48; IMPROVEMENT: 7;
  INCREASE: 16; TRUTH: 88;
  UNITY: 32
Guthrie, Guthry, UNITY: 32
Guthry, INCREASE: 16; PIETY: 23;
  TRUTH: 88; UNITY: 32
Guy, GIFTS and GIVING: 11
Gwilt, FAIRNESS: 5
Gwinnett, NOBILITY: 29; VIRTUE: 295
Gwyn, WEAPONS: 48
Gwyn (of Ford Abbey),
  ENDURANCE: 23; HOPE: 57

Gwyn (of Pant-y-cored), FORCE: 34
Gwyn-Holford, FORCE: 34
Gwynne, WEAPONS: 48
Gyll, COURAGE: 266; GLORY: 61

H

Haberdashers' Company (London),
   SERVICE: 50; TRADES: 31
Hacket, FORTITUDE: 10; PRUDENCE: 22
Hackney B. C., U.K., JUSTICE: 74;
   LOCAL GOVERNMENT: 203
Hadden, SUFFERING: 10
Hadderwick, FEAR: 50
Haddington (E.), PERSEVERANCE: 75
Hadley, DIVINE GUIDANCE: 266
Hadley (U.S.), DIVINE GUIDANCE: 267
Hadwen, VICTORY: 19
Hagerstown Business College,
   Hagerstown Business College,
   FUTURE, THE: 18; SCHOOL
   MOTTOES: 197
Haggard, GUIDANCE: 11;
   MODERATION: 20; TRUTH: 16
Haggard (of Bradenham, Co.
   Norfolk), SHINING: 22
Hague, SEASONS: 3
Haig (of Bemerside), FATE: 36
Haige, VIRTUE: 186
Haileybury College, U.K.,
   HAPPINESS: 66; SCHOOL MOTTOES: 307
Haines, WILL: 5
Hains (U.S.), ADVERSITY: 85;
   STEADFASTNESS: 139; WILL: 5
Haire, DIVINITY: 269; TRUST: 71
Hairstanes, FIDELITY: 312
Halcrow, RISK: 11
Halden, SUFFERING: 10
Hale, LEADERSHIP: 6
Hale, Landon, TRUTH: 114
Hale U. D. C., U.K., LOCAL
   GOVERNMENT: 20; POWER: 1
Hales, LOCAL GOVERNMENT: 402;
   STATE MOTTOES: 61; STRENGTH: 184;
   UNITY: 122
Halesowen B.C., U.K., LOCAL
   GOVERNMENT: 309; TIME: 47
Halford, ACTION: 25; GLORY: 38, 39;
   SILENCE: 12, 13; VIRTUE: 278
Halford (Bt.), HUMILITY: 7
Haliburton, ASPIRATION: 56

Halifax C. B. C., U.K., DIVINE
   GUIDANCE: 231; LOCAL
   GOVERNMENT: 109

Halkerston, ADVERSITY: 31

Halket, HONESTY: 15

Halket (Bt.), FAITH: 113; HONESTY: 13

Halket (co. Warwick), FAITH: 113

Halkett, HONESTY: 13

Halkett (co. Fife), FAITH: 113

Hall, ADVERSITY: 60; ASPIRATION: 64;
   DILIGENCE: 48; FORCE: 4, 42;
   FORTITUDE: 6; HONOR: 8;
   INDUSTRIOUSNESS: 9; LIFE: 49; LOCAL
   GOVERNMENT: 18; PEACE: 7;
   PERSEVERANCE: 61; PREPAREDNESS: 3;
   REST: 19; TRUTH: 175; WAR: 5

Hall (Bt.), DESPAIR: 8; REST: 3

Hall of Farnham Castle, Hampshire,
   England, FAITH: 11; HOME: 3

Hall (of Grappenhall), FINISH: 7

Hall (of Jamaica), MEMORY: 24

Halliday, HEALING and HEALTH: 26

Hallyday, VIRTUE: 413

Halsey, WORDS: 28

Haltemprice U. D. C., U.K.,
   ASPIRATION: 49; LOCAL
   GOVERNMENT: 168

Halyburton (of Pitcur, Newmains,
   etc.), VIGILANCE: 115

Hamborough, HONOR: 65

Hambrough (of Steephill Castle, Isle of
   Wight), FORESIGHT: 2; HONOR: 66

Hamburgh Merchants, DIVINE
   GUIDANCE: 184

Hamerton (of Hellifield),
   ADVERSITY: 22; STEADFASTNESS: 56

Hamilto, ADVERSITY: 19; FIDELITY: 120

Hamilton, AGGRESSION: 13;
ANCESTRY: 12; COUNTRY: 41, 55;
COURAGE: 108, 139, 140;
COURTESY: 4; DEATH: 90;
DEDICATION: 10; DEFENSE: 31;
DILIGENCE: 58; DIVINE GIFTS: 11;
FIDELITY: 137, 184; FLORA: 11;
FLOURISHING: 70, 88, 95; FORCE: 17;
FORTITUDE: 22; FORTUNE: 91;
GRATITUDE: 15; GROWTH: 6, 22;
GUILT: 4; HONOR: 64, 178;
HOPE: 124; IMPROVEMENT: 31;
LAW: 4; LIBERTY: 106;
PERSEVERANCE: 76, 80;
PREPAREDNESS: 54; STATUS: 4;
STRENGTH: 2; TRUST: 19;
UNCLASSIFIED: 56; VIRTUE: 200, 201;
VISION: 8; WAY: 4; WORTHINESS: 39
Hamilton (Co. Meath, etc.),
ADVANCE: 56
Hamilton (D.), ADVANCE: 56
Hamilton (of Abbotstown),
CONSISTENCY: 7
Hamilton (of Bangour),
ENDURANCE: 36
Hamilton (of Barns, Scotland),
FIDELITY: 87
Hamilton (of Binning), DIVINE
GUIDANCE: 425
Hamilton (of Brecon, bt.),
ADVANCE: 56
Hamilton (of Cairness), FAITH: 179
Hamilton (of Colquot), LOVE: 105
Hamilton (of Daichmont),
FIDELITY: 243
Hamilton (of Dalziel), REST: 25;
SHADE: 8
Hamilton (of Edinburgh), RISK: 3
Hamilton (of Kilbrackmont),
FLOURISHING: 17
Hamilton (of Little Ernock),
COURAGE: 164
Hamilton (of Mount Hamilton),
COURAGE: 4; PRUDENCE: 1
Hamilton (of Preston), COUNTRY: 100;
PATRIOTISM: 46
Hamilton (of Rosehill), NAVIGATION: 2
Hamilton (of Silverston, bt.),
ADVANCE: 56
Hamilton (of Silverton), NOBILITY: 22;
VIRTUE: 185

Hamilton (of Somelston),
DECEPTION: 5
Hamilton (of the Mount, Co.
Middlesex, bt.), ADVANCE: 56
Hamilton (of Udstoun), FIDELITY: 327
Hamilton (of Westburn), VIRTUE: 46;
WEAPONS: 35
Hamilton (of Westport), STRENGTH: 1
Hamilton (of Woodbrook, bt.),
ADVANCE: 56; PROPER NAMES: 3
Hamilton-Tyndal-Bruce, FIDELITY: 25
Hamlet, DIVINE GUIDANCE: 74
Hamlyn, CAUTION: 15
Hammersley, HONOR: 81; LOVE: 56
Hammersmith B. C., U.K., DEEDS: 87;
LOCAL GOVERNMENT: 360
Hammerton, INTEGRITY: 10; SCHOOL
MOTTOES: 94
Hammick (Bt.), PRAISE: 5
Hammond, PERSEVERANCE: 74
Hamond (Bt.), FIDELITY: 246;
PREPAREDNESS: 47
Hamond (of St. Albans Court),
PATRIOTISM: 65; ROYALTY: 81
Hampden, STEADFASTNESS: 143
Hampson (Bt.), PRESENT, THE: 7
Hampstead B. C., U.K., LOCAL
GOVERNMENT: 252;
UNSELFISHNESS: 18
Hampton, DIVINE GIFTS: 3; ROYALTY: 1
Hanbury, REWARD: 20
Hancock (U.S.), PRINCELINESS: 7
Hancocks, TIME: 43
Handcock, LOCAL GOVERNMENT: 397;
VIGILANCE: 103
Handfield, JUSTICE: 88
Handley, FAIRNESS: 7
Handyside, COURAGE: 155;
GENEROSITY: 13
Hanercroft, FAITH: 255; HOPE: 294;
TRADITION: 7
Hanford, DEATH: 45; MEMORY: 19
Hanger, ART: 10
Hankinson, COURAGE: 228;
STRENGTH: 162
Hanman, ADVERSITY: 60;
ASPIRATION: 64
Hanmer, HONOR: 46
Hannay, HOPE: 17; INCREASE: 10
Hannay (Bt.), ADVERSITY: 60;
ASPIRATION: 64

Hannibal-LaGrange College,
Hannibal, Missouri,
KNOWLEDGE: 35; SCHOOL
MOTTOES: 154; SERVICE: 28

Hanover College, Hanover, Indiana,
PIETY: 15; SCHOOL MOTTOES: 223;
WISDOM: 48

Hanoverian Guelphic Order,
ADVERSITY: 47

Hanrott, PERSEVERANCE: 56; STATE
MOTTOES: 40

Hansard, WAR: 29

Hansler (of Eastwood),
INDUSTRIOUSNESS: 176; WISDOM: 69

Hansom (U.S.), VIRTUE: 187

Hanson, OBEDIENCE: 14; VIRTUE: 182,
186

Hapgood (U.S.), FRUIT: 6

Hara, REPUTATION: 10; VIRTUE: 374

Harben, STRENGTH: 136

Harberton (V.), COURAGE: 265;
FORTUNE: 117

Harborne, DIVINE GUIDANCE: 132;
INDUSTRIOUSNESS: 26

Harboro, EQUANIMITY: 3

Harcourt, DEEDS: 52; WORDS: 20

Harcourt (of Aukerwycke),
PROSPERITY: 21

Hardcastle, DIVINE GUIDANCE: 139

Hardenbrook (U.S.), GIFTS and
GIVING: 15

Hardie, AUDACITY: 96; COURAGE: 203

Harding, AUDACITY: 25; ENDURANCE: 5

Harding (of Petherton, b.),
VIGILANCE: 89

Harding University, Searcy, Arkansas,
KNOWLEDGE: 91; LIBERTY: 115;
SCHOOL MOTTOES: 340; TRUTH: 106

Hardinge, ANCESTRY: 27; PROPER
NAMES: 42

Hardinge (Bt.), PROPER NAMES: 8

Hardinge (U.S.), VIGILANCE: 93

Hardinge (V.), ADMIRATION: 3;
EQUANIMITY: 11

Hardness, DIVINITY: 418; TRUST: 101

Hardress, COURAGE: 135; SILENCE: 9

Hardwicke (E.), DESIRE: 13; FEAR: 36;
MODERATION: 23

Hardy, DIVINITY: 399; HOPE: 245

Hare, PROFANITY: 2;
STEADFASTNESS: 17; VIGILANCE: 9

Hare (Bt.), INTEGRITY: 31

Hare (of Docking, Co. Norfolk),
CHRIST, JESUS: 72; SALVATION: 40

Harewood (E.), SALVATION: 31

Hargreaves, COUNTRY: 140;
FORTITUDE: 10; LOVE: 117;
PATRIOTISM: 93; PRUDENCE: 22

Harison (U.S.), SELF-RELIANCE: 10

Harker, ASSISTANCE: 2; LISTENING: 2

Harkness, DIVINITY: 221; HOPE: 73

Harland, ADVERSITY: 68;
STEADFASTNESS: 22

Harland (Bt.), FORTITUDE: 25

Harland (Co. York), ADVERSITY: 10;
PERSEVERANCE: 10

Harley, COURAGE: 243; FAITH: 252

Harleyford, COUNTRY: 32;
DIVINITY: 181; ROYALTY: 40

Harleyford, Buckinghamshire,
England, OBEDIENCE: 4; PEACE: 67

Harlow Development Corp., U.K.,
INTER-RELATEDNESS: 2

Harnage (Bt.), CONFIDENCE: 10;
DIVINE GUIDANCE: 87; FIDELITY: 98

Harow School, U.K., SCHOOL
MOTTOES: 302

Harpenden U. D. C., U.K., FAITH: 65;
INDUSTRIOUSNESS: 42; LOCAL
GOVERNMENT: 125

Harpending (U.S.), GIFTS and GIVING: 9

Harper, COURAGE: 61; ENJOYMENT: 13;
GIFTS and GIVING: 27; PRAISE: 14

Harries, DIVINE GIFTS: 30;
INTEGRITY: 17; WORDS: 27

Harrington, SECURITY: 35

Harrington (Bt.), SECURITY: 35

Harrington (E.), DIVINE GIFTS: 3;
ROYALTY: 1

Harris, COUNTRY: 136; DIVINE
GUIDANCE: 314; DIVINITY: 286;
GOVERNMENT: 8; HOSPITALITY: 4;
INDUSTRIOUSNESS: 78;
MODERATION: 8; RELIGION: 18;
SECURITY: 23; TRUTH: 37;
UNCLASSIFIED: 21; VIRTUE: 182, 186

Harris (B.), PATRIOTISM: 19;
PRINCELINESS: 6

Harrison, CONQUEST: 51;
COURAGE: 273; ENDURANCE: 58;
FEAR: 53; FRIENDSHIP: 7;
LIVELINESS: 9; PRIDE: 17;
PROVIDENCE: 6; PRUDENCE: 35;
REVERENCE: 3

Hawtin, HONOR: 109; REWARD: 11

Hawtyn, HONOR: 109; REWARD: 11

Haxton, REBIRTH: 30

Hay, CONQUEST: 12; COURAGE: 196; DESPAIR: 5; DILIGENCE: 29; DIVINITY: 144, 395; GENEROSITY: 16; GROWTH: 4; HOPE: 214; OBEDIENCE: 12; REBIRTH: 23; REWARD: 17; RISK: 9; STRENGTH: 36, 69; UNITY: 37

Hay (Bt.), COUNTRY: 100; PATRIOTISM: 46

Hay (of Cardenie), HONOR: 49

Hay (of Glenluce, bt.), SERVICE: 48

Hay (of Leith), PREPAREDNESS: 37

Hay (of Lethim), FAITH: 53

Hay (of Leys, Co. Perth), ORIGIN: 7

Hay (of Linplum), EVIL: 3

Hay (of Locheloy), SERVICE: 49

Hay (of London), STRENGTH: 157

Hay (of Park, bt.), SERVICE: 48

Hay (of Woodcockdale), INCREASE: 18

Haydon, FAITH: 52

Hayes, AUDACITY: 3

Hayes and Harlington U. D. C., U.K., IMPROVEMENT: 13; LOCAL GOVERNMENT: 160

Hayes (Bt.), DIVINE GUIDANCE: 181

Hayman (of South Abbey), PARADISE: 8

Haynes, NAVIGATION: 4

Hayter, FORCE: 24

Hazard, SINCERITY: 16

Hazlerigge (Bt.), HOME: 19; RELIGION: 19

Head (Bt.), KNOWLEDGE: 82; SILENCE: 20

Headfort (M.), SUCCESS: 2

Headlam, INNOCENCE: 10; MIND: 19

Headley (B.), COURAGE: 247

Heald, CROSS, THE: 77; GLORY: 35

Heard, RECTITUDE: 61; SALVATION: 35; WISDOM: 55

Hearne, LAW: 17

Heart, FIDELITY: 94; LOVE: 49

Heath, HOPE: 52

Heath (Bt.), INDUSTRIOUSNESS: 66; REWARD: 15

Heathcoat-Amory (Bt.), LOVE: 16

Heathcote, DEEDS: 35; DIVINE GUIDANCE: 151; HOPE: 58

Heathcote-Amory, LOVE: 16

Heathcote-Drummond-Willoughby, FIDELITY: 231

Heaton, FORTIFICATIONS: 2; WAR: 5

Heaton-Ellis, AUDACITY: 52; FIDELITY: 172

Heaven, IMMORTALITY: 8

Hebbert, BRIGHTNESS: 2; FIDELITY: 309; PERSEVERANCE: 83

Hebden (of Appleton), WORTHINESS: 58

Heber (Co. York), PREPAREDNESS: 56

Heddle, COURAGE: 247

Hedwig Sophie, Landgravine of Hesse-Cassel (1623–83), HONOR: 134; VIRTUE: 103

Heignie, FIDELITY: 165; STEADFASTNESS: 46

Heinrich, Count Reuss zu Schleiz (1563–1616), SECURITY: 32

Heinrich, Duke of Braunschweig and Danneberg (1533–98), DIVINITY: 23

Heinrich, Duke of Saxony (d. 1585), DIVINITY: 112

Heinrich, Duke of Saxony-Römhild (1650–1710); Caldicote, DIVINE GUIDANCE: 405

Heinrich II, Count Reuss (1575–1639), BLESSING: 2; DIVINE GUIDANCE: 20

Heinrich II, Duke of Münsterberg (1507–48), BRIGHTNESS: 10

Heinrich II, the Younger, Duke of Braunschweig-Wolfenbüttel (1489–1568), DIVINE GUIDANCE: 291; RIGHTEOUSNESS: 6, 11

Heinrich III, Count Reuss (1578–1616), DIVINE GUIDANCE: 284; GRACE: 15

Heinrich Julius, Duke of Braunschweig-Wolfenbüttel (1564–1613), CHRIST, JESUS: 21; COUNTRY: 40, 102; DEATH: 44; DIVINE GUIDANCE: 21; DIVINITY: 165; ENDURANCE: 57; ENVY: 4; EVIL: 5; FAITH: 208; FATE: 9; HOME: 18; HONOR: 63; HOPE: 266; HOSPITALITY: 2; INDUSTRIOUSNESS: 175; INTEGRITY: 26; JUSTICE: 40; PATRIOTISM: 48; REST: 24; SUFFERING: 3; TRUTH: 68, 146; UNITY: 99; VICTORY: 49

Heinrich Julius, Duke of
Braunschweig-Wolfenbüttel
(1564–1613); abbreviated form, D.
C. S. C., used by Julius Ernst, Duke
of Braunschweig-Lüneburg-
Danneberg (1571–1636),
OPPOSITION: 4

Heinrich Posthumus (1572–1635),
RIGHTEOUSNESS: 13; USEFULNESS: 6

Heinrich Posthumus, Count Reuss
(1572–1635), DIVINITY: 222

Heinrich the Pious, Duke of Saxony
(1473–1541), DIVINE GUIDANCE: 111;
SCRIPTURES: 16

Heinrich V, Count Reuss (1602–67),
COURAGE: 207; SELF-CONTROL: 10

Heinrich VIII, Count Reuss
(1652–1711), PIETY: 21; VIRTUE: 141

Heinrich X, Count Reuss (1662–1711),
PIETY: 19; PRUDENCE: 37

Helham, SERVICE: 33; UBIQUITY: 6

Hellier, PATRIOTISM: 72

Helme, PROTECTION: 4; VIRTUE: 21

Helps, GUIDANCE: 2

Helyer, INDUSTRIOUSNESS: 84; REST: 8

Hemel Hempstead Development
Corp., U.K., GREATNESS: 5

Hemming, VIRTUE: 2

Hemphill (B.), FIDELITY: 47

Hemsworth (of Shropham, co.
Norfolk), HANDS: 23; HOSTILITY: 13

Henderson, DANGER: 18;
DECEPTION: 11; NOBILITY: 20, 29;
SECURITY: 54; TRANSIENCE: 16;
VIRTUE: 295, 335

Henderson (Bt.), NOBILITY: 23;
VIRTUE: 189

Hendon B. C., U.K., EFFORT: 9;
LOCAL GOVERNMENT: 102

Heneage, STEADFASTNESS: 36

Heneage (of Hainton), STRENGTH: 146

Henley, PERSEVERANCE: 56; STATE
MOTTOES: 40; VIRTUE: 182

Henley (B.), PRUDENCE: 81

Henn, DIVINITY: 187

Hennessy, FORCE: 45; WEAPONS: 104

Hennidge, DIVINE GUIDANCE: 80;
LOCAL GOVERNMENT: 84

Henniker (B.), DIVINITY: 111;
EXCELLENCE: 11

Henrison, NOBILITY: 34; VIRTUE: 339

Henry, FIDELITY: 137

Henry Chadwick, (re. baseball),
HONESTY: 27

Henry Ford, MANNER: 2

Henry IV of Navarre, COURAGE: 3

Henry VIII., SECURITY: 1

Henshaw, ADVERSITY: 63

Henslowe, COURTESY: 3

Henvill, NOBILITY: 28; VIRTUE: 272

Henville, NOBILITY: 35; VIRTUE: 351

Henzey, DIVINE GUIDANCE: 400

Hepburn, EXPECTATION: 5;
PRUDENCE: 85; SIZE: 4; TRUST: 78;
VIRTUE: 384

Hepburn (Bt.), TRUST: 79

Hepburn (of Colquhalzie), TRUST: 81

Hepburn (of Smeaton, Bt.), REBIRTH: 5

Heppesley, COUNTRY: 57;
PATRIOTISM: 25

Hepworth (of Pontefract),
FIDELITY: 218

Herbert, FORTITUDE: 2, 10;
PRUDENCE: 22; SERVICE: 71;
STEADFASTNESS: 26

Herbert (of Llanarth Court),
CONSCIENCE: 2; DEFENSE: 5

Herbertstone, DIVINITY: 117; HOPE: 28

Hereford City Council, U.K.,
FIDELITY: 205; LOCAL
GOVERNMENT: 197

Hereford (E.), FIDELITY: 206

Hereford (V.), ENVY: 16

Herefordshire C. C., U.K., DIVINE
GIFTS: 48; LOCAL GOVERNMENT: 300

Hereford(V.), FIDELITY: 21; VIRTUE: 20

Heriot, FIDELITY: 320; MIND: 13, 14

Herklott, DEFENSE: 19

Hermann Fortunatus, Margrave of
Baden-Rodemachern (1596–1664),
DEATH: 78; STEADFASTNESS: 101

Hermon, FEAR: 17; TRUST: 38

Hern, or Heron, COURAGE: 39

Herne, MODERATION: 33; RELIGION: 33

Herne Bay U. D. C., U.K.,
ADVERSITY: 50; LOCAL
GOVERNMENT: 236

Heron, COURAGE: 172; DESPAIR: 5

Heron (Bt.), ASPIRATION: 33; BIRDS: 7;
DESPAIR: 5

Herrick, NOBILITY: 32; VIRTUE: 299

Herries, UNCLASSIFIED: 64

Herschel (Bt.), EXPLORATION: 1

Hertford B. C., U.K., FAITH: 188;
FUTURE, THE: 21; LOCAL
GOVERNMENT: 284; PRESENT,
THE: 10; PRIDE: 10
Hertford (M.), FIDELITY: 94; LOVE: 49
Hertford R. D. C., U.K.,
COUNTRY: 115; LOCAL
GOVERNMENT: 296
Hertslet, FATE: 12; VIRTUE: 54
Hervey (Bt.), MEMORY: 12
Hervey (of Killiane), MEMORY: 12
Hervie, RISING: 5
Hesketh, DEEDS: 77
Hesketh (of Gwyrch Castle), Neate,
DIVINITY: 242
Hesse, LISTENING: 3; SILENCE: 21;
WISDOM: 64
Heston and Isleworth B. C., U.K.,
LOCAL GOVERNMENT: 386;
STRENGTH: 153; UNITY: 103
Hewetson, ABILITY: 1; HANDS: 1;
WORDS: 25
Hewett (Bt.), LIMITATION: 5
Hewitson, CAUTION: 29
Hewitt, DARKNESS: 1; FAITH: 39;
FEAR: 3; JUSTICE: 9; LIFE: 5;
LIGHT: 2; LIMITATION: 5; LOCAL
GOVERNMENT: 45
Hewitt (Co. Glamorgan), FAITH: 239
Hewlett, DIVINE GUIDANCE: 362
Hewson, DIVINITY: 325; LIGHT: 63, 64
Hewson (of Emusmore), LIGHT: 63
Heyes (Co. Chester), DEEDS: 43
Heygate (Bt.), PROPER NAMES: 12
Heyrick, NOBILITY: 32; VIRTUE: 299
Heytesbury (B.), INDUSTRIOUSNESS: 52
Heywood, MEASURE: 8
Heywood B. C., U.K., LOFTINESS: 3
Heywood (Bt.), LOFTINESS: 3
Hibbert, FAITH: 81
Hickman, ANCESTRY: 38;
FIDELITY: 312; PERSEVERANCE: 74
Hickman (Bt.), FIRE: 7
Hicks, GIFTS and GIVING: 14;
PROVIDENCE: 1
Hicks (Bt.), TIME: 69
Hicks (of Watton, Co. Norfolk),
TIME: 69
Hicks (U.S.), COMMERCE: 5;
CROWN: 26; JUDGMENT: 8; LAW: 49;
LIBERTY: 94
Hickson, FAITH: 61; FORTITUDE: 3

Hide, DIVINE GIFTS: 26; LOCAL
GOVERNMENT: 90; TRANQUILLITY: 3
Higga, PEACE: 64
Higginbotham, PURPOSE: 5
Higginbottom, NOURISHMENT: 8
Higgins, COUNTRY: 77, 100, 107;
DEFENSE: 49, 52; FIDELITY: 86;
PATRIOTISM: 37, 46, 55; VIRTUE: 117,
160
Higginson, DEATH: 40; DISGRACE: 10
High Wycombe, INDUSTRIOUSNESS: 64
Highgate School, U.K., DIVINE
GUIDANCE: 17; SCHOOL MOTTOES: 11
Highland Light Infantry, EFFORT: 1
Hill, ACCEPTANCE: 3;
ACCOMPLISHMENT: 11, 12; DIVINE
GUIDANCE: 368; FEAR: 11;
HONOR: 84; INDUSTRIOUSNESS: 56;
INTEGRITY: 10; KNOWLEDGE: 47;
PROSPERITY: 48; RECTITUDE: 20;
SCHOOL MOTTOES: 94; STATUS: 8;
TRUSTWORTHINESS: 1; TRUTH: 140;
WEAPONS: 79
Hill (Bt.), ACCOMPLISHMENT: 12;
ADVANCE: 5; NOBILITY: 22;
VIRTUE: 185
Hill (of Edinburgh), TRUTH: 139
Hill (of Gressenhall Hall, co. Norfolk),
HOPE: 184
Hill (of Oxon), FIDELITY: 110
Hillary, VIRTUE: 403
Hillary (Bt.), COURAGE: 263
Hillas, POSSESSION: 20; WEAPONS: 80
Hillasdon, REASON: 24
Hills, FAITH: 104; PARADISE: 30;
TRUST: 44
Hillyard, MEASURE: 5
Hilton, POSSIBILITY: 11
Hinckley U. D. C., U.K., FEELINGS: 1;
LOCAL GOVERNMENT: 25
Hincks (of Breckenbrough), CROSS,
THE: 59; HOPE: 90
Hind, COURAGE: 81; FIDELITY: 179
Hinde, ASSISTANCE: 17; DIVINITY: 314;
KINDNESS: 15; LOCAL
GOVERNMENT: 243; SECURITY: 74;
STRENGTH: 149
Hindley U. D. C., U.K., LOCAL
GOVERNMENT: 290; SERVICE: 40
Hindmarsh, COUNTRY: 52;
PATRIOTISM: 21
Hinds, DIVINITY: 41

Hine, HONOR: 55; SECURITY: 38

Hines (U.S.), NOURISHMENT: 2

Hippisley (Bt.), FRIENDSHIP: 5;
VIRTUE: 11

Hippisley (Co. Berks, Bt.),
COUNTRY: 54; PATRIOTISM: 23

Hirst, FLOURISHING: 12

Hislop (Bt.), PROPER NAMES: 29

Hitch, ANCESTRY: 1

Hitchin U. D. C., U.K., ANCESTRY: 15;
LOCAL GOVERNMENT: 106

Hives, INDUSTRIOUSNESS: 70;
RECTITUDE: 30

Hoadly, COUNTRY: 137; TRUTH: 119

Hoare, HONOR: 27; HOPE: 35;
LOFTINESS: 12; STATE MOTTOES: 11

Hoare (Bt.), HONOR: 27; HOPE: 35;
STATE MOTTOES: 11; TIME: 71

Hoare (of Cork, Dunmanway,
Annabella, Factory-Hill, etc., all in
the county of Cork, Ireland),
TIME: 71

Hobart, GIFTS and GIVING: 5

Hobhouse, CHANGE: 11

Hoblyn, ENJOYMENT: 5; LIBERTY: 109;
REST: 28

Hobson, FORTITUDE: 6

Hockin, DIVINITY: 219

Hodder, CONQUEST: 15, 27

Hodge, KNOWLEDGE: 63; POWER: 20

Hodges, EVIL: 1; HUMILITY: 4;
LIGHT: 7; SELF-KNOWLEDGE: 10

Hodges (of Hemsted), FORESIGHT: 5

Hodges (U.S.), INCREASE: 4

Hodgeson, FEAR: 34; PROSPERITY: 25

Hodgetts, TRUST: 8

Hodgkinson, DIVINITY: 379; LOCAL
GOVERNMENT: 332

Hodgson, ASSISTANCE: 17; BIRDS: 17;
DIVINITY: 144; KINDNESS: 15;
PEACE: 14

Hodilow, DIVINITY: 28

Hodson (Bt.), LOVE: 99; PEACE: 46

Hoey, FIDELITY: 148; FORTUNE: 26

Hoffman, TRUTH: 96

Hofstra University School of Law,
Hempstead, New York,
MAINTENANCE: 3; SCHOOL
MOTTOES: 148

Hog, GLORY: 11

Hogan, SPEED: 30

Hogart, COURAGE: 199

Hogarth, STRENGTH: 14; TRUTH: 7

Hogg, 2Hogue, GLORY: 11

Holborn B. C., U.K., KNOWLEDGE: 51;
LOCAL GOVERNMENT: 234

Holburne (Bt.), HONOR: 21; VIRTUE: 37

Holburton, DIVINE GUIDANCE: 359;
INDUSTRIOUSNESS: 150

Holden, MODERATION: 24;
POSSESSION: 6; UNCLASSIFIED: 27

Holdich (of Mardwell, co.
Northampton), FORTUNE: 104

Hole, HONOR: 109; REWARD: 11

Holford (of Buckland), FIDELITY: 312

Holl, INTEGRITY: 18

Holland, CONQUEST: 69; JUSTICE: 29;
PEACE: 15; TIME: 22, 48

Holland (B.), SACRIFICE: 1; TRUTH: 19

Holles, COUNTRY: 139; LOVE: 116;
PATRIOTISM: 92

Hollingsworth, CONSISTENCY: 9;
LIGHT: 36; LOCAL GOVERNMENT: 338

Hollingworth (of Hollingworth),
ENDURANCE: 14

Hollis, HOPE: 234

Hollist, CONSERVATION: 5; RUNNING: 1

Holloway, DIVINE GIFTS: 5; LIGHT: 1

Holloway (U.S.), DIVINITY: 78;
LIGHT: 9

Holme, DIVINITY: 178

Holme (of Paull-Holme),
FLOURISHING: 46

Holmes, ANCESTRY: 3; JUSTICE: 80;
PURPOSE: 10; UNCLASSIFIED: 78

Holmes (U.S.), ORDER: 7;
STRENGTH: 99

Holt, DESIRE: 21; HEALING and
HEALTH: 38

Holte (of Erdington), EXALTATION: 3;
HUMILITY: 3

Holyoke (U.S.), FOLLOWING: 2

Homan (Bt.), BEING, SELF: 1

Homan (Bt.), Mann, Manns,
HOSTILITY: 7

Home, FIDELITY: 322

Home (Bt.), FINISH: 16

Home (E.), FIDELITY: 322; HOME: 1

Home (of Kames), TRUTH: 84

Home (of Staines), VIRTUE: 365

Home of the French architect, Puget,
in Marseilles, France,
INDUSTRIOUSNESS: 145

Home (of Wedderburn), MEMORY: 23

House in Stoke Bishop, Gloucestershire, England, HOME: 21

House near Cheltenham, Gloucestershire, England, INDUSTRIOUSNESS: 131

the house of John Knox, Edinburgh, Scotland, LOVE: 87

House of Rossini, Bologna, Italy, HOME: 14

Houston, DEEDS: 22; LOCAL GOVERNMENT: 97; SCHOOL MOTTOES: 143; TIME: 26

Houston (B.), SCHOOL MOTTOES: 143; TIME: 26

Hove B. C., U.K., FLOURISHING: 30; LOCAL GOVERNMENT: 141

How, DIVINITY: 431; JUSTICE: 86; PURPOSE: 12

Howales, ADVANCE: 19

Howard, COURAGE: 63; FAITH: 56, 184, 194; FEAR: 81; GIFTS and GIVING: 1; GOALS: 2; IMPROVEMENT: 39; REST: 4; VIRTUE: 334; WILLINGNESS: 12

Howard (Bt.), Wicklow (E.), SERVICE: 25

Howard de Walden (B.), MANNER: 6

Howard (of Corby Castle), VIRTUE: 186

Howard (of Effingham, b.), VIRTUE: 294

Howard (of Greystoke), VIRTUE: 186

Howden (B.), CONQUEST: 40; PROPER NAMES: 17; UNCLASSIFIED: 4

Howdon, DEFENSE: 19

Howe, DIVINITY: 431; TRUTH: 84

Howe (E.), POSSESSION: 11

Howell, COURAGE: 237; PERSEVERANCE: 56; STATE MOTTOES: 40

Howes (of Morningthorpe, Co. Norfolk), FORTUNE: 101

Howett, COURAGE: 12; PRUDENCE: 4

Howie, RISING: 5

Howison, ASPIRATION: 84; PROFANITY: 1

Howitt, AUDACITY: 26

Howlastone, ENJOYMENT: 10

Howman (of Bexwell, Co. Norfolk), TIMELINESS: 6

Howson, FIDELITY: 2

Howth (E.), THOUGHT: 21

Hoyle (Co. York), DEEDS: 38; WORDS: 9

Hoyle (of Denton Hall), EQUANIMITY: 2

Hubbard, ANIMALS: 10; VIGILANCE: 15

Hubbard (U.S.), PARADISE: 47; SUN: 7

Huddart, DIVINITY: 168

Huddersfield C. B. C., U.K., DILIGENCE: 40; DIVINE GUIDANCE: 325; LOCAL GOVERNMENT: 204

Huddleston (of Sawston), DIVINITY: 392

Huddlestone, ABILITY: 17; STRENGTH: 76

Hudson's Bay Company, HUNTING: 5

Hugar, COUNTRY: 135; LIBERTY: 117

Hugel (U.S.), RISK: 2

Huggard, HOPE: 106; PARADISE: 35

Hughan, SEA: 6; WORTHINESS: 8

Hughes, COURAGE: 265; DIVINE GUIDANCE: 10, 403; FORTUNE: 117; HOPE: 171; PROPER NAMES: 26; PROTECTION: 33

Hughes (of Alltwyd), ANIMALS: 61; AUDACITY: 103; RIGHTEOUSNESS: 20

Hughes (of Clapham), VIGILANCE: 63

Hughes (of Kinmel), DIVINITY: 218

Hughes (of Plas Coch), BIRDS: 14; DIVINE GUIDANCE: 224

Hughes (of Wexford), COUNTRY: 138; LOVE: 115; PATRIOTISM: 91

Hulburn, HONOR: 21; VIRTUE: 37

Hulton, MIND: 28

Hume, PERSEVERANCE: 55

Hume (Bt.), FIDELITY: 322

Hume (of Humewood), FIDELITY: 322

Humfrey, FUTURE, THE: 27

Humphery, DIVINE GUIDANCE: 152

Humphreys, HOPE: 153

Humphries (U.S.), PERSEVERANCE: 30

Humphry, PERSEVERANCE: 73

Hungerford, DIVINE GUIDANCE: 230

Hunt (of Co. Somerset), MIND: 8; NOBILITY: 4

Hunter, ABILITY: 6, 8; ACCOMPLISHMENT: 7; CONFIDENCE: 8; COURAGE: 24; DIVINE GUIDANCE: 172; ENJOYMENT: 18, 36; FLOURISHING: 19, 20; HONOR: 27; HOPE: 35; REBIRTH: 18; RUNNING: 4; SECURITY: 20; SPEED: 22; STATE MOTTOES: 11; STRENGTH: 166; VIGILANCE: 96

Hunt-Grubbe, JUSTICE: 87

Huntingdon (E.), HONOR: 77
Huntingdonshire C. C., U.K.,
   FLOURISHING: 54;
   INDUSTRIOUSNESS: 106; LOCAL
   GOVERNMENT: 210
Huntingfield (B.), JUSTICE: 21
Huntley, RECTITUDE: 36
Huntly (M.), LOCATION: 9
Hurd (U.S.), GOODNESS: 2
Hurley, CROSS, THE: 49
Hurry, PURITY: 19
Hurst, COURAGE: 229; STRENGTH: 165;
   TRADES: 41
Hurt, HUNTING: 4
Husdell, DIVINITY: 418; TRUST: 101
Huskinson, HOPE: 229
Huskisson, REST: 1, 33
Hussey, DEEDS: 93; FAITH: 234;
   MIND: 8; NOBILITY: 4; POSSESSION: 31;
   STRENGTH: 151
Hussey (Co. Dublin),
   STEADFASTNESS: 29
Hussey (Co. Sussex), POSSESSION: 31
Hussey (of Wood Walton, Co.
   Huntingdon), PROPER NAMES: 23
Hustler, ACCOMPLISHMENT: 4;
   ATTEMPT: 1
Huston-Tillotson College, Austin,
   Texas, SCHOOL MOTTOES: 145;
   STRENGTH: 84; UNITY: 44
Hustwick (of Hull), DIVINITY: 336
Hutchins, COURAGE: 48
Hutchinson, ASPIRATION: 83;
   AUDACITY: 56; FIDELITY: 181;
   PARADISE: 4; STARS: 35;
   STEADFASTNESS: 30; SUCCESS: 5;
   WISDOM: 67
Hutchinson (Bt.), CROSS, THE: 55
Hutchinson (of Edinburgh),
   ATTENTIVENESS: 6
Hutchinson (of Whitton),
   HUMANITY: 8; MANLINESS: 3
Hutchinson (U.S.), ADVANCE: 44;
   SUCCESS: 9
Hutchison, INDUSTRIOUSNESS: 179;
   KNOWLEDGE: 68; RISING: 14
Hutchon, LOCAL GOVERNMENT: 154;
   STRENGTH: 56; TRUTH: 27
Huth, MIND: 4
Hutton, DIVINE GUIDANCE: 155;
   HOPE: 215

Hutton (of Marske), LIFE: 26;
   SPIRIT: 14; WEAPONS: 91
Huxley, DIVINITY: 245
Hyatt, DEEDS: 35; HOPE: 58
Hyde, STRENGTH: 126; TRUTH: 15
Hyde B. C., U.K., IMPROVEMENT: 29;
   LOCAL GOVERNMENT: 263
Hyett, STEADFASTNESS: 29
Hymers College, Hull, U.K., SCHOOL
   MOTTOES: 126; WORTHINESS: 16
Hynde, MERCY: 23
Hyndman, FIDELITY: 321
Hynes, STRENGTH: 147
Hyslop, GROWTH: 11

I

Ibbetson (Bt.), LEADERSHIP: 26;
   LIBERTY: 135
Ilbert (Co. Devon), FLORA: 26;
   IRONY: 2
Ilchester (E.), DEEDS: 43
Ilford B. C., U.K., LOCAL
   GOVERNMENT: 194; UNITY: 45
Iliff (of Newington Butts), LIFE: 49
Ilkeston B. C., INDUSTRIOUSNESS: 116;
   LOCAL GOVERNMENT: 211; SCHOOL
   MOTTOES: 161; STATE MOTTOES: 26
Illidge, BIRDS: 5; STATUS: 1
Illinois Wesleyan University,
   Bloomington, Illinois,
   KNOWLEDGE: 72; SCHOOL
   MOTTOES: 275; WISDOM: 90
Imbrie, AGRICULTURE: 2
Imry, DESPAIR: 5
Inchbold, FAME: 19
Independence Community College,
   Independence, Kansas,
   KNOWLEDGE: 92; SCHOOL
   MOTTOES: 341; TRUTH: 107;
   WISDOM: 101
Independent Company of Cadets,
   Prince William County, Virginia,
   LIBERTY: 4
Indian River Community College, Ft.
   Pierce, Florida, FELLOWSHIP: 2;
   KNOWLEDGE: 20; LEADERSHIP: 11;
   SCHOOL MOTTOES: 92
Indiana Northern Graduate School of
   Professional Management,
   INTEGRITY: 16; SCHOOL
   MOTTOES: 141

Indiana University, Division of Allied Health Sciences, Bloomington, Indiana, KNOWLEDGE: 16; SCHOOL MOTTOES: 85; SERVICE: 15

Indiana Vocational Technical College, OPPORTUNITY: 13; SCHOOL MOTTOES: 333

Infantleroy, OFFSPRING: 2

Ingersoll (U.S.), FAME: 10; VIRTUE: 53

Ingilby (Bt.), RECTITUDE: 46

Ingledew, LIGHT: 12

Inglis, DARKNESS: 5; DIVINITY: 314; LIGHT: 26; LOCAL GOVERNMENT: 243; MERCY: 11

Inglis (Bt.), ANGER: 5; ANIMALS: 39; JUSTICE: 109; NOBILITY: 10; SECURITY: 48

Inglis (of Stewart, Buchanan, etc.), ANGER: 5; ANIMALS: 39; NOBILITY: 10

Ingoldsby, CONFIDENCE: 11; FIDELITY: 152

Ingram, COURAGE: 260; GREATNESS: 2

Innes, CAUTION: 35; DECORATION: 3; ENJOYMENT: 12; FIDELITY: 23; GIFTS and GIVING: 20; HONESTY: 22; HONOR: 116; INDUSTRIOUSNESS: 31, 139, 169; LEADERSHIP: 16; POWER: 18; PRUDENCE: 67; SECURITY: 64; STARS: 52; VIRTUE: 248, 344

Innes (Bt.), ANCESTRY: 16; EXCELLENCE: 14; FIDELITY: 23

Innes (of Edinburgh), FIDELITY: 70

Innes (of Innes), FIDELITY: 24

Innholders' Company, HOPE: 68

The Inquisition, JUDGMENT: 3

Interdenominational Theological Center, Atlanta, Georgia, CHRIST, JESUS: 64; SCHOOL MOTTOES: 209

International Fine Arts College, Miami, Florida, ART: 18; HONOR: 100; SCHOOL MOTTOES: 131

Inverarity, FLOURISHING: 68

Inwards, ENVY: 6

Iona College, New Rochelle, New York, SCHOOL MOTTOES: 36; WAR: 11

Irby, FIDELITY: 193; HONOR: 98, 113; REWARD: 9, 13; VIRTUE: 81

Ireland, LOVE: 19; PEACE: 2

Ireton, DEEDS: 51

Ironmongers' Company, DIVINE GUIDANCE: 270; ENDURANCE: 4

Ironside, CONQUEST: 19

Irton (of Irton), FIDELITY: 285

Irvine, ADVERSITY: 53; COUNTRY: 12; DIVINE GUIDANCE: 37; DIVINITY: 48; EARTH: 16; ENDURANCE: 31; FAITH: 17, 92; FIRE: 15; FLOURISHING: 80; GREATNESS: 2; INCREASE: 25; MODERATION: 18; ROYALTY: 11; SHADE: 4, 10, 11; SPIRIT: 16; SUN: 6, 21, 22, 26; WATER: 17

Irvine (Bt.), SELF-KNOWLEDGE: 5

Irvine (of Artamford), FLOURISHING: 81; SUN: 23

Irvine (of Cairnfield), ENDURANCE: 25

Irvine (of Inchray), ANCESTRY: 35

Irvine (of Kinconssie), COUNTRY: 13; DIVINITY: 49; ROYALTY: 12

Irvine (of Murthill), INCREASE: 25; SHADE: 11; SUN: 22

Irving, FLOURISHING: 80; SHADE: 10; STEADFASTNESS: 61; SUN: 21

Irwin (Co. Sligo), PROVOCATION: 2

Irwin (of Calder Abbey), STEADFASTNESS: 61

Irwine, FAIRNESS: 4; FLOURISHING: 80; SHADE: 10; SUN: 21

Isham (Bt.), BOASTFULNESS: 6; GLORY: 41; TRANSIENCE: 11

Isle of Man, RESULTS: 2

Isle of Wight, FAITH: 38

Isle of Wight C. C., U.K., BEAUTY: 1; DIVINITY: 14; LOCAL GOVERNMENT: 13

The Isle of Man, LOCAL GOVERNMENT: 362; STEADFASTNESS: 120

Islington B. C., U.K., DIVINITY: 116; LOCAL GOVERNMENT: 92

Isothermal Community College, Spindale, North Carolina, KNOWLEDGE: 21; REWARD: 5; SCHOOL MOTTOES: 93

Source Information

J

J. W. von Goethe, PERSEVERANCE: 43
Jack, SHADE: 7; SUN: 10
Jackson, ASPIRATION: 76; AUDACITY: 40,
  56; DIVINE GUIDANCE: 208;
  FIDELITY: 181; HONOR: 176;
  PRIMACY: 2; SPEED: 6;
  STRENGTH: 133; SUCCESS: 5;
  VIRTUE: 233
Jackson (Bt.), DEATH: 4; INNOCENCE: 8
Jackson (of Preston), DEATH: 40;
  DISGRACE: 10
Jackson (U.S.), HONESTY: 3
Jacob, PRIDE: 15; UNSELFISHNESS: 9
Jacob, Margrave of Baden-Hochberg
  (1562–90), DIVINE GUIDANCE: 413;
  RIGHTEOUSNESS: 3
Jacob Gimbel (1876–1943), merchant
  and philanthropist who devoted part
  of his wealth to the education of
  talented boys, STRENGTH: 9
Jacob (of Bromley), ACQUISITION: 5;
  DEFENSE: 39
Jacoby, DEEDS: 67; SHINING: 23
Jadewine, DIVINITY: 374
Jaffray, SUN: 10
Jafrey, SUN: 10
Jaggard, PRUDENCE: 57
Jamaica, NATIONAL MOTTOES: 21;
  UNITY: 58
James, COUNTRY: 140; DIVINE
  GUIDANCE: 115; FIDELITY: 93;
  FORTUNE: 21; INJURY: 7; LOVE: 62,
  117; PATRIOTISM: 93; PEACE: 4; SELF-
  KNOWLEDGE: 9
James (Bt.), COUNTRY: 100; LOVE: 65;
  PATRIOTISM: 46
James (Co. Kent), FIDELITY: 96
James (of Dublin, Bt.), COUNTRY: 88;
  DIVINITY: 346; ROYALTY: 63;
  STEADFASTNESS: 3
James (of Eltham), CONQUEST: 48
James (of Otterburn), DIVINITY: 87;
  TRUST: 27
James Otis, American patriot,
  LIBERTY: 136
Jameson, COURAGE: 204
Jamieson, DESTINATION: 2
Jane Seymour, 3rd wife of Henry
  VIII., OBEDIENCE: 5; SERVICE: 5

Janssen, DIVINITY: 162; HOPE: 47
Janvim, ROYALTY: 62
Jardin, HONOR: 41; VIGILANCE: 11;
  VIRTUE: 51
Jardine (Bt.), VIGILANCE: 11
Jarrett, FACTUALITY: 4
Jarrow B. C., U.K.,
  INDUSTRIOUSNESS: 103; LOCAL
  GOVERNMENT: 209
Jarvis (U.S.), SALVATION: 21;
  SERVICE: 23
Jary (of Burlingham), MIND: 25;
  RECTITUDE: 43
Jauncey (U.S.), VIRTUE: 168
Jay (U.S.), DIVINE GUIDANCE: 90;
  PERSEVERANCE: 11
Jayne (U.S.), HONOR: 83; JUSTICE: 41
Jean Jacques Rousseau (1712–1778),
  SACRIFICE: 9; TRUTH: 176
Jeanne d'Albret, mother of Henry IV
  of Navarre, COURAGE: 3
Jebb, HOPE: 180
Jefferay, DEEDS: 58
Jefferson (Co. York), CROSS, THE: 2;
  SALVATION: 2
Jeffery (U.S.), SECURITY: 26; TRUTH: 41
Jeffrey, DARKNESS: 14; LIGHT: 69
Jeffreys, HOPE: 283
Jeffries, FEAR: 11; RECTITUDE: 20
Jehangier, SHINING: 1
Jejeebhoy (Bt.), GENEROSITY: 9;
  INDUSTRIOUSNESS: 80
Jemmett, MODERATION: 11
Jenings (U.S.), HUMANITY: 4;
  MANLINESS: 2
Jenkins, FIDELITY: 154; PROPER
  NAMES: 35
Jenkins (of Bicton), ADVANCE: 45
Jenkinson (Bt.), OBEDIENCE: 10
Jenks (Bt.), HONOR: 20
Jenks (U.S.), AUDACITY: 15; CAUTION: 2
Jenner, PERSEVERANCE: 27;
  REWARD: 16
Jennings, ANIMALS: 60;
  CONSERVATION: 3; COURAGE: 279;
  USEFULNESS: 19
Jennings (of Hartwell), FUTURE,
  THE: 11
Jenyns, IDLENESS: 1
Jephson, FIDELITY: 226; SERVICE: 31;
  VIRTUE: 342
Jephson (Bt.), TRUTH: 127

Jerningham, GIFTS and GIVING: 1

Jerrney, DIVINE GUIDANCE: 140

Jersey (E.), CROSS, THE: 53; TRUTH: 23

Jervis, ACQUISITION: 9; FRIENDSHIP: 52; INTEGRITY: 42; UNCLASSIFIED: 69; VIRTUE: 371

Jervoise (Bt.), PRAISE: 15; VIRTUE: 447

Jesham, HANDS: 21

Jesson (of Oakwood), SILENCE: 3

Jessop, LOVE: 99; PEACE: 46

Jewell, ROYALTY: 119

Jewish Theological Seminary of America, New York City, New York, FIRE: 1; SCHOOL MOTTOES: 14

Jex-Blake, HEART: 2; PREPAREDNESS: 9

Joachim, Margrave of Brandenburg (1583–1600), CHRIST, JESUS: 17; FEAR: 26; FIDELITY: 49; HOPE: 12; SINCERITY: 3; WISDOM: 33

Joachim, Prince of Anhalt (1509–61), DIVINITY: 10

Joachim Ernst, Duke of Schleswig-Holstein (1595–1671), GLORY: 15

Joachim Ernst, Margrave of Brandenburg-Anspach (1583–1625), DIVINE GUIDANCE: 283

Joachim Ernst, Margrave of Brandenburg-Anspach (1583–1625); his son, DIVINE GUIDANCE: 107

Joachim Ernst, Prince of Anhalt (1592–1615), COURAGE: 146; DIVINE GUIDANCE: 243; HOPE: 115; SILENCE: 10

Joachim I, Elector of Brandenburg (1484–1535), JUDGMENT: 9

Joachim II, Elector of Brandenburg (1505–71), ROYALTY: 105

Joachim Karl, Duke of Braunschweig (1573–1615), PIETY: 14; TIME: 68; VICTORY: 49

Joass, LOVE: 38

Jobling, COUNTRY: 34; PATRIOTISM: 14

Jocelyn, DUTY: 11

Jockel, CONFIDENCE: 12; DILIGENCE: 36

Jodrell (Bt.), COUNTRY: 58; PATRIOTISM: 26

Johann, Duke of Braunschweig-Lüneburg (1583–1628), RIGHTEOUSNESS: 13; USEFULNESS: 6

Johann, Duke of Braunschweig-Lüneburg-Harburg (1573–1625), VIRTUE: 304; WEAPONS: 98

Johann, Duke of Holstein-Gottorp (1606–55), PROSPERITY: 60; VIRTUE: 209, 218

Johann, Duke of Saxony-Weimar (1570–1605), ABILITY: 22; DIVINE GUIDANCE: 200; LAW: 63; PEOPLE: 20; SCRIPTURES: 4; VIRTUE: 156

Johann, Duke of Schleswig-Holstein (1545–1622), DEATH: 107

Johann, Elector of Saxony (1467–1532), SCRIPTURES: 16

Johann, Margrave of Brandenburg (1597–1628), CHRIST, JESUS: 79; DEATH: 79; HOPE: 254; VIRTUE: 144

Johann, Prince of Anhalt-Zerbst (1621–67), CHRIST, JESUS: 15, 23

Johann Adolf, Duke of Schleswig-Holstein-Gottorp (1575–1616), LOCAL GOVERNMENT: 403; VIRTUE: 453

Johann Adolf, Duke of Schleswig-Holstein-Sonderburg-Plön (1634–1704), FIDELITY: 258; REBIRTH: 11; VIRTUE: 158

Johann Adolf I, Duke of Saxony-Weissenfels (1649–97), GLORY: 31; IMPROVEMENT: 33; SALVATION: 26

Johann Adolf II, Duke of Saxony-Weissenfels (1649–97), DIVINITY: 305; RIGHTEOUSNESS: 13; TRUST: 86; USEFULNESS: 6

Johann Albert II, Duke of Mecklenburg-Güstrow (1590–1636), DESIRE: 16

Johann August, Count of the Palatinate of Veldenz (1575–1611), FEAR: 26; WISDOM: 33

Johann Casimir, Count of the Palatinate of Lantern (1543–92), FIDELITY: 49; SINCERITY: 3

Johann Casimir, Duke of Saxony-Coburg (1564–1633), DEATH: 104; VIRTUE: 306

Johann Casimir, Prince of Anhalt-Dessau (1596–1660), FEAR: 63; FIDELITY: 49; SINCERITY: 3

Johann Christian, Duke of Brieg (1591–1639), DIVINE GUIDANCE: 15; PRESENT, THE: 2; TIME: 68

Source Information

Jones, CONSCIENCE: 2; DEATH: 60;
DEFENSE: 5; DESPAIR: 5;
DEVOTION: 2; DIVINE GUIDANCE: 70,
148, 453; DIVINITY: 96, 385;
FAITH: 174; FIDELITY: 77;
HAPPINESS: 71; HONOR: 40;
HOPE: 197; INTEGRITY: 20;
JUSTICE: 83; PAST, THE: 5;
PATRIOTISM: 53; PERSEVERANCE: 59;
PURPOSE: 11; REWARD: 60;
ROYALTY: 21, 72; STEADFASTNESS: 59;
TRUTH: 22; VIRTUE: 445

Jones (Co. Lancaster), FUTURE,
THE: 30; GOODNESS: 44

Jones College, Jacksonville, Florida,
LIBERTY: 124

Jones (Co. of Carmarthen),
DIVINITY: 147

Jones (Co. Salop, Bt.), SUN: 3

Jones (of Bealanamore), DIVINE
GUIDANCE: 128

Jones (of Cranmer Hall, Co. Norfolk,
bt.), ART: 23; COURAGE: 149; PROPER
NAMES: 37

Jones (of Hartsheath, co. Flint),
DIVINE GUIDANCE: 301

Jones (of Idrial), TRADITION: 3

Jones (of Thurston), HOPE: 34;
ORIGIN: 1

Jones (of Ystrad), DIVINITY: 218

Jones (U.S.), COUNTRYSIDE: 1;
FATE: 20; PEACE: 52;
TRANQUILLITY: 6; VIRTUE: 93

Jordan, ABILITY: 9; REBIRTH: 16

Jornlin, DEEDS: 44

Joseph, UNITY: 38

Joseph Clemens, Duke of Bavaria
(1671–1723), DIVINITY: 367

Joseph I, Emperor of Germany
(1678–1711), FRIENDSHIP: 28

Jossey, HANDS: 22

Jossey (of Westpans), VISION: 7

Jowett, COURAGE: 12; PRUDENCE: 4

Joy, COUNTRY: 103; HAPPINESS: 72;
LIBERTY: 98; PATRIOTISM: 50

Joyce, DEATH: 53; HONOR: 138

Joynt, PRUDENCE: 29

Judah (U.S.), FORTITUDE: 17;
JUSTICE: 34

Judd (U.S.), DIVINE GUIDANCE: 104

Judge, PROVIDENCE: 29

Juliane Ursula, Margravine of Baden
(D. 1614), DIVINE GUIDANCE: 299

Julius, Duke of Braunschweig-
Wolfenbüttel (1529–89), EVIL: 6;
FEAR: 25; PROVIDENCE: 9; SERVICE: 1

Julius August, Duke of Braunschweig
(1578–1617), MODERATION: 18

Julius Ernst, Duke of Braunschweig-
Lüneberg-Danneberg (1571–1636),
UNITY: 11

Julius Ernst, Duke of Braunschweig-
Lüneberg-Danneburg (1571–1636),
FEAR: 70; ROYALTY: 118

Julius Franz, Duke of Saxony-
Lauenburg (1641–89), FEAR: 69;
RECTITUDE: 76

Julius Friedrich, Duke of
Württemberg (1588–1635),
FORCE: 33; VIRTUE: 226

Julius Heinrich, Duke of Saxony-
Lauenburg (1586–1665), BEAUTY: 19;
COUNTRY: 62; COURAGE: 168; DIVINE
GUIDANCE: 308; TIME: 38, 68

Justice, CAUSATION: 5

Justus II, Count of Mansfeld
(1558–1619), HOPE: 113; SILENCE: 8;
STRENGTH: 80

K

Kadie, ASSISTANCE: 20

Kadle, ASSISTANCE: 20

Kadwell, VIGILANCE: 81

Kalamazoo Valley Comunity College,
Kalamazoo, Michigan,
OPPORTUNITY: 6; SCHOOL
MOTTOES: 210

Kane, GENTLENESS: 4

Karl, Count of the Palatinate of
Birkenfeld (1560–1600),
RIGHTEOUSNESS: 4; SUFFERING: 11

Karl, Duke of Braunschweig-Bevern
(1713–80), STEADFASTNESS: 96

Karl, Duke of Mecklenburg (D. 1610),
VIRTUE: 156

Karl, Elector of the Palatinate
(1651–85), DIVINE GUIDANCE: 420

Karl, Margrave of Baden (1598–1625),
FEAR: 76; RECTITUDE: 78;
VIRTUE: 360

Kempe (U.S.), INDUSTRIOUSNESS: 121; REST: 10

Kemper Military School and College, Boonville, Missouri, PREPAREDNESS: 41; SCHOOL MOTTOES: 207

Kempsey, DIVINE GUIDANCE: 412

Kempt, PREPAREDNESS: 61

Kenah, FIDELITY: 110

Kenan, ACCOMPLISHMENT: 13

Kendal B. C., U.K., COMMERCE: 3; LOCAL GOVERNMENT: 269

Kendall, ASPIRATION: 32; BIRDS: 6; SUN: 1; VIRTUE: 262

Kenmare (E.), FIDELITY: 222

Kennard, HOPE: 6

Kennard (B.), SUFFERING: 7

Kennaway (Bt.), ASPIRATION: 35

Kennedar, ADVANCE: 25

Kennedy, DIVINE GUIDANCE: 252; FINISH: 10; FRUIT: 9; HANDS: 34; HAPPINESS: 43; LAUGHTER: 1; PAST, THE: 3; PURPOSE: 3; STRENGTH: 144; TRUTH: 132

Kennedy (Bt.), VIRTUE: 4

Kennedy (of Clowburn), DECEPTION: 9; POWER: 26; TRUTH: 169

Kennedy (of Kirkmichael), HONESTY: 28

Kenny (of Ballyflower, Co. Roscommon), COURAGE: 213; FLOURISHING: 83; VIRTUE: 204; WORTHINESS: 61

Kenny (of Kilcloghar and Correndos, Co. Galway), COURAGE: 213; FLOURISHING: 83; VIRTUE: 204; WORTHINESS: 61

Kenrick, HONOR: 186; VIRTUE: 238

Kensington (B.), FAITH: 133

Kensington B. C., U.K., ADVERSITY: 77; LOCAL GOVERNMENT: 303

Kent C. C., U.K., LOCAL GOVERNMENT: 196; MERCY: 9

Kentucky State University, Frankfort, Kentucky, ASPIRATION: 63; TRUTH: 64

Kenyon, PROVIDENCE: 26

Kenyon (B.), CROSS, THE: 76

Keogh, DEFIANCE: 11

Keppel, ADVERSITY: 50; LOCAL GOVERNMENT: 236

Ker, ADVANCE: 19; COUNTRY: 85; SATISFACTION: 9; SCHOOL MOTTOES: 237; VIRTUE: 234

Ker (of Abbot Rule), ADVANCE: 34

Ker (of Moristoun), COUNTRY: 27; DANGER: 6

Ker (of Sutherland Hall), COURAGE: 1

Kerr, ABILITY: 15; DIVINE GUIDANCE: 161; DIVINITY: 344; INDUSTRIOUSNESS: 83; UNCLASSIFIED: 7

Kerr (of Kerrislande), DIVINITY: 344

Kerrick (of Gelderston), PREPAREDNESS: 41

Kerrison, INTEGRITY: 34

Kerrison (Bt.), DIVINITY: 373

Kerry, IMMORTALITY: 9

Kersey, EFFORT: 26

Kerslake (of Banner Hall, co. Norfolk), FIDELITY: 2

Kerwan (Co. Galway), COUNTRY: 50; DIVINITY: 303; ROYALTY: 53

Kesteven C. C., U.K., CONQUEST: 30; LOCAL GOVERNMENT: 274; PERSEVERANCE: 68; RESTRAINT: 1

Keswick U. D. C., U.K., GUIDANCE: 21; LOCAL GOVERNMENT: 232

Ketchum (U.S.), UNITY: 31

Kett, UNIQUENESS: 5

Kettering B. C., U.K., FRIENDSHIP: 47; IMPROVEMENT: 38; LAW: 42

Kettle, GOODNESS: 7; WORTHINESS: 56

Kettle (U.S.), COUNTRY: 5; LIBERTY: 8; LIFE: 3

Kettlewell, ANIMALS: 53

Key, DIVINITY: 248; HOPE: 94

Keydon, PURPOSE: 4

Kidd, FULLNESS: 2; INDUSTRIOUSNESS: 136; SCHOOL MOTTOES: 199

Kidder, UNCLASSIFIED: 62

Kidderminster B. C., U.K., ART: 16; DIVINE GUIDANCE: 72; INDUSTRIOUSNESS: 21; LOCAL GOVERNMENT: 81

Kidson, LAW: 55; LOCAL GOVERNMENT: 294; ROYALTY: 79

Kildahl, ASSISTANCE: 10

Kirkburton U. D. C., U.K., DIVINE
GUIDANCE: 99; LOCAL
GOVERNMENT: 86
Kirke, EFFORT: 5
Kirkham U. D. C., U.K., LOCAL
GOVERNMENT: 133; SECURITY: 10
Kirkland, HOME: 19; RELIGION: 19
Kirkman, DIVINITY: 230; TRUST: 48
Kirkpatric, ENTRAPMENT: 1
Kirkpatrick, SECURITY: 17
Kirkpatrick (Bt.), SECURITY: 16
Kirkwood, DIVINITY: 402; HOPE: 260
Kirsop, MIND: 25; RECTITUDE: 43
Kirsopp, FAITH: 23
Kirvin, COUNTRY: 44; DIVINITY: 276;
ROYALTY: 46
Kiveton Park R. D. C., COURAGE: 44;
LOCAL GOVERNMENT: 65; WISDOM: 10
Knapton, CROWN: 22; REWARD: 37
Knatchbull (Bt.), CROSS, THE: 72;
GLORY: 30
Knatchbull-Hugessen, CROSS, THE: 28;
GLORY: 10
Knight, FOLLOWING: 24, 30;
JUSTICE: 23; PREPAREDNESS: 41, 78;
VIRTUE: 328
Knight (of Clopton), GLORY: 19
Knightley, FATE: 21; FORTUNE: 72
Knightley (Bt.), FORTUNE: 71
Knights Templars, DIVINITY: 319
Knottingley U. D. C.,
INDUSTRIOUSNESS: 64
Knottingley U. D. C., Widnes B. C.,
Radcliffe B. C., High Wycombe,
Sideserf, Reath, Wauchop, (of
Niddry), Waugh, Vanderplante. B.
C., U.K., LOCAL GOVERNMENT: 183
Knowles (Bt.), PREPAREDNESS: 72;
SCHOOL MOTTOES: 283
Knowlys (of Heysham), DILIGENCE: 45
Knox, ACTION: 14; CONCILIATION: 7
Knox (of Belleck Abbey),
CONQUEST: 19
Knox (U.S.), IMPROVEMENT: 26
Knoye, ASSISTANCE: 13
Knyfton, DIVINITY: 268
Knyvitt, MODERATION: 29
Koecker (U.S.), HONESTY: 37
Koehler, ASSISTANCE: 13
Korda, RECTITUDE: 5
Kramer, FATE: 16
Kroye, ASSISTANCE: 12

Kunigunde Juliane, Landgravine of
Hesse (1608–56), BEAUTY: 22;
VIRTUE: 216
Kunigunde Juliane, Princess of Anhalt
(1608–56), BEAUTY: 22; VIRTUE: 216
Kuyfton, CONQUEST: 19
Kyan, VIRTUE: 87
Kyd, SEASONS: 5
Kyd (of Craigie), FULLNESS: 2
Kyle, GIFTS and GIVING: 28
Kyle, Park (of Fulfordlies),
PROVIDENCE: 21
Kynaston, HONOR: 102
Kynnersley, OPPRESSION: 4
Kynsey, PERSEVERANCE: 42;
STEADFASTNESS: 92
Kynymound, WEAPONS: 71
Kyrle (of Much Marcle),
STEADFASTNESS: 86

L

La Beaume, VICTORY: 55
La Fountaine (Bt.), ORIGIN: 2
La Fout, ANGER: 8
La Rochefoucault, ENJOYMENT: 3
La Roche-Jaquelin, ADVANCE: 54;
DEATH: 91; FOLLOWING: 22;
LEADERSHIP: 23; VENGEANCE: 8
La Serre, ETERNITY: 5
La Touche, TRUTH: 76
La Trobe-Bateman,
ACCOMPLISHMENT: 21
Lace, DEATH: 18; HOPE: 33
Lachlan, MUSIC: 2
Lackerstein, DIVINITY: 68; VIRTUE: 38
Lacock, HONESTY: 52; HONOR: 183
Lacon, SELF-KNOWLEDGE: 4
Lacon (Bt.), HONESTY: 38; HONOR: 156
Lacy (Bt.), HONOR: 137
Ladbrooke (Lynn, co. Norfolk), CROSS,
THE: 54; FLOURISHING: 27
Ladies' Tea-room in the British House
of Commons, KNOWLEDGE: 27
Ladykirk and Kindeace, co. Ross),
COURAGE: 266; GLORY: 61
Lafayette College, Easton,
Pennsylvania, LIBERTY: 125; SCHOOL
MOTTOES: 354; TRUTH: 123
Laffan (Bt.), SCHOOL MOTTOES: 361;
TRUTH: 167
Laforey, FIDELITY: 221

Leechaman, GIFTS and GIVING: 19;
INDUSTRIOUSNESS: 65
Leeds (Bt.), VIGILANCE: 102
Leeds City and C. B. C., U.K.,
LAW: 55; LOCAL GOVERNMENT: 294;
ROYALTY: 79
Leeds (D.), FIDELITY: 187;
LIBERTY: 27; PEACE: 53; WAR: 54
Leek U. D. C., U.K., ABILITY: 7;
LOCAL GOVERNMENT: 33
Leeke (Co. Salop), PRUDENCE: 2
Leeper, PATRIOTISM: 84; ROYALTY: 99
Lees, RECTITUDE: 29
Lees (Bt.), ACCOMPLISHMENT: 8
Leeson, BRIGHTNESS: 6
Leeward Community College, Pearl
City, Hawaii, ASSISTANCE: 22;
KNOWLEDGE: 88; SCHOOL
MOTTOES: 329
Lefevre, CHANGE: 17
Lefroy, CHANGE: 11;
INDUSTRIOUSNESS: 146
Legard (Bt.), CROSS, THE: 91;
PARADISE: 51
Legat, CHRIST, JESUS: 49
Legge, VIRTUE: 70
Legge, Stawell (B.), WORDS: 6
Legh-Keck, FAITH: 35
Leicester, DIVINITY: 420;
PATRIOTISM: 65; ROYALTY: 81
Leicester City and C. B. C., U.K.,
CONSISTENCY: 9; LOCAL
GOVERNMENT: 338
Leicester (E.), PATIENCE: 42;
PRUDENCE: 50
Leicestershire C. C., U.K.,
IMPROVEMENT: 12; LOCAL
GOVERNMENT: 152
Leigh, AUDACITY: 84; FIDELITY: 264;
GOODNESS: 34; PRUDENCE: 47
Leigh (B.), DIVINITY: 416
Leigh B. C., U.K., SPEED: 2
Leigh (Co. Chester), DIVINITY: 340;
EARTH: 13
Leigh (of Bardon), LAW: 19
Leigh (of Belmont, co. Chester),
LAW: 18
Leigh (of West Hall), STRENGTH: 42;
VIRTUE: 61
Leighton (Bt.), DISGRACE: 3
Leighton (of Shrewsbury), DISGRACE: 3

Leinster (D.), DEFIANCE: 3;
GRATITUDE: 13
Leith, VIRTUE: 359
Leith (of Craighill), TRUST: 99
Leith (of Over-Barns), FIDELITY: 293
Leith (of Whitehaugh), CHRIST,
JESUS: 72; FIDELITY: 153;
SALVATION: 40
Leithbridge (Bt.), DIVINITY: 402;
HOPE: 260; TRUTH: 98
Leith-Hay, TRUST: 100
Leitrim (E.), VIRTUE: 135
Lempriere, BIRDS: 24; FEAR: 73;
NOBILITY: 26; OFFSPRING: 3
Lend-a-Hand Club, HUMANITY: 5
Lendrum, PEACE: 25
Lennard, GOODNESS: 14
Lennon, ANCESTRY: 32
Lennox, DEFENSE: 23; FLORA: 13;
FLOURISHING: 16
Lenoir Community College, Kinston,
North Carolina, KNOWLEDGE: 90;
SCHOOL MOTTOES: 335
Lentaigne, COUNTRY: 96; FAITH: 198;
ROYALTY: 69
Lenthall (of Oxon), PROPER NAMES: 2, 9
Leopold Ebrehard, Duke of
Württemberg-Mümpelgart
(1670–1723), WISDOM: 21
Leopold Ludwig, Count of the
Palatinate of Veldenz (1625–94),
SCRIPTURES: 16
Le-Poer Trench, PRUDENCE: 10;
WISDOM: 14
Le-Poer-Trench, DIVINE
GUIDANCE: 185
Lepper, DIVINE GUIDANCE: 221
Leppington, ANCESTRY: 5
Lermitte, DIVINE GUIDANCE: 179
Lerrier, GOODNESS: 8; RECTITUDE: 10;
USEFULNESS: 1
Lesley, FAITH: 221
Leslie, FAITH: 221; HOPE: 63;
PATRIOTISM: 65; ROYALTY: 81
Leslie (Bt.), STEADFASTNESS: 60
Leslie (Co. Antrim, and Aberdeen),
STEADFASTNESS: 60
Leslie (of Surrey), MIND: 26
Leslie (of Wardes), STEADFASTNESS: 47
Lesly, DIVINITY: 389; HONESTY: 35;
STEADFASTNESS: 62

Lesly (of Aberdden), DIVINE
GUIDANCE: 154; SCHOOL
MOTTOES: 63
Lesly (of Aberdeen), DIVINE
GUIDANCE: 264
Lesly (of Burdsbank),
STEADFASTNESS: 77
Lesly (of Colpnay), EFFORT: 6
Lesly (of Finrassie), STRENGTH: 33
Lesly (of Kincraige), HOPE: 63
Lesly (of Kinivie), STRENGTH: 105;
UNITY: 60
Lesotho, PEACE: 23
L'Estrange, CONSISTENCY: 8
L'Estrange (of Moystown),
MEMORY: 15
Letchworth, DEEDS: 92
Letchworth U. D. C., U.K., FUTURE,
THE: 23; LOCAL GOVERNMENT: 299;
PRUDENCE: 49
Levant Company, COUNTRY: 14;
DIVINITY: 52; FRIENDSHIP: 23
Leven (E.), PATRIOTISM: 65;
ROYALTY: 81
Leveson, STEADFASTNESS: 59
Levinge, STEADFASTNESS: 94
Levinge (Bt.), STEADFASTNESS: 143
Levy, POSSESSION: 18
Lewin, COURAGE: 42; DIVINITY: 135,
402; HOPE: 260; PRUDENCE: 9
Lewis, ANIMALS: 5; BIRDS: 9;
DIRECTNESS: 15; DIVINE GIFTS: 3;
FATE: 33; FORTUNE: 75;
HARMLESSNESS: 1; HOPE: 277;
LIBERTY: 53; MEMORY: 5; NATIONAL
MOTTOES: 13; PERSEVERANCE: 23;
ROYALTY: 1; WISDOM: 4
Lewis (Bt.), DEATH: 33; DUTY: 17;
FIDELITY: 82
Lewis (Co. Glamorgan), COUNTRY: 72;
FIDELITY: 250; PATRIOTISM: 33
Lewis (of Gilfach), FEAR: 4;
RIGHTEOUSNESS: 2
Lewis (of Greenmeadow, Co.
Glamorgan), FEAR: 54
Lewis (of St. Pierre), FAITH: 138
Lewisham B. C., LAW: 62; LOCAL
GOVERNMENT: 329; PEOPLE: 19
Lewthwait, TRUTH: 96
Lewthwaite, VIRTUE: 202
Ley, SHINING: 12

Leycester (of White Place), DIVINE
GUIDANCE: 210; SCHOOL
MOTTOES: 71
Leyland, DIVINE GUIDANCE: 260
Leyland U. D. C., U.K.,
IMPROVEMENT: 44; LOCAL
GOVERNMENT: 341
Leys School, Cambridge, U.K.,
FAITH: 152; SCHOOL MOTTOES: 136
Leyton B. C., U.K., LOCAL
GOVERNMENT: 229; SERVICE: 32
Liberator, The (abolitionist journal,
William Lloyd Garrison, editor),
HUMANITY: 9; MANLINESS: 4
Liberty Baptist College, Lynchburg,
Virginia, KNOWLEDGE: 32; SCHOOL
MOTTOES: 151
Liberty Bell, LIBERTY: 91
Lichfield City Council, U.K., LOCAL
GOVERNMENT: 330; PARENTS: 4
Lichfield (E.), DESPAIR: 5
Liddel (of Edinburgh), FRAGRANCE: 5;
HEALING and HEALTH: 12
Liddell, FAME: 11
Lidderdale (of St. Mary Isle,
Scotland), FORESIGHT: 3
Liddersdale, VIGILANCE: 56; WAR: 59
Lidiard, VIGILANCE: 46
Lidwell, LOCAL GOVERNMENT: 402;
STATE MOTTOES: 61; STRENGTH: 184;
UNITY: 122
Lievre, RISK: 4
Lightbody, BRIGHTNESS: 7;
DARKNESS: 2; LIGHT: 11
Lighton, VIRTUE: 137
Lighton (Bt.), FORTITUDE: 10;
PRUDENCE: 22
Lighton (of Ullishaven),
UNCLASSIFIED: 39
Ligonier, CONQUEST: 1; ROYALTY: 2
Lilburne, STRENGTH: 185
Lilford (B.), ACQUISITION: 5;
DEFENSE: 39
Lilford (V.), FEAR: 3; JUSTICE: 9;
LOCAL GOVERNMENT: 45
Limerick (E.), COURAGE: 255
Lincoln College, Canterbury, New
Zealand, DILIGENCE: 50;
KNOWLEDGE: 70; RECTITUDE: 68;
SCHOOL MOTTOES: 273

Lincoln University, Jefferson City, Missouri, INDUSTRIOUSNESS: 93; SCHOOL MOTTOES: 159

Lincolne, FORCE: 16; MIND: 40

Lind, VIRTUE: 175

Lindesay (of Warmiston), PATIENCE: 36

Lindoe, STEADFASTNESS: 73

Lindon, COUNTRY: 68; LIBERTY: 88

Lindsay, ENDURANCE: 18; GROWTH: 16; HONOR: 50; LOVE: 67, 80, 91; REBIRTH: 7; RECTITUDE: 58; STEADFASTNESS: 54

Lindsay (Bt.), DIVINE GUIDANCE: 29; STARS: 10

Lindsay (of Blackholm), REBIRTH: 15

Lindsay (of Cairnie), WEAPONS: 75

Lindsay (of Cavill), COURAGE: 206

Lindsay (of Culsh), STEADFASTNESS: 50

Lindsay (of The Byres, Scotland), LIFE: 15

Lindsay (U.S.), ADVERSITY: 79

Lindsey, DIVINE GUIDANCE: 29; ENDURANCE: 38; FAITH: 47; HOPE: 60; STARS: 10

Lindsey C. C., U.K., LOCAL GOVERNMENT: 346; SERVICE: 57

Lindsey (E.), FIDELITY: 232

Linlithgow (Scotland), PARADISE: 16

Linskill, CONQUEST: 48

Lippincott, DANGER: 17; PROSPERITY: 50; RECTITUDE: 69

Lisburne (E.), VENGEANCE: 6

Lisle, ANIMALS: 28; CROSS, THE: 64; FAITH: 148

Lisle (Bt.), WAR: 9

Lisle (U.S.), LAW: 21

Lismore (V.), AUDACITY: 50; FIDELITY: 157

Lister, DEATH: 40; DISGRACE: 10; MODERATION: 4

Lister (of Armytage Park), ANCESTRY: 34

Listowel (E.), PROFANITY: 2

Litchfield, PREPAREDNESS: 74

Litster, CONFIDENCE: 14; DIVINITY: 384; INDUSTRIOUSNESS: 98

Little, BEAUTY: 17; SIZE: 3, 4

Little Lever U. D. C., U.K., FEAR: 35; LOCAL GOVERNMENT: 235; STEADFASTNESS: 81

Littlehampton U. D. C., U.K., IMPROVEMENT: 35; LOCAL GOVERNMENT: 291

Littlejohn, AGGRESSION: 4

Littler, PROPER NAMES: 19, 30; STARS: 11

Litton, GLORY: 47; PRUDENCE: 70

Livere, VIGILANCE: 43

Liverpool City and C. B. C., U.K., DIVINE GIFTS: 26

Liverpool College, U.K., ABILITY: 21; LOCAL GOVERNMENT: 253; SCHOOL MOTTOES: 204; VIRTUE: 127

Liverpool (E.), INDUSTRIOUSNESS: 155; REWARD: 24; STEADFASTNESS: 16, 32

Livingston (of Glentarran), POSSIBILITY: 13

Livingston (U.S.), PROSPERITY: 44; WISDOM: 49

Livingstone, HOME: 9; HONOR: 140; HOPE: 181

Livingstone (of Aberdeen), COURAGE: 79; JUSTICE: 33

Livingstone (of Miltoun, etc.), POSSIBILITY: 10

Llanover (of Llanover and Abercarn, b.), INTENTION: 5

Llewellin, NOBILITY: 28; VIRTUE: 272

Lloyd, ACCEPTANCE: 7; ACTION: 21; DIVINE GUIDANCE: 44, 46, 47; DIVINITY: 138, 224; FEAR: 43; HOPE: 31; JUSTICE: 27; LOFTINESS: 8, 11; LOVE: 59; RECTITUDE: 37; VENGEANCE: 3; VIRTUE: 203, 320; WILLINGNESS: 7

Lloyd (of Coedmore), FAITH: 61; FORTITUDE: 3

Lloyd (of Dan-yr-alt), DIVINITY: 218

Lloyd (of Dolobran), VIGILANCE: 29

Lloyd (of Ferney Hall), DEATH: 22; DISGRACE: 5

Lloyd (of Gloucester), TIME: 46

Lloyd (of Leaton-knolls), ANCESTRY: 34

Lloyd (of Rosindale and Aston), FAME: 16; PROSPERITY: 17

Lloyd (of Seaton), REPUTATION: 9

Lloyd (U.S.), GLORY: 52; SALVATION: 36

Lloyd-Verney, FAITH: 242; SUN: 28; UNITY: 91

Lluellin, DEATH: 60; FAITH: 174

Loades, OBEDIENCE: 9

Loch (of Drylaw and Rachan),
   DILIGENCE: 8; SCHOOL MOTTOES: 26
Lochlan, MUSIC: 2
Locke, MIND: 34; WAR: 41
Locker, DIVINITY: 169
Lockett, POSSESSION: 27
Lockhart, FEELINGS: 3; SECURITY: 15
Lockhart (B.), COUNTRY: 129;
   PATRIOTISM: 88
Lockhart (Bt.), FEELINGS: 4
Lockhart (of Birkhill), ANIMALS: 22;
   AUDACITY: 46; FIERCENESS: 1
Lockhart (of Cleghorn), FAITH: 216
Locock (Bt.), VICTORY: 55
Lodder, DIVINITY: 232
Loftus, ACCEPTANCE: 4;
   CONSISTENCY: 12; FIDELITY: 218, 221
Loftus (Bt.), FIDELITY: 218
Loftus (Co. Norfolk), FIDELITY: 218
Logan, ANCESTRY: 20
Logan College of Chiropractic,
   Chesterfield, Missouri,
   EXCELLENCE: 15; HEALING and
   HEALTH: 37; SCHOOL MOTTOES: 304
Loghlan, MUSIC: 2
Logie, WAR: 68
Login, DIVINE GUIDANCE: 51; GRACE: 2
Lomax, RECTITUDE: 48
Lomax (of Clayton), FATE: 14;
   PRUDENCE: 20
Londesborough (B.), ADVERSITY: 3;
   VIRTUE: 5
The London School of Economics and
   Political Science, CAUSATION: 7;
   SCHOOL MOTTOES: 254
Londonderry (M.), FEAR: 33
Lone, SOLITUDE: 1
Long, ADVANCE: 4; ANGER: 4;
   ANIMALS: 30; CONFIDENCE: 5;
   COURAGE: 182; FOLLOWING: 25;
   PIETY: 43, 45
Long Island University, Brooklyn,
   New York, EARTH: 24; SCHOOL
   MOTTOES: 347
Long (of Carshalton), MANNERS: 4
Longbottom, COURAGE: 97
Longcroft, PRESENT, THE: 9
Longe, COUNTRY: 94; FAITH: 196
Longe (of Spixworth), LOVE: 109
Longeville-Clarke, MILITARY
   DISTINCTION: 4; REWARD: 19
Longfield, MERCY: 29

Longford (E.), GLORY: 24
Longley, INTEGRITY: 10; SCHOOL
   MOTTOES: 94
Longmore, KINDNESS: 11
Longstaff, VIGILANCE: 102
Longworth, FIDELITY: 105
Lonsdale (E.), OFFICE: 2
Lookyer, DILIGENCE: 52;
   PROSPERITY: 53
Lopes, DEEDS: 78
Lorain, FLORA: 19; REBIRTH: 14;
   RIGHTS: 6
Loraine, WEAPONS: 86
Loraine (Bt.), RISING: 7
Loras College, Dubuque, Iowa,
   COUNTRY: 92; DIVINITY: 357; SCHOOL
   MOTTOES: 240
Lord, COURAGE: 89
The Lord Audley (reign of Henry
   VIII), FORTUNE: 81
Lord Beaumont, IMPROVEMENT: 23
The Lord Prior of St. John of
   Jerusalem, STATUS: 10
Lord Waveney, VICTORY: 29
Loretto School, U.K., DUTY: 29;
   SCHOOL MOTTOES: 298
Lorimer, ADVANCE: 37; COURAGE: 266;
   GLORY: 61; RISING: 22; WAR: 46
Lorton (V.), HOPE: 272
Los Angeles Baptist College, Newhall,
   California, GROWTH: 1; SCHOOL
   MOTTOES: 19
Loseley House, near Guildford,
   Surrey, England, CONCILIATION: 2
Lotbiniere (U.S.), FORTUNE: 27;
   VIRTUE: 63
Lothian (M.), ADVANCE: 22
Loughborough B. C., U.K., LOCAL
   GOVERNMENT: 195; TRUTH: 43;
   VICTORY: 22
Loughnan, COURAGE: 82;
   TRUSTWORTHINESS: 2
Louis, ADVERSITY: 56; MANNER: 1
Louis (Bt.), Duckworth (Bt.), PROPER
   NAMES: 49
Louis de la Trémouille (1460–1525),
   AGE: 1
Louis XII., ROYALTY: 111; WEAPONS: 84
Louis XIII (1601–43), KNOWLEDGE: 19;
   WARNING: 5
Louis XIV of France, EQUALITY: 6

Ludwig VIII, Landgrave of Hesse-
Darmstadt (1691–1768),
PROSPERITY: 12; RECTITUDE: 7;
STEADFASTNESS: 9

Luise Amalie, Princess of Anhalt
(1606–35), BLESSING: 12;
DIVINITY: 363; FORTUNE: 94;
HOPE: 167

Luise Henriette, Electress of
Brandenburg (1627–67), CHRIST,
JESUS: 50; ETERNITY: 4; HOPE: 133

Luise Juliane, daughter of Prince of
Orange (B. 1576), PURITY: 17;
SINCERITY: 12

Luke, FOLLOWING: 23

Lumisden, LOVE: 22

Lumley, CONSCIENCE: 7; PROPER
NAMES: 4

Lumm, LIBERTY: 134

Lumsdaine, VIGILANCE: 5

Lumsden, CONQUEST: 14; DEATH: 29;
FAITH: 68; PERSEVERANCE: 17;
TRUST: 105; VIGILANCE: 5

Lumsden (of Pitcaple and Cushnie),
DIVINE GIFTS: 15

Lund, FORTUNE: 14

Lunden, ANCESTRY: 40; VIRTUE: 199

Lundin, CONFIDENCE: 3; DIVINE
GIFTS: 15

Lurgan (B.), INTEGRITY: 10; SCHOOL
MOTTOES: 94

Lusado, GUIDANCE: 16; HONOR: 99

Luscombe, DEATH: 64

Lushington, FAITH: 106; TRUTH: 26

Lushington (of Pool and Kent),
PATIENCE: 42; PRUDENCE: 50

Lutefoot (of Scotland), BIRDS: 2

Luther, DEATH: 36; HAPPINESS: 39

Luther Theological Seminary, St.
Paul, Minnesota, CHRIST, JESUS: 65;
GRACE: 20; SCHOOL MOTTOES: 120,
219; TRUTH: 30

Luton B. C., U.K.,
INDUSTRIOUSNESS: 178;
KNOWLEDGE: 67; LOCAL
GOVERNMENT: 335

Luttrell, ART: 30; DIVINITY: 151;
TRUST: 28; WAR: 67

Luxmore, WEAPONS: 88

Lyall, DILIGENCE: 54; HONESTY: 49

Lydall, TIME: 18

Lyde, COURAGE: 72; UNSELFISHNESS: 15

Lyell, COURAGE: 72; DILIGENCE: 55;
DIVINE GUIDANCE: 30; HONOR: 163;
PROTECTION: 27

Lyell (of Dysart), DEFENSE: 51

Lyle, COURAGE: 72; DEFENSE: 51

Lynch, ASPIRATION: 57; FIDELITY: 285;
PURITY: 7

Lynch (Bt.), FIDELITY: 289

Lynde (U.S.), PATRIOTISM: 39;
ROYALTY: 60

Lyndhurst (B.), ADVANCE: 58

Lyndon B. Johnson, REASON: 4

Lynedoch (B.), DIRECTNESS: 7

Lynes, FAITH: 121; RIGHTS: 3;
ROYALTY: 39

Lynes (of Tooley Park), DUTY: 15;
FAITH: 126; ROYALTY: 41

Lyon, COURAGE: 12; HONOR: 133;
HOPE: 213; PATRIOTISM: 65;
PRUDENCE: 4; REST: 11; ROYALTY: 81;
STRENGTH: 78; TRUTH: 38

Lyon (of Auldabar), DIVINITY: 269;
TRUST: 71

Lyons, COURAGE: 244; FIDELITY: 340;
HOPE: 213

Lyons (B.), ANIMALS: 42;
PROVOCATION: 4

Lyons (of Ledestown), ANIMALS: 42;
PROVOCATION: 4

Lysaght, WAR: 9

Lysons (of Hemsted), VICTORY: 53

Lyster, FIDELITY: 221; REPUTATION: 9

Lyster (of Rowton Castle),
FIDELITY: 218

Lyte, HAPPINESS: 38; IMMORTALITY: 4

Lytham-St. Annes B. C., LAW: 62;
LOCAL GOVERNMENT: 329;
PEOPLE: 19

Lyttelton, REBIRTH: 24

Lyttleton, DIVINITY: 423;
ROYALTY: 120; UNITY: 80

M

Maberly, SALVATION: 20

Mac Causland, HONOR: 11

Mac Inroy, FOLLOWING: 20

Macadam, CONQUEST: 19

Macalester, SEA: 20

Macartney, HOPE: 182

Macartney (Bt.), MIND: 25;
RECTITUDE: 43

Macloide, STEADFASTNESS: 62
MacMillan, ASSISTANCE: 17;
    KINDNESS: 15
Macmillan-Scott, ASSISTANCE: 18;
    KINDNESS: 16
MacMoran, REWARD: 56; VIRTUE: 357
MacMoran, or McMoran, SPORT: 4
Mac-Murdoch, FORTUNE: 89
Macnab (Bt.), COURAGE: 219
Macnaghten, DIVINITY: 227; HOPE: 81
MacNeil, COURAGE: 177;
    KNOWLEDGE: 56
Macneill (of Barra), CONQUEST: 62;
    DEATH: 102
Maconochie (of Meadowbank),
    ASSISTANCE: 9
MacPeter, DEEDS: 31
MacPharlin, DEFENSE: 47
MacPherson, ANIMALS: 55;
    TOUCH: 3, 4; UNCLASSIFIED: 5
Macpherson (of Cluny), ANIMALS: 38;
    TOUCH: 1
MacQuarie, DIVINE GUIDANCE: 429
MacQuay, LIMITATION: 3
Macqueen, COURAGE: 236;
    FIDELITY: 42; PARADISE: 55
Macrae, INTEGRITY: 28
Macre, LIBERTY: 25
Macrea, ENJOYMENT: 6
MacSween, PROVIDENCE: 2
Mactier, COUNTRY: 38; HANDS: 13;
    PATRIOTISM: 15
MacWilliams (U.S.), REBIRTH: 19
Madan, FAITH: 61; FORTITUDE: 3
Madden, AUDACITY: 82; STRENGTH: 50;
    VIRTUE: 161
Maddison, FEAR: 78
Maddock, ANIMALS: 43; DIVINITY: 316
Magan, HONESTY: 54; INTEGRITY: 43;
    VIRTUE: 383, 414
Magawly, DEFIANCE: 7; HANDS: 17
Magdalen College School, Oxford,
    U.K., FLORA: 41; SCHOOL
    MOTTOES: 291
Magdalene, Princess of Anhalt
    (1585–1657), DIVINE GUIDANCE: 303
Magdalene Auguste, Duchess of
    Saxony-Gotha and Altenburg
    (1679–1740), FEAR: 75; WISDOM: 100
Magdalene Sibylle, Duchess of Saxony-
    Gotha and Altenburg (1648–81),
    HAPPINESS: 11

Magdalene Sibylle, Electress of Saxony
    (1612–87), DIVINITY: 20; GLORY: 3
Magenis, DIVINITY: 387
Magens, ADVERSITY: 36; VIRTUE: 86
Magnus, Duke of Braunschweig-
    Lüneburg (1577–1632), DIVINITY: 6;
    PIETY: 28; VIRTUE: 143
Magrath, FAITH: 205; SALVATION: 38
Maguire, ART: 23; COUNTRY: 92;
    COURAGE: 149; DIVINITY: 358;
    FORTITUDE: 18, 24; JUSTICE: 35, 69;
    SCHOOL MOTTOES: 241
Maharishi International University,
    Fairfield, Iowa, KNOWLEDGE: 37;
    SCHOOL MOTTOES: 156
Maher, AUDACITY: 73; DANGER: 10;
    PARADISE: 23
Mahon, ADVERSITY: 65; FORTITUDE: 25;
    RISING: 10
Mahon (Bt.), IMPROVEMENT: 25
Mahoney, VICTORY: 25
Maidenhead B. C., U.K., BEAUTY: 13;
    LOCAL GOVERNMENT: 198
Maidstone B. C., U.K.,
    AGRICULTURE: 1; COMMERCE: 1;
    LOCAL GOVERNMENT: 10; STATE
    MOTTOES: 1
Main, UNCLASSIFIED: 55
Maine, DANGER: 21; VIRTUE: 230
Mainwaring, PRIMACY: 2
Mainwaring (Bt.), PRIMACY: 2
Mair, BEAUTY: 18; FORTITUDE: 27;
    HOPE: 240; LOVE: 35
Mairis, DIVINE GUIDANCE: 404
Maitland, ADVERSITY: 43; DIVINE
    GUIDANCE: 99, 100; FINISH: 14;
    INTEGRITY: 10; LOCAL
    GOVERNMENT: 86;
    PERSEVERANCE: 19; SCHOOL
    MOTTOES: 94; TRANQUILLITY: 1;
    TRUST: 40
Maitland, Walrond, PEACE: 35
Maitland (Bt.), COURAGE: 44; LOCAL
    GOVERNMENT: 65; WISDOM: 10
Majendie, CONSISTENCY: 7
Makepeace, HOPE: 215
Makgill, FINISH: 14
Makins (Bt.), LIGHT: 22; SHINING: 8
Malawi, LIBERTY: 121; NATIONAL
    MOTTOES: 41; UNITY: 114
Malaysia, STRENGTH: 7; UNITY: 3
Malcolm, DIVINE GUIDANCE: 156

Malcolm (Bt.), ASPIRATION: 34

Malcolm (of Burnfort), ADVERSITY: 33

Malcolm (of Poltalloch),
ACCOMPLISHMENT: 9; ADVERSITY: 32;
SEARCH and DISCOVERY: 6

Malden, ASSISTANCE: 15; KINDNESS: 13

Malden and Coombe B. C., U.K.,
LOCAL GOVERNMENT: 98; LOVE: 44

Malet, STRENGTH: 89

Malim, FAITH: 116

Malins, DIVINE GUIDANCE: 4

Mallet, DIVINITY: 150; FIDELITY: 281;
PARADISE: 7; STRENGTH: 13, 43

Malloch, SELF-RELIANCE: 2

Malmesbury (E.), COUNTRY: 136;
MAINTENANCE: 2

Malone, FIDELITY: 112

Malta, PERSEVERANCE: 84; VIRTUE: 375

Malvern College, U.K., FORESIGHT: 9;
SCHOOL MOTTOES: 261; WISDOM: 70

Malvern U. D. C., U.K.,
ASPIRATION: 55

Man, COURAGE: 161

Manatee Jr. College, Bradenton,
Florida, LIBERTY: 128; SCHOOL
MOTTOES: 356; TRUTH: 126

Manbey, FAITH: 77

Manchester City and C. B. C., U.K.,
GUIDANCE: 5; INDUSTRIOUSNESS: 14;
LOCAL GOVERNMENT: 62

Manchester (D.), Montague,
CHANGE: 4

Manders, DIVINITY: 362

Mandit, LAW: 55; LOCAL
GOVERNMENT: 294; ROYALTY: 79

Manigault (U.S.), THOUGHT: 17;
VENGEANCE: 7

Manley, HANDS: 23; HOSTILITY: 13

Manly, COUNTRY: 108; DEATH: 86;
PATRIOTISM: 57

Mann, BEING, SELF: 1; ENVY: 12, 14;
VIRTUE: 356, 425

Mann (of Ditchingham, co. Suffolk),
ADVERSITY: 63

Manners (B.), ACCOMPLISHMENT: 17

Manners (of Goadby Marwood Park),
ACCOMPLISHMENT: 17

Manning, LIFE: 48

Manningham, ASPIRATION: 31;
EXCELLENCE: 1

Manns, BEING, SELF: 1

Mannsell, HONOR: 77

Mansel, STEADFASTNESS: 129

Mansfield, STEADFASTNESS: 129;
STRENGTH: 148

Mansfield B. C., U.K.,
FLOURISHING: 74;
INDUSTRIOUSNESS: 182; LOCAL
GOVERNMENT: 347

Mansfield (E.), VIRTUE: 207

Manson, ORIGIN: 6

Mant, LIGHT: 35

Manvers (E.), CONFIDENCE: 16

Mappin, INCENTIVE: 3, 4

Marblers' Company, London,
INDUSTRIOUSNESS: 53; TRADES: 14

Margar, SEARCH and DISCOVERY: 3

Margarethe, Countess of Mansfeld (b.
1534), DIVINITY: 202

Margate B. C., U.K., HEALING and
HEALTH: 24; LOCAL
GOVERNMENT: 278; SEA: 25

Margesson, FIDELITY: 228

Margetson, DIVINE GUIDANCE: 363

Margrave of Brandenburg
(1587–1665), HOPE: 254

Marian College, Indianapolis,
Indiana, SCHOOL MOTTOES: 280;
WISDOM: 91

Marie, Margravine of Brandenburg
(1579–1649), DIVINE GUIDANCE: 21

Marie Eleonore, Margravine of
Brandenburg (1599–1655), DIVINE
GUIDANCE: 285, 289; GRACE: 16

Marie Elisabeth, DIVINE
GUIDANCE: 317; FATE: 18;
SALVATION: 30

Marie Elisabeth, Landgravine of Hesse
(1634–65), HAPPINESS: 5; HEART: 3

Marie Elizabeth, Duchess of Saxony-
Coburg (1638–87), FEAR: 57

Maris, INTEGRITY: 10; SCHOOL
MOTTOES: 94

Marishall, VIRTUE: 175

Marjoribanks, CONSERVATION: 4;
PREPAREDNESS: 14; VIGILANCE: 21

Marjoribanks (Bt.), ADVANCE: 2;
COURAGE: 6

Market Harborough U. D. C., U.K.,
ENVY: 1; HONOR: 117; LOCAL
GOVERNMENT: 177

Markham, AUDACITY: 77;
GENTLENESS: 10

Markoe (U.S.), HOPE: 187

Matherson, DEEDS: 35; HOPE: 58

Matheson, FEELINGS: 15; HANDS: 15

Mathew, COUNTRY: 120;
EQUANIMITY: 2; PATRIOTISM: 79;
PROPER NAMES: 53

Mathil, INTEGRITY: 10; SCHOOL
MOTTOES: 94

Mathison, FLOURISHING: 96

Matthew, DIVINE GUIDANCE: 10

Matthew (of Coggeshall, Co. Essex),
ANIMALS: 13; CROSS, THE: 18;
TRUST: 20

Matthews, COUNTRY: 64; HOME: 15

Matthias, Emperor of Germany
(1557–1619), SADNESS: 1; VICTORY: 2

Maturin, HOSTILITY: 14

Maude, LOFTINESS: 7

Mauduit, DIVINE GUIDANCE: 134

Maughan, FORTUNE: 28

Maule, COURAGE: 40, 132; MERCY: 2, 4,
7

Mauleverer (Co. York), FAITH: 35

Maundy, UNCLASSIFIED: 54

Maunsell (Bt.), DESIRE: 21

Mauritius, STARS: 41

Mawbey, LIBERTY: 2

Mawbey (of Surrey), HUMANITY: 2;
PRUDENCE: 7

Maximilian, Archduke of Austria
(1558–1620), WAR: 43

Maximilian, Elector of Bavaria
(1573–1651), FATE: 11

Maximilian, Prince-Elector of Bavaria
(1573–1651), HOPE: 13;
PROTECTION: 5

Maximilian Emanuel, Elector of
Bavaria (1662–1726), HOPE: 13;
PROTECTION: 5; WISDOM: 19

Maximilian I, Emperor of Germany
(1459–1519), ADVERSITY: 72;
CAUTION: 1; MODERATION: 6, 34

Maximilian II, Emperor of Germany
(1527–76), DIVINE GUIDANCE: 217

Maxton, FAITH: 93

Maxtone, PRUDENCE: 46

Maxwell, ASPIRATION: 87; CROSS,
THE: 96; FLOURISHING: 64, 71, 93;
HOPE: 222; LIGHT: 77;
PREPAREDNESS: 34; REBIRTH: 32;
RISING: 24; STARS: 45;
STRENGTH: 125; UNCLASSIFIED: 29;
USEFULNESS: 4; VIGILANCE: 20;
VIRTUE: 402; WAKEFULNESS: 5, 9

Maxwell (Bt.), FLOURISHING: 67;
PREPAREDNESS: 24

Maxwell (of Calderwood, Bt.),
THOUGHT: 28

Maxwell (of Everingham),
FLOURISHING: 65

Maxwell (of Maxwell),
FLOURISHING: 67

May, COURAGE: 81; FIDELITY: 179

Mayer (U.S.), BIRDS: 15; CHRIST,
JESUS: 36

Maynard, FEELINGS: 24; HANDS: 32

Maynard (of Harlesey Hall), HANDS: 24

Maynard (V.), HANDS: 24

Mayne, DAY: 6

Mayne (of Powis, etc.), COURAGE: 261;
FORTUNE: 116

Mayo (E.), CROSS, THE: 2;
SALVATION: 2

Mayor, CHRIST, JESUS: 54

Mays, PEACE: 28

Maysey, COUNTRY: 99; LIBERTY: 97

Maze, PROTECTION: 14

Mazyck (U.S.), ENTRAPMENT: 7

Mazzinghi (of London, originally from
Germany), DEEDS: 4

McAdam, CROSS, THE: 42;
EQUANIMITY: 17; PEACE: 39;
PROSPERITY: 39; REST: 2; VIRTUE: 136

McAdam (of Ballochmorrie),
EQUANIMITY: 7

McAlister, COURAGE: 97; SEA: 20

McAlla, DANGER: 5

McAllum, ADVERSITY: 33

McAlpin, DEATH: 12; FIDELITY: 280,
281

McAlpine, DEEDS: 30

McAlpine (Bt.), DEPENDABILITY: 2

McAndrew, DIVINITY: 168;
FORTUNE: 45

McArthur, FAITH: 67;
INDUSTRIOUSNESS: 43

McAul, DEFENSE: 19

McBarnet, STARS: 37

McBean, ANIMALS: 55; TOUCH: 4
McBeth, COURAGE: 41; FORTUNE: 10
McBrayne, ANIMALS: 26, 54;
  AUDACITY: 94; FIDELITY: 177;
  RIGHTEOUSNESS: 16; STRENGTH: 55
McCabin, PRIDE: 7
McCall, DANGER: 5; DEFENSE: 19
McCalle, PRIDE: 7
McCallem, ADVERSITY: 33
McCammond, JUSTICE: 82
McCarlie, CONQUEST: 19
McCarthy, COURAGE: 69;
  FIDELITY: 175; FIERCENESS: 4;
  NAME: 4; OFFICE: 3; SPEED: 27;
  STRENGTH: 59
McCartnay, DECORATION: 4
McCartney, REWARD: 44; VIRTUE: 194
McCasker, HANDS: 21
McCausland, AUDACITY: 5
McCay, HANDS: 21
McClambroch, DIVINITY: 172
McClauchlan, COURAGE: 82;
  TRUSTWORTHINESS: 2
McCleish (of Maryfield), LOVE: 79
McClellan, WISDOM: 89
McClelland, WISDOM: 89
McColl, RIGHTEOUSNESS: 5; STARS: 19
McConnel, CONQUEST: 49;
  DIVINITY: 434
McConnell, PREPAREDNESS: 78
McCook Community College,
  McCook, Nebraska,
  IMPROVEMENT: 28; SCHOOL
  MOTTOES: 202
McCorda, FIDELITY: 337
McCorgusdell, ROYALTY: 128
McCormack, COURAGE: 205
McCormick, COURAGE: 205
McCorquodill, ROYALTY: 128
McCoul, CONQUEST: 59
McCowan, PARADISE: 63
McCracken, RIGHTEOUSNESS: 12
McCrae, ENJOYMENT: 6; FORTITUDE: 6
McCray, COURAGE: 97; FORTITUDE: 6
McCree, ENJOYMENT: 6
McCrire, INDUSTRIOUSNESS: 60;
  SCHOOL MOTTOES: 135
McCrobie, EARTH: 1
McCrombie, ANIMALS: 55; TOUCH: 4
McCrummen, WAR: 15
McCrummin, DIVINITY: 338

McCubbin, PATRIOTISM: 65;
  ROYALTY: 81
McCulloch, COURAGE: 228;
  DILIGENCE: 59; PURITY: 22;
  STRENGTH: 162; TRUTH: 163
McDonagh, COURAGE: 266; GLORY: 61
McDonald, ASPIRATION: 41;
  FOLLOWING: 1; FORTUNE: 85;
  OPPOSITION: 3; PARADISE: 5
McDonegh, COURAGE: 266; GLORY: 61
McDonnel, ASSISTANCE: 5;
  FEELINGS: 12; ROYALTY: 9
McDougal, DIVINITY: 168
McDougall, CONQUEST: 54;
  COURAGE: 89; DEATH: 100
McDowal, COURAGE: 238
McDowall, CONQUEST: 54, 62, 63;
  COUNTRY: 90; COURAGE: 89;
  DEATH: 97, 100, 102, 103;
  DIVINITY: 348; HUMILITY: 8;
  ROYALTY: 65; VICTORY: 63
McDowall (of Logan), ROYALTY: 87
McDowell, DIVINITY: 168
McDuff, DIVINE GUIDANCE: 133
McEntire, ADVERSITY: 59
McEwen, RECTITUDE: 53;
  STEADFASTNESS: 100
McFall, REBIRTH: 30
McFarlane, DEFENSE: 47
McFarquhar, FAITH: 61; FORTITUDE: 3
McFell, ATTENTIVENESS: 6
McGassock, INDUSTRIOUSNESS: 68
McGee, DEEDS: 35; HOPE: 58
McGell, HONOR: 67
McGilchrist, WAR: 16
McGill, DIVINITY: 255; FINISH: 14;
  TRUST: 61
McGilleray, ANIMALS: 55; TOUCH: 4
McGillycuddy, ASPIRATION: 84
McGouan, WEAPONS: 55;
  WORTHINESS: 20
McGougan, CONQUEST: 62; DEATH: 102
McGrea, DIVINE GUIDANCE: 341;
  GRACE: 23
McGregor, DEEDS: 28, 31
McGregor (Bt.), FLORA: 4
McGregor (of Camden Hill, Bt.),
  FIDELITY: 281
McGuarie, DIVINE GUIDANCE: 429
McGuire, FORTITUDE: 29; VIRTUE: 269
McHado, VIGILANCE: 105
McHardie, AUDACITY: 95

McTavish, FORGETTING: 7, 9
McTurk, WAR: 48
McVicar, DIVINE GUIDANCE: 217
McWhirter, PRAISE: 14
Meade, PREPAREDNESS: 78
Meadows (Co. Suffolk), VIRTUE: 110
Meares, PROVIDENCE: 12
Meason, STEADFASTNESS: 42
Meath (E.), DIVINE GUIDANCE: 443
Mecham, FORTITUDE: 1
Medhurst, ADVERSITY: 3; VIRTUE: 5
Medley, DIVINITY: 239; TRUST: 55
Medlicott (Bt.), VIGILANCE: 23
Meek, INTEGRITY: 38
Megget, CERTAINTY: 3
Meigh, PROVIDENCE: 1
Meik, UNITY: 47
Meiklejohn, DIVINITY: 400; HOPE: 252
Melbourne, REPUTATION: 8
Melbourne (V.), COURAGE: 243;
  FAITH: 252
Meldrum, ENDURANCE: 40;
  STEADFASTNESS: 80
Melksham U. D. C., U.K., LOCAL
  GOVERNMENT: 390; UNITY: 116
Melliar, ASPIRATION: 43
Mellor, COURAGE: 12; FIDELITY: 136;
  FORTUNE: 79; PRUDENCE: 4;
  VIRTUE: 112
Melvil, PARADISE: 19
Melvile (of Raith), PARADISE: 18
Melvill, PARADISE: 18
Melvill (E.), PARADISE: 18
Melville, FORESIGHT: 10; PARADISE: 17
Melville, 2Whytt, VIRTUE: 411
Melville (V.), DEEDS: 75
Memorial University of
  Newfoundland, Canada, SCHOOL
  MOTTOES: 247
Menzes, DEATH: 40; DISGRACE: 10
Menzies, CHRIST, JESUS: 75; DIVINE
  GUIDANCE: 449; FORTUNE: 30;
  GOALS: 7; HOPE: 215; INCREASE: 27;
  JUDGMENT: 4, 5
Menzies (Bt.), DIVINE GUIDANCE: 439
Merced College, Merced, California,
  KNOWLEDGE: 86; SCHOOL
  MOTTOES: 323
Mercer, CROSS, THE: 32; CROWN: 6;
  DIVINITY: 279; UNCLASSIFIED: 66, 81

Mercer University, Macon, Georgia,
  ART: 31; KNOWLEDGE: 76;
  RELIGION: 28; SCHOOL MOTTOES: 279
Mercers' Company, HONOR: 80
Merchant Taylors' Company,
  TRADES: 9; UNITY: 15
Merchants of Bristol, PROSPERITY: 18
Merchants of Exeter, DIVINE
  GUIDANCE: 83; FORTUNE: 16
Mercier, FIDELITY: 312
Mercier (of Northumberland),
  WARNING: 1
Meredith (Bt.), DIVINITY: 218
Meredyth (Bt.), DIVINE GUIDANCE: 238
Meres, COURAGE: 204
Merewether, FORCE: 27
Merioneth C. C., U.K., LOCAL
  GOVERNMENT: 378; SEA: 37
Merle, BIRDS: 21; LIBERTY: 45
Merrick (U.S.), LIBERTY: 10;
  SERVICE: 7
Merritt (U.S.), WORTHINESS: 25
Merrman (of Kensington),
  GOODNESS: 41
Merry, DEEDS: 68; ENJOYMENT: 32, 33;
  HANDS: 31; HOPE: 162, 164;
  STEADFASTNESS: 99; STRENGTH: 139
Mersar, CROSS, THE: 32; CROWN: 6
Merthyr Tydfil C. B. C., U.K.,
  FELLOWSHIP: 6; LOCAL
  GOVERNMENT: 240
Merton and Morden U. D. C., U.K.,
  LIBERTY: 42; LOCAL
  GOVERNMENT: 188; STRENGTH: 77
Mervyn, DIVINE GIFTS: 13
Messeury, COURAGE: 30
Messiah College, Grantham,
  Pennsylvania, CHRIST, JESUS: 14;
  SCHOOL MOTTOES: 42
Messinger (U.S.), VIGILANCE: 1
Metaxa-Anzolato, AUTHORITY: 6;
  LAW: 64
Metcalfe (Bt.), HAPPINESS: 7
Methen (of Craiglownie), WAR: 37
Methuen (B.), ENVY: 11; VIRTUE: 286
Metropolitan State College, Denver,
  Colorado, SCHOOL MOTTOES: 317
Metropolitan Water Board, London,
  U.K., WATER: 7
Metterville (V.), CROSS, THE: 27;
  HOPE: 20
Mewburn (of Darlington), CAUTION: 24

Minn, ASPIRATION: 14
Minnitt, STATE MOTTOES: 60;
    VIRTUE: 373; WEAPONS: 99
Minot State College, Minot, North
    Dakota, SCHOOL MOTTOES: 285;
    SERVICE: 55
Minshull, DEEDS: 54; SHINING: 6;
    WEAPONS: 50
Minshull (Co. Chester), INCREASE: 21
Minshull (U.S.), HAPPINESS: 19;
    STRENGTH: 63
Minto (E.), DISCIPLINE: 6;
    GENTLENESS: 16; WEAPONS: 71
Minturn (U.S.), INTEGRITY: 9
Mirehouse, CONSISTENCY: 7
Mirfield U. D. C., U.K., FRUIT: 5;
    LOCAL GOVERNMENT: 161
Mississippi College, Clinton,
    Mississippi, SCHOOL MOTTOES: 353;
    TRUTH: 120; VIRTUE: 213
Mitchael (of Alderstoun), INCREASE: 8
Mitchell, CONTEMPT: 6; DEATH: 46;
    DILIGENCE: 46; DIVINE
    GUIDANCE: 63, 234; DIVINITY: 252;
    HONOR: 118; HOPE: 97;
    INNOCENCE: 14; MODERATION: 24
Mitchell (Bt.), INDUSTRIOUSNESS: 176;
    WISDOM: 69
Mitchell Community College,
    Statesville, North Carolina,
    EXCELLENCE: 16; SCHOOL
    MOTTOES: 310
Mitchell (of Barry),
    INDUSTRIOUSNESS: 176; WISDOM: 69
Mitchell (of Filligrige), SECURITY: 52
Mitchell (of Landath),
    INDUSTRIOUSNESS: 112
Mitchell (U.S.), PATIENCE: 40
Mitchelson, GOODNESS: 10; INCREASE: 5
Mitford, CONSISTENCY: 1;
    DILIGENCE: 1; EVIL: 10;
    WEAPONS: 105
Mitford (of Pitshill), DIVINE
    GUIDANCE: 257
M'Kenzie, VIGILANCE: 39
M'Kenzie (Co. Inverness), FIDELITY: 9
M'Laren, DESTRUCTION: 3
M'Laurin, OFFSPRING: 1
Moat (U.S.), DESPAIR: 4
Moffat, HOPE: 222
Mogg, PIETY: 4
Moil, FORGETTING: 11

Moilliet, LIGHT: 17; TRUTH: 29
Moir, DIVINE GIFTS: 22;
    FORGETTING: 11; HOPE: 284;
    MODERATION: 14; UNSELFISHNESS: 16
Moir (of Hilton), VIRTUE: 404
Moir (of Stonniewood),
    WORTHINESS: 22
Moises, VIRTUE: 121
Molesworth (Bt.), FIDELITY: 298
Molesworth (V.), COUNTRY: 140;
    LOVE: 117; PATRIOTISM: 93
Molineux, RECTITUDE: 18
Molleson, GLORY: 17
Molony (Co. Clare), DIVINITY: 256;
    HOPE: 101
Molyneux, CONQUEST: 72;
    COUNTRY: 31, 73; FIDELITY: 88, 251;
    PATRIOTISM: 34
Molyneux (Bt.), FORTUNE: 102;
    VIRTUE: 193
Mompesson (Co. Norfolk),
    HAPPINESS: 46
Monastic Order of St. Benedict,
    DIVINITY: 59
Monck (V.), AUDACITY: 56;
    FIDELITY: 181; SUCCESS: 5
Moncrief, FLOURISHING: 90; HOPE: 64
Moncrief (of Edinburgh),
    DILIGENCE: 23
Moncrieff, HOPE: 100
Moncrieff (Bt.), FLOURISHING: 90;
    HOPE: 284
Moncrieffe (Bt.), HOPE: 284
Money, DEEDS: 40; STEADFASTNESS: 86;
    WORDS: 10
Monins, MODERATION: 13
Monk Bretton (B.), DIVINE
    GUIDANCE: 50
Monkhouse (of Newcastle-on-Tyne),
    SALVATION: 34
Monk-Mason (of Mason-Brook),
    HONOR: 27; HOPE: 35; STATE
    MOTTOES: 11
Monks, ZEALOUSNESS: 2
Monmouth B. C., U.K.,
    GUIDANCE: 18; LOCAL
    GOVERNMENT: 230; PROTECTION: 20
Monmouthshire C. C., U.K.,
    FIDELITY: 331; LOCAL
    GOVERNMENT: 393
Monnet (U.S.), FLOURISHING: 39

Morgan (U.S.), REPUTATION: 3; VIRTUE: 52

Morice, HONOR: 27; HOPE: 35; STATE MOTTOES: 11

Morison, PRUDENCE: 43, 73; STRENGTH: 154; UNITY: 67

Morison (U.S.), PRUDENCE: 41

Moritz, Count of the Palatinate of Rhein (B. 1620), DIVINE GUIDANCE: 296; GRACE: 19

Moritz, Duke of Saxony-Zeitz (1619–81), DIVINITY: 355

Moritz, Elector of Saxony (1521–53), FORTUNE: 31

Moritz, Landgrave of Hesse-Cassel (1572–1632), LAW: 28; RIGHTEOUSNESS: 10; SELF-KNOWLEDGE: 6

Moritz Wilhelm, Duke of Saxony-Zeitz (1664–1718), MODERATION: 18

Morley, STEADFASTNESS: 137

Morley B. C., U.K., INDUSTRIOUSNESS: 75; LOCAL GOVERNMENT: 185

Morley (E.), FIDELITY: 106

Morley (of Marrick Park, Yorkshire), DEFENSE: 45

Mornington (E.), NECESSITY: 2

Morocco, DIVINE GUIDANCE: 311; NATIONAL MOTTOES: 10

Morpeth B. C., U.K., LOCAL GOVERNMENT: 191; LOCATION: 2

Morrall, TRUTH: 62

Morrell, COURAGE: 37

Morres, DIVINE GUIDANCE: 145

Morrice, TRADITION: 2

Morris, ACTION: 21; COURAGE: 245; FIDELITY: 207; FORTITUDE: 31; HONOR: 27; HOPE: 35; LIFE: 44; LOVE: 107; MUSIC: 7; ROYALTY: 92; SCRIPTURES: 1; STATE MOTTOES: 11; WAR: 5, 39

Morris Brown College, Atlanta, Georgia, DIVINITY: 195; SCHOOL MOTTOES: 118

Morris (Bt.), FAITH: 209

Morris (U.S.), CONQUEST: 35; FAITH: 108; GLORY: 46

Morrison, TRUTH: 168

Morrogh, VIRTUE: 283

Morse, DIVINITY: 80; WEAPONS: 29

Morse (U.S.), DIVINITY: 243

Morse-Boycott, DIVINITY: 80; WEAPONS: 29

Mortimer, ADVANCE: 48

Mortimer (of Auchenbody), DEFENSE: 1

Mortimer (U.S.), ANCESTRY: 45; VIRTUE: 396

Mortlake, ADVERSITY: 27

Morton, GIFTS and GIVING: 4; PERSEVERANCE: 56; STATE MOTTOES: 40

Morton (E.), CERTAINTY: 3

Morton (of Scarborough), HOPE: 267

Morton (U.S.), DIVINITY: 90

Moseley, FEAR: 20; HONOR: 78; LOVE: 55

Moseley (of Owsden), DIVINE GIFTS: 41; INCREASE: 20

Moseley (U.S.), GRADUALNESS: 5

Mosley (Bt.), LAW: 33

Moss, UNSELFISHNESS: 9

Mosse, CONQUEST: 19

Mossley B. C., INDUSTRIOUSNESS: 50; LOCAL GOVERNMENT: 149; PROSPERITY: 10

Mossman, FORTUNE: 80

Mostyn, PRESENT, THE: 3

Mostyn (B.), DIVINE GUIDANCE: 44; DIVINITY: 218; VENGEANCE: 3

Motley (U.S.), ANIMALS: 23; FAITH: 101

Mott, ACTION: 21

Motteux, DESIRE: 19

motto on a coin of 1633, DIVINE GUIDANCE: 435

Moubray, ADVERSITY: 25

Moulson, FIDELITY: 274; ROYALTY: 97

Moultray, FIDELITY: 244

Moultrie, FIDELITY: 244

Mounsey, BEAUTY: 7; PREPAREDNESS: 72; SCHOOL MOTTOES: 283

Mount Edgecumbe (E.), DIVINE GUIDANCE: 31

Mount Saint Mary's College, Emmitsburg, Maryland, HOPE: 268; SCHOOL MOTTOES: 299

Mount Stephen (B.), AUDACITY: 42; OPPOSITION: 1

Mountain, CROSS, THE: 48; SALVATION: 14

Mylne, COURAGE: 189;
    INDUSTRIOUSNESS: 33; PRUDENCE: 65
Mynors, DEEDS: 35; FAITH: 218;
    HOPE: 58, 225
Myrton, SUPPORT: 9
Mytton, STRENGTH: 83

N

Nafleur, PATIENCE: 36
Nagel (U.S.), STEADFASTNESS: 33
Nagle, ADVANCE: 39; FIDELITY: 190;
    GRATITUDE: 9; HOSTILITY: 10
Nagle (Bt.), DESIRE: 17
Nairn, SERIOUSNESS: 8
Nairn (of Greenyards), HOPE: 273
Nairn (of St. Ford), HOPE: 130
Nairne (B.), HOPE: 130
Napair (of Milliken, Bt.), PURITY: 19
Napier, COURAGE: 252; GLORY: 60;
    TRUTH: 61, 168; UNCLASSIFIED: 73;
    VIRTUE: 441
Napier (B.), PREPAREDNESS: 66
Napier (Bt.), FIDELITY: 151; VISION: 15
Napier (of Balwhaple), FIDELITY: 330
Napier (of Blackstone), PURITY: 19
Napier (of Falside), PURITY: 1
Napier (of Tayock), PATIENCE: 36
Nash, FIDELITY: 204; TRUTH: 63
Nasmyth (Bt.), WAR: 45
Nassau, HOPE: 237
Nassu, MODERATION: 28; WISDOM: 42
National College of Chiropractic,
    Lombard, Illinois, INTEGRITY: 10;
    SCHOOL MOTTOES: 94
National Order of France,
    REWARD: 39; VIRTUE: 159
National Society of the Daughters of
    the American Revolution,
    COUNTRY: 39; HOME: 12
Naughten, DIVINITY: 227; HOPE: 81
Naunton, CONQUEST: 41
Naval Postgraduate School, Monterey,
    California, EXCELLENCE: 8; SCHOOL
    MOTTOES: 101
2nd Dragoons (Royal Scots Greys),
    PRIMACY: 10
102nd Foot (Royal Dublin Fusiliers),
    DEEDS: 87; JUDGMENT: 13
2nd Regiment of Infantry of South
    Carolina, DEATH: 38; LIBERTY: 75
Neasmith, ART: 24; WEAPONS: 65

Neave, INDUSTRIOUSNESS: 76
Neave (Bt.), GOODNESS: 39
Neaves, HOPE: 179;
    INDUSTRIOUSNESS: 186
Needham, PRESENT, THE: 7
Neel, FAITH: 177; ROYALTY: 57
Neeld (Bt.), DEEDS: 65; NAME: 8
Neil, CONQUEST: 62; DEATH: 102
Neill, CONQUEST: 62; DEATH: 102;
    DIVINE GUIDANCE: 244;
    EQUANIMITY: 17
Neilson, CROWN: 11; GREATNESS: 9;
    PATRIOTISM: 41; PREPAREDNESS: 52;
    SERVICE: 22
Neilson (of Manwood), VIRTUE: 391
Nelson B. C., U.K.,
    INDUSTRIOUSNESS: 10; INTEGRITY: 3;
    LOCAL GOVERNMENT: 51
Nelson (E.), FAITH: 48; PROPER
    NAMES: 45, 54; WORTHINESS: 49
Nelson (of Beeston, co. Norfolk),
    FRIENDSHIP: 5; VIRTUE: 11
Nemehard, PEACE: 58; WAR: 55
Nepean, THOUGHT: 22
Nesbett, TRUTH: 4
Nesbitt, RECTITUDE: 35
Nesbitt (of Lismore), MAINTENANCE: 2
Nesham (of Stockton), HONOR: 175;
    HOPE: 227
Netherwood, AGGRESSION: 9
Nettles (of Nettleville, Co. Cork),
    PROVOCATION: 2
Neve, ASPIRATION: 31; EXCELLENCE: 1
Nevile, WORTHINESS: 34
Nevile (of Thornley), WORTHINESS: 36
Nevill, WORTHINESS: 36
Nevill (Lord Abergavenny),
    NOBILITY: 2
Neville-Rolfe, INCREASE: 9
Nevoy, ART: 23; COURAGE: 149
New College, Oxford, MANNERS: 5;
    SCHOOL MOTTOES: 183
New French Merchant Adventurers'
    Company, DUE: 4
New Mexico, GROWTH: 3
New Mexico Highlands University, Las
    Vegas, New Mexico, ART: 11;
    SCHOOL MOTTOES: 24
New York State University College at
    Potsdam, New York,
    EXCELLENCE: 2; SCHOOL
    MOTTOES: 27

Nisbet, FORTUNE: 87; HONOR: 48;
  HOPE: 82; RESULTS: 1; SHARING: 2;
  VIRTUE: 125, 126; WEAPONS: 49
Nisbet (Bt.), PATIENCE: 15
Nisbet (of Dirletoun), JUSTICE: 18
Nisbett, PATIENCE: 15
Niven, HOPE: 297; LIFE: 51
Nivison, RESULTS: 1
Noble, COURAGE: 250; VIRTUE: 388
Noble (of Reresbie), FAITH: 61;
  FORTITUDE: 3
Noel, DUE: 1; GOODNESS: 32;
  THOUGHT: 15
Noguier, WORTHINESS: 57
Norbury (B.), COUNTRY: 124;
  FIDELITY: 273; ROYALTY: 96
Norcliffe, PURITY: 22
Norden, PROVIDENCE: 26
Norfolk C. C., U.K., LOCAL
  GOVERNMENT: 178; SERVICE: 24
Norfolk (D.), VIRTUE: 186
Norfolk State University, Norfolk,
  Virginia, SCHOOL MOTTOES: 2
Norgate, ACTION: 24; VIRTUE: 259
Norie, HOME: 7
Norman (Co. Sussex), DIVINE
  GUIDANCE: 118
Normanby (M.), COURAGE: 259
Normand, DIVINE GUIDANCE: 42
Normanton (E.), SECURITY: 79
Norreys, FIDELITY: 226; SERVICE: 19,
  31
Norris, EQUANIMITY: 17; SERVICE: 19
Norris (Co. Norfolk), FIDELITY: 144
North, COURAGE: 11; DEFENSE: 34;
  FAITH: 5; LOCAL GOVERNMENT: 26;
  NOBILITY: 9; VIRTUE: 101
North Carolina Agricultural and
  Technical State University,
  Greensboro, North Carolina,
  HANDS: 25; MIND: 27; SCHOOL
  MOTTOES: 188
North Dakota State School of Science,
  Wahpeton, North Dakota,
  KNOWLEDGE: 98; SCHOOL
  MOTTOES: 371
North Walsham U. D. C., U.K.,
  LOCAL GOVERNMENT: 248;
  UNSELFISHNESS: 8
Northampton C. B. C., U.K., LOCAL
  GOVERNMENT: 57; STRENGTH: 15;
  UNITY: 7

Northamptonshire C. C., U.K.,
  FLORA: 32; LOCAL
  GOVERNMENT: 317; UNITY: 64
Northcote, SPEED: 16
Northcote (Bt.), CROSS, THE: 6;
  LIGHT: 4
Northeast Louisiana University,
  Monroe, Louisiana, SCHOOL
  MOTTOES: 281; TRUTH: 82
Northen, EQUANIMITY: 17
Northesk (E.), PROPER NAMES: 54;
  VICTORY: 8
Northmore, EQUANIMITY: 13
Northumberland (D.), DIVINITY: 163;
  HOPE: 49
Northwest College of the Assemblies of
  God, Kirkland, Washington,
  LIGHT: 29; SCHOOL MOTTOES: 167;
  SHINING: 13
Northwestern College of Chiropractic,
  St. Paul, Minnesota,
  KNOWLEDGE: 65; SCHOOL
  MOTTOES: 270
Northwestern State University,
  Natchitoches, Louisiana,
  CONFIDENCE: 21; JUSTICE: 123;
  SCHOOL MOTTOES: 343; UNITY: 94
Northwich U. D. C., U.K., LIFE: 30;
  LOCAL GOVERNMENT: 322
Northwick (B.), MEASURE: 12
Norton, ANCESTRY: 1; FORCE: 3
Norton (B.), JUSTICE: 1; LAW: 1
Norton (of Elmham, Co. Norfolk),
  DIVINITY: 133; WEAPONS: 30
Norton (of Kings-Norton),
  AUDACITY: 62; FIDELITY: 183
Norvill (of Boghall), HOPE: 190
Norwich University, Northfield,
  Vermont, EFFORT: 20; SCHOOL
  MOTTOES: 146
Norwood, CROSS, THE: 109
Notley, DECEPTION: 7
Nott, CROWN: 18; OPPOSITION: 12;
  PEACE: 29, 63
Nottingham City and C. B. C., U.K.,
  LOCAL GOVERNMENT: 403;
  VIRTUE: 453
Nottinghamshire C. C., U.K.,
  IMPROVEMENT: 43; LOCAL
  GOVERNMENT: 334
The Nova-Scotia Baronets, GLORY: 17
Nova Scotia Knights, DEFENSE: 36

Oldham C. B. C., U.K., LOCAL
GOVERNMENT: 333; WISDOM: 63

O'Learie, CROWN: 15; SEA: 11

Oliffe, DIVINE GUIDANCE: 229

Oliphant, COURAGE: 192; FORTUNE: 88;
HONOR: 53; HOPE: 71, 85

Oliphant (Co. Perth), PRUDENCE: 6

Oliphant (of Bachiltoun), TIME: 74

Oliphant (of Clasbury, Langtoun,
etc.), ENLIGHTENMENT: 2

Oliphant (of Newton, co. Perth),
ASPIRATION: 25; SCHOOL MOTTOES: 13

Oliveira, AUDACITY: 33

Oliver, CONCILIATION: 1; DEEDS: 37,
57; DIVINE GUIDANCE: 183;
DIVINITY: 382; FLORA: 28;
HAPPINESS: 58; RELIGION: 29;
SATISFACTION: 5

Olivet College, Olivet, Michigan,
CHRIST, JESUS: 66; SCHOOL
MOTTOES: 236

Olivet Nazarene College, Kankakee,
Illinois, JUSTICE: 75; TRUTH: 48

O'Loghlen (Bt.), SECURITY: 3

O'Malley (Bt.), POWER: 23; SEA: 36

O'Mallun, PATIENCE: 11

O'Meara, PROSPERITY: 36

Omond, TIME: 9

O'Moran, DARKNESS: 7; LIGHT: 34;
SHINING: 15

O'More, COURAGE: 202; FIDELITY: 292

O'Mulley, DEATH: 40; DISGRACE: 10

O'Mulloy, FORTUNE: 58;
OPPORTUNITY: 4

On a building in Louvigny, France,
FEAR: 74; SECURITY: 65

on a farmhouse in Lucerne,
Switzerland, PEACE: 85

on coins of the United States,
DIVINITY: 263; TRUST: 66

On coronet of Garter King-at-Arms,
GOODNESS: 16; MERCY: 22

On the first American flag of the
Revolutionary War, WARNING: 4

on the first Eddystone Lighthouse,
Devonshire, England; Hewatt,
DARKNESS: 16; LIGHT: 72

on the Great Seal of the Northwest
Territory, IMPROVEMENT: 22; STATE
MOTTOES: 33

on the Seal of the State of South
Carolina, IMPROVEMENT: 22; STATE
MOTTOES: 33

O'Naghten, AUDACITY: 88; WISDOM: 59

O'Neil, COUNTRY: 130; PATRIOTISM: 90

O'Neill, COUNTRY: 96; DEFENSE: 22;
DEFIANCE: 6; FAITH: 198; HANDS: 16;
INJURY: 3; ROYALTY: 69

O'Neill (of Bunowen), HANDS: 33

Ongley (B.), FUTURE, THE: 16

Onslow, CAUTION: 24; PRAISE: 7

Onslow (Bt.), CAUTION: 24

Onslow (E.), FIDELITY: 289

Oral Roberts University, Tulsa,
Oklahoma, MIND: 37; SCHOOL
MOTTOES: 192; SPIRIT: 13

Oranmore and Browne (B.),
AUDACITY: 62; FIDELITY: 183

Ord, COURAGE: 150, 152;
GENTLENESS: 11; MILITARY
DISTINCTION: 3

Orde, COURAGE: 153; GENTLENESS: 12

Ordell, DIVINE GUIDANCE: 42

Order of Amaranta, MEMORY: 2

Order of Charles III (Spain),
COURAGE: 248; WORTHINESS: 63

Order of Christian Charity,
SERVICE: 37

Order of Concord, UNITY: 8

Order of Cyprus, SECURITY: 57

Order of Danebrog (Denmark),
REBIRTH: 27

Order of Death's Head, DEATH: 44;
MEMORY: 16

Order of Ermine, DEATH: 40;
DISGRACE: 10

Order of Francis of the Two Sicilies,
WORTHINESS: 44

Order of Generosity (Prussia),
GENEROSITY: 11

Order of Hubert, FAITH: 167

Order of Ladies Slaves to Virtue,
VICTORY: 45

Order of Leopold (Austria),
CROWN: 17; PROSPERITY: 35

Order of Leopold (Belgium),
POWER: 10; UNITY: 51

Order of Maria Eleonora, DEATH: 82

Order of Mary Magdalen, LOVE: 72;
PEACE: 24

Order of Maximilian Joseph of Bavaria, COUNTRY: 143; COURAGE: 264

Order of Merit of St. Michael (Bavaria), DIVINITY: 367

Order of Merit of the Bavarian Crown, HONOR: 193; VIRTUE: 270

Order of Military Merit, MILITARY DISTINCTION: 5

Order of Military Merit (Hesse Cassel), COURAGE: 185; FIDELITY: 263

Order of Neighborly Love, LOVE: 25

Order of our Redeemer, SADNESS: 7

Order of Prince Ernst of Saxe-Coburg-Gotha, FIDELITY: 141

Order of Re-Union, GOVERNMENT: 13

Order of Saint Catherine (Russia), DUTY: 1

Order of St. Andrew of Scotland, PROVOCATION: 2

Order of St. Anna, PROTECTION: 29

Order of St. Anne (Schleswig-Holstein), FAITH: 4; JUSTICE: 3; PIETY: 1

Order of St. Anne (Sleswick), FAITH: 3; JUSTICE: 2

Order of St. Catharine (Russia), COUNTRY: 66; FIDELITY: 247; LOVE: 97; PATRIOTISM: 30

Order of St. Constantine, CONQUEST: 19

Order of St. Elizabeth (Brazil), ASSISTANCE: 21; KINDNESS: 19

Order of St. Ferdinand, PATRIOTISM: 12; ROYALTY: 29

Order of St. Ferdinand and of Merit (Sicily), FIDELITY: 261

Order of St. George (Bavaria), FAITH: 150; FLOURISHING: 53; JUSTICE: 45; RIGHTEOUSNESS: 8; STRENGTH: 74

Order of St. George of Bavaria, PURITY: 27

Order of St. Henry of Saxony, COURAGE: 262; WAR: 77

Order of St. Henry (Saxony), COURAGE: 179; PIETY: 33

Order of St. Herminigilde (Spain), MILITARY DISTINCTION: 1; REWARD: 1

Order of St. Hubert, FIDELITY: 38

Order of St. Hubert of Loraine and of Bar, HONOR: 193; VIRTUE: 270

Order of St. James of the Sword, WEAPONS: 85

Order of St. Januarius (of Naples), DEVOTION: 8

Order of St. Joachim, GOODNESS: 10; INCREASE: 5

Order of St. Joachim (Germany), FRIENDSHIP: 39; LOVE: 69

Order of St. Louis and The Legion of Honour (France), COURAGE: 34

Order of St. Mark, PEACE: 60

Order of St. Mary the Glorious, CONQUEST: 18

Order of St. Michael (France), SEA: 9

Order of St. Nicholas (Russia), TIME: 35; TRUST: 90

Order of St. Patrick, UNITY: 62

Order of St. Stanislaus (Russia), REWARD: 29

Order of St. Stephen, LOVE: 111

Order of St. Stephen (Austria), REWARD: 41; SERVICE: 42

Order of the Bath (Britain), UNITY: 76

Order of the Bee (France), SIZE: 1

Order of the Belgic Lion for Civil Merit, NOBILITY: 29; VIRTUE: 295

Order of the Black Eagle of Prussia, DUE: 4

Order of the Crescent, FULLNESS: 4

Order of the Danebrog (Denmark), DIVINITY: 212; ROYALTY: 44

Order of the Dog and Cock, Montmorency (France), DIVINE GUIDANCE: 169

Order of the Ear of Corn and Ermine, FIDELITY: 10

Order of the Fan, UNITY: 48

Order of the Garter (Britain), DISGRACE: 7

Order of the Golden Fleece (Austria and Spain), INDUSTRIOUSNESS: 164; REWARD: 36

Order of the Golden Fleece (Spain), FIDELITY: 18; TIMELINESS: 3

Order of the Golden Lion, FIDELITY: 341; VIRTUE: 430

Order of the Golden Lion (Hesse-Cassel), COURAGE: 244; FIDELITY: 340

Order of the Guelph (Britain), ADVERSITY: 48

Order of the Holy Ghost (France),
  GUIDANCE: 10
Order of the Hospitallers of St. Hubert
  (Bavaria), FIDELITY: 203
Order of the Indian Empire,
  SUPPORT: 4
Order of the Iron Crown (Austria),
  HONOR: 6
Order of the Knights of Christ of
  Portugal, founded 1317, WAR: 13
Order of the Lamb of God (Sweden),
  DIVINE GUIDANCE: 153
Order of the Legion of Honor
  (France), COUNTRY: 42; HONOR: 68;
  MILITARY DISTINCTION: 5
Order of the Lion of Lembourg,
  NOBILITY: 7; VIRTUE: 428;
  WORTHINESS: 17
Order of the Lion of Lembourg, and
  St. Charles of Wurtemberg,
  WORTHINESS: 4
Order of the Noble Passion,
  HONOR: 128; VIRTUE: 96
Order of the Polar Star, STARS: 27
Order of the Porcupine (France),
  WAR: 17
Order of the Red Eagle
  (Brandenburg), CONSISTENCY: 14
Order of the Red Eagle (Prussia),
  SINCERITY: 15; STEADFASTNESS: 116
Order of the Redeemer (Greece),
  DIVINITY: 404
Order of the Royal-Crown, founded
  802, CROWN: 4
Order of the Royal Red Cross,
  FAITH: 44; HOPE: 59; KINDNESS: 7
Order of the Seraphim (Sweden),
  CHRIST, JESUS: 49
Order of the Star of India (founded
  1861), GUIDANCE: 14; LOCAL
  GOVERNMENT: 169; PARADISE: 27
Order of the Star of Sicily, STARS: 25
Order of the Star of the Cross
  (Austria), GLORY: 53; SALVATION: 37
Order of the Sword (Sweden),
  COUNTRY: 100
Order of the Thistle of Bourbon,
  HOPE: 48
Order of the Tower and Sword,
  COURAGE: 224; FIDELITY: 332

Order of the Two Sicilies,
  COUNTRY: 116; COURAGE: 186;
  DEVOTION: 8; HAPPINESS: 15; STATE
  MOTTOES: 19
Order of the White Eagle (Polish),
  FAITH: 195; LAW: 41; ROYALTY: 68
Order of the White Elephant,
  GREATNESS: 3
Order of the White Falcon (Saxe-
  Weimar), VICTORY: 69;
  VIGILANCE: 78
Order of the White Rose, MEMORY: 23
Order of Wilhelm (Netherlands),
  COURAGE: 275; FIDELITY: 343;
  PRUDENCE: 86
O'Reilly, HONOR: 27; HOPE: 35; STATE
  MOTTOES: 11
O'Reilly (of Knock Abbey),
  FORTITUDE: 10; PRUDENCE: 22
Orford (E.), WORDS: 18
Original motto of the Innholders'
  Company, London, HOSPITALITY: 1
Original State seal of Nevada, STATE
  MOTTOES: 62; WILLINGNESS: 9
Orkney (E.), WAR: 23
Orme, COURAGE: 81; FIDELITY: 179
Ormerod, GIFTS and GIVING: 13
Ormiston, FORTUNE: 25
Ormonde (M.), SEARCH and
  DISCOVERY: 4
Ormsby, COURAGE: 93; PRUDENCE: 21
O'Rourke, GOVERNMENT: 10;
  SERVICE: 61; VICTORY: 64
Orpen, TRUTH: 168
Orpen (of Glancrough), TRUTH: 144
Orr, ACCEPTANCE: 2; COURAGE: 87,
  261; FIDELITY: 322; FORTUNE: 116;
  UNITY: 28; VIGILANCE: 36
Orr (of Barrowfield), GOODNESS: 3
Orrock, ART: 8; CHRIST, JESUS: 76;
  FAITH: 10
Osbaldeston, STEADFASTNESS: 20
Osborn, INCREASE: 22
Osborne (Bt.), INSIGNIFICANCE: 5
Osborne (of Newtown, Bt.),
  PEACE: 53; WAR: 54
Osbourne, INCREASE: 22
O'Shee, TRUTH: 168
Osmand, FAITH: 85
O'Sullivan, DEFIANCE: 8; HANDS: 18;
  VICTORY: 27

Oswald, CLEVERNESS: 6; COURAGE: 70; FOLLOWING: 16; PARADISE: 25; SERVICE: 34; STARS: 24

Otto, Landgrave of Hesse (1594–1617), JUSTICE: 100; PIETY: 34, 39; PRUDENCE: 40

Otto Heinrich, Count of the Palatinate of Sulzbach (1556–1604), DIVINITY: 101; ROYALTY: 24

Otto Heinrich, Elector of the Palatinate (1502–59), TIME: 31

Otto the Younger, Duke of Braunschweig-Lüneburg-Harburg (1528–1603), FEAR: 39; HOPE: 115, 147; PATIENCE: 8; SILENCE: 10; TIME: 13; VICTORY: 49

Otway, DIVINE GUIDANCE: 404

Oughton, PAST, THE: 6

Our Lady of Holy Cross College, New Orleans, Louisiana, HOPE: 274; SCHOOL MOTTOES: 300

Ouseley (Bt.), ANIMALS: 36; DEATH: 58

Outhwaite, DIVINITY: 61

Outram (Bt.), FIDELITY: 240

Ouvry, JUSTICE: 27

over a bedroom door in Loseley House, near Guildford, Surrey, England, ENVY: 5; FRIENDSHIP: 37

Over a door in a house in Clontra Shankill, Ireland, DIVINE GUIDANCE: 446

over a door in the Palazzo Borghese, Rome, ACCOMPLISHMENT: 20

Over a stairway in a house in Edinburgh, Scotland, DIVINE GUIDANCE: 423

over the doorway of Holy Trinity Hospital at West Croydon, England, KINDNESS: 21

over the drawing-room door, Loseley House, near Guildford, Surrey, England, GOODNESS: 33

over the entrance door of a house in Edinburgh, Scotland, ENDURANCE: 35

Ovington, FINISH: 13

Owen, MODERATION: 24; STEADFASTNESS: 59; VIRTUE: 183

Owen (Bt.), HONESTY: 11

Owens, FORCE: 7

Oxford City and C. B. C., U.K., LOCAL GOVERNMENT: 154; STRENGTH: 56; TRUTH: 27

Oxford (E.), COURAGE: 243; FAITH: 252

Oxford University, Oxford, U.K., DIVINITY: 143; SCHOOL MOTTOES: 72

Oxfordshire C. C., LOCAL GOVERNMENT: 333; WISDOM: 63

Oxley, RELIGION: 31

P

Pack, FIDELITY: 155

Packe, CROWN: 16; LIBERTY: 62

Packwood, GOODNESS: 23; GREATNESS: 7

Page, CROSS, THE: 41; HONOR: 70; PEACE: 76

Pagen, FEAR: 42

Paget, OPPOSITION: 8; REWARD: 28

Paget (Bt.), HOPE: 51; PERSEVERANCE: 15

Paget (Co. Somerset), WORDS: 2

Pagit (of Hadley), DIVINITY: 83

Paignton U. D. C., U.K., HOSPITALITY: 5; LOCAL GOVERNMENT: 337

Pain, DEATH: 40; DISGRACE: 10

Painters' Company, LOVE: 18, 26; OBEDIENCE: 2, 3; TRADES: 4, 5

Pakenham, GLORY: 24

Pakington, VIRTUE: 134

Palazzo Borghese, Rome, ABILITY: 20; LIMITATION: 9

Palgrave, DIVINITY: 289; PRAISE: 4

Palles, DIVINE GUIDANCE: 86; FORTUNE: 17

Palliser, COURAGE: 62; DIVINE GUIDANCE: 106

Palmer, FLOURISHING: 51; FORGETTING: 19; REWARD: 25, 42; SUFFERING: 1; VIRTUE: 133

Palmer (Bt.), DIVINITY: 233; TRUST: 50

Palmer (of Carlton, Bt.), INDUSTRIOUSNESS: 156; SUCCESS: 8

Palmer (of Fairfield, Bt.), REWARD: 25; VIRTUE: 133

Palmer (of Kilmare), INDUSTRIOUSNESS: 156; SUCCESS: 8

Palmer (of Wingham, Bt.), REWARD: 25; VIRTUE: 133

Palmerston (V.), FLEXIBILITY: 3

Source Information

Provan, COUNTRY: 100; PATRIOTISM: 46
Prudham, FIDELITY: 266;
  PRUDENCE: 76
Prudhoe (B.), DIVINITY: 163; HOPE: 49
Pryce, ANCESTRY: 1; DIVINITY: 148,
  229; TRUST: 47
Pryce (Bt.), DIVINE GUIDANCE: 225
Pryme (of Cambridge), COURAGE: 14;
  FORTUNE: 4
Prytherch, DIVINITY: 146
Pudsey, FORTUNE: 41
Pudsey B. C., U.K., FEAR: 3;
  JUSTICE: 9; LOCAL GOVERNMENT: 45
Pugh, ENVY: 9; IMMORTALITY: 9
Pughe (of Ty Gwyn), HEALING and
  HEALTH: 18
Puleston (Bt.), BRIGHTNESS: 6
Pulleine, INNOCENCE: 14
Pulteney, TRUTH: 79
Purcell, DEATH: 6; VICTORY: 7
Purchon, PRUDENCE: 68; VIGILANCE: 58
Purdie, FIDELITY: 127
Purdon, HOME: 19; RELIGION: 19
Purefoy (of Leicestershire), FAITH: 201
Purie, TIME: 72
Purton, FRUIT: 2
Purves, BRIGHTNESS: 7
Purvis, BRIGHTNESS: 7;
  MODERATION: 24; SUN: 10
Pybus (U.S.), CONVENIENCE: 3
Pye, CROSS, THE: 14, 61; GLORY: 9, 29;
  PIETY: 41
Pyke, DIVINE GUIDANCE: 96

Q

Quain, STEADFASTNESS: 75
Quantock, GRATITUDE: 13
Quatherine, DESTINATION: 2
Quayle, HOPE: 166
Queen Elizabeth I., CONSISTENCY: 9;
  FLORA: 39; LOCAL GOVERNMENT: 338
Queen Mary (1516–1558), TRUTH: 141
Queen Mary of England,
  PROTECTION: 24
Queens College, Charlotte, North
  Carolina, SCHOOL MOTTOES: 201;
  SERVICE: 35
Queen's Own (Royal West Kent
  Regiment), U.K., MERCY: 9
Queen's Own (Roy. West Kent)
  Regiment, U.K., DUTY: 26

Queen's (Royal W. Surrey) Regiment,
  VICTORY: 54
Queen's University, Kingston, Ontario,
  Canada, RECTITUDE: 72; SCHOOL
  MOTTOES: 296
Queensbury (M.), ADVANCE: 19
Queensland Agricultural College,
  Lawes, Queensland, Australia,
  SCHOOL MOTTOES: 269
Queenstown Harbour, Cork, Ireland,
  LOCAL GOVERNMENT: 364;
  PROTECTION: 28
Quin, ASPIRATION: 71; PARADISE: 55
Quinan, COUNTRY: 121; LOVE: 103;
  PATRIOTISM: 80
Quincy (U.S.), DISCRETION: 5;
  VIRTUE: 40
Quinsigamond Community College,
  Worcester, Massachusetts,
  INTEGRITY: 27; KNOWLEDGE: 43;
  SCHOOL MOTTOES: 165; SERVICE: 29

R

Rabett, VIRTUE: 197
Radcliffe, GOODNESS: 9; POSSIBILITY: 9
Radcliffe B. C., INDUSTRIOUSNESS: 64
Radcliffe (Bt.), VIRTUE: 317
Radcliffe (of Fox-Denton and
  Ordshall), PROPER NAMES: 14
Radnorshire C. C., U.K.,
  ASPIRATION: 47; LOCAL
  GOVERNMENT: 108
Radstock (B.), PROPER NAMES: 51
Rae, HONOR: 51; PRAISE: 3
Rae (Bt.), PREPAREDNESS: 27
Raeburn, COURAGE: 220; DIVINE
  GUIDANCE: 386; SECURITY: 78;
  STRENGTH: 118
Raffles, CROSS, THE: 68
Raikes, FUTURE, THE: 9
Raikes (of Welton), HONESTY: 16
Raines, CONQUEST: 44; JUDGMENT: 10
Rainier, FLORA: 20
Raisbeck, KINDNESS: 2; SUCCESS: 1
Rait, HOPE: 142, 201, 222;
  IMPROVEMENT: 21
Ralph, FIDELITY: 137
Ralston, FIDELITY: 101
Ram, DEEDS: 70, 71, 81
Ramadge, COURAGE: 44; LOCAL
  GOVERNMENT: 65; WISDOM: 10

Ramage, MEASURE: 15; TRUTH: 177

Ramsay, ASPIRATION: 82; EFFORT: 29;
EMERGENCE: 2; FEAR: 14; GRACE: 28;
INNOCENCE: 15; MANNER: 9;
PERSEVERANCE: 16; PIETY: 8;
PRUDENCE: 59; STEADFASTNESS: 34;
VICTORY: 37

Ramsay (Bt.), ASPIRATION: 40

Ramsay (of Banff House, Bt.),
DANGER: 19; VIRTUE: 192

Ramsay (of Idington), CHANGE: 5

Ramsay (of Methven), FOLLOWING: 28;
PARADISE: 62

Ramsay (of Whitehill), CONQUEST: 33

Ramsay-Fairfax-Lucy (Bt.), WORDS: 13

Ramsbottom, COURAGE: 64;
FIDELITY: 102

Ramsden, CHANGE: 3; MIND: 6

Ramsey, VENGEANCE: 4

Ramsgate B. C., U.K., LOCAL
GOVERNMENT: 326; SECURITY: 49

Ramsgate College, U.K.,
CONQUEST: 17; SCHOOL
MOTTOES: 132

Rancliffe (B.), AUDACITY: 71

Rand (U.S.), IMMORTALITY: 7

Randall, TIME: 34

Randles, TIME: 52

Ranelagh (V.), PARADISE: 6;
STRENGTH: 12

Ranfurley (E.), ACTION: 14;
CONCILIATION: 7

Ranfurly (E.), PROPER NAMES: 34;
PROSPERITY: 28

Ranken, UNCLASSIFIED: 36;
VIRTUE: 314

Rankin, AUDACITY: 64; COURAGE: 190;
PROVIDENCE: 23; PRUDENCE: 69;
RECTITUDE: 26; VIRTUE: 162

Rankine, INCREASE: 28

Rant, ANIMALS: 51

Rasch (Bt.), RECTITUDE: 22

Ratcliff, FEAR: 66; HOPE: 208

Rathbone, DISCIPLINE: 6;
GENTLENESS: 16

Rathdowne (E.), AUDACITY: 56;
FIDELITY: 181; SUCCESS: 5

Ratray, LIBERTY: 34

Rattary (of Scotland), VICTORY: 17

Rattray, PARADISE: 58

Rattray (of Craighill), DESIRE: 23;
STARS: 44

Raven, LIFE: 12

Ravens, BIRDS: 26; NOURISHMENT: 6

Ravenscroft, FIDELITY: 254;
INDUSTRIOUSNESS: 160;
PERSEVERANCE: 63

Ravenshaw, DIVINE GUIDANCE: 148

Ravensworth, IDENTITY: 2

Ravensworth (B.), FAME: 11

Rawdon-Hastings (Marquis of
Hastings), TRUST: 103

Rawlings (Co. Cornwall), SELF-
KNOWLEDGE: 3

Rawlins, CHANGE: 13; FEAR: 38, 49;
FORCE: 11

Rawlinson, COUNTRY: 24;
DEVOTION: 7; ROYALTY: 27

Rawlinson (knt.), CAUTION: 24

Rawson, DEEDS: 61; DIVINE
GUIDANCE: 26; SECURITY: 4;
VIRTUE: 100

Rawtenstall B. C., U.K.,
INDUSTRIOUSNESS: 50; LOCAL
GOVERNMENT: 149; PROSPERITY: 10

Ray, JUSTICE: 24, 55; TRUTH: 18

Ray (U.S.), DIVINITY: 282; HOPE: 126

Ray-Clayton (of Norwich),
HONESTY: 17

Raymond, BIRDS: 28; ENVY: 8;
EQUANIMITY: 2; GIFTS and GIVING: 5;
REBIRTH: 25

Raymond (U.S.), ROYALTY: 109

Rayson, ETERNITY: 1

23rd Foot (Royal Welsh Fusiliers),
ADVERSITY: 47

3rd (King's Own) Hussars,
ADVERSITY: 47

Read, LAW: 9; PEACE: 44;
PROSPERITY: 40

Read (Bt.)., STATE MOTTOES: 7;
WEAPONS: 21

Read (U.S.), FEAR: 40; HOPE: 148;
VIGILANCE: 51

Reade, FEAR: 2; LOVE: 27;
USEFULNESS: 17

Readhead (Bt.), EFFORT: 21

Reading School, U.K., ART: 4; SCHOOL
MOTTOES: 23

Reath, INDUSTRIOUSNESS: 64

Reay, PREPAREDNESS: 26

Reay (B.), HANDS: 21

Republic of Tunisia, JUSTICE: 93;
LIBERTY: 85; NATIONAL MOTTOES: 20;
ORDER: 6
Republic of Upper Volta,
INDUSTRIOUSNESS: 194; JUSTICE: 126;
NATIONAL MOTTOES: 36; UNITY: 107
Republic of Zambia, NATIONAL
MOTTOES: 19; UNITY: 57
Reveley (of Bryn y Gwin), SPORT: 3;
STARS: 29
Revere (U.S.), COUNTRY: 119;
PATRIOTISM: 77
Reynardson, VIRTUE: 268
Reynell, FAITH: 149
Reynell (Bt.), STRANGER: 6;
STRENGTH: 92
Reynolds, ACTION: 21; DIVINITY: 178;
RIGHTS: 5
Reynolds (of Great Yarmouth and
Necton, Co. Norfolk), DIVINE
GUIDANCE: 232
Reynolds (U.S.), COUNTRY: 118;
PATRIOTISM: 76; VIRTUE: 187
Rhet, HOPE: 222
Rhodes, DIVINE GUIDANCE: 387;
MIND: 5; STRENGTH: 119
Rhodes (of Bellair), CHANGE: 2
Rhodesia, NATIONAL MOTTOES: 16;
WORTHINESS: 38
Riall, HOPE: 170
Riblesdale (B.), ANCESTRY: 34
Ribton (Bt.), LIBERTY: 43
Rice, AUDACITY: 89; FAITH: 105
Rich, FAITH: 135, 137
Rich (Bt.), FAITH: 133
Richard, Count of the Palatinate
(1521–98), DIVINE GIFTS: 42
Richard I., CHRIST, JESUS: 10
Richard III., FIDELITY: 228
Richards, HONOR: 81;
INDUSTRIOUSNESS: 180; LIBERTY: 64;
LOVE: 56; MODERATION: 24;
VIRTUE: 105
Richardson, ADVERSITY: 73;
DIVINITY: 234, 275; FIDELITY: 289;
HONESTY: 46; HONOR: 199, 201;
INDUSTRIOUSNESS: 119; KINDNESS: 4;
MEMORY: 20; OPPOSITION: 10;
PROVIDENCE: 3; STEADFASTNESS: 53,
115; STRENGTH: 176, 178;
TRANSIENCE: 3; TRUST: 12, 51, 74;
VIRTUE: 109, 301, 364, 394, 412

Richardson (Bt.), HONOR: 199;
VIRTUE: 364
Richardson (U.S.), PRUDENCE: 42
Richie, HONOR: 199; VIRTUE: 364
Richmond B. C., U.K., DIVINITY: 2;
LOCAL GOVERNMENT: 4
Richmond (D.), FLORA: 13;
FLOURISHING: 16
Rickart, PREPAREDNESS: 50;
WARNING: 8
Ricketson, BEING, SELF: 2
Ricketts, DIVINE GUIDANCE: 80; LOCAL
GOVERNMENT: 84
Ricketts (Bt.), ACCEPTANCE: 4
Ricketts (of Combe), TRUTH: 75
Rickford (of Aylesbury), DEEDS: 8;
WORDS: 1
Rickinghall (Co. Suffolk),
DIVINITY: 133; WEAPONS: 30
Riddel, VIRTUE: 292
Riddell, HOPE: 76; NAVIGATION: 1;
SHARING: 4; VIRTUE: 292
Riddell (Bt.), HOPE: 82; SHARING: 2;
USEFULNESS: 15
Riddell (of Felton), DIVINE
GUIDANCE: 162
Riddock, ADVERSITY: 87
Rideout, OFFICE: 4
Rider, INCREASE: 14
Ridgeley (U.S.), ANIMALS: 8
Ridgeway, DIVINITY: 301
Ridley (Bt.), FAITH: 18; FIDELITY: 40
Ridley (V.), FAITH: 18; FIDELITY: 40
Ridsdale, DIVINITY: 107; HOPE: 26
Rig, COURAGE: 247
Rigg, COURAGE: 247; LIFE: 7; MUSIC: 3
Rigge, CAUTION: 24
Rind, FRAGRANCE: 2
Ripley (U.S.), FINISH: 11
Ripon (E.), FAITH: 128
Rippon (Co. Northumberland),
HOPE: 154
Rishton U. D. C., U.K., LOCAL
GOVERNMENT: 312; REBIRTH: 33
Ritchie, BOASTFULNESS: 6; HONOR: 199;
VIRTUE: 364
Riverdale (B.), FIDELITY: 199
Rivers (B.), EQUANIMITY: 2
Rivers (Bt.), WATER: 16
Riversdale, OPPOSITION: 5
Riversdale (B.), HANDS: 23;
HOSTILITY: 13

Robe, DIRECTNESS: 9; HONOR: 15
Robeck, COURAGE: 95
Roberson, FIDELITY: 221
Robert (U.S.), DIVINITY: 25
Robertoun (of Ernock), SECURITY: 11
Roberts, CONSCIENCE: 4;
    DILIGENCE: 43; DIVINITY: 196;
    IMPROVEMENT: 11; LOVE: 106;
    PARADISE: 54; SUCCESS: 17
Roberts (of Beechfield), HONOR: 27;
    HOPE: 35; STATE MOTTOES: 11
Roberts (of Crofton Hall, Co. Salop),
    DIVINE GUIDANCE: 71; FORTUNE: 15
Robertson, COURAGE: 272; DEATH: 81;
    DIVINITY: 94; DUTY: 32; FAITH: 156;
    FEAR: 60; JUSTICE: 108;
    LEADERSHIP: 10; ORIGIN: 9;
    PERSEVERANCE: 69; REWARD: 8;
    SHINING: 24; STRENGTH: 110, 111;
    VIRTUE: 72, 146, 363; WISDOM: 57
Robertson (of Auchleeks), GLORY: 23
Robertson (of Glasgow), GLORY: 49;
    LAW: 57
Robertson (of Lude), ANIMALS: 15;
    WAKEFULNESS: 2
Robertson (of Oakridge (B.), WAR: 26
Robertson (of Strowan, COURAGE: 266;
    GLORY: 61
Robertstoun (of Bedley), SECURITY: 58
Robins, DIVINE GUIDANCE: 145
Robinson, CAUTION: 33; COUNTRY: 28;
    COURAGE: 257; DIVINITY: 386;
    FAITH: 123, 128; FIDELITY: 84;
    GOODNESS: 43; LOVE: 45;
    PATRIOTISM: 11; SALVATION: 44;
    SEARCH and DISCOVERY: 5; SPEED: 42;
    STATE MOTTOES: 16; SUN: 10;
    VIRTUE: 313
Robinson (Bt.), DIVINITY: 386;
    HOPE: 261
Robison, SECURITY: 67
Robson, FEAR: 31; JUSTICE: 84
Roch, FAITH: 109
Rochdale C. B. C., U.K., LOCAL
    GOVERNMENT: 72; SIGN: 1; TRUST: 17
Roche, DIVINITY: 304
Roche (Bt.), DIVINE GUIDANCE: 174
Rochead, COUNTRY: 100; COURAGE: 64;
    FIDELITY: 102; PATRIOTISM: 46
Rochester Community College,
    Rochester, Minnesota, SCHOOL
    MOTTOES: 338; TRUTH: 103

Rochford, Walmesley, HOPE: 237
Rochfort, FAITH: 220; FORCE: 43;
    GENTLENESS: 19; STRENGTH: 14;
    TRUTH: 7
Rocke, DIVINITY: 244; HOPE: 93
The Rockefeller University, New York,
    New York, HUMANITY: 10; SCHOOL
    MOTTOES: 235
Rockford College, Rockford, Illinois,
    GLORY: 12; SCHOOL MOTTOES: 56;
    TRUTH: 10
Rockhurst College, Kansas City,
    Missouri, SCHOOL MOTTOES: 262;
    WISDOM: 76
Rodd, DIVINE GUIDANCE: 383, 384
Roddam (of Roddam),
    UNCLASSIFIED: 46
Roden, TRUTH: 56
Roden (E.), DUTY: 11
Roderich, Duke of Württemberg
    (1618–51), SATISFACTION: 4
Roderick (of Gateacre), LOVE: 95
Rodie, HOPE: 222
Rodney (B.), BIRDS: 24; OFFSPRING: 3
Rodwell, HONOR: 27; HOPE: 35; STATE
    MOTTOES: 11
Roe, IMPROVEMENT: 28
Roe (Bt.), WAY: 10
Rogers, CHRIST, JESUS: 53;
    CONSCIENCE: 8; GUILT: 2;
    INNOCENCE: 12; LIGHT: 50;
    RELIGION: 12; ROYALTY: 50;
    SPEED: 14; VIGILANCE: 75
Rogers (Bt.), DIVINITY: 323
Rogers (of Yarlington Lodge),
    FEAR: 30; JUSTICE: 81
Rogers (U.S.), DIVINITY: 320
Rogers-Harrison, VIRTUE: 1
Rogerson, FORTUNE: 83; MANNERS: 6
Rokeby, DECISION: 3
Rokeby (B.), DIVINITY: 386;
    UNSELFISHNESS: 11
Rolfe, SUN: 10
Rolland, HOPE: 249; PROVIDENCE: 28
Rolland (of Disblair), PERMANENCE: 3
Rolle (B.), PEOPLE: 3; ROYALTY: 55
Rolleston, ASPIRATION: 15
Rollins College, Winter Park, Florida,
    LIGHT: 15; SCHOOL MOTTOES: 105
Rollo (B.), FORTUNE: 75
Rollo (of Powhouse), COURAGE: 225;
    FORTUNE: 106

Rolls, SPEED: 9; TRUTH: 8

Rolt, INTEGRITY: 2

Rolt (Co. Kent), CROWN: 8;
WEAPONS: 25

Romanis, LOVE: 100

Romans, ADVANCE: 46

Rome, ENJOYMENT: 29

Romer, COURAGE: 58

Romford B. C., U.K., LOCAL
GOVERNMENT: 344; SERVICE: 53

Romney (E.), COUNTRY: 57;
PATRIOTISM: 25

Ronald, VIRTUE: 178

Ronan, ORIGIN: 5

Rooke, DIVINE GUIDANCE: 344

Rooke (of Carlisle, Akenhead and
Wigtoun), FLOURISHING: 13

Rooper, LIGHT: 41

Roosevelt (U.S.), AGRICULTURE: 6

Roper, DIVINE GUIDANCE: 164;
DIVINITY: 402; HOPE: 260; TRUTH: 13

Ropner (Bt.), FAITH: 96; FORTITUDE: 4

Rosborough, DIVINE GUIDANCE: 269

Rosborough-Colclough, DIVINE
GUIDANCE: 269

Roscommon (E.), DIVINE GUIDANCE: 42

Roscow, SPEED: 4; WISDOM: 7

Rose, DEFENSE: 4; FLORA: 5, 6, 35;
FLOURISHING: 43; FRAGRANCE: 7;
HONESTY: 42; INTEGRITY: 36;
IRONY: 1; THOUGHT: 9

Rose (of Houghton Conquest, Co.
Beds.), AUDACITY: 34

Rose (of Kilravock), FIDELITY: 43

Rose (of Worighton),
STEADFASTNESS: 28

Roseberry (E.), CONFIDENCE: 10;
FIDELITY: 98

Rose-Cleland, SPORT: 2

Rose-Hulman Institute of Technology,
Terre Haute, Indiana,
INDUSTRIOUSNESS: 109;
KNOWLEDGE: 40; SCHOOL
MOTTOES: 160

Rosher, FINISH: 5

Roskell (Co. Flint, Lancaster, and
York), PARADISE: 56

Ross, ANGER: 7; ANIMALS: 40; CHRIST,
JESUS: 13; DIVINE GUIDANCE: 23;
DIVINITY: 405; FLORA: 33;
FRAGRANCE: 7; HOPE: 233;
INDUSTRIOUSNESS: 49, 206; MIND: 22,
39; NOBILITY: 12; PROSPERITY: 10,
30; STARS: 49; THOUGHT: 28;
UNCLASSIFIED: 40; VIRTUE: 236, 249

Ross (of Auchlossen), REPUTATION: 1

Ross (of Balnagowan, Bt.), HOPE: 194;
SUCCESS: 15

Ross (of Belfast), FIDELITY: 43

Ross (of Craigie), VIRTUE: 139

Ross (of Kindies), CAUTION: 10

Ross (of Marchinch), IRONY: 3

Ross (of Morinchie), HOPE: 177

Rossall School, U.K., MIND: 23;
SCHOOL MOTTOES: 186

Rosse (E.), DIVINITY: 361

Rosse (E.), ROYALTY: 67

Rosslyn (E.), VISION: 6; WAR: 23

Rossmore (B.), HONOR: 150

Roster, FAITH: 93

Rotherham C. B. C., U.K.,
FLOURISHING: 75;
INDUSTRIOUSNESS: 183; LOCAL
GOVERNMENT: 348

Rothery, CAUTION: 24

Rothes (E.), STEADFASTNESS: 60

Rothschild, INDUSTRIOUSNESS: 15;
INTEGRITY: 4; UNITY: 9

Rothwell, CONSCIENCE: 8; GUILT: 2;
INNOCENCE: 12

Round, INTEGRITY: 10; SCHOOL
MOTTOES: 94

Roundell, WORTHINESS: 26

Rounder, STEADFASTNESS: 137

Roupell, FIDELITY: 103

Rous, CHRIST, JESUS: 60; FLORA: 35;
HOPE: 128

Rous (of Devon), CHRIST, JESUS: 83

Rouse, DIVINITY: 269; TRUST: 71

Rousseau, SACRIFICE: 1; TRUTH: 19

Roussell, FIDELITY: 103

Row, PERSEVERANCE: 41;
STEADFASTNESS: 88

Rowan, CROSS, THE: 9; INCREASE: 11;
INDUSTRIOUSNESS: 158

Rowand, INDUSTRIOUSNESS: 54

Rowe, INNOCENCE: 3; PRUDENCE: 2

Rowe (U.S.), LIBERTY: 48

Rowley, VIRTUE: 102

Rowley (Bt.), FORTUNE: 108
Rowley (of Lawton), SELF-CONTROL: 4
Rowley Regis B. C., U.K.,
  FIDELITY: 219;
  INDUSTRIOUSNESS: 124; LOCAL
  GOVERNMENT: 219
Roxburgh, COURAGE: 212;
  FIDELITY: 306; PARADISE: 12
Roxburghe (B.), FIDELITY: 23
Roxburghe (D.), CHRIST, JESUS: 67;
  COUNTRY: 86
Roxby, PERSEVERANCE: 56; STATE
  MOTTOES: 40
Roy, DESTINATION: 6
Royal Artillery, Royal Engineers,
  UBIQUITY: 10
Royal Artillery, U.K., DUTY: 26
Royal Asiatic Society, FLORA: 44
Royal Engineers, U.K., DUTY: 26;
  EARTH: 14; INDUSTRIOUSNESS: 173
Royal Exchange, London, EARTH: 22
Royal Exchange Assurance,
  COMMERCE: 8; NAVIGATION: 3
Royal Fishery Company, HARVEST: 4
Royal Humane Society, U.K.,
  OBSCURITY: 3
Royal Institution of Great Britain,
  CONVENIENCE: 5
Royal Marine Forces, U.K., SEA: 19
Royal Naval School, Eltham, U.K.,
  ENDURANCE: 20; SCHOOL
  MOTTOES: 96
Royal Naval School, U.K., SCHOOL
  MOTTOES: 215; WORTHINESS: 48
Royall (U.S.), PURITY: 13
Royden (Bt.), DUTY: 3; ROYALTY: 4
Roydes, PREPAREDNESS: 72; SCHOOL
  MOTTOES: 283
Royston U. D. C., U.K.,
  IMPROVEMENT: 1; LOCAL
  GOVERNMENT: 1
Ruck, ROYALTY: 3
Ruddiman, STRENGTH: 185
Rudge, Glendening, CROSS, THE: 60;
  FAITH: 146
Rudolf, Prince of Anhalt-Zerbst
  (1576–1621), CONSCIENCE: 6;
  FAITH: 173; WAR: 42
Rudolf, Prince of Anstalt-Zerbst
  (1576–1621), DEATH: 44

Rudolf August, Duke of
  Braunschweig-Wolfenbüttel
  (1627–1704), SECURITY: 8; UNITY: 43;
  WILL: 4
Rudolf II, Emperor of Germany
  (1552–1612), DIVINE GUIDANCE: 353;
  SPEED: 37; VIGILANCE: 19
Rudolf Maximilian, Duke of Saxony
  (1595–1647), DIVINE GUIDANCE: 388;
  LOVE: 122; WAR: 80
Rudolph August, Duke of
  Braunschweig-Wolfenbüttel
  (1627–1704), UNITY: 27
Rugby B. C., U.K., FLOURISHING: 34;
  LOCAL GOVERNMENT: 144; SPORT: 1
Rugby School, U.K., DIVINE
  GUIDANCE: 360;
  INDUSTRIOUSNESS: 151; SCHOOL
  MOTTOES: 212
Rugeley, TRUST: 4
Ruggles-Brise (of Spains Hall),
  EFFORT: 34
Ruislip-Northwood U. D. C.,
  IMPROVEMENT: 28; LOCAL
  GOVERNMENT: 250
Rule, FEELINGS: 26; HANDS: 36
Rumbold, RISING: 23
Rumbold (Bt.), ACTION: 26;
  VIRTUE: 443
Rumford, FORCE: 36
Rumney, DEATH: 54; REST: 13
Rumsey, FORCE: 40; VIRTUE: 407
Rumsey (U.S.), HONOR: 189;
  VIRTUE: 241
Runciman (V.), SEA: 3
Rundall, STRENGTH: 152; TRADES: 39;
  UNITY: 100
Rundle, GOODNESS: 42; LIGHT: 87
Rupert, Count of the Palatinate of
  Rhein (1619–82), FIDELITY: 49;
  SINCERITY: 3
Rush, DIVINITY: 123, 425; FAITH: 30,
  235, 241; LAW: 70; ROYALTY: 26,
  122, 126; UNITY: 82, 90
Rushbrooke, SPEED: 24
Rushout, ANCESTRY: 29
Rushout (Bt.), MEASURE: 12
Rushton, ENDURANCE: 33; PATIENCE: 12
Rushton (of Elswick), FLOURISHING: 67
Russel, LOVE: 5; PREPAREDNESS: 61

S

Salmon P. Chase College of Law of
  Northern Kentucky University,
  Covington, Kentucky,
  FIDELITY: 132; INTEGRITY: 14;
  SCHOOL MOTTOES: 107; TRUTH: 25
Salmond, RECTITUDE: 50; WISDOM: 46
Salmons, DIVINE GUIDANCE: 70
Salop C. C., FLOURISHING: 35; LOCAL
  GOVERNMENT: 145
Salt (Bt.), SECURITY: 24
Salt (Co. York), DIVINE GUIDANCE: 379
Saltburn and Maske-by-the-Sea U. D.
  C., U.K., LOCAL GOVERNMENT: 370;
  RISING: 18
Salter, REST: 26
Salters' Company, VIRTUE: 171
Saltmarshe (Co. York), STARS: 6;
  VIRTUE: 3
Saltoun (B.), DIVINITY: 258
Salusbury (Bt.), ANIMALS: 50;
  SATISFACTION: 8
Salve Regina—The Newport College,
  Newport, Rhode Island, MERCY: 19;
  SCHOOL MOTTOES: 190
Salvin, CHANGE: 8
Salwey, DIVINE GUIDANCE: 241
Sampson, FAITH: 37
Sampson (of Henbury), DEATH: 73;
  DISGRACE: 13
Sampson Technical College, Clinton,
  North Carolina, IMPROVEMENT: 27;
  KNOWLEDGE: 17; SCHOOL
  MOTTOES: 86, 195
Samson, Scheffeld (kt. of Rhodes,
  reign of Henry VIII), DIVINE
  GUIDANCE: 310
Samuel, ROYALTY: 45; STARS: 17
Samuel (Bt.), DEDICATION: 1
Samuel Gridley Howe, SCHOOL
  MOTTOES: 208
Samuels, SIZE: 2
Samwell (of Upton Hall), CHRIST,
  JESUS: 29
San Francisco Law School, San
  Francisco, California, LAW: 25;
  SCHOOL MOTTOES: 168
Sandberg, FAITH: 212
Sandby, ADVANCE: 19
Sanderlands, HOPE: 222
Sanderman, TRUTH: 87
Sanders, INNOCENCE: 13; SUN: 16

Sanderson, BRIGHTNESS: 8;
  COUNTRY: 47; COURAGE: 198;
  INDUSTRIOUSNESS: 148; LIBERTY: 56
Sanderson (B.), PEACE: 8
Sandes, FORTUNE: 111; VIRTUE: 275
Sandford, HEART: 6; MODERATION: 24;
  UNITY: 24
Sandilands, RIGHTEOUSNESS: 5;
  STARS: 19; VICTORY: 61
Sandwich (E.), SECURITY: 38
Sandys (B.), HONESTY: 44
Sanford, FAITH: 52; PAST, THE: 3
Sangster, or Songster, DIVINE
  GUIDANCE: 376
Sankey, FAITH: 206; PARADISE: 57
Sargeant (U.S.), TRANSIENCE: 2
Sargent (U.S.), HONOR: 142;
  NOBILITY: 6; STRENGTH: 53
Sarsfield, VIRTUE: 298
Saul or Saule, FIDELITY: 107
Saumarez, EARTH: 11
Saunders, BIRTH: 1; DIVINITY: 402;
  ENVY: 3; HOPE: 260
Saunderson, DIVINITY: 379; LOCAL
  GOVERNMENT: 332; VIGILANCE: 54
Sautry, FIDELITY: 212; LAW: 22;
  ROYALTY: 47
Savage, ASSISTANCE: 19; GIFTS and
  GIVING: 4; KINDNESS: 18;
  UNCLASSIFIED: 63; VIGILANCE: 110
Savage (of Dublin), COURAGE: 74;
  FIDELITY: 176
Savage (U.S.), DEATH: 52
Savary, EVIL: 4
Savile (of Rufford), STEADFASTNESS: 11
Saville-Onley, UNSELFISHNESS: 2
Saward, PAST, THE: 8
Sawers, COURAGE: 257
Sawrey, DEEDS: 11; SIMPLICITY: 1
Sawtell, PARADISE: 13
Sawyer, SEARCH and DISCOVERY: 2
Saxby, LOCAL GOVERNMENT: 353;
  STRENGTH: 123
Say and Sele (B.), MIND: 13
Say (of Swaffham, Co. Norfolk),
  WORDS: 14
Sayle, SERVICE: 76
Scaife, HOPE: 228
Scales, MEASURE: 13
Scalter, CROSS, THE: 51

Scarborough B. C., U.K., ADVERSITY: 70; GLORY: 44; LOCAL GOVERNMENT: 273

Scarborough (E.), CONSCIENCE: 7

Scarsdale (B.), GENTLENESS: 13; JUSTICE: 105

Scarth, LOFTINESS: 26

Scepter, DEEDS: 35; HOPE: 58

Schermerhorn (U.S.), INDUSTRIOUSNESS: 77

Schiefflin (U.S.), FAITH: 182

Scholefield, ACTION: 21

School for the Instruction of the Blind, Boston, Mass, SCHOOL MOTTOES: 208

The School of the Ozarks, Point Lookout, Missouri, KNOWLEDGE: 1; PATRIOTISM: 1; SCHOOL MOTTOES: 1; SPIRIT: 1

Schrieber, TRUTH: 14

Schuster (Bt.), DIVINITY: 264

Scobell, SALVATION: 27

Scopholine, HOPE: 222

Scot, COUNTRY: 84; FIDELITY: 127; HOPE: 201; INCREASE: 6, 19; LOVE: 8, 102; PATRIOTISM: 43; SHINING: 20; VIRTUE: 13, 149

Scot, Scott, COURAGE: 195; DANGER: 16; WORDS: 12

Scot (of Bonholm), COURAGE: 85

Scot (of Broadmeadows), LOVE: 96; PEACE: 30

Scot (of Harwood), LOVE: 32

Scot (of Hundilshope), PREPAREDNESS: 24

Scot (of Orkney), DEEDS: 23

Scot (of Vogry), LOVE: 92

Scot's Company, MERCY: 1

Scots Guards, CONQUEST: 37; COURAGE: 217; DESTRUCTION: 1; FAITH: 155; FEAR: 68

Scots Guards, 2nd Battalion, STRENGTH: 152; TRADES: 39; UNITY: 100

Scots Guards, 1st battalion, U.K., HOSTILITY: 2

Scots Guards, U.K., COURAGE: 137; DEATH: 74; FEAR: 22; HONOR: 88; REASON: 14; UNITY: 36

Scott, ACTION: 13; ANCESTRY: 30; ASPIRATION: 83; ASSISTANCE: 18; COUNTRY: 76, 84, 100; DARKNESS: 6; DEEDS: 23; DIVINE GUIDANCE: 180, 331; GENIUS: 4; HONOR: 123; HOPE: 278; INCREASE: 6; INTER-RELATEDNESS: 3; KINDNESS: 16; LIBERTY: 29; LIGHT: 27; LOVE: 7, 98, 102; PATRIOTISM: 4, 36, 43, 46; PROSPERITY: 26; PURITY: 24; RISING: 16; SECURITY: 13; STRENGTH: 90; VICTORY: 34; VIGILANCE: 116; VIRTUE: 13, 149; WORDS: 39; WORTHINESS: 6

Scott (Bt.), FULLNESS: 3; WORDS: 39

Scott (of Abbotsford, Bt.), VIGILANCE: 114

Scott (of Abbotsford (Bt.), REBIRTH: 26

Scott (of Betton), FEAR: 60; JUSTICE: 108

Scott (of Castle House, bt.), COURAGE: 65; FIDELITY: 158

Scott (of Comeston), ACTION: 4; SILENCE: 2

Scott (of Dunninald), HOPE: 279

Scott (of Edinburgh), FIDELITY: 127

Scott (of Great Barr, bt.), COUNTRY: 125; FIDELITY: 276; ROYALTY: 100

Scott (of Highchester), LOVE: 96; PEACE: 30

Scott (of Hussindene), TRUST: 104

Scott (of Pitlochie), DARKNESS: 20; LIGHT: 83

Scott (of Raeburn and Harden), REBIRTH: 26

Scott (of Silwood Park, Bt.), HOPE: 279

Scott (of Stourbridge), LIBERTY: 84

Scott (of Thirlestane), PREPAREDNESS: 66

Scott (U.S.), DIVINITY: 263; HAPPINESS: 25; TRUST: 66

Scott-Ker, STRENGTH: 108

Scougal, FULLNESS: 7

Scougall, DECORATION: 1

Scourfield (Bt.), AUDACITY: 49; FIDELITY: 138; SUCCESS: 4

Scribner (U.S.), AUTHORITY: 7; TRUTH: 137

Scrimgeour, UNCLASSIFIED: 10

Scripps (U.S.), VISION: 13

Scriveners' Company, ABILITY: 28;
TRADES: 30
Scrogie, REBIRTH: 6
Scrope, GRACE: 9; HOPE: 46;
PRIMACY: 2; UBIQUITY: 7
Scrugall, DECORATION: 2
Scrymgeour (of Dundee),
UNCLASSIFIED: 10
Scudamore (of Ditchingham, co.
Norfolk), DIVINE GUIDANCE: 393
Scudmore (Bt.), DIVINE GIFTS: 3;
ROYALTY: 1
Scunthorpe B. C., U.K., DEEDS: 84;
LOCAL GOVERNMENT: 307
Scurfield, CONQUEST: 52
Seabees, United States Navy,
INDUSTRIOUSNESS: 204
Seabright, MIND: 42
Seabury (U.S.), ASPIRATION: 81;
FIDELITY: 192
Seaford (B.), MANNER: 6
Seaforth Highlanders, ANIMALS: 6
Seaforth Highlanders, U.K.,
ASSISTANCE: 5; ROYALTY: 9
Seaham U. D. C., U.K., COURAGE: 38;
FAITH: 12; LOCAL GOVERNMENT: 50
Seal of State of South Carolina, STATE
MOTTOES: 41; UNITY: 61
Seal of State of Texas, MEMORY: 25;
STATE MOTTOES: 45, 52; UNITY: 68
Seal of State of Virginia,
PERSEVERANCE: 56; STATE
MOTTOES: 40
Seal of State of West Virginia,
FIDELITY: 215; LIBERTY: 55; STATE
MOTTOES: 28
Seal of Virginia, 1776–1779,
LIBERTY: 16; STATE MOTTOES: 9
Seale (Bt.), SALVATION: 24
Sealy, HOPE: 14
Seaman, STARS: 26
Searle, DIVINITY: 166; GRATITUDE: 2
Sears, FAITH: 140; HONOR: 90
Sears (U.S.), HUMILITY: 2; INCREASE: 1
Seaton, ADVANCE: 13; ANCESTRY: 24;
DIVINE GUIDANCE: 172; MUSIC: 1
Seaton (B.), ADVERSITY: 82; HOPE: 211
Seaver, ACQUISITION: 8; MIND: 43;
PRIDE: 14
Sebag, DIVINE GUIDANCE: 92;
INDUSTRIOUSNESS: 24
Seckham, HOPE: 289

Sefton (E.), CONQUEST: 72
Segrave (B.), DIVINE GUIDANCE: 170
Seisdon R. D. C., U.K., EFFORT: 15;
IMPROVEMENT: 16; LOCAL
GOVERNMENT: 173
Selby, AUDACITY: 53; FIDELITY: 173;
PREPAREDNESS: 61
Selby (of Biddleston and Earle),
WISDOM: 93
Selkirk (E.), PREPAREDNESS: 19;
STATUS: 4; STRENGTH: 38
Selma University, Selma, Alabama,
SERVICE: 3
Selon, SHINING: 16
Selsey (B.), ATTENTIVENESS: 7;
FIDELITY: 239
Sempill, TRUST: 81
Semple, DILIGENCE: 28; FIDELITY: 201;
VIGILANCE: 24
Semple (of Cathcart, etc.), TRUST: 81
Senhouse, DIVINITY: 76; GRATITUDE: 1
Senhouse (of Nether Hall),
CONQUEST: 42
Senior, SECURITY: 33
Senior, Heinrich, Count Reuss zu
Schleiz (1563–1616),
MODERATION: 16
Seras, LOFTINESS: 26
Seton, ADVANCE: 13, 31; ANCESTRY: 42;
CROWN: 12; DEDICATION: 15;
FIDELITY: 283; GUIDANCE: 29;
HONOR: 124; MUSIC: 1; PURSUIT: 5;
SACRIFICE: 7; VIRTUE: 94, 266
Seton (Bt.), INDUSTRIOUSNESS: 128;
REWARD: 18
Seton (of Abercorn, Bt.),
VIGILANCE: 48
Seton (of Culbeg and Tough,
Scotland), ADVANCE: 23
Seton (of Fordingbridge),
UNCLASSIFIED: 60
Seton Viscount Kingstoun,
POSSESSION: 7
Seton-Karr, ADVANCE: 7; COURAGE: 32
17th (Duke of Cambridge's Own)
Lancers, GLORY: 42
7th Regiment of National Guard, State
of New York (U.S. Civil War),
COUNTRY: 104; HONOR: 157;
PATRIOTISM: 51
Severne, SECURITY: 84; VIRTUE: 311,
323

Sewall (U.S.), ACTION: 27; LIFE: 45

Seward, PAST, THE: 8

Seymour, DUTY: 16; FAITH: 129; FIDELITY: 6; FRIENDSHIP: 2

Seys, OPPRESSION: 1; VIRTUE: 34

Shadforth, TIME: 21

Shadwell, FIDELITY: 218

Shaftesbury (E.), LOVE: 81; SERVICE: 30

Shakerley (Bt.), DEATH: 47; LIFE: 23

Shakerly (Bt.), HONOR: 4

Shakespear, LOCAL GOVERNMENT: 251; RIGHTS: 8

Shand, COURAGE: 241; FORTUNE: 112

Shand (of the Burn, co. Forfar), GUIDANCE: 30; VIRTUE: 370

Shank, HOPE: 215

Shanke (of Castlerig), HOPE: 215

Shanly, COUNTRY: 106; PATRIOTISM: 54; RELIGION: 24

Shannon, GUIDANCE: 30; VIRTUE: 370

Shannon (E.), ACTION: 21; LOCAL GOVERNMENT: 403; VIRTUE: 453

Shardlow R. D. C., U.K., LOCAL GOVERNMENT: 302; WISDOM: 53

Sharp, ADVANCE: 52; HONOR: 27; HOPE: 35, 117; STATE MOTTOES: 11; VIGILANCE: 109; VIRTUE: 390

Sharpe, AGGRESSION: 5; CROWN: 27; KNOWLEDGE: 36; POWER: 9; REST: 29; SCHOOL MOTTOES: 155; SHADE: 14; WEAPONS: 93

Sharpless (U.S.), ENDURANCE: 47; TRUTH: 72

Shatt, DIVINE GUIDANCE: 99; LOCAL GOVERNMENT: 86

Shaw, DEATH: 5; ENDURANCE: 40; FACTUALITY: 2; HAPPINESS: 38; HONESTY: 1; HONOR: 5; IMMORTALITY: 4; MIND: 29; STEADFASTNESS: 80; WORTHINESS: 3

Shaw (Bt.), ENDURANCE: 58; HOPE: 222; INTENTION: 2

Shaw (of Dublin, Bt.), SELF-KNOWLEDGE: 12

Sheath, SUPPORT: 5

Sheddon, FAITH: 80; FIDELITY: 146

Shee, CROSS, THE: 20; SALVATION: 8; TRUTH: 168

Sheffield, PREPAREDNESS: 53

Sheffield (Bt.), COURTESY: 1

Sheffield City and C. B. C., U.K., DIVINE GUIDANCE: 73; INDUSTRIOUSNESS: 22; LOCAL GOVERNMENT: 82

Sheffield (E.), DIVINE GUIDANCE: 377

Sheffinham, IMPROVEMENT: 4

Sheldon, SUFFERING: 5

Shelley (Bt.), FAITH: 54; FIDELITY: 91

Shelton, PRIDE: 2; STRENGTH: 31

Shepherd, ANIMALS: 21; FIDELITY: 110; NOURISHMENT: 3

Shepherd College, Shepherdstown, West Virginia, SCHOOL MOTTOES: 227

Sheppard, GUIDANCE: 9; PROTECTION: 9

Sheppard (U.S.), SPEED: 35; STRENGTH: 94

Shepperd, LOVE: 4

Shepperson, WATER: 11

Sherard, COUNTRY: 45; ROYALTY: 51

Sherborne (B.), FAITH: 211

Sherborne School, U.K. (founded 1550), DIVINITY: 132; NATIONAL MOTTOES: 3; SCHOOL MOTTOES: 65

Sherbrooke, FORCE: 41

Sherburne (U.S.), MANNER: 10

Sheriff, INTEGRITY: 10; SCHOOL MOTTOES: 94

Sherman (U.S.), DEATH: 10; VIRTUE: 29

Shevill, DUTY: 22

Shield, CROWN: 24; LAW: 43; PEOPLE: 8; PROTECTION: 26; WEAPONS: 87

Shiell, ENDURANCE: 2

Shiels, FIDELITY: 23

Shipley, HAPPINESS: 48

Shippard (Bt.), FEAR: 42

Shippersdon (of Pidding Hall, and Murton, Co. Durham), SHADE: 2

Shipwrights' Company, SECURITY: 89; TRADES: 45

Shirley, FIDELITY: 227; HONOR: 109; REWARD: 11; SELF-CONTROL: 1

Shivez, FORCE: 40; VIRTUE: 407

Shore (of Norton Hall), WAKEFULNESS: 7

Shoreditch B. C., U.K., LIGHT: 61; LOCAL GOVERNMENT: 233; POWER: 12

Short, SINCERITY: 16

Short (of Borrowstoun), HOPE: 246

Shorter College, North Little Rock, Arkansas, SCHOOL MOTTOES: 46; THOUGHT: 3

Shrewsbury B. C., U.K., FLOURISHING: 35; LOCAL GOVERNMENT: 145

Shrewsbury (E.), PREPAREDNESS: 56

Shrewsbury School, U.K., RECTITUDE: 33; SCHOOL MOTTOES: 144

Shrubb, CROSS, THE: 107

Shubrick (U.S.), OPPRESSION: 3

Shuckburgh, LOCAL GOVERNMENT: 397; VIGILANCE: 103

Shuckburgh (Bt.), COUNTRY: 38; HANDS: 13; PATRIOTISM: 15

Shuldham, SUN: 10

Shute, AGGRESSION: 12

Shuttleworth, SPEED: 21; USEFULNESS: 14

Shuttleworth (Bt.), EQUANIMITY: 3

Sibbald, AUDACITY: 87

Sibbald (of Balgony), JUSTICE: 62

Sibbald (of Kips, Scotland), DEATH: 42

Sibthorp, CONSCIENCE: 8; GUILT: 2; INNOCENCE: 12

Sibthorpe, DIVINITY: 140

Sibylle, Electress of Saxony (1512–54), FRIENDSHIP: 33

Sibylle, Margravine of Baden (1620–79), VIRTUE: 114

Sibylle Christine, Princess of Anhalt (1603–86), DIVINITY: 223

Sibylle Elisabeth, Duchess of Braunschweig (1576–1630), CHRIST, JESUS: 79; DIVINE GUIDANCE: 434; HOPE: 254

Sick and Hurt Office, London, DEEDS: 36

Sicklemore (of Wetheringsett), EQUALITY: 8

Siddell, IDENTITY: 2

Siddon, GIFTS and GIVING: 24

Siddons, NECESSITY: 3

Sideserf, INDUSTRIOUSNESS: 64; VIRTUE: 177

Sideserf (of Rochlaw), ADVANCE: 59; VIRTUE: 415

Sidmouth (V.), CROWN: 16; LIBERTY: 62

Sidney, DIVINITY: 211; GRATITUDE: 7

Sidney (Bt.), FATE: 29

Sier, ACTION: 25; VIRTUE: 278

Sierra Leone, JUSTICE: 127; LIBERTY: 120; NATIONAL MOTTOES: 39; UNITY: 112

Sigismund, Margrave of Brandenburg (1592–1640), DIVINE GUIDANCE: 219; DIVINITY: 5, 254; HOPE: 99; THOUGHT: 18

Sikes (of Berwick), DEEDS: 73

Silk Trowersters' Company, DIVINITY: 198

Sillifant, MIND: 25; RECTITUDE: 43

Silney, HOPE: 200

Silver, DESPAIR: 5

Simeon, SERVICE: 60

Simeon (Bt.), MODERATION: 24

Simmons, ACTION: 13; HONOR: 123; STEADFASTNESS: 118; VICTORY: 47

Simon, DIVINE GIFTS: 35; VICTORY: 18

Simon (Brittany), ENJOYMENT: 3

Simon VII, Count von der Lippe (1588–1627), VIRTUE: 368

Simonet, DIVINE GUIDANCE: 160

Simons, RISING: 22

Simpson, DESPAIR: 5; FIDELITY: 277; FULLNESS: 7; PREPAREDNESS: 34; ROYALTY: 101; SADNESS: 9

Simpson (Co. Durham), PERSEVERANCE: 69

Simpson College, San Francisco, California, SCHOOL MOTTOES: 117; SERVICE: 20

Simpson (of Sittingbourn), FORGETTING: 14

Simpson (of Udock), NOURISHMENT: 1

Simpson (U.S.), GOODNESS: 21

Sims, DEFENSE: 19

Sims (U.S.), JUSTICE: 46; VIRTUE: 92

Sinclair, CONQUEST: 16, 25; CROSS, THE: 11, 36, 111; DESTINATION: 7; DEVOTION: 1; DIVINITY: 173; ENTRAPMENT: 6; FAITH: 23; HONOR: 165; PREPAREDNESS: 62; SALVATION: 12; VIRTUE: 138

Sinclair (B.), WAR: 23

Sinclair (Bt.), CAUTION: 4; DIRECTNESS: 4; GUIDANCE: 27; LOVE: 1, 63; VIRTUE: 19

Sinclair (of Brimmes), COURAGE: 54

Singapore, IMPROVEMENT: 18

Singleton, HONESTY: 2; INDUSTRIOUSNESS: 146

Smith, AGGRESSION: 15; CONQUEST: 28, 34; DEATH: 56; DIVINE GUIDANCE: 218; DIVINITY: 296; ENTRAPMENT: 4; EXHORTATION: 2; FAITH: 225; FIDELITY: 308; FIRE: 12; FORCE: 13; FRIENDSHIP: 20; GENEROSITY: 5; HONOR: 27, 60; HOPE: 35, 138, 222; KNOWLEDGE: 11; LIBERTY: 79; LIFE: 25; LIGHT: 55; MANNERS: 8; PATRIOTISM: 66; PERSEVERANCE: 54, 82; PROPER NAMES: 16; PROSPERITY: 11; PURPOSE: 18; ROYALTY: 82; SEARCH and DISCOVERY: 8; SELF-RELIANCE: 7; SHINING: 19, 21; STATE MOTTOES: 11; STEADFASTNESS: 62; STRENGTH: 188; TIME: 29; UNCLASSIFIED: 46; VICTORY: 39, 50, 65; VIGILANCE: 35, 81

Smith (Bt.), DIVINITY: 153; GIFTS and GIVING: 8; HOPE: 40; SHINING: 25

Smith (Co. Essex, Bt.), CLEVERNESS: 5; WAR: 38

Smith (Co. Meath), COUNTRY: 7

Smith (of Berdodc), WORTHINESS: 40

Smith (of Dirleton), CONVENIENCE: 2; ENJOYMENT: 15

Smith (of Dorchester), PROVIDENCE: 1

Smith (of East Stoke, Bt.), FAITH: 224; PERSEVERANCE: 81

Smith (of Giblston), FULLNESS: 1

Smith (of Gloucestershire), AUDACITY: 92; GENTLENESS: 15

Smith (of Lydiate), MODERATION: 7; SECURITY: 22

Smith (of Preston, Bt.), PATRIOTISM: 65; ROYALTY: 81

Smith (of Sydling, Bt.), FIDELITY: 289

Smith (U.S.), BEAUTY: 2; DIRECTNESS: 13; GOALS: 6; GRACE: 1; IMPROVEMENT: 30; UNIQUENESS: 2

Smith-Ryland, STATUS: 6

Smiths' Company, Exeter, ABILITY: 31; TRADES: 37

Smithson, JUSTICE: 60

Smollet, UNCLASSIFIED: 64

Smollett, FLOURISHING: 2

Smyth, CONQUEST: 61; FRIENDSHIP: 20; SECURITY: 9; WEAPONS: 40

Smyth (Bt.), ENTRAPMENT: 3; PREPAREDNESS: 78

Smyth (Co. Clare), ASSISTANCE: 16; KINDNESS: 14

Smyth (Co. Perth), TRANQUILLITY: 5

Smyth (of Drumcree), HOME: 6; HONOR: 12

Smyth (of Graybrook), HONOR: 35

Smythe, ART: 7; INDUSTRIOUSNESS: 5; LOCAL GOVERNMENT: 275; PERSEVERANCE: 70

Smythe (Bt.), FIDELITY: 278; ROYALTY: 104

Smythe-Owen, FORESIGHT: 12; IMPROVEMENT: 49

Snead State Junior College, Boaz, Alabama, HANDS: 8; HEART: 7; KNOWLEDGE: 6; MIND: 10; SCHOOL MOTTOES: 57

Snell, CROSS, THE: 69; HOME: 19; RELIGION: 19; VICTORY: 20

Sneyd (of Ashcomb), OPPRESSION: 4

Soapmakers' Company, DIVINE GUIDANCE: 189; ROYALTY: 28

Society of Jesus, DIVINITY: 3

Sohier, CHRIST, JESUS: 81; STARS: 40

Soke of Peterborough C. C., U.K., HEART: 5; LOCAL GOVERNMENT: 70; UNITY: 23

Solihull U. D. C., U.K., COUNTRYSIDE: 5; LOCAL GOVERNMENT: 391

Solosborough, HONOR: 81; LOVE: 56

Soltau, ASSISTANCE: 17; KINDNESS: 15

Somaster, STATUS: 9

Somers (E.)., GOODNESS: 34

Somerset, CHANGE: 12; FEAR: 35

Somerset (D.), DUTY: 16; FAITH: 129

Somersetshire College, Bath, U.K., SCHOOL MOTTOES: 95

Somervil, FULLNESS: 3

Somervill, AUDACITY: 2

Somerville, DIVINITY: 176

Somerville (B.), DIVINITY: 175

Somerville (of Drum), DIVINITY: 175

Sommerville, FULLNESS: 3

Sondes (B.), INTEGRITY: 12

Sonoma State University, Rohnert Park, California, LIGHT: 51; MIND: 21; SCHOOL MOTTOES: 180; WORLD: 2

Sons of Veterans of the United States of America, DIVINE GUIDANCE: 297

Soote, FIDELITY: 118;
PREPAREDNESS: 18

Sophie, consort of Georg Friedrich,
Margrave of Brandenburg-Anspach
(1563–1639), DIVINE GUIDANCE: 333

Sophie, Duchess of Schleswig-Holstein
(1579–1618), DIVINE GUIDANCE: 21

Sophie, Electress of Hanover
(1630–1714), FORTUNE: 19;
VIRTUE: 39

Sophie, Margravine of Brandenburg
(1614–46), DIVINE GUIDANCE: 329;
HAPPINESS: 31

Sophie, Princess of Anhalt
(1654–1724), AGE: 2; FEAR: 18, 26;
VIRTUE: 71; WISDOM: 33

Sophie Charlotte, Queen of Prussia
(1668–1705), DUTY: 21

Sophie Eleonore, Landgravine of Hesse
(1609–71), DIVINITY: 157; HOPE: 41

Sophie Elisabeth, Countess of
Schwarzenburg (1565–1621), DIVINE
GUIDANCE: 302

Sophie Ursula, Countess of Oldenburg
(1601–41), DIVINITY: 160; TRUST: 30

Sorel, FAITH: 237; LAW: 67; UNITY: 84

Sotheby, WORTHINESS: 47

Sotherne, ASPIRATION: 19

South Carolina State College,
Orangeburg, South Carolina,
DUTY: 18; HONOR: 131;
KNOWLEDGE: 33; SCHOOL
MOTTOES: 152

South Dakota School of Mines and
Technology, Rapid City, South
Dakota, SCHOOL MOTTOES: 90

South Kesteven R. D. C., U.K.,
DIVINE GUIDANCE: 358; LOCAL
GOVERNMENT: 267

South Molton B. C., U.K.,
JUSTICE: 25; LOCAL
GOVERNMENT: 121

South Mountain Community College,
Arizona, KNOWLEDGE: 34; LIFE: 11;
SCHOOL MOTTOES: 153

South Sea Company, DIRECTION: 1

South Shields C. B. C., U.K.,
COMMERCE: 2; COURAGE: 47; LOCAL
GOVERNMENT: 71

Southall B. C., U.K., LOCAL
GOVERNMENT: 151; SHARING: 1

Southam, HONOR: 107; JUSTICE: 44;
TRUTH: 34

Southampton (B.), HONOR: 34;
RECTITUDE: 19; REWARD: 6

Southby, LIBERTY: 60; VIRTUE: 406

Southend-on-Sea C. B. C., U.K.,
LOCAL GOVERNMENT: 272; SEA: 22

Southern Missionary College,
Collegedale, Tennessee, SCHOOL
MOTTOES: 358; TRUTH: 145

Southgate B. C., U.K., GROWTH: 8;
LOCAL GOVERNMENT: 110

Southport C. B. C., U.K., LOCAL
GOVERNMENT: 327; PEOPLE: 17

Southwark B. C., U.K., LOCAL
GOVERNMENT: 388; UNITY: 109

Southwell (V.), Southwell,
REPUTATION: 6

Southwestern Christian College,
Terrell, Texas, CHRIST, JESUS: 5;
SCHOOL MOTTOES: 34

Southwestern College in Kansas,
Winfield, Kansas, LIGHT: 42;
SCHOOL MOTTOES: 174

Southwold B. C., U.K., DEFENSE: 46;
LOCAL GOVERNMENT: 377

Sovereigns of Great Britain (since
Henry VI), DIVINITY: 132; NATIONAL
MOTTOES: 3; SCHOOL MOTTOES: 65

Spalding, SALVATION: 20

Spalding U. D. C., U.K.,
GUIDANCE: 28; LOCAL
GOVERNMENT: 396

Spange, FATE: 8

The Spanish State, LIBERTY: 119;
NATIONAL MOTTOES: 32

Sparkes, HOPE: 222

Sparling, HONOR: 206

Sparrow, HAPPINESS: 33; HOPE: 215;
SALVATION: 29

Sparrow (of Redhill), HONESTY: 11

Spearman (of Thornley), HONOR: 27;
HOPE: 35; STATE MOTTOES: 11

Spectacle-makers' Company,
BLESSING: 1

Spedding, USEFULNESS: 14

Speid, DIVINE GUIDANCE: 33; SPEED: 51

Speir, ADVANCE: 19

Spenborough U. D. C., U.K.,
INDUSTRIOUSNESS: 82; LOCAL
GOVERNMENT: 187

Spence, AUDACITY: 38; DILIGENCE: 15;
DIVINE GUIDANCE: 406;
DIVINITY: 177; FIDELITY: 291;
HAPPINESS: 16; HONOR: 190, 199;
PEACE: 13; PERSEVERANCE: 9;
SPIRIT: 17; VIRTUE: 245, 364

Spence (of Kerbuster), DEEDS: 14

Spencer (E.), DIVINE GUIDANCE: 172

Spennymoor U. D. C., U.K.,
HOPE: 196; LOCAL GOVERNMENT: 361

Spens, FIDELITY: 339; FORTITUDE: 30;
VIRTUE: 274

Spens (of Lathallan), DIVINE
GUIDANCE: 406

Spense, COURAGE: 49

Sperling, INDUSTRIOUSNESS: 176;
WISDOM: 69

Spickernell, TRANSIENCE: 17

Spiers, DIVINE GUIDANCE: 389;
ENDURANCE: 13

Spiers (of Eldershe), ADVANCE: 1;
LOCAL GOVERNMENT: 8

Splatt, COUNTRY: 111; PATRIOTISM: 60

Spode, DIVINE GUIDANCE: 419;
FIDELITY: 272; RECTITUDE: 60

Spofforth, TIME: 62

Spoight, COURAGE: 229;
STRENGTH: 165; TRADES: 41

Spooner (U.S.), REASON: 7

Spoor, FIDELITY: 285

Spottiswood, ASSISTANCE: 23;
ENDURANCE: 45; ENJOYMENT: 25

Sprewell, ENDURANCE: 39

Spring, COUNTRY: 54; PATRIOTISM: 23;
PURITY: 15; WATER: 15

Springe, COUNTRY: 54; PATRIOTISM: 23

Sproston, HONESTY: 55

Sprot, ENJOYMENT: 23

Spry, HONOR: 27; HOPE: 35;
SIMPLICITY: 11; STATE MOTTOES: 11;
WISDOM: 99

Spurdens, CLARITY: 2

Spurgeon (of Gressenhall, Co.
Norfolk), PEOPLE: 4

Spurrier, INCENTIVE: 2

Squarey, AUDACITY: 81; CROSS, THE: 93

Squire, STEADFASTNESS: 140

St. Albans (D.), DEDICATION: 2

St. Albyn, DIVINE GUIDANCE: 137

St. Andrews Presbyterian College,
Laurinburg, North Carolina,
CHRIST, JESUS: 37; EXCELLENCE: 7;
SCHOOL MOTTOES: 100

St. Aubyn, SELF-RELIANCE: 8

St. Barbe, LIFE: 19; VISION: 9

St. Clair, FAITH: 117; REBIRTH: 34;
WAR: 23, 24; WISDOM: 20

St. Clair-Erskine (Earl of Rosslyn),
REBIRTH: 34

St. Edmund's School, Canterbury,
U.K., RELIGION: 7; SCHOOL
MOTTOES: 77

St. Edward's School, Oxford, U.K.,
PARENTS: 3; SCHOOL MOTTOES: 226

101st Foot (Royal Munster Fusiliers),
DEEDS: 87; JUDGMENT: 13

St. George, PARADISE: 24

St. George (Bt.), PARADISE: 23

St. Germains (E.), FOLLOWING: 11;
SHADE: 3

St. Gregory's College, Shawnee,
Oklahoma, FAITH: 102; LIGHT: 16;
SCHOOL MOTTOES: 108

St. Helens (B.), HONOR: 125

St. Helens C. B. C., U.K., LIGHT: 14;
LOCAL GOVERNMENT: 112

St. Hill, FINISH: 15

St. Ives B. C., U.K.,
INDUSTRIOUSNESS: 188; LOCAL
GOVERNMENT: 367

St. John, HONOR: 141

St. John (B.), FATE: 4

St. Joseph's Seminary, Yonkers, New
York, CHRIST, JESUS: 56; SCHOOL
MOTTOES: 191

St. Lawrence, HEALING and
HEALTH: 27; THOUGHT: 20

St. Leger, LOFTINESS: 10

St. Leonards (B.),
INDUSTRIOUSNESS: 111

St. Louis University, St. Louis,
Missouri, RELIGION: 26; SCHOOL
MOTTOES: 252

St. Mark's School, Windsor, U.K.,
FLOURISHING: 38; LOCAL
GOVERNMENT: 148; SCHOOL
MOTTOES: 111

St. Marylebone B. C., U.K., DIVINE
GUIDANCE: 240; LOCAL
GOVERNMENT: 122; SCRIPTURES: 5

St. Mary's Church, Persey, Berkshire, England, KINDNESS: 22

St. Pancras B. C., U.K., COURAGE: 277; LOCAL GOVERNMENT: 409; WISDOM: 114

St. Paul, INTEGRITY: 10; SCHOOL MOTTOES: 94

St. Paul (Bt.), INTEGRITY: 10; SCHOOL MOTTOES: 94

St. Paul's School, London, FAITH: 66; SCHOOL MOTTOES: 106

St. Peter's School, York, U.K., SCHOOL MOTTOES: 306; TRADITION: 4

1st Royal Dragoons, DEEDS: 87; JUDGMENT: 13

St. Vincent (V.), UNCLASSIFIED: 69

Stacey, DIVINE GIFTS: 21

Stackpole, COUNTRY: 93; DIVINITY: 360

Stacpole, DEATH: 30

Stacy, DARKNESS: 9; DAY: 7

Stafford, ASPIRATION: 15; NAME: 12; STRENGTH: 143

Stafford (B.), VIRTUE: 257

Staffordshire C. C., U.K., LOCAL GOVERNMENT: 376; UNITY: 70

Stahlschmidt, DIVINE GUIDANCE: 98; ROYALTY: 19

Staines U. D. C., U.K., LOCAL GOVERNMENT: 7; TIME: 1

Stainforth, WORTHINESS: 40

Stair (E.), STEADFASTNESS: 42

Stalybridge B. C., INDUSTRIOUSNESS: 1

Stalying, HAPPINESS: 24

Stamer, HAPPINESS: 35

Stamer (Bt.), COURAGE: 250; VIRTUE: 388

Stamford (E.), LOCAL GOVERNMENT: 20; POWER: 1

Standbridge, CONSERVATION: 6

Standish, NOBILITY: 21; VIRTUE: 184

Standish (of Duxburg), FIDELITY: 45

Stanfield (of Esholt and Burley Wood), SELF-KNOWLEDGE: 9

Stanford (U.S.), TRUTH: 158

Stanhope, DIVINITY: 65; PRAISE: 7; RESULTS: 1; ROYALTY: 15; SEARCH and DISCOVERY: 9

Stanhope (Bt.), CONQUEST: 19

Stanhope (E.), DIVINE GIFTS: 3; ROYALTY: 1

Stanier-Philip-Broade, PIETY: 38; STRENGTH: 102

Stanley (of Alderley, B.), CHANGE: 17

Stanley (of Dalegarth), CHANGE: 17

Stannus, STRENGTH: 24; VIRTUE: 48

Stansfield, DEATH: 105; FIDELITY: 216; LOVE: 83; VIRTUE: 307

Stanton, HONOR: 27; HOPE: 35; STATE MOTTOES: 11

Staple Merchants' Company, DIVINE GUIDANCE: 255

Staples, POSSESSION: 24

Stapleton, DIVINITY: 178; GOVERNMENT: 6; IMPROVEMENT: 24; WORTHINESS: 35

Stapleton (Bt.), GOVERNMENT: 6

Stark, COURAGE: 73

Starke, PROPER NAMES: 40

Starkey, DIVINE GUIDANCE: 306; EXPECTATION: 10

Starky (of Spye Park and Bromham), FAME: 5

Starr, HOPE: 295

State Area Vocational-Technical Schools System, Tennessee, OPPORTUNITY: 7; SCHOOL MOTTOES: 211

State of Alabama, DEFENSE: 6; STATE MOTTOES: 6

State of Alabama, 1868–1939, REST: 6; STATE MOTTOES: 22

State of Alaska, FUTURE, THE: 19; STATE MOTTOES: 37

State of Arizona, DIVINE GUIDANCE: 196

State of Arkansas, PEOPLE: 16; STATE MOTTOES: 44

State of California, SEARCH and DISCOVERY: 5; STATE MOTTOES: 16

State of Colorado, DIVINITY: 312; SCHOOL MOTTOES: 200; STATE MOTTOES: 35

State of Connecticut, ENDURANCE: 48; STATE MOTTOES: 42

State of Delaware, LEADERSHIP: 15; LIBERTY: 72; STARS: 22; STATE MOTTOES: 29

State of Florida, DIVINITY: 263; STATE MOTTOES: 25; TRUST: 66

State of Georgia, JUSTICE: 130; MODERATION: 36; STATE MOTTOES: 63; WISDOM: 108

State of Hawaii, RIGHTEOUSNESS: 17; STATE MOTTOES: 55

State of Idaho, ENDURANCE: 22
State of Illinois, STATE MOTTOES: 50; UNITY: 66
State of Indiana, LOCATION: 1; STATE MOTTOES: 8
State of Iowa, LIBERTY: 86; RIGHTS: 10; STATE MOTTOES: 39
State of Kansas, ADVERSITY: 2; ASPIRATION: 8; STARS: 4
State of Louisiana, CONFIDENCE: 20; JUSTICE: 122; STATE MOTTOES: 57; UNITY: 93
State of Maine, GUIDANCE: 8; STATE MOTTOES: 10
State of Maryland, DEEDS: 49; DIVINE GUIDANCE: 394; STATE MOTTOES: 18, 47
State of Massachusetts, LIBERTY: 21; PEACE: 11; STATE MOTTOES: 12; WEAPONS: 34
State of Michigan, DEFENSE: 48; SEARCH and DISCOVERY: 11; STATE MOTTOES: 49, 54
State of Minnesota, STARS: 21; STATE MOTTOES: 27
State of Mississippi, STATE MOTTOES: 60; VIRTUE: 373; WEAPONS: 99
State of Missouri, LAW: 63; PEOPLE: 20; STATE MOTTOES: 46
State of Montana, PROSPERITY: 37; STATE MOTTOES: 38
State of Nebraska, EQUALITY: 3; STATE MOTTOES: 13
State of Nevada, COUNTRY: 1; PATRIOTISM: 2; STATE MOTTOES: 4
State of New Hampshire, LIBERTY: 76; STARS: 23; STATE MOTTOES: 32
State of New Jersey, LIBERTY: 73; PROSPERITY: 22; STATE MOTTOES: 30
State of New York, ASPIRATION: 48
State of North Carolina, INTEGRITY: 11; STATE MOTTOES: 15
State of North Dakota, LIBERTY: 74; STATE MOTTOES: 31; UNITY: 49
State of Ohio, DIVINE GUIDANCE: 452; STATE MOTTOES: 64
State of Oklahoma, INDUSTRIOUSNESS: 116; LOCAL GOVERNMENT: 211; SCHOOL MOTTOES: 161; STATE MOTTOES: 26

State of Oregon, STATE MOTTOES: 53; UNITY: 72
State of Oregon, 1848–1858, SELF-DETERMINATION: 1; STATE MOTTOES: 2
State of Pennsylvania, LIBERTY: 131; STARS: 48; STATE MOTTOES: 59; VIRTUE: 237
State of Pennsylvania; Barton (U.S.), LEADERSHIP: 25
State of Rhode Island, HOPE: 70
State of South Carolina, HOPE: 35; MIND: 2; PREPAREDNESS: 4; STARS: 15; STATE MOTTOES: 5
State of South Dakota, PEOPLE: 23; STATE MOTTOES: 56
State of Tennessee, AGRICULTURE: 1; COMMERCE: 1; LOCAL GOVERNMENT: 10; STATE MOTTOES: 1
State of Texas, FRIENDSHIP: 34; STATE MOTTOES: 21
State of Utah, INDUSTRIOUSNESS: 79; STATE MOTTOES: 24
State of Vermont, LIBERTY: 31; STATE MOTTOES: 20; UNITY: 39
State of Virginia, OPPRESSION: 7; STATE MOTTOES: 48
State of Washington, STATE MOTTOES: 3; TIME: 3
State of West Virginia, LIBERTY: 78; STATE MOTTOES: 34
State of Wisconsin, IMPROVEMENT: 13; LOCAL GOVERNMENT: 160
State of Wyoming, EQUALITY: 4; STATE MOTTOES: 14
State University of New York, KNOWLEDGE: 89; SCHOOL MOTTOES: 331; SEARCH and DISCOVERY: 17; SERVICE: 70
The States-General, UNITY: 18
States of Kentucky and Missouri, SCHOOL MOTTOES: 346; STATE MOTTOES: 58; UNITY: 110
Stationers' Company, SCRIPTURES: 16
Stauffer (U.S.), UTENSILS: 3
Staunton, FAITH: 37
Staunton (co. Warwick), FAITH: 35
Staveley, ANIMALS: 57
Stawell, VIGILANCE: 91
Stebbing (of Woodrising), REST: 20
Steddert, LIGHT: 70; SHADE: 6
Stedman, SELF-RELIANCE: 3

Steed College, Johnson City, Tennessee, DILIGENCE: 17; DISCIPLINE: 2; INTEGRITY: 6; SCHOOL MOTTOES: 66

Steedman, SECURITY: 11

Steel, COURAGE: 187; ENDURANCE: 30; PERSEVERANCE: 55; PRUDENCE: 60; WEAPONS: 92

Steel (Bt.), BIRDS: 5; STATUS: 1; STRENGTH: 40

Steele, LOVE: 60; WAR: 34

Steele (Bt.), INDUSTRIOUSNESS: 1

Steele-Graves, LOVE: 60; WAR: 34

Steere, ADVERSITY: 87; OPPOSITION: 13

Stein, DESTINATION: 1

Steinman, EXPECTATION: 3

Steinthal, ASPIRATION: 48

Stenhouse, COURAGE: 67, 88; FIDELITY: 171, 180

Stephens, DIVINITY: 109; FAITH: 112; HOPE: 128; WEAPONS: 24; WISDOM: 11

Stephens (of Radnorshire), LIBERTY: 105

Stephens (of Tregenna), LOVE: 120; VIRTUE: 438

Stephenson, PROTECTION: 32; VIRTUE: 348

Stephenson-Hamilton, GRATITUDE: 15

Stepney B. C., U.K., IMPROVEMENT: 3; LOCAL GOVERNMENT: 19

Stepney (Bt.), DEEDS: 39; FAITH: 71; VIGILANCE: 32

Sterling, ADVANCE: 27

Stetson (U.S.), NOBILITY: 31; VIRTUE: 297

Steuart, ADVERSITY: 40; COURAGE: 145; FRIENDSHIP: 20; HAPPINESS: 65

Steuart (of Allanton), COURAGE: 267; WAR: 78

Steuart (of Auchlunkart), FEELINGS: 6; HANDS: 4

Steuart (of Ballechin), FIDELITY: 289

Steuart (of Coltness, bt.), ADVERSITY: 41; FORTUNE: 74

Stevenage Development Corp., U.K., PURPOSE: 6

Stevens, ABILITY: 33; DESTINATION: 1; FIDELITY: 8; STRENGTH: 163

Stevens (U.S.), ENDURANCE: 12

Stevenson, FIDELITY: 160, 161; RUNNING: 6; VIRTUE: 349

Stevenson (of Newcastle-on-Tyne), PARADISE: 8

Stevensone, VIRTUE: 350

Steward (of Nottingham), NOBILITY: 14; VIRTUE: 123

Stewart, ADVANCE: 41; ADVERSITY: 41, 83; ANCESTRY: 39; AUDACITY: 3, 23; CHRIST, JESUS: 19, 73, 77; CONSERVATION: 2; COURAGE: 33, 261; DANGER: 1; DEATH: 30; DEEDS: 7; DESPAIR: 5; DIVINE GUIDANCE: 102, 277; DIVINITY: 391; FAITH: 67; FAME: 2; FEAR: 33; FIDELITY: 289, 307; FLOURISHING: 75, 90, 91, 92, 102; FORTUNE: 64, 74, 116; HOPE: 221, 222; INCREASE: 12; INDUSTRIOUSNESS: 43, 183; INJURY: 4, 16; INTEGRITY: 22; LOCAL GOVERNMENT: 348; PATRIOTISM: 65; PEACE: 4, 39; PERSEVERANCE: 77; POWER: 19; PREPAREDNESS: 38; PROSPERITY: 39, 55; PROVIDENCE: 27; RECTITUDE: 6; ROYALTY: 81; SALVATION: 41; SIGN: 7; STEADFASTNESS: 109, 134; SUN: 19; VIRTUE: 136, 409; WAY: 8

Stewart (Bt.), ADVANCE: 6; DESPAIR: 7; INTENTION: 2

Stewart de Rothsay (B.), ANCESTRY: 8

Stewart (of Appin), DIRECTION: 6

Stewart (of Athenry, Bt.), ADVANCE: 19

Stewart (of Binny), DIRECTNESS: 3

Stewart (of Blacaskie), CAUTION: 30; PREPAREDNESS: 44

Stewart (of Burgh), TIME: 53

Stewart (of Carnousie), FEELINGS: 6; HANDS: 4

Stewart (of Castlestewart and St. Fort), FEAR: 51

Stewart (of Dalguise), RISING: 5

Stewart (of Dundee), FELLOWSHIP: 8

Stewart (of Edinglassie), ANCESTRY: 21; HONOR: 59

Stewart (of Fincastle), LAW: 55; LOCAL GOVERNMENT: 294; ROYALTY: 79

Stewart (of Fornese), PROVIDENCE: 19

Stewart (of Grandtully, Bt.), PROVIDENCE: 13

Stewart (of Greenock), OPPOSITION: 7

Stewart (of Inchbrock),
PREPAREDNESS: 72; SCHOOL
MOTTOES: 283
Stewart (of Newhall), REBIRTH: 28
Stewart (of Overton), REWARD: 59;
VIRTUE: 444
Stewart (of Rosling),
STEADFASTNESS: 55
Stewart (of Tillicoultry, bt.),
ANGER: 6; NOBILITY: 11
Stewart (U.S.), DESTINATION: 8
Stillé (U.S.), INNOCENCE: 6;
PATIENCE: 18; STEADFASTNESS: 69
Stillingfleet, TRUTH: 55
Stirling, FIDELITY: 151, 299;
FORTIFICATIONS: 1; STRENGTH: 70,
141; TRUSTWORTHINESS: 3
Stirling (Bt.), ADVANCE: 19, 26
Stirling (of Achoyle), ADVANCE: 26
Stirling (of Calden), HEALING and
HEALTH: 5
Stirling (of Denchray), RECTITUDE: 23
Stirling (of Dundee), FORTUNE: 23
Stirling (of Gorat, Bt.), FIDELITY: 289
Stith (U.S.), VIRTUE: 169
Stiven, INCREASE: 8
Stockenstrom (Bt.), RECTITUDE: 25;
STRENGTH: 65
Stockes, COURAGE: 92; FIERCENESS: 5
Stockport C. B. C., U.K.,
COURAGE: 11; FAITH: 6; LOCAL
GOVERNMENT: 26
Stockton, DIVINE GUIDANCE: 352
Stockton-on-Tees B. C., U.K.,
ENDURANCE: 32; HOPE: 65; LOCAL
GOVERNMENT: 159
Stodart, BRIGHTNESS: 12; DARKNESS: 18
Stoddart, HONOR: 22
Stoke Newington B. C., LOCAL
GOVERNMENT: 311; TIME: 49
Stoke-on-Trent City and C. B. C.,
U.K., LOCAL GOVERNMENT: 402;
STATE MOTTOES: 61; STRENGTH: 184;
UNITY: 122
Stokes, COURAGE: 92; FIERCENESS: 5;
VIRTUE: 228
Stokes (Bt.), ADVANCE: 33;
ADVERSITY: 39
Stokes (U.S.), LAW: 31; LIBERTY: 54
Stone, RECTITUDE: 73; STRENGTH: 129
Stone mantelpiece in Lower Soughton,
Flintshire, Wales, FRIENDSHIP: 54

Stone U. D. C., U.K., LOCAL
GOVERNMENT: 353; STRENGTH: 123
Stonyhurst College, EFFORT: 30;
SCHOOL MOTTOES: 248
Stopford, COUNTRY: 73; FIDELITY: 251;
PATRIOTISM: 34
Storey, NOBILITY: 24; VIRTUE: 190
Storie, COURAGE: 51; FAILURE: 1;
HOPE: 15; INDUSTRIOUSNESS: 129,
130; SADNESS: 5; WORTHINESS: 28
Stork, COURAGE: 73
Story, UNCLASSIFIED: 16
Story (U.S.), FAITH: 115
Stothard, SHADE: 5
Stott, ASPIRATION: 18
Stoughton, HONOR: 52
Stourbridge B. C., U.K., HEART: 10;
LOCAL GOVERNMENT: 261; UNITY: 55
Stourton (B.), FIDELITY: 224
Stow, FAITH: 223
Stowe State College, St. Louis,
Missouri, EXCELLENCE: 12; SCHOOL
MOTTOES: 205
Stowe (U.S.), CROSS, THE: 74;
CROWN: 13
Strachan, ADVANCE: 19; CAUTION: 29;
DILIGENCE: 39; DIVINE
GUIDANCE: 323
Strachan (Bt.), CAUTION: 29;
EQUANIMITY: 18
Strachen (Bt.), ADVANCE: 17
Strachey, LIGHT: 31; VIRTUE: 107
Strachey (Bt.), CHANGE: 2
Strachy (Bt.), DIVINE GIFTS: 3;
ROYALTY: 1
Stradbroke (E.), HOPE: 128
Strafford (B.)., DEFENSE: 48; PROPER
NAMES: 33; STATE MOTTOES: 54
Straingways, HOPE: 54
Straiton, REBIRTH: 29
Straker, DIVINE GUIDANCE: 125
Straloch, HOPE: 79
Strang, USEFULNESS: 2
Strange, FEAR: 3; JUSTICE: 9; LOCAL
GOVERNMENT: 45
Strangford (V.), POWER: 27;
VIRTUE: 279
Strangways (of Well), FAITH: 176
Stratford (B.), ADVERSITY: 51
Strathallan (v.), DIVINITY: 292
Strathcona (B.), LEADERSHIP: 1

T

Thelluson, HONOR: 132;
INDUSTRIOUSNESS: 99
Thesiger, PEACE: 42; WAR: 52
Thicknesse, VICTORY: 41
Thiel College, Greenville,
Pennsylvania, LIGHT: 53; SCHOOL
MOTTOES: 181; WORLD: 3
Thirley, ENVY: 7
13th Hussars, FLOURISHING: 94
39th Foot (Dorsetshire) Regiment,
PRIMACY: 7
Thom, HONOR: 28; HOPE: 36
Thomas, COURAGE: 255; DIVINE
GIFTS: 2; EQUANIMITY: 14;
PATRIOTISM: 53; ROYALTY: 72;
TRANQUILLITY: 7
Thomas (Bt.), GLORY: 59; VIRTUE: 284
Thomas County Community College,
Thomasville, Georgia, SCHOOL
MOTTOES: 288; SERVICE: 59
Thomas Jefferson, OBEDIENCE: 13;
OPPOSITION: 11
Thomas Nelson Community College,
Hampton, Virginia, SCHOOL
MOTTOES: 305; SUCCESS: 18
Thomas (of Yapton, bt.), HONESTY: 19
Thomlinson, COUNTRY: 57;
PATRIOTISM: 25
Thomond (M.), STRENGTH: 169
Thompson, COURAGE: 89;
DIVINITY: 262; FAIRNESS: 8;
FRIENDSHIP: 29; LIGHT: 23;
LOVE: 124; PATIENCE: 39; SHINING: 9;
TRUST: 65; TRUTH: 65; VIRTUE: 454
Thompson (Bt.), GOALS: 2; MANNER: 6;
PROPER NAMES: 38
Thompson (co. Durham), HONOR: 27;
HOPE: 35; STATE MOTTOES: 11
Thompson (Co. York), VIGILANCE: 45
Thompson (U.S.), SELF-
DETERMINATION: 3; VICTORY: 5
Thomson, CAUTION: 20; CHRIST,
JESUS: 27; COUNTRY: 67;
DILIGENCE: 42; FAIRNESS: 8;
FAITH: 180; FATE: 3; HONESTY: 14;
INDUSTRIOUSNESS: 74; MEMORY: 18;
PROTECTION: 19; PROVIDENCE: 25;
TRUTH: 65; UNCLASSIFIED: 59;
VIRTUE: 12
Thomson (of Banchory), DUE: 4
Thomson (of Edinburgh), HONESTY: 18

Thomson (of Fleet, B.),
STEADFASTNESS: 83
Thorburn, HOPE: 296, 298
Thores, CONTEMPT: 3
Thoresby, COURAGE: 135; SILENCE: 9
Thorlby, CONFIDENCE: 10;
FIDELITY: 98
Thorn, FLORA: 40; GLORY: 2; IRONY: 5
Thornaby-on-Tees B. C., U.K.,
IMPROVEMENT: 2; LOCAL
GOVERNMENT: 17
Thornburgh, FEAR: 32; LOVE: 86
Thorndike (U.S.), IRONY: 4
Thorneycroft, STRENGTH: 64
Thornhill, FLORA: 1
Thornicroft, STRENGTH: 64
Thornton, DANGER: 21; DIVINITY: 88;
FIDELITY: 145; HANDS: 11; HOPE: 23;
PIETY: 46; ROYALTY: 88; VIRTUE: 230
Thornton Cleveleys U. D. C., U.K.,
EARTH: 19; LOCAL
GOVERNMENT: 375; SEA: 34
Thornton (U.S.), DIVINITY: 89;
HOPE: 24
Thorold (Bt.), ANIMALS: 11; LIBERTY: 9
Thoroton, DIVINE GUIDANCE: 159;
SALVATION: 17
Thorp, CROSS, THE: 51; DIVINITY: 31;
PAST, THE: 11
Thoyts, ROYALTY: 92
Thrale, CROSS, THE: 58; TRUST: 45
Thriepland, COURAGE: 18; FORTUNE: 5
Thriepland (Bt.), COURAGE: 8;
FORTUNE: 3
Throckmorton (Bt.), MANNERS: 9;
NOBILITY: 33; VIRTUE: 338
Thruston (of Cranbrook), ADVANCE: 57
Thurburn, AGGRESSION: 3
Thurlow (B.), FATE: 29
Thurlow (B.), Thurlow, FAITH: 164;
JUSTICE: 65
Thurston (of Talgarth), INTEGRITY: 10;
SCHOOL MOTTOES: 94
Thurston (of Weston, Co. Suffolk),
INTEGRITY: 10; SCHOOL MOTTOES: 94
Thynne, CAUSATION: 2
Tibbetts, INDUSTRIOUSNESS: 158
Tichborne (Bt.), PATRIOTISM: 75;
WAR: 63
Tichburn, COUNTRY: 43; STRENGTH: 81
Tiffin, COUNTRY: 71, 75;
FIDELITY: 249; PATRIOTISM: 32

Tighe (of Woodstock), EQUANIMITY: 20

Tillard, DISCRETION: 1; SILENCE: 1

Tilney, HOPE: 54

Timperley, FORESIGHT: 4

Tindal, SELF-KNOWLEDGE: 9

Tin-plate Workers' and Wire-workers' Company, LOVE: 17; TRADES: 3; UNITY: 1

Tippet, HOPE: 150

Tippet (of Truro), FORCE: 14

Tipping, FIDELITY: 57; WEAPONS: 26

Tipton B. C., LAW: 62; LOCAL GOVERNMENT: 329; PEOPLE: 19

Tirwhit, FLOURISHING: 59

Tisdall, CROWN: 31; WEAPONS: 94

Toash, FAITH: 21

Todd, DEEDS: 43; VIGILANCE: 63

Todd (of Tranby), LIFE: 27

Todd (U.S.), CLEVERNESS: 2

Toke (of Godinton), Tooke, WAR: 44

Toler, JUSTICE: 111; RECTITUDE: 65

Tollemache, TRUST: 8

Tollet, FORESIGHT: 8

Tollet (of Betley), ADVERSITY: 75; PRUDENCE: 71

Tolson (of Bridekirk, Co. Cumberland), WEAPONS: 37

Tomlin, INDUSTRIOUSNESS: 149; PROSPERITY: 33

Tomlins, VIRTUE: 138

Tomlinson, COUNTRY: 56; PATRIOTISM: 24

Tonbridge School, U.K., CHRIST, JESUS: 40; SCHOOL MOTTOES: 133

Tonbridge U. D. C., Willenhall U. D. C., U.K., LAW: 62; LOCAL GOVERNMENT: 329; PEOPLE: 19

Tonge, EQUANIMITY: 17

Tonkin, DIVINITY: 287

Tonson, HANDS: 23; HOSTILITY: 13

Toole, HOPE: 215

Tooth, PERSEVERANCE: 66; REWARD: 26

Topham, CROSS, THE: 19; PRUDENCE: 14

Torpichen (B.), HOPE: 222

Torquay B. C., HAPPINESS: 56; HEALING and HEALTH: 31; LOCAL GOVERNMENT: 325

Torr, ASPIRATION: 27

Torrance, SALVATION: 32

Torre, DIVINE GUIDANCE: 430

Torrens, DIVINITY: 110; LIGHT: 10

Torrey (U.S.), DIVINE GUIDANCE: 451

Torrington (V.), DEFENSE: 48; STATE MOTTOES: 54

Tottenham B. C., U.K., DEEDS: 22; LOCAL GOVERNMENT: 97

Tottenham (Co. Wexford), ASPIRATION: 9; STARS: 5

Touchet, POSSESSION: 10

Tounley-Balfour (of Tounley Hall), COUNTRY: 62; COURAGE: 168

Touzel, ZEALOUSNESS: 3

Tovy, DIVINITY: 230; TRUST: 48

Tower, DIVINE GUIDANCE: 209

Towers, DIVINE GUIDANCE: 432; DIVINITY: 314; LOCAL GOVERNMENT: 243; UNITY: 5

Towle, LOVE: 9; PEACE: 1; VIRTUE: 13

Town of Aberdeen, FELLOWSHIP: 1

Town of Anstruther, U.K., LOCAL GOVERNMENT: 401; VIRTUE: 416

Town of Cambrai, France, LOCAL GOVERNMENT: 55; PEACE: 6

Town of Dijon, France, GENEROSITY: 10; JUSTICE: 63; LOCAL GOVERNMENT: 202

Town of Doncaster (U.K.), HAPPINESS: 61; LOCAL GOVERNMENT: 359

Town of Dumbarton, FIDELITY: 186; FORTITUDE: 16; LOCAL GOVERNMENT: 158

Town of Dundee, DIVINE GIFTS: 16

Town of Gateshead, LOFTINESS: 6

Town of Glasgow, FLOURISHING: 58; LOCAL GOVERNMENT: 218

Town of Liverpool, DIVINE GIFTS: 26

Town of Liverpool, Bolger, LOCAL GOVERNMENT: 90; TRANQUILLITY: 3

Town of Lyons, France, DIVINITY: 428; LAW: 69; ROYALTY: 124; UNITY: 86

Town of Marseilles, France, FAME: 13; LOCAL GOVERNMENT: 117

Town of Montrose, FLORA: 24; LOCAL GOVERNMENT: 224; SEA: 13

Town of Nantes, France, DIVINITY: 273; LOCAL GOVERNMENT: 192

Town of Newcastle-on-Tyne, DEFENSE: 20

Town of Peebles, LOCAL GOVERNMENT: 69; PROSPERITY: 4

U

Underwood, ANIMALS: 41;
ENJOYMENT: 22; PROVOCATION: 3
Underwood (U.S.), UTENSILS: 1
Undey, DIVINITY: 12; HOPE: 2
Unett, REBIRTH: 4
Uniacke, UNIQUENESS: 7
Uniacke (U.S.), AUDACITY: 45;
FIDELITY: 85
Union of Burma, HAPPINESS: 28;
NATIONAL MOTTOES: 8;
PROSPERITY: 14; UNITY: 41
Union of Soviet Socialist Republics,
NATIONAL MOTTOES: 45; UNITY: 124
Union Theological Seminary, New
York, New York, KINDNESS: 26;
SCHOOL MOTTOES: 345; TRUTH: 112;
UNITY: 101
United Church of Christ, UNITY: 69
United Daughters of the Confederacy,
LIFE: 14; LOVE: 78; RISK: 5;
UBIQUITY: 5
United Kingdom of Great Britain and
Northern Ireland, DIVINITY: 132;
NATIONAL MOTTOES: 3; SCHOOL
MOTTOES: 65
United Republic of Tanzania,
LIBERTY: 118; NATIONAL
MOTTOES: 31; UNITY: 78
United States Coast Guard,
PREPAREDNESS: 72; SCHOOL
MOTTOES: 283
United States Marine Corps,
FIDELITY: 289; WAR: 81
United States Naval Academy,
Annapolis, Maryland,
KNOWLEDGE: 23; SCHOOL
MOTTOES: 104
United States of America, UNITY: 29
University College School, London,
GRADUALNESS: 4; SCHOOL
MOTTOES: 217
University of Alaska, Fairbanks,
Alaska, ASPIRATION: 12; SCHOOL
MOTTOES: 4
University of Arkansas for Medical
Sciences, Arkansas, HEALING and
HEALTH: 16; SCHOOL MOTTOES: 185
University of Bristol, Bristol, U.K.,
POWER: 24; SCHOOL MOTTOES: 360
University of Central Florida,
Orlando, Florida, ASPIRATION: 72;
SCHOOL MOTTOES: 250; STARS: 34

University of Chicago, Chicago,
Illinois, KNOWLEDGE: 46; SCHOOL
MOTTOES: 166
University of Dayton School of Law,
Dayton, Ohio, COUNTRY: 92;
DIVINITY: 357; SCHOOL MOTTOES: 240
University of Georgia, Athens,
Georgia, KNOWLEDGE: 22; SCHOOL
MOTTOES: 97
University of Houston, Houston,
Texas, SCHOOL MOTTOES: 143;
TIME: 26
University of Illinois, Urbana-
Champaign, Illinois,
INDUSTRIOUSNESS: 122;
KNOWLEDGE: 41; SCHOOL
MOTTOES: 163
University of Manchester, Manchester,
U.K., LOFTINESS: 5; SCHOOL
MOTTOES: 21; SUN: 2
University of Melbourne, Melbourne,
Australia, OFFSPRING: 4; PRAISE: 11;
SCHOOL MOTTOES: 229
University of Montevallo, Montevallo,
Alabama, SCHOOL MOTTOES: 8
The University of New England,
Australia, SCHOOL MOTTOES: 139;
WISDOM: 36
University of North Carolina School of
Nursing, Chapel Hill, North
Carolina, LIBERTY: 77; LIGHT: 49;
SCHOOL MOTTOES: 179
University of Northern Iowa, Cedar
Falls, Iowa, LIGHT: 39; SCHOOL
MOTTOES: 173
University of Oxford, DIVINE
GUIDANCE: 210; HAPPINESS: 57;
SCHOOL MOTTOES: 71, 266;
WISDOM: 83
University of Paris, SCHOOL
MOTTOES: 125; UBIQUITY: 3
University of Redlands, Redlands,
California, SCHOOL MOTTOES: 18;
UNIQUENESS: 1
University of Salford, Salford, U.K.,
ASPIRATION: 21; SCHOOL MOTTOES: 12
University of Science and Arts of
Oklahoma, Chickasha, Oklahoma,
HEALING and HEALTH: 22; SCHOOL
MOTTOES: 224

V

Vanderplante B. C., U.K.,
  INDUSTRIOUSNESS: 64
Vane, LIBERTY: 100; MODERATION: 24
Vanneck, JUSTICE: 22
Varnum (U.S.), FLOURISHING: 60
Varty, DIVINITY: 401; HOPE: 257
Vassal-Fox, WORTHINESS: 58
Vassall (of Milford), PATRIOTISM: 86;
  ROYALTY: 114
Vassall (of Milford Co. Southampton),
  FATE: 5
Vaudin, COUNTRY: 82; LIBERTY: 90
Vaughan, CHRIST, JESUS: 28;
  CONSCIENCE: 2; DEFENSE: 5;
  DIVINITY: 146; HARMLESSNESS: 4;
  LIBERTY: 11; PURITY: 11;
  SIMPLICITY: 3; WISDOM: 96
Vaughan (of Lettleton, kt.),
  COURAGE: 50
Vaughan (U.S.), LIBERTY: 10;
  PRUDENCE: 25, 54; SERVICE: 7;
  SIMPLICITY: 2, 6
Vaux (B.), ANIMALS: 37; LIFE: 24;
  PRESENT, THE: 3
Veale, SACRIFICE: 8
Veel, DEEDS: 34; SILENCE: 4
Veevers, VIGILANCE: 72; VIRTUE: 223
Veitch, FAME: 8
Velasquez de la Cadena (U.S.),
  FAITH: 86
Venables, CONQUEST: 43; MIND: 3;
  STRENGTH: 4; WEAPONS: 95
Venning, FIDELITY: 100; INTEGRITY: 13
Ventry (B.), CONQUEST: 72
Verdon, DIVINITY: 159
Vere, TRUTH: 154
Vere (of Craigie Hall), TRUTH: 155
Verelst, EQUANIMITY: 17
Vermont Law School, South Royalton,
  Vermont, LAUGHTER: 2; LAW: 29;
  SCHOOL MOTTOES: 170
Verner, COUNTRY: 85; SCHOOL
  MOTTOES: 237
Verney, FAITH: 242; SOLITUDE: 7;
  SUN: 28; UNIQUENESS: 6; UNITY: 91
Verney, Willoughby de Broke (B.),
  VIRTUE: 217
Vernon, FOLLOWING: 15
Vernon (B.), FLOURISHING: 86
Vernon (of Hanbury Hall),
  FLOURISHING: 86
Verschoyle, STEADFASTNESS: 135

Verst, VIRTUE: 349
Verulam (E.), MODERATION: 12
Vibert, FORCE: 30; LIBERTY: 129
Vicars, VIRTUE: 229
Vicary, HONESTY: 38; HONOR: 156
Vickers, LIVELINESS: 7; STRENGTH: 167
The Victoria Cross, COURAGE: 119
Vilant, FAITH: 118
Villers, CROSS, THE: 53; TRUTH: 23
Vincennes University, Vincennes,
  Indiana, SCHOOL MOTTOES: 293;
  SERVICE: 67
Vincent, CONQUEST: 58; FORCE: 39;
  VIRTUE: 362
Vincent (Bt.), CONQUEST: 56
Vincent (U.S.), CONQUEST: 57;
  REWARD: 52
Viner, HONOR: 132;
  INDUSTRIOUSNESS: 99
Vintners' Company, HAPPINESS: 69
Virginia, DEATH: 38; LIBERTY: 75
Virginia Merchants, MEASURE: 2
Visme, COURAGE: 241; FORTUNE: 112
Vivian, LIFE: 46; REBIRTH: 38
Vivian (B.), MIND: 8; NOBILITY: 4
Vivian (of Pencalenick), LIFE: 49
Vosper, HAPPINESS: 68
Vowe (of Hallaton), DEDICATION: 18
Vynne, UNSELFISHNESS: 17
Vyse, VIRTUE: 294
Vyvyan, LIFE: 5

W

Waddel, TRUTH: 1
Waddell, TRUTH: 66
Waddilove, INTEGRITY: 1;
  LIMITATION: 12
Waddington (U.S.), DUE: 3
Waddy, COUNTRY: 60; LEADERSHIP: 19
Wade, HOPE: 116
Wadge, HOPE: 248
Wadman, FLORA: 37
Wainman, GOODNESS: 27; LOCAL
  GOVERNMENT: 259
Wainwright, DIVINITY: 402; HOPE: 260
Wait, HOME: 19; RELIGION: 19
Waithman, PERSEVERANCE: 72
Wake (Bt.), VIGILANCE: 75

Wake Forest University, Winston-Salem, North Carolina, HUMANITY: 11; SCHOOL MOTTOES: 245

Wakefield, HOPE: 215; LIBERTY: 113; TRUTH: 101

Wakeman, VIGILANCE: 31

Wakeman (Bt.), MODERATION: 24

Walch, AMBITION: 2

Walcot, JUSTICE: 104; LIBERTY: 83

Waldegrave, ADVANCE: 40; MIND: 5

Waldegrave (E.), CHANGE: 2

Waldorf College, Forest City, Iowa, LIGHT: 47; SCHOOL MOTTOES: 177; TRUTH: 52

Waldron, COURAGE: 250; SPEED: 26; STRENGTH: 58; VIRTUE: 388

Waldy, FIDELITY: 110

Walford, DUE: 6; FIDELITY: 246; PREPAREDNESS: 47; SELF-KNOWLEDGE: 9; THOUGHT: 21

Walker, CONSCIENCE: 8; DEDICATION: 9; DIVINITY: 255; FEAR: 82; FIDELITY: 140, 233, 270; FORTUNE: 67; GUIDANCE: 23; GUILT: 2; HEALING and HEALTH: 19; HONOR: 27, 54, 149; HOPE: 35; INNOCENCE: 12; MODERATION: 24; POWER: 8; PREPAREDNESS: 67; STATE MOTTOES: 11; TRUST: 61; UNITY: 46; VIGILANCE: 63; WALKING: 1, 4

Walker (Bt.), DESPAIR: 5; PROPER NAMES: 2, 39

Walker (of Dalry), INDUSTRIOUSNESS: 20

Walker (of Newcastle-on-Tyne), SECURITY: 36

Walker-Heneage, DIVINITY: 437

Walkingshaw, SEASONS: 2

Wall, DEATH: 3; FIDELITY: 29; LIBERTY: 5; ROYALTY: 5

Wall (of Wortley Park), STEADFASTNESS: 42

Wall (U.S.), UNCLASSIFIED: 52

Wallace, CONSISTENCY: 6; HOPE: 179, 202; INDUSTRIOUSNESS: 186; LOVE: 68; SACRIFICE: 3

Wallace (Bt.), HOPE: 48, 202

Wallace (of Kelly), LIBERTY: 93

Wallace (U.S.), HOPE: 203; MEASURE: 1

Wallange, UNCLASSIFIED: 35

Wallasey C. B. C., U.K., AUDACITY: 30; CAUTION: 3; LOCAL GOVERNMENT: 38

Waller (Bt.), COURAGE: 125, 126; HONOR: 96; PROPER NAMES: 2, 9; TRUST: 42

Walley, DESPAIR: 3

Wallington, AUDACITY: 78, 79; FIDELITY: 312

Wallop, TRUTH: 17

Wallscourt (B.), NOBILITY: 34; VIRTUE: 339

Wallsend B. C., U.K., LOCAL GOVERNMENT: 355; LOCATION: 8

Walmesley, INDUSTRIOUSNESS: 94

Walmsley, DIVINITY: 152; HOPE: 39

Walpole, WORDS: 17, 18, 19

Walrond, FORGETTING: 5; LOCAL GOVERNMENT: 349; UNSELFISHNESS: 24; VENGEANCE: 2

Walsh, HOPE: 141; IMPROVEMENT: 20; INJURY: 10; TRUTH: 121; VIRTUE: 214

Walsh (Bt.), STEADFASTNESS: 42

Walsham (Bt.), ASPIRATION: 60; DIVINE GUIDANCE: 10; LIBERTY: 109; REST: 28

Walsingham (B.), LIVELINESS: 2

Walter (U.S.), HAPPINESS: 19; STRENGTH: 63

Walters, COUNTRY: 36; DIVINITY: 184

Waltham, WORTHINESS: 30

Waltham U. D. C., U.K., CONQUEST: 19

Walthamstow B. C., FELLOWSHIP: 3; LOCAL GOVERNMENT: 119

Walton and Weybridge U. D. C., U.K., LOCAL GOVERNMENT: 100; WATER: 6

Walton (of Clifton, Gloucestershire), VIRTUE: 113

Walton-le-Dale U. D. C., U.K., FEELINGS: 14; LOCAL GOVERNMENT: 76

Walworth (U.S.), LAW: 65

Walwyn, ANCESTRY: 14

Walwyn (Co. Herts.), WORTHINESS: 40

Wandesford, RELIGION: 16, 32

Wandsworth B. C., U.K., LOCAL GOVERNMENT: 406; SERVICE: 75

Wanstead and Woodford B. C., U.K., COURAGE: 43; LOCAL GOVERNMENT: 64; WISDOM: 9

Wayne County Community College,
Detroit, Michigan,
OPPORTUNITY: 11; SCHOOL
MOTTOES: 287; SERVICE: 58
Waynflete, INNOCENCE: 14
Weare, STEADFASTNESS: 132
Weare (of Hampton), BEING, SELF: 5
Weaver-Hazelton, CROSS, THE: 3
Weavers' Company (London),
TRADES: 44; TRUTH: 179
Webb, ASPIRATION: 52; CHRIST,
JESUS: 30; CONSCIENCE: 8; CROWN: 5;
GUILT: 2; IMPROVEMENT: 42;
INNOCENCE: 12; STRENGTH: 109;
UNSELFISHNESS: 5; VICTORY: 57;
VIRTUE: 234
Webb (U.S.), PRINCIPLES: 2
Webber, FLORA: 22; WEAPONS: 61
Webley, PERSEVERANCE: 55
Webster, EMERGENCE: 1; FAITH: 110;
OPPORTUNITY: 1; PURITY: 8, 26;
TIME: 10; TRUTH: 117, 168
Webster (Bt.), FAITH: 98; JUSTICE: 31;
LOCAL GOVERNMENT: 128
Webster (U.S.), TRUTH: 156
Weddeburn, BIRDS: 5; STATUS: 1
Weddell, CONSISTENCY: 7; TRUTH: 66
Wedderburn, FIDELITY: 2; VISION: 6
Wedderburn (Bt.), GOODNESS: 22
Wednesbury B. C., U.K., ABILITY: 2;
COURAGE: 22; LIVELINESS: 1; LOCAL
GOVERNMENT: 31
Weekes, DIVINITY: 26, 54
Weeks, VIRTUE: 451
Weems, THOUGHT: 2; VIRTUE: 264
Wegg, VIGILANCE: 91
Weir, TRUTH: 60
Welbey (Bt.), FIRE: 11; WEAPONS: 81
Welby, HAPPINESS: 62
Weld (of Lulworth), DIVINITY: 312;
SCHOOL MOTTOES: 200; STATE
MOTTOES: 35
Weldon, ACCOMPLISHMENT: 6;
WORTHINESS: 5
Welford, FIDELITY: 298
Weller, EQUANIMITY: 17
Welles, PREPAREDNESS: 72; SCHOOL
MOTTOES: 283
Wellesley, VIRTUE: 208
Wellesley (M.), NECESSITY: 2
Wellingborough U. D. C., U.K.,
LOCAL GOVERNMENT: 35; TIME: 8

Wellington College, U.K.,
ANCESTRY: 18; COURAGE: 265;
FORTUNE: 117; SCHOOL
MOTTOES: 124
Wellington (D.), COURAGE: 265;
FORTUNE: 117
Wellington U. D. C., U.K., DIVINE
GUIDANCE: 69; LOCAL
GOVERNMENT: 80
Wells, ACTION: 14; BLESSING: 5;
CONCILIATION: 7; DEEDS: 2;
HONOR: 200; VIRTUE: 376
Wells (Bt.), ART: 20; HONESTY: 24;
TRUTH: 39
Wells City Council, U.K., LOCAL
GOVERNMENT: 170; PROSPERITY: 15
Wells (of Grebly Hall),
PREPAREDNESS: 72; SCHOOL
MOTTOES: 283
Wells (of Sporle, co. Norfolk),
DEEDS: 38; WORDS: 9
Wellwood, EFFORT: 24
Welman (of Poundsford Park), DIVINE
GUIDANCE: 67; PROVIDENCE: 5
Welsh, COURAGE: 181; DIVINE
GUIDANCE: 36; REWARD: 38
Welsted, SECURITY: 77
Wembley B. C., IMPROVEMENT: 45;
LOCAL GOVERNMENT: 373
Wemyss, POWER: 13
Wemyss (E.), ADVANCE: 19
Wendell Phillips, abolitionist,
PIETY: 13
Wenley, TRUTH: 166; VIGILANCE: 86
Wenlock (B.), CHRIST, JESUS: 4; DIVINE
GUIDANCE: 32; FAIRNESS: 9
Wenman, GOODNESS: 27; LOCAL
GOVERNMENT: 259
Wentworth, GOODNESS: 32;
THOUGHT: 15
Wentworth (co. York), DIVINITY: 154;
SCHOOL MOTTOES: 89
Wentworth Military Academy,
Lexington, Missouri, DIVINITY: 154;
SCHOOL MOTTOES: 89
Wenzel Adam Posthumus, Duke of
Teschen (1524–79), BLESSING: 7
Were (of Wellington), PAST, THE: 3
Wesley, DIVINITY: 200
Wesleyan College, Macon, Georgia,
KNOWLEDGE: 71; PIETY: 49; SCHOOL
MOTTOES: 274

West, PEACE: 38; PROSPERITY: 38;
  REASON: 5; WISDOM: 47
West, (of Delawarr, e.), DAY: 3
West Ham C. B. C., U.K.,
  DIVINITY: 56; LOCAL
  GOVERNMENT: 83; TRUST: 23
West Hartlepool C. B. C., U.K.,
  INDUSTRIOUSNESS: 32; LOCAL
  GOVERNMENT: 101; SEA: 7
West (of Tonbridge Wells, Co. Kent),
  DAY: 11
West Point U.S. Military Academy,
  West Point, New York,
  COUNTRY: 30; DUTY: 10; HONOR: 29;
  SCHOOL MOTTOES: 73
West Riding C. C., U.K.,
  GUIDANCE: 1; PROVOCATION: 1
Westby, DIVINITY: 285
Westby (of Thornhill), WILLINGNESS: 5
Westcote, REBIRTH: 24
Westerman, HONOR: 27; HOPE: 35;
  STATE MOTTOES: 11
Western (B.), MODERATION: 24
Western Evangelical Seminary,
  Portland, Oregon, SCHOOL
  MOTTOES: 22; SCRIPTURES: 2;
  SPIRIT: 7
Western State University College of
  Law, Fullerton and San Diego,
  California, JUSTICE: 38; LAW: 6;
  LIBERTY: 33; SCHOOL MOTTOES: 115
Western Wisconsin Technical
  Institute, Wisconsin,
  KNOWLEDGE: 97; SCHOOL
  MOTTOES: 369
Westmacott, DISGRACE: 4
Westminster City Council, U.K.,
  DIVINE GUIDANCE: 59; LOCAL
  GOVERNMENT: 74
Westminster College, New
  Wilmington, Pennsylvania, LAW: 2;
  SCHOOL MOTTOES: 31
Westminster (M.), NOBILITY: 16;
  VIRTUE: 124, 244
Westminster School, U.K., DIVINE
  GIFTS: 10; SCHOOL MOTTOES: 54
Westmont College, Santa Barbara,
  California, CHRIST, JESUS: 26;
  SCHOOL MOTTOES: 43
Westmore, MIND: 25; RECTITUDE: 43
Westmoreland (E.), WORTHINESS: 35

Weston, BIRDS: 5; DISGRACE: 1;
  DIVINITY: 192; GLORY: 22; STATUS: 1
Weston-super-Mare, U.K.,
  IMPROVEMENT: 9; LOCAL
  GOVERNMENT: 107
Westropp, DIRECTION: 2
Westropp-Dawson, DIRECTION: 10
Wetherby R. D. C., U.K.,
  GOVERNMENT: 3; OBSCURITY: 1
Wetmore (U.S.), COUNTRY: 142;
  LIBERTY: 132; VIRTUE: 291
Weyland (of Woodrising, Co.
  Norfolk), FEELINGS: 16
Weymiss (E.), THOUGHT: 8
Whalley, DIVINITY: 161, 189
Whalley (Co. Somerset and Hants),
  SEA: 17
Whannell, PEACE: 27
Wharncliffe (B.), ANCESTRY: 8
Wharton, DIVINE GUIDANCE: 193;
  ENDURANCE: 23; HOPE: 57;
  JUSTICE: 49; MANNERS: 2; WORDS: 21,
  24
Whatley, FEAR: 55
Whatman, WORTHINESS: 55
Whatton, CROSS, THE: 53; TRUTH: 23
Wheatley, PATRIOTISM: 65;
  ROYALTY: 81
Wheatly, DIVINITY: 275; TRUST: 74
Wheeler, ANCESTRY: 4;
  STEADFASTNESS: 6
Wheelton, DIVINE GUIDANCE: 84
Wheelwrights' Company, DIVINE
  GIFTS: 37; UNITY: 40
Wheler (Co. Warwick),
  COUNTENANCE: 2
Whetham, DIVINITY: 278
Whettnall, COURAGE: 245;
  FORTITUDE: 31
Whewell, FIRE: 8
Whichcote (Bt.), HONESTY: 26;
  JUSTICE: 53
Whieldon, VIRTUE: 311
Whimper, STEADFASTNESS: 59
Whitaker, FAITH: 204; STRENGTH: 116
Whitbread, COURAGE: 255
Whitburn, VIRTUE: 263
Whitby, VIRTUE: 358
Whitby U. D. C., U.K., LOCAL
  GOVERNMENT: 162; PAST, THE: 4

Wilhelm Ludwig, Duke of
Württemberg (1647–77),
DIVINITY: 254, 334; HOPE: 99;
TIME: 37

Wilhelm Ludwig, Prince of Anhalt-
Köthen (1638–65), DIVINE
GUIDANCE: 199, 328; SCRIPTURES: 11

Wilhelm V, Duke of Bavaria
(1548–1626), DIVINE GUIDANCE: 49;
FEELINGS: 22; FIDELITY: 54;
PATIENCE: 5; RECTITUDE: 8

Wilhelm V, Landgrave of Hesse-Cassel
(1602–37), CHANGE: 1; DEATH: 1;
DEEDS: 47; FATE: 6; FRUIT: 1;
GOALS: 5; SILENCE: 5;
STEADFASTNESS: 7; SUCCESS: 12;
SUFFERING: 9; TRUST: 33

Wilhelm VI, Landgrave of Hesse-
Cassel (1629–63), FIDELITY: 255;
HONOR: 134; JUSTICE: 98; PIETY: 30;
VIRTUE: 103

Wilhelm VI, Landgrave of Hesse-
Cassel (1629–63): on a coin struck in
memory of the death of his son in
1670, LIFE: 54

Wilkes, WEAPONS: 2

Wilkie, DIVINE GUIDANCE: 232

Wilkins, PRUDENCE: 19; SELF-
KNOWLEDGE: 11

Wilkinson, INTEGRITY: 8; PEOPLE: 3;
PERSEVERANCE: 25; RECTITUDE: 75;
ROYALTY: 55; TIME: 17

Willard (U.S.), KNOWLEDGE: 49

Willesden B. C., U.K.,
INDUSTRIOUSNESS: 92

Willet, DIVINITY: 131; DUTY: 7

William III and Mary, sovereigns of
England, MAINTENANCE: 2

William Jennings Bryan College,
Dayton, Tennessee, CHRIST, JESUS: 6;
SCHOOL MOTTOES: 37

William Jewell College, Liberty,
Missouri, DIVINITY: 73;
INDUSTRIOUSNESS: 25; SCHOOL
MOTTOES: 61; TRUST: 26

William Lloyd Garrison, abolitionist
and editor of The Liberator,
STEADFASTNESS: 72

Williams, DEATH: 24; DIVINE
GUIDANCE: 70, 74; DIVINITY: 218,
255, 309; GOODNESS: 19;
INDUSTRIOUSNESS: 146; POWER: 28;
PROTECTION: 32; SUFFERING: 12;
TRUST: 61; VIGILANCE: 63;
VIRTUE: 348

Williams and Norgate, publishers,
London, UNCLASSIFIED: 13

Williams (Bt.), PROPER NAMES: 24

Williams (Co. Brecon and Herts.),
DIVINE GIFTS: 24; TRANQUILLITY: 2

Williams (Co. Cardigan),
DIVINITY: 331

Williams (Co. Dorset), TRANSIENCE: 7

Williams (Co. Monmouth), TRUTH: 17

Williams (of Clovelly Court, Bt.),
VIRTUE: 111

Williams (of Colebrook),
LIMITATION: 11

Williams (of Eltham), HONOR: 195;
VIRTUE: 280

Williams (of Lee), DISCIPLINE: 7;
GENTLENESS: 18

Williams (of Temple House), DIVINE
GUIDANCE: 148

Williams (U.S.), AUDACITY: 74;
FLORA: 16; FRIENDSHIP: 3;
LIBERTY: 3; PREPAREDNESS: 29;
STRENGTH: 82; TIMELINESS: 5

Williamson, CONSCIENCE: 7;
DEFENSE: 24; OBSCURITY: 6;
STEADFASTNESS: 27

Williamson (of Hutchinfield),
INCREASE: 23

Williamson (of Kirkaldy),
INCREASE: 24

Willington, STRENGTH: 169

Willis, UNCLASSIFIED: 48

Willmott, UNCLASSIFIED: 41

Willoughby, COURAGE: 52; FEAR: 80;
HOPE: 37; TRUTH: 152

Willoughby de Eresby (B.),
EQUANIMITY: 5

Wills, HEART: 6; PERSEVERANCE: 47;
UNITY: 24; WORTHINESS: 33

Willsher, COURAGE: 111;
GENTLENESS: 8

Willshire (Bt.), PROPER NAMES: 15, 25

Willson, JUDGMENT: 2

Willyams, DIVINE GUIDANCE: 334;
DIVINITY: 255; GRACE: 22; TRUST: 61

Wolfgang Wilhelm, Count of the
Palatinate of Rhein zu Neuburg
(1578–1653), DIVINITY: 241
Wollaston (of Shenton), TRUTH: 59
Wolley (of Allen Hill), AUDACITY: 71
Wolrige, STRENGTH: 134
Wolsele, DEATH: 62
Wolseley, REASON: 13
Wolseley (Bt.), DEATH: 62; REASON: 13
Wolseley (of Wolseley, bt.),
ANIMALS: 27; HOSTILITY: 6
Wolstenholme, ADVERSITY: 34;
VIRTUE: 85
Wolverhampton C. B. C., U.K.,
DARKNESS: 12; LIGHT: 65; LOCAL
GOVERNMENT: 268
Wolverton (B.), FAITH: 74
Wombwell (Bt.), VIGILANCE: 53
Wombwell U. D. C., U.K., LOCAL
GOVERNMENT: 336; VIGILANCE: 61
Wood, AUDACITY: 91; COUNTRY: 71;
CROSS, THE: 8; FIDELITY: 249;
FLOURISHING: 10; GIFTS and
GIVING: 10; PATRIOTISM: 32;
RESULTS: 4; TRUST: 18
Wood Green B. C., U.K., LOCAL
GOVERNMENT: 254; STRANGER: 8;
STRENGTH: 95
Wood (of Barnsley, Bt.),
PERSEVERANCE: 56; STATE
MOTTOES: 40
Wood (of Boneytown), DEFENSE: 10
Wood (of Brownhills), DIVINE
GUIDANCE: 157
Wood (of co. Gloucester, bt.),
DEFENSE: 10
Wood (of Grangehaugh),
STRENGTH: 20
Wood (of Holm Hull), COUNTRY: 100;
PATRIOTISM: 46
Wood (of Mount House),
COURAGE: 142
Wood (of Singleton Lodge),
LIBERTY: 12; RELIGION: 4
Woodbridge (U.S.), VIRTUE: 322
Woodburne, AUDACITY: 22
Woodcock, DEEDS: 52; WORDS: 20
Woodcock (of Coventry),
INTEGRITY: 10; SCHOOL MOTTOES: 94
Woodd, UNSELFISHNESS: 4
Woodford, HOME: 19; RELIGION: 19
Woodford (Bt.), LIBERTY: 67

Woodhouse (Co. Stafford), SIGN: 2
Woodmongers' Company,
STRENGTH: 152; TRADES: 35, 39;
UNITY: 100; UTENSILS: 4
Woodroffe, WISDOM: 97
Woodrooffe, ACQUISITION: 7
Woods, COURAGE: 78; FLORA: 3;
INDUSTRIOUSNESS: 101;
PERSEVERANCE: 35; STRANGER: 12;
STRENGTH: 62, 115
Woodstock B. C., U.K., ANIMALS: 49;
LOCAL GOVERNMENT: 304
Woodward, VIRTUE: 325, 326
Wooldridge, CROSS, THE: 4
Woolfe, ADVERSITY: 21; FAITH: 99
Woolnough (of London), EFFORT: 19
Woolwich B. C., U.K., LOCAL
GOVERNMENT: 60; WEAPONS: 22
Worcester City and C. B. C., U.K.,
FIDELITY: 33, 168, 290;
FLOURISHING: 36; LOCAL
GOVERNMENT: 58, 146, 340; WAR: 14
Wordie, WORTHINESS: 37
Workington B. C., U.K.,
ASPIRATION: 55
Workman, INDUSTRIOUSNESS: 137;
PEOPLE: 5
Workman-Macnaghten (Bt.),
INDUSTRIOUSNESS: 137; PEOPLE: 5
Worksop B. C., U.K., DIVINITY: 379;
LOCAL GOVERNMENT: 332
Worksop R. D. C., U.K.,
INDUSTRIOUSNESS: 207; LOCAL
GOVERNMENT: 410
Wormeley (U.S.), DEDICATION: 8
Worrall, ABILITY: 15;
INDUSTRIOUSNESS: 83
Worsley, HONOR: 168; NAME: 10
Worsley (Bt.), GOODNESS: 35
Worth, CROSS, THE: 16
Worthing B. C., U.K., EARTH: 6;
FULLNESS: 5; HEALING and HEALTH: 7;
LOCAL GOVERNMENT: 111
Worthington, EXPECTATION: 6
Worthinton, ANCESTRY: 44
Wrangham, SEASONS: 1
Wray, JUSTICE: 24; TRUTH: 18
Wren, COURAGE: 261; FORTUNE: 116
Wren-Hoskyns (Harewood House,
Herefordshire), MEASURE: 11

Wrexham B. C., U.K., DIVINITY: 170; LOCAL GOVERNMENT: 118; ROYALTY: 34

Wrexham R. D. C., U.K., DUE: 7; LOCAL GOVERNMENT: 371

Wrey (Bt.), PROSPERITY: 21

Wright, ABILITY: 29; ASPIRATION: 77; AUDACITY: 19; BIRDS: 5; COURAGE: 97; DANGER: 3; DESIRE: 20; DIRECTNESS: 1, 2; ENDURANCE: 17, 56; FLORA: 30; FORTUNE: 12; HOPE: 43, 285; JUSTICE: 5; MIND: 25; RECTITUDE: 43; ROYALTY: 89; STATUS: 1; STRENGTH: 140; VIGILANCE: 107

Wright (Bt.), MIND: 31; RECTITUDE: 44

Wright (U.S.), PROTECTION: 12; RECTITUDE: 27

Wriothesley, UNITY: 89

Wrowe-Walton, VIRTUE: 433

Wyatt, ENDURANCE: 17; FORCE: 22; HONOR: 185; HOPE: 43; REASON: 24; VIRTUE: 45

Wyatt-Edgell, PROSPERITY: 16

Wybergh (of Clifton Hall), HOSTILITY: 5

Wyborn, FAME: 9; GENTLENESS: 13; JUSTICE: 105

Wyggesden School, Leicester, U.K., GIFTS and GIVING: 12; SCHOOL MOTTOES: 55

Wykeham (Bishop of Winchester and Lord Chancellor of England, founder of New College, Oxford, in 1379), MANNERS: 5; SCHOOL MOTTOES: 183

Wyld, SPEED: 58; VIGILANCE: 85

Wylie, MIND: 35; RECTITUDE: 45

Wylie (Bt.), INDUSTRIOUSNESS: 103

Wyllie, HOPE: 226

Wyllie (of Forfar), FAITH: 93

Wyndham, EXPECTATION: 1; FAITH: 254; STRENGTH: 180

Wynford (B.), LAW: 32; LIBERTY: 59

Wynkoop (U.S.), VIRTUE: 400

Wynn, DEEDS: 89; MANNER: 12

Wynne (Bt.), MEMORY: 22

Wynne (of Pengwern), BIRDS: 16; COURAGE: 55

Wynn-Williams, ASPIRATION: 46; BIRDS: 16; POWER: 28

Wyrley-Birch (of Wretham, Co. Norfolk), PRUDENCE: 74; SIMPLICITY: 8

Wyvill (Bt.), DIVINE GUIDANCE: 364

X

Ximenes, JUSTICE: 128; TRUTH: 147

Y

Yaldwyn, DEATH: 48; REASON: 11

Yale University, New Haven, Connecticut, LIGHT: 47; SCHOOL MOTTOES: 178; TRUTH: 53

Yankton College, Yankton, South Dakota, CHRIST, JESUS: 7; SCHOOL MOTTOES: 38

Yarburgh, DARKNESS: 10

Yarburgh (of Heslington), VICTORY: 31

Yarker (of Leyburn), FINISH: 9

Yate (of Bromesberrow), COURAGE: 193

Yate (of Whimper, Co. Suffolk), COURAGE: 193

Yates, FIDELITY: 301; JUDGMENT: 11; SECURITY: 60

Yates (U.S.), UNSELFISHNESS: 3

Yatman, COURAGE: 103

Yea (Bt.), FIDELITY: 79

Yeldham, FIDELITY: 147

Yelverton, FAITH: 127

Yeoman, WEAPONS: 89

Yerburgh, AUDACITY: 102; VICTORY: 71

Yester, GENEROSITY: 16

Yonge, FIDELITY: 35; LIFE: 28; LOVE: 39

York, DESIRE: 13; FEAR: 36; MODERATION: 23

Yorke (of Erddig), DESIRE: 13; FEAR: 36; MODERATION: 23

Youl, COURAGE: 176; STRENGTH: 100

Young, ABILITY: 25; AGE: 9; ENDURANCE: 49; FORTITUDE: 28; HOPE: 200; PRUDENCE: 57, 78; STRENGTH: 114; UNCLASSIFIED: 15; VICTORY: 56; VIRTUE: 221

Young (Co. Bucks, Bt.), PERSEVERANCE: 5

Young (kt., Garter king-at-arms), HOSTILITY: 8

Young (of Marlow, bt.), ADVANCE: 49

Z